Birds of Prey

Birds of Prey

Blue Ribbon Techniques

(Carving Projects)

William Veasey

Schiffer Publishing Ltd

1469 Morstein Road, West Chester, Pennsylvania

Other books by William Veasey

Power Tool Carving: Blue Ribbon Techniques
Burning and Texturing Methods: Blue Ribbon Techniques
Waterfowl Carving: Blue Ribbon Techniques, with Cary Schuler Hull
Waterfowl Painting: Blue Ribbon Techniques
Bills and Feet: An Artisan's Handbook, with Sina Kurman
Blue Ribbon Pattern Series
Full Size Decorative Decoy Patterns I
Miniature Decoy Patterns II
Head Patterns III
Song Bird Patterns IV
Shore Bird Patterns V
Miniature Decorative Patterns VI
Hunting Birds VII

Books by Tricia Veasey

Waterfowl Illustrated, by Tricia Veasey
Championship Carving, by Tricia Veasey and Tom Johnson

Photography of live birds by Leonard Soucy, founder of the Raptor Trust of New Jersey.

Library of Congress Catalog Number: 85-61704.

Printed in the United States of America.
ISBN: 0-88740-052-3
Published by Schiffer Publishing Ltd. 1469 Morstein Road, West Chester, Pennsylvania 19380

This book may be purchased from the publisher.
Please include $1.50 postage.
Try your bookstore first.

The person who risks nothing
does nothing
has nothing
is nothing
Author unknown

DEDICATION

I would like to dedicate this work to three of my closest associates; my daughter Tricia Veasey, Debra Norvell and Paul Suarez. The superb talents and personal dedication to excellance of these three have made it possible for me to become an author, without them it would have been quite impossible.

Acknowledgments

Thanks to Len Soucy and the New Jersey Raptor Trust for being generous. A special thanks to David Biddle, Jeff Ebel, Jack Hemphill, Vicky Herron, Genille McDyre, Jeff Moore, Debra Norvell, Paul Suarez and Tricia Veasey for the outstanding carvings done as projects in this book. Appreciation to Peter Schiffer for sticking tenaciously with the project.

A very special thanks to Paul Suarez for being project director and creating the step-by-step process of carving and painting.

Contents

Introduction

Some years ago I decided to create a series of pattern books for carvers. One of the projected books was to be on birds of prey, raptors.

As time went by it became apparent that what was needed was a step-by-step project book which would present information in a manner usable by novice and intermediate carvers on fun projects. Finally the idea for this book was born and the work began.

It has always been my intention to present mateial in such a way as to cover the subject yet at the same time allow the student a wide latitude in his own creativity.

Throughout this book you will encounter the name of Len Soucy and the New Jersey Raptor Trust several times, this is not coincidental, the large contribution Len Soucy has made cannot be measured. His interest, his ability and his willingness to share is truly incredible. The photos of real, live birds came from his personal files and were a result of his great ability as a photographer. His knowledge of raptors is overwhelming.

When you study the photographs of live birds in this book remember Len Soucy and that he cares. "IF HE DID NOT CARE" you and I would not have this wonderful piece of source material and so if you care you may want to make a small contribution to the New Jersey Raptor Trust at 1390 White Bridge Road, Millington, New Jersey 07946 so that Len and his associates can continue this wonderful, exciting and important work which benefits us all.

Bill Veasey

Foreword

Leonard J. Soucy, Jr.
Founder — The Raptor Trust
1390 White Bridge Road
Millington, NJ 07946

Raptors are a spectacular group of birds that have inspired writers and artists throughout history. Their beauty, agility, daring and predatory nature have evoked in man a wide range of feelings towards them — everything from adulation to hatred. Unfortunately, however we have viewed them, humanity has historically been of little help to these marvelous creatures.

Worldwide, there are over 400 species of raptors, or birds of prey. They inhabit every continent (except Antarctica) and many of the world's islands. Scientifically they have been divided into two major groups, or orders: the 280 species of diurnal hawks, eagles, falcons and vultures are in the order *Falconiformes* and the nocturnal owls, some 134 species, are in the order *Strigiformes*. In North America (north of Mexico), 39 species of diurnal raptors and 18 species of owls occur.

Because of their hooked beaks, curved talons and similar life styles, hawks and owls were once classified together. We now know they are actually unrelated. But the two groups do furnish a good example of convergent evolution whereby birds of separate origin have developed similar features because of their way of life.

Even though raptors have many features in common, there are considerable variations among them. Generally, the sexes are more or less alike in appearance but in some species, like the Northern Harrier and the American Kestrel, there is a conspicuous difference. Very few can be described as colorful, compared to many other groups of birds, but nevertheless many are strikingly marked and many others display beautiful, subtle blends of colors in their plumage. In almost all species, females are larger than males.

Raptor sizes vary greatly. The world's smallest owl, the Elf Owl, has a wingspan of 14 inches and weighs in at about 1½ ounces, while the Eagle Owl, the world's largest owl, has a 6 foot wingspan and tips the scales at 8½ pounds. Even greater size differences occur in the diurnal raptors. The Red-legged Falconet of Asia is the size of a small sparrow. It has a wingspan of barely 6 inches and weighs 1/10th pound. The Andeon Condor has a wingspan of over 10 feet and weighs 25 pounds — 250 times as much as the falconet!

Raptors throughout the world have suffered a serious decline in numbers in recent history. This decline has been caused almost entirely by man's influence, whether direct or indirect. Habitat loss, the indiscriminate use of toxic chemicals, shooting, poisoning, and exploitation all have negatively impacted their numbers. But lately there has been an increasing awareness of the plight of raptors, and many individuals and groups are working on their behalf.

Many of the photographs used to illustrate this book were taken at The Raptor Trust in Millington, N.J. The Trust is a private, non-profit, tax-exempt corporation dedicated to the preservation and well-being of birds of prey. Licensed by the State of New Jersey and the U.S. Fish and Wildlife Service, The Raptor Trust is qualified to deal with all raptor-related matters.

The organization operates a rehabilitation center in Millington where injured and orphaned birds are cared for with the goal of releasing them back into the wild. Many birds are crippled by their injuries and cannot be returned to freedom. Some of these damaged birds are kept permanently at the center, trained to tolerate people, and are used in educational programs. Interested groups and individuals can arrange appointments to visit The Raptor Trust and see live hawks and owls close up and personal. Over the years many painters, sculptors and carvers have used these birds as models

Raptors are in peril. They need and deserve our help. They are important to save because of their biological significance alone. But beyond that, these unique and beautiful birds add quality to our own lives. The need is for understanding and tolerance to replace biased attitudes of the past. The destiny of raptors is in our hands. Let history show that we cared.

Biography of Carvers

David Biddle was born and grew up on the Elk River in Port Herman, Maryland. He came from a family of hunters and outdoorsmen and grew up with a great appreciation of nature.

Very early David showed great apptitude for drawing and painting, particularly in cartooning. His ready wit lends itself to this form of art.

He later became interested in carving decoys but did not care very much for the super detail of today's decorative carvers. Instead, he chose to stylize antique waterfowl which he has done with great success. His work is found throughout the country in many galleries and private collections. He continues to create art quite different from the main stream, thus keeping his work in great demand.

Jeff Ebel grew up in Iowa hunting upland game birds and waterfowl. He learned to recognize wildlife in parks and refuges that he has visited. At a young age, he saw his first decoy competition at the Mississippi Valley Fair. Jeff studied computer science and business systems in college, but he found he did his best work and earned his best grades in art. In May 1982, Jeff attended a three day seminar at Veasey Studios. Shortly thereafter he joined as an associate. He won his first blue ribbon as an amateur at the Chestertown, Maryland show in 1985 and plans to make his living carving and teaching.

Jack Hemphill is from Wilmington, Delaware and has been involved in sales for the last twenty-eight years for a large pharmaceutical company. He got interested in carving in 1980 after taking his son John, Jr., who started carving at ten years of age, back and forth for carving lessons. After two years Jack decided to join John in his hobby. This turned out to be a good decision as he won his first competition ribbon during the show season of 1981. At present his commission work is keeping him quite busy. He plans to continue his carving as an avocation at this time and as a vocation after retirement.

Vicky Herron was born and raised in Elkton, Maryland. A 1976 graduate of Elkton High School, Vicky is a housewife and mother of a five year old son, Tommy. Her husband Tom learned to carve with William Veasey. While watching him carve and attending the shows, she developed an interest in carving. In 1982 she began working in the Veasey studio. Vicky says, "The opportunity to be a part of this book is really a thrill. I am learning a great deal and I will continue to learn. In general, carving has become an important part of my life."

Genille McDyre, resident free-lance artist and carver at Veasey Studios, lives on the North East River at Carpenter's Point and draws mainly on the indigenous waterfowl for her work.

The Snowy Owl is her first carving of a bird of prey. It follows many waterfowl carvings, most recently a wood sculpture of a Blue Hen, the state bird of Delaware (collection of William Buck).

Ms. McDyre has studied at Veasey Studios for eight years. She works in the studio with a wide range of duties. In addition to her carving experience, Genille has studied with Carol White at Cecil Community College in the areas of pottery, color theory, oil painting, serigraphy and design, and slide photography with Kristi Esinberg. She has donated time to the Cecil County Arts Council and to Cecil County Ducks Unlimited. Genille McDyre is the daughter of Marlin and Donna Tusha of Osprey, Florida, wife of Michael McDyre, a photo journalist, and mother of 13-year old Simon Smith, who is also an award-winning carver. Genille's work is found in many private collections throughout the country.

Jeff Moore was born in Wilmington, Delaware and has lived in Newark, Delaware all his life. He is a 1984 graduate of Newark High School who enjoys fishing, hunting and carving. He started carving in 1984 working at Veasey Studios part-time. It seemed almost unbelieveable to

Jeff what could be done with a block of wood. After a time his interest grew and he began to take lessons from William Veasey. He is currently an integral member of the Veasey team working both in the studio and at shows.

Debra Norvel was born in London, England and has family in England and the United States. Since her father was in the Air Force, Debbie has traveled extensively throughout the world living and visiting in such places as Taiwan, Japan, the Middle Eastern countries and England. Having moved to Delaware in 1974, Debbie began as an apprentice in 1976 at Veasey Studios and began teaching full time in 1977. Currently at the age of twenty five, Debbie has been carving and competing for ten years, professionally for six years. She is currently studying classical sculpture with sculptor Angelo Frudakis at the Frudakis Academy of the Fine Arts in Philadelphia, Pennsylvania. She is also studying drawing and watercolor with artist and watercolorist Jean Lanyon and figure drawing at Barnstone Studios in Allentown, Pennsylvania. She has worked with sculptor Charles Parks of Wilmington, Delaware.

Debbie travels extensively teaching classes in England, conducting weekend seminars as an associate of Veasey Studios, teaching wildfowl carving twice a week.

Debbie's future goals: to become a sculptor in figure and portraiture as well as wildfowl carving.

Paul A. Suarez was born March 14, 1961. He was a scholarship student at the Delaware Art Museum at the age of thirteen and was an accomplished potter and artist in high school, at which time he was also taking college art courses. In 1979 he began an apprenticeship under William Veasey and worked full time at Veasey Studios. He started teaching at the studio in 1980 and began doing his own work in earnest. In 1982 he received an invitation to the Ward Foundation's 15th Annual Wildfowl Carving and Art Exhibit. He is an active supporter of Ducks Unlimited. His work can be found in many private and public collections throughout the country.

Tricia Veasey has studied at the University of Delaware and was individually instructed in creative photography by the well known photographer and author James Warner. She has had her photos extensively published in *Waterfowl Carving, Blue Ribbon Techniques*, by William Veasey in 1982 and in her first solo book *Waterfowl Illustrated* in 1983. The latter is a complete source book of North American waterfowl photographs for carvers, taxidermists, ornithologists, bird watchers and all waterfowl enthusiasts.

With photographer Tom Johnson, she has done the first book of pictures recording the winners of the World Championship carving competition *Championship Carving* in 1984. This first volume contains all the winners of the Best in World categories as well as blue ribbon winners in novice, amateur and professional categories. It contains tips from and biographies of many of the carvers whose birds appear in the book. She had the honor of taking the pictures for the biography of Lem Ward told by his daughter *Lem Ward* by Ida Ward and Glen Lawson in 1984.

Tricia is a writer, photographer, professional carver, author and carving teacher. She has assisted in many seminars for Veasey Studios School of Carving and has taught complete carving classes in the United States and Great Britain. Her own carvings are in many public and private collections. Tricia accepts commissions for wildfowl carvings and family or pet portraits.

Gray Screech Perched (Wall Mount)

Carved by Vicky Herron

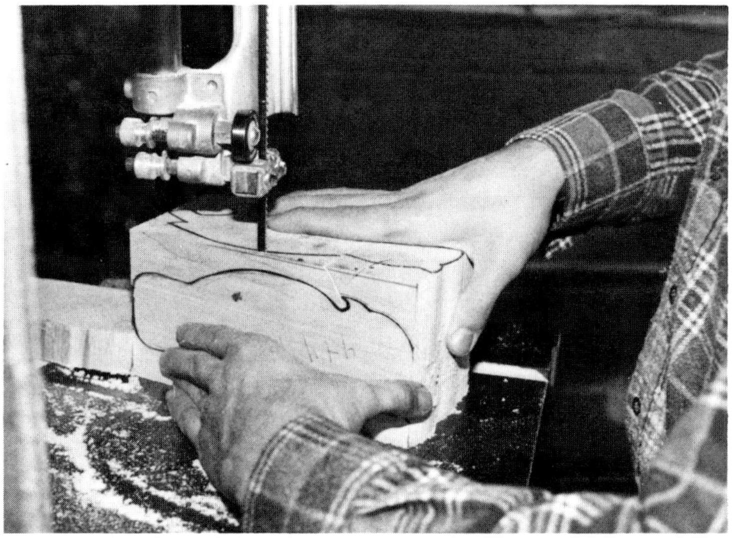

Band sawing profile view

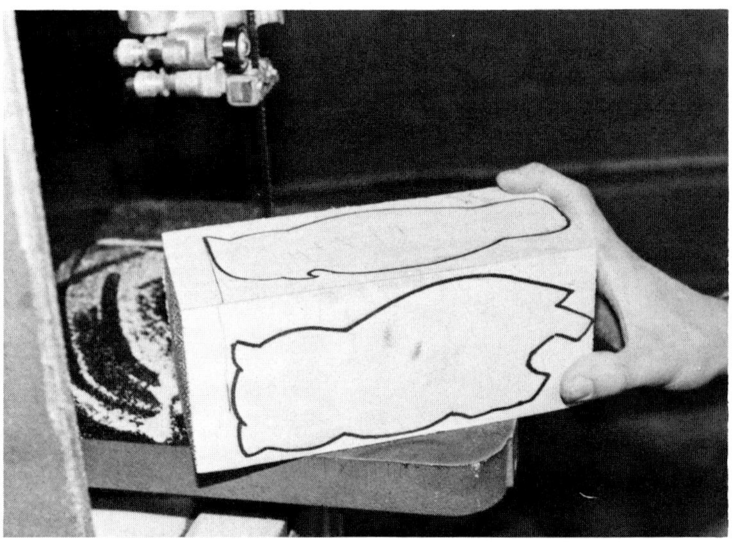

Band sawing plan or top view

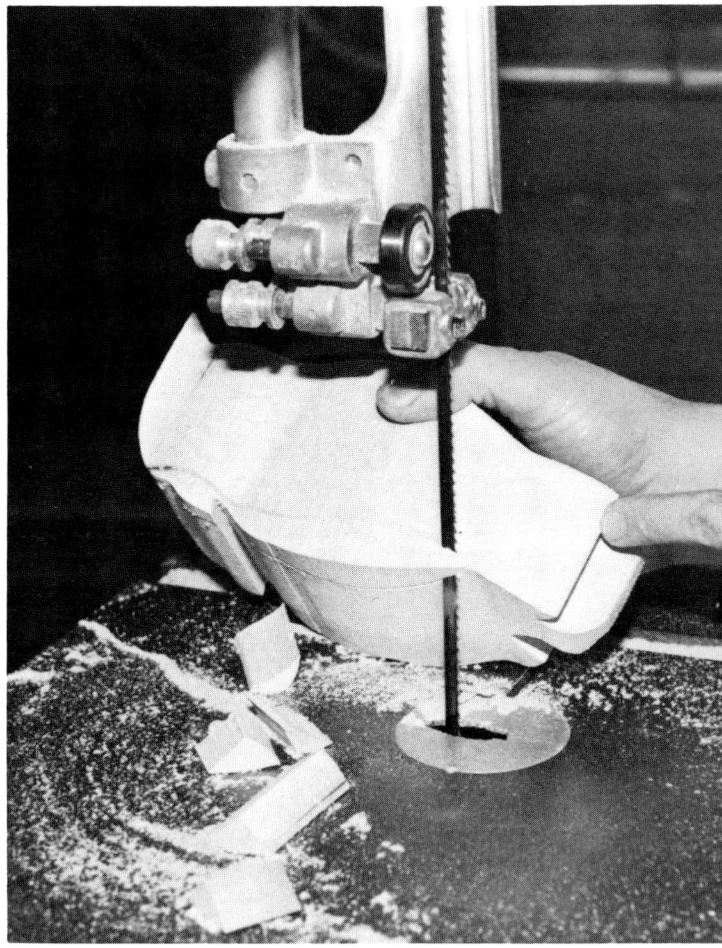

Trimming excess wood on band saw

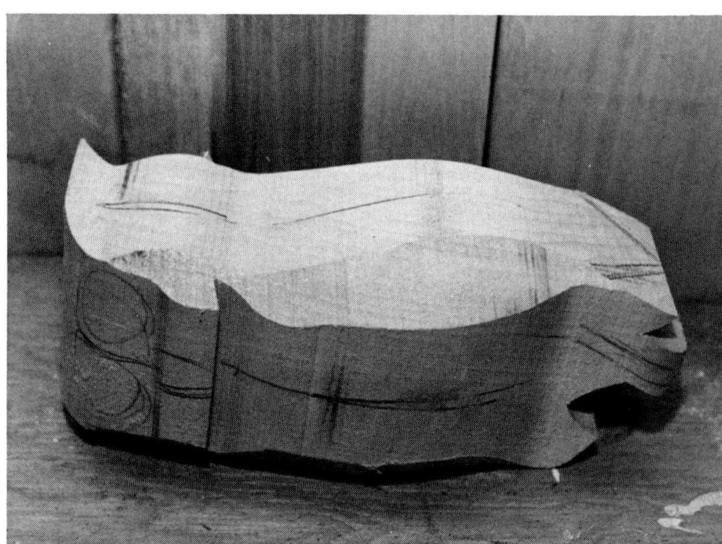

Trimmed blank ready for carving

(See page 137 for painting instructions and page 266 for patterns)

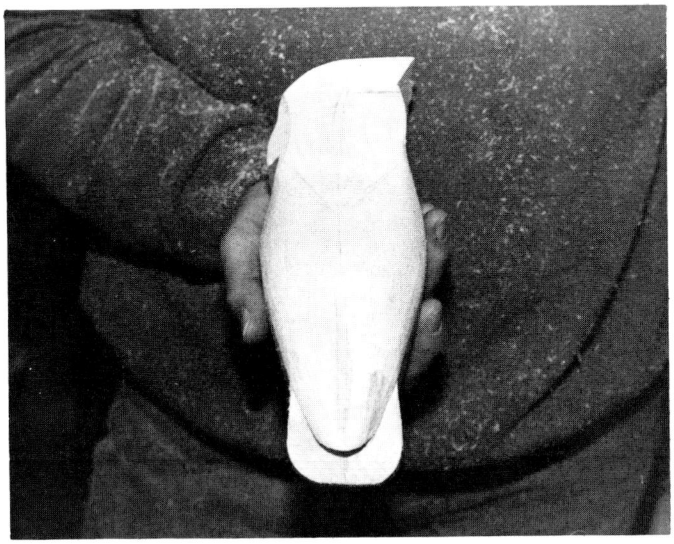
Back shaped—note: smooth rounded lines

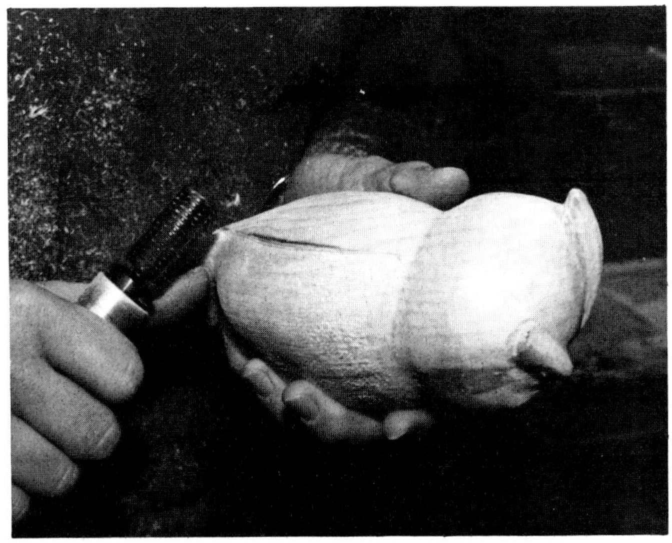
Shaping wing area and back of head

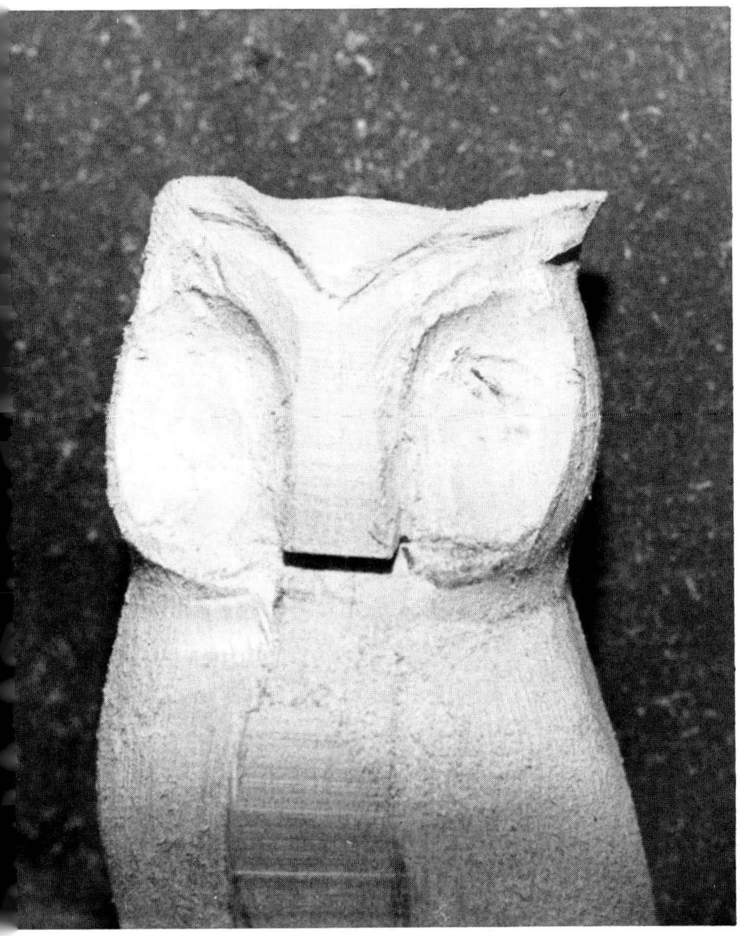
Front view of face plate being shaped

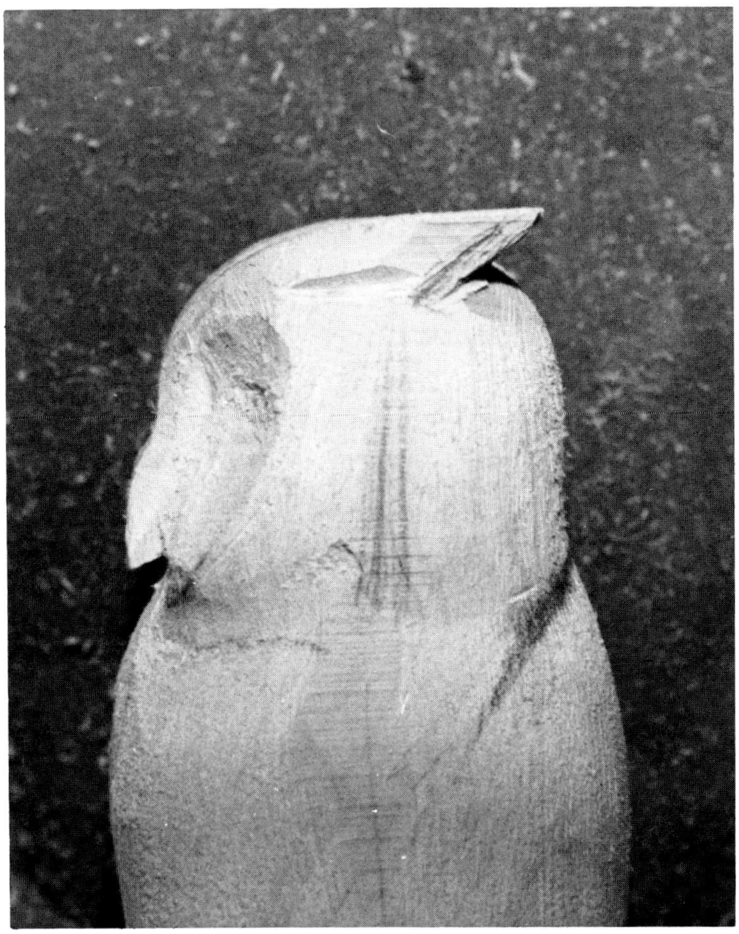
Side view of facial discs and beak

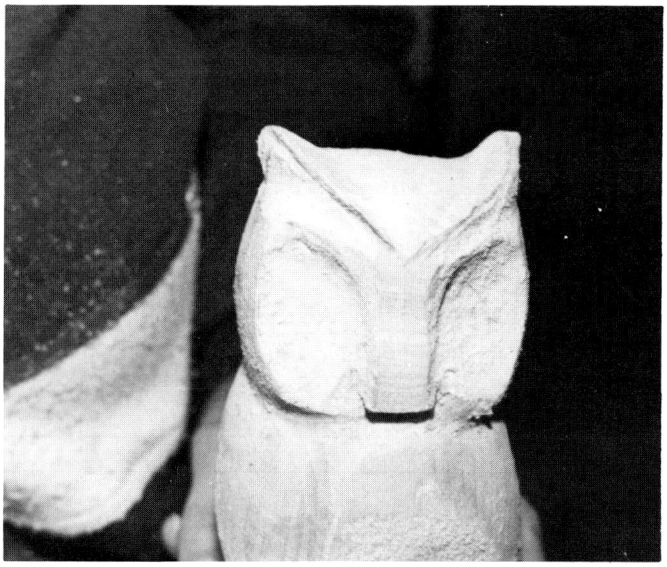

Front view of facial area—note: tufts

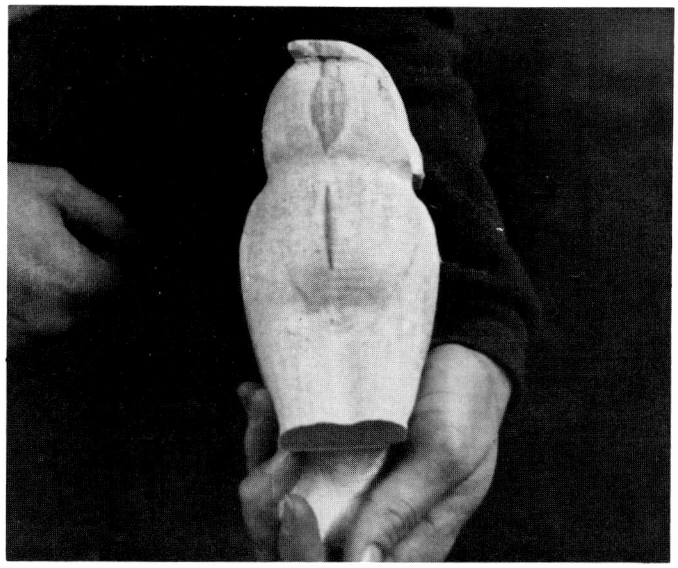

Side view of head and belly—note: indentation of leg area

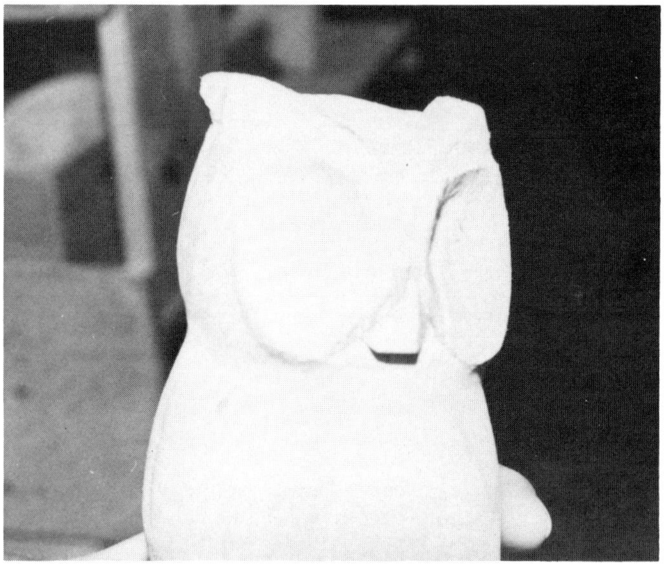

Front view of emerging beak

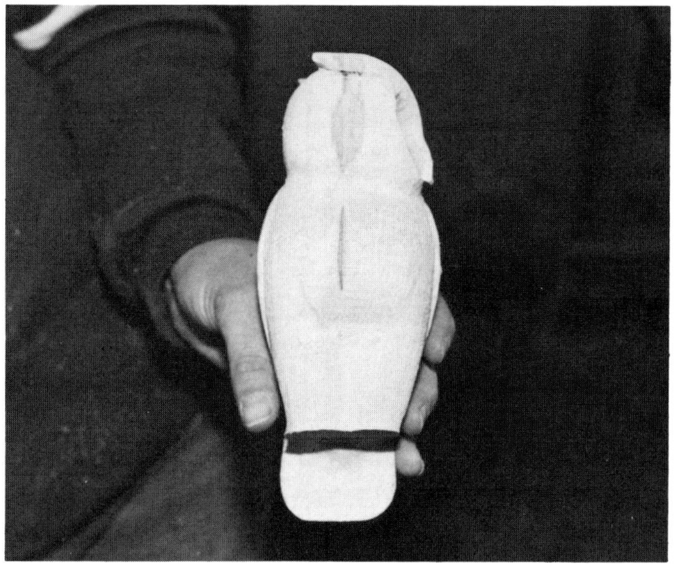

Side view of head, belly and tail areas

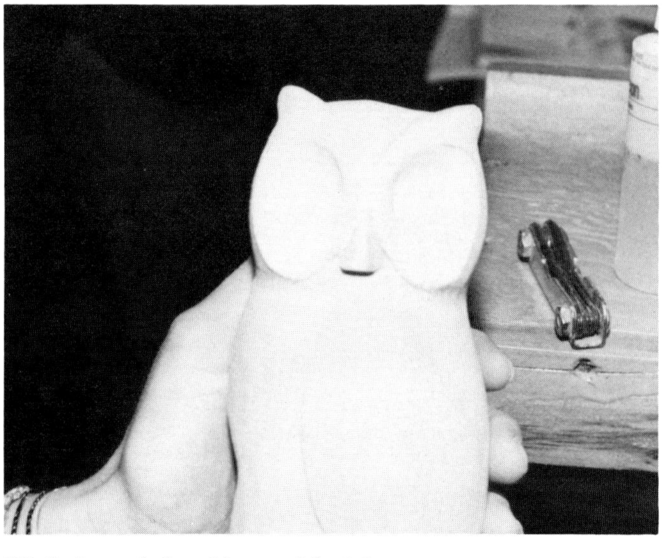

Well shaped shoulder and facial areas

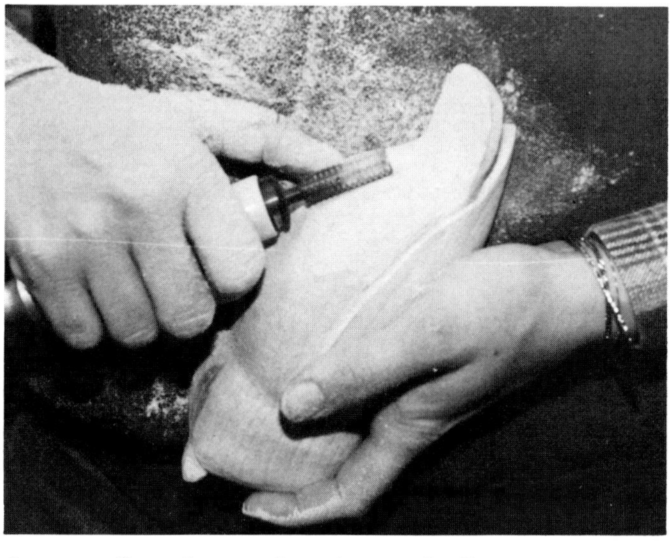

Leg area flows into under wings and tail

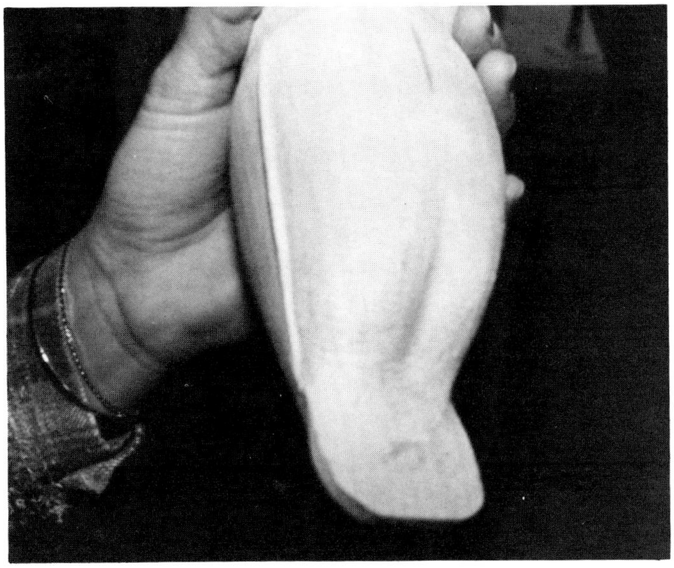

Indentations between legs

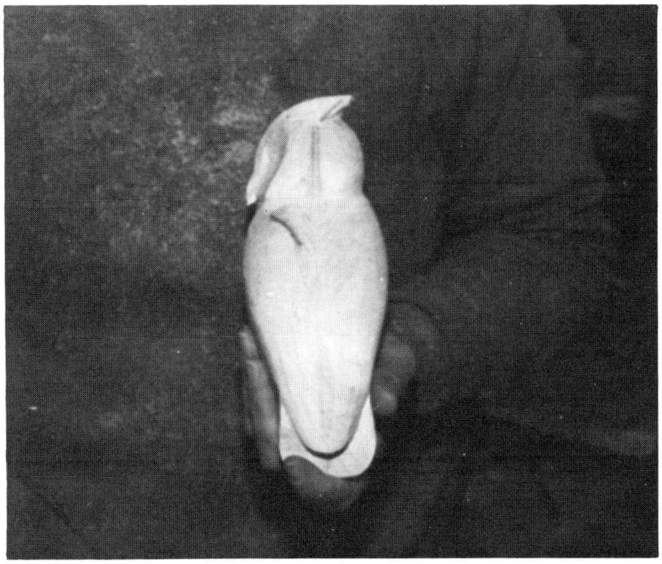

Bird ready for feather lay out

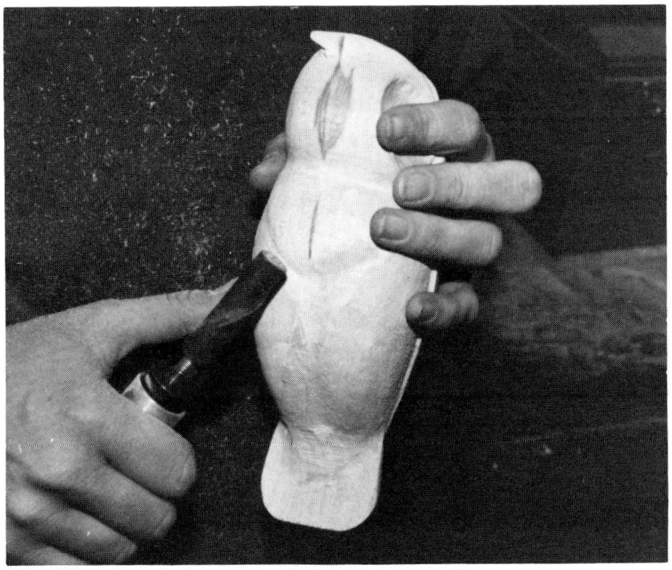

Indentations (V) area of chest

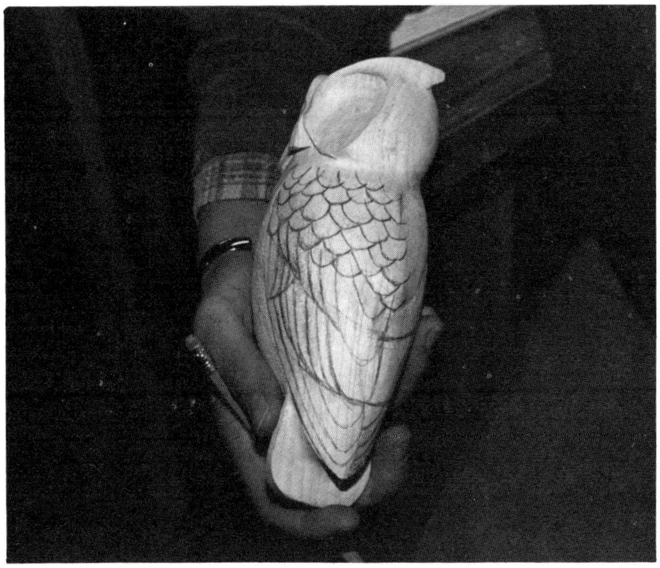

Feather lay out on back (wing area)

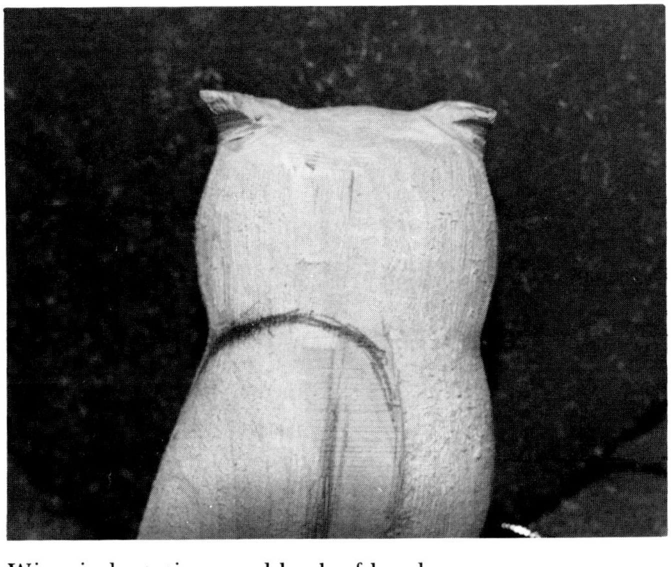

Wing indentations and back of head

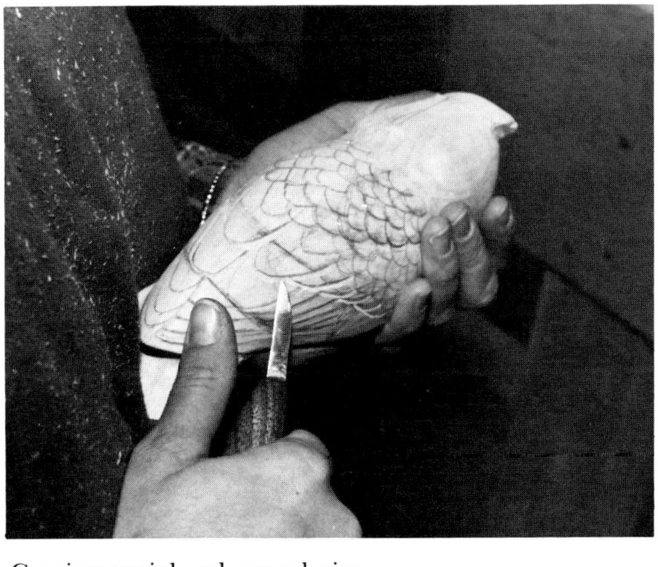

Carving tertial and secondaries

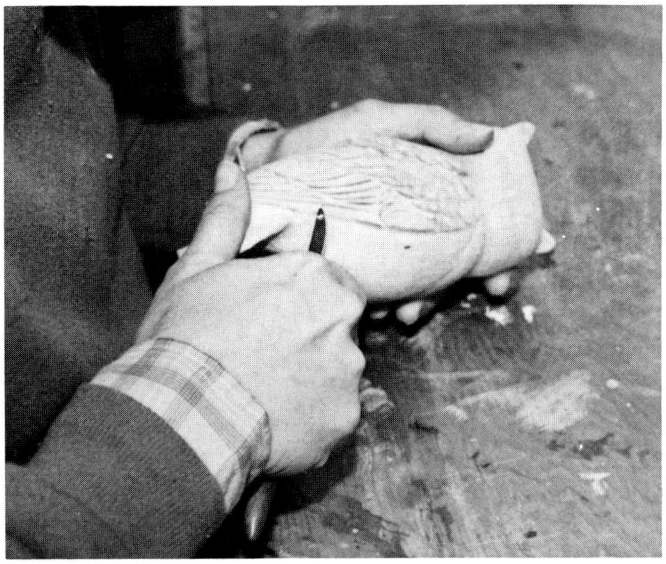

Trimming feather to smooth out carving

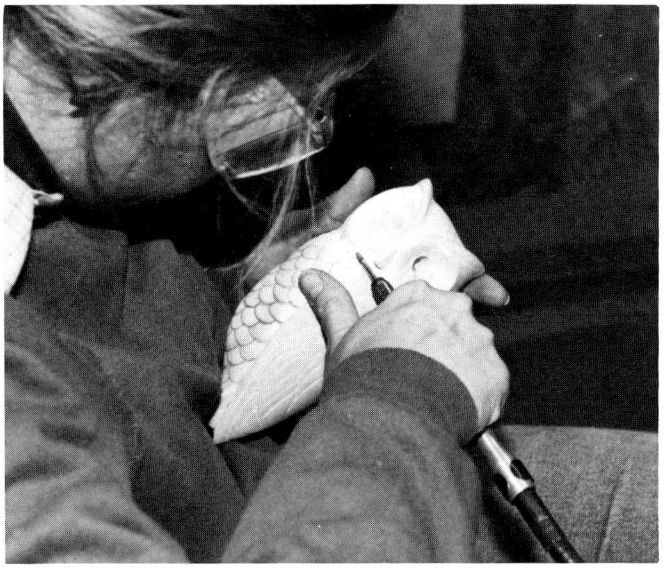

Ruby carving belly feathers to create roll or lumps and bumps

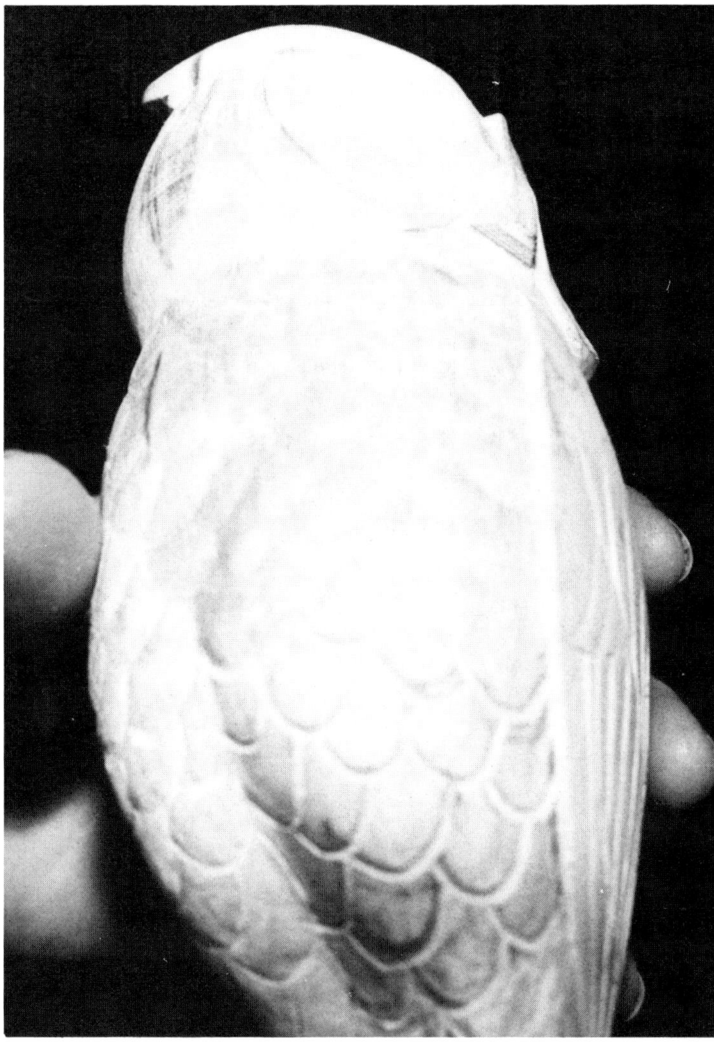

Example of ruby carved feathers top sanded lower not sanded

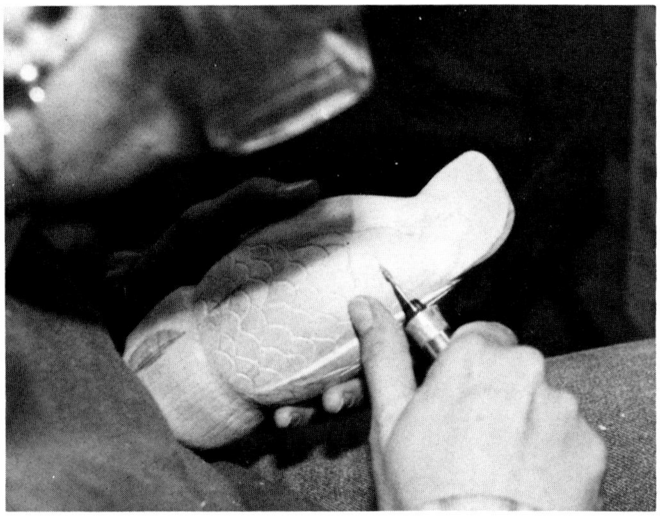

More ruby carving of feathers

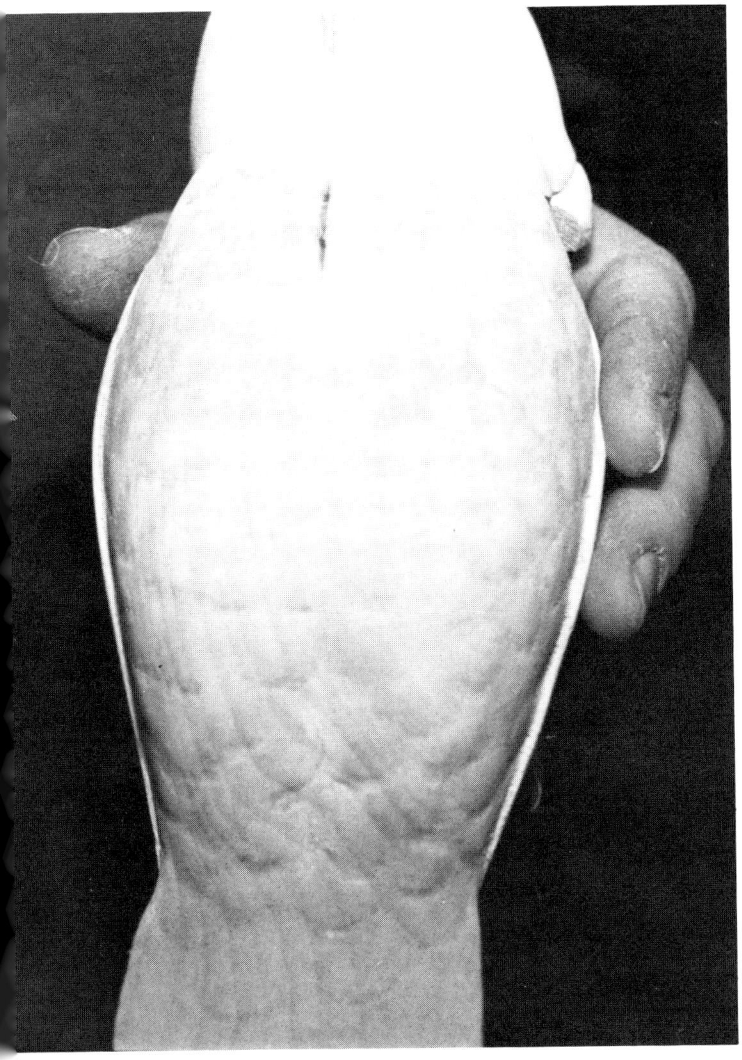

Belly and chest carved and sanded

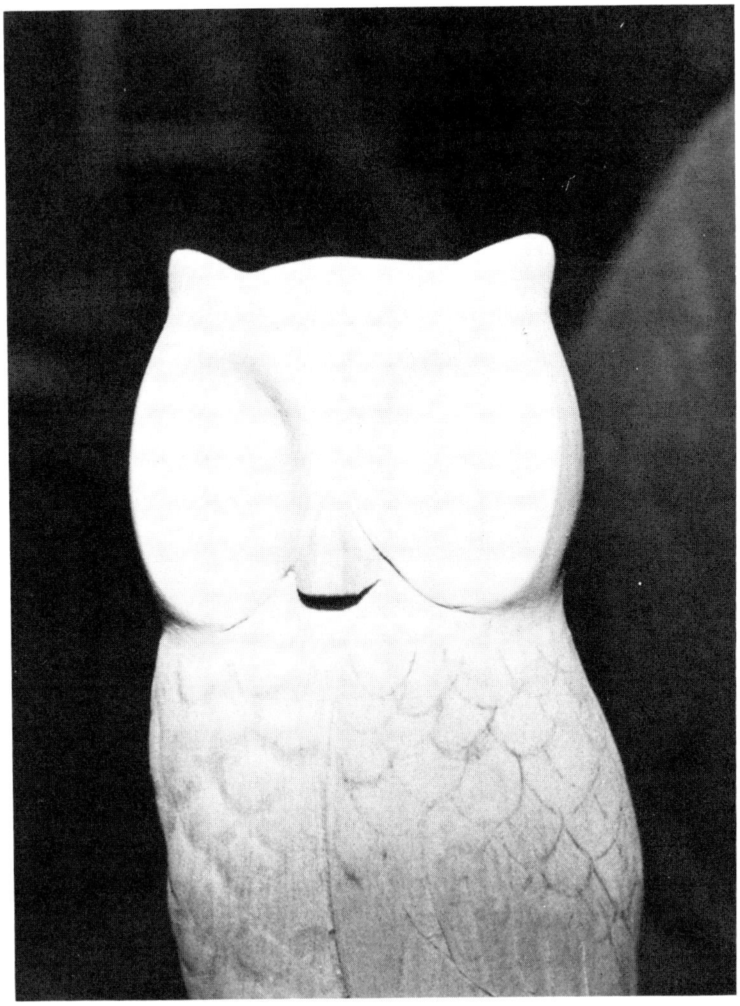

Carving finished except for beak

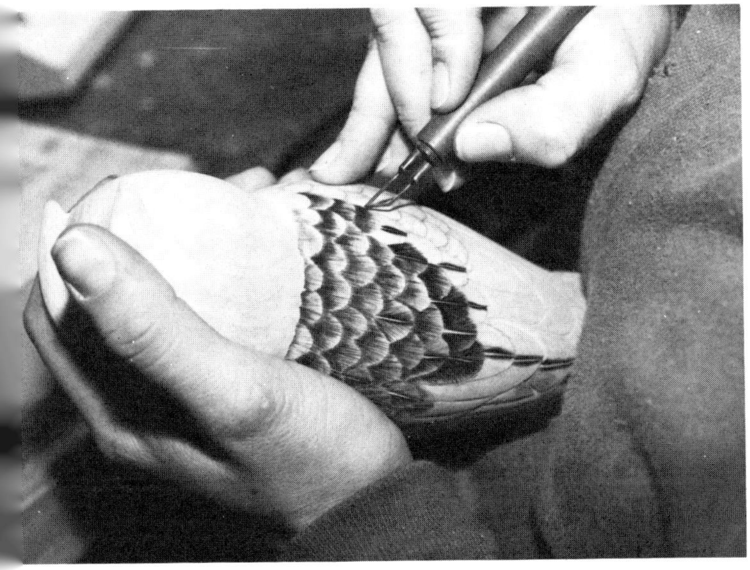

Burning feathers on back

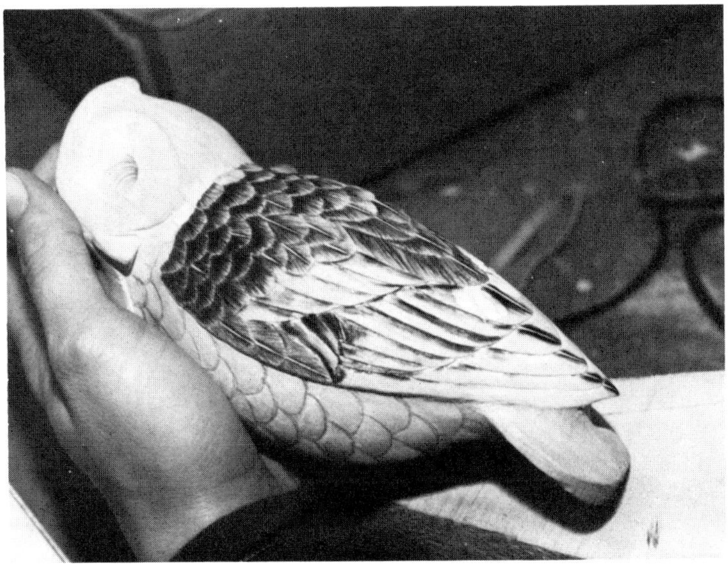

Wing area partially burned and eye holes drilled—beak carved

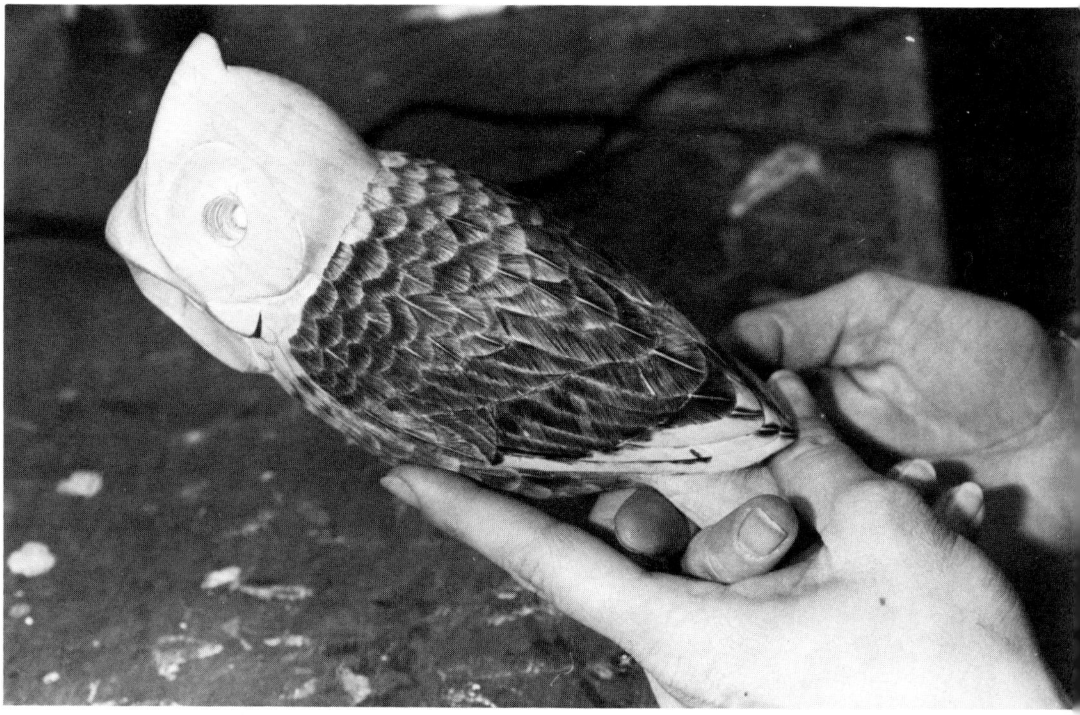

Study burning techniques

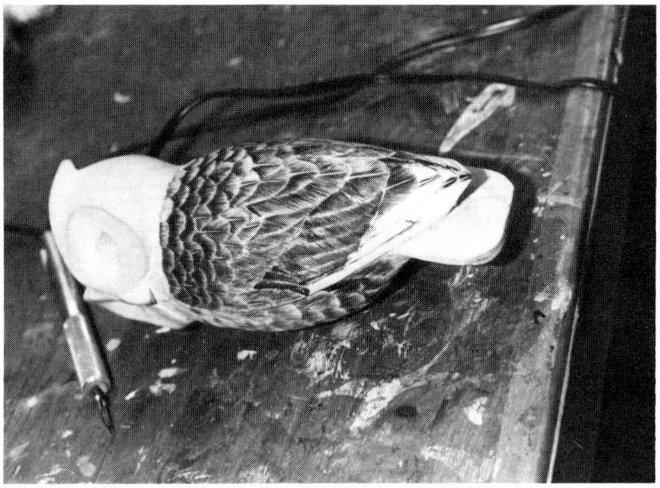

Note feather lay out

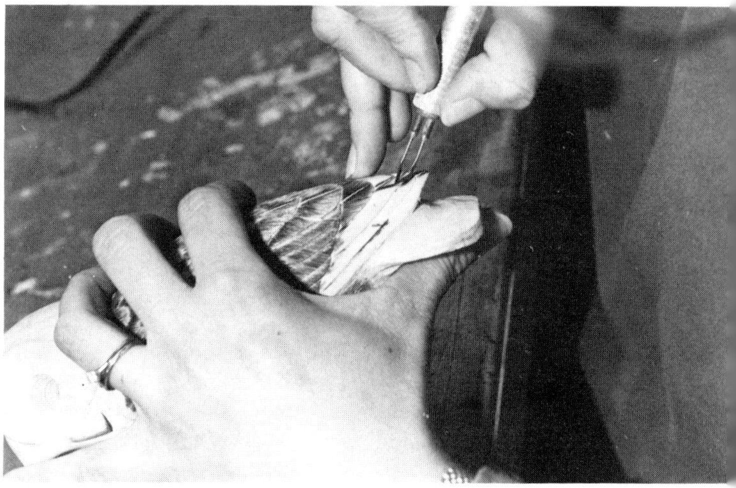

Note burning techniques

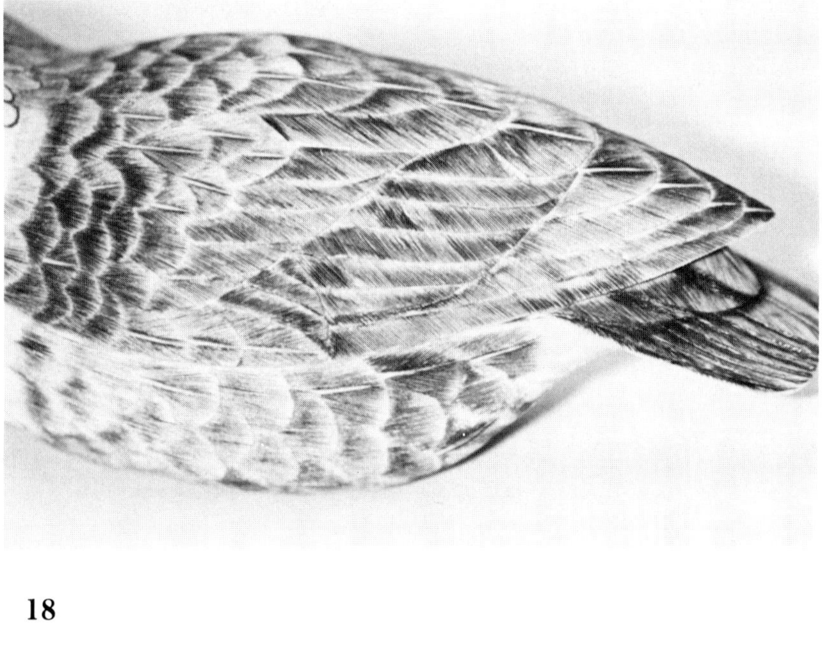

Back, tail and belly burned

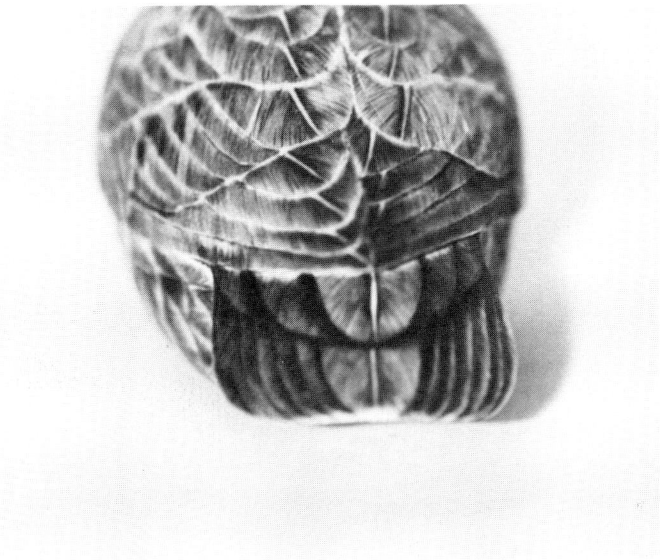

Entire back burned

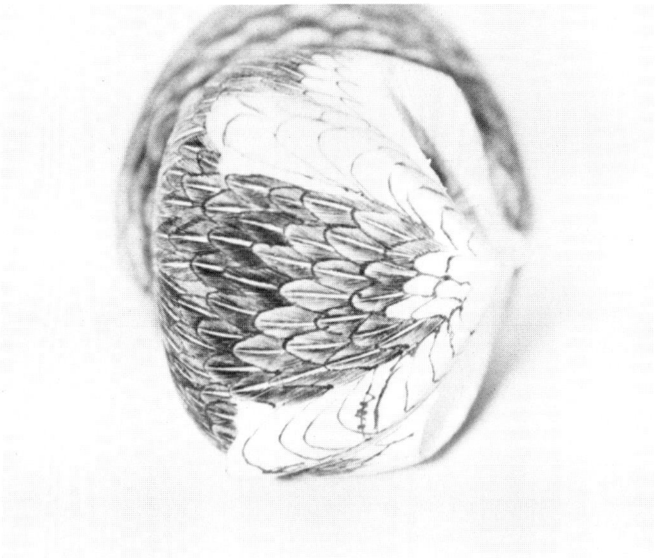

Top view of head burned except "ears"

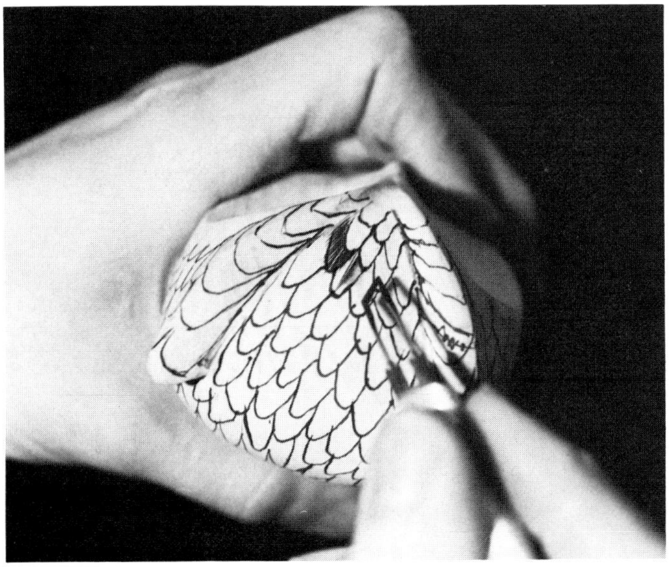

Feather lay out of head including "ears"

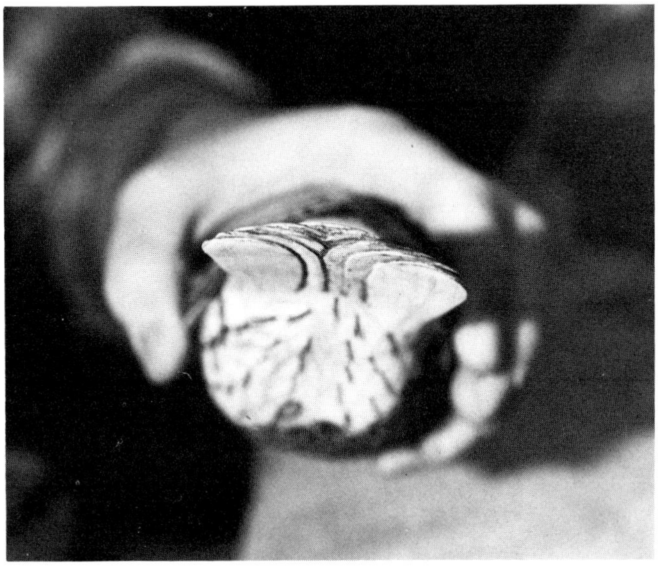

End view of tail carved

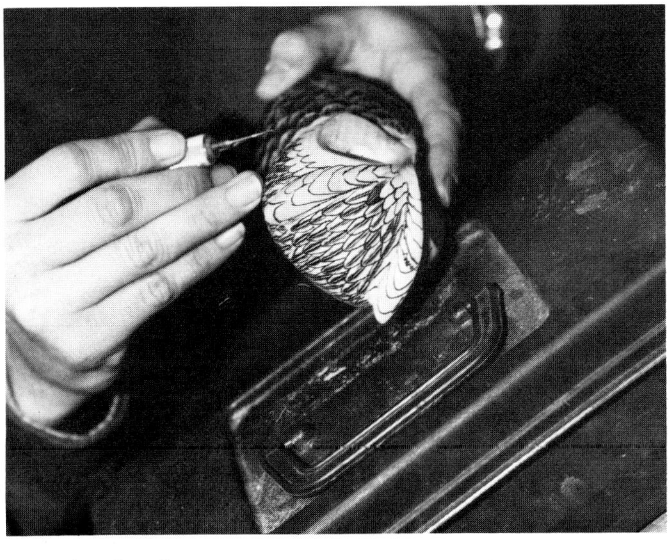

Burning head

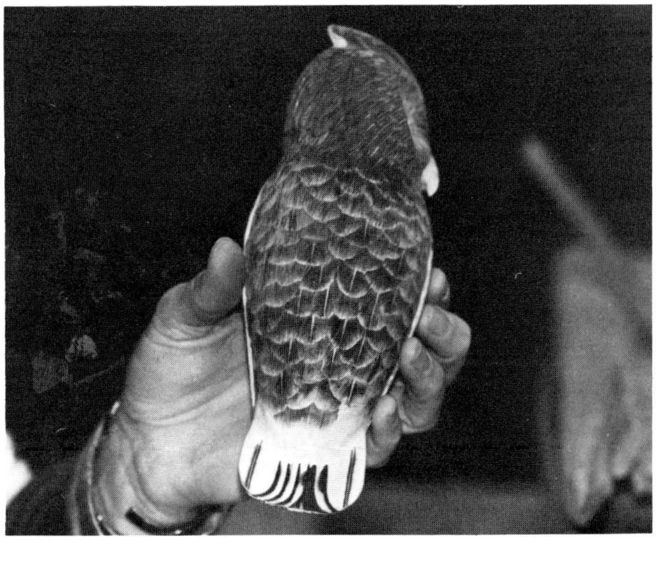

Bottom view of tail carved with burner

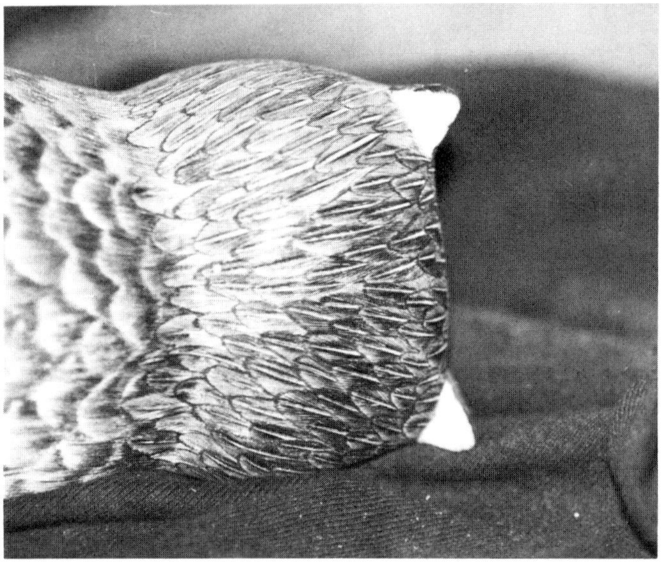

Back of head burned

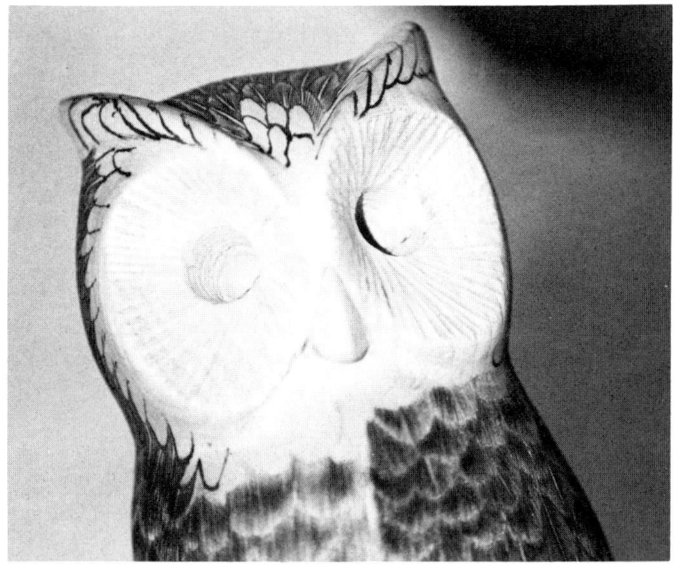

Another view of bottom left photograph

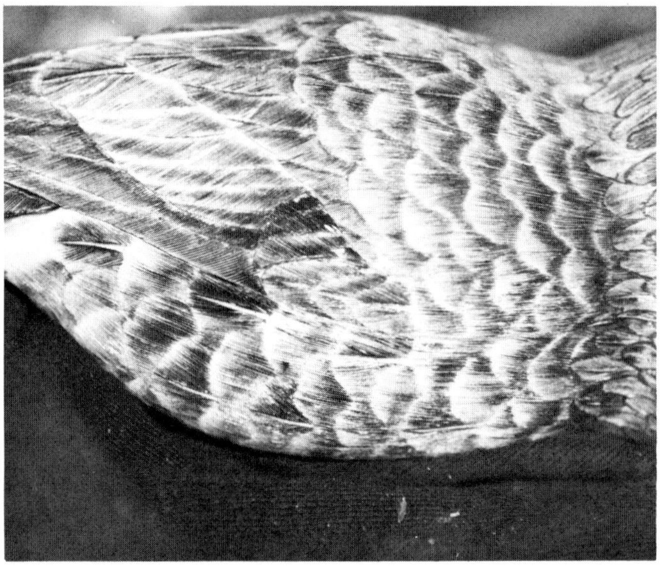

Side view of bird burned

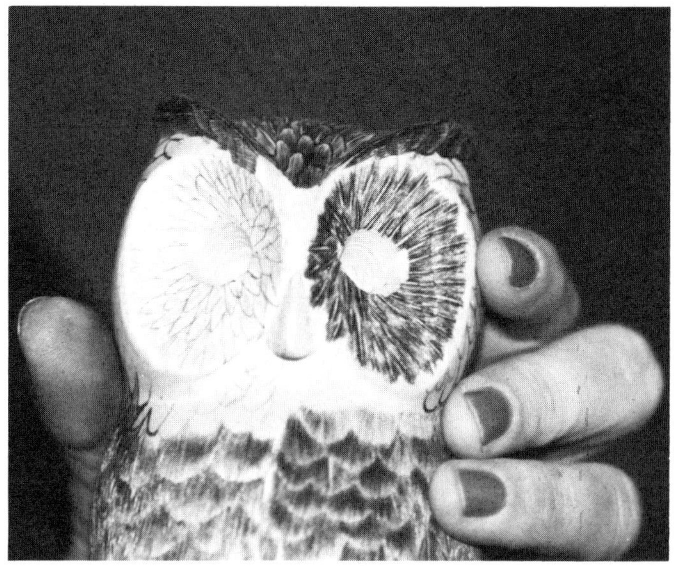

Facial plate feathers burned

Front view of head showing texturing direction on facial discs

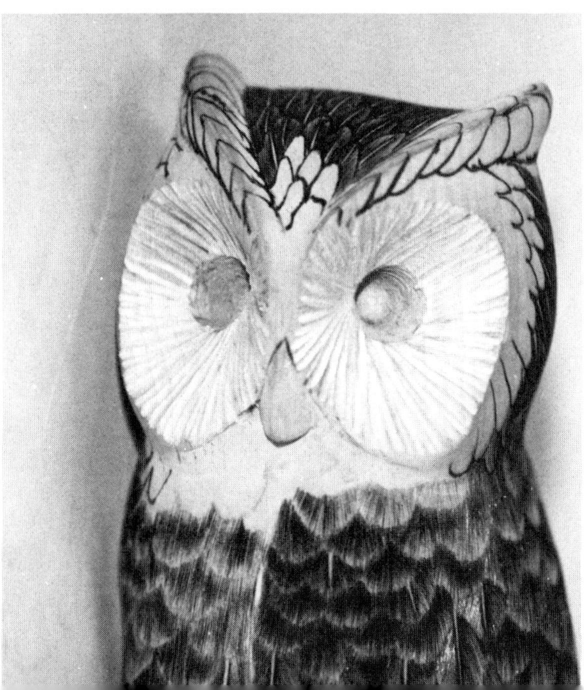

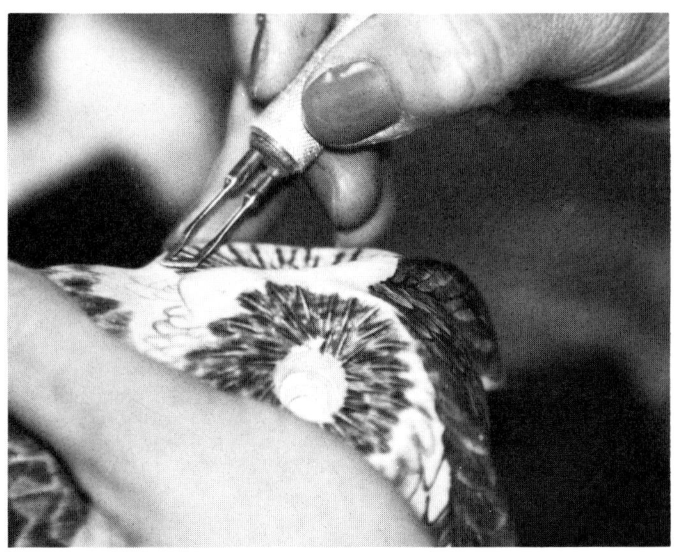

Note: burning techniques of burning face plates

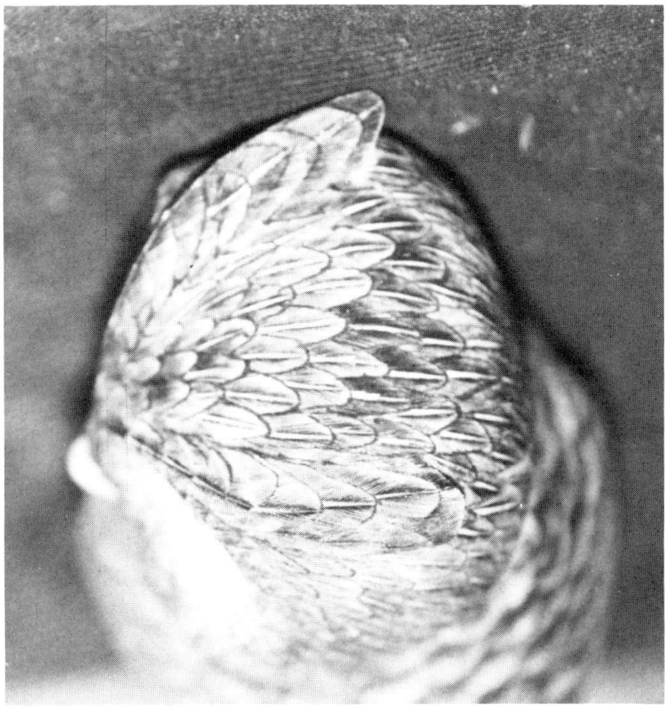

Top of head burned (study lay out and burning techniques)

Side and back of head

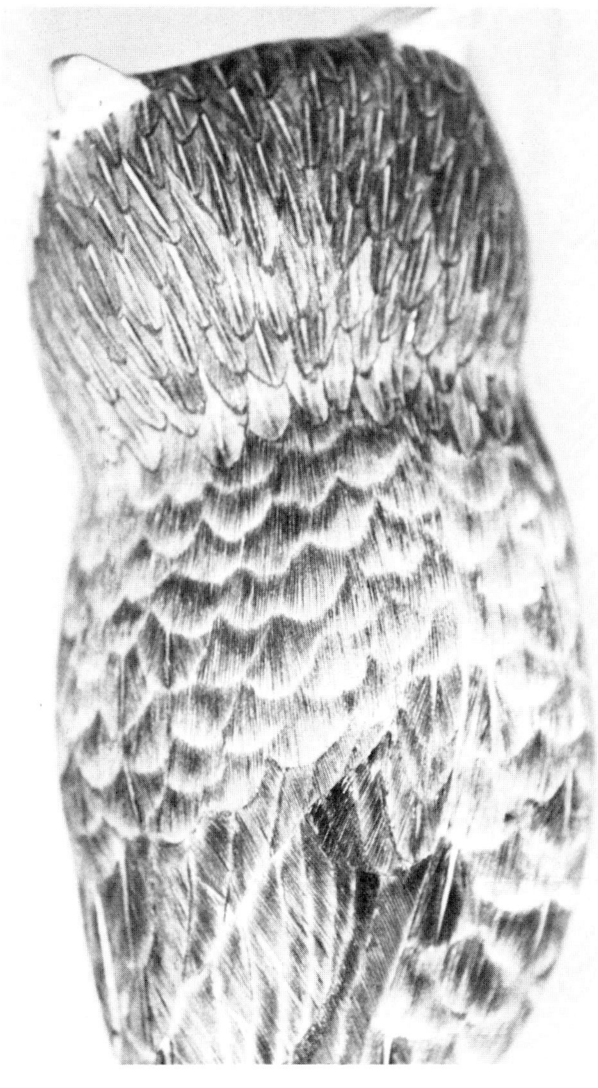

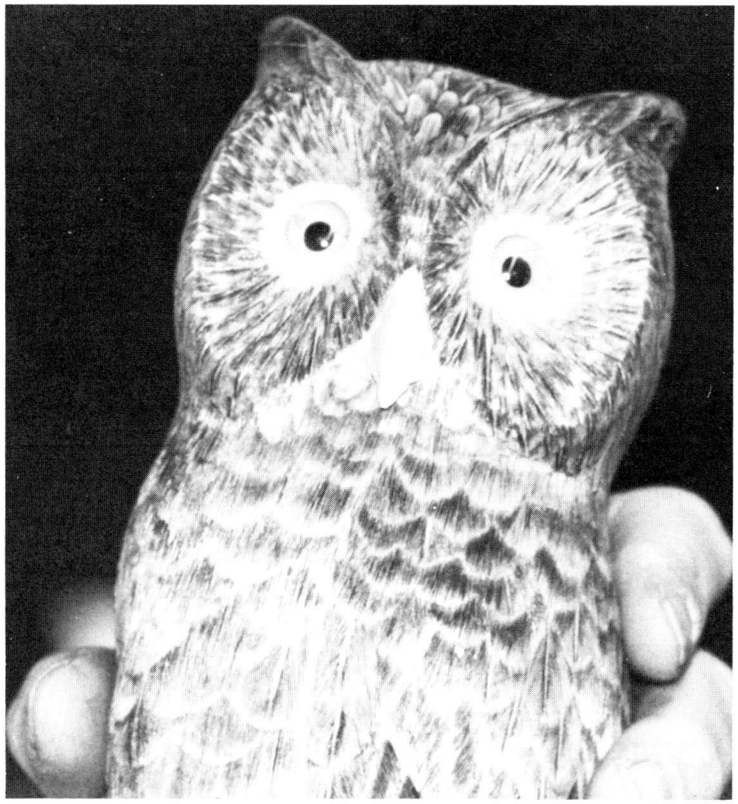

Front view of face with eyes set using epoxy putty to shape eyelids

Close up of eye set

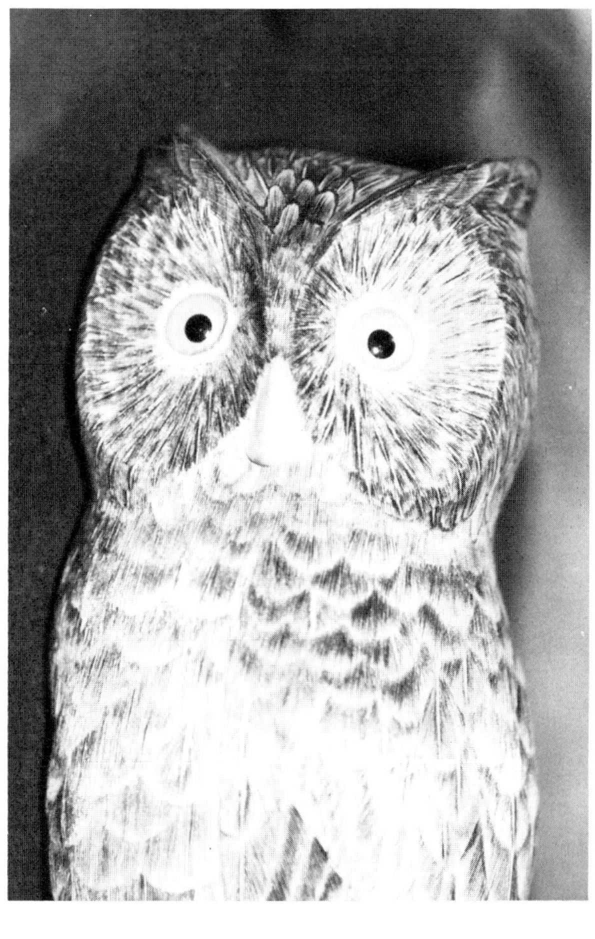

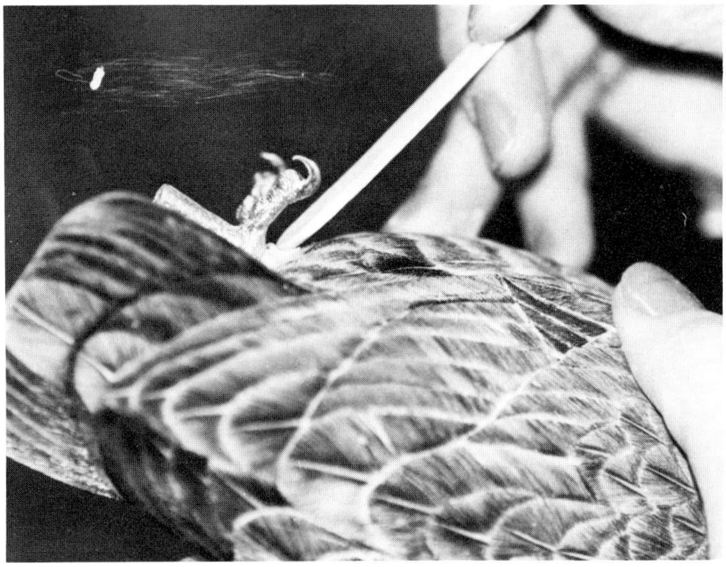

Setting cast feet with five-minute epoxy and epoxy putty to shape at body

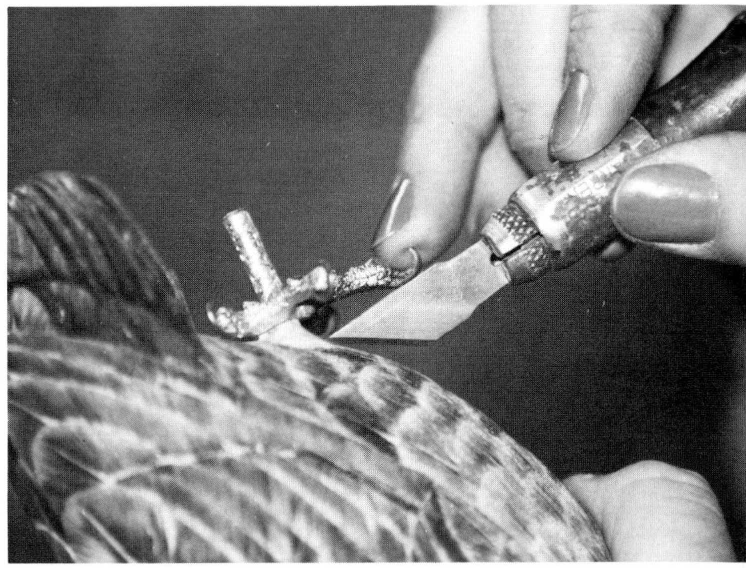

Texturing putty with knife

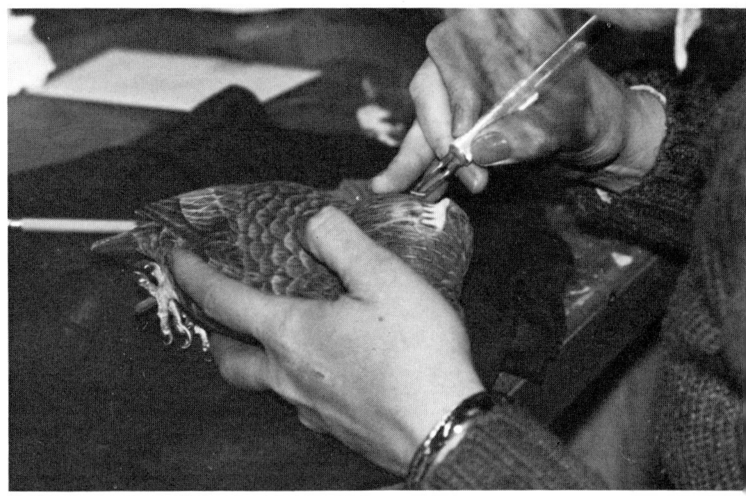

Touch up burning

Undercoating—preparation to painting

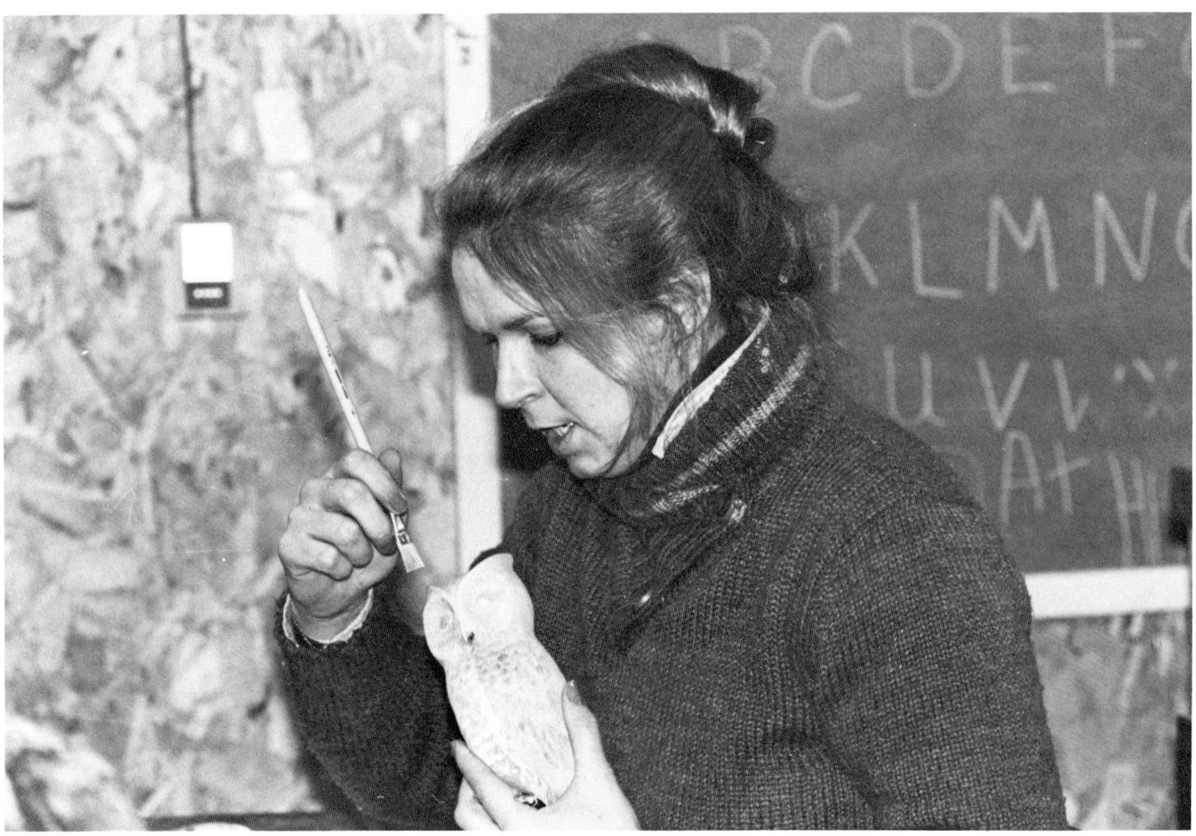

Red Screech Owl in Flight

Carved by Debra Norvell

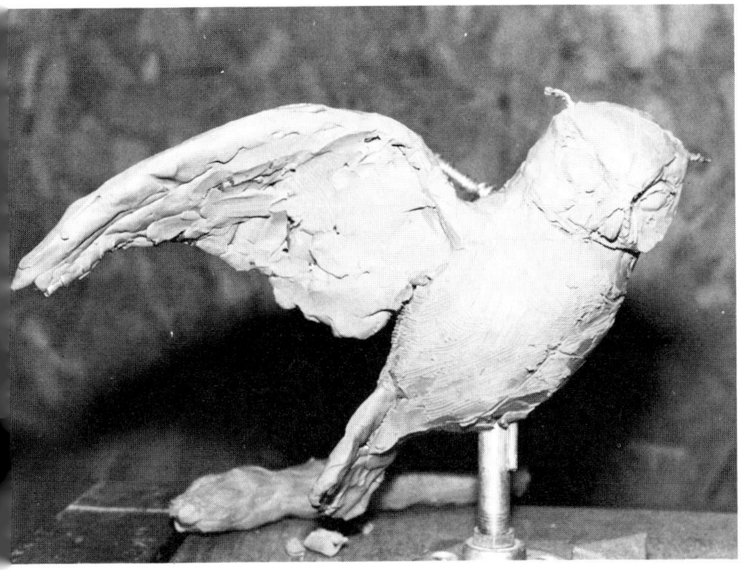

Front view of head and right wing in clay sculpture as model for carving

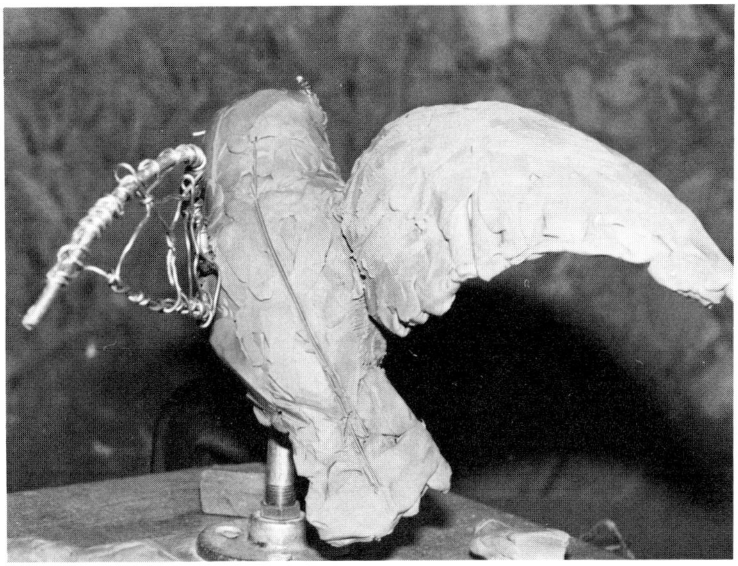

Back view of clay sculpture showing left wing armature

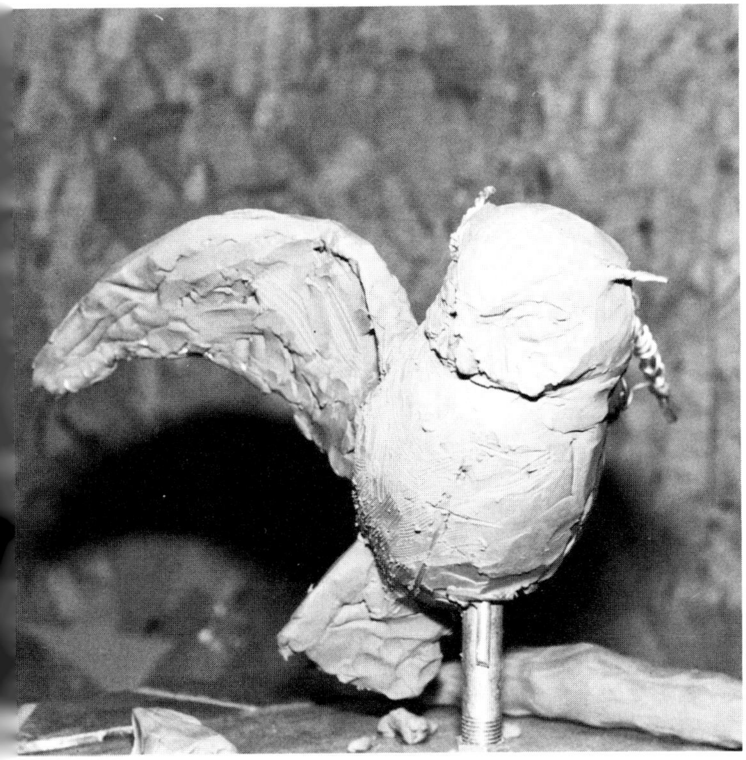

Another view of above

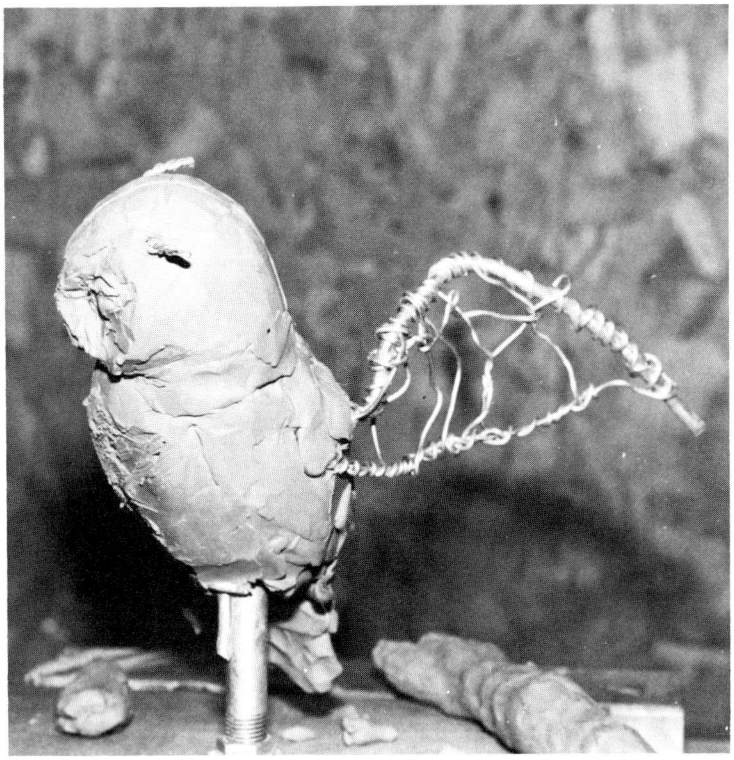

Under side of left wing armature and profile of head

(See page 145 for painting instructions and page 267 for patterns)

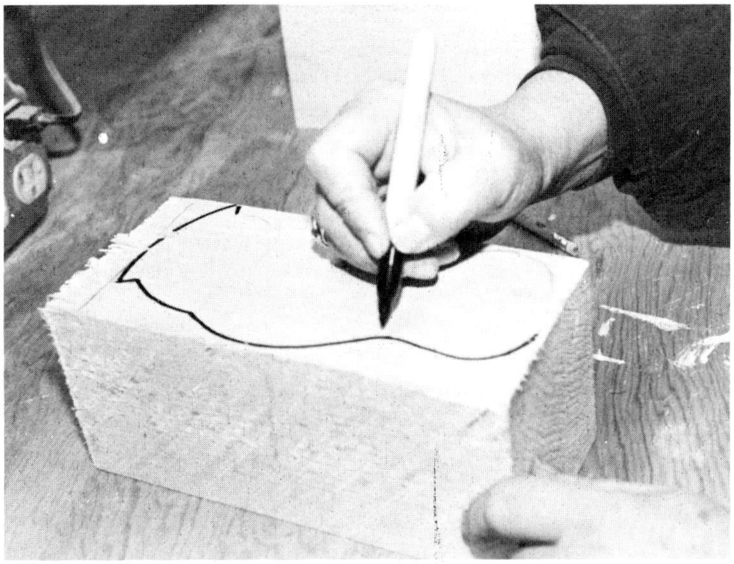

Tracing pattern onto wood preparatory to band sawing

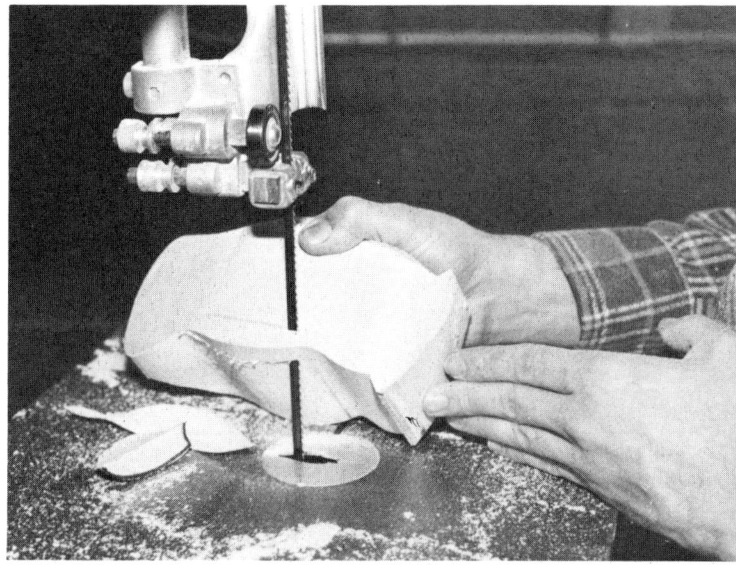

Trimming excess wood from rough cut on 45°

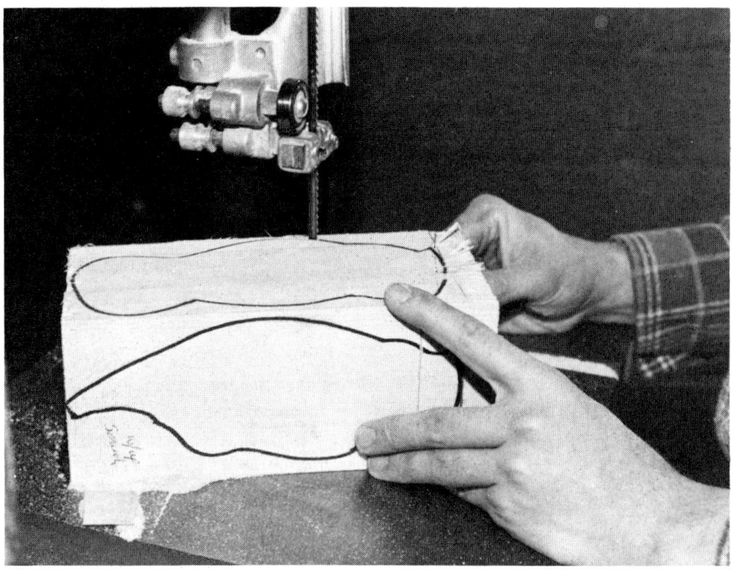

Band sawing plan view

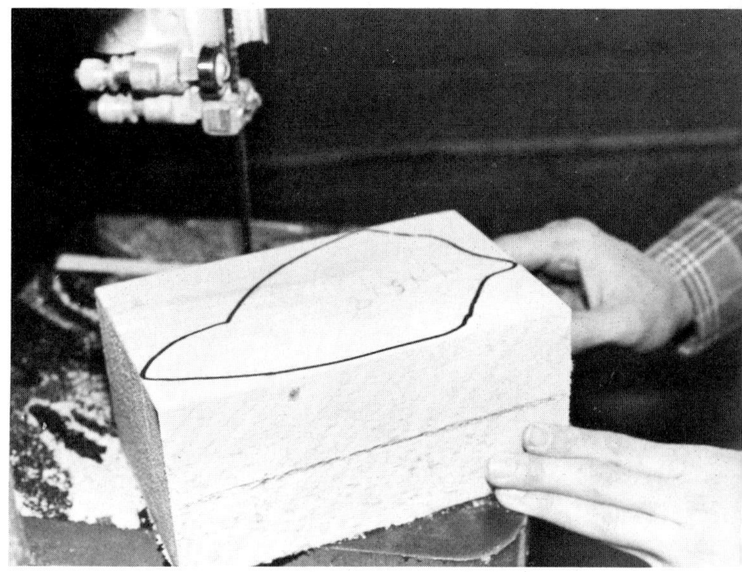

Band sawing plan view of wings

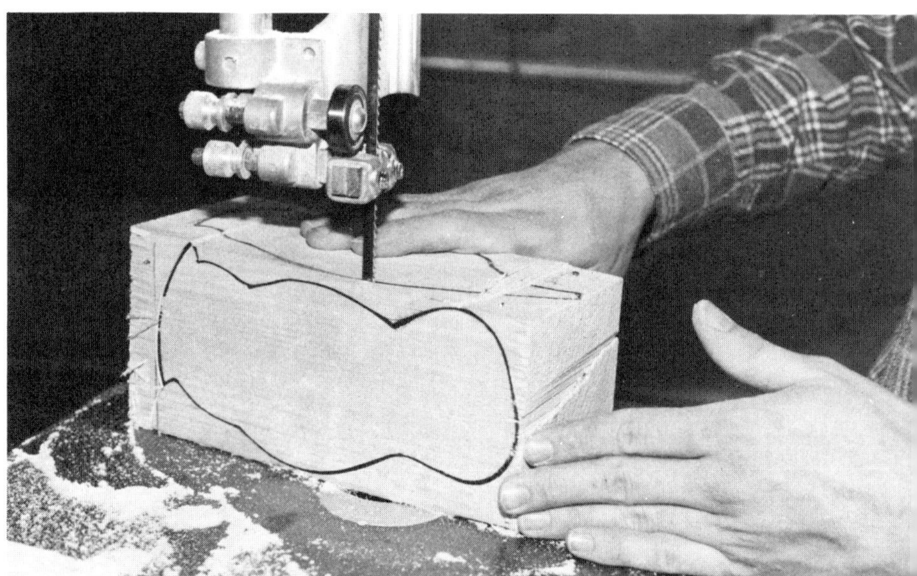

Band sawing profile

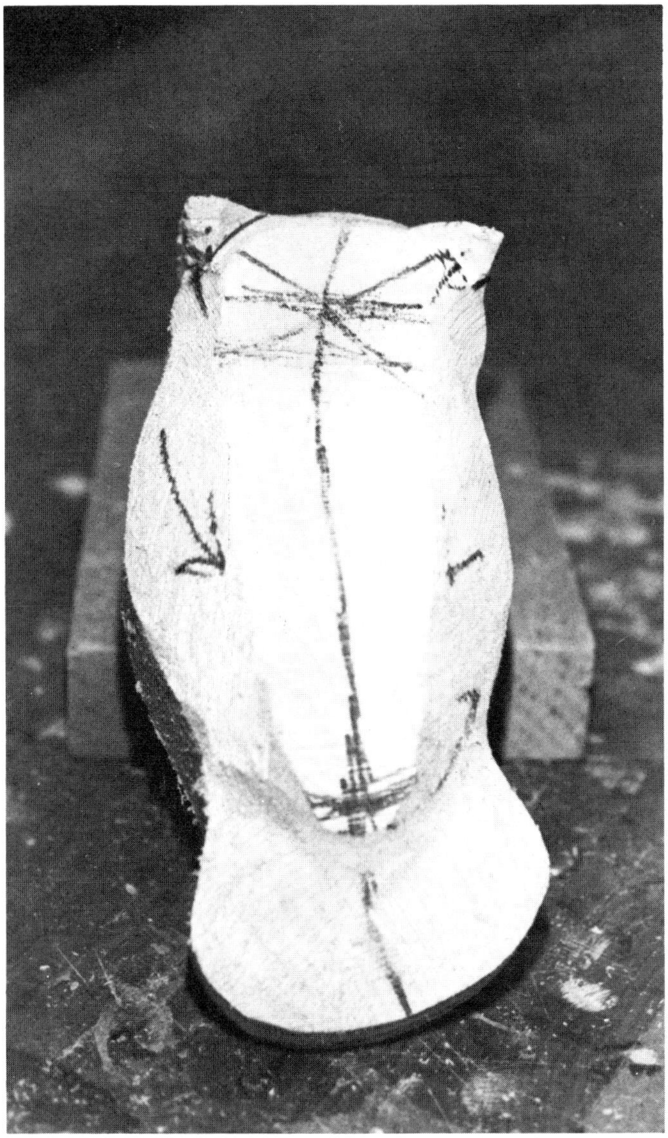

View of roughed out belly—note: guide lines and arc of body

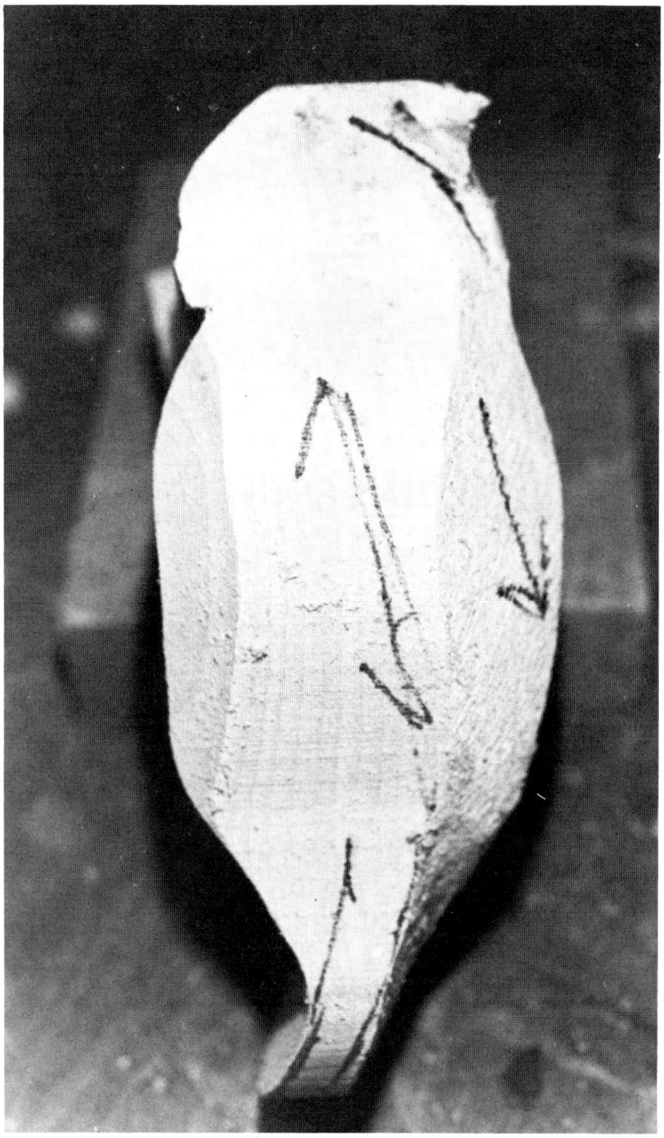

Guide marks on profile of rough out

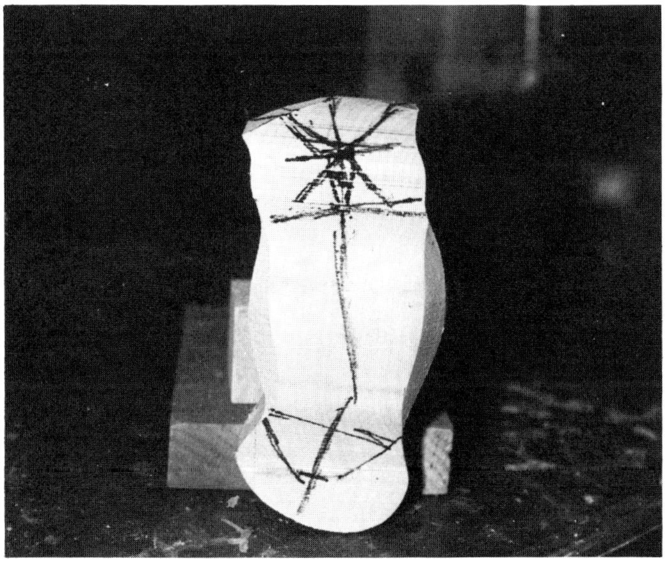

Guide marks on back of bird

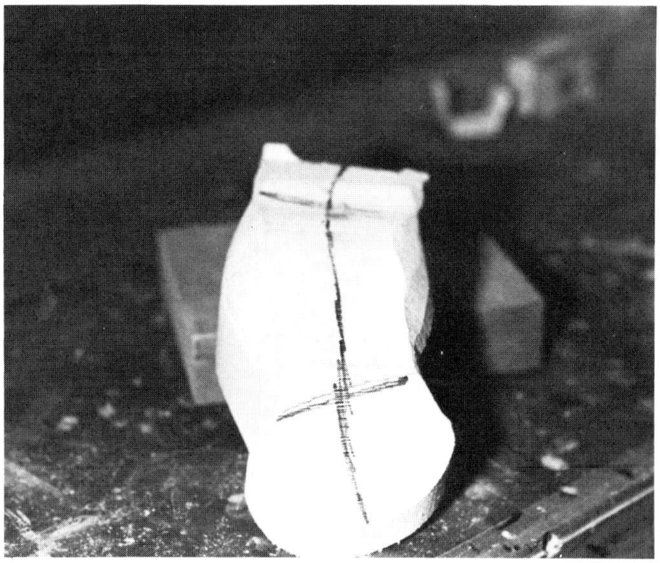

Guide marks on belly

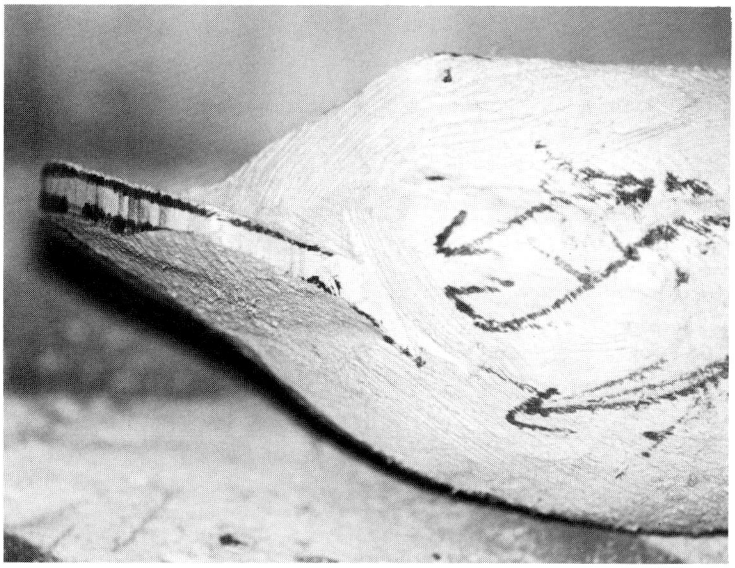

Note: tail thickness at this point on carving and direction of cut for rasp

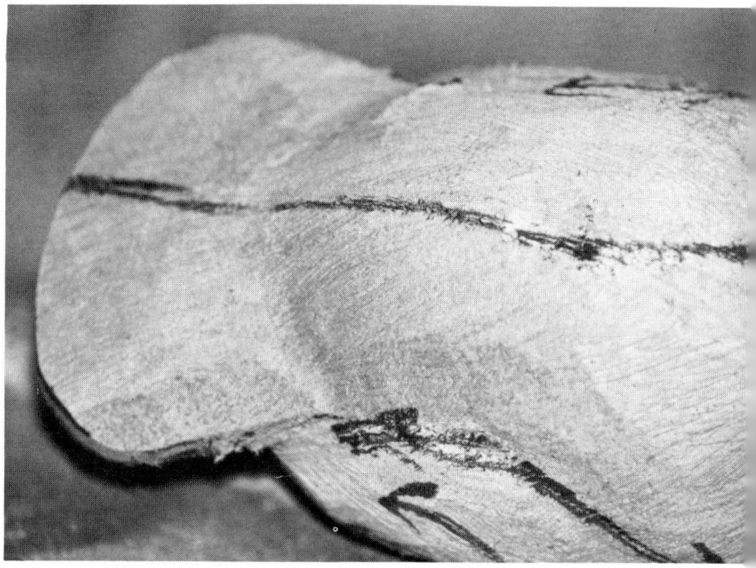

Upperside of tail

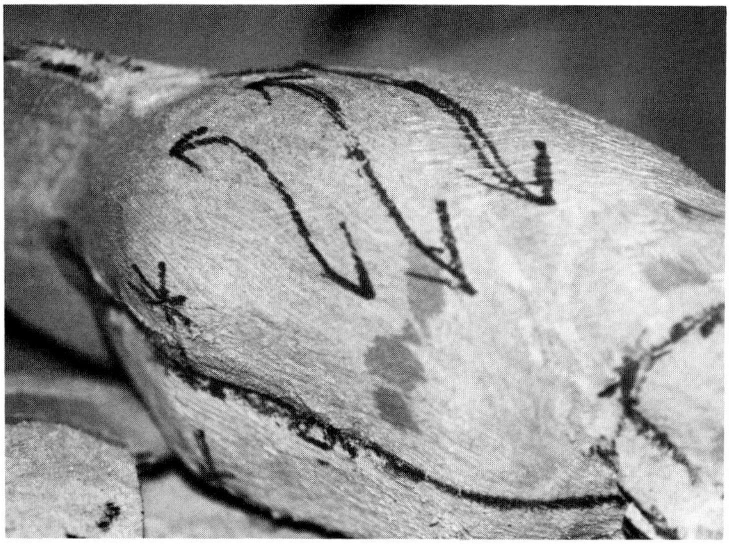

Flow line on side of carving

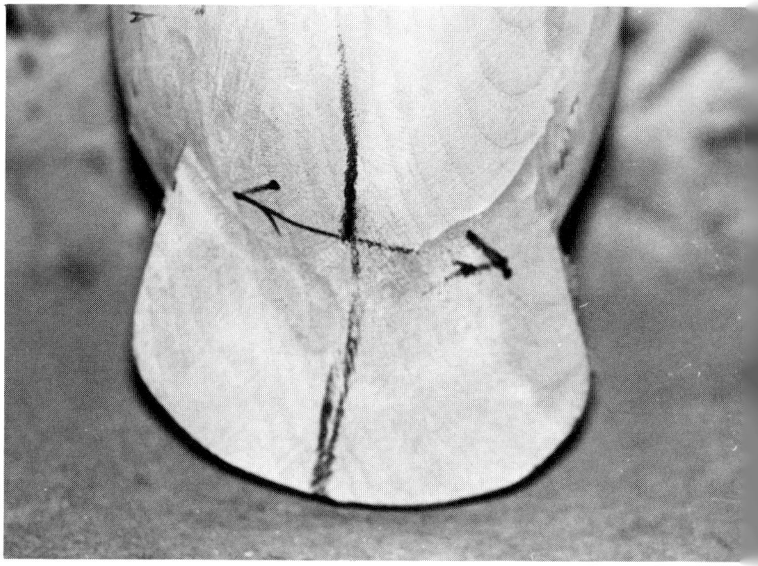

Upperside of tail refining rump

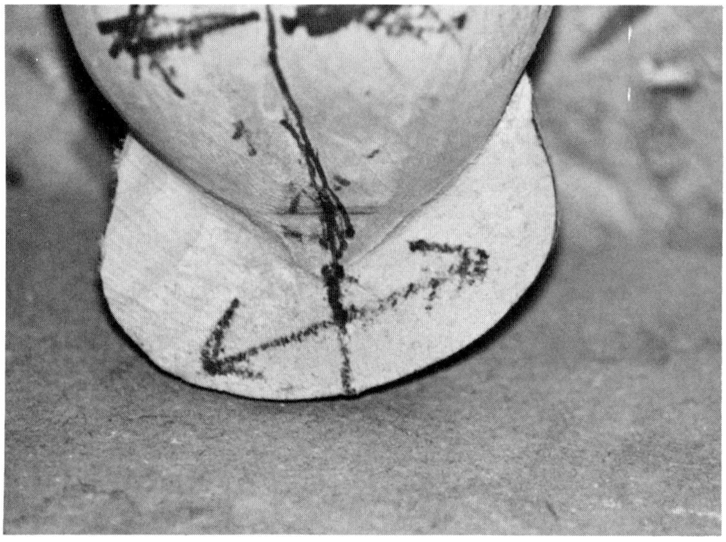

Underside of tail

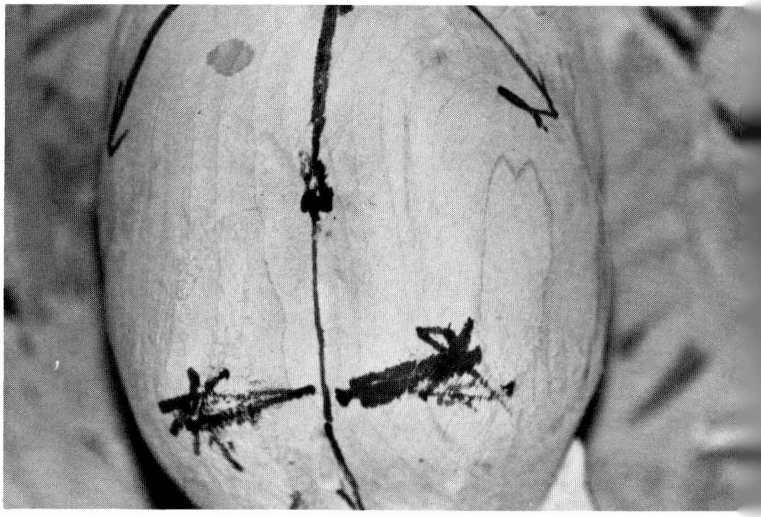

Leg placement

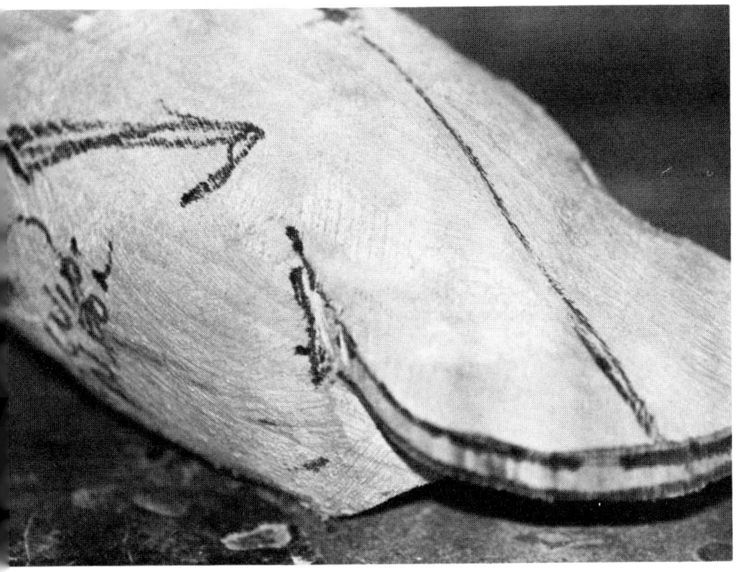

Carve sides flowing toward center line and then to tail

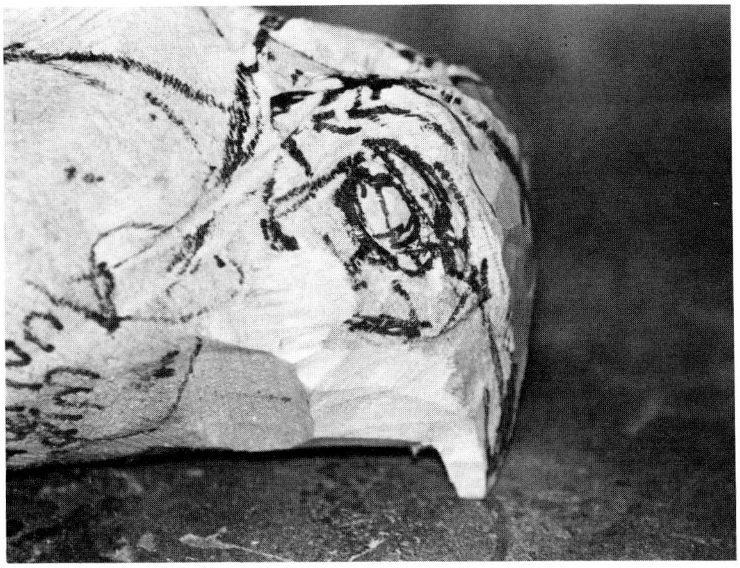

Facial disc lay out—note: direction of cut

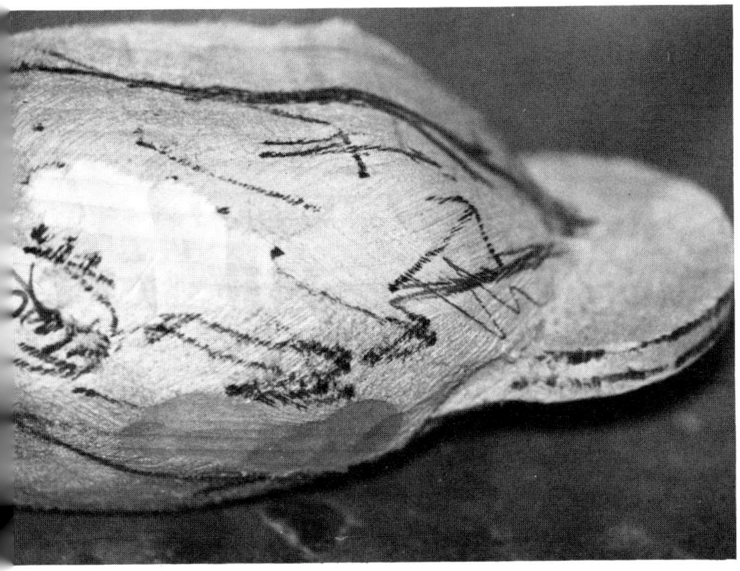

Begin shaping around leg area

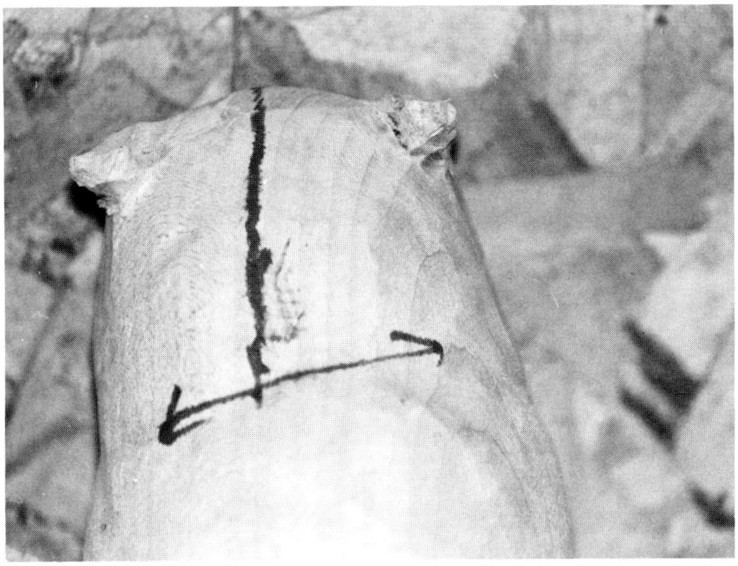

Shaping neck area behind neck

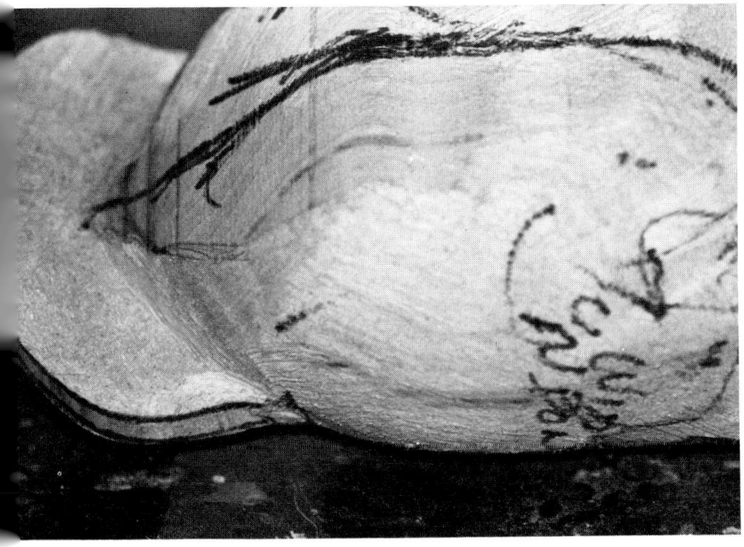

Work out flat area of under rump

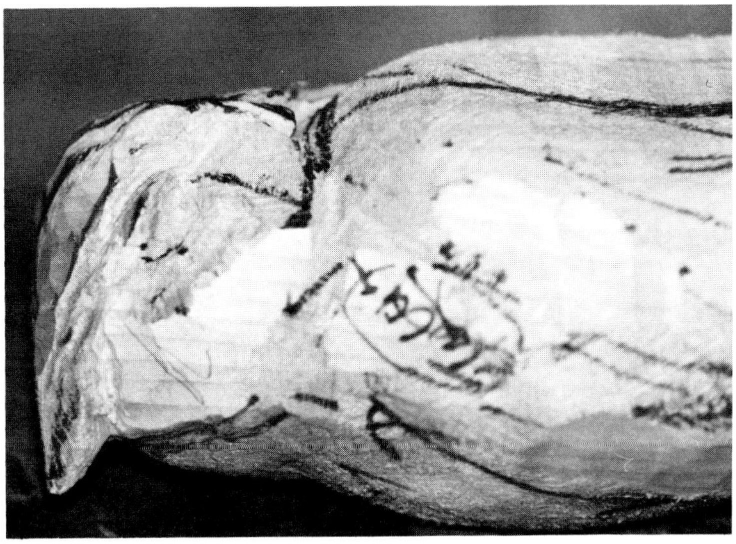

Side view flowing into neck

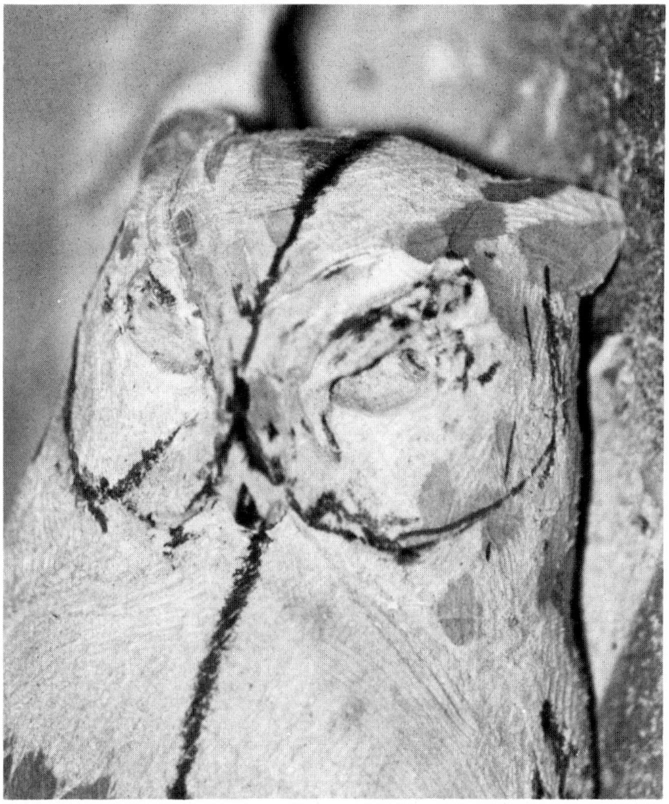

Basic facial carving

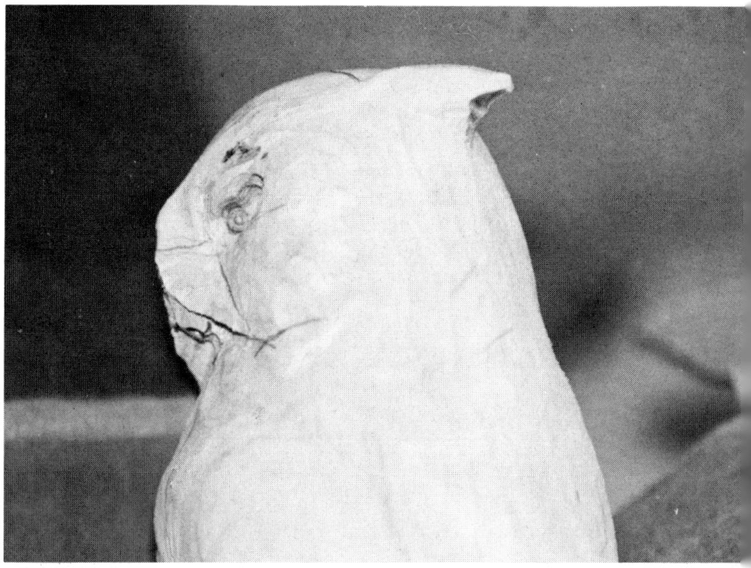

Profile of face—note: beak area

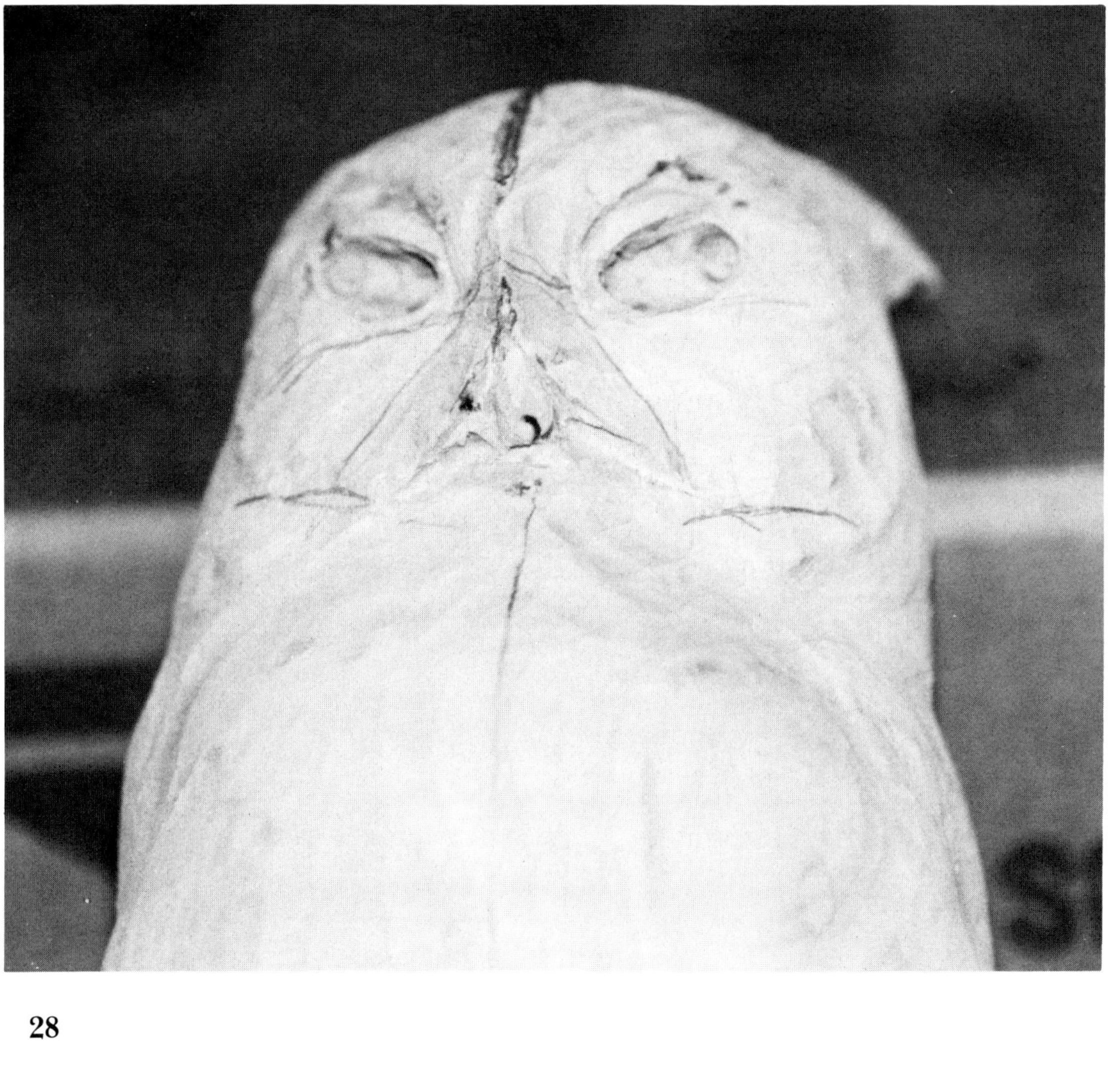

Eyes drilled more
detail of facial discs

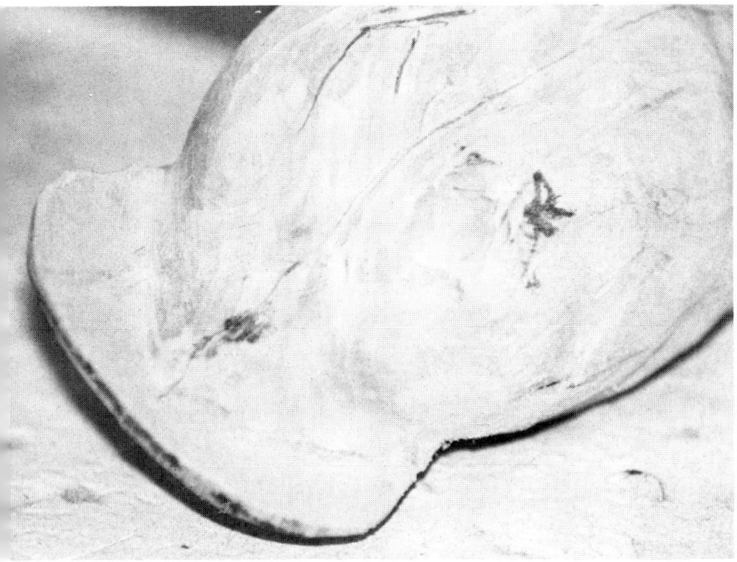

Detail of feather groups on belly

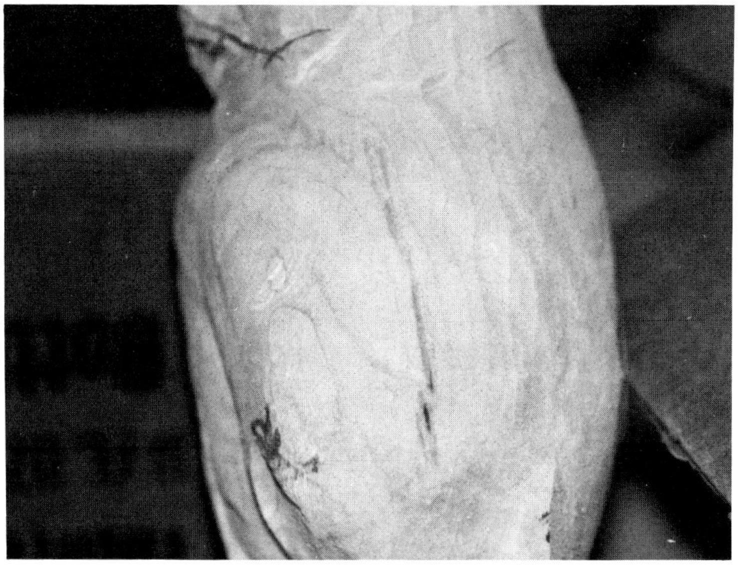

Shoulder area

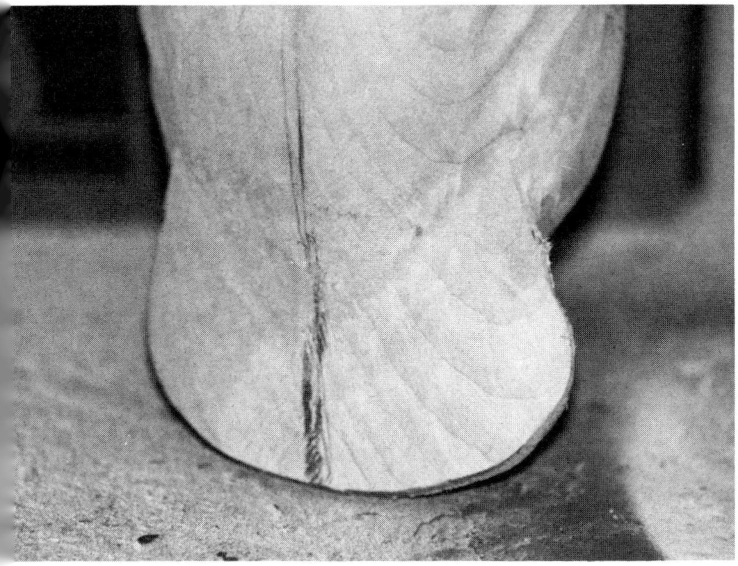

Upper tail shaped

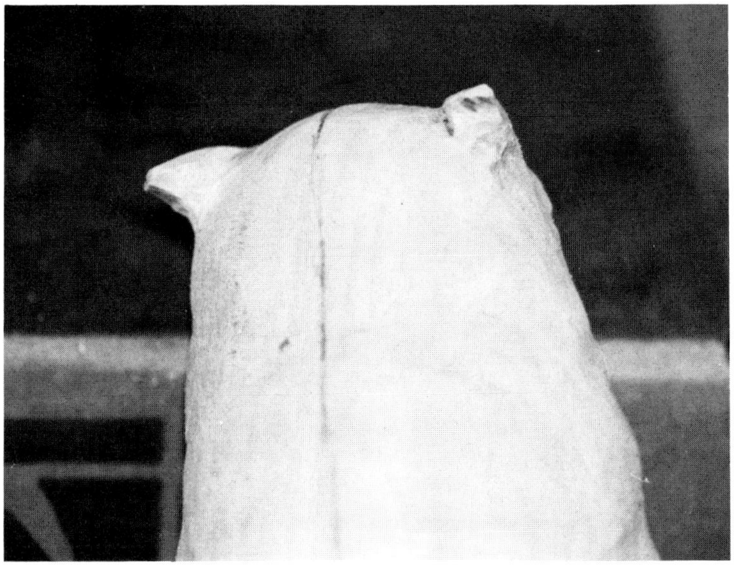

Back of head view

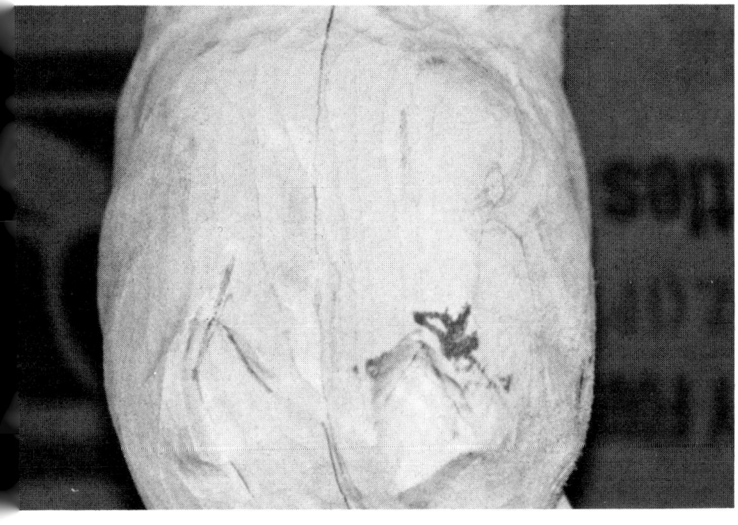

Belly and leg areas defined—note: legs are off set slightly to create a sense of motion

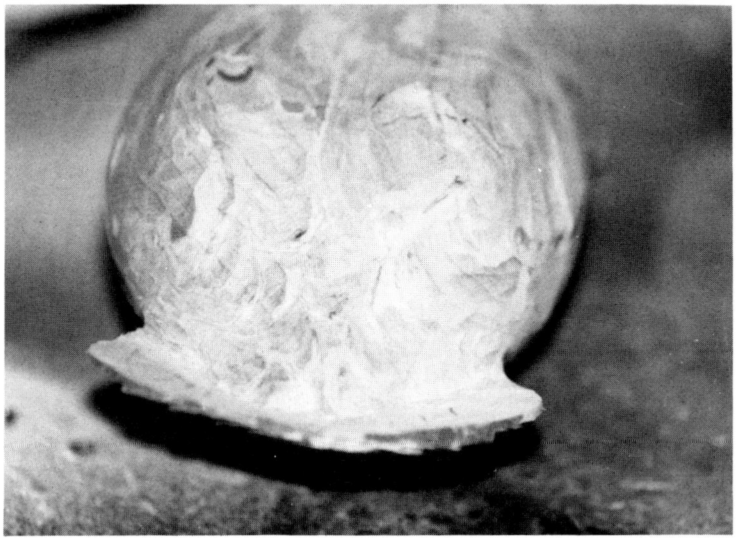

End view of tail

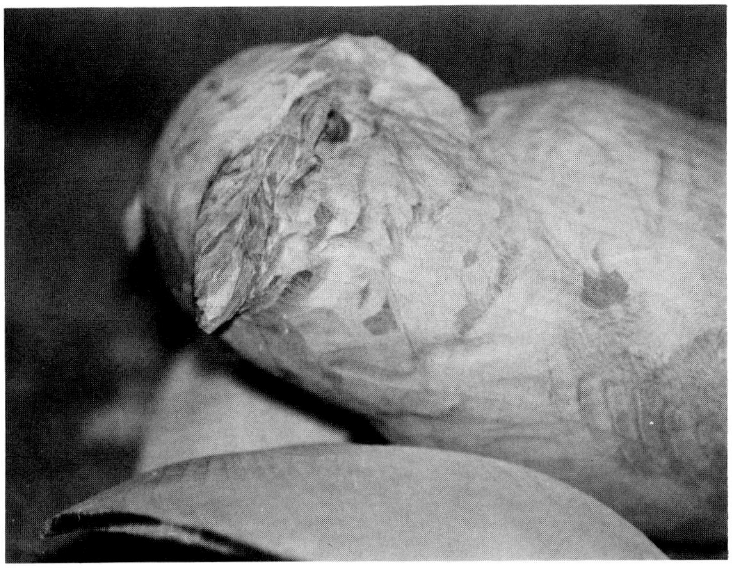

Right side of head detail

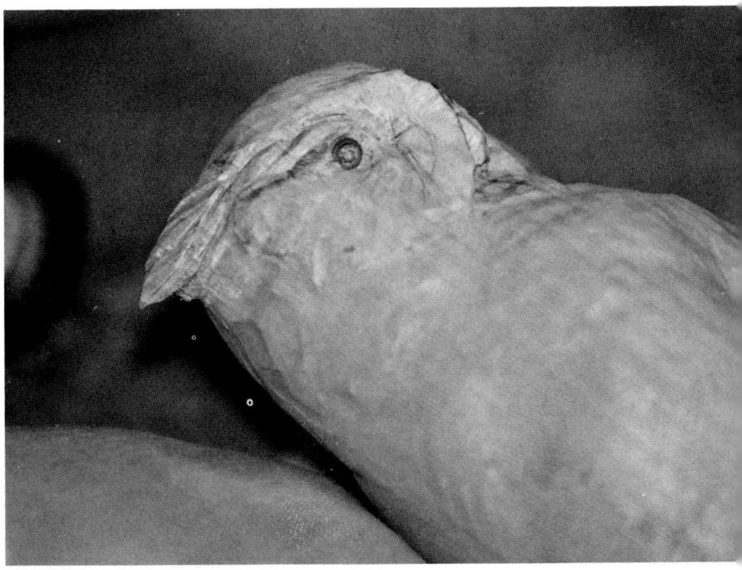

Right side of head detail and chest area

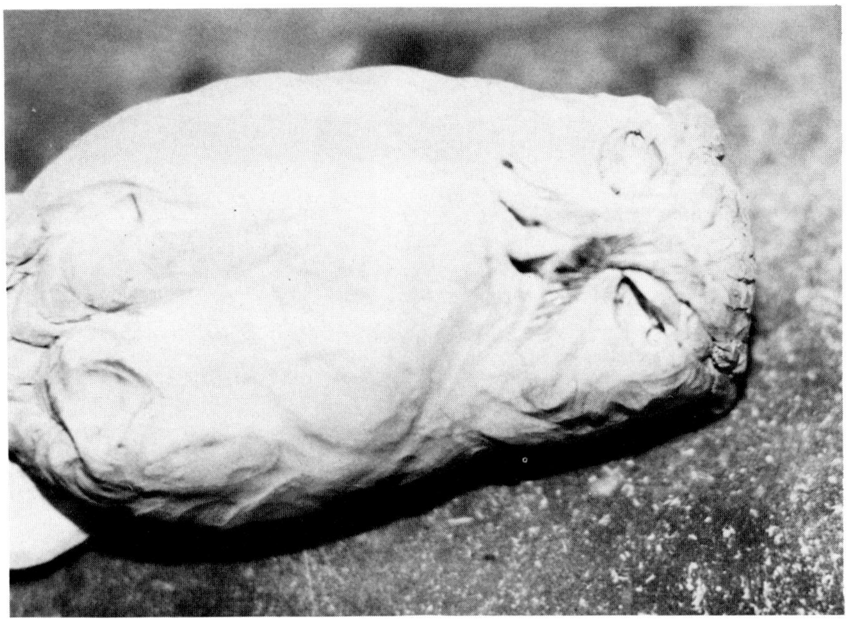

Full front detail

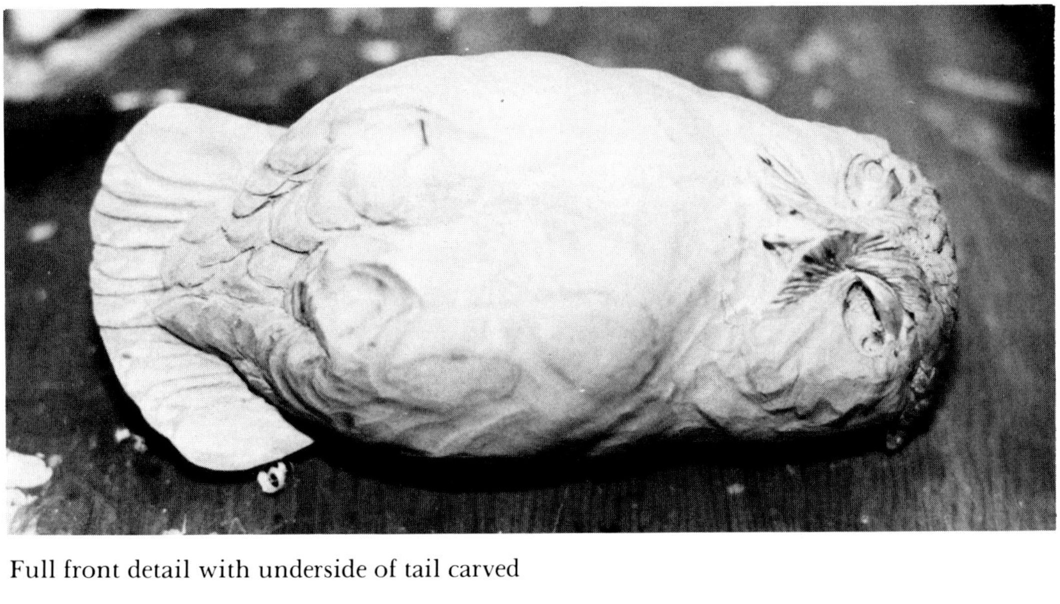

Full front detail with underside of tail carved

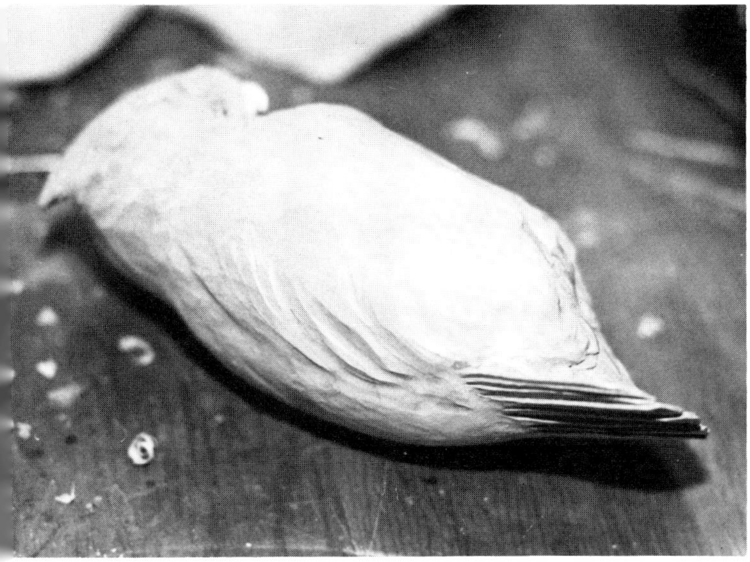

Indentations on right side

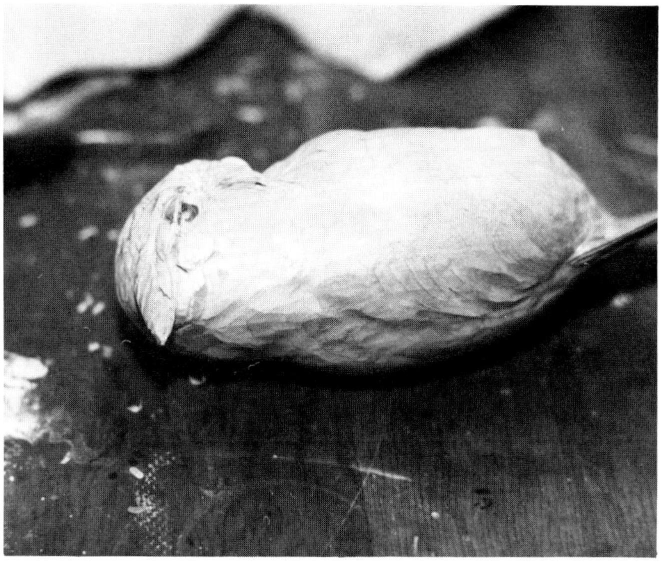

Full right side profile

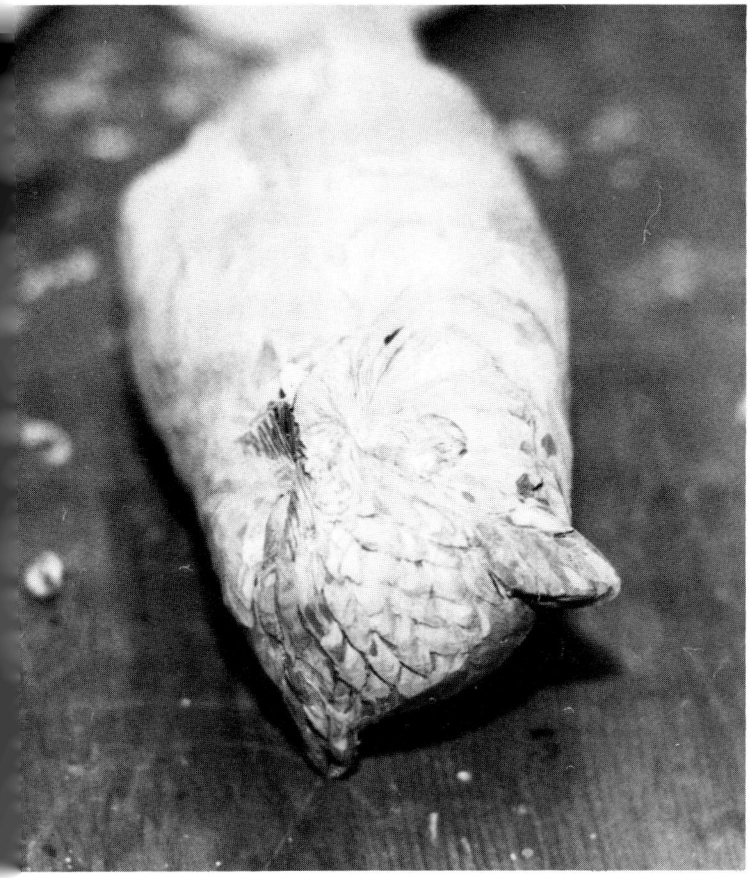

Top of head detail with feather lay out

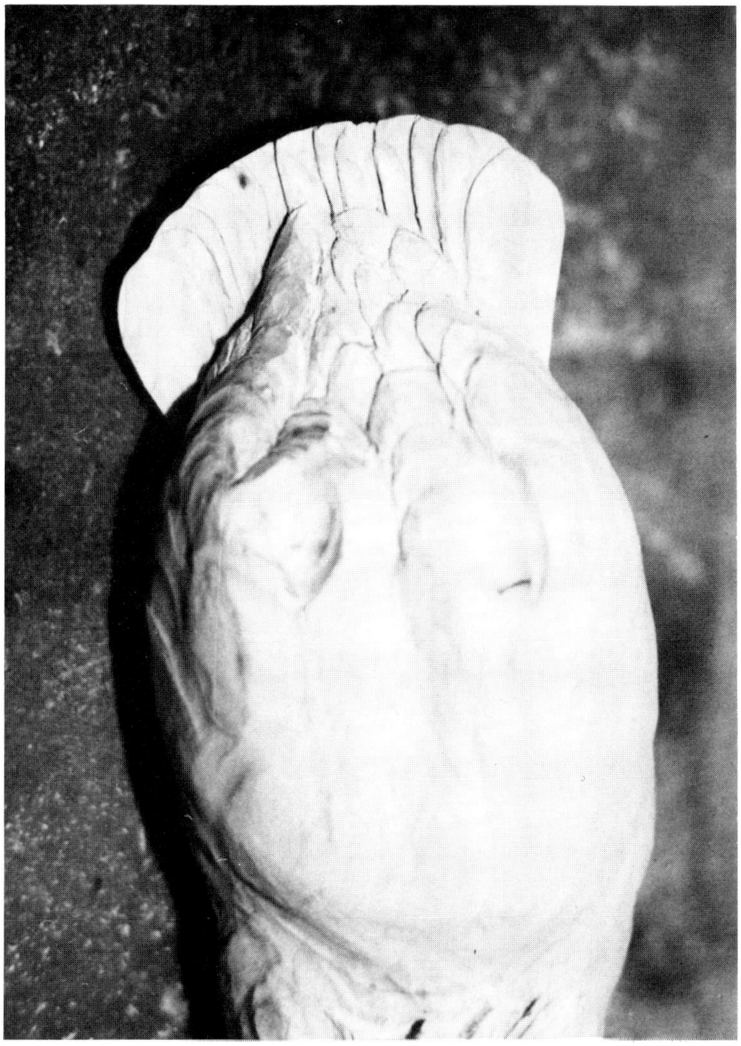

Underside of tail and rump carved—note: rump carving detail

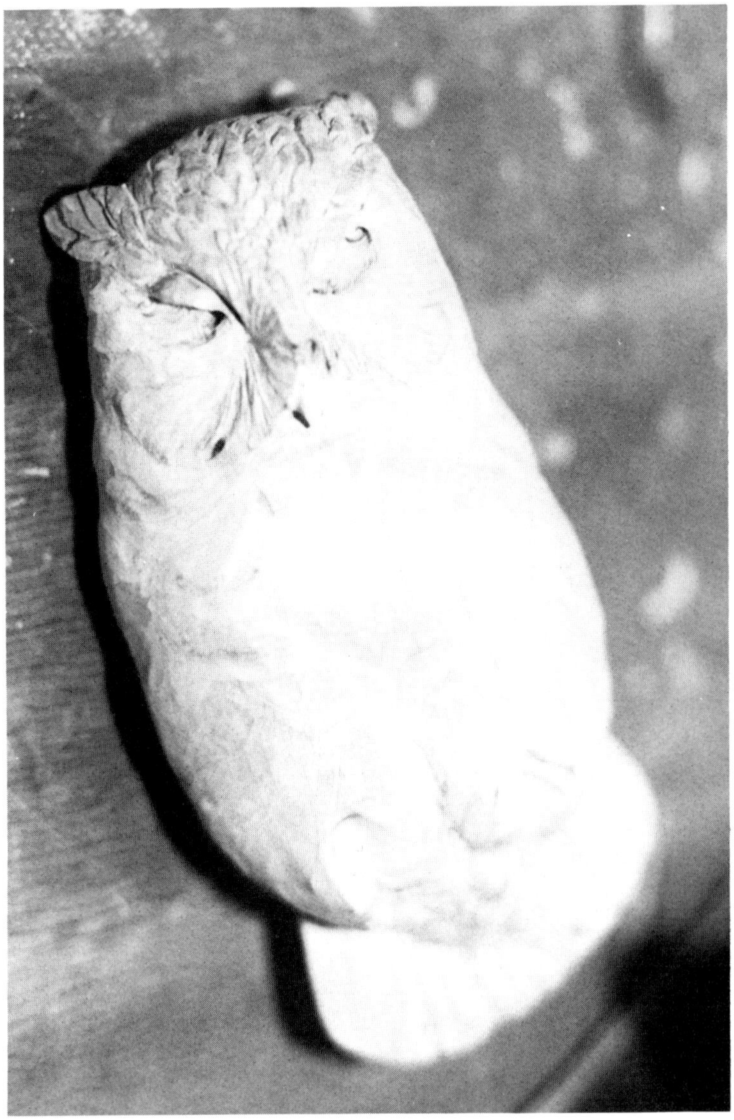

Belly and head detail—note: head detail

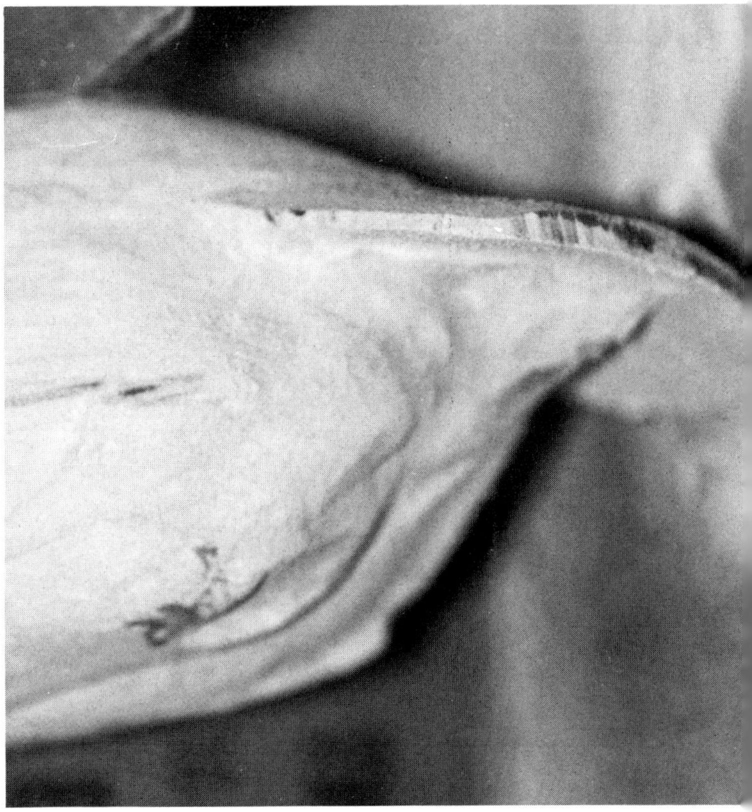

Rump and tail detail

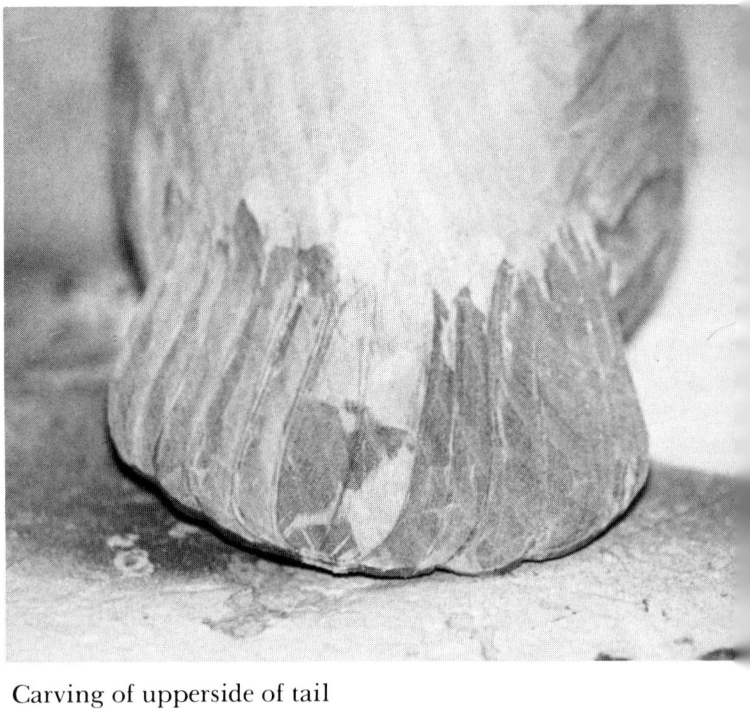

Carving of upperside of tail

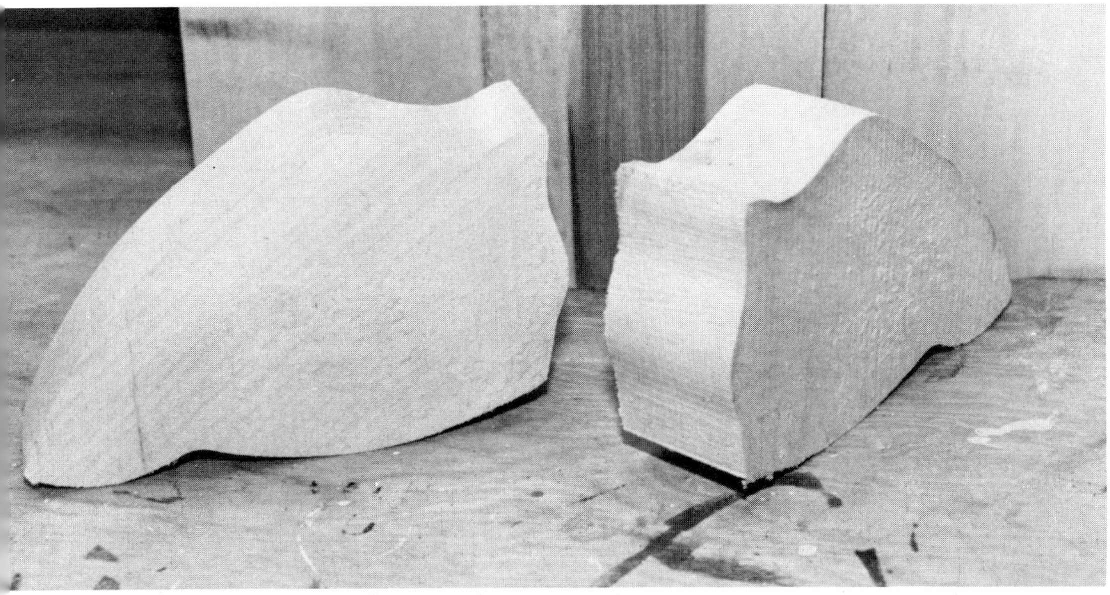

Wing rough outs ready to carve

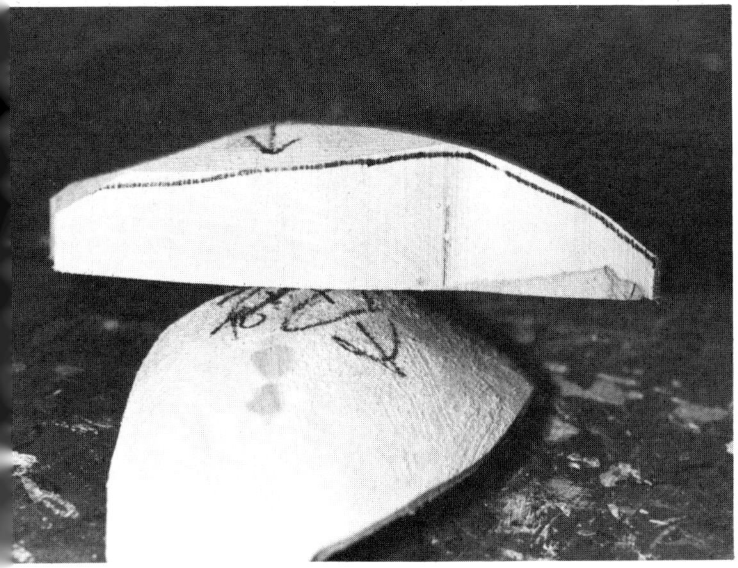

Top side of wing shaped—note: arc line

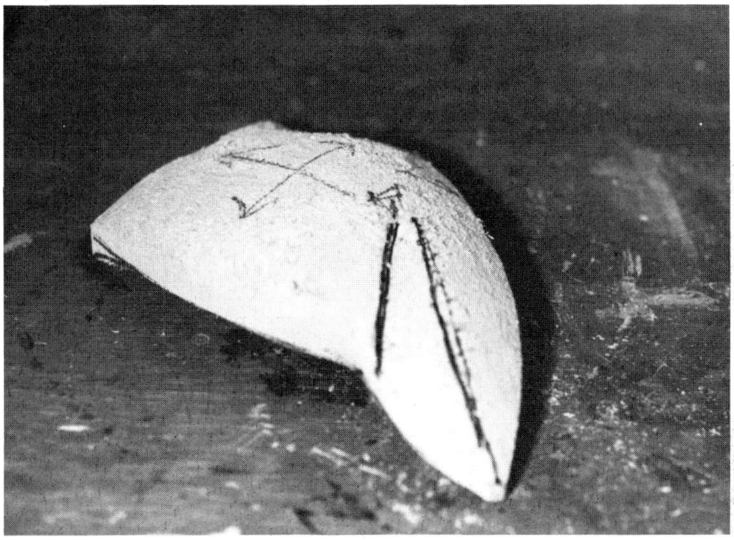

View of primary feather area—note: Pencil lines in direction of roll

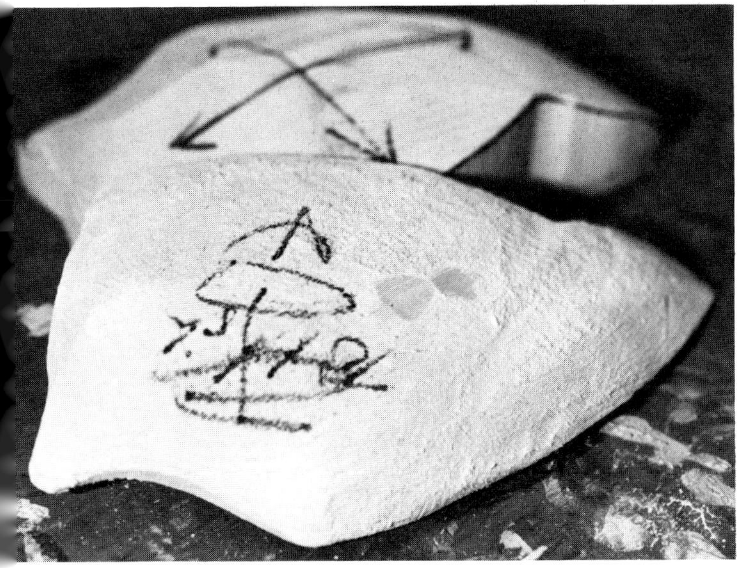

Wings shaped—note: arcing in both directions

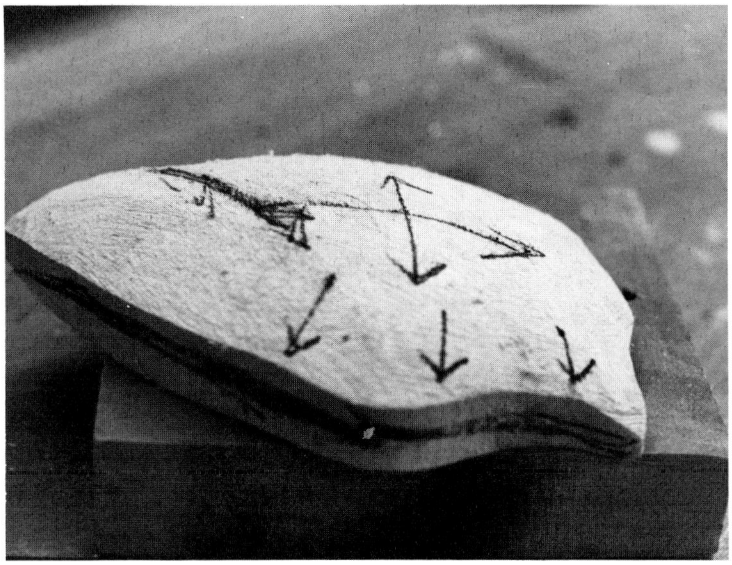

Top of wing showing direction of roll

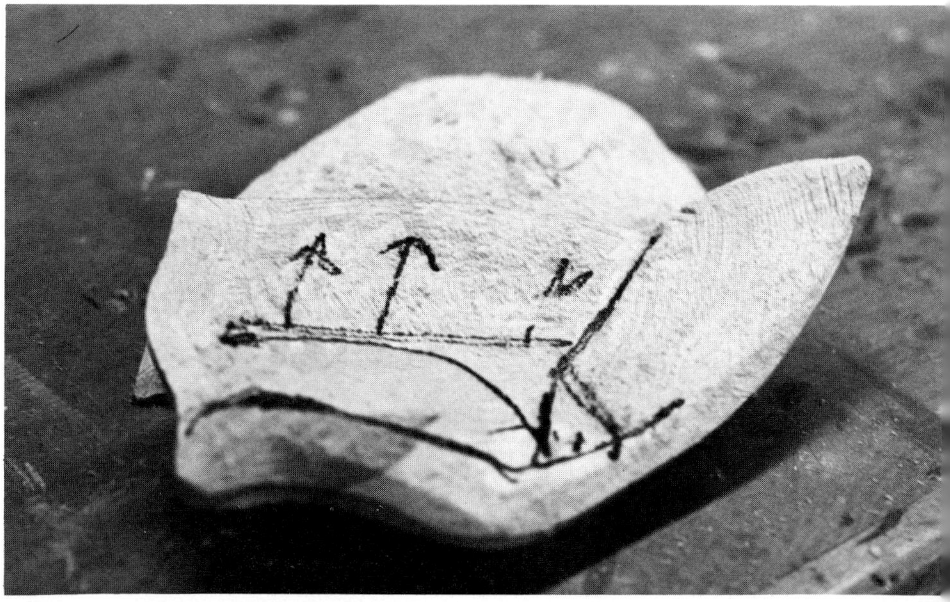

Underside of wing to be hollowed

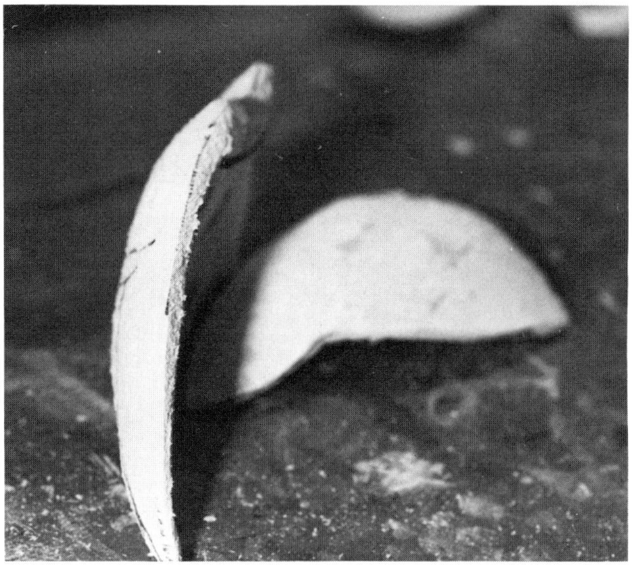

End view showing arc of wing

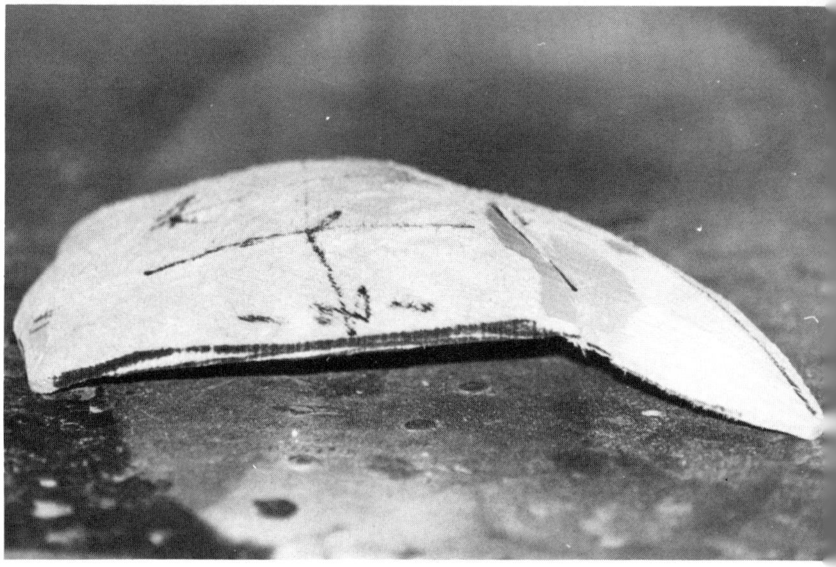

End view showing secondary area

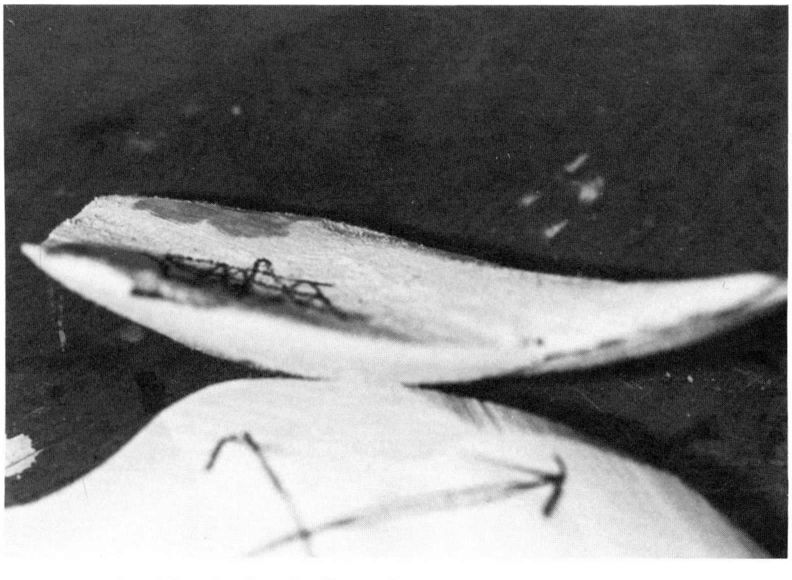

Underside of wing hollowed

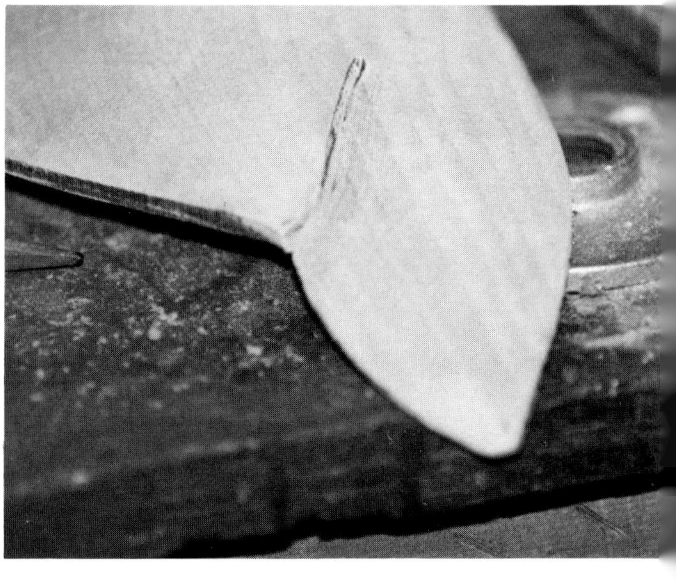

Top of wing sanded and ready for detailing

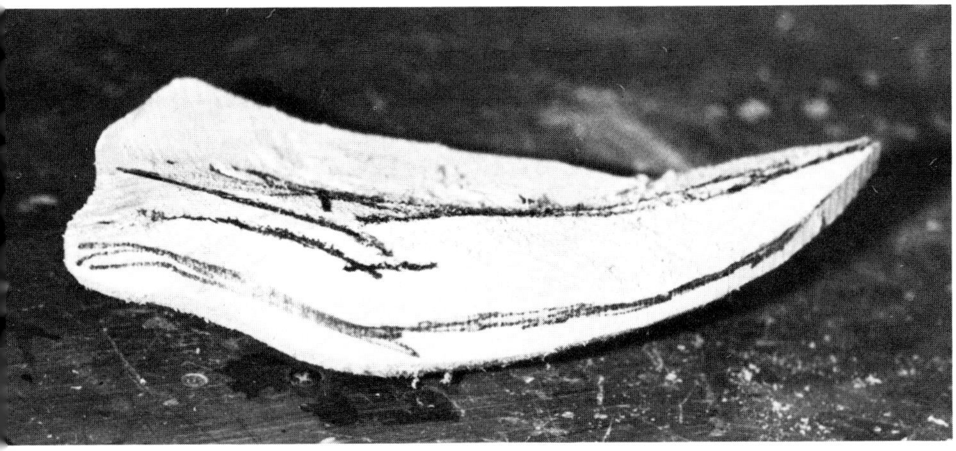
Underside of wing to be refined

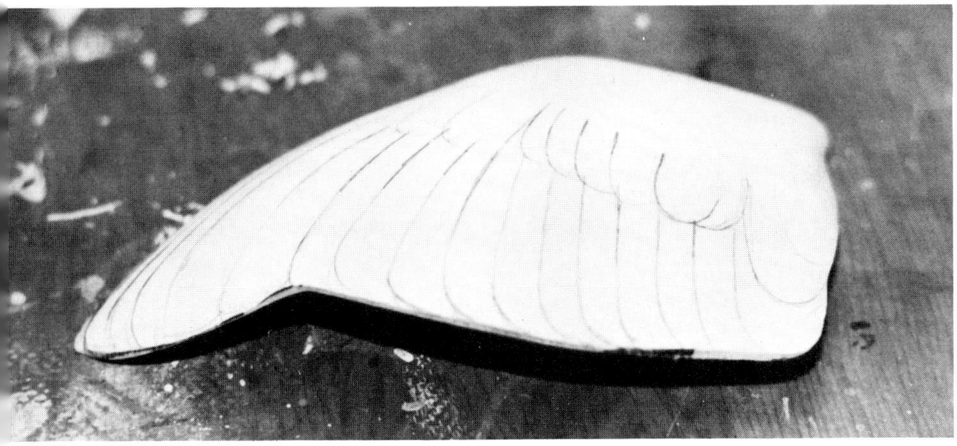
Upperside of wing feather lay out ready to carve

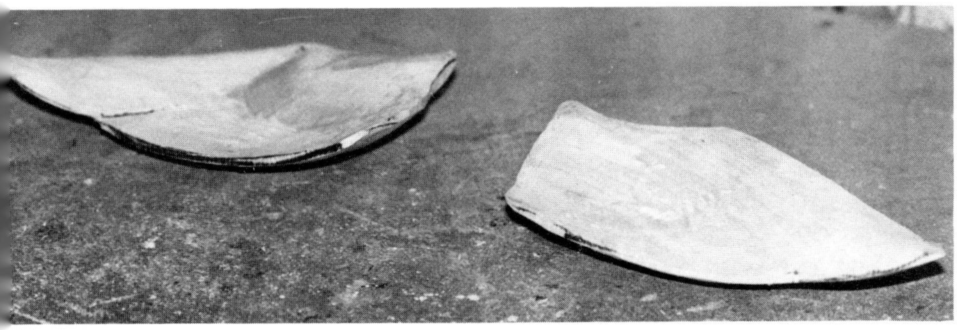
Underside of wing hollowed

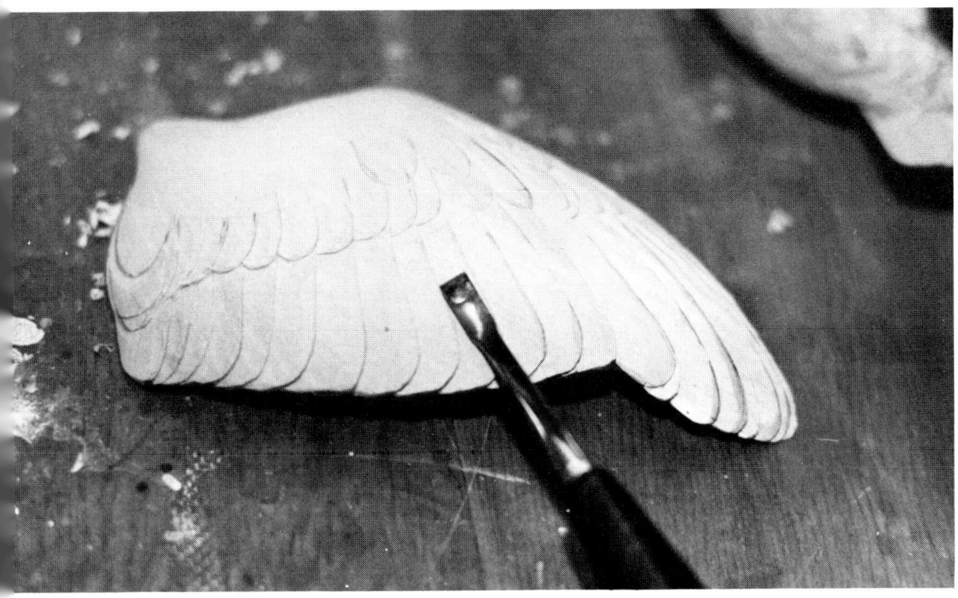
Carving primary and secondary feathers

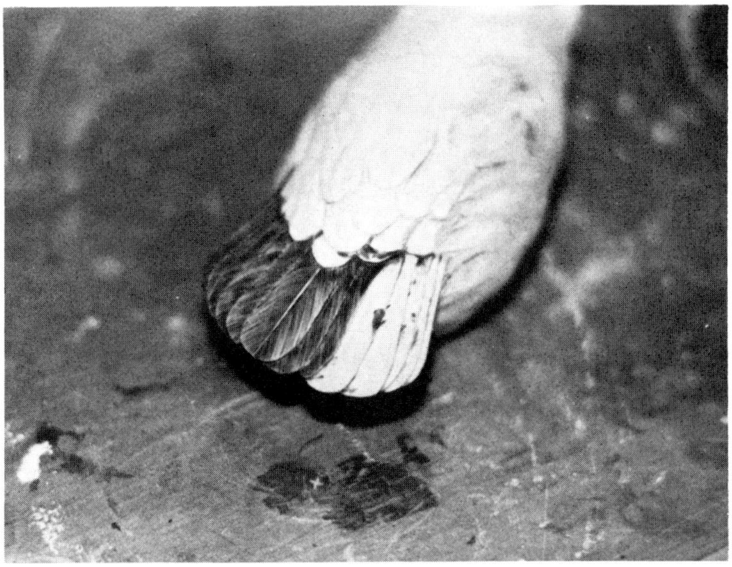

Upper side of tail partially burned

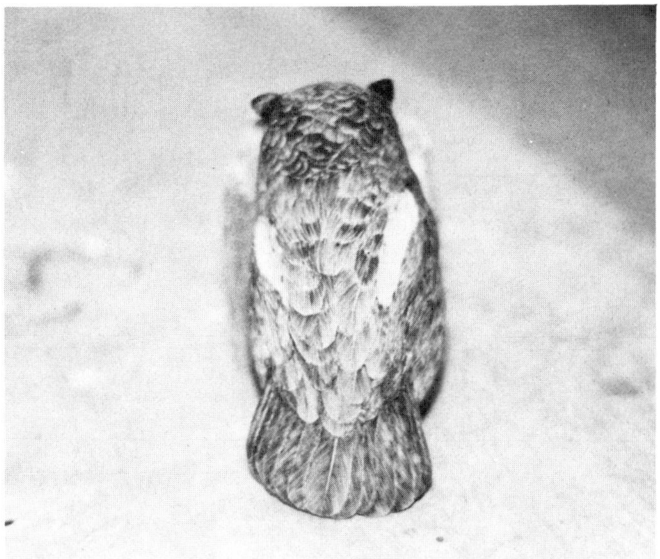

Back and tail completely burned

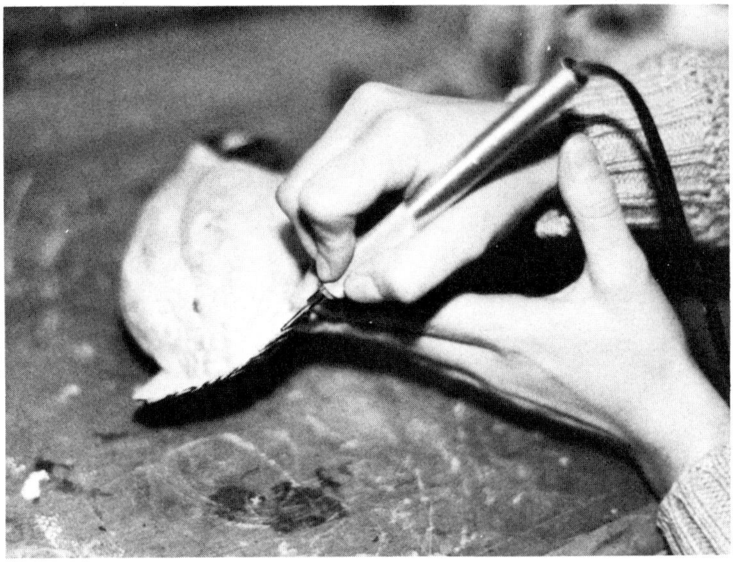

Separating ends of tail feathers with burner

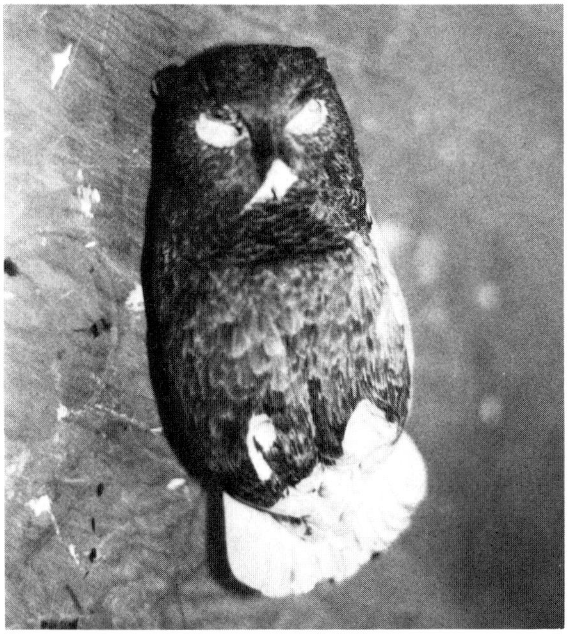

Face, chest, and belly burned, note feather patterns

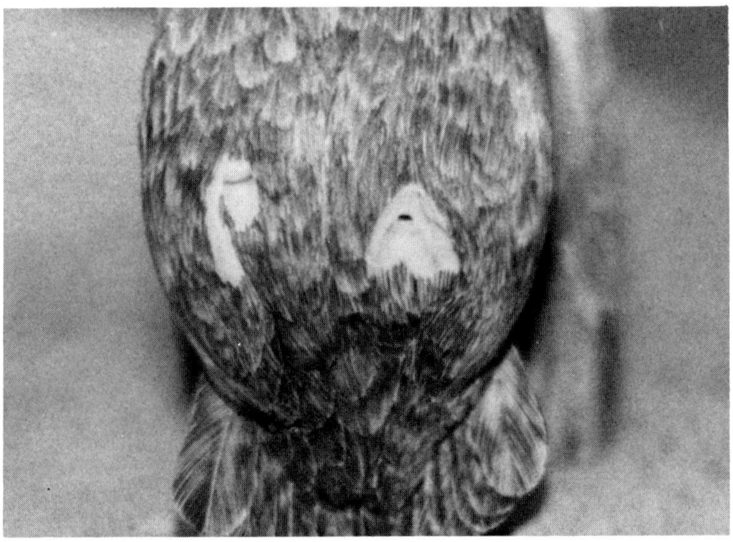

Underside of rump and tail burned

Eyes set: note carved and burned feather patches over eyes

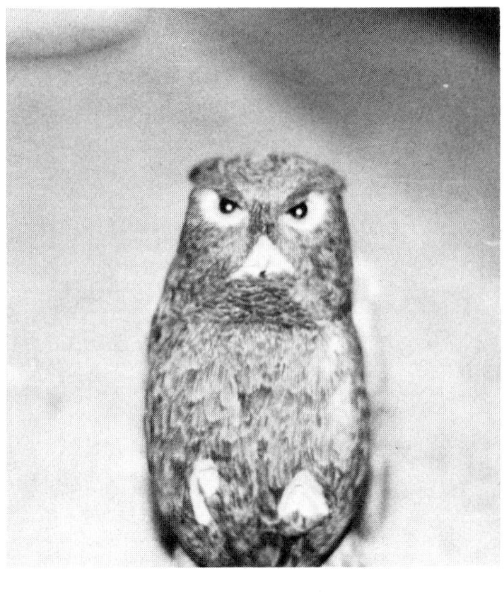

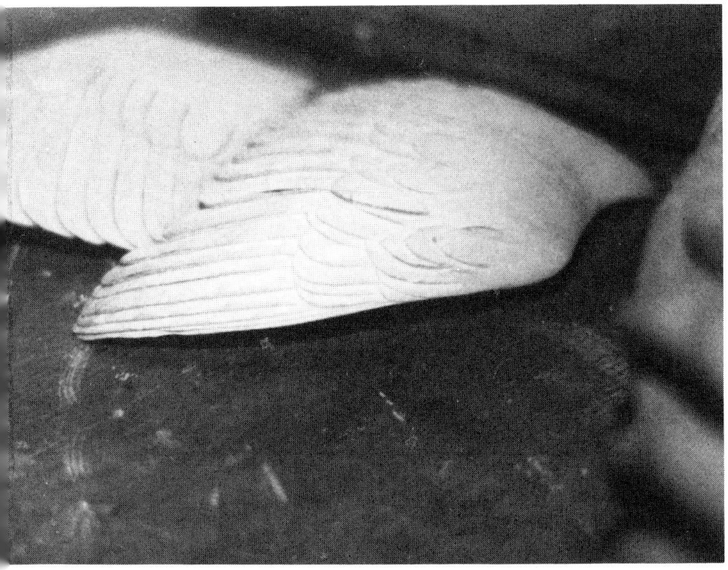

Upper side of wings completely carved

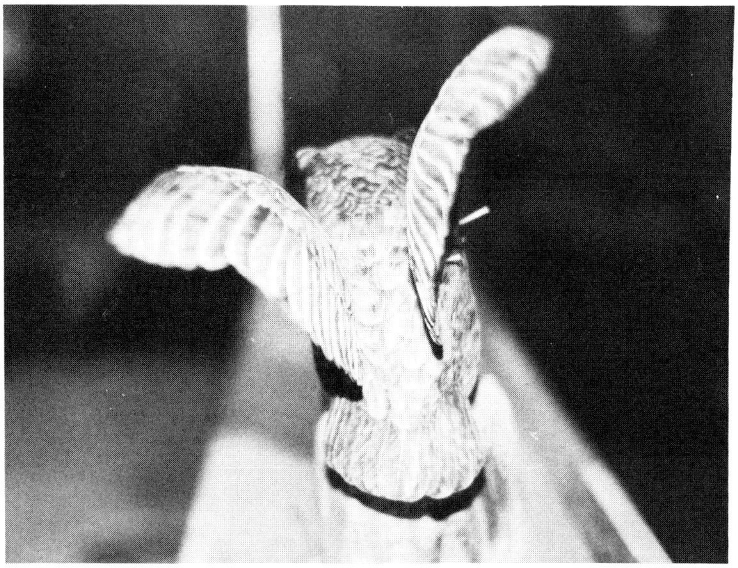

Bird completely burned and temporarily perched with wings set (Note wooden pins holding wings in place)

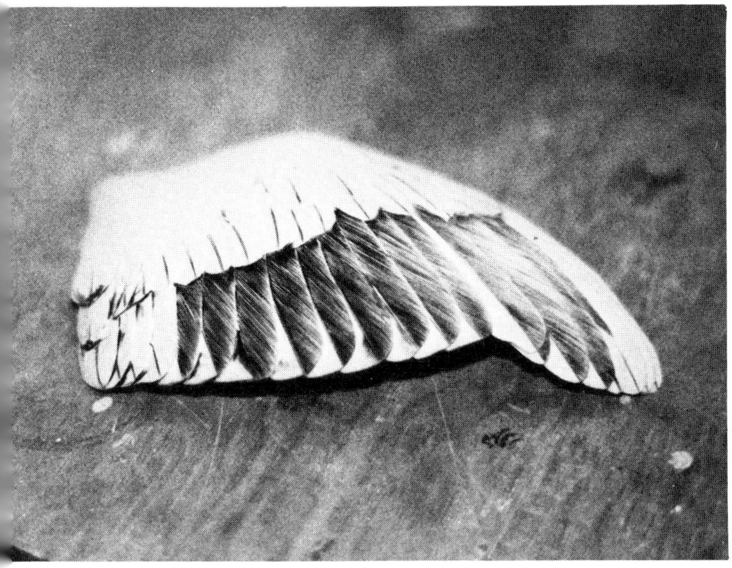

Upper side of wing partially burned

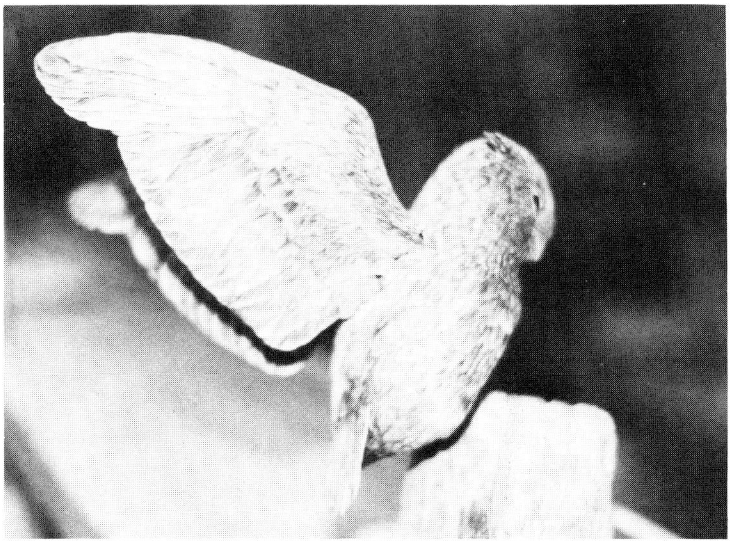

Finished bird ready to paint

Under side of wing partially burned

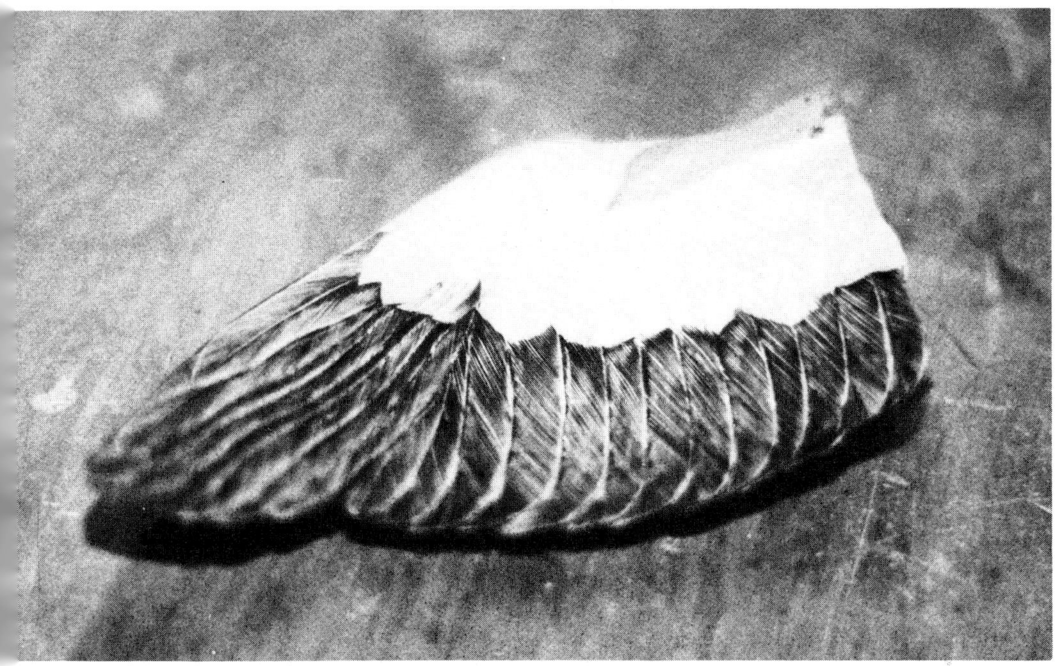

Saw-Whet Owl

Carved by Tricia Veasey

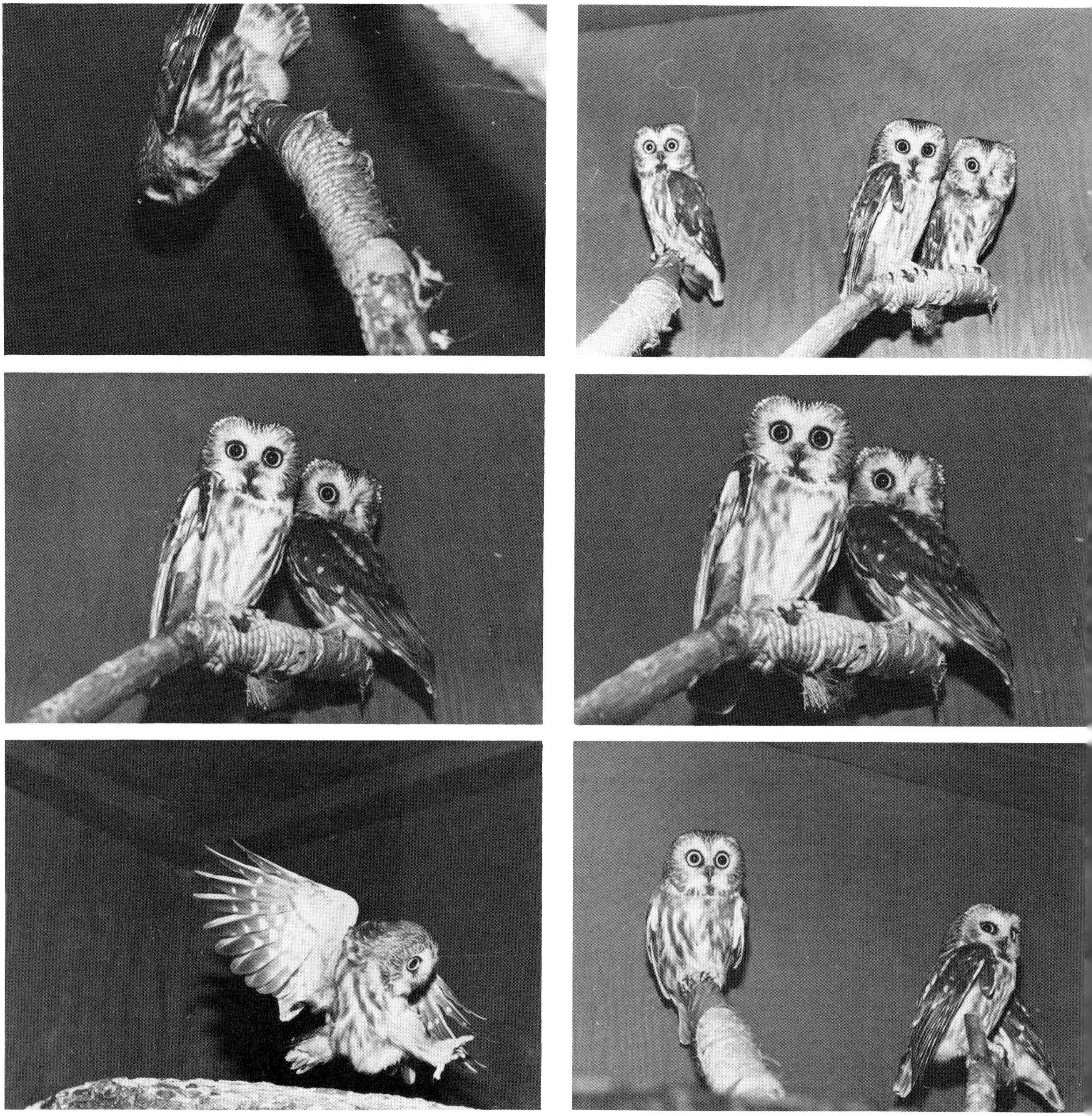

Saw-whet owls living at New Jersey Raptor Trust

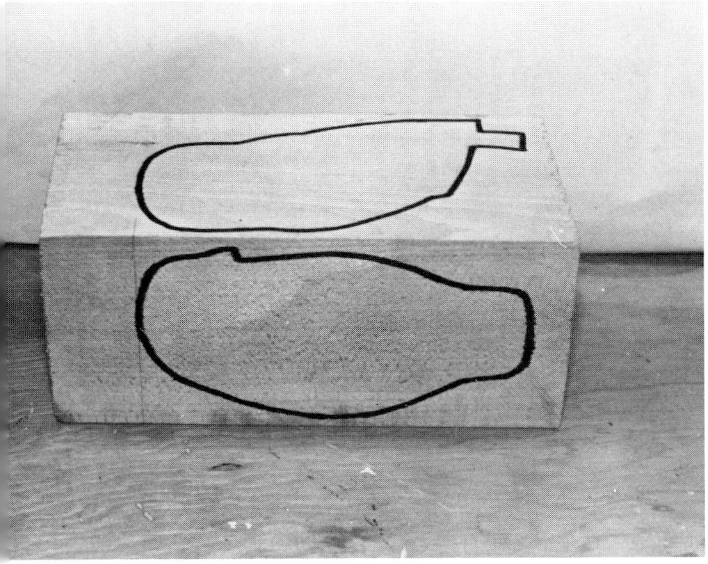

Block with plan view and profile pattern

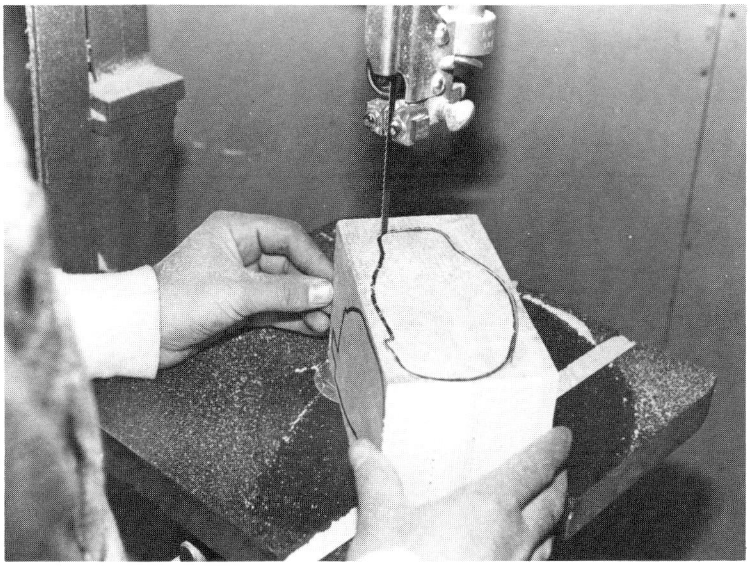

Band sawing plan view

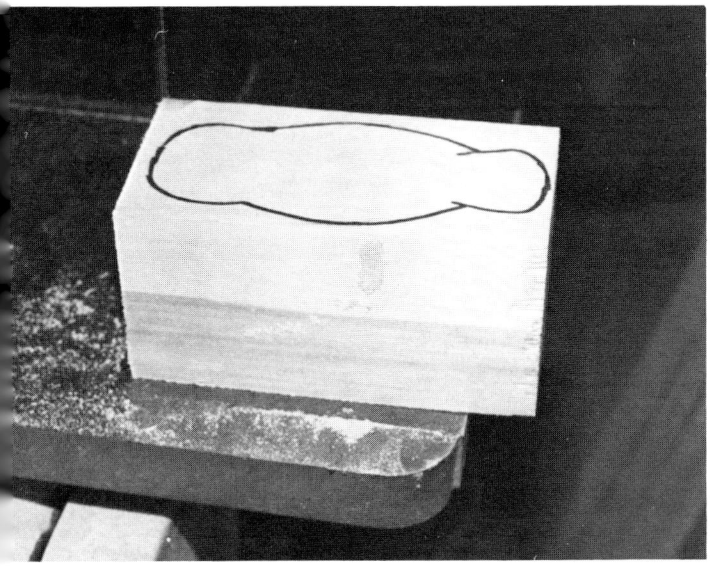

Band sawing plan view

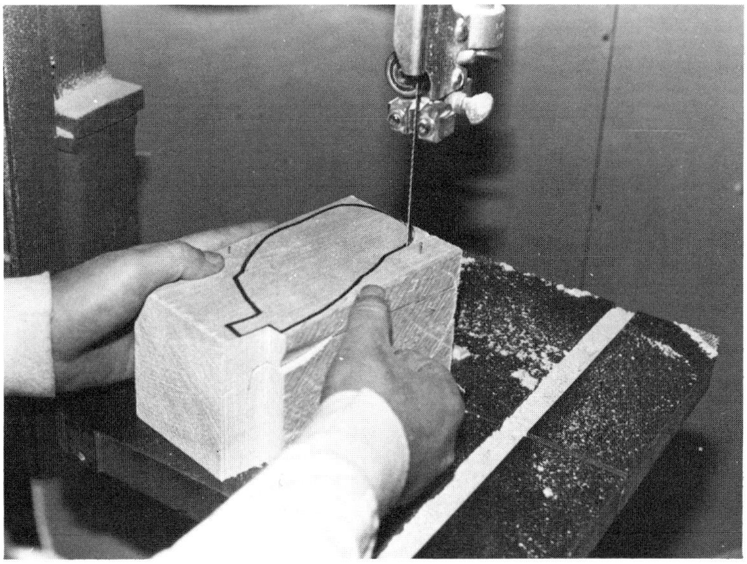

Band sawing profile

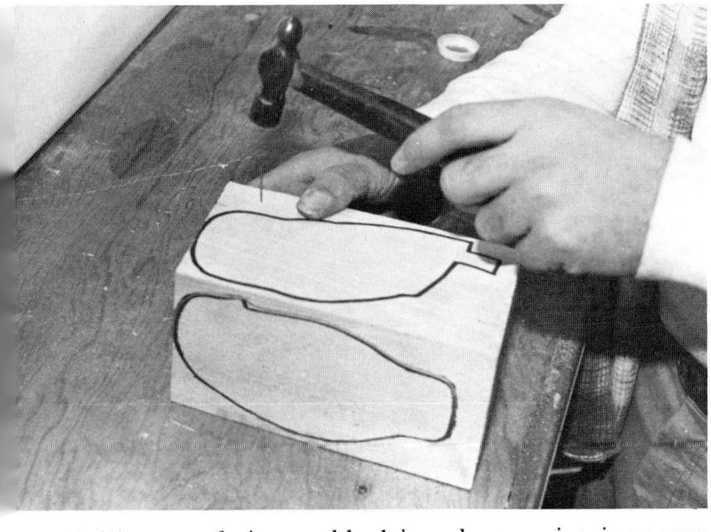

Nailing sawed pieces to block in order to maintain square for cutting

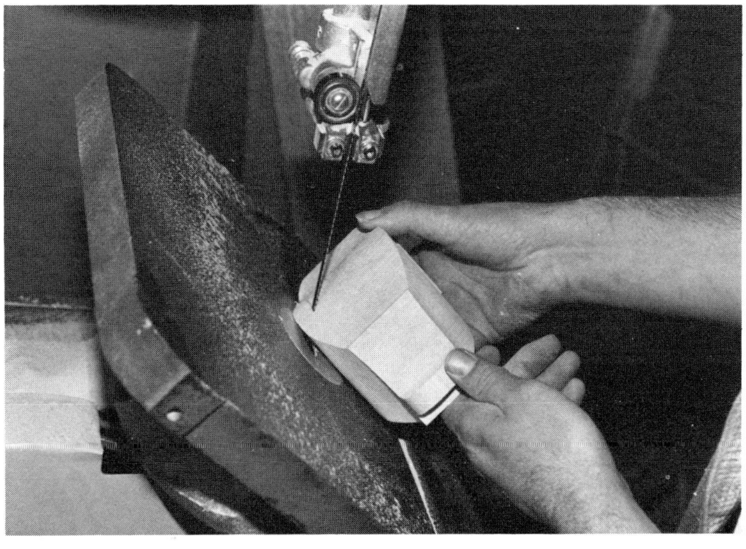

Trimming band-sawed blank

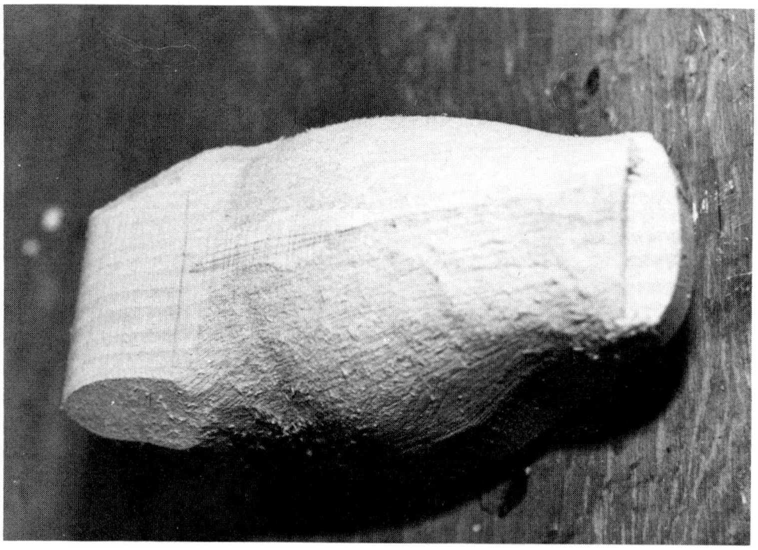

Begin by rounding body with rasp on flexible shaft machine

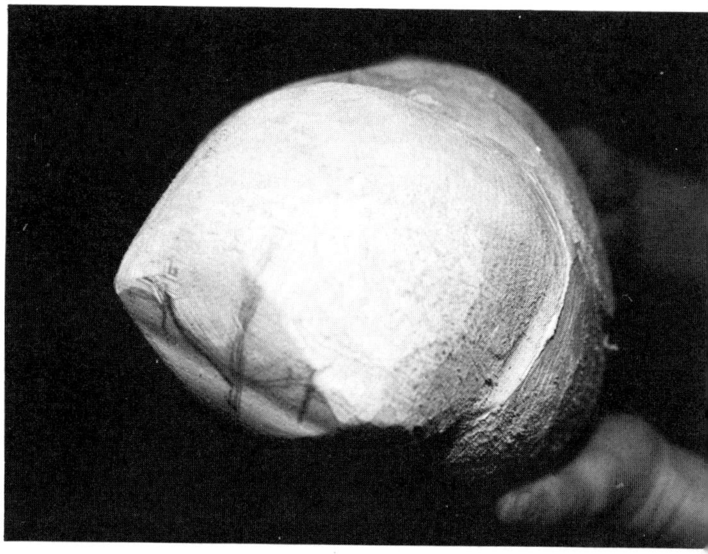

Top of head view

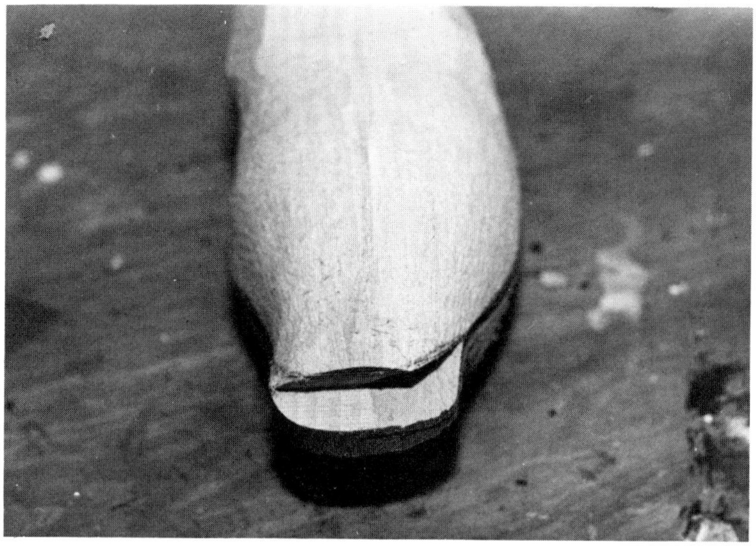

Back view of rounded body

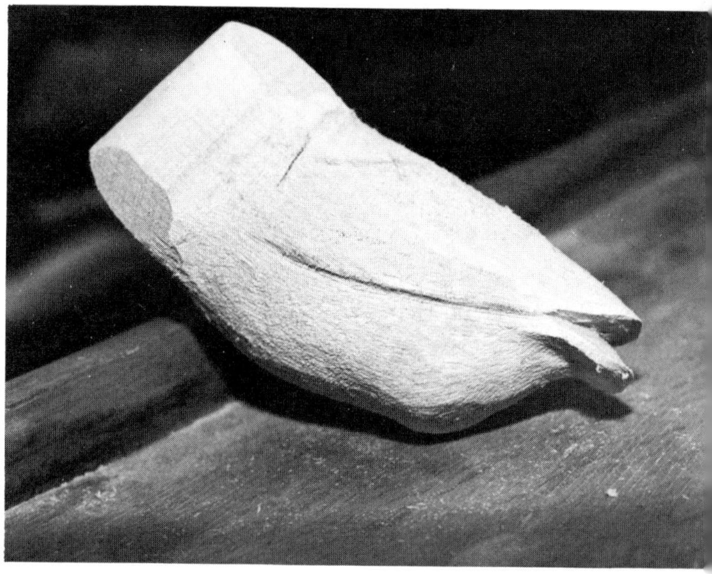

Side view, showing wing cut in

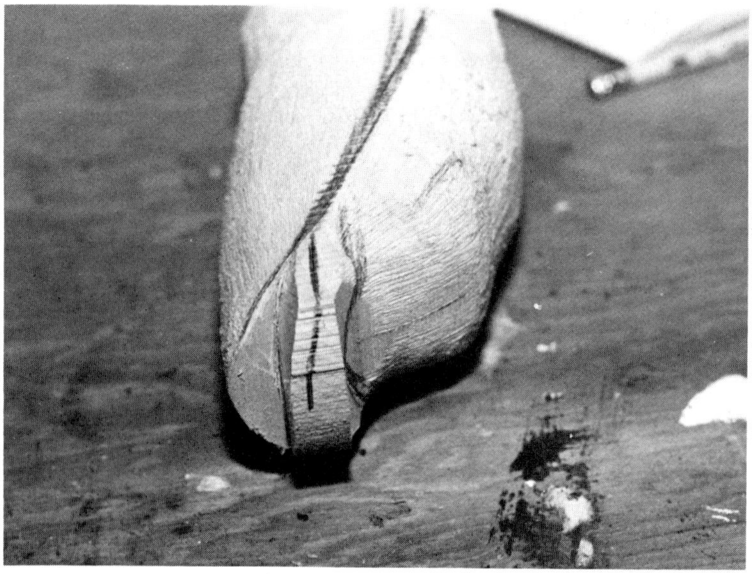

Side and belly view

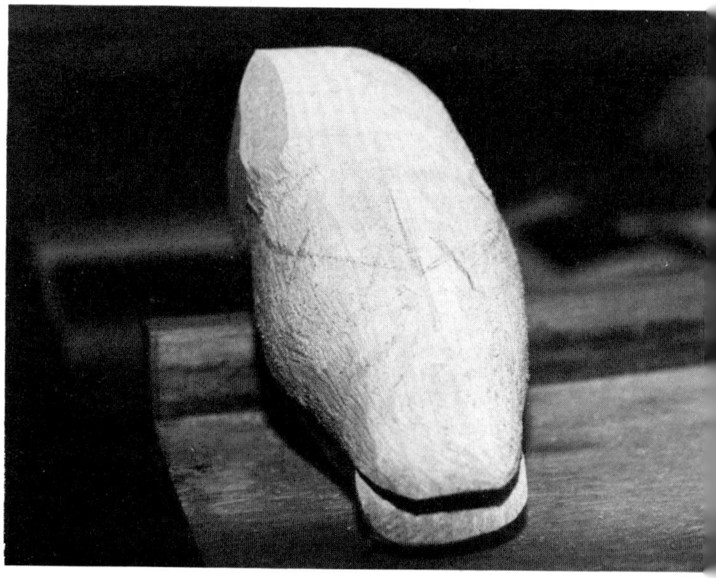

Back view and flow into head

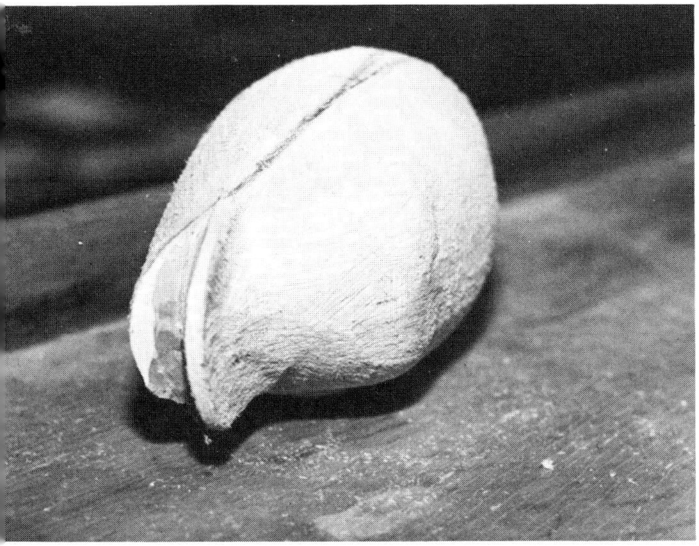

Under tail shape

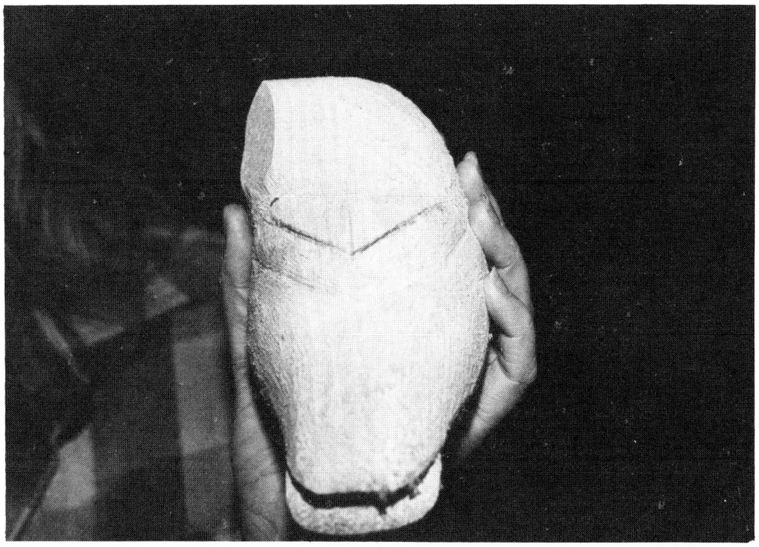

Cape area indented

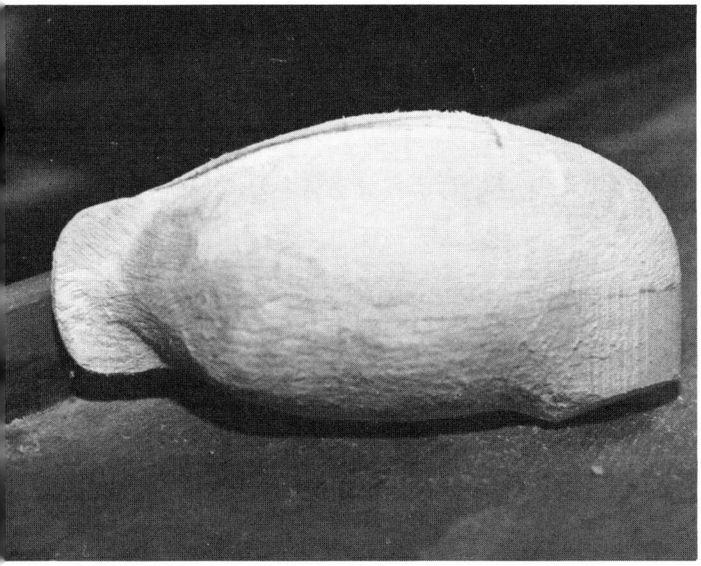

Belly shape—note: curve of head

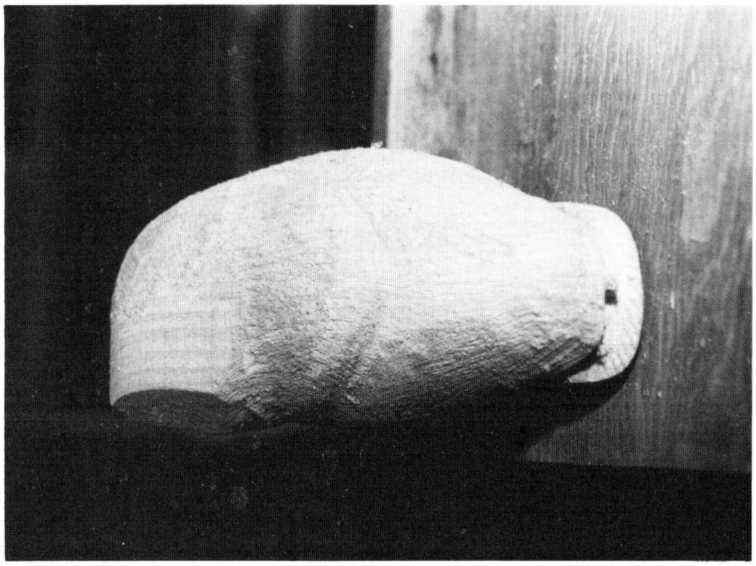

Cape area indentation smoothed out

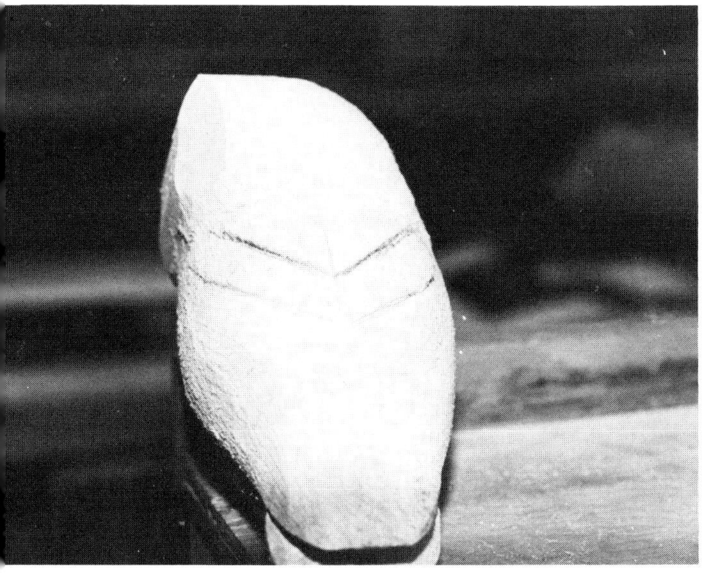

Cape area pencilled in

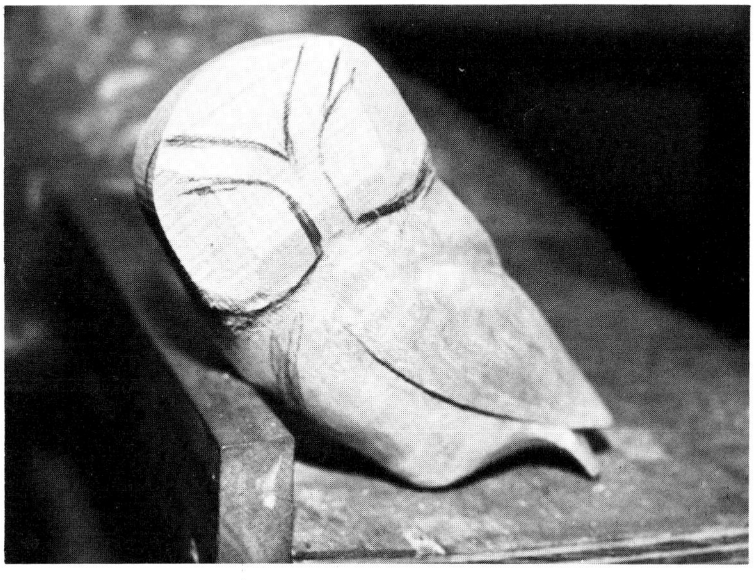

Facial plate (discs) pencilled in (leave wide area for beak)

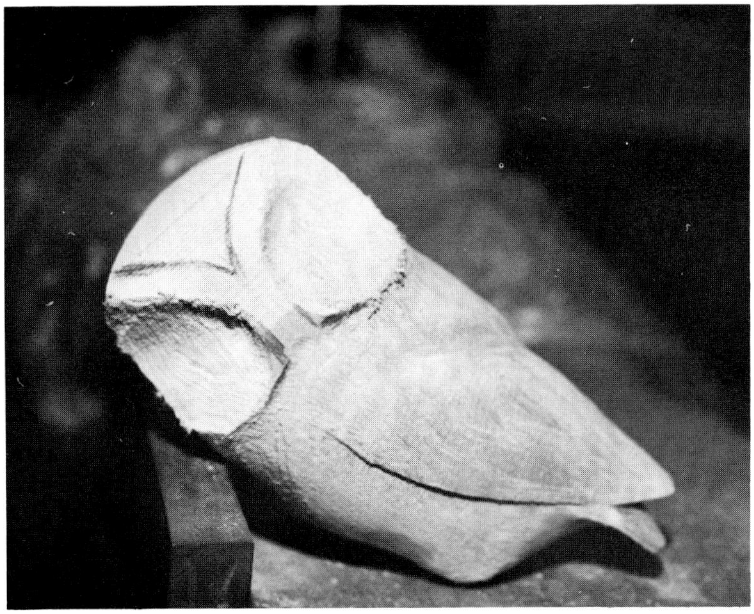

Carving of facial discs

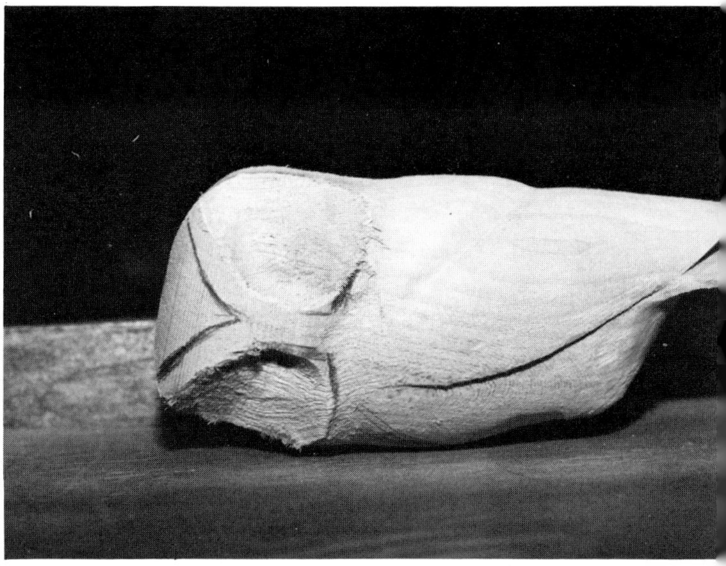

Face, wing and cape areas defined

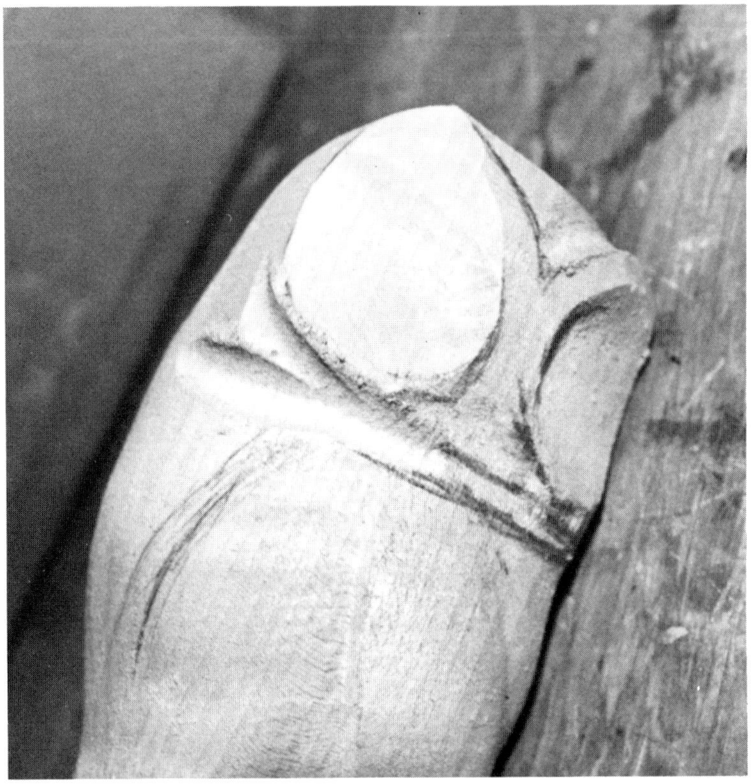

Cut in around facial discs is accomplished with a 1/2" rasp as this radius works well

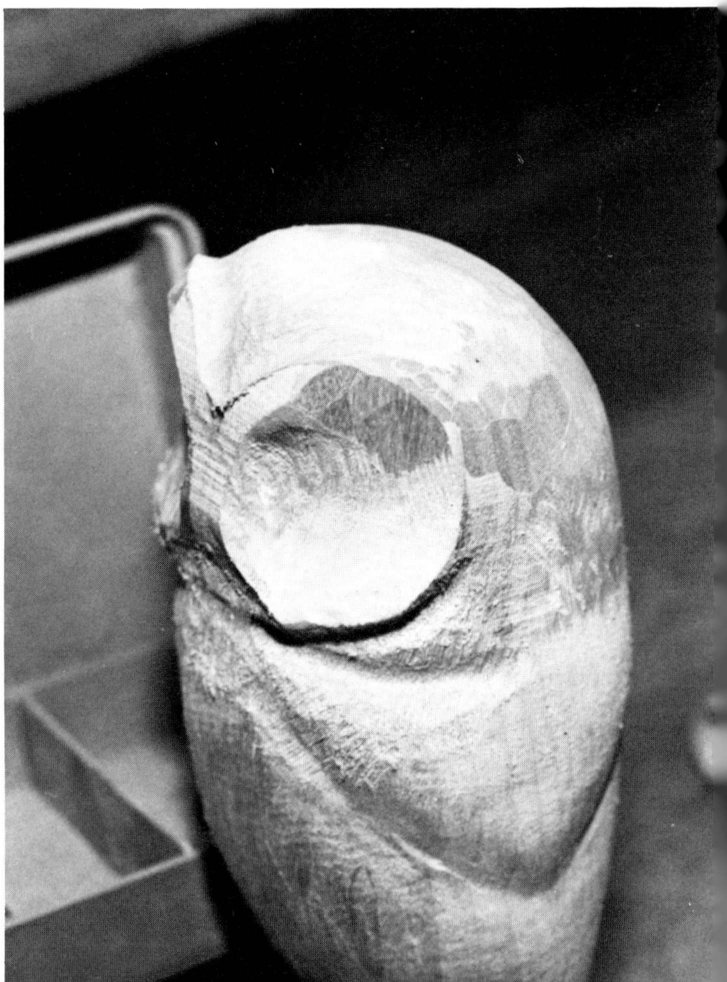

Depth of facial discs, cape area and roundness of head

(See page 148 for painting instructions and page 270 for patterns)

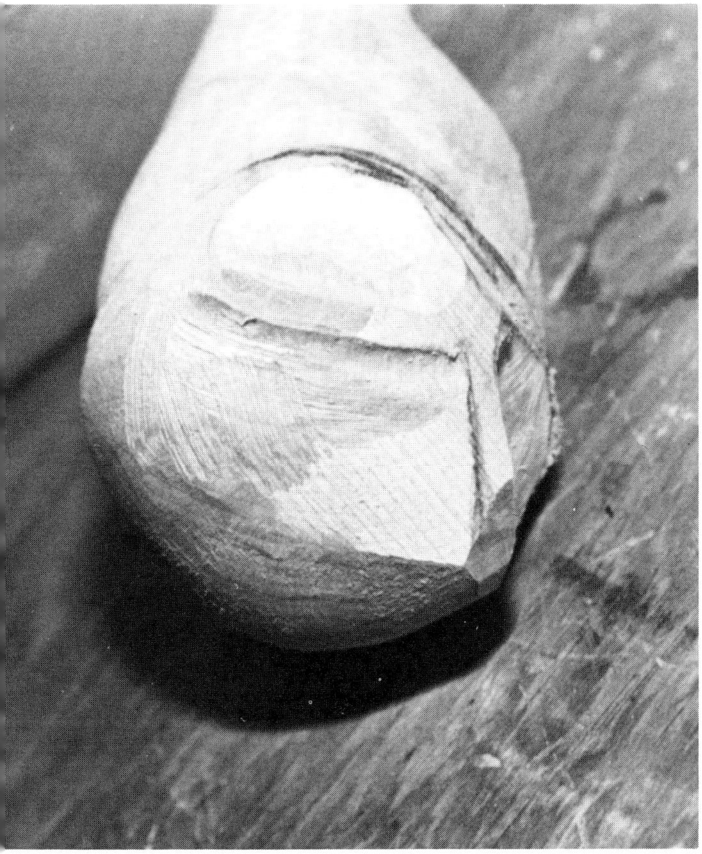

Top view of head

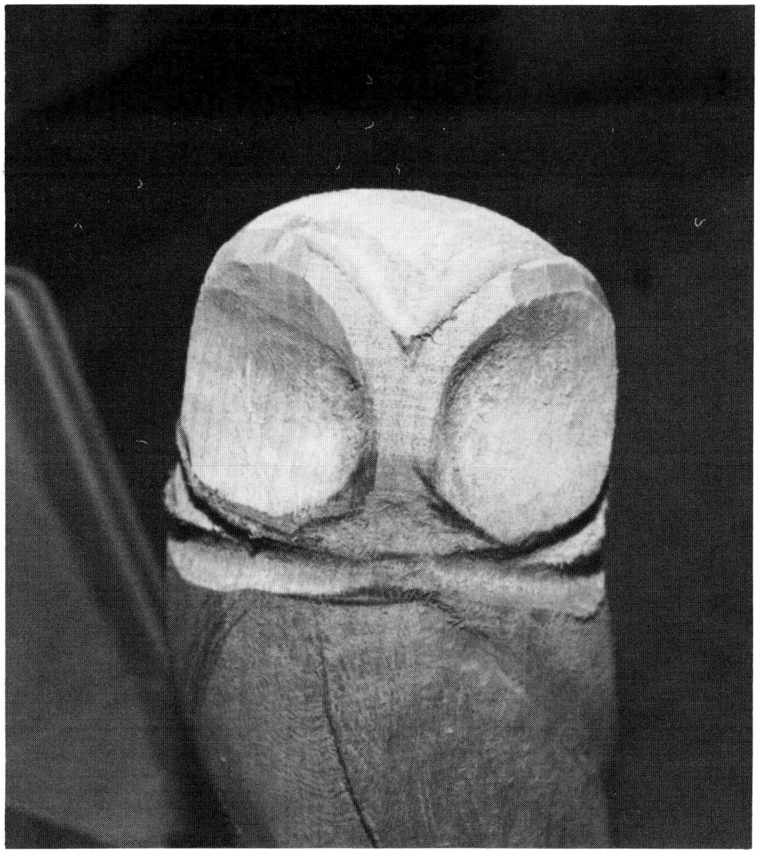

Front view of face, left side of body

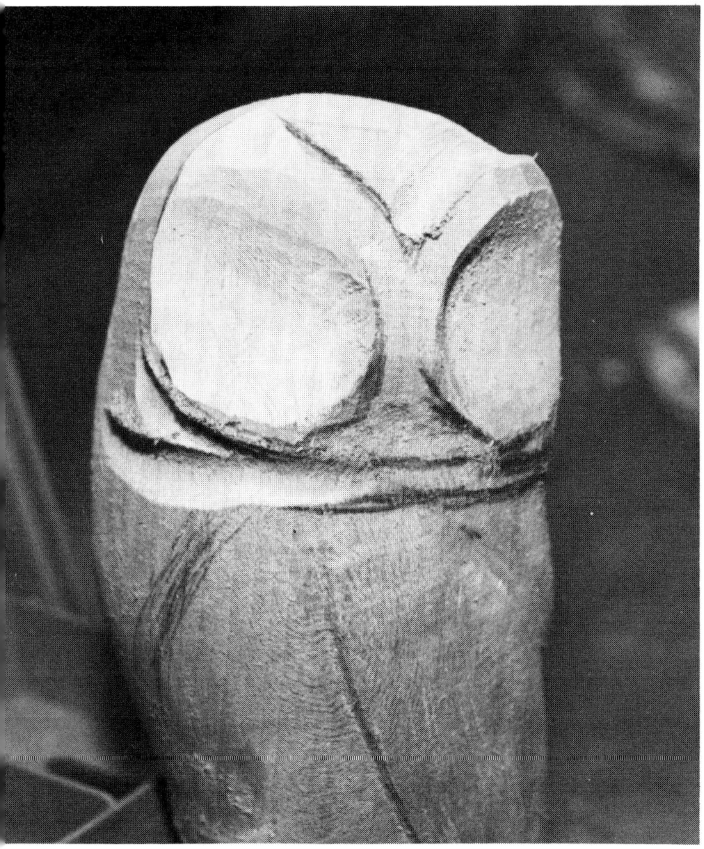

Right side view face and belly

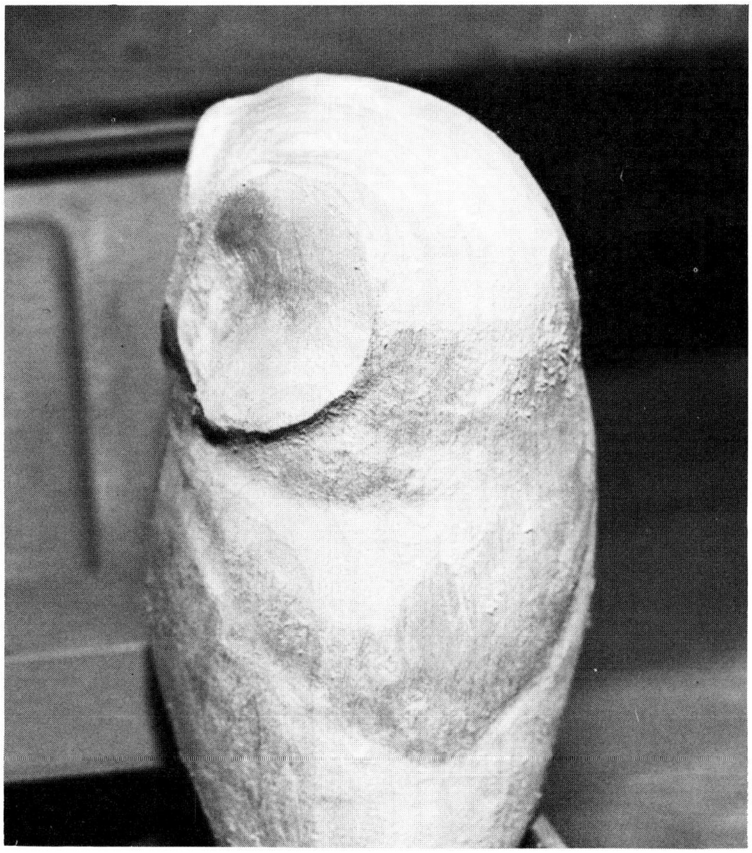

Left side of face plate and cape area

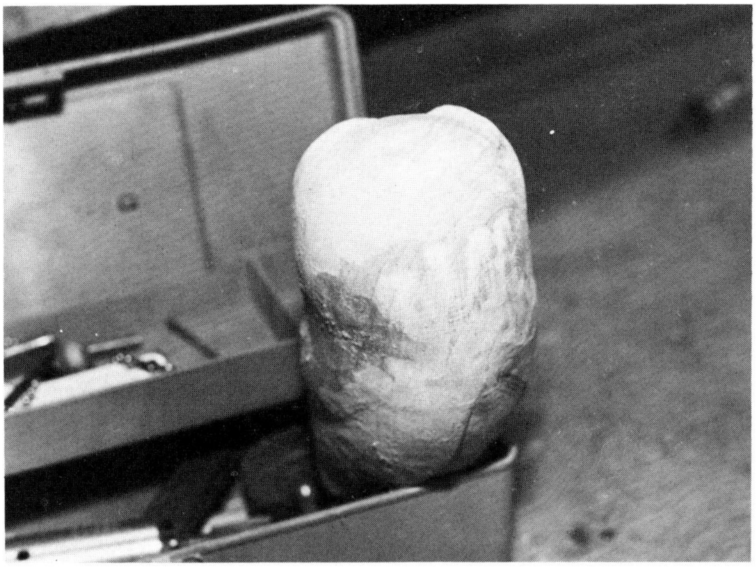

Back of head view

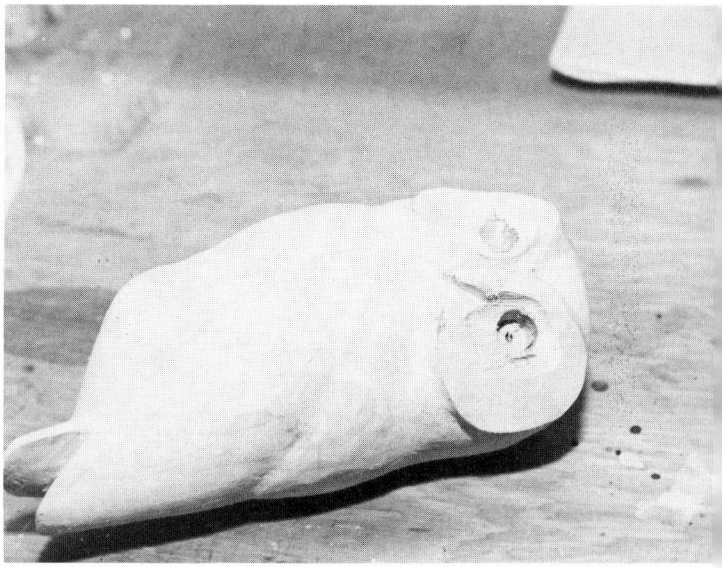

Front view of face

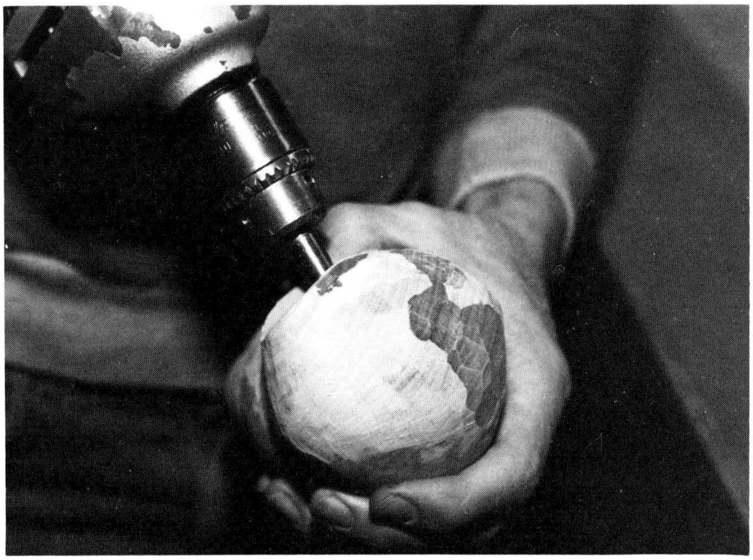

Drilling eye holes

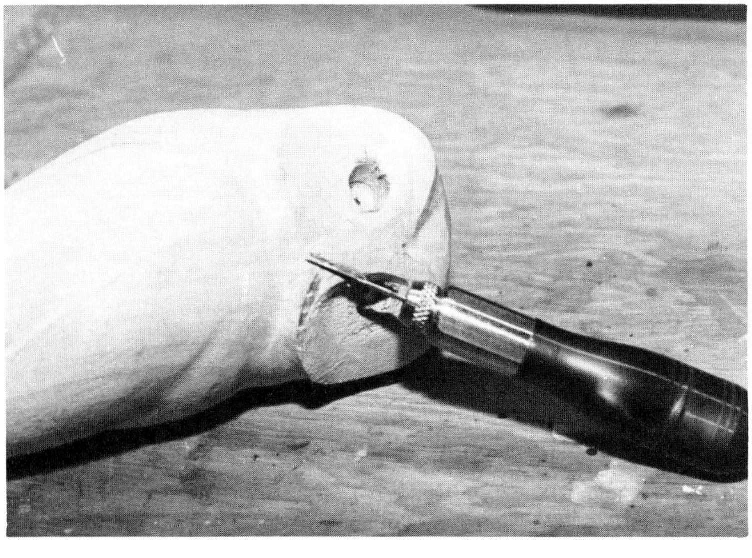

Detailing beak with knife

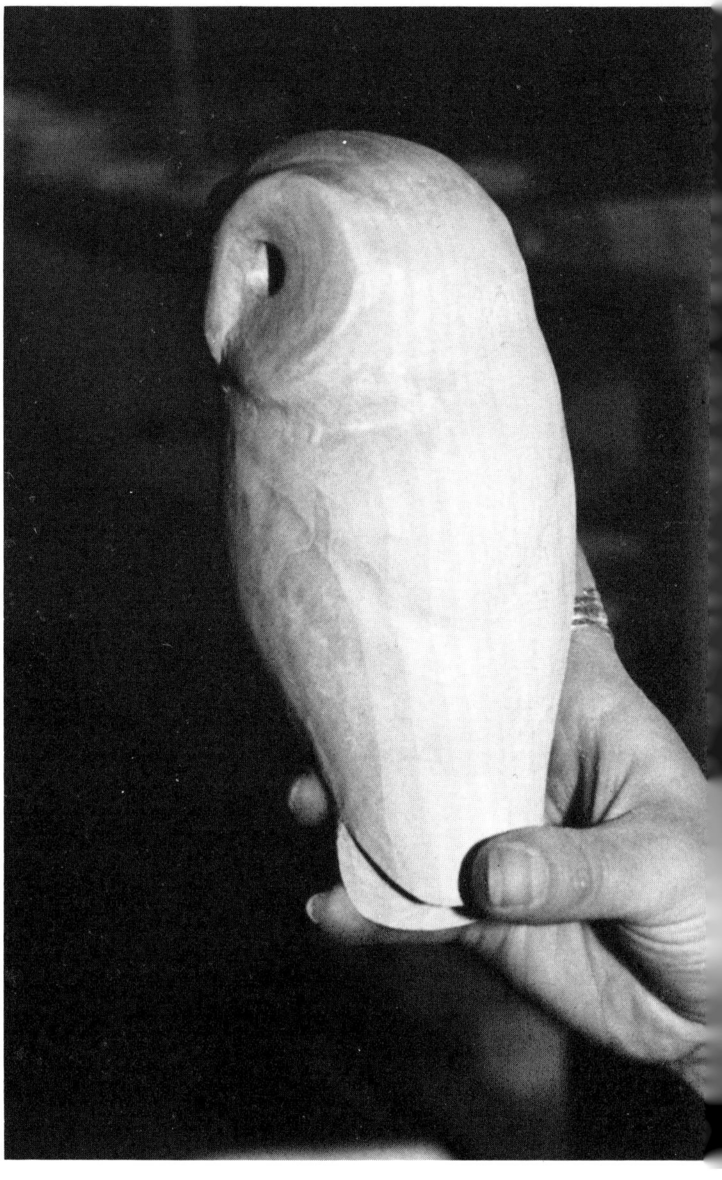

Back and left face profile

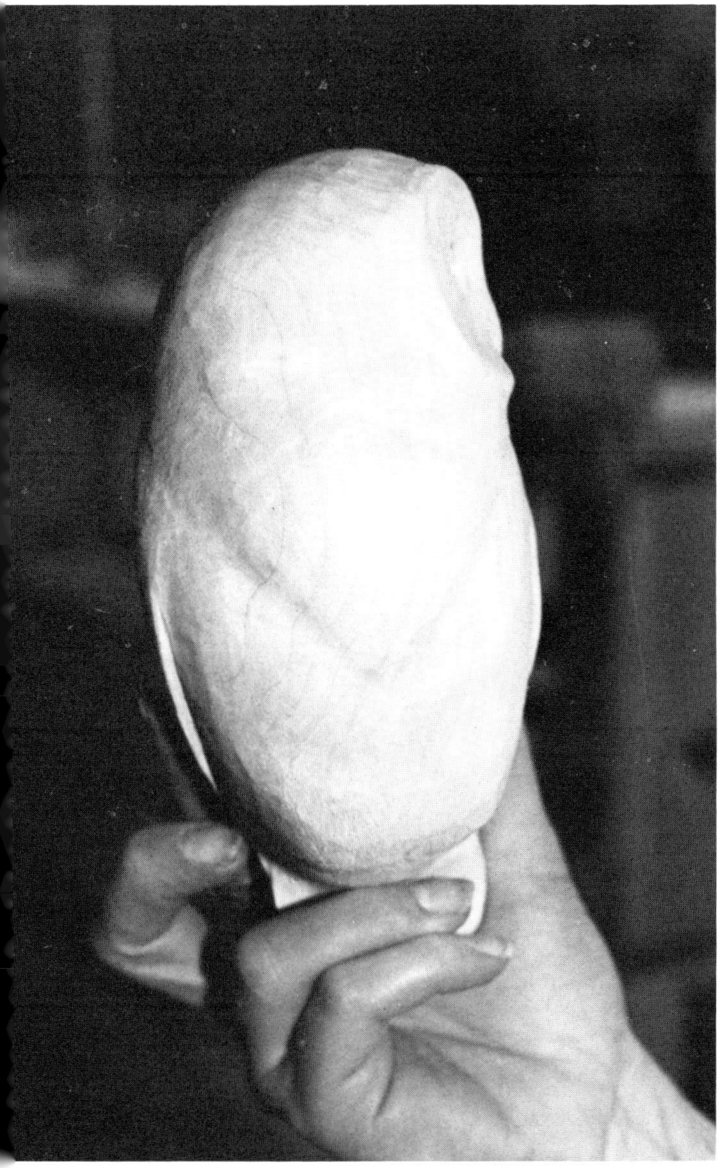

Belly and chest—right profile of face

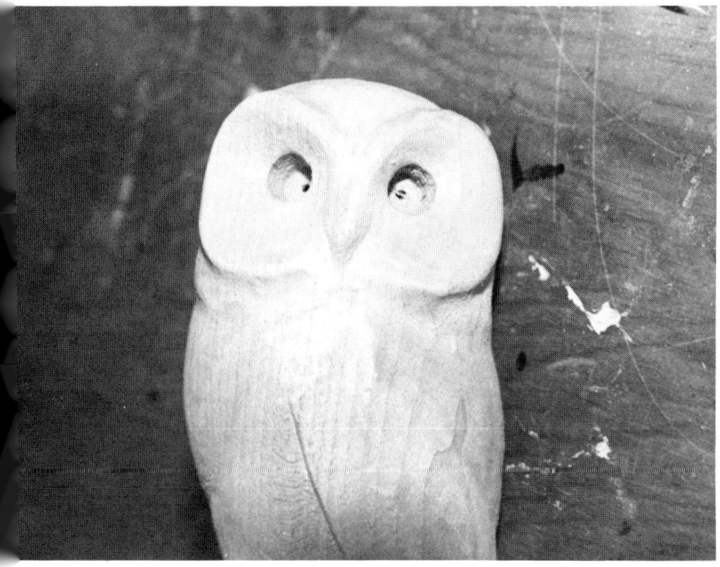

Front view of face ready to texture

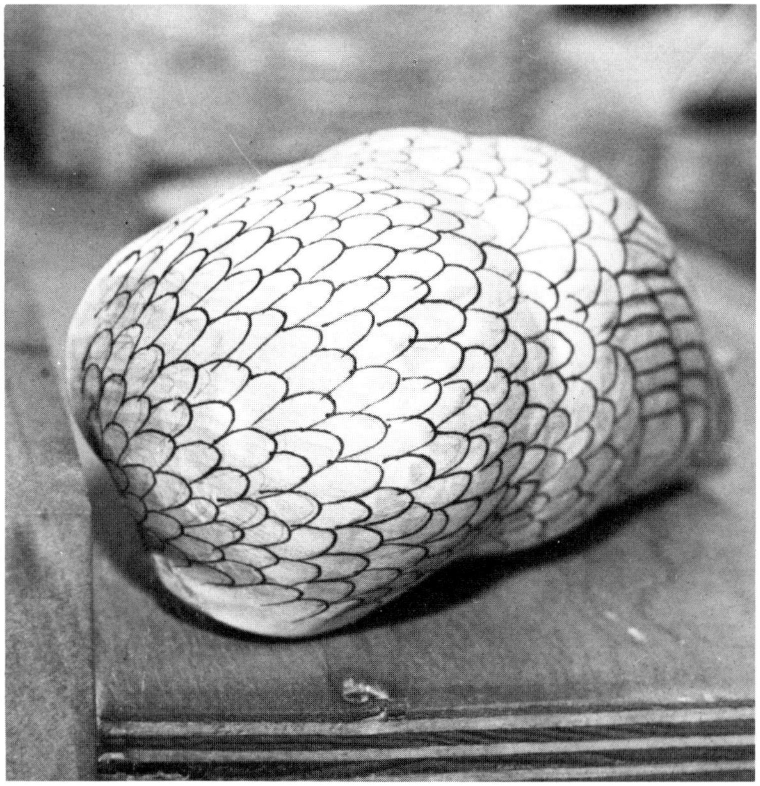

Feather pattern back of head

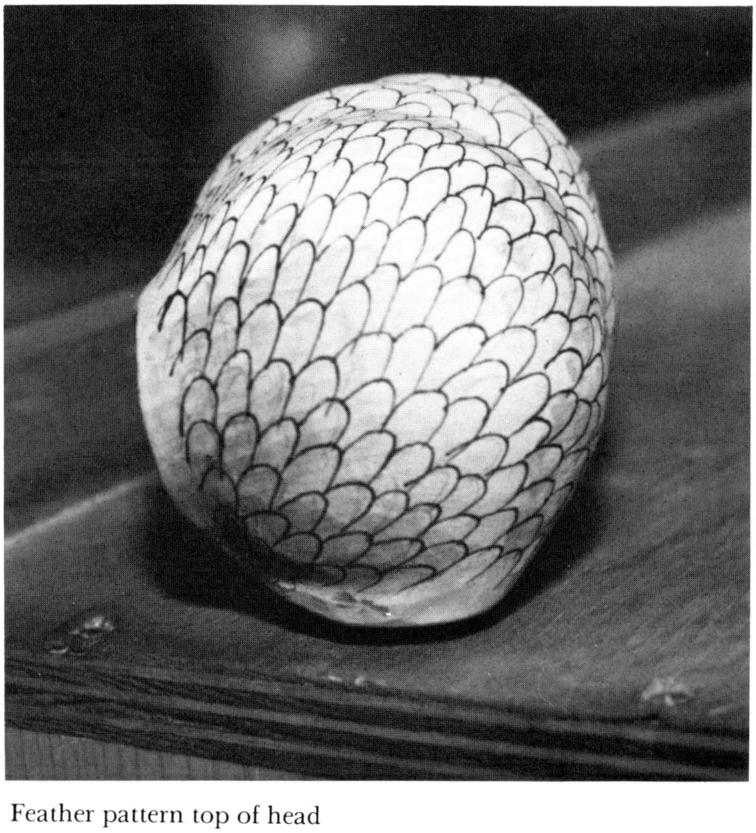

Feather pattern top of head

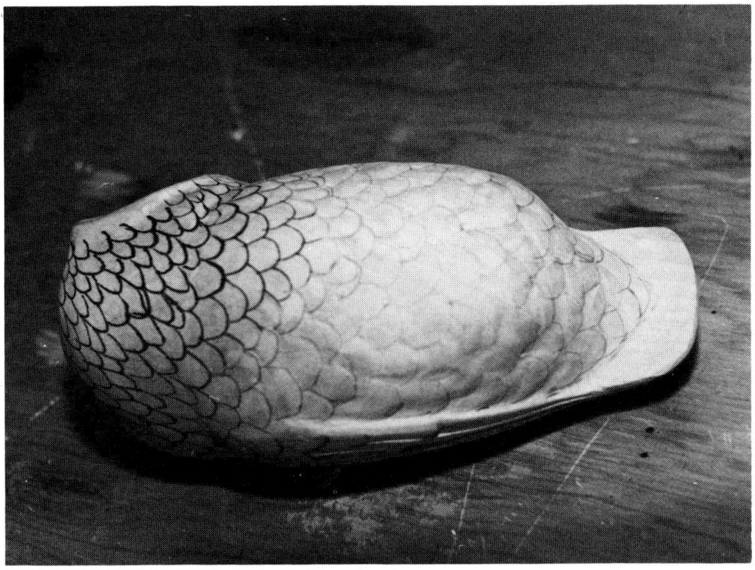

Feather pattern side of head

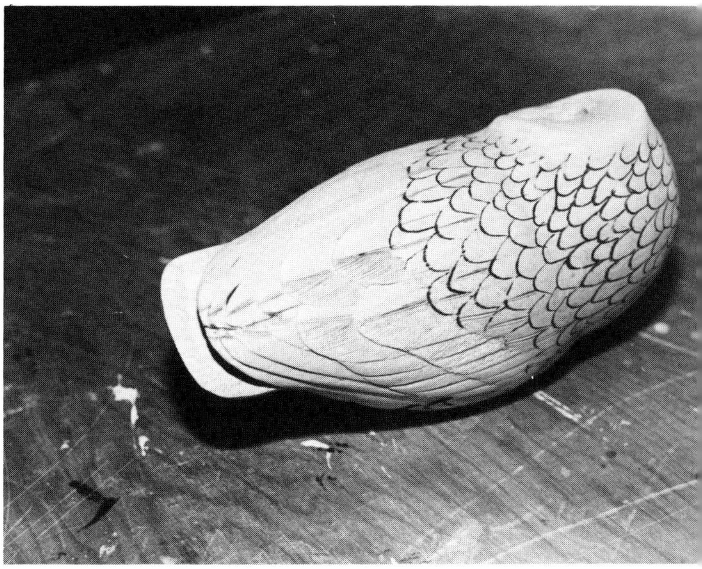

Carved feather of secondaries—secondary coverts and primaries

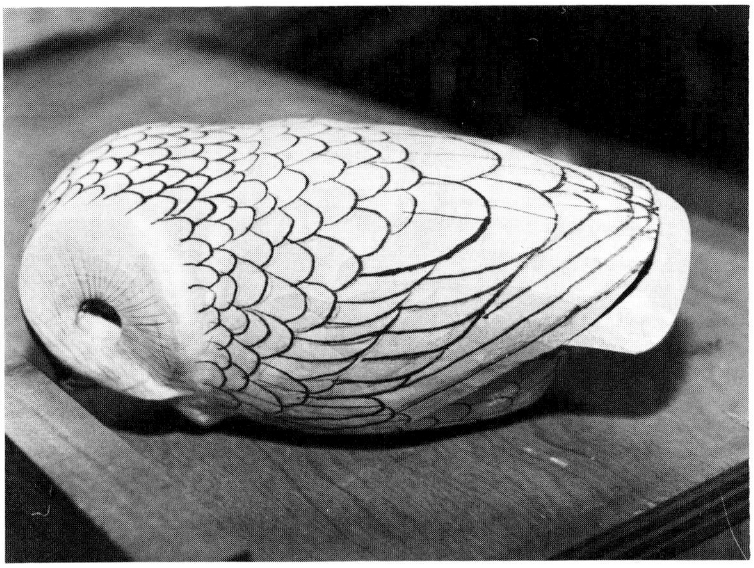

Feather lay out on cape back and wings

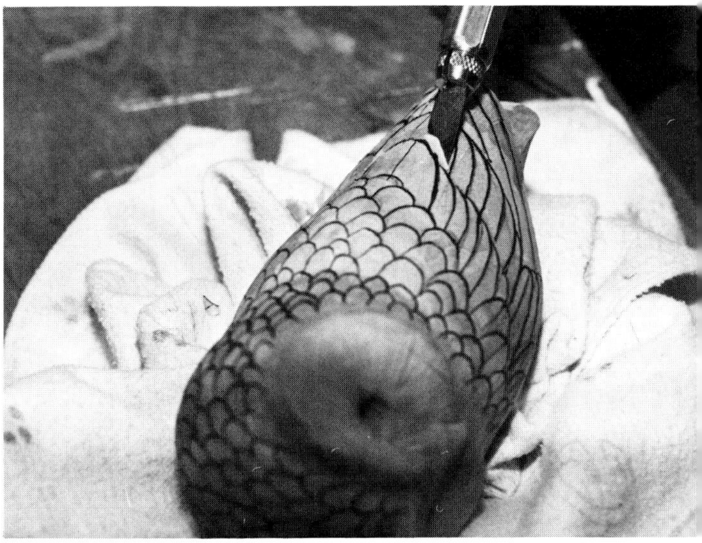

Carving secondary coverts

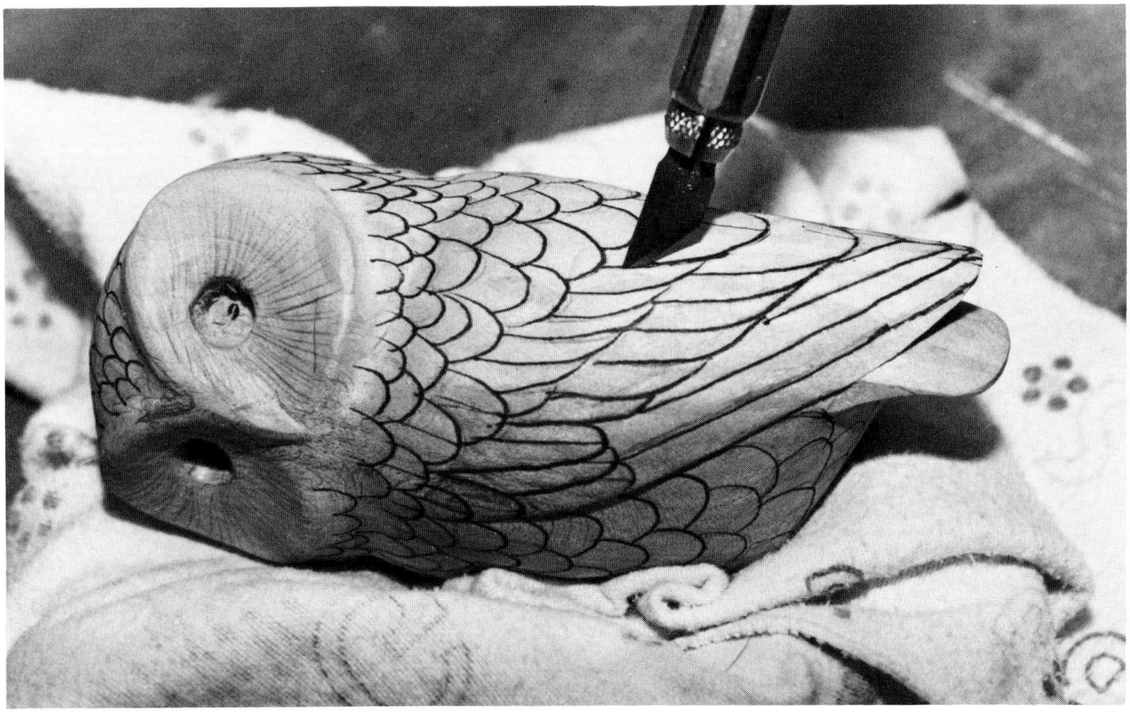

Carving major feather groups

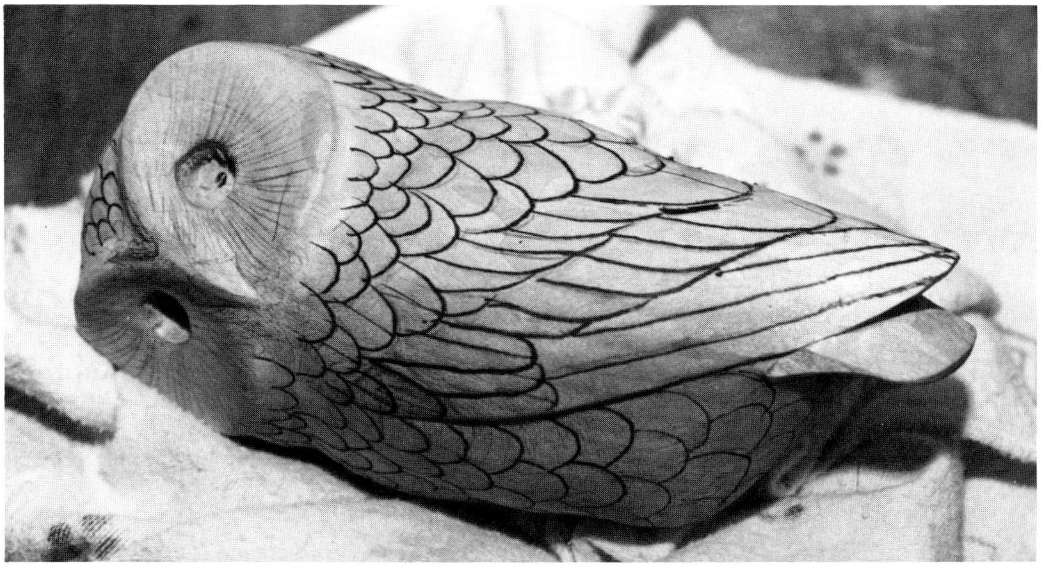

Lay out for carving and texturing

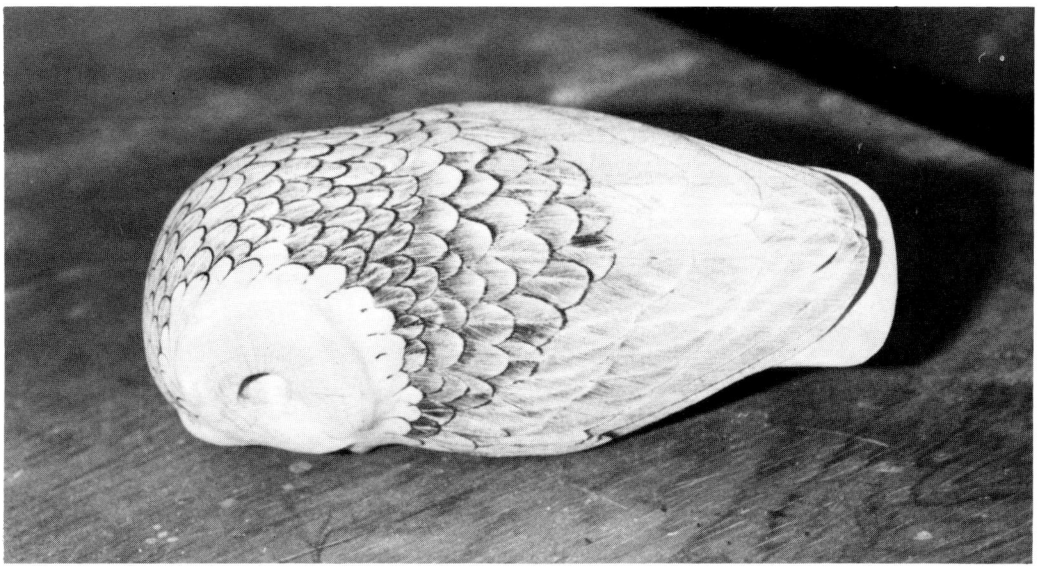

Cape and head burned

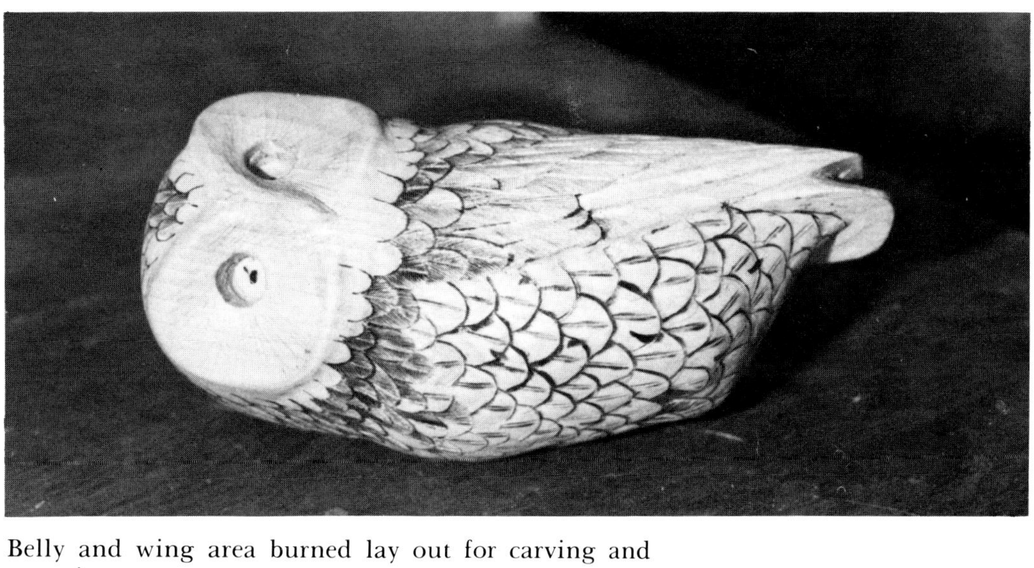

Belly and wing area burned lay out for carving and texturing

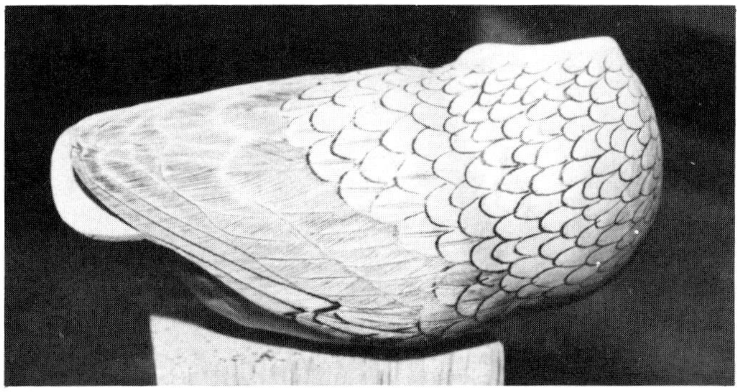

Major feather groups burned

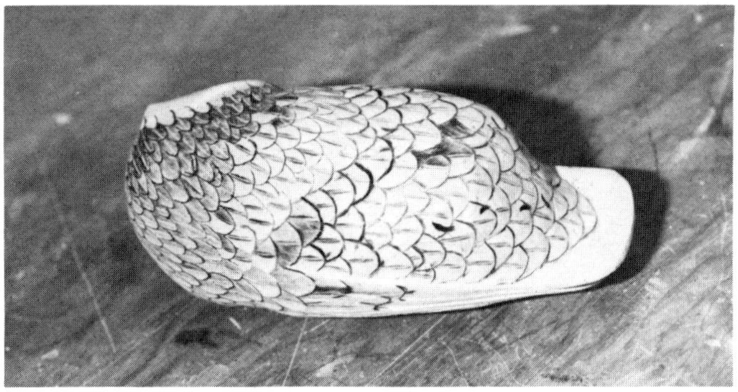

Left side of head and under belly—feather detail

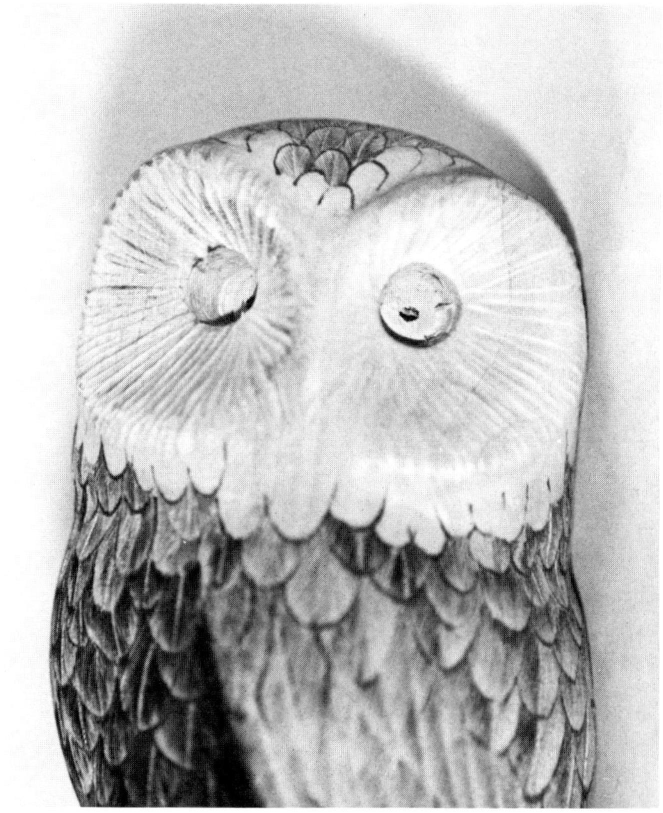

Front view textured with stone

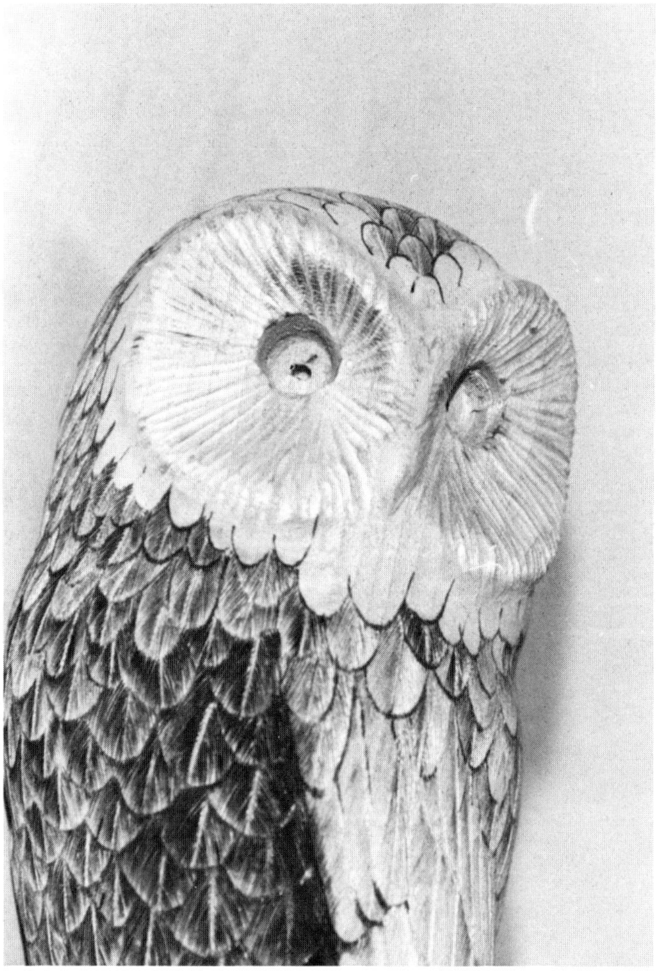

Face plate textured with stone

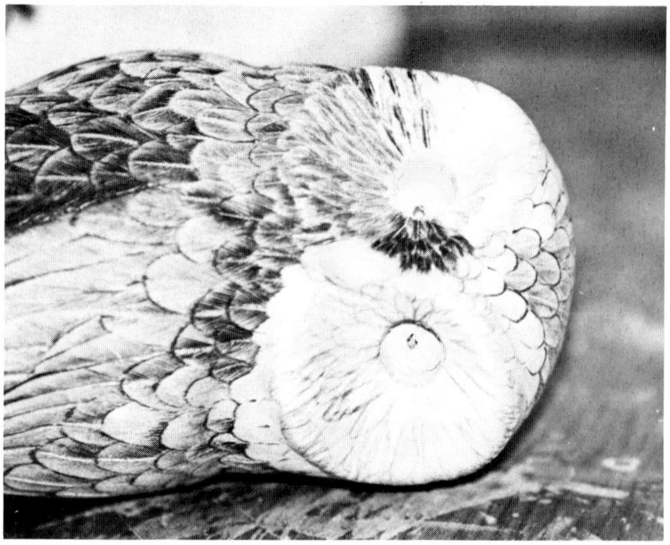

Facial disc partially burned in feather pattern over stoning

Facial discs burned

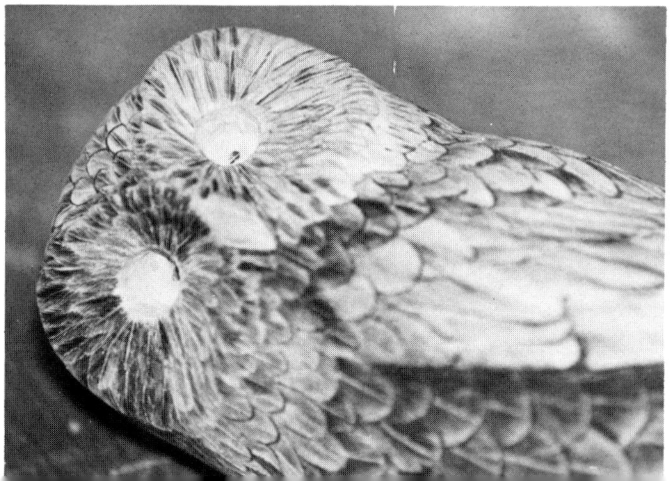

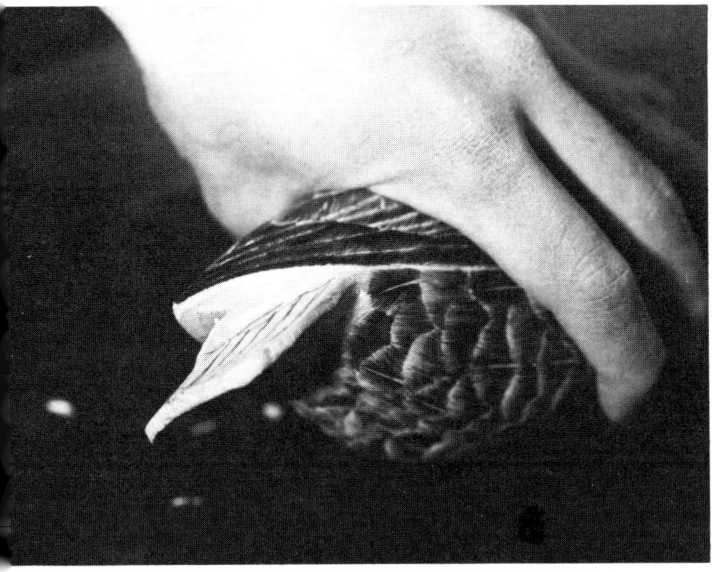

Tail area ready for burning

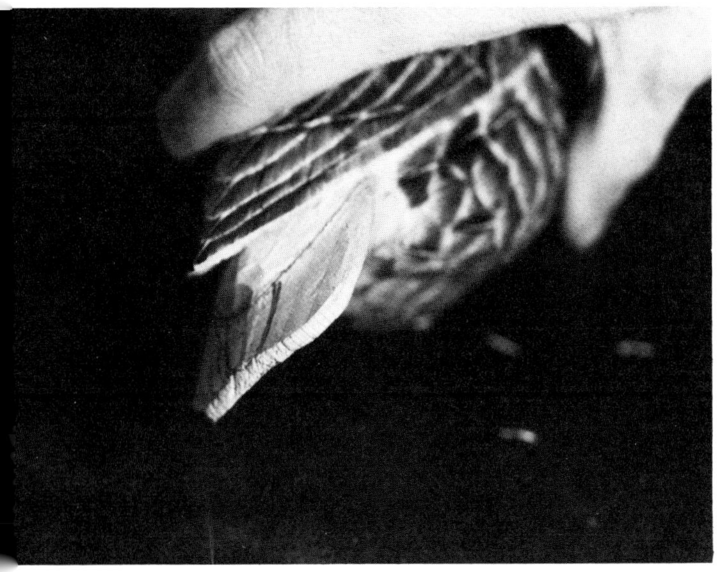

Another view of above

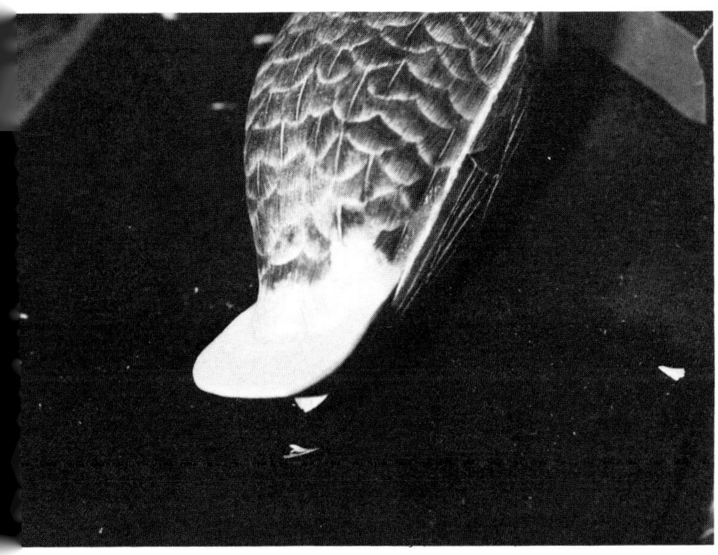

Underside of tail

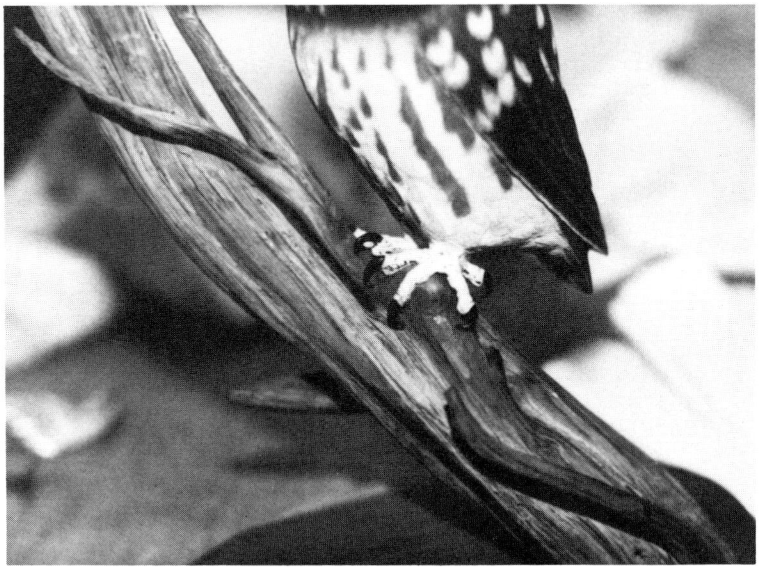

Cast feet set in bird and fitted around mounting branch

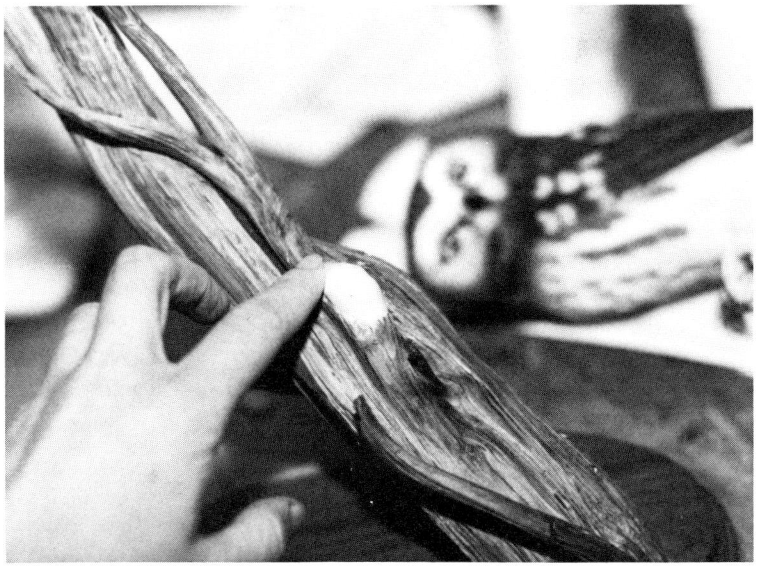

Slight build up of moldable epoxy (which will then be painted) so that owl will stand properly on mount

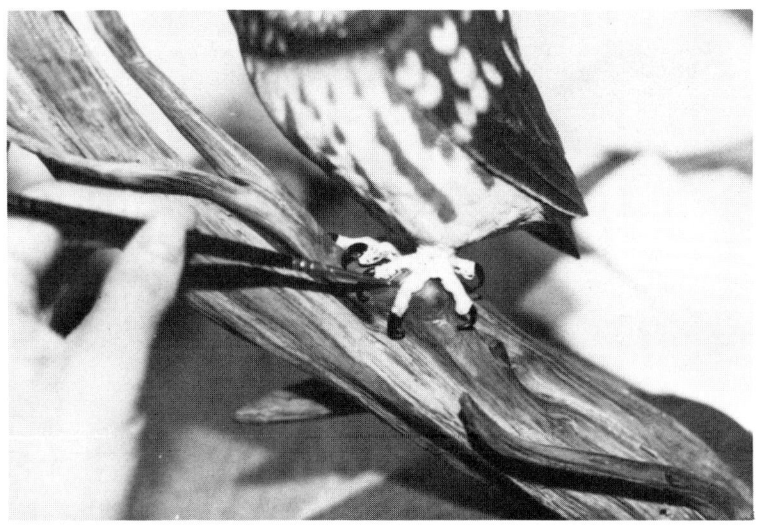

Finished owl mount

Snowy Owl

Carved by Genille McDyre

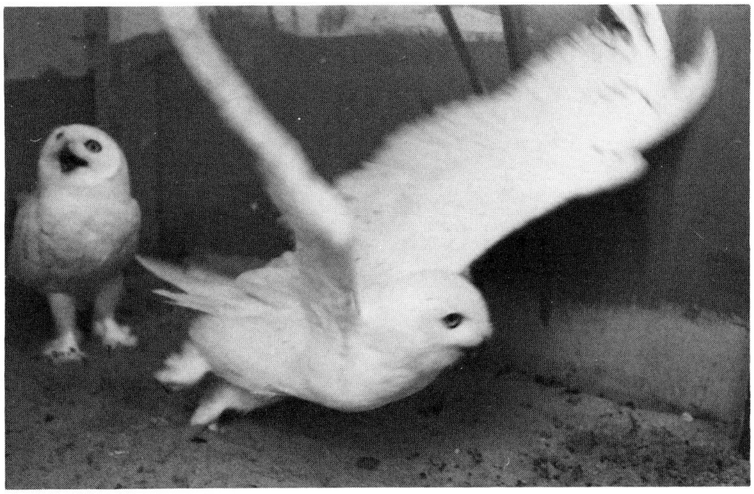

Pair of live Snowy Owls at New Jersey Raptor Trust

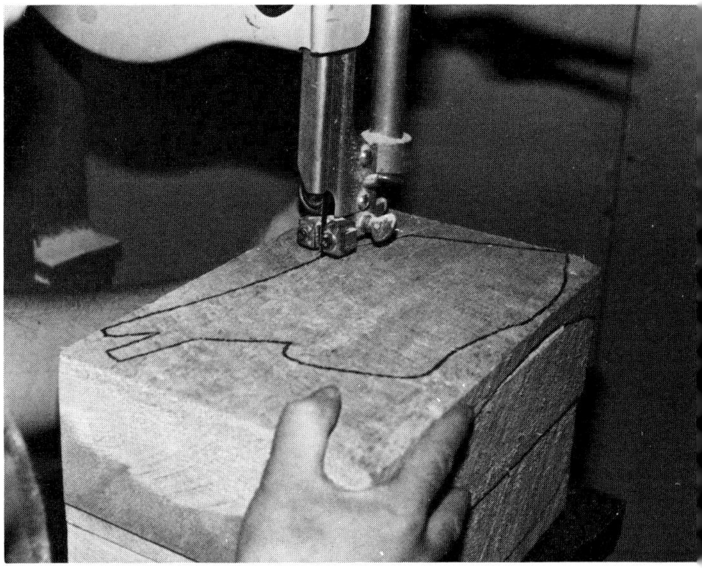

Body pattern being band sawed (plan view being sawed first, profile second)

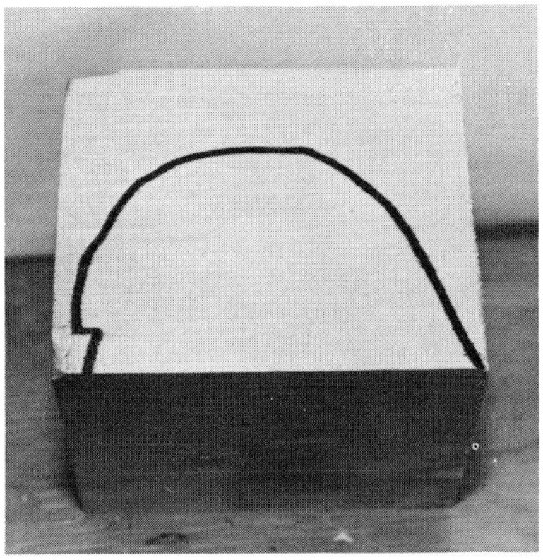

Head pattern on block

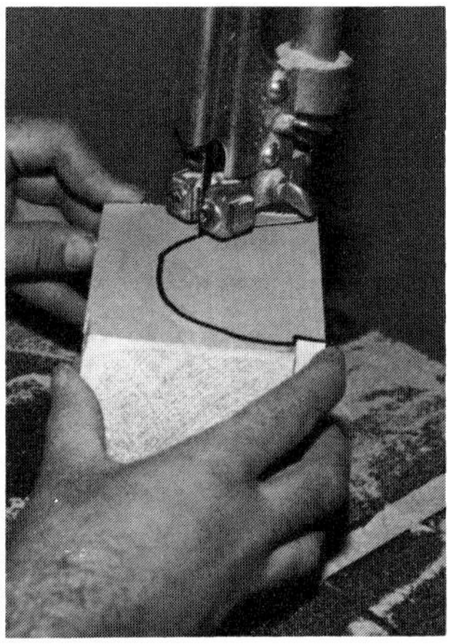

Head being band sawed

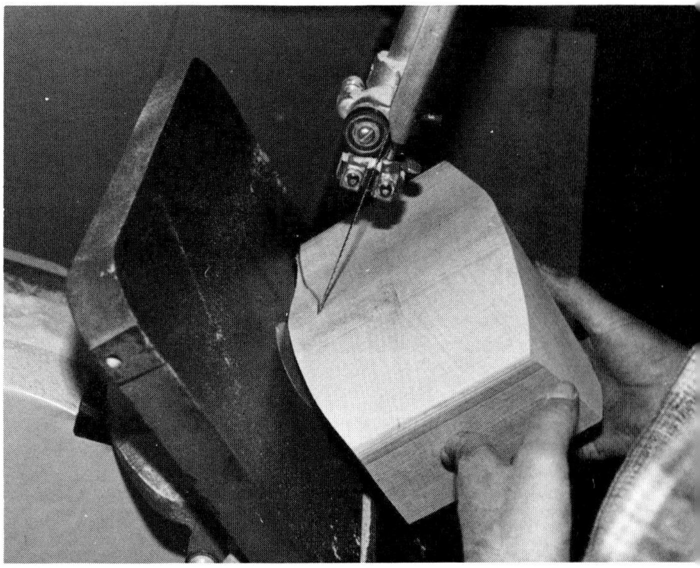

Trimming excess wood from band sawed block

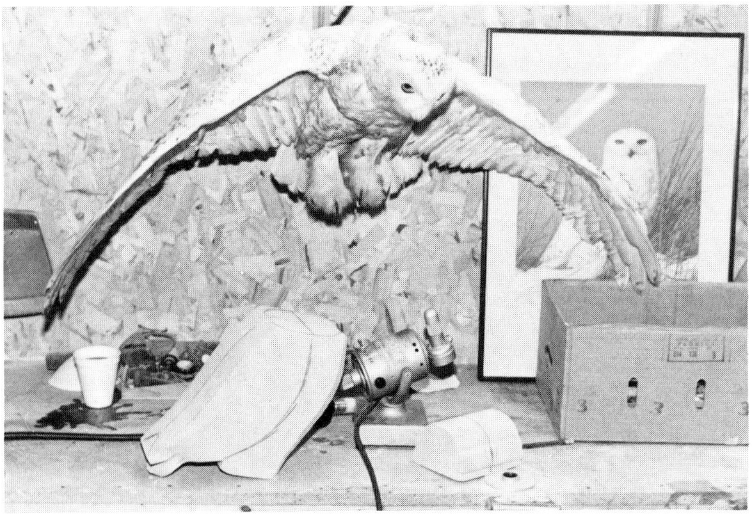

Band sawed block wth mounted owl and photo

(See page 152 for painting instructions and page 271 for patterns)

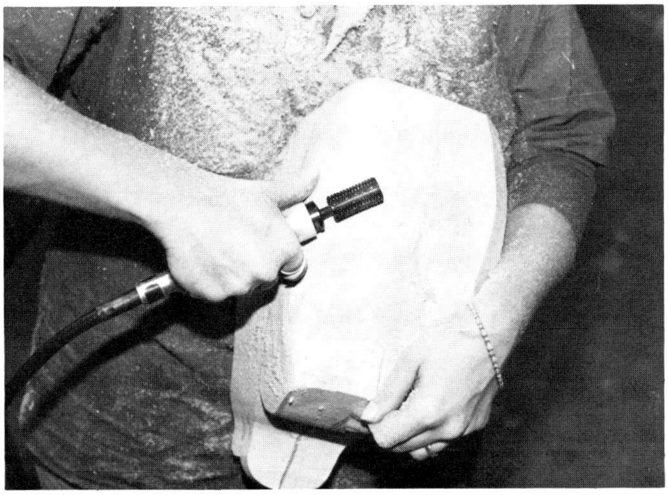

Removing excess wood with flexible shaft machine to "round" body

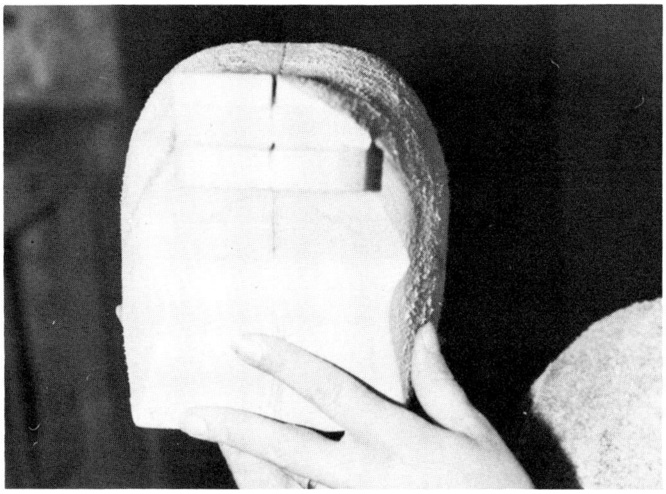

Example of roundness on right side of body as opposed to squarish left side

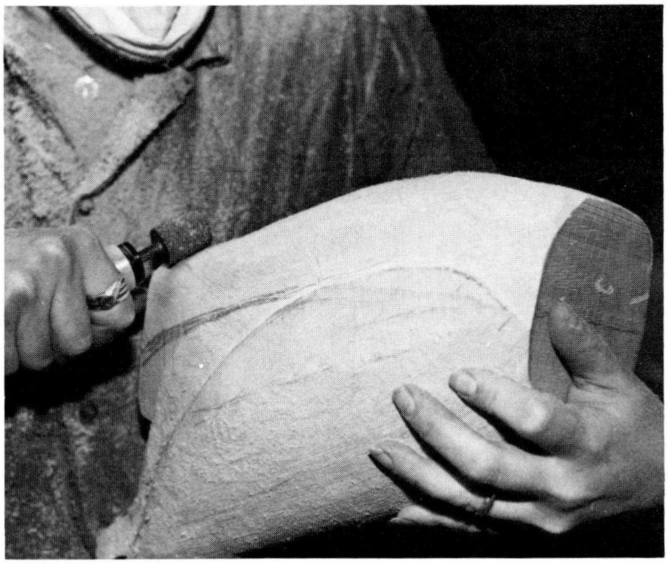

Further shaping with large carbide bit which removes wood quickly

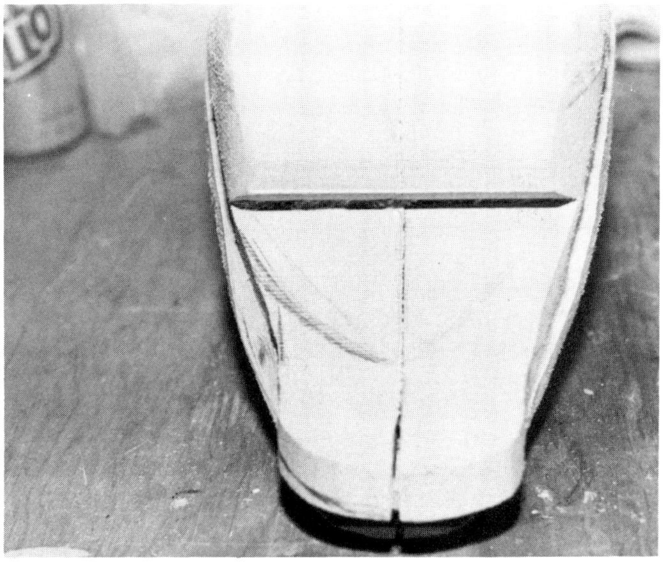

Note wing cut in and shaping of left side of rump

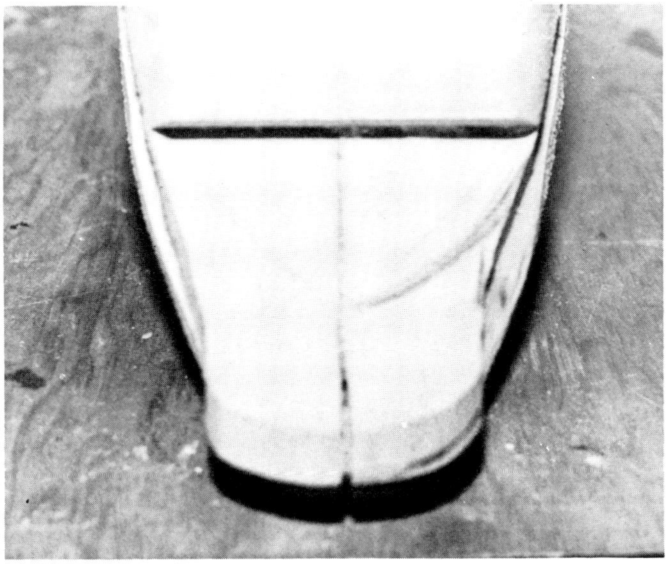

Basic guide marks on underside of tail

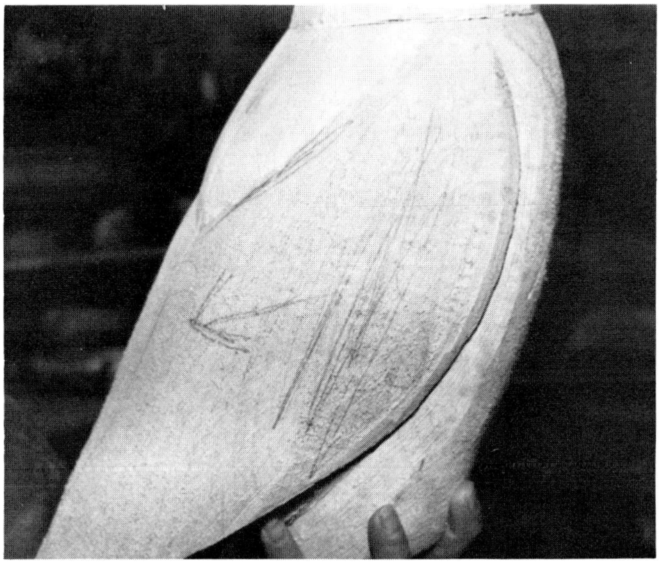

Wing cut in and cape area defined

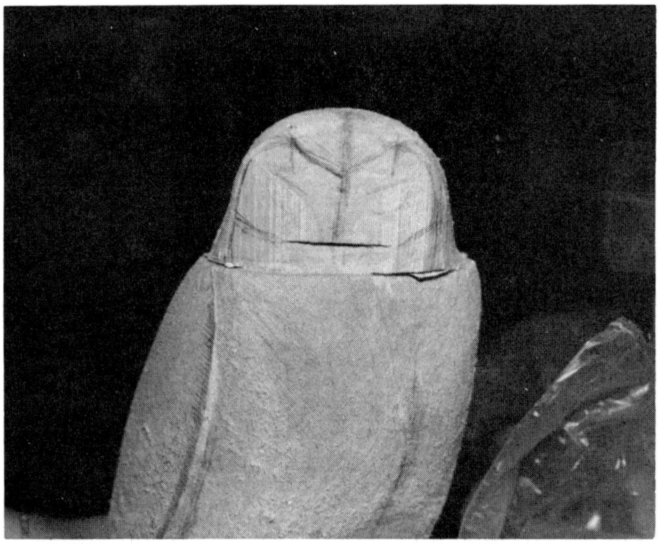

Roughed-out head set to body, slightly turned

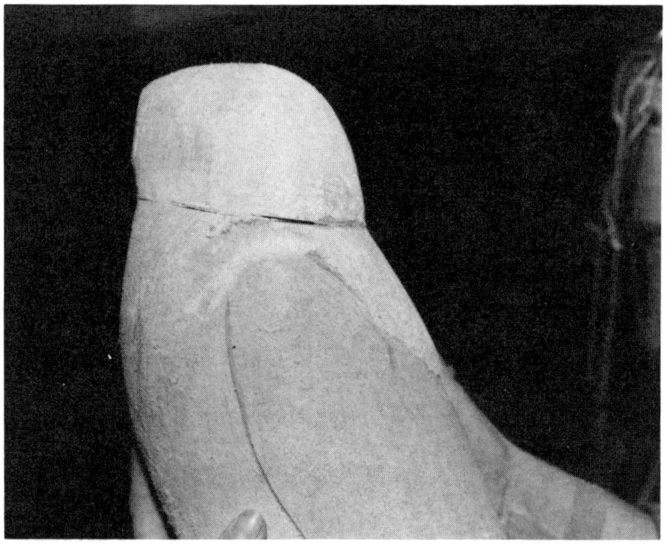

Back view of set head

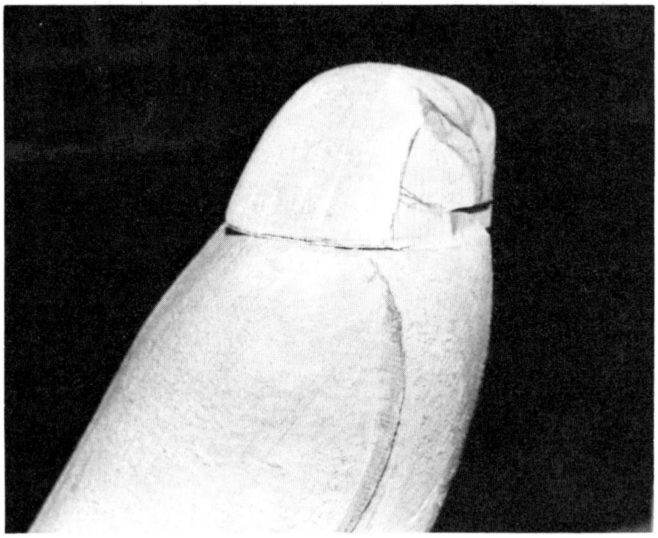

Side view of above

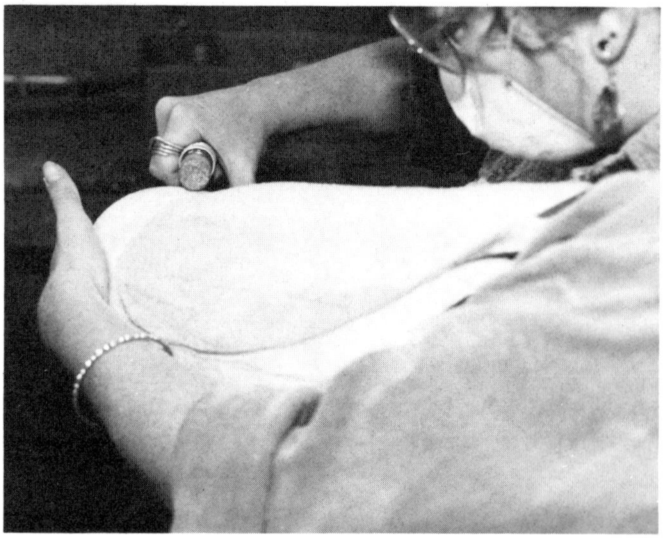

Shaping head to body

Deep indentation of cape line and roll in to deepest point

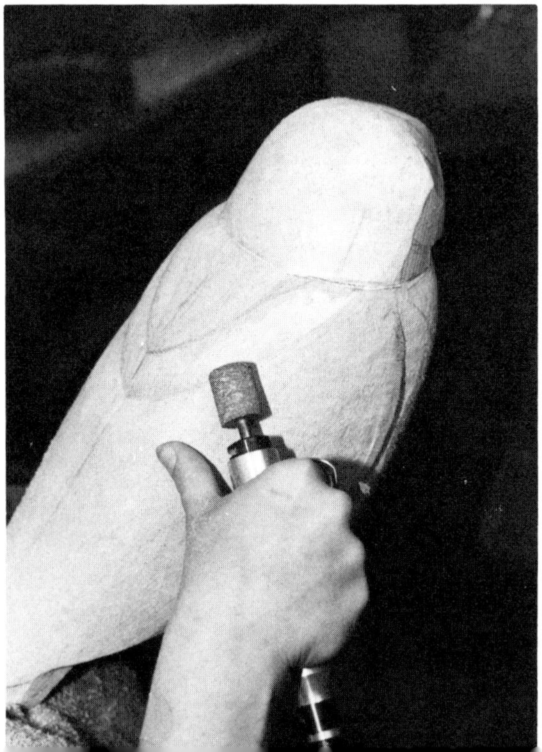

Full shaped cape area and flow through to head

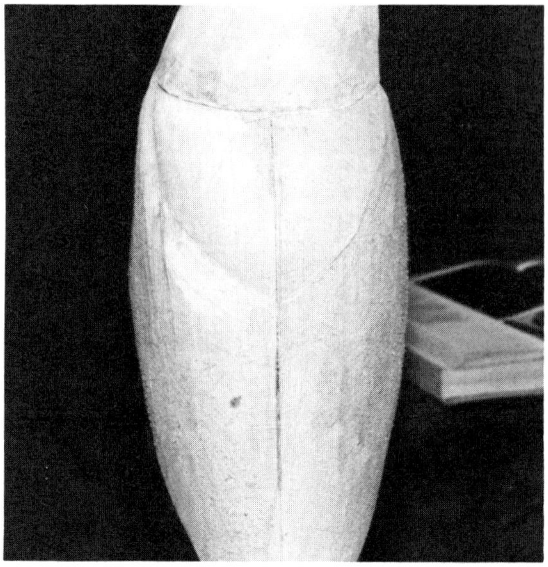

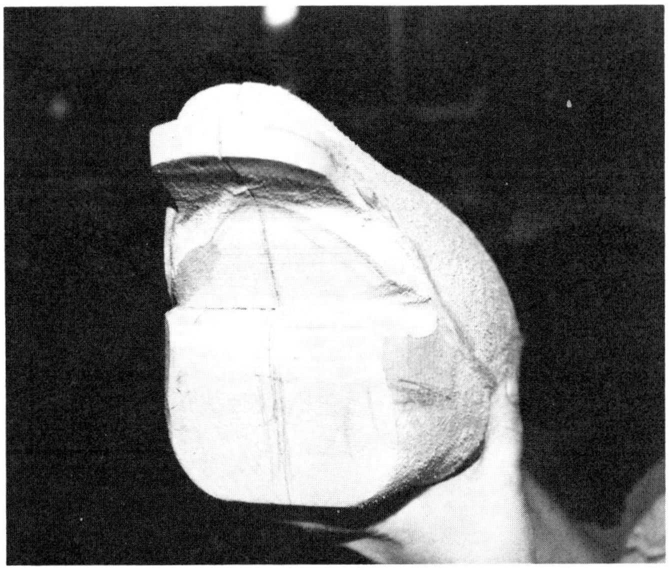

Initial cut in for under rump area

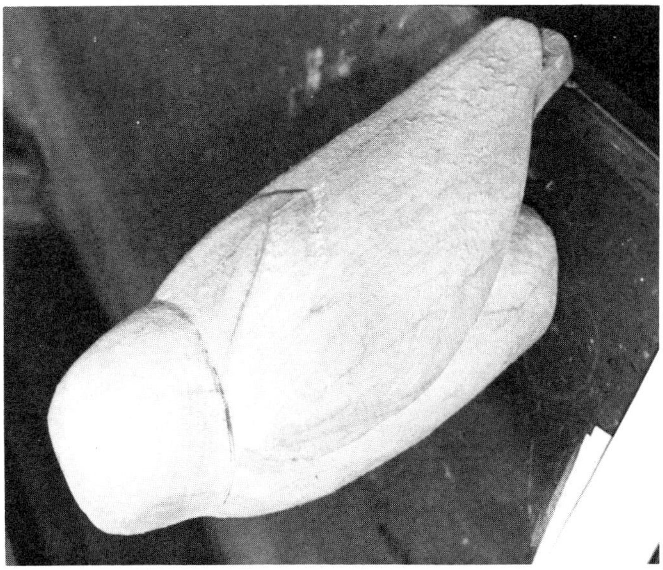

Shows back of head, cape and full wing shape

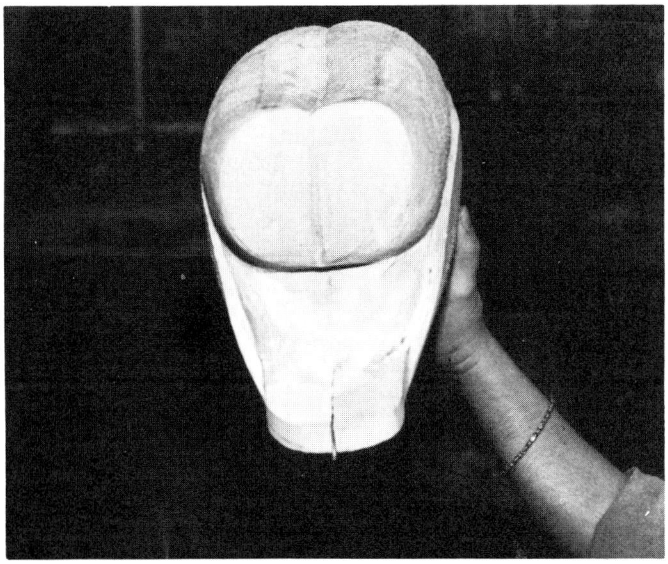

Fully shaped under rump and belly indent

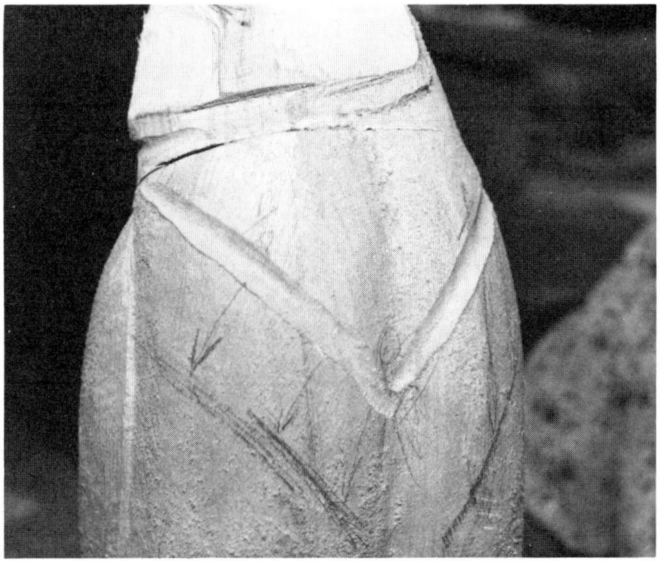

Breast indentations to create musculature

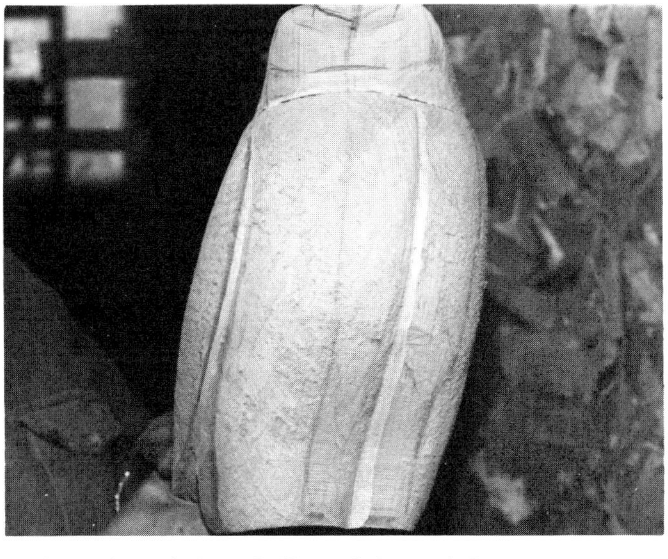

Indentation of chest, belly and through legs

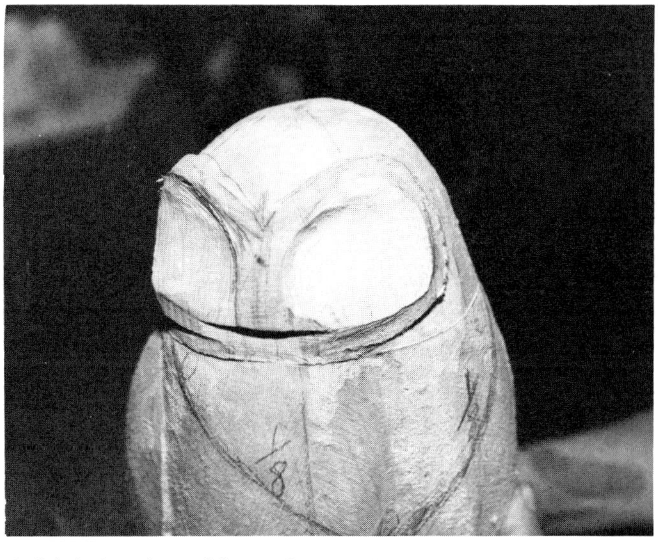

Initial shaping of face plate or discs

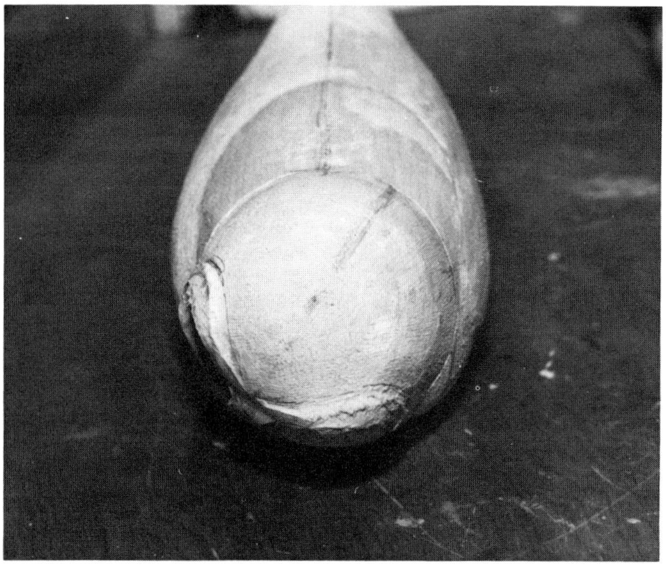

Top view of head (note face plate ridges)

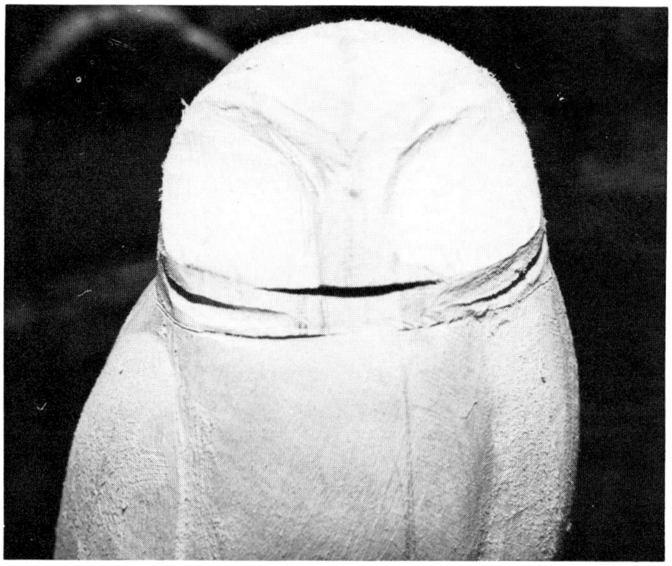

Shaping of facial discs

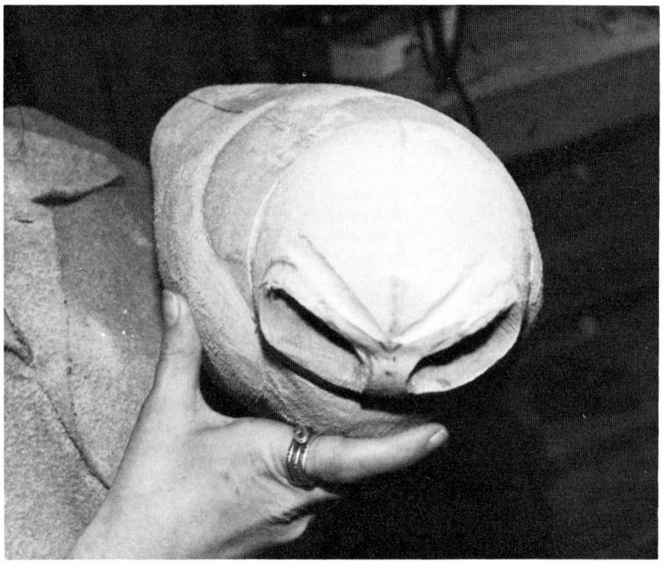

Note indentations to create ridges in head behind face plate

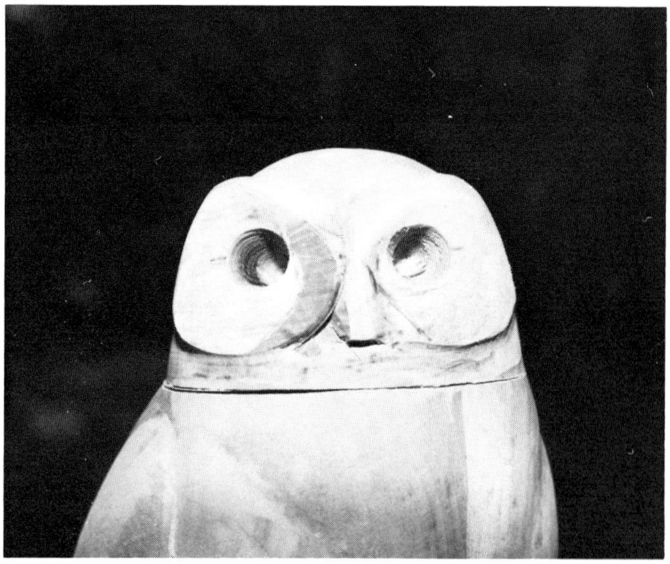

Eye sockets drilled and preliminary beak shaping

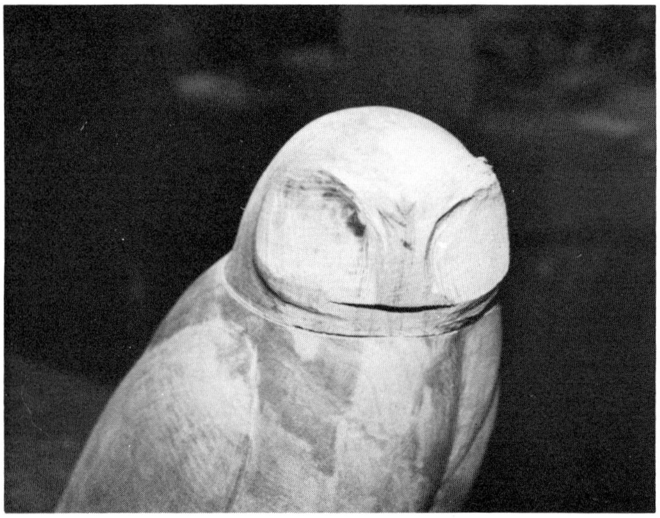

Further shaping of facial plates

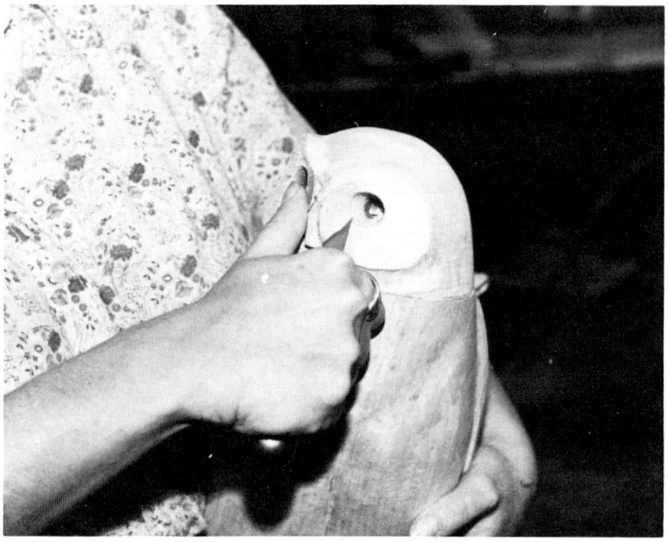

Refining facial discs and beak

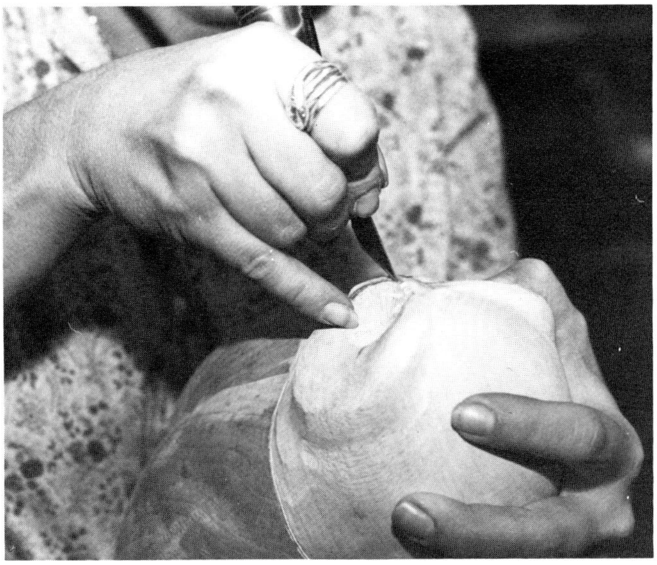

Detailing beak (note head has been sanded)

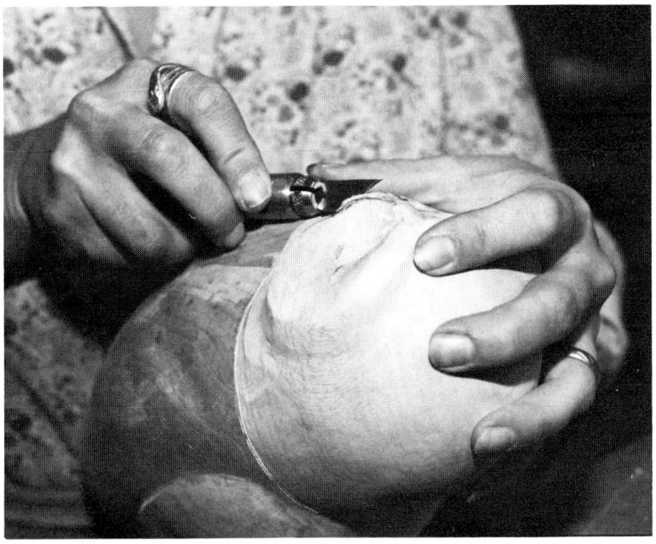

Continued refining of beak

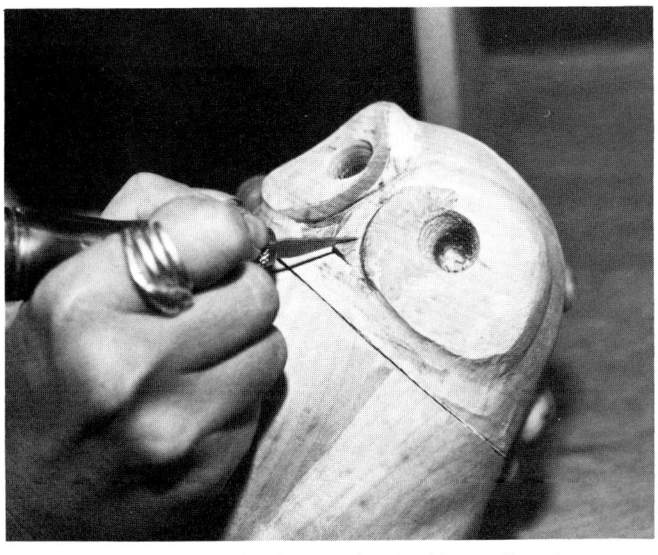

Delicate beak work is done with knife or fine burrs on flexible shaft machine

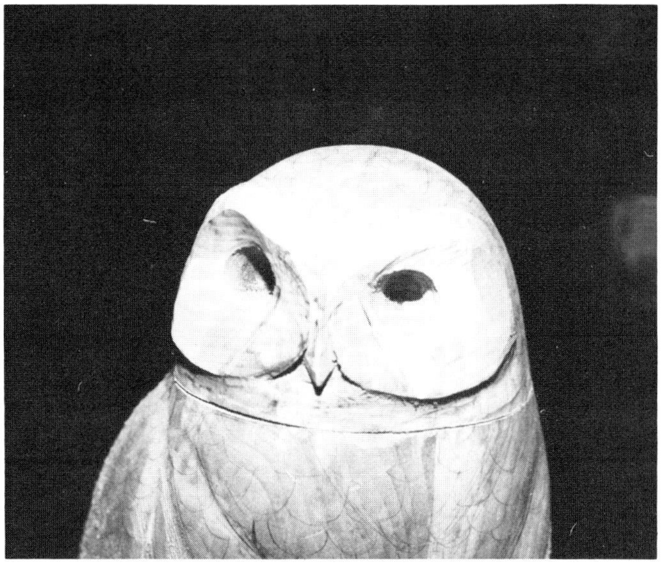

Facial discs and beak area basically finished and ready for texturing

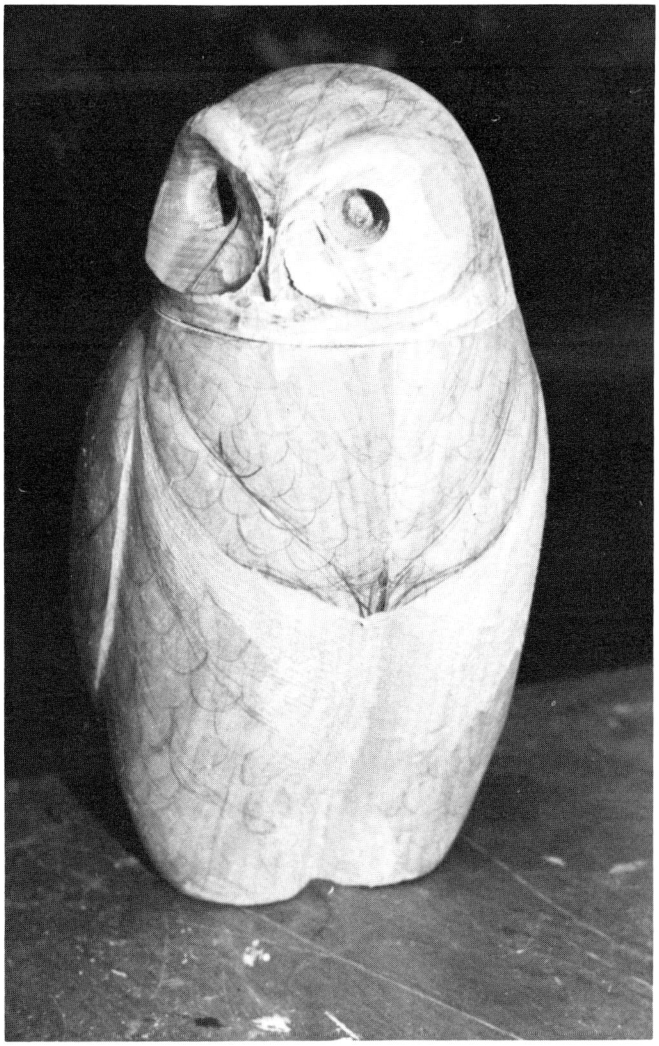

Chest area shaped

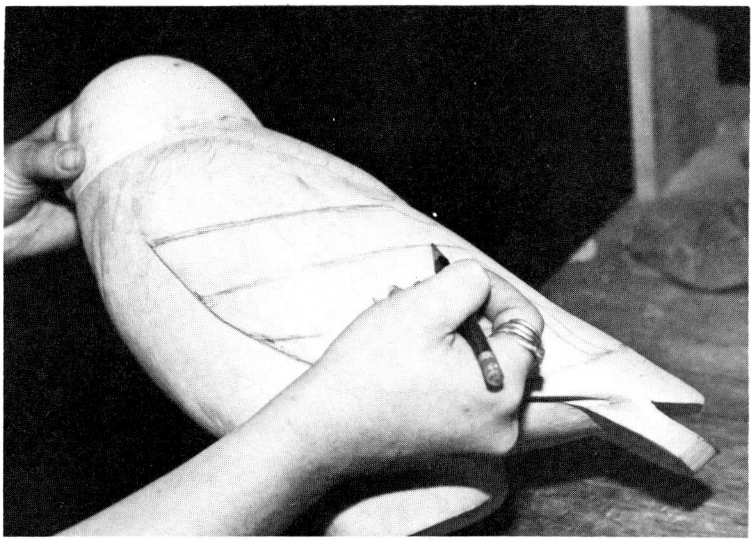

Feather layout in wing area

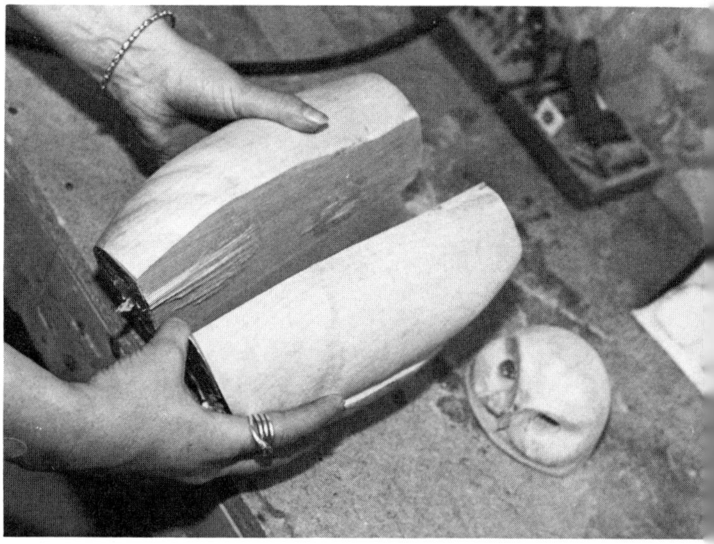

Head removed and body blocks separated for hollowing to lighten bird

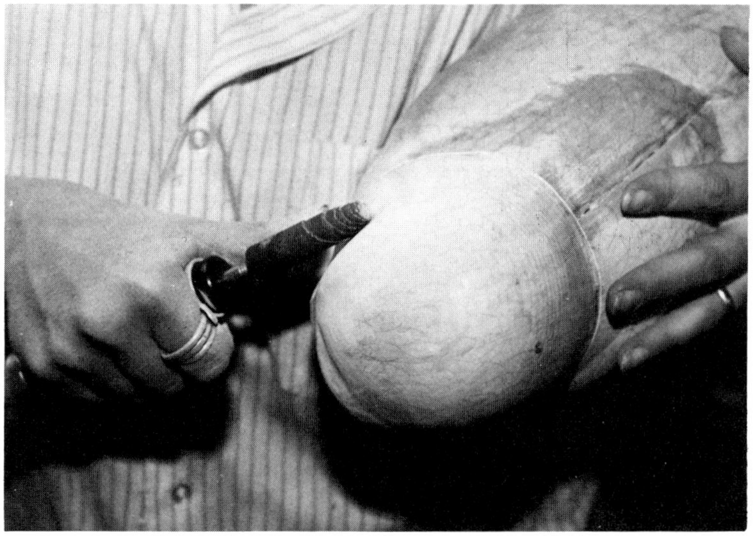

Rough sanding with cartridge roll (referred to as tootsie roll)

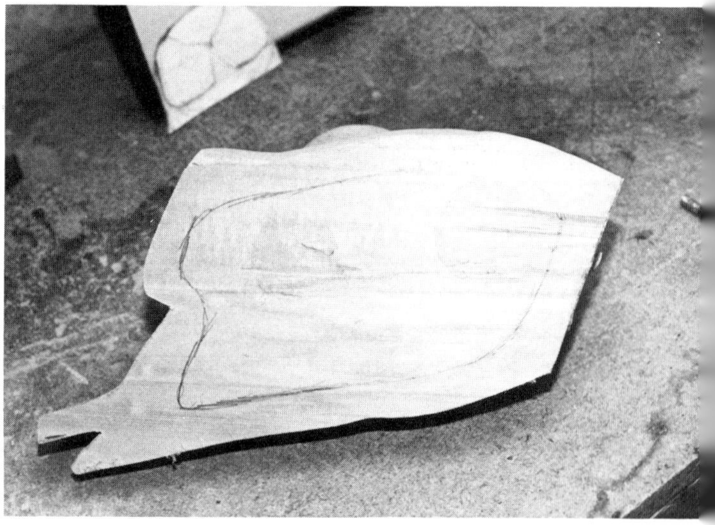

Area to be drilled out

Drilling excess wood—to lighten and to remove internal stresses to lessen probability of checking and cracking

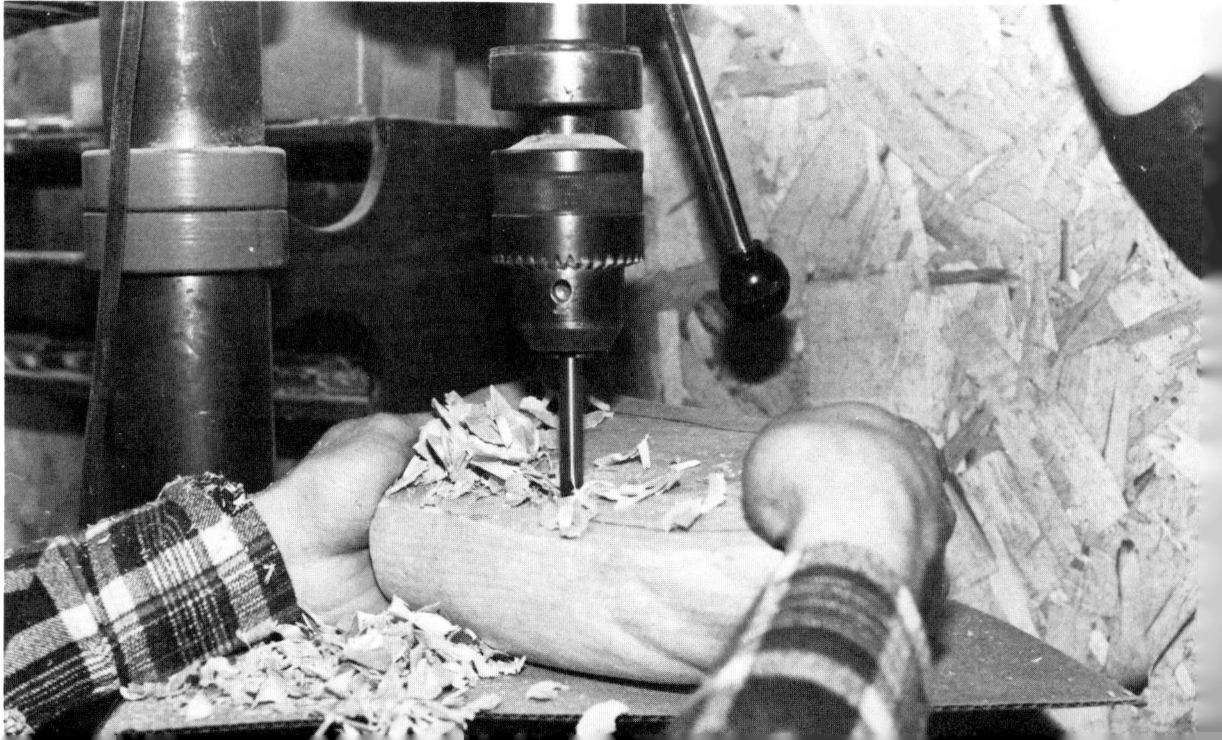

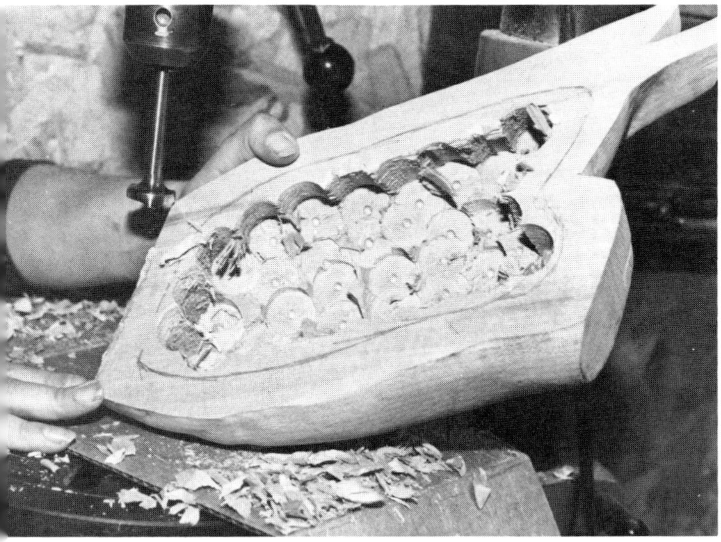

Hollowed half of body, at this point it is advisable to detail each half separately as it is easier to handle this way

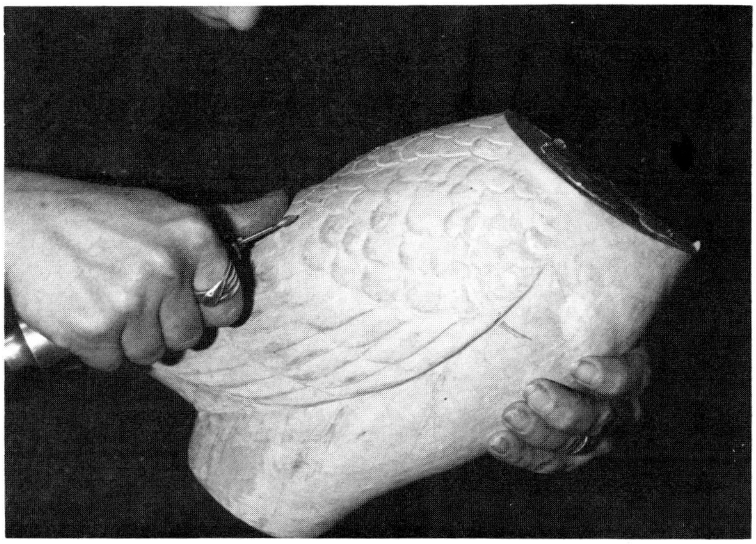

More ruby carver work, this creates an undulating effect

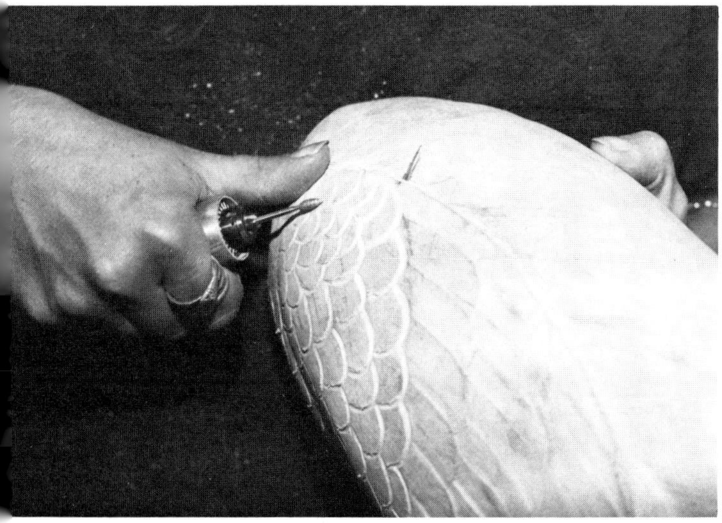

Creating "lumps and bumps" by rolling each feather in both directions with ruby carver

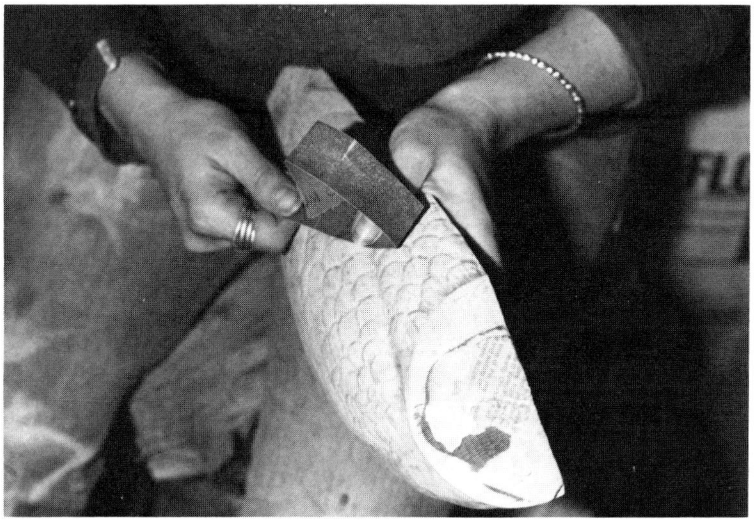

Hand sanding with strip paper (coated abrasive 120 grit)

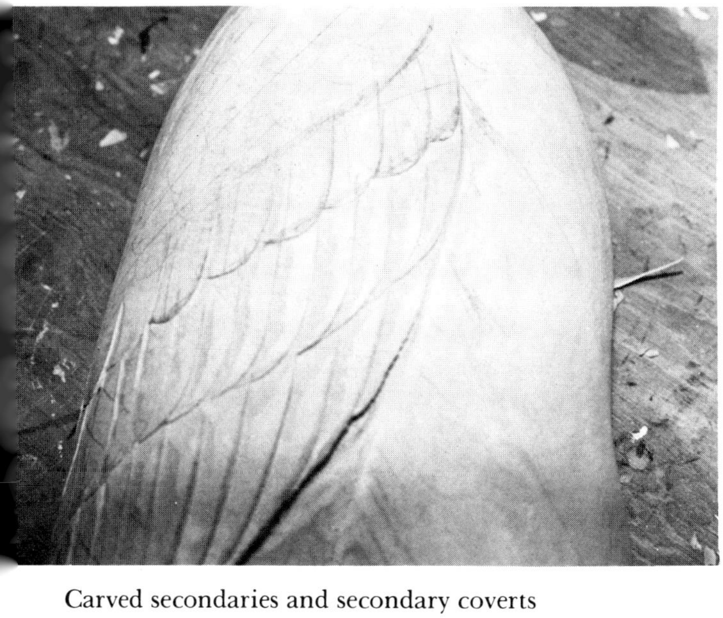

Carved secondaries and secondary coverts

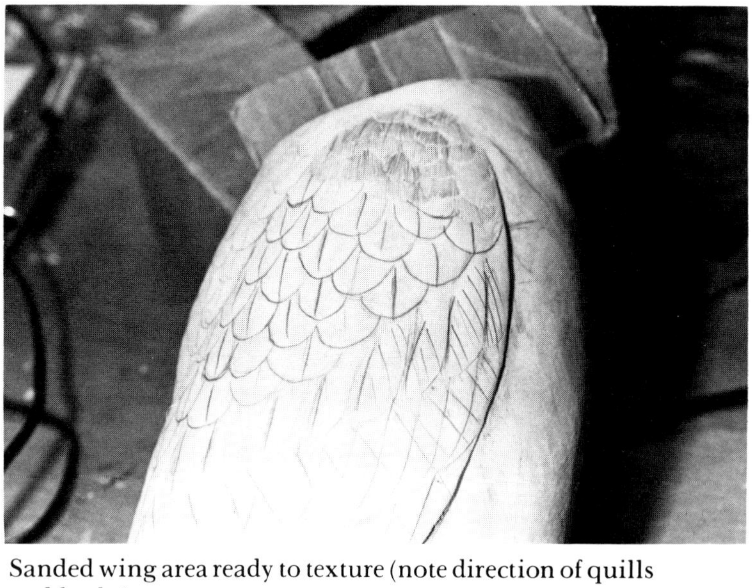

Sanded wing area ready to texture (note direction of quills and barbs)

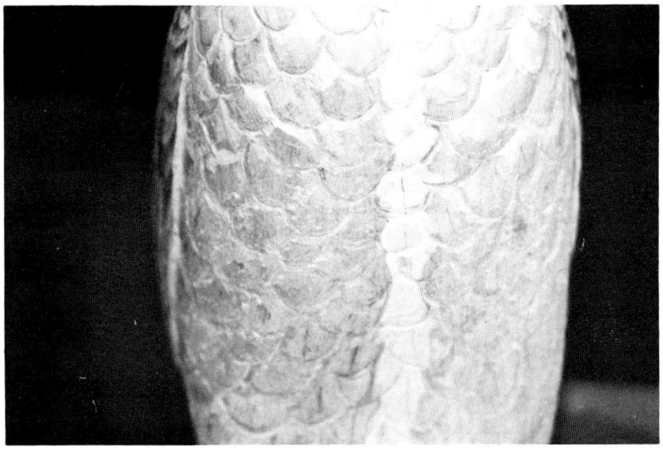

Carved belly and chest, note wide seam of fill material (wood dough with large amounts of acetone to break down air gaps)

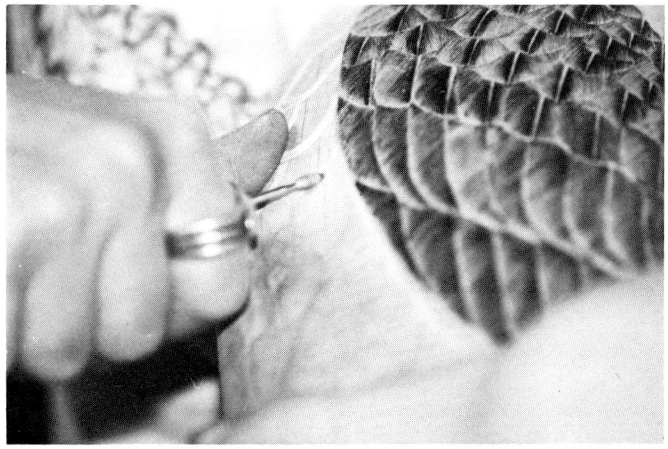

More carving by ruby carver, note burned wing area with raised quills (shafts)

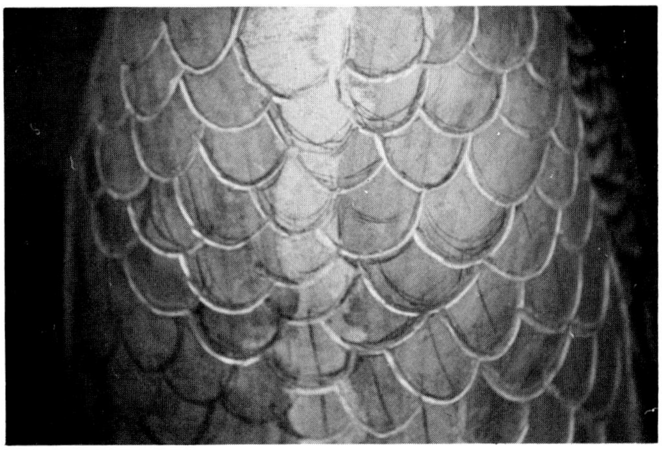

Chest area carved with ruby carver

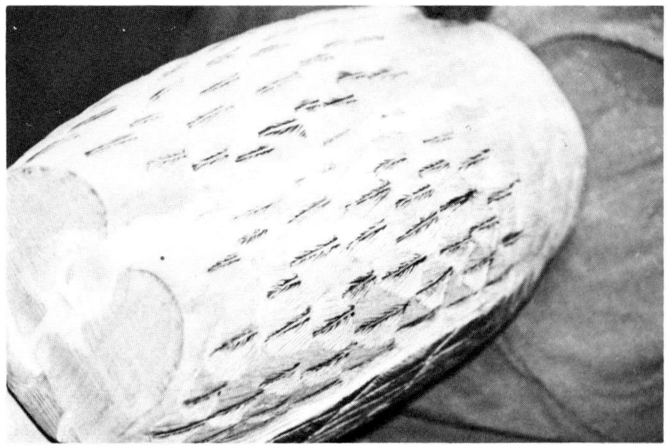

Quills (shafts) are raised by first tracing shaft with burner then flat edging with flat side of burner edge

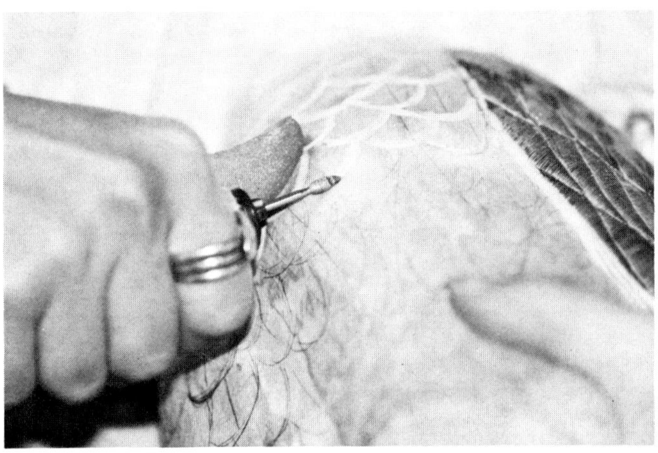

Carving feathers with small ruby carver

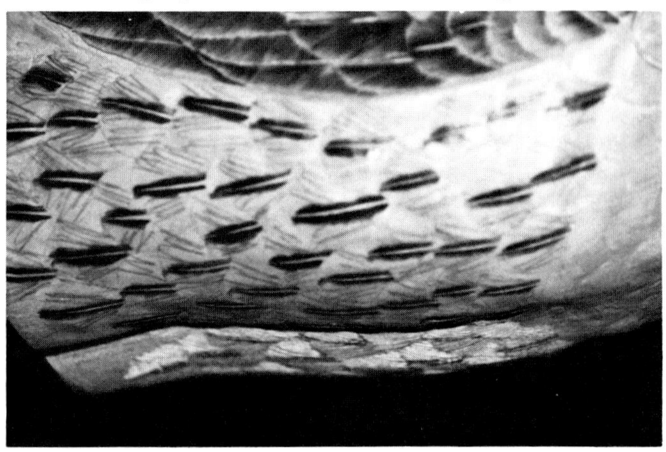

Close up of raised quills

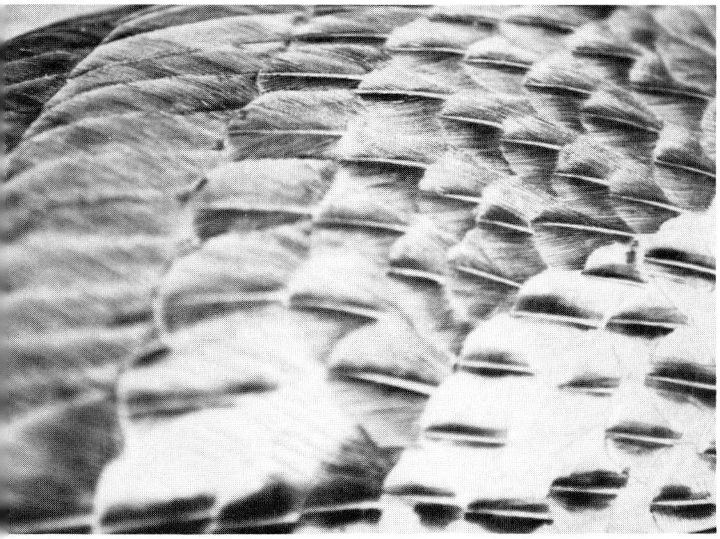

Raised quills and burned feathers (note how tight burning is)

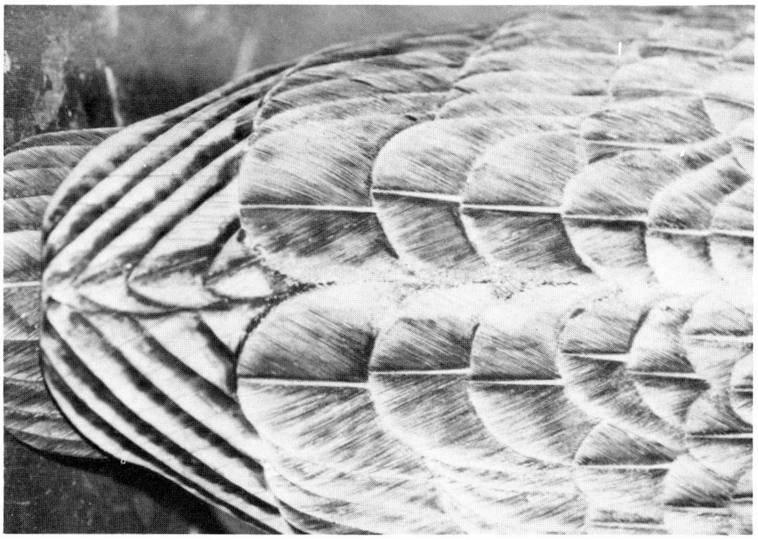

Burned belly (note feather layout)

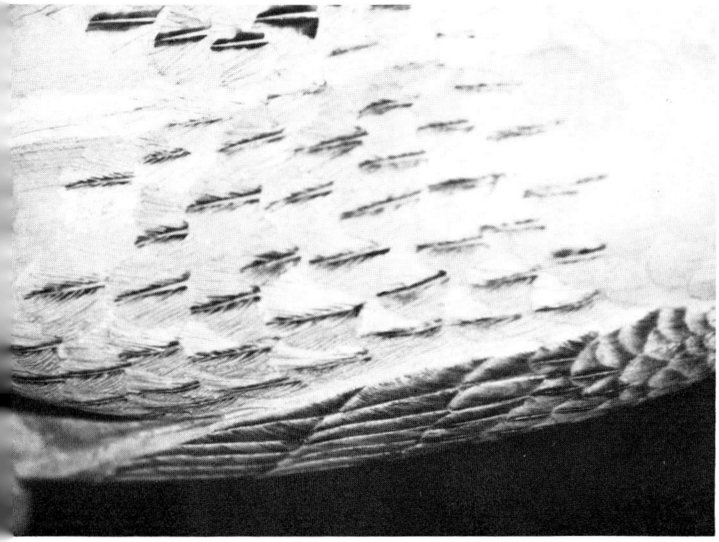

Raised quills on legs and belly

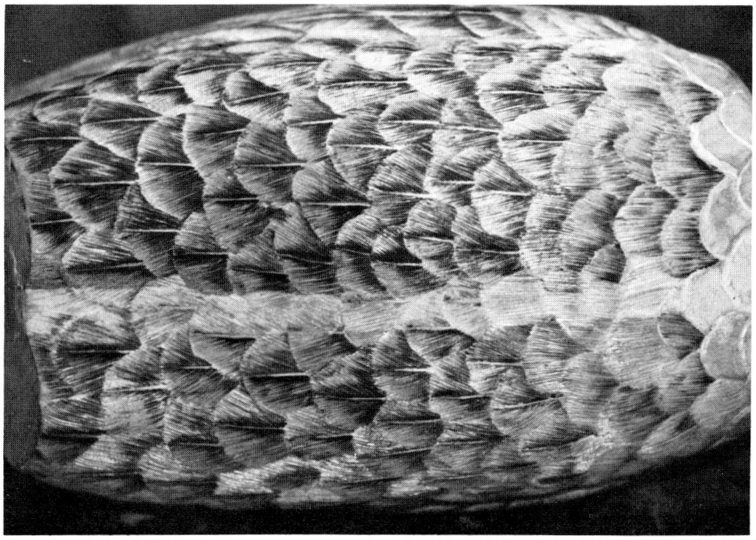

Burned feather groups—tertials, secondaries, primaries and tail

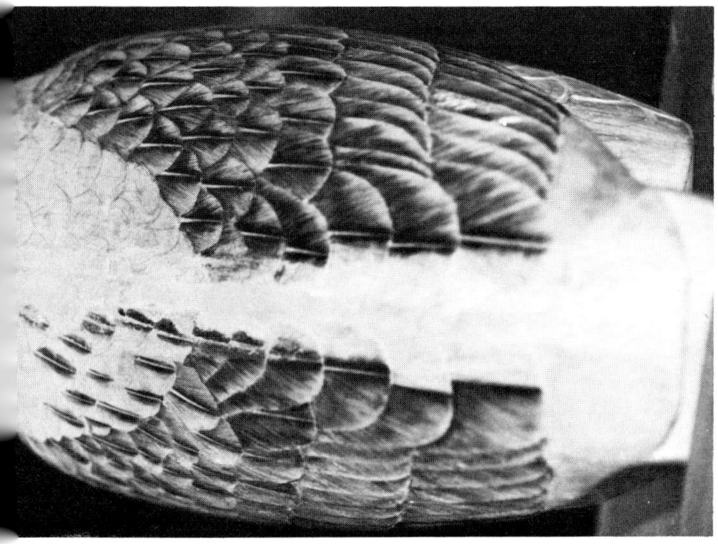

Burned back (note feather layout)

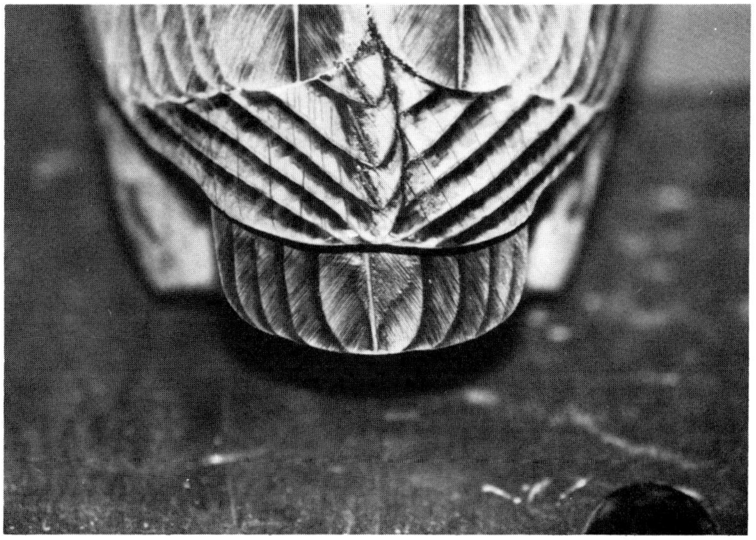

Same as above—different view

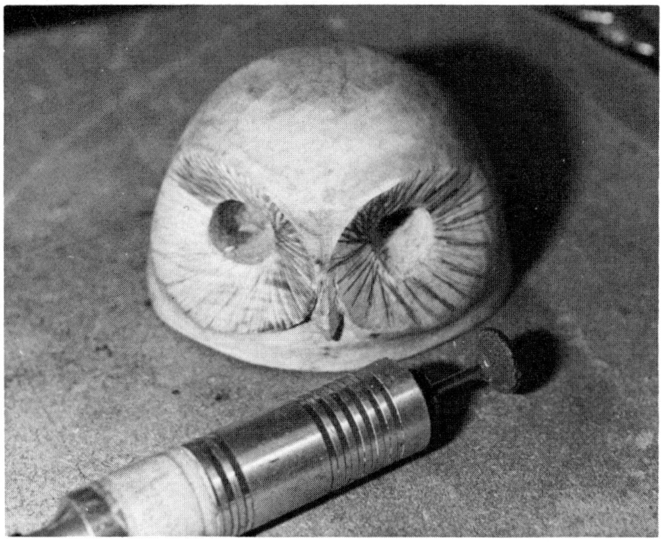

Deep stoning of face plate

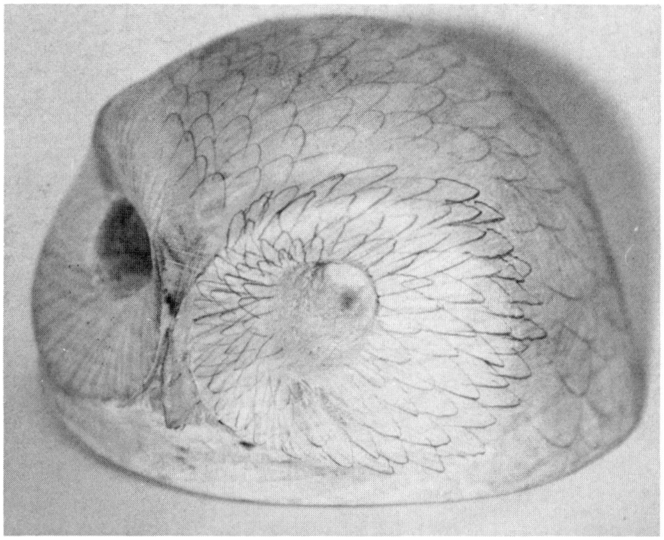

Feather layout on facial disc and head

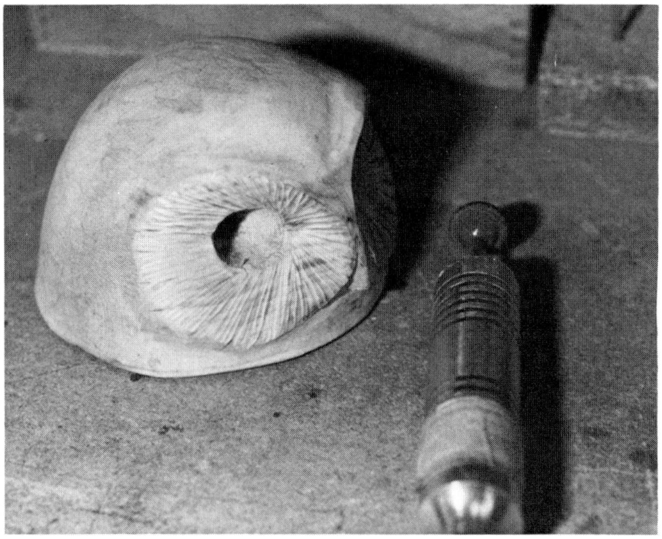

Another view of above

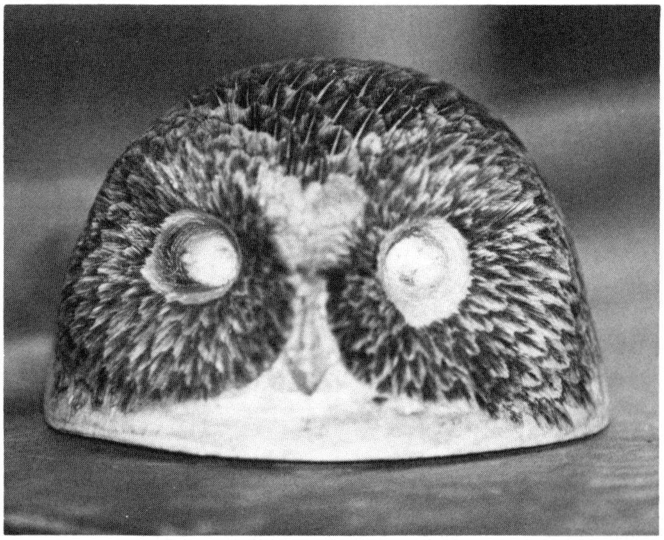

Burned face and head

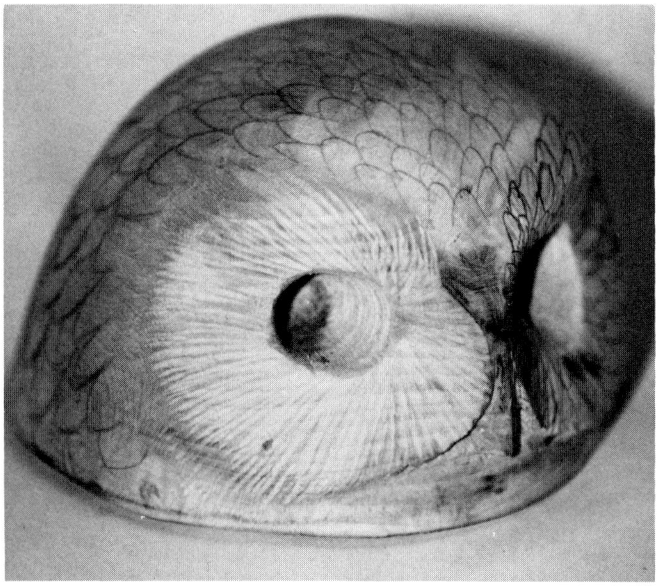

Texture direction on facial disc

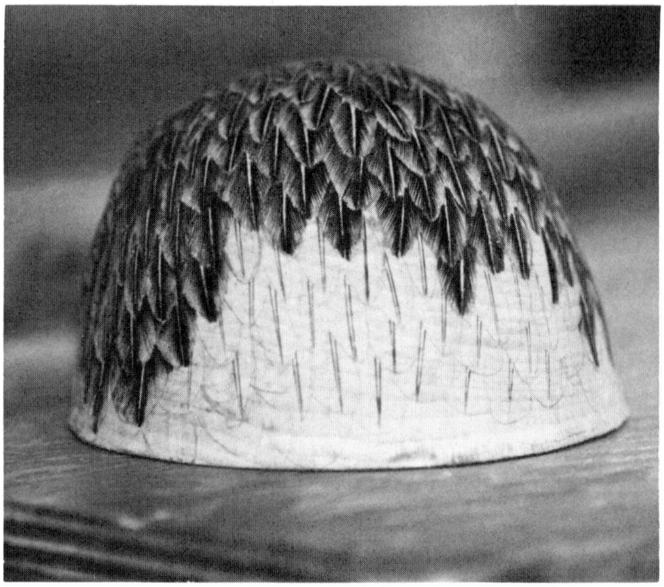

Back of head layout and example of burning

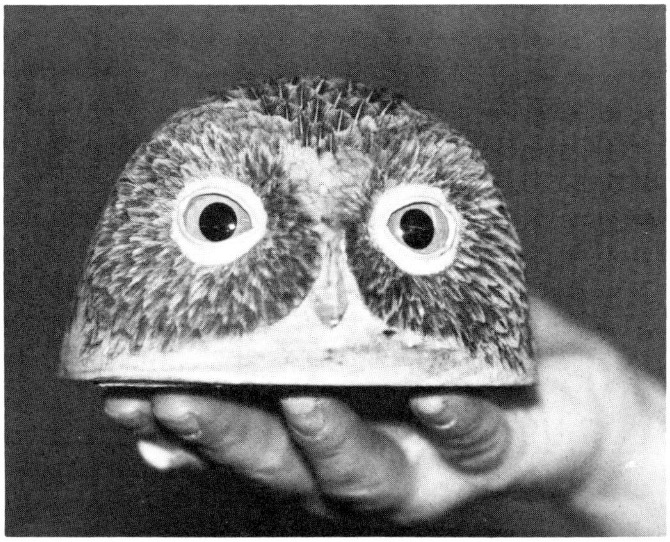

Setting of eyes using epoxy putty to sculpt eyelids, this is water workable with finger and brush for about 1/2 hour (note the eyes and lids are almond shaped)

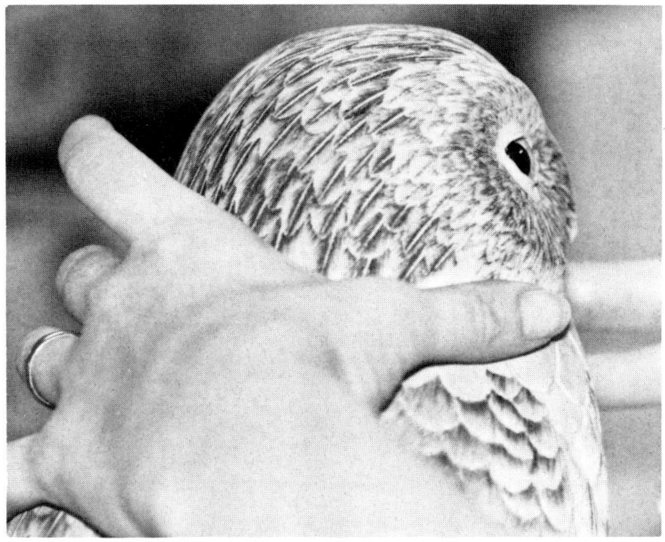

Neck joint is filled with wood dough with liberal amounts of acetone. Maintain wide band of fill material to hide seam

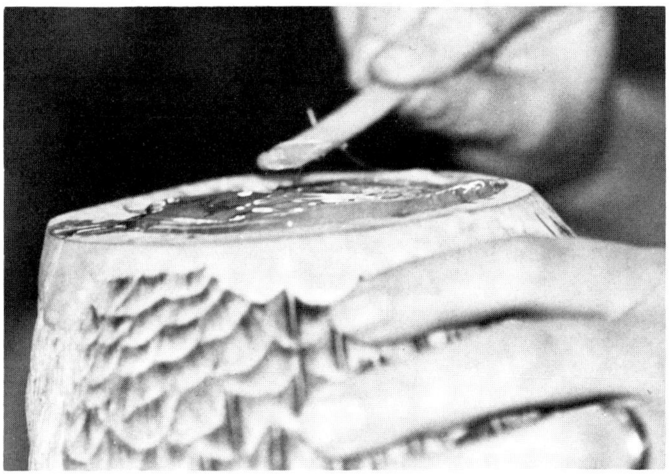

Head attached to body with 5-minute epoxy

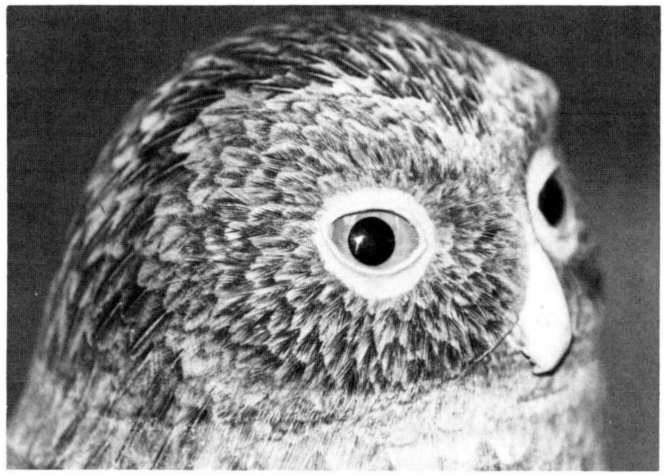

Neck joint after burning

Neck joint in back of head

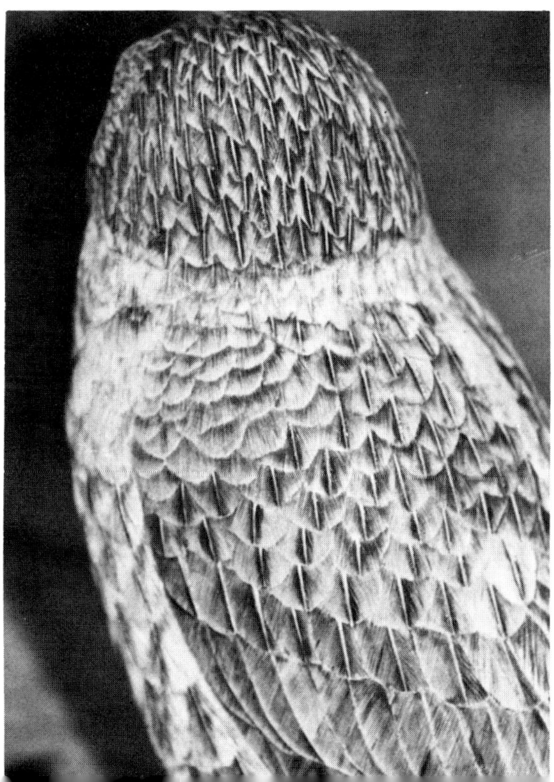

Burned wing and leg area

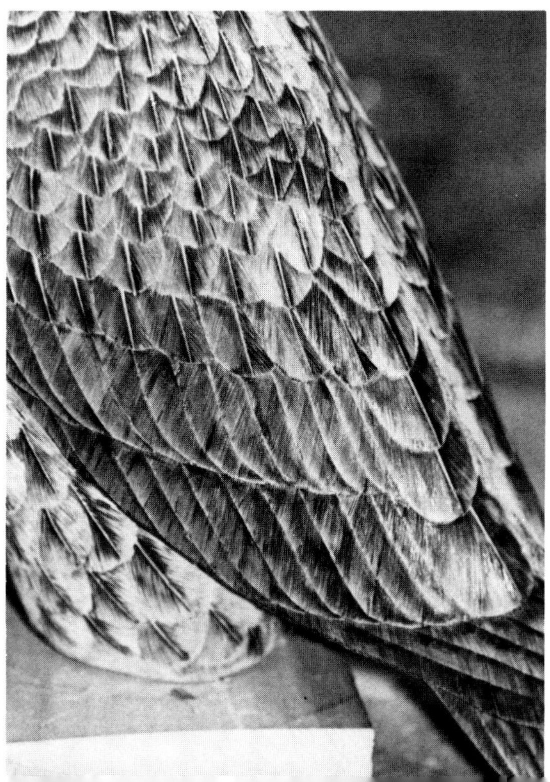

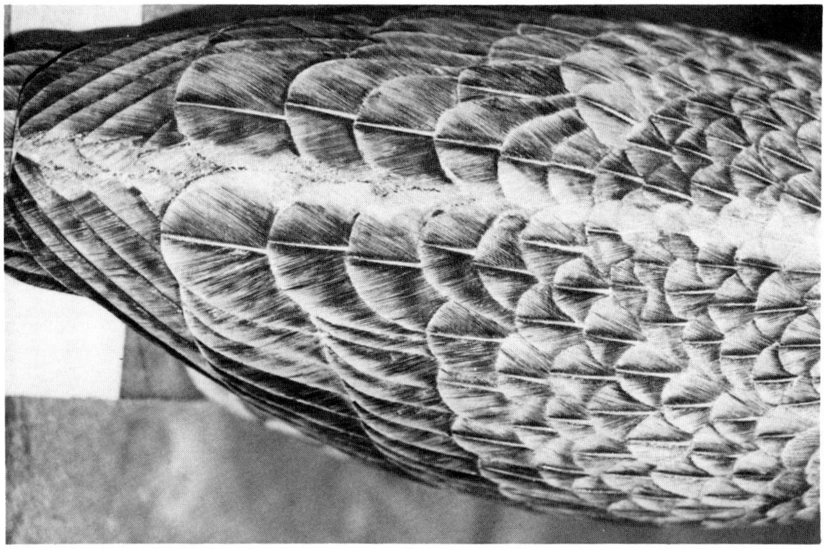

Back of bird burned

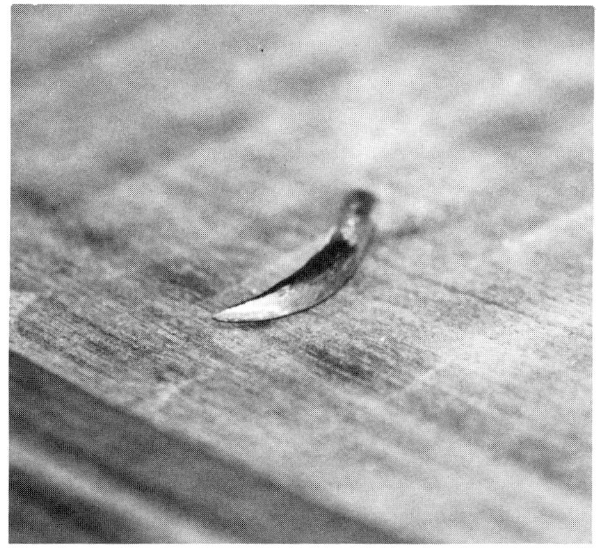

Completed talon

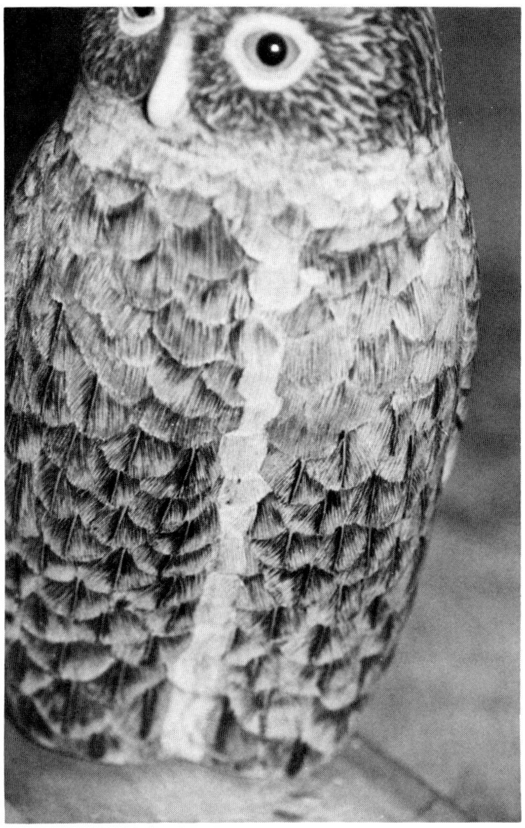

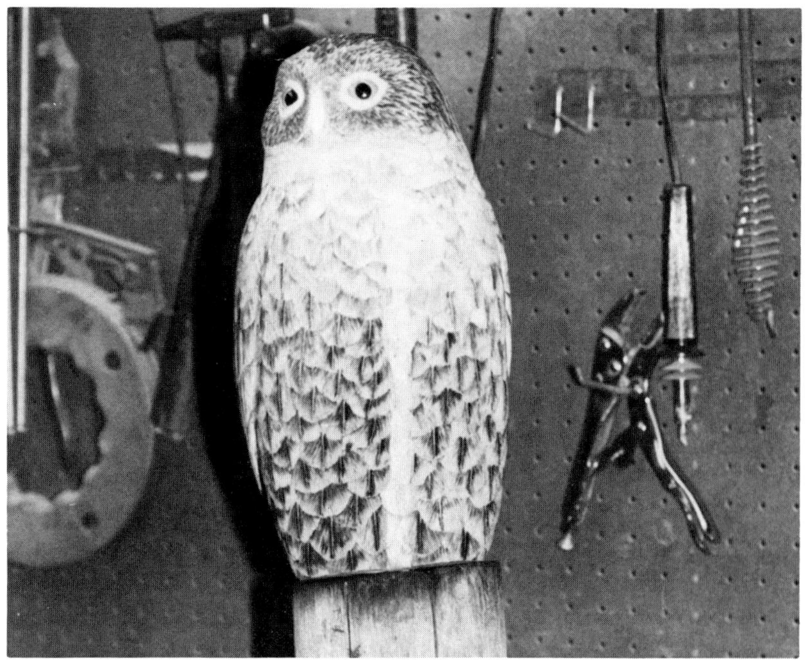

Preparing perch

Area where legs meet perch

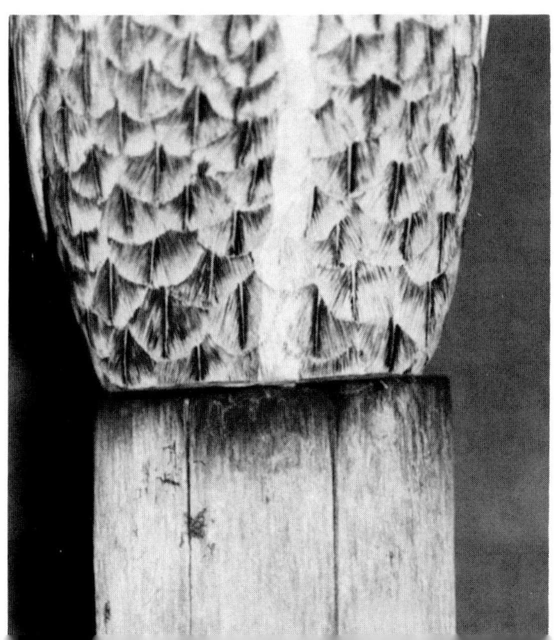

Belly of bird burned

Making talon out of brass

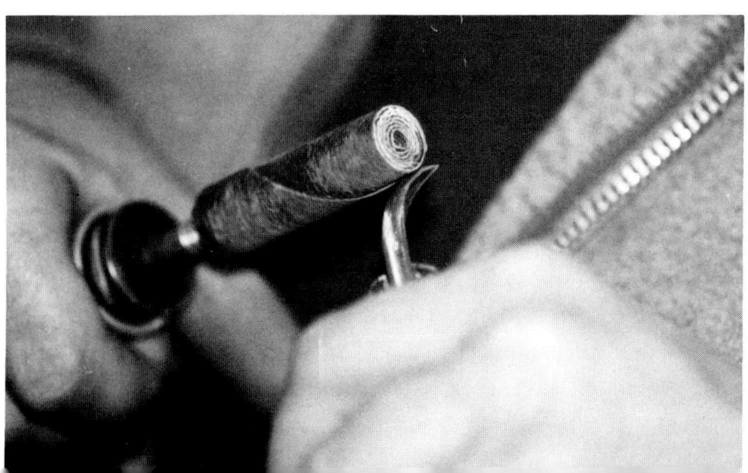

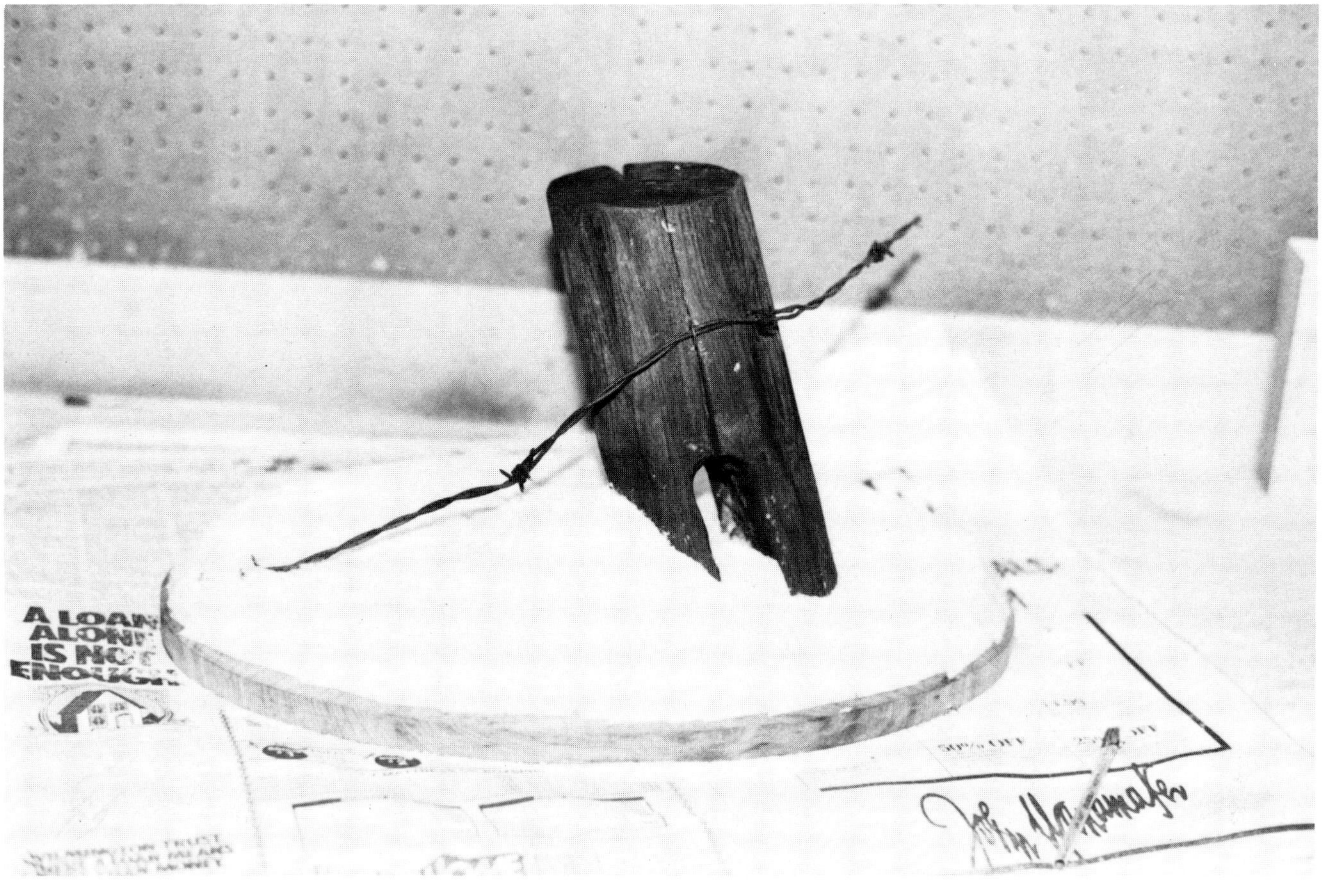

Barbed wire fence post (cut down), snow (glue and crushed glass) on walnut base

Base after several coats of glue and glass

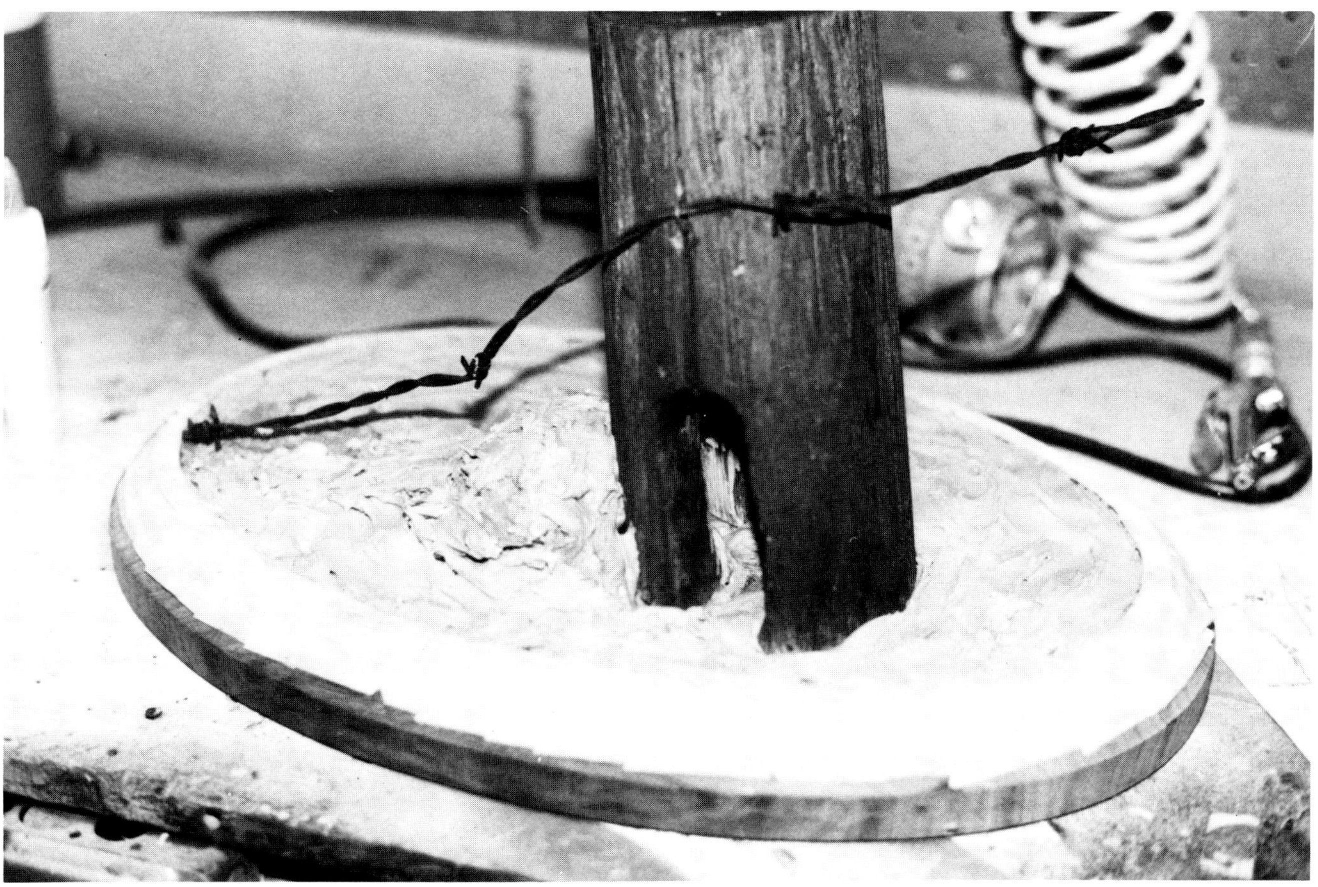

Osprey

TWO-THIRDS SIZE
Carved by Jeff Ebel

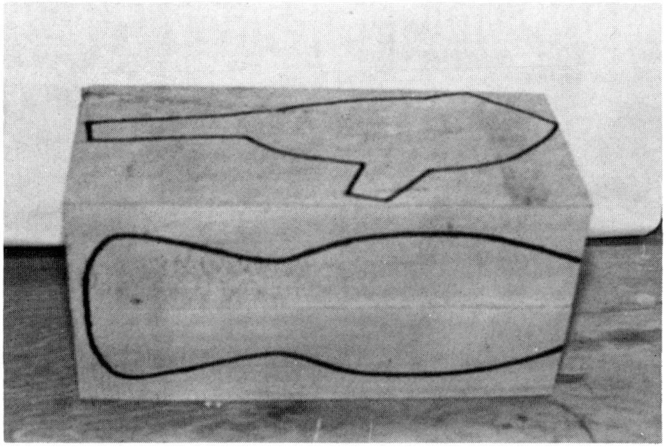

Plan and profile views of pattern on block

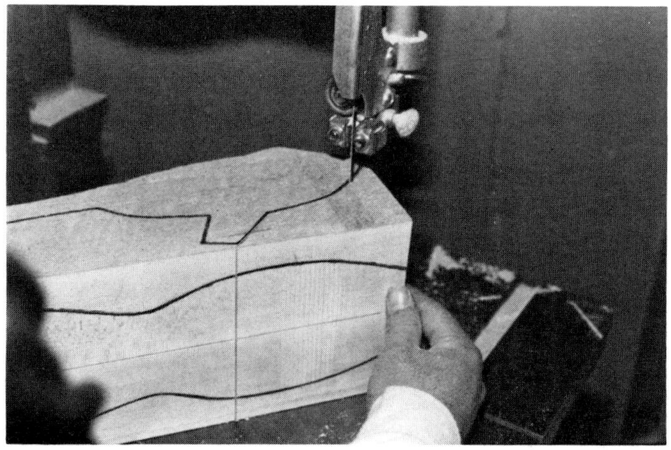

Cutting profile on band-saw

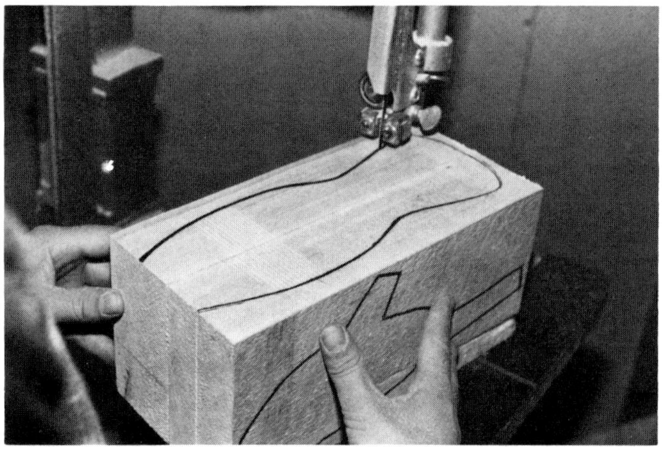

Cutting plan view on band-sawed

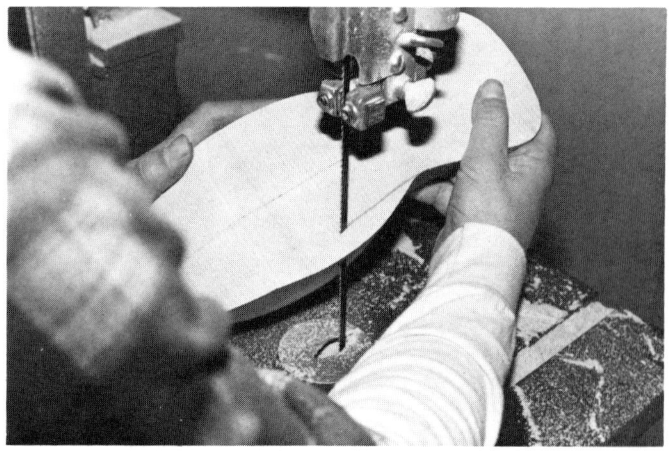

Trimming roughed out block on band-saw

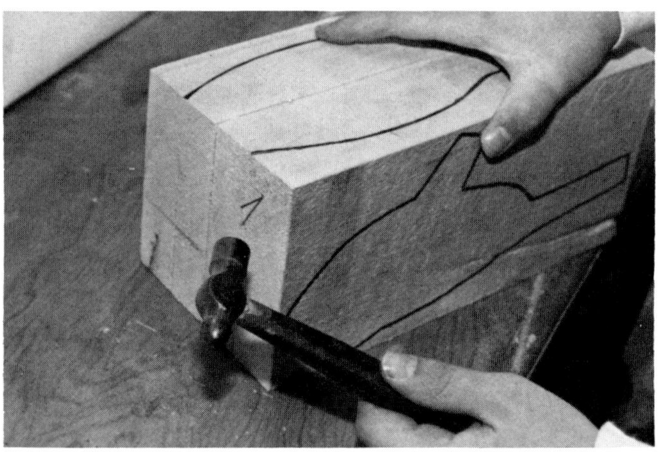

Nailing pieces together to maintain a square for safe and accurate cutting

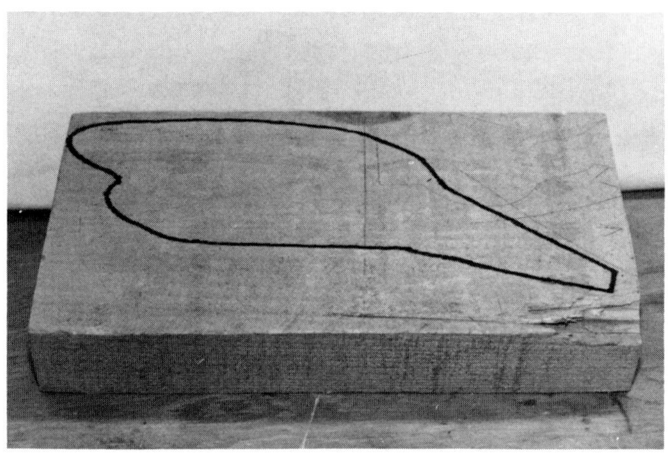

Plan view of wing (2" stock)

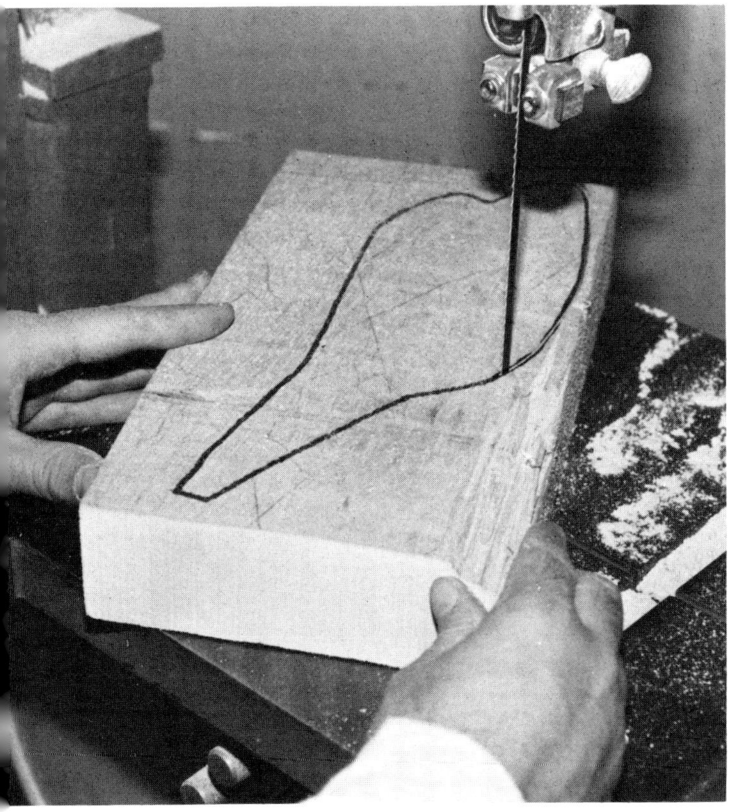

Cutting out wing on band saw

(See page 156 for painting instructions and page 278 for patterns)

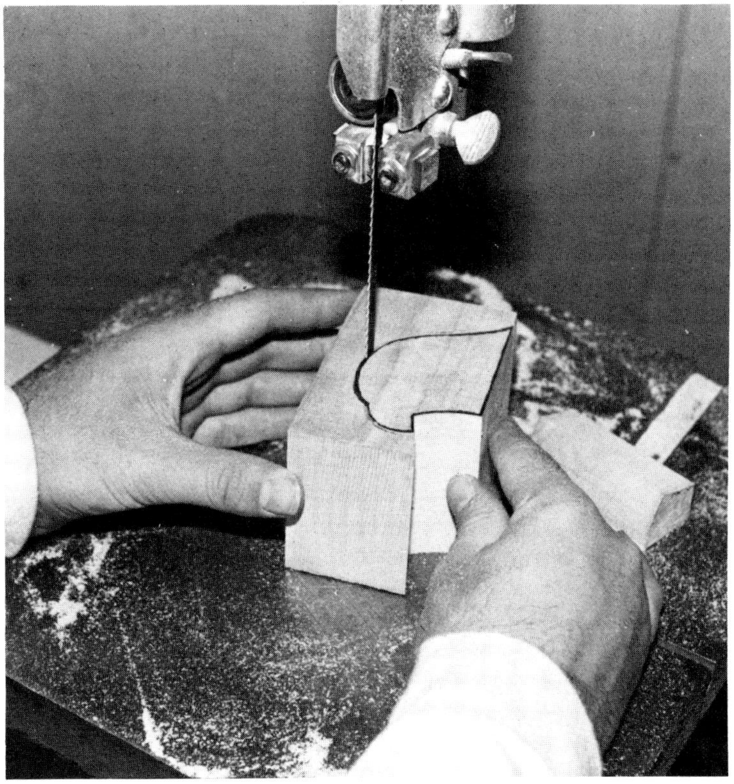

Cutting head profile on band saw

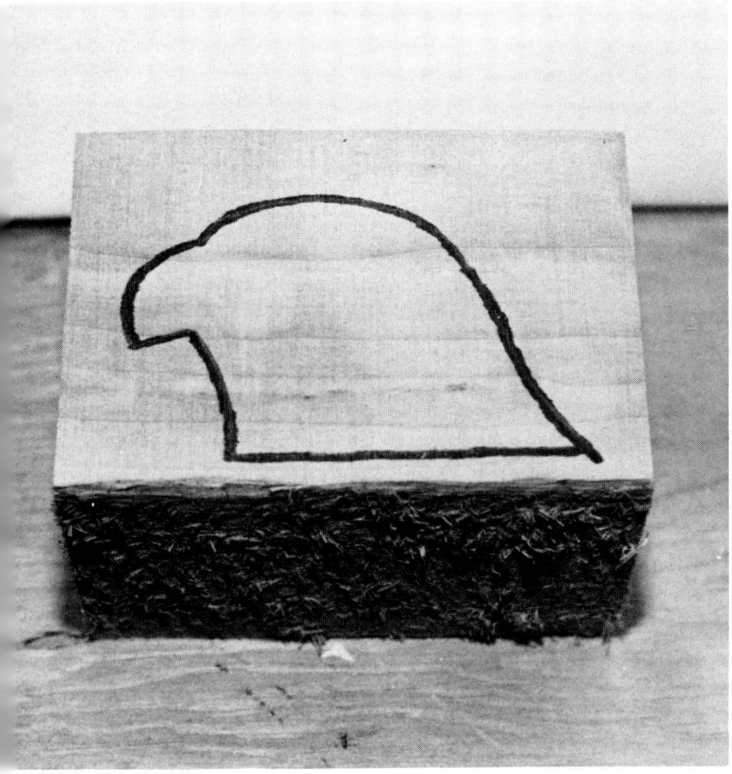

Profile of head pattern on block

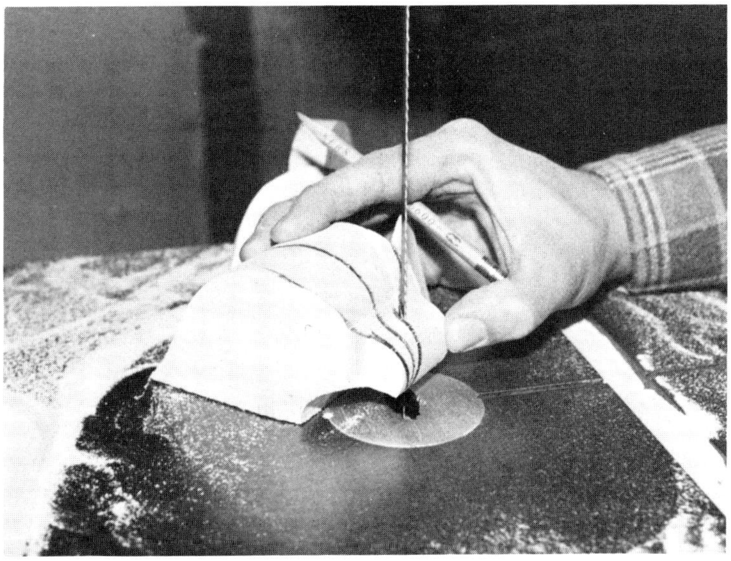

Cutting plan view of head on band saw

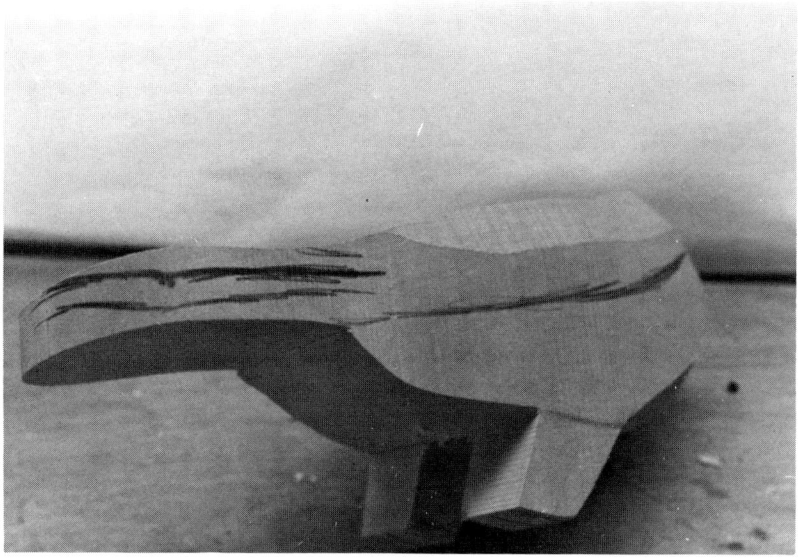

Body rough cut with pencil guide lines, note: arc in tail

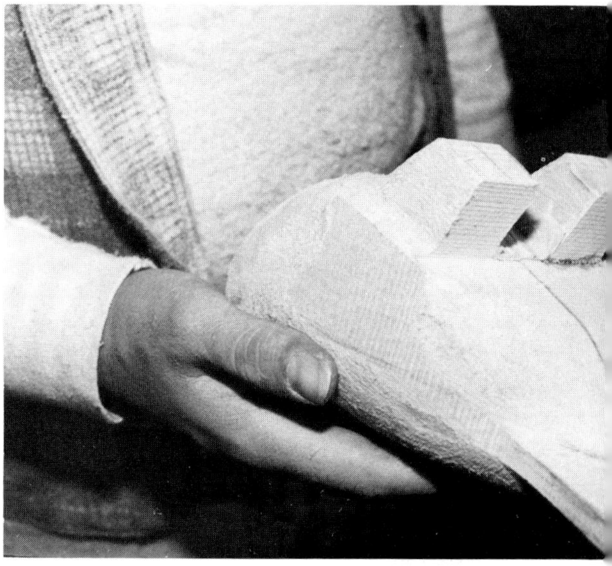

Legs notched for separation on band saw

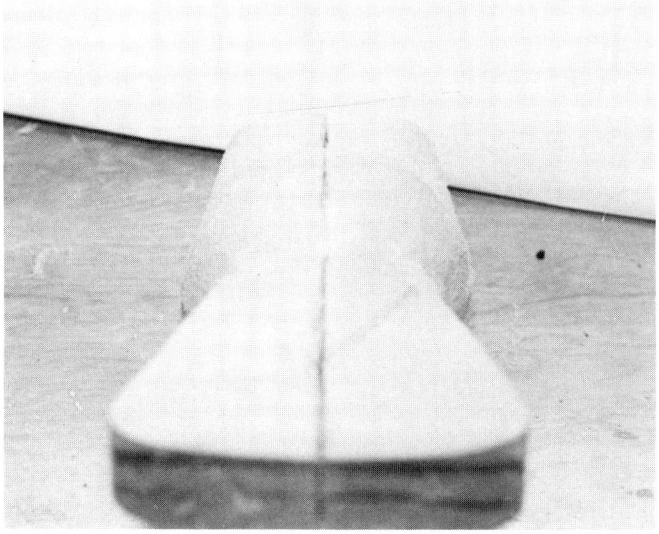

Body rounded used rasp or carbide bit with flexible shaft machine

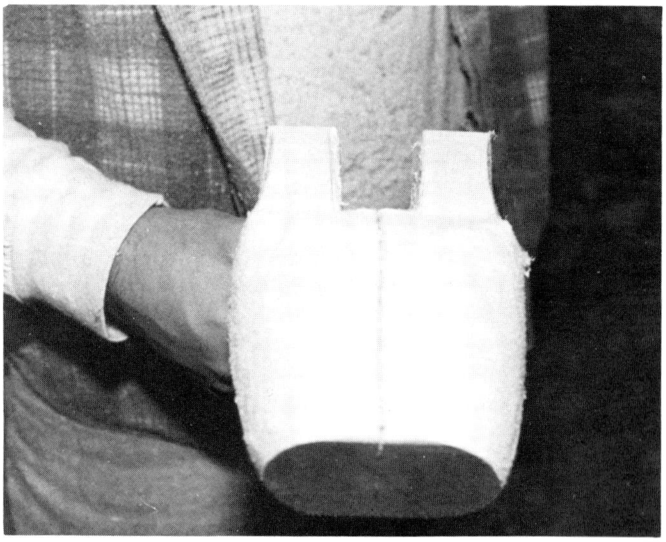

Front view of legs with center removed to make separation

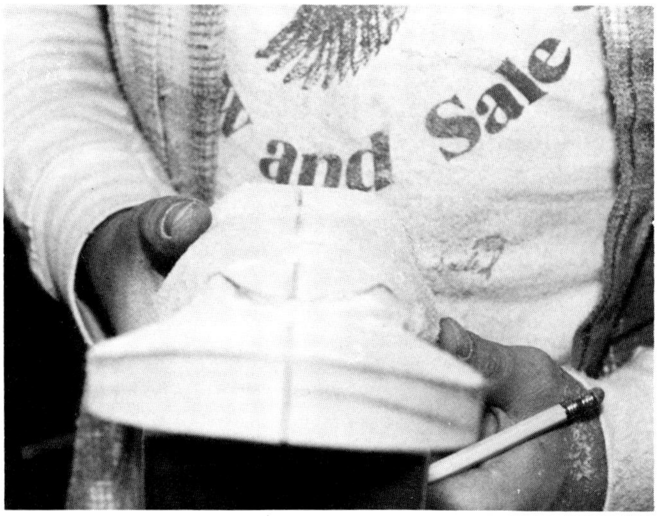

Arc of tail—make accurate pencil guides, they are very important

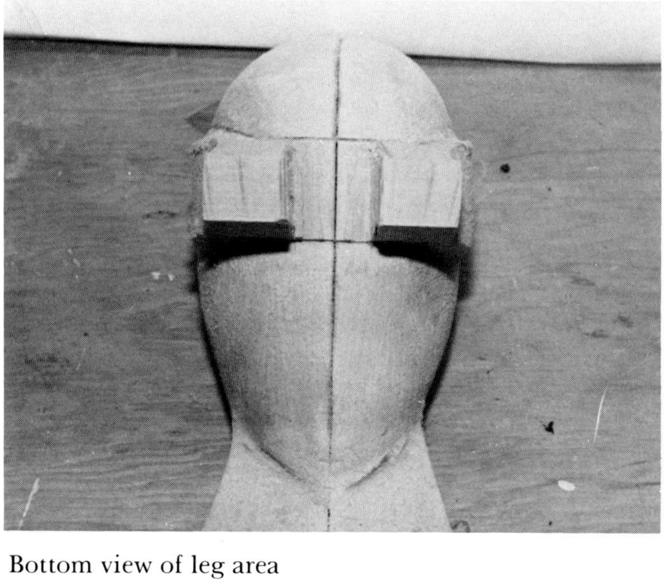

Bottom view of leg area

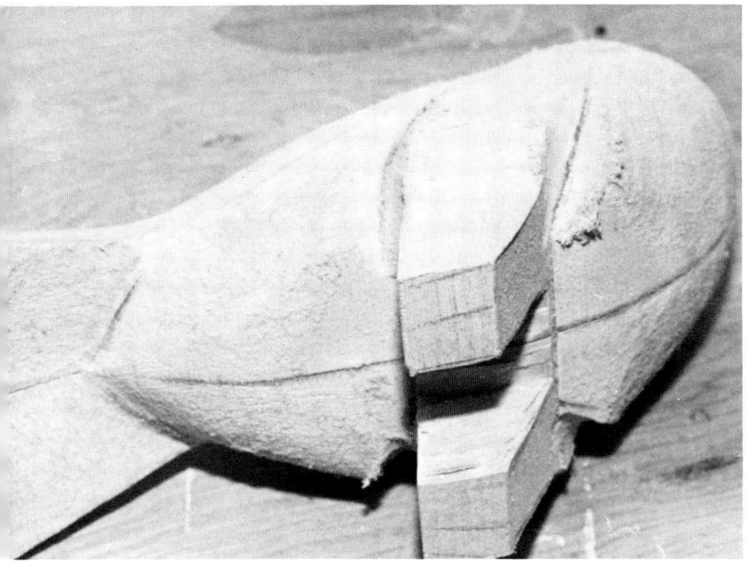

Shaping under rump

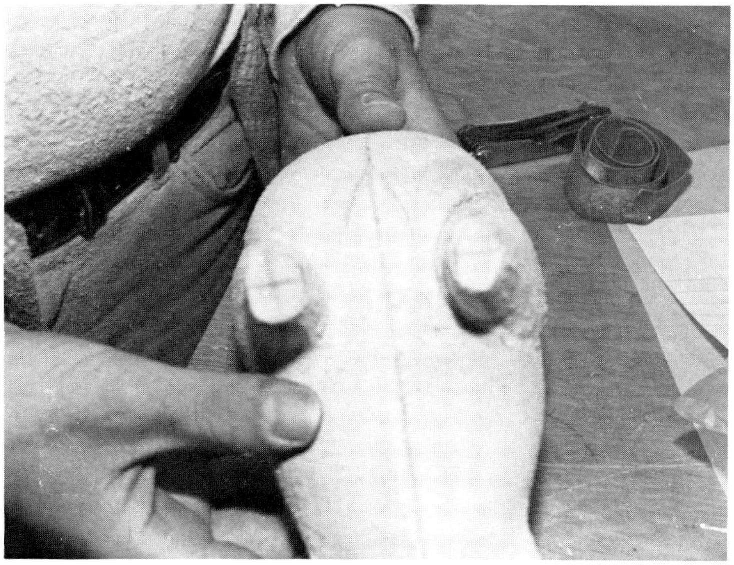

Legs shaped

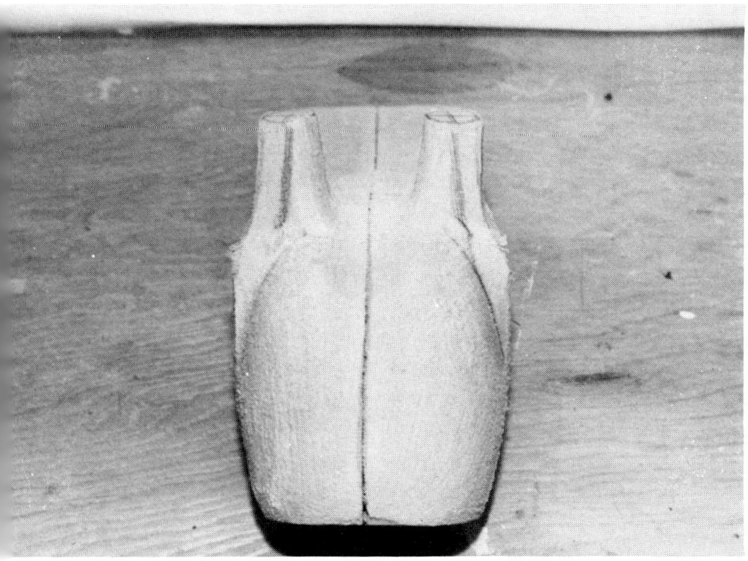

Legs shaped (note: guide line) belly flowing into legs

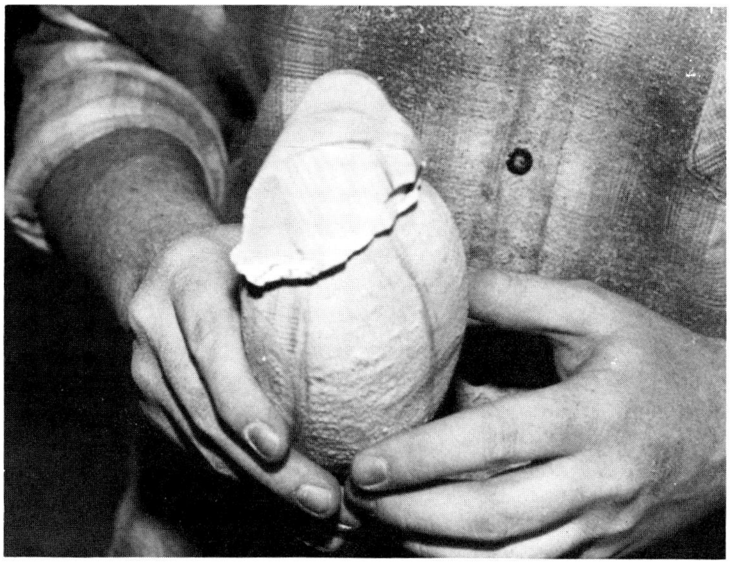

Roughed out head set temporarily to be shaped

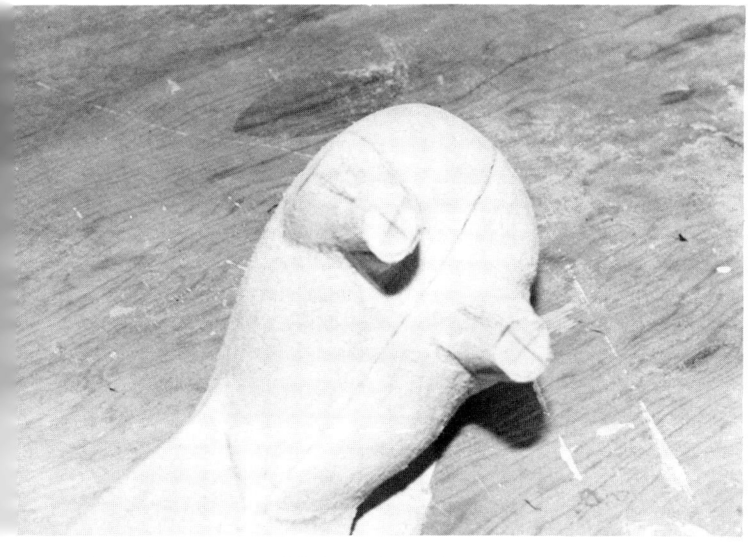

Legs in process of being shaped

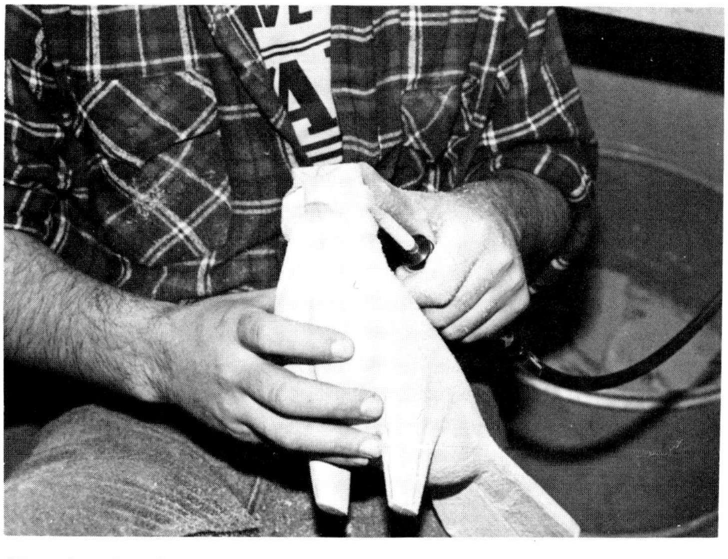

Shaping head

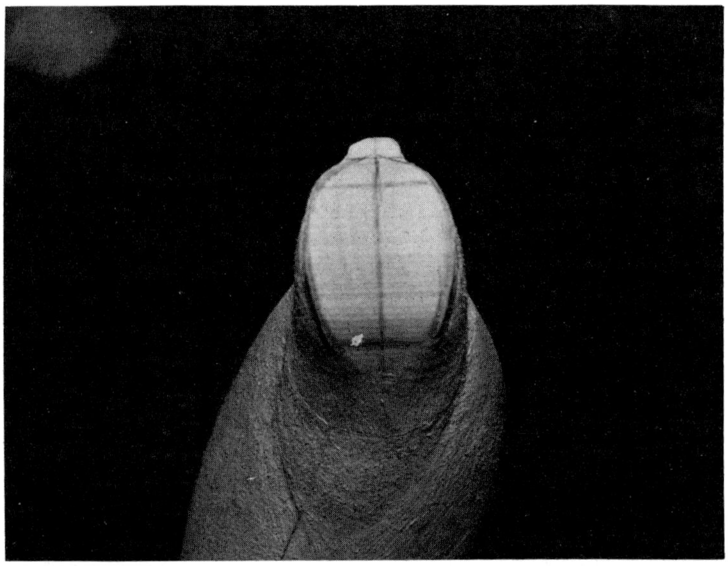

Top of head and neck flowing into cape area

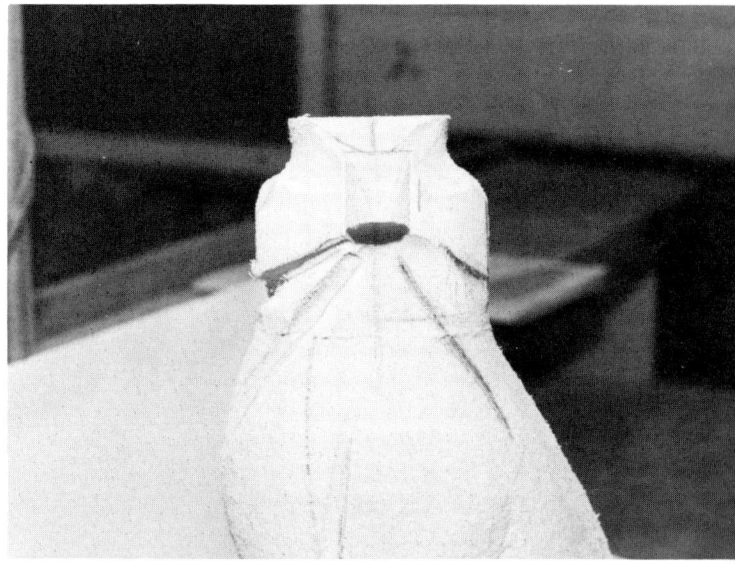

Front view of eye channels note: flow to beak

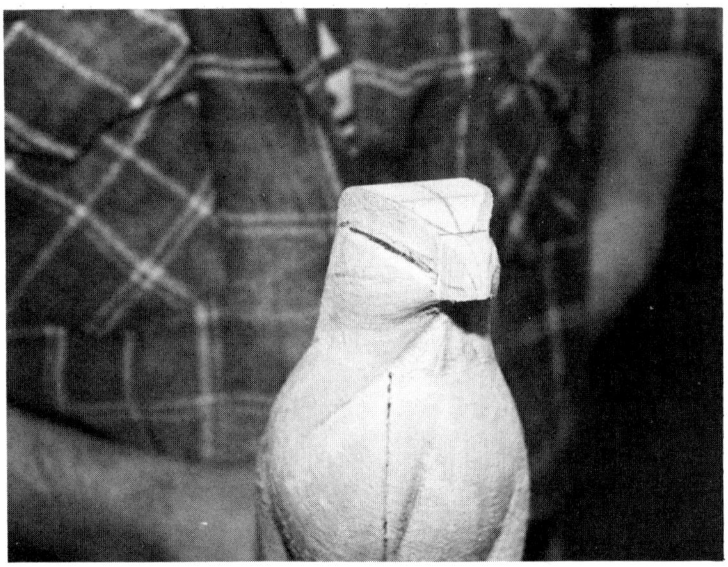

Line for eye channel indentation

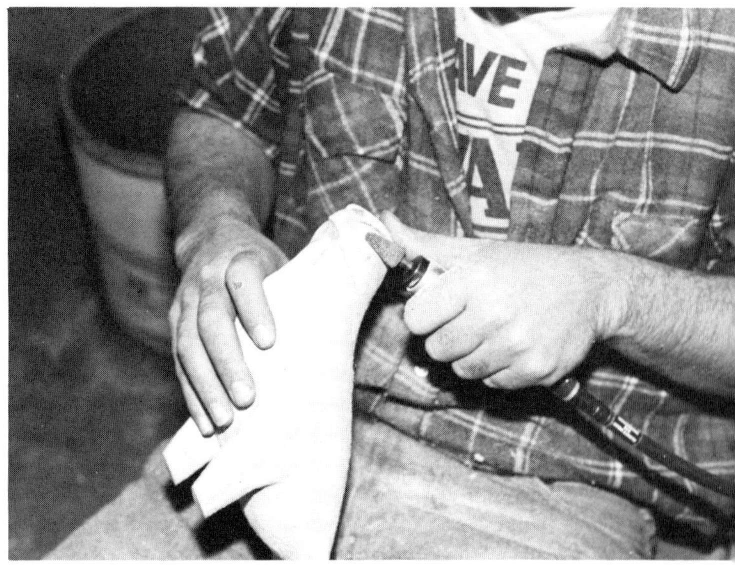

Further refining of eye channel for smooth flow

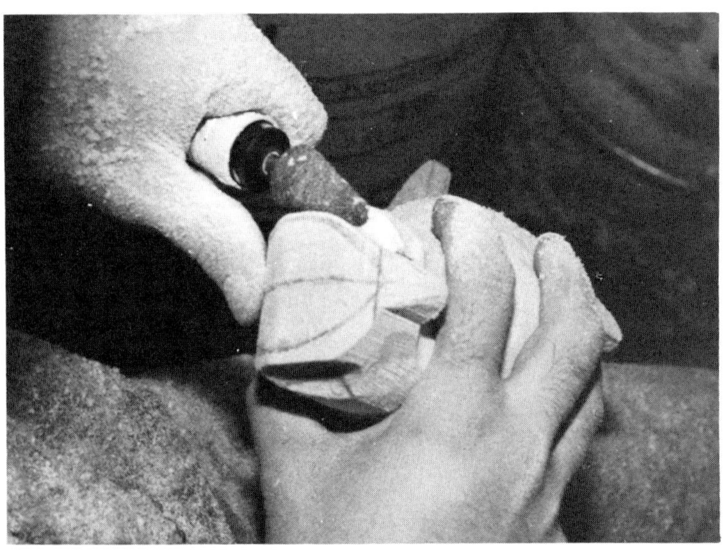

Carving eye channel

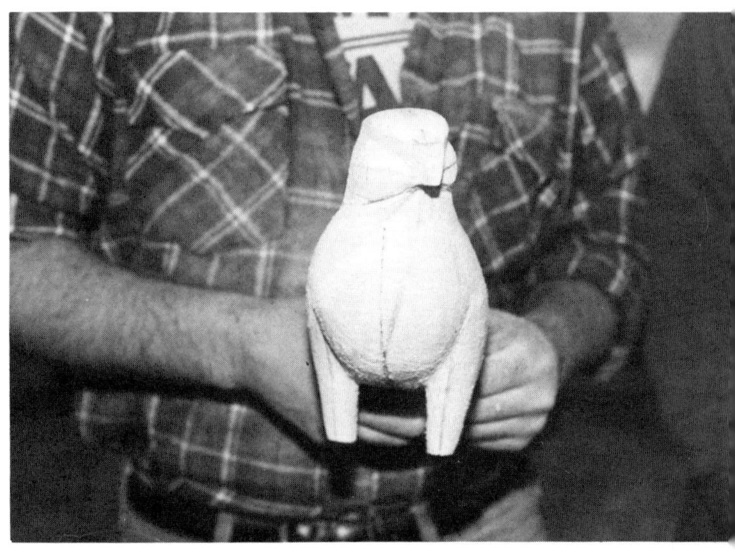

Head basically carved—note: slightly rounded crown

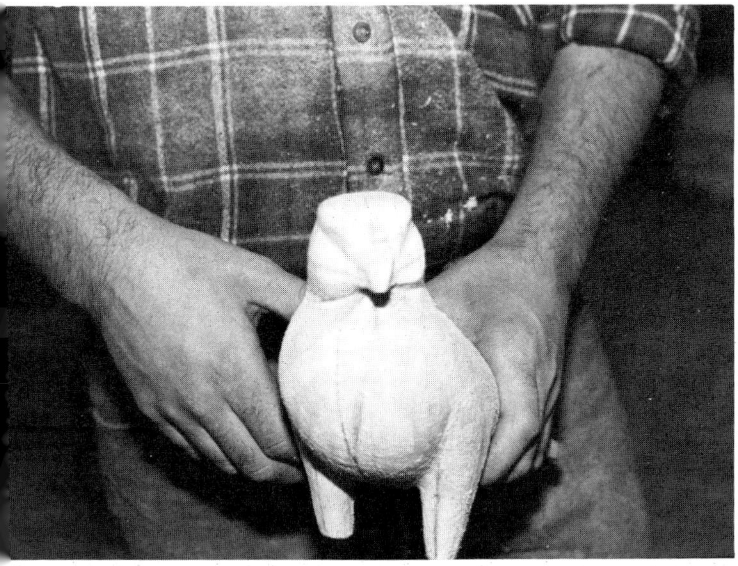

Front view of head

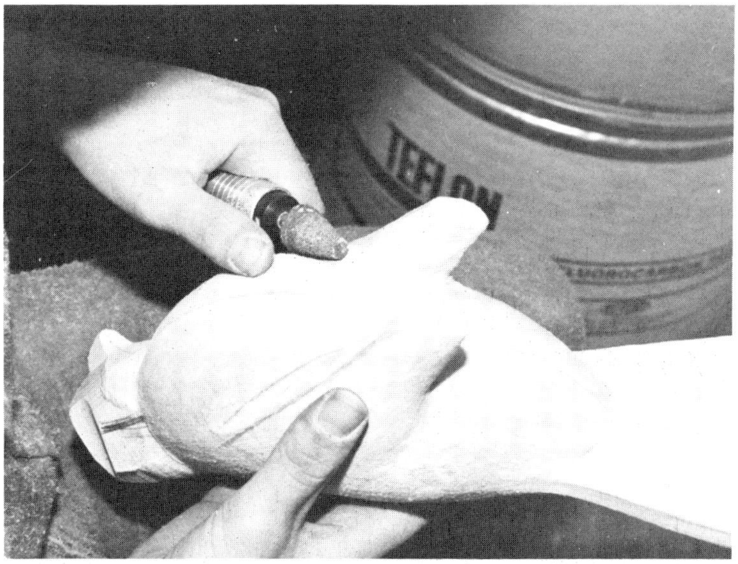

Cutting in of breast lines

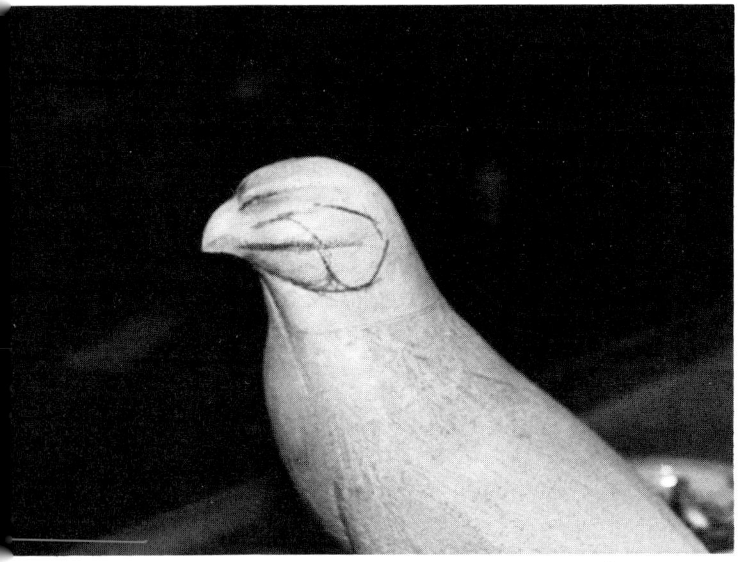

Egg shaped cheek area—note: slight undercut of cheek

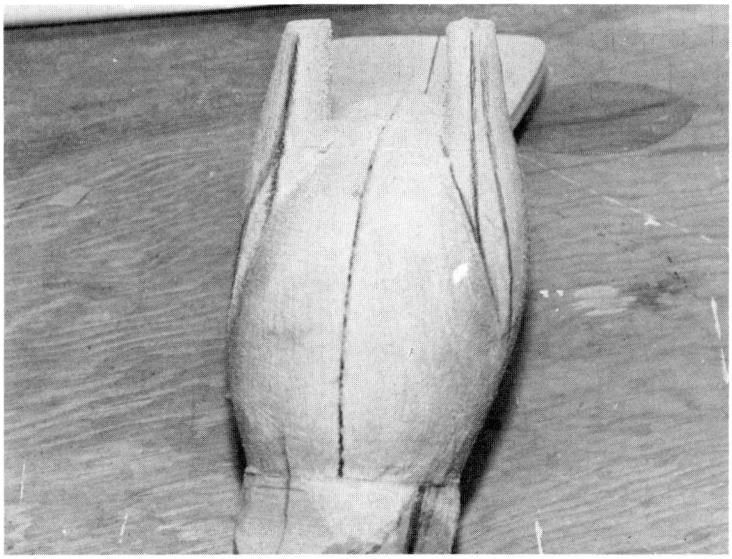

Breast lines defined

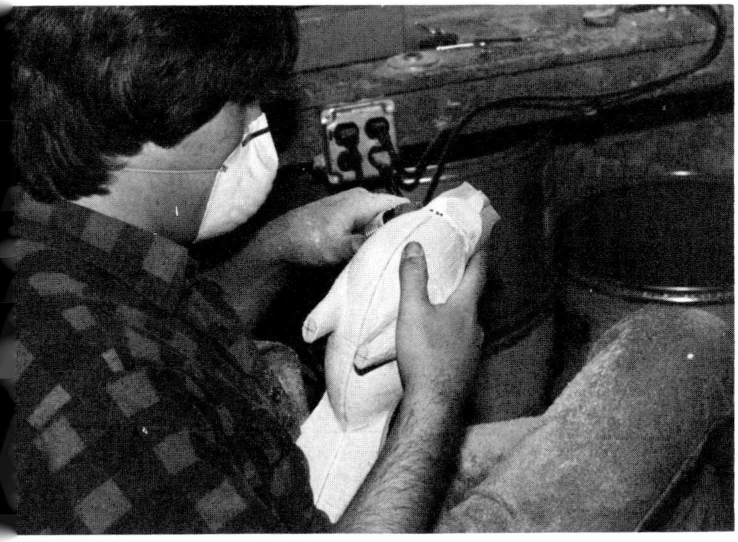

Flowing head into body

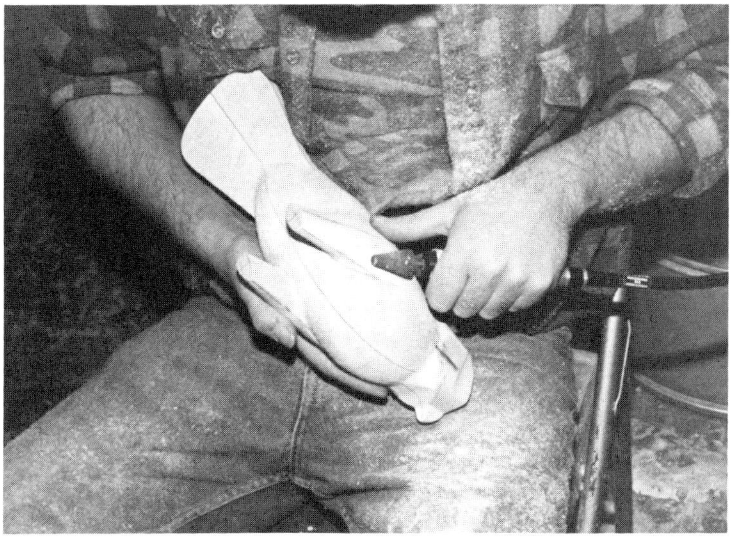

Gently flow body to legs

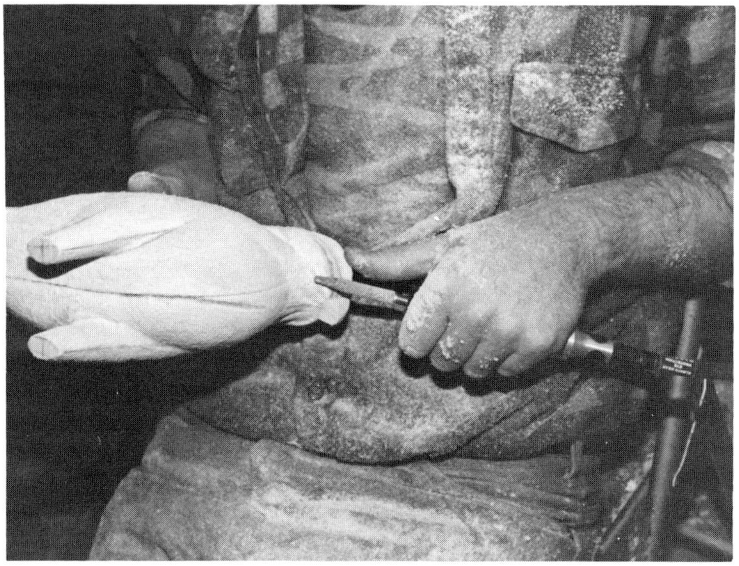

Final shaping of head

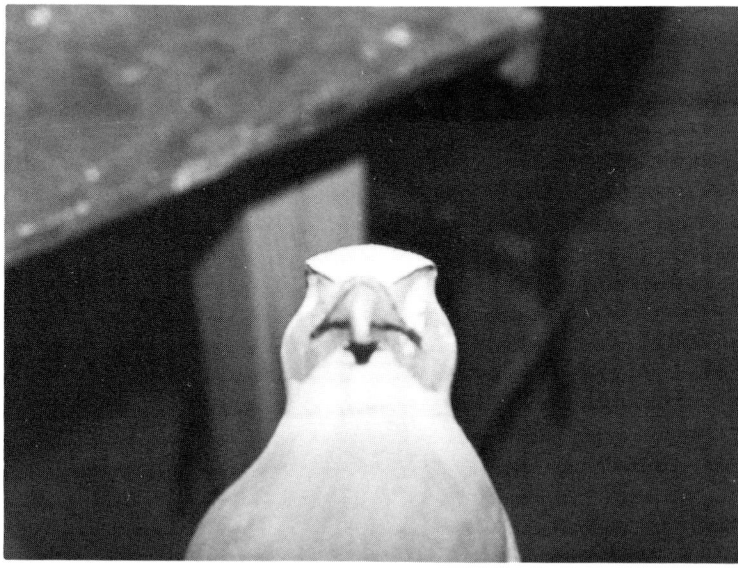

Front view of head

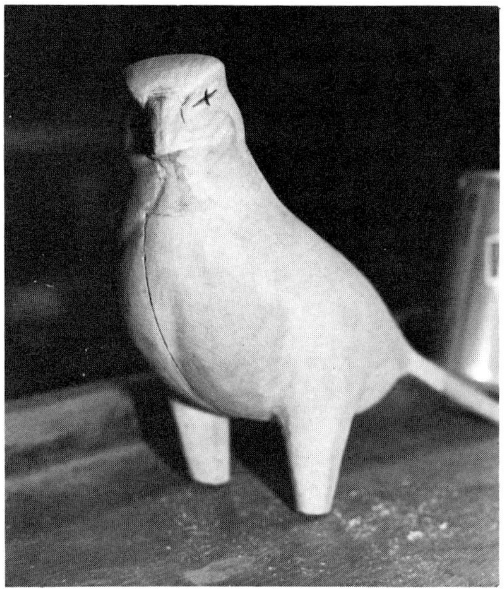

Head and body ready for detailing

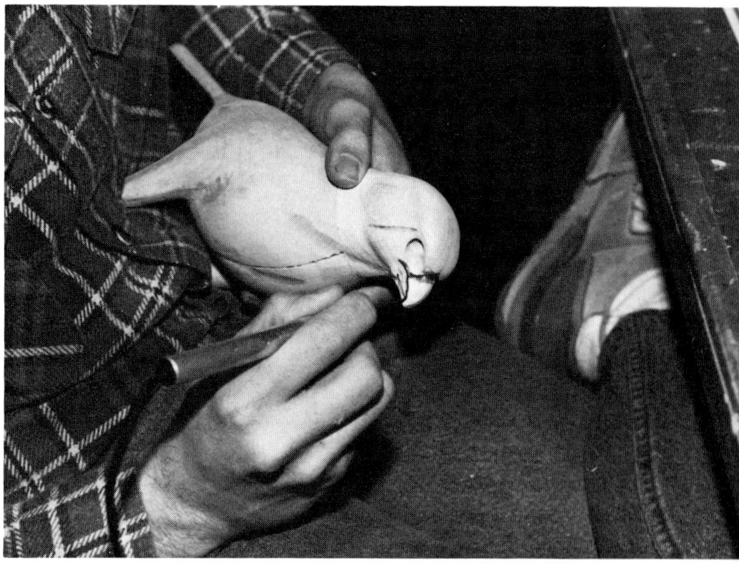

Detailing beak

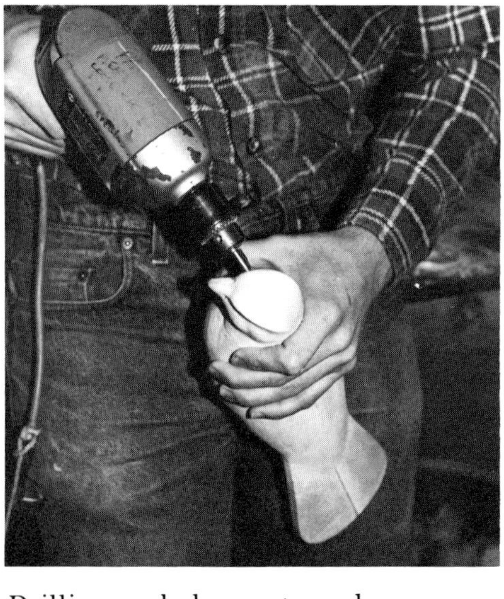

Drilling eye holes—note angle

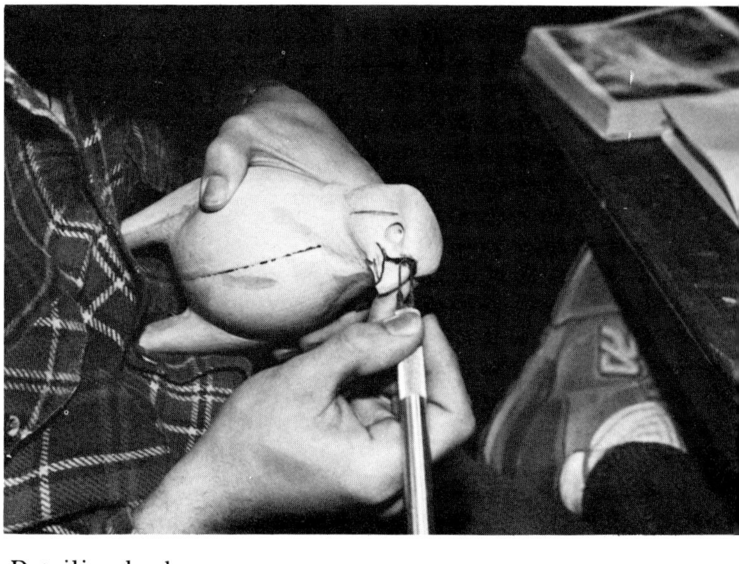

Detailing beak

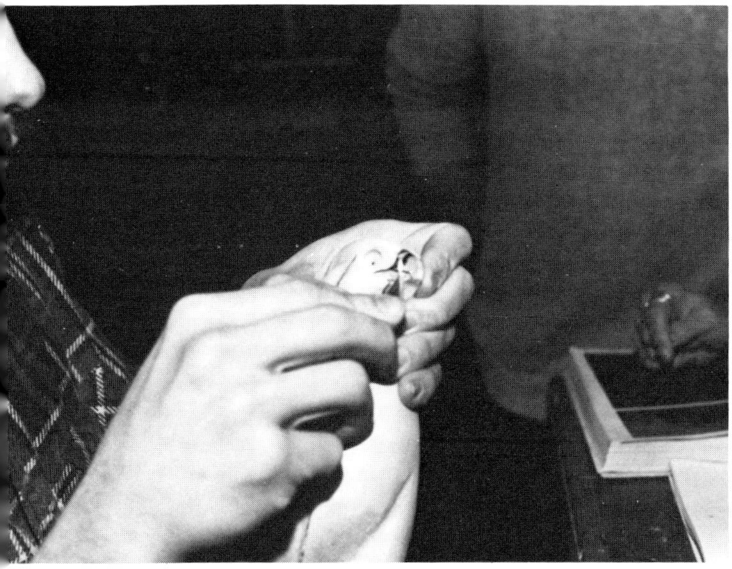

Carving underside of head

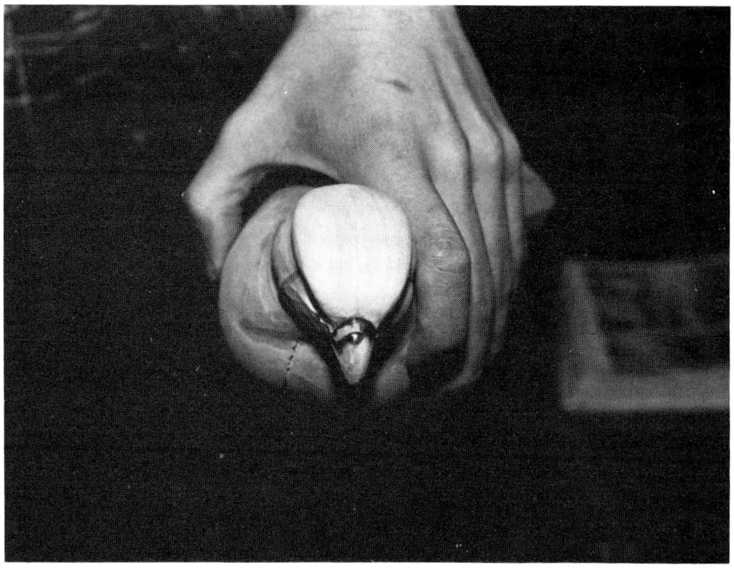

Top view of detailed beak

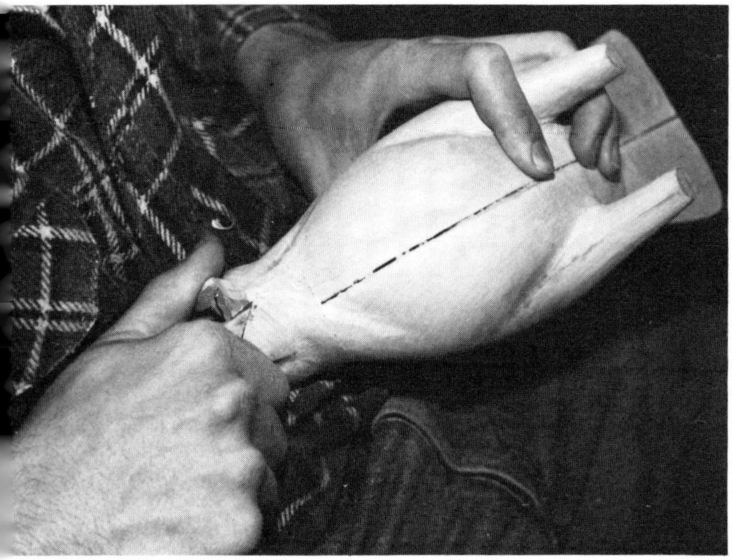

Carving underside of head

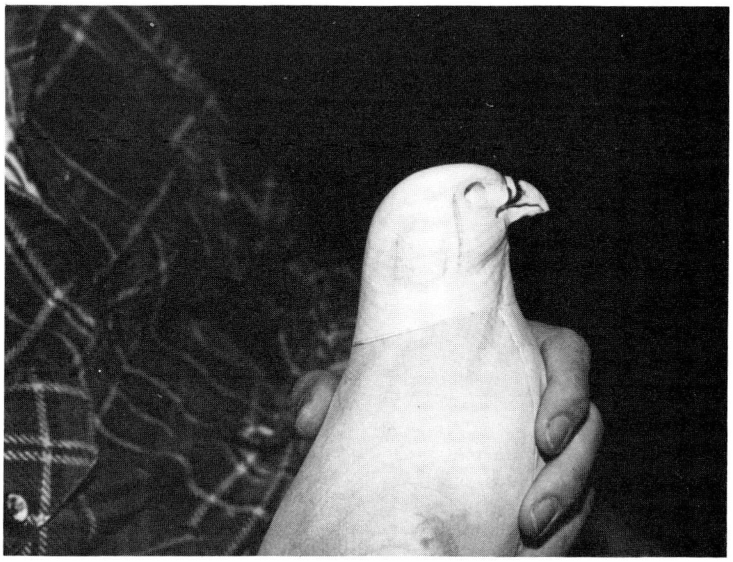

Profile of detailed beak

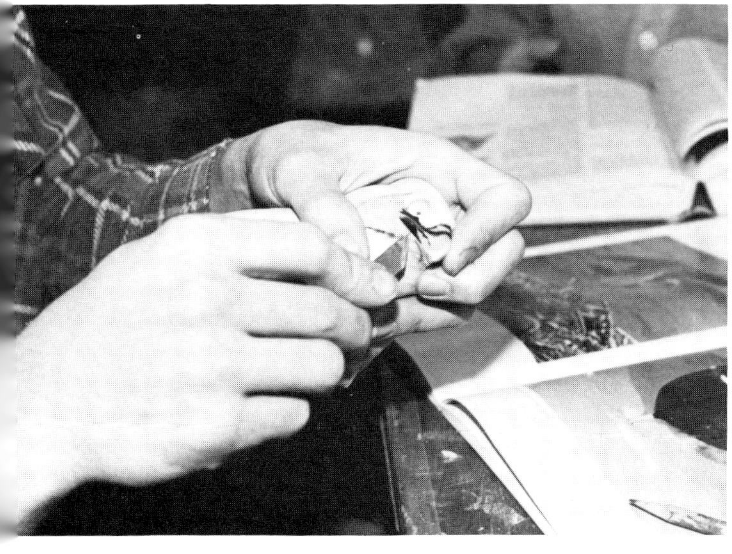

Carving underside of head

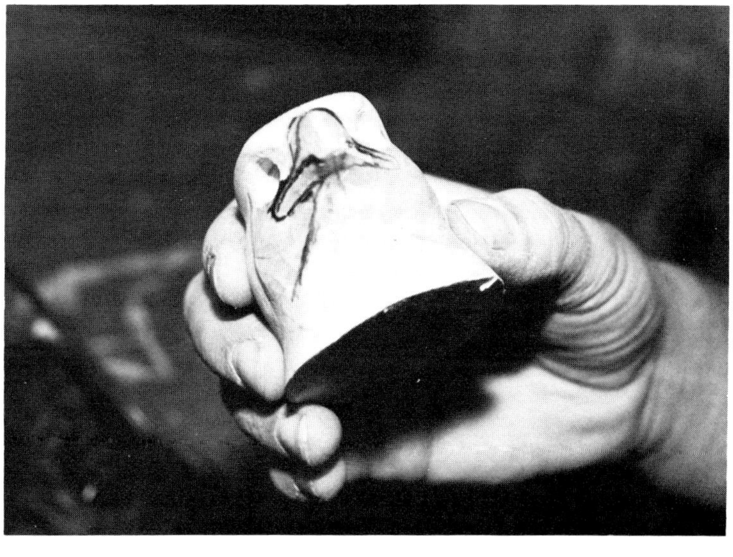

Head removed from body for ease in detailing

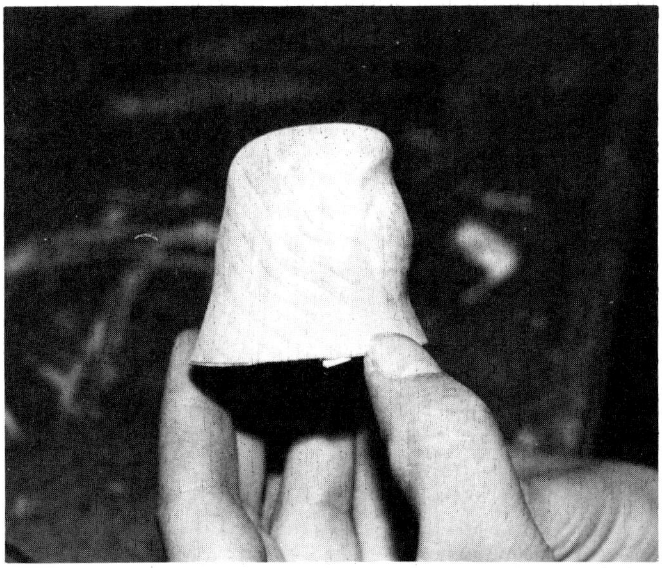
Back view of head

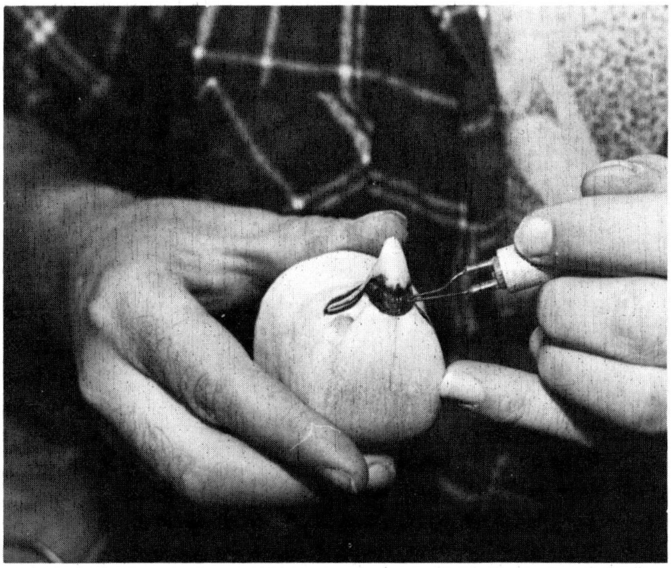
Burning detail into head

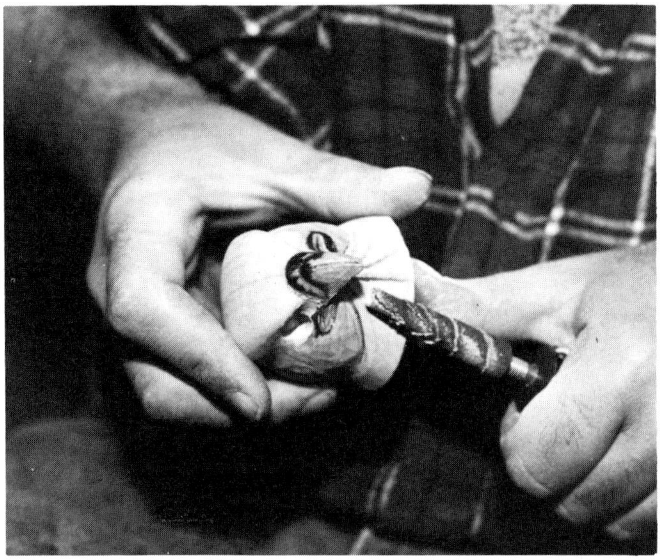
Indentation on neck

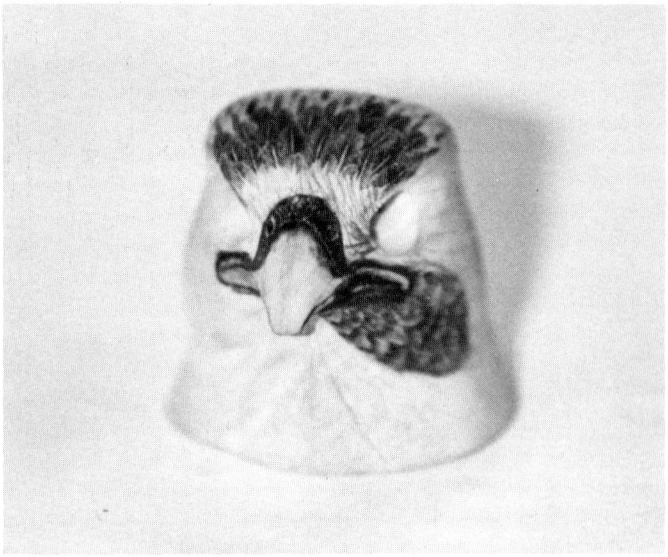
Feather pattern on crown and in cheek area

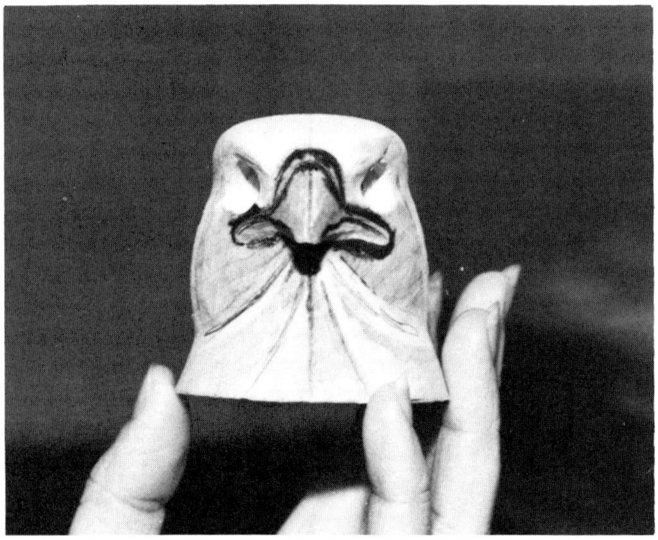
Head ready for burning

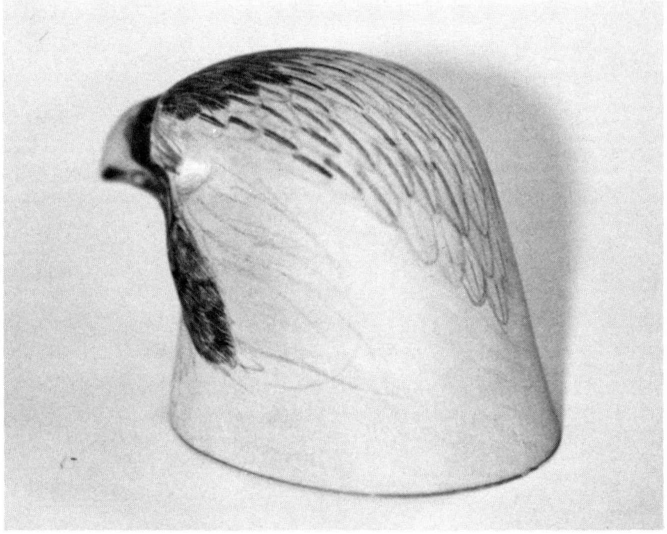
Back of head feather pattern

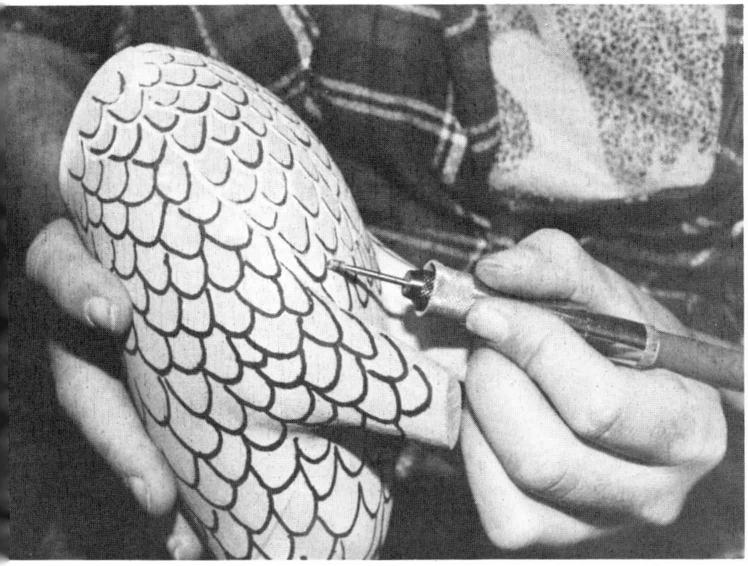

Feather pattern side and belly

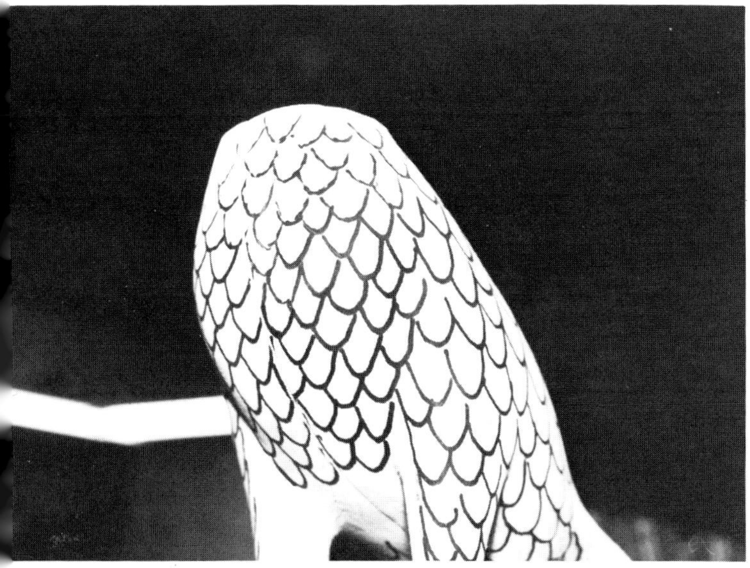

Feather pattern belly and leg

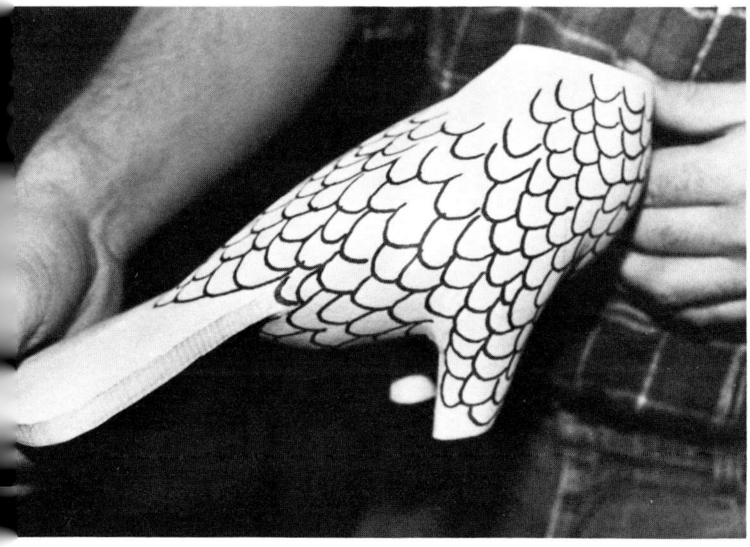

Feather pattern right side

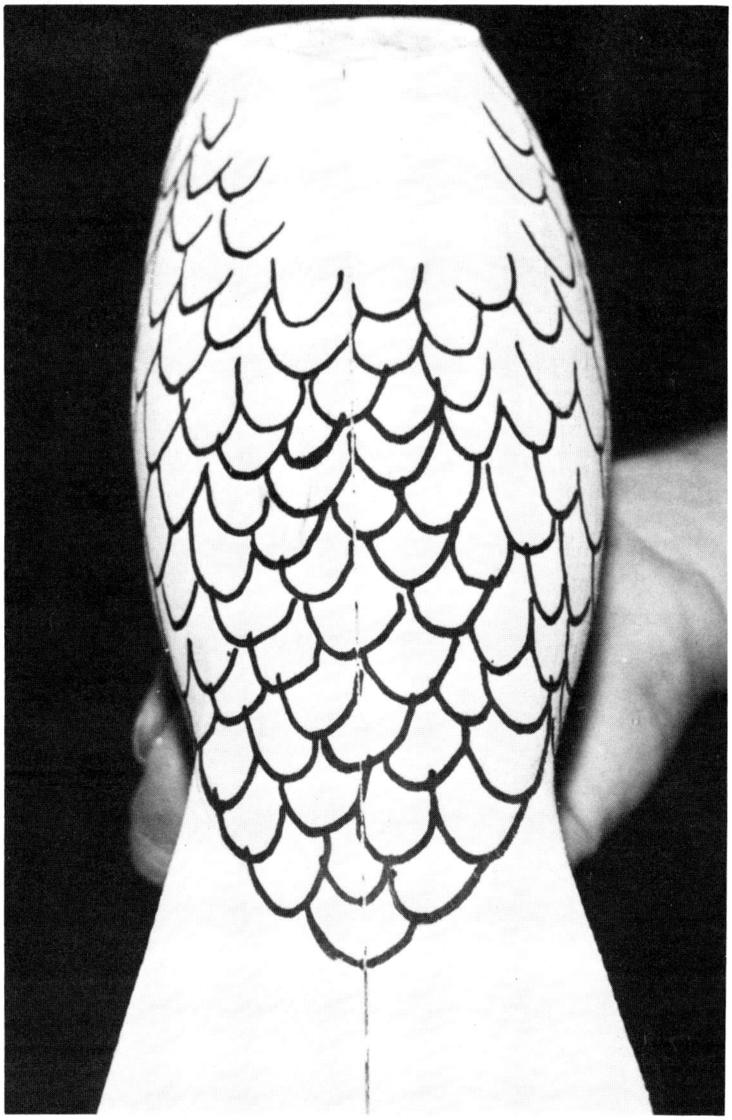

Feather pattern back

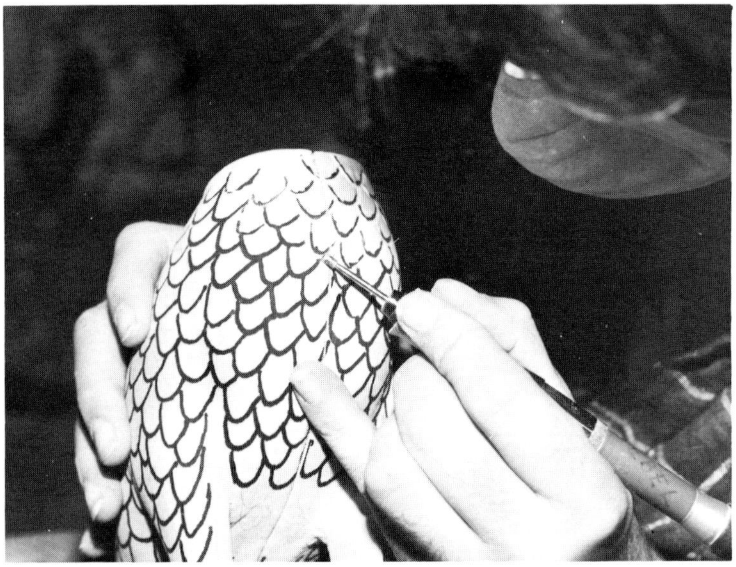

Carving feathers with ruby carver

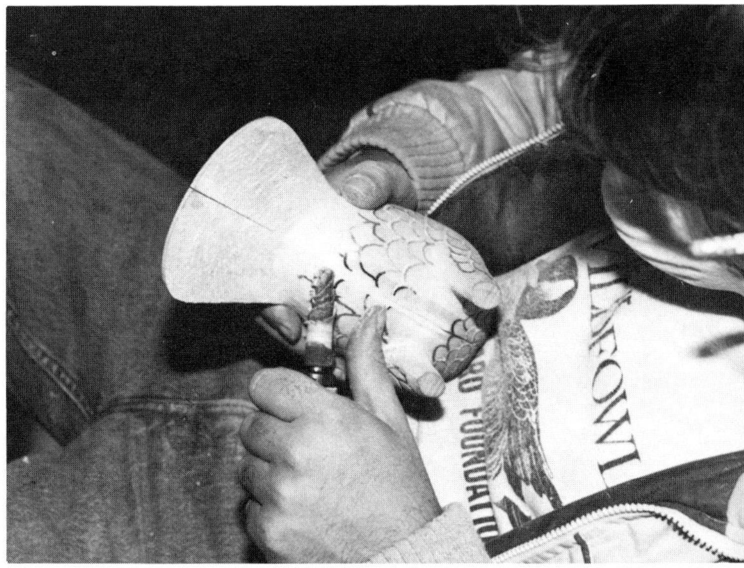

Another view of feather that has been ruby carved

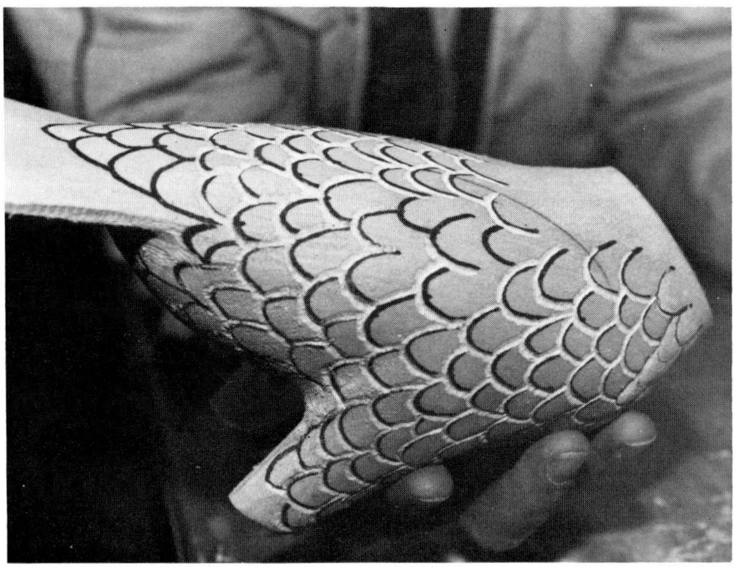

Feathers carved with ruby carver

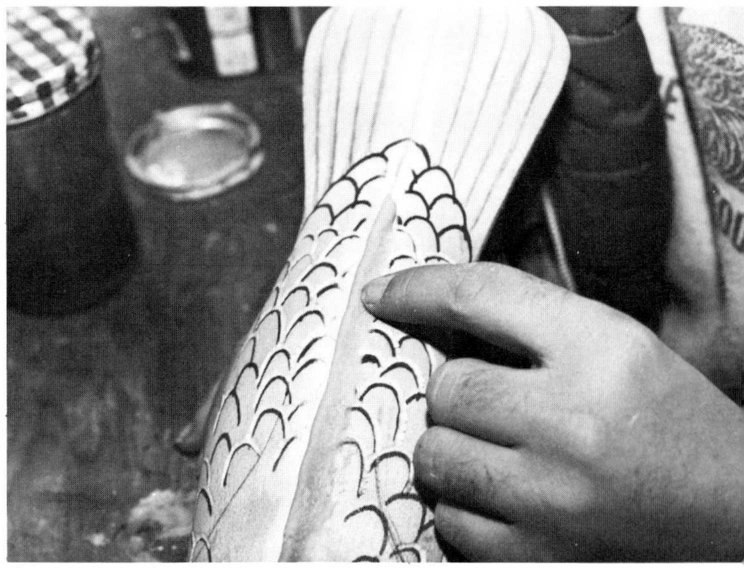

Glue joint being filled with wood dough (use a lot of acetone to break down air gaps and smooth wood dough into wood)

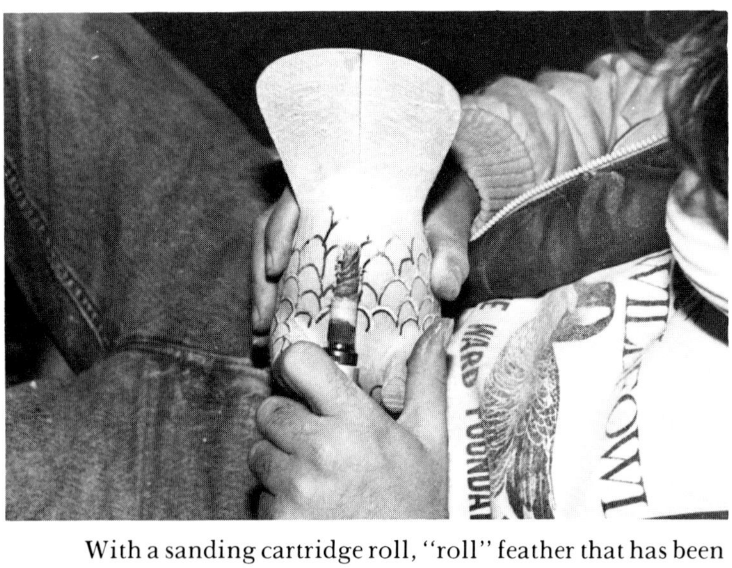

With a sanding cartridge roll, "roll" feather that has been ruby carved

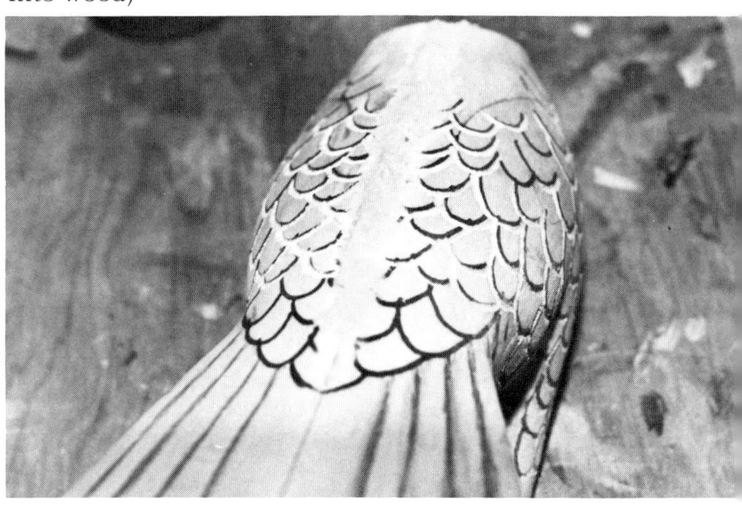

Same joint with wood dough

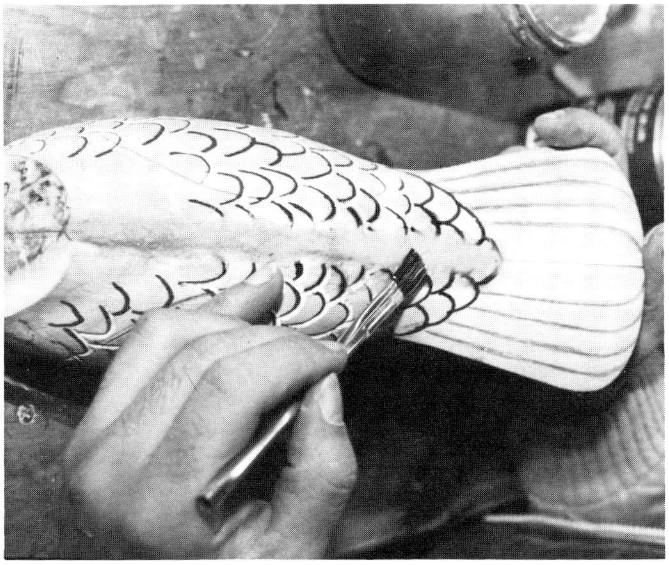

"Painting" wood dough over seam with flux brush

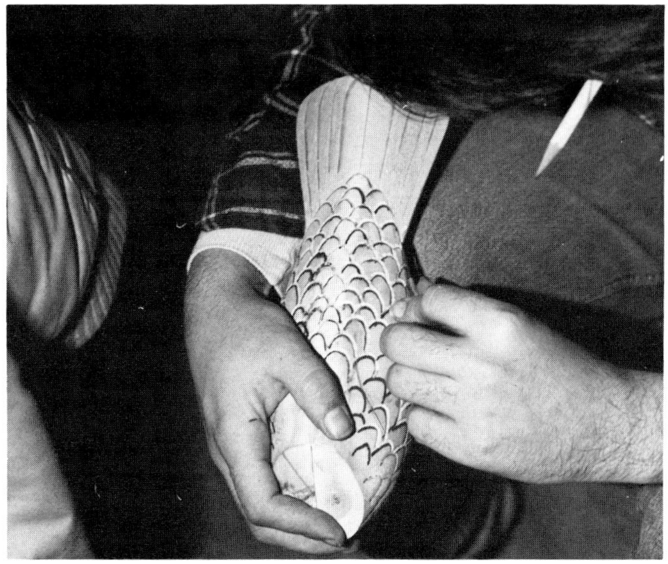

Sanding feathers

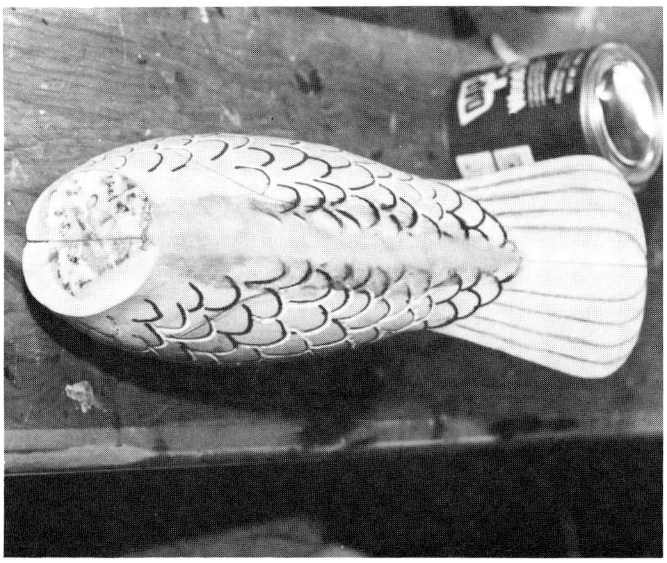

Finished seam area

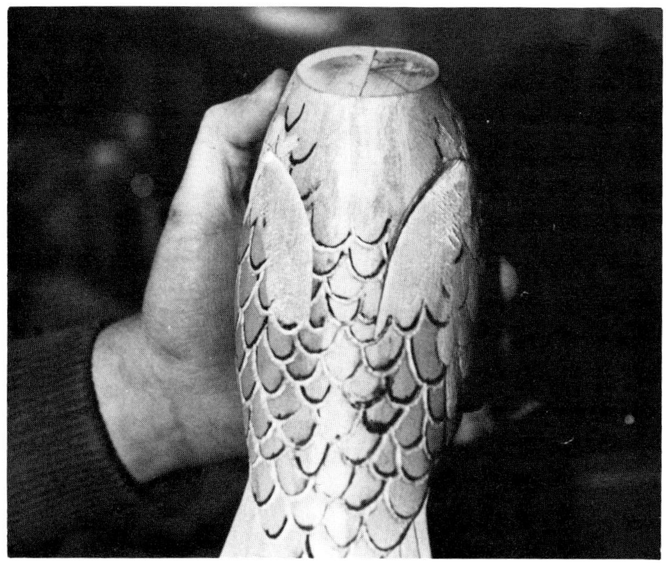

Back view showing cut in

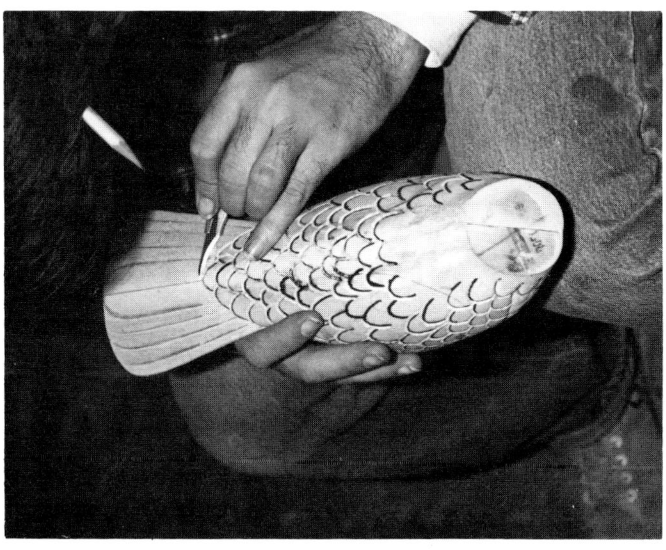

Carving feathers

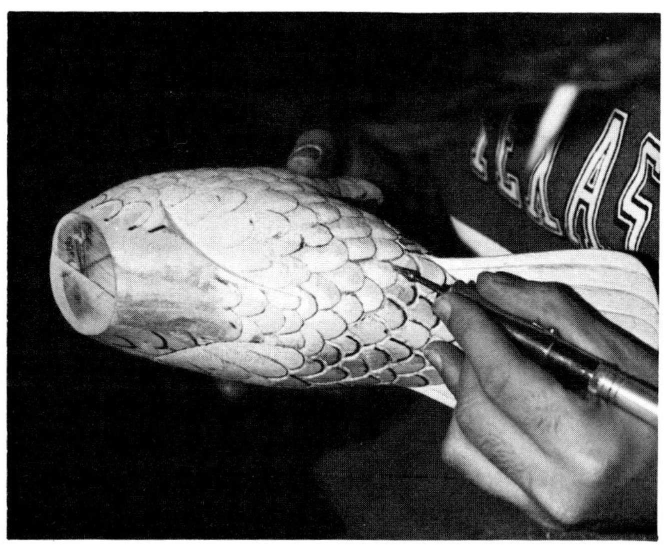

Carving feathers with ruby carver

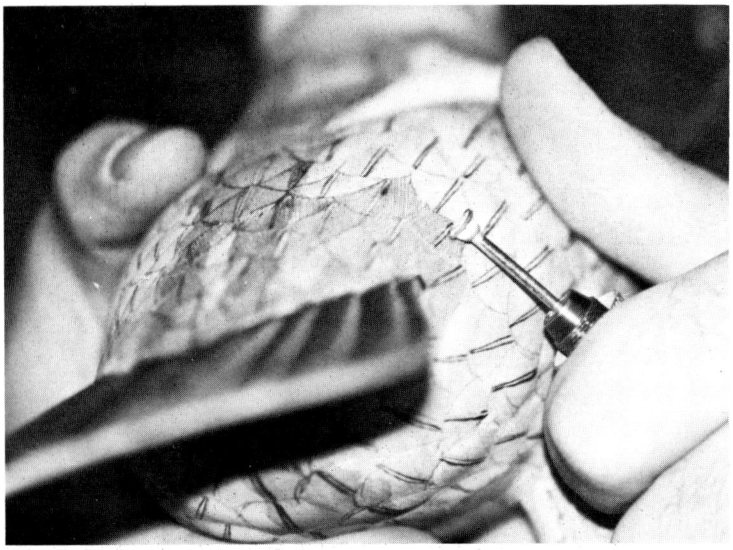

Stoning feathers with white stone

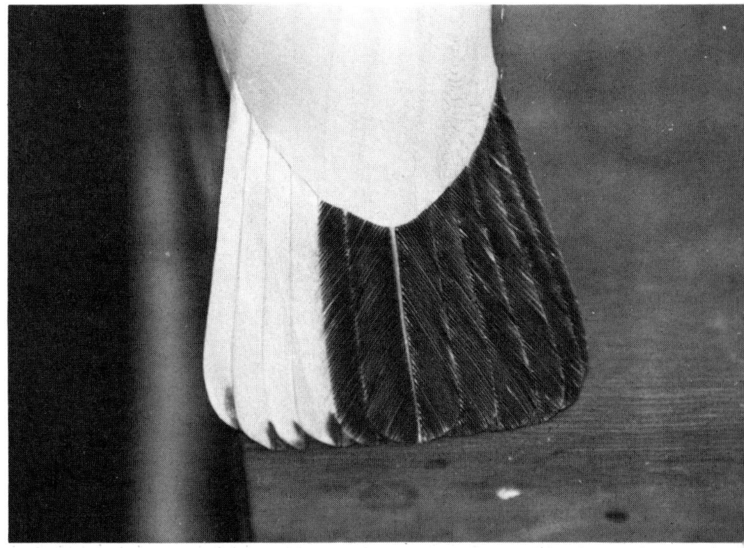

Upper side of tail partially burned—note: splits burned into feathers

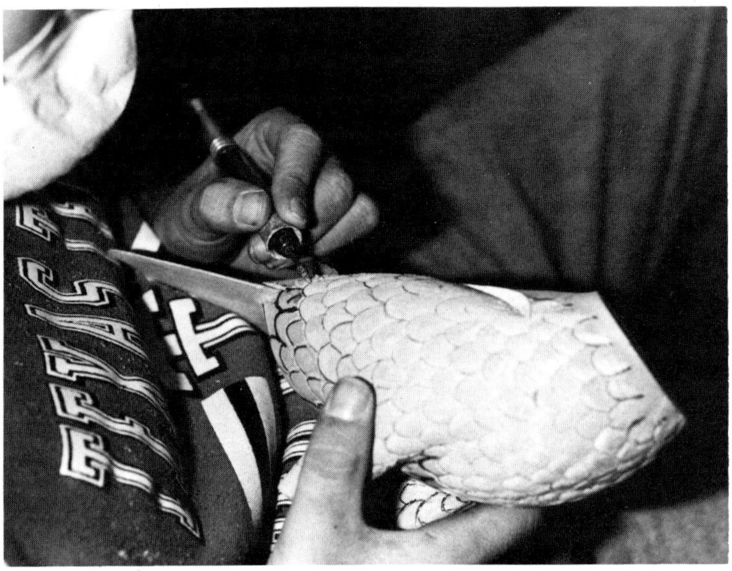

Carving feathers with ruby carver—note: #8 handpiece used like a pencil

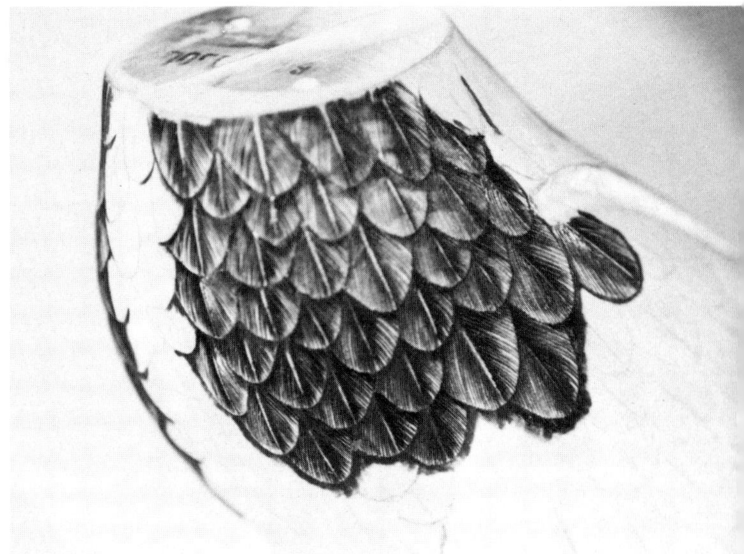

Chest area burned

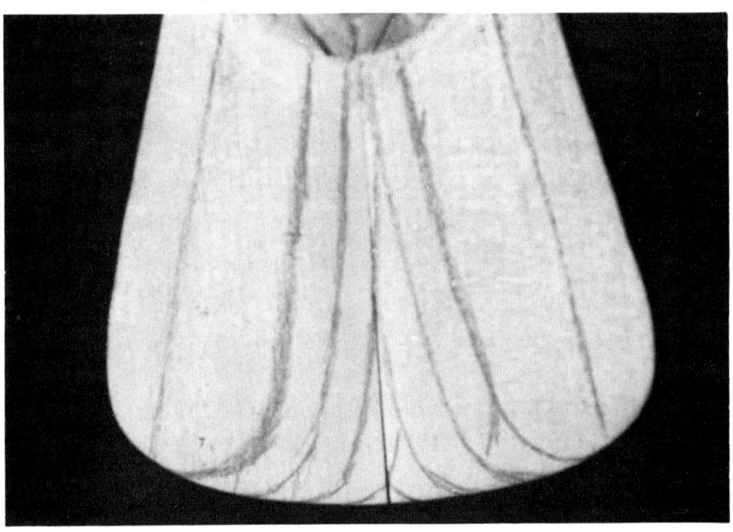

Underside of tail lay out

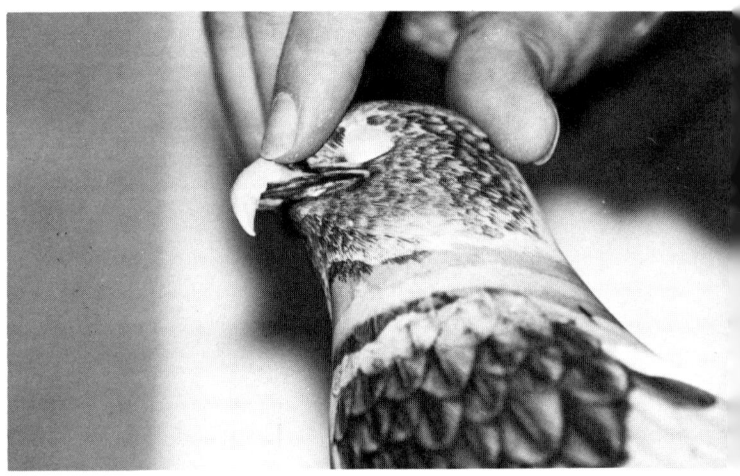

Head being set with five-minute epoxy and joint line filled with wood dough, use same techniques discussed on seam of body

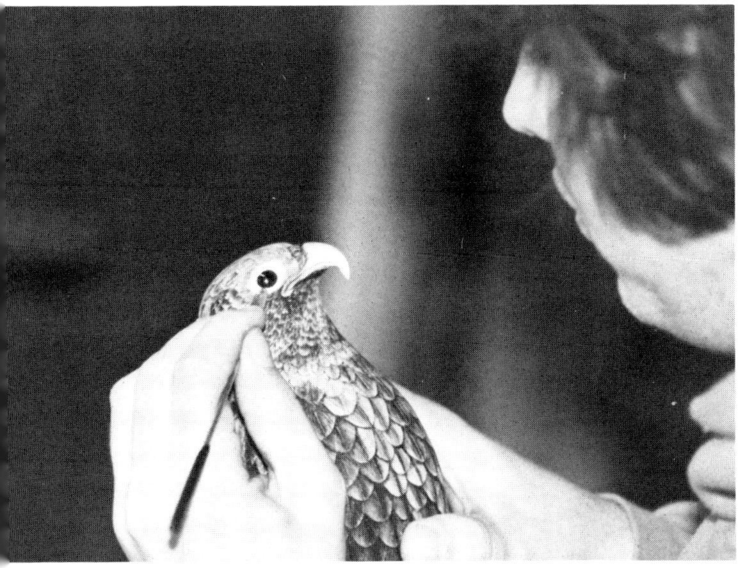

Eye lid being made using moldable epoxy after basic shaping use small paint brush to smooth out lid

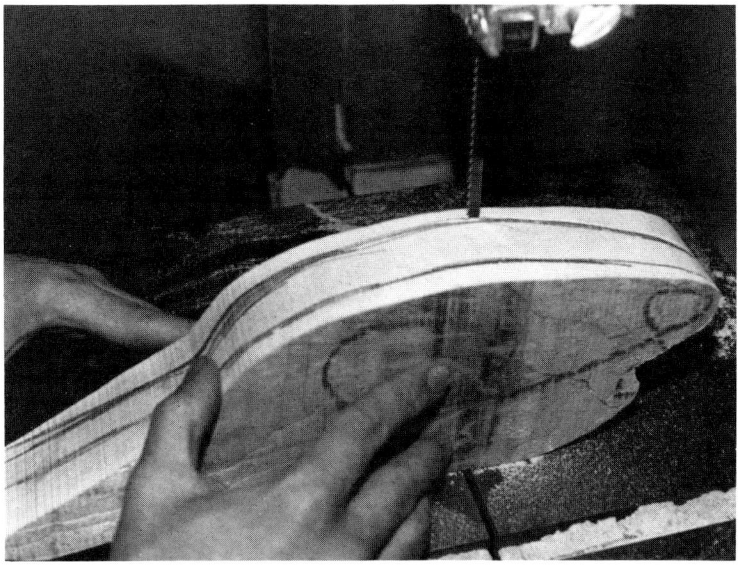

Wing profile being set on band saw

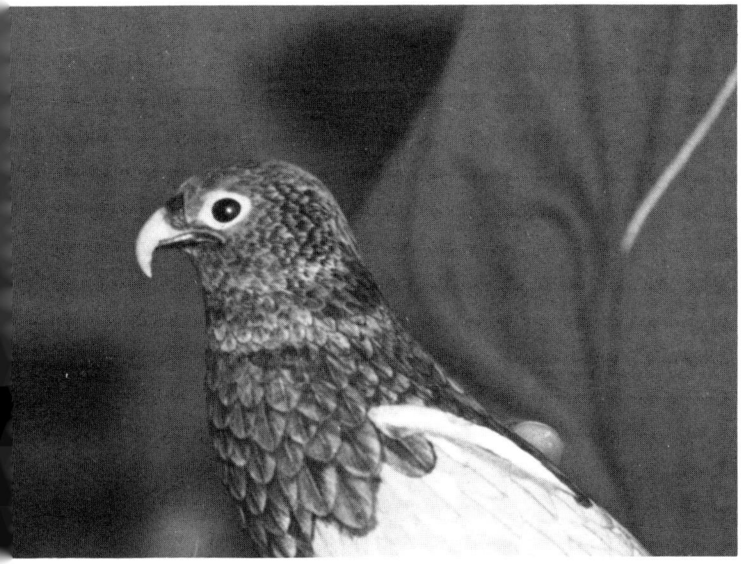

Completed head

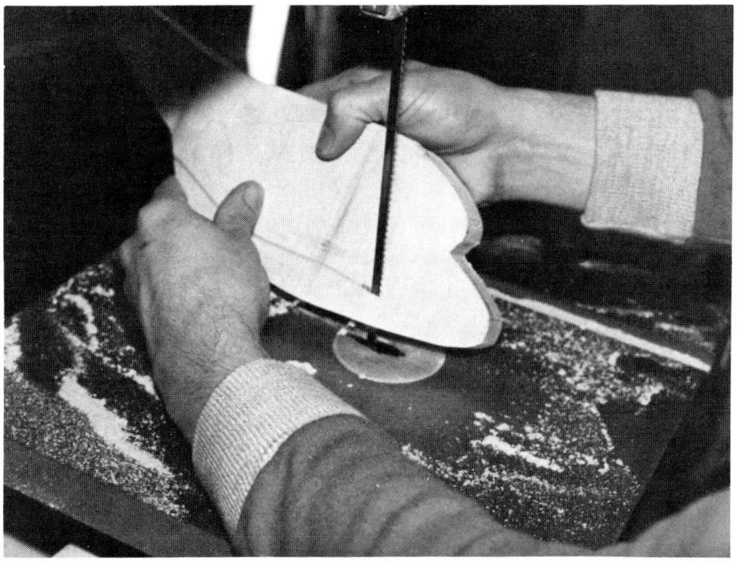

Wing being trimmed on band saw

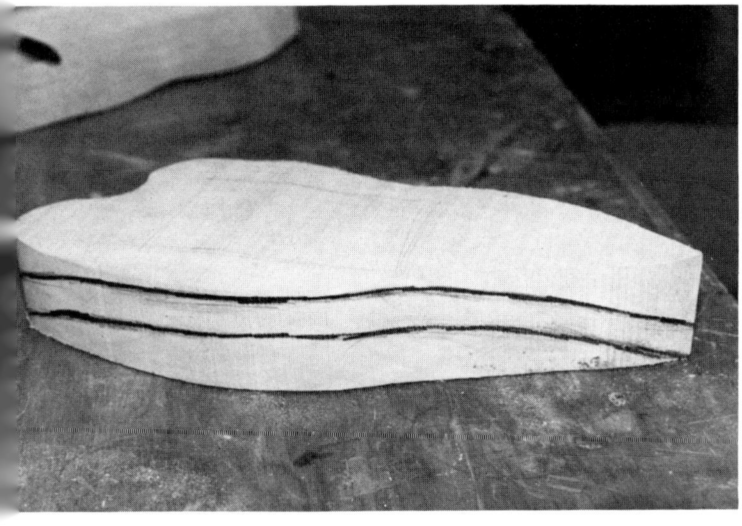

Wing profile

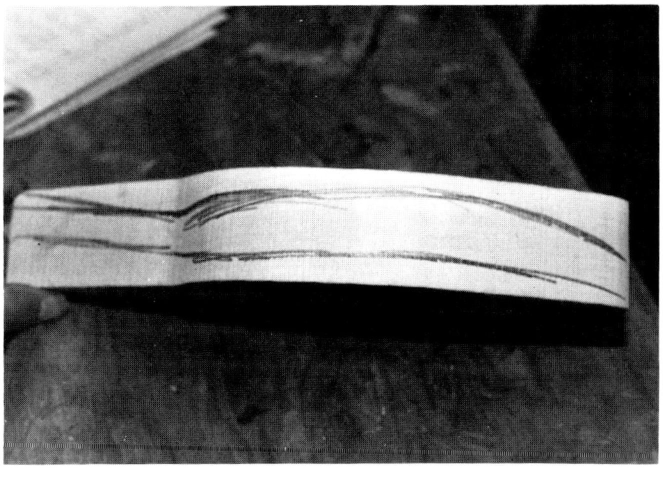

Shape of wing

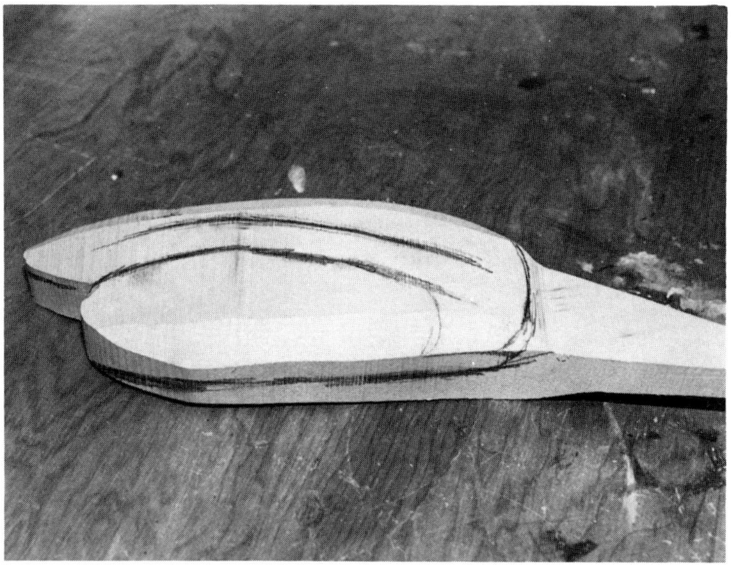

Roughed out wing ready for carving—note: guide lines

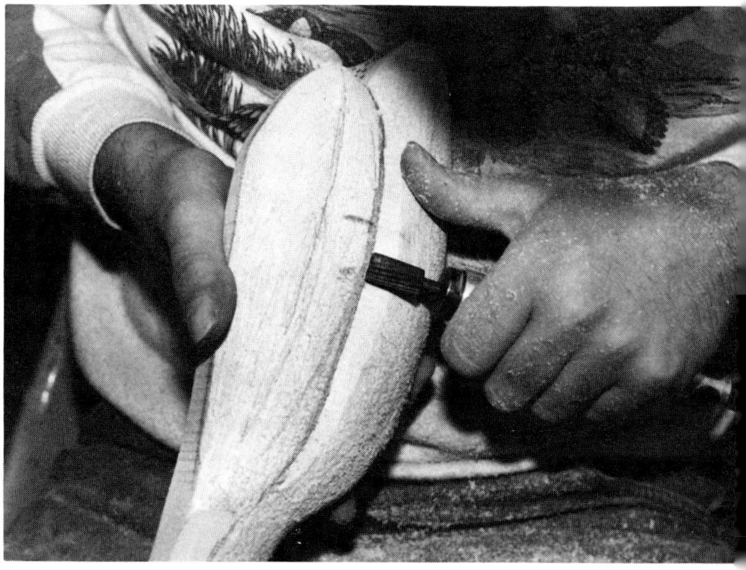

Carving deep roll in

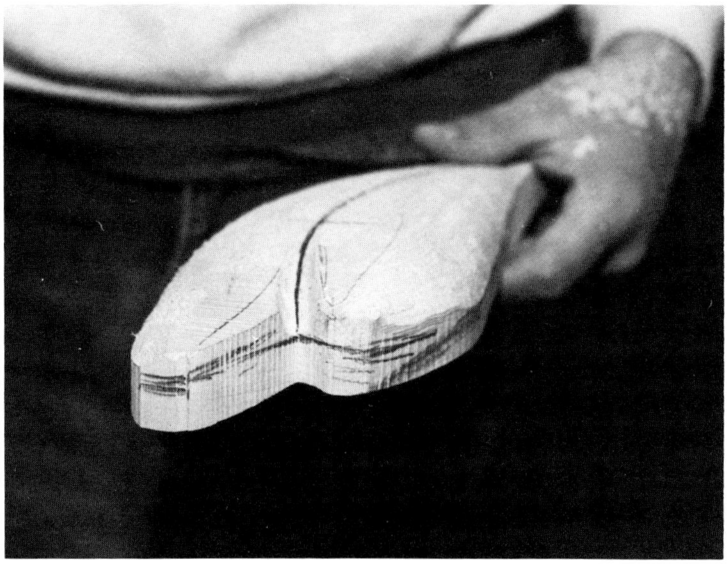

Top of wing partially shaped—note: guide line for indentation

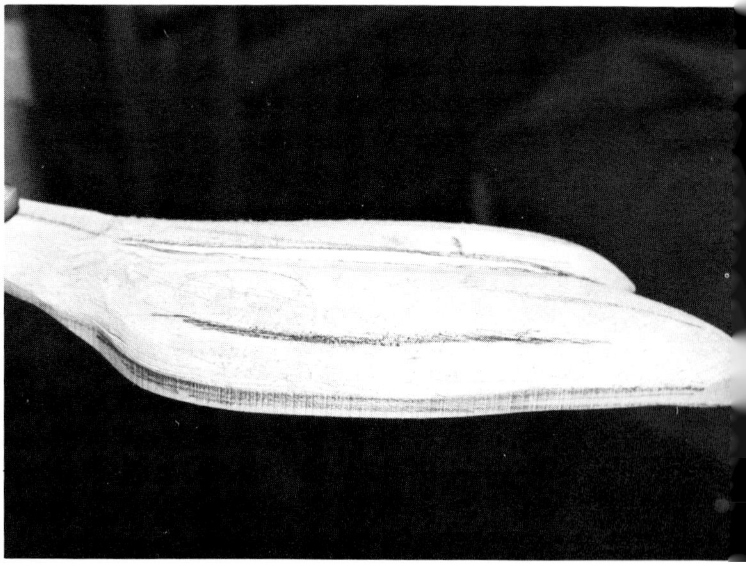

Top of wing basically shaped

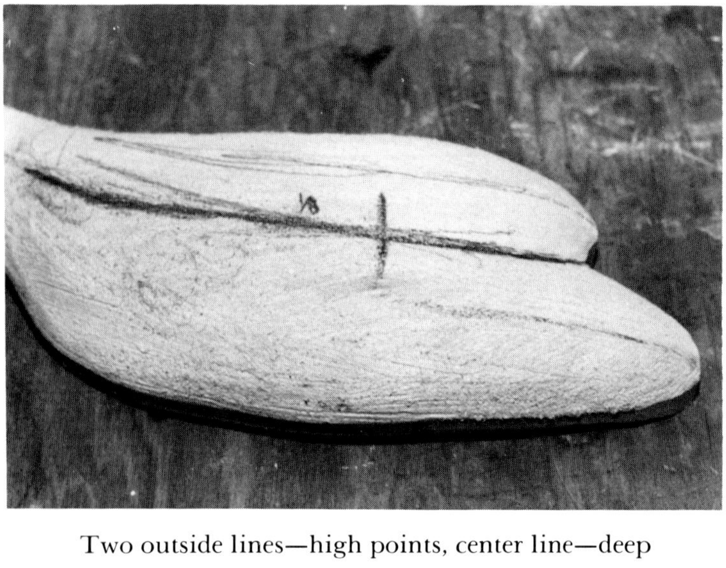

Two outside lines—high points, center line—deep

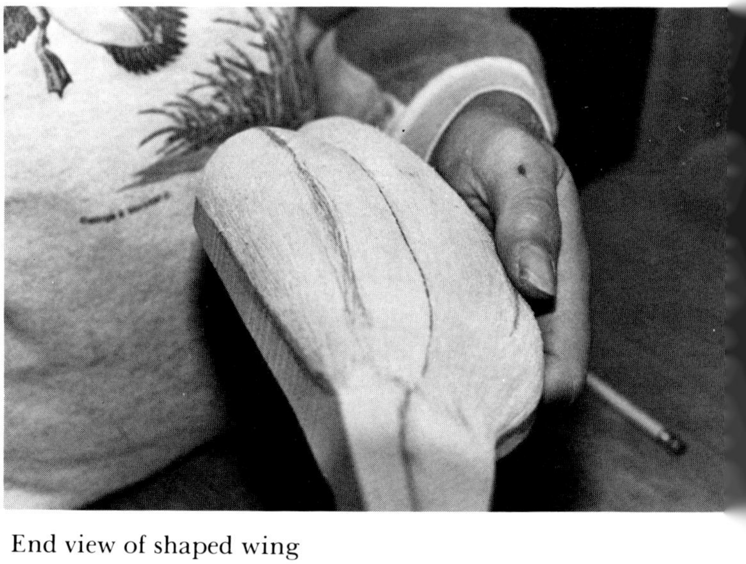

End view of shaped wing

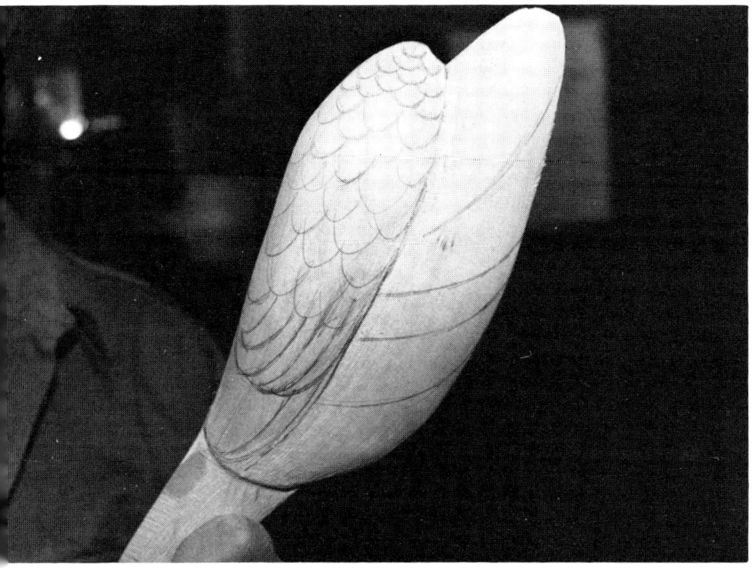

Feather lay out on top side

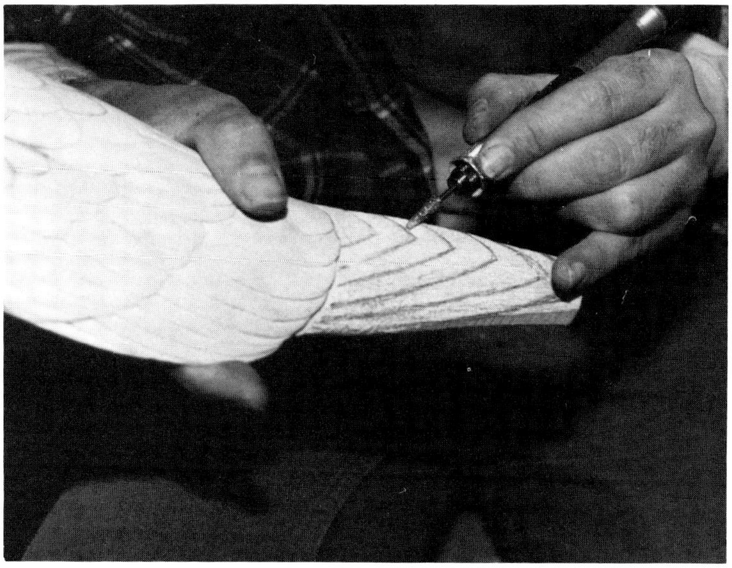

Burning in primary feather

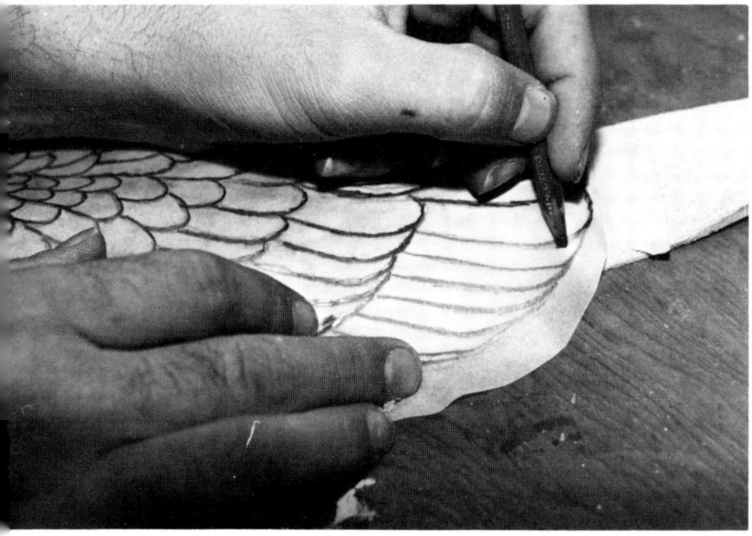

Paper tracing of wing lay out—turn over tracing paper for other wing lay out to match

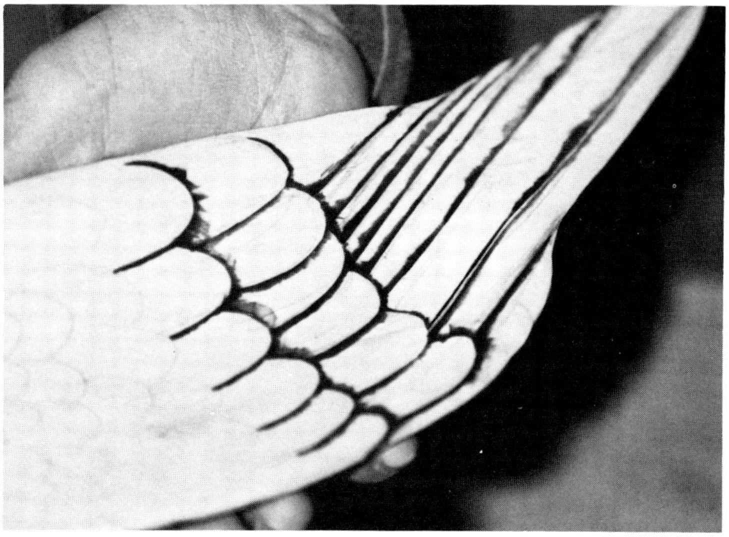

Primaries and coverts burned in on underside of wing

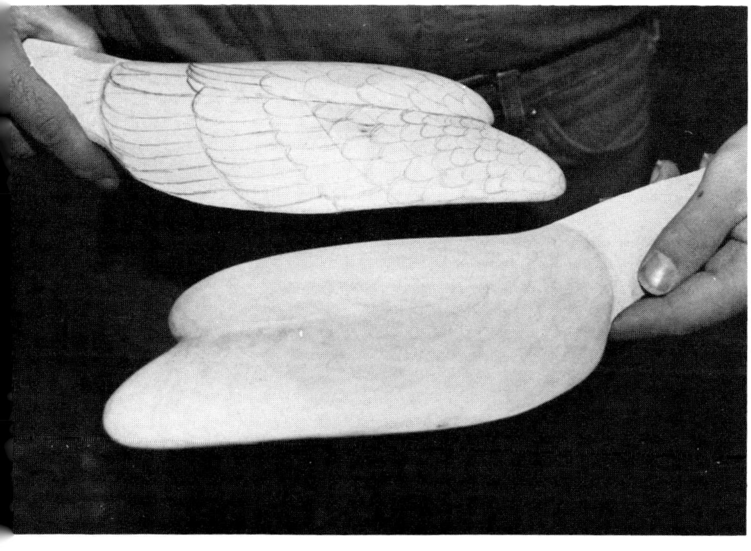

One wing with lay out and other ready for tracing

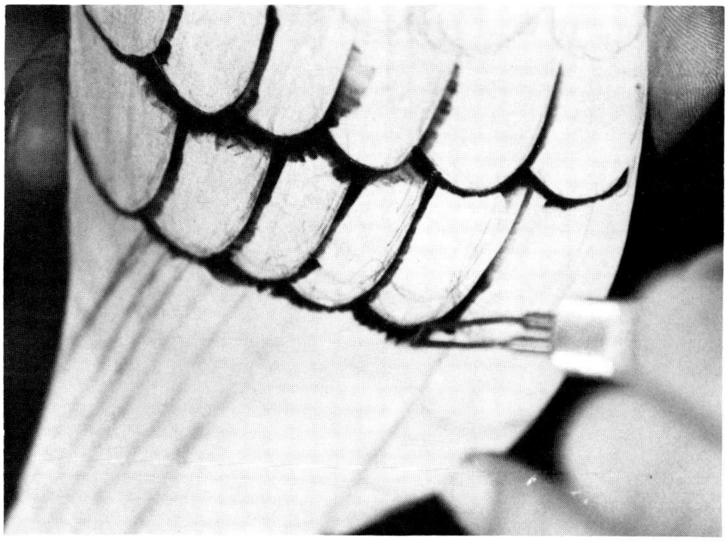

Another view of primaries and coverts burned

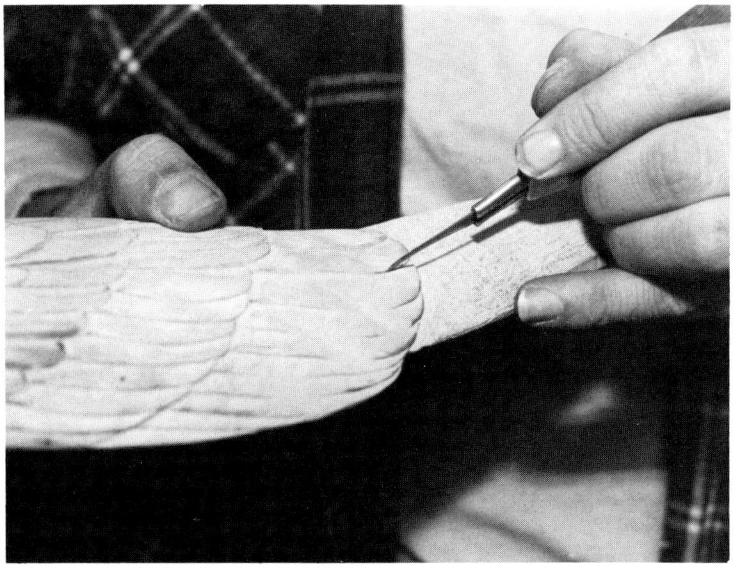

Carving in detail of secondaries

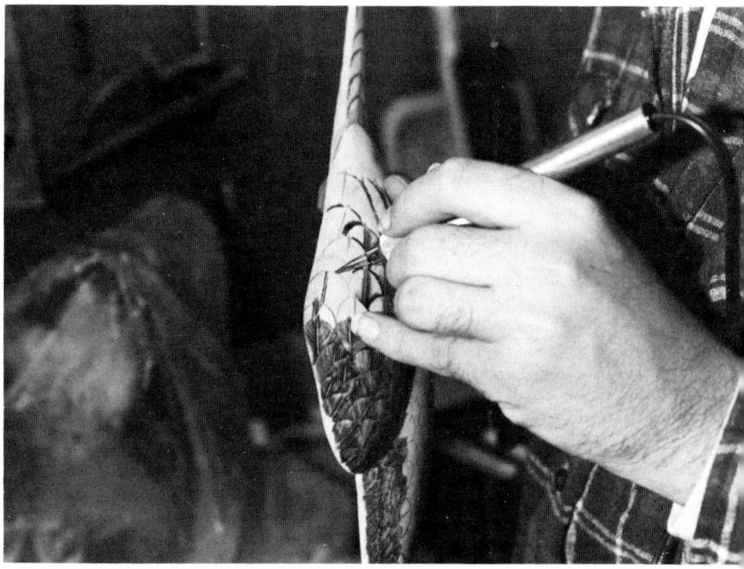

Burning feathers—note: little finger being used as guide

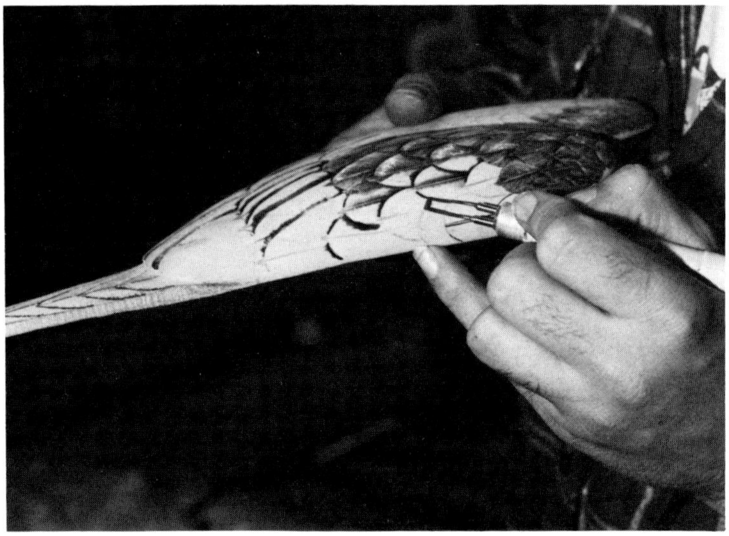

Burning in quills

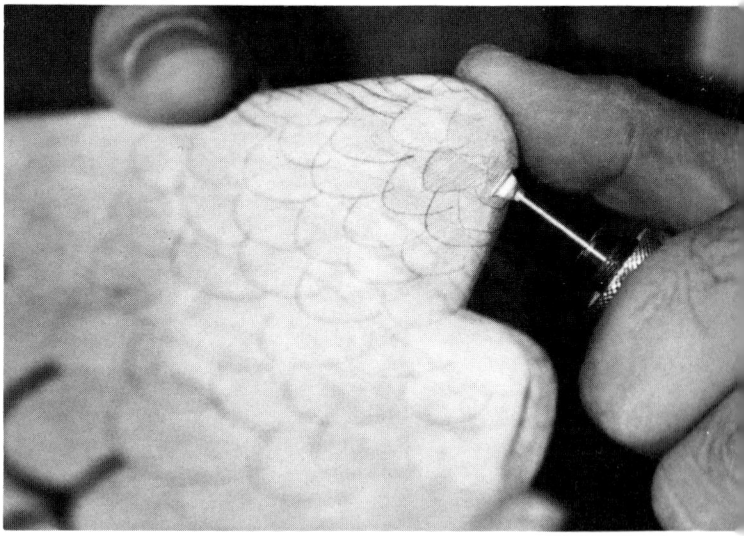

Small feathers being textured with white stone

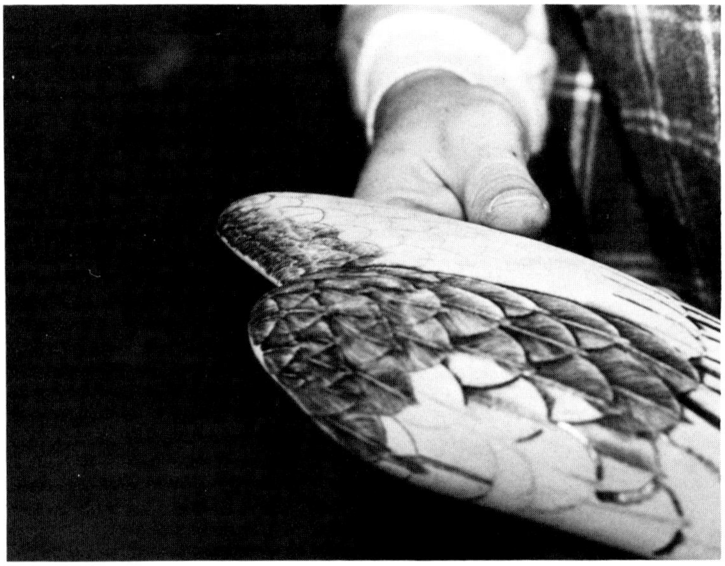

Large feather on wing burned

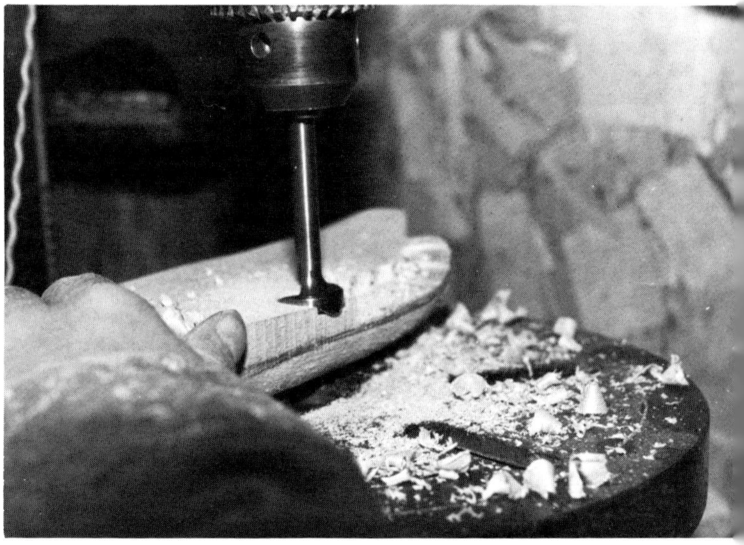

Underside of wing being hollowed with drill press to quickly get rid of excess wood

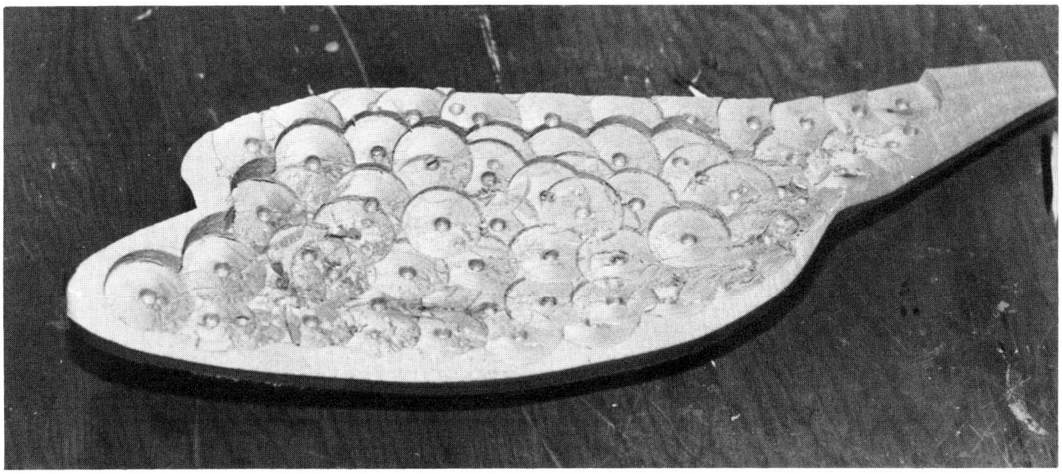

Underside of wing drilled with forstner bit

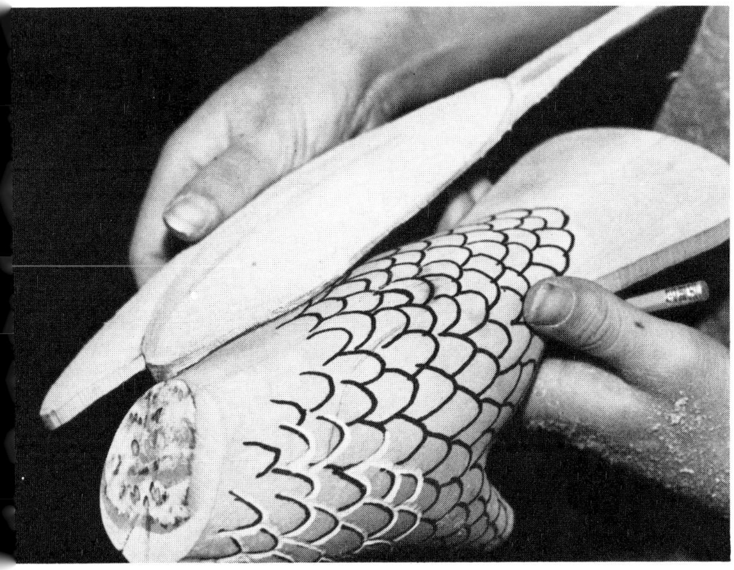

Wing being fitted to body

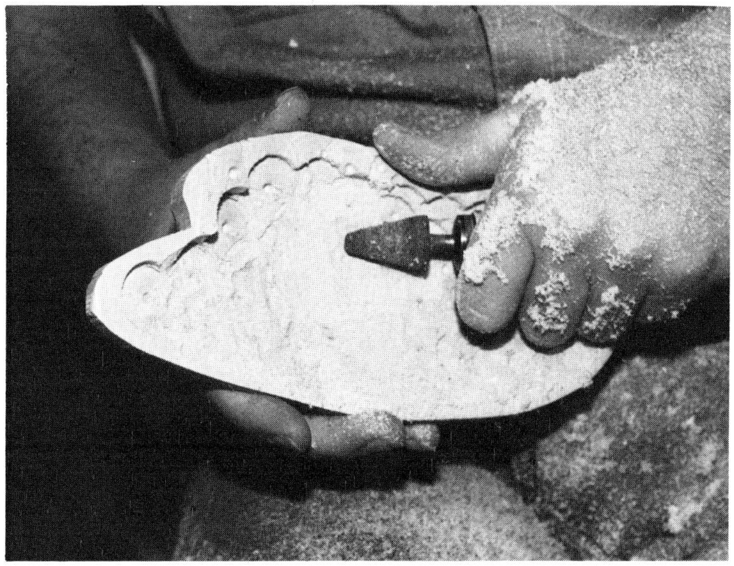

Underside of wing being smooth carved with a carbide bit

View of other side of wing being fitted to body

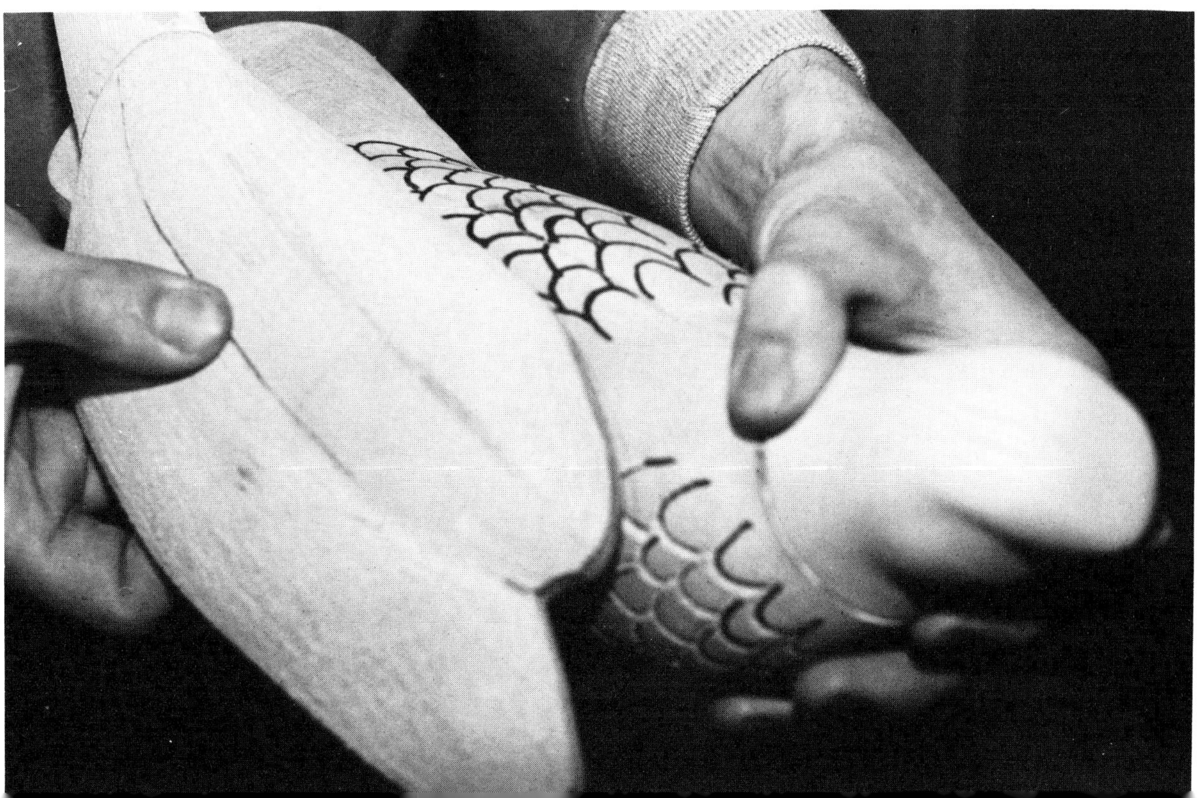

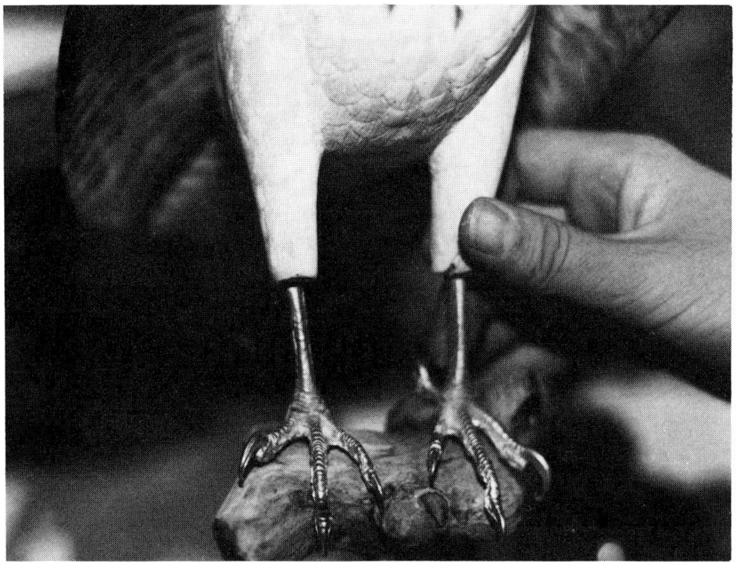

Cast feet being fitted to bird and to mount. Feet and wings are attached after bird is painted

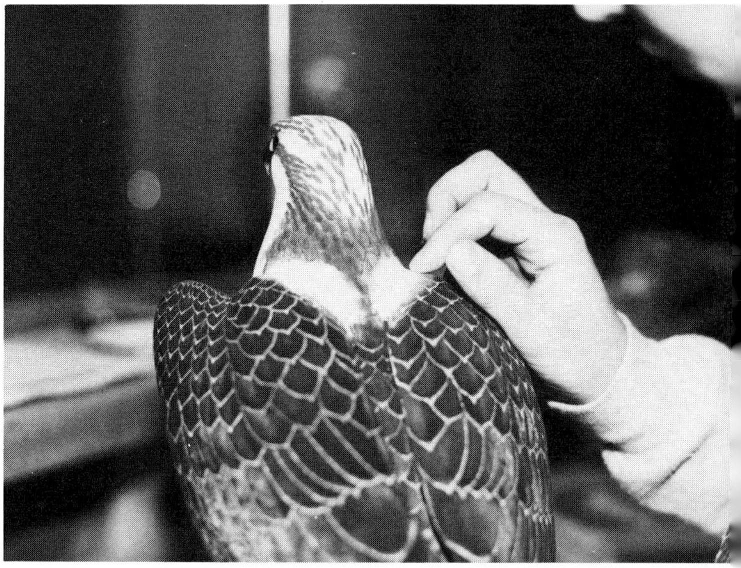

Wings set with five-minute epoxy and filled with moldable epoxy

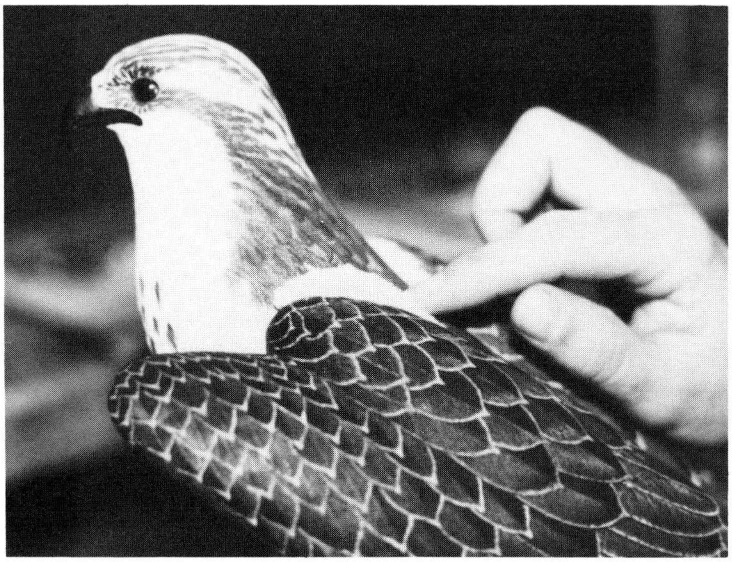

Smoothing epoxy with fingers and water

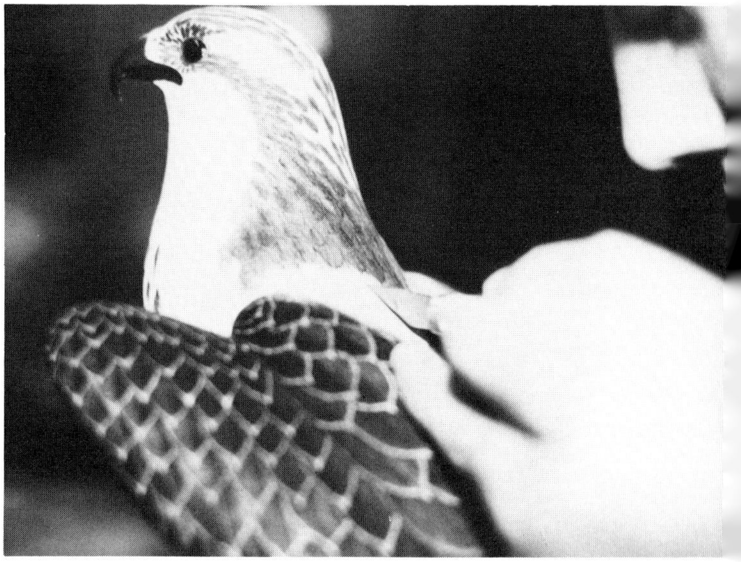

With knife texture fill area before it hardens

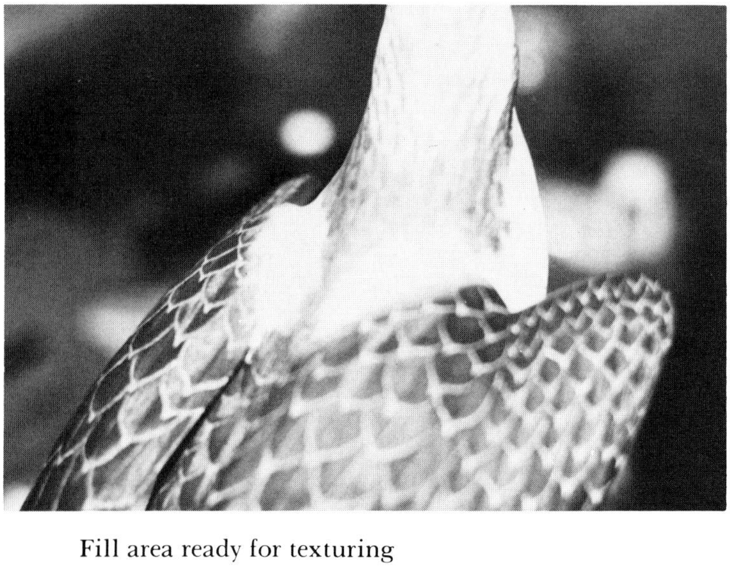

Fill area ready for texturing

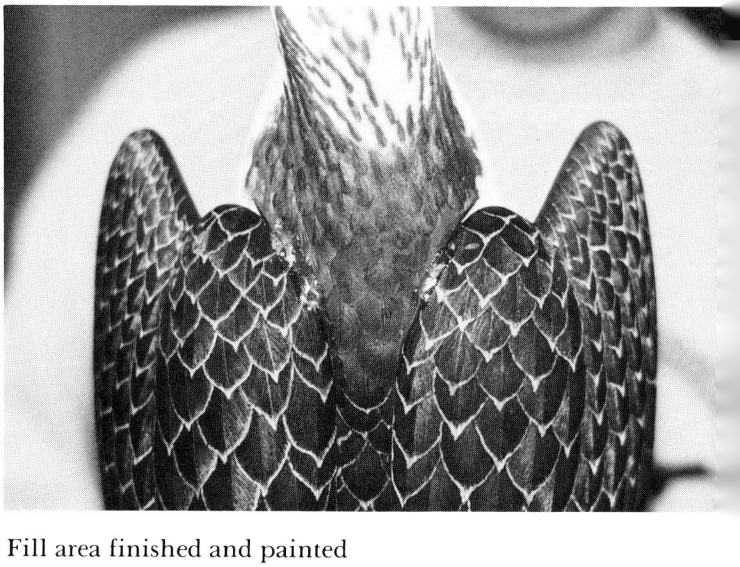

Fill area finished and painted

American Kestrel

Carved by Jeff Moore

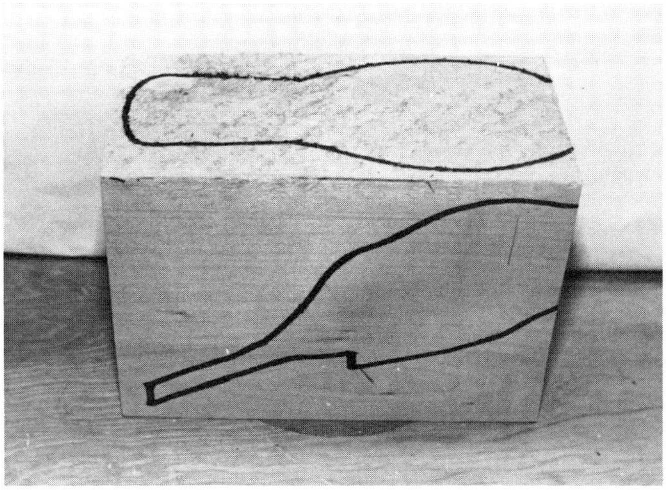

Plan and profile views of body on block

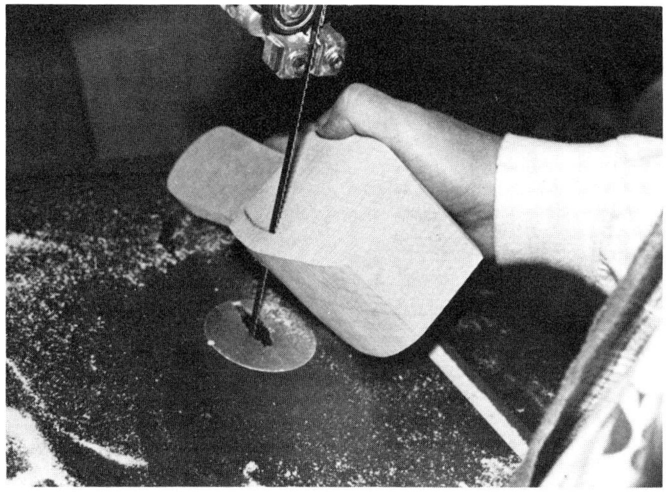

Trimming excess on band saw

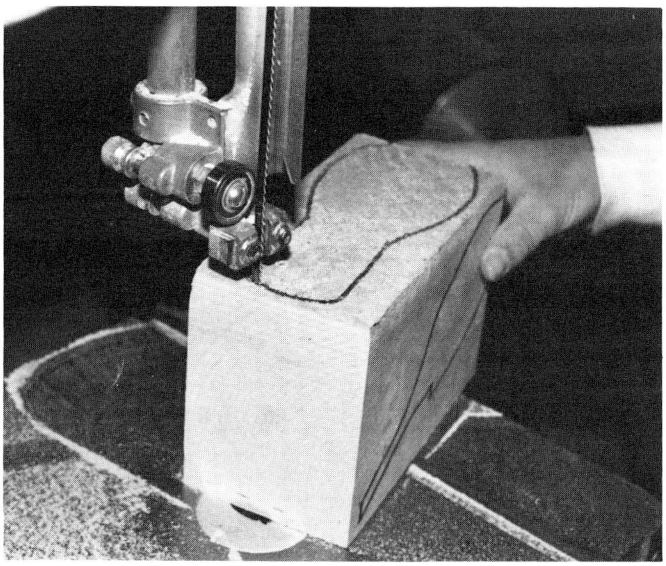

Band sawing plan view

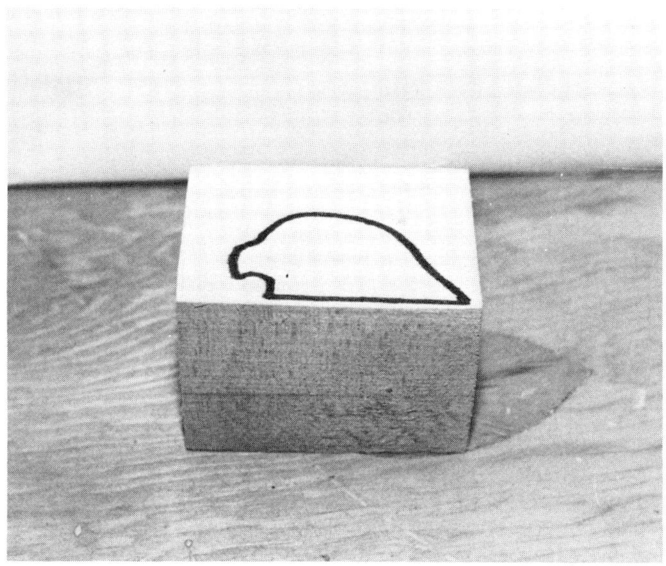

Profile of head on block

Band sawing profile view

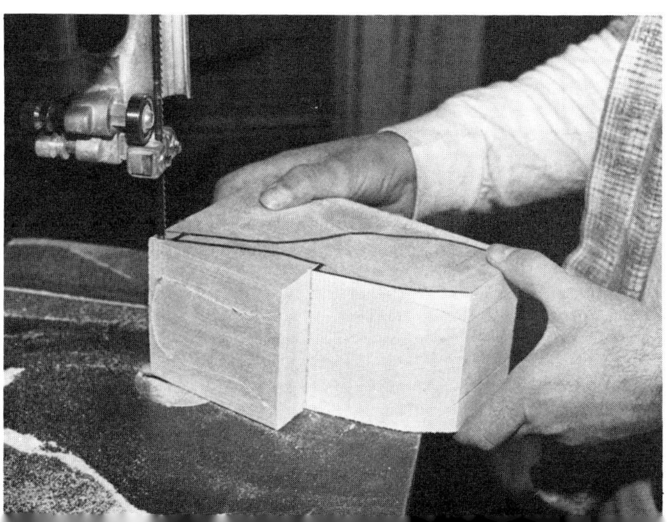

Band sawing head

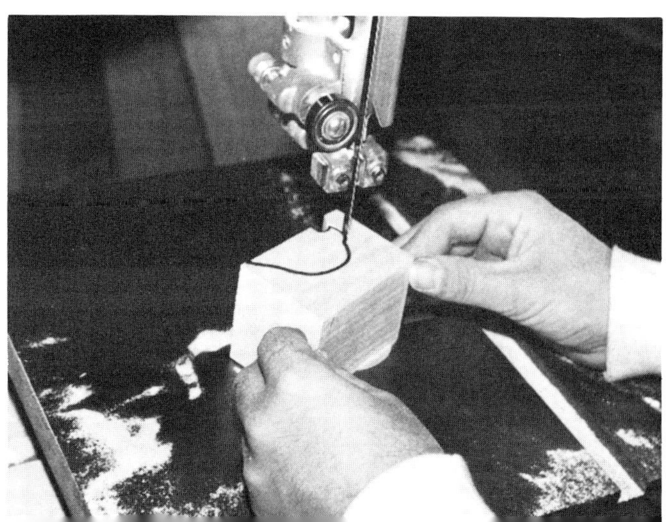

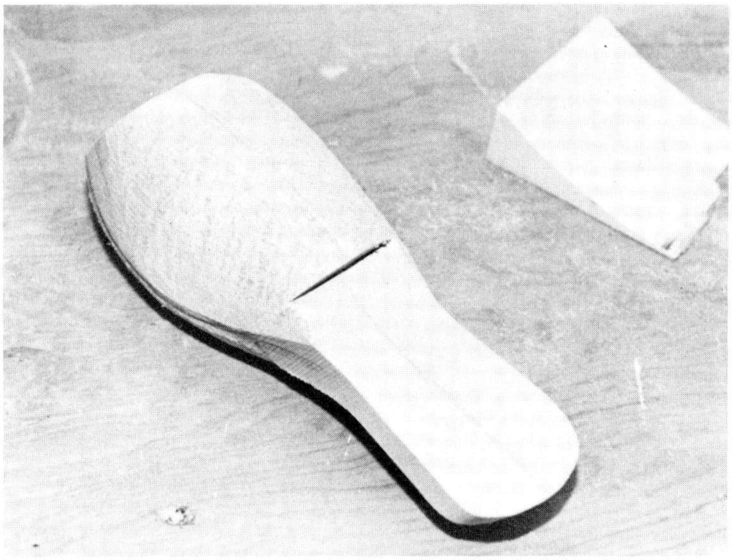

Body shaped

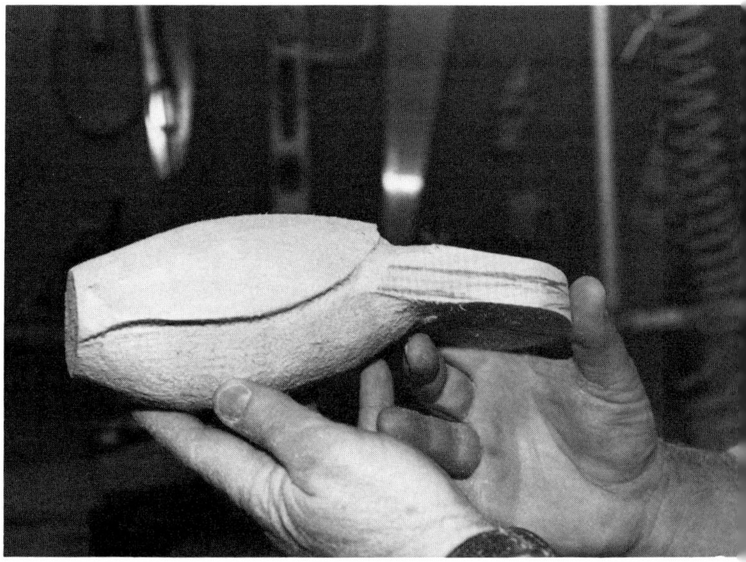

Cut in of wing area

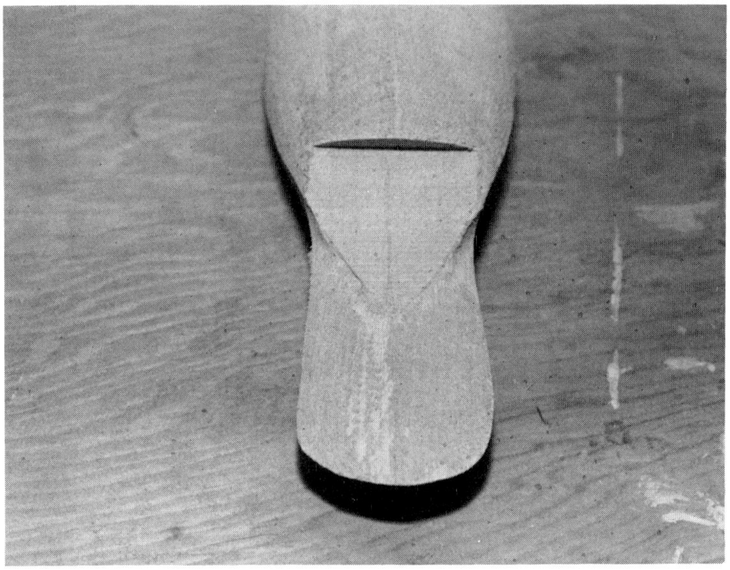

Rump and upper tail shaped

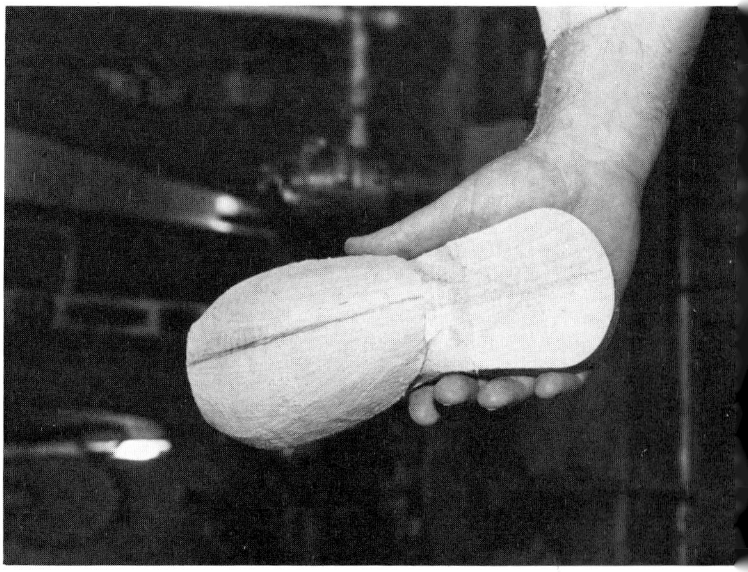

Back shaped and flowed smoothly into tail

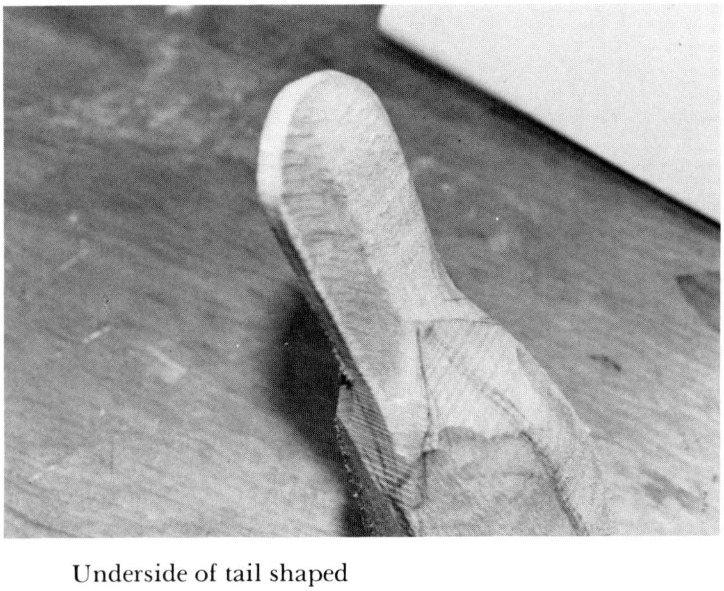

Underside of tail shaped

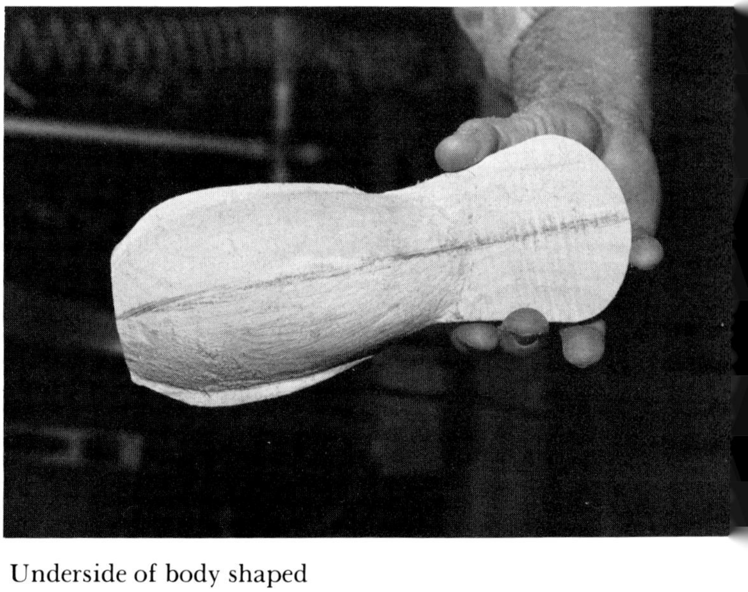

Underside of body shaped

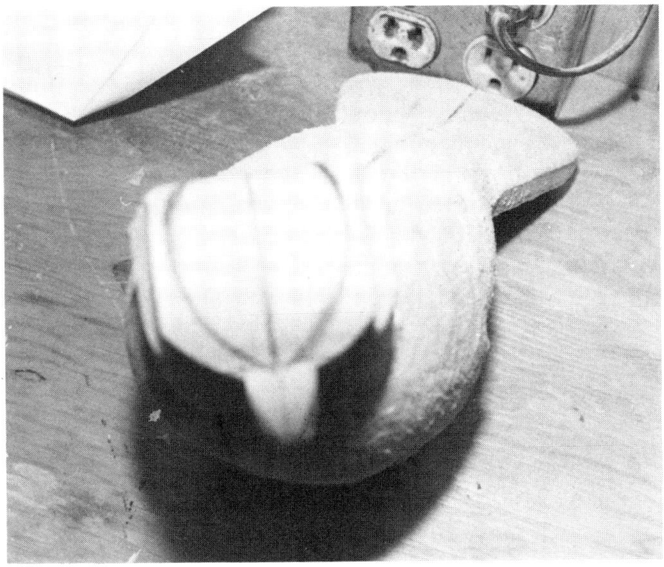

Head set temporarily onto body showing crown lines

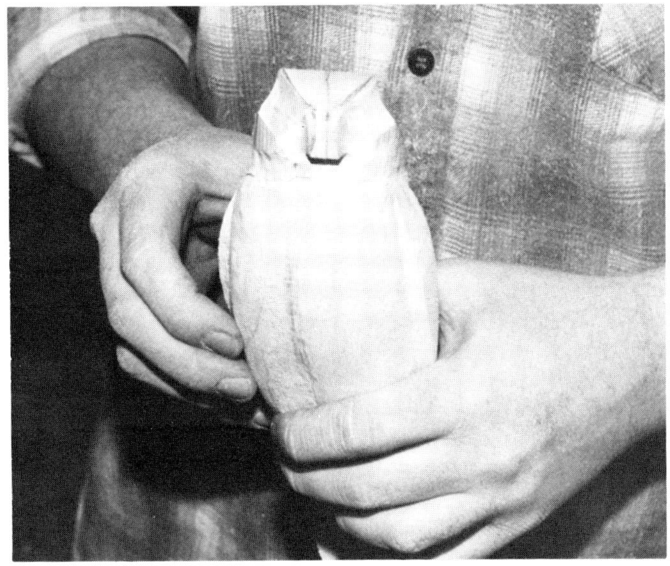

Eye channels flowing into beak

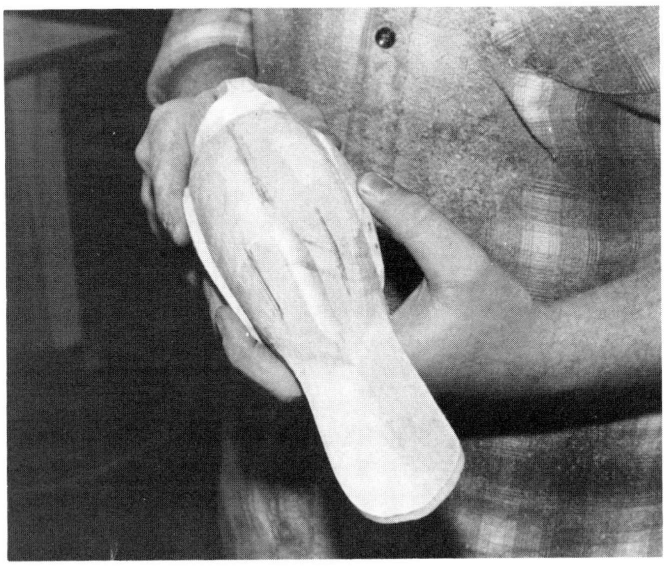

Belly showing leg separation

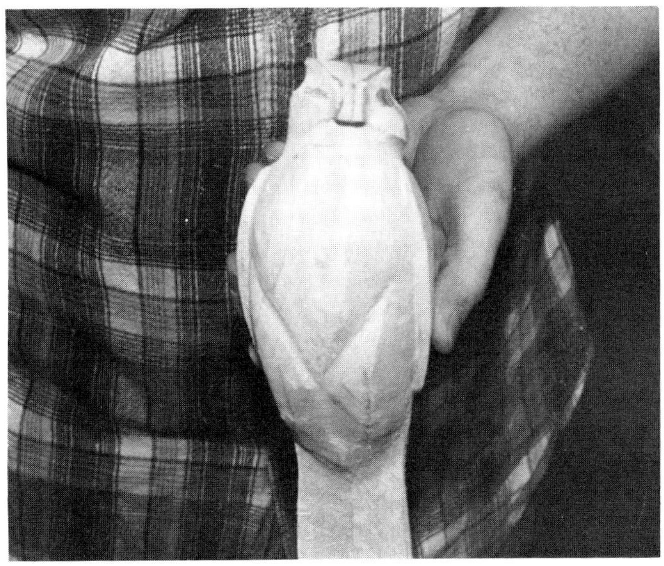

Belly and breast indentation

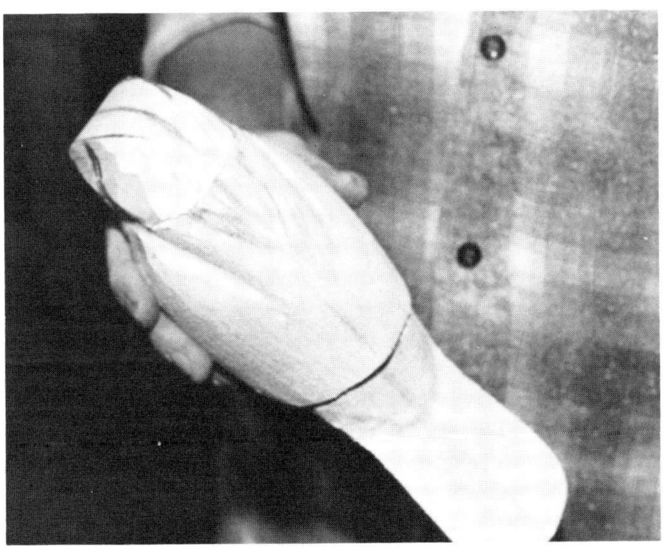

Cape area shaped

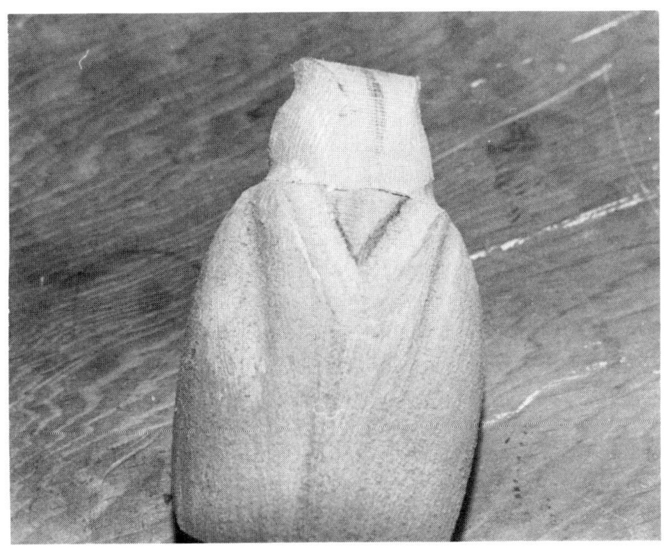

Cape area flowing smoothly into head

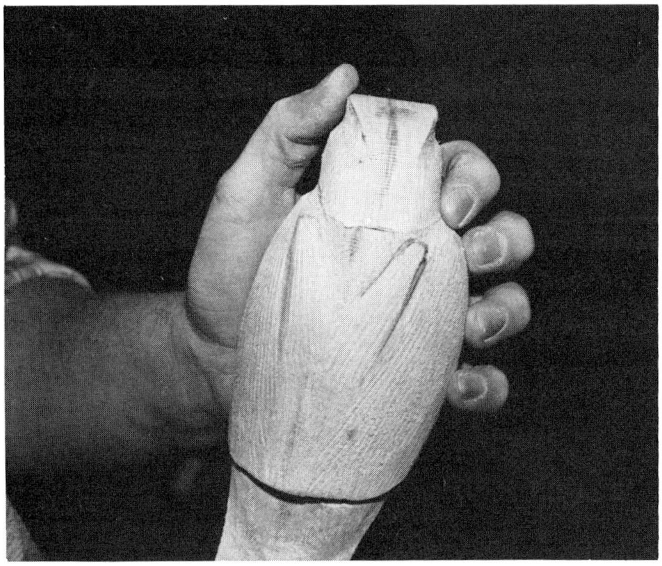

Guide lines for wings

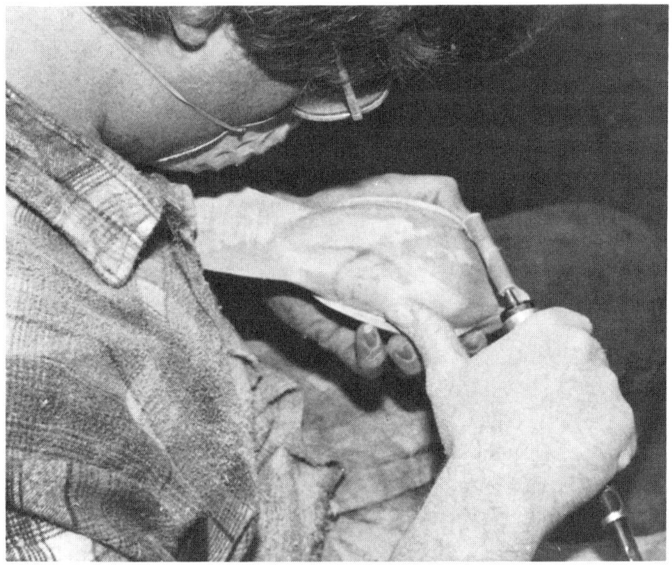

Shaping belly area

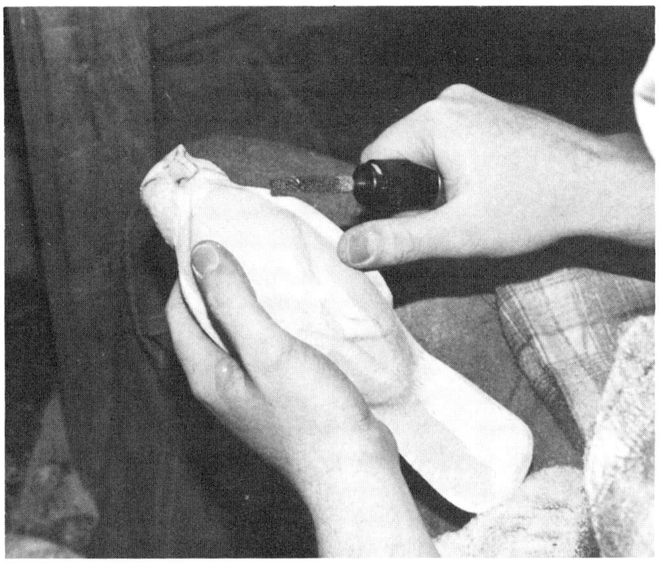

Shaping breast area

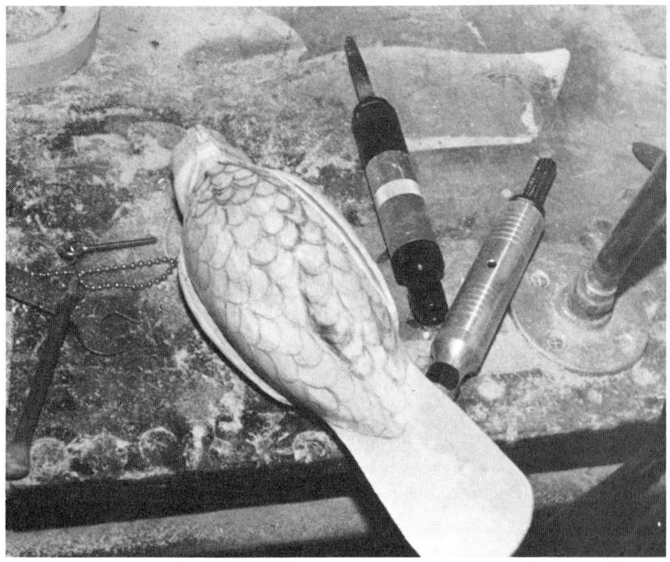

Feather layout on breast and belly

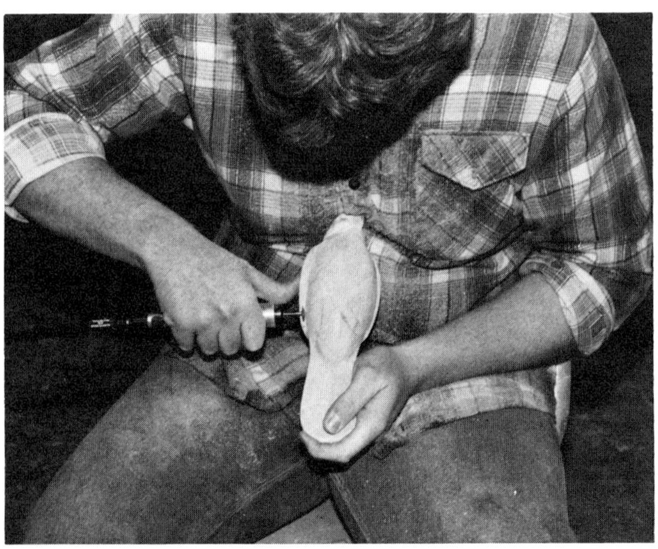

Cutting channel between wing and body

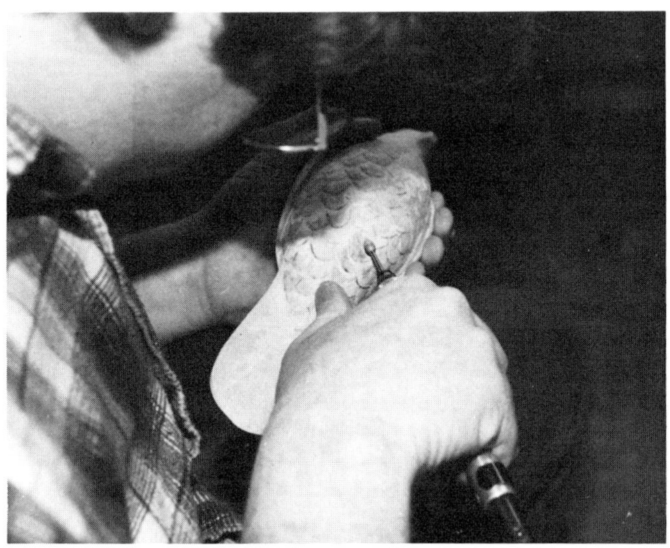

Ruby carving feathers to create roll on each one

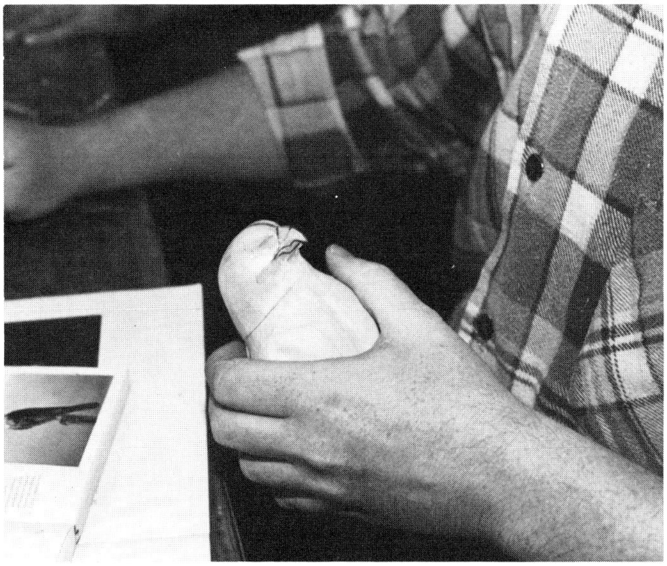

Shaping beak

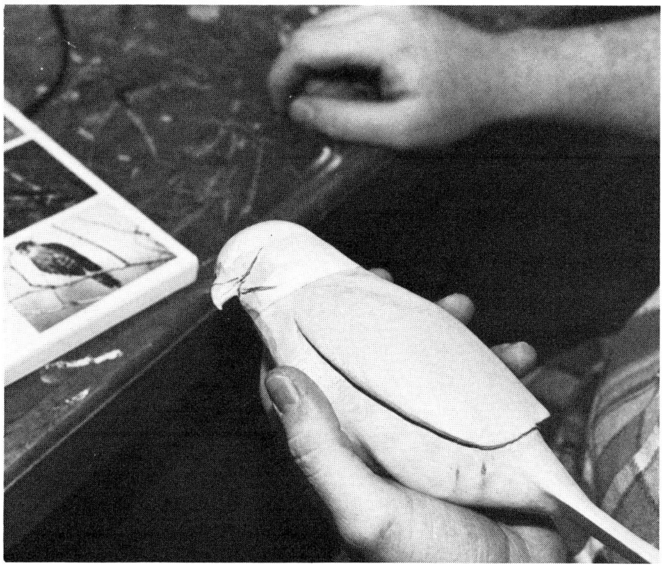

Profile of head and wing areas

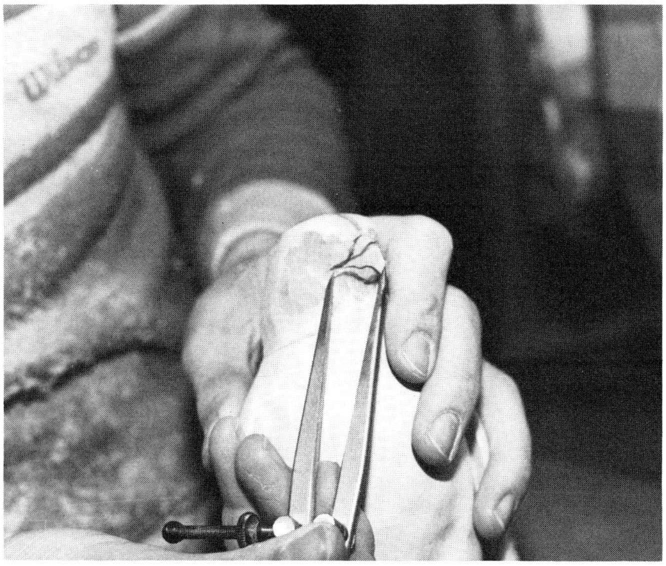

Measuring beak

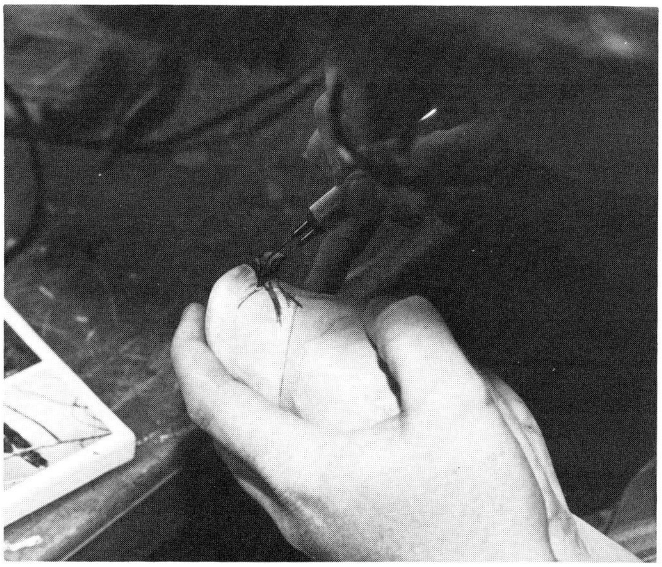

Burning detail into beak and head area

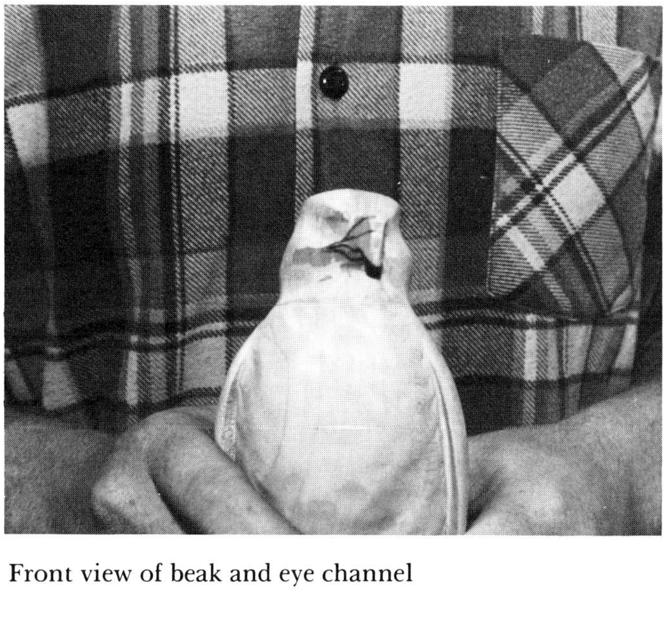

Front view of beak and eye channel

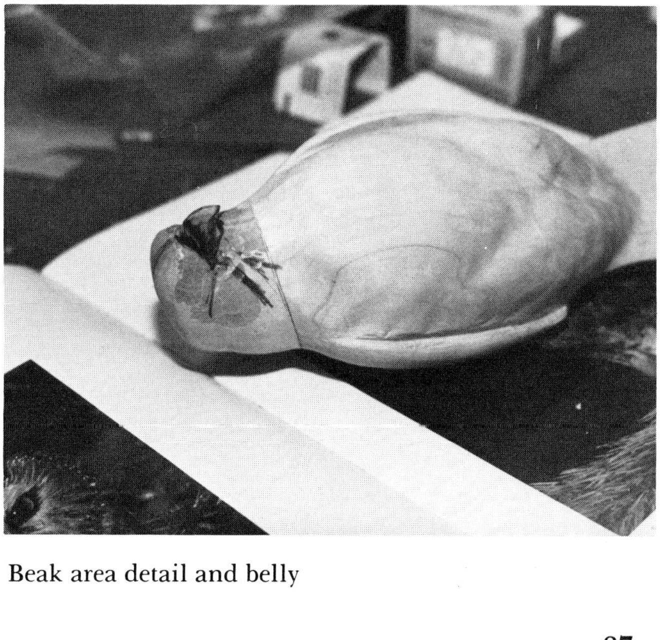

Beak area detail and belly

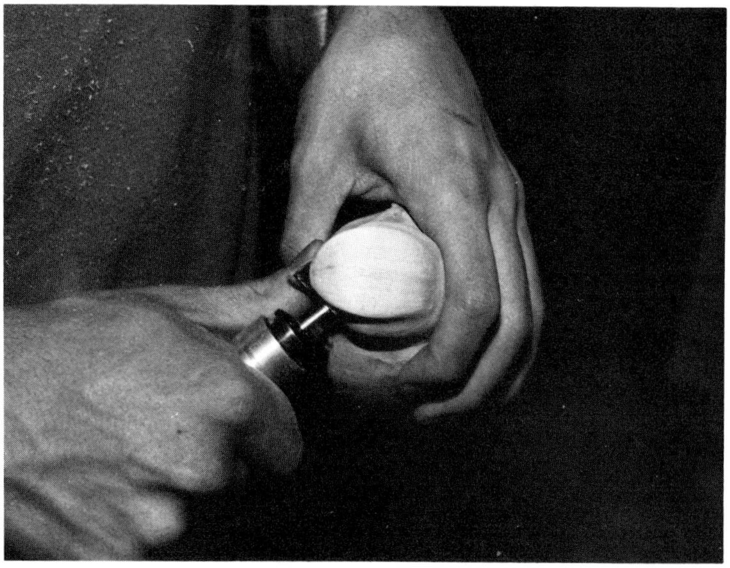

Drilling eye holes (note angle)

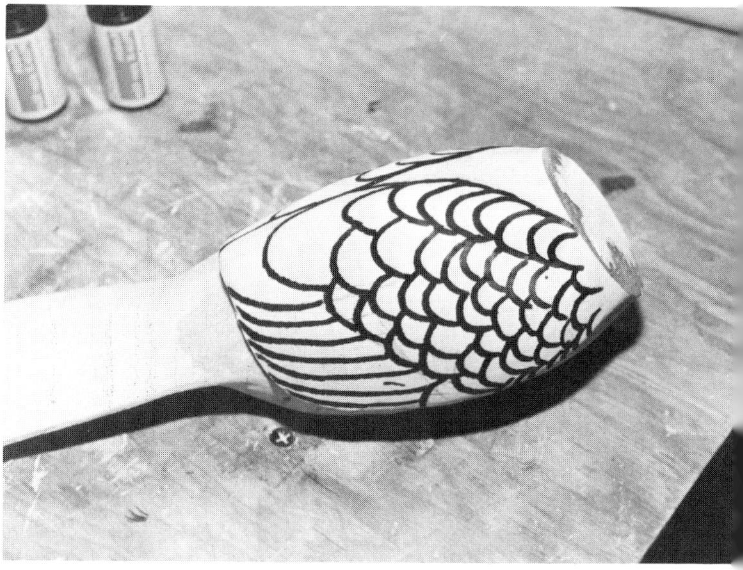

Feather layout on wing

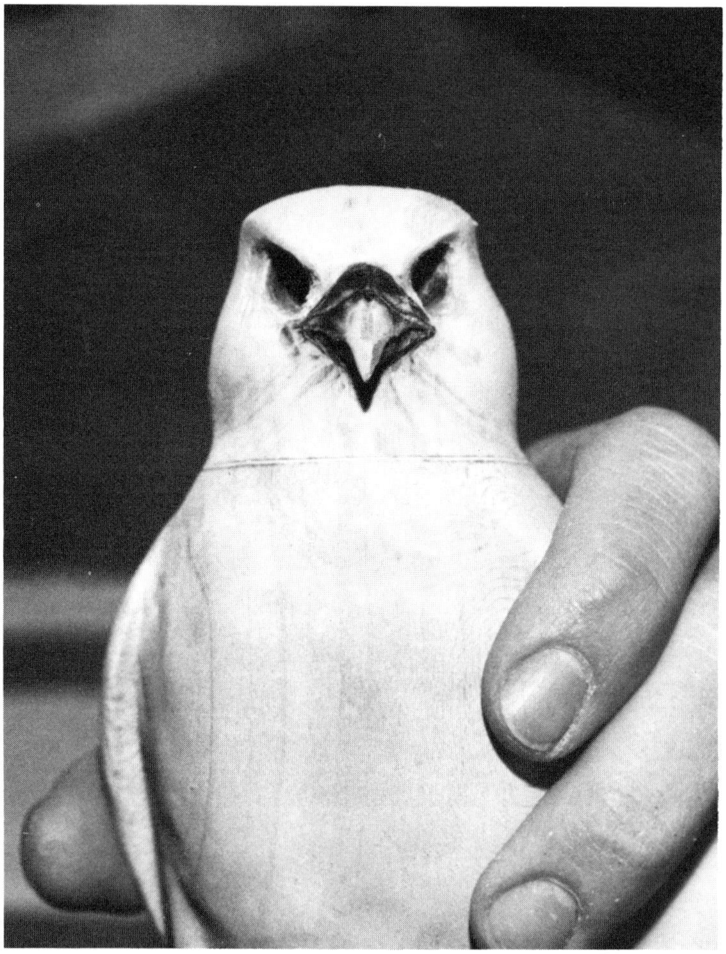

Front view eye holes drilled, beak carved and detailed

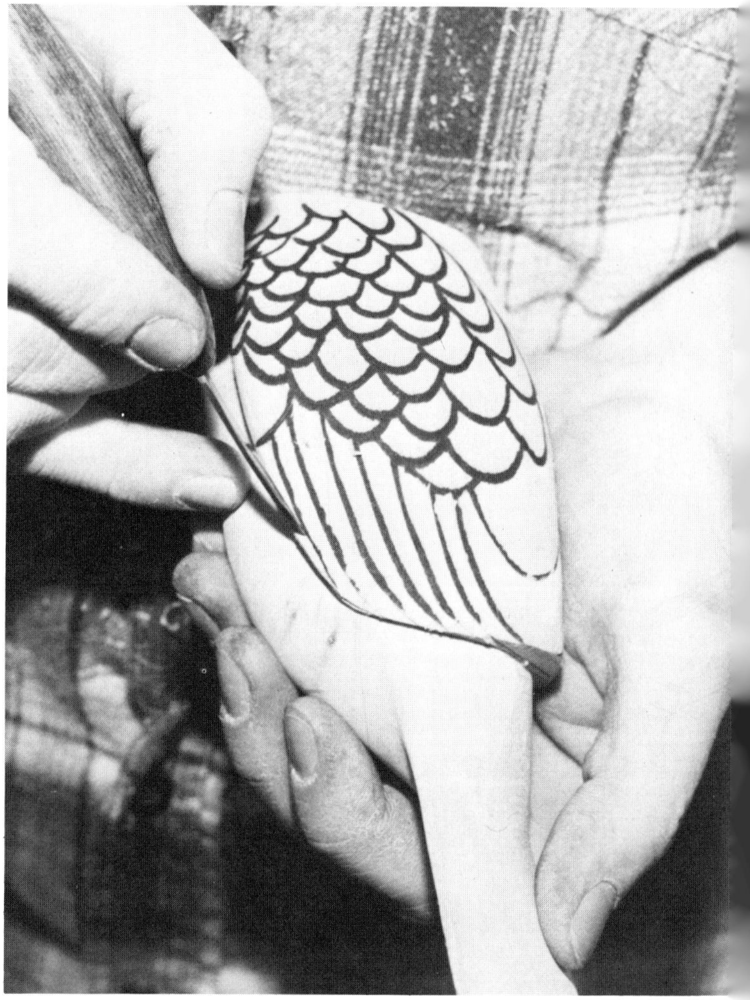

Carving feather detail

(See page 162 for painting instructions and page 283 for patterns)

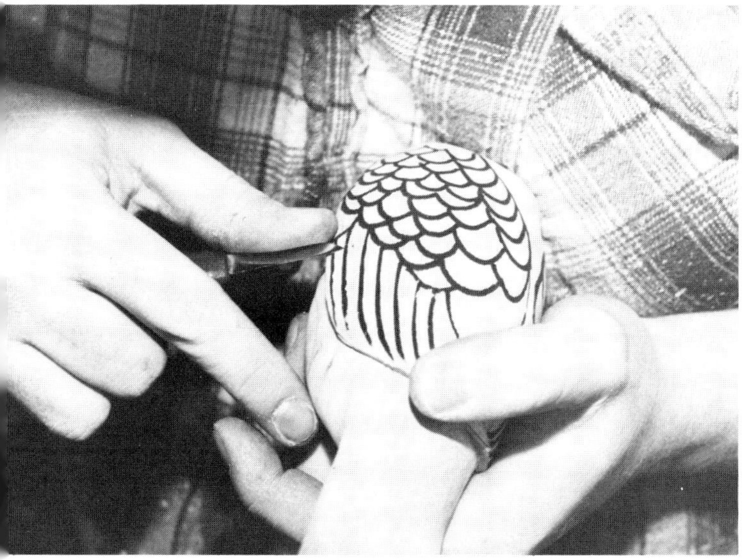

Carving secondaries

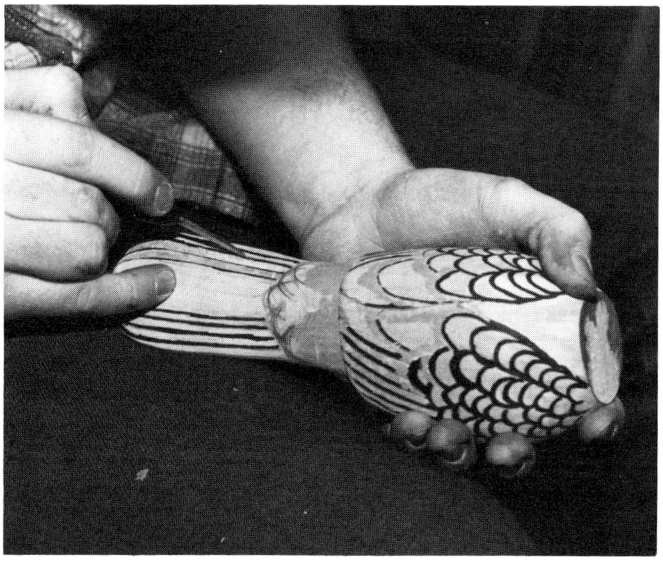

Carving tail detail

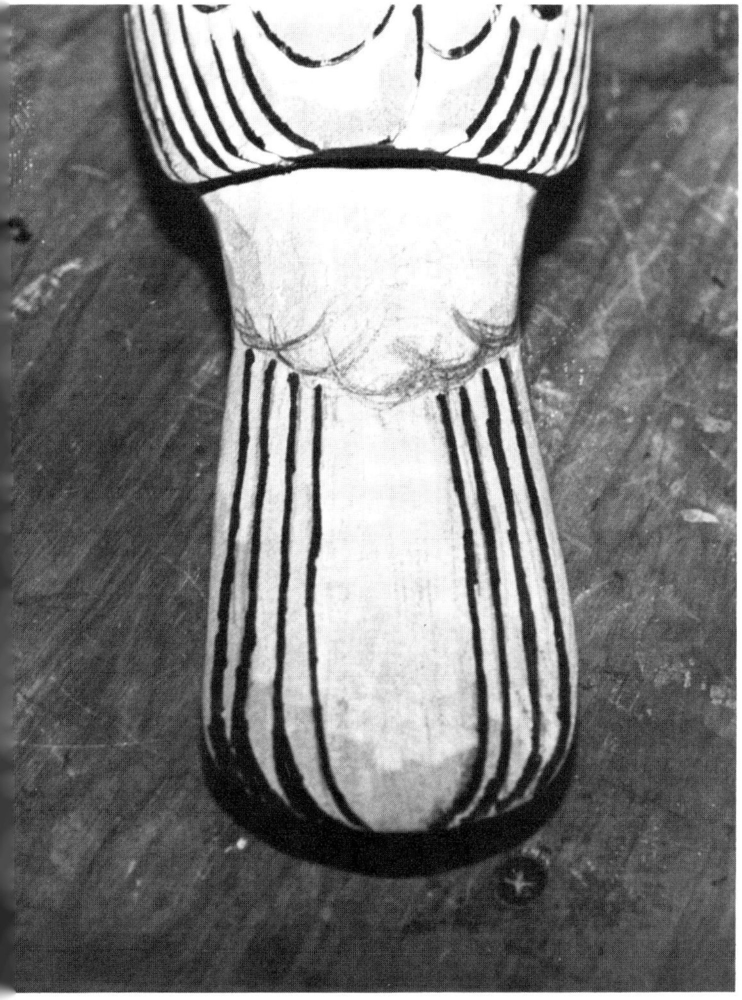

Upper tail layouts

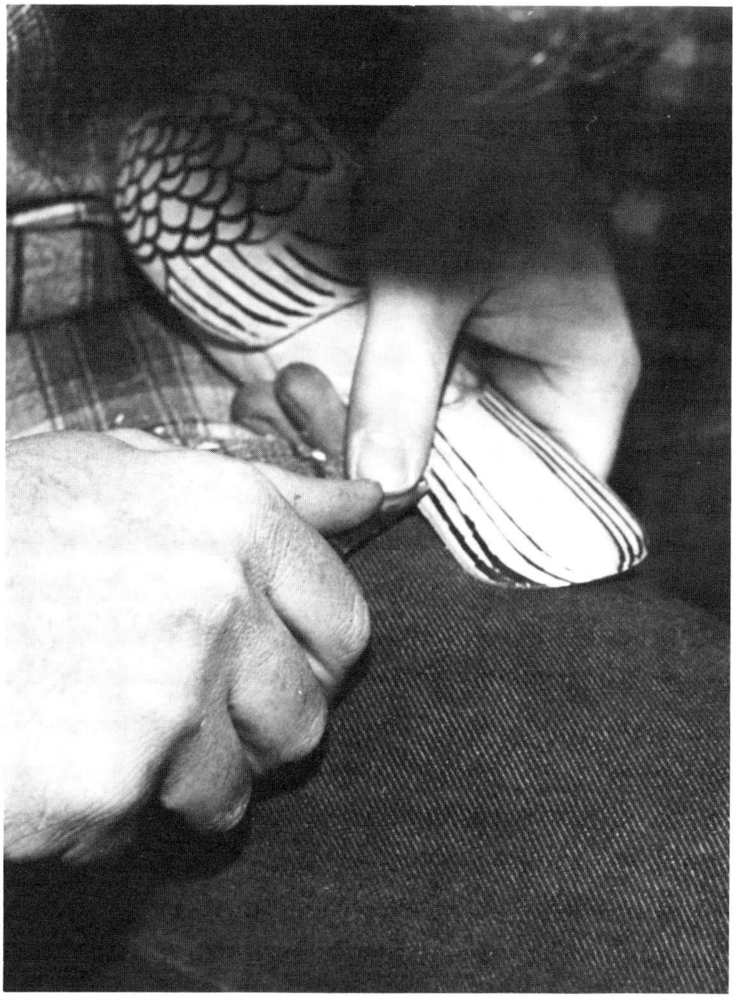

Carving tail detail

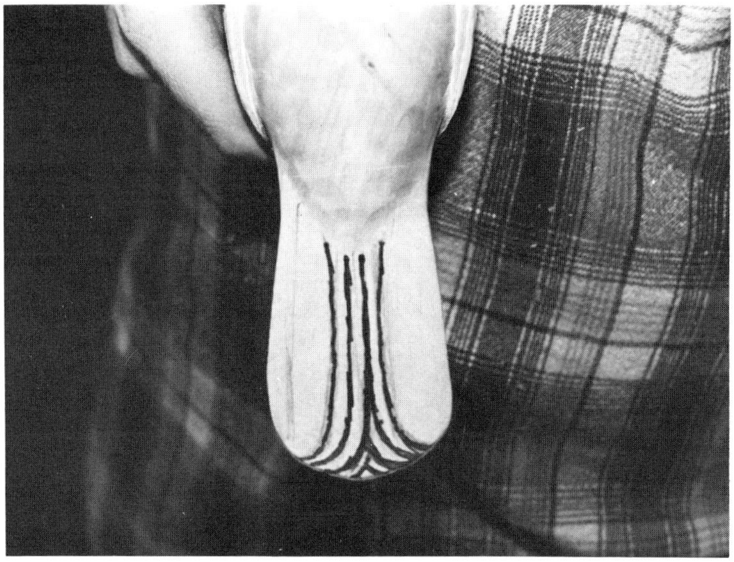

Underside of tail layout

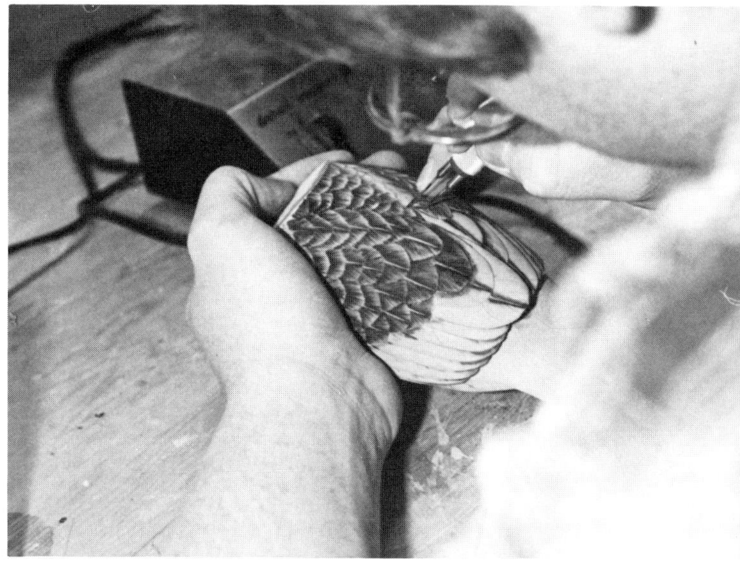

Burning cape and wings

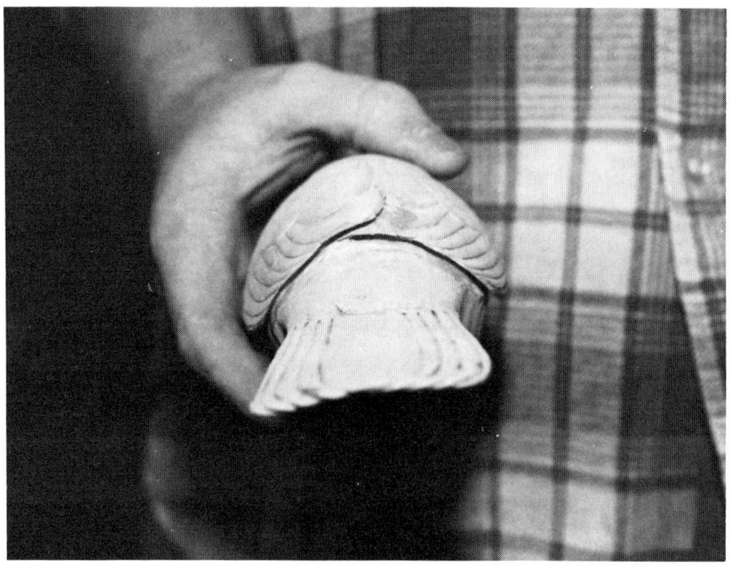

Upperside of tail and wing channels for inserts

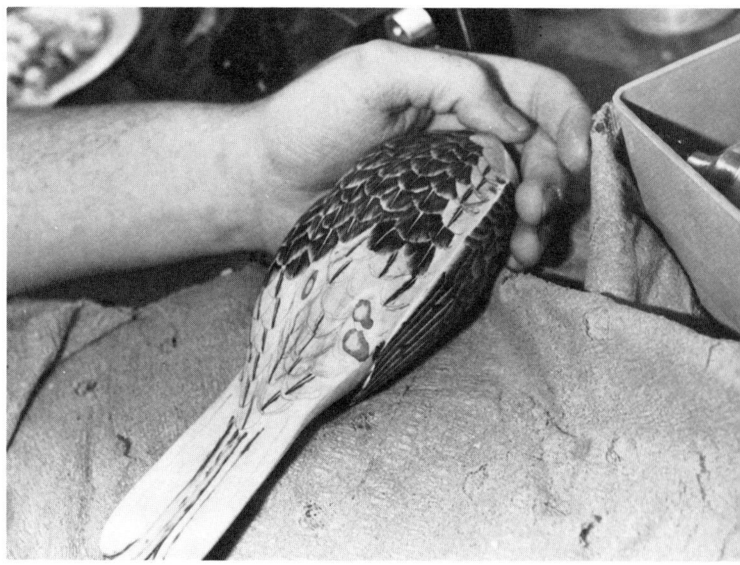

Burning (note raised quills)

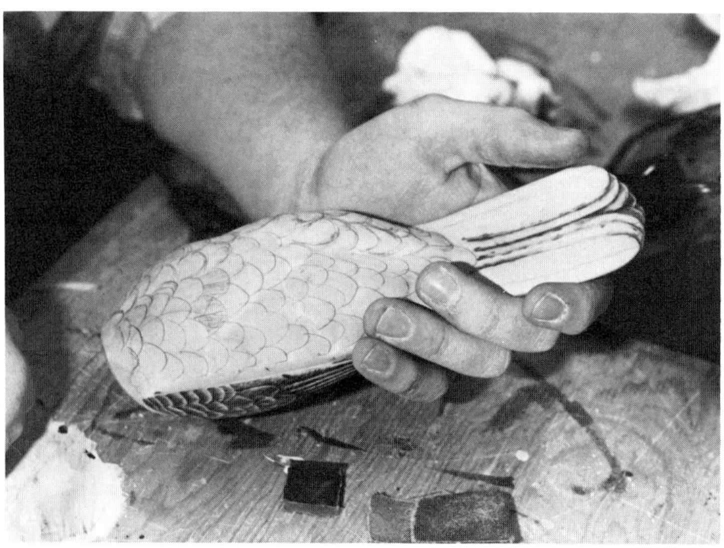

Under tail and belly carved

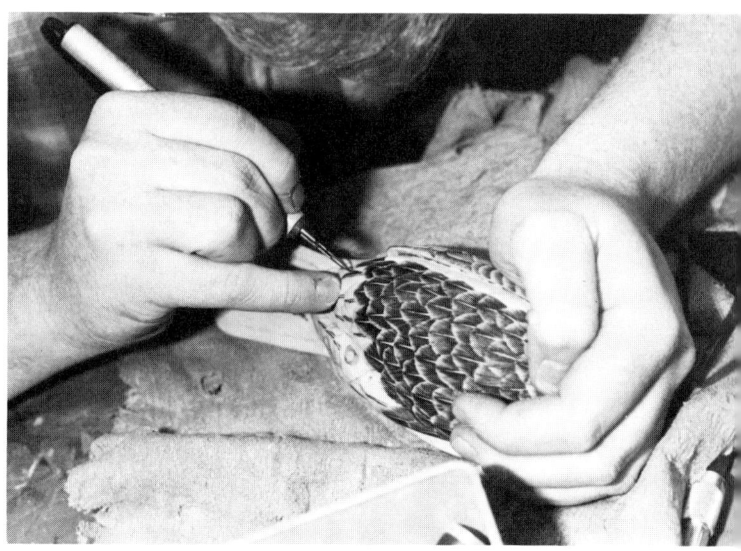

Burnings wings

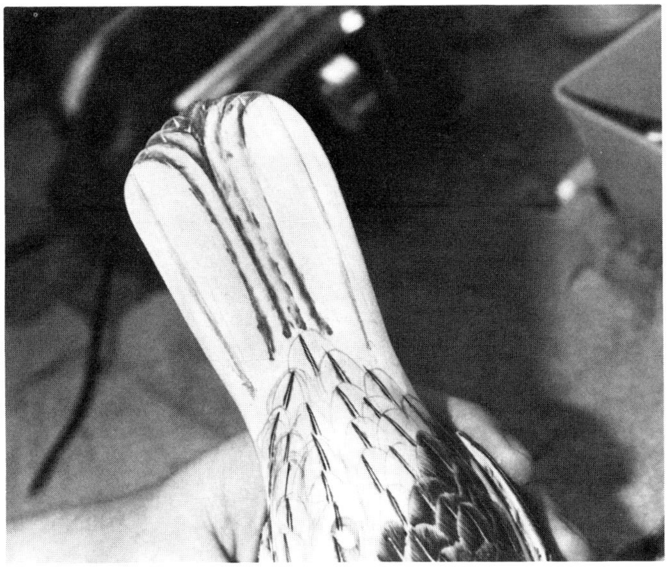

Underside of tail carved

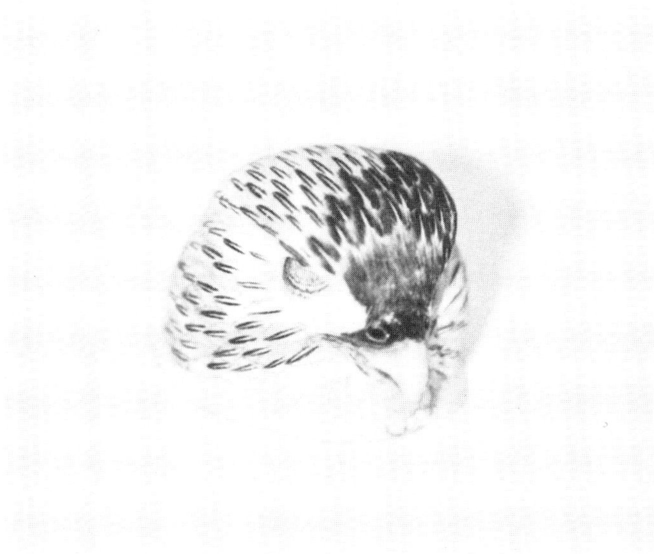

Head layout

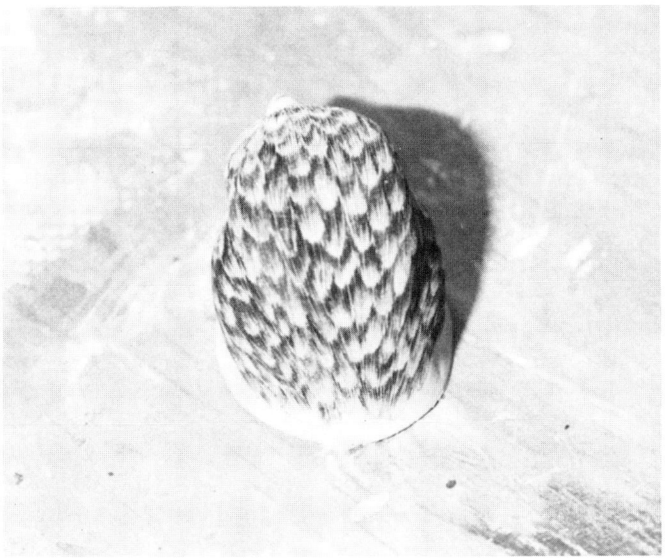

Back of head and crown detailed

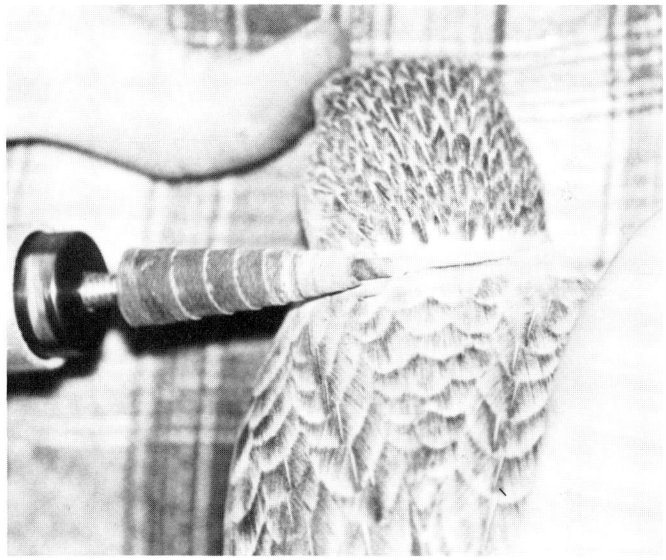

Head set and channel cut for fill

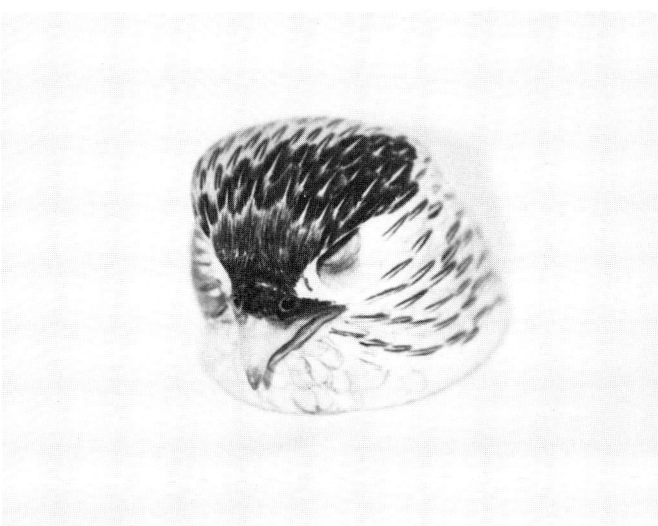

Crown detailed

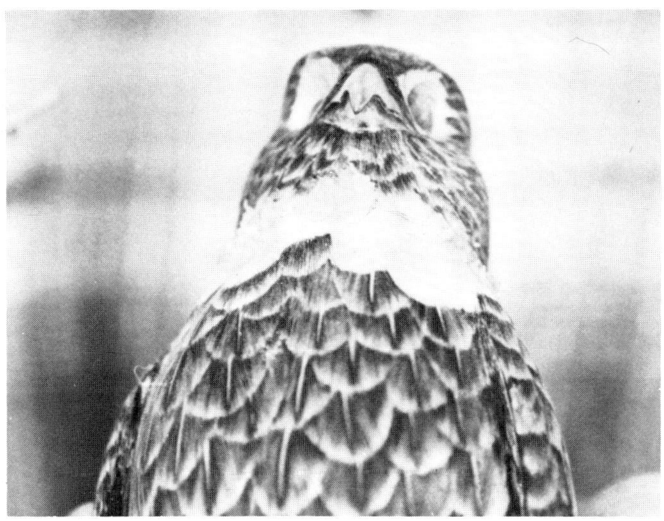

Neck joint filled with wood dough using a lot of acetone to break down air gaps

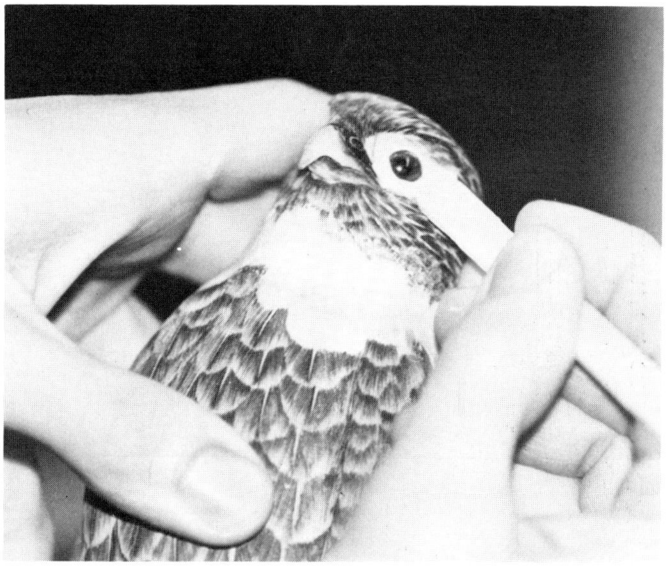

Set eyes, crimp fill material (epoxy putty) with craft stick

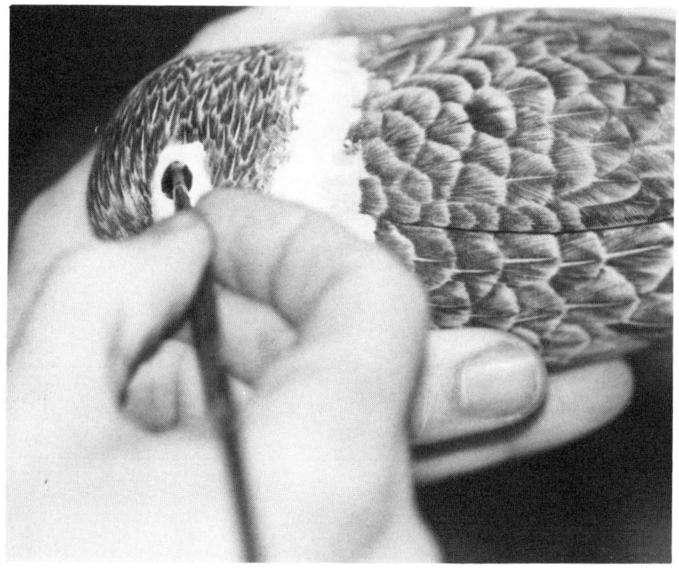

Use small paint brush to finish eye lid

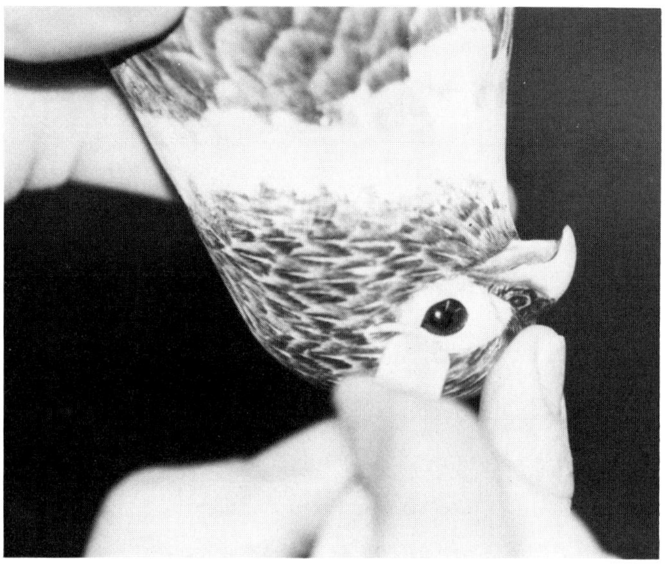

Fashion basic eye lid with craft stick (caution—use small amount of material)

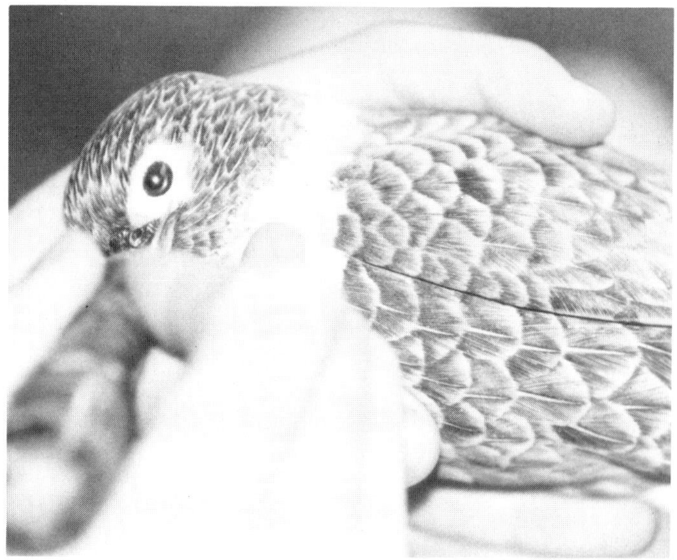

Texture excess putty with knife (dampen blade so it does not drag putty)

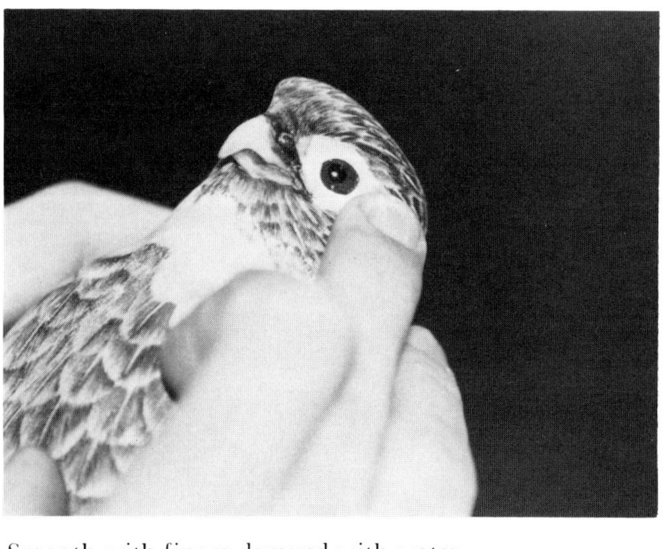

Smooth with finger damped with water

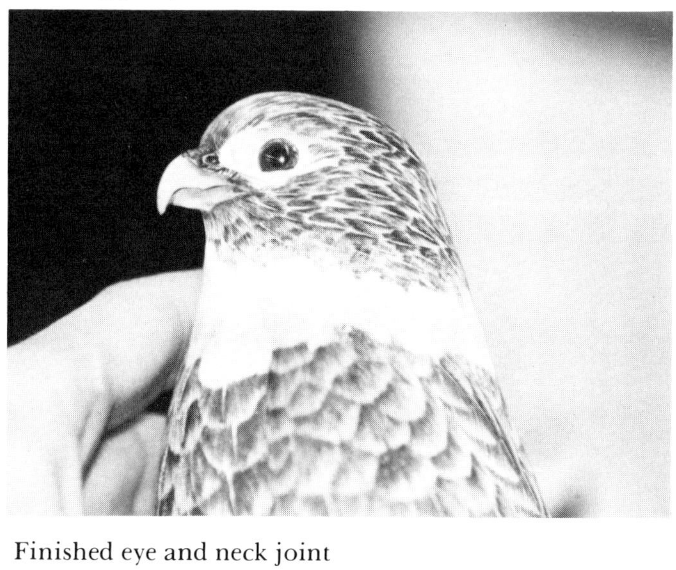

Finished eye and neck joint

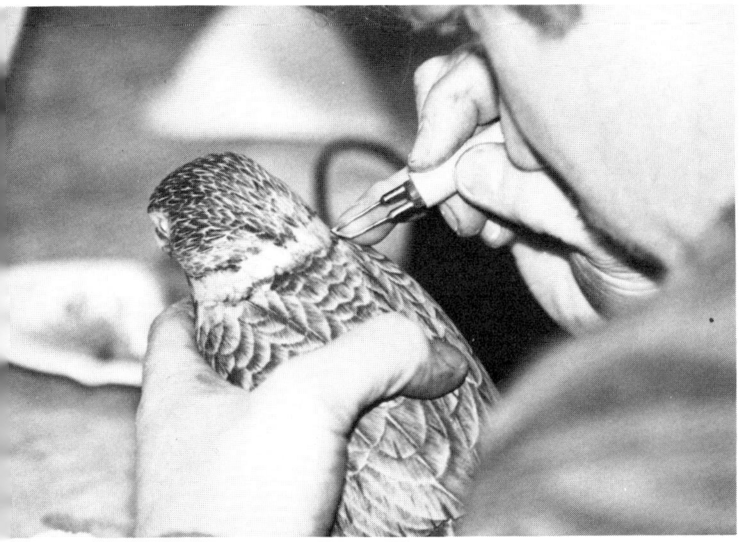

Burning fill material, use very low heat or wood dough will melt

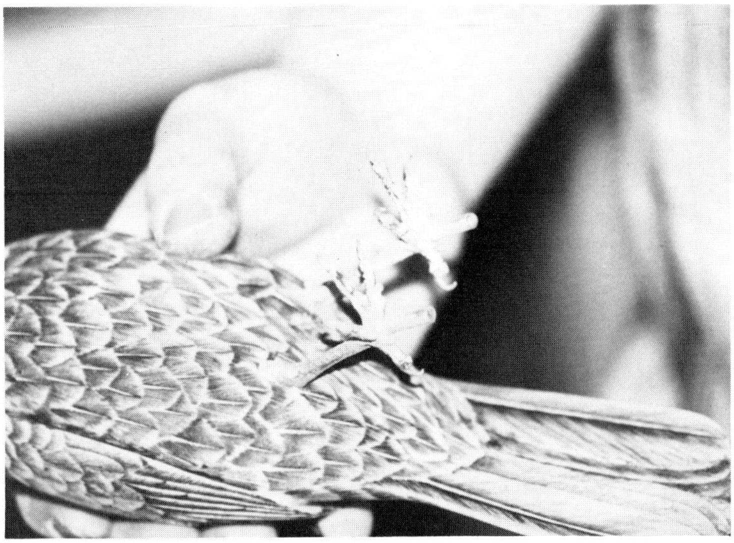

Glue legs with 5-minute epoxy and fill at junction to body with small amount of moldable epoxy

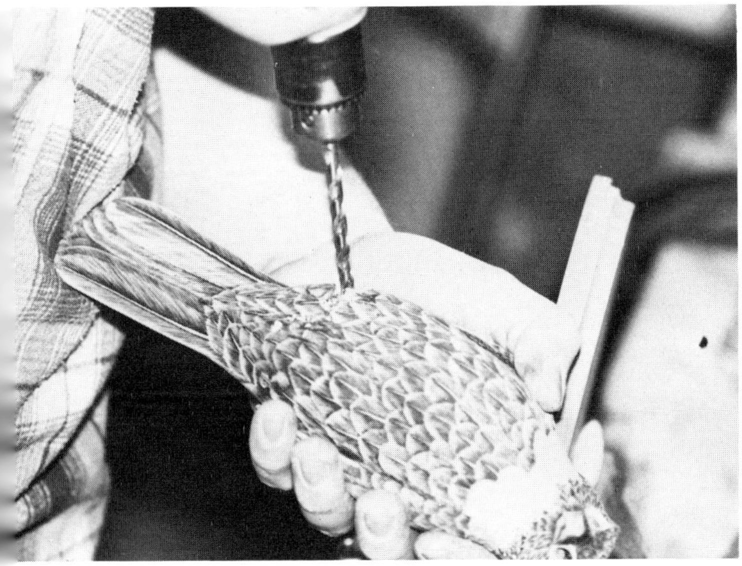

Drill holes for legs (note angle to start)

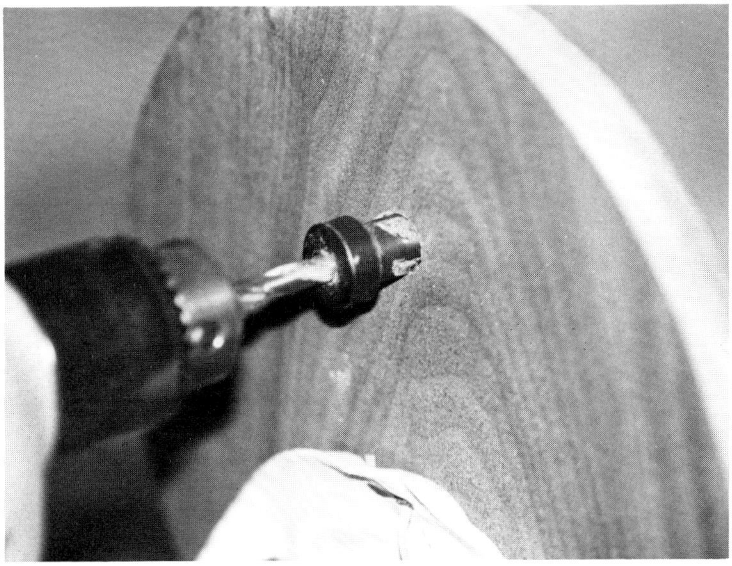

Countersink hole in bottom for screw head

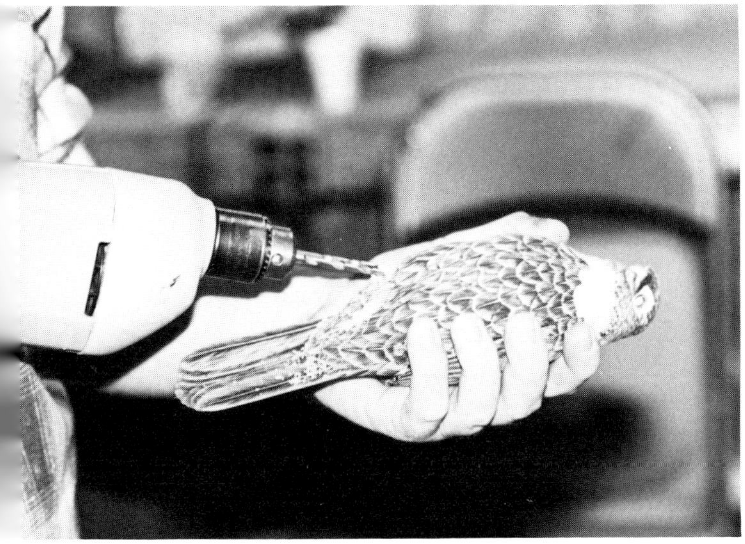

Change angle after start (fig. 2)

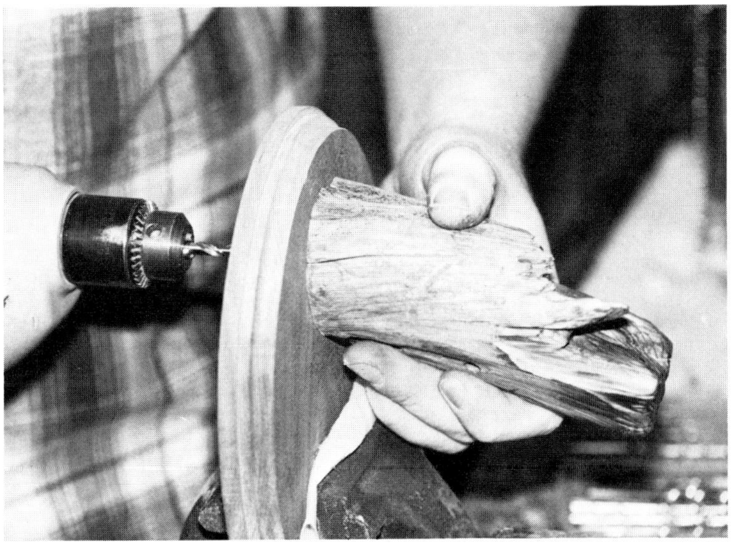

Attach driftwood and set bird

Female Merlin

Carved by Jack Hemphill

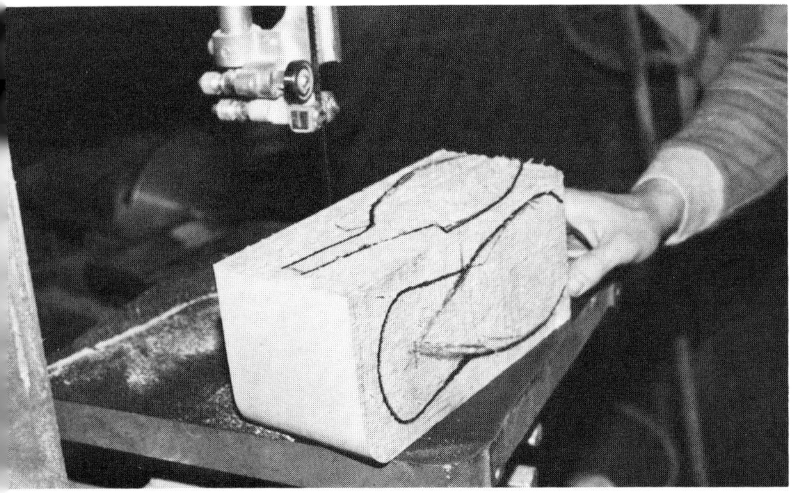

Body pattern on block

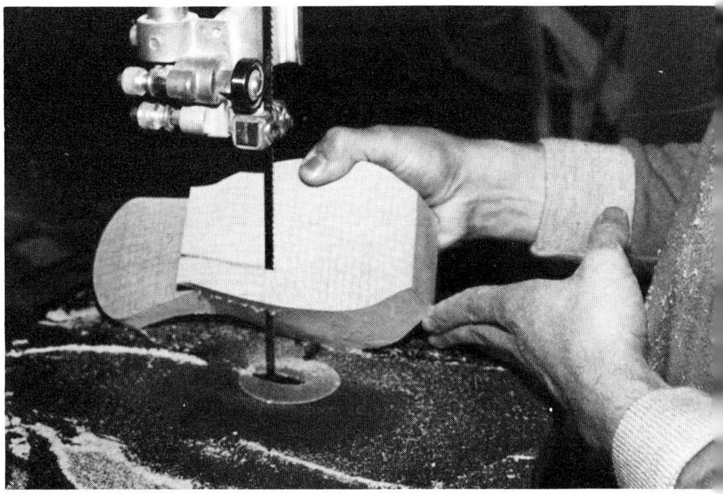

Trimming body block

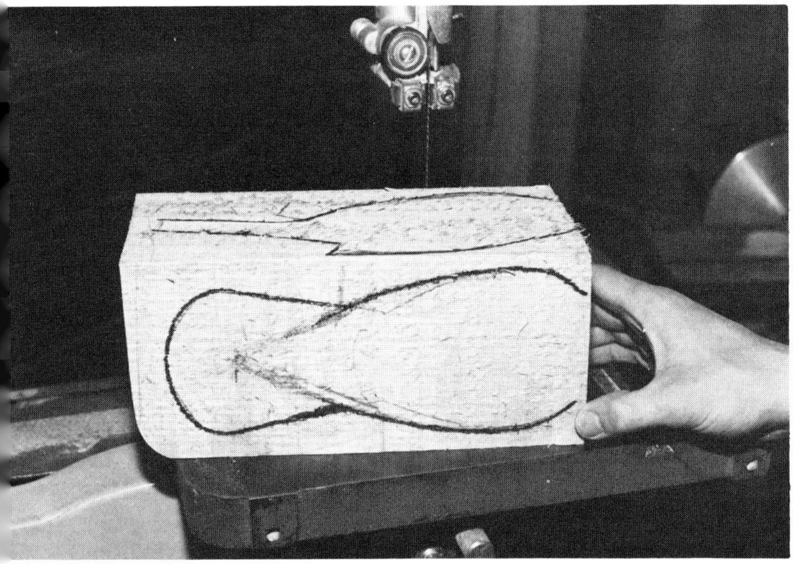

Another view of pattern on block

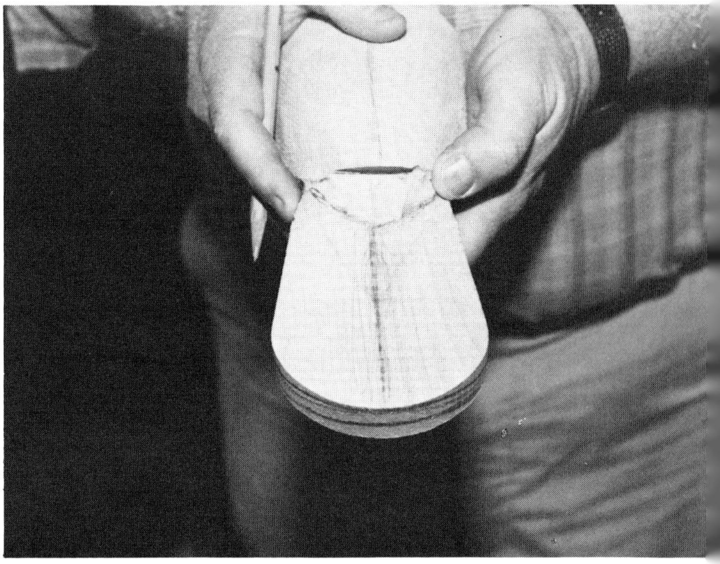

Rounding body with guide lines

Band sawing body pattern

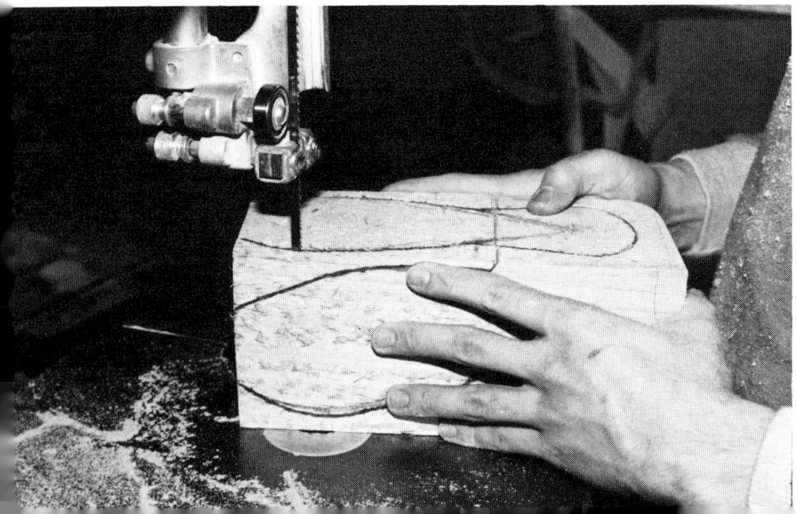

Tail lines, note shelf for primary inserts

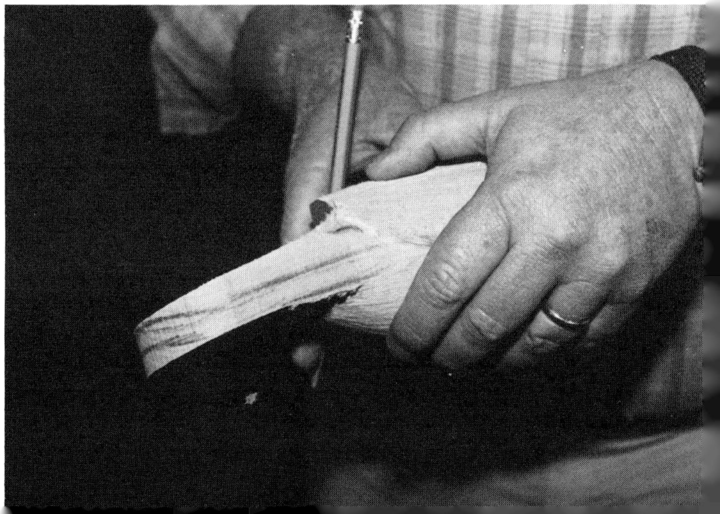

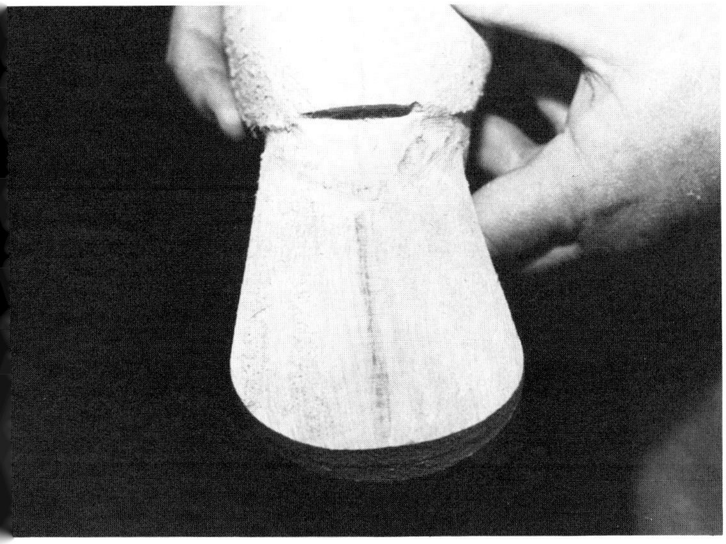

Top side of tail shaped

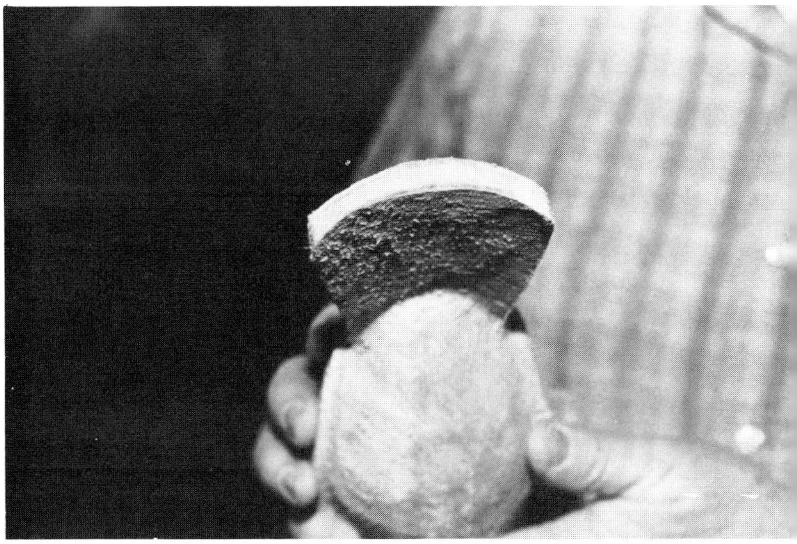

Underside of tail shaped

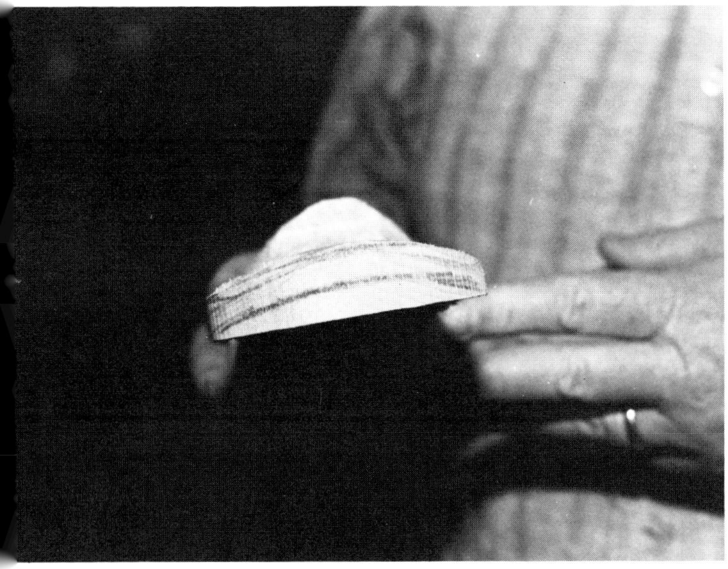

End view of tail

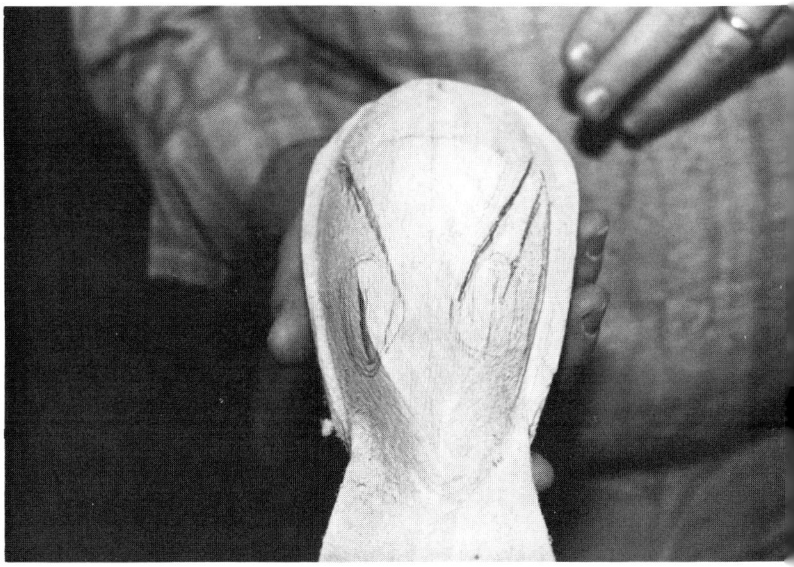

V—in chest area

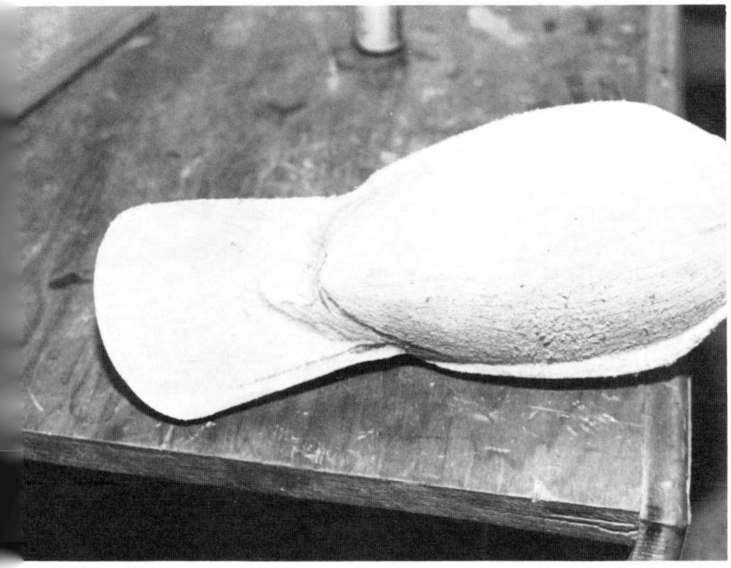

Belly view showing wing under-cuts

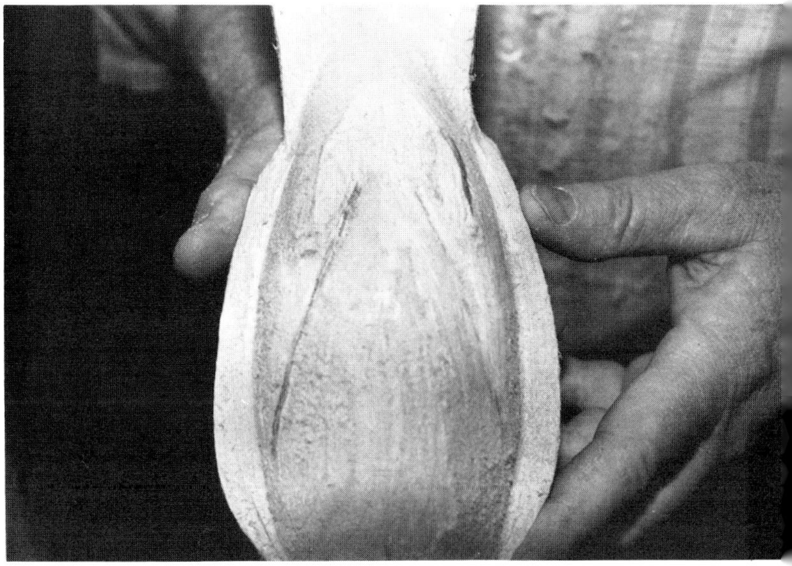

Leg area shaped

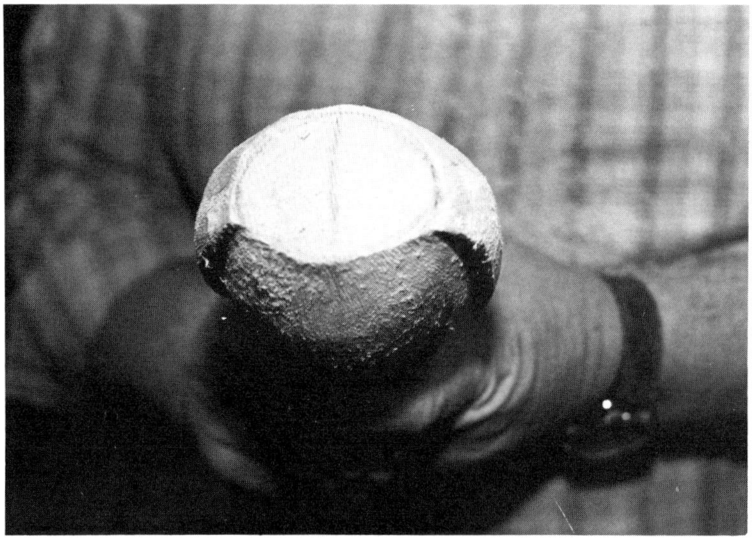

Top view where head will be set

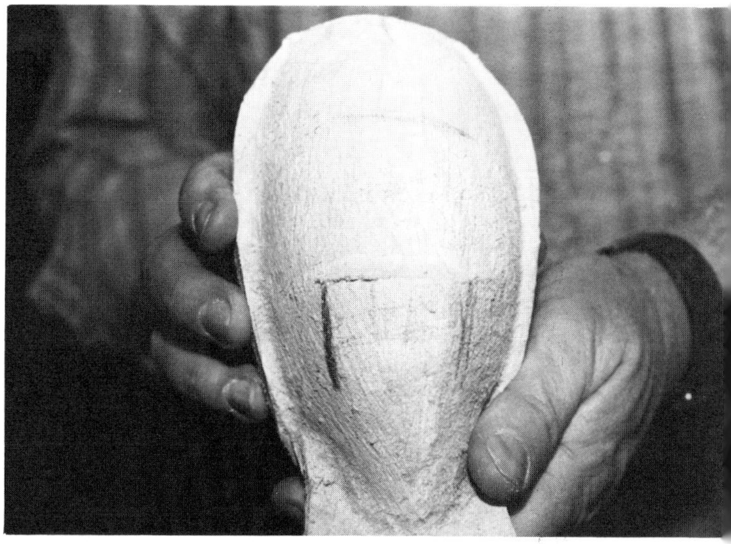

Leg area

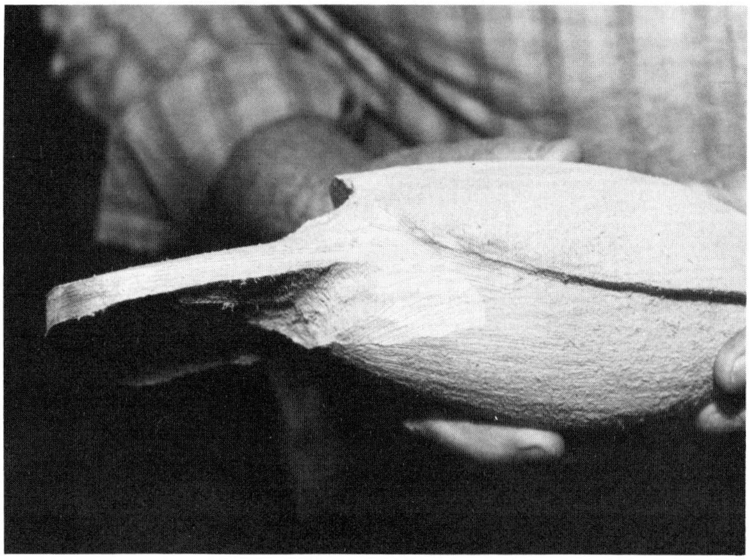

Profile

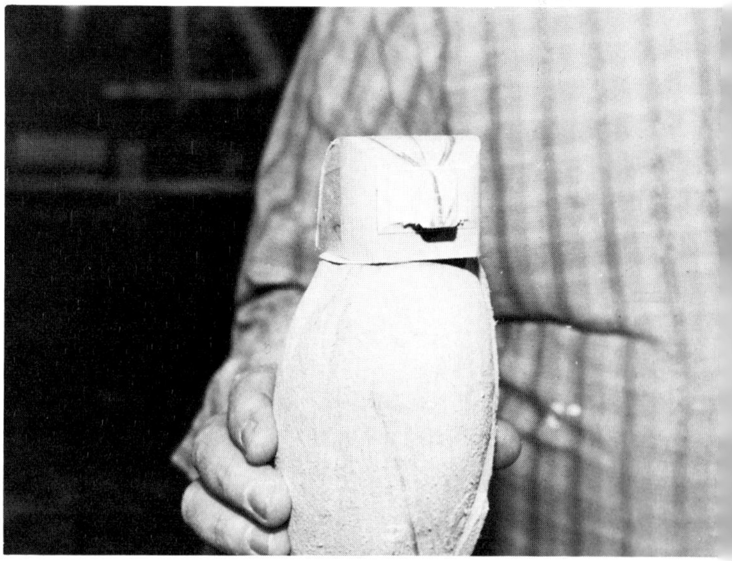

Head set temporarily with paper

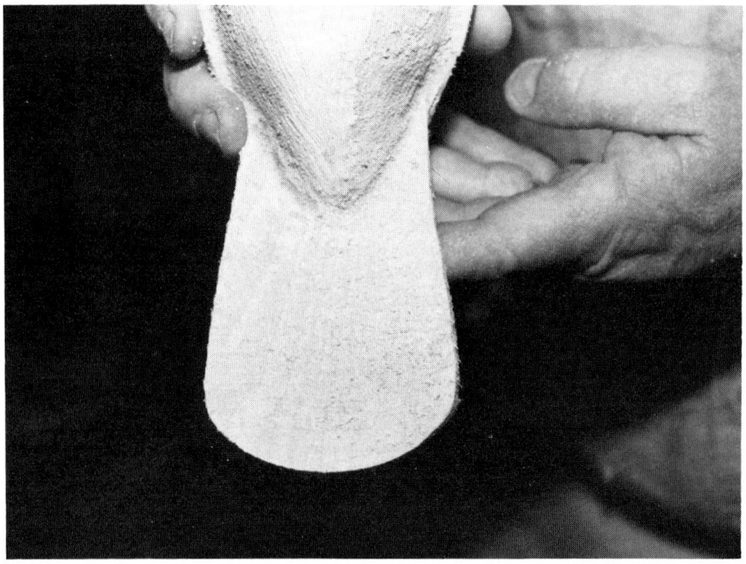

Underside of tail and under rump

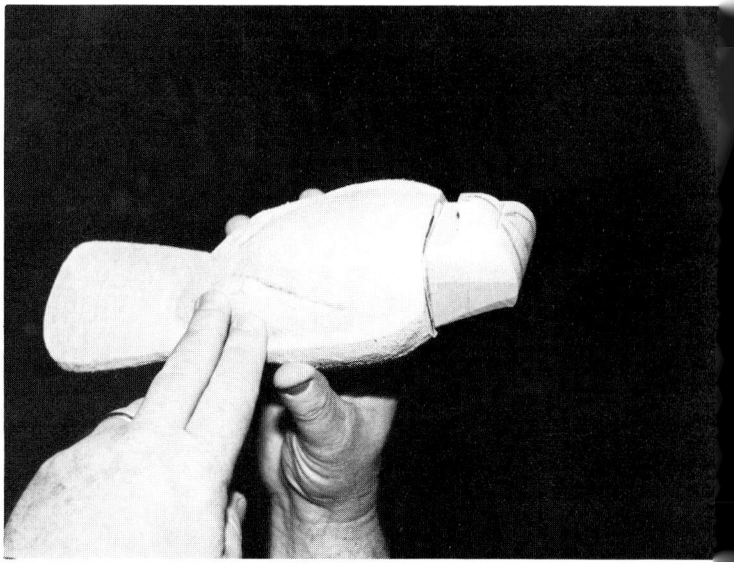

Another view of head set ready to shape

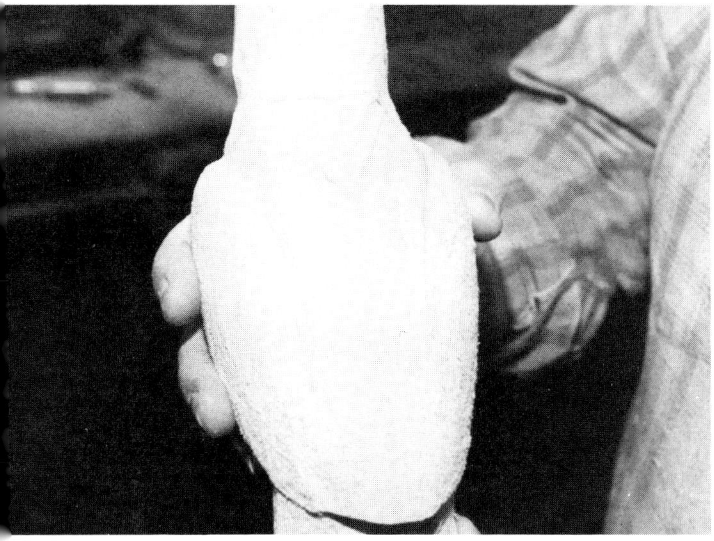

Cape area shaped

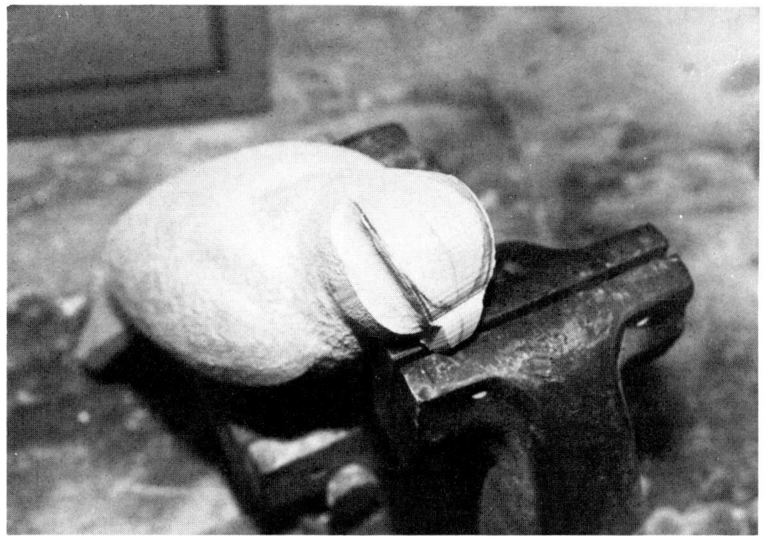

Eye channel carved

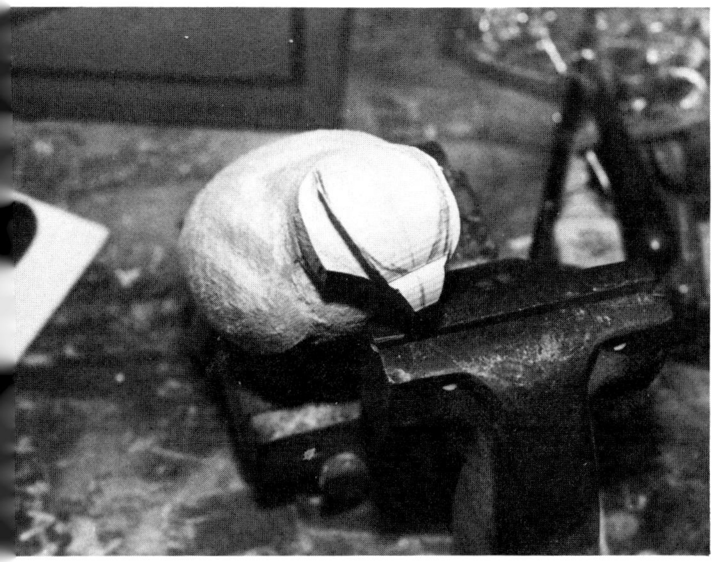

Top view of crown

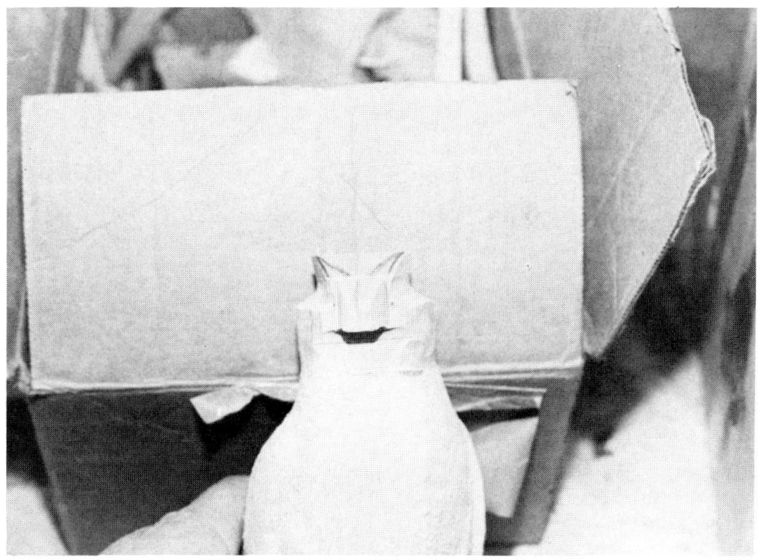

Front view, note eye channels

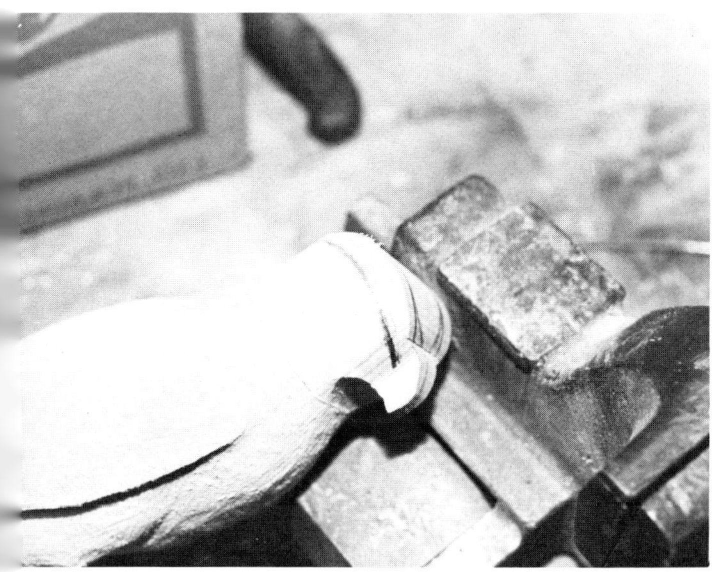

Eye channel marked

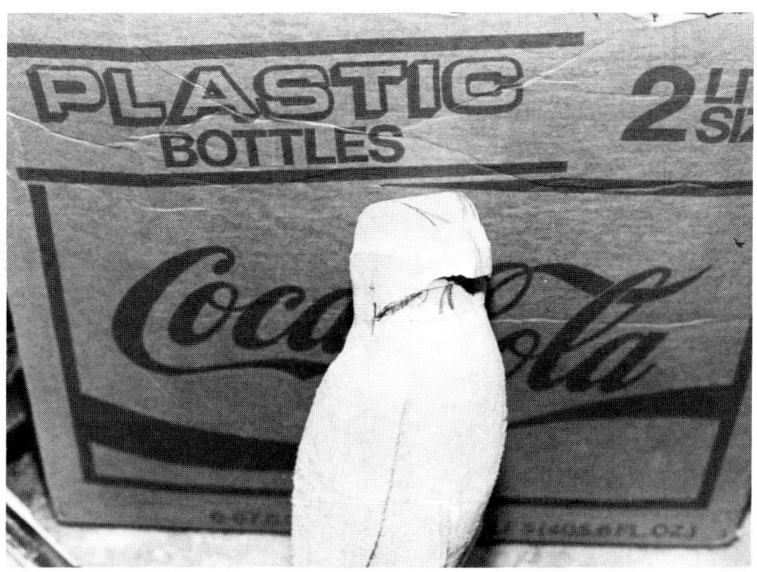

Note cut under cheek and neck flowing into body

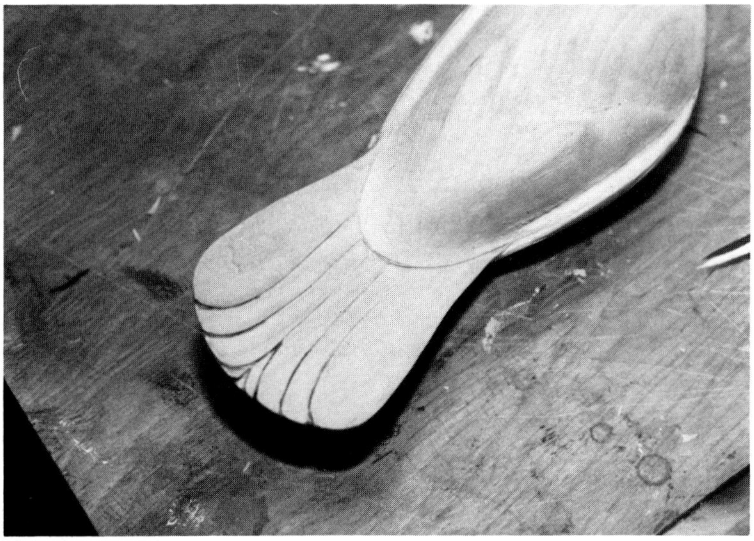

Underside of tail layout

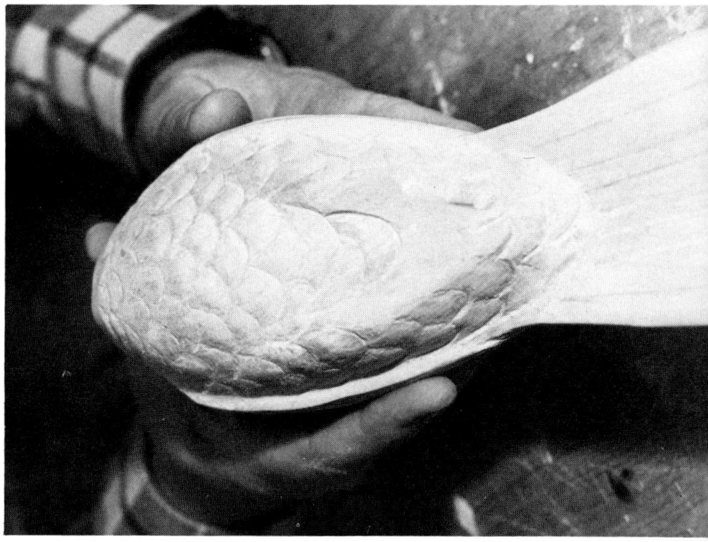

Feather layout of belly and leg area

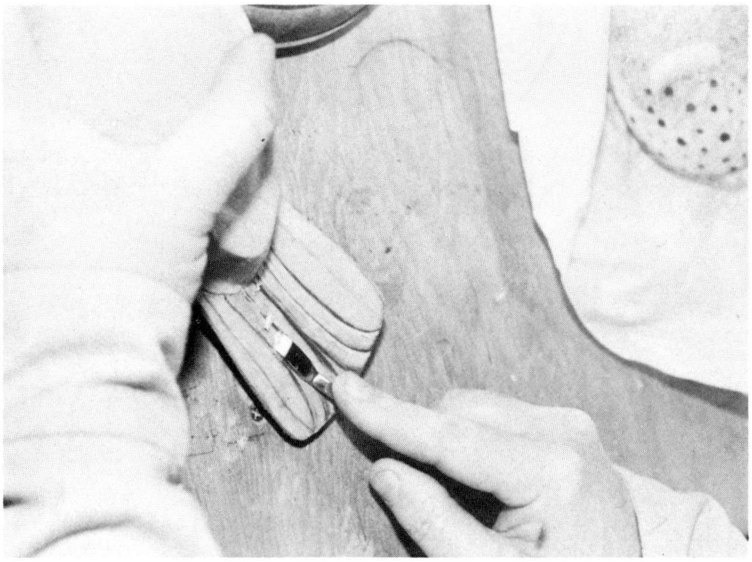

Carving underside of tail

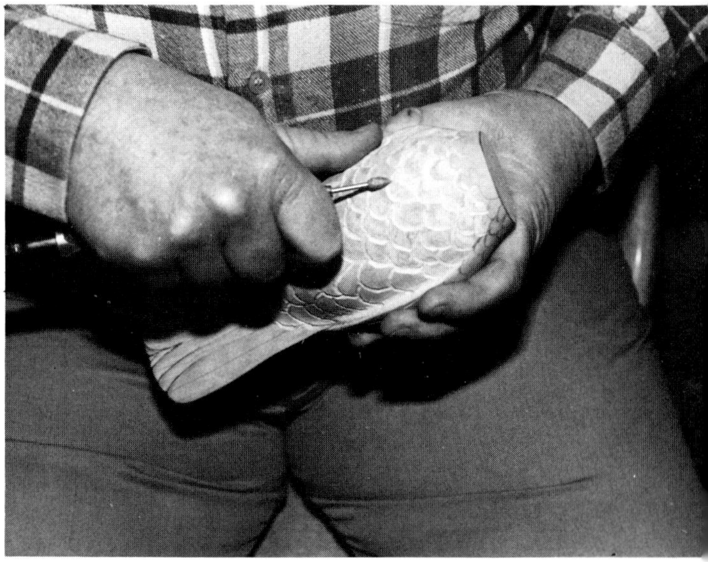

Ruby carving on belly

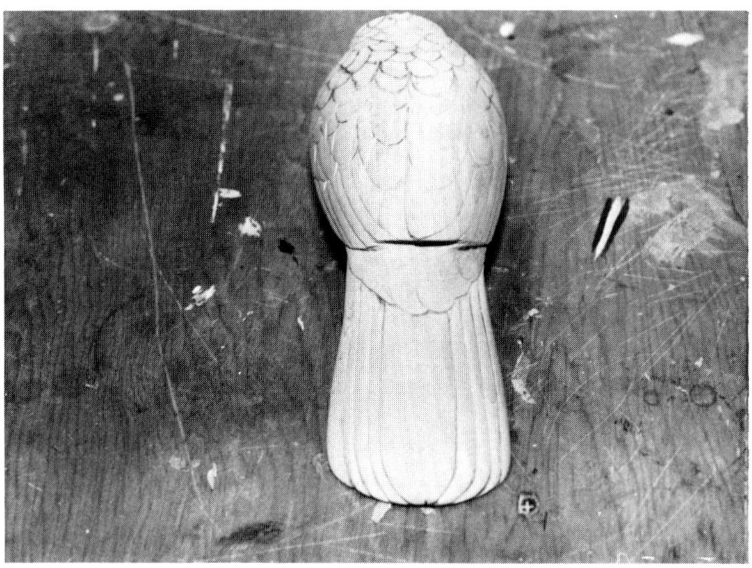

Upper tail layout

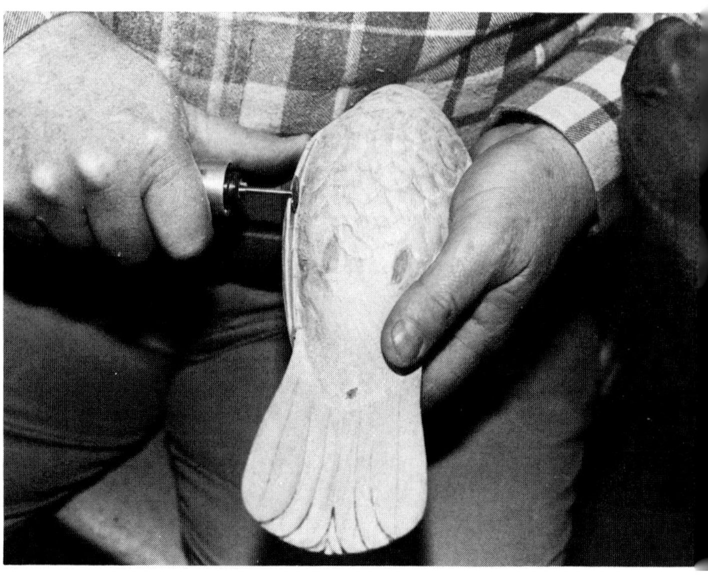

Cutting channel between wing and body

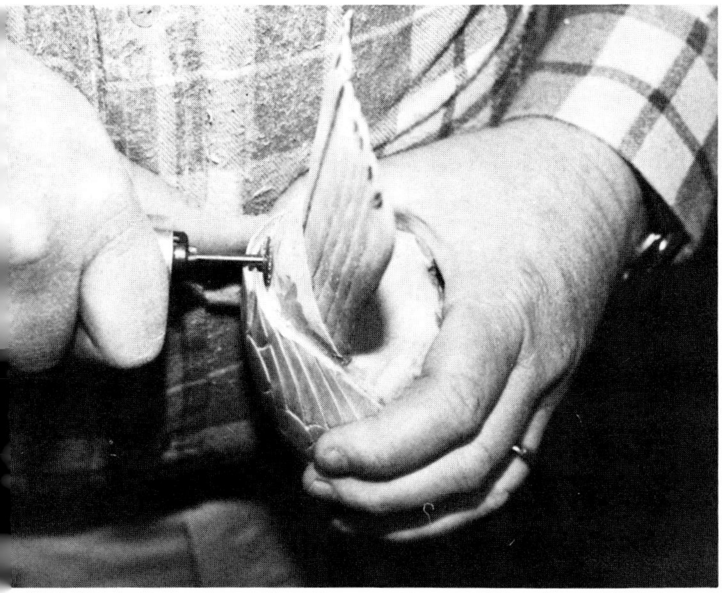

Cutting channel for primary inserts

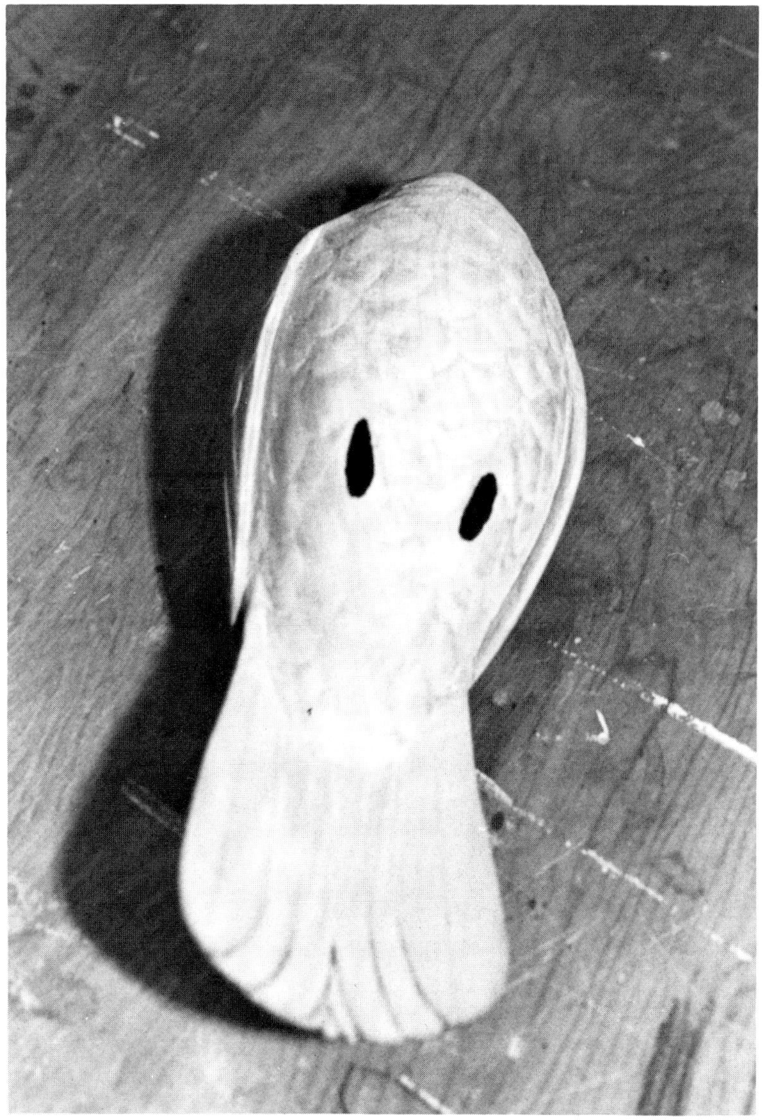

Leg placement

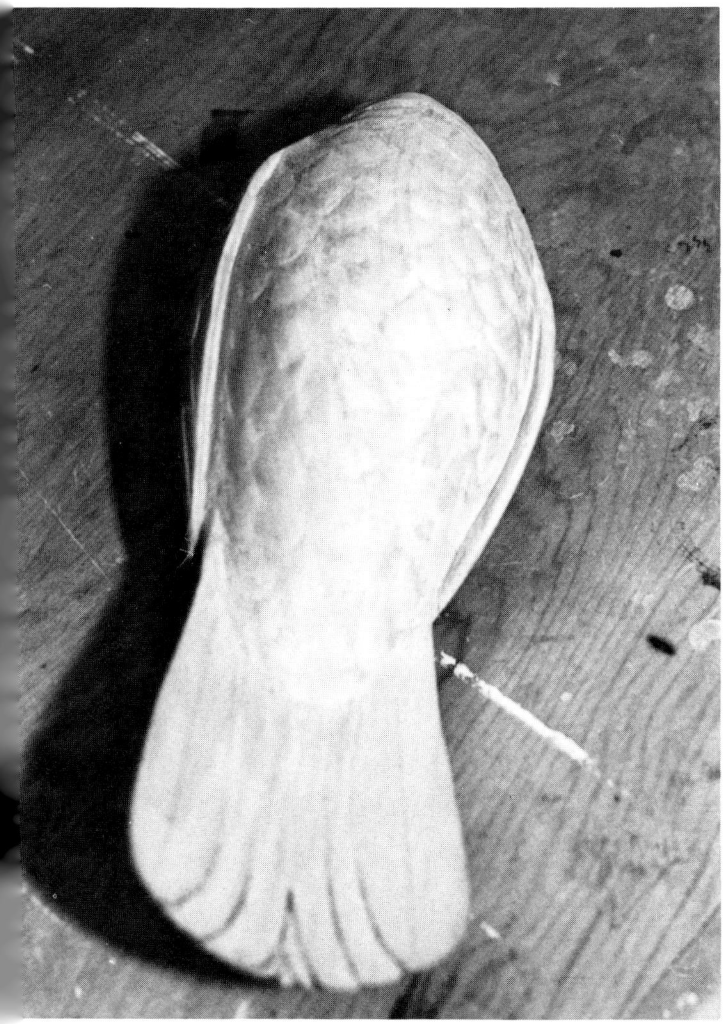

Underside carved

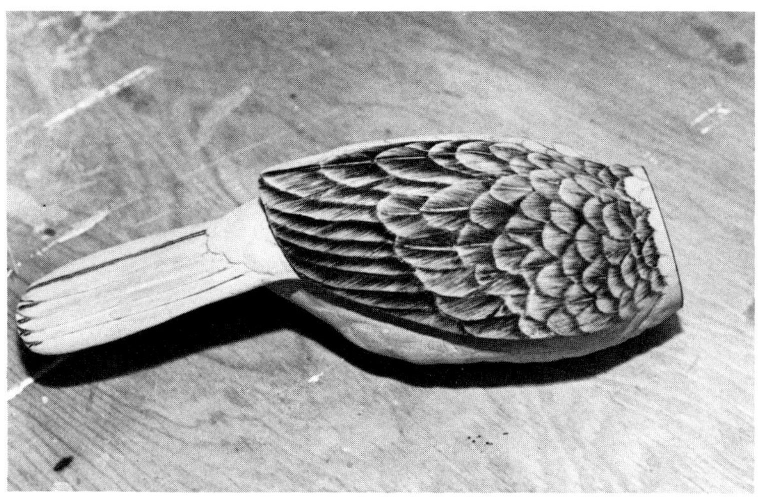

Wing area burned

(See page 167 for painting instructions and page 285 for patterns)

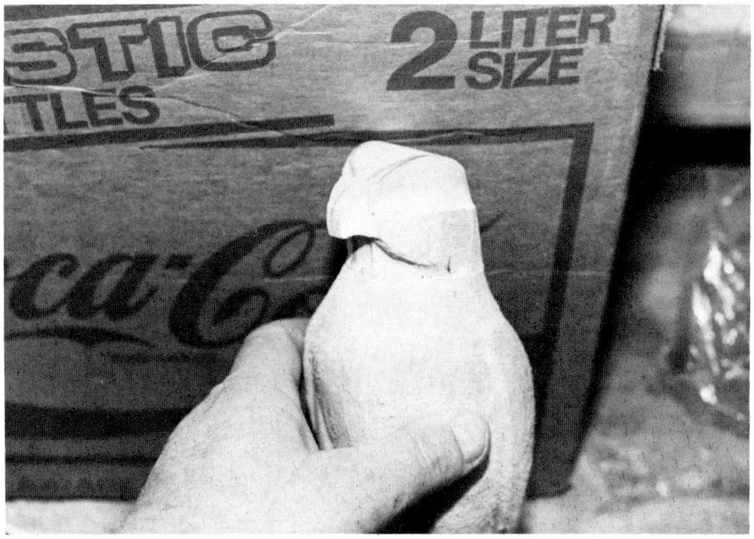

Side view of cheek area

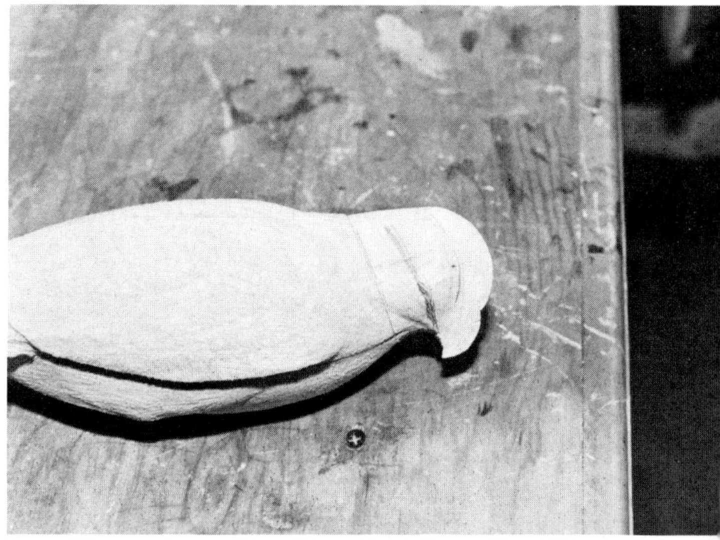

Side view of cheek showing classic egg shape of cheek area

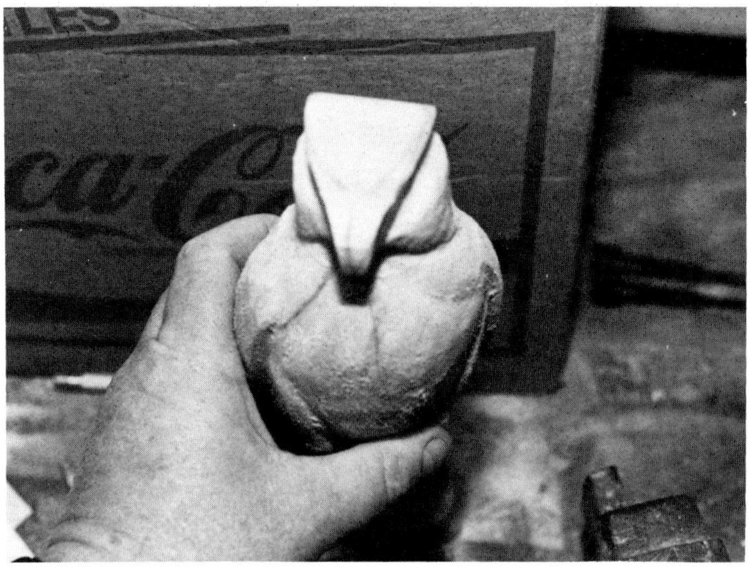

Top view of head

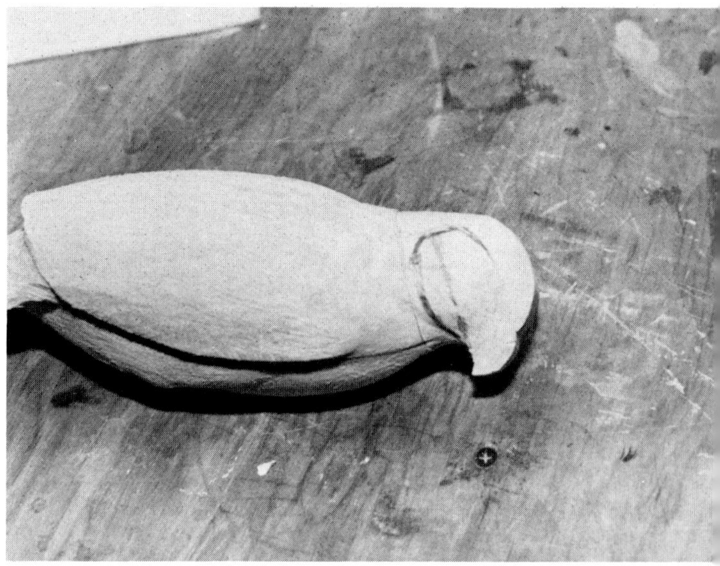

Egg shape of cheek cut in

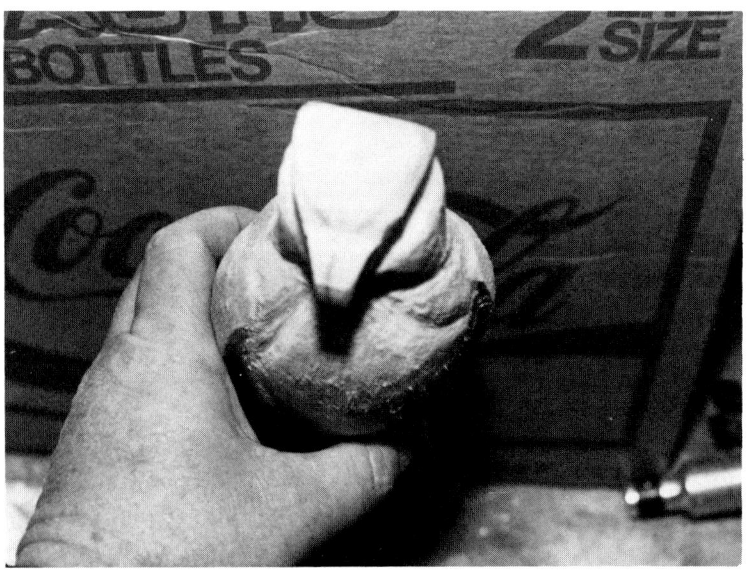

Top view of head showing breast cut in

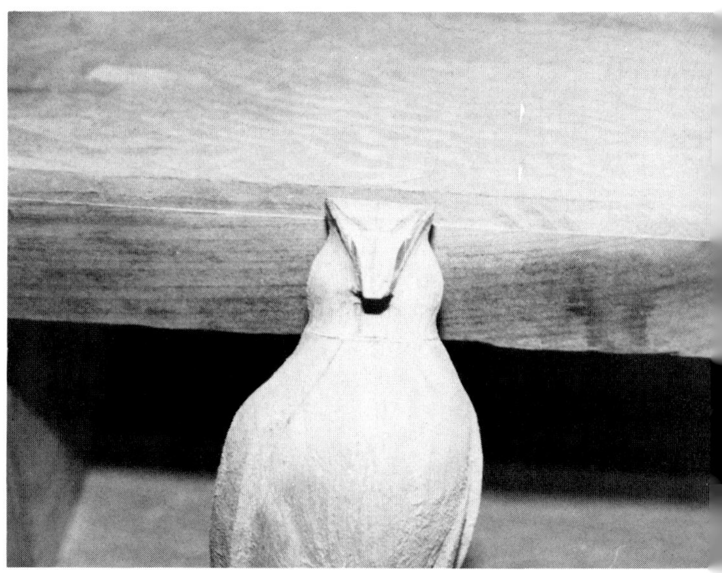

Neck and cheek area flowing together

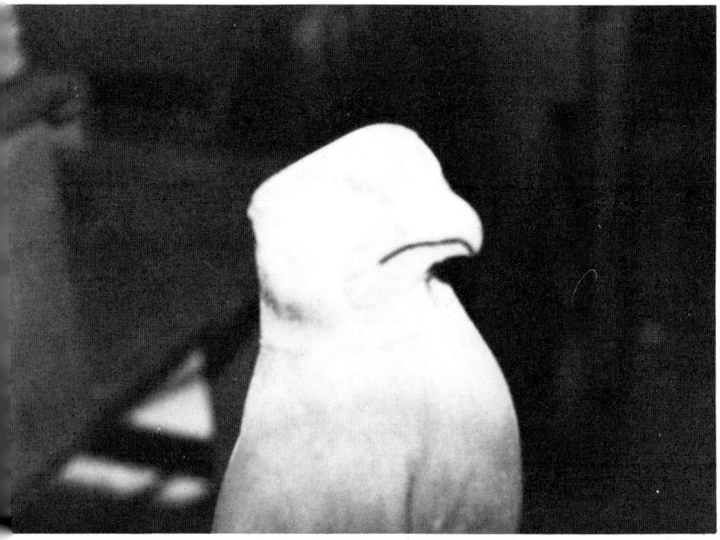

Beak separation penciled in

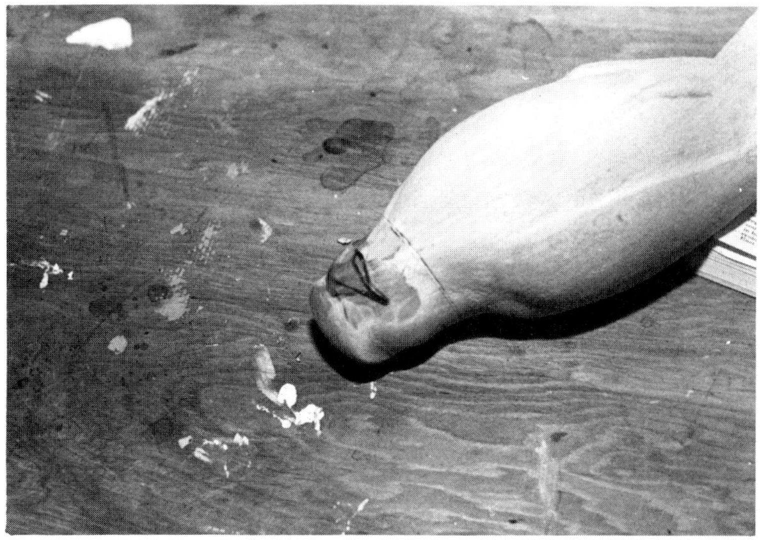

Side view of beak detail

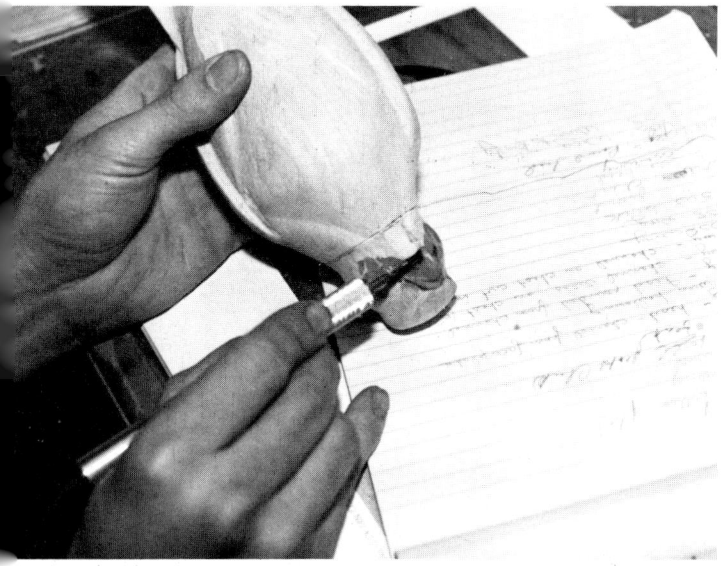

Burning in beak detail

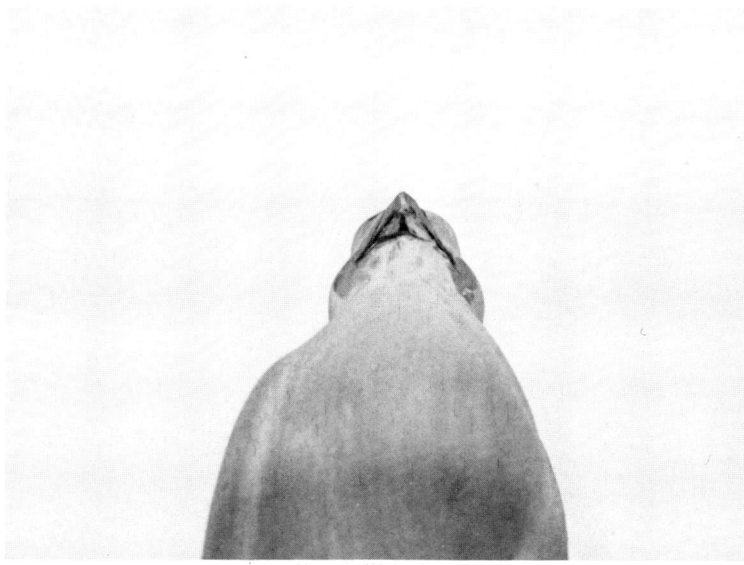

Underside of beak detail

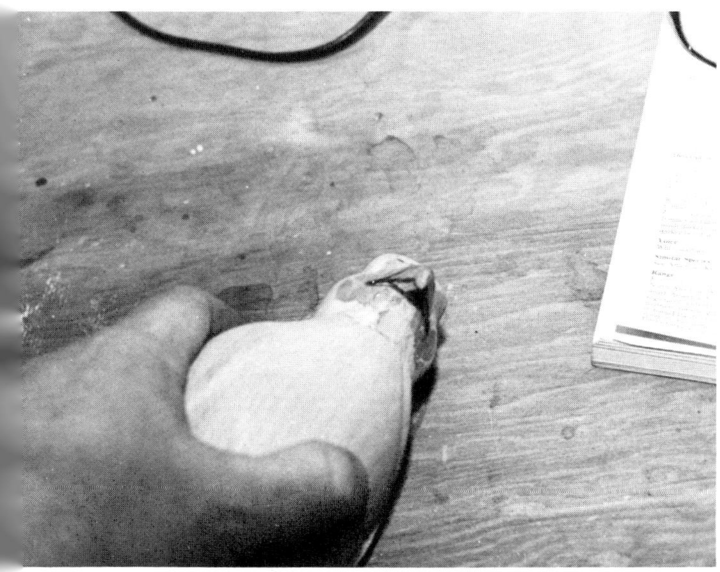

Showing underside of beak

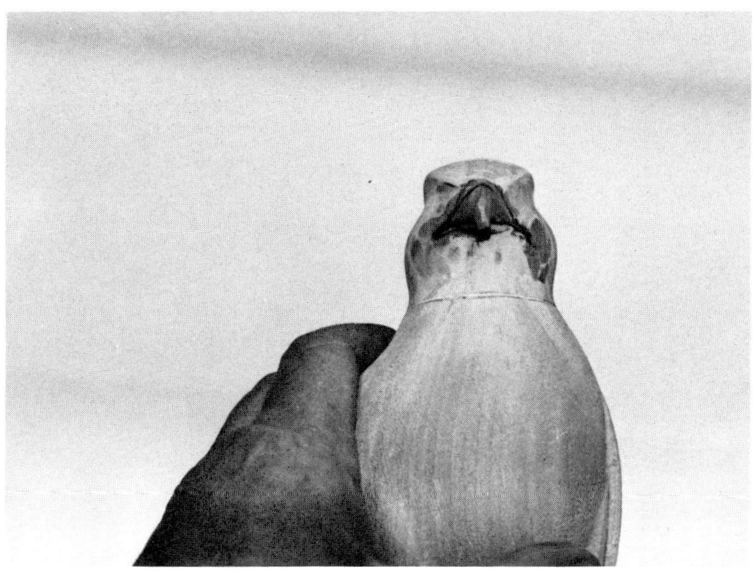

Front view of beak detail

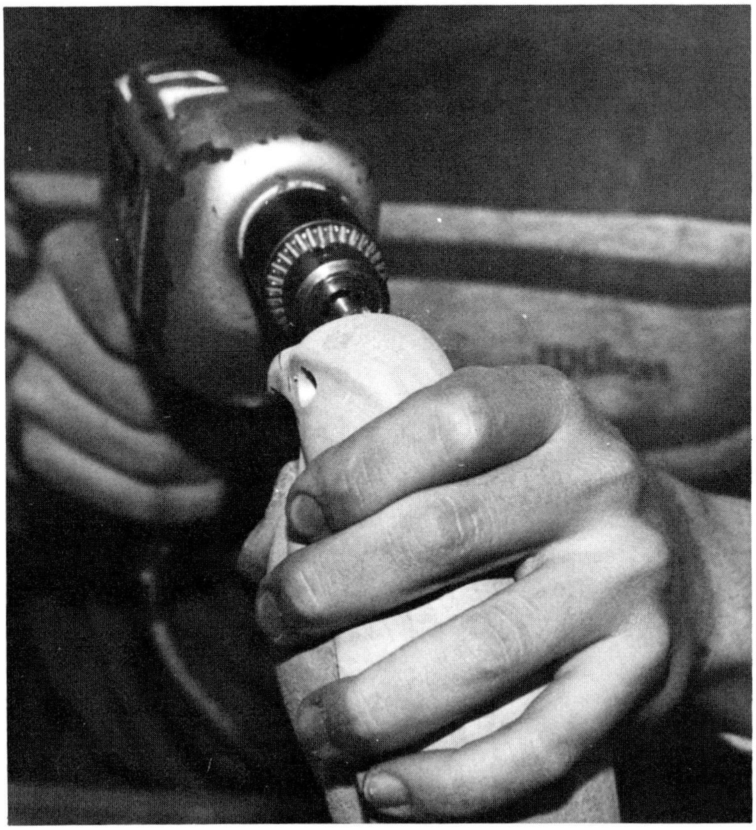

Drilling eye sockets

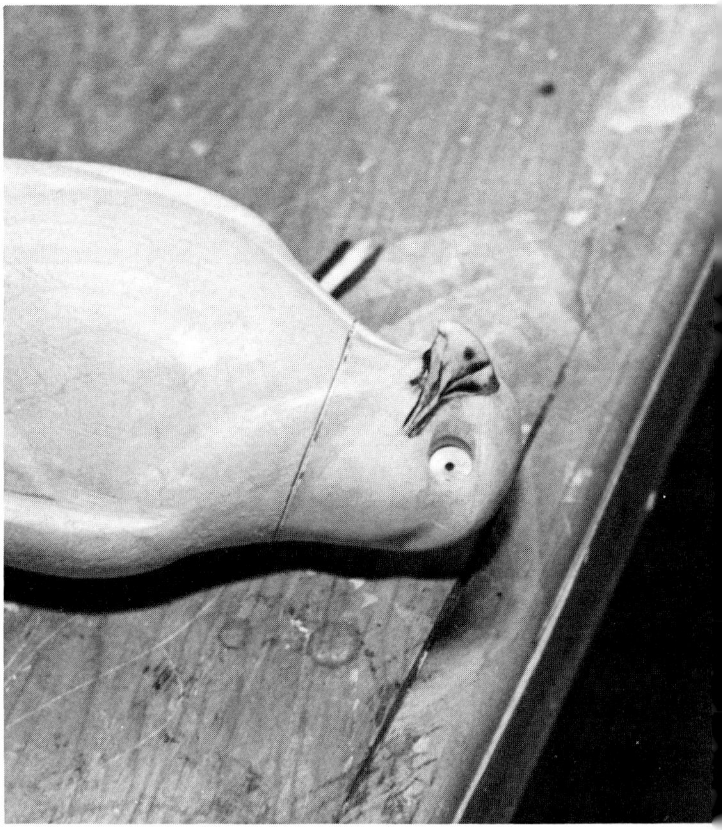

Beak detail and eye sockets drilled

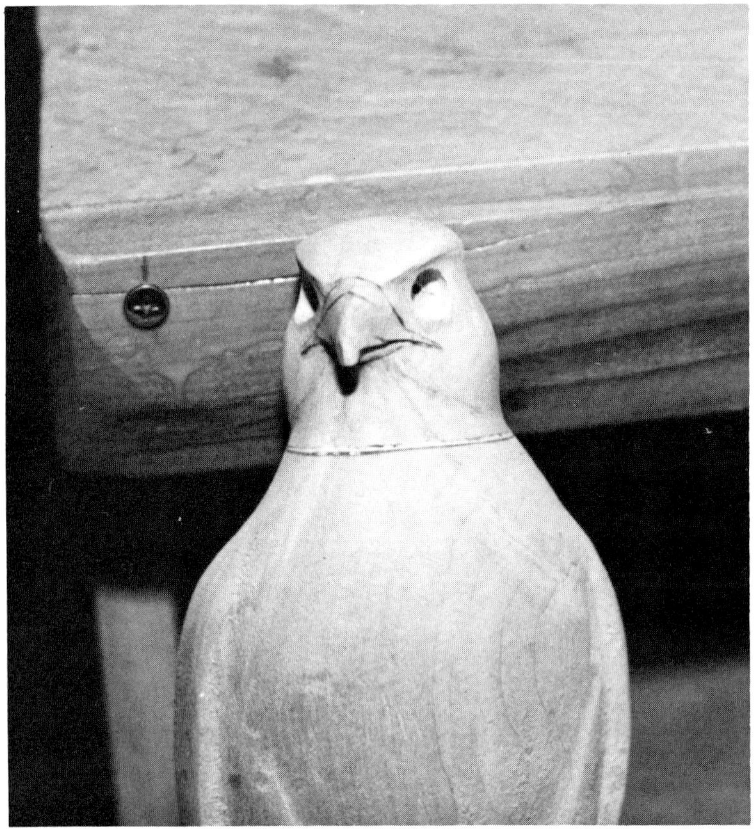

Eyes drilled (note forward set)

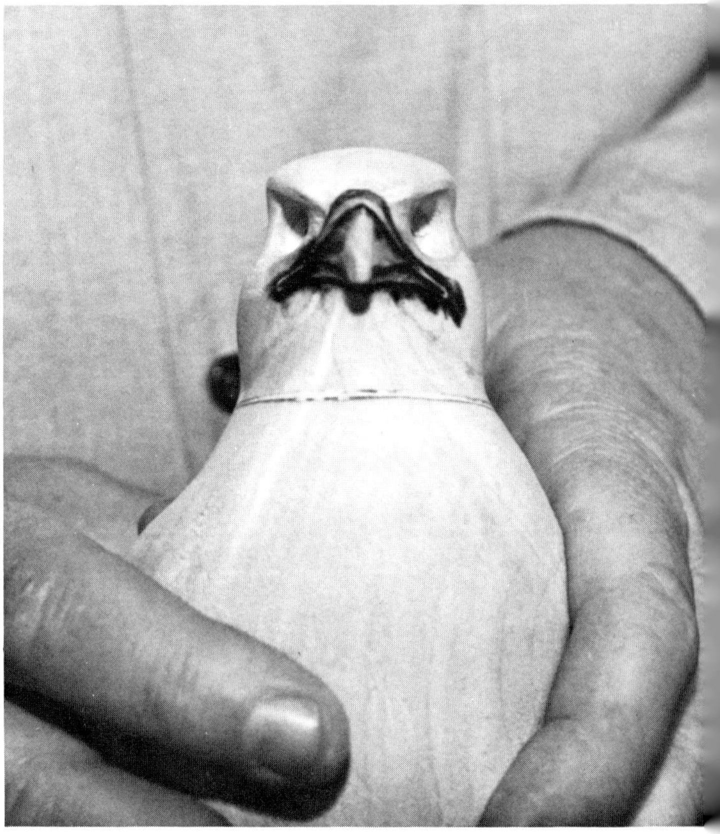

Head and body detail

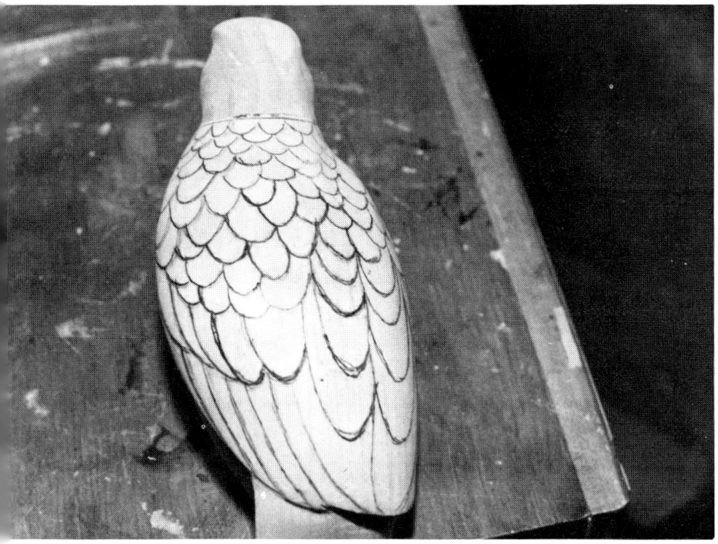

Feather layout on body

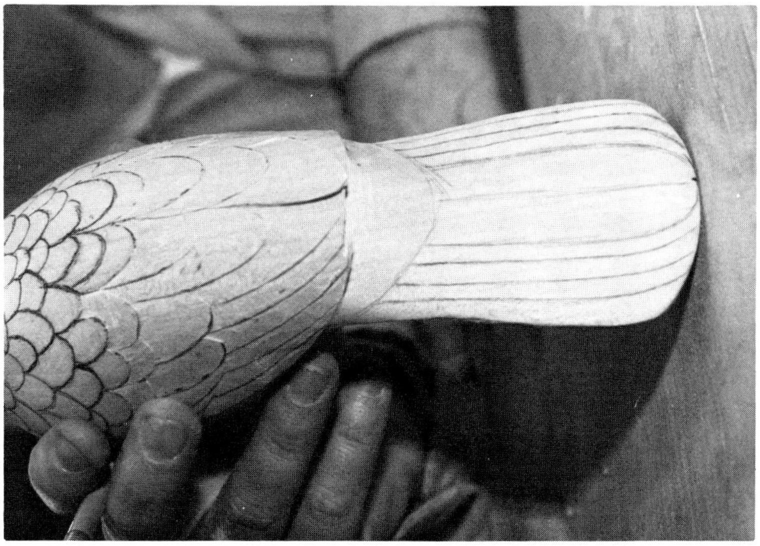

Back and tail layout

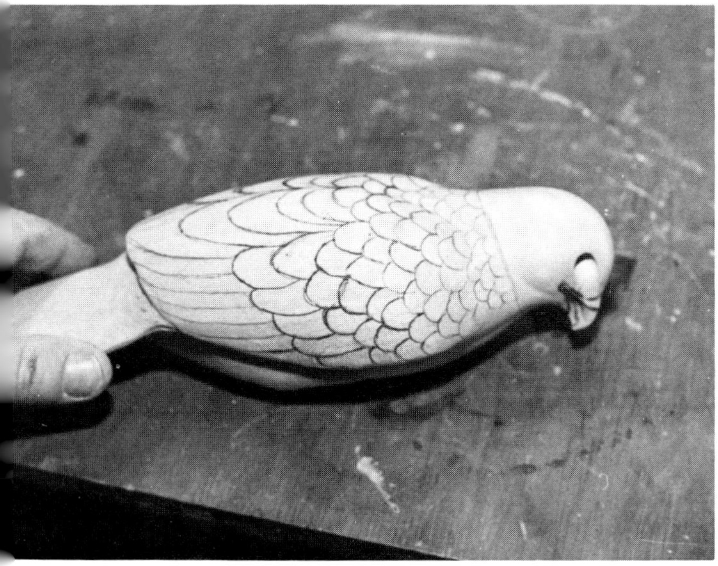

Side view of feather layout

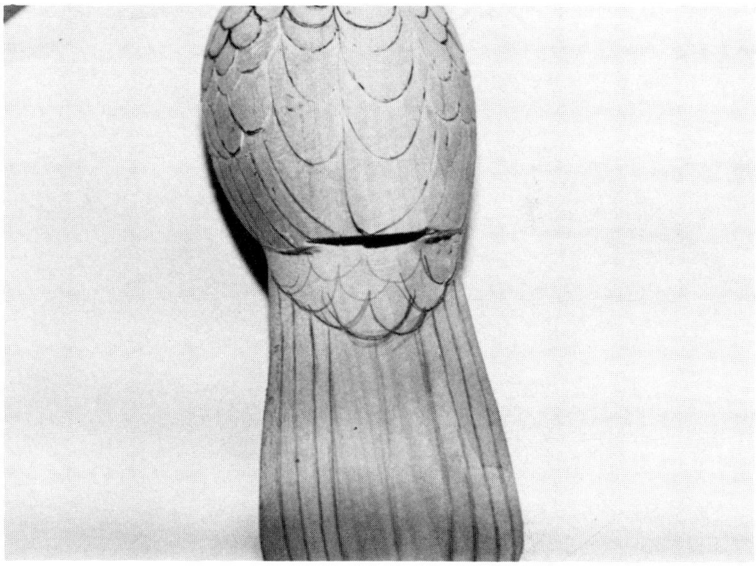

Back and tail layout

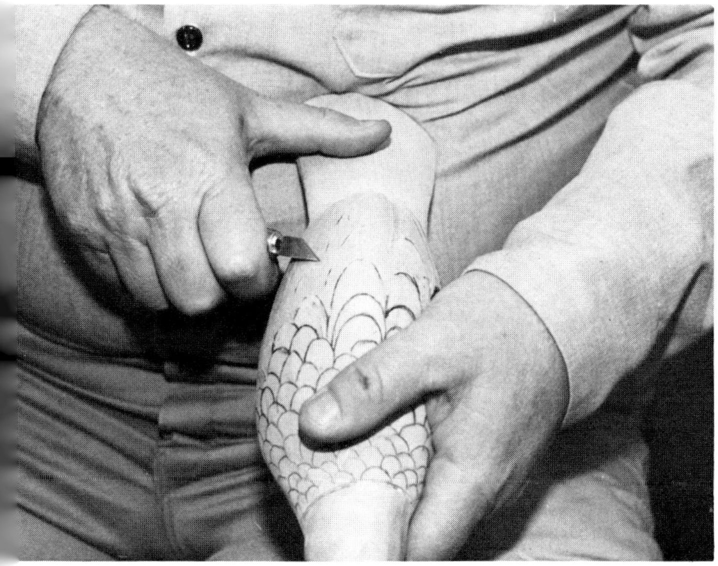

Carving tertials and secondaries

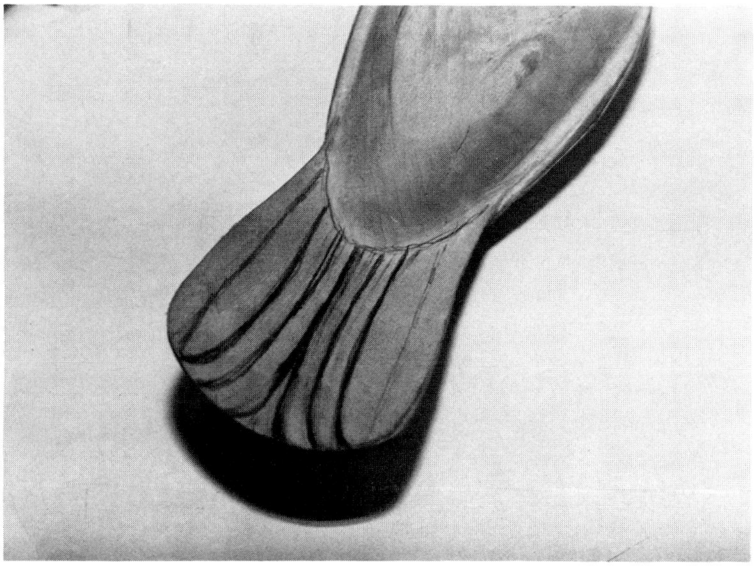

Under tail layout

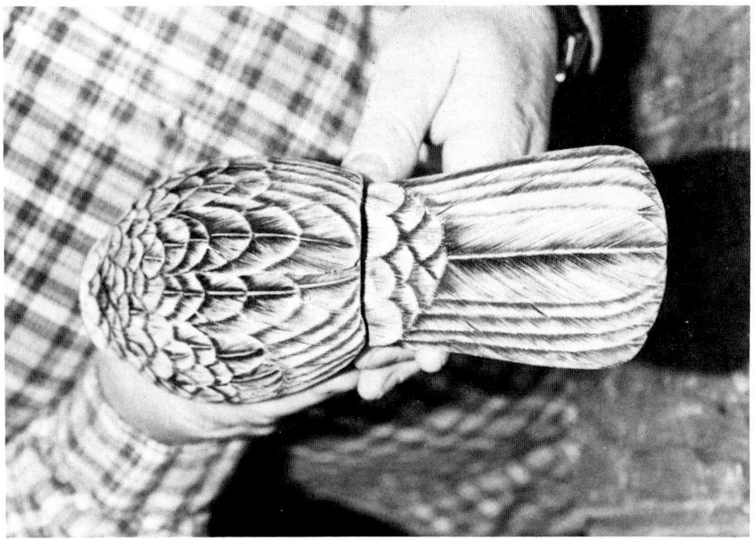

Wings and tail burned

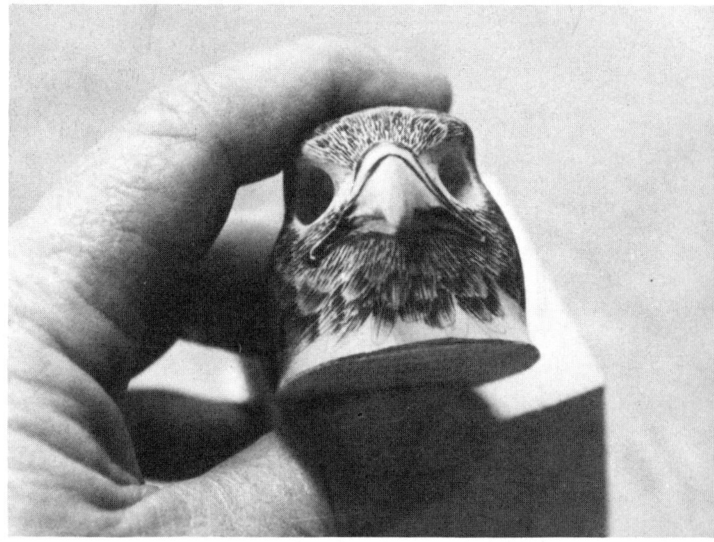

Head burned

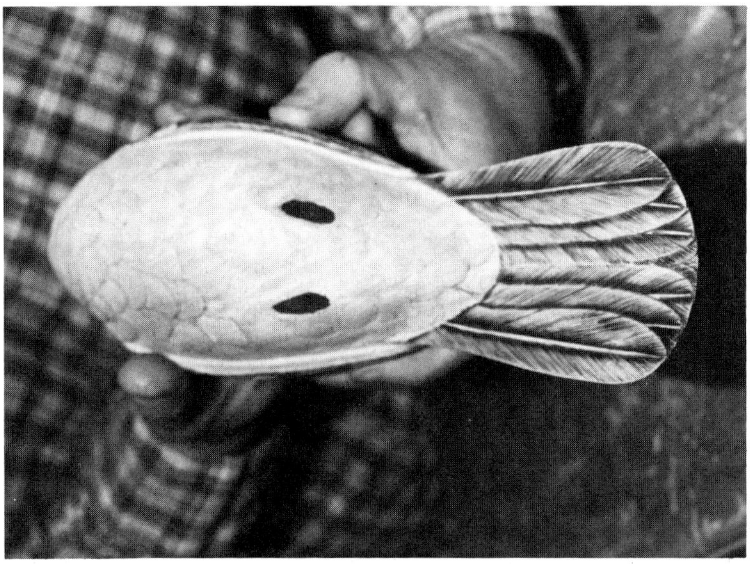

Under tail burned

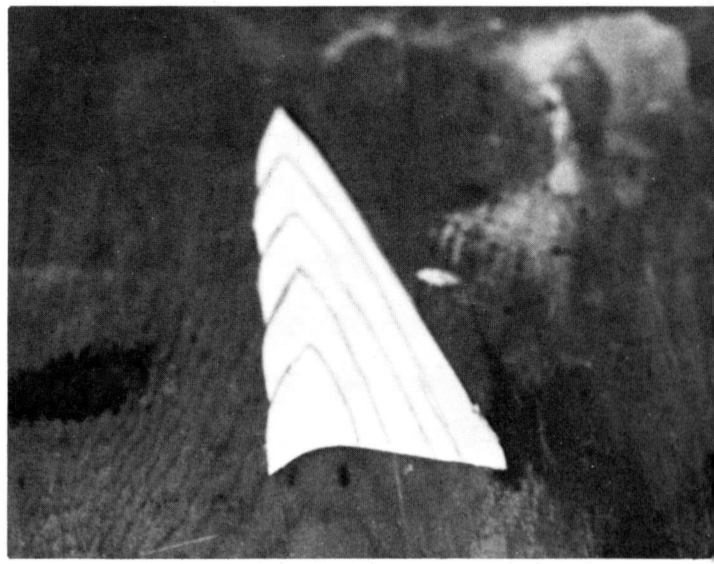

Primary feather insert as a block

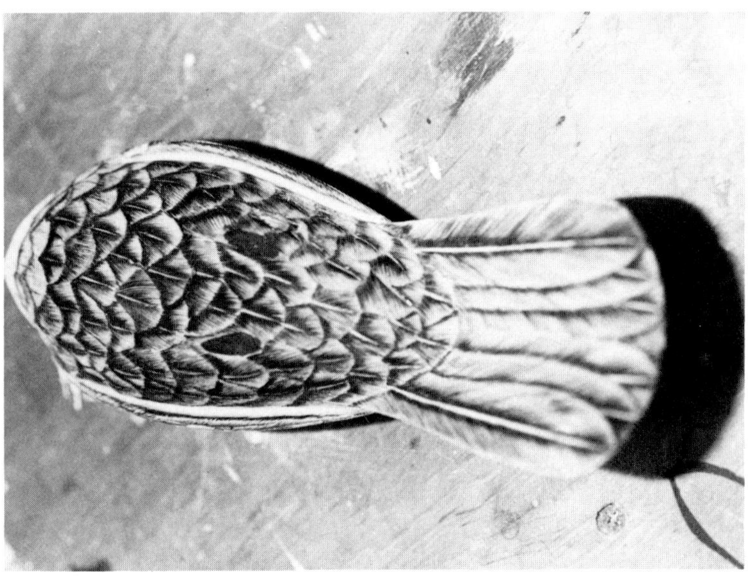

Under belly and tail burned

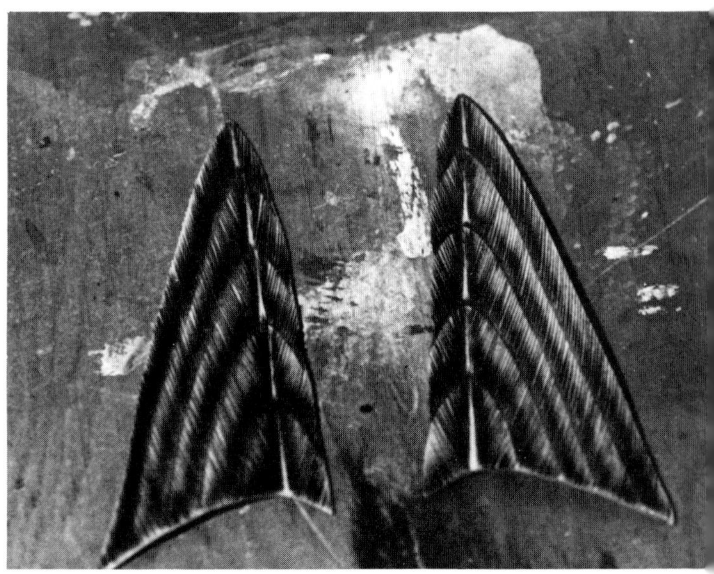

Primary blocks burned

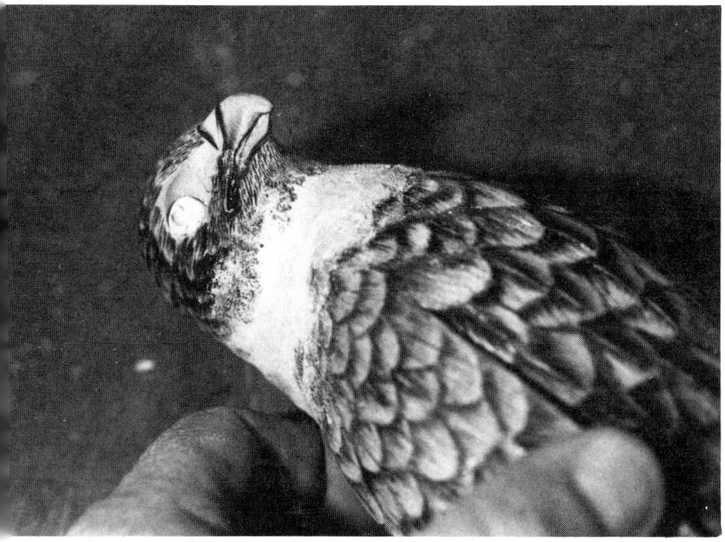

Eye sockets filled with moldable epoxy and neck joint filled with wood dough, use a lot of acetone to break down air gaps

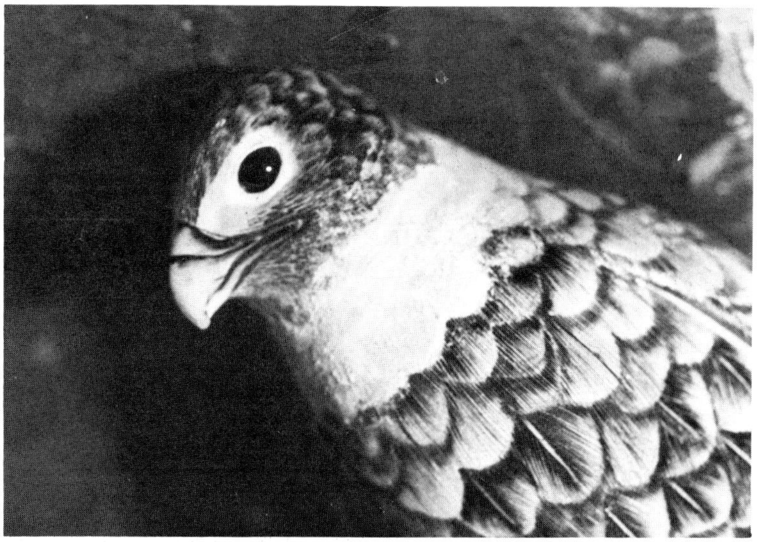

Eye lids, use moldable epoxy

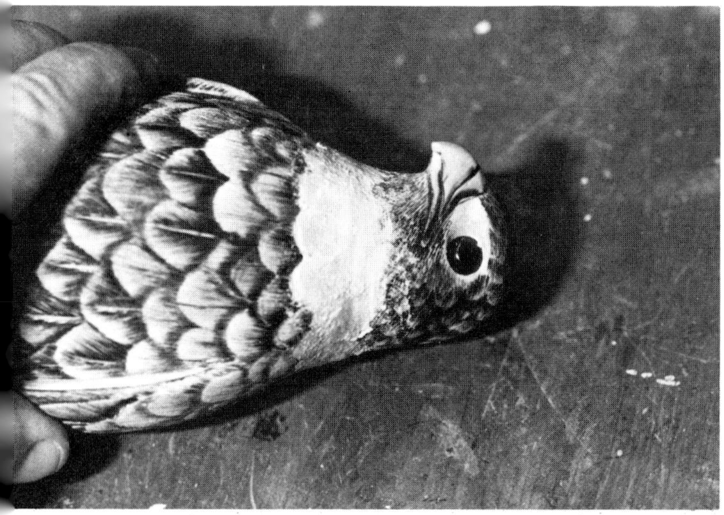

Eyes set

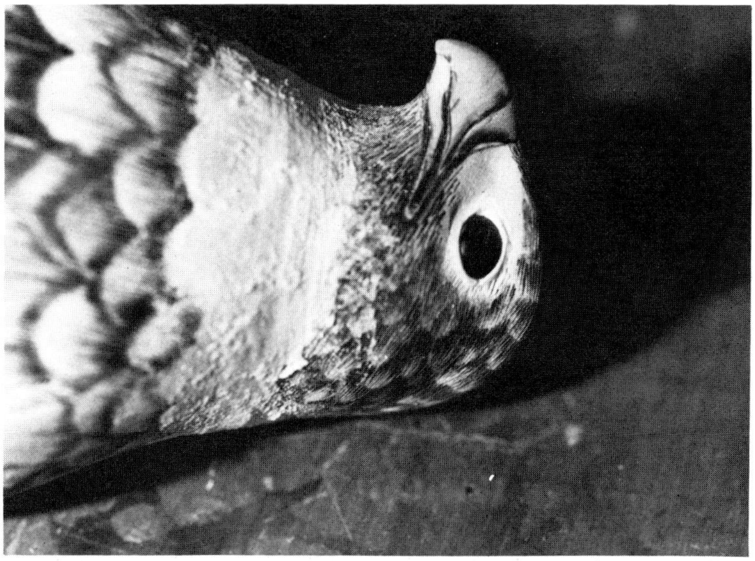

Eye lids—close view

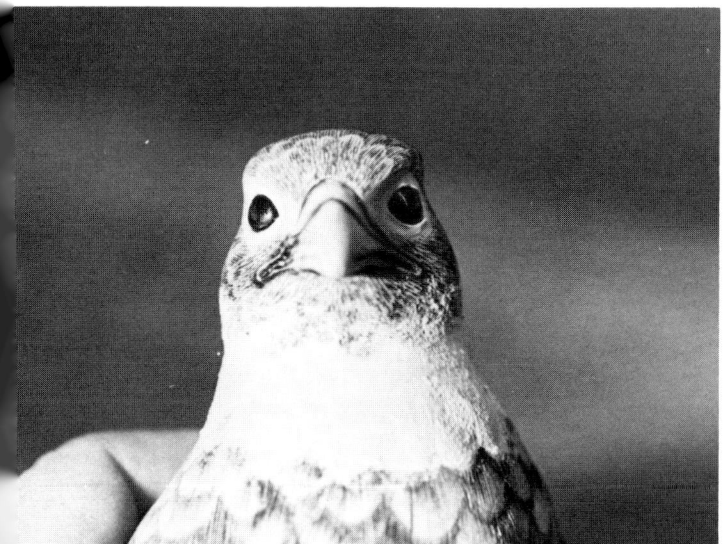

Front view eyes set—note angle

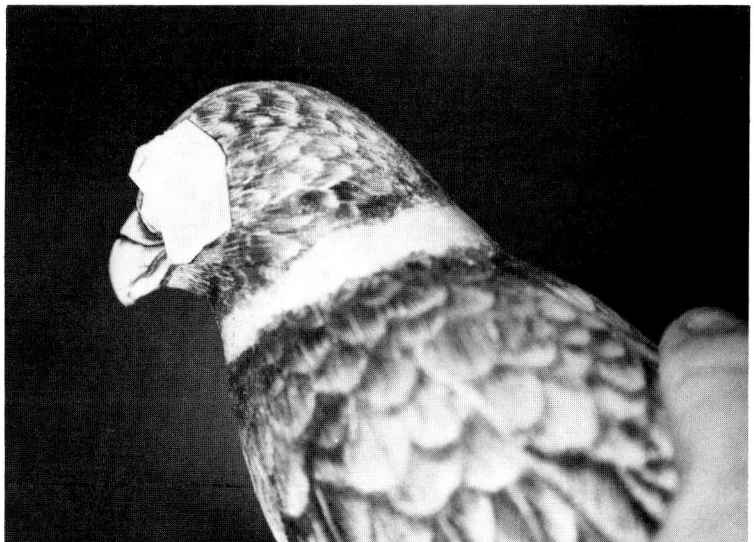

Tape eyes to protect

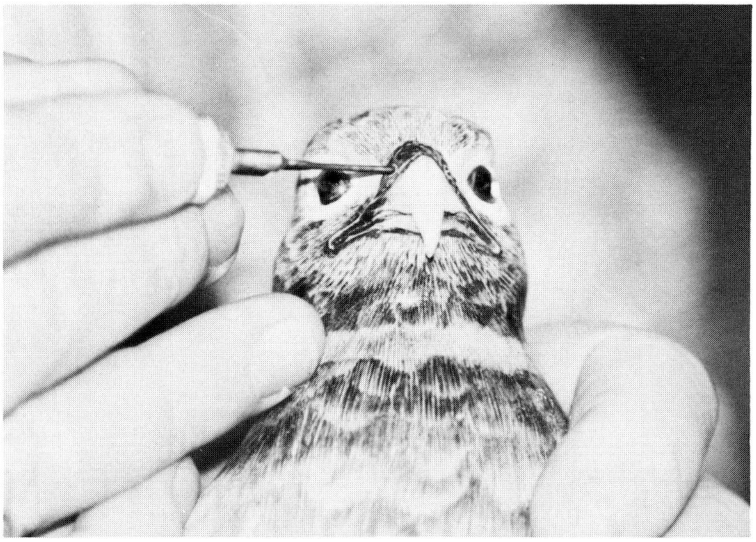

Burn detail on beak

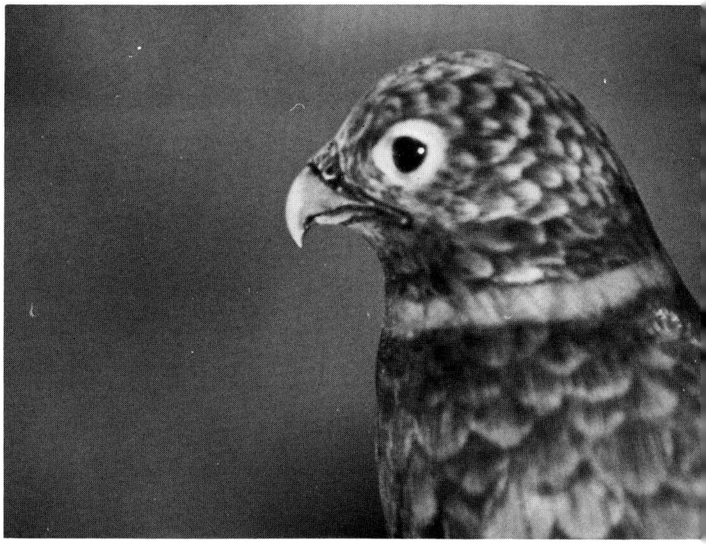

Profile and finished neck joint

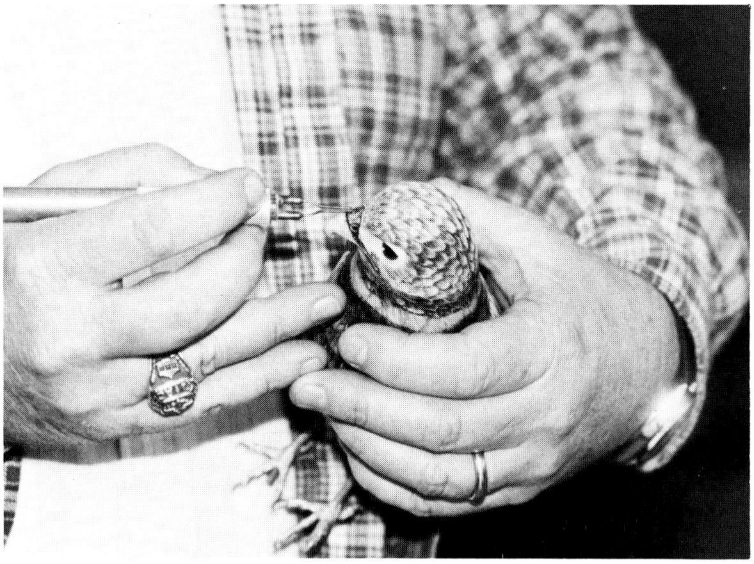

Burnishing beak area

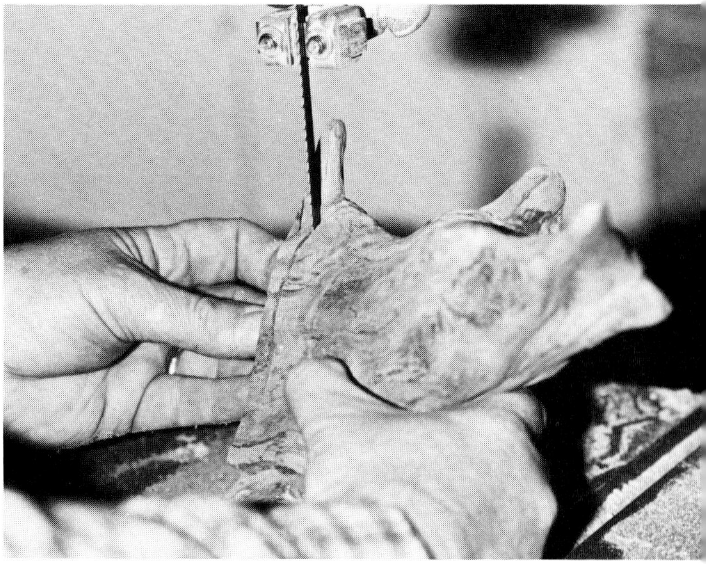

Cutting driftwood—use care and concentration as you will be cutting without a squared surface

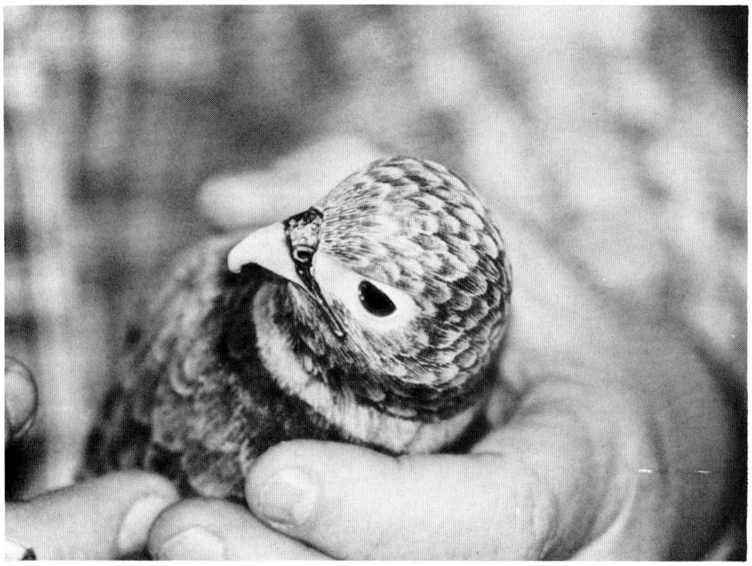

Note nares (nostrils)

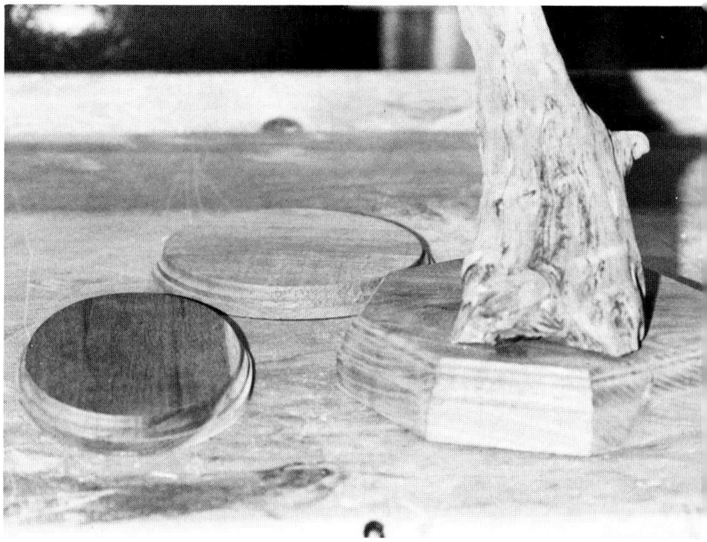

Driftwood moulded on walnut base

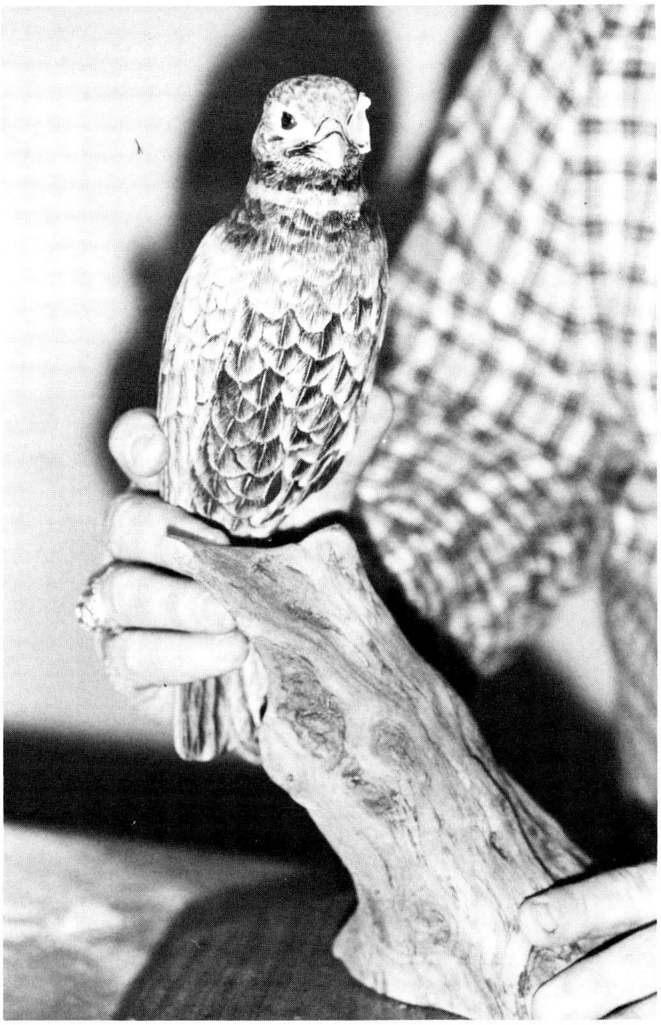

Testing various positions

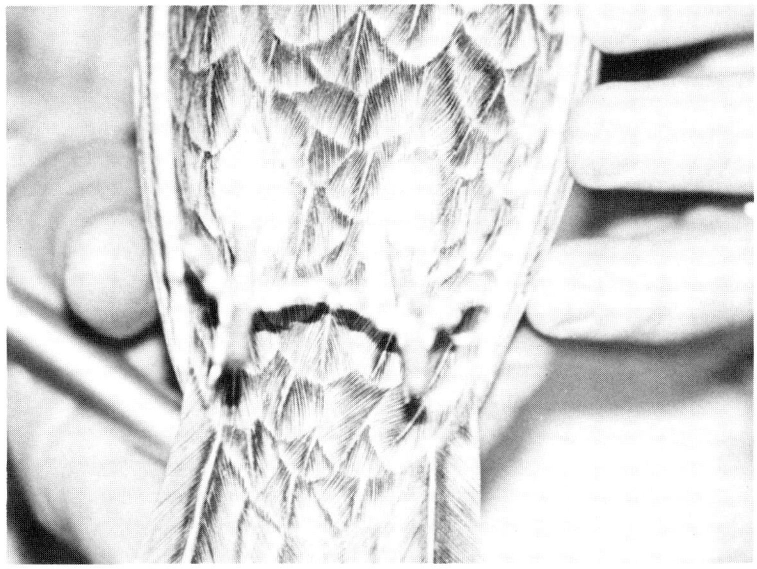

Cast feet—note small amount of fill material where legs enter body

Drilling on driftwood

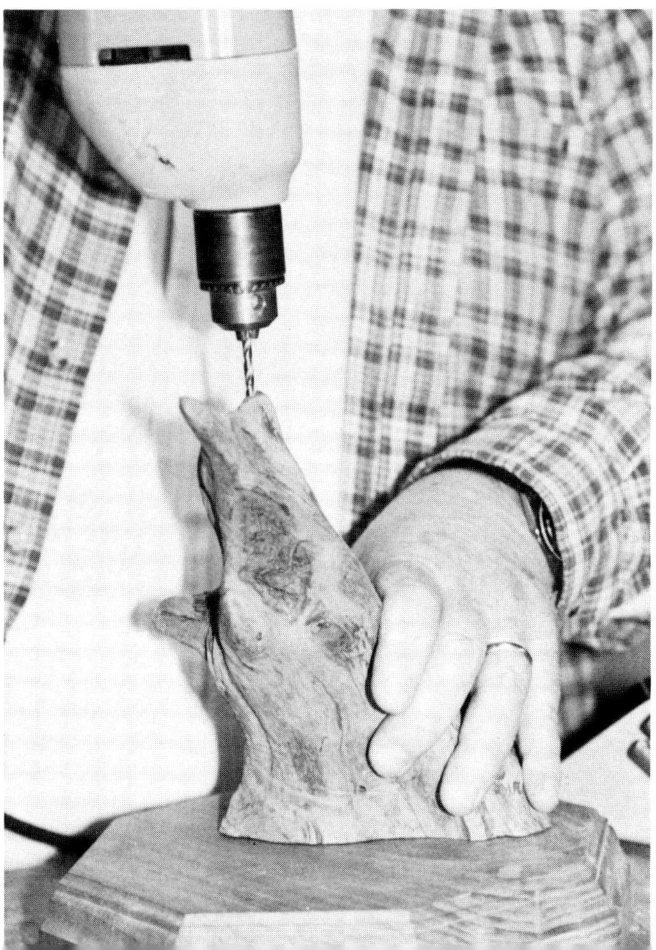

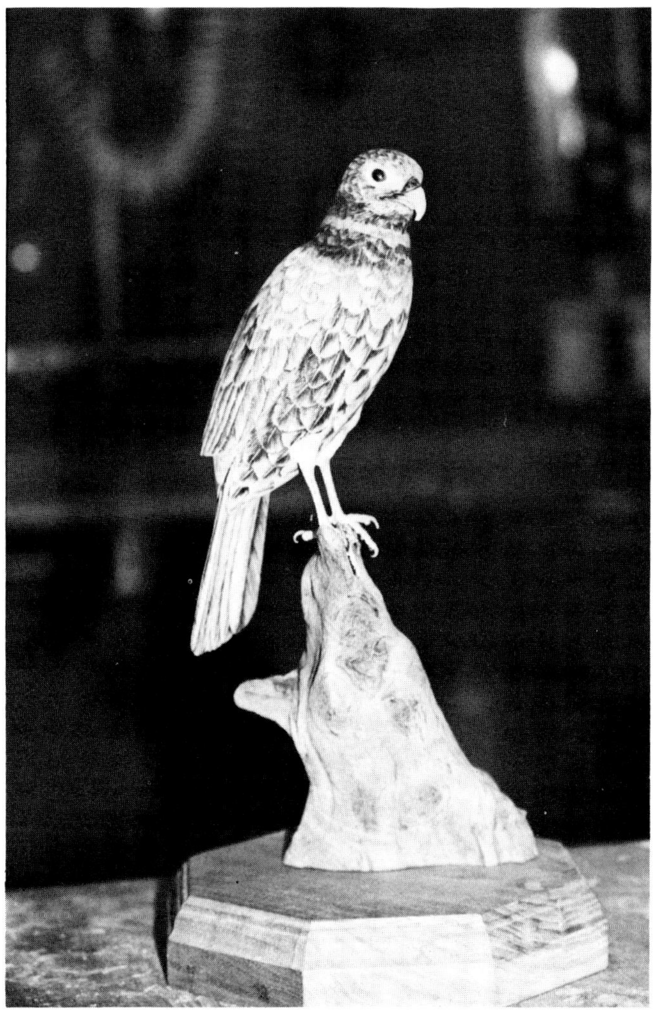

Mounted Merlin ready to paint

Miniature Flying Peregrine Falcon

Carved by Paul Suarez

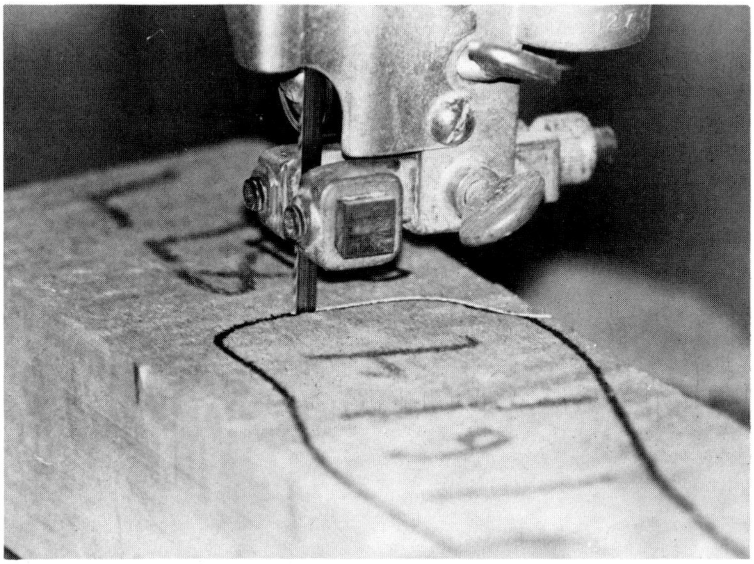

Band sawing wing

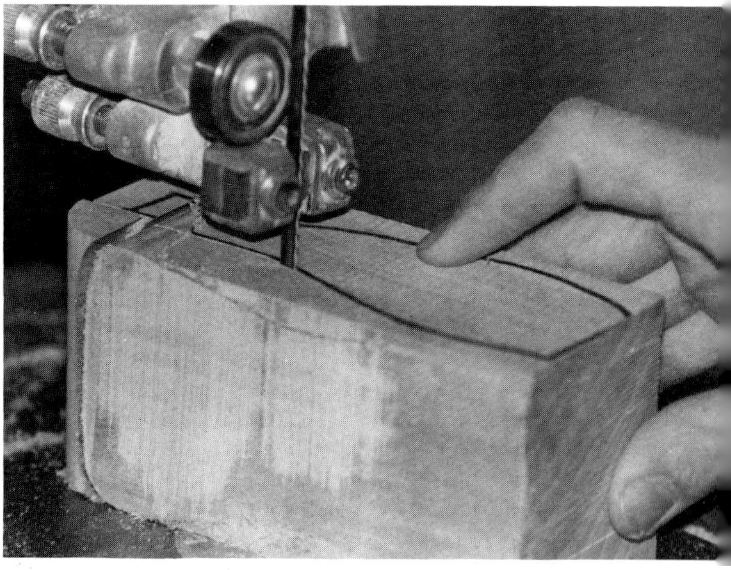

Band sawing body

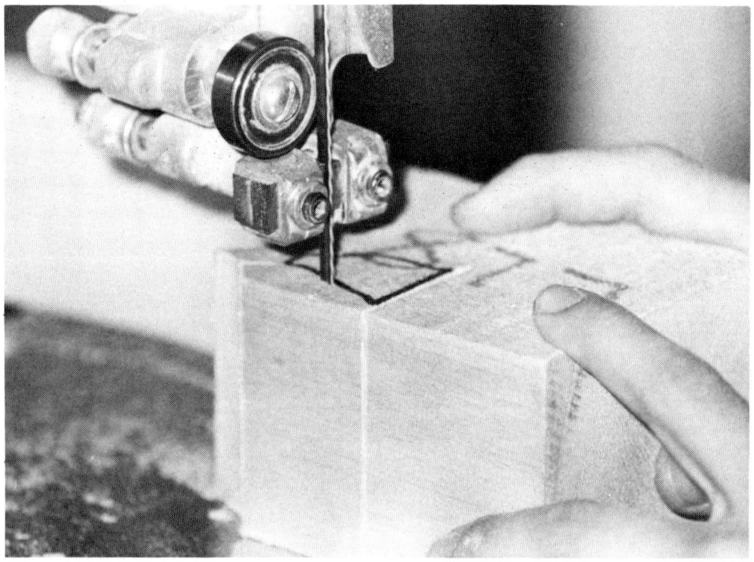

Band sawing head

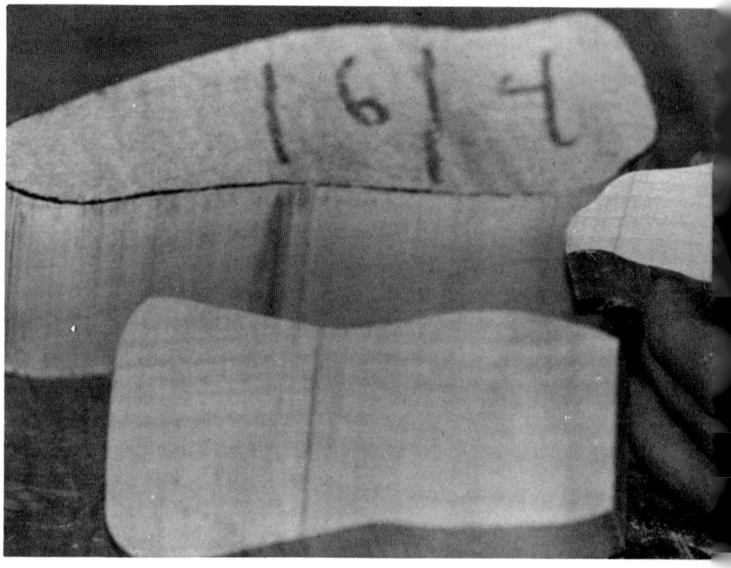

Band sawed parts

(See page 172 for painting instructions and page 287 for patterns)

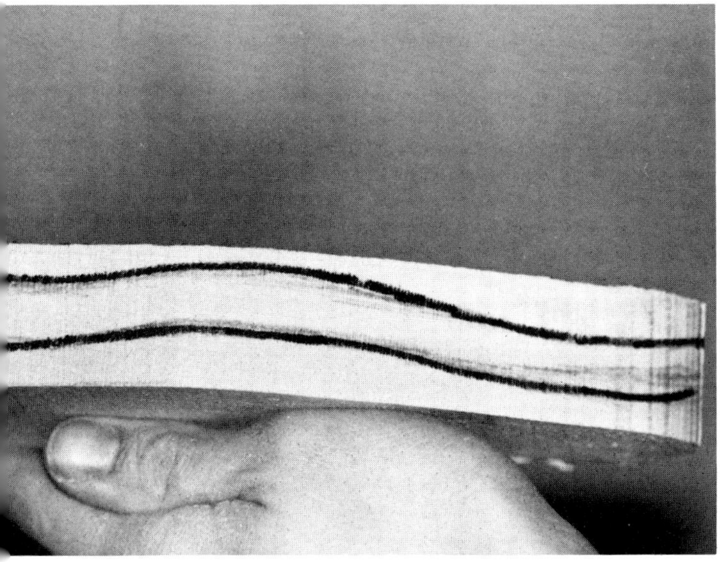

Wing shape (profile)

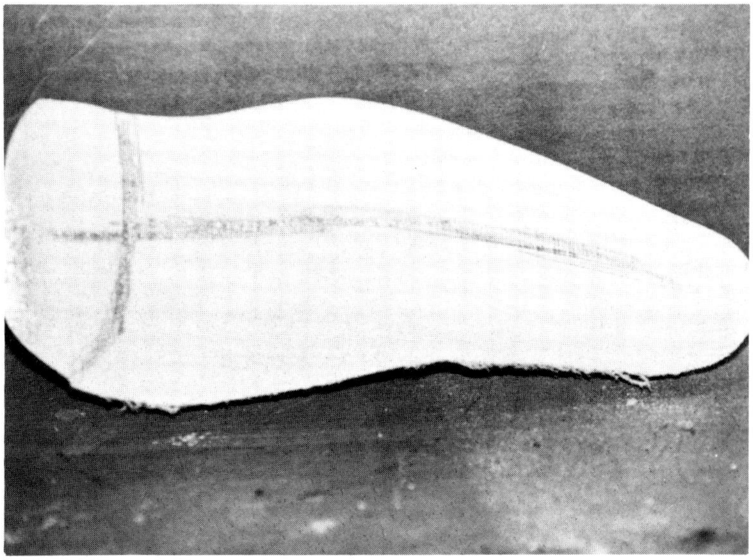

Guide marks on underside of wing

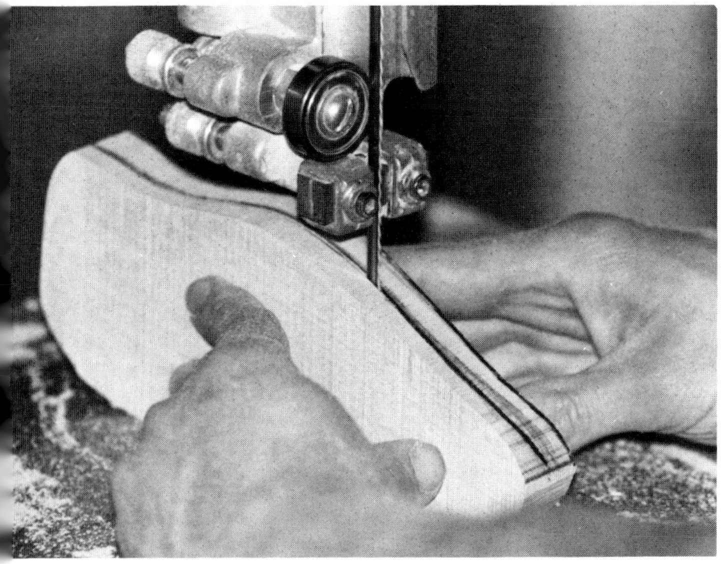

Cutting profile on band saw

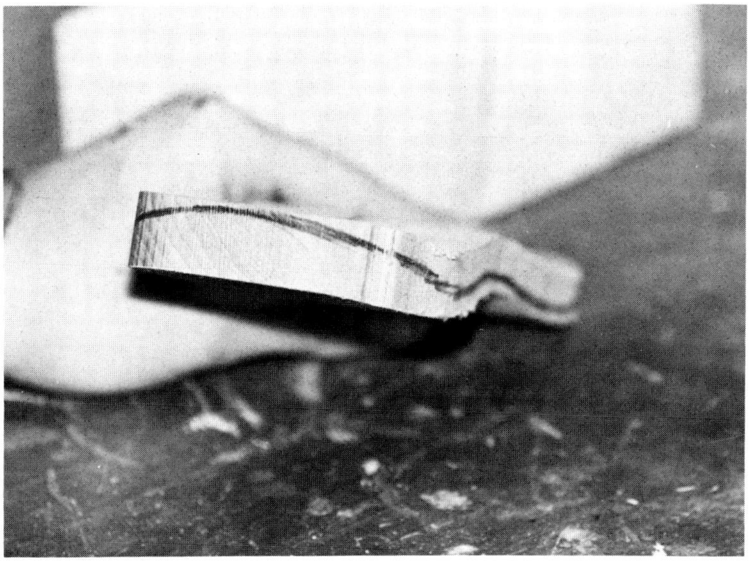

Arc and wing end view

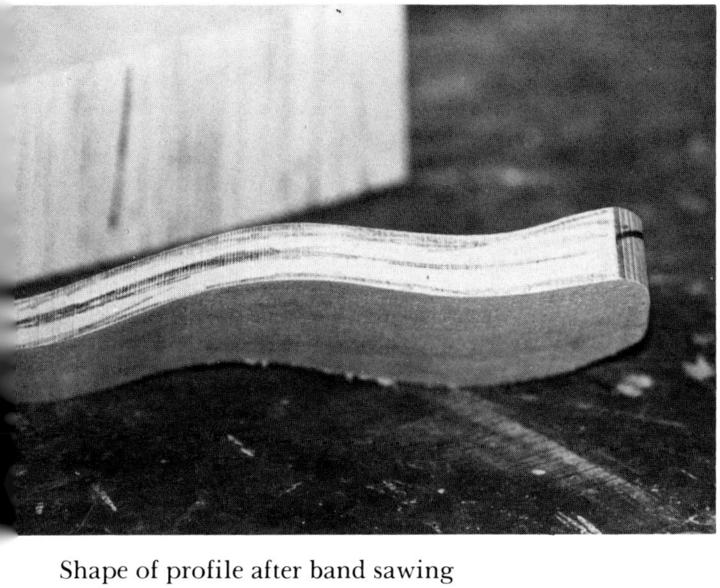

Shape of profile after band sawing

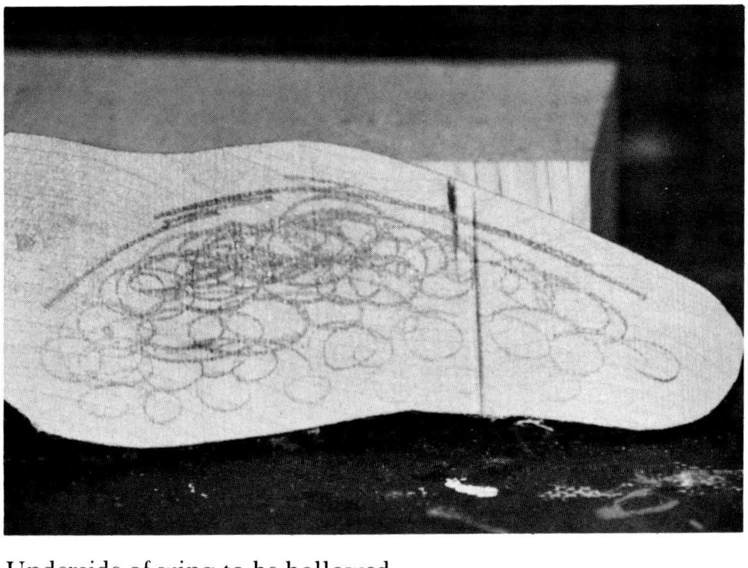

Underside of wing to be hollowed

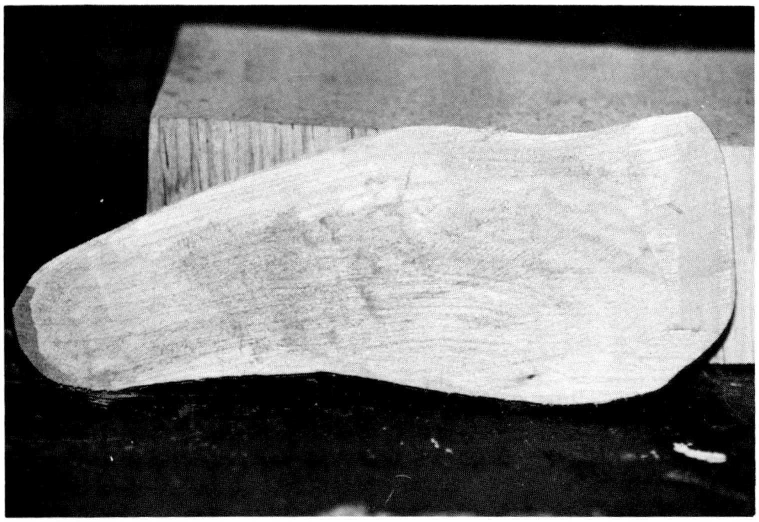

General shaping of wing with rasp

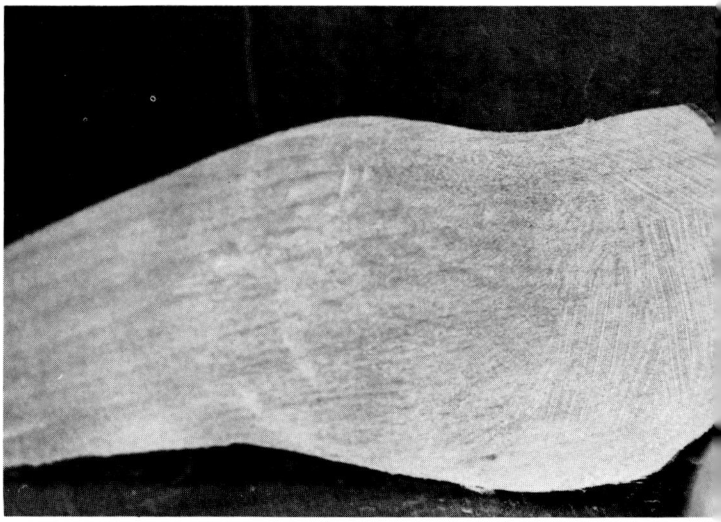

Under side hollowed

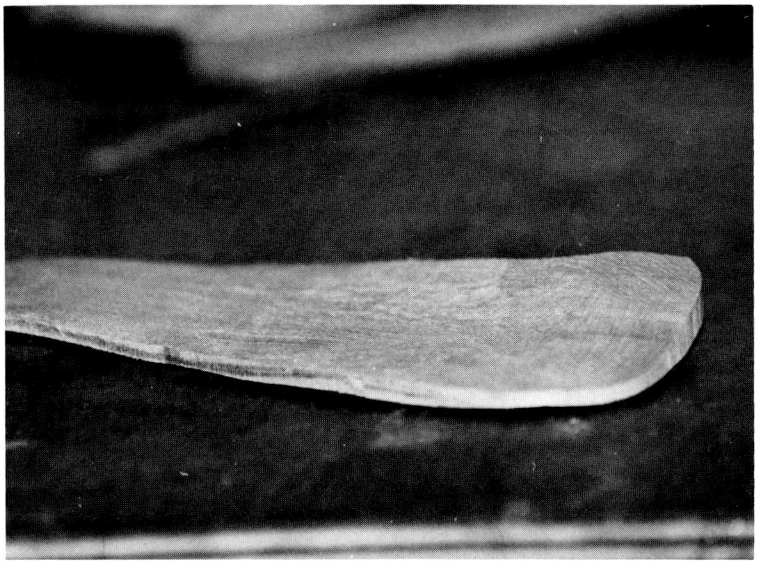

Further shaping of wing with rasp

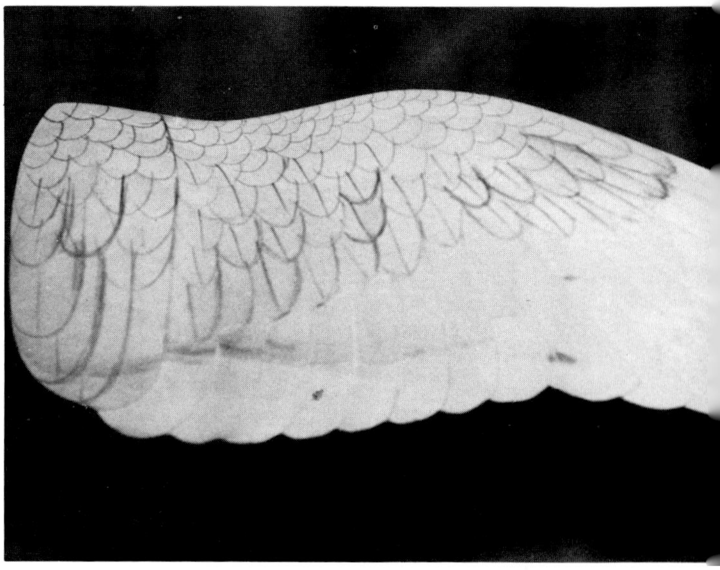

Feather lay out upperside of wing

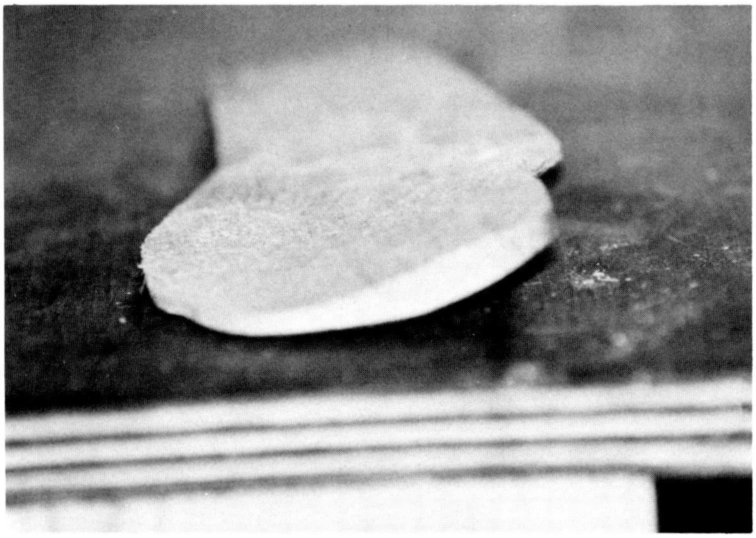

End view showing twist in wing

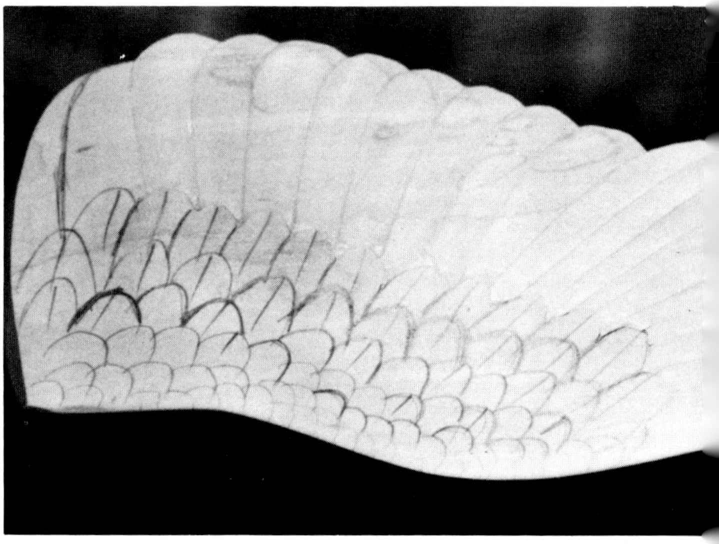

Feather lay out underside of wing

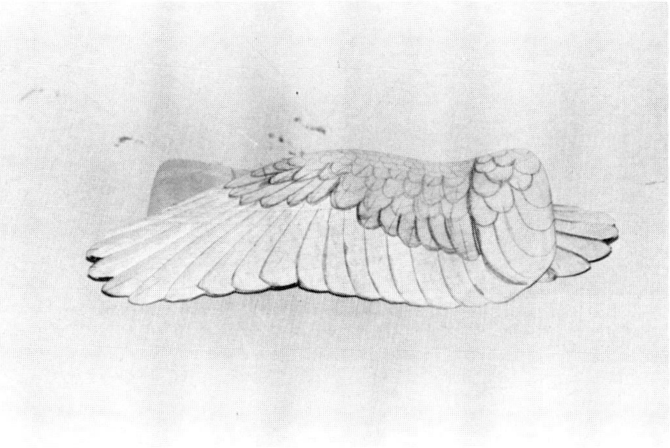

Underside of wing carved

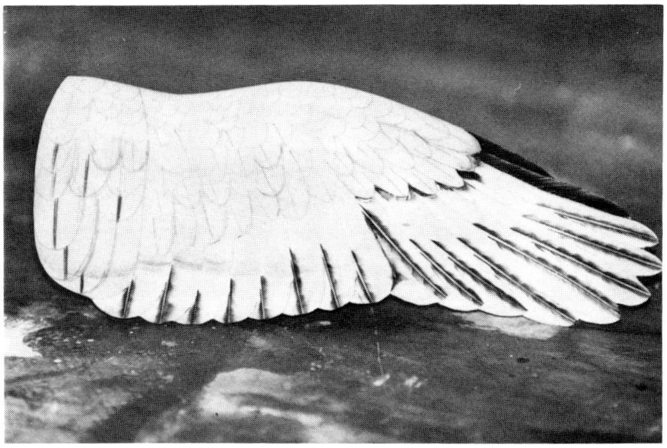

Underside burned in

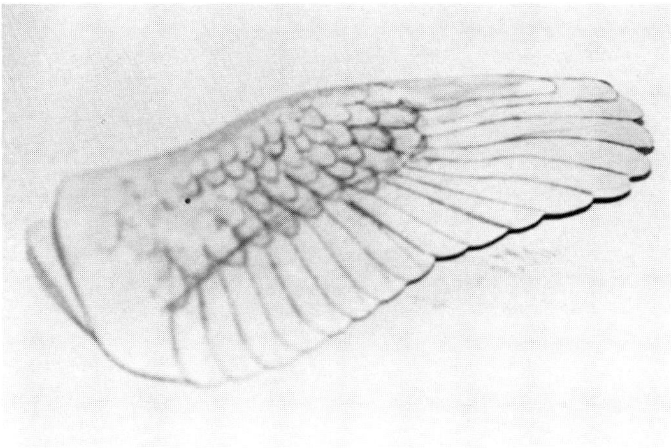

Upper side of wing laid out

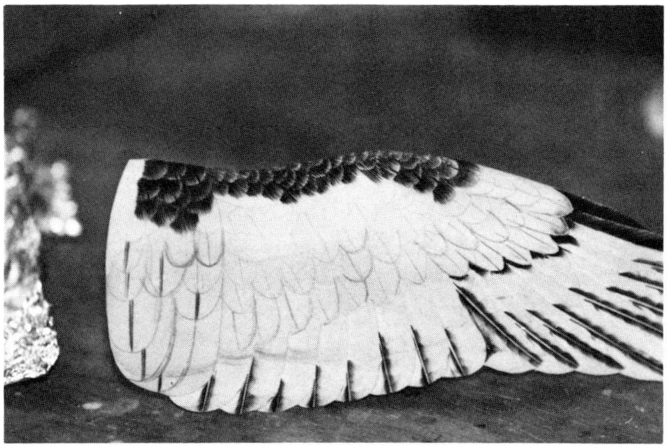

Upper side of wing partially burned

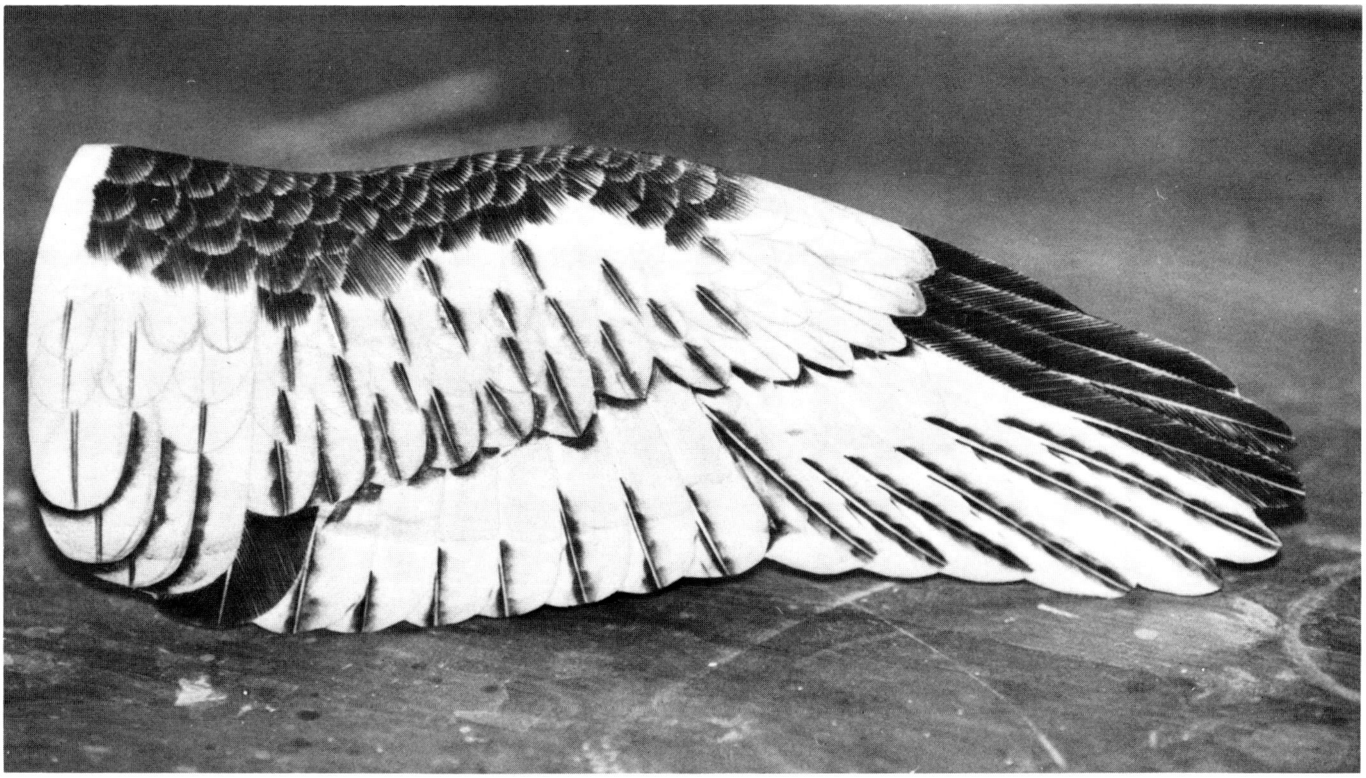

Further burning on upper wing

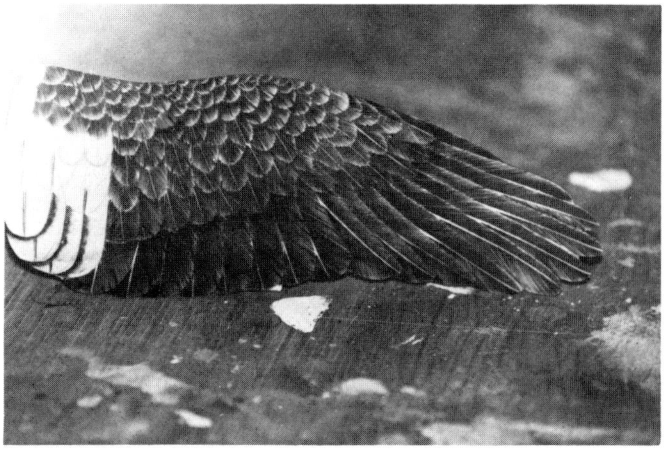

Upper wing burned

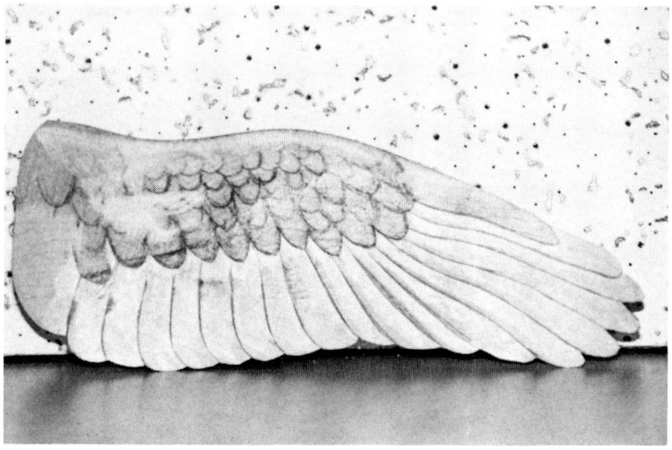

Under wing carved

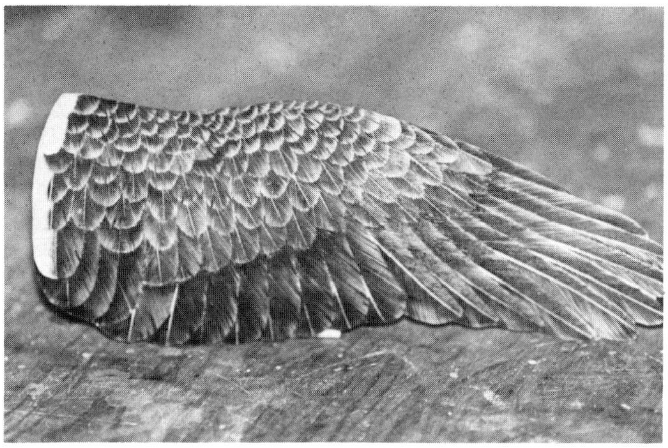

Upper wing burned except joint area

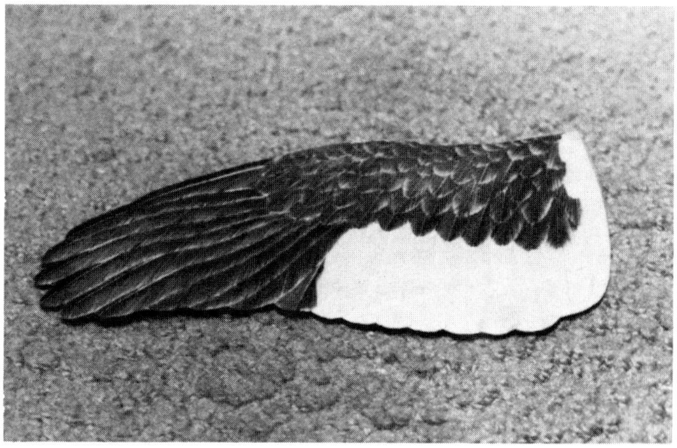

Under wing partially burned

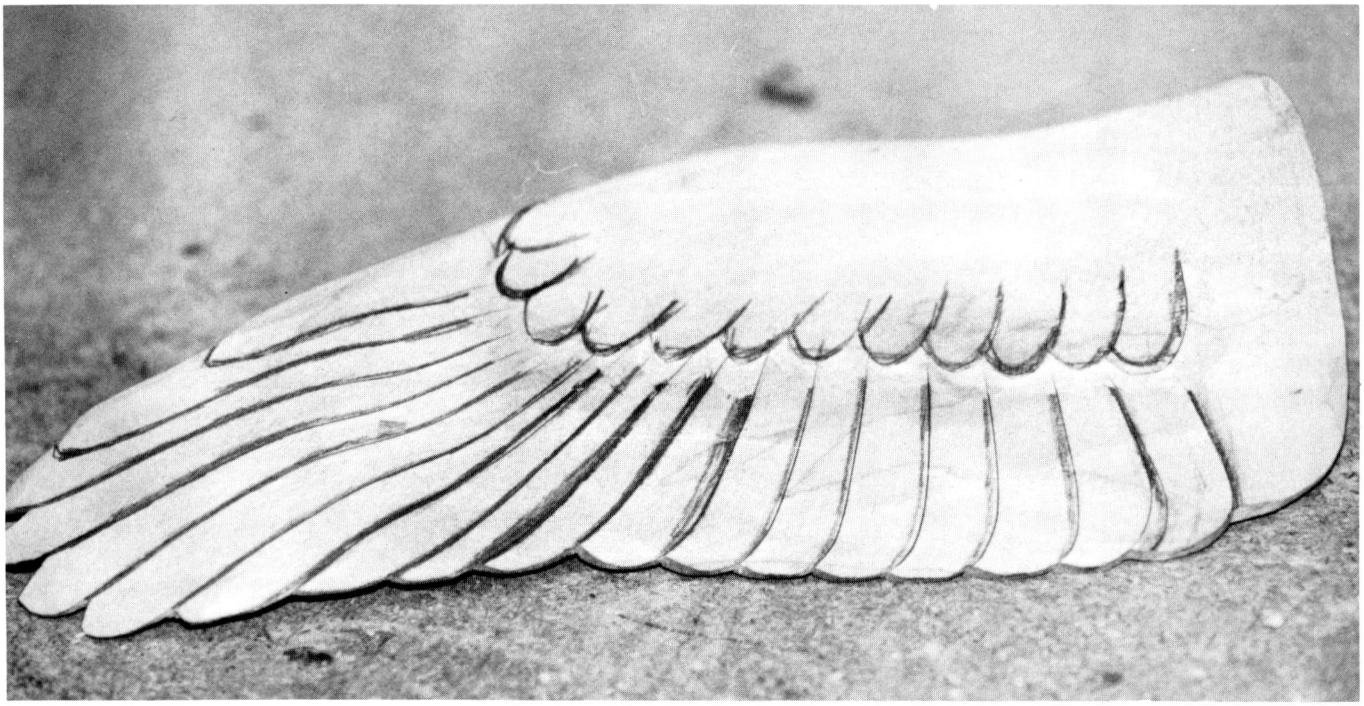

Underside of wing feather lay out

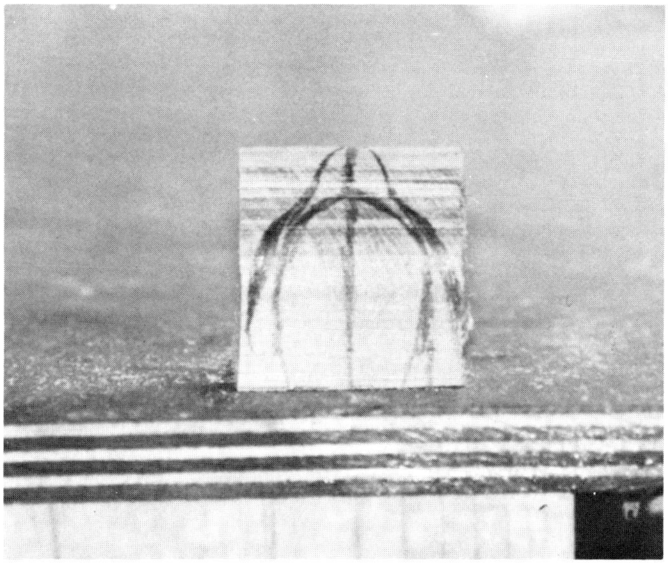
Head plan view

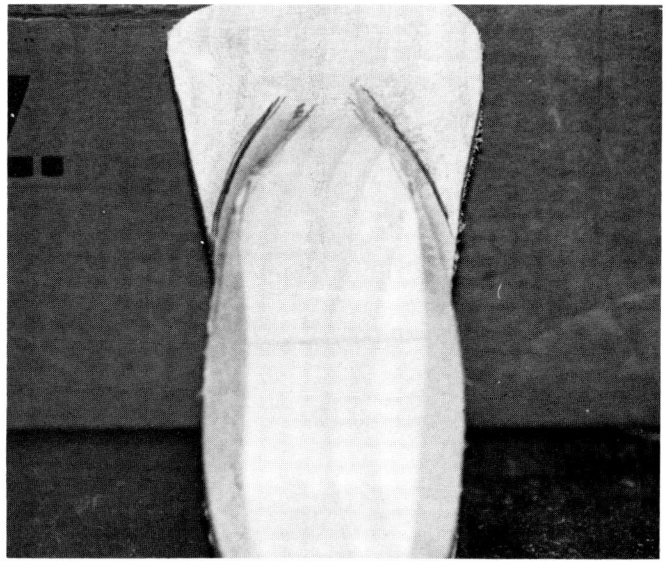
Under side of tail and rump area being shaped with rasp

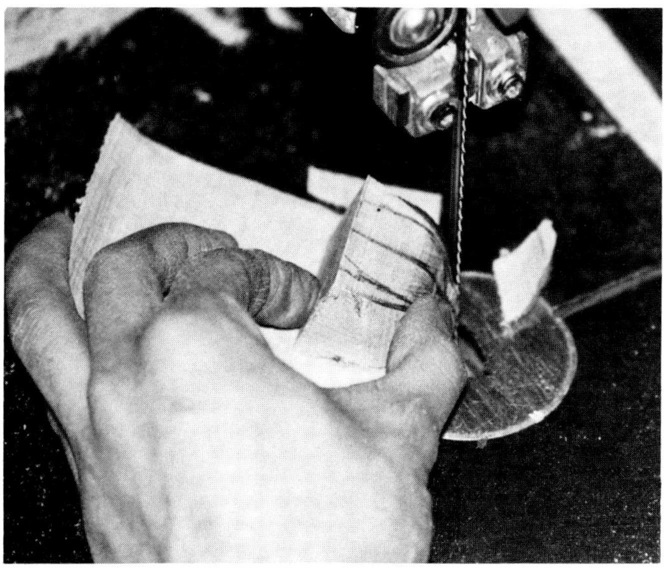
Head plan view being band sawed

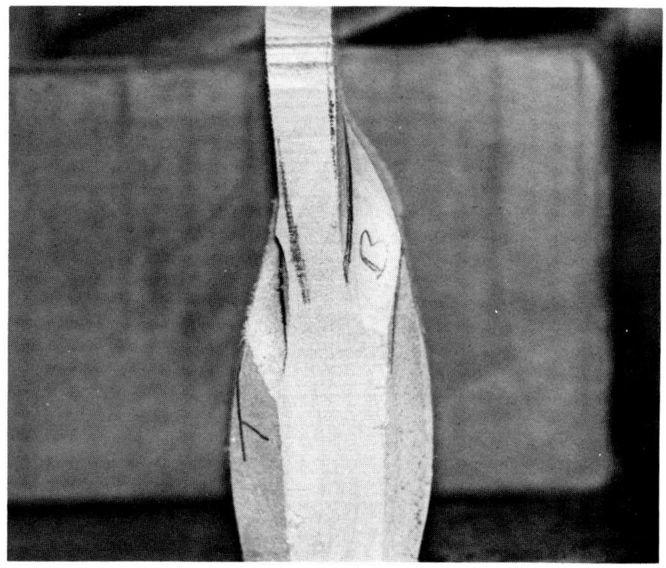
Profile of tail and rump areas

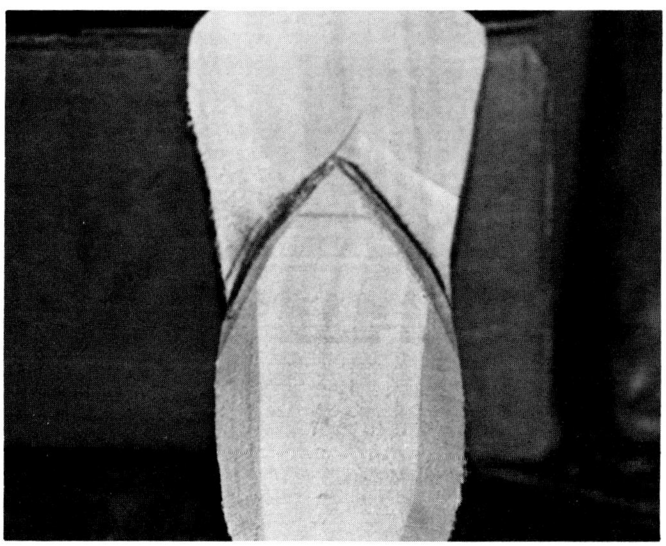
Upper side of tail and rump area being shaped with rasp

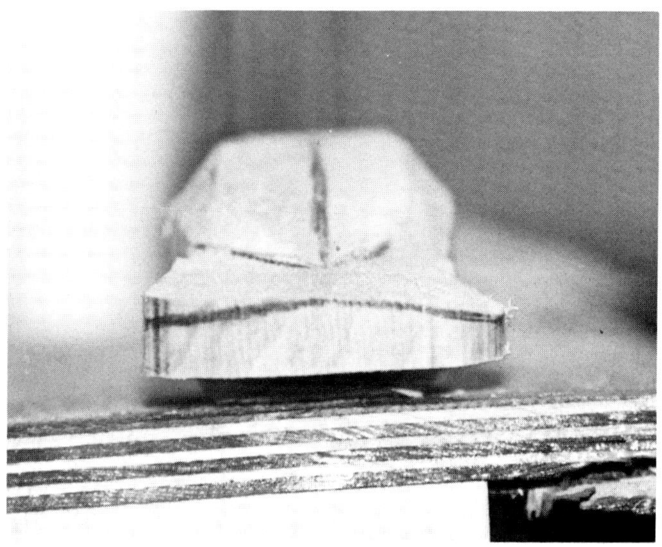
End view of tail—note: arc

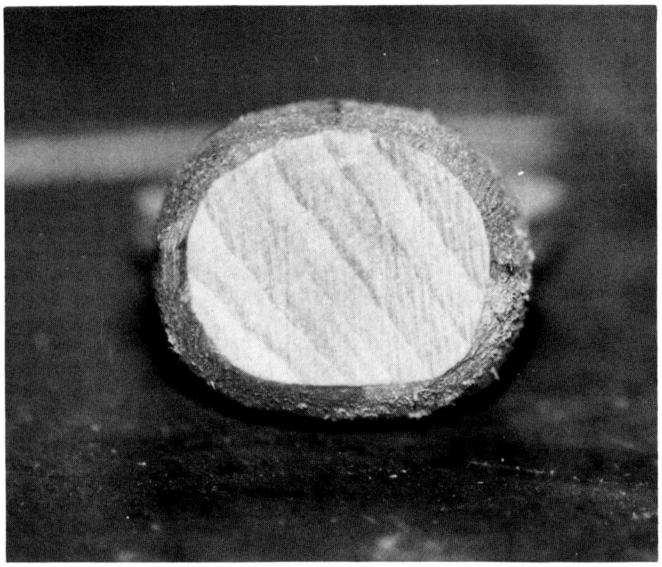

End view of area where head will set

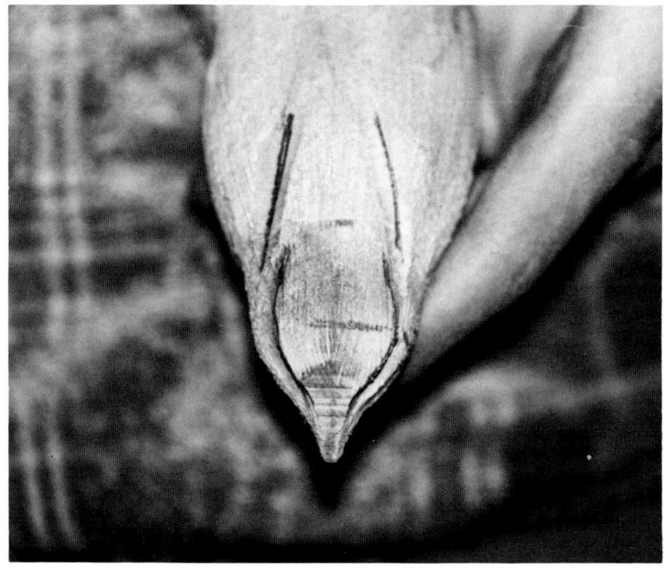

Crown and cape area flowing together

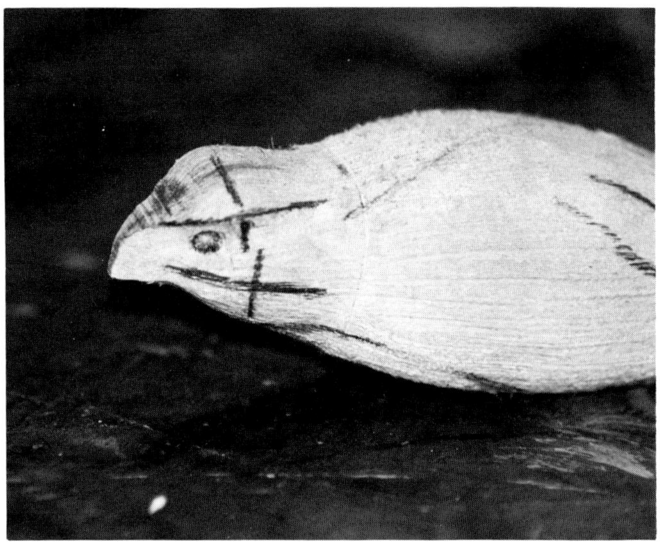

Profile of head with guide marks including eye crown and cheek areas

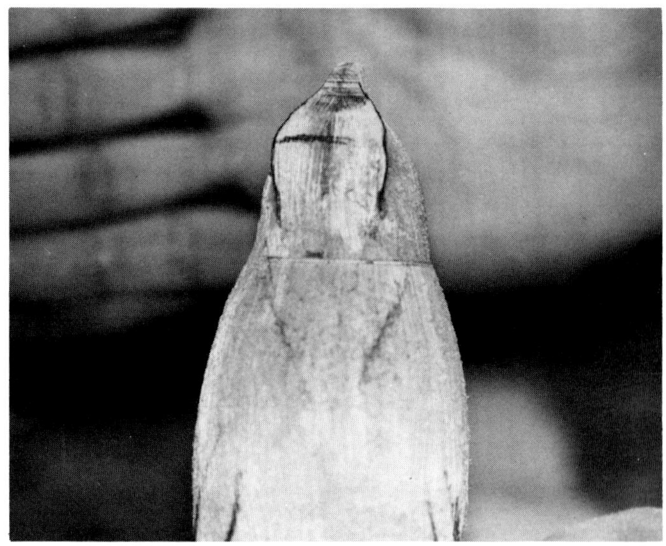

Another view of crown and cape area

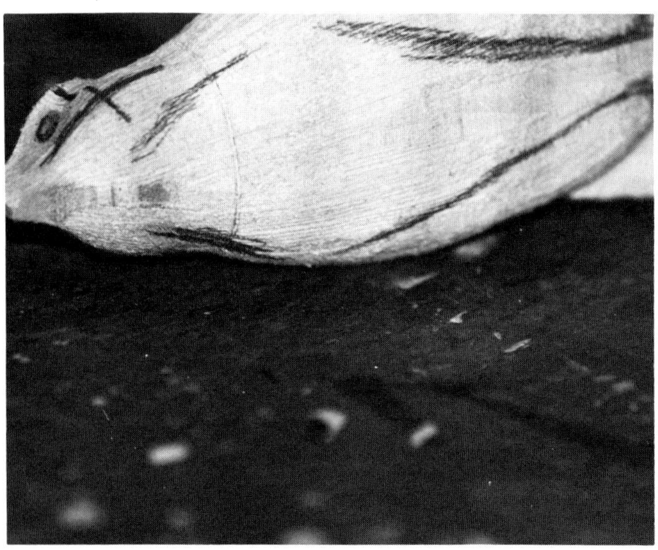

Belly and leg areas to be rough carved

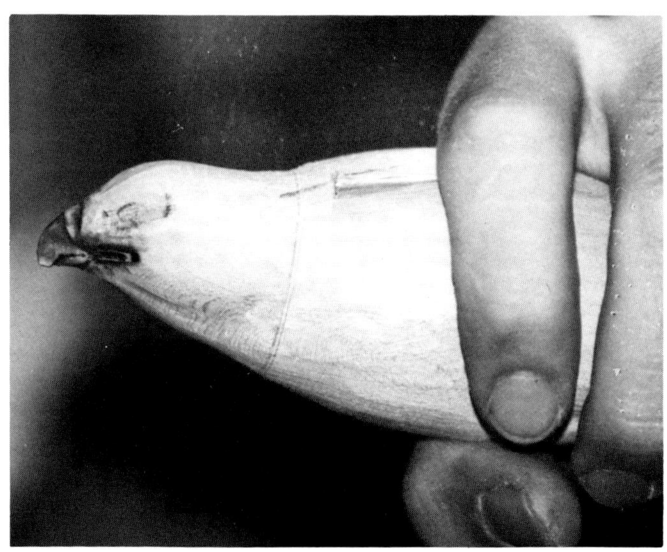

Profile of beak detail

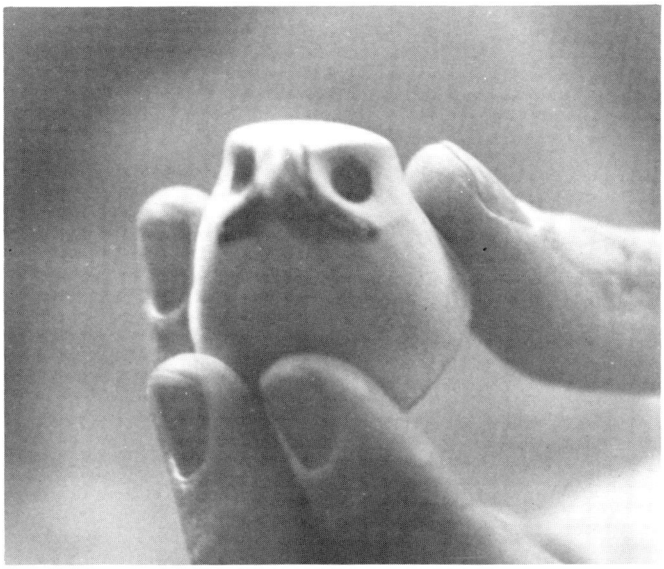

Front view of head with eye holes drilled—note: angle

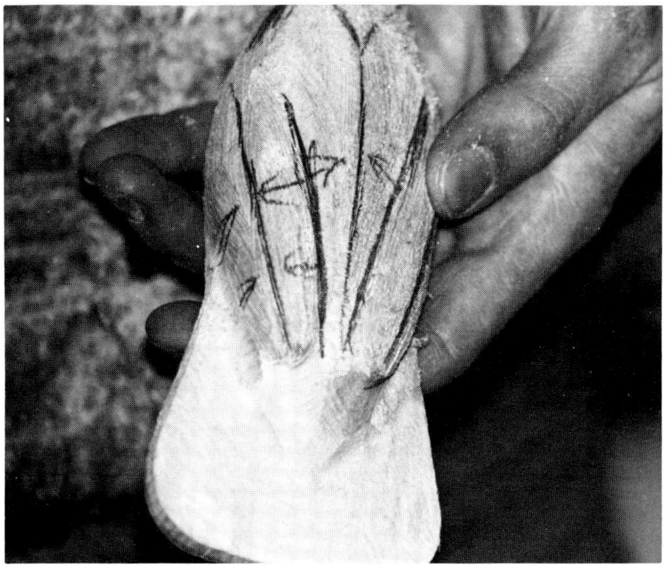

Leg areas tight to body in flight

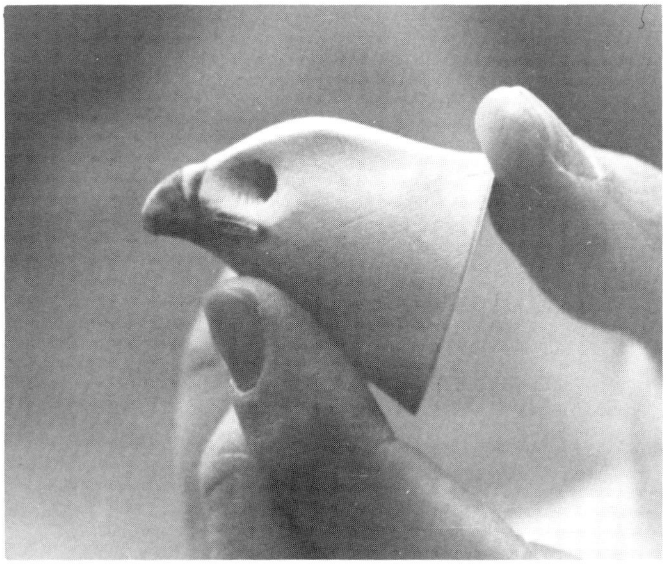

Profile of head with beak detail and eye hole drilled

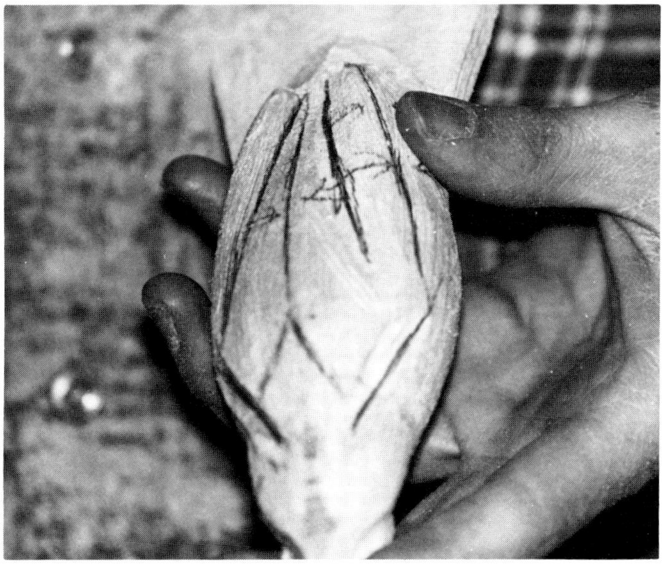

Other side of leg areas

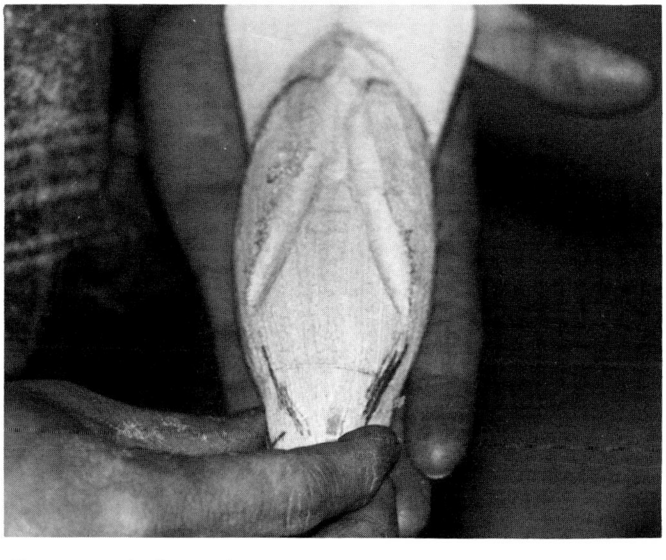

Cape area indentations

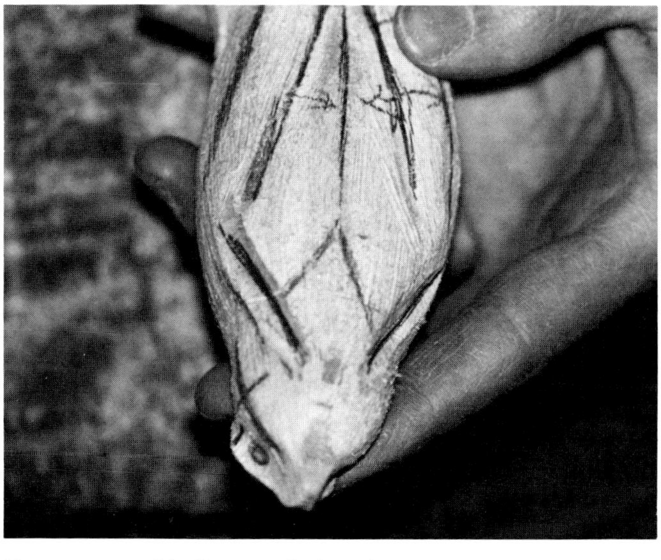

Leg areas guide lines and chest indentations

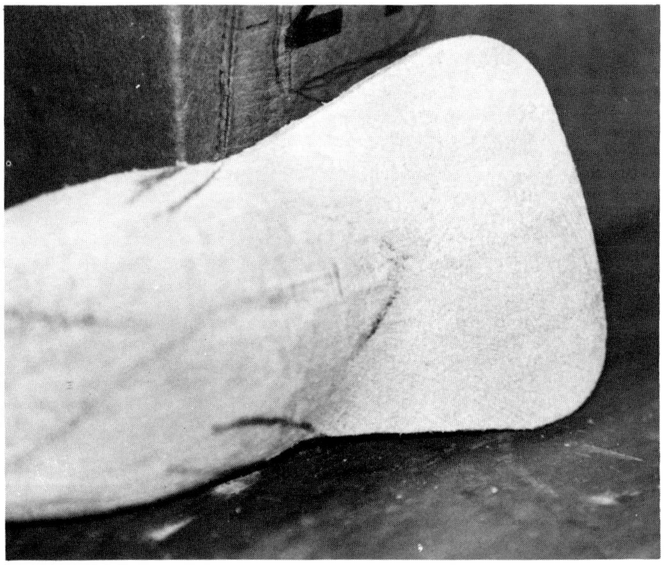

Upper side of tail

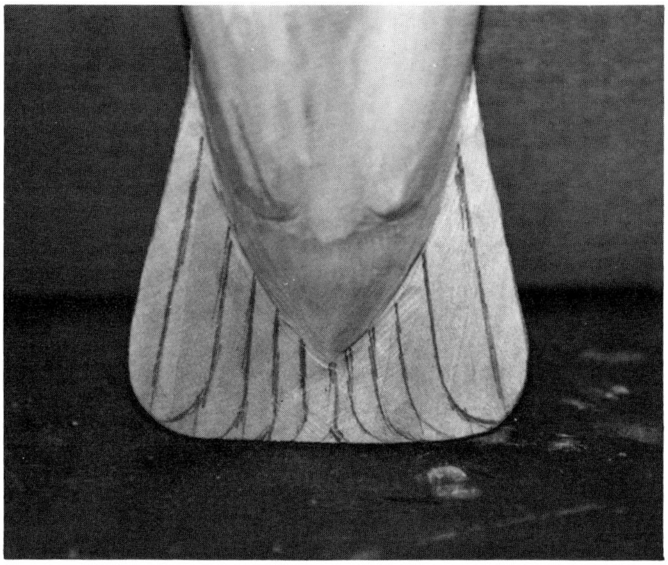

Detail and feather lay out on under side of tail

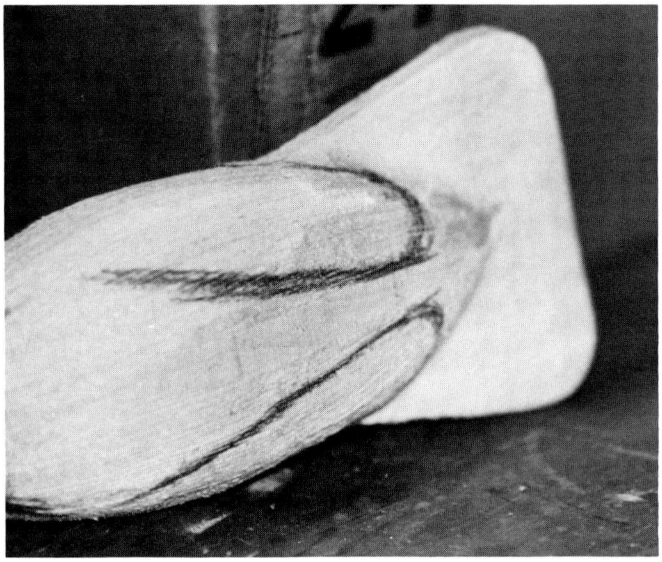

Under side of tail

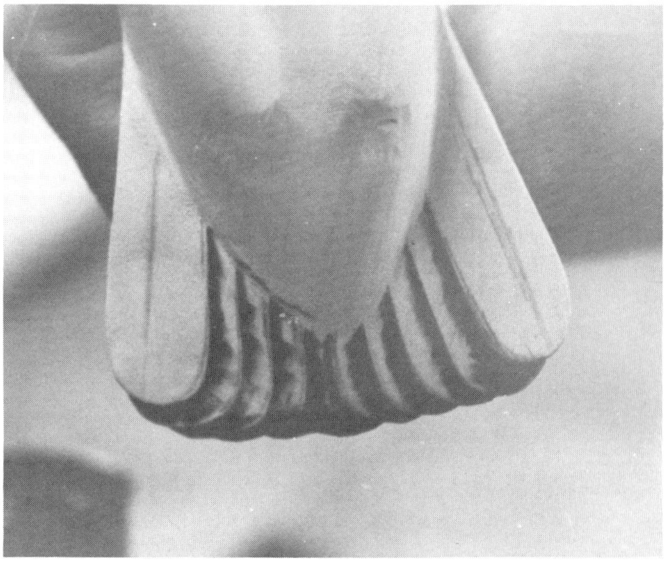

Underside of feathers carved in with burner

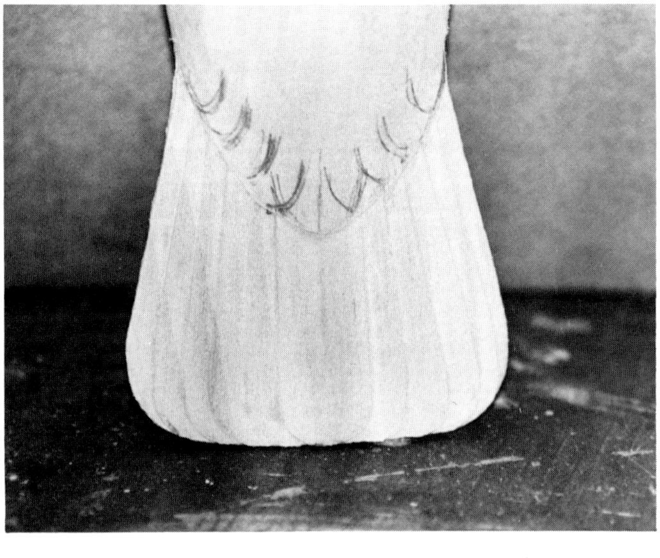

Detail and feather lay out on upper side of tail

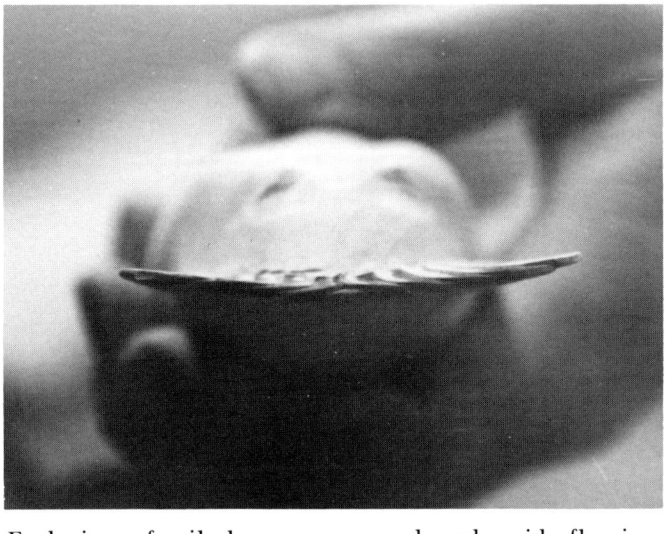

End view of tail shows upper and under side flowing together

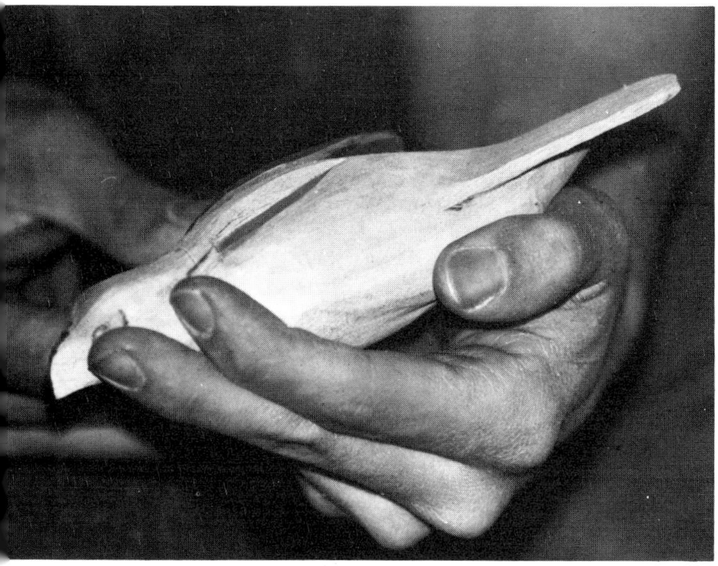

Notches for wings

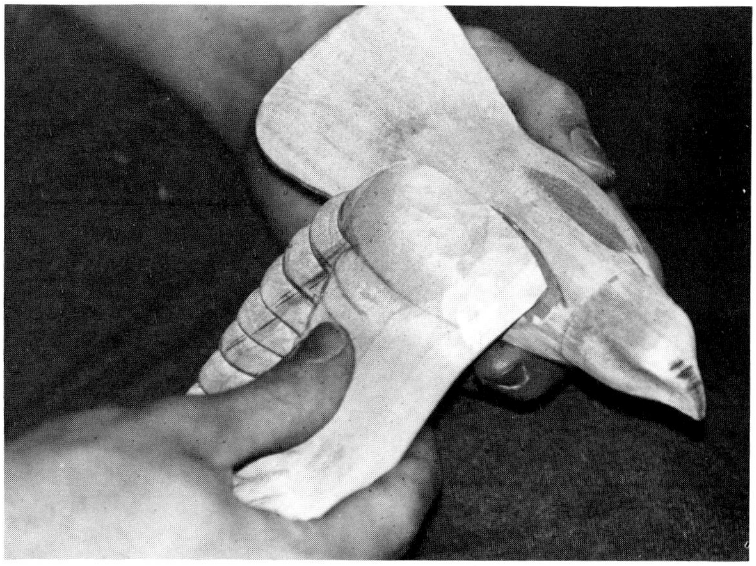

Fitting wing to body

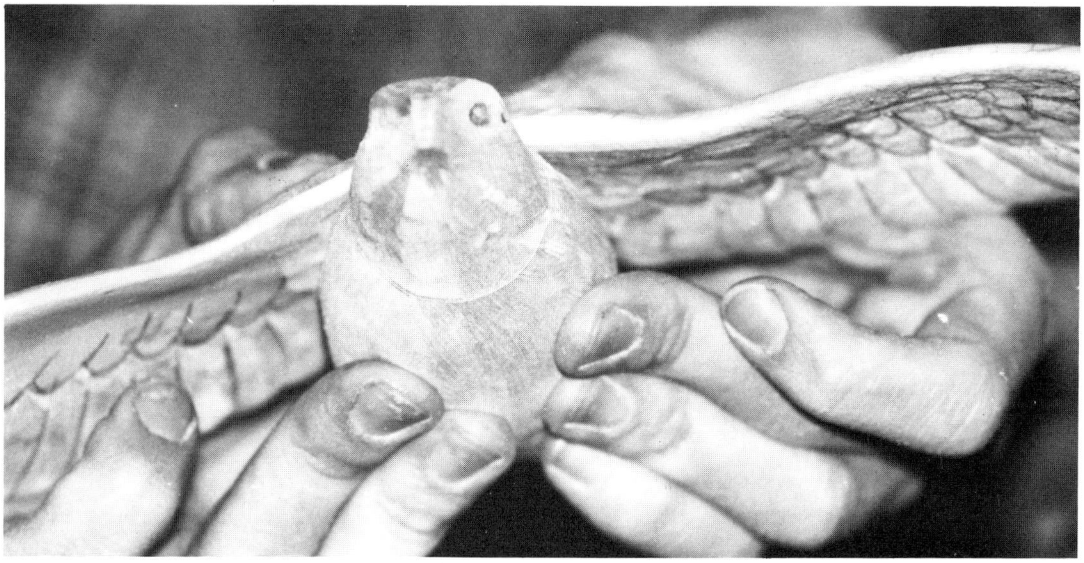

Fitting both wings to body bottom view

Fitting wings to body top view

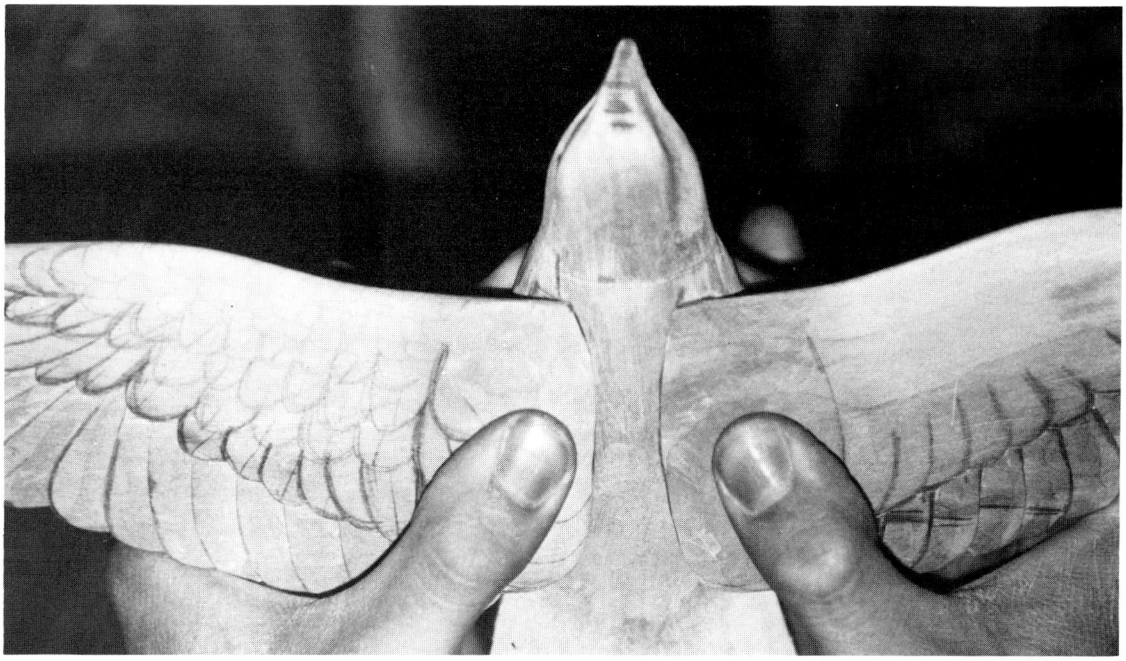

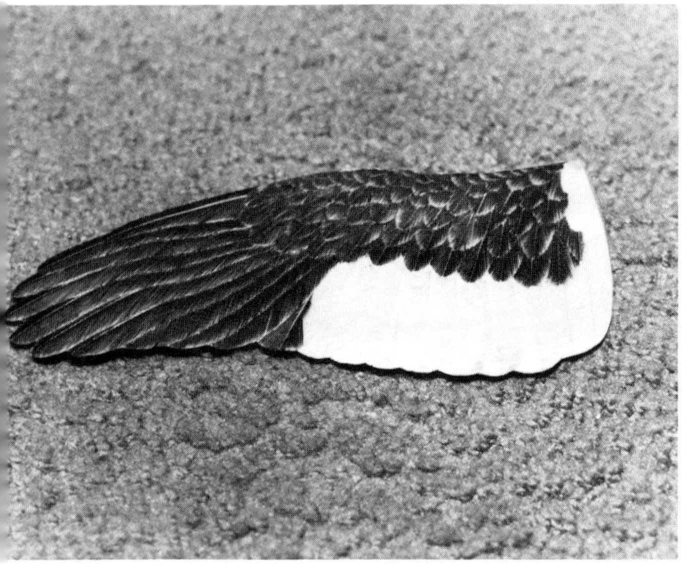

Underside of wing partially burned

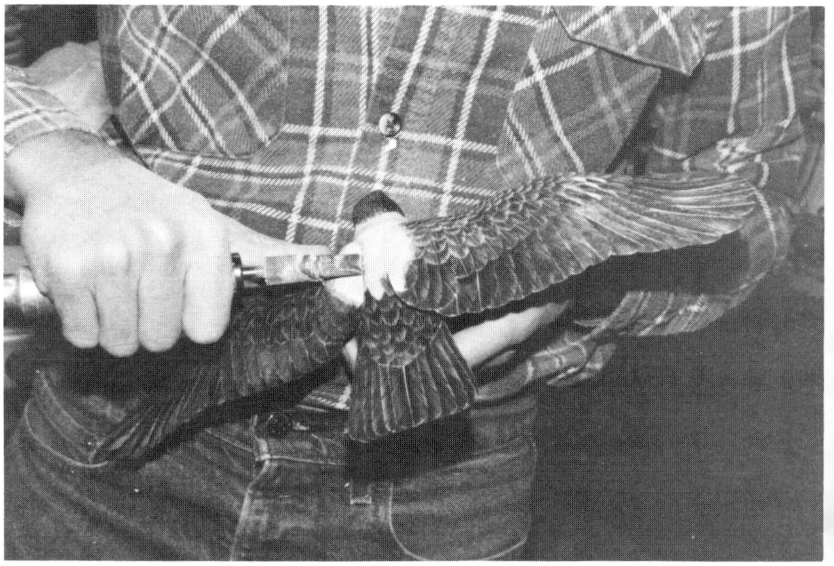

Shaping wings to body with sanding cartridge

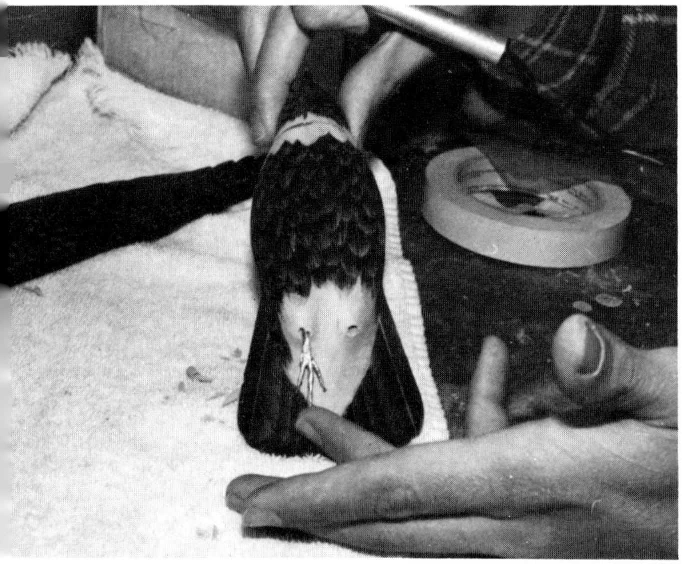

Belly and undertail burned—setting legs and feet

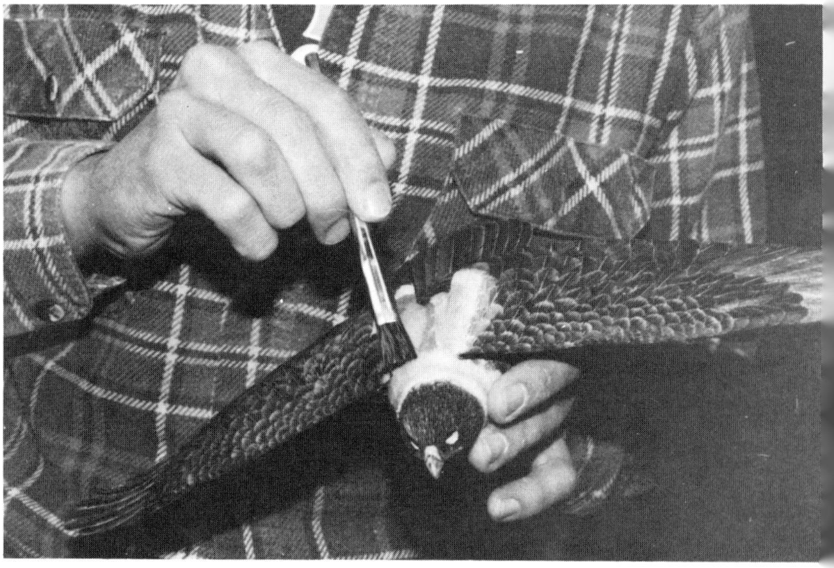

Filling wing and neck joints with wood dough (use large amounts of acetone to smooth the wood dough into wood—it also breaks down air gaps

Wings fitted and set with five-minute epoxy

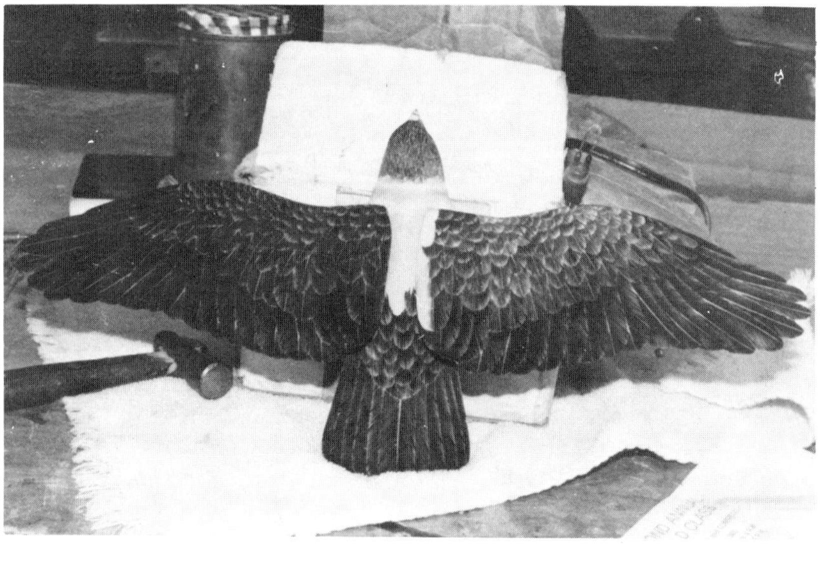

Eyes set and eye lids fashioned

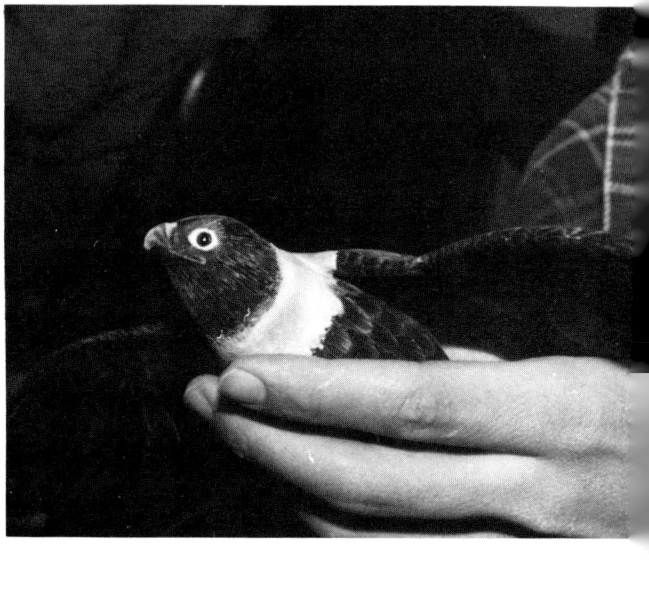

Antiqued Goshawk

Carved by David Biddle

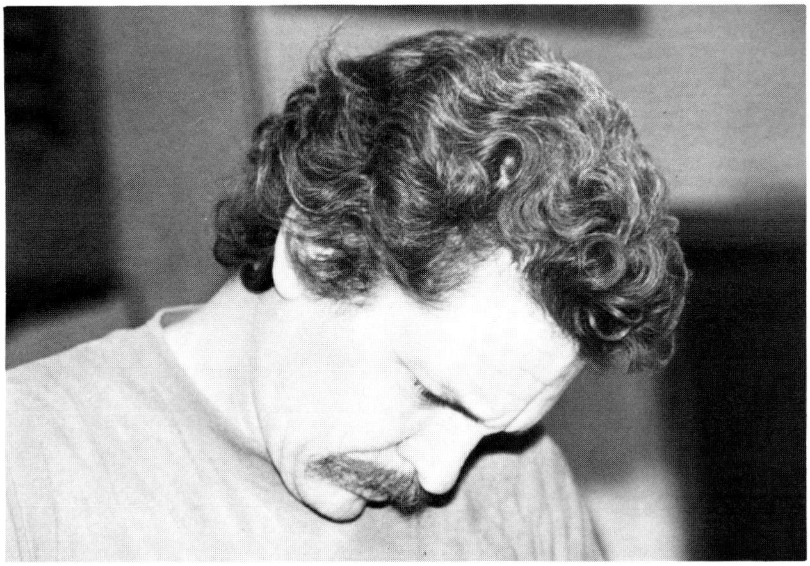

Portrait of an artist

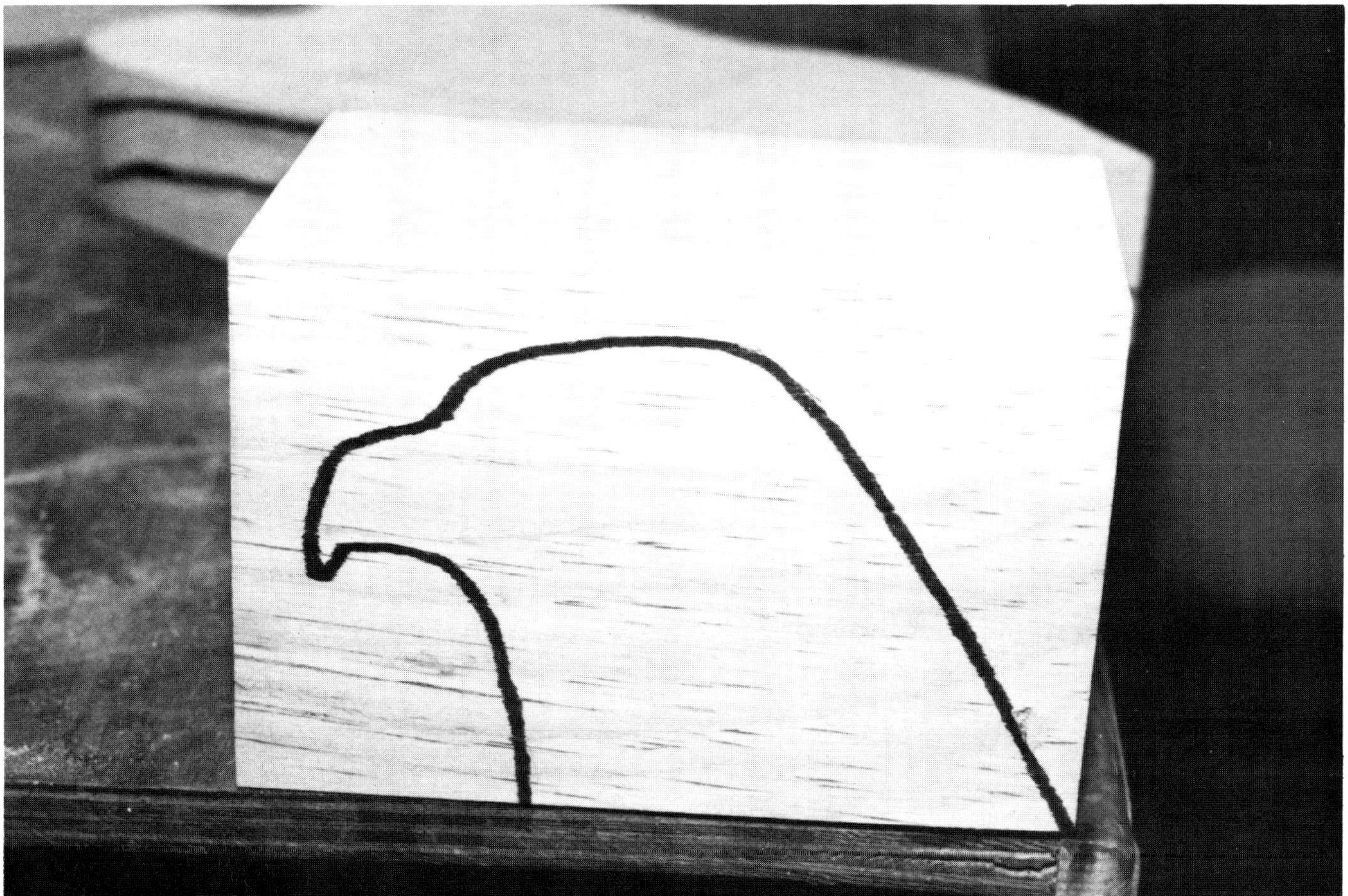

Profile of head pattern on block to be band-sawed

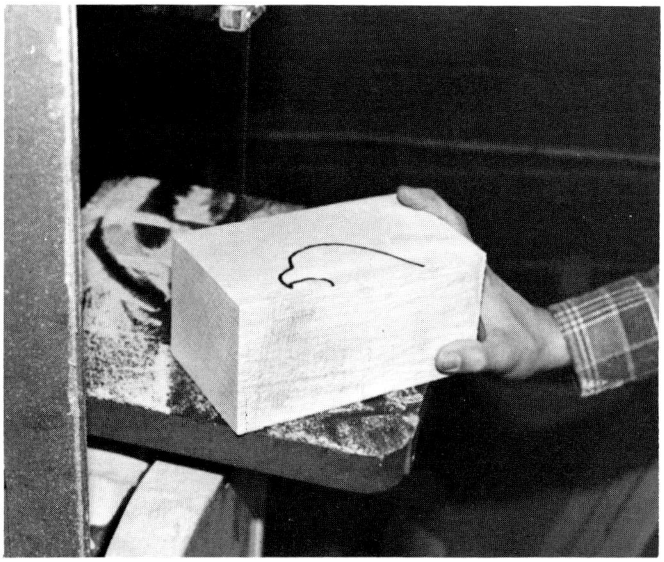

Head pattern of pine

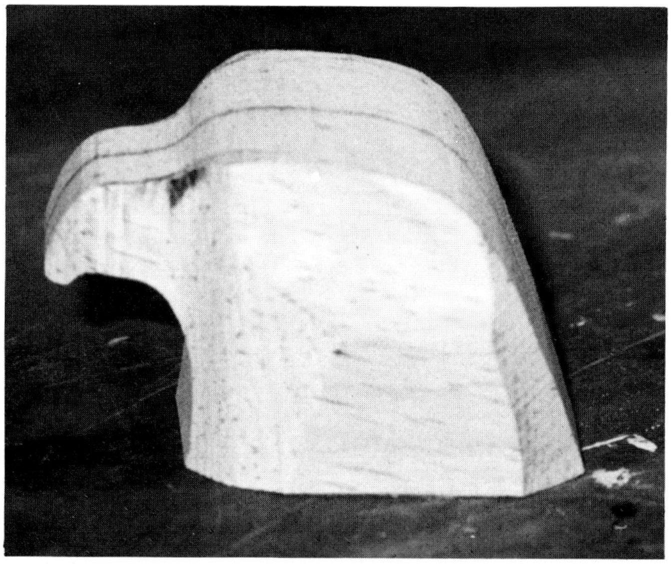

Band-sawed head ready to be carved

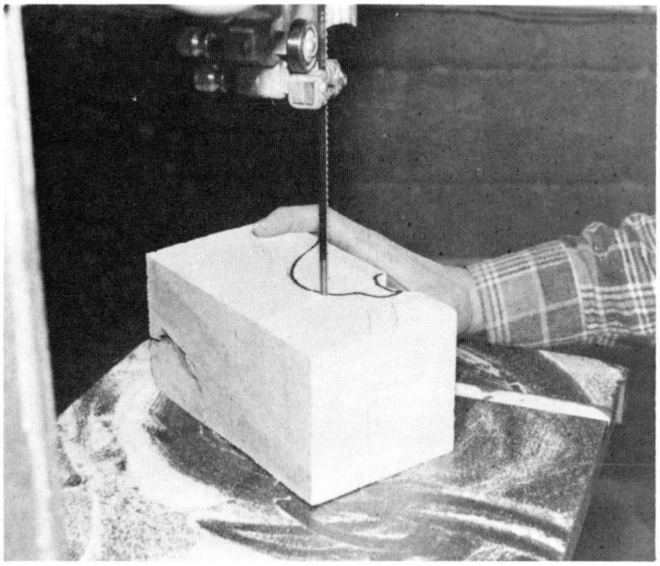

Head pattern being band-sawed

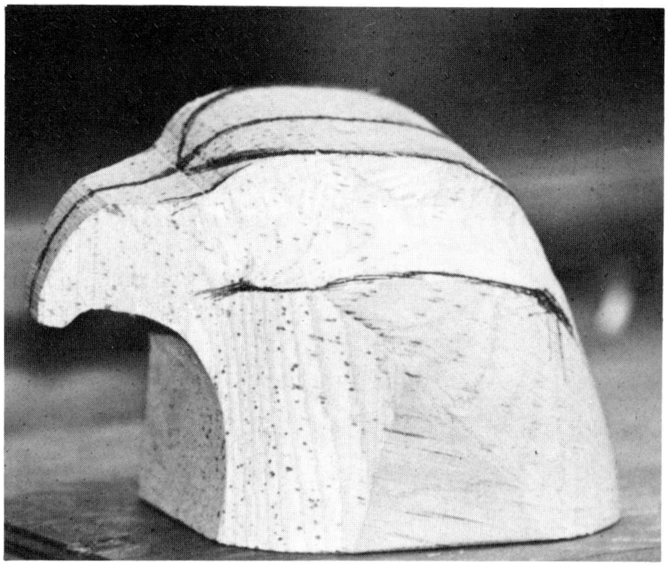

Eye channel carved

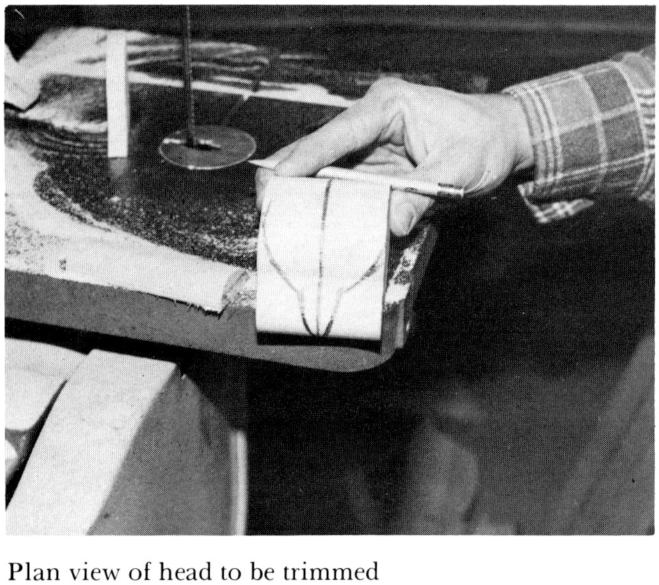

Plan view of head to be trimmed

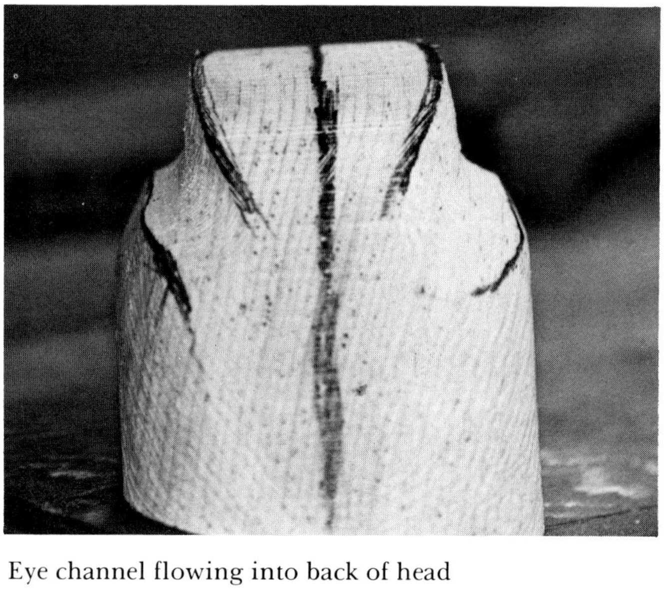

Eye channel flowing into back of head

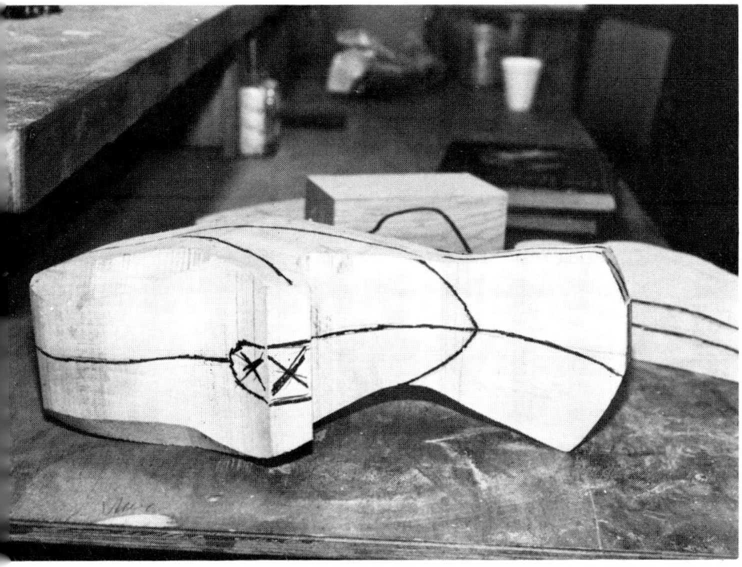

Belly view—note: (XX) area to be removed between legs and twist in tail

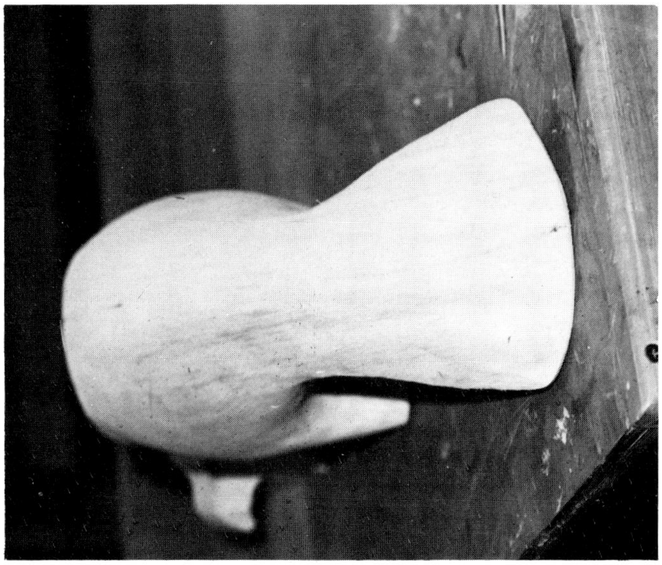

Back view of body after shaping

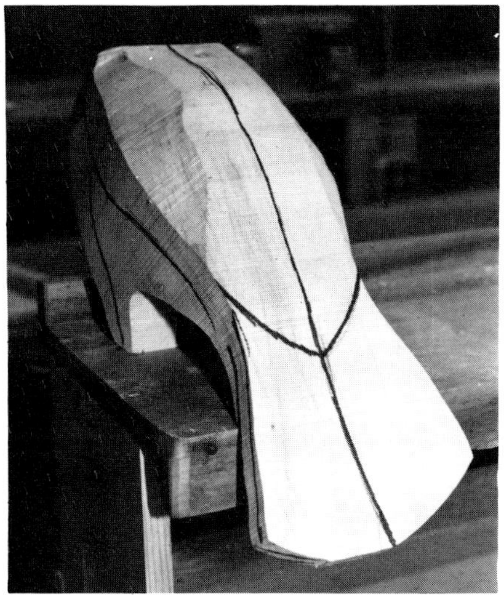

Profile of body with guide lines (high points)

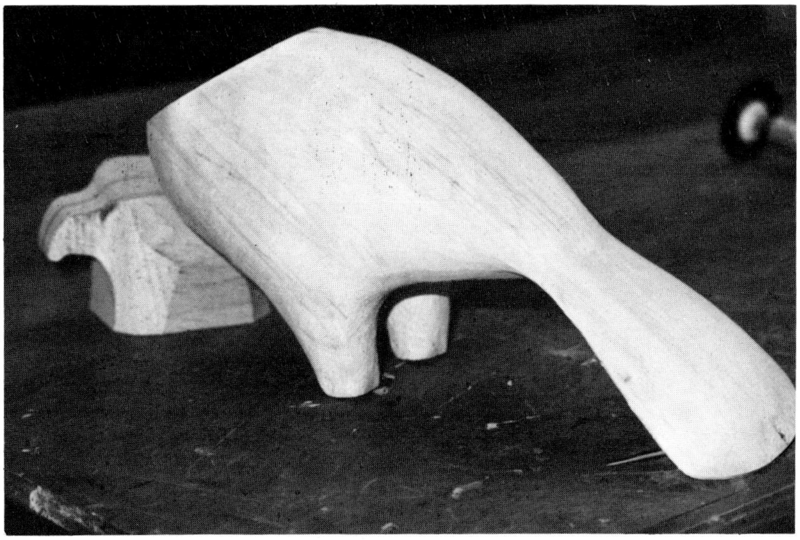

Side view of body after shaping

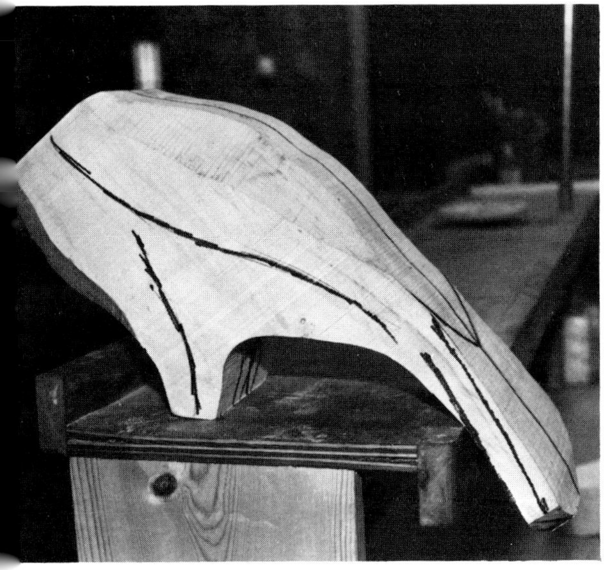

Plan view—note: guide lines

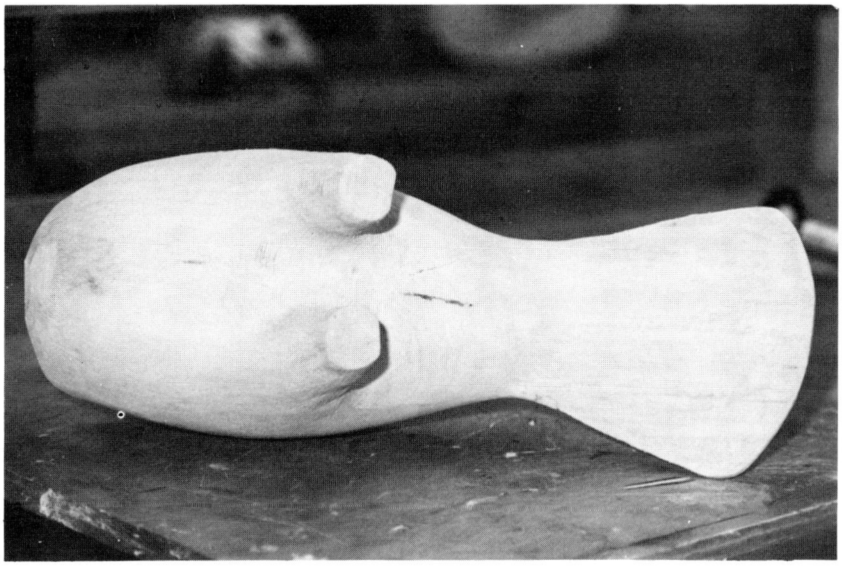

Belly view of body after shaping

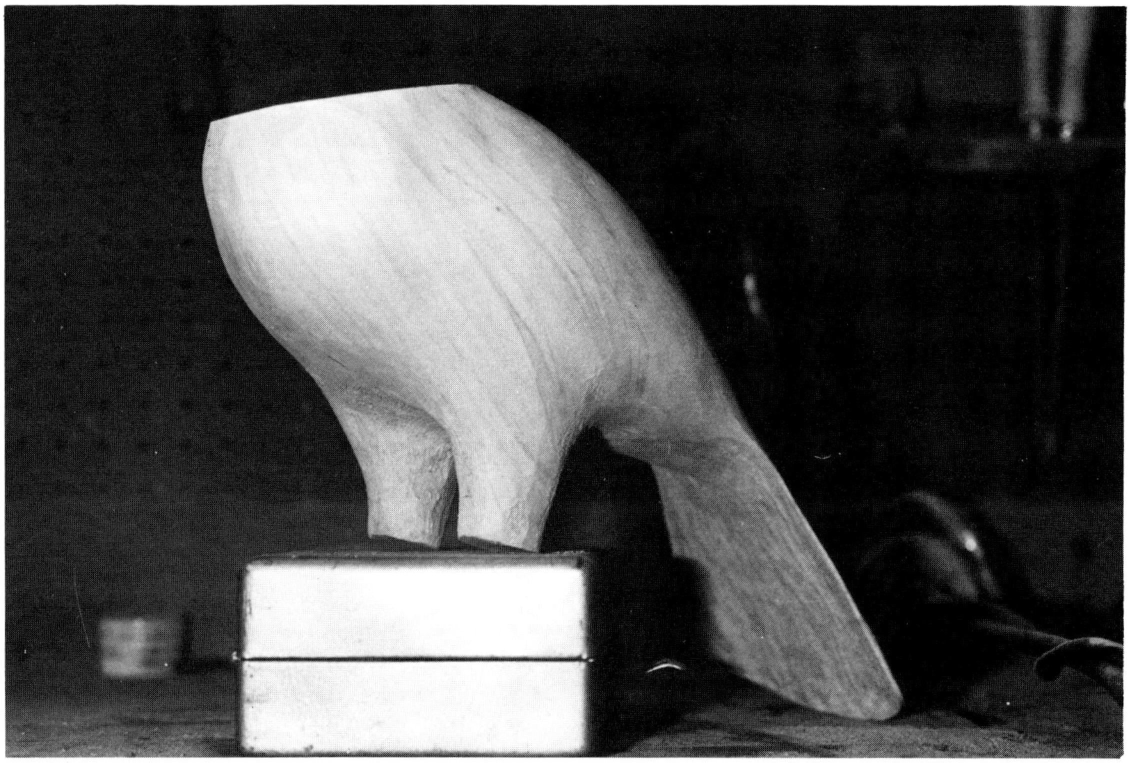

Front view of carved body

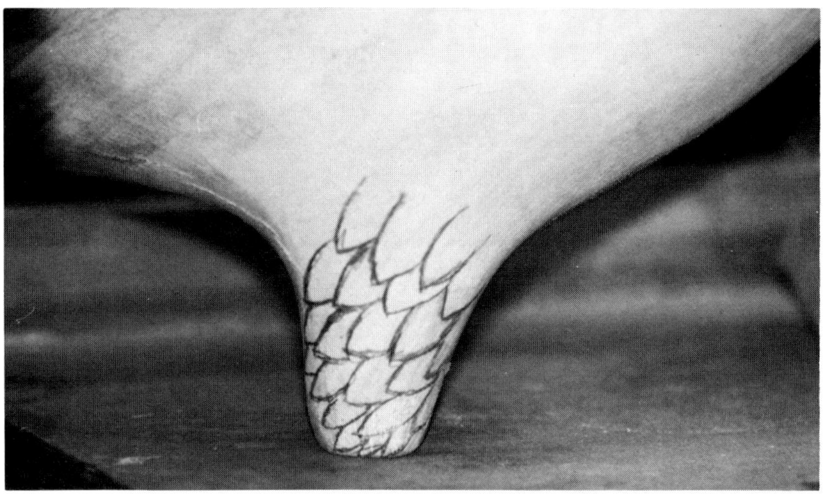

Feather detail on leg

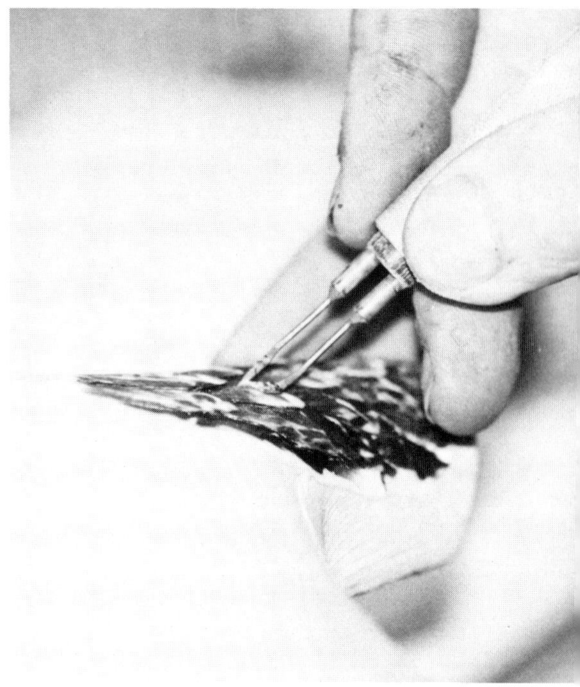

Completed leg detail

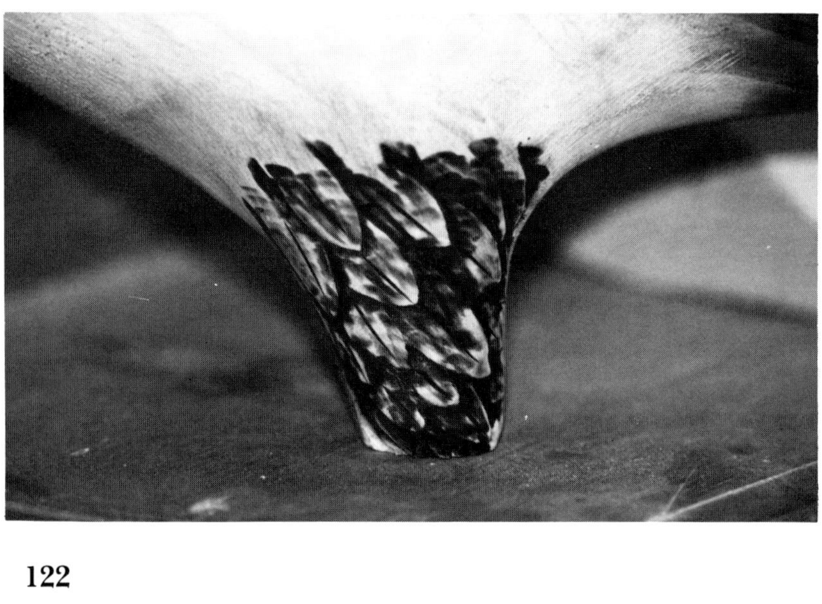

Burning feather detail on leg

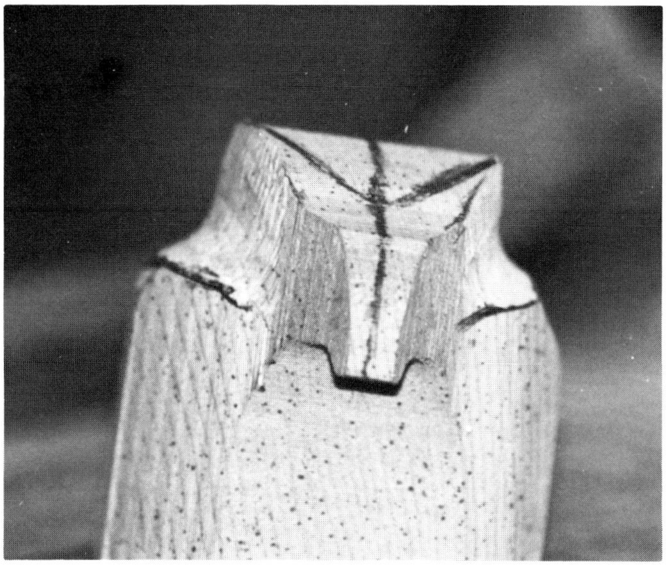

Eye channel flows into beak

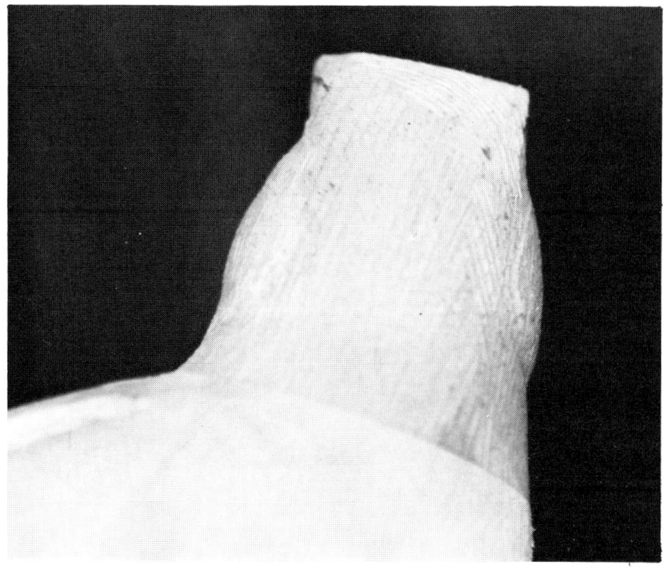

Back view of head flowing into body

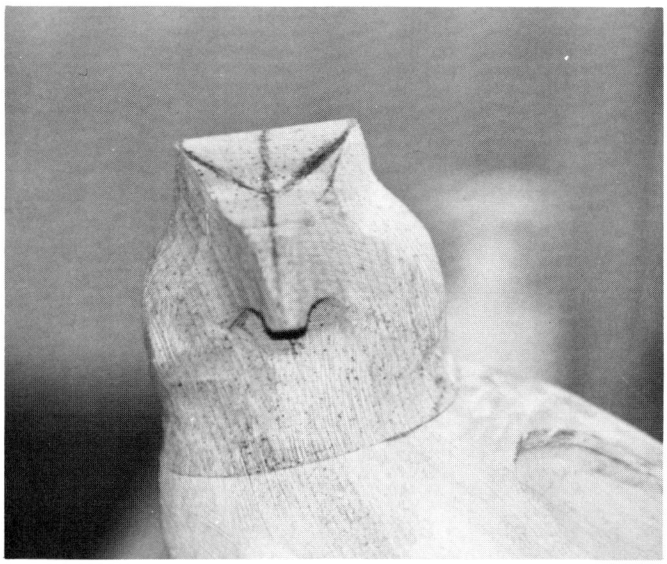

Head flowing into body

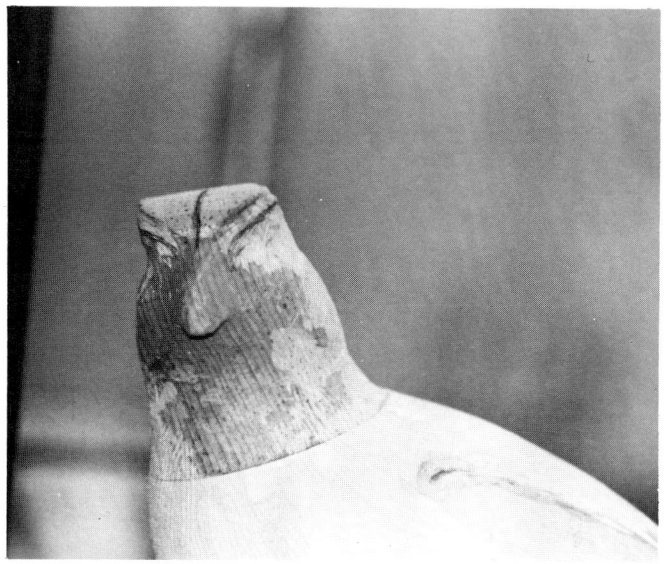

Front view of head flowing into body

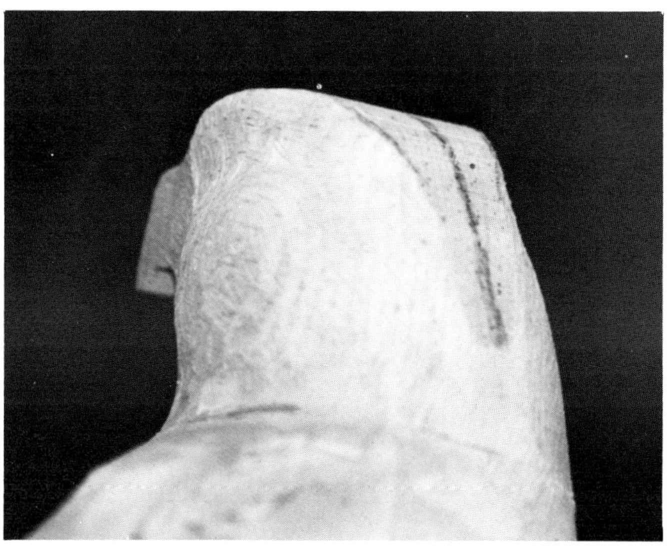

Side view of head flowing into body

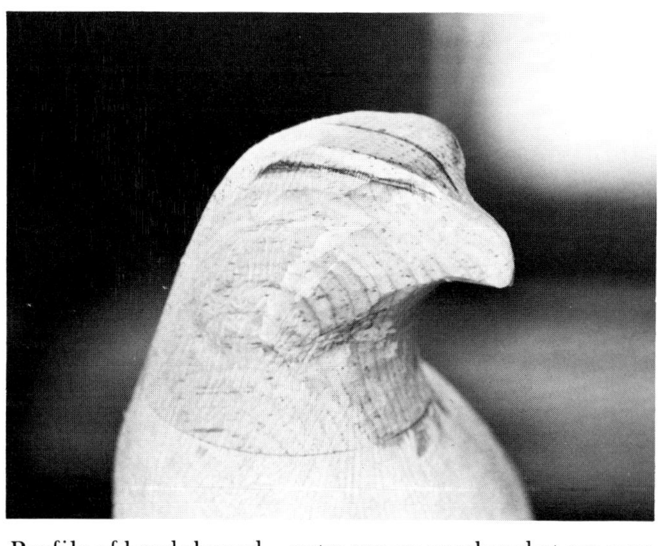

Profile of head shaped—note: crown overhand at eye area which creates the so called "mean" look

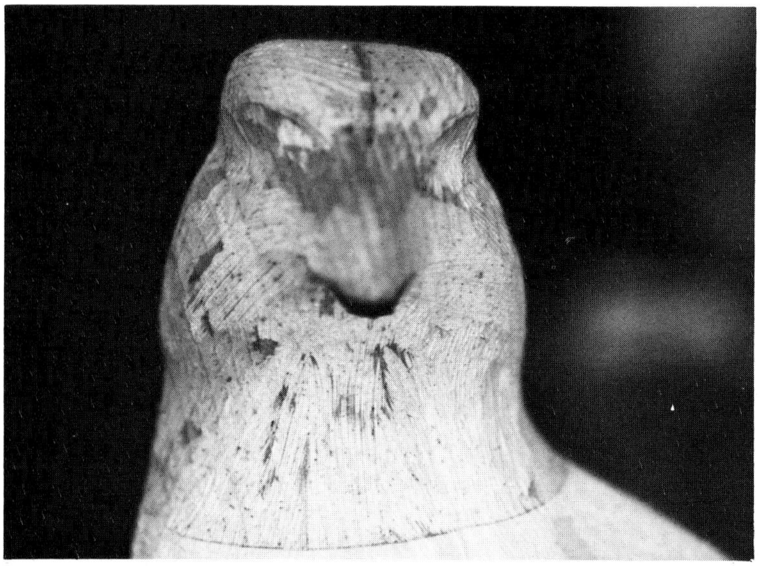

Front view of head—note: eye channel

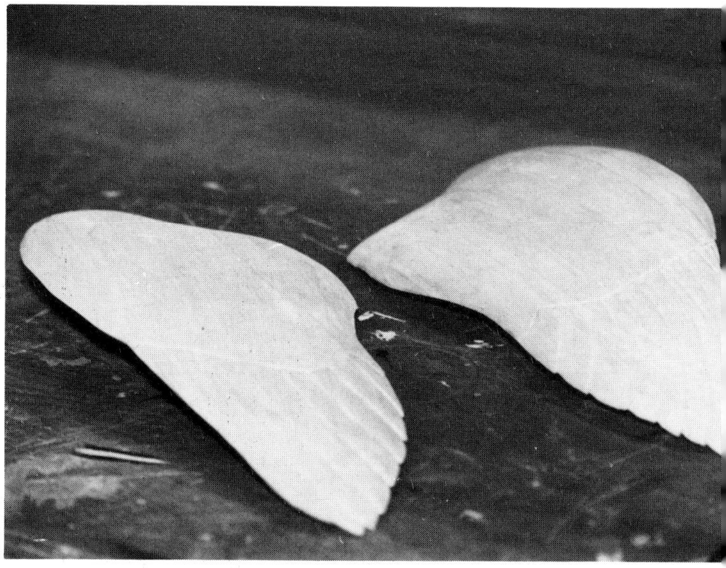

Carved wings—note: carved primary feathers

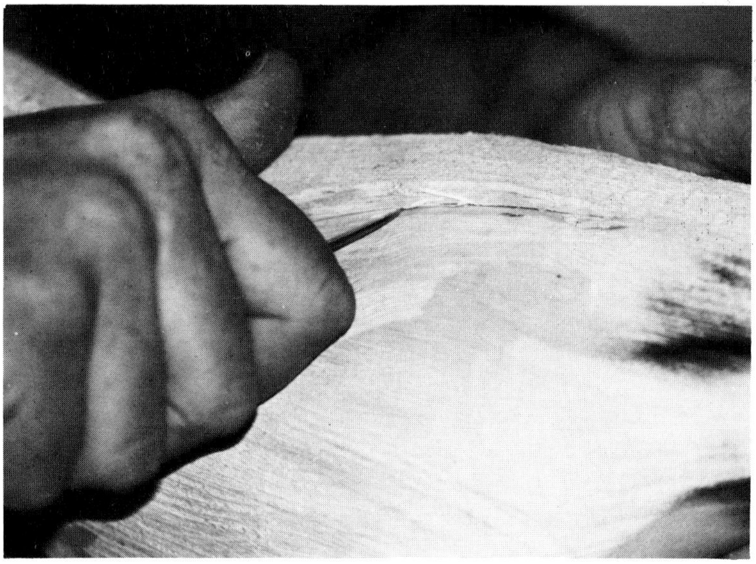

Cutting notch for wings to fit body

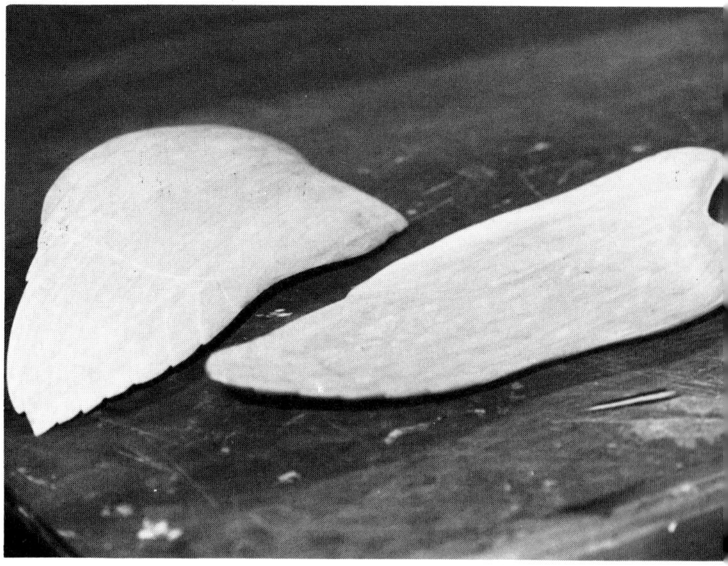

Carved wings

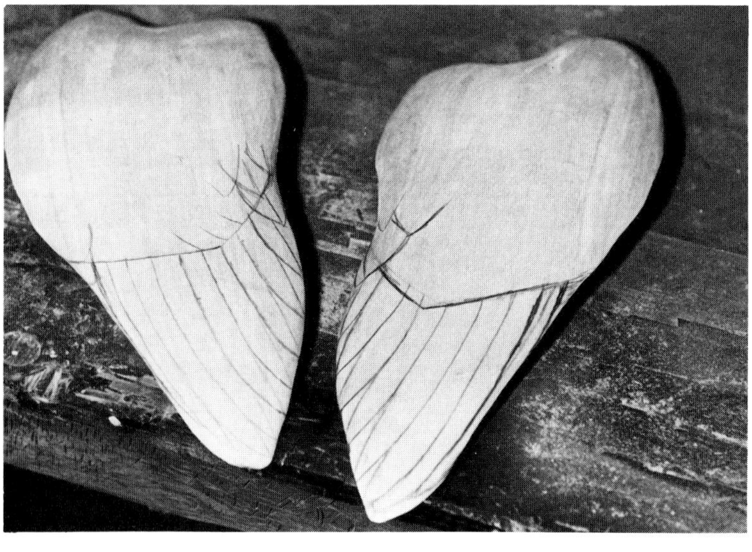

Primary feather lay out

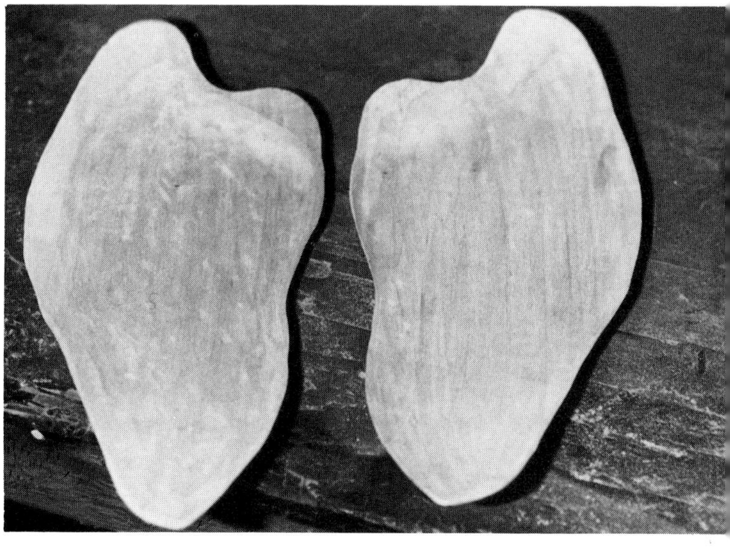

Under side of wings slightly hollow

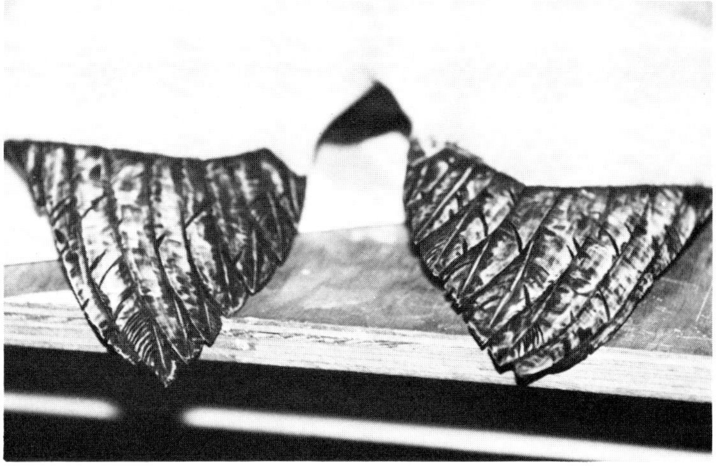

Primary feathers burned minimum detail

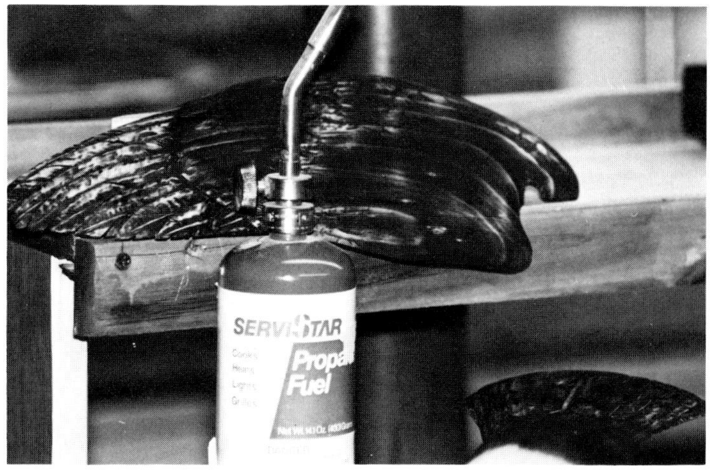

Torch wings to raise grain

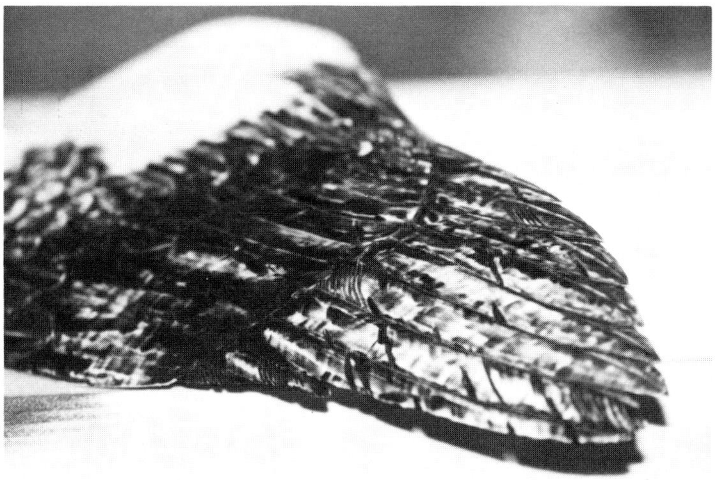

Primary coverts burned

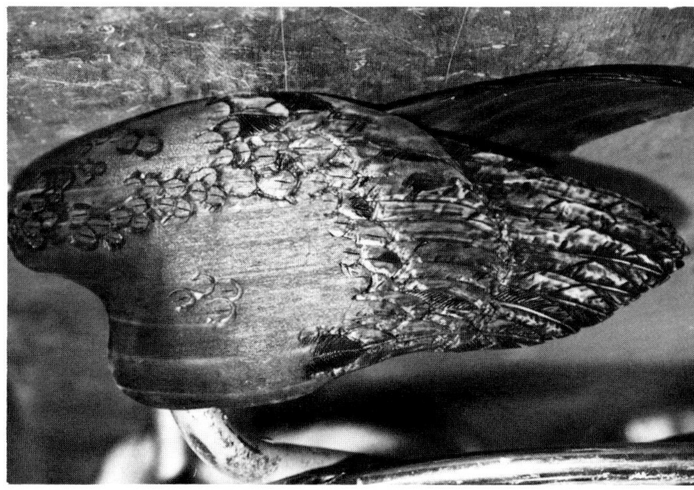

Torched wing

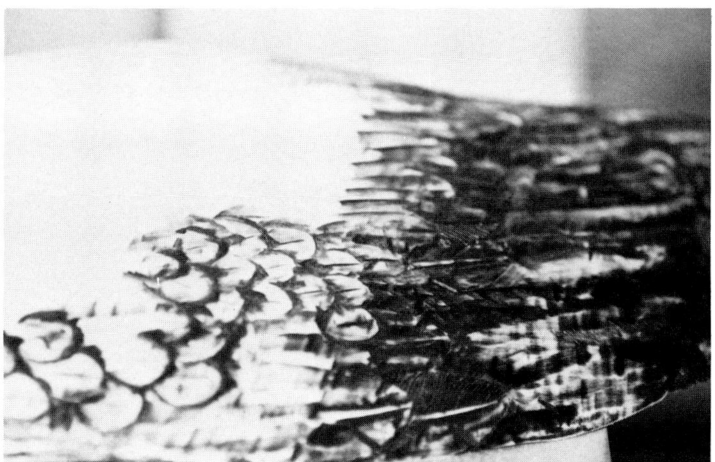

Some detail on wings

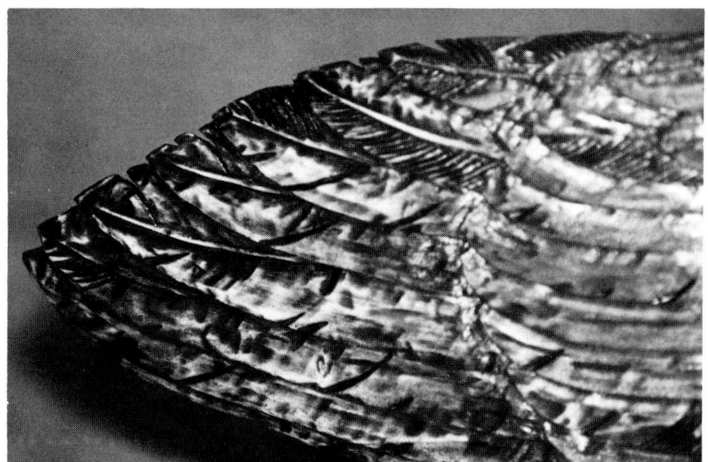

Close up primary detail

(See page 180 for painting instructions and page 289 for patterns)

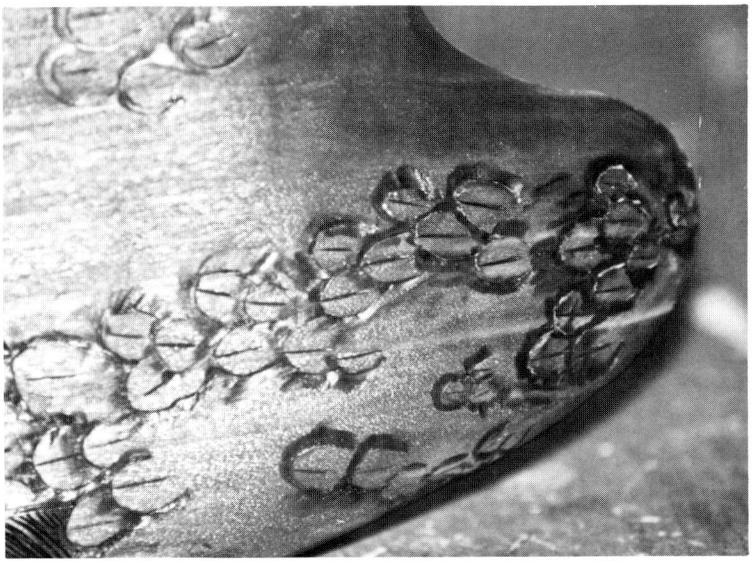

Detail on wing

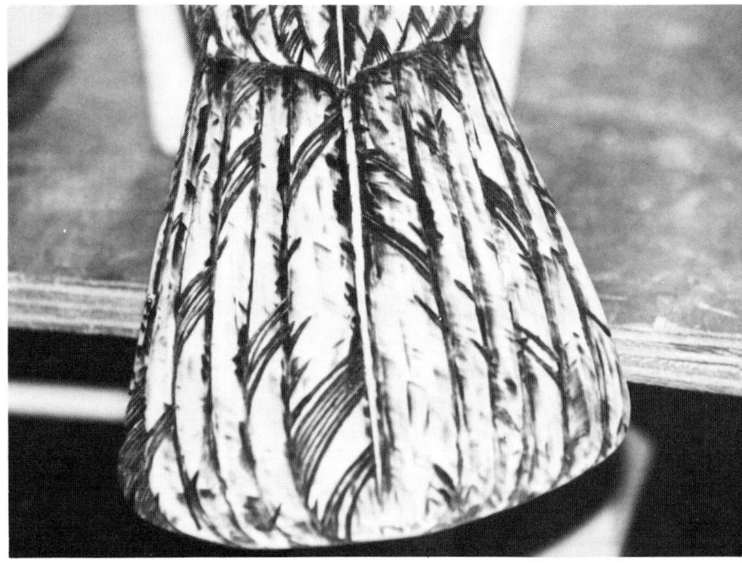

Detail on tail

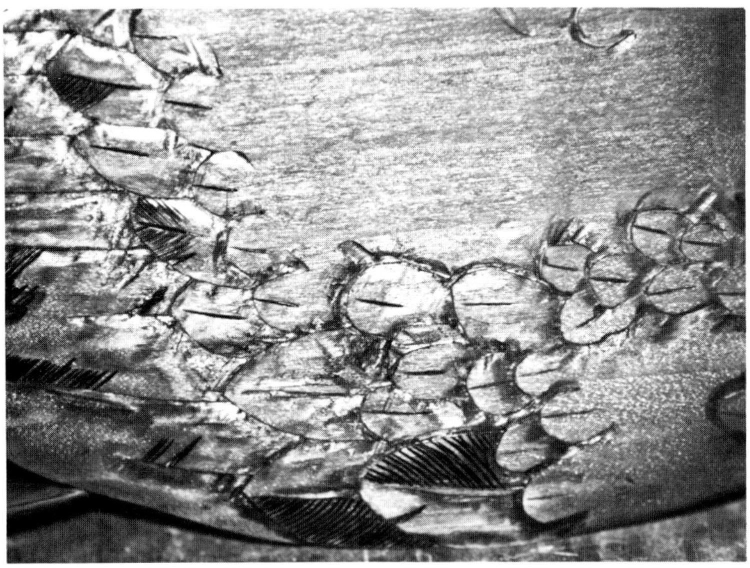

Close up detail on wing

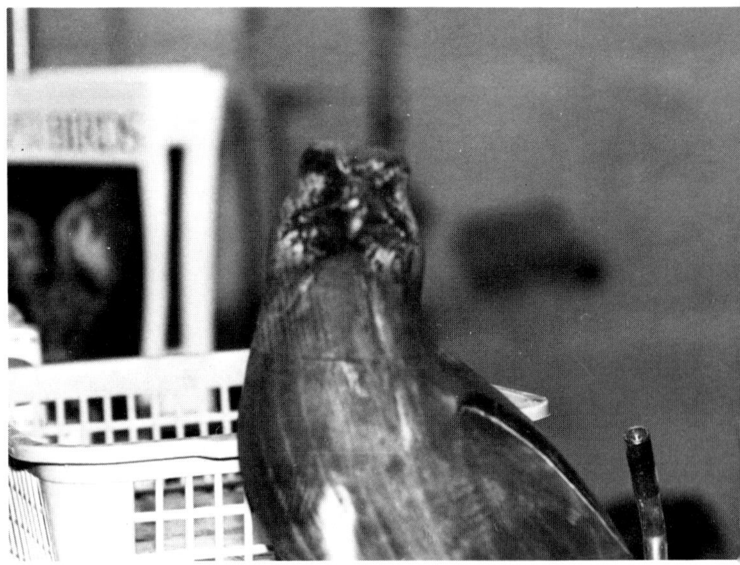

Head and body torched

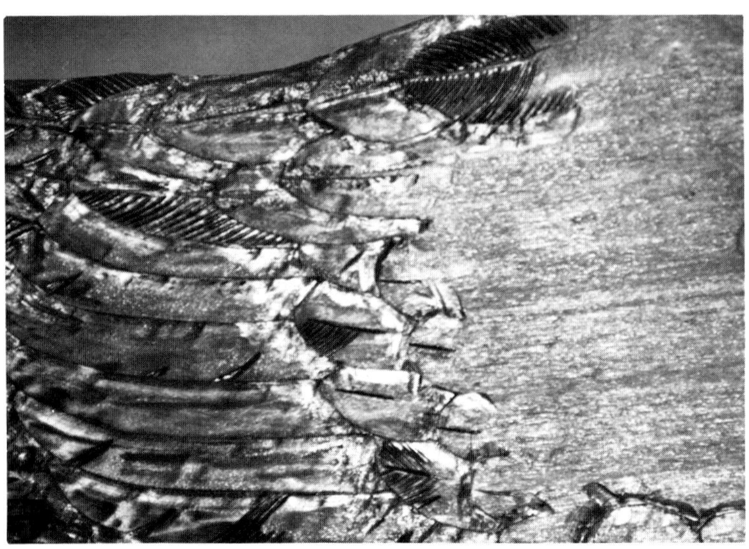

Further detail on wing

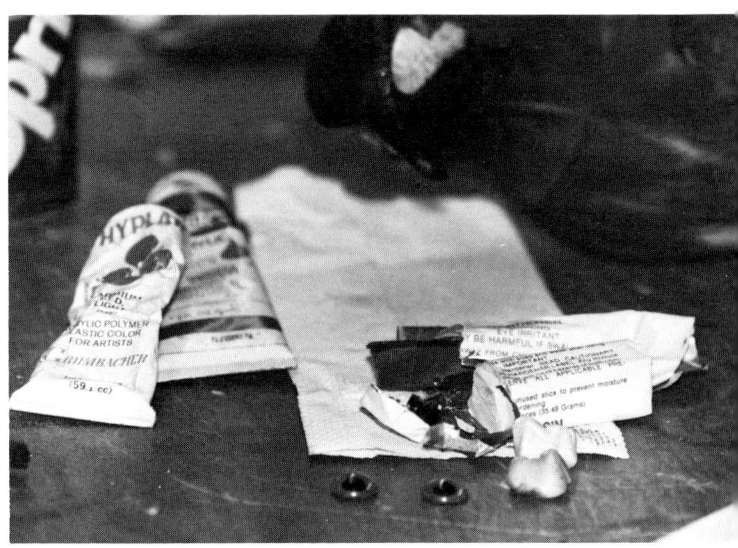

Putting in eye sockets and eye ready to set

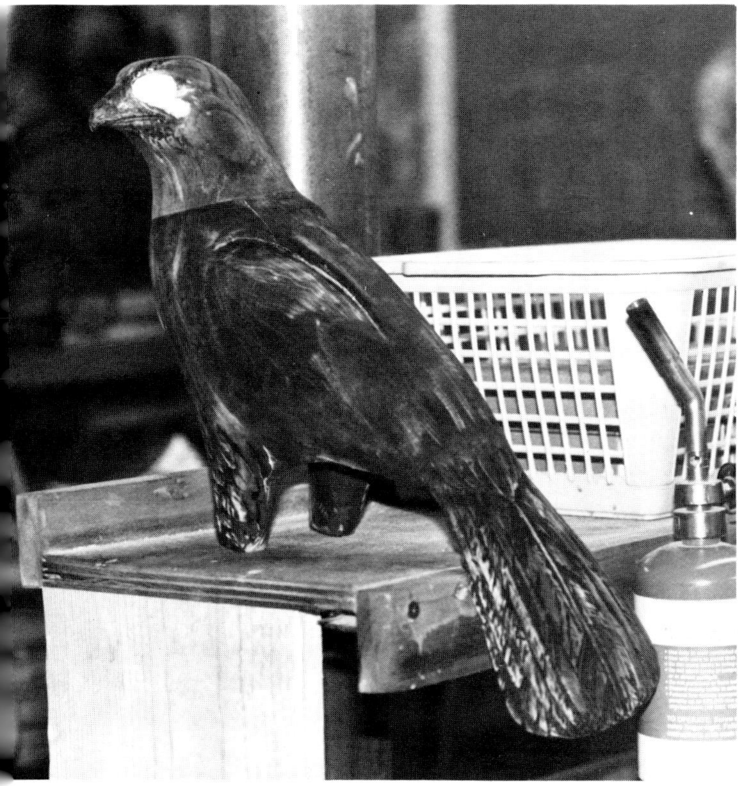

Full body burned and ready for eyes

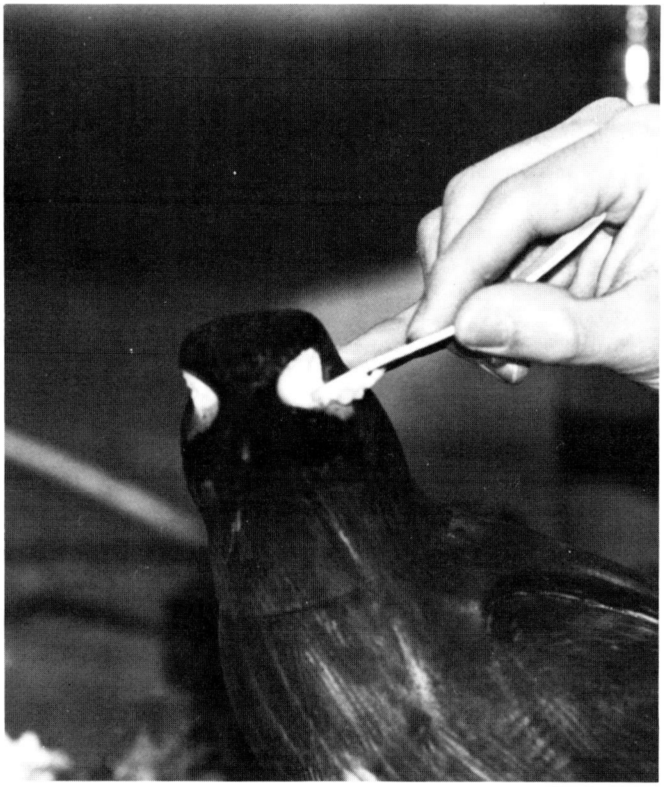

Removing excess putty with craft stick

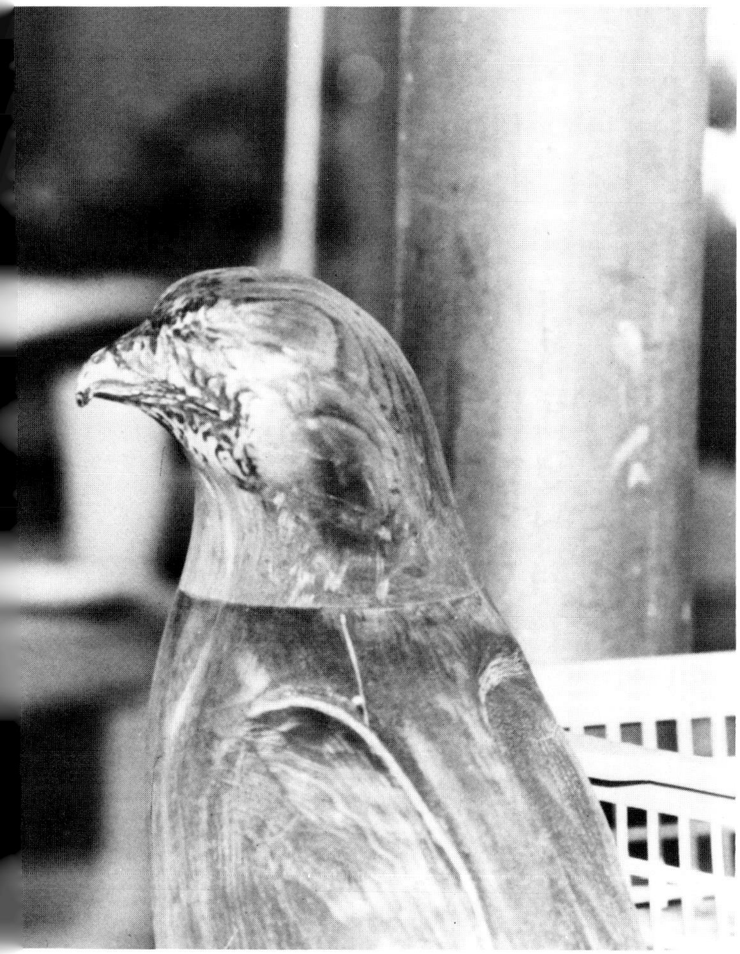

Another view of body burned and ready for eyes

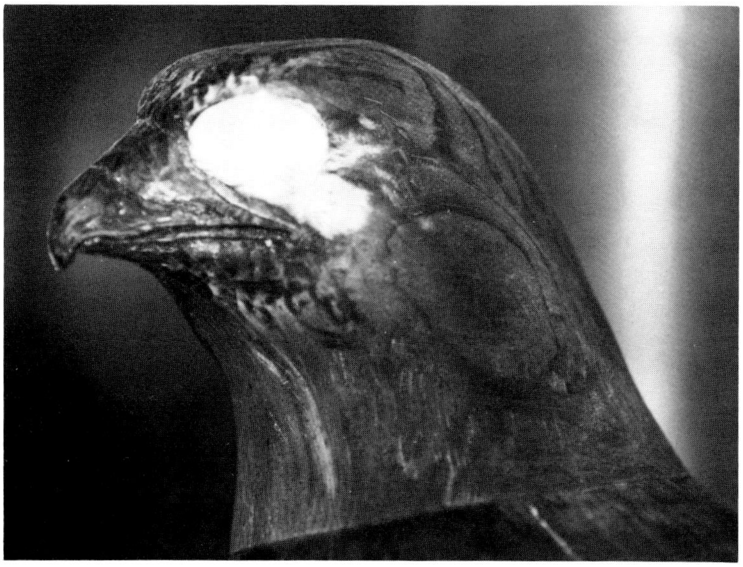

Close up of head ready for eyes

Red-Tailed Hawk

Carved by Paul Suarez

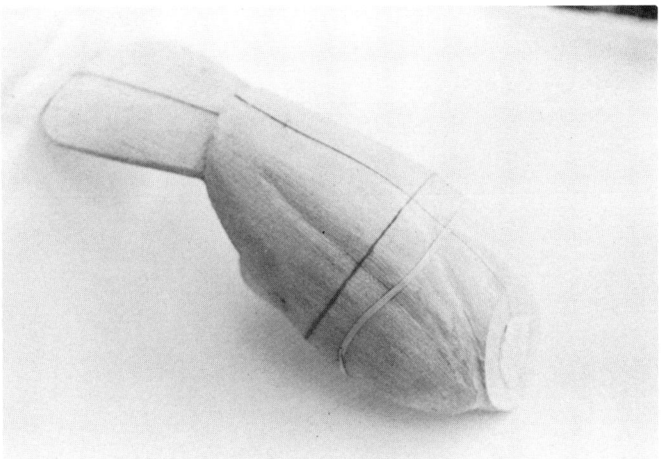

Two piece block tacked together with dots of epoxy so the body may be shaped prior to hollowing

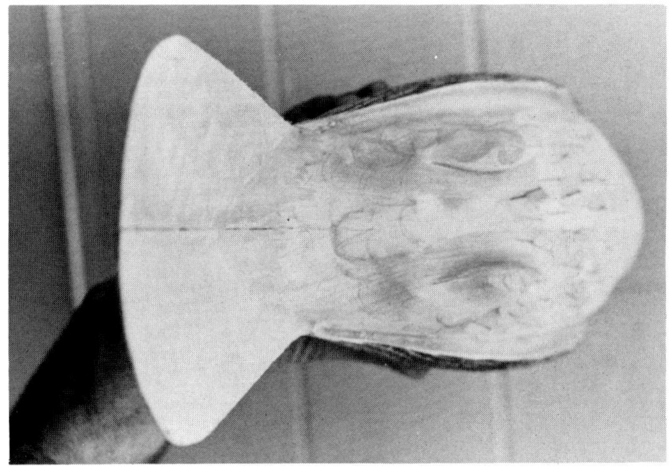

Two pieces back together

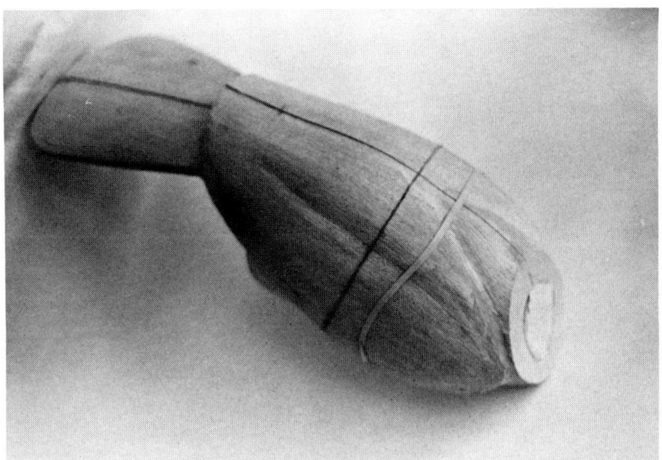

Another view of above

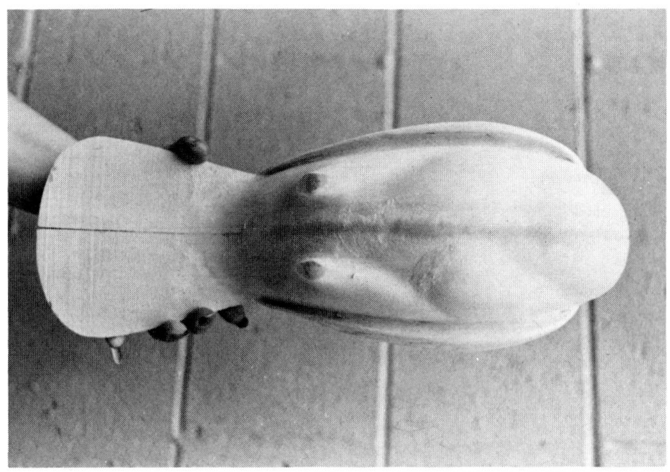

Body shaped and sanded

Separated blocks for hollowing to lighten weight and to relieve internal stress of wood

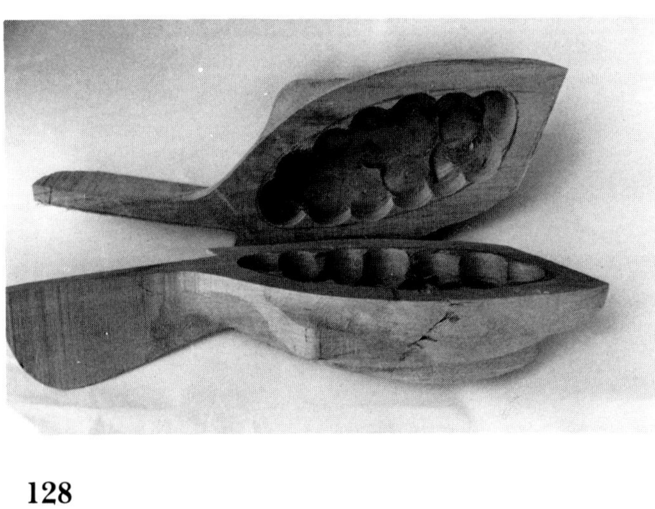

Two pieces held together with rubber bands

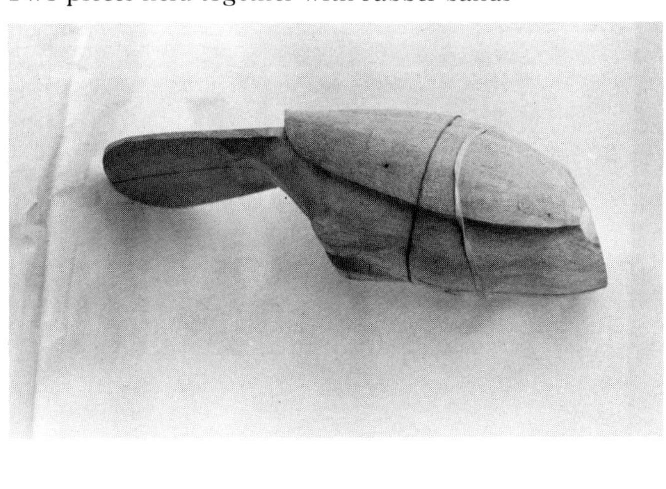

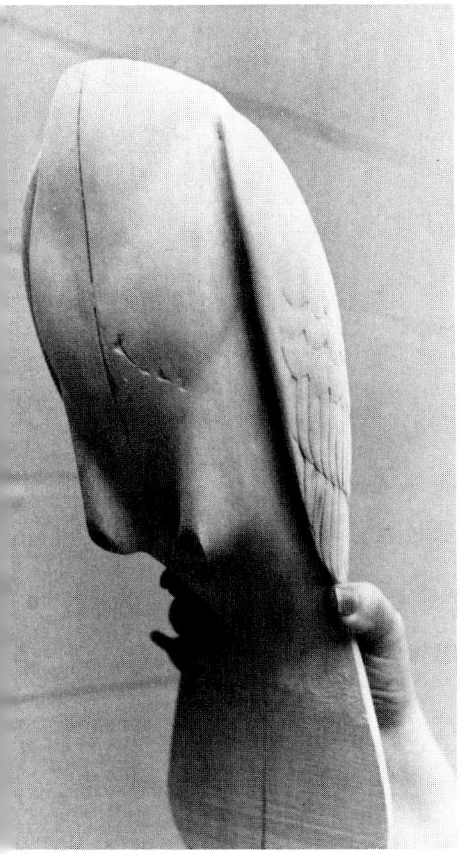

Front view of sanded body

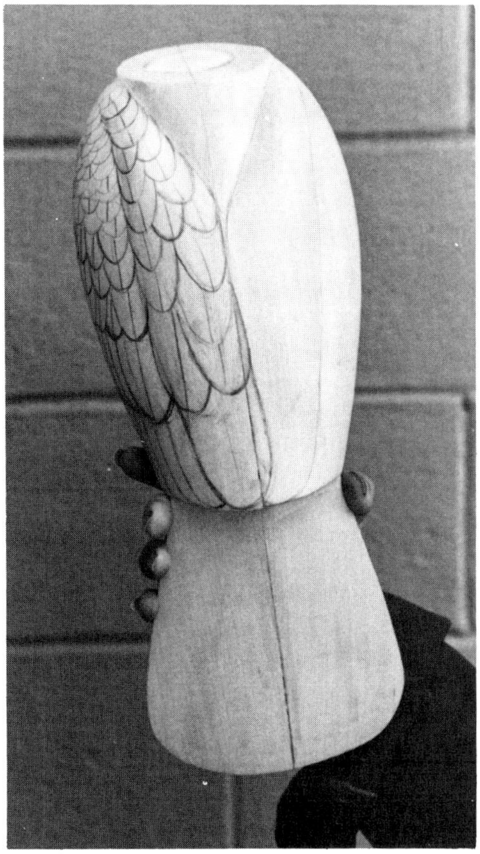

Pencil lay out on back (wing)

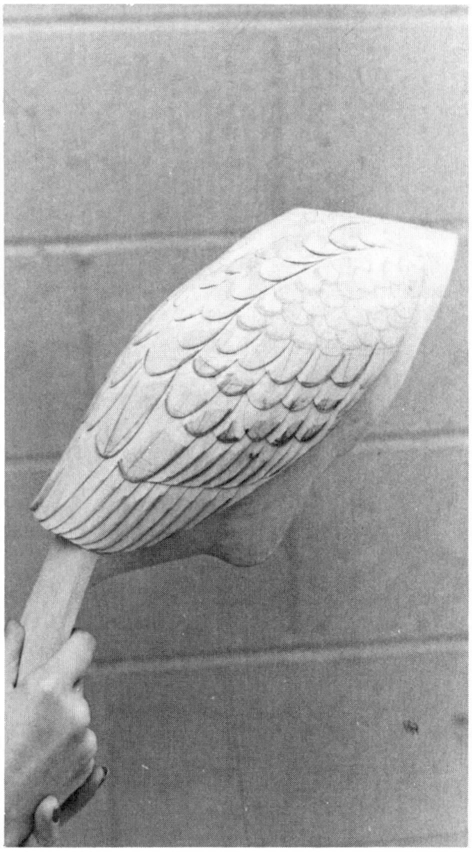

Side of wing carved

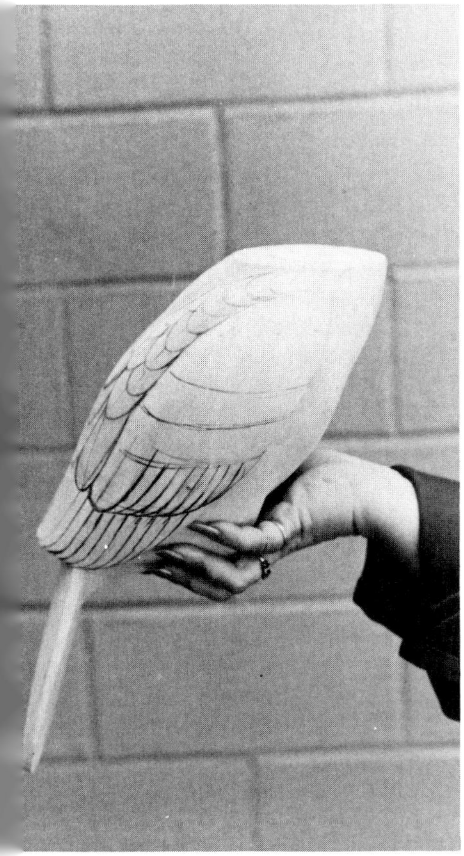

Pencil lay out on wing

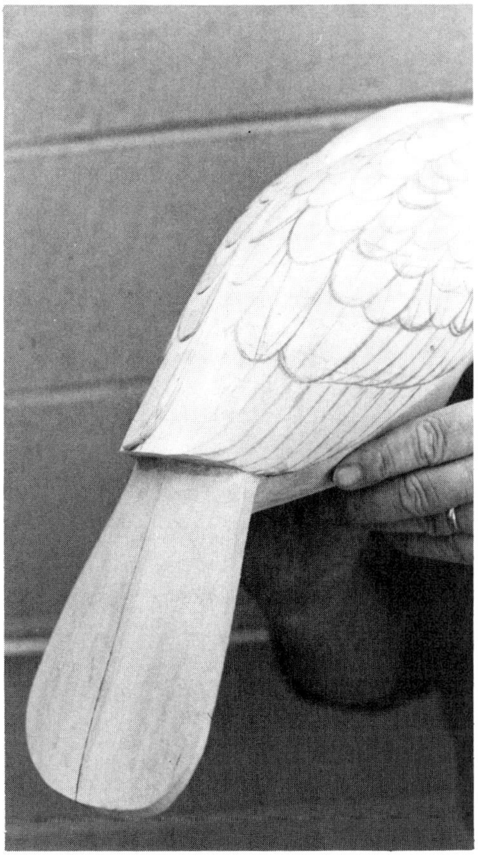

Close up of tertial and secondary areas

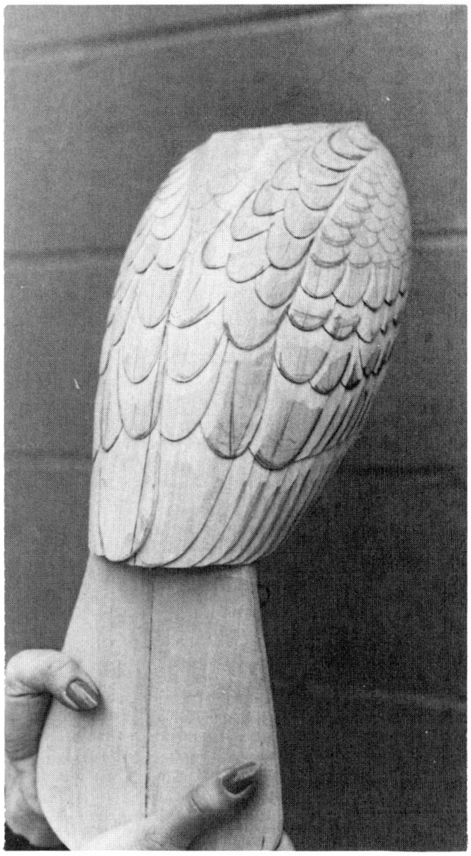

Side and back of wing carved

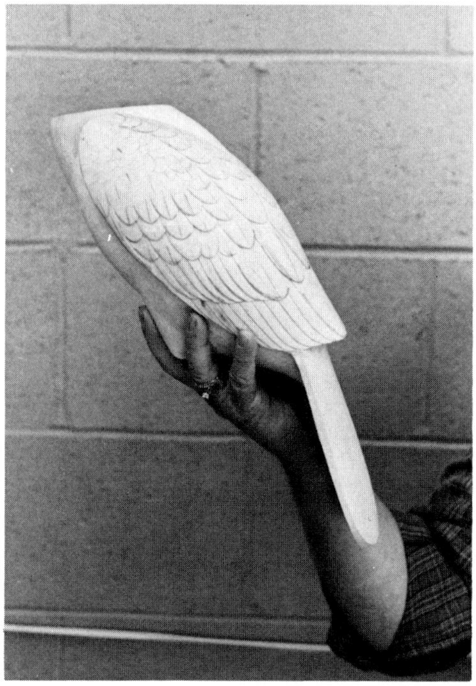

Profile with feather lay out on wing

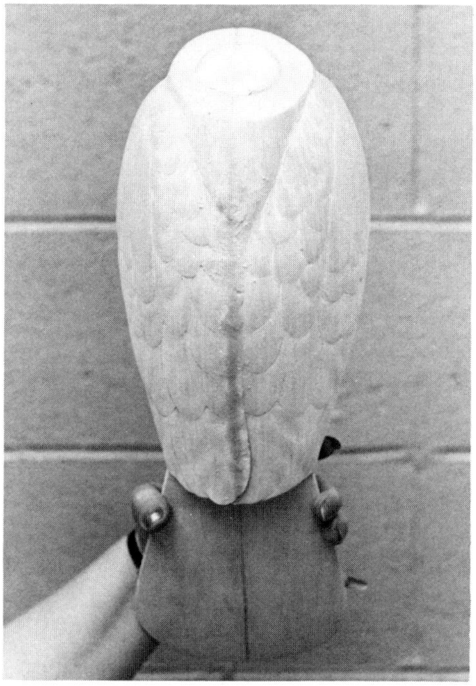

Back view with contoured feathers (ruby carvers) sanded

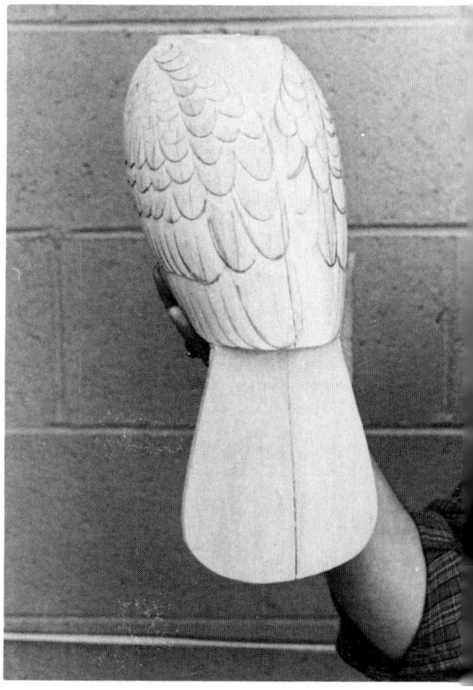

Another view of back

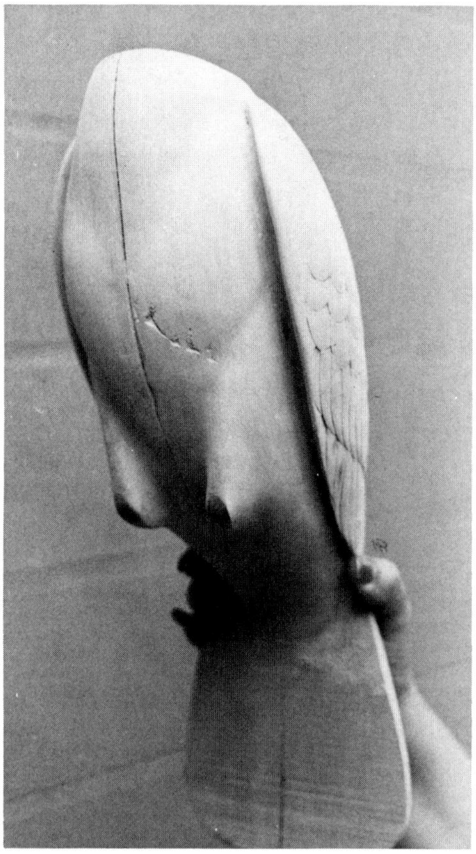

Sanded body showing leg shanks

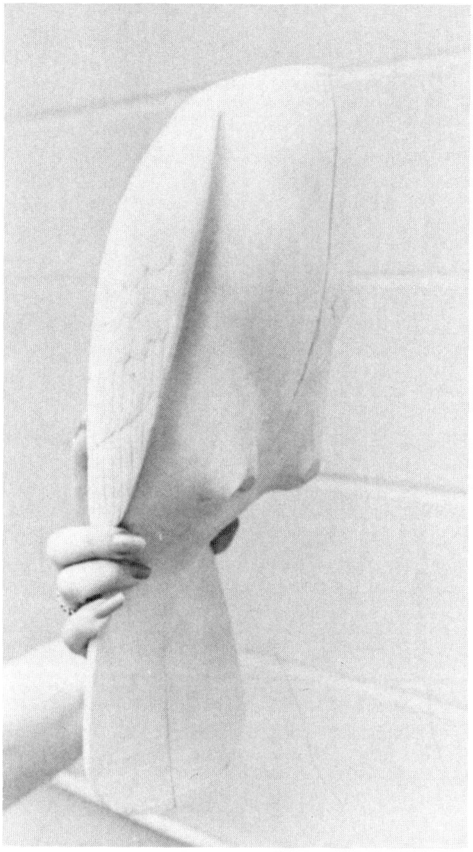

Sanded body showing leg shanks on right side

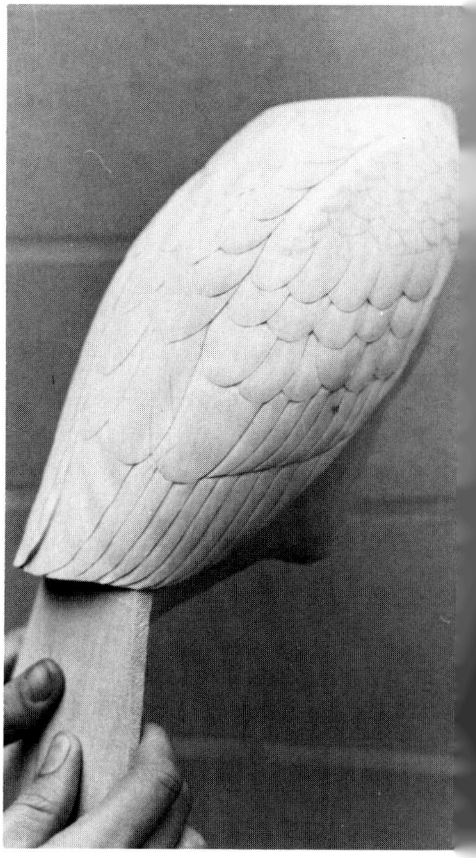

Side and back showing carved feathers—note: raised left tertial group to accommodate crossed primaries

(See page 174 for painting instructions and page 298 for patterns)

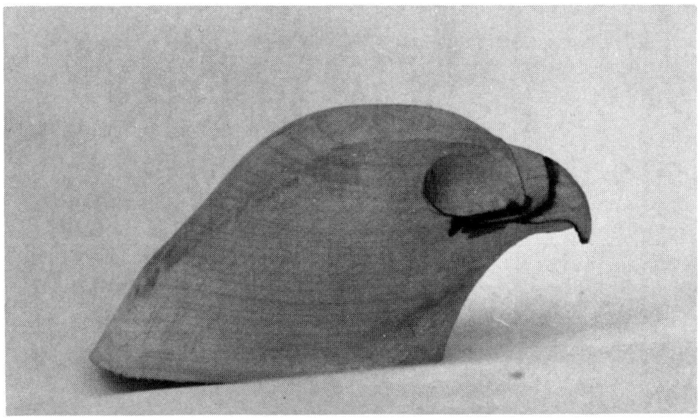

Profile of head carved and sanded with eye holes drilled

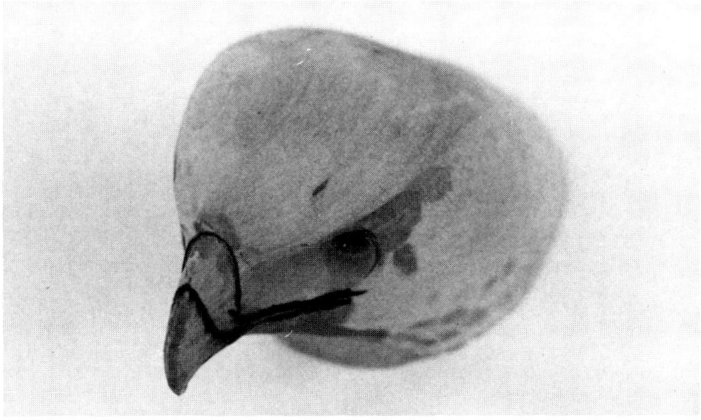

Top view of head with bill detail

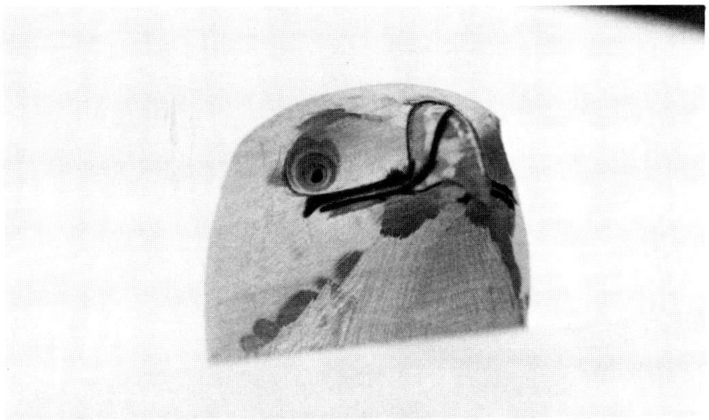

Front view of head with beak detail—note: angle of eye holes

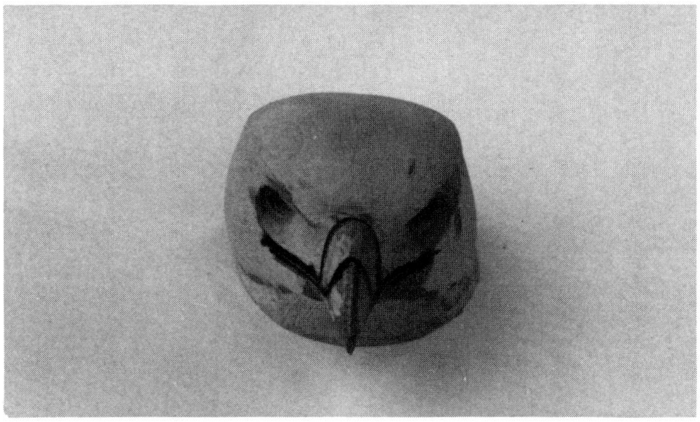

Front view of head with both eye holes

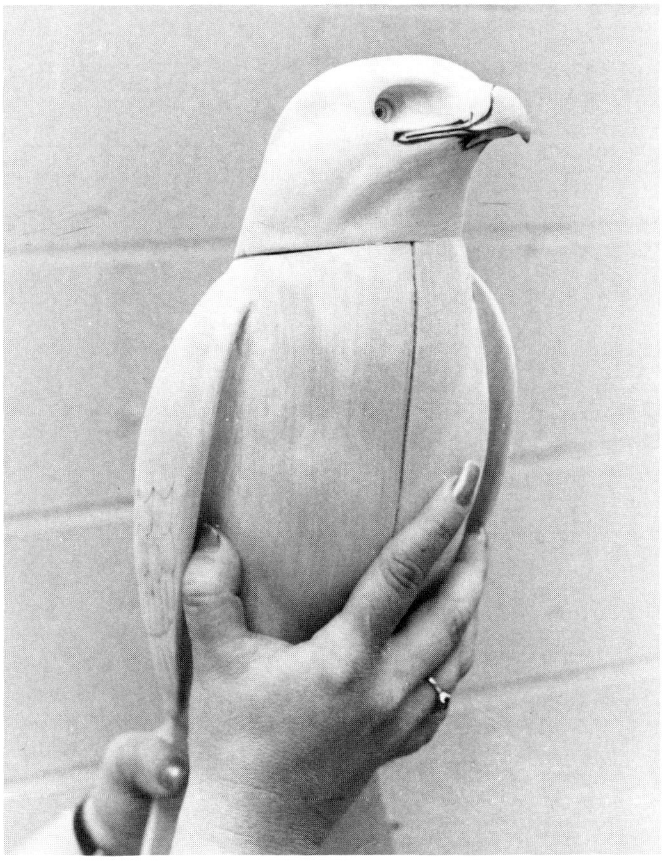

Temporary head set in order to shape and flow into body

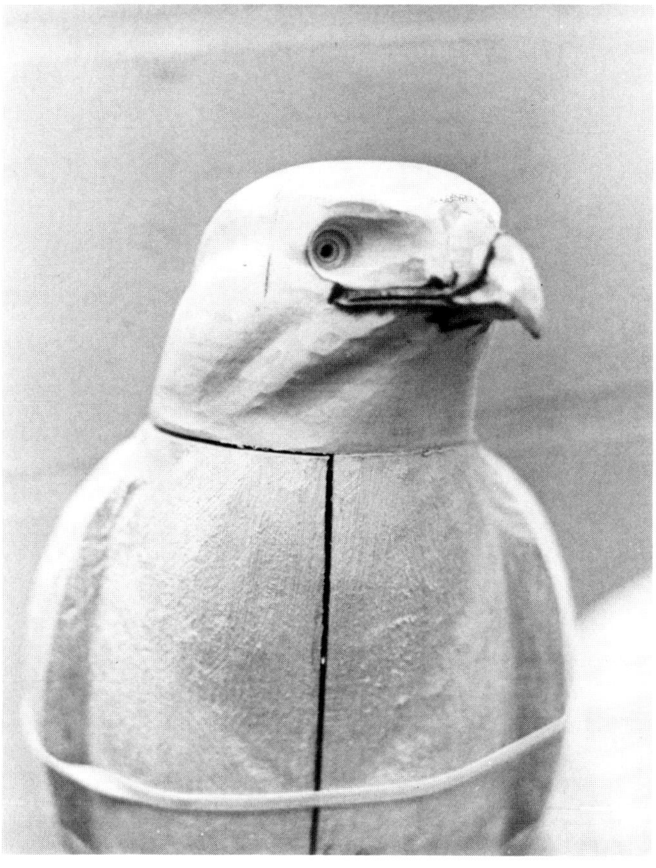

Close profile of head joining body

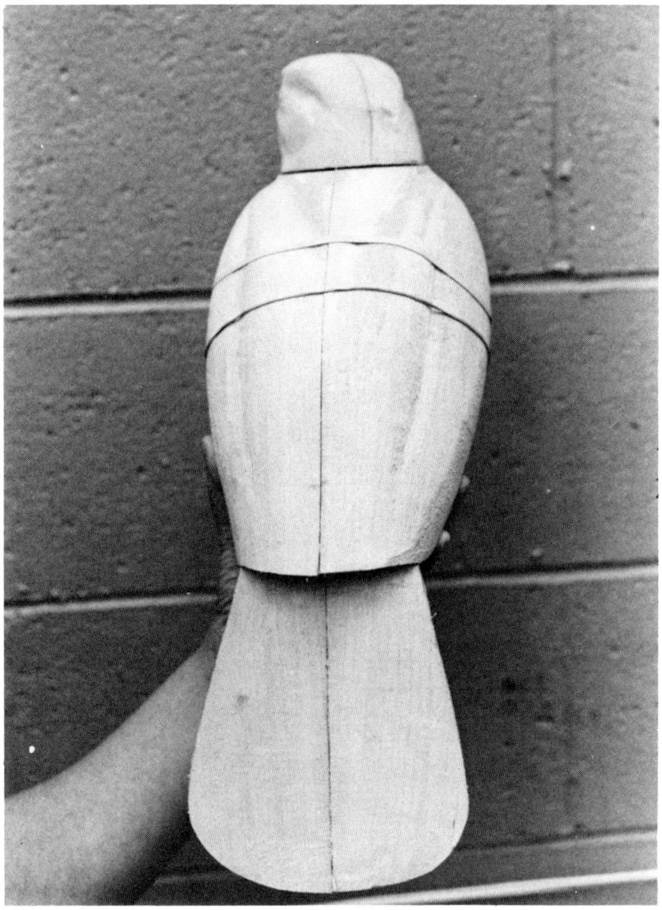

Back view of head flowing into body

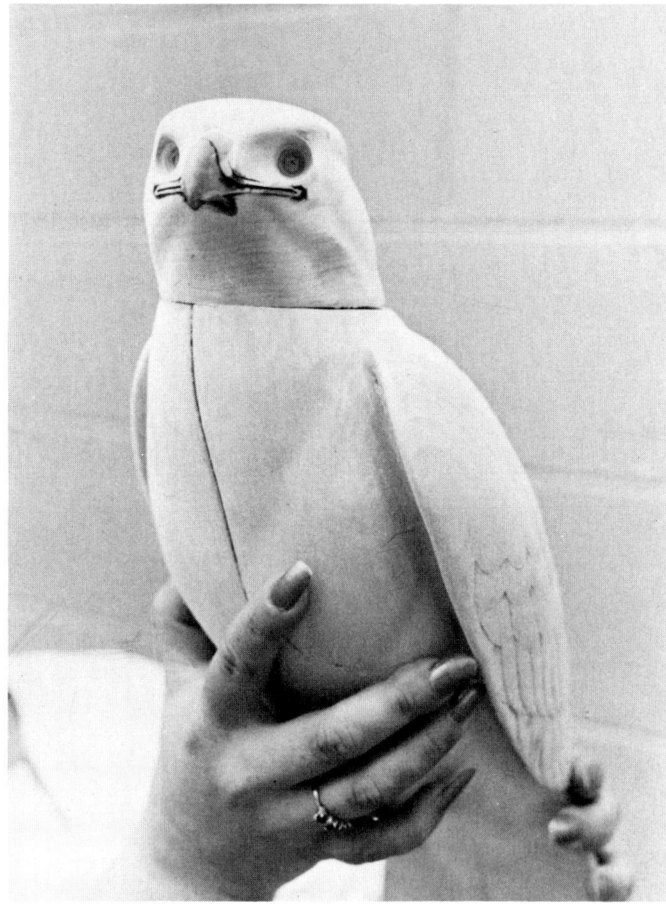

Left front view of head—note: musculature in cheek and neck areas

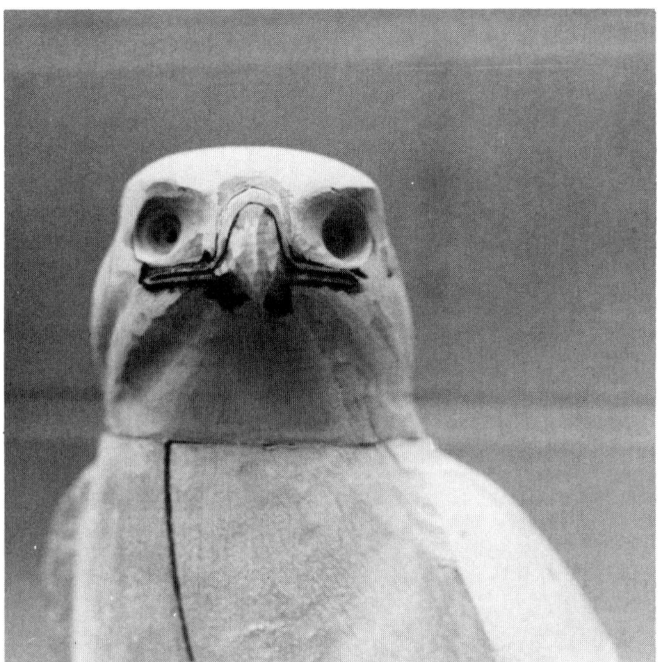

Front view of head with beak detail flowing into body

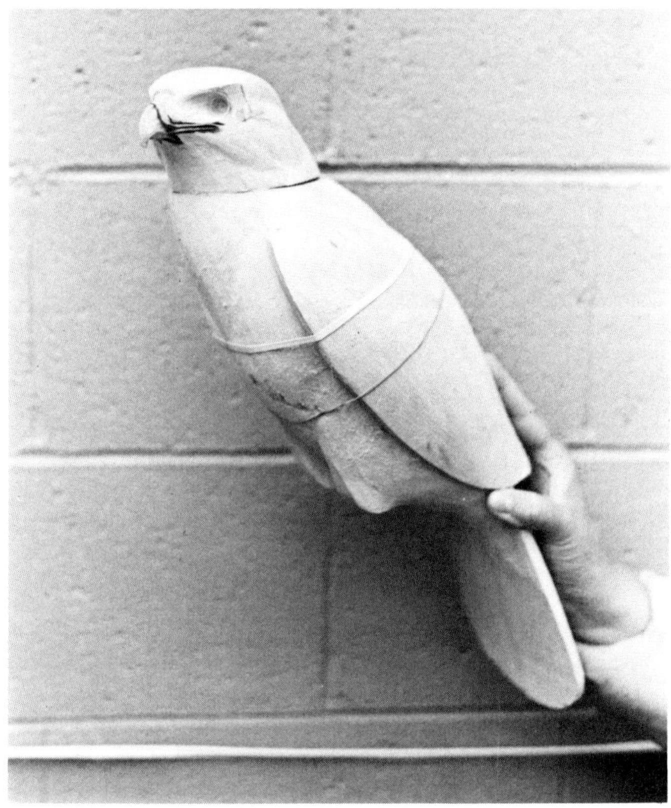

Profile of head and body

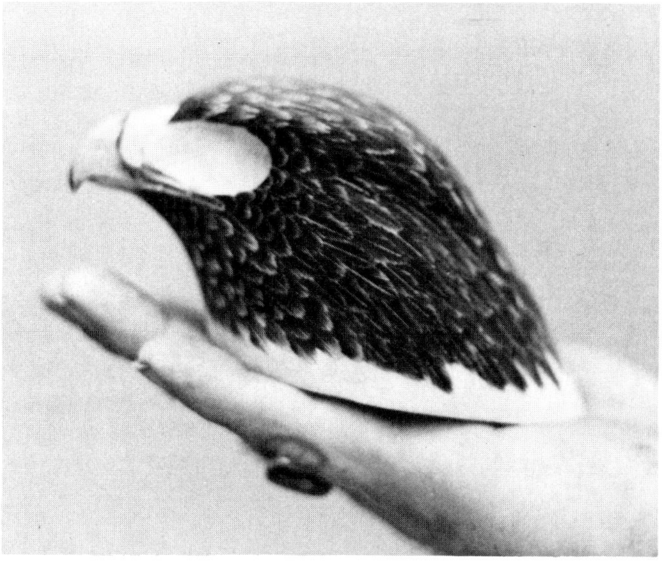

Head burned and eye holes fill with epoxy putty, preparatory to setting eyes

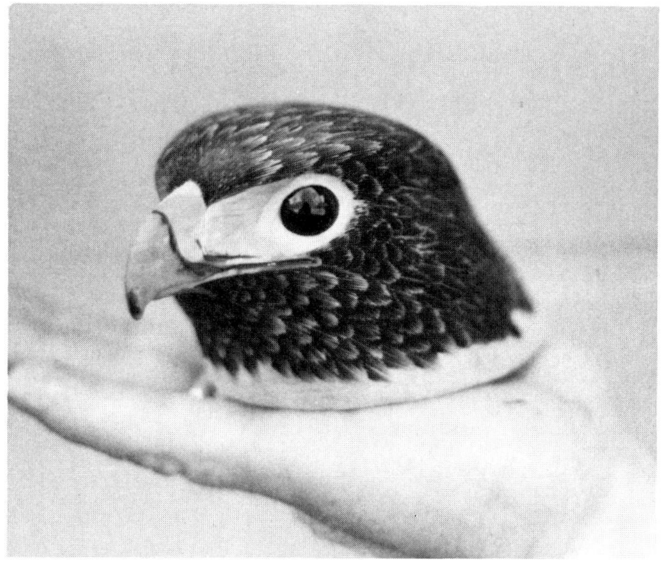

Eyes set—note: angle left side

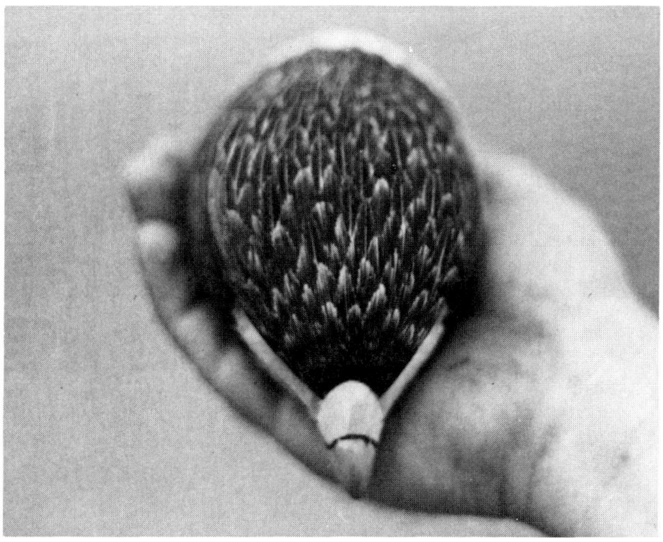

Top view of head burned—note: feather pattern

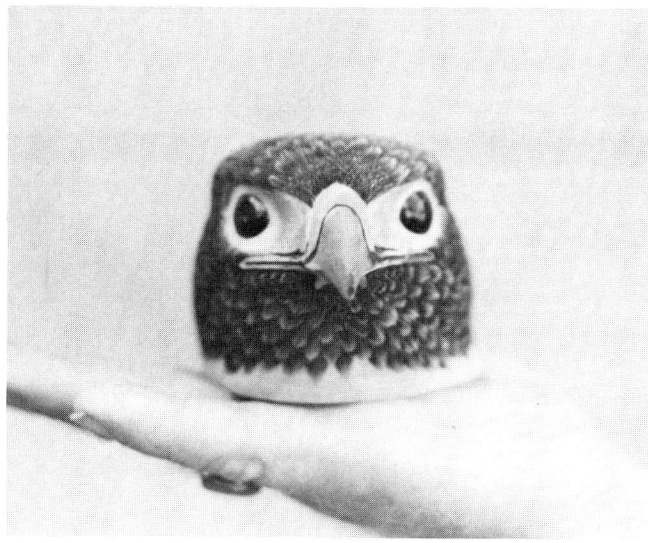

Front view of eyes

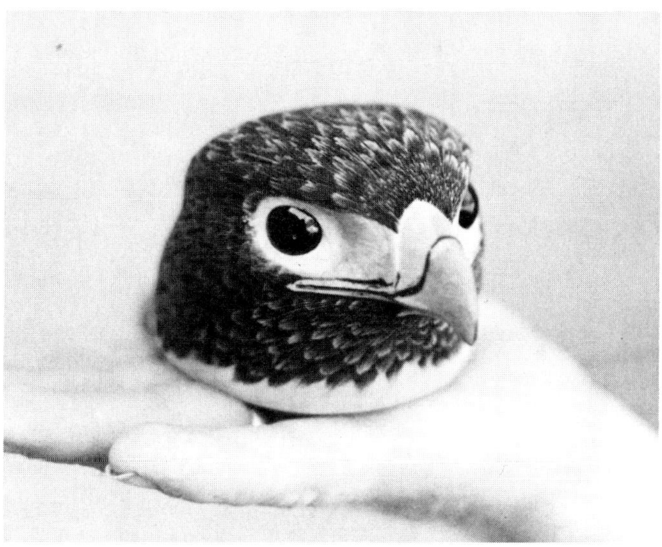

Eye set—note: angle right side

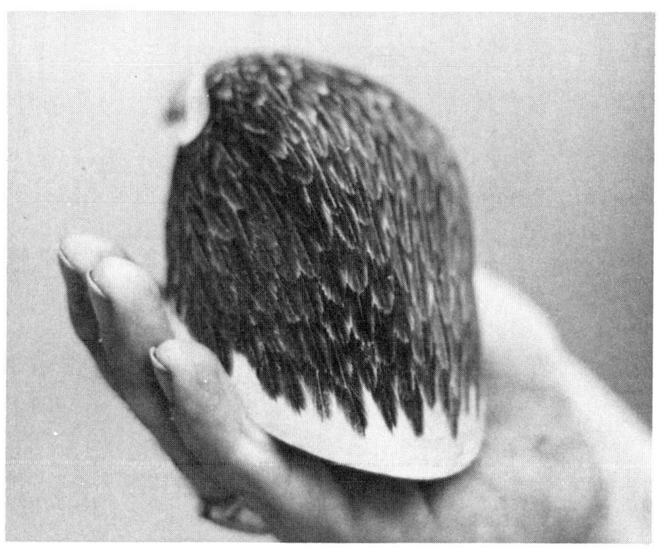

Eyes taped to protect them from being scratched

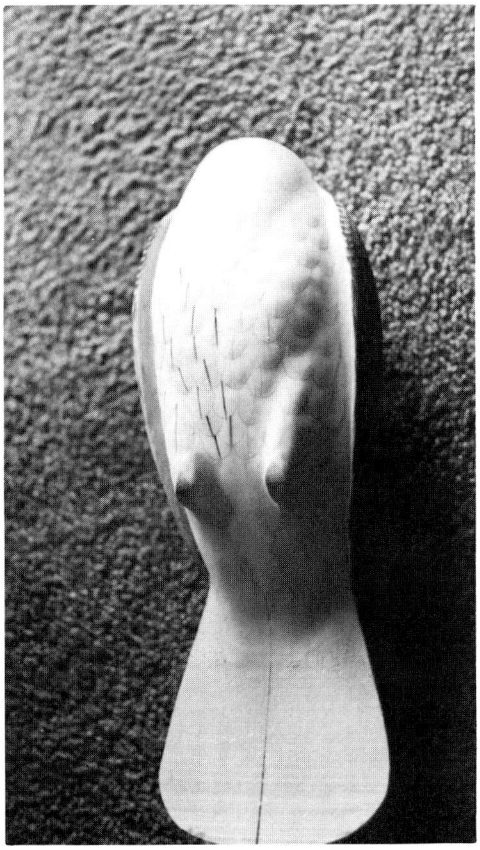

Belly carved and sanded—note: gentle roundness of each feather this is achieved by using ruby carvers

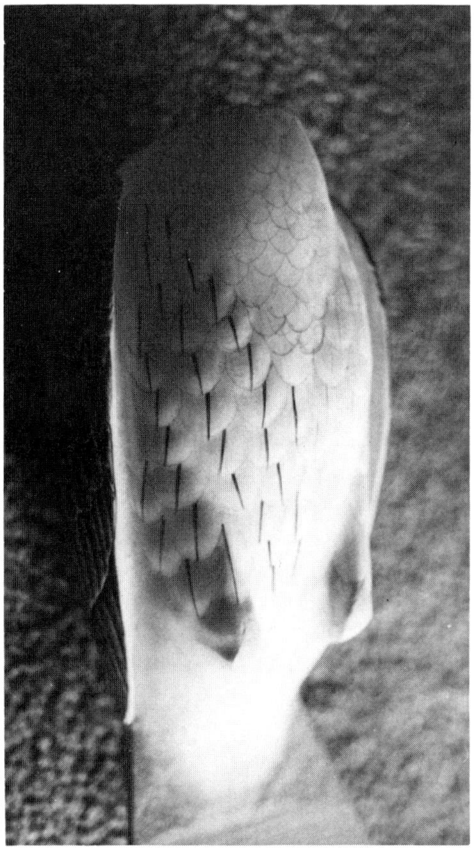

Another view of quills burned in on the belly

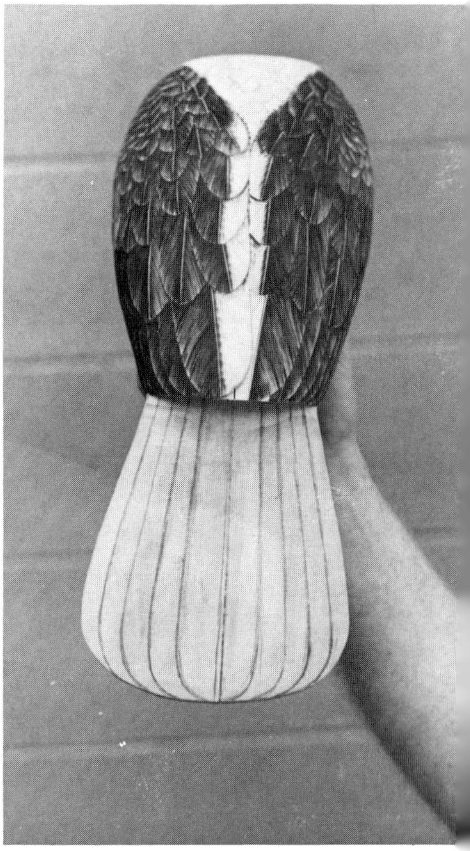

Upper side of tail carved

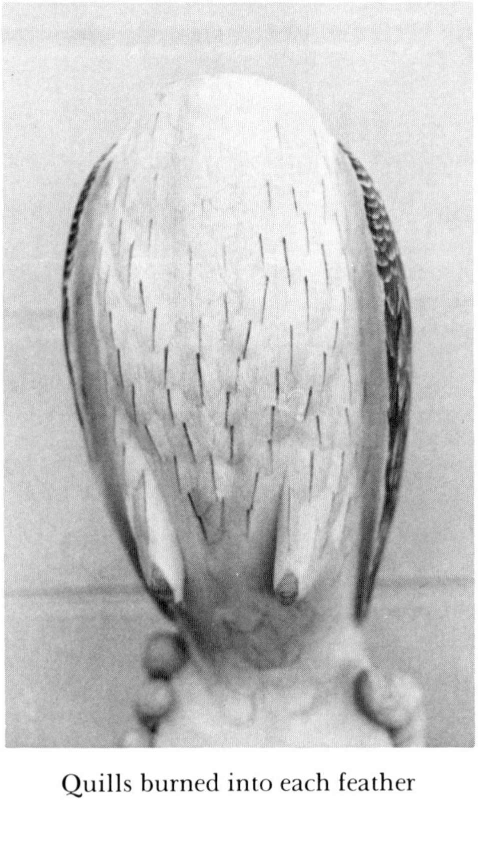

Quills burned into each feather

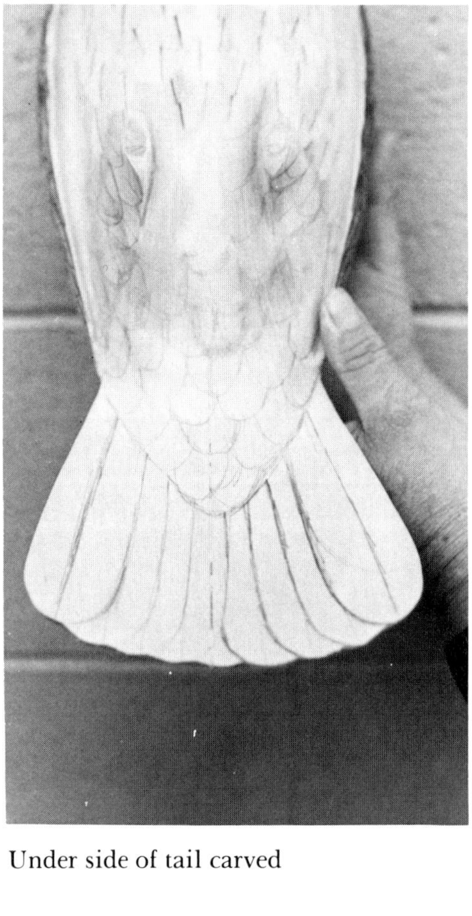

Under side of tail carved

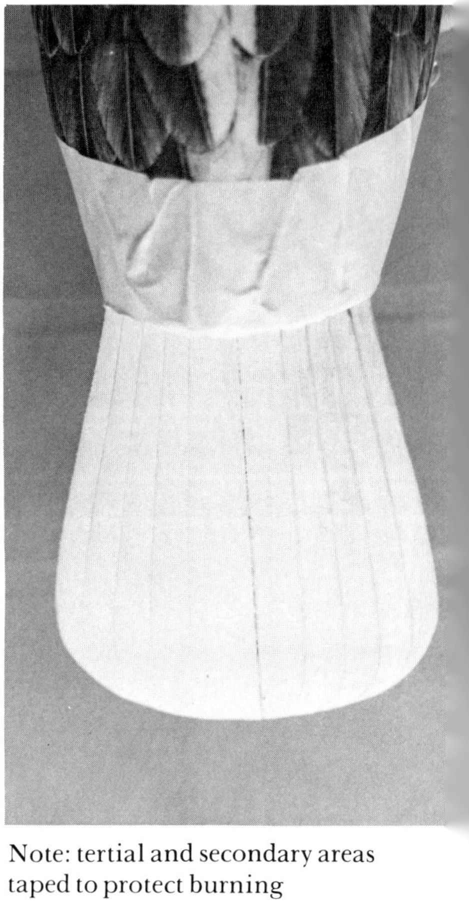

Note: tertial and secondary areas taped to protect burning

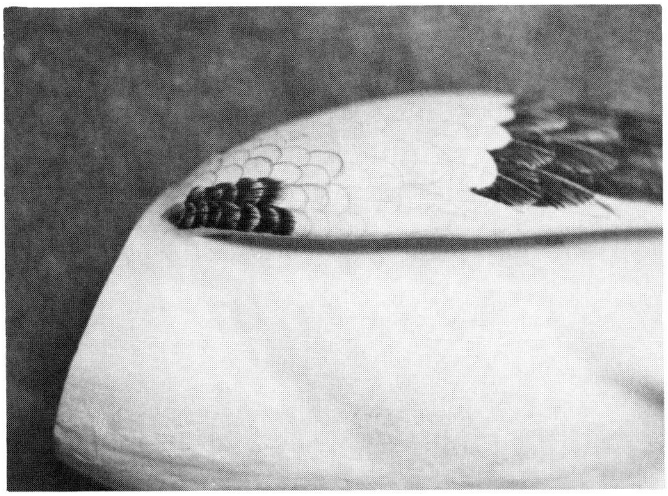

Burning of feather pattern on wing

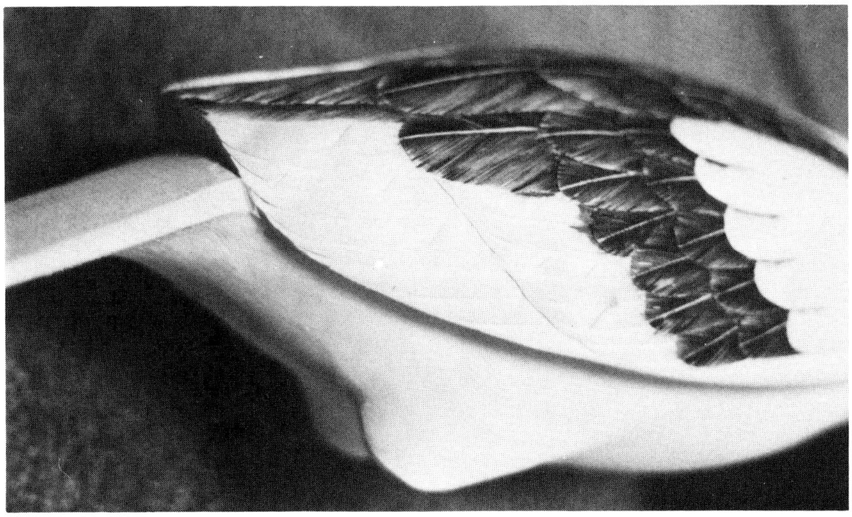

Carved secondaries and coverts scapulars burned

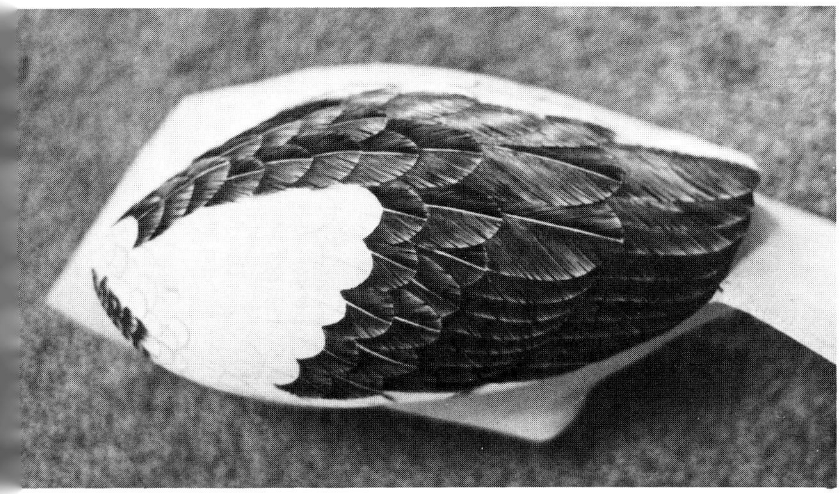

Wing burning in progress

Entire wing burned

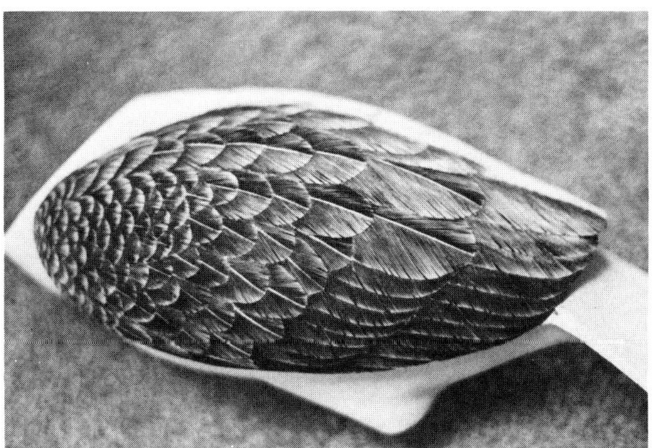

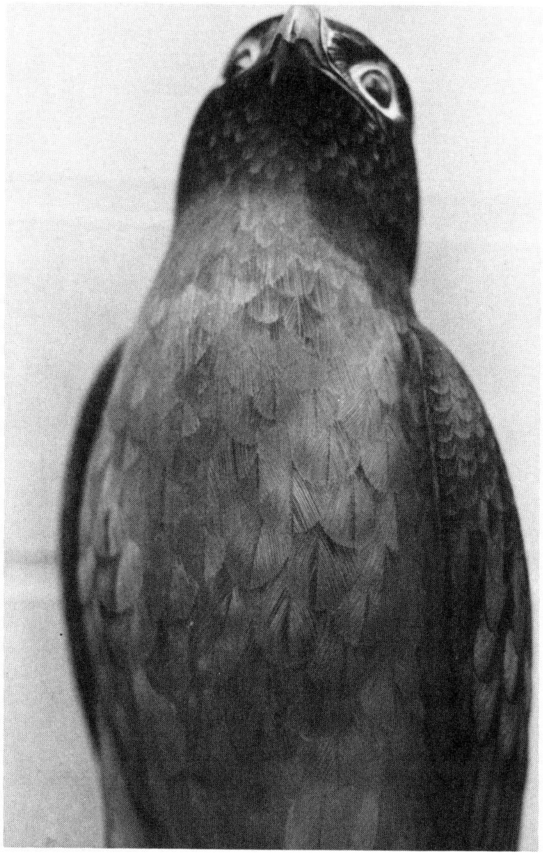

Head set and filled with wood dough (use lots of acetone to break down all air gaps) belly stoned

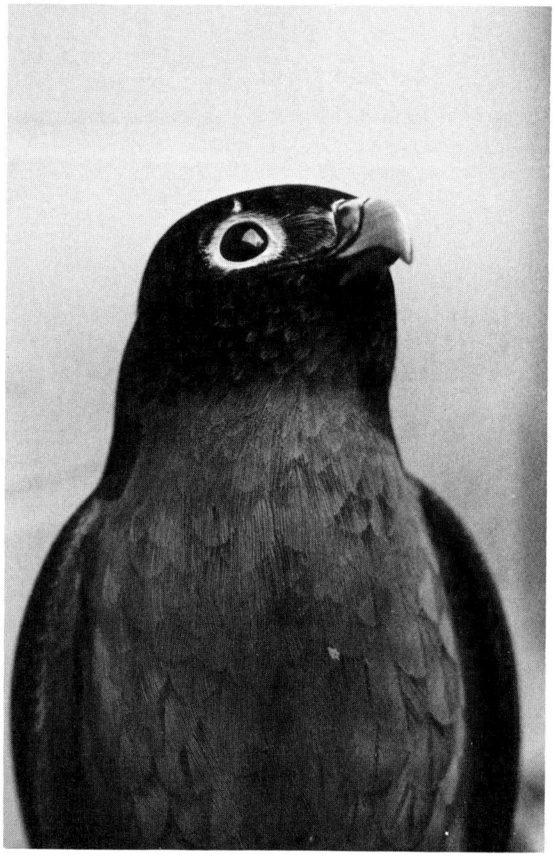

Chest area stoned

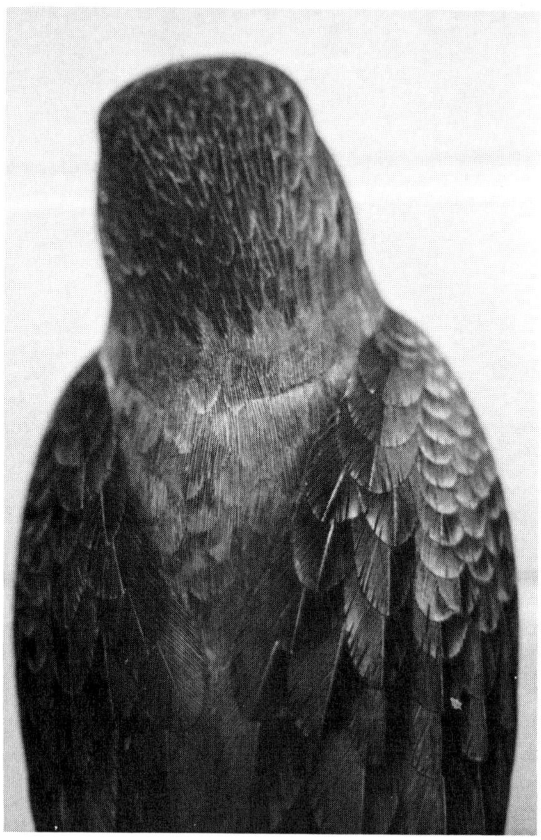

Back view burned

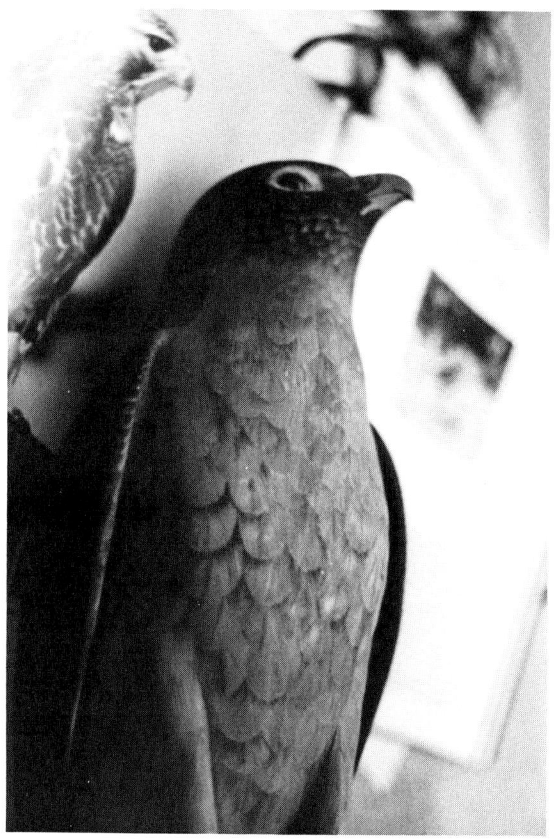

Note: under cutting of wings to create separation from body, bird is ready to paint

Color Charts

Painting Instructions

GRAY SCREECH OWL

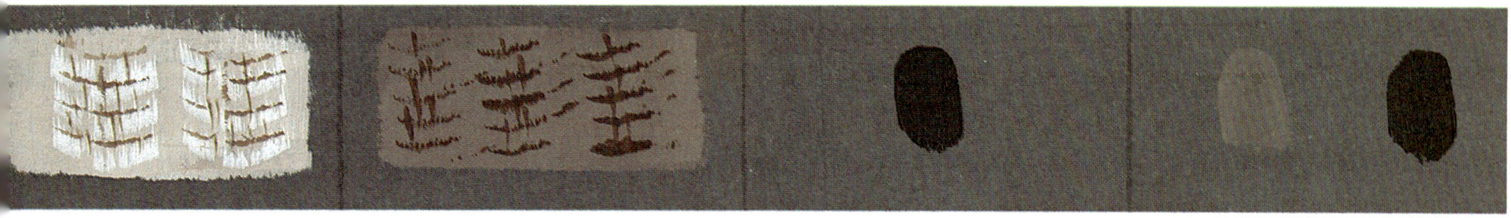

1-Belly
Undercoat with white & gesso & burnt umber (light tan)—edge with white & put in thin brown bars

2-Back, head & tail
Undercoat with darker tan (same mix only add more burnt umber plus tiny amount of black
Burnt umber bars & streaks to resemble vermiculation

3-Beak
Black

4-Feet
Tannish
Black—talons

RED SCREECH OWL

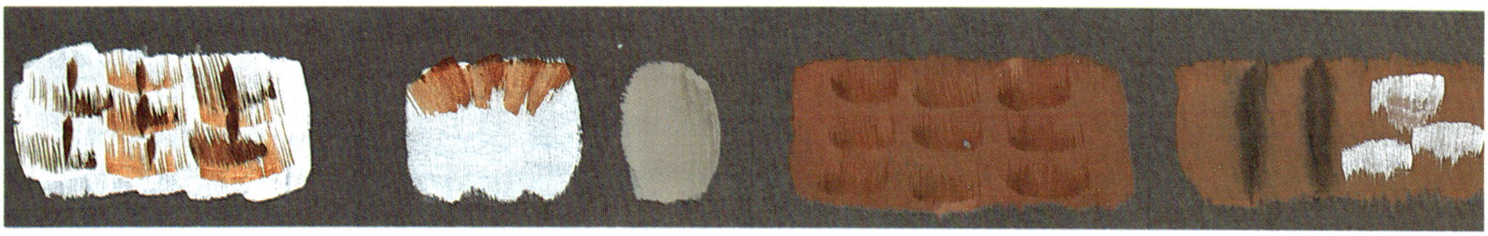

1-Belly
White & gesso
Edgings of burnt sienna & burnt umber

2-Face & back
White
Edge with burnt sienna
Bone color (Raw umber & white)

3-Head & neck
Burnt sienna mixed with white—edged with burnt sienna

4-Upper wing
Burnt sienna with white
Black bars

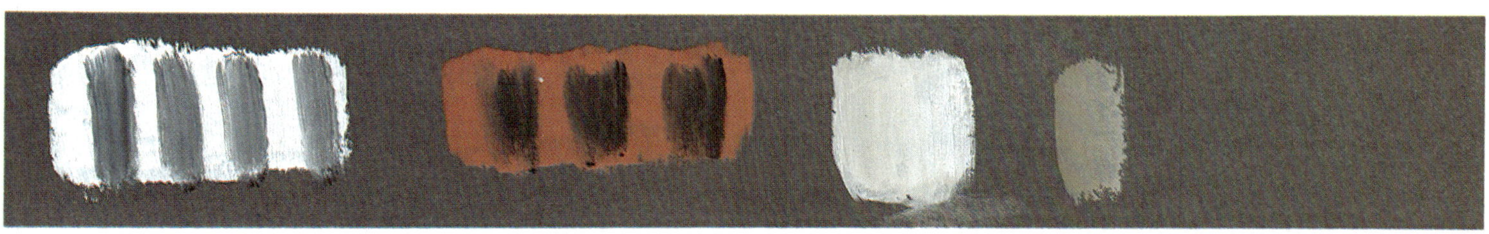

5-Under wing
White & gesso
Black bars

6-Upper tail
Burnt sienna & white
Faint black bars

7-Feet & talons
Whitish—feet
Gray—talons

SAW-WHET OWL

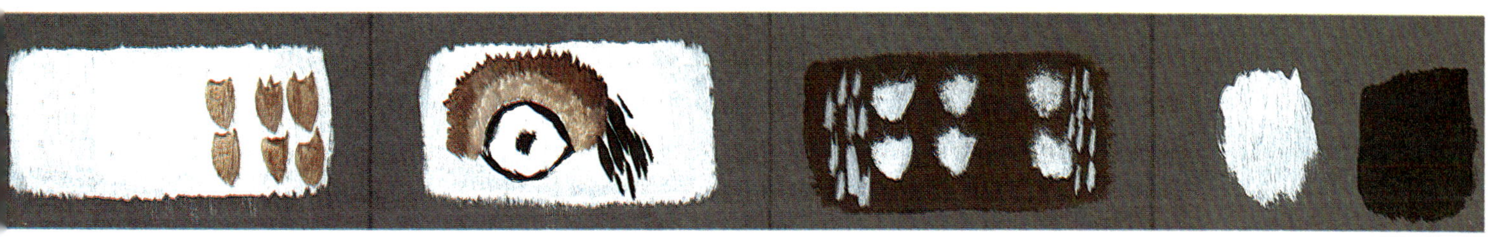

1-Belly
Gesso & white
Thin burnt umber
Spots

2-Facial discs
White & gesso
Thin burnt umber
Outer ring full
Burnt umber
Black streaks

3-Back & Head
Burnt umber
Streaks & spots
White

4-Feet & talons
Feet—white
Talons—black

SNOWY OWL

1-Entire bird
Burnt umber & gesso (tan)

2-Entire bird
Tan undercoat
White feather edging

3-Head, cape & tail
Burnt umber bars

4-Talons & Beak
Black

OSPREY

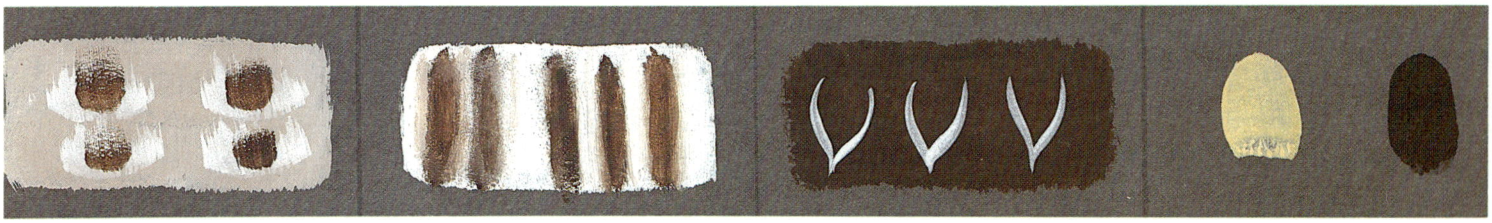

1-Chest, belly & head
Tan undercoat
Gesso & burnt umber
Edged with white then washed with white & gesso
Burnt umber on interiors of some of chest feathers

2-Underwing & tail
White/burnt umber
Stippled

3-Back & top of wings
Burnt umber
Edged with white

4-Beak
Yellow ochre & white
Black

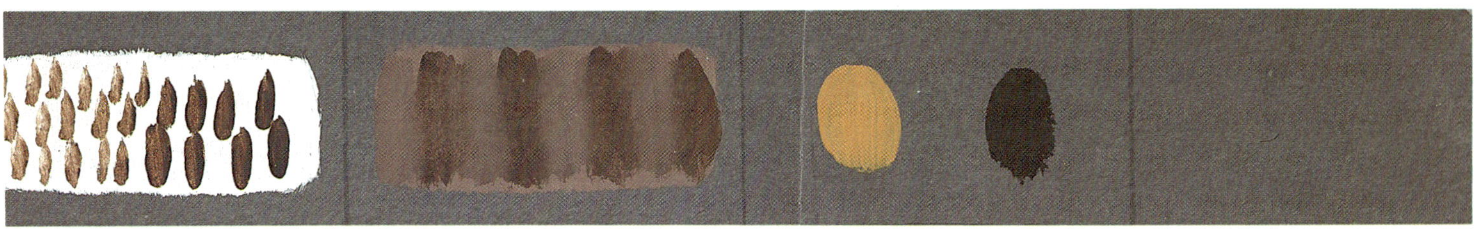

5-Head
Undercoat white & gesso

6-Upper tail
Tan (white & burnt umber) and brown (burnt umber)
Bars

7-Feet & talons
Feet—yellow ochre
Talons—black

AMERICAN KESTREL

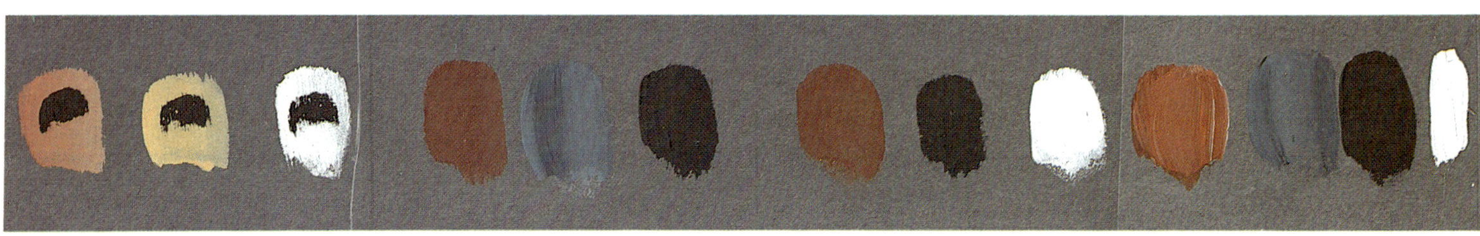

1-Belly
Burnt sienna
Yellow ochre with white
White
Black

2-Back
Burnt sienna
Paynes gray & white
Black

3-Tail
Burnt sienna
Black & white

4-Head
Burnt sienna
Paynes gray & white
Black & white

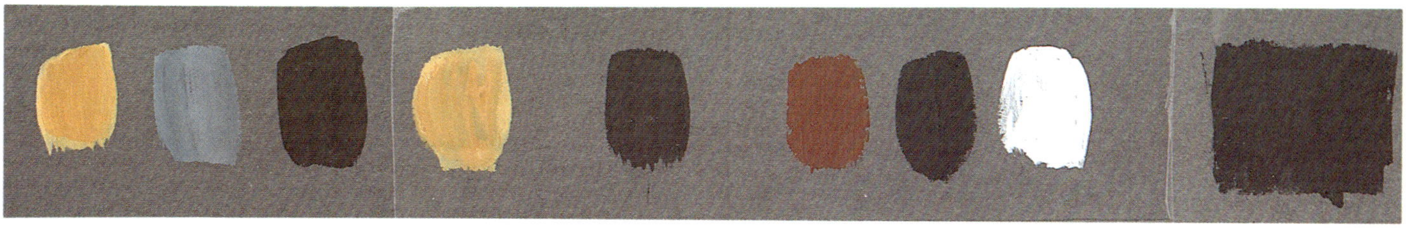

5-Beak
Yellow ochre & white
Paynes gray & white
Black

6-Feet
Yellow ochre
Black

7-Under tail
Burnt sienna
Black
White

8-Primaries
Black

FEMALE MERLIN

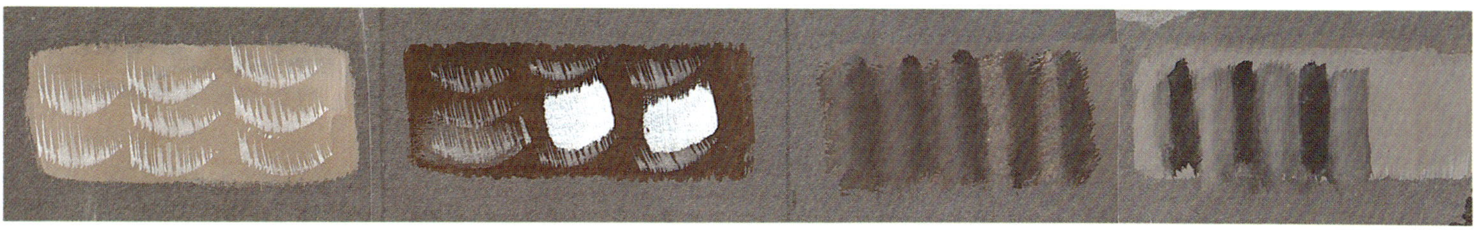

1-Belly
White & gesso
Burnt umber mixed to make
pale tan feathers edged with white.

2-Back & wings
Burnt umber
Some feathers spotted with white

3-Tail
Tan & grown bars

4-Underside tail
Black & white bars

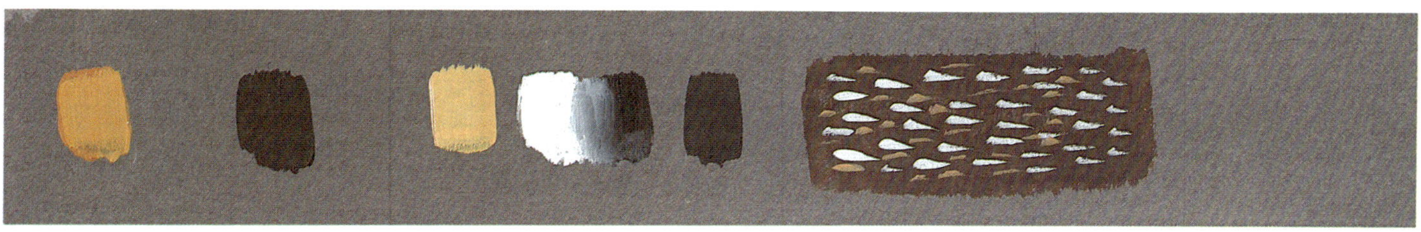

5-Feet & talons
Feet—yellow ochre
Talons—black

6-Beak
Yellow ochre
Paynes gray & white
Edged with raw sienna & white

7-Head
Burnt umber
Streaked with white

PEREGRIN FALCON

1-Chest & belly
White gesso mixed with
raw sienna
Wash with yellow ochre

2-Under wings
Black
White
Gray

3-Under tail
Black
White
Gray

4-Beak
Yellow ochre with whtie
Paynes gray with white
Black

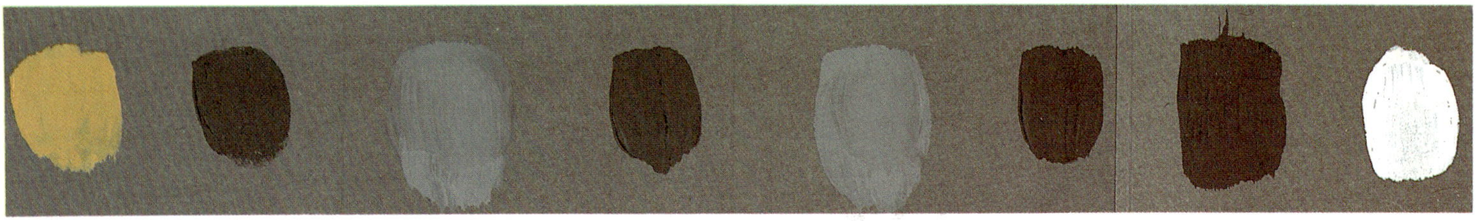

5-Feet & talons
Yellow ochre
Talons—black

6-Upper wings & back
Gray—black
(Burnt umber, Paynes gray
& white

7-Under tail
Gray—black
(Burnt umber, Paynes gray
& white

8-Head
Black
White with yellow ochre

ANTIQUED GOSHAWK

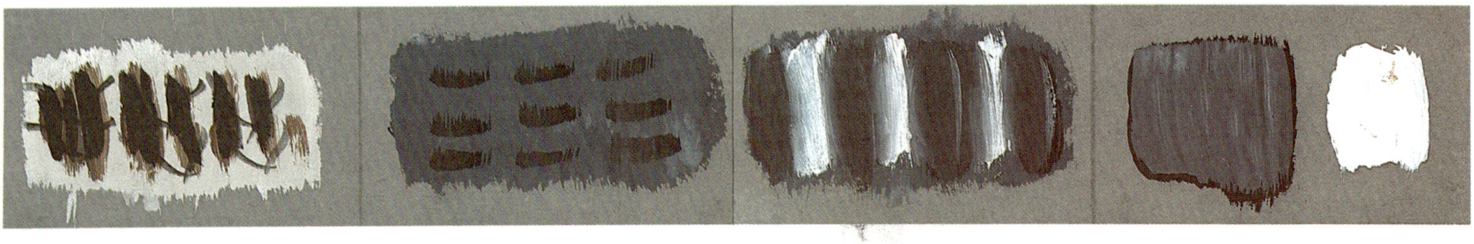

1-Belly
Whitish
White & raw umber streaked
with black

2-Back & Upper wing
Paynes gray & white
Some black

3-Under wings
Paynes gray & white

4-Head
Dark gray & white

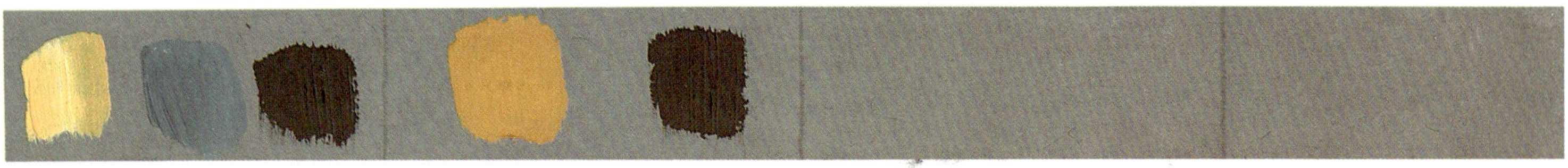

5-Beak
Yellow ochre with white.
Paynes gray with white
Black

6-Feet & talons
Yellow ochre—feet
Talons—black

Final wash of oil paints—black & raw sienna with turpentine for Antiqueing process.

RED-TAILED HAWK

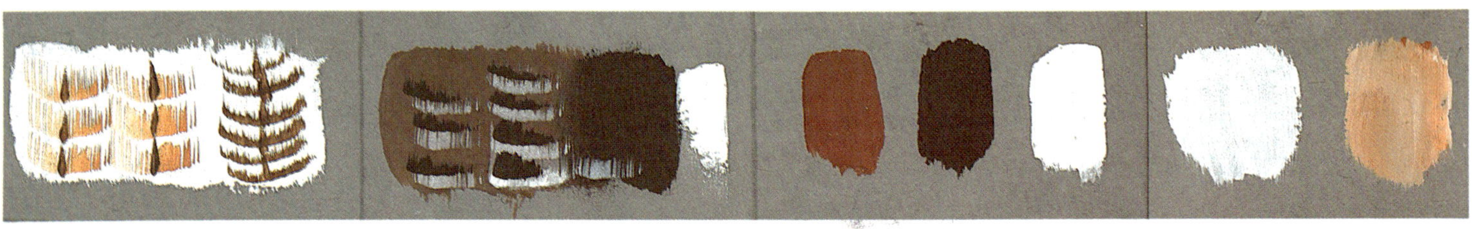

1-Belly
White with gesso edged with
raw sienna & white. Interiors
of burnt umber. Some edgings of
burnt umber

2-Black
Burnt umber with white.
Blackish bars edged with white

3-Upper tail
Burnt sienna with white.
Black banded with white

4-Under tail
White, edged with
raw sienna

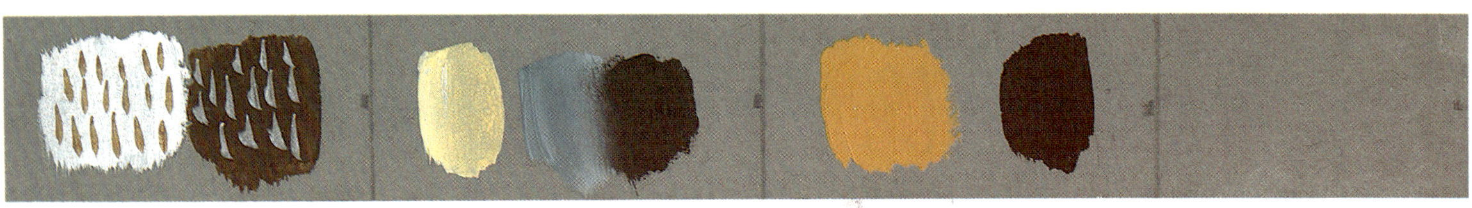

5-Head
Cheek—whitish
streaked with burnt umber.
Crown—burnt umber streaked
with white

6-Beak
Yellow ochre with white.
Paynes gray with white
Black

7-Feet & talons
Yellow ochre—feet
Talons—black

Gray Screech Perched (Wall Mount)

Color list: Black, Titanium white, Burnt umber, Gesso

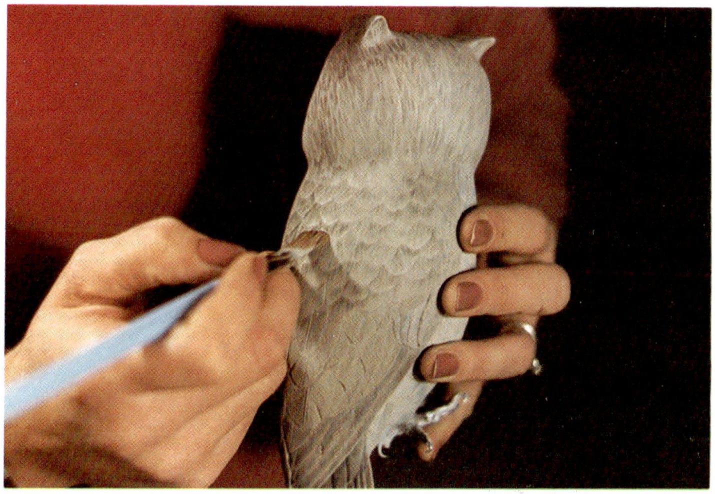

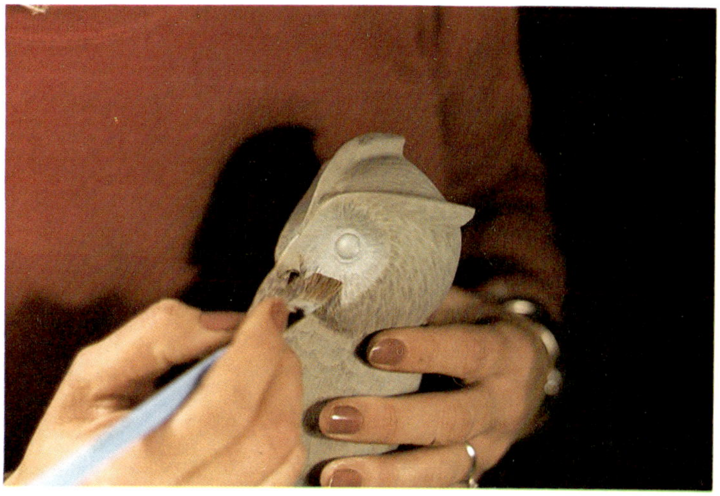

After sealing — coat entire bird with light tan made by mixing white, gesso and burnt umber

Lighten facial discs

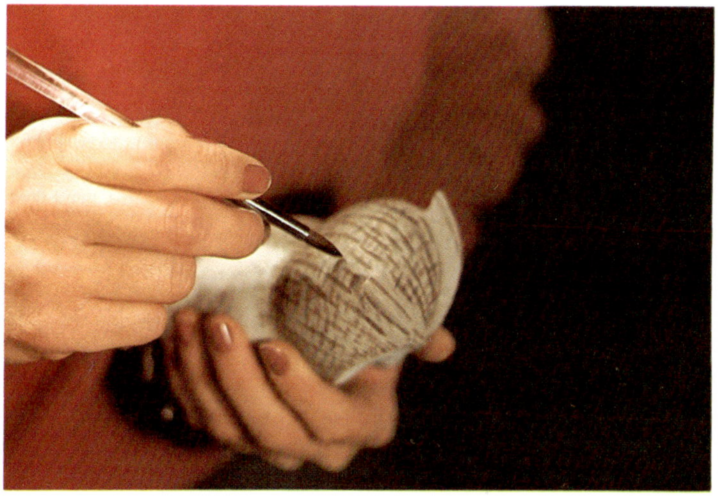

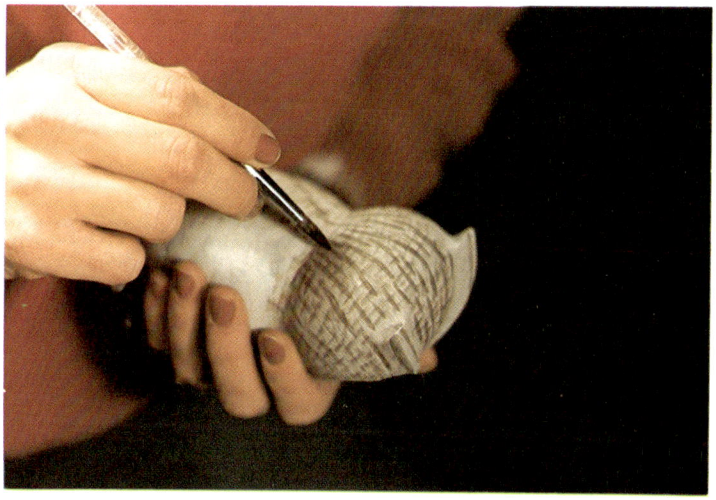

Begin streaking quill lines with burnt umber (add touch of black to gain opacity)

With 1/2" or 3/4" wash brush slightly thicken paint and put in cross mark (almost like vermiculation) in each feather on head and back (cape, wings, rump and tail)

Further streaking

Continue with cross marks and then wash border areas of burnt umber around quill line to create a three tone effect

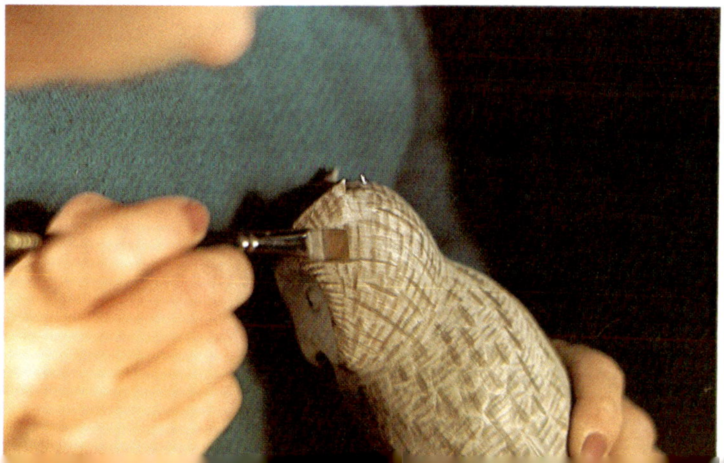

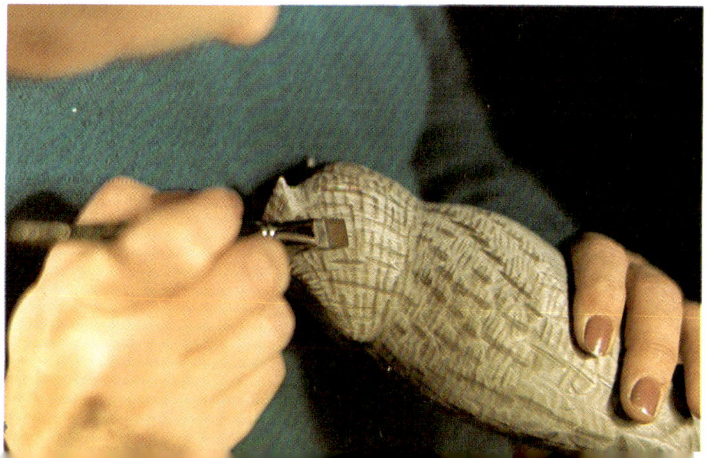

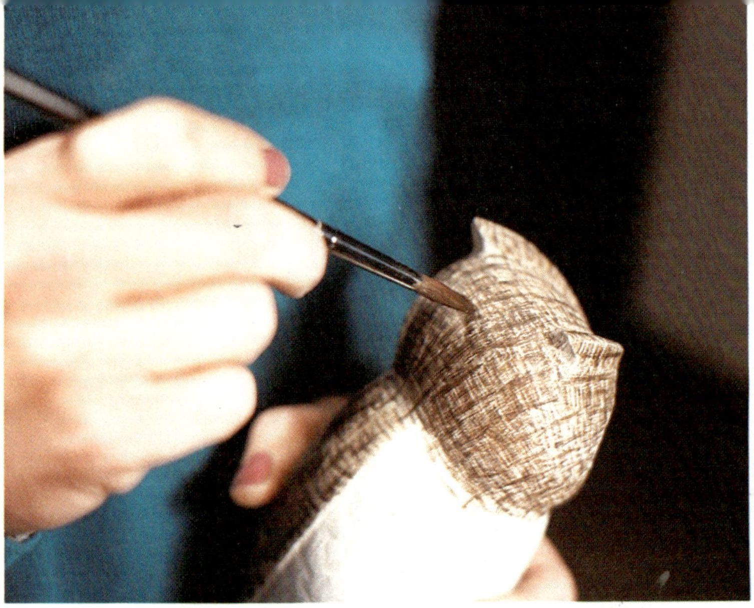

Cross marks on head

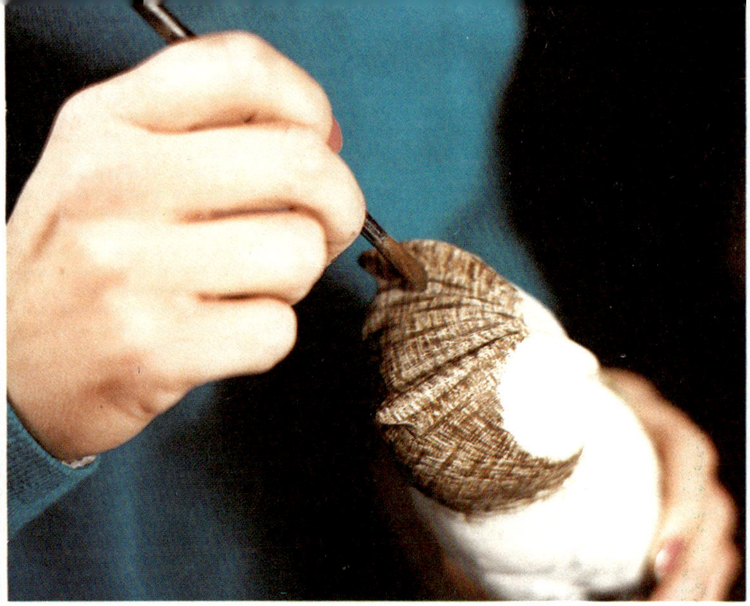

Cross marks up the "ear" line

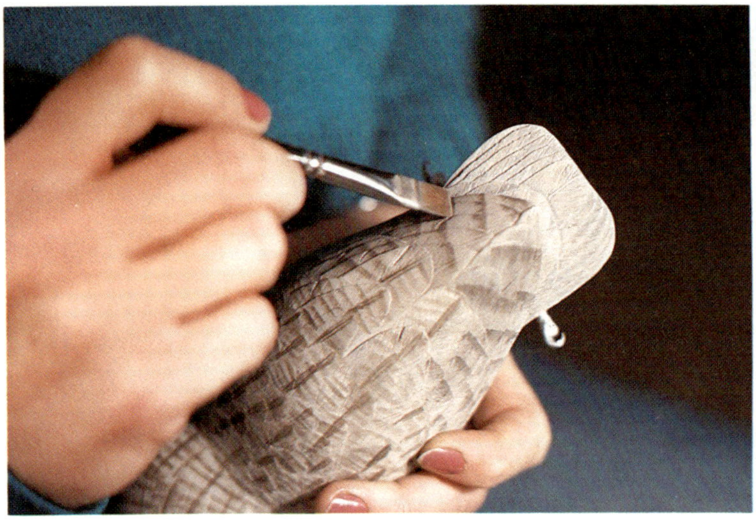

Broader cross marks on primaries

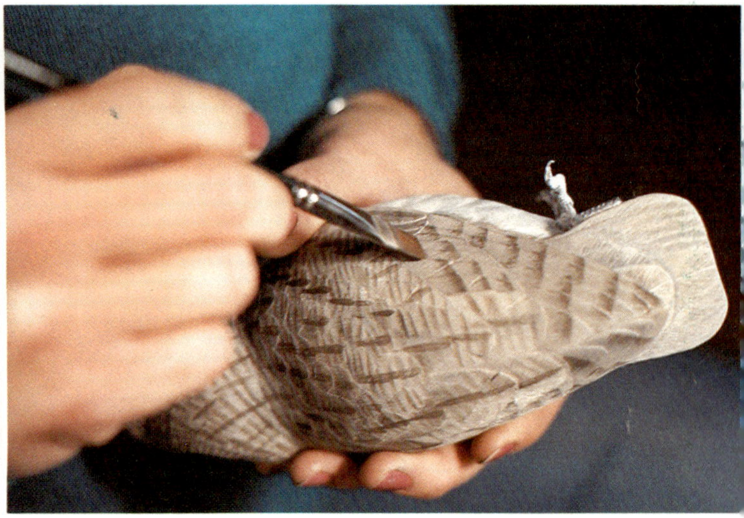

Broader cross marks on secondaries

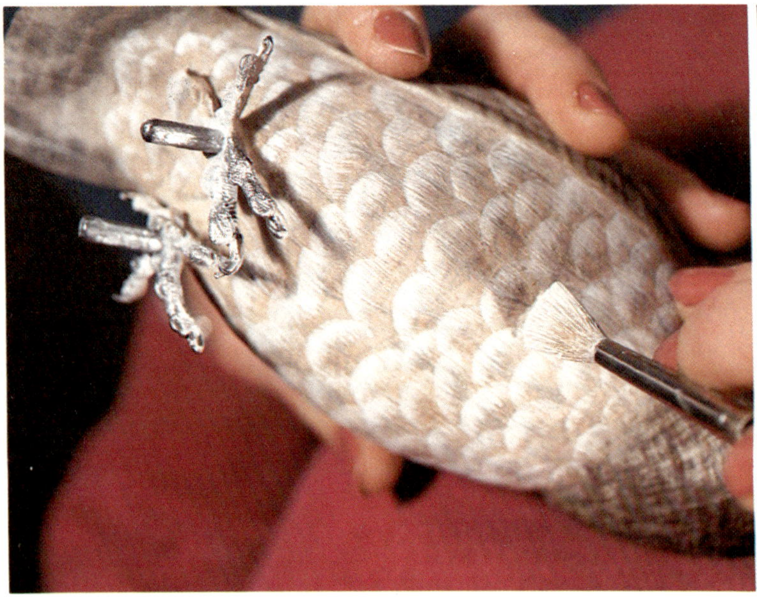

White edging belly (tan undercoat)

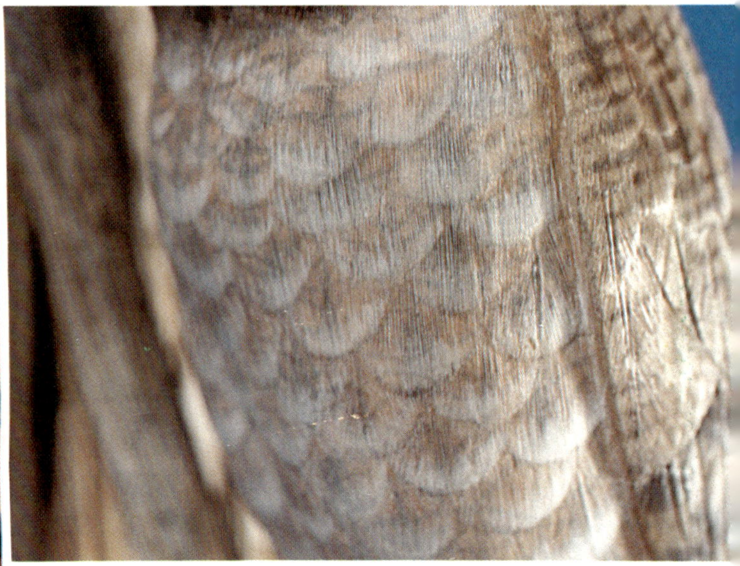

After several edgings of white a white wash will turn the tan to a soft gray

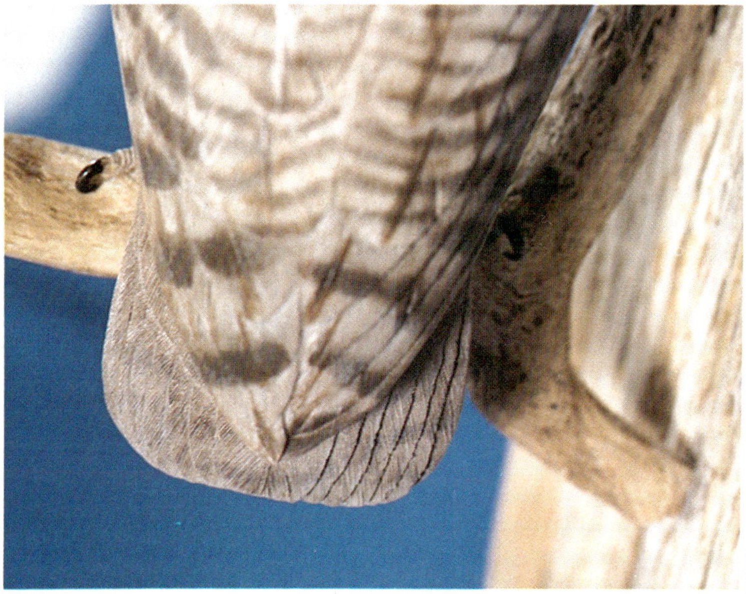

Primary secondary tertial and tail detail — Note: darker color of marks this is achieved by adding a little black to brown

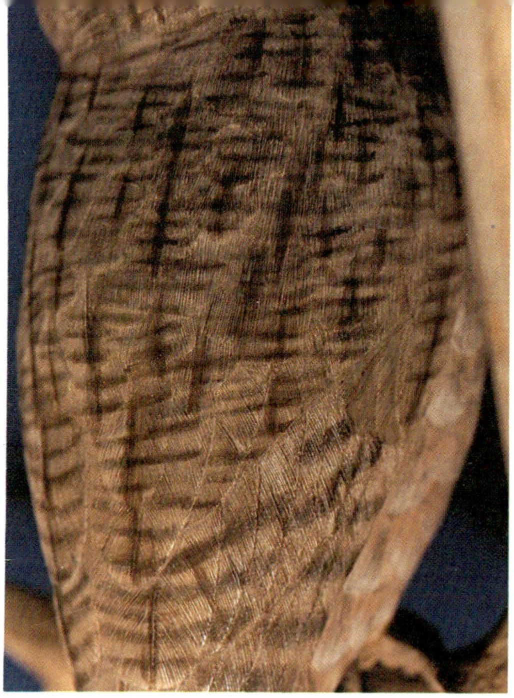

Finished back area — Note: soft blending of dark to light. This is achieved by constantly stippling and wiping excess paint away

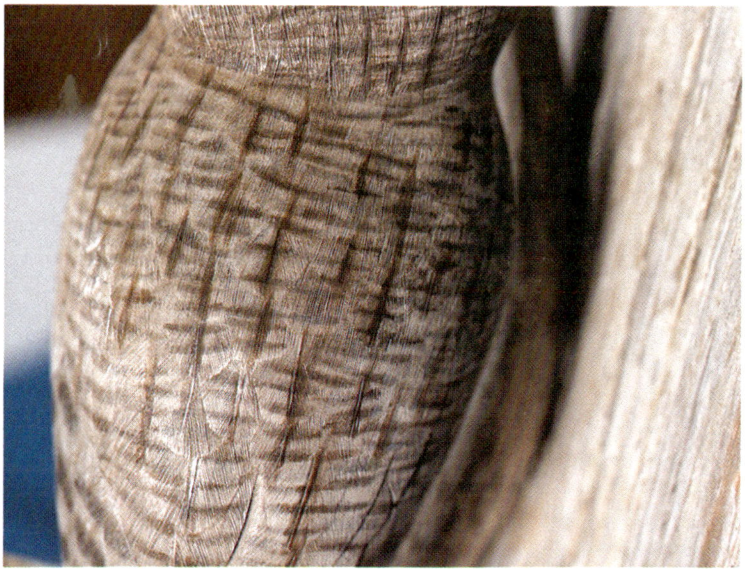

Close up of finished back

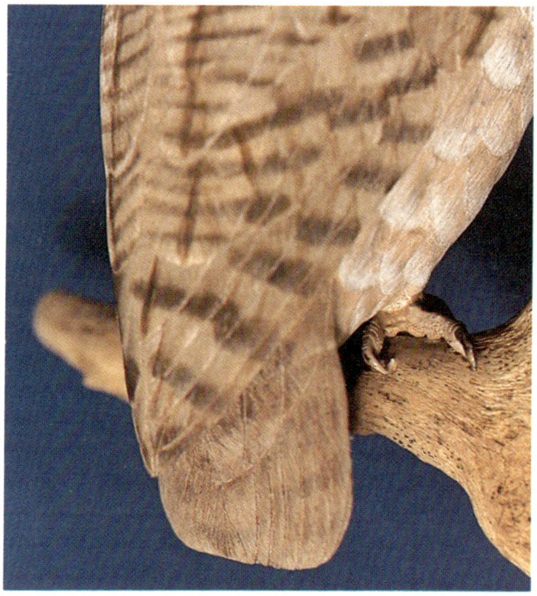

Close up of finished wing and tail area

Close up of finished chest and wing

Close up of feet (whittish with black talons) Note: grayish belly with white edgings.

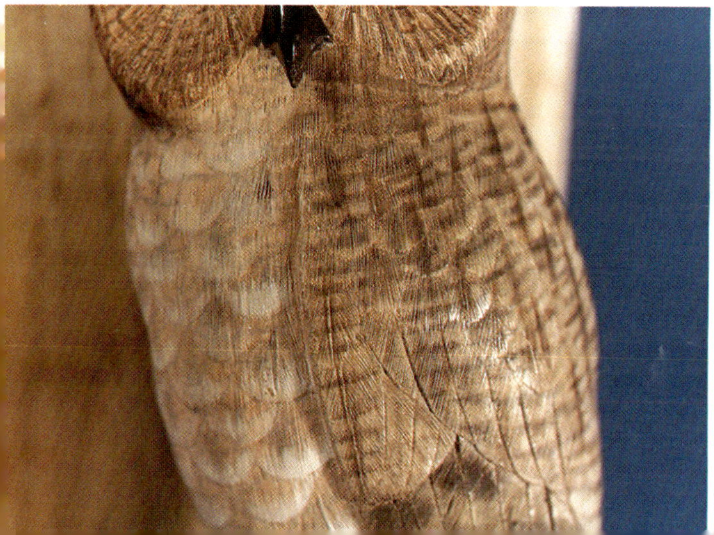

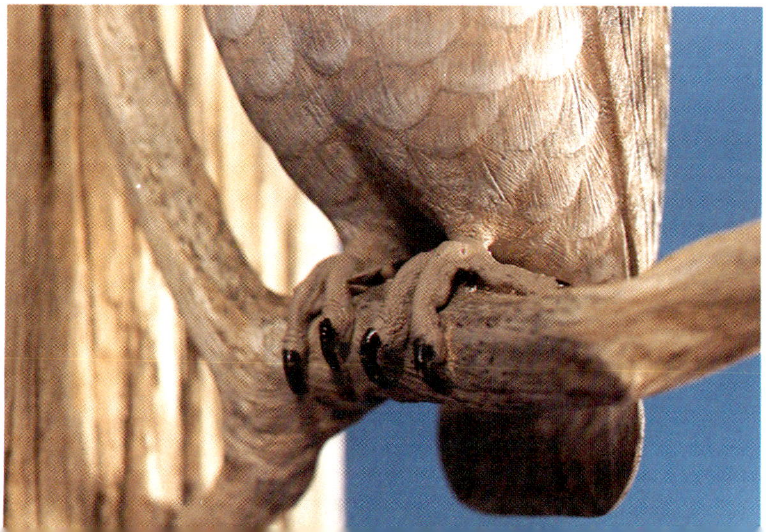

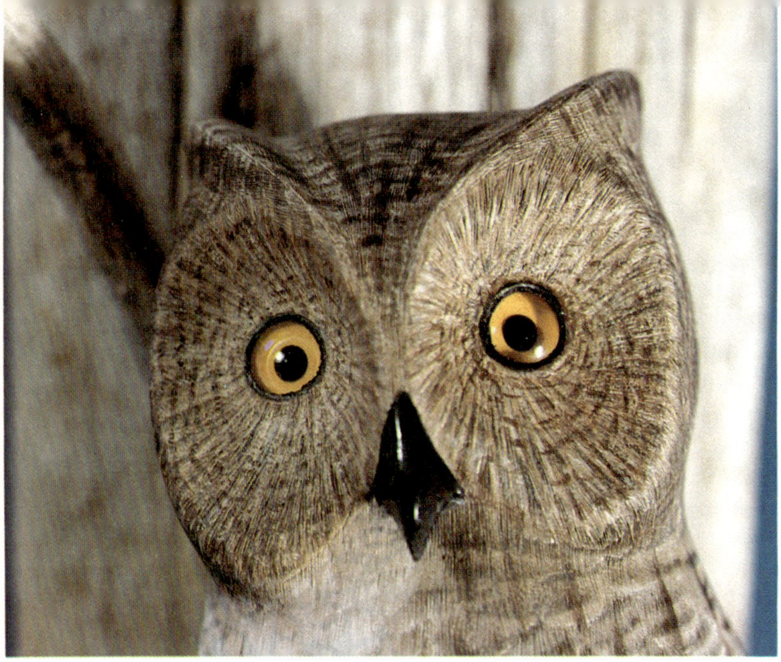

Front view of finished head — Note: black eyelids

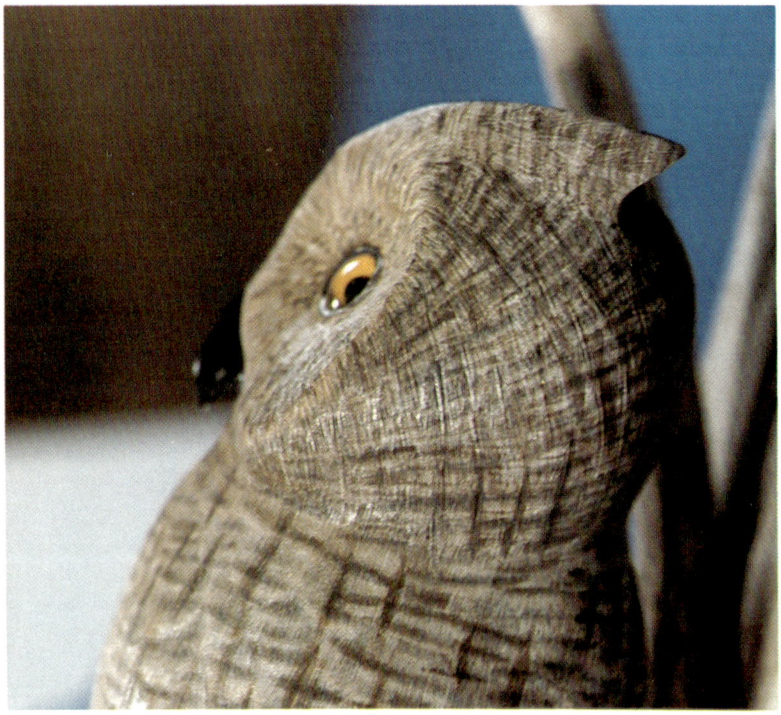

Profile of head finished

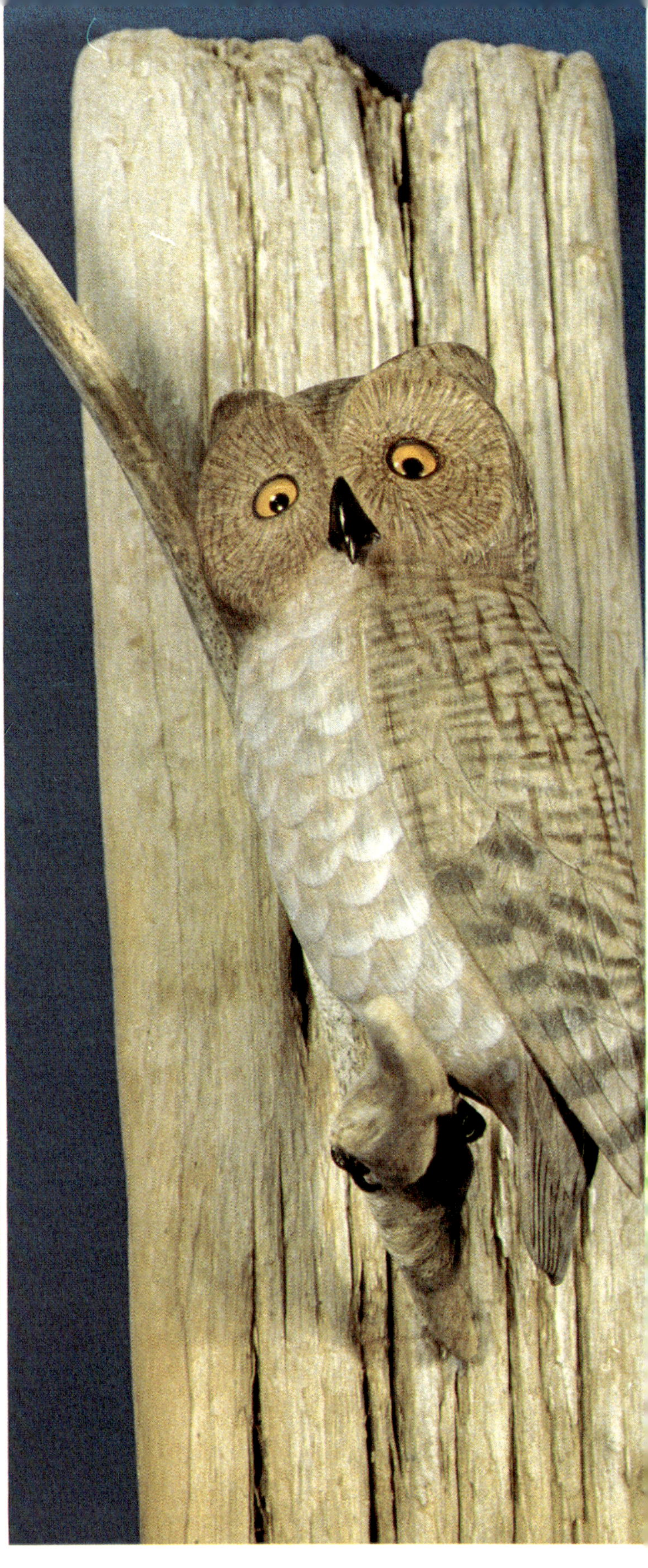

Wall mount of finished carving by Vicky Herron. This is Vickys first carving.

Red Screech Owl

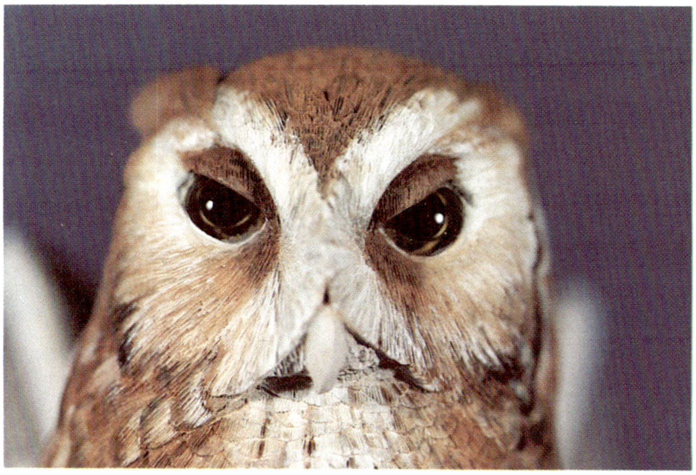

Facial discs and belly washed with white mixed with gesso—outer edges of discs washed with thin burnt sienna. Eye lids darker hue of burnt sienna. Beak—bone color (raw umber and white mixed)

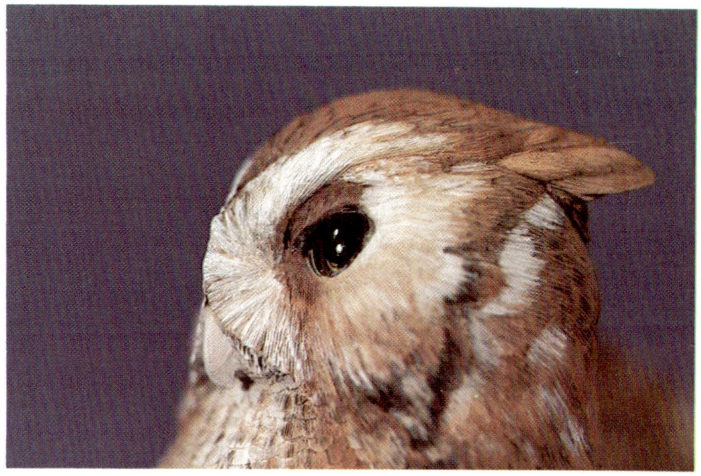

Side view of head. Note—reddish (burnt sienna) color in corners of eye and blend of white to reddish from belly to back

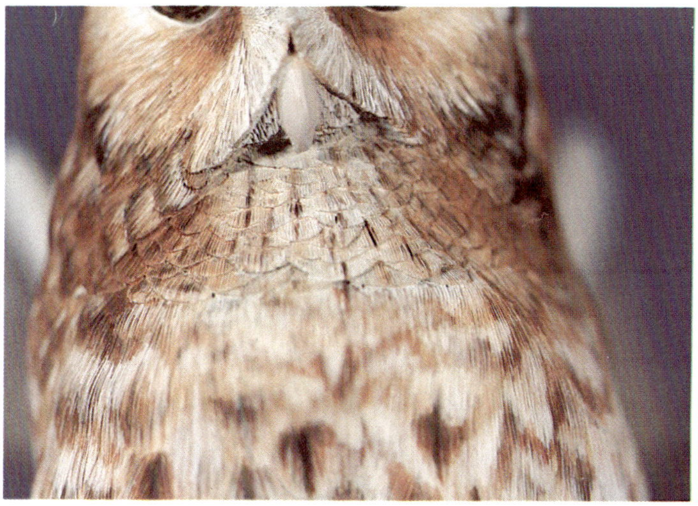

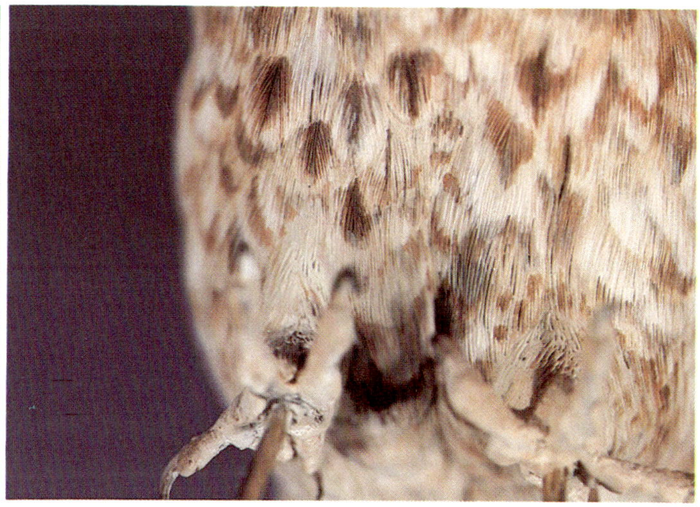

Belly and underrump washed with white mixed with gesso until opaque. Then interiors of feathers washed with burnt sienna and in center of feathers along quill washed with burnt umber

Underside of tail washed with white mixed with gesso and small amount of burnt umber until opaque. Then a wet coat of same and darker bars of burnt umber stippled to create soft transition of color

Underside of wing—same colors and same procedure as underside of tail

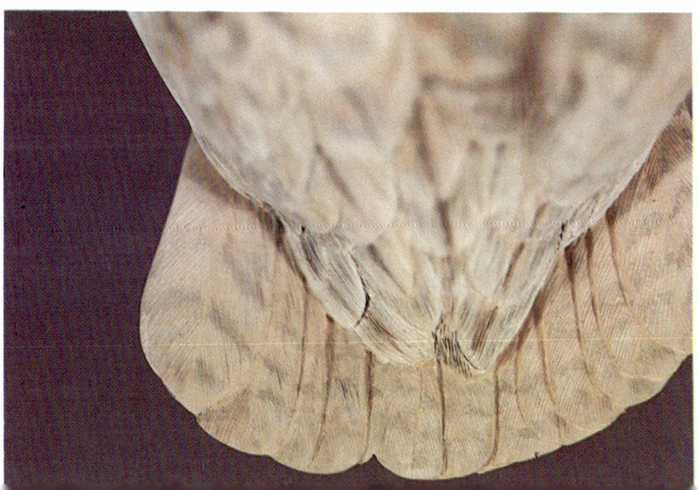

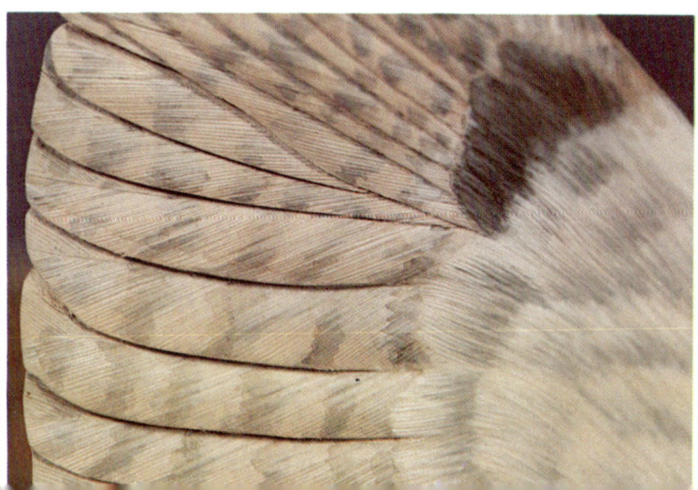

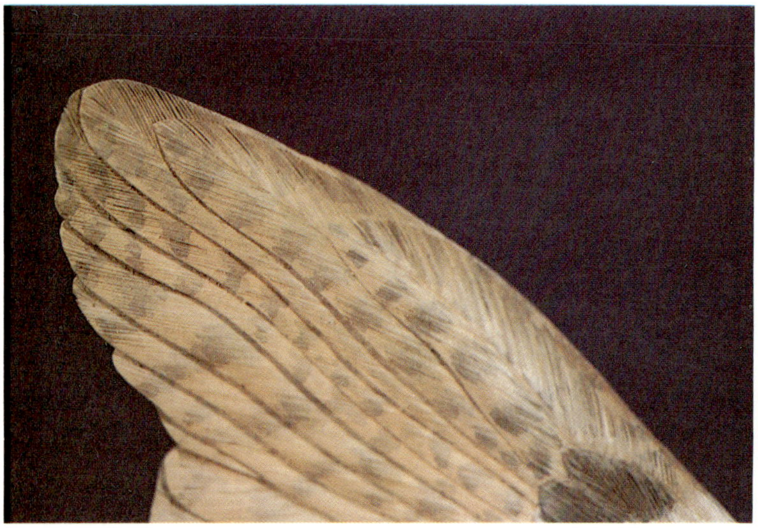

Underside of primaries same as underside of wing. Note—darker area at base of first four primaries

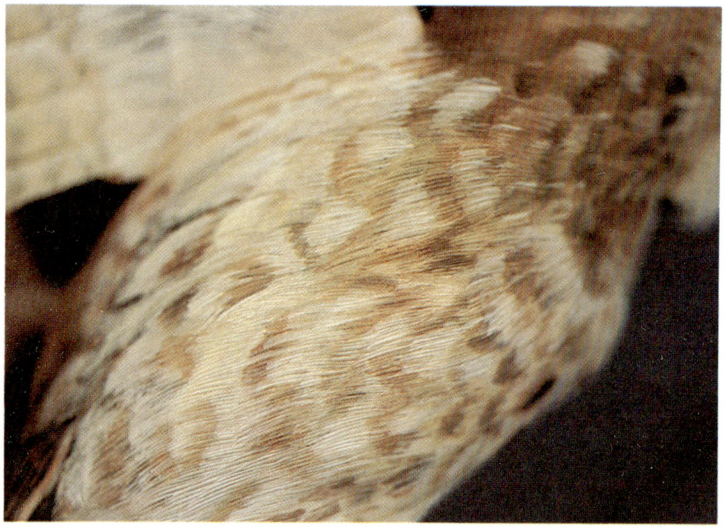

Sides of body white mixed with gesso and spotted with burnt sienna, occasional burnt umber spots

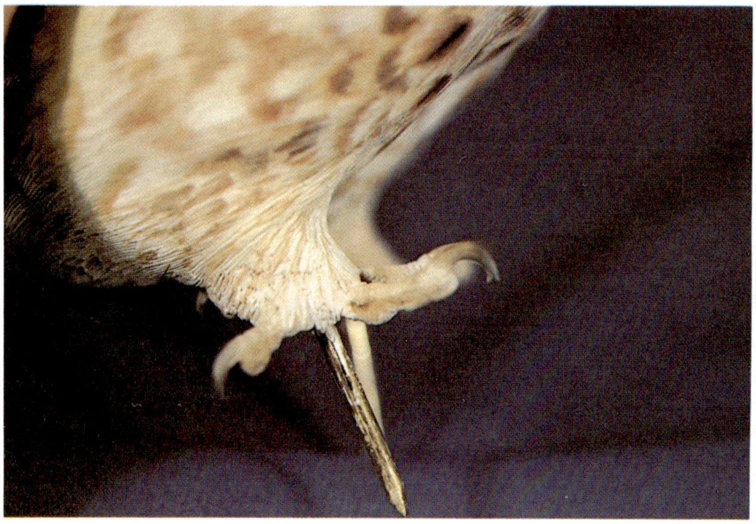

Feet whitish with gray talons

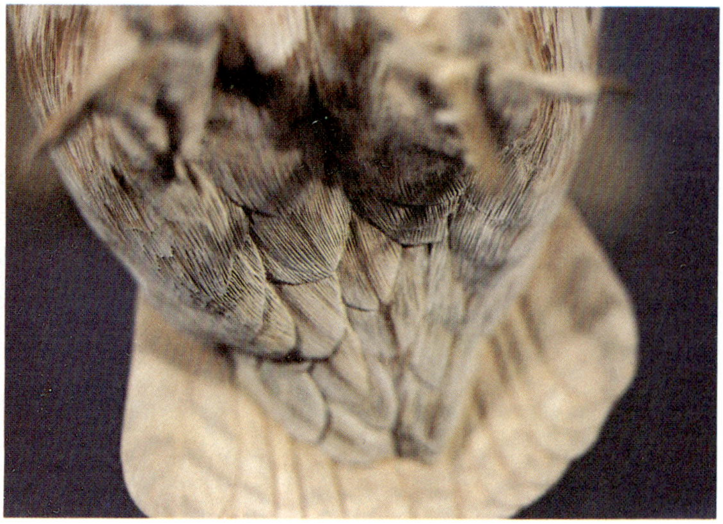

Underside of rump, base color is white mixed with gesso, stippled burnt umber interiors

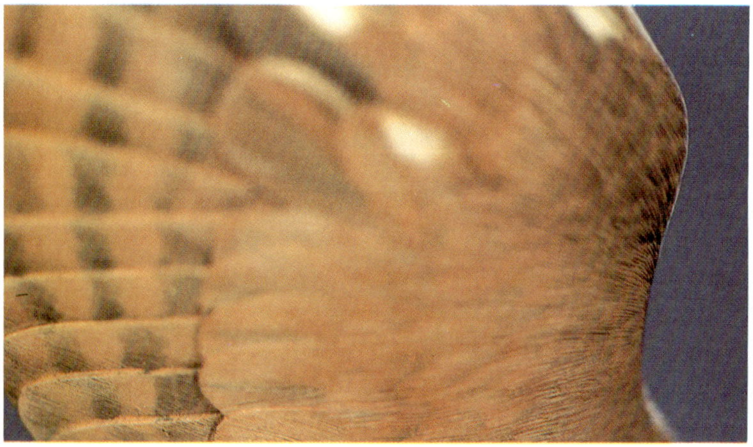

Upper side of wing and secondaries base color is burnt sienna mixed with small amount of white, bars of burnt umber stippled edges for blend, occasional white spots on wings

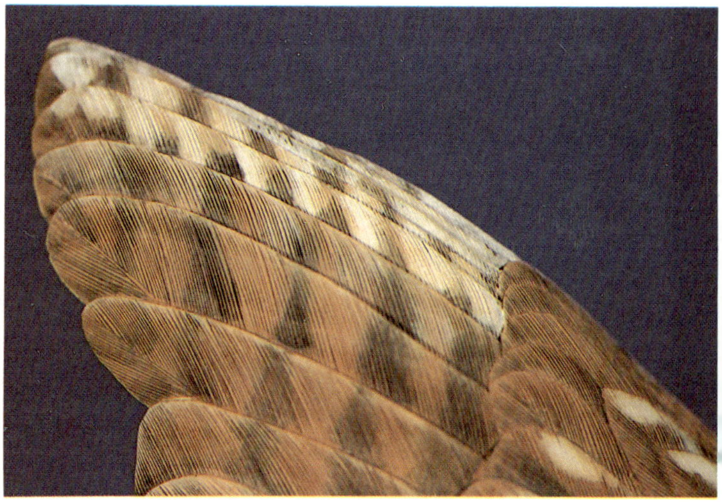

Primaries base color burnt sienna mixed with tiny amount of white barred with burnt umber stipple blended

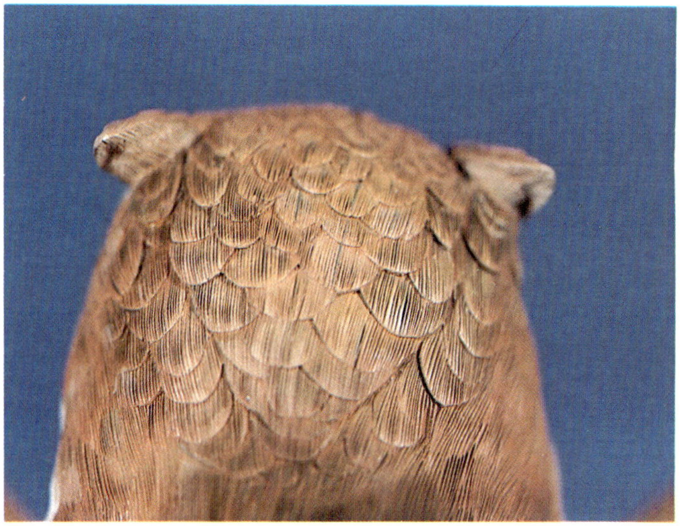

Back of head—burnt sienna mixed with tiny amount of yellow ochre—interior of feathers, small wash of burnt umber

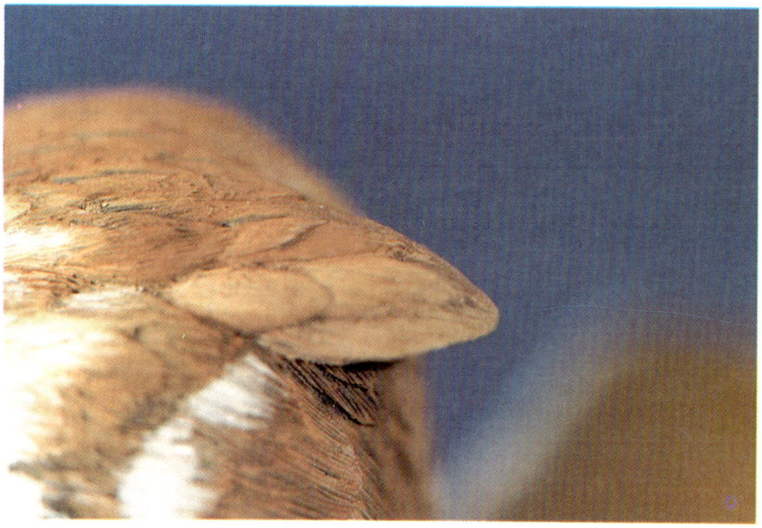

Ears burnt sienna lightened with yellow ochre—burnt umber centers

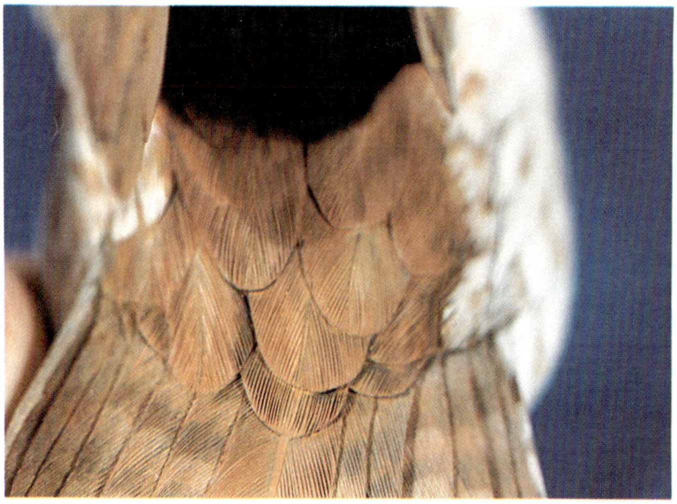

Back—burnt sienna

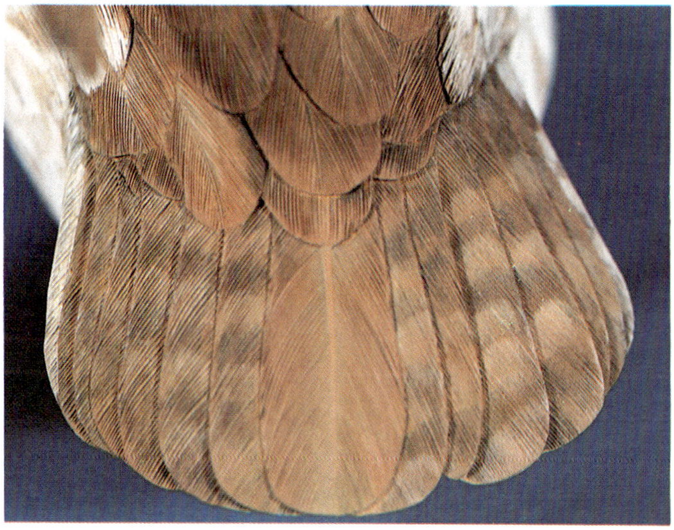

Upper side of tail burnt sienna barred with burnt umber stipple blended

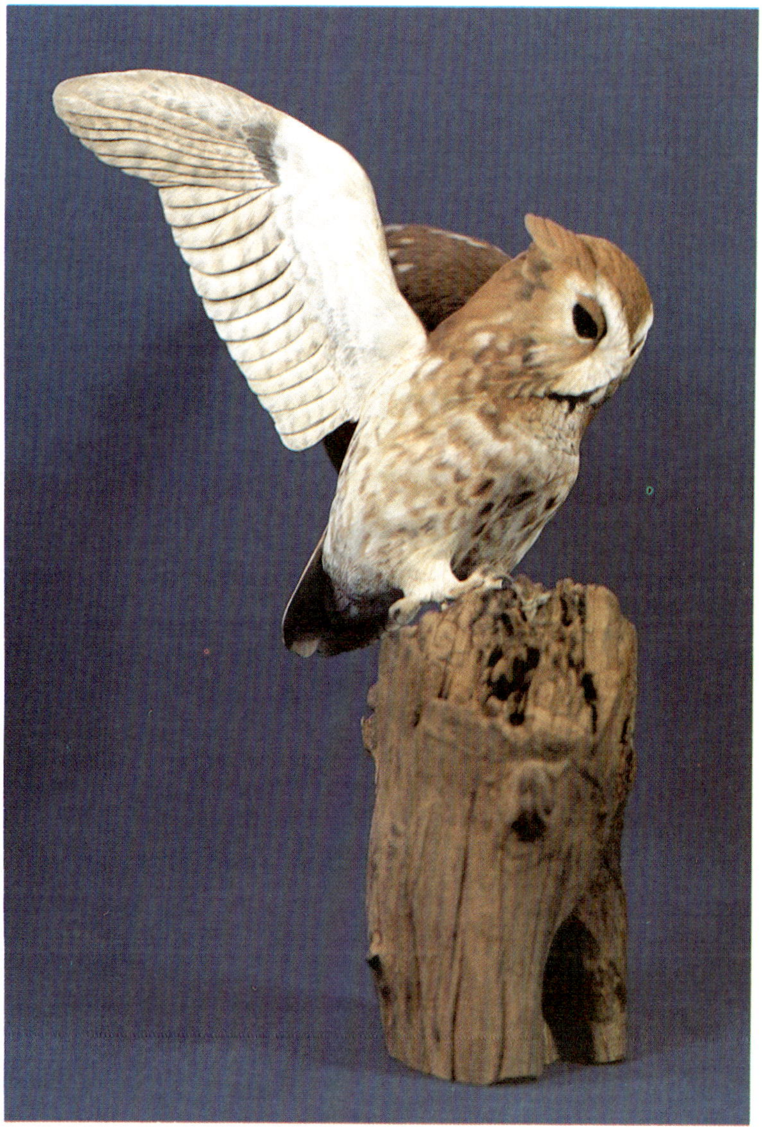

Finished carving

Saw-Whet Owl

Color list: Burnt umber, Black, Titanium white, Gesso

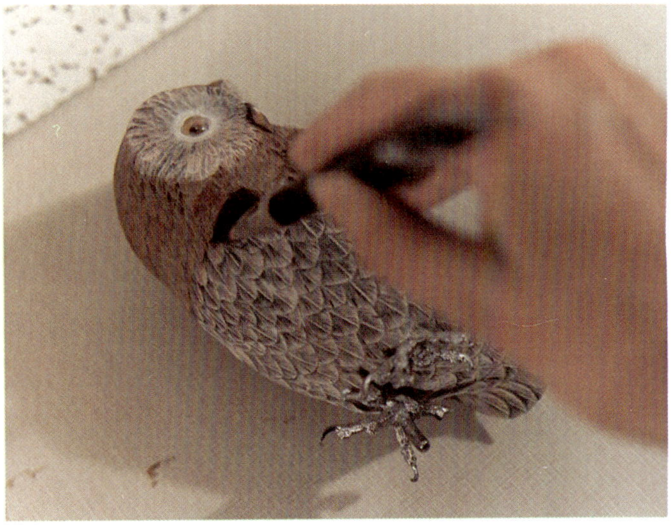

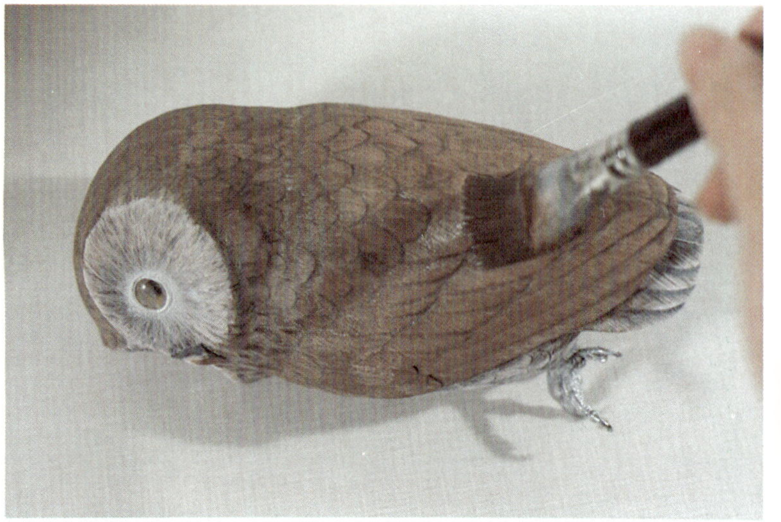

Wash belly and facial discs with light tan using burnt umber and white (when using white in washes it is best to mix white and gesso 50/50. This helps keep color flat.

Wash back and rest of head with burnt umber until areas are opaque

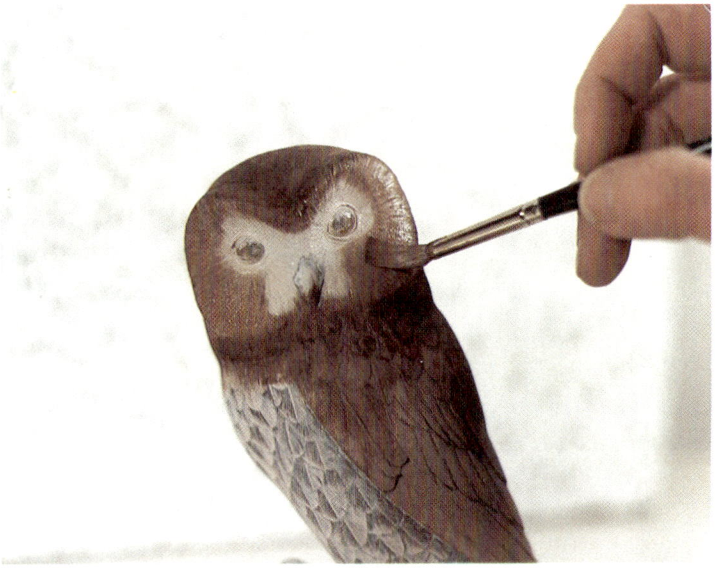

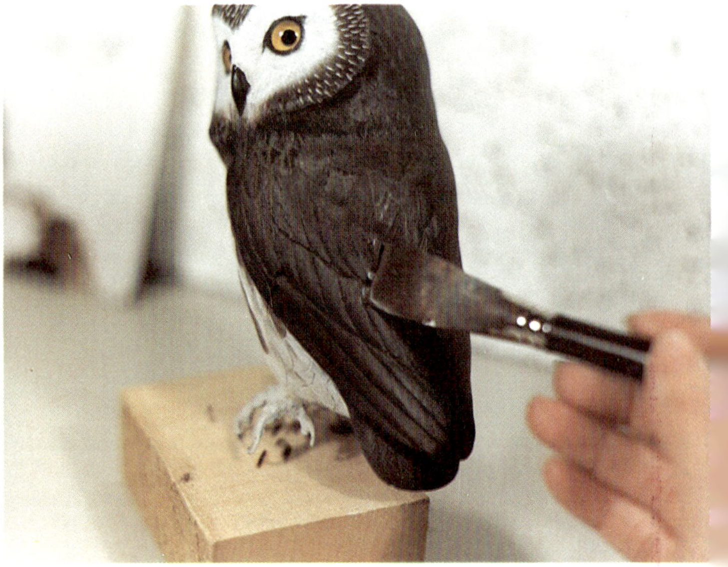

Outer rings of facial disc washed with burnt umber

All belly feathers are edged with white (white mixed with gesso) several times then washed with white

More burnt umber washed — Note: white flecks on outer ring of facial discs.

White flecks on quill lines of head feathers using #4 script brush

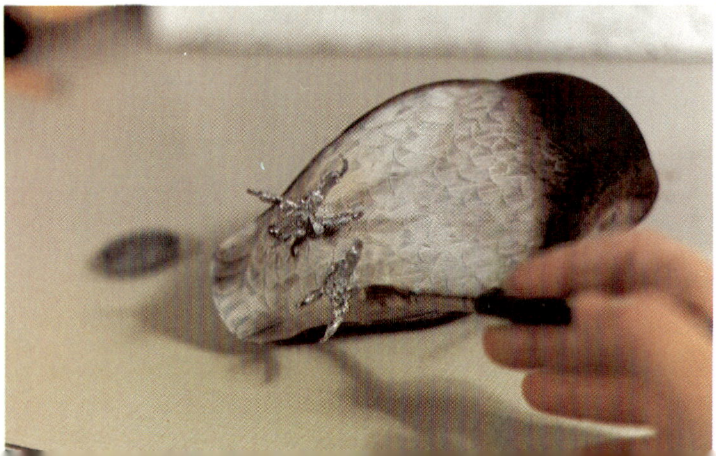

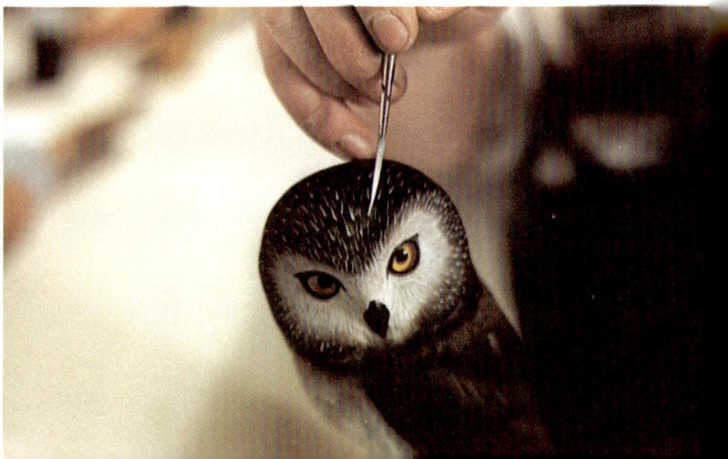

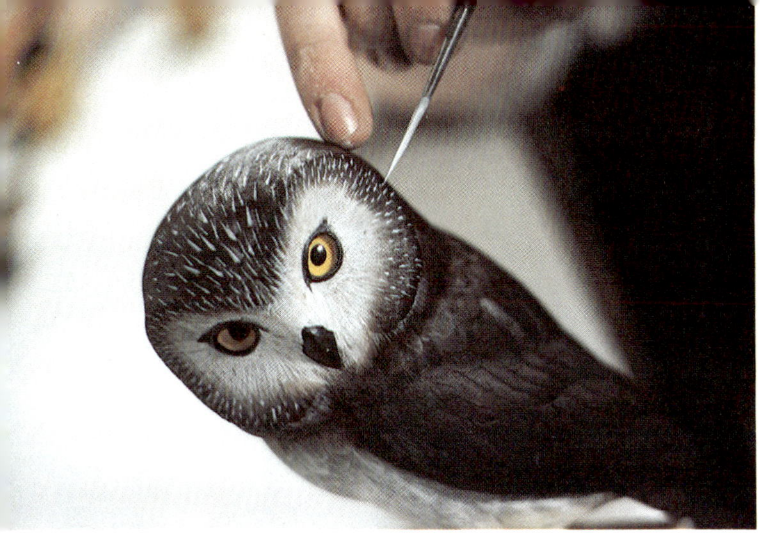

Further flecking on head

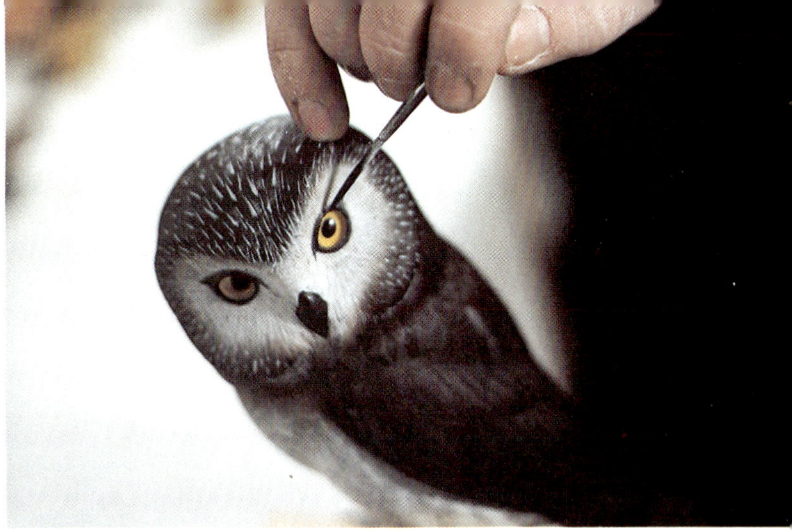

Painting black eyelid

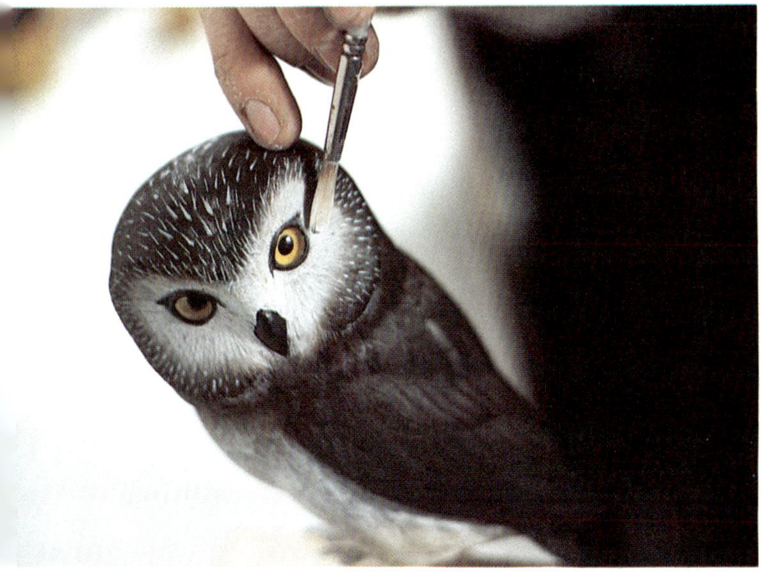

Highlighting white area of facial discs

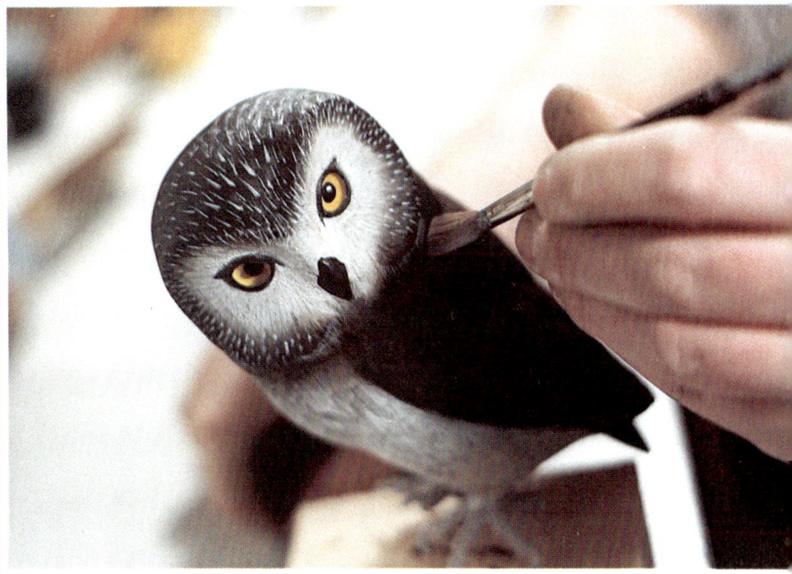

Retouching burnt umber (brown) areas

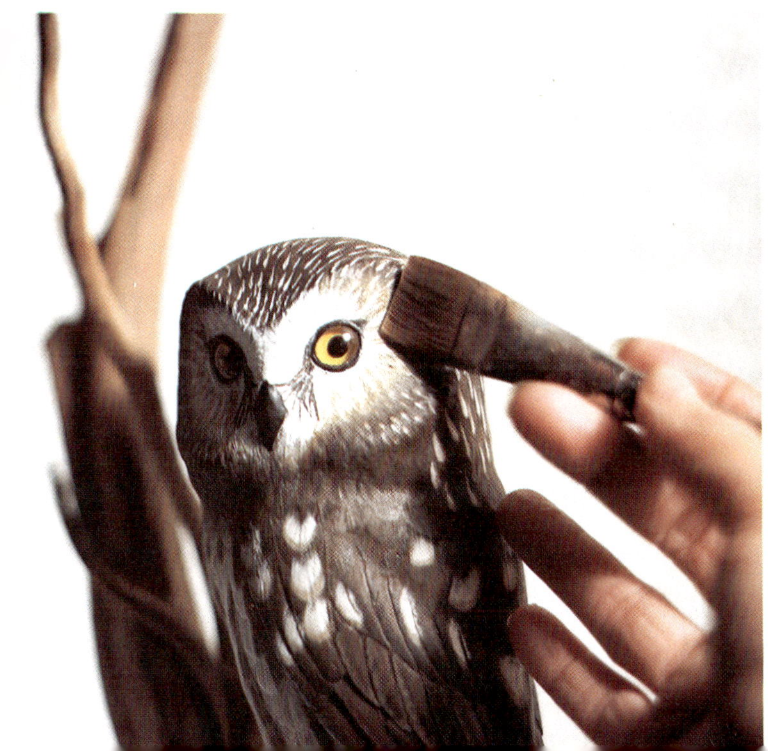

Thin wash of burnt umber to soften facial disc area

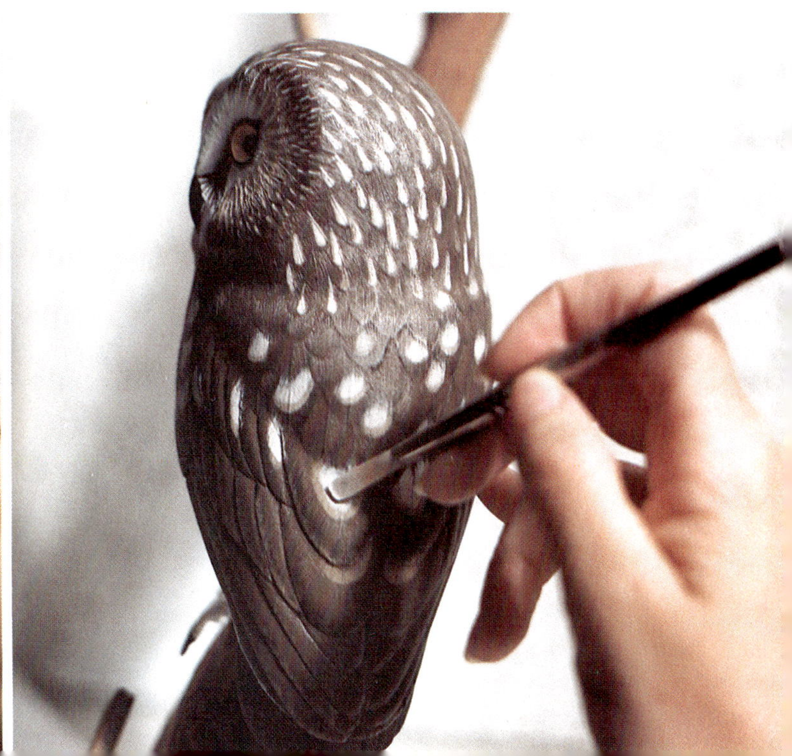

White spotting areas on cape and wing areas — Note: that outer band of light tan (burnt umber and white) surrounds white spots

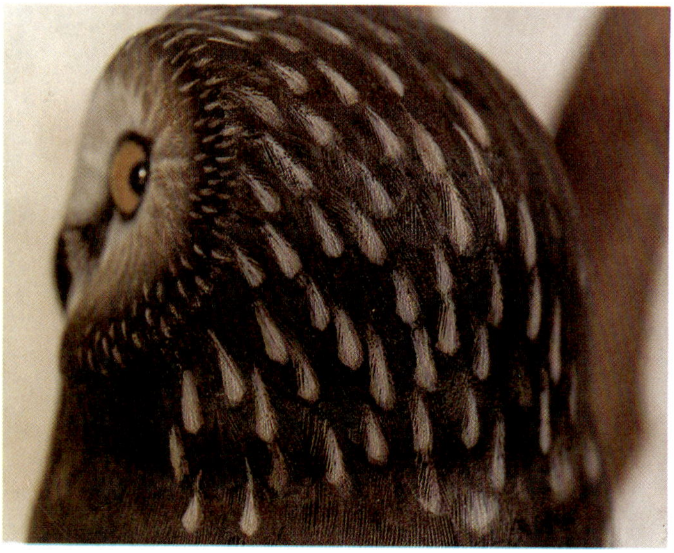

Close up of white spots (elongated tear drop shaped) on back of head

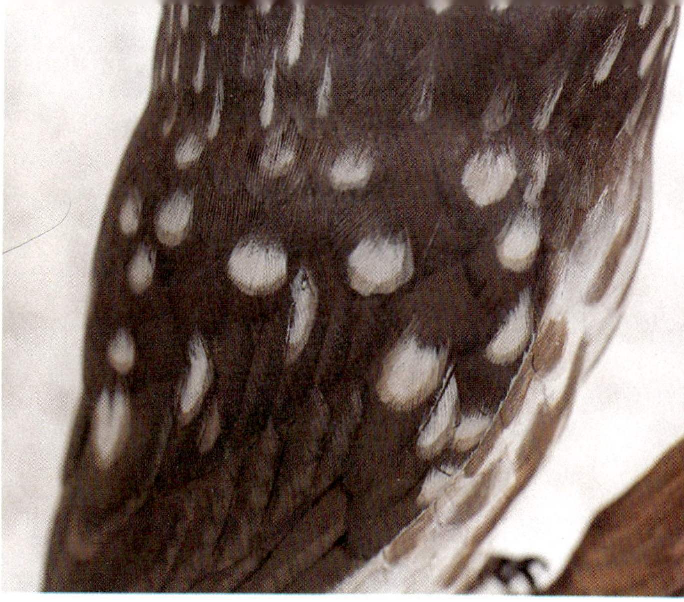

Close up of white spot locations on cape and wings

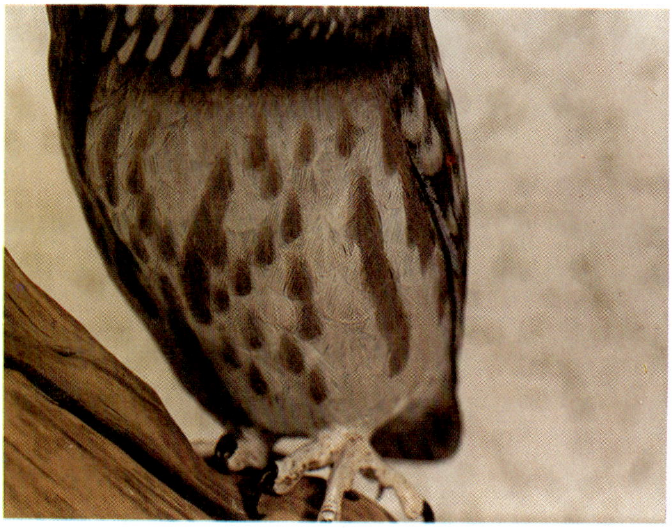

Brown (large tear drops) spots on chest and belly (burnt umber thin washes — not quite opaque)

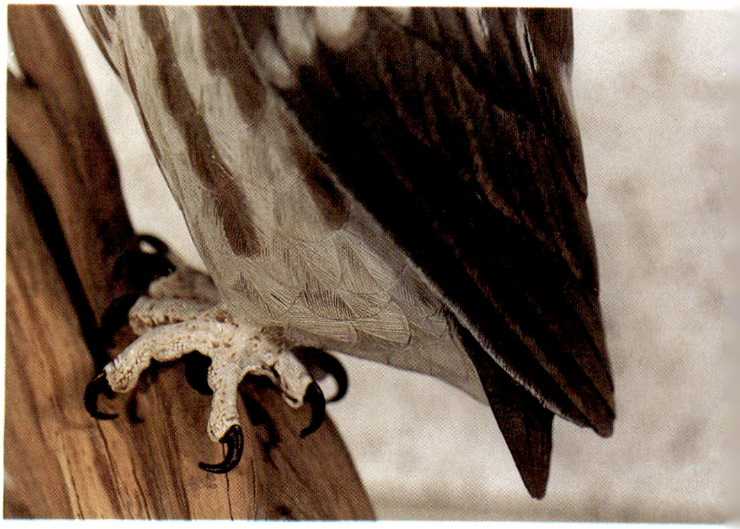

Feet whitish with black talons — Note: light tan edgings of primaries secondaries

Close view of cape and wings

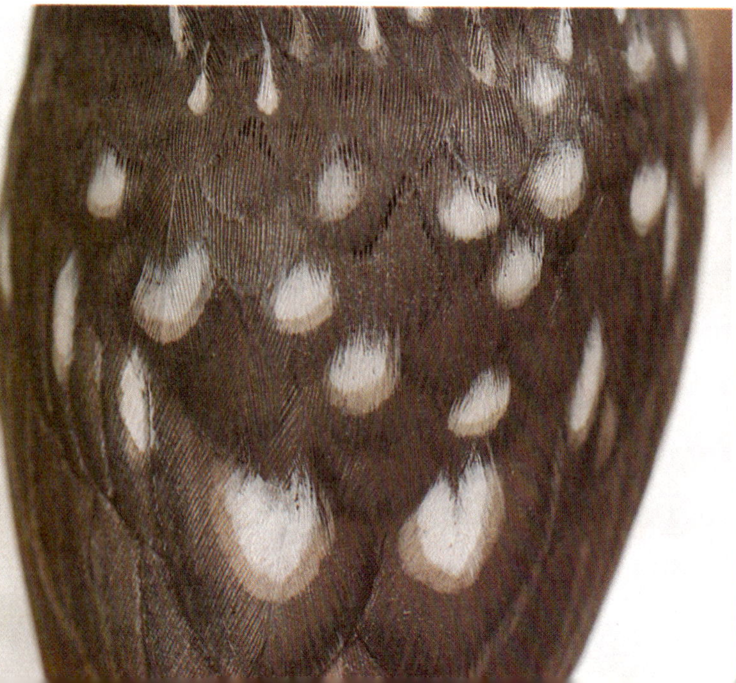

Front face and body profile — Note: black beak and graduation of color from white surrounding eyes to tan to brown flecked with white in facial discs.

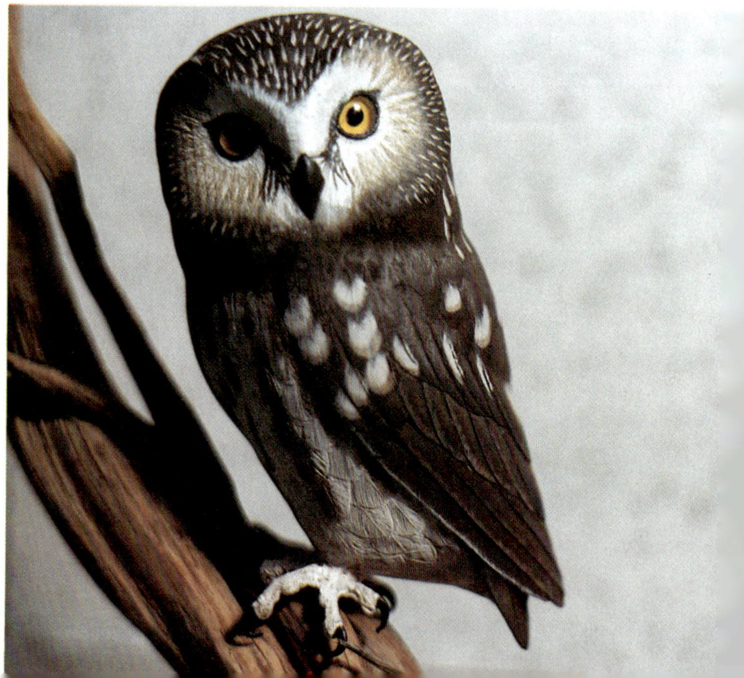

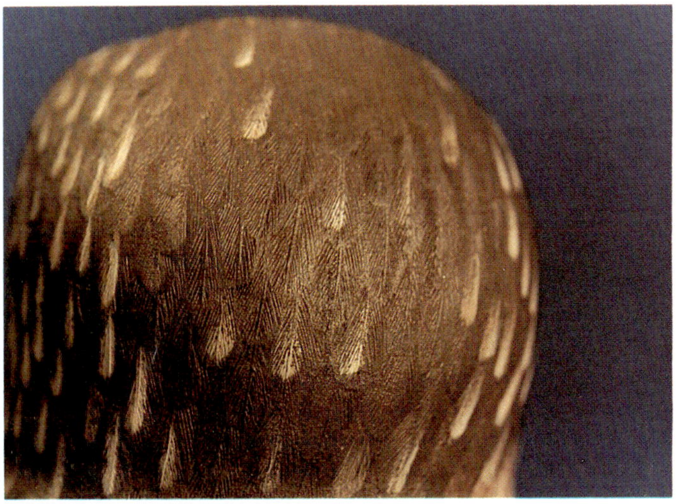

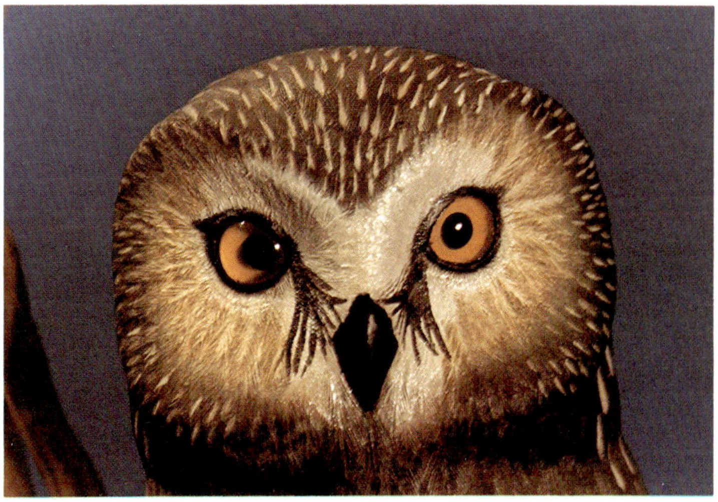

Back of head washed with burnt umber for soft effect (make toning washes ultra thin) (See *Waterfowl Painting, Blue Ribbon Techniques)*

Study detail location in close up of face

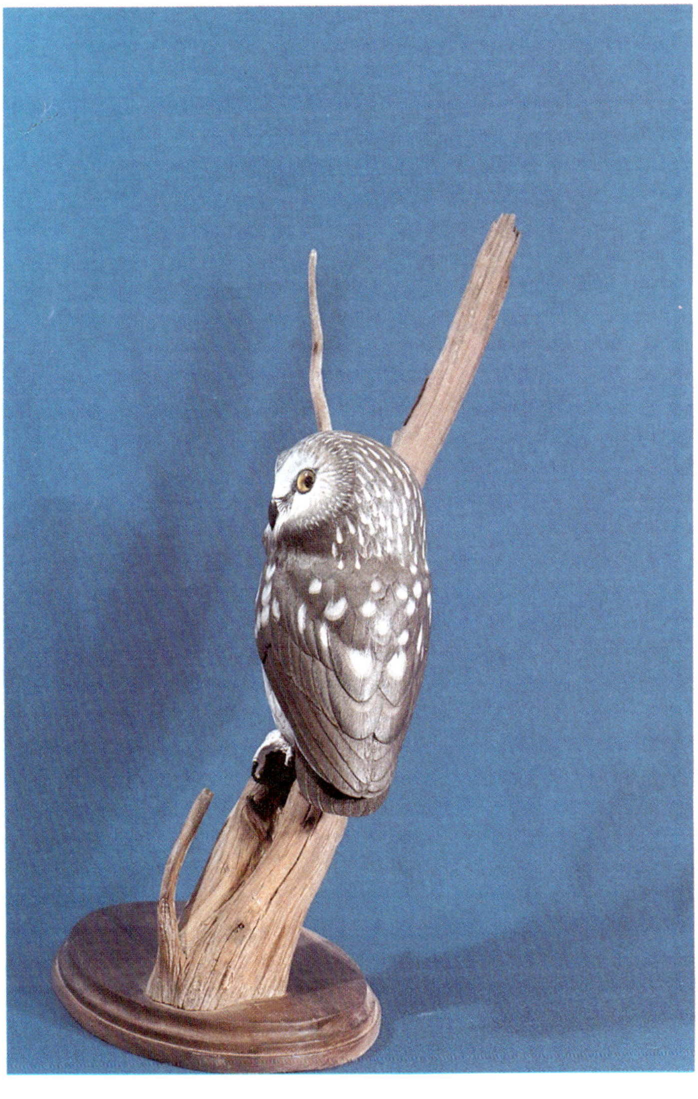

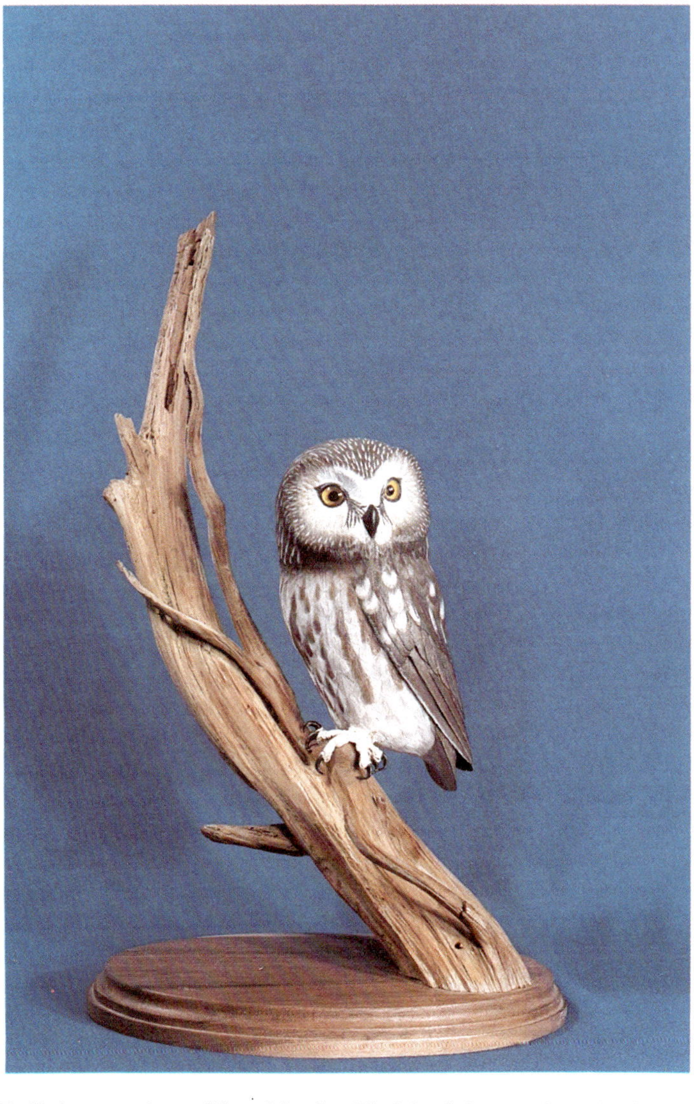

Profile of face and full back

Full face and profile of body. Finished Saw-Whet Owl mounted by Tricia Veasey

Snowy Owl

Color list: Burnt umber, Black, White, Gesso

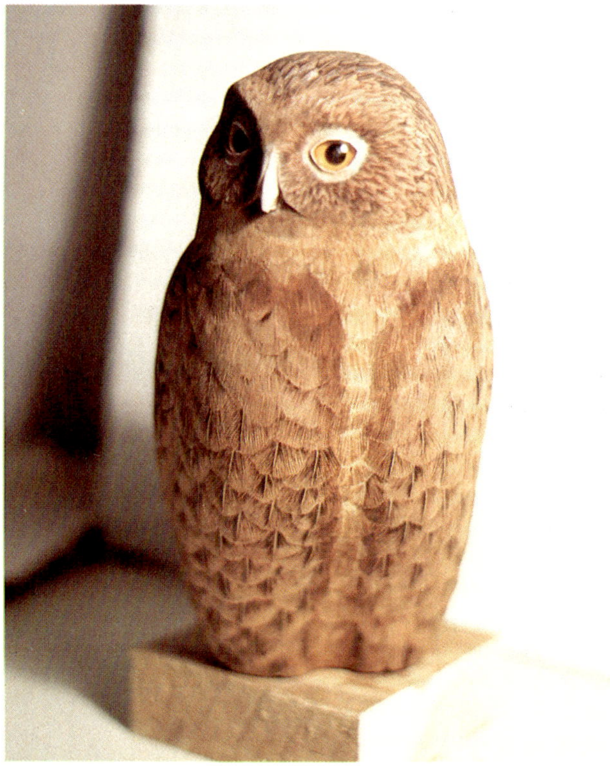

Snowy owl to seal burnings use Krylon or you may also use spray deft

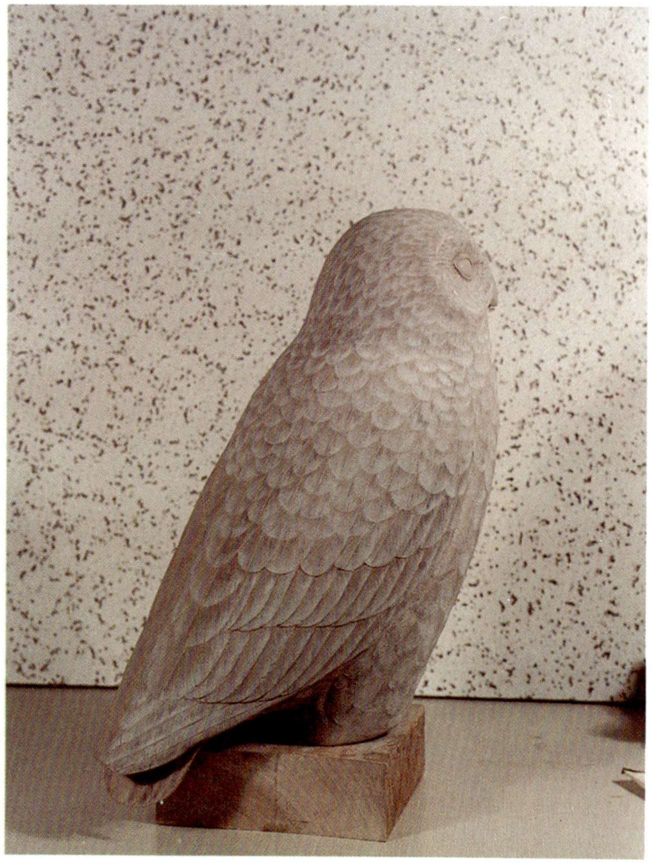

Edge each feather several times with white and gesso mixed. This creates shadows on the interior of each feather with a graduation of color from gray interior to white edge. After several edgings wash with combination of white and gesso to desired effect. Note: brown fleckings on cape area

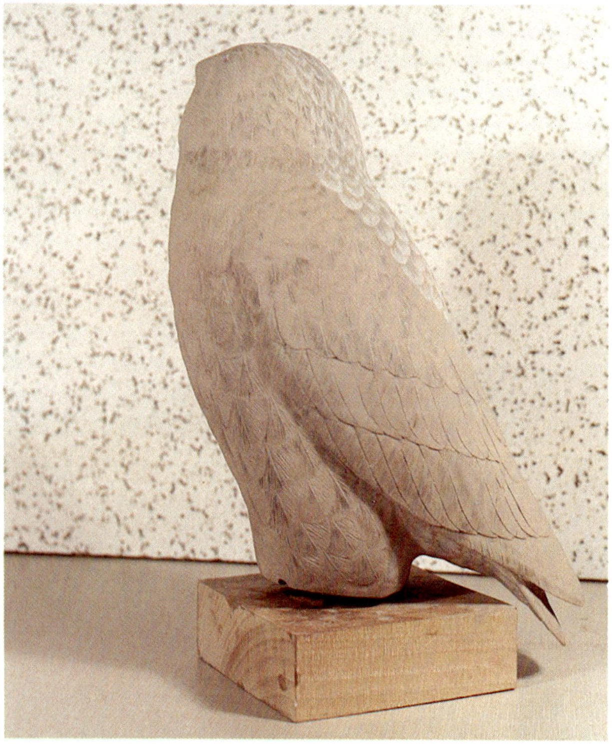

Wash entire bird with light tan made with burnt umber, titanium white and gesso. Continue until surface is opaque.

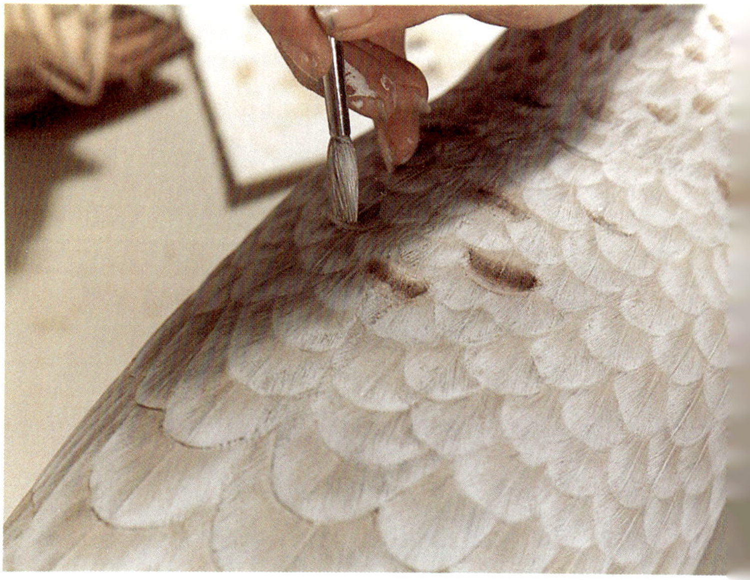

Continued white edging

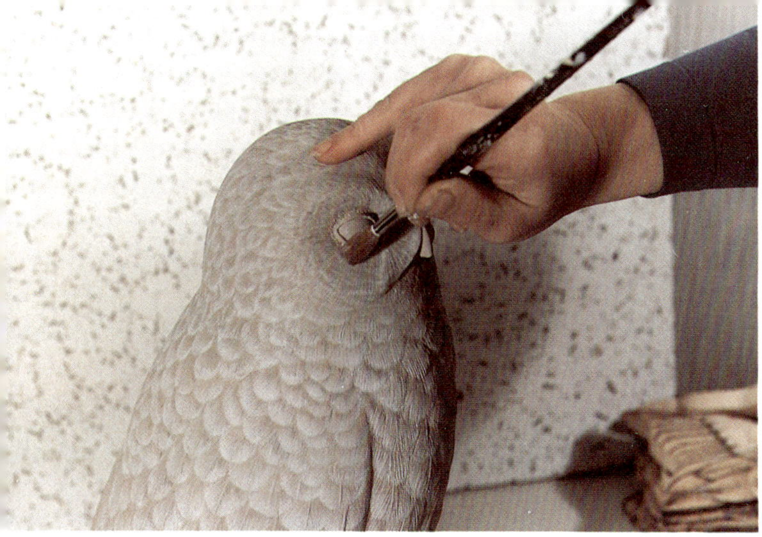

Washing facial discs

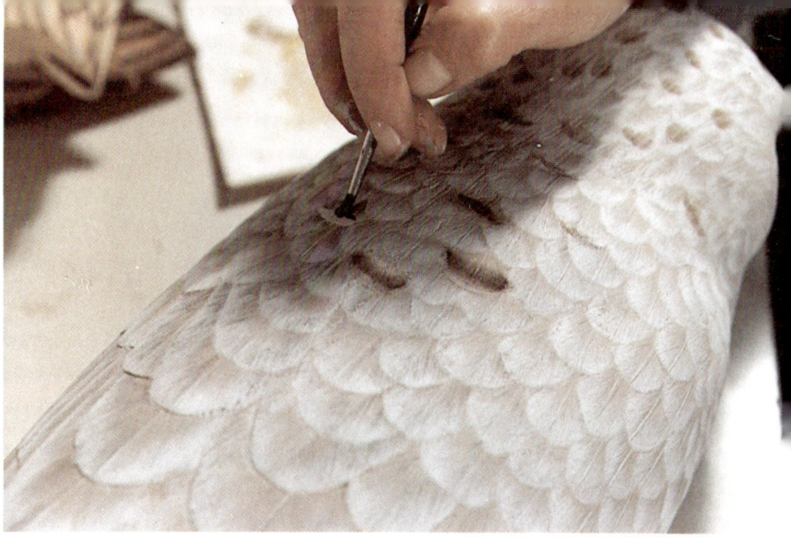

Brown flecking in cape and back of head — keep slightly translucent

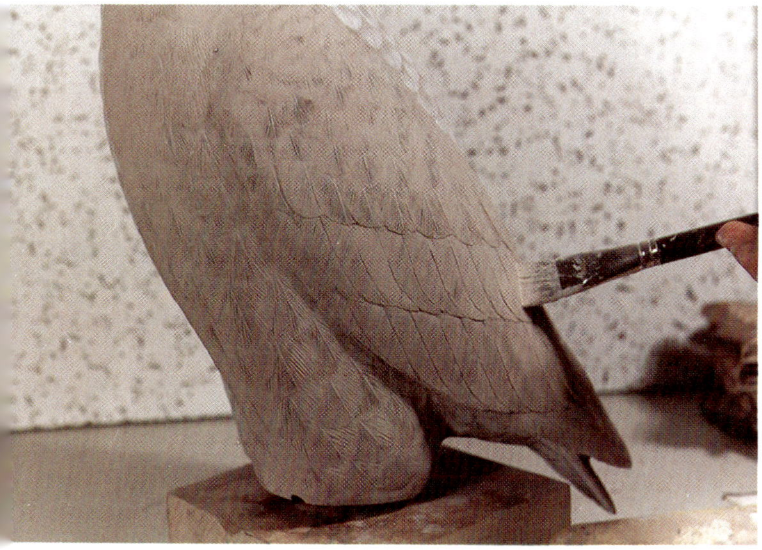

Washing entire bird with combination of white and gesso — very thick.

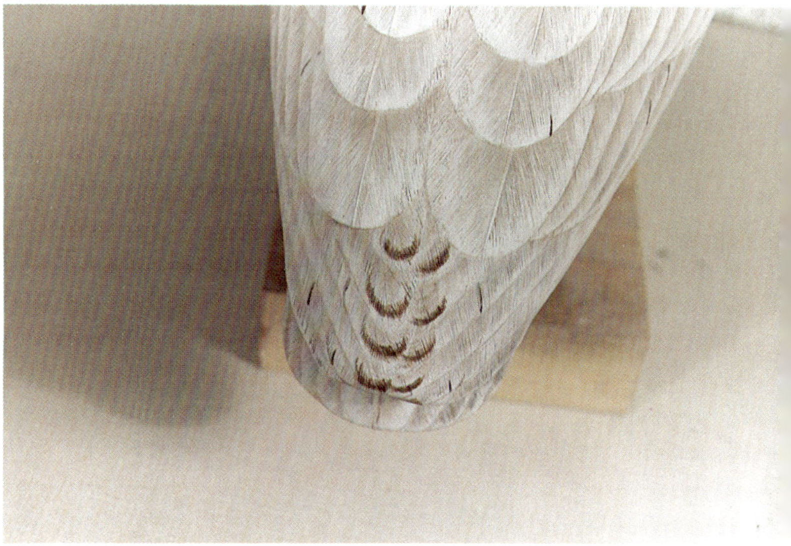

Note: feathers edged in white and darker interiors. Also note: brown fleckings in tail area and primaries — these marks generally disappear in male — the female has them throughout life

Washing with combination of white and gesso

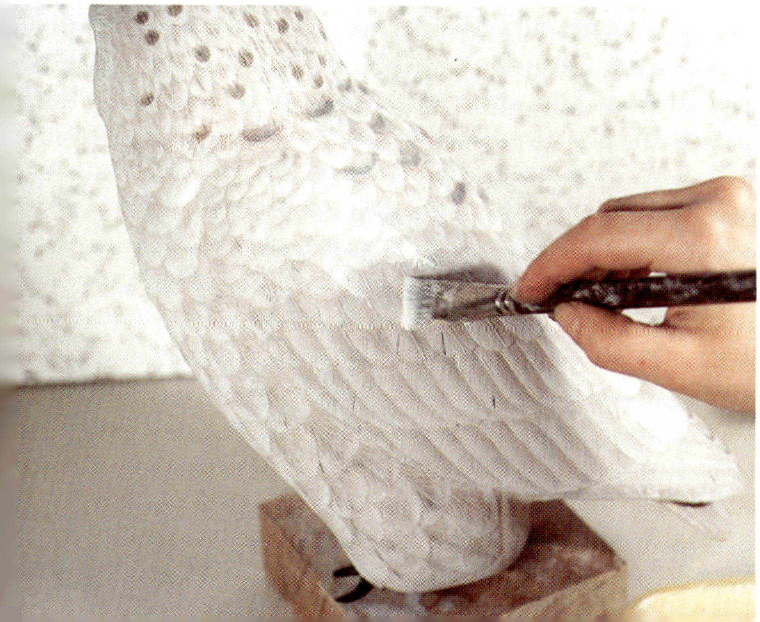

Bringing bird to "life" by scraping eye — when doing this trace around inside of eyelid first so when scraping you will not "tear" paint over eyelid.

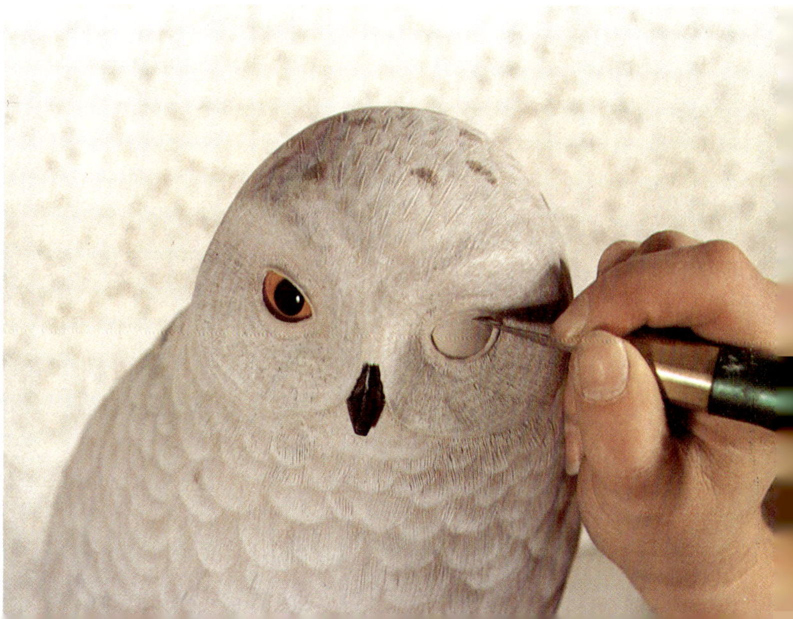

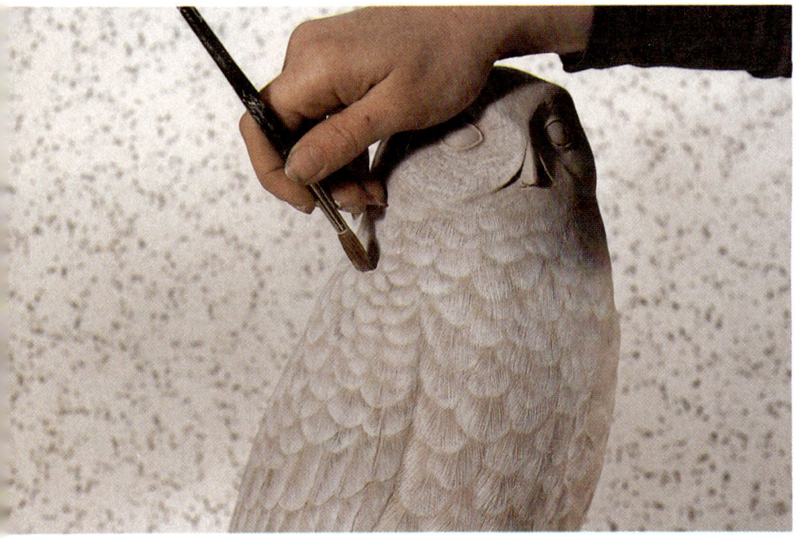

Edging wing area

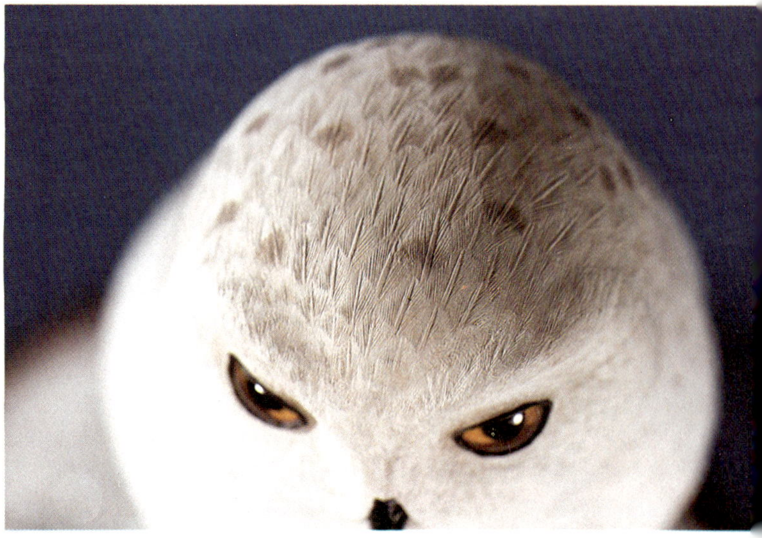

Top of head showing light brown flecks — black beak and black eyelids — Note: almond shaped eyes

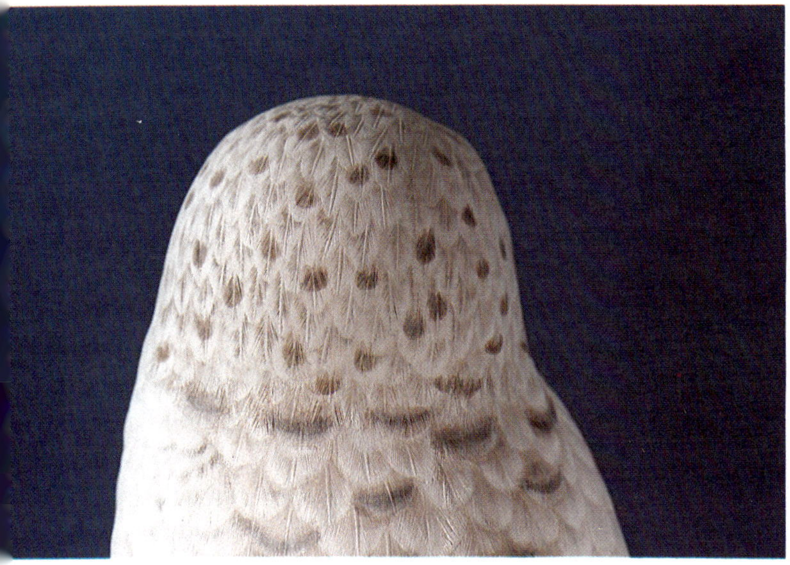

Note: location of brown flecks and white edgings on back of head

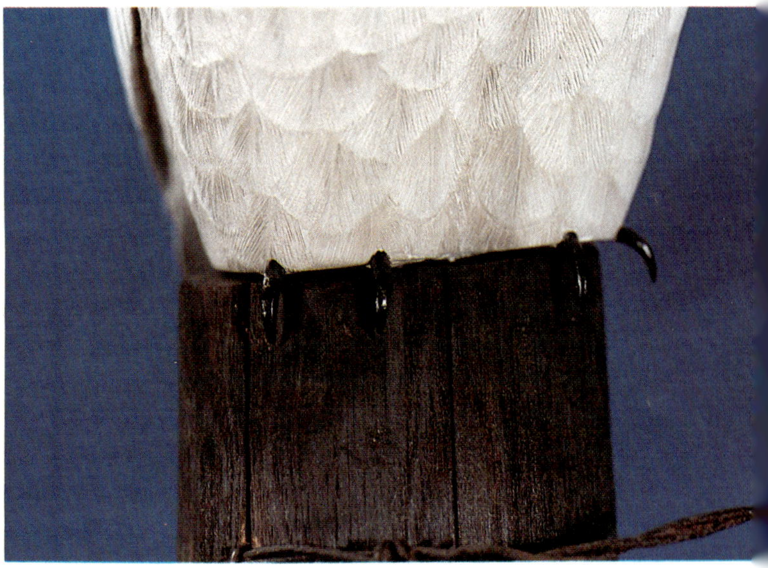

Leg area showing black talons gripping post

Wing area completed

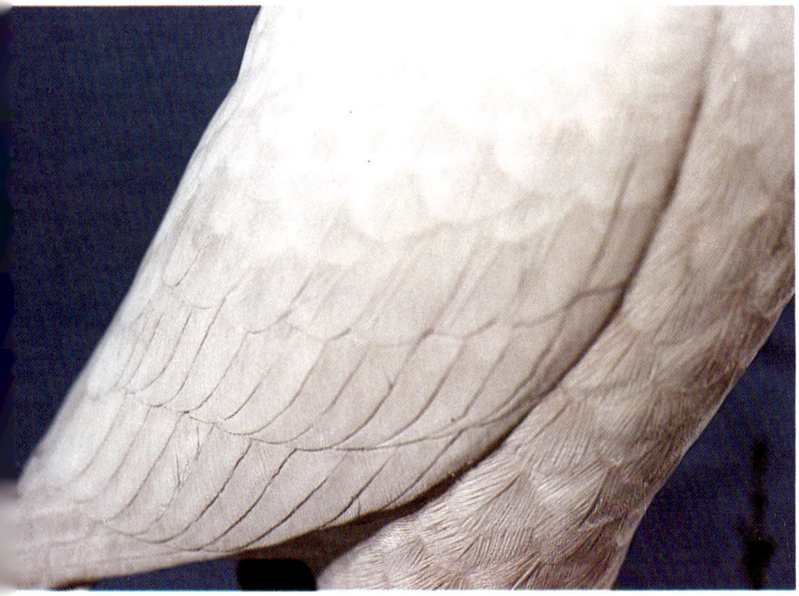

Chest area completed

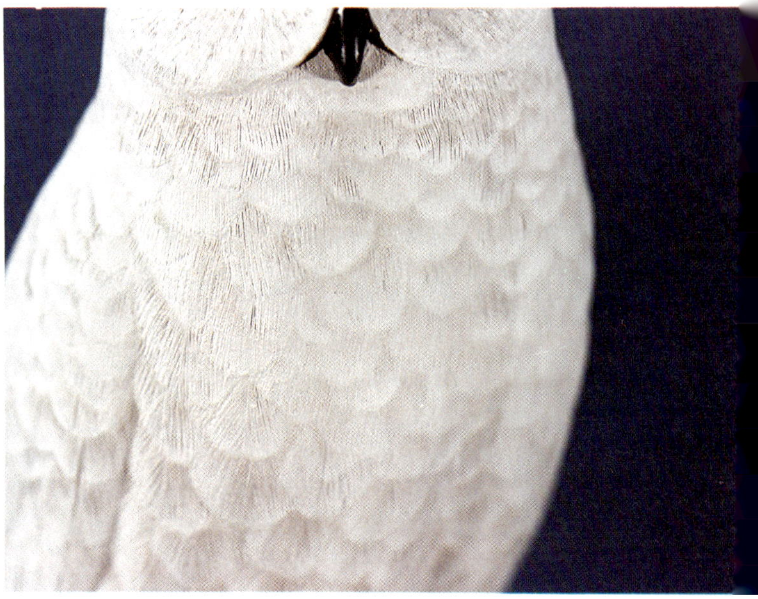

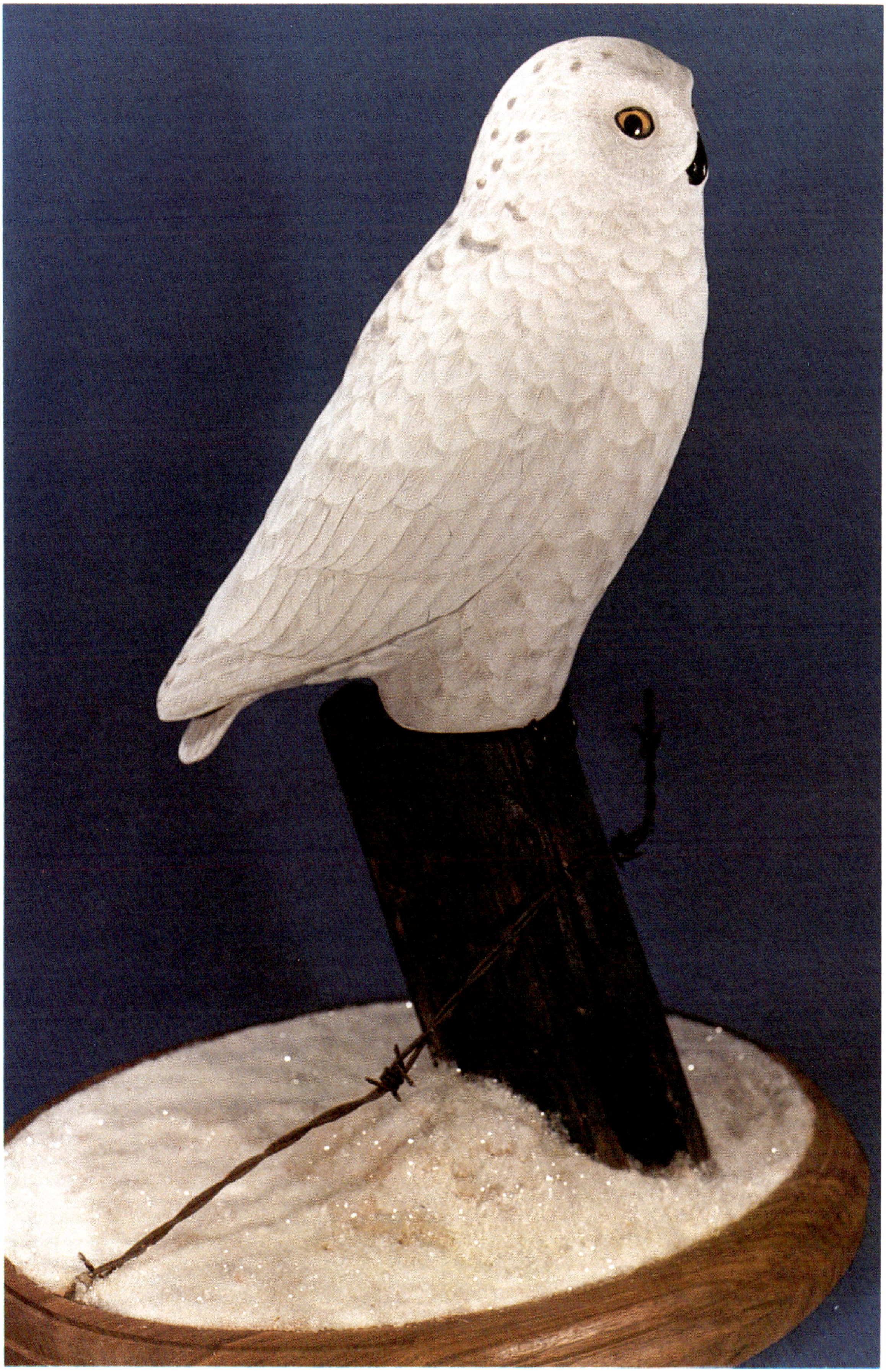

Completed carving of snowy owl by Genille McDyre — The setting compliments carving and presents a whole or complete picture

Osprey

Color list: Black, Burnt umber, White, Yellow ochre, Gesso

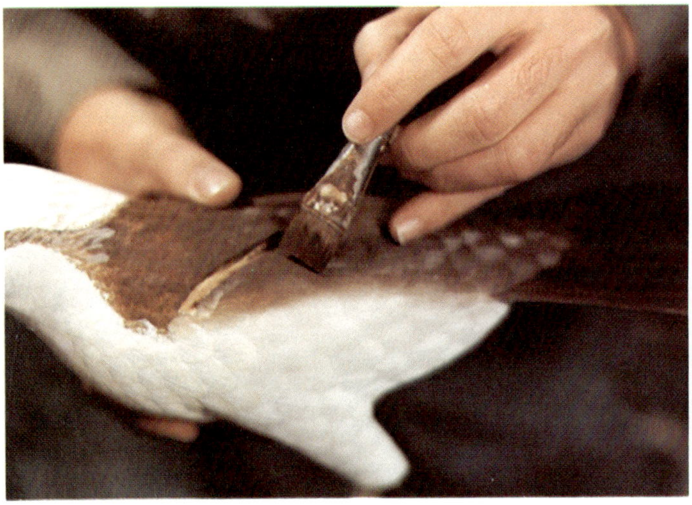

Wash back and upper side of tail with several washes of burnt umber until area is opaque

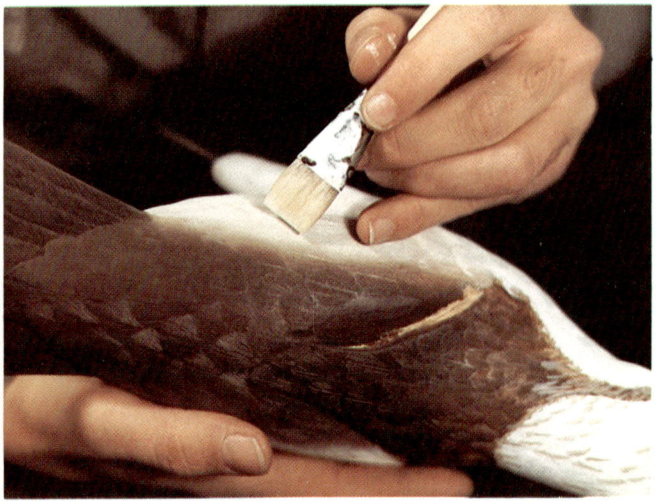

Wash head, side, chest and belly and under tail with combination of white and gesso (50/50)

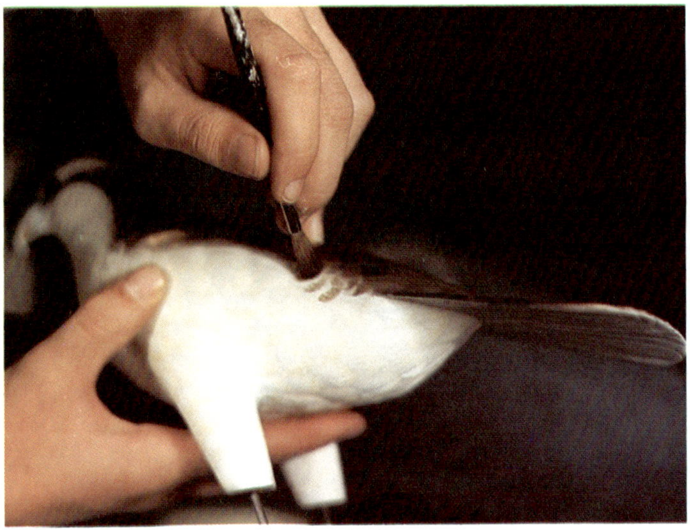

Feather edgings with burnt umber

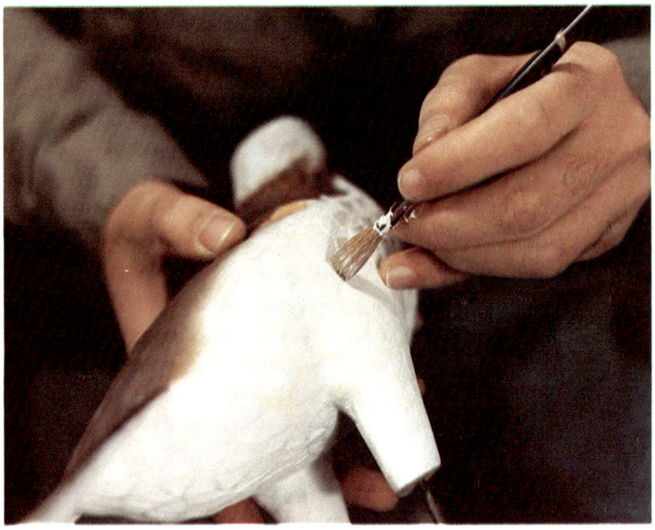

Further edgings

Edging back feathers lightly with black and burnt umber mixed

Streaking head and eyeline with burnt umber with small amount of black mixed in

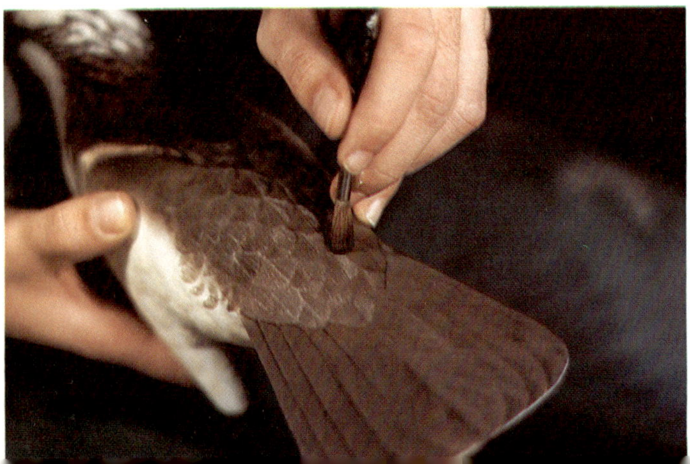

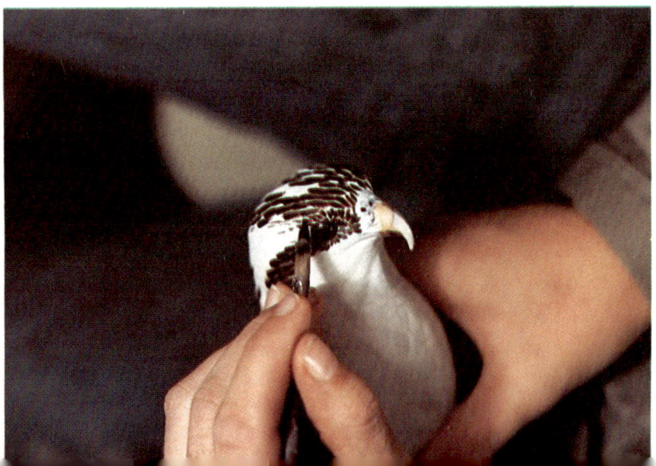

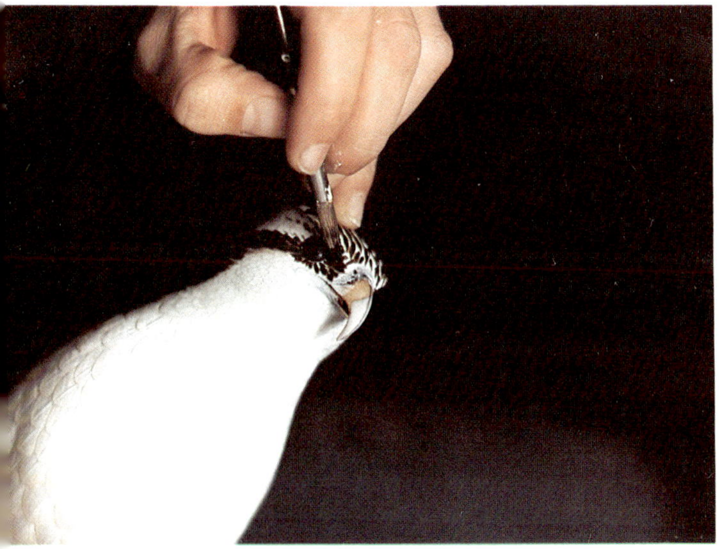

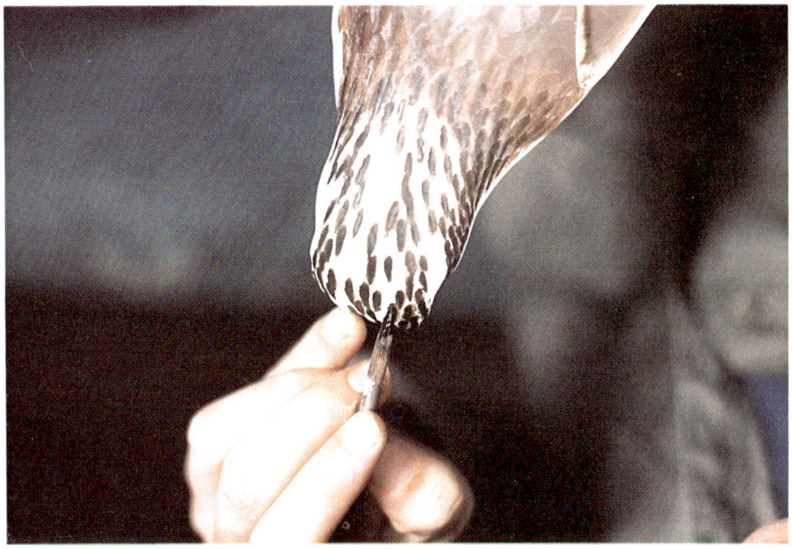

Edging eyeline

Tear drop markings on head

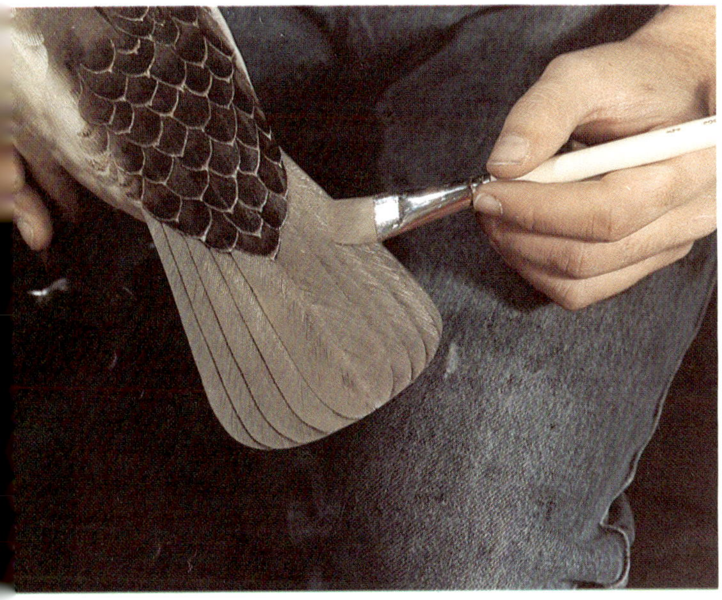

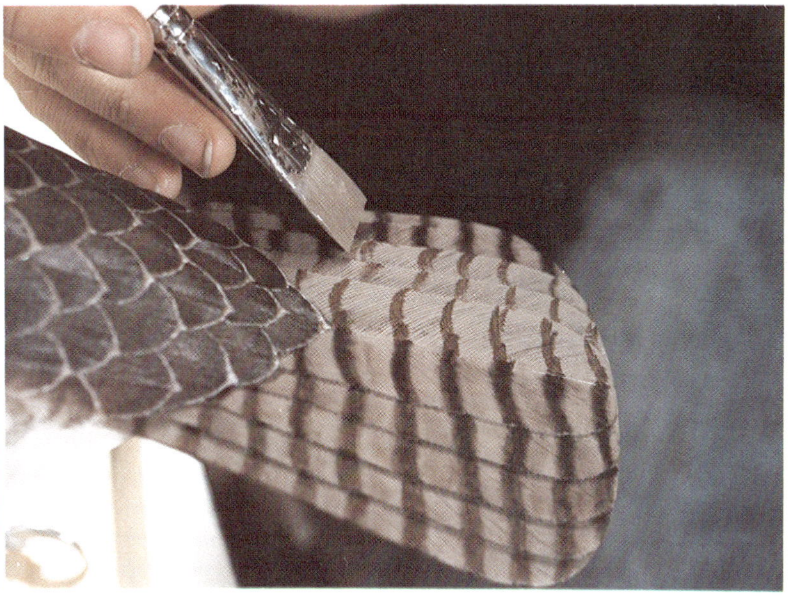

Wash tail with medium tan using burnt umber and white to make the tan

Put black bars in tail side by side with coat of tan, then stipple blend while wet

Continue to blend for softness

Edge back feathers with faint band of white also paint center tail feather quill white

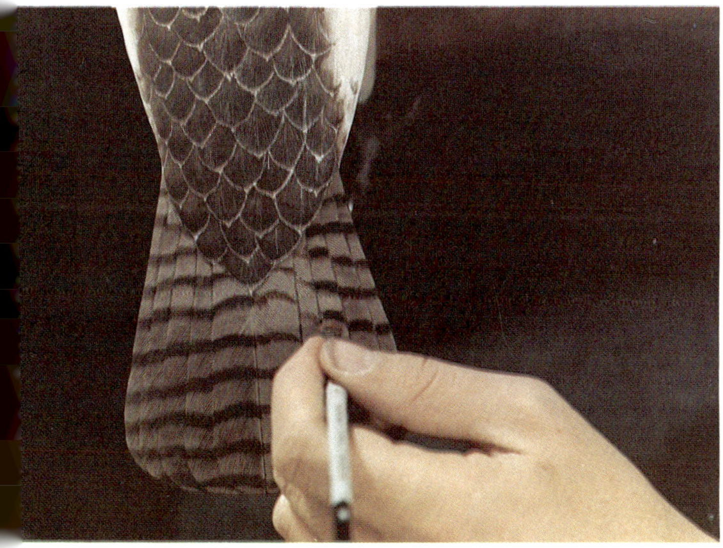

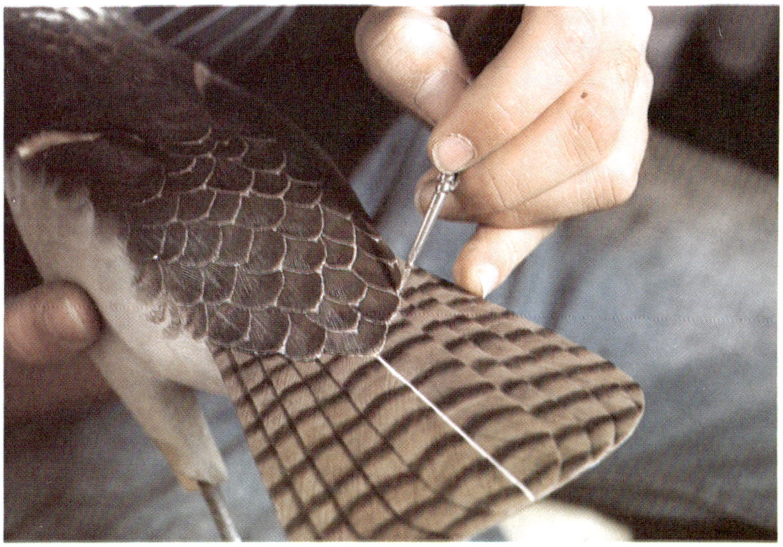

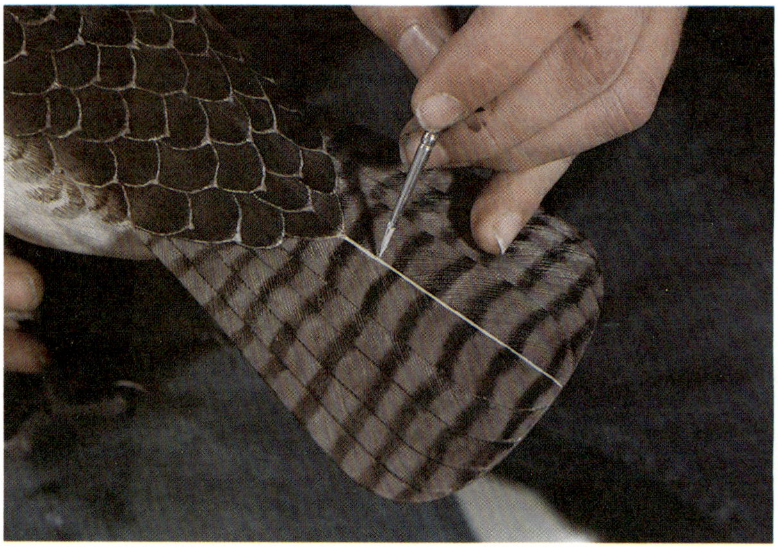

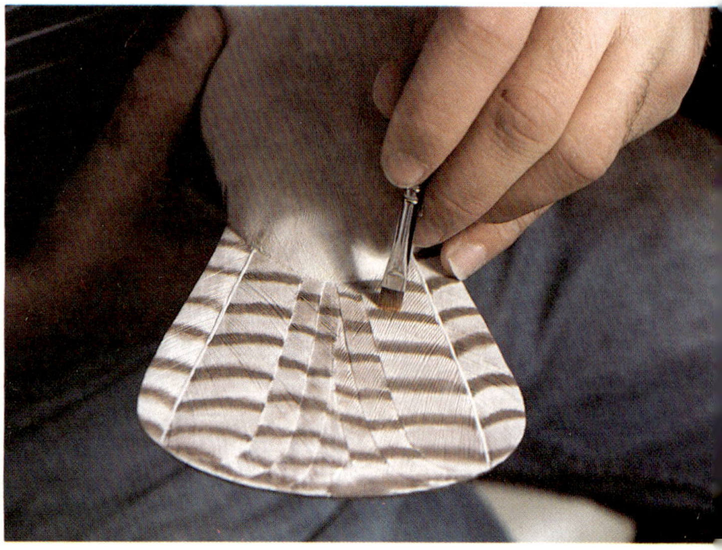

Painting quill or center tail feather

Underside of tail with brown bars, same procedure as topside, wet white and wet brown, heavy cream consistancy and stipple blended

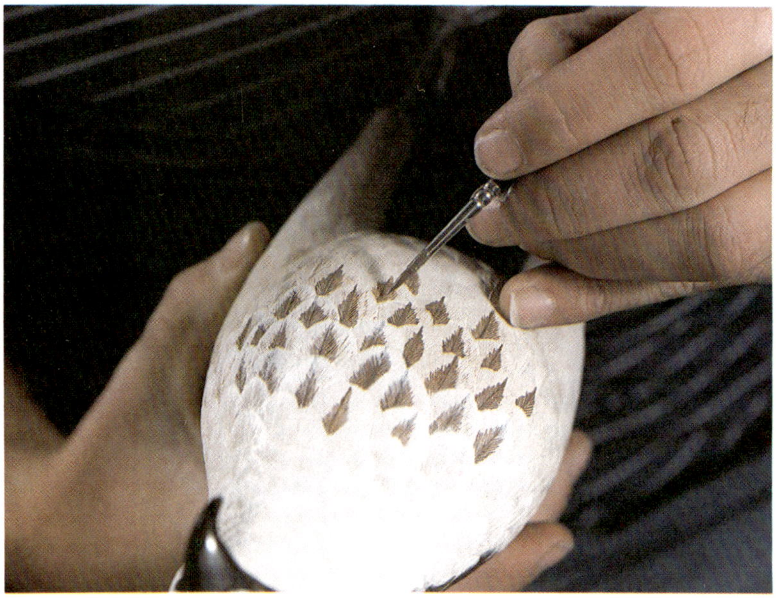

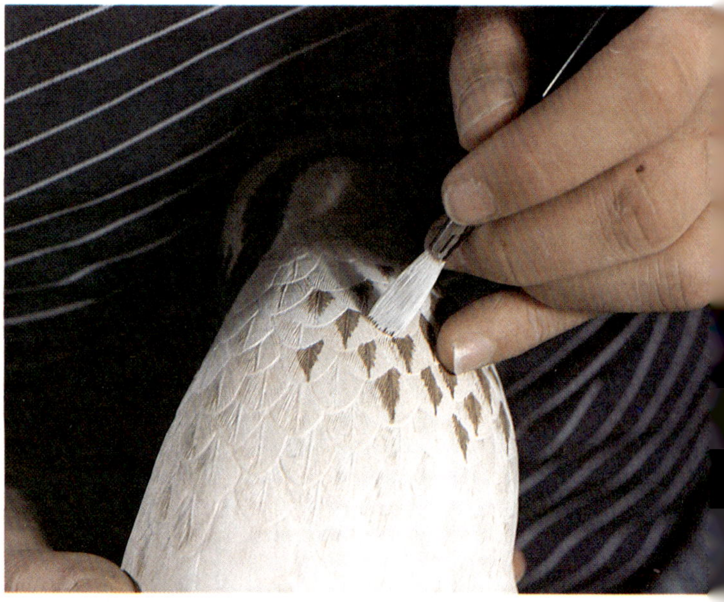

Chest feathers white with light brown interiors (burnt umber applied thinly and kept somewhat translucent)

White edging chest feathers

Under wing white body blended into brown primaries

Upper side of wing washed with burnt umber and edged with black

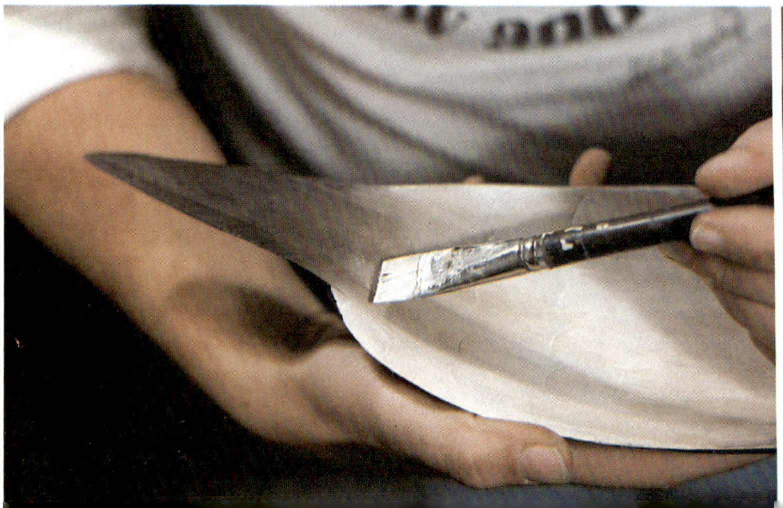

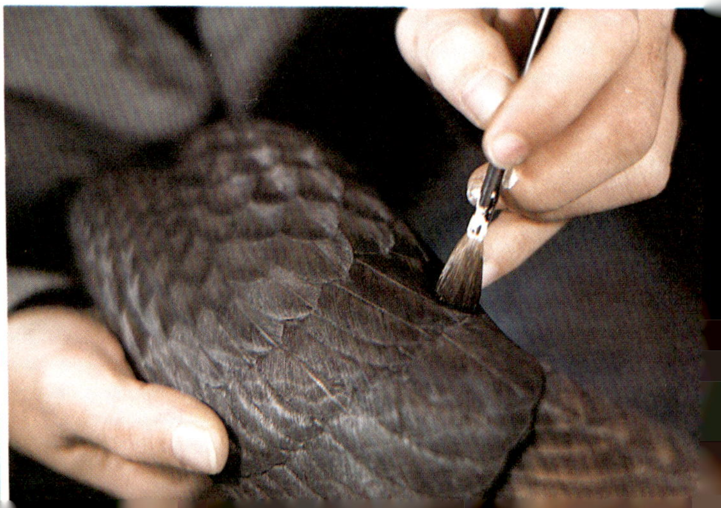

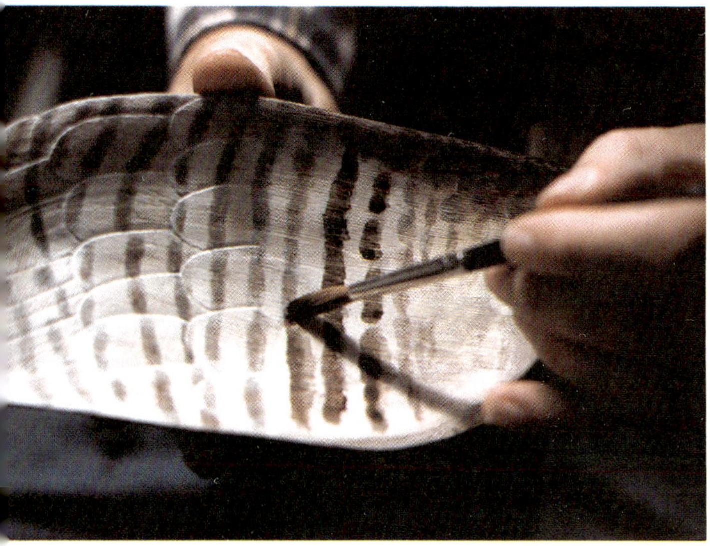

Underside of wing feathers whitish, barred with burnt umber stipple blended

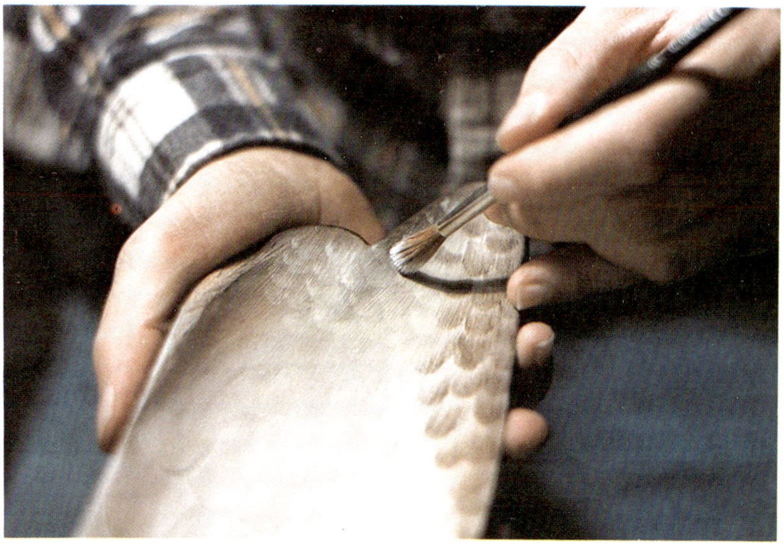

Along edge of wing on underside, some cupped feathers with brown edging

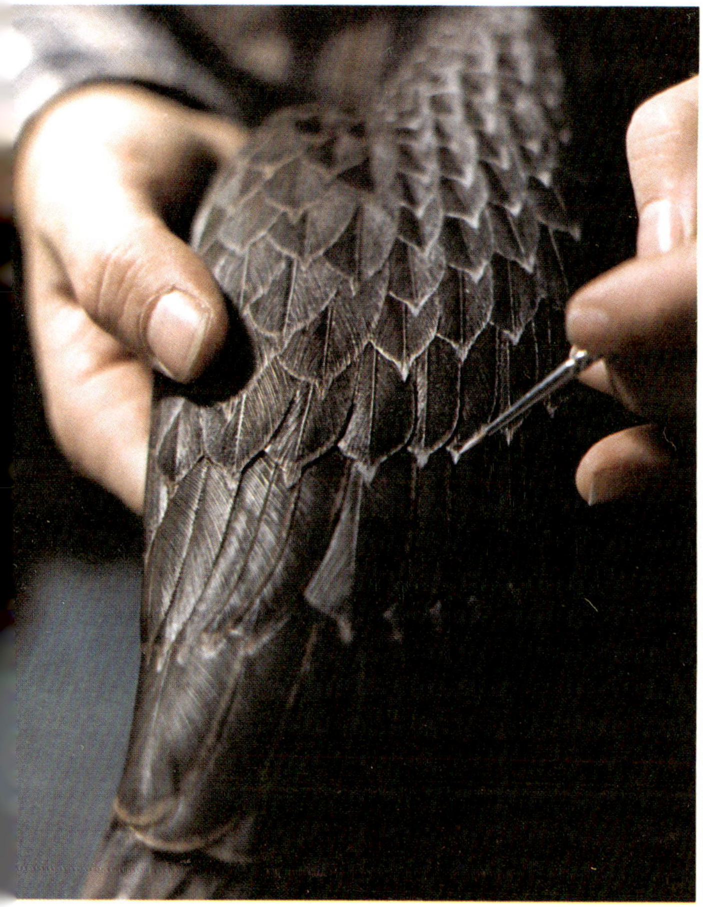

Upper side of wing light, narrow edging in white, note exact shape of feathers as this is the way Osprey wing feathers are shaped

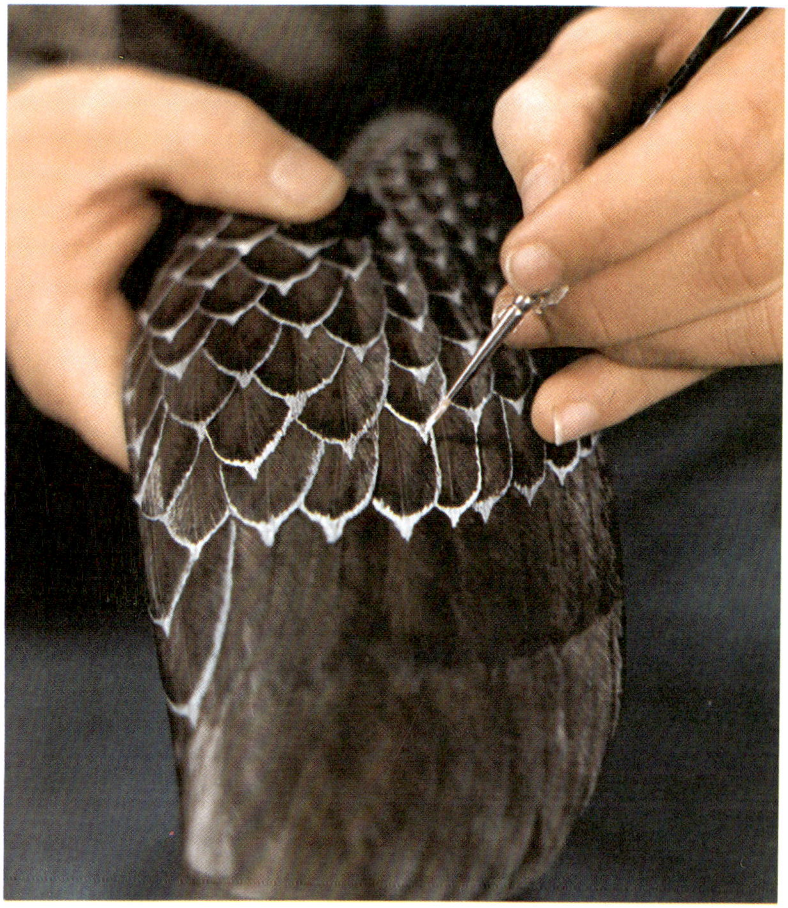

White edging of wing feathers after several edgings to intensify color

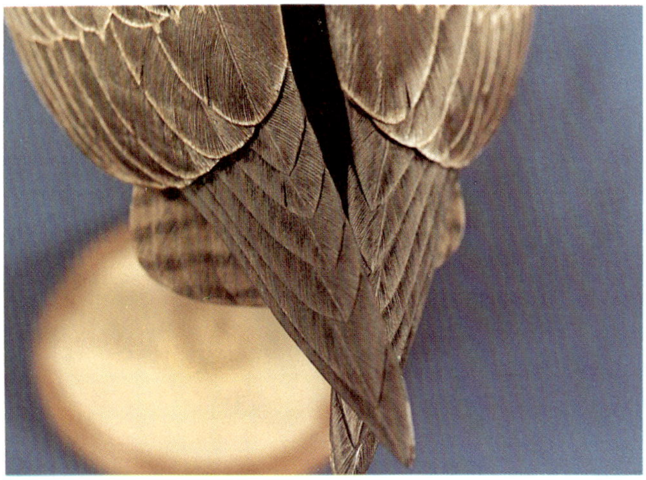

Tertials, secondaries, primaries and tail sections. Note light edgings and dark bars on tail

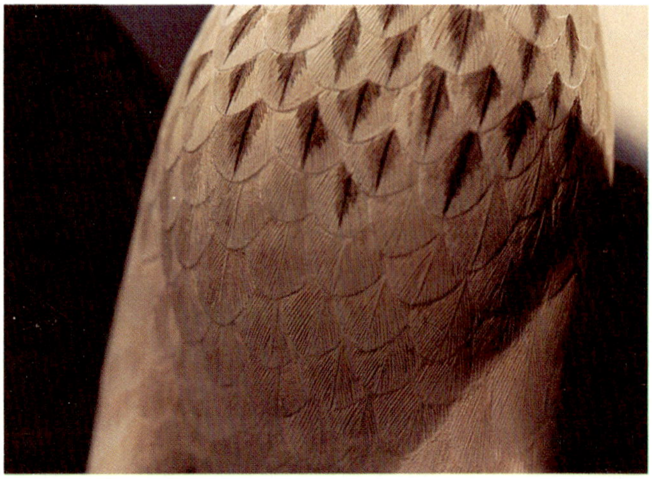

Brown interiors on chest feathers with darker quill lines

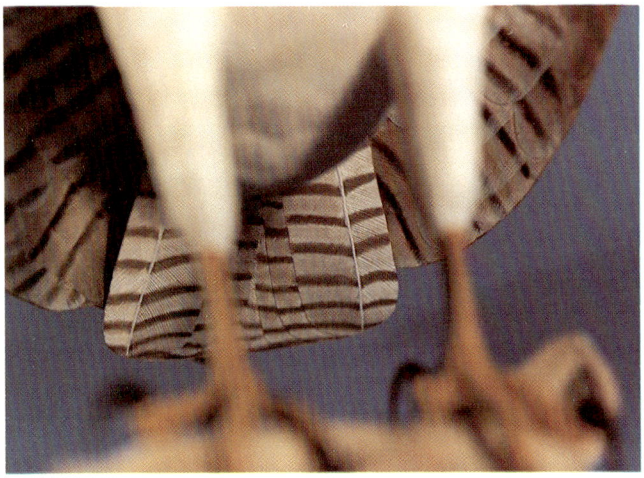

Under tail white with dark brown bars (burnt umber)

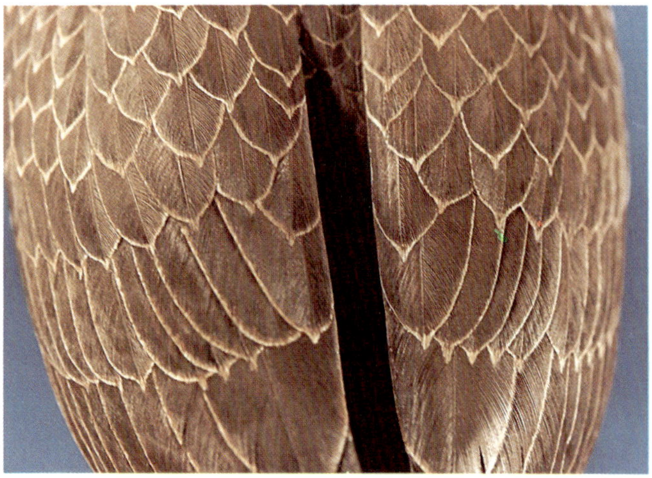

Top of wings edged—note paint on feathers

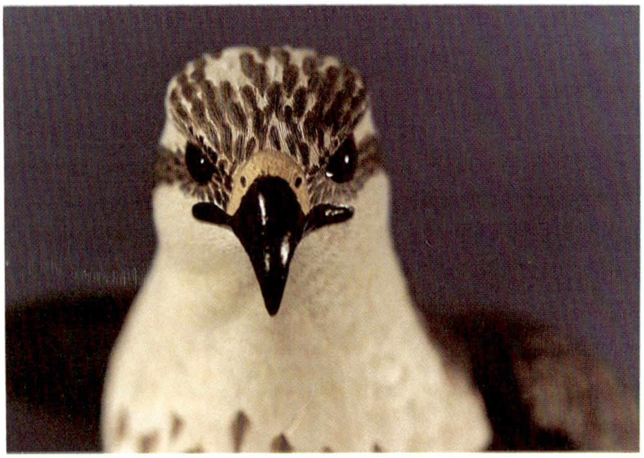

Head detail—black beak with yellow ochre patch at base. Crown feathers white with dark brown interior, dark brown eye line

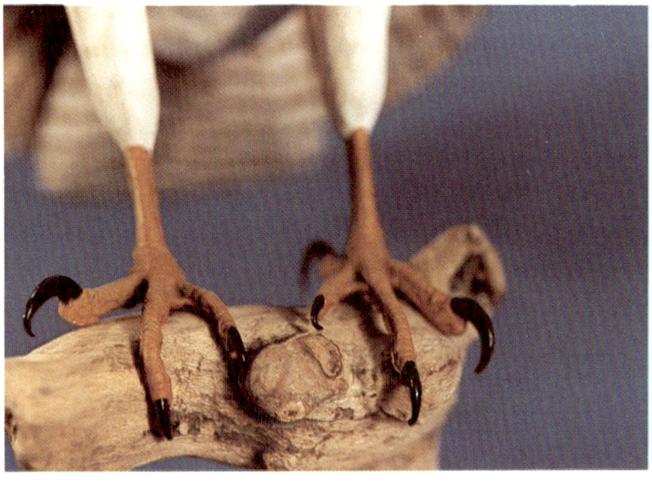

Feet—yellow ochre washed with thin wash of black. Black talons

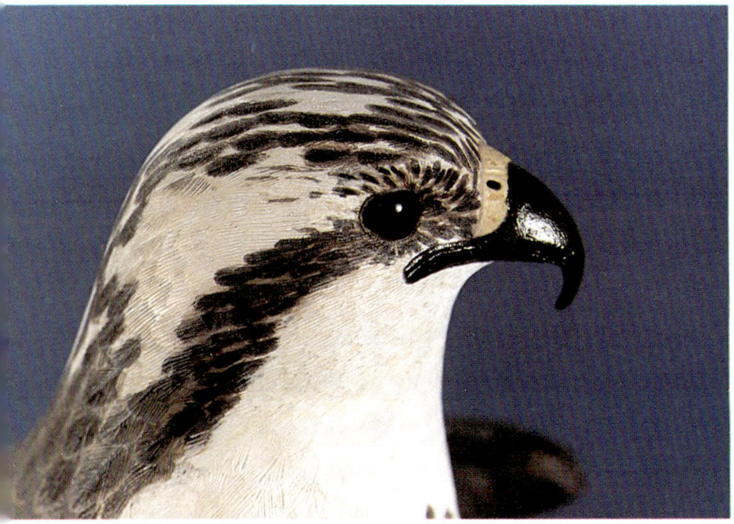

Head detail profile—note direction of dark eye line

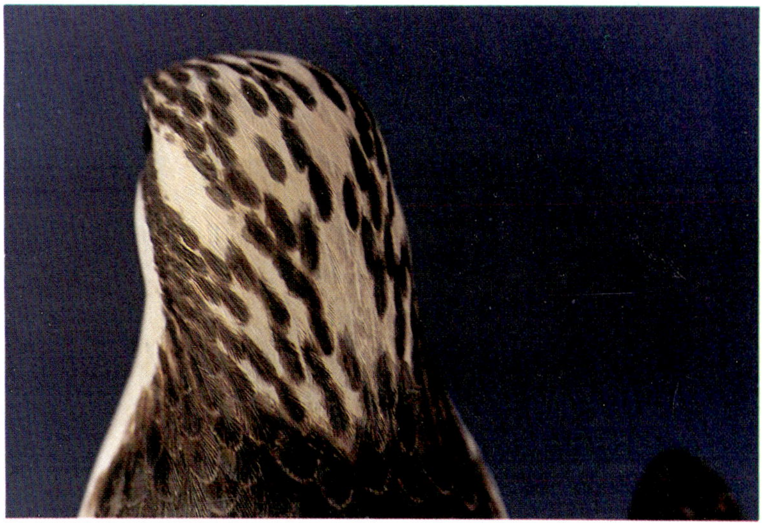

Back of head detail flowing into cape area

Finished carving perched on mount.

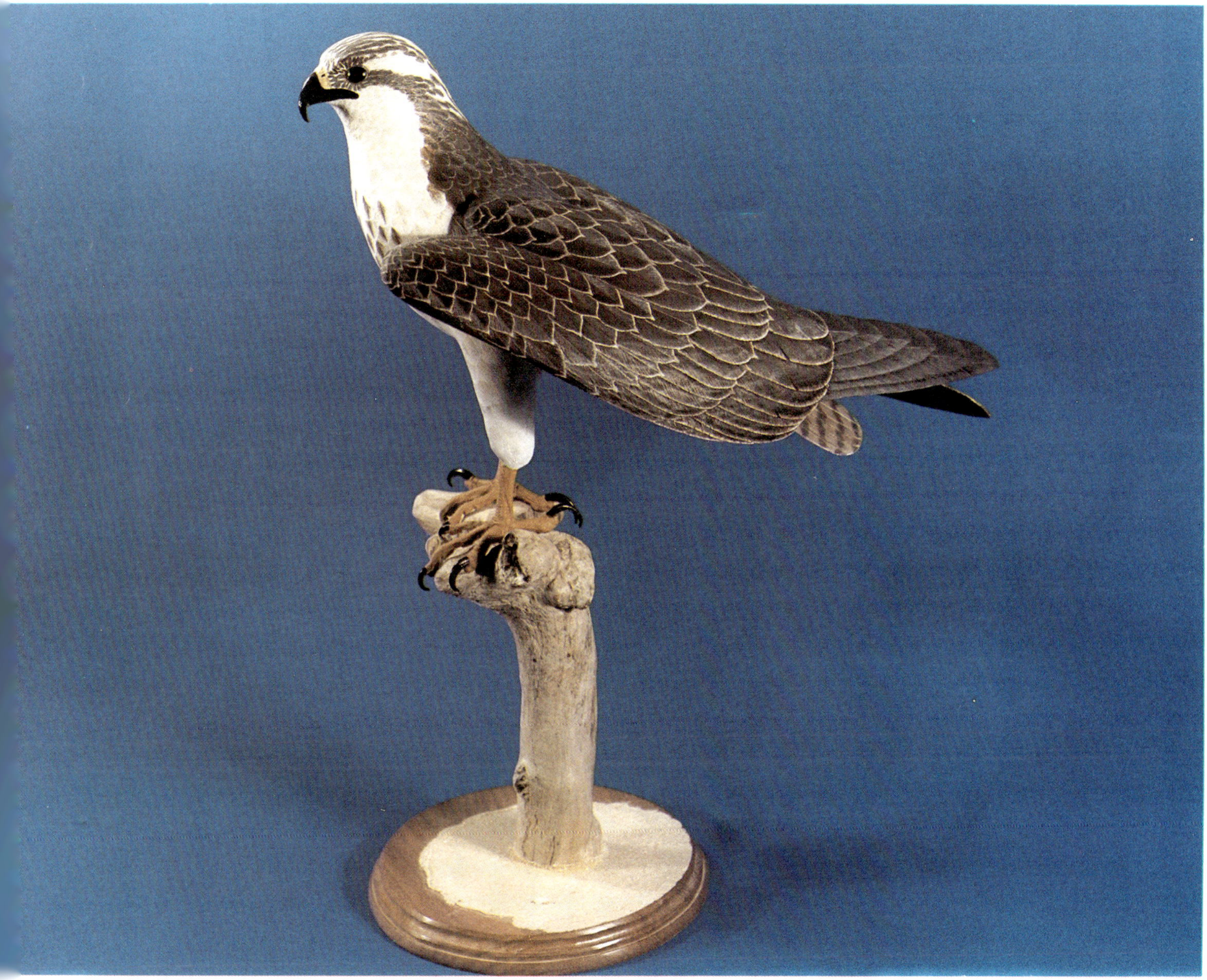

American Kestrel

Color list: Paynes gray, Titanium white, Gesso, Yellow ochre, Burnt umber, Raw sienna, and Burnt sienna

A. Always mix white and gesso (50/50) to make white
B. Use Paynes gray and burnt umber to make black
C. Use Paynes gry and white for bluish gray

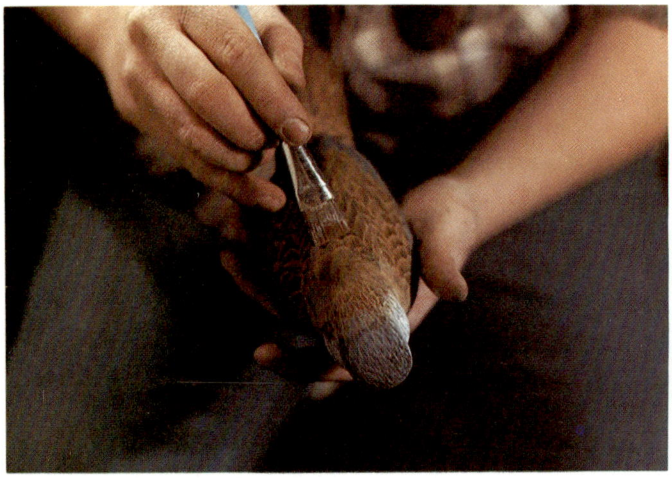

With thin washes lay in basic colors in general areas —back and cape

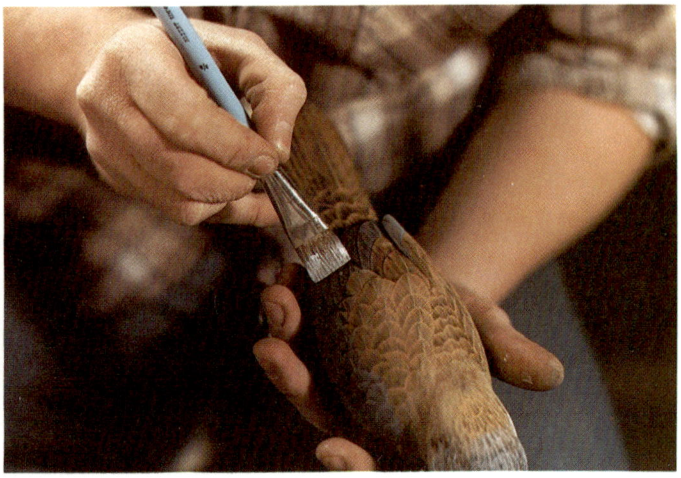

Wing areas, as basic colors are laid in also lay in black spots so as to "bleed somewhat". This way there will be no harsh line of demarkation.

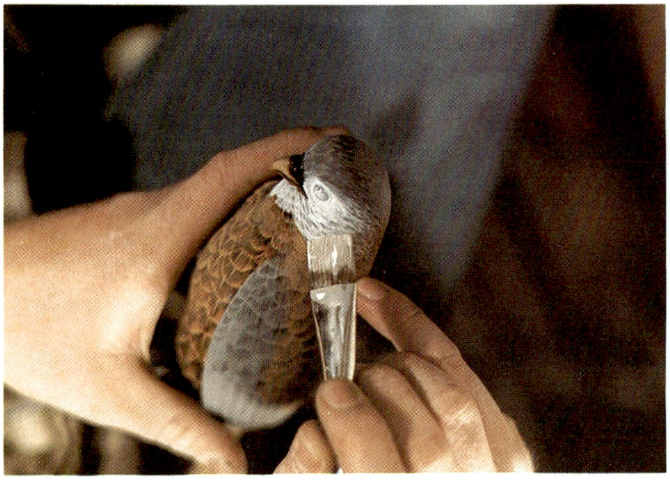

White area on head

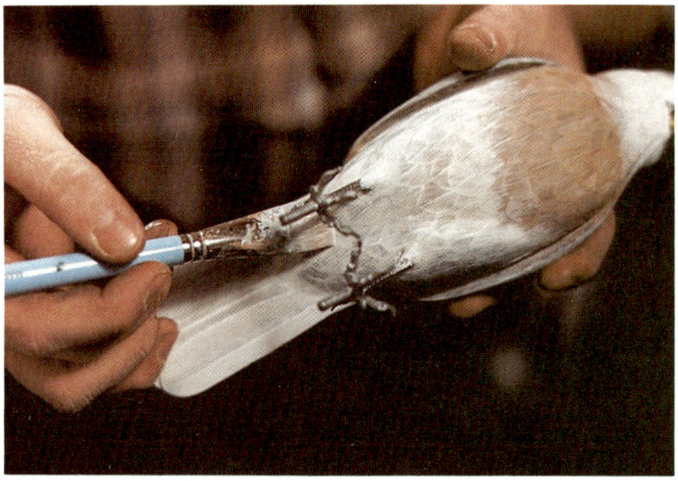

Buff color of chest (raw sienna and white)

Burnt sienna with small amount of yellow ochre on underside of tail Note: white band at end of tail

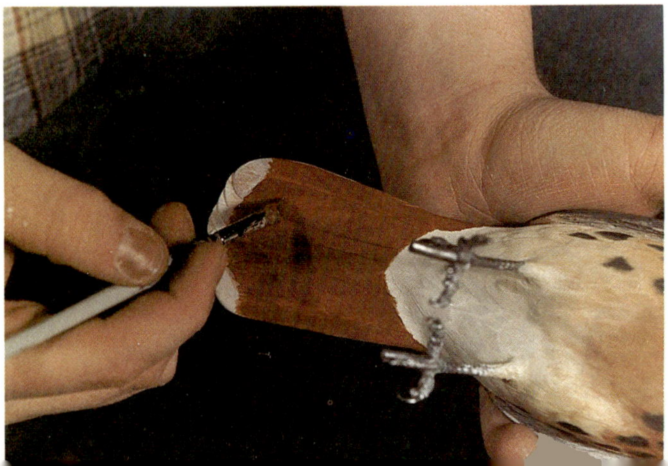

Top side of tail white band — black then burnt sienna with small amount of yellow ochre

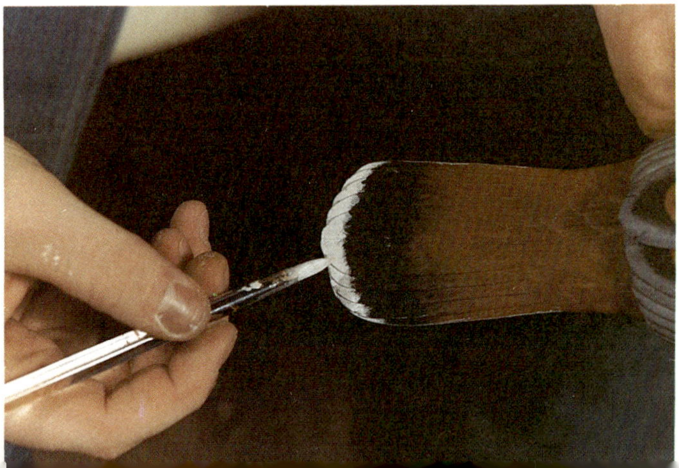

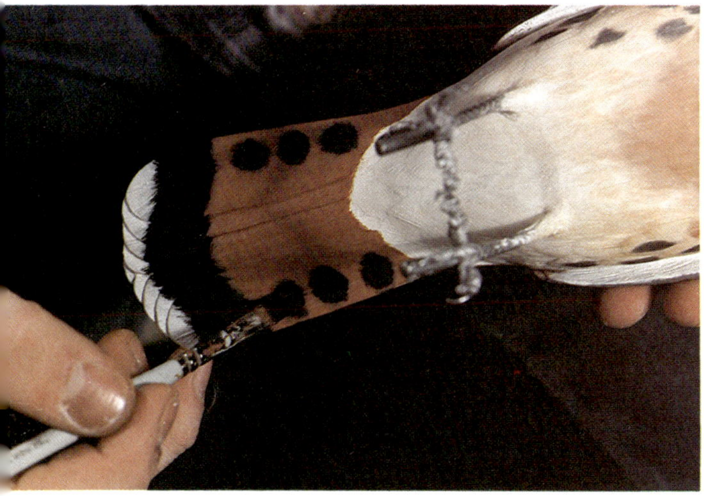

Black spots on underside of outer tail feathers (Keep lines soft with gentle stipple blend. This necessitates using paint at the consistency of heavy cream)

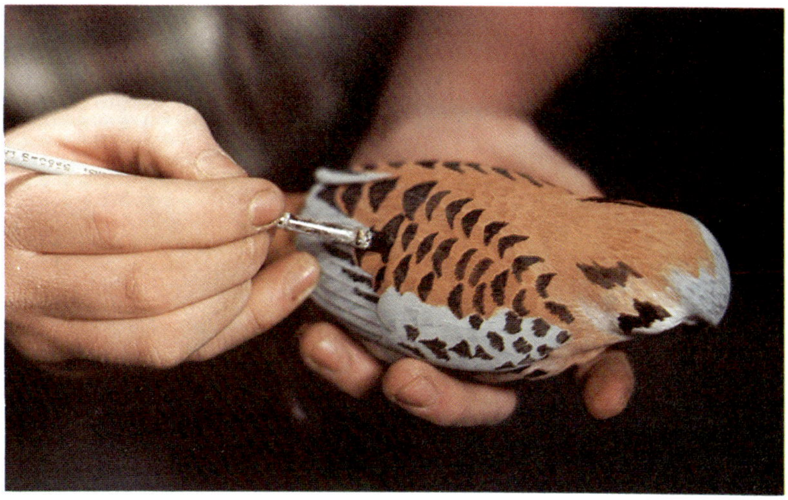

Back bars laid in on wings and cape area; this is accomplished by wet next to wet with repeated layers of color. Burnt sienna and yellow ochre mixed with black stippled together to create soft color transaction.

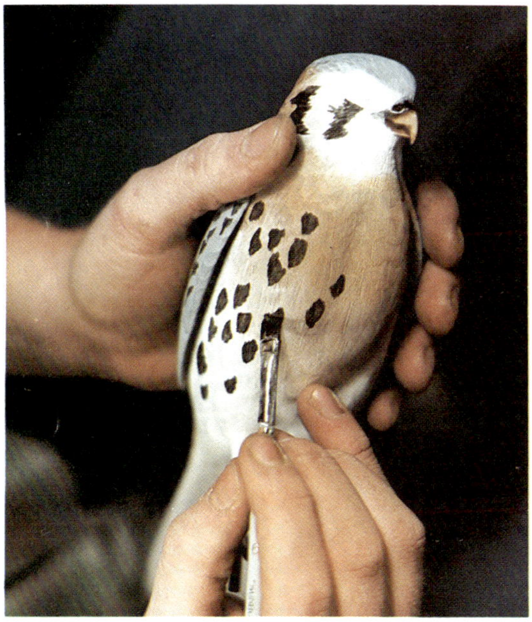

Black spots on chest and belly (These spots amost always disappear as the bird gets older, however, in a carving the slightly immature bird has a little more color

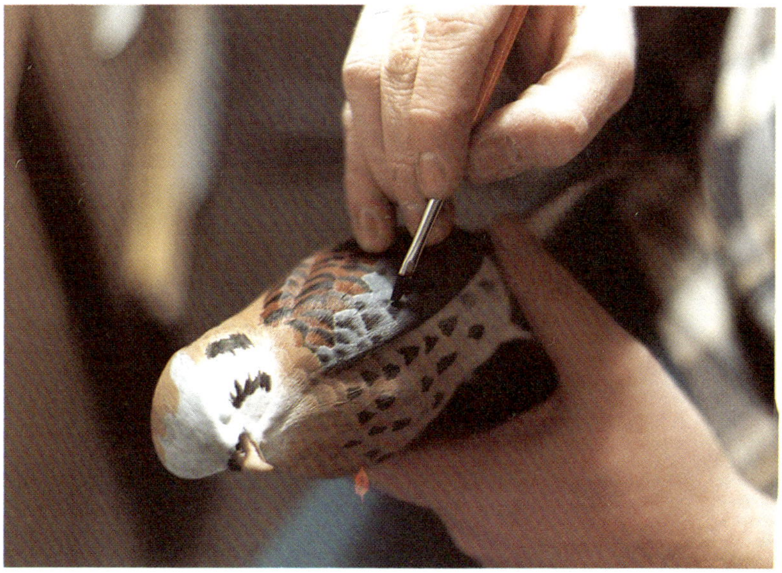

Black spotting in blue gray area of wing same techniques as in reddish area

Back of head detail — blue gray and reddish areas

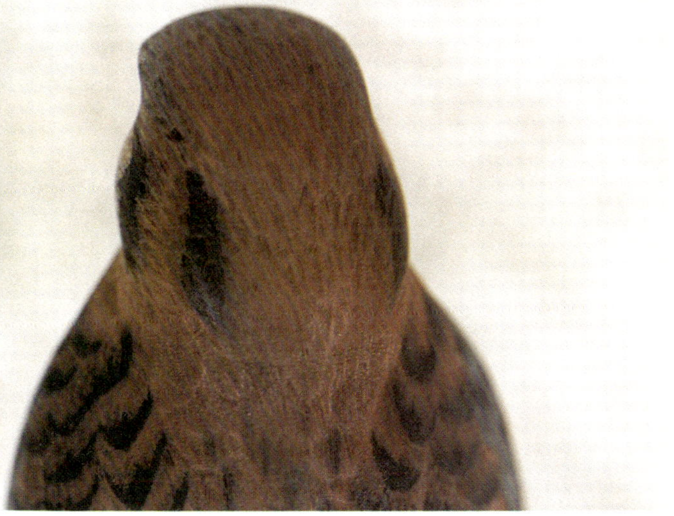

Chest buff color blended with black spotting using above techniques

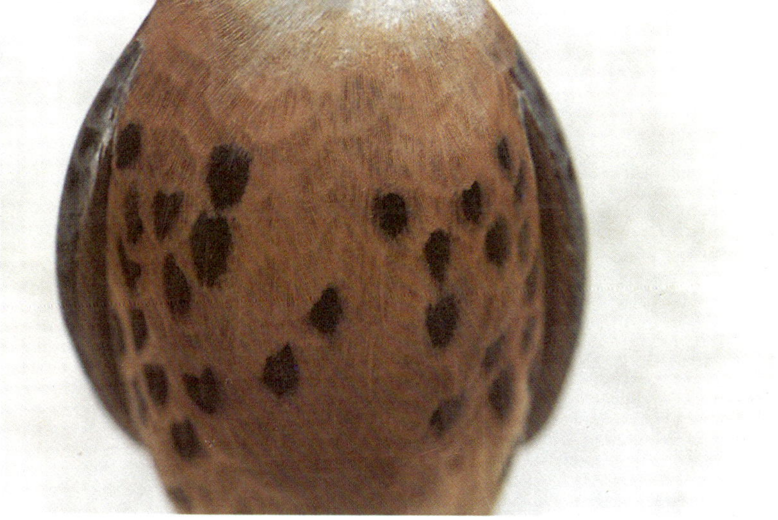

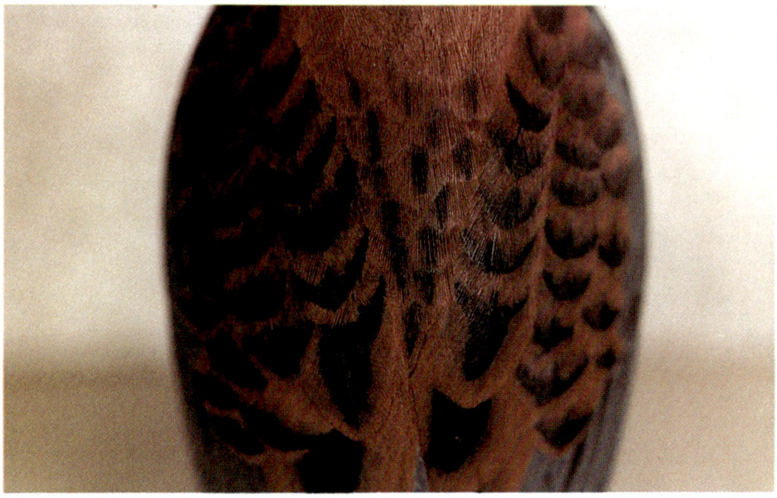

Full back at about half way points. Note: the blendings are still not quite soft enough

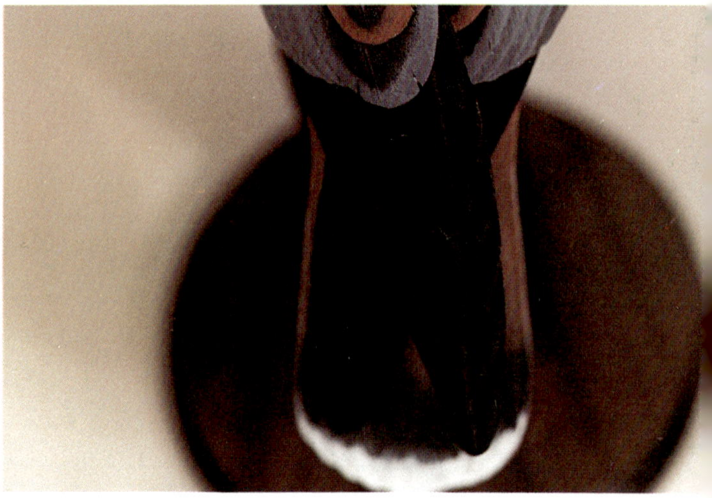

Tail area — Note: light edging of primary feathers

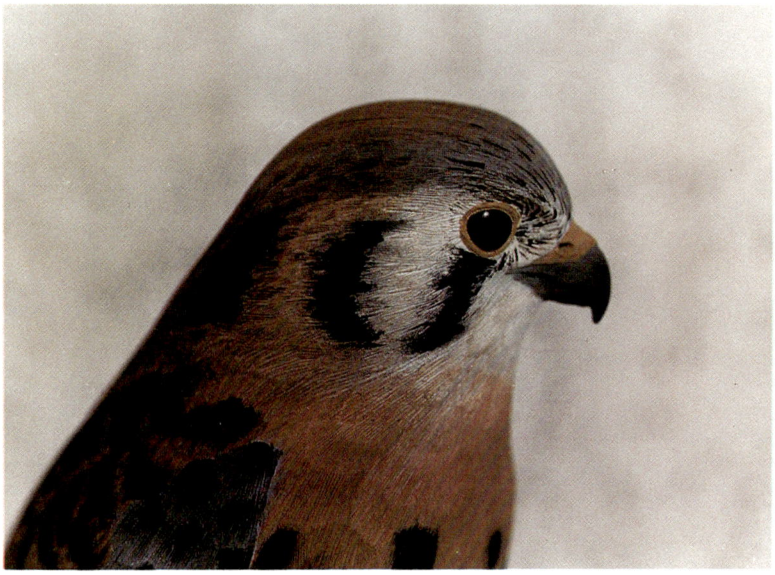

Profile of head — thin black streaks through crown — black bars in cheek (very jagged) — yellow ochre eyelid — beak yellow ochre at base blended to blue gray to almost black at tip

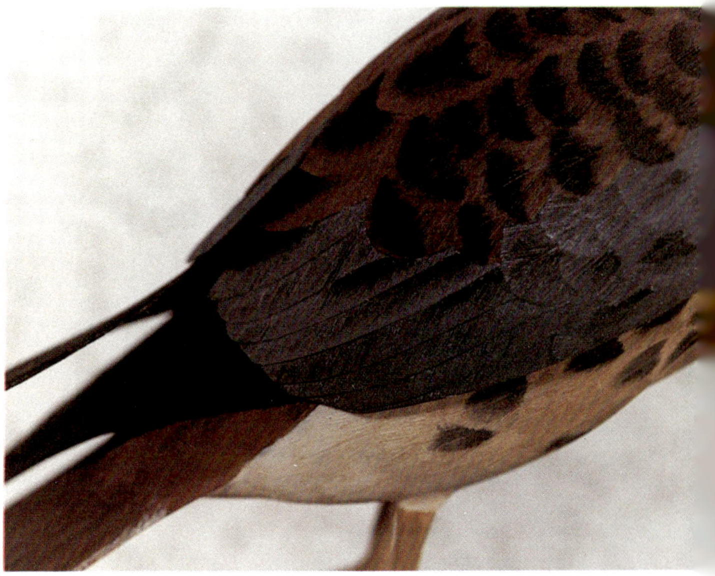

Side view of finished wing area

Under tail and side of belly area

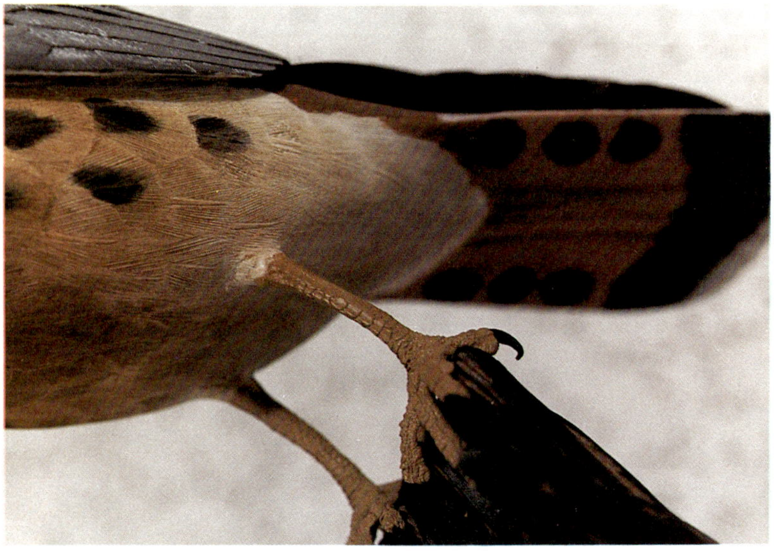

Front view of head and chest — Note: fine black streaks in head and black nostrils

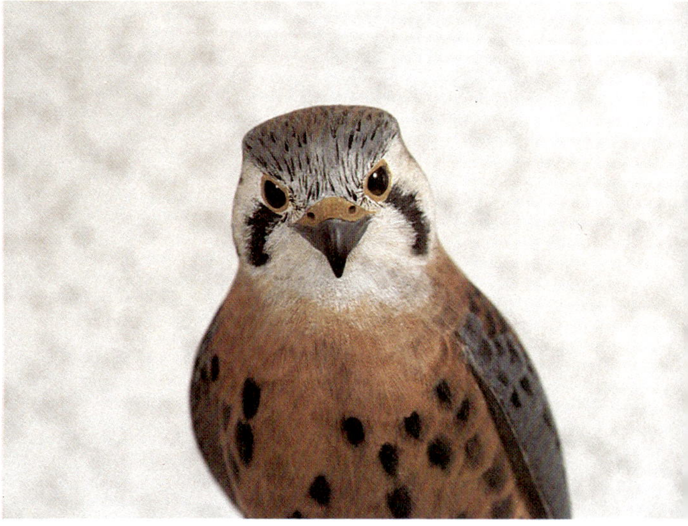

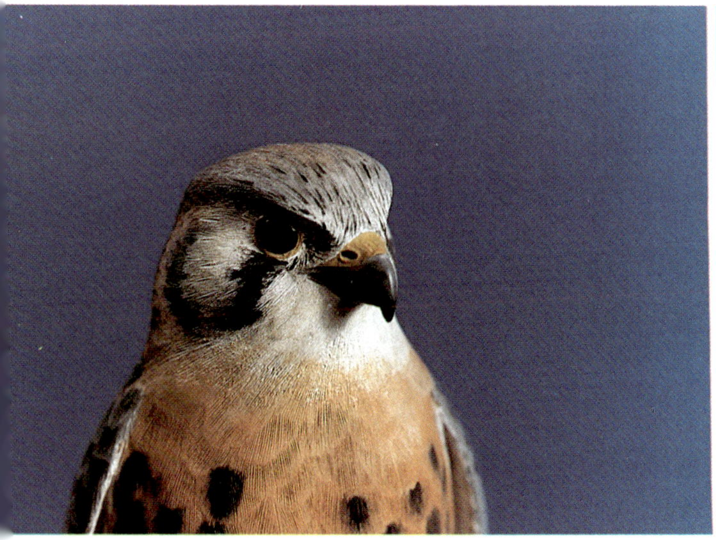

Front view of finished head and chest

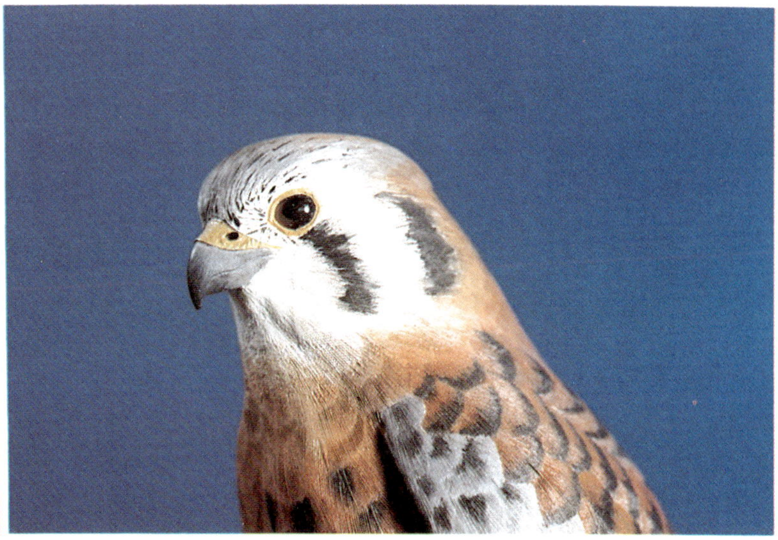

Profile of finished head and shoulder area

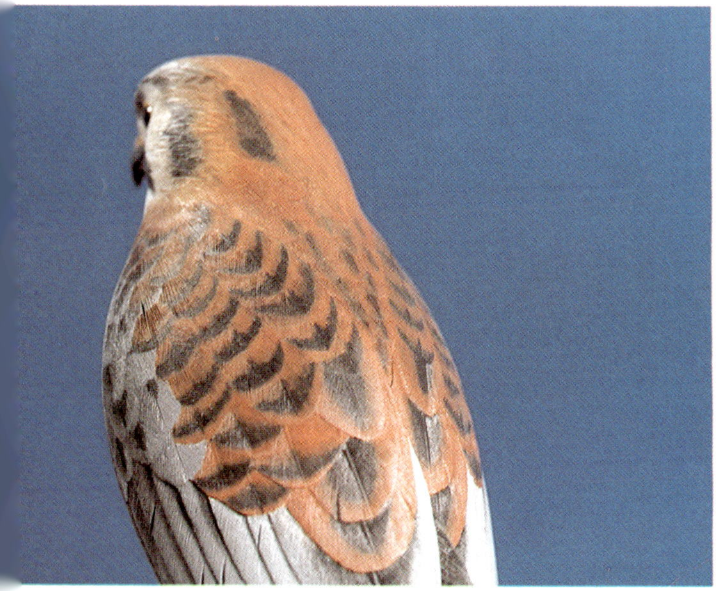

Back view of finished back area — Note: how soft repeated coats have made it.

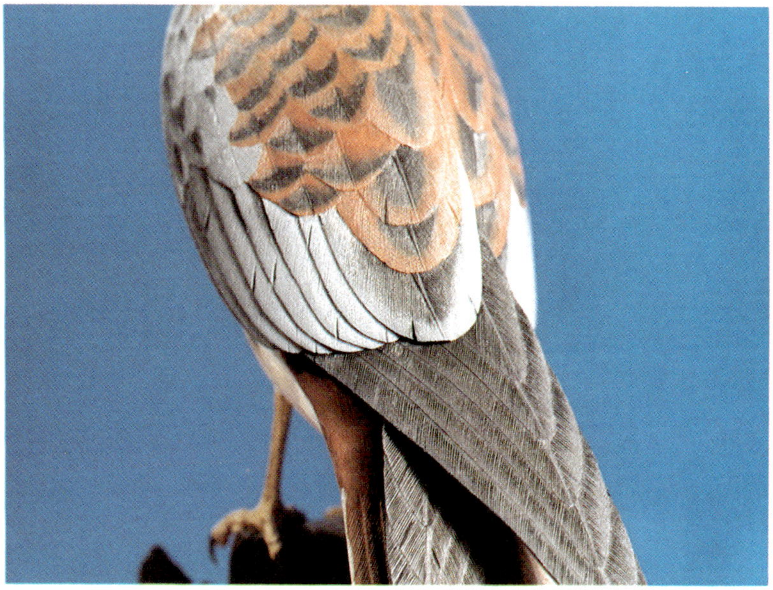

Finished wing with primary area

Finished chest area

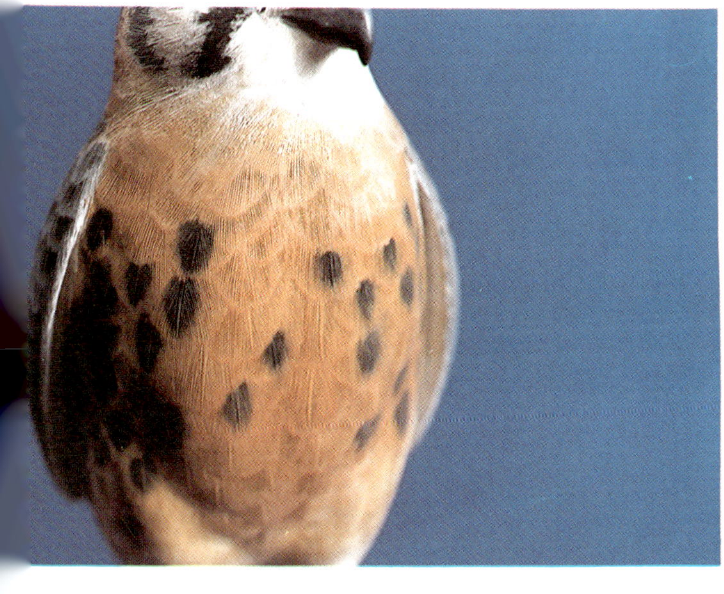

Finished tail and primary area

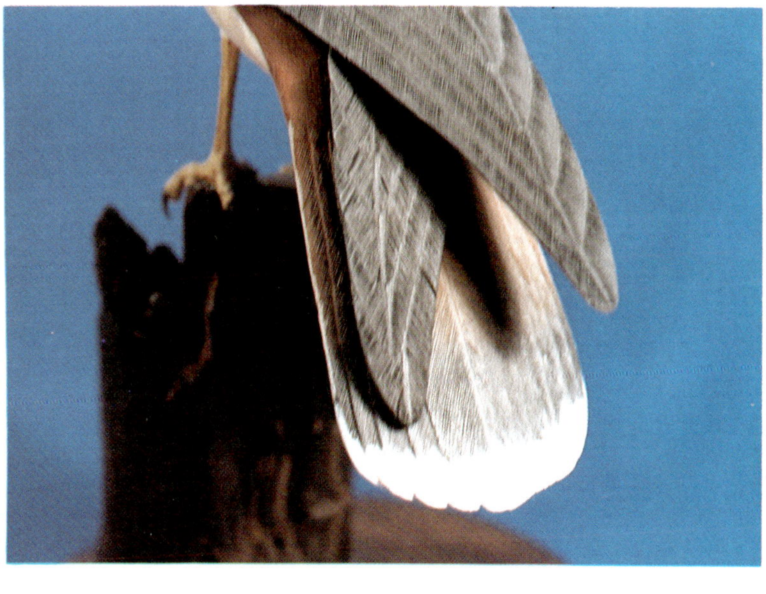

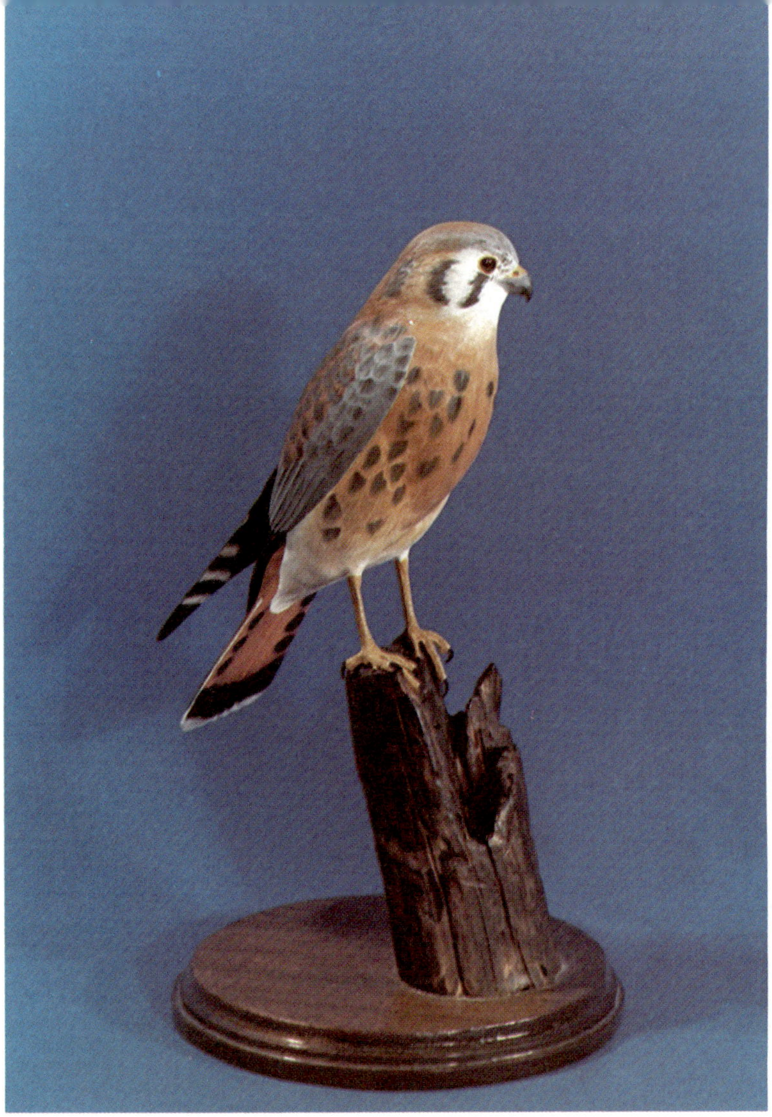

Finished carving by Jeff Moore. This is Jeffs' first carving

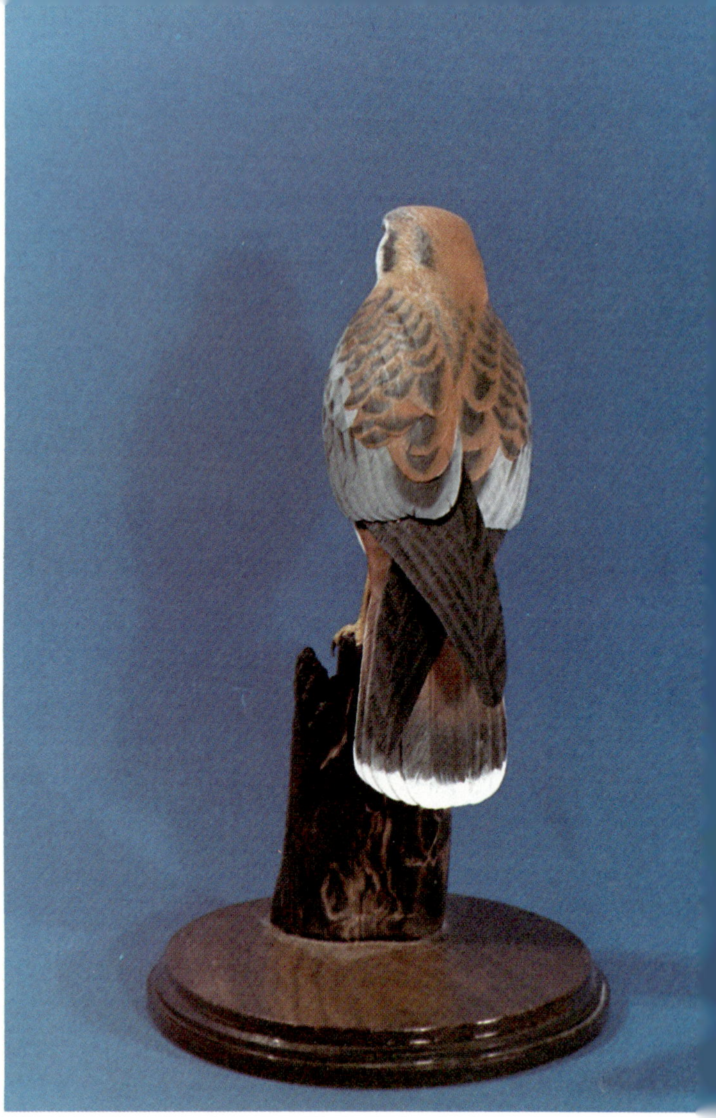

Back view of finished carving mounted on driftwood on walnut base

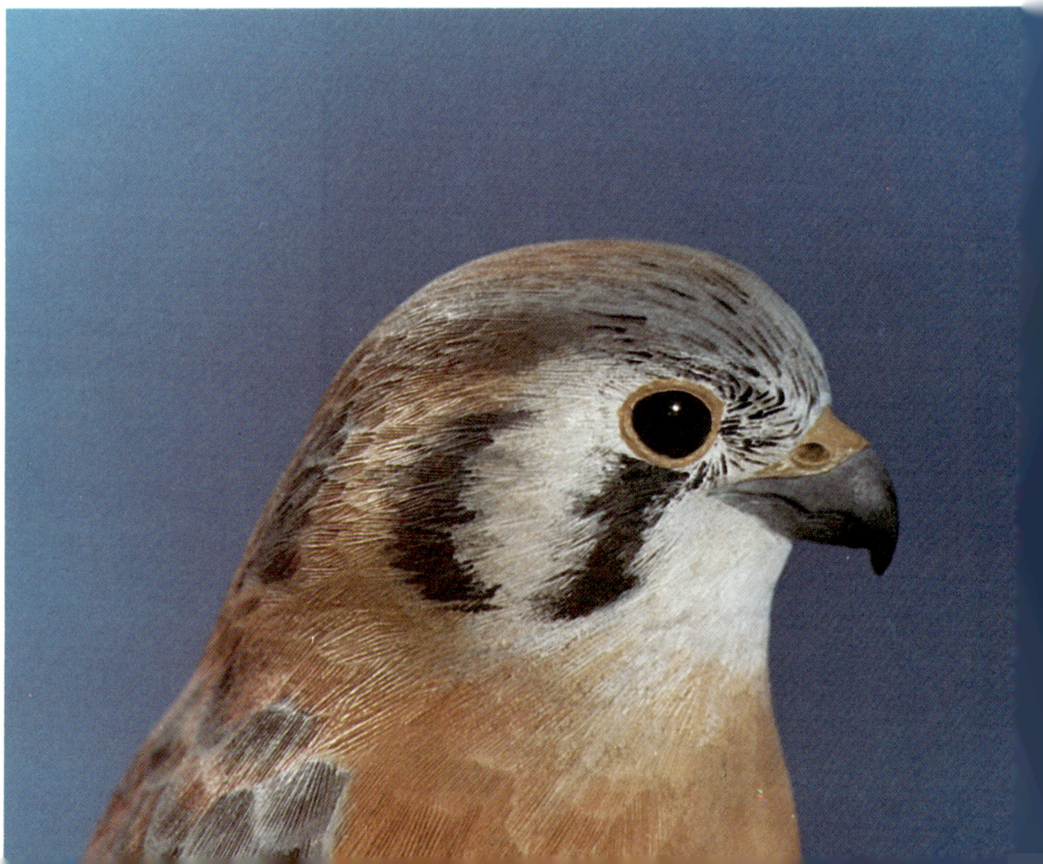

Head view of finished carving

Female Merlin

Color list: Burnt umber, White, Gesso, Black, and Yellow ochre

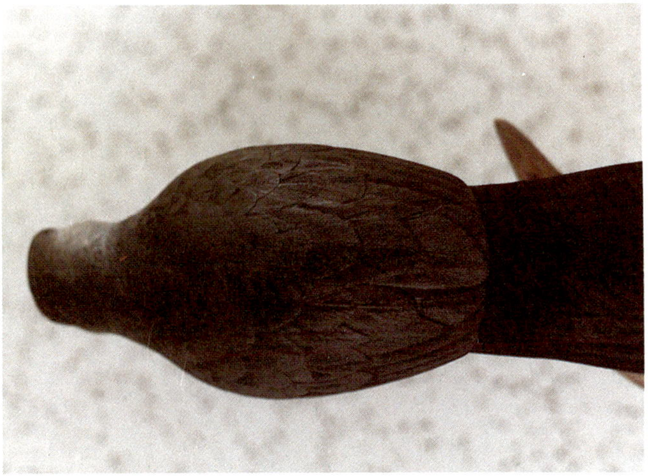

Crown and entire back washed with burnt umber until opaque.

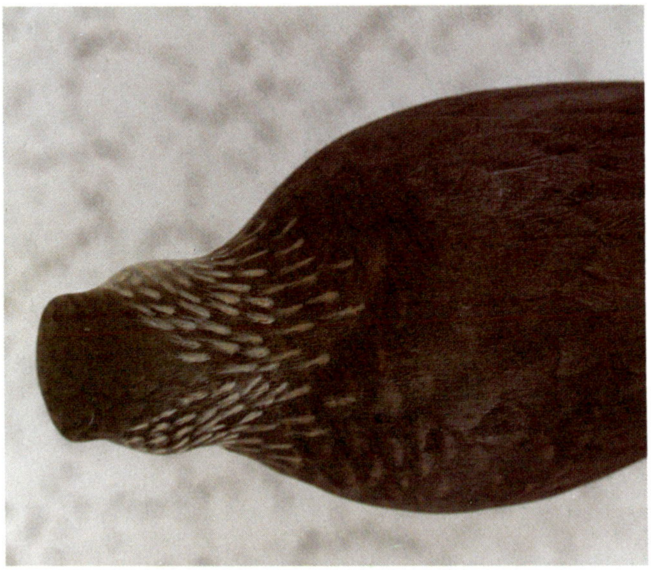

White tear drop marks on sides of head flowing into cape area edged with white and edged with burnt umber

Belly and tail washed with white and gesso 50/50 then black bands stipple blended on tail, cheek area also washed with white and blended to crown line

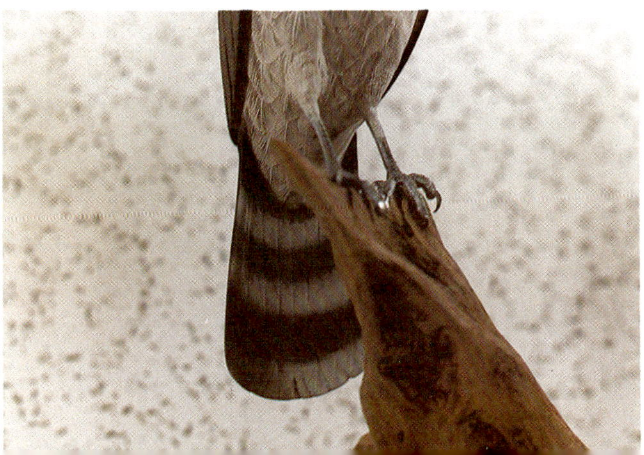

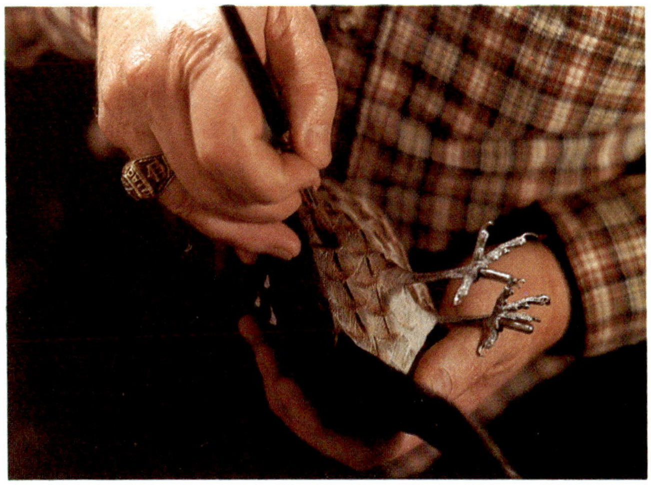

Chest and belly feather edged with burnt umber and interiors of each feather washed in large tear drop shapes with burnt umber, keep these areas somewhat translucent. On quill lines add black to burnt umber to make quills opaque

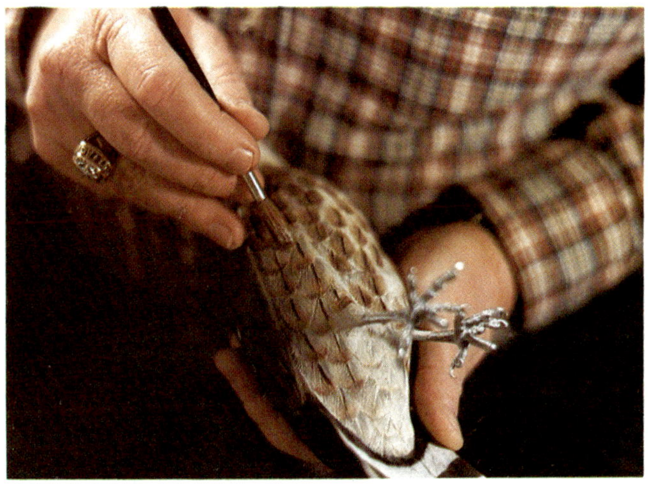

Another view of above

Finished chest and tail area (to soften this area wash with ultra thin wash of burnt umber using clear water)

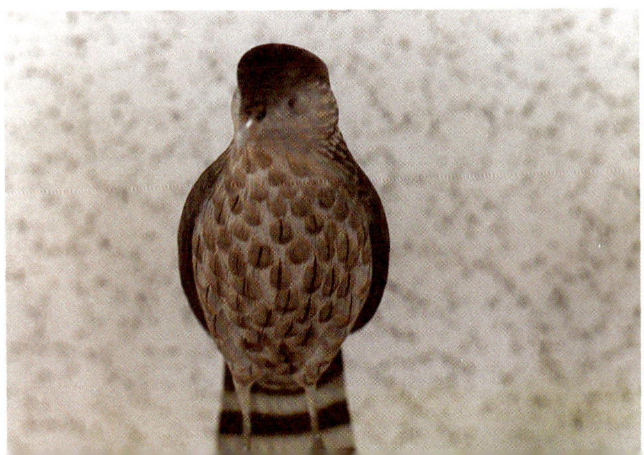

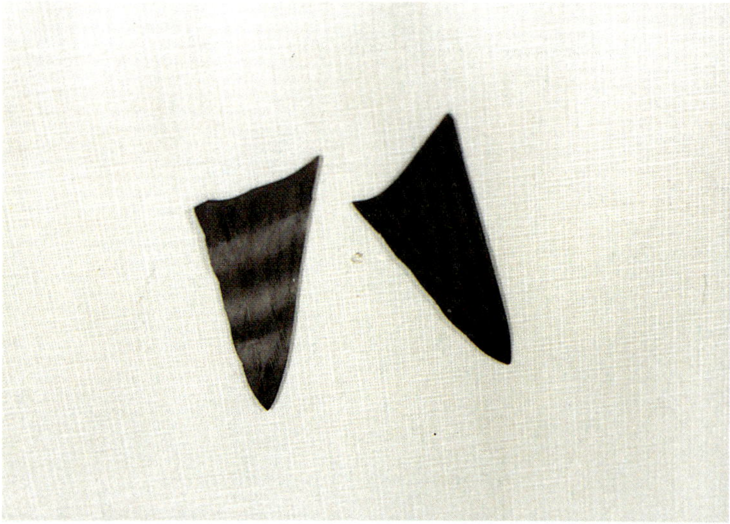

Upper side of primaries lightly edged — bottom barred with soft blend of color by stippling

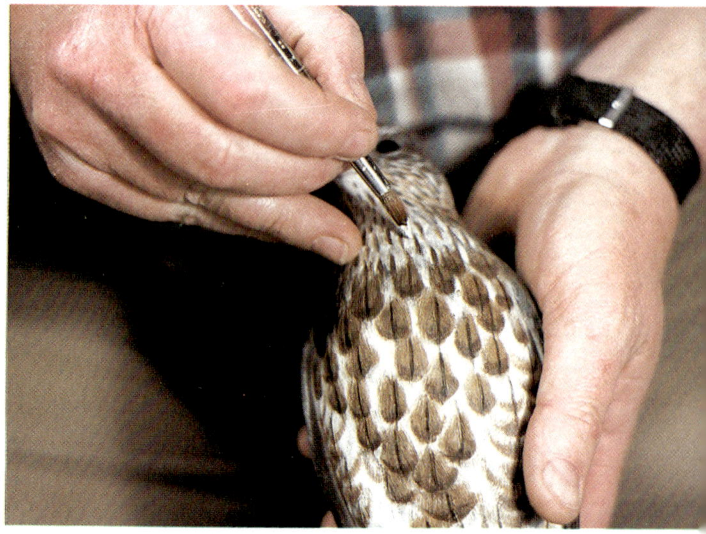

Dark brown streaking in chest and neck area

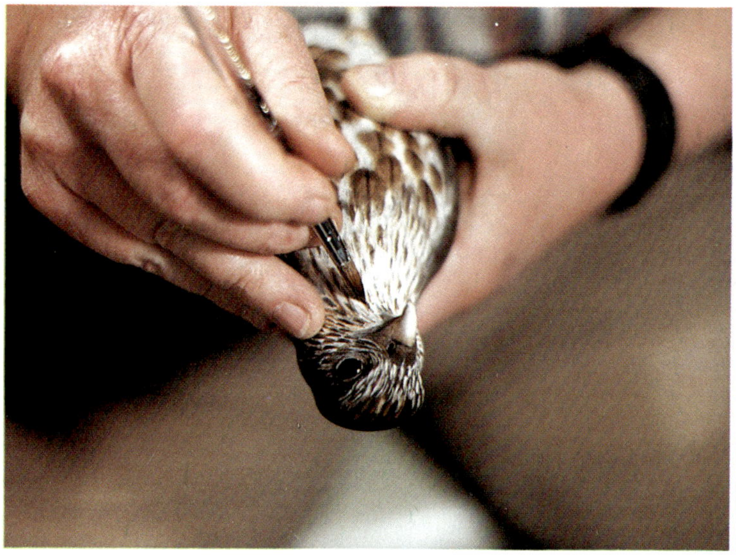

Dark brown streaking in chin area

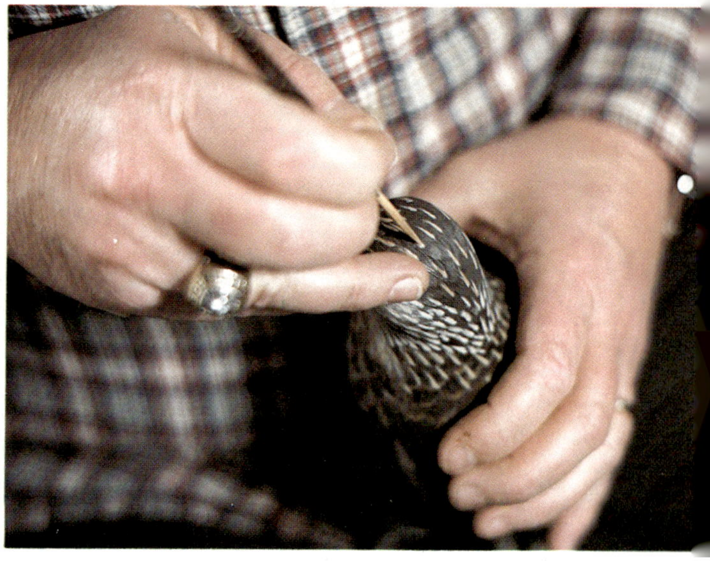

White tear drop streaking in head, use white

Back of head final light streaking

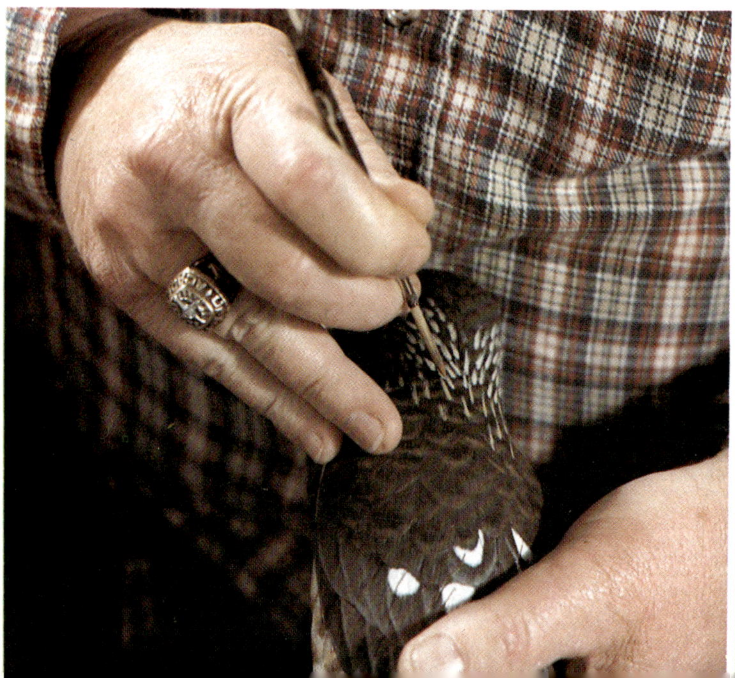

White spotting on wing area

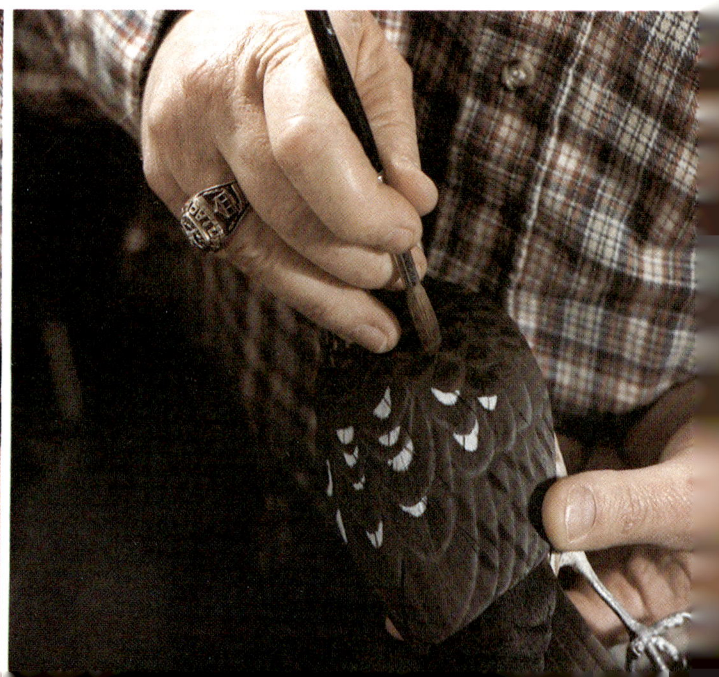

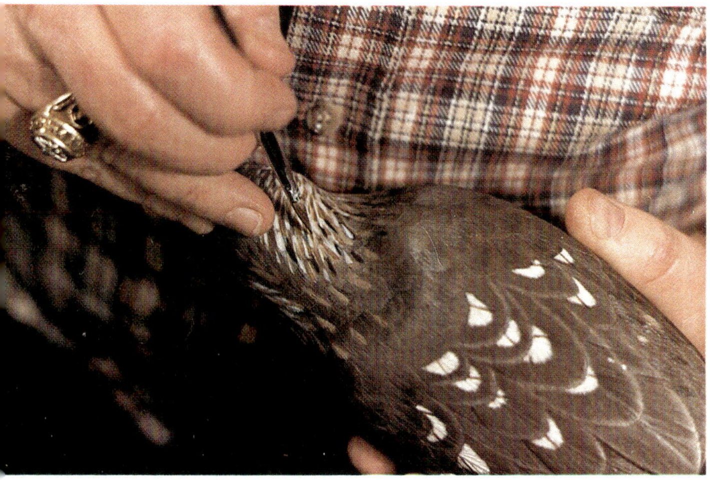

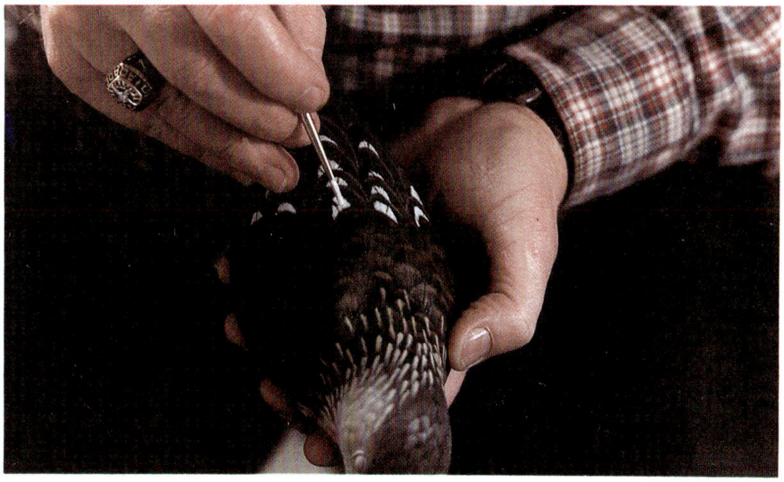

Dark brown streaking in side of head (add some black to burnt umber)

White spotting on back

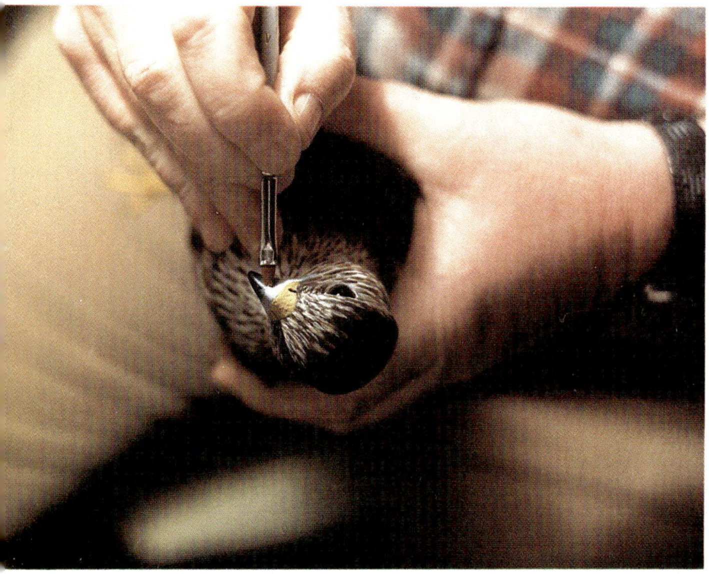

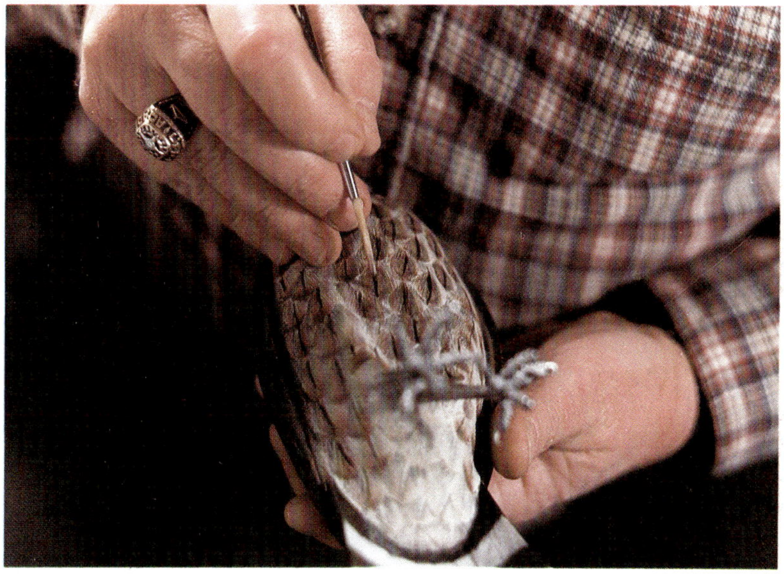

Painting beak—yellow ochre blended to light blue-gray to black at tip

Streaking quill line

Blending upper side of tail, black and burnt umber stippled for soft blend

Applying paint for blending

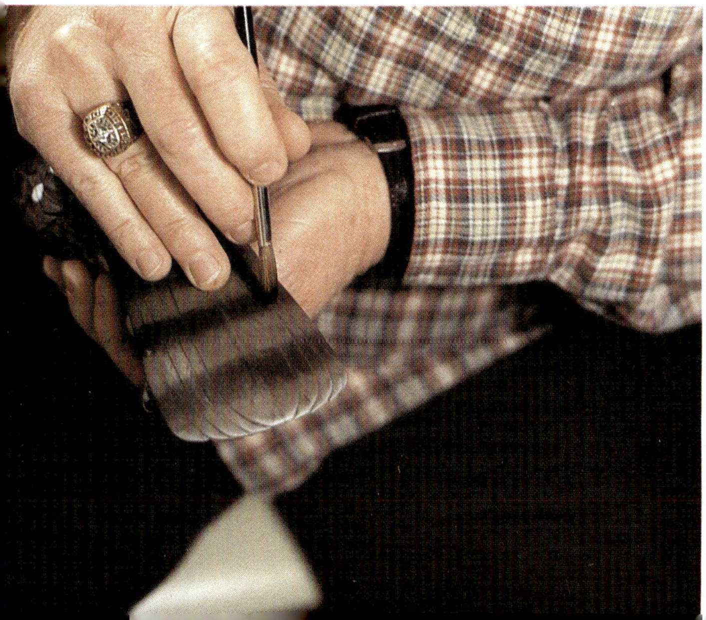

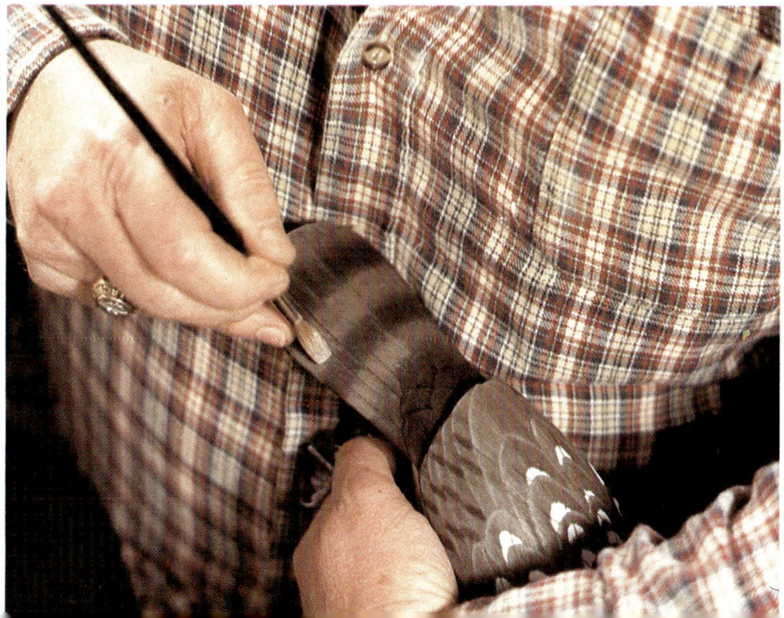

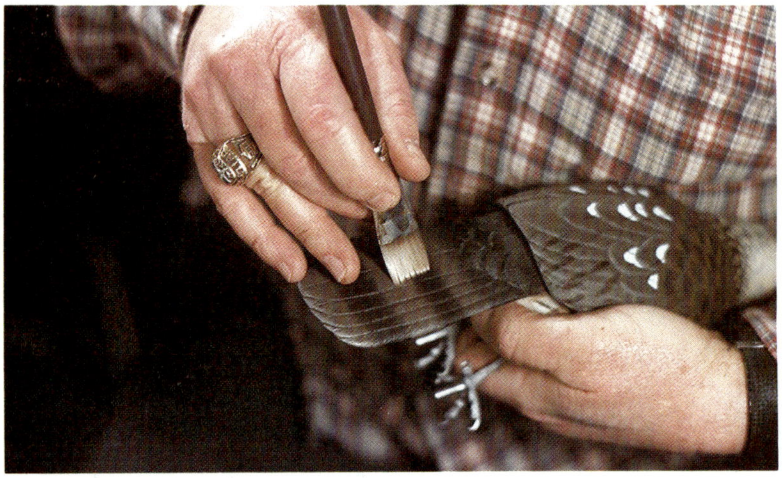

Blending in upper side of tail

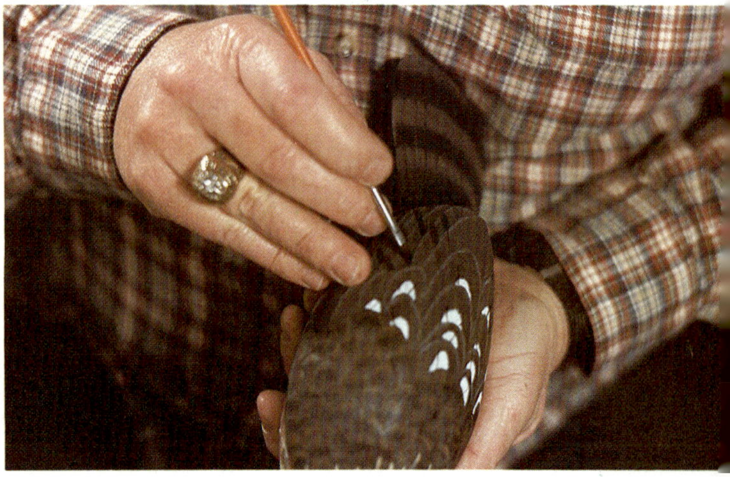

Dark streaks on secondaries

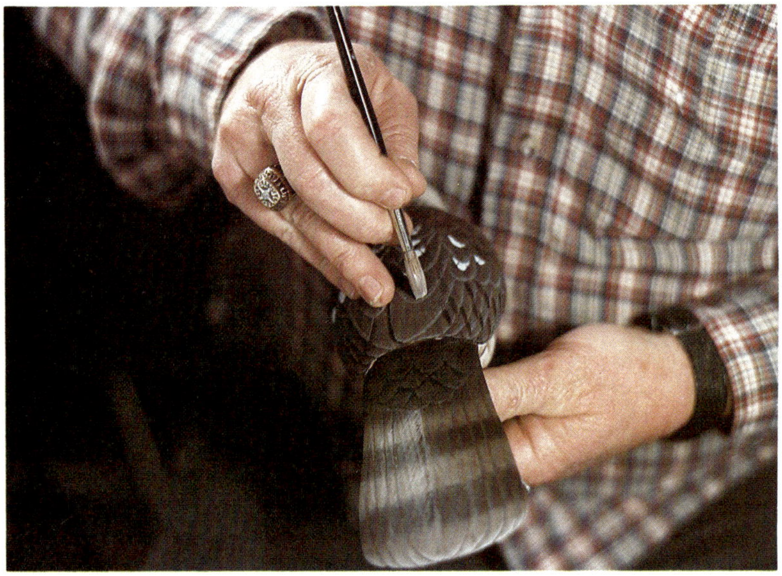

White spotting on wing areas

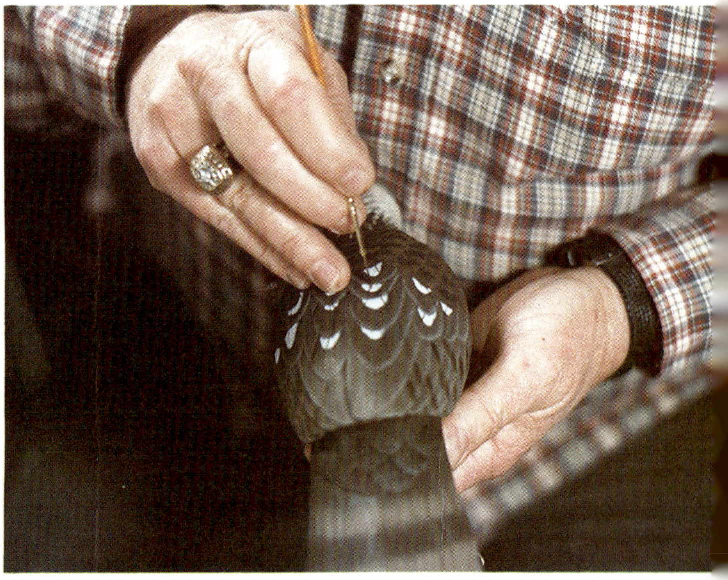

More white spotting

Finished chest and belly areas (note darker edgings to light brown to white)

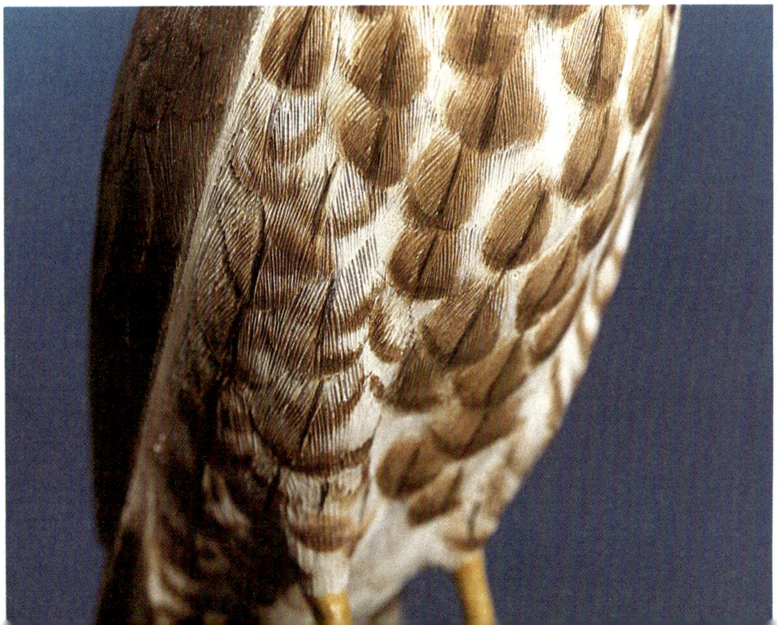

Primaries lightly edged with white and washed (note soft edges of tail)

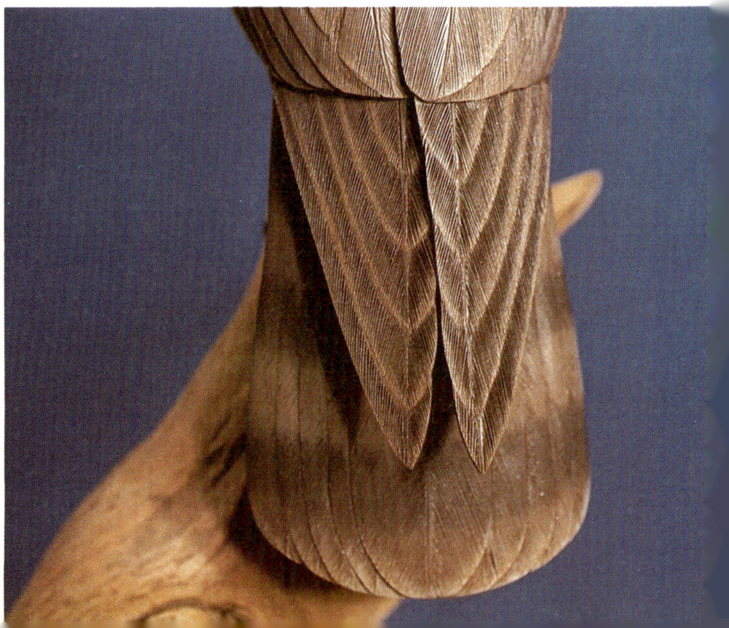

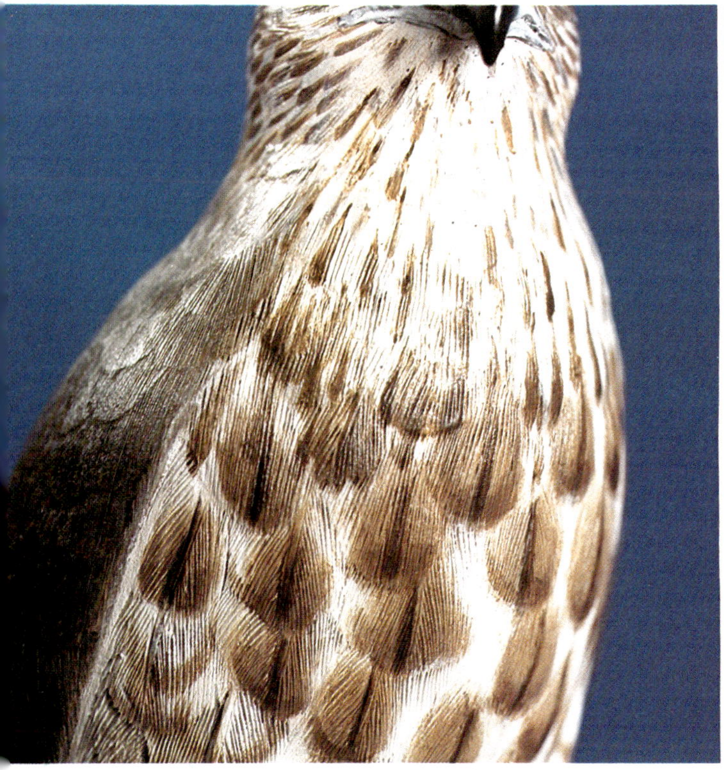
Chest area finished

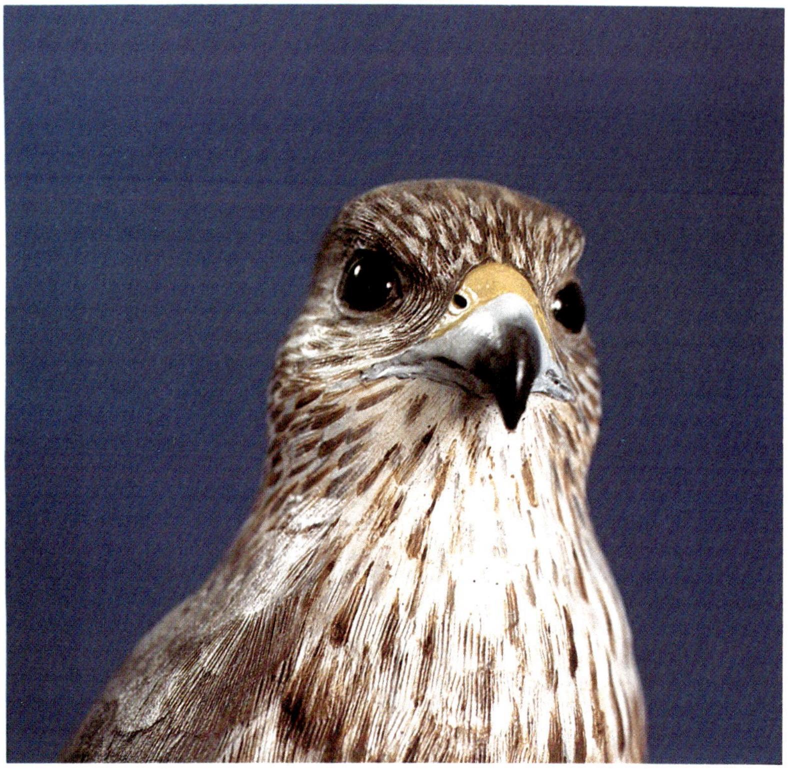
Head and beak area finished

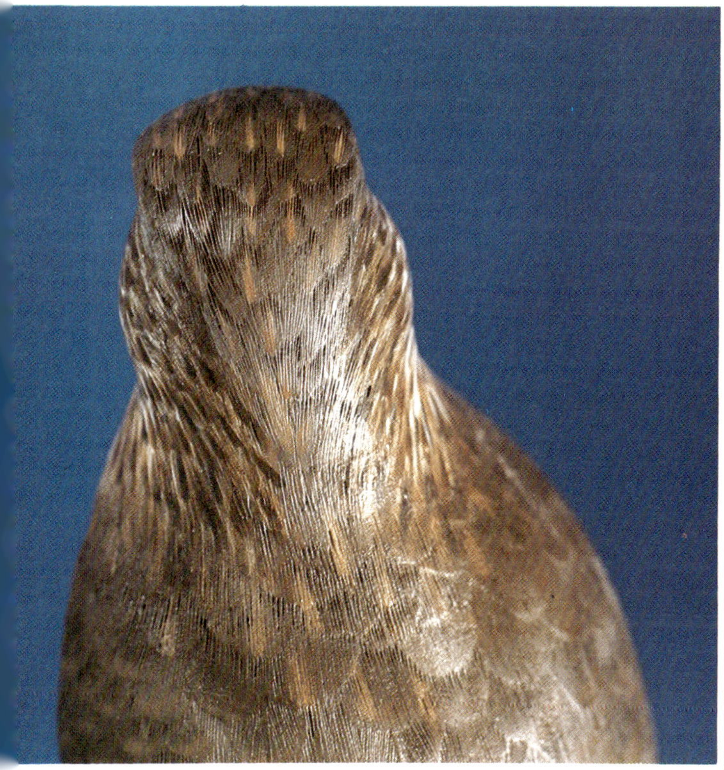
Back of head finished, note light and dark streaks

Finished carving of female Merlin by John Hemphill

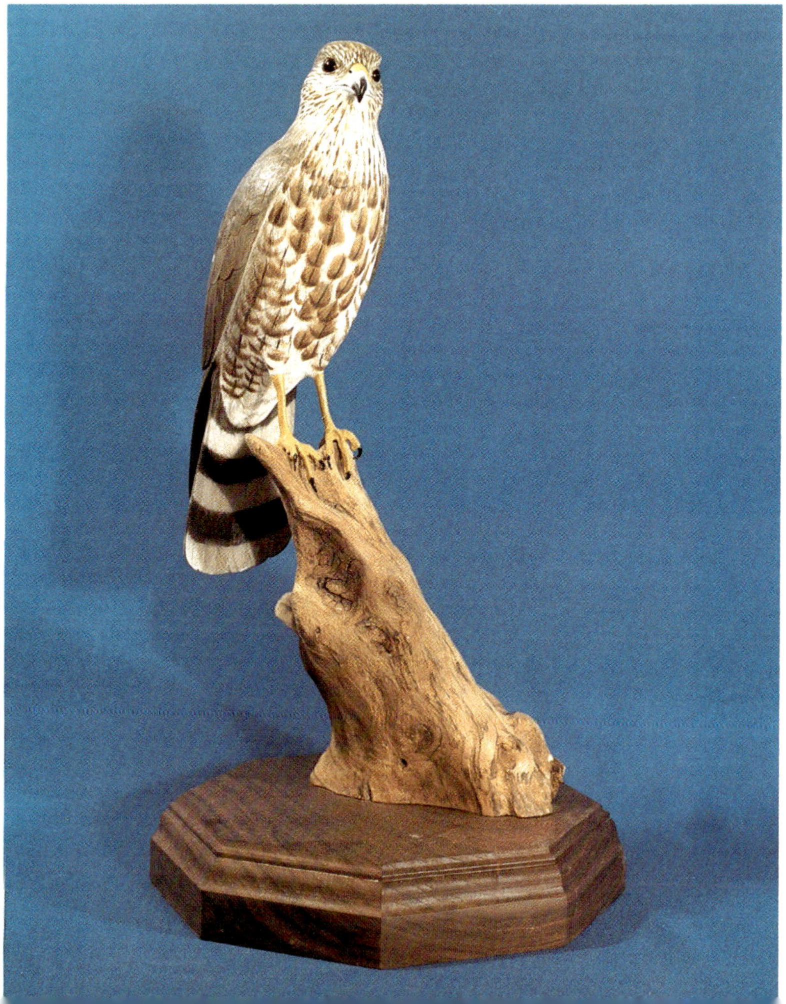

Miniature Flying Peregrine Falcon

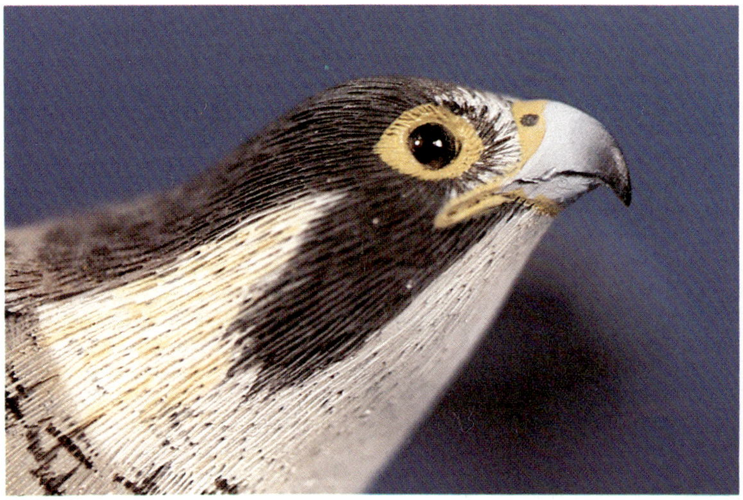

Head black with yellow ochre mixed with white around eye and at base of beak. Beak—blue gray (Paynes gray and white mixed to black base

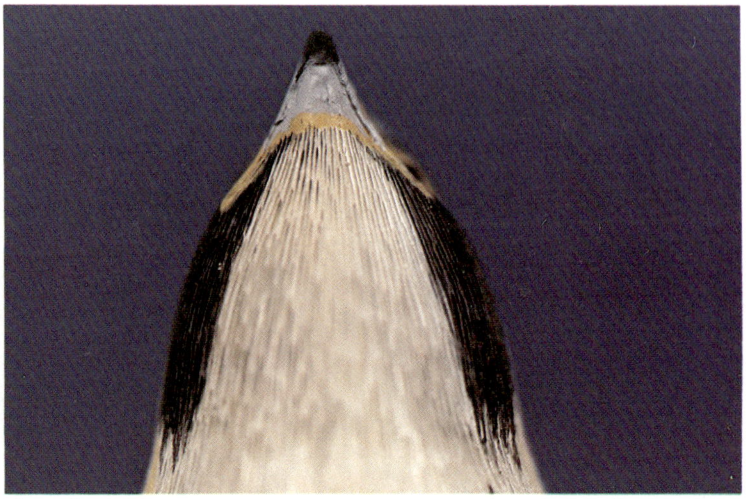

Underside of head—white mixed with gesso

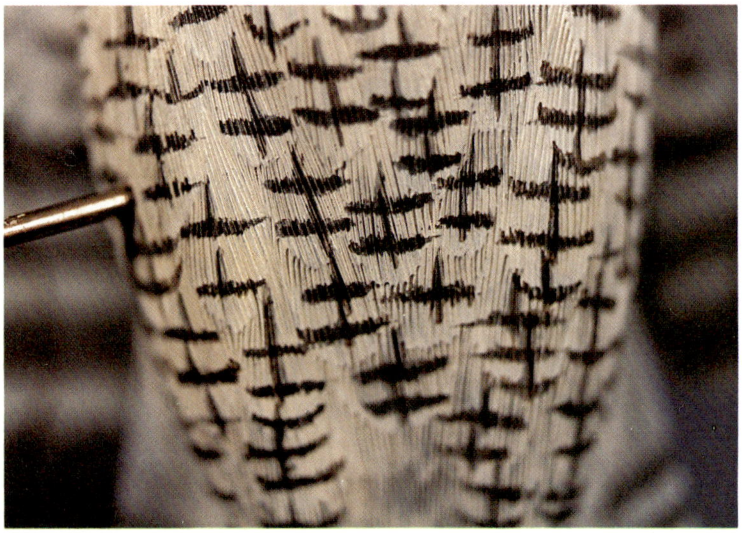

Belly and legs white mixed with gesso, yellow ochre wash, black bars

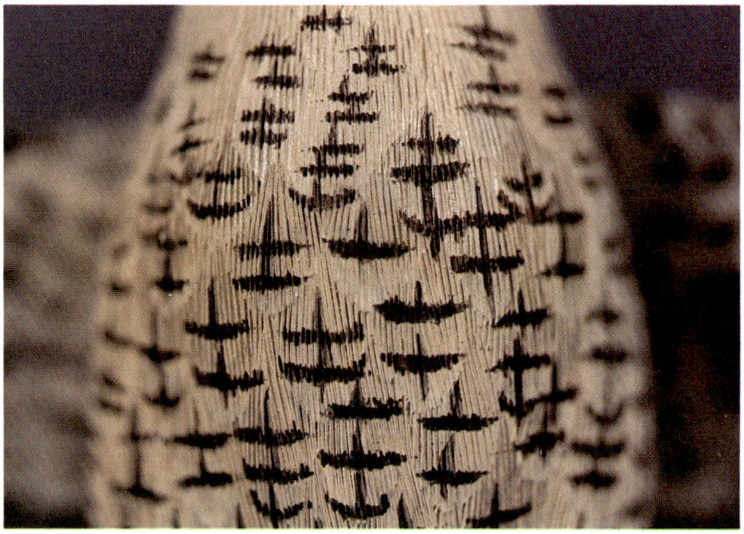

Chest same as belly

Rump area blue gray with black interiors and quills

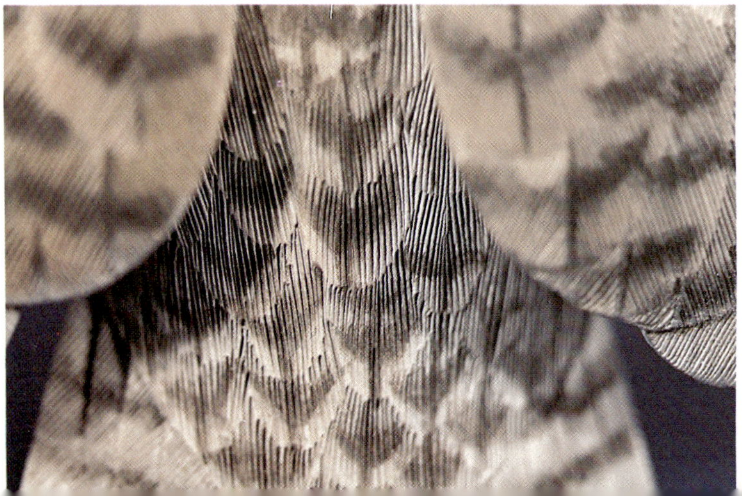

Shoulder area same as rump area

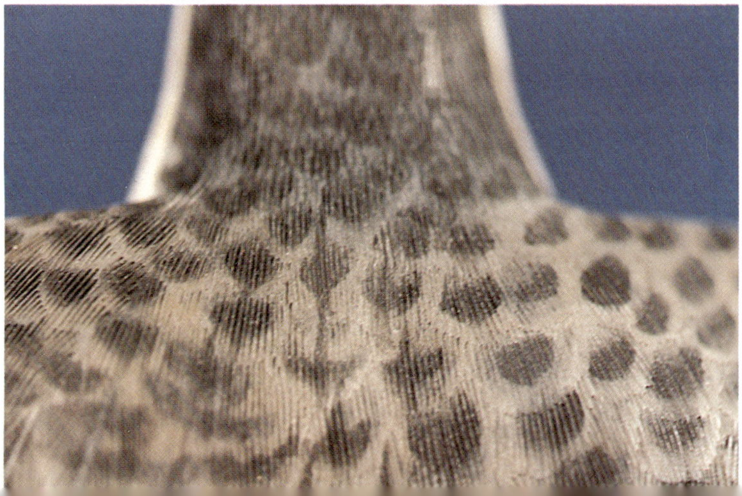

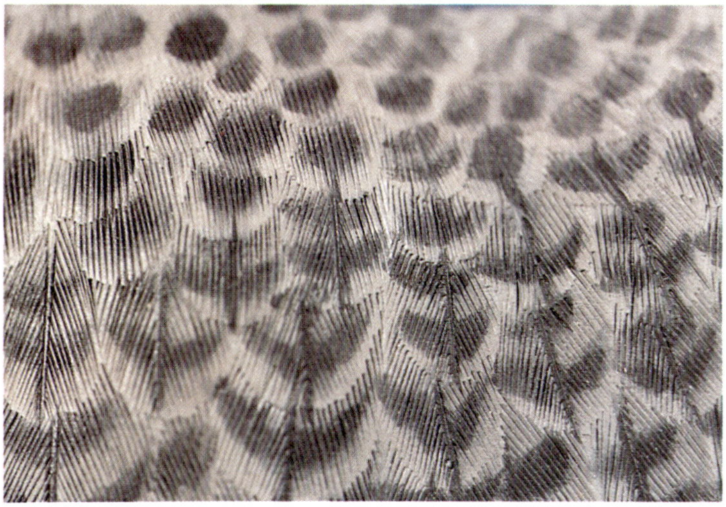

Upper side of wing bluish gray (Paynes gray and white with burnt umber) base coat lighter towards leading edge of wing—black bars and interior markings V-shaped and quill lines

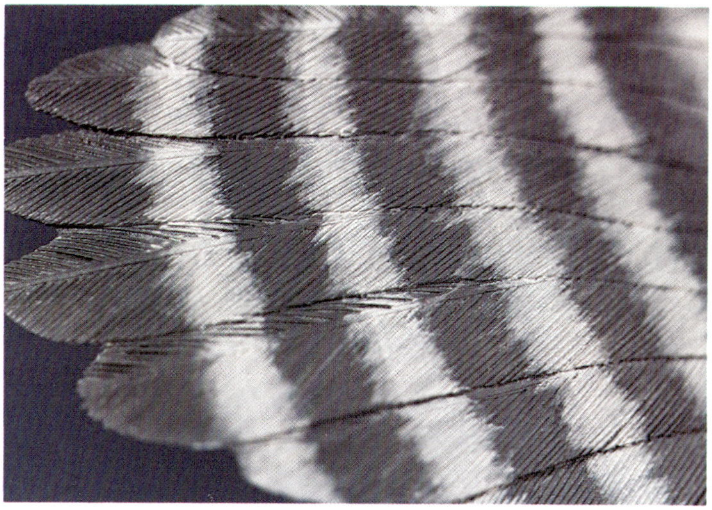

Primaries gray with black bars

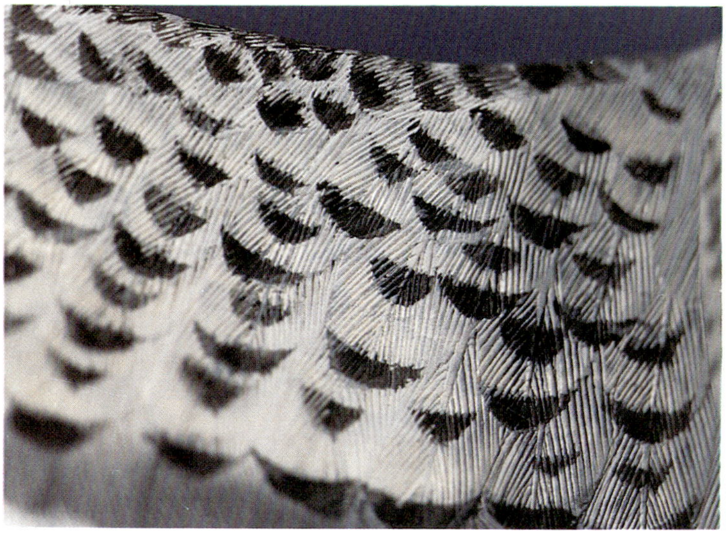

Underside of wing base color white mixed with gesso and tiny amount of yellow ochre

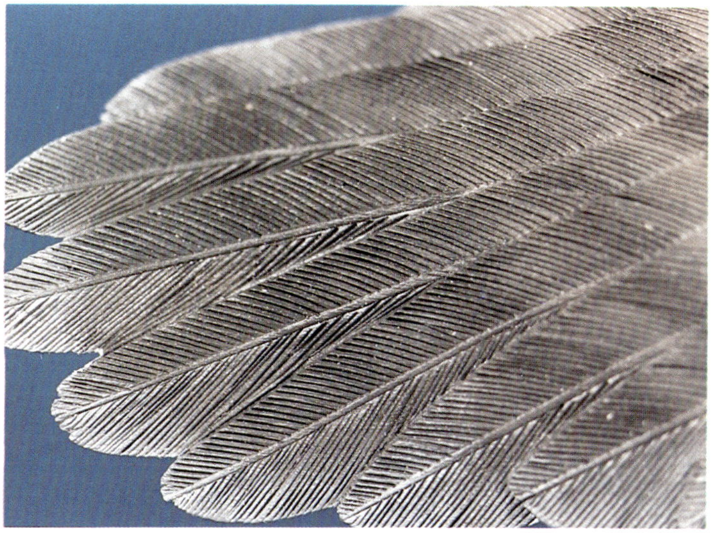

Underside of primaries gray and white bars

Underside of completed bird. Note—feet yellow ochre with black talons

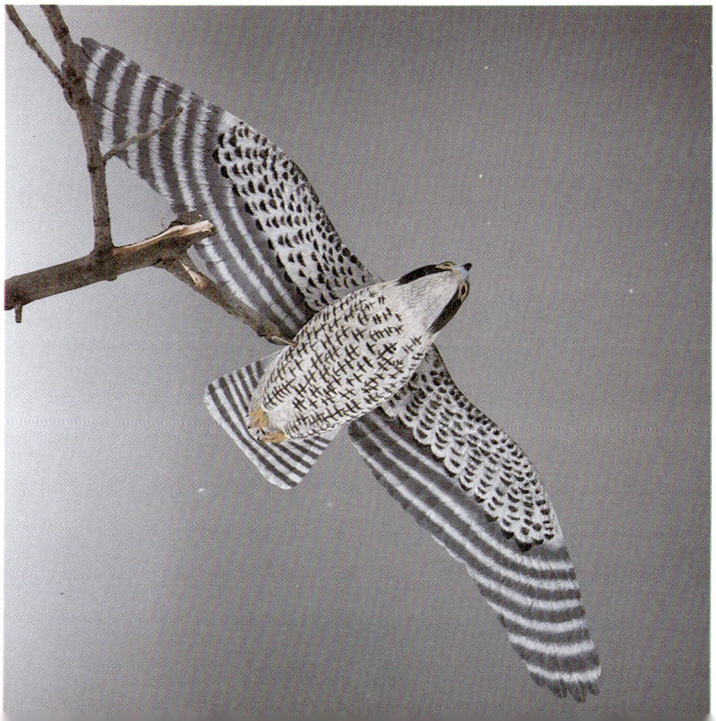

Upper side of completed bird

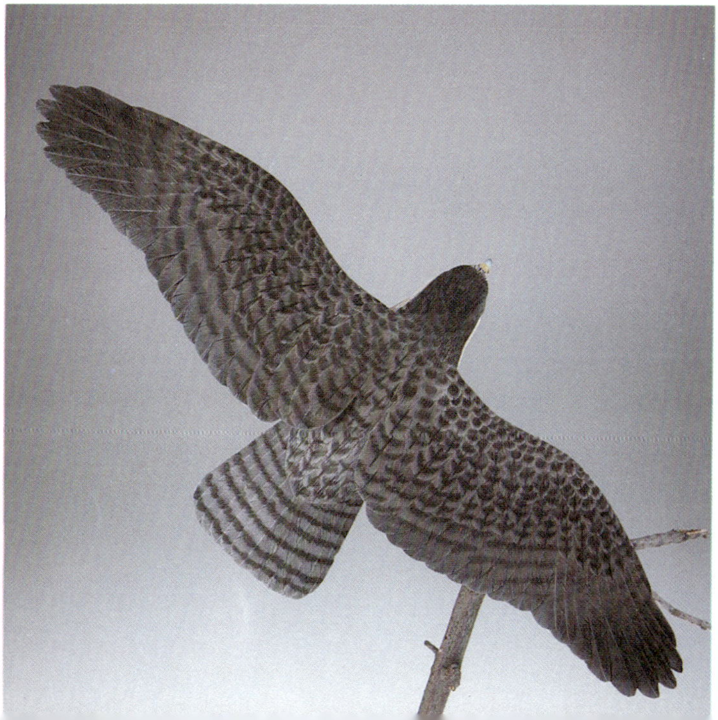

Red-Tailed Hawk

White, Gesso, Burnt umber, Black, Burnt sienna, Yellow ochre, Paynes gray

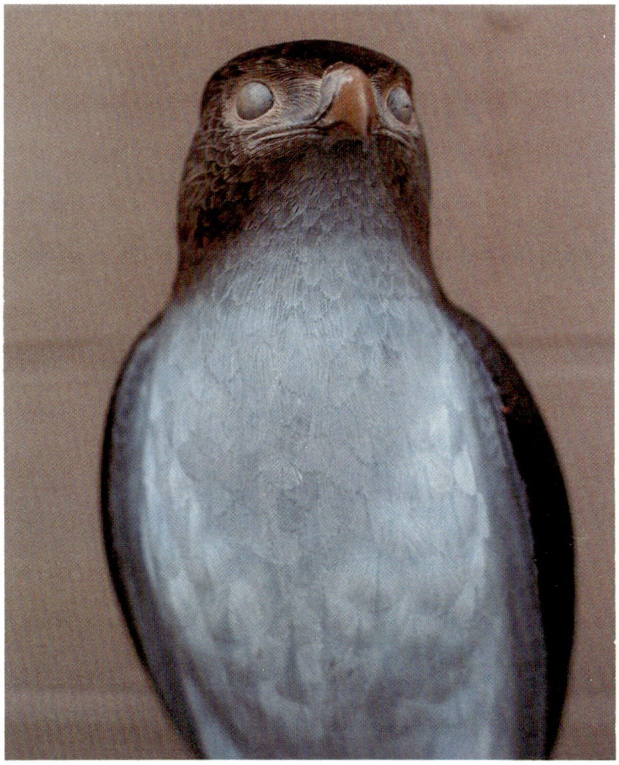

White-wash chest and belly using white and gesso 50/50
Wash crown and back with burnt umber

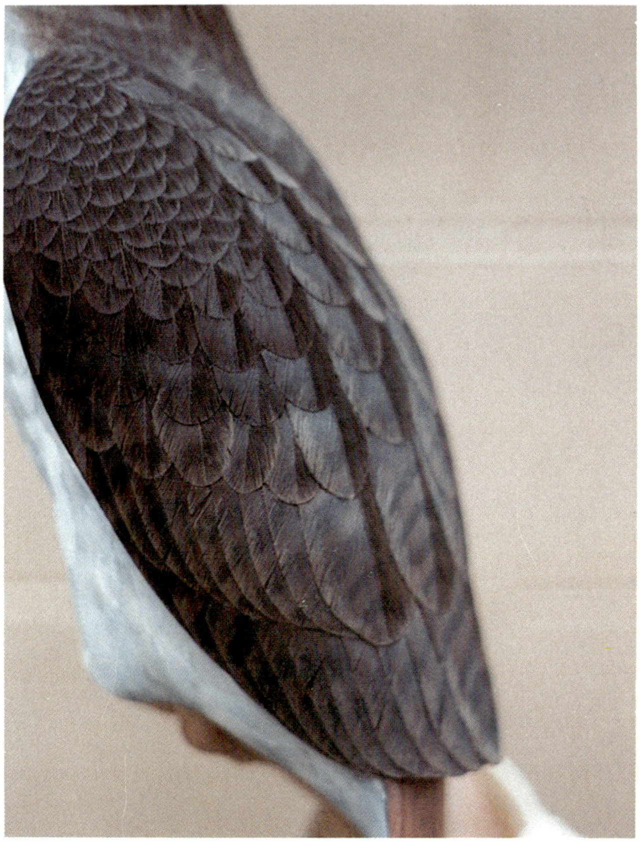

Back edged with white and darker bars in each feather (darker bars; combination of burnt umber and black, stipple blended with brown, both colors need to be wet, about consistancy of heavy cream, then edged with white and splits painted in with script brush using dark brown)

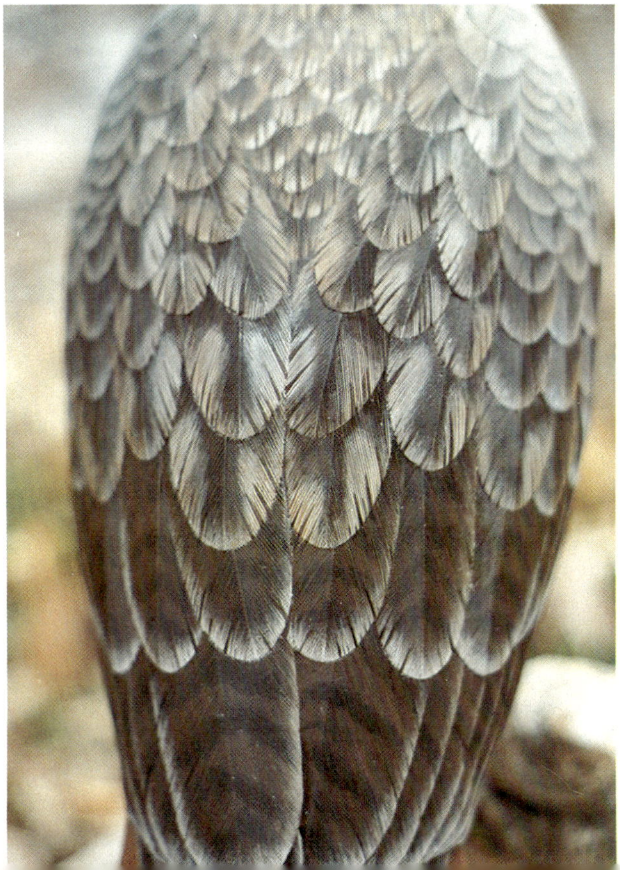

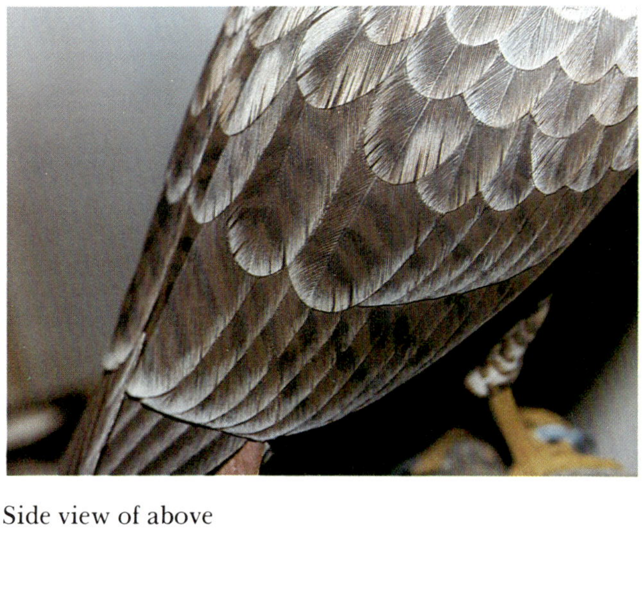

Side view of above

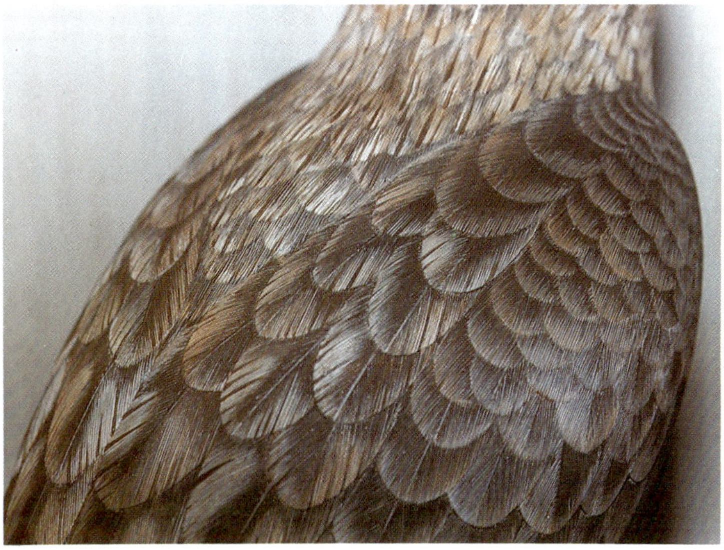

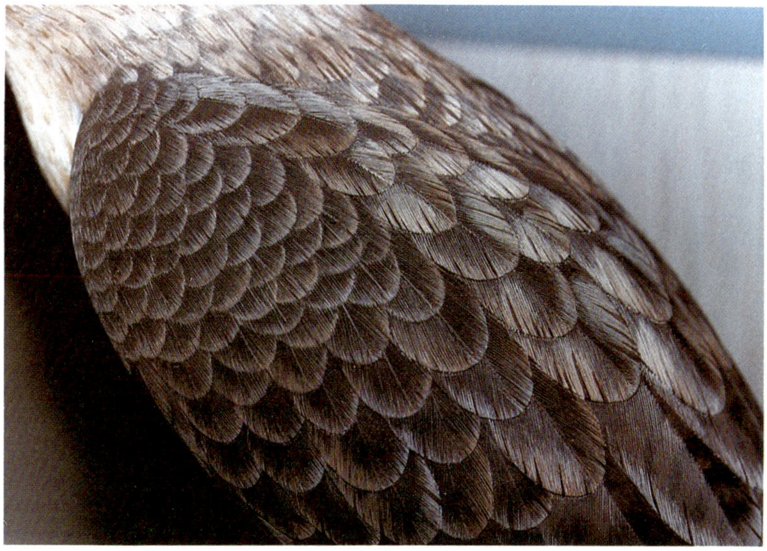

Shoulder area and back of neck, note light quills on back and dark ones on head

Wing and shoulder area — feather edgings are best done with a #8 round red sable brush (Grumbacher series 190 —some people prefer Katz tongue or Filbert type brushes). Best technique is to place bristles on edge of feather at a 90 degree angle, pull and lift toward interior of feather

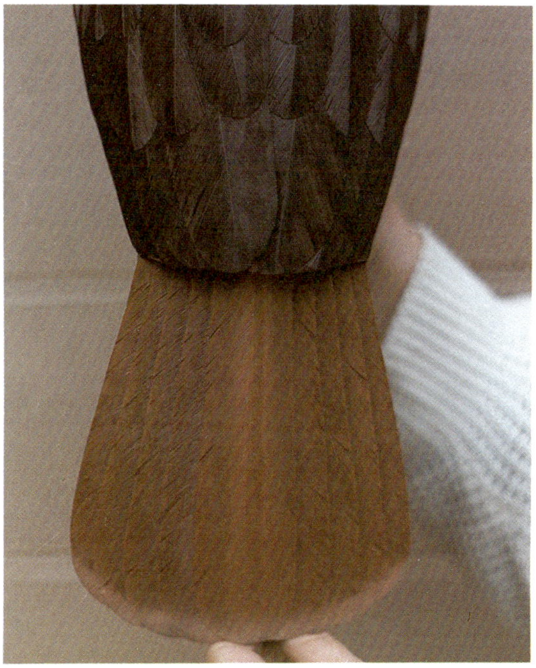

Wash tail with burnt sienna

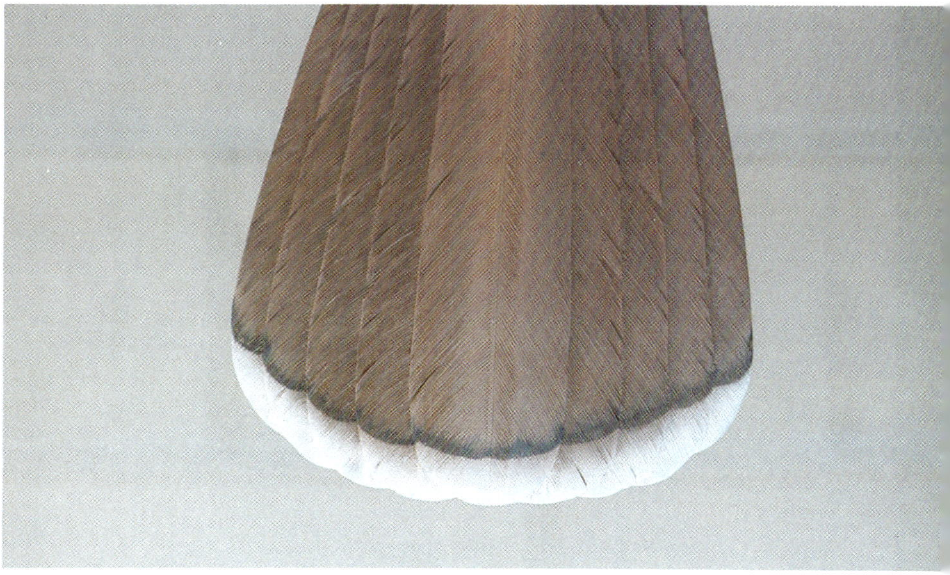

Wash tail with burnt sienna and a small amount of yellow ochre, note edged with white and black band

Underside of tail white with light burnt sienna edgings

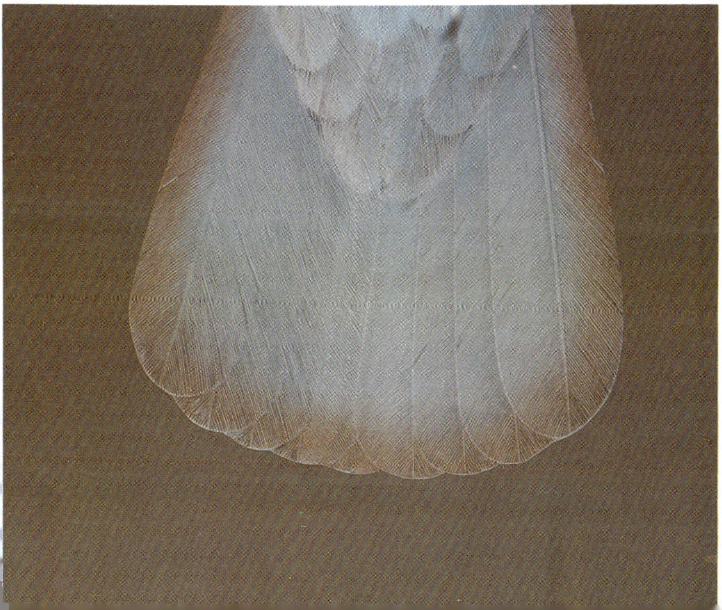

Primary feathers dark brown, faint edged with white

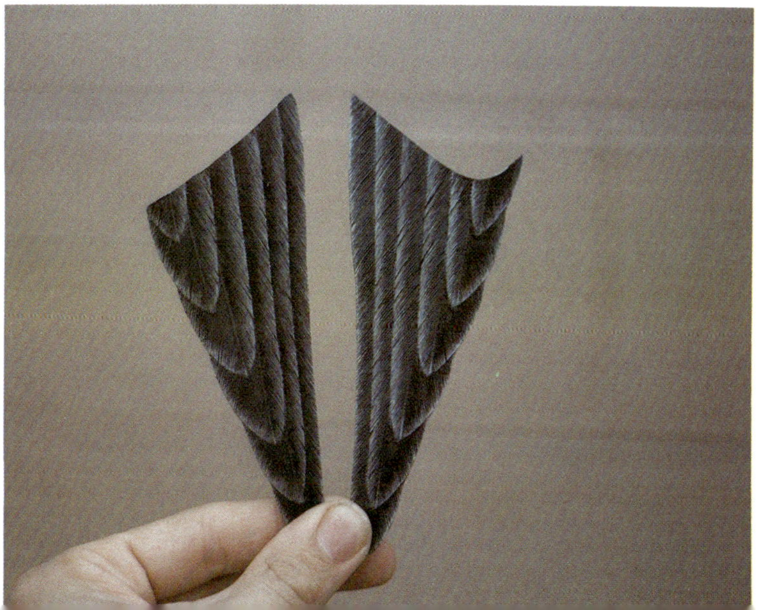

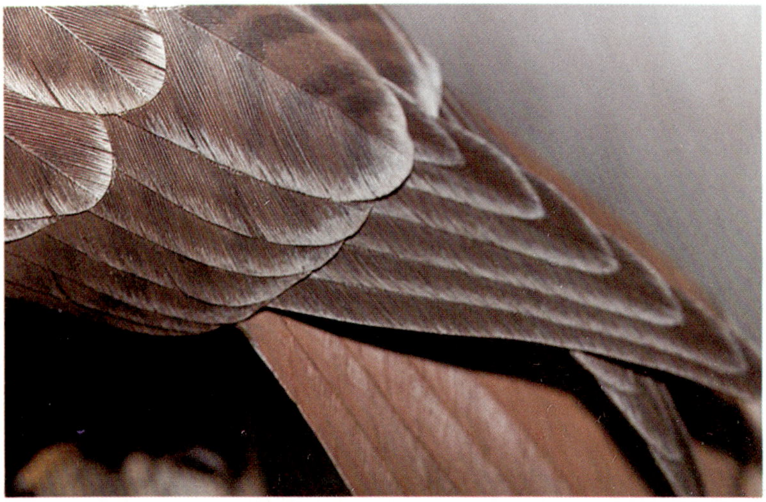

Primary, secondary, tertial and tail areas

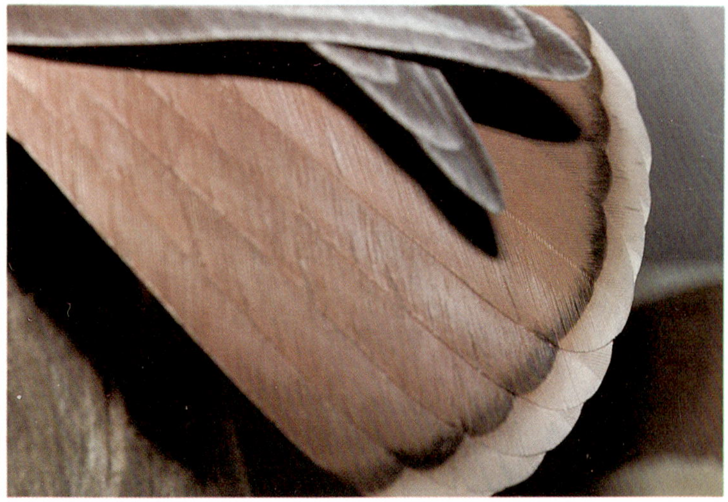

Primaries and tail are red, note blendings of burnt sienna black and white of tail

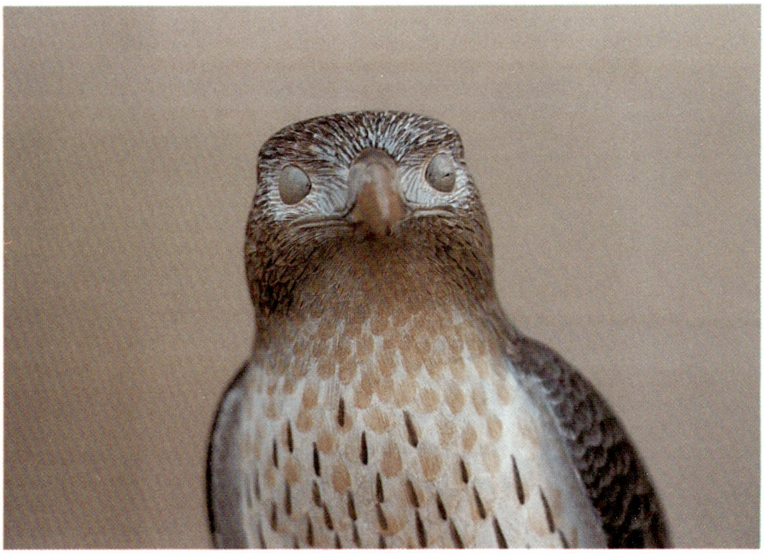

Chest feathers edged with raw sienna and white mixed to a bright color and tear drop shapes on interiors of feathers with burnt umber

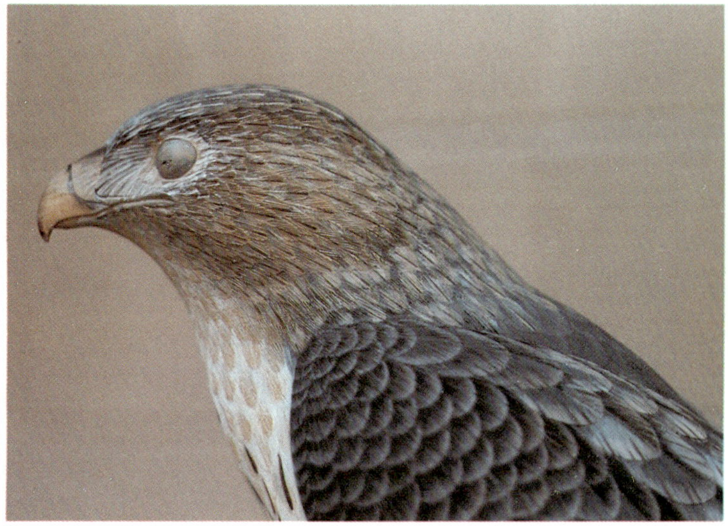

Cheek area washed with buff color (raw sienna and white), then streaked with burnt umber

Back of head feathers edged with buff color and streaked with fine white streaks

Back of head, another view

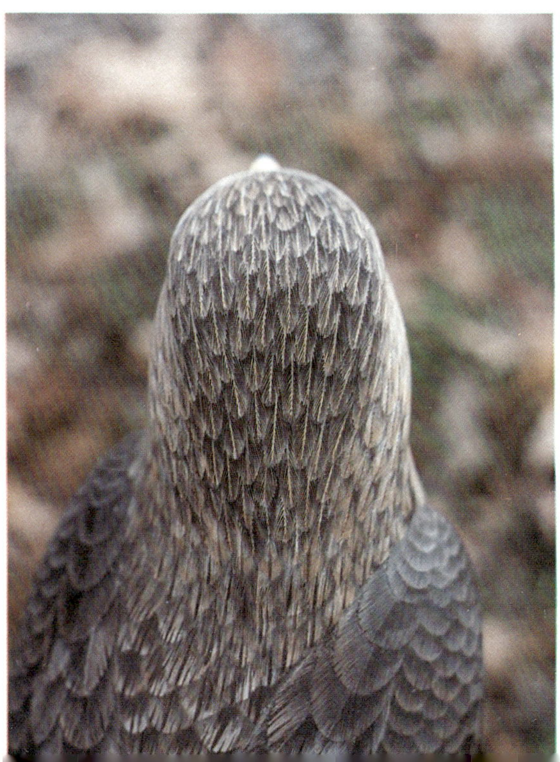

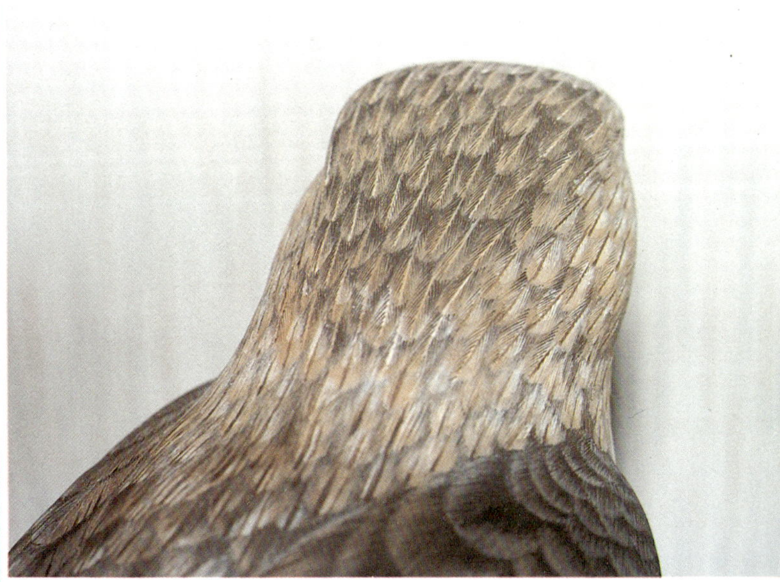

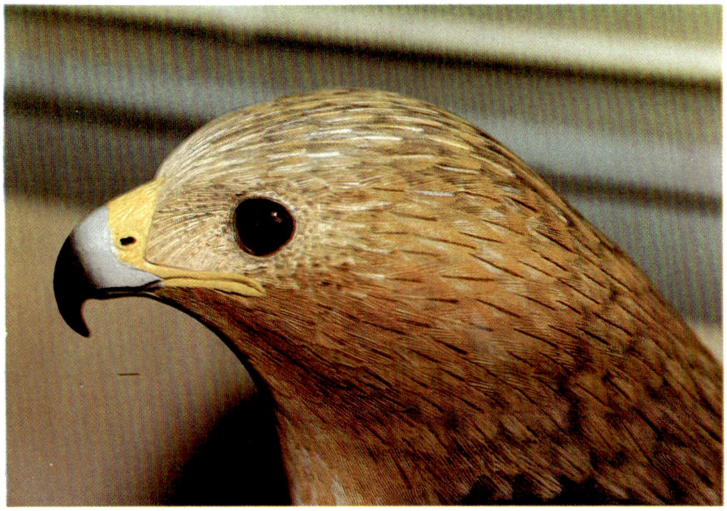

Profile — note faint white edges of cheek feathers, beak color yellow ochre at base blended to blue-ish gray (paynes gray and white mixed) blended to black at tip

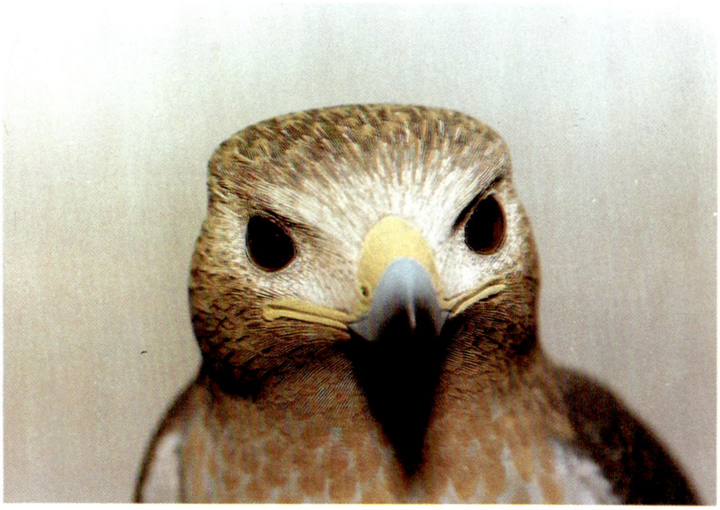

Front view of head showing whitish face with brown dots around eye

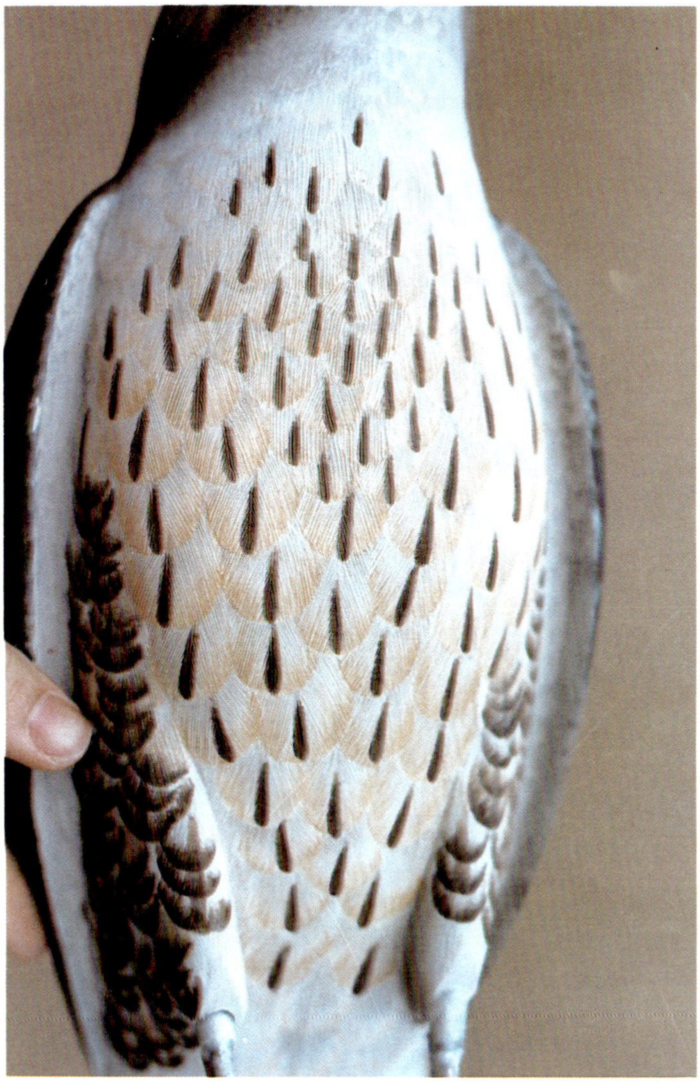

Chest and belly edged with buff color, dark interiors

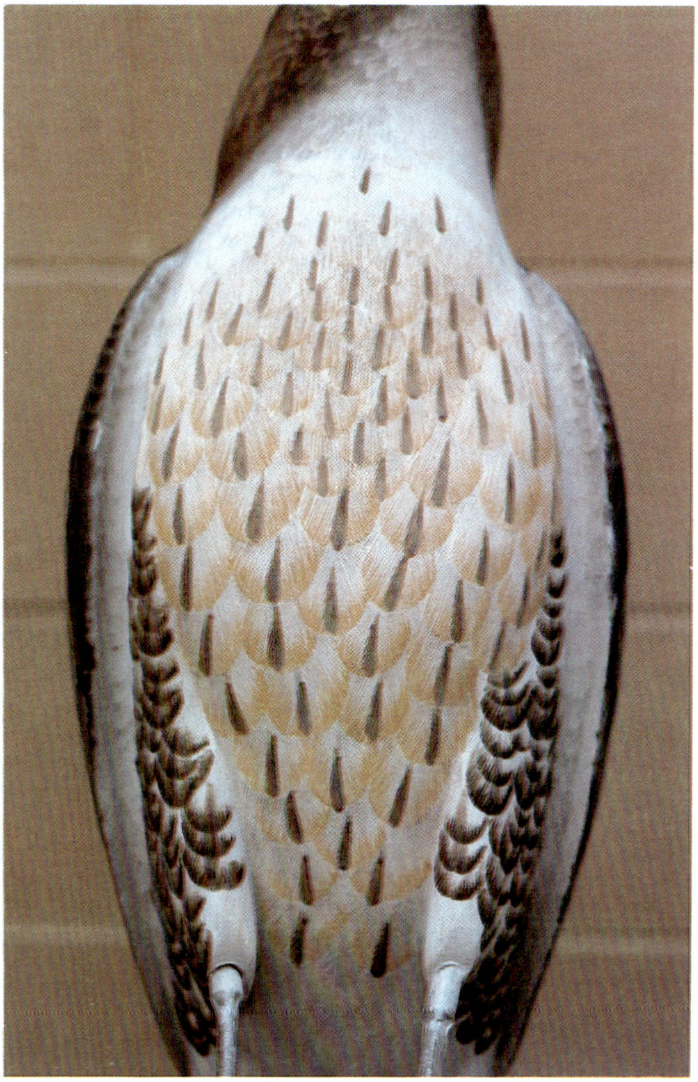

Same areas with leg feathers

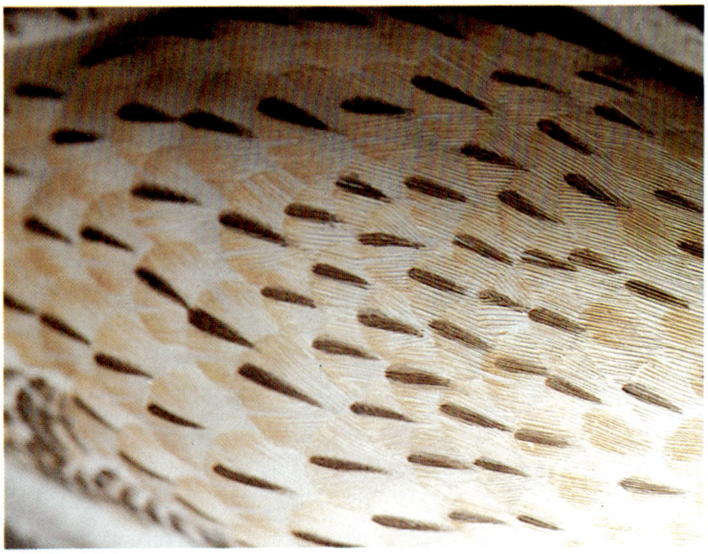

Close-up of belly

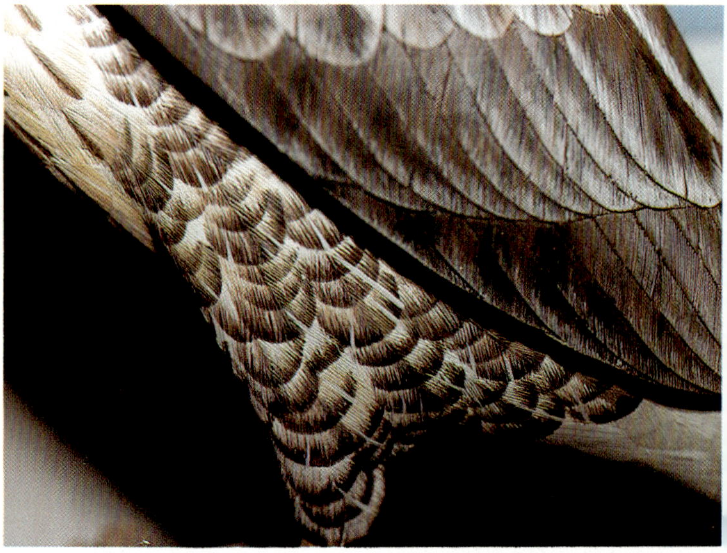

Leg and side area — feathers edged with burnt umber, note white splits in feathers, this is done with a #4 script brush

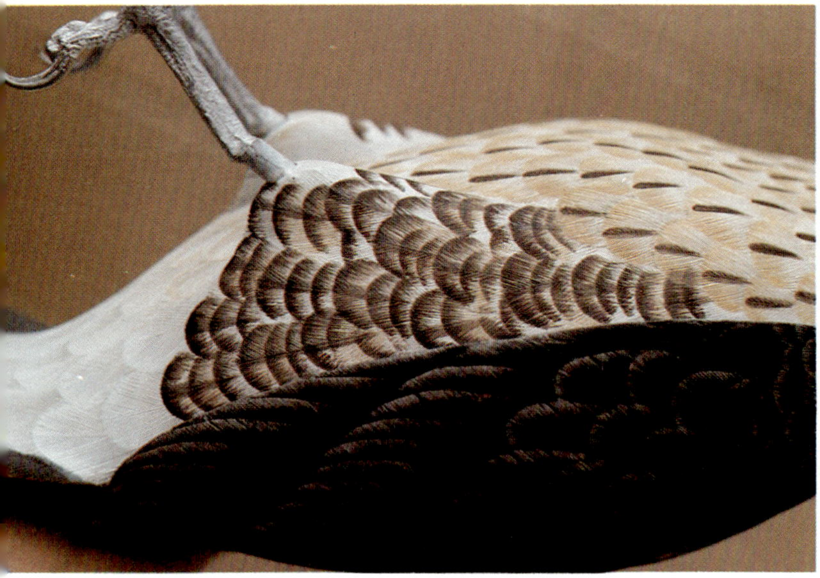

Leg and side feathers, note darker centers

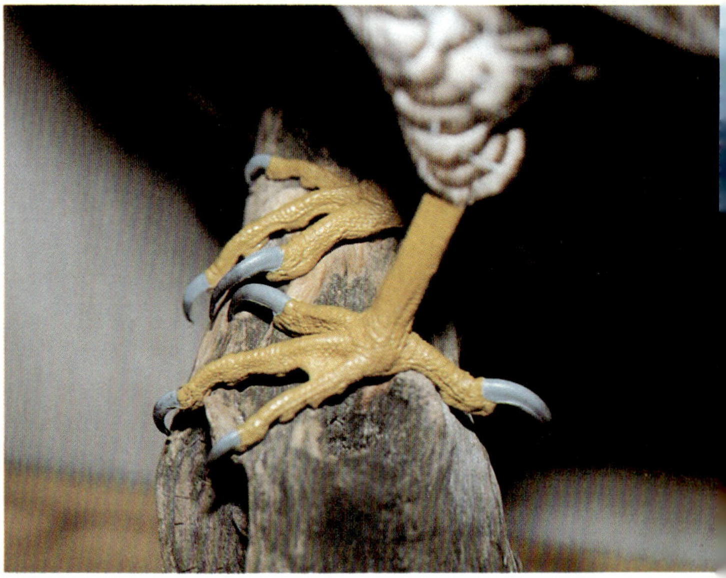

Feet and legs yellow ochre, talons blue-ish gray to black at tips

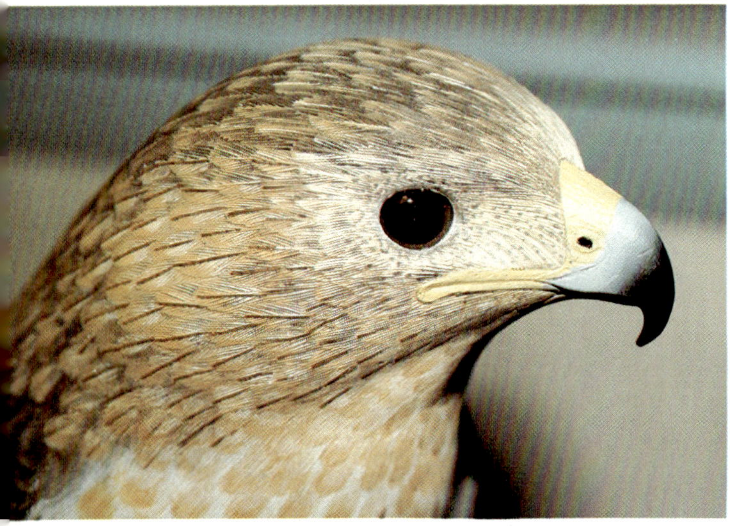

Finished head right profile

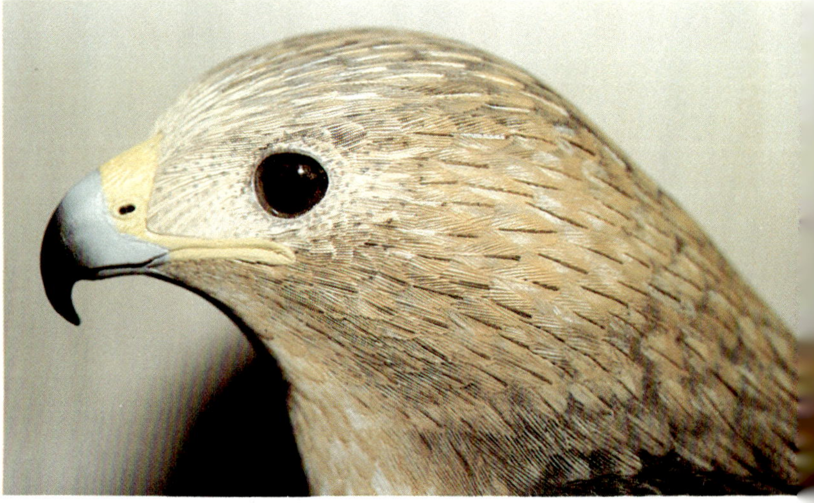

Finished head left profile

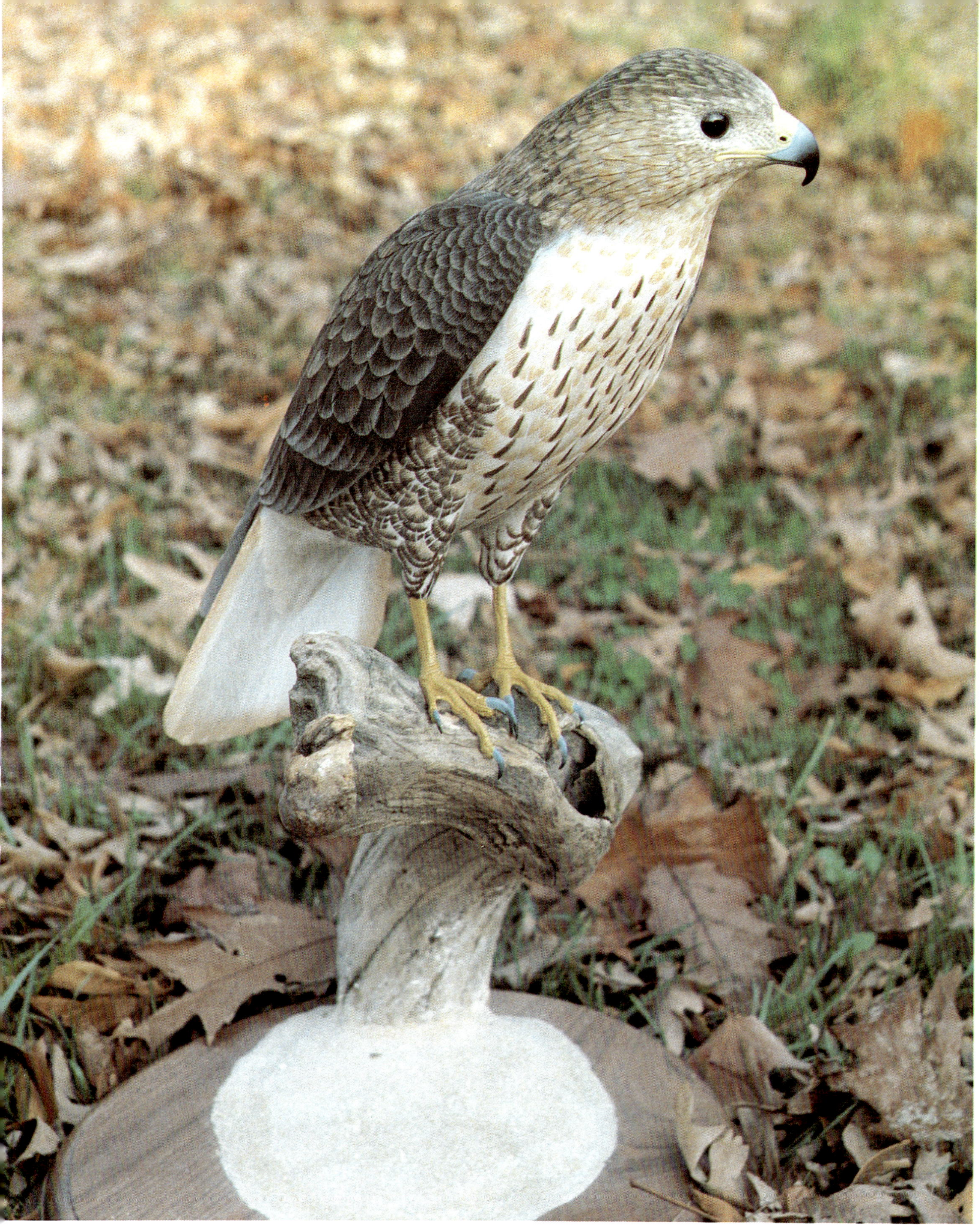

Finished carving by Paul Suarez, project director of the book

Antiqued Goshawk

Color list: Paynes gray, White, Black, Yellow ochre

Prepare carving by sealing with shelac cut with 50% alcohol

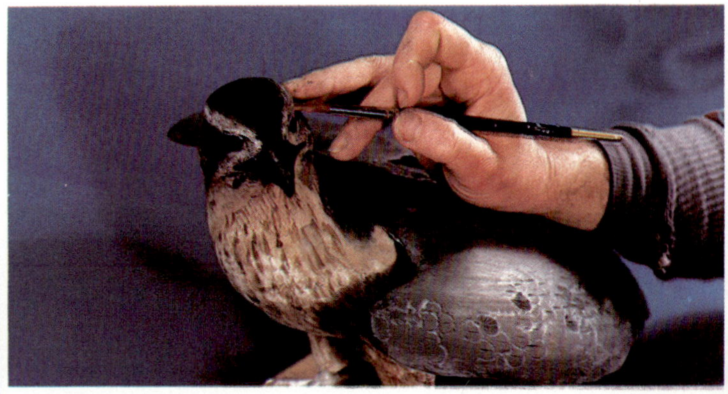

Crown and back of cheek black wipe, put in white streaks using heavy paint then wipe

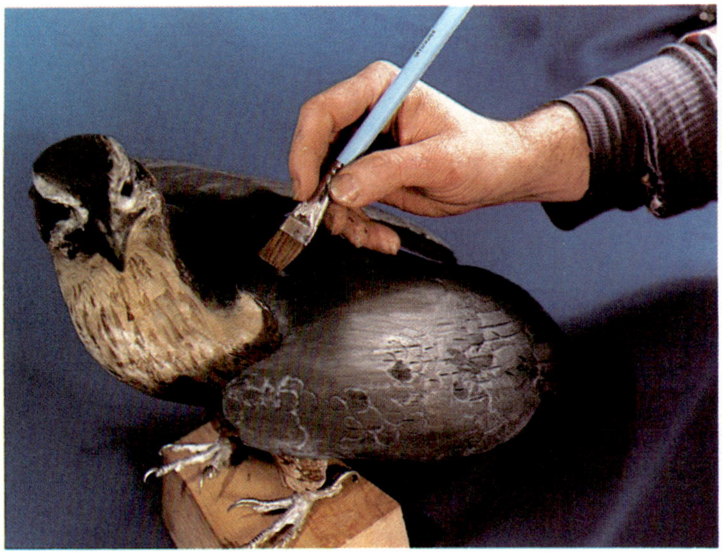

Paint upper wings bluish gray using paynes gray and white, then wipe white wet with paper towel so some of the brown char is left

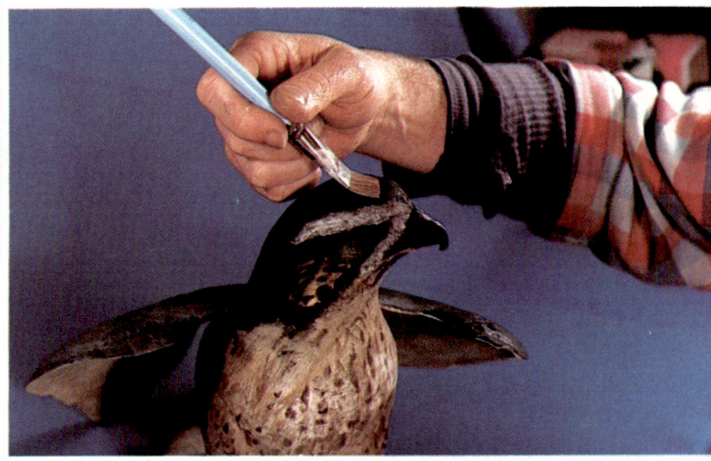

Wash entire head with black — beak dull yellow to black — legs yellow ochre washed with black, talons black

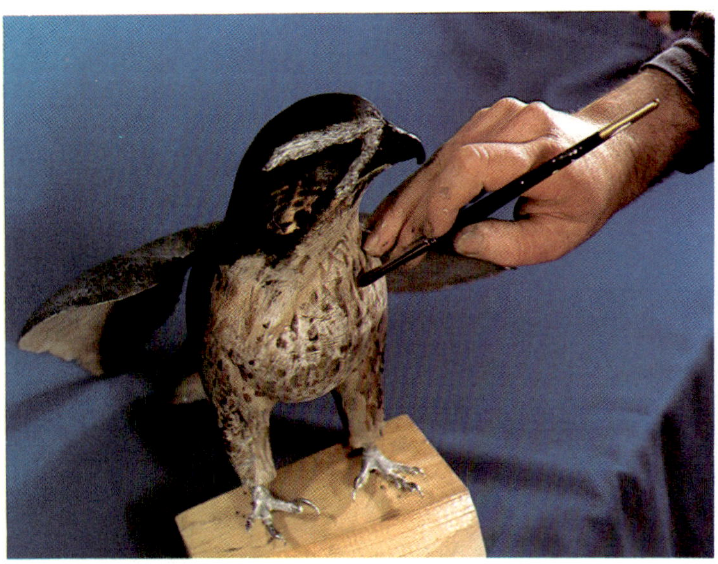

Undercoat chest and sides with white and wipe, then wash spot burnt umber and wipe to create streaked effect

Finished carving by David Biddle

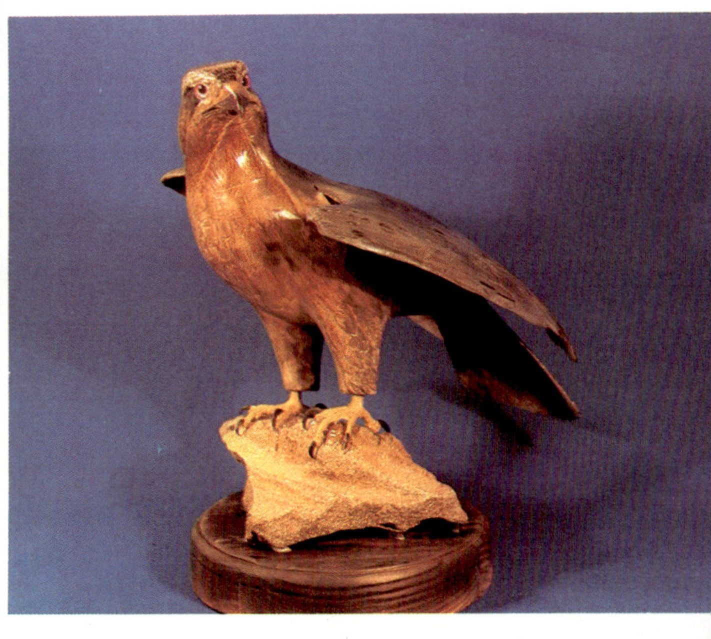

Gallery of Live Birds

Barn Owl

Tyto alba

Barn Owls, sometimes called "Monkeyfaced" owls because of their heart-shaped faces, are strictly nocturnal. As their name suggests, they commonly select man-made structures in which to live: silos, water tanks, church towers and barns are favored sites.

They are 14 to 20 inches tall with a wingspan of 40 to 45 inches. Their color is tawny or golden above and white or pale cinnamon below. They have long, broad wings and are graceful and somewhat moth-like in flight.

Barn Owls do not hoot, but are very vocal nevertheless. Their various sounds include hissing, screeching, beak snapping, and a cry best described as a maniacal shriek.

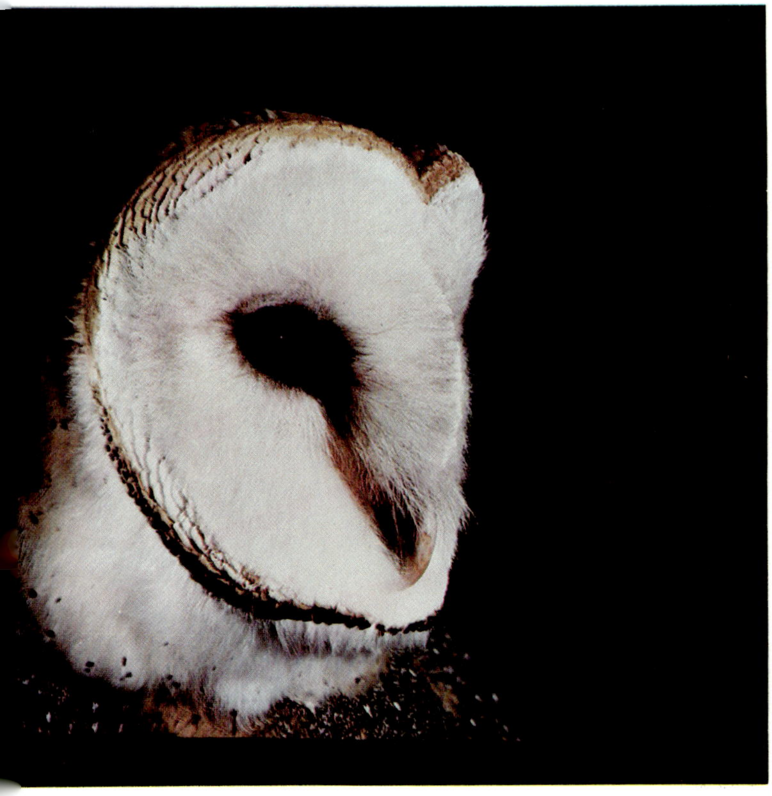

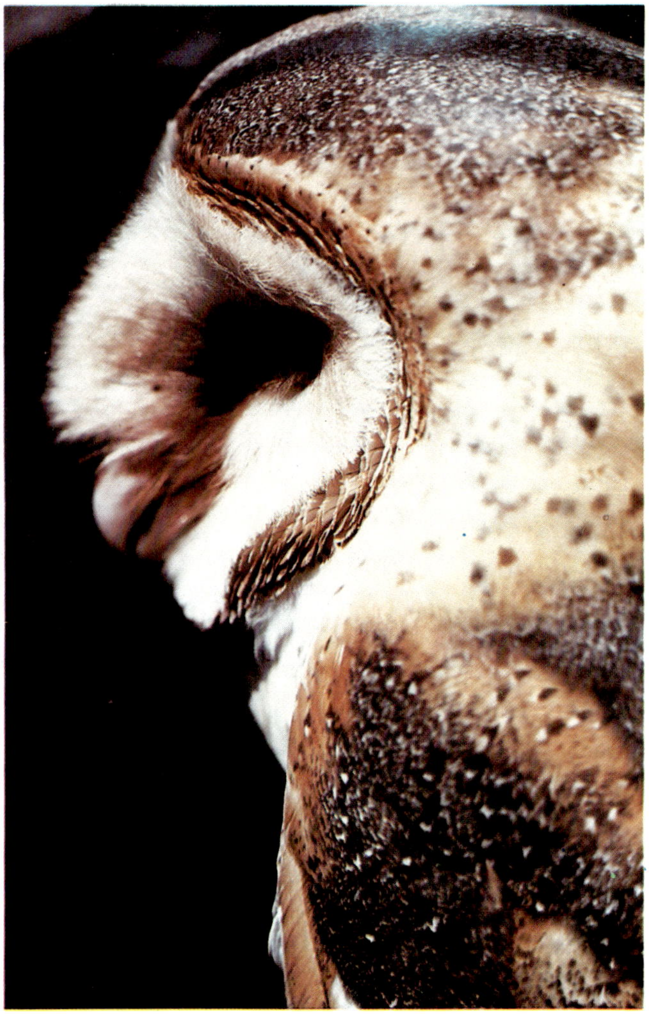

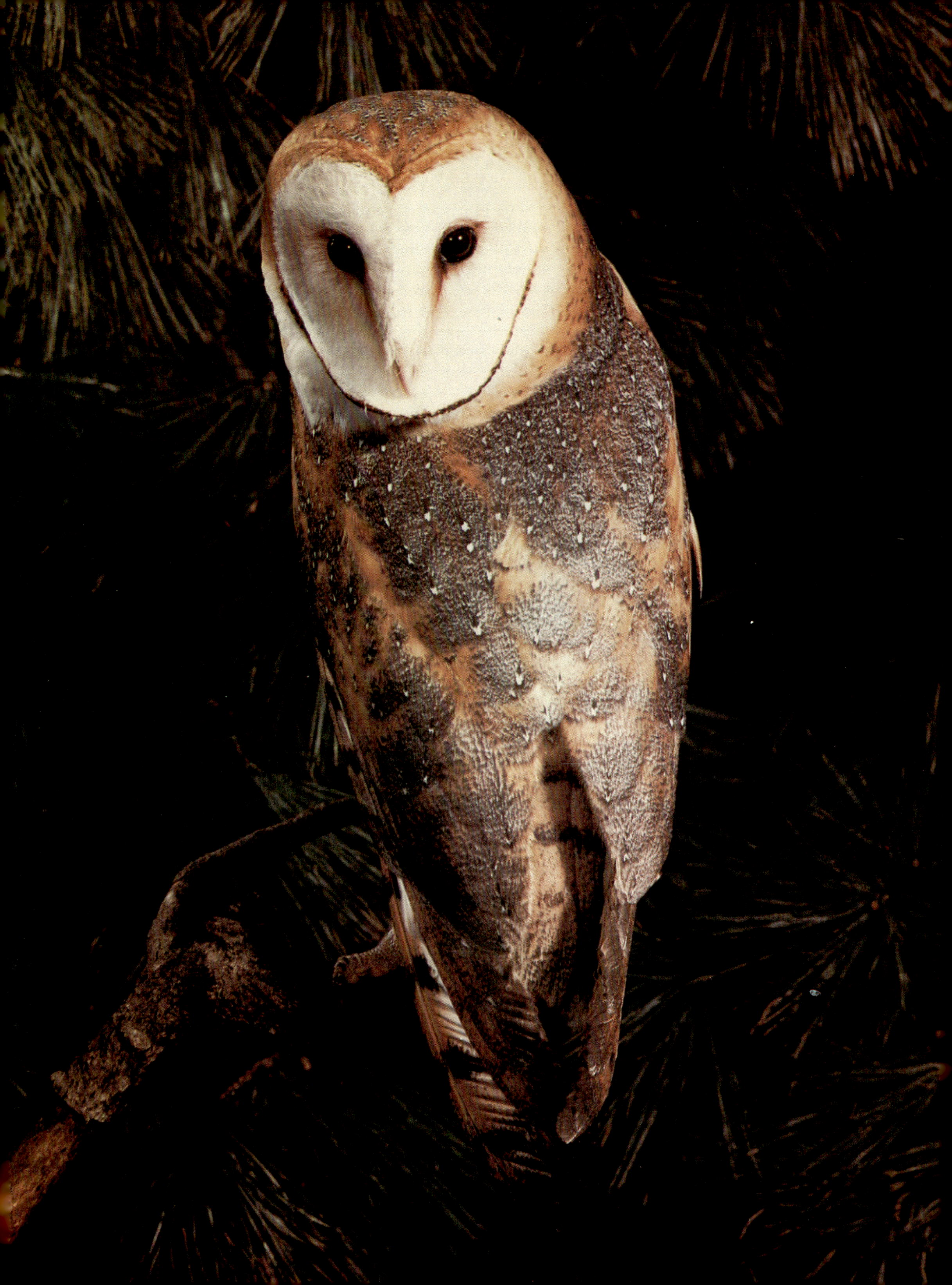

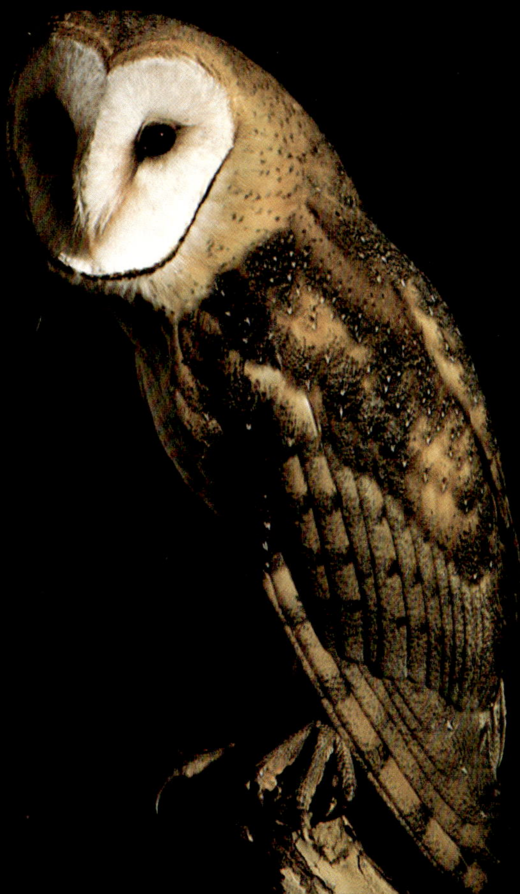
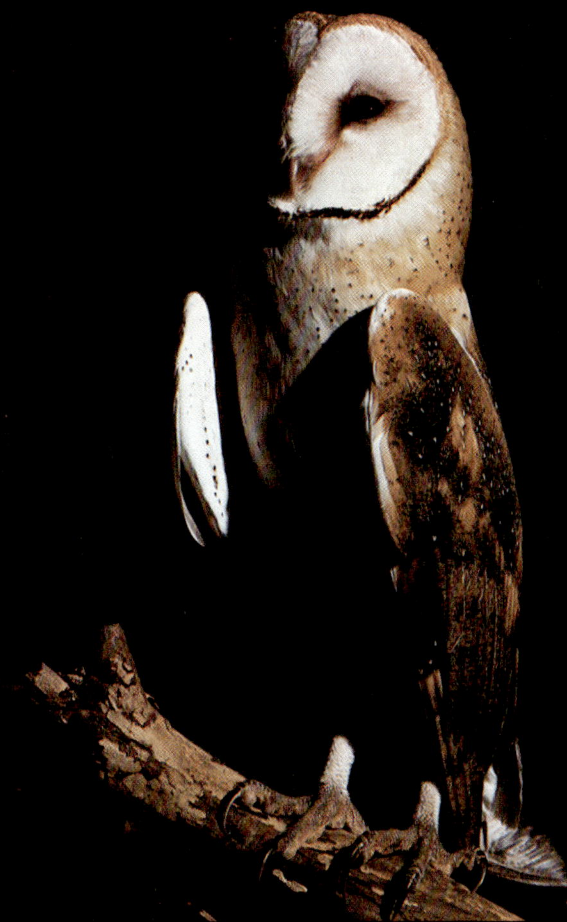
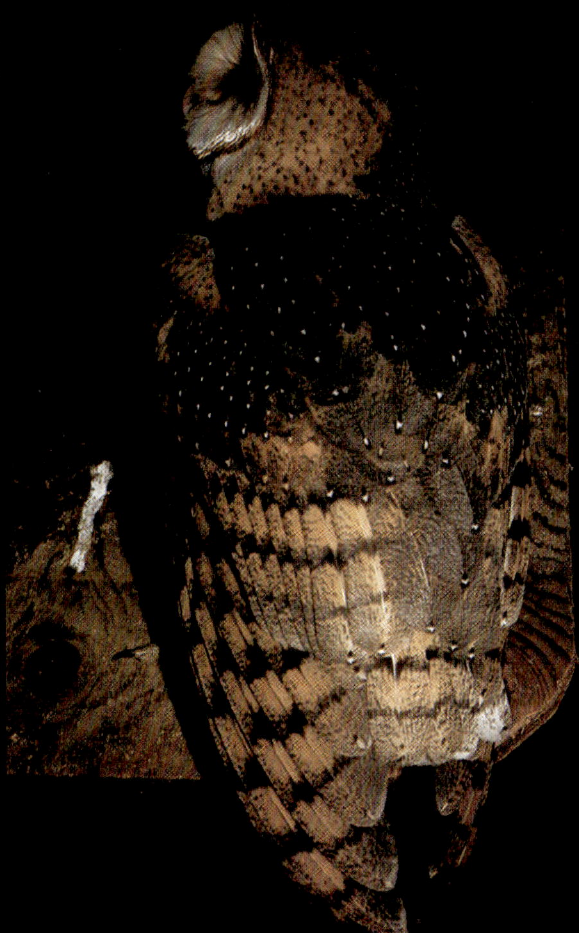
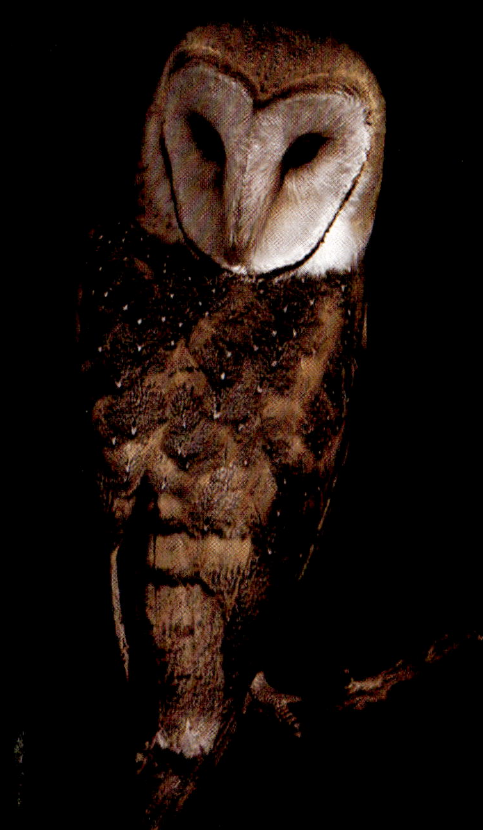

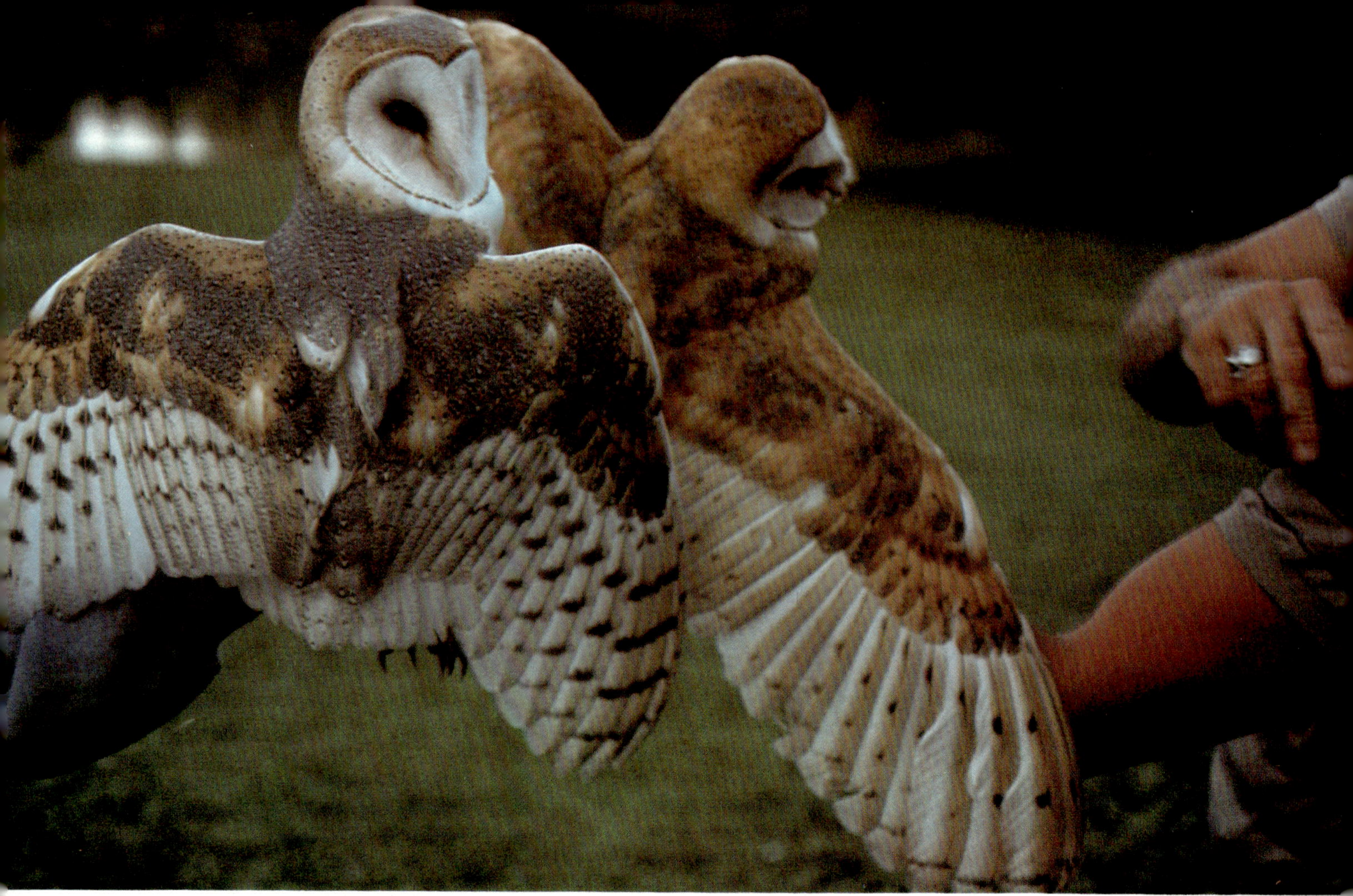

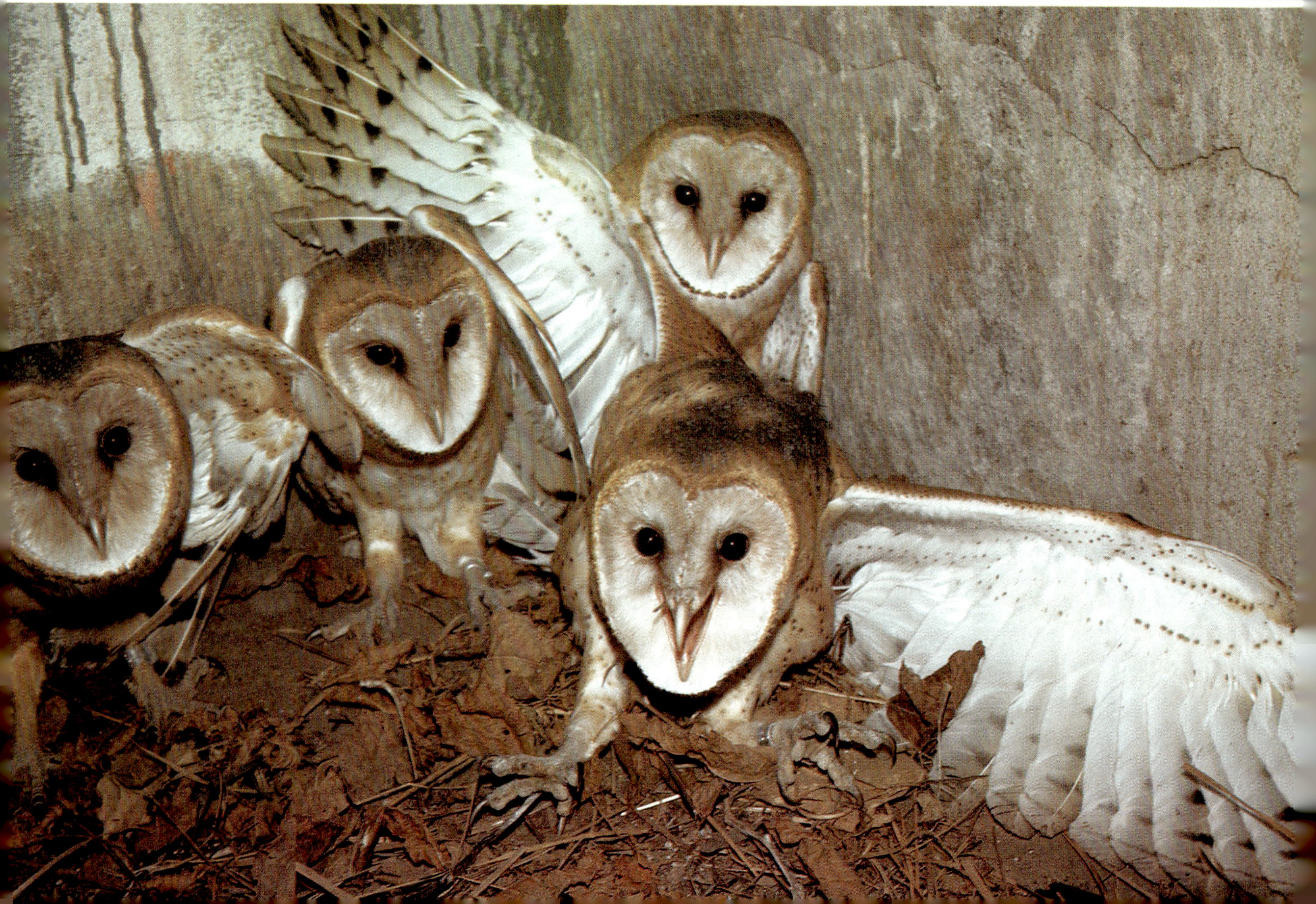

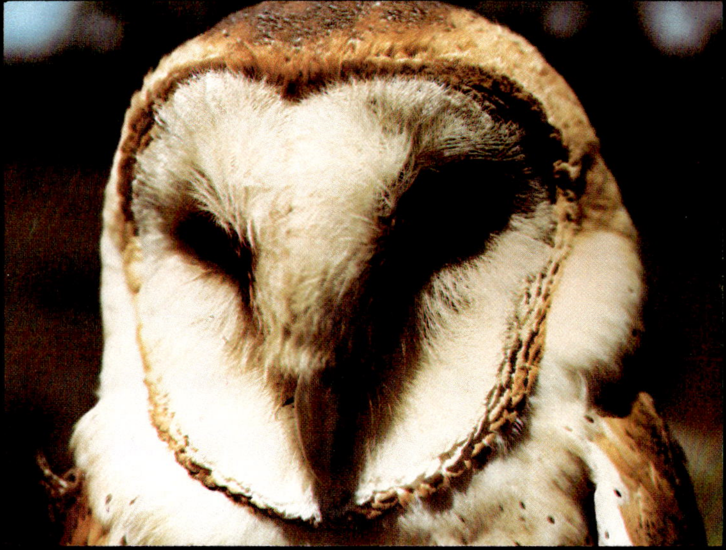

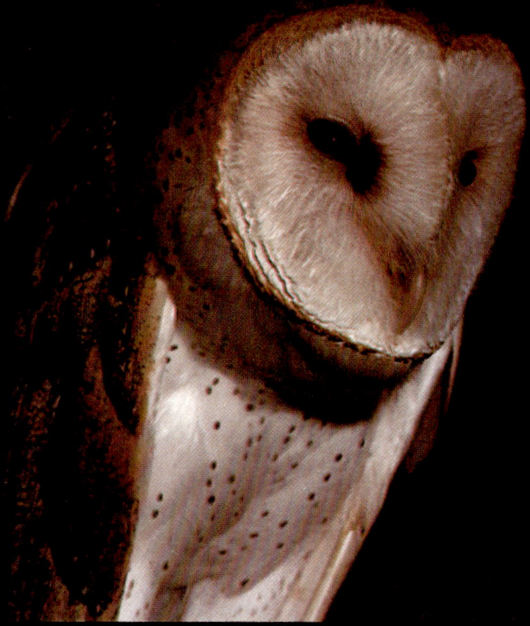

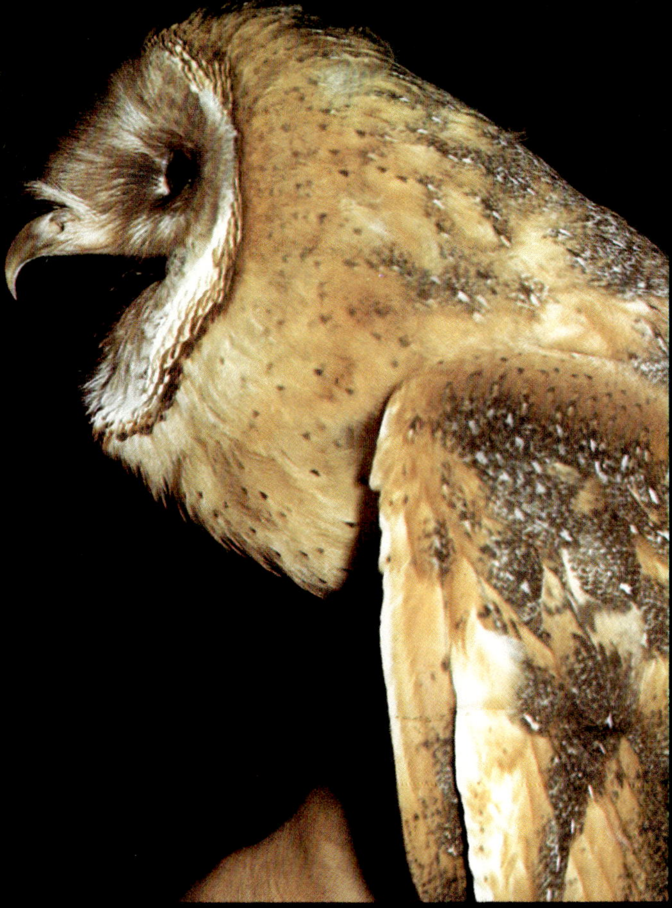

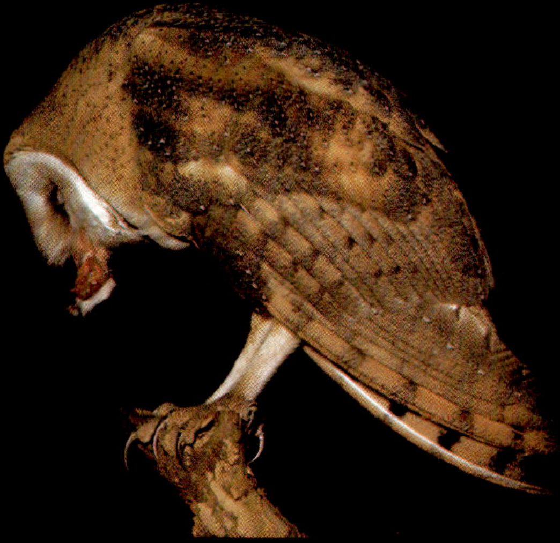

Great Horned Owl

Bubo virginianus

The Great-horned Owl is New Jersey's most impressive owl. Standing 18 to 25 inches tall, with a wingspan of 48 to 60 inches, it is indeed a powerful and fearless bird of prey. Its distinguishing characteristics are long feather tufts, large bright yellow eyes, and a white "collar" around the throat.

This owl is commonly called the "Hoot-Owl". Its deep-pitched, booming notes, "Whoo-whoo-whoo", repeated three to eight times, can be heard for miles on a still night.

The Great-horned Owl is primarily a woodland species, but is occasionally found in parks and orchards. It is non-migratory and occurs throughout the state in good numbers year round.

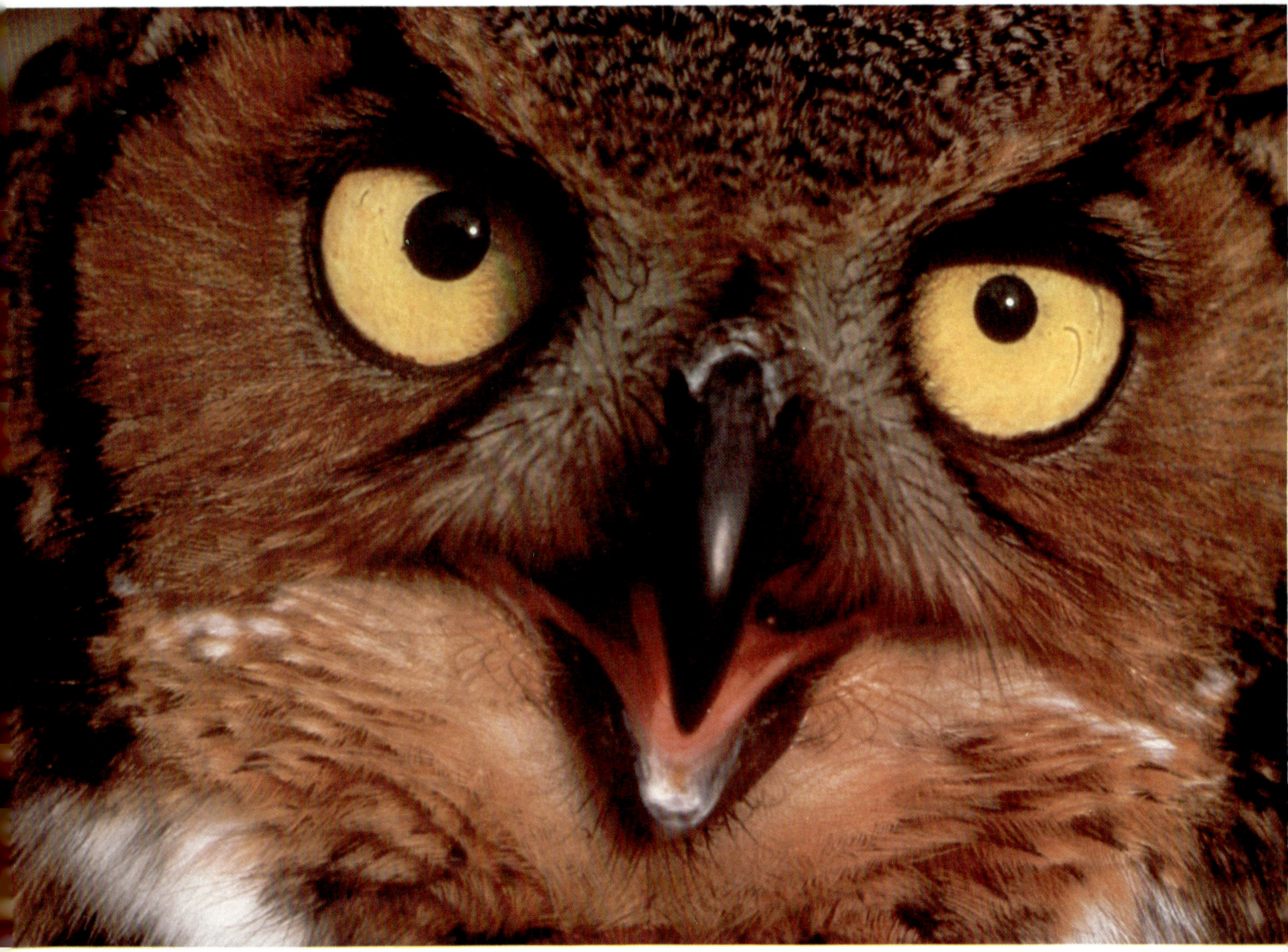

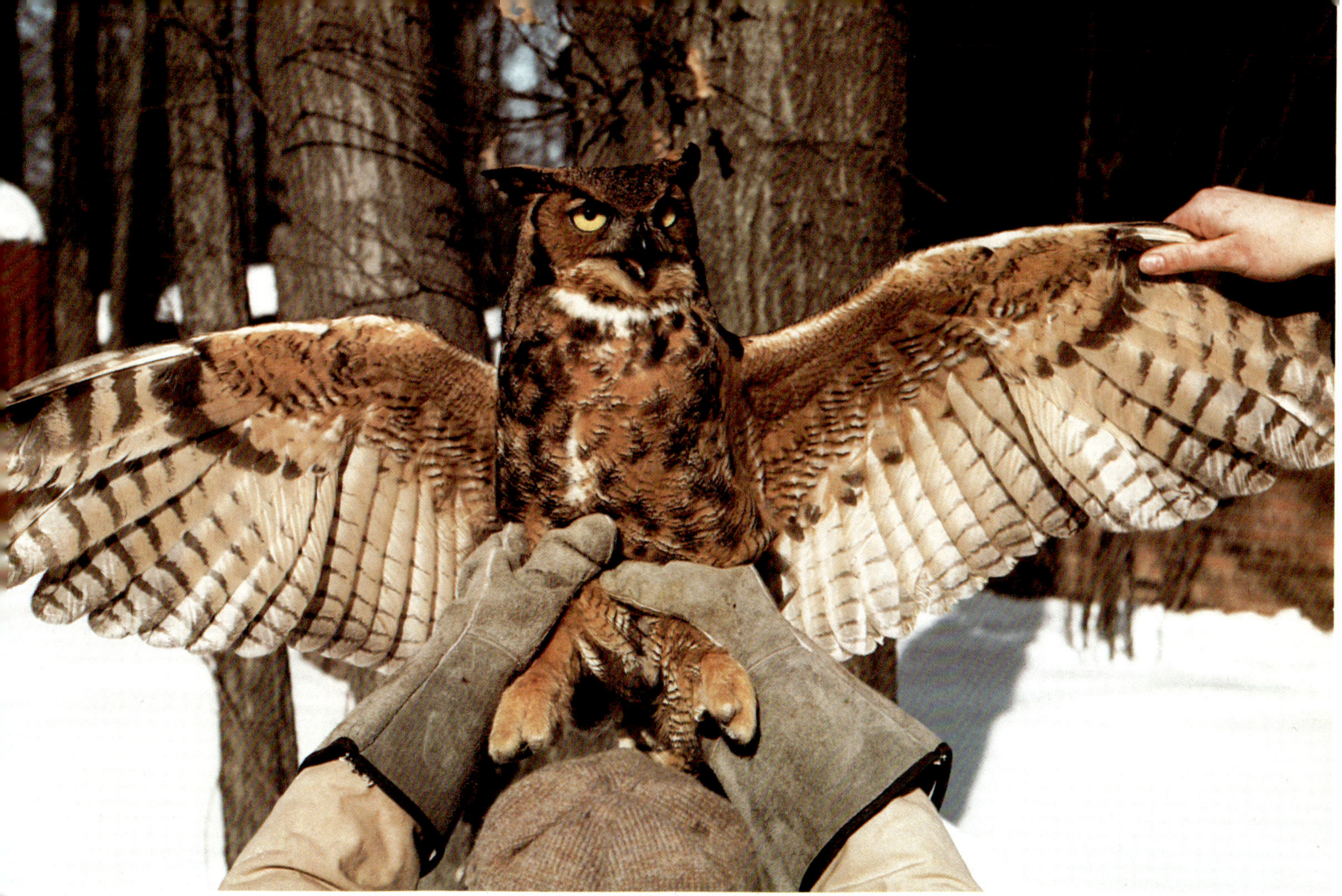

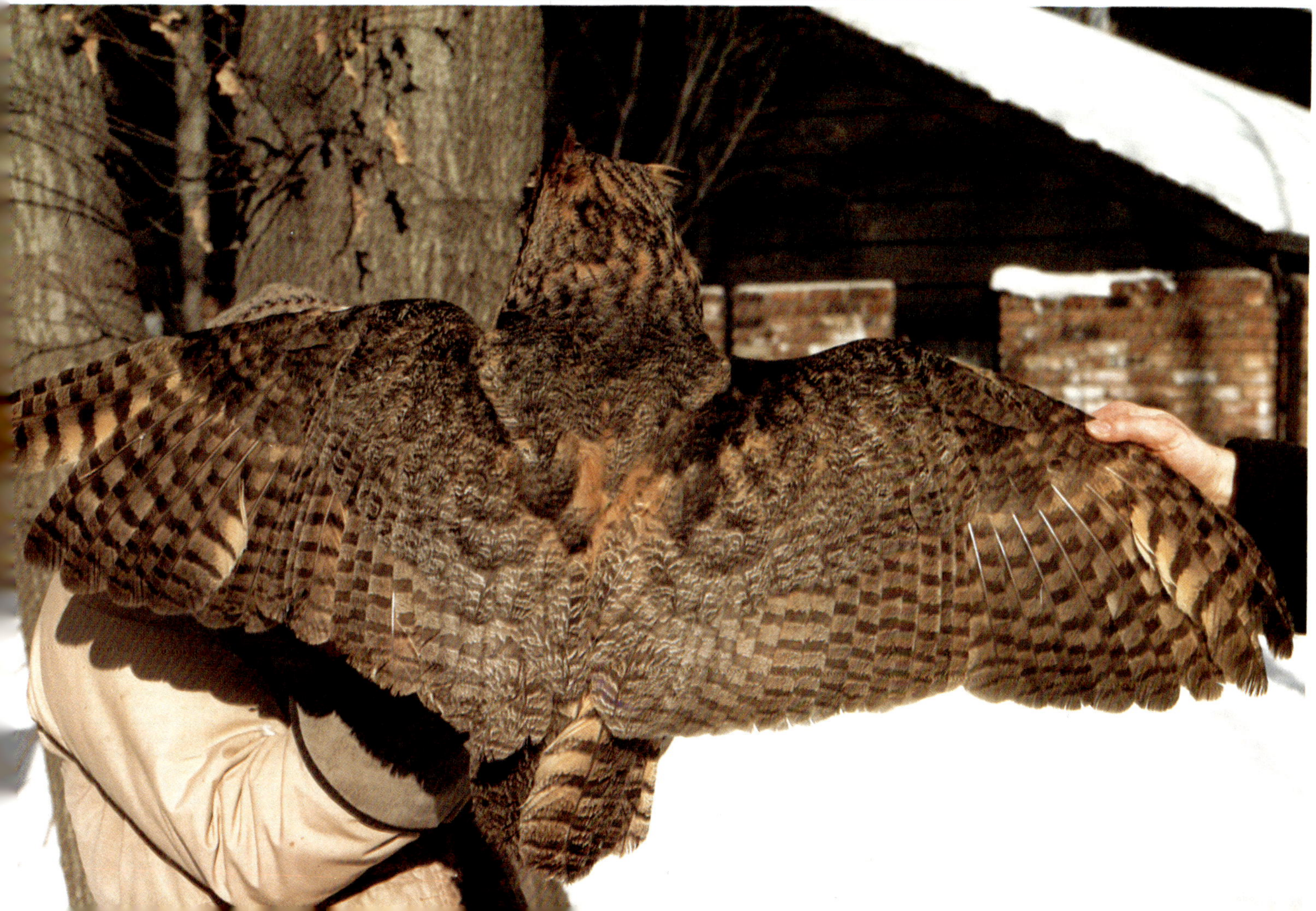

Screech Owl

Otus asio

The Screech Owl is one of the most common breeding owls and is a permanent, year round resident. Preferring open woodland terrain,l it lives in rural suburbs, farming districts, city parks and apple orchards. It is small, 7 to 10 inches tall with a wingspan of 18 to 24 inches, and occurs in two color phases, or morphs: gray and red. It has prominent, wide-set feather tufts and bright yellow eyes.

Its name is misleading as a description of its voice. Rather than a screech, its call is a plaintive, mellow trill, descending in tone, said to resemble the whinny of a horse.

The Screech Owl eats a wide variety of prey including small rodents, amphibians and fish. In summer, large quantities of insects are consumed.

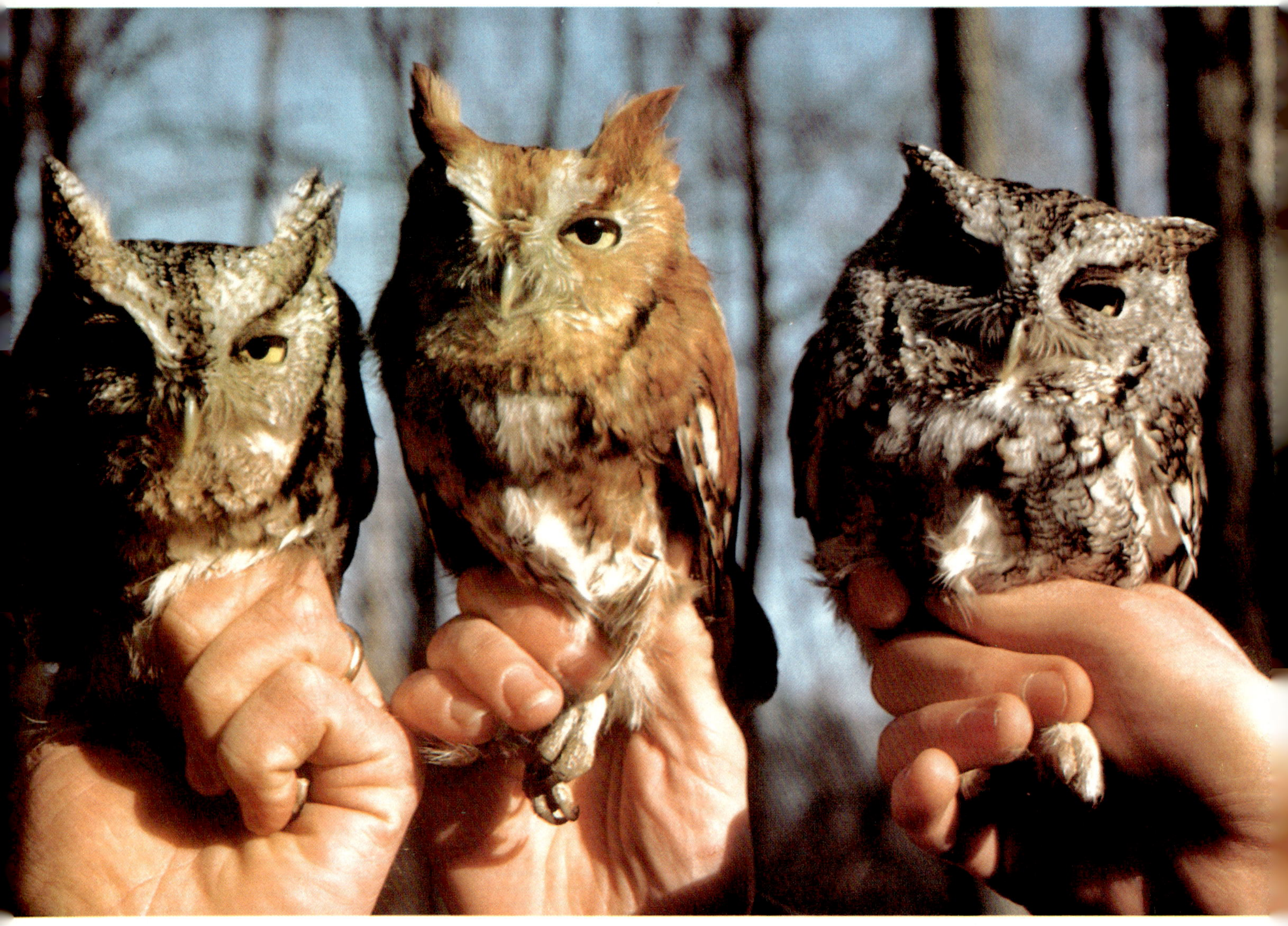

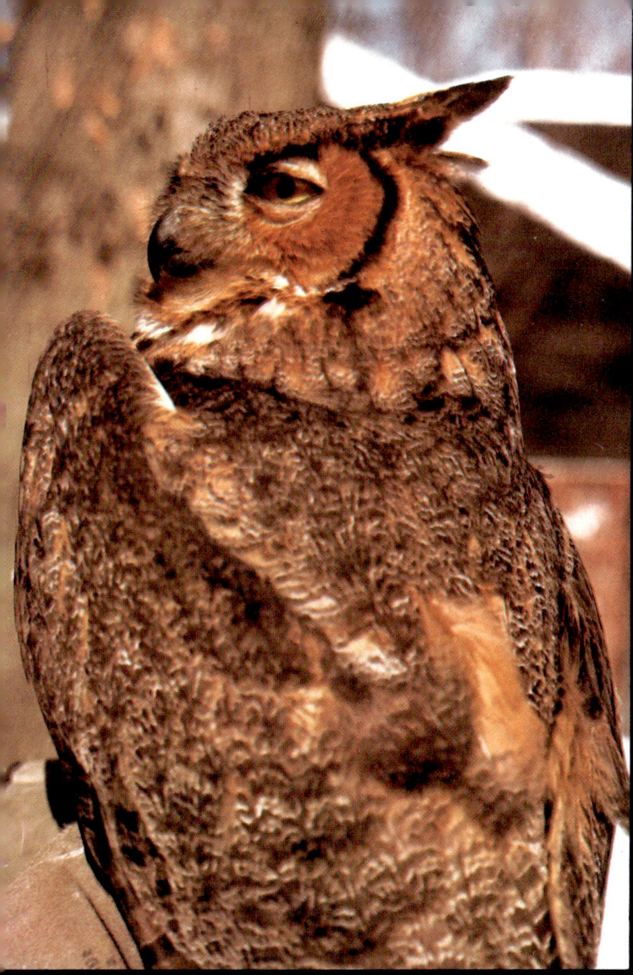
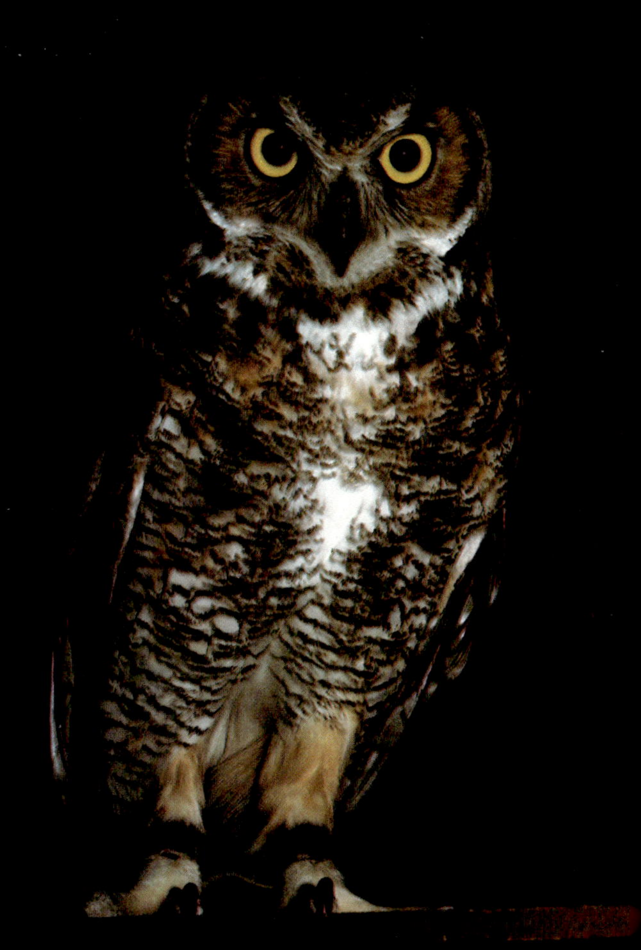
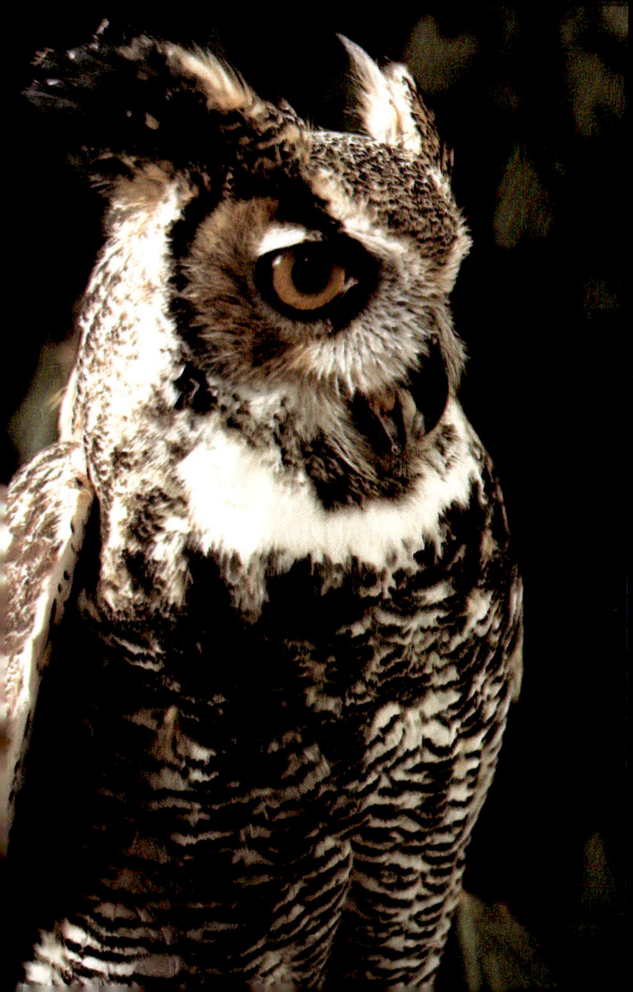
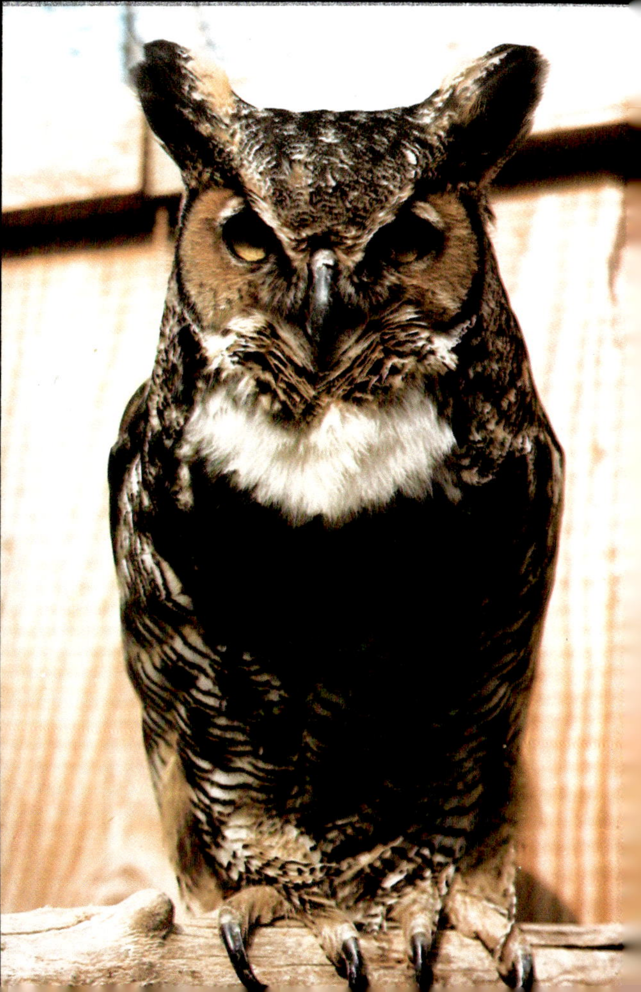

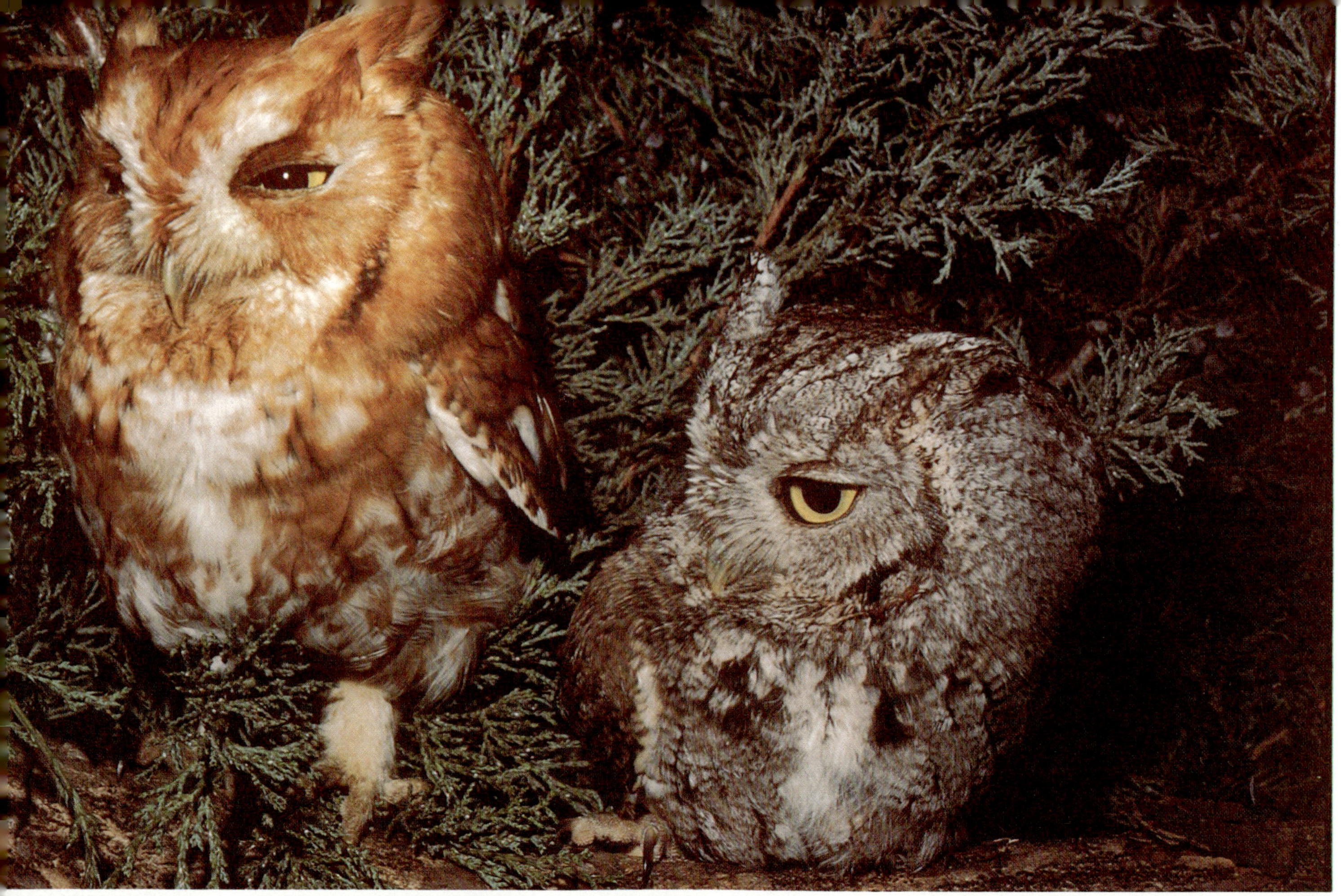

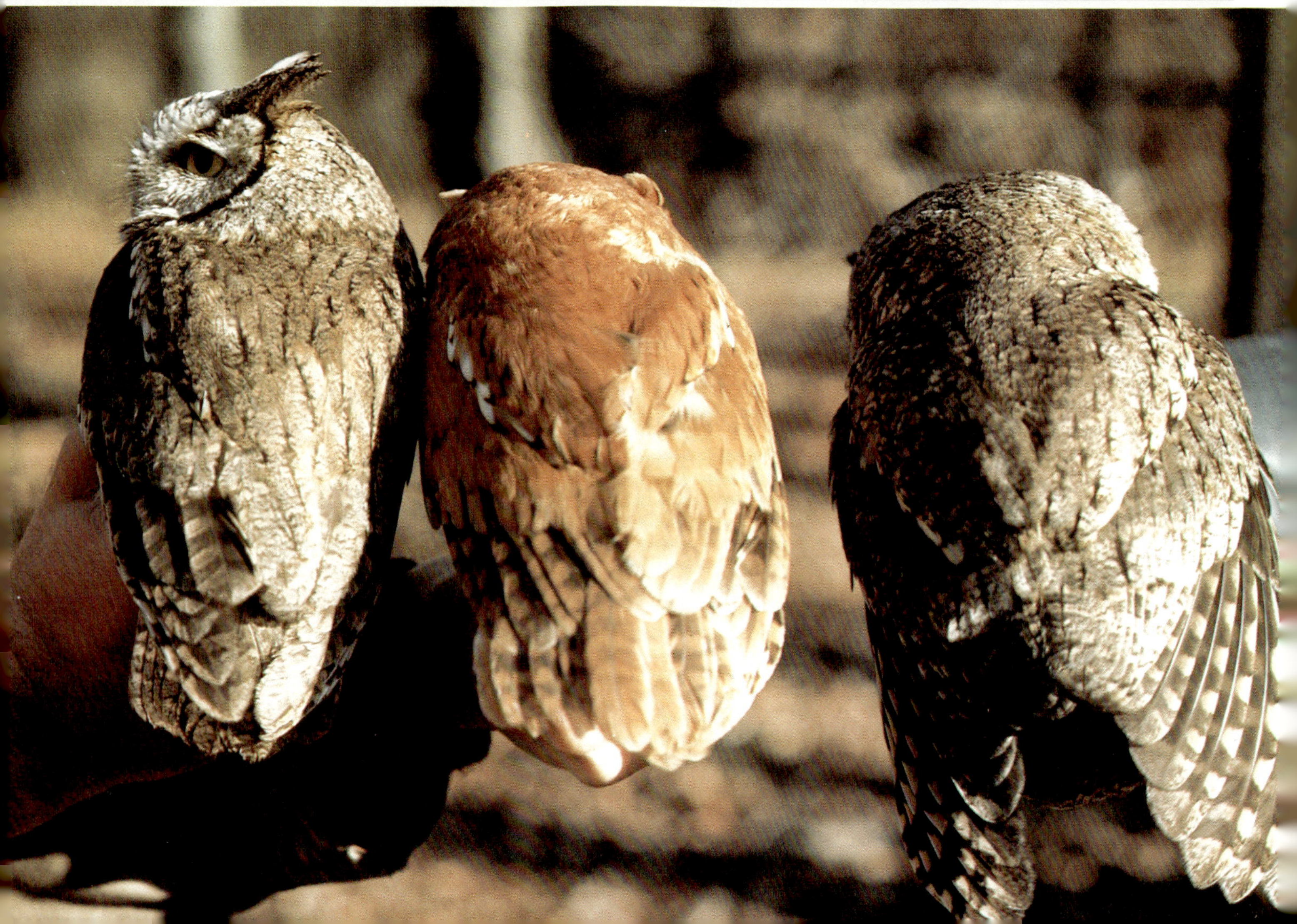

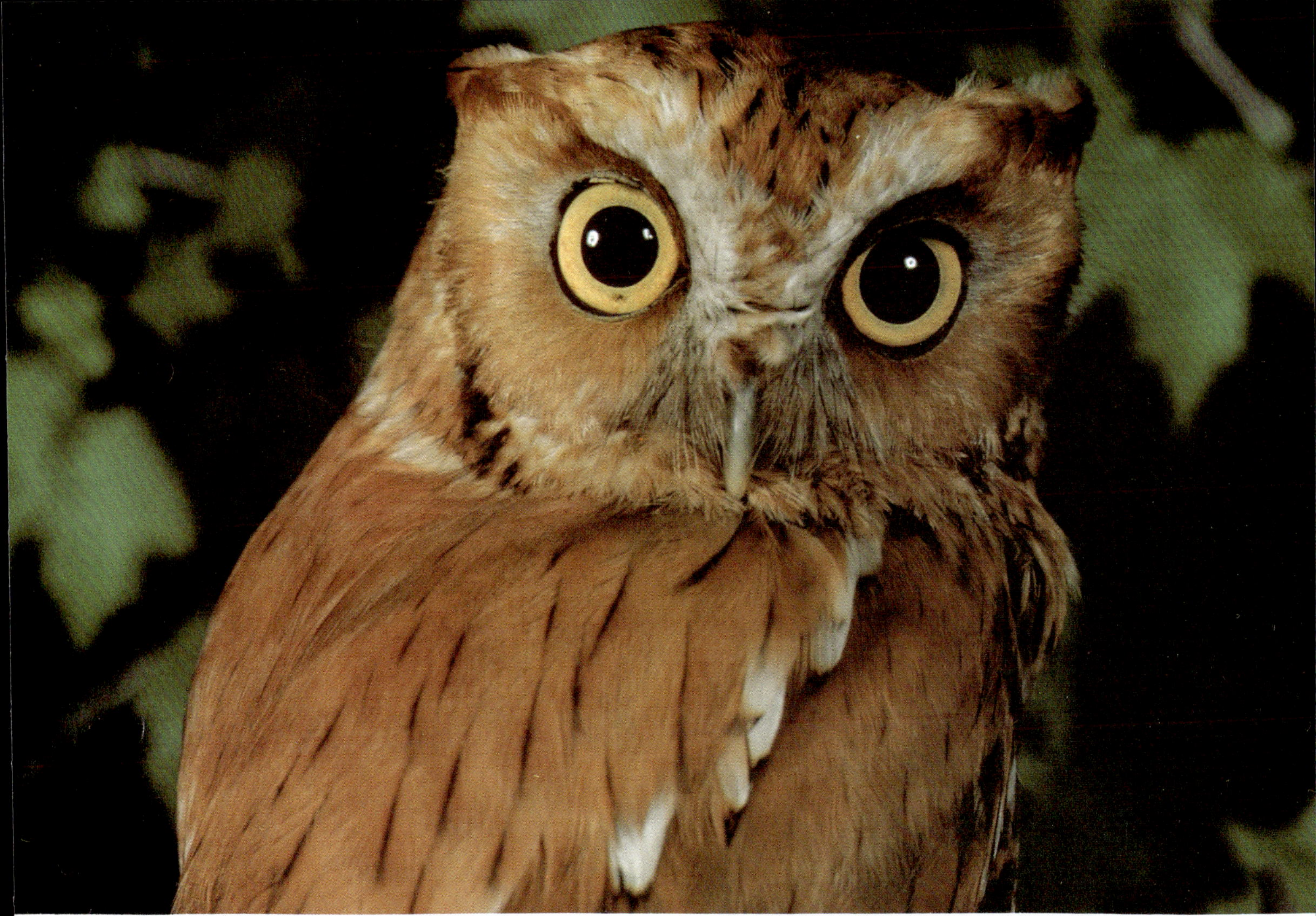

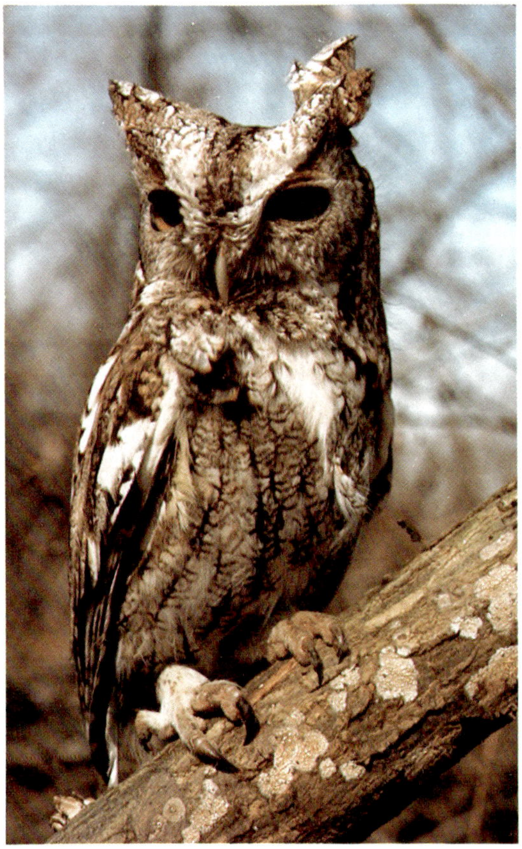

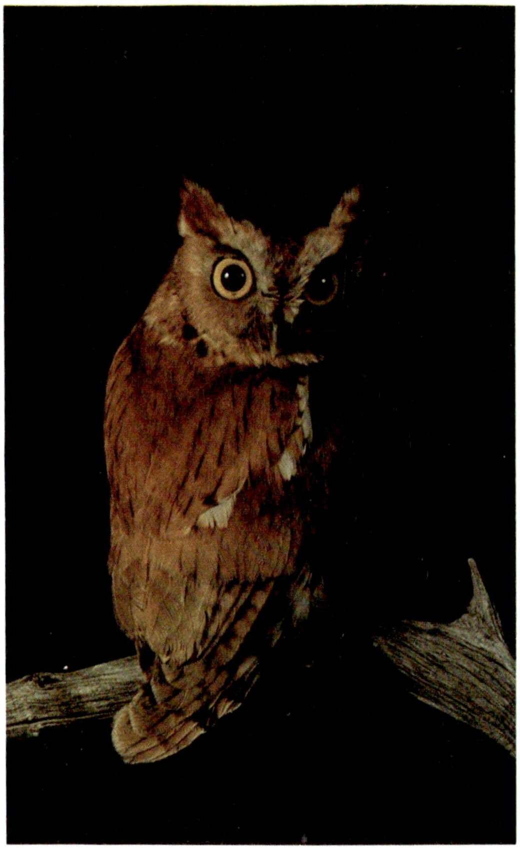

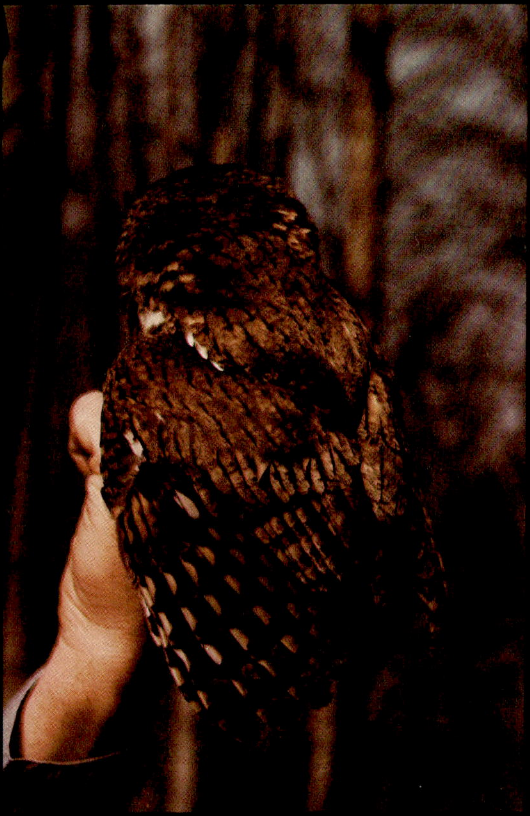

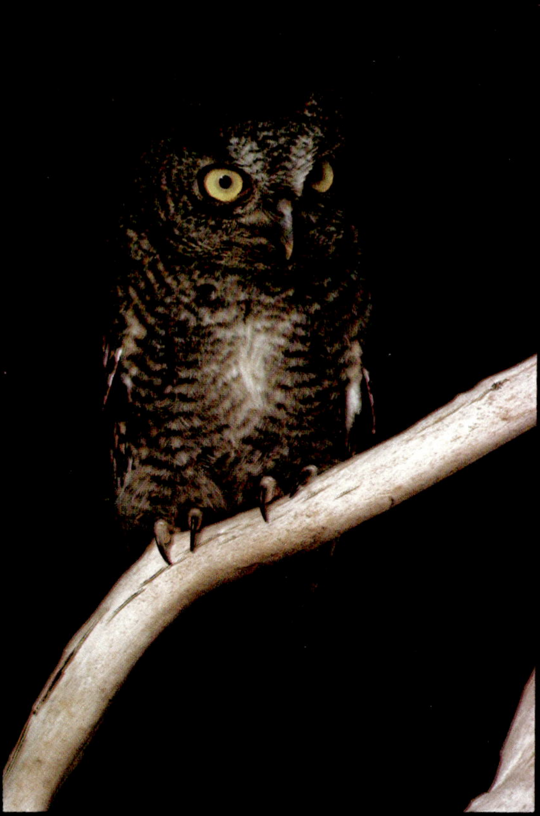

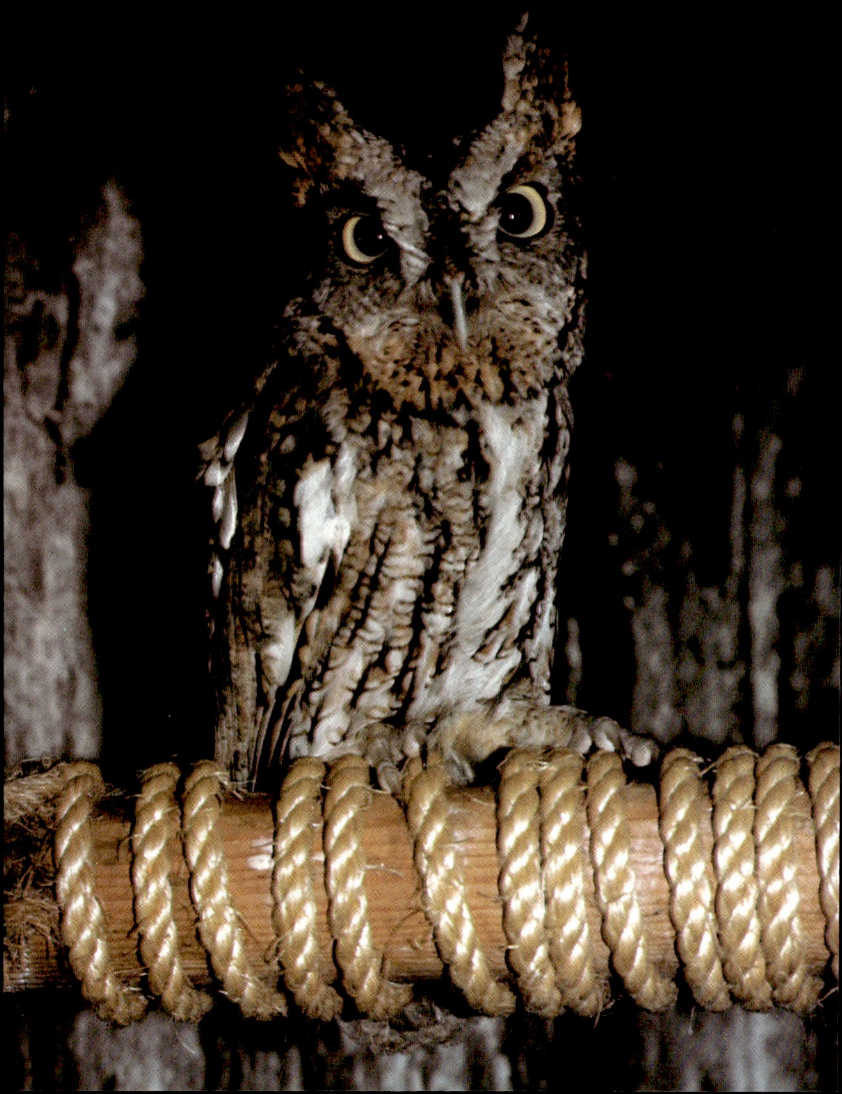

Specialized Information

OWL FACTS
From information provided by the Raptor Trust
1390 White Bridge Road, Millington, NJ 07946

Have you ever heard that an owl can turn its head completely around? Or that owls are blind in daylight? Or that the feather tufts of an owl's head are its ears? Or that if you hear an owl it means bad luck?

These are all misconceptions that have been passed down through generations. Let's set the record straight.

Owls can rotate their heads three-quarters of the way around. They cannot move their eyes from side to side but have extremely flexible necks and can move their heads rather quickly — thus the illusion of a complete turn.

Owls see perfectly well during the day and exceptionally well at night.

Owls have the best hearing of all birds. Their ears are located on the sides of their heads and are hidden by feathers. The so-called "ear-tufts" on the top of their heads aid in camouflage and recognition between individuals and have nothing to do with hearing.

Finally, if you hear an owl calling, consider yourself fortunate . . . even more fortunate to observe one in the wild.

Owls are predators — they catch, kill and eat other animals in order to survive. This predation is neither cruel nor wasteful and has been going on for millions of years. It seldom upsets anything except perhaps a few people. An owl killing and eating another animal is no different from a robin eating a worm or a gull eating fish. Although some owl species are diurnal (active by day), most owls hunt at night and are seldom observed by humans. Because of this nocturnal (nighttime) existence, they are little known and often misunderstood, even though some owls live their entire lives in close proximity to man.

Hunting at night, owls use their extraordinary vision and excellent hearing to locate their prey. Special adaptations such as wide wings, lightweight bodies and unusually soft, fluffy feathers allow them to fly silently. Owls seize their prey, usually a rodent or other small mammal, and kill it with their powerful feet. If the prey is small enough, it is swallowed whole; otherwise the food is torn apart by the owl's strong, hooked beak.

The owl's digestive system assimilates the nutritious portions of the prey; the undigested parts (hair, bones, claws, teech, etc.) are regurgitated in the form of pellets. These pellets, found at roosting sites, can be examined to determine the owl's diet.

There are eighteen species of owls in North America; eight of these can be found in our area. Some species, like the Screech Owl and Great-horned Owl, live here year-round; others like the Snowy Owl and the Saw-whet Owl, are winter visitors.

Even though we live in a part of the country that is densely inhabited, most of our native owl populations appear stable. There have been some adverse effects on certain species due mainly to habitat loss and other environmental factors. The Barred Owl, for example, a year-round dweller in swamps and deep woods is on the Threatened Species list in some areas because of diminishing habitat.

All owls are protected by state and federal regulations. It is illegal to kill or capture an owl; it is also illegal to possess an owl, living or dead, without the proper permits from both the U.S. Fish and Wildlife Service and the State.

Owls pose no threat to humans, although adult birds will defend their territory and their young against any intruders, human or otherwise. Unfortunately, superstitions and untruths about owls still persist which have subjected this group of birds to unwarranted suspicion and persecution. We hope, with knowledge and understanding of the owl's true character, these fears and misgivings will be replaced by tolerance and respect for these unique birds.

Barn Owl
Tyto alba

Barn Owls, sometimes called "Monkeyfaced" owls because of their heart-shaped faces, are strictly nocturnal. As their name suggests, they commonly select man-made structures in which

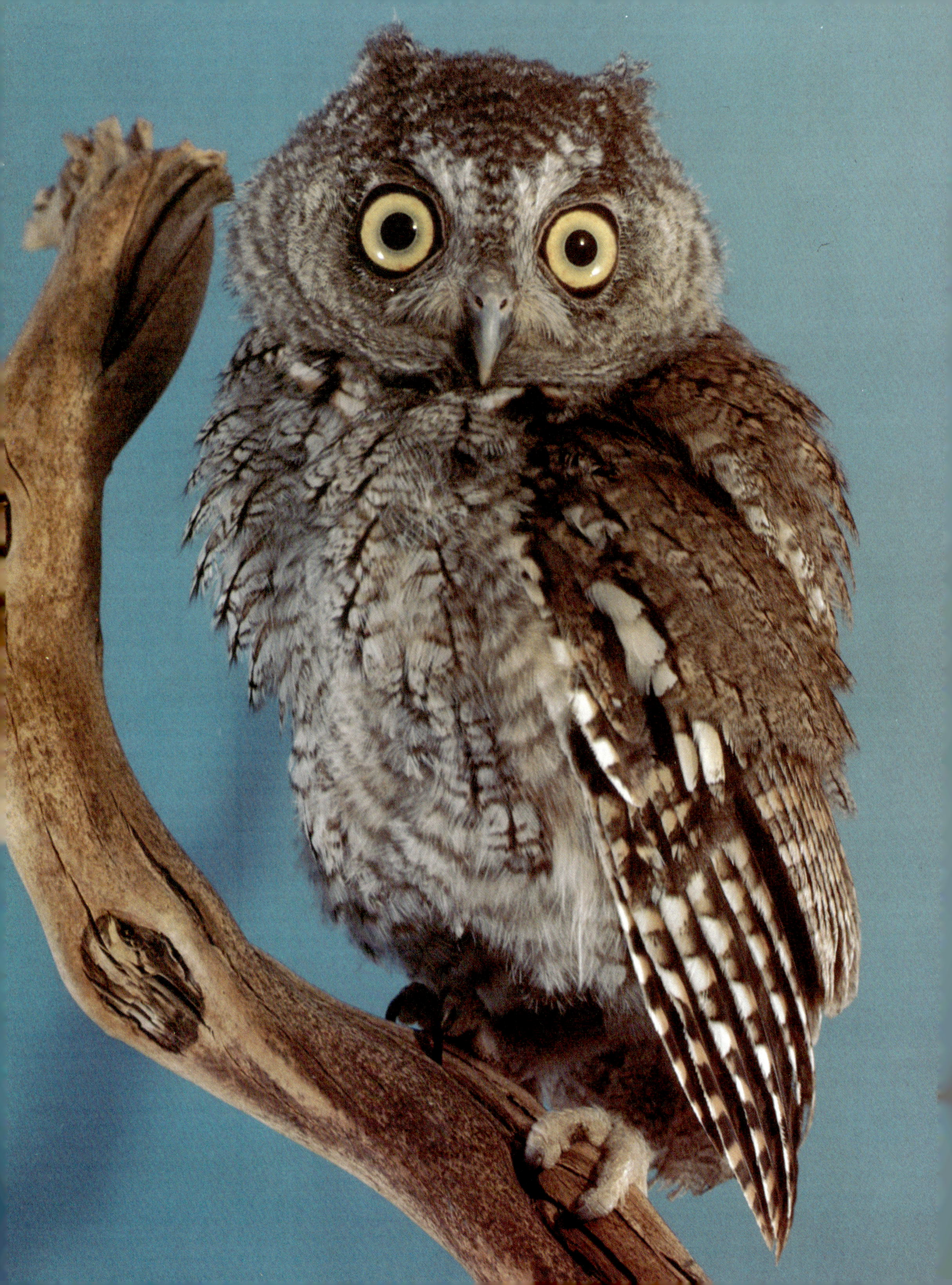

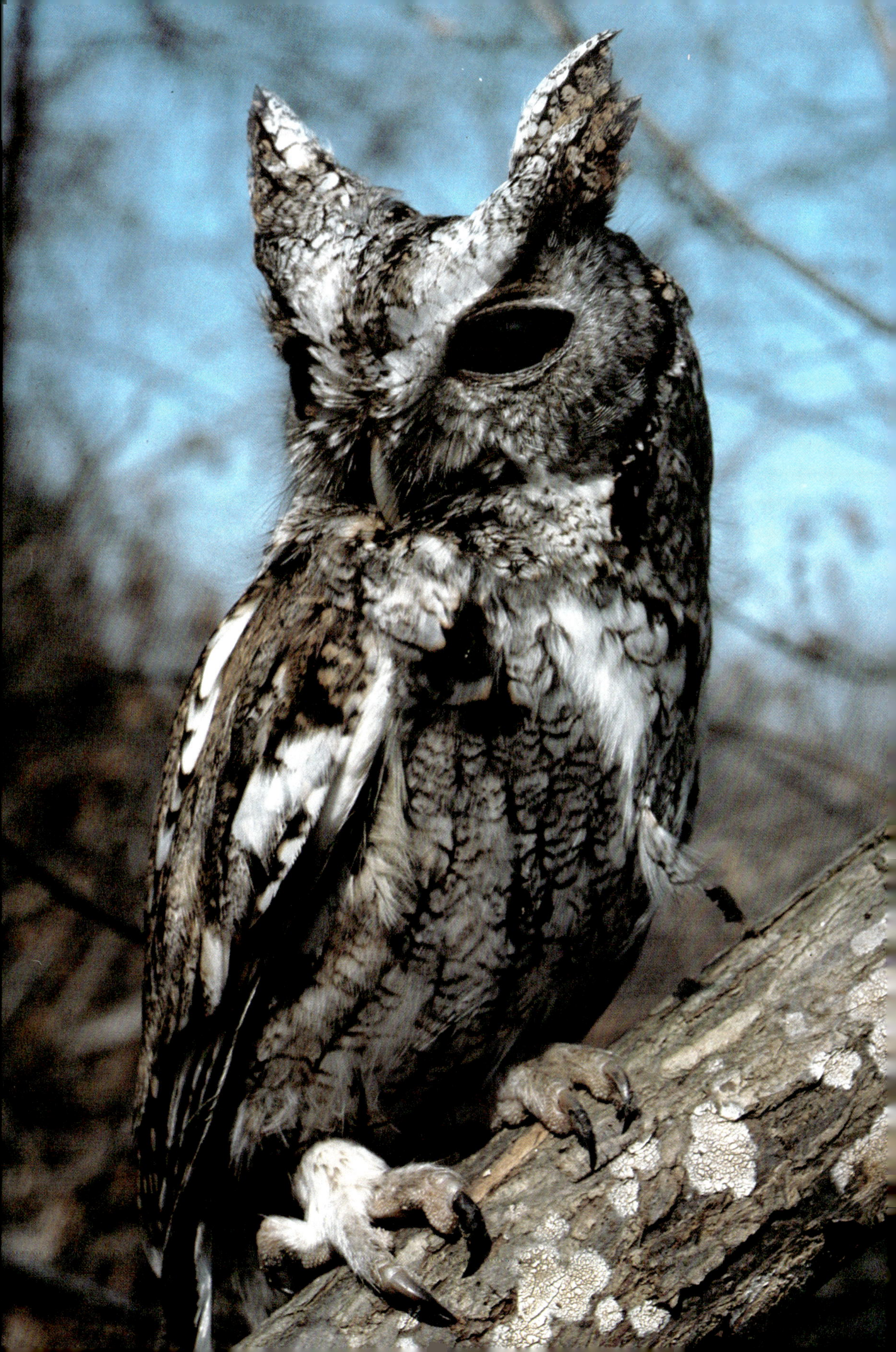

to live: silos, water tanks, church towers and barns are favored sites.

They are 14 to 20 inches tall with a wingspan of 40 to 45 inches. Their color is tawny or golden above and white or pale cinnamon below. They have long, broad wings and are graceful and somewhat moth-like in flight.

Barn Owls do not hoot, but are very vocal nevertheless. Their various sounds include hissing, screeching, beak snapping, and a cry best described as a maniacal shriek.

Great-Horned Owl

Bubo virginianus

The Great-horned Owl is a most impressive owl. Standing 18 to 25 inches tall, with a wingspan of 48 to 60 inches, it is indeed a powerful and fearless bird of prey. Its distinguishing characteristics are long feather tufts, large bright yellow eyes, and a white "collar" around the throat.

This owl is commonly called the "Hoot-Owl". Its deep-pitched, booming notes, "Whoo-whoo-whoo", repeated three to eight times, can be heard for miles on a still night.

The Great-horned Owl is primarily a woodland species, but is occasionally found in parks and orchards. It is non-migratory and occurs throughout the state in good numbers year round.

Screech Owl

Otus asio

The Screech Owl is one of the most common breeding owls and is a permanent, year round resident. Preferring open woodland terrain,l it lives in rural suburbs, farming districts, city parks and apple orchards. It is small, 7 to 10 inches tall with a wingspan of 18 to 24 inches, and occurs in two color phases, or morphs: gray and red. It has prominent, wide-set feather tufts and bright yellow eyes.

Its name is misleading as a description of its voice. Rather than a screech, its call is a plaintive, mellow trill, descending in tone, said to resemble the whinny of a horse.

The Screech Owl eats a wide variety of prey including small rodents, amphibians and fish. In summer, large quantities of insects are consumed.

Barred Owl

Strix varia

The Barred Owl is one of our largest owls, 16 to 23 inches tall with a 38 to 45 inch wingspan. It can be recognized by its large rounded head, lack of feather tufts, and dark brown eyes.

This owl is predominantly nocturnal and lives in deep woods and swamps. It is our most vocal owl, and is heard more often than seen. It has a wide variety of calls, many impossible to describe. The most often heard call is the "eight-hooter," given in two groups of four hoots: "Hoo-hoo-hoo-hoo; hoo-hoo-hoo-hoowah." The last note slides downward in tone.

The bird feeds mainly on small mammals, but being an opportunist, it also consumes fish, snakes and frogs.

Long-Eared Owl

Asio otus

The Long-eared Owl, a nocturnal bird about the size of a crow, has a 36 to 42 inch wingspan. Long feather tufts set close together on the head and bright yellow eyes are distinguishing features.

This owl lives in deep woodlands, preferring dense groves of conifers.

Rodents, mainly meadow voles, mice and shrews, are its major food. It is a hoot owl with a soft, deep, "Hoo-ooo" call, repeated several times.

Short-Eared Owl

Asio flammeus

The Short-eared Owl lives in open fields, marshes and meadows, and nests on the ground, well hidden in the reeds and grasses. It is often seen on the wing in daylight, flying low to the ground in a zig-zagging moth-like manner. Many times it can be found at airports, where runways and surrounding open areas suit its lifestyle.

Medium sized, 13 to 17 inches tall with a wingspan of 39 to 44 inches, the Short-eared Owl has a rounded head with small inconspicuous feather tufts, and bright yellow eyes. It feeds primarily on rodents, specifically field mice.

Saw-Whet Owl

Aegolius acadicus

The Saw-whet Owl is one of our smallest bird of prey. Only 7 to 8 inches tall with a wingspan of 18 to 21 inches, this mini-owl weighs a mere 4 ounces. That's about the size of a "quarter-pounder." It has a wide rounded head with no feather tufts, and bright yellow eyes.

Saw-whets are seldom observed because of their small size, their nocturnal habits, and the dense, deep woods in which they live. When discovered, however, they are amazingly tame and easily approached.

Snowy Owl
Nyctea scandiaca

The Snowy Owl is one of the most beautiful of all birds of prey. It is a large bird, 21 to 28 inches tall, and has a wingspan of 50 to 65 inches. When perched, the bird has a smooth, heavy appearance. Its head is rounded and lacks feather tufts. It has bright yellow eyes, a black beak, and thickly feathered legs and feet.

Male and female Snowys can be told apart, something which is not always possible in other species. The female is larger than the male, as in all owls, but the recognizable difference is that the adult male is almost pure white, while the female has dark, heavy flecking.

The Snowy Owl is a bird of the Canadian tundra. It prefers open country such as fields, pastures, coastal beaches and airports.

These winter visits to our state depend on the availability of food in its Arctic home, not on the severe weather there, which the bird is well equipped to endure. Periodically, in cycles of from four to eight years, the populations of the Snowy's usual northern prey species decline. Then these owls begin a southward movement in search of food, and we are afforded a chance to see one of nature's masterpieces.

HAWK FACTS

From information provided by the Raptor Trust
1390 White Bridge Road, Millington, NJ 07946

"Hawk" is a general term used to describe the entire group of diurnal (active by day) predatory birds. Worldwide there are approximately 270 species of carnivorous birds that comprise the order *Falconiformes* — the scientific name for hawks. All are classified as birds of prey, or raptors. We present in formation on 16 species here.

Although all hawks have certain basic similarities such as keen eyesight, hooked beaks and taloned feet, a wide diversity of forms and sizes exists among them. For instance, an American Kestrel weighs only 4 ounces, while a Bald Eagle can weigh 13 pounds — 52 times as much.

Hawks are efficient predators. They catch, kill, and eat a wide variety of other animals in order to survive. This predation is not mean or cruel. It has been going on for millions of years and is, in fact, a necessary function which helps to maintain nature's balance.

Hawks are strong, powerful birds. Their feet are equipped with sharp, curved talons for capturing prey, and their strong beaks are hooked for biting and tearing flesh. Swift fliers, some hawks can attain speeds of over 150 mph when diving. Some species undertake long migrational journeys, traveling thousands of miles each year — a testimony to their strength and stamina.

Their sense of hearing is excellent, and their eyesight the best in the entire animal world. Not only can hawks see greater distances than humans, but their visual acuity (the ability to see clearly) is eight times that of ours. Hawks also see in color.

In many animal species the males are larger and stronger, but in hawks the difference in size between the sexes is reversed, and females are larger. This sexual size difference is often appreciable. In some species, such as Sharp-shinned Hawks, females can weigh *twice* as much as males.

In the northeast, hawks typically breed in the late spring or early summer. Most hawks pair for life, but if one partner dies, the other will quickly find a new mate. Some pairs remain together year round; others may separate after the breeding season. The allegiance to the breeding site is strong, however, and even those that migrate or disperse will normally return to the same nesting territory and the same mate each year.

Large hawks lay only one or two eggs each year, small hawks from three to five. Incubation takes three to six weeks, depending on the species. After hatching, the young hawks "grow up" very quickly. Small hawks, like Kestrels and Sharpshins, grow to full size in one month; large species, like eagles, are full grown in only 11 weeks. The young leave the nest (fledge) at this time, but often remain with their parents for

Long-Eared Owl

Asio otus

The Long-eared Owl, a nocturnal bird about the size of a crow, has a 36 to 42 inch wingspan. Long feather tufts set close together on the head and bright yellow eyes are distinguishing features.

This owl lives in deep woodlands, preferring dense groves of conifers.

Rodents, mainly meadow voles, mice and shrews, are its major food. It is a hoot owl with a soft, deep, "Hoo-ooo" call, repeated several times.

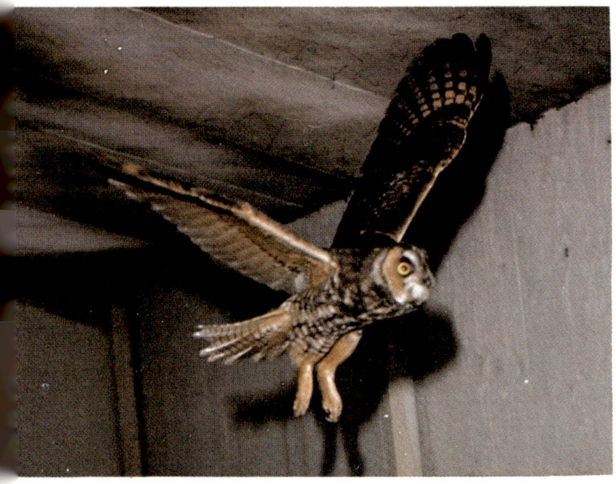

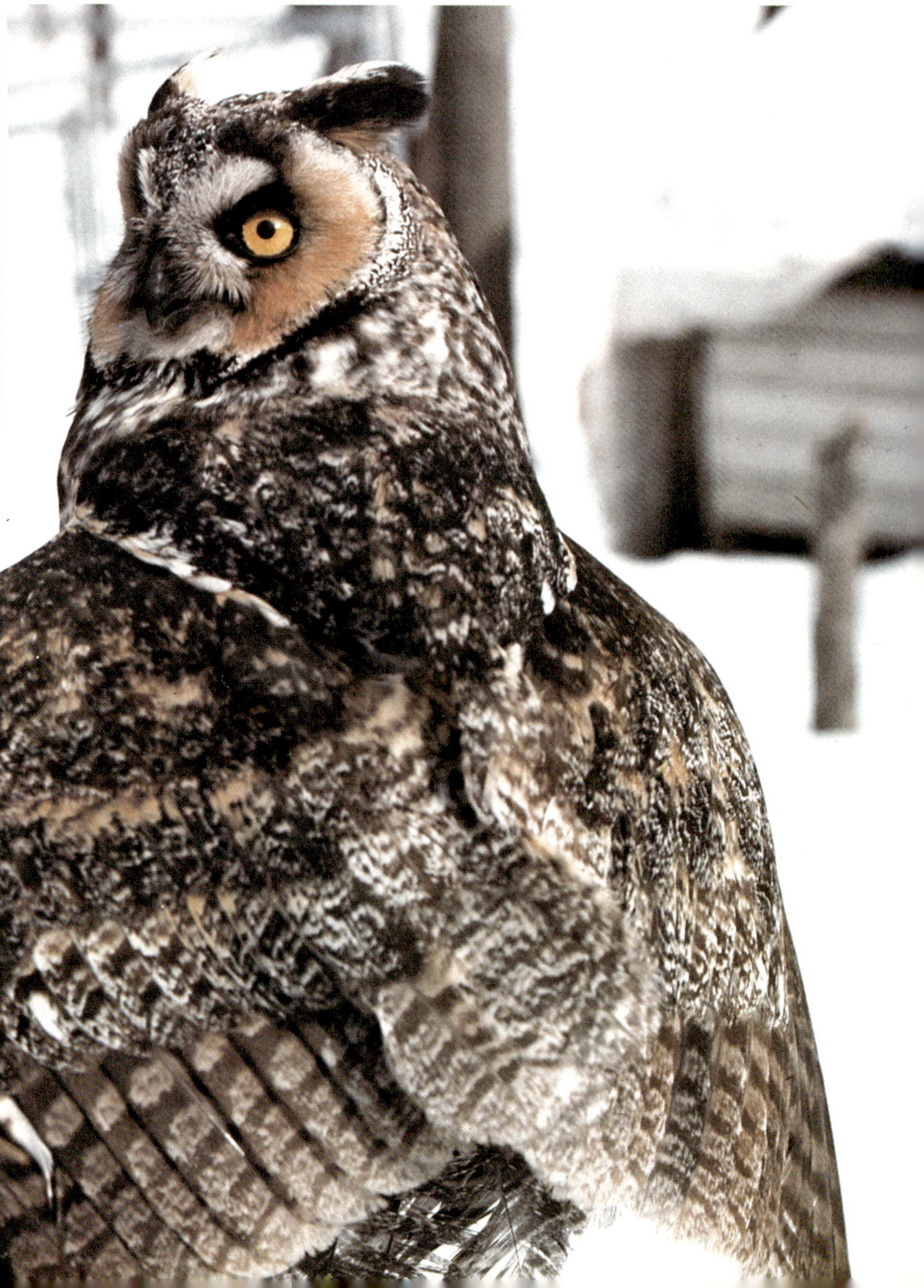

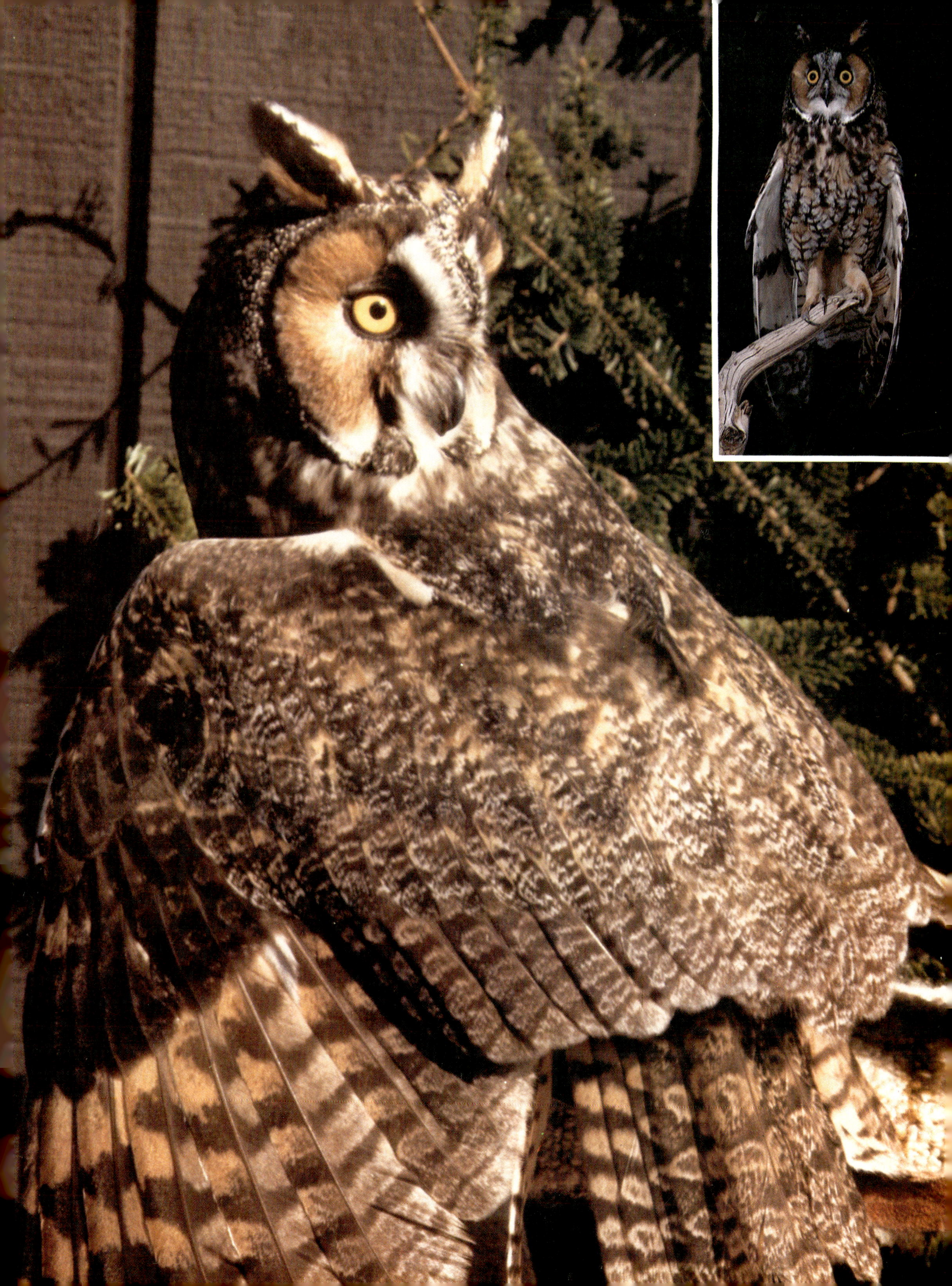

several more weeks before attaining total independence.

All hawks are protected by state and federal laws. It is illegal to capture or kill a hawk, or to possess a hawk, alive or dead, without the proper permits from both the State and the U.S. Fish and Wildlife Service.

Because they are predators, hawks have historically been regarded by many people as vermin. In the past, they were seen as wanton killers — cruel and harmful creatures. Fortunately, with our increased ecological knowledge we now realize that hawks are neither harmful nor cruel. They are, like all living things, important parts of a diverse and intricate natural world. The protection of that natural world is of paramount importance to their well-being, and to ours.

Ospreys

Ospreys are large raptors that feed exclusively on fish. Although they are widely distributed throughout the world, the entire group is comprised of but a single species.

Osprey
Pandion haliaetus

This hawk is a highly specialized fish eater, seldom found far from water. The Osprey plunges feet first into the water to capture fish swimming near the surface. Rough sandpaper-like spicules on the bottoms of its feet allow the Osprey a good grip on slippery prey.

It is a large bird measuring 21 to 24 inches long with a wingspan from 4½ to 6 feet. Soaring in the air the Osprey resembles a gull. Its long, narrow wings are bent in the shape of a stretched out "M." Seen from below, the hawk is white with a black patch at the bend of each wing. Its head is white with a broad dark stripe through the cheeks, and its upperparts are dark brown.

In the past few decades Ospreys have declined in numbers, due mainly to the indiscriminate use of pesticides. Our breeding population has made a striking recovery in recent years. Restricted pesticide use and successful management plans are helping the Osprey to once again attain a healthy status. Their large stick nests, constructed in trees or atop high platforms specially provided for them, are once again visible from major highways along the shore.

Falcons

Falcons are streamlined fast-flying hawks. They have long, narrow, pointed wings and long narrow tails. They feed primarily on other birds and usually capture their prey in mid-air. Birds of open areas, falcons are seldom found in woods. They often live and breed in cities and towns in close proximity to humans.

American Kestrel
Falco sparverius

The American Kestrel, sometimes called the Sparrow Hawk, is our smallest and most common falcon. Although this bird is easily seen, it is often not recognized as a hawk because of its resemblance to a songbird. Perched, it is similar to a dove or robin. From head to tail the Kestrel measures only 9 to 12 inches, but its wings are long, spanning up to 2 feet.

Unlike most other birds of prey, in which the sexes are alike, male and female Kestrels have different color plumages. Females have rufous backs and wings, barred with black, while males have rufous backs and blue-gray wings.

Kestrels catch most of their prey on the ground. They are often seen perched on telephone poles and wires, like sentinels of the road, searching the terrain below. They also hunt on the wing, characteristically hovering over grassy areas. Grasshoppers, crickets and other insects are eaten in great numbers when available; but mice, voles, snakes and songbirds are also taken.

Kestrels are unique among our falcons in that they are hole-nesters, using natural cavities in trees and small openings in buildings. They are the only North American hawks that will nest in bird boxes.

Merlin
Falco columbarius

Merlins are small dark falcons just slightly larger than Kestrels. They measure 10 to 13½ inches long and have wingspans of 24 to 27 inches. Immature Merlins are brown above, while adults are blue-gray; both young and adult birds have heavy dark brown vertical streaks on their underparts. Their tails are long with prominent dark bands. When flying and perched, a Merlin resembles a dark pigeon.

Like other falcons, Merlins are birds of open country and generally avoid wooded areas. They are fast-flying aerial acrobats and hunt primarily on the wing, catching other birds (their main food), some insects and occasionally small mammals.

Peregrine Falcon
Falco peregrinus

This mighty falcon's scientific name *peregrinus* means "wandering," and indeed. Peregrines are among the most widely distributed birds in the world. Although they inhabit every continent except Antarctica, Peregrine populations have suffered drastic declines during the past 40 years due to the effects of pesticides. The species is presently classified as endangered throughout the world. Recently, through conservation programs on their behalf, they are making a comeback throughout their breeding range.

Peregrines are large falcons, 15 to 20 inches long, with a wingspan of 3½ feet. They have a distinctive facial pattern with a dark "mustache" mark on the cheeks. Adult Peregrines have slate blue backs.

Their favored nesting sites are generally high, rocky cliff ledges in remote places overlooking a lake, stream, or river, but they have been known to nest on the rooftops or ledges of city buildings and in the steelwork of bridges.

Peregrines feed mainly on other birds, catching whatever is available, from small songbirds to large ducks. They dive at incredible speeds, approaching 200 miles an hour, to capture their prey in mid-air.

Buteos

Buteos are robust hawks with long, broad, rounded wings and short broad tails. Because they are easily observed soaring in wide, lazy circles or perched in a conspicuous place, they are among the best known hawks. They hunt mainly from perches, dropping to the ground to capture their prey.

Broad-Winged Hawk

Buteo platypterus

The Broad-winged Hawk is one of the smallest buteos, about the size of a crow. It is 14 to 19 inches long, with a wingspan of about 3 feet. Its relatively short wings and tail give the bird a chunky appearance in flight.

The adult is grayish-brown on the back, and its underparts are white, heavily barred with reddish-brown. Its tail is dark, with two or three equally wide white bands. The immature is brown-backed, and its underparts are whitish with vertical brown streaks. The barring in the tail of the young bird is not as prominent as in the adult.

Broad-winged Hawks breed throughout eastern North America, from Canada to Florida. Many nest in areas where proper habitat still exists, primarily deep deciduous forests. In early autumn they begin a spectacular migration southward, some going as far as South America. During this time huge concentrations of these hawks can be seen along the mountain and coastal flyways of our state.

Their diet consists of a wide variety of prey animals including small mammals, snakes, frogs and toads, grasshoppers and catepillars.

Red-Shouldered Hawk

Buteo lineatus

Red-shouldered Hawks are medium-sized slender buteos, larger than Broad-wings but smaller than Red-tails. They have body lengths of 18 to 24 inches and wingspans of 3½ to 4 feet. Their backs are brown, flecked with white, and their shoulders are rufous. Immature birds have brown teardrop-shaped streaks on their white breasts; adults have pale robin-red underparts.

Red-shouldered Hawks inhabit low, wet, open woodlands usually near a river, stream or swamp. They prey upon the wide variety of animal life found there: small mammals, frogs, snakes, lizards, insects and birds.

Red-Tailed Hawk

Buteo jamaicensis

The Red-tail is named for the rufous color of the adult's tail. These buteos are often seen soaring in wide circles or perched conspicuously in trees along roadsides. Vocal hawks, their distinctive call — a high, shrill "kree-e-e" — is usually uttered in flight.

Red-tails stand about 2 feet tall and have wingspans of 4½ to 5 feet. They are dark brown above, white to cinnamon below, and usually have a band of dark streaks across the belly. Immature birds are similar to adults in plumage except for their tails — the young have brown tails for their first year. When they molt, these brown feathers are replaced by the characteristic red of the species.

Red-tailed Hawks are found throughout North America. They prefer a habitat of fields and pastures mixed with open woodlands. Their large stick nests are usually built in the tallest available tree. From one to three young are raised each year.

Their diet consists mainly of mammals and includes mice, voles, squirrels and rabbits.

Rough-Legged Hawk

Buteo lagopus

The Rough-legged Hawk breeds in the far north. Like many northern species, it is protected from the cold by feathers that cover even its legs and toes. Its common and scientific names both

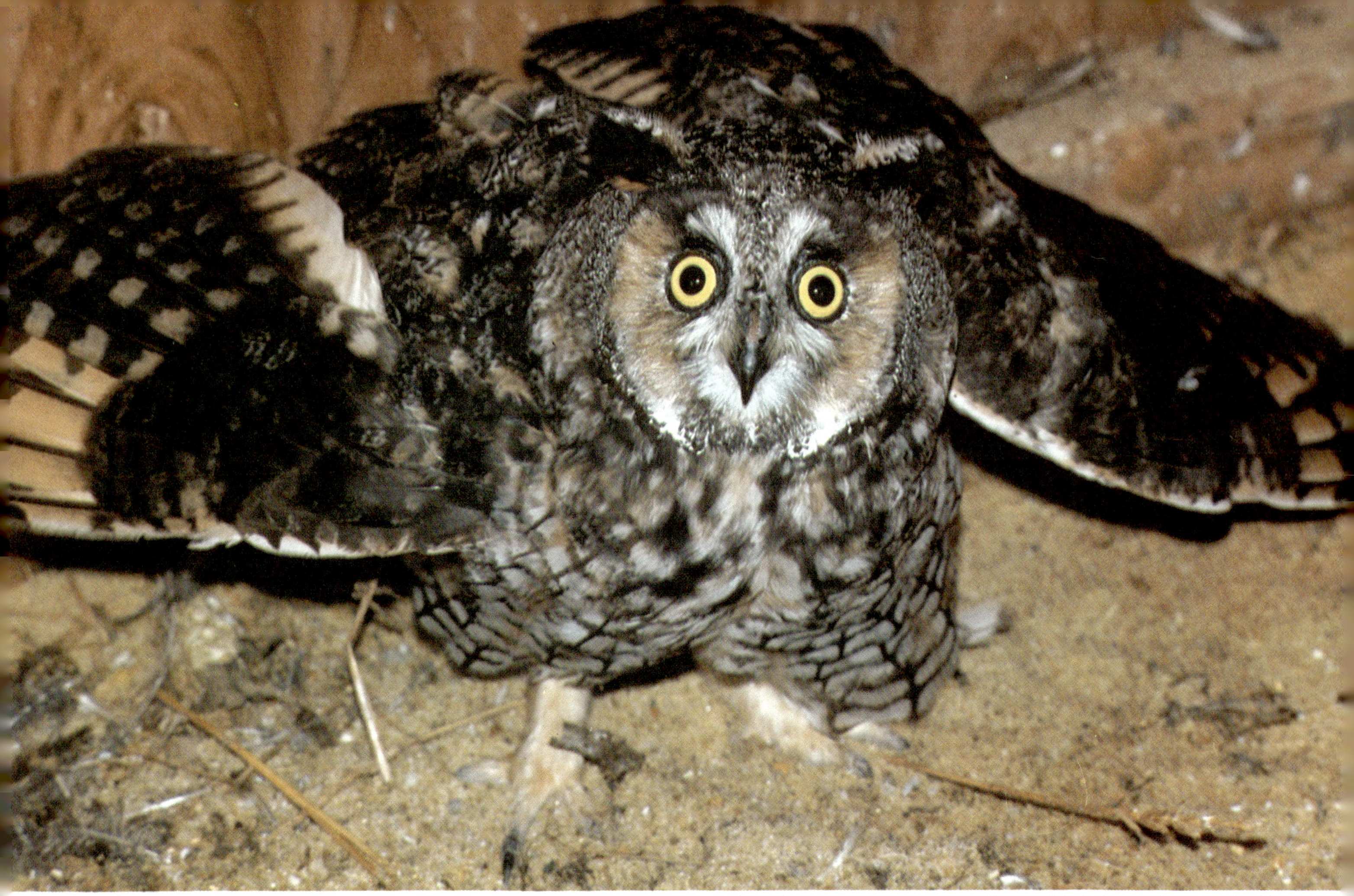

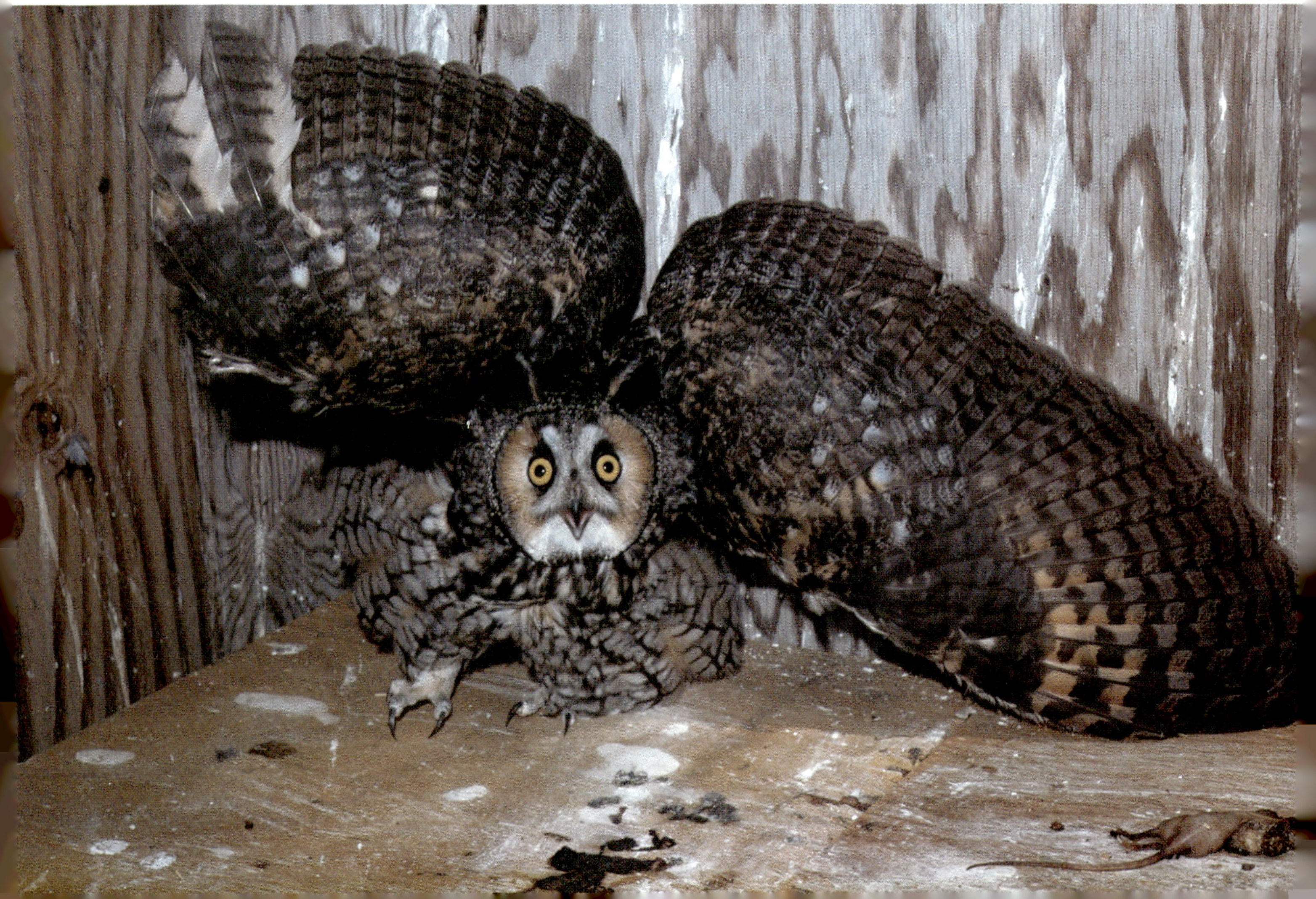

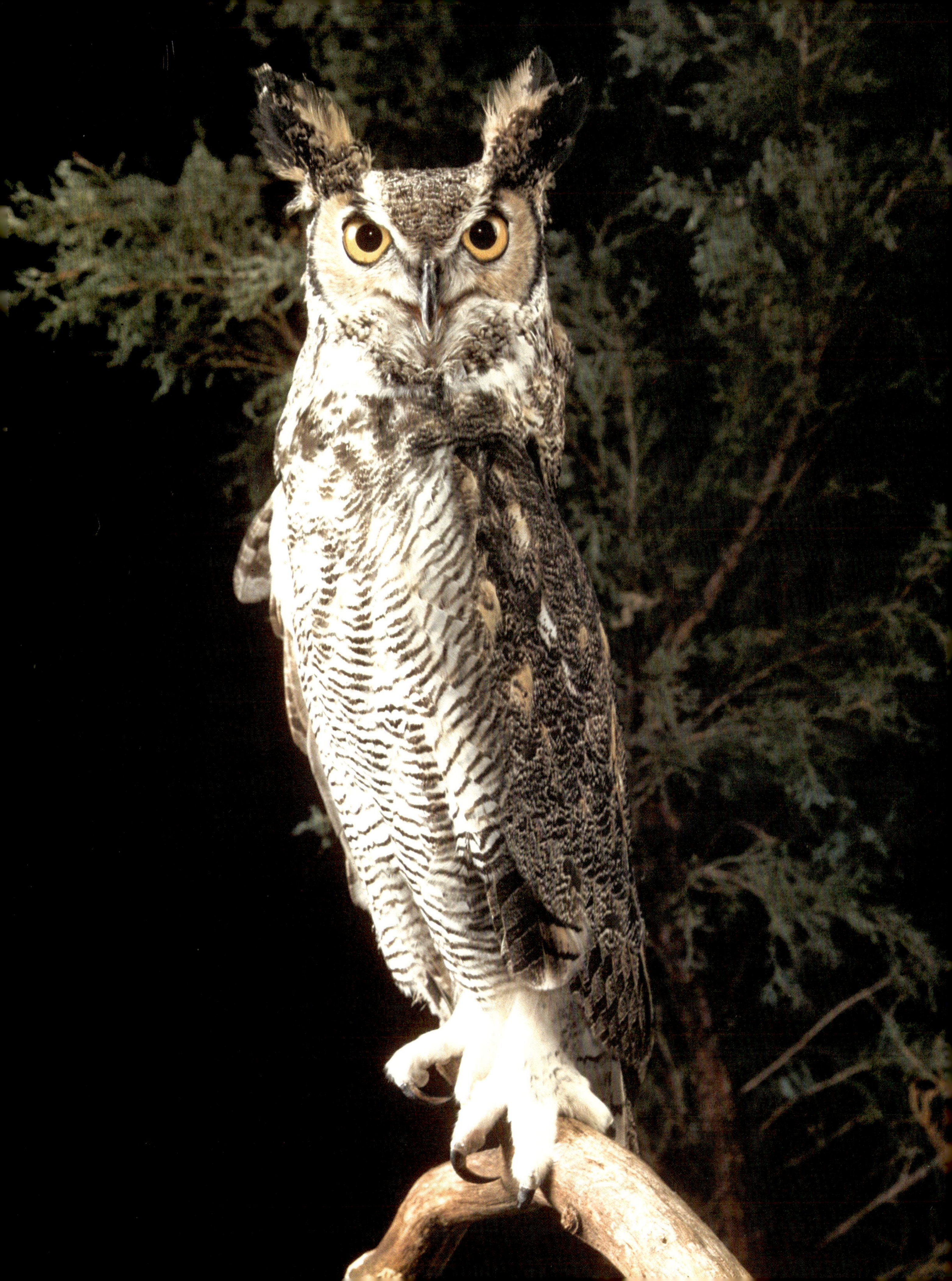

refer to the furry appearance of its legs; the Greek word *lagopus* means "hare-footed."

Rough-legged Hawks are large, about 2 feet long with wingspans of 4½ feet. Plumage color varies greatly in this species from light to very dark (melanistic) individuals. All have a conspicuous white rump patch and a wide, dark band at the tip of the tail.

Birds of open country and graceful soarers, Rough-legs can be distinguished from other buteos in flight by their longer wings and tails. They have a habit of hovering in one spot, as Kestrels and Ospreys do.

Rough-legged Hawks are rodent eaters and feed on small animals, primarily meadow voles.

Eagles

The Golden and Bald eagles are the largest birds of prey in North America except for the California Condor.

Bald Eagle

Haliaeetus leucocephalus

Our national emblem, the Bald Eagle is familiar to nearly everyone. The adult bird, with its snowy white head and tail and contrasting dark brown body, is unmistakable. The term "Bald" as used here means white, rather than featherless; and its scientific name *leucocephalus* means "white head." The immature Bald Eagle, however, lacks the distinctive white markings of the adult. The young bird is an overall brown color for several years before its head and tail become pure white; for this reason it can be mistaken for a Golden Eagle.

A large bird, measuring approximately three feet high with a wingspan of up to 7½ feet, this eagle is an efficient hunter and also a scavenger. It feeds primarily on fish and waterfowl which it catches alive, but will readily eat carrion when available.

Although a well-known symbol, the Bald Eagle is rarely seen. Its population across North America has drastically declined in the past forty years, due primarily to loss of habitat and DDT poisoning.

Golden Eagle

Aquila chrysaetos

The Golden eagle is a huge bird weighing up to thirteen pounds, measuring approximately three feet in length, with a wingspan of 6½ to 7½ feet. The entire bird appears dark brown in color, but at closer view a gold wash of feathers on the back of its neck and head can be seen —hence the common name. Young birds can be distinguished from adults by their white-based tail feathers and white patches in their wings.

Golden Eagles range across the entire Northern Hemisphere and in North America they are most common in the west. Their large stick nests are usually constructed on high, inaccessible cliff ledges in remote mountainous areas. The same nest site, or eyrie, may be used year after year.

These large and powerful birds hunt while flying, dropping suddenly on prey which they have surprised in the open. Their diet is varied, but consists mainly of rabbits and other small mammals.

Although primarily a western species, some Golden Eagles do breed in eastern Canada, northern New England, and a few in New York state.

Accipiters

Accipiters are hawks that inhabit deeply wooded areas. They have short rounded wings and long rudder-like tails which allow them to maneuver among the trees. Their recognizable flight pattern consists of several rapid flaps and then a glide. As a group, accipiters are secretive and are observed less frequently than most other hawks.

Sharp-Shinned Hawk

Accipiter striatus

Sharp-shinned Hawks are the smallest of the three North American accipiters. They measure 10 to 14 inches long and have wingspans of about 2 feet, yet weigh only 3½ to 7 ounces.

Young Sharp-shins are brown backed and have brown streaks on their white breasts. As they mature, the colors change: their backs become slate-gray, and their breasts become barred with reddish-brown. Even their eye color changes with age — from yellow to deep red.

The Sharp-shinned Hawk gets its common name from the "shins" of its legs which are not round, but oval and rather sharp. The small head is round, and the long, square-tipped tail has narrow black and gray bands.

They are swift, agile hawks well adapted to flying in heavily forested areas. Their prey, predominantly small birds, is captured in dashing, headlong pursuits.

Cooper's Hawk

Accipiter cooperii

The Cooper's Hawk is a larger version of the Sharp-shinned Hawk, and the two are very much alike in color and markings. The Cooper's is crow-sized, 15 to 20 inches long, and has a wingspan of 27 to 36 inches.

The Cooper's Hawk is chiefly a bird-eating hawk, and almost any bird up to the size of a pheasant qualifies as prey. In addition to birds, it also captures mammals, including squirrels and rabbits, and occasionally takes lizards and amphibians.

During this century the Cooper's Hawk has decreased in numbers over much of its range. The reasons for its decline are not positively known, but habitat loss, nesting failures from the effects of pesticides, and direct persecution by man could be contributing factors.

Northern Goshawk

Accipiter gentilis

The Goshawk is a powerful raptor and the largest of the North American accipiters. It is 20 to 26 inches long with a wingspan of 3½ to 4 feet. The immature is brown above with brown streaking on its white underside, and closely resembles an immature Cooper's Hawk. The adult Goshawk is bluish-gray above, and its underside is white with a fine black herringbone pattern. All have a white streak above the eye.

Their prey consist largely of birds, from songbirds to ducks and grouse. They also capture numbers of mammals, ranging from mice and chipmunks to rabbits and woodchucks. Hunting from perches or on the wing, Goshawks are aggressive and persistent in pursuit of food and have been known to chase prey on foot.

The Goshawk is a northern bird. They are secretive by nature and prefer to live in dense wooded areas; hence, Goshawks are seldom observed.

Harriers

Harriers are slender hawks with distinctive owl-like faces. This facial shape aids their sense of hearing and allows them to locate rodent prey by sound. Harriers are found throughout the world, but the only representative of this group in North America is the Northern Harrier.

Northern Harrier

Circus cyaneus

Northern Harriers, also known as Marsh Hawks, are long-winged, long-tailed birds of open terrain. They can be seen coursing low over fields, pastures, and marshes in search of prey. Their buoyant, veering flight is very distinctive.

Harriers are slender birds, 18 to 23 inches in length, with wingspans of about 4 feet. Although large, they are light in weight, weighing approximately one pound. Adult male Harriers are silvery-blue with black wingtips; adult females are dark brown above and have streaks on their white underparts. The young (both male and female) resemble the adult females. All Harriers have a white rump patch.

Their diet consists chiefly of small mammals, especially meadow voles, but also include frogs, insects, and small birds.

Unlike most hawks, Harriers nest on the ground. Their nests are built of dry grasses and small sticks and are hidden among the weeds and vegetation of fields and marshes. Most Harriers are migrants. They are present in large numbers along the coastline during migration.

Vultures

Vultures are large dark-plumaged birds with small bare heads. Although classified as birds of prey, they seldom kill their own food and are primarily scavengers, feeding on dead animals. Their featherless heads and necks allow them to feed neatly on dead carcasses. Vultures serve an important function as part of nature's clean-up crew.

Turkey Vulture

Cathartes aura

Turkey Vultures, sometimes mistakenly called buzzards, are large, dark birds common throughout most of North America. They are the master soarers of the raptor world, effortlessly gliding on air currents and thermals for long periods of time. Their distinctive flight — veering and tilting with the wings held in a shallow "V" —makes them easy to identify.

Turkey Vultures are approximately two feet tall and have wingspans of up to six feet. The undersides of their wings are two-toned, blackish in front and silver-gray on the rear half. They have small featherless heads which are black when the birds are young and red when they are adults.

These birds eat carrion and will feed on any dead animal, large or small.

Vultures are social raptors — roosting, feeding and often soaring together. They are probably the most commonly seen bird of prey in the state.

Black Vulture

Coragyps atratus

Primarily a southern bird, the Black Vulture is expanding its range northward and is becoming more common in the northeast.

Short-Eared Owl

Asio flammeus

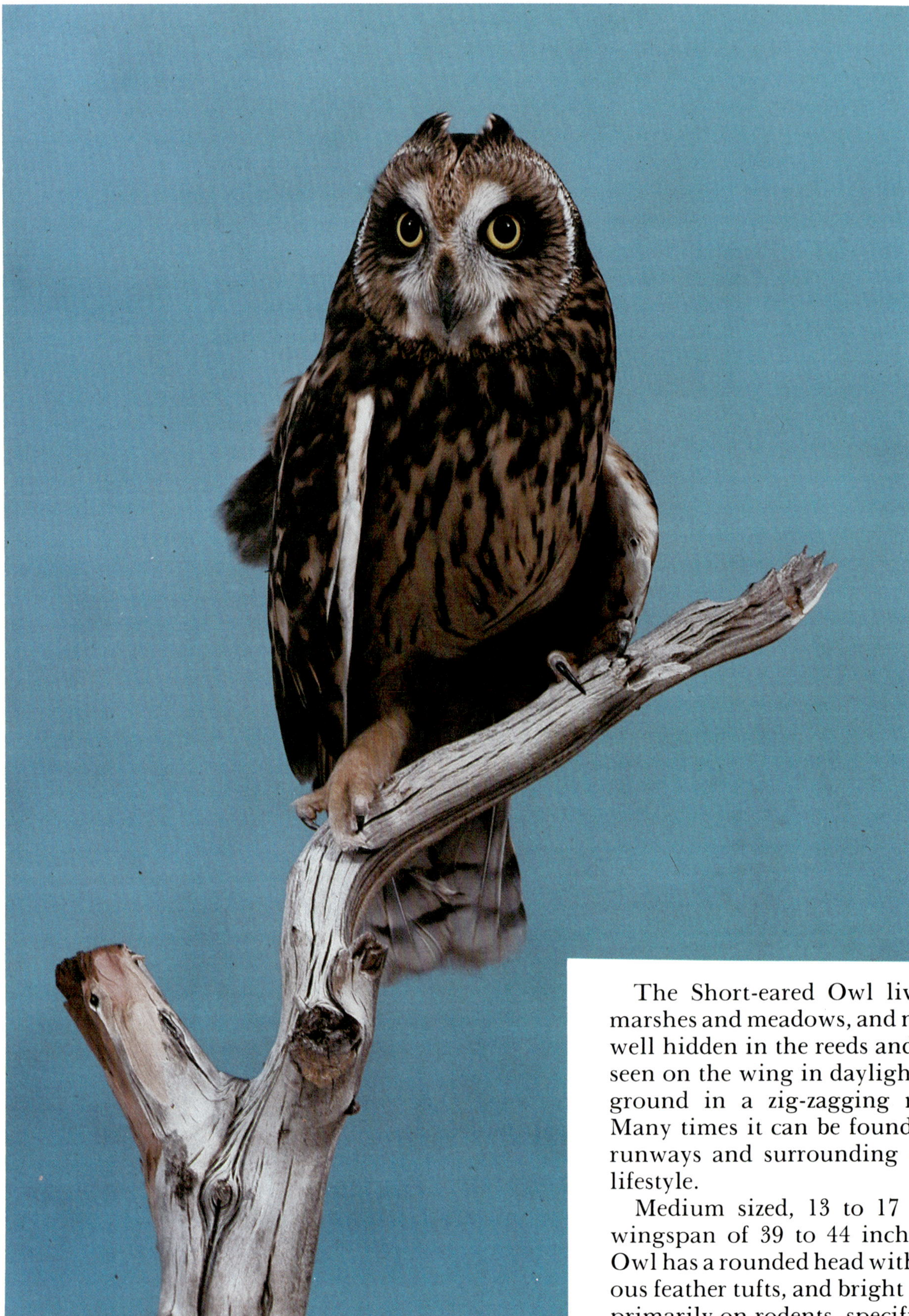

The Short-eared Owl lives in open fields, marshes and meadows, and nests on the ground, well hidden in the reeds and grasses. It is often seen on the wing in daylight, flying low to the ground in a zig-zagging moth-like manner. Many times it can be found at airports, where runways and surrounding open areas suit its lifestyle.

Medium sized, 13 to 17 inches tall with a wingspan of 39 to 44 inches, the Short-eared Owl has a rounded head with small inconspicuous feather tufts, and bright yellow eyes. It feeds primarily on rodents, specifically field mice.

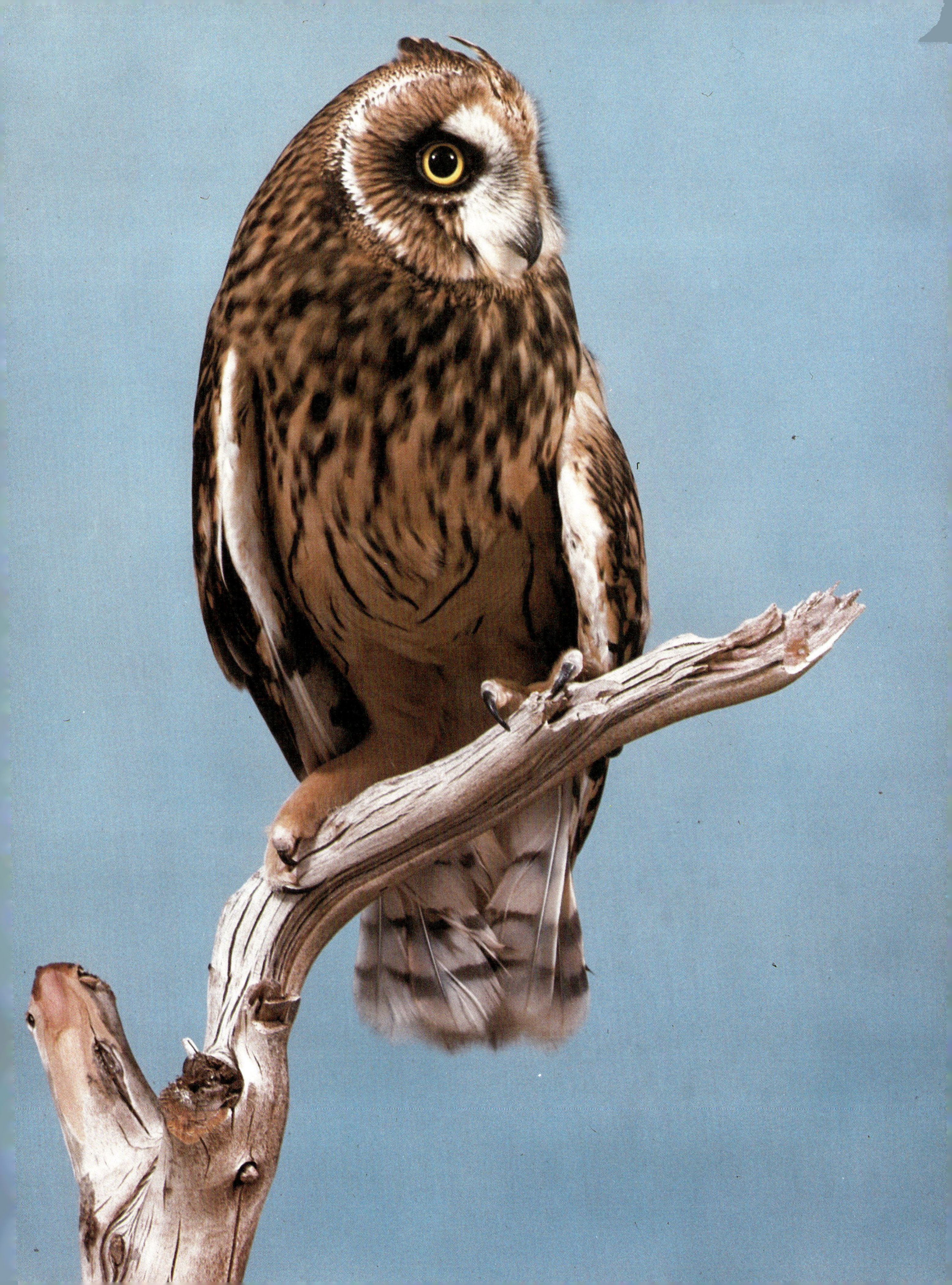

With a wingspan of about five feet, the Black Vulture is slightly smaller than the Turkey Vulture. The bird is dull black in color, including its bare head. Each wingtip has a large, whitish patch visible only when the wing is open. In flight Black Vultures can be identified by these wingpatches and by their short, square tails. They tend to flap more than Turkey Vultures and when soaring, hold their wings straight out, not upward in a "V".

Like most vultures, this species is gregarious by nature and often roosts in large flocks. They are primarily scavengers, but do occasionally capture living prey. An unusual trait of this raptor is that its diet also includes vegetable matter.

More Facts

BARN OWL
Eye color—Brown
Eye size—14mm
Height—14 to 20"
Wing span—40 to 45"

GREAT HORNED OWL
Eye color—Yellow
Eye size—20mm
Height—18½ to 25"
Wing span—48 to 60"

SCREECH OWL
Eye color—Straw
Eye size—14mm
Height—7 to 10"
Wing span—18 to 24"

BARRED OWL
Eye color—Dark Brown
Eye size—18mm
Height—16 to 23"
Wing span—38 to 45"

LONG-EARRED OWL
Eye color—Yellow
Eye size—14mm
Height—13 to 16"
Wing span—36 to 42"

SHORT-EARRED OWL
Eye color—Yellow
Eye size—14mm
Height—13½ to 17"
Wing span—39 to 44"

SAW-WHET OWL
Eye color—Straw
Eye size—12mm
Height—7 to 8½"
Wing span—18 to 21"

SNOWY OWL
Eye color—Straw
Eye size—18mm
Height—21 to 28"
Wing span—50 to 65"

OSPREY
Eye color—Yellow
Eye size—14mm
Height—21 to 24"
Wing span—4½ to 6'

AMERICAN KESTREL
Eye color—Brown
Eye size—8mm
Height—9 to 12"
Wing span—Up to 2'

PEREGRINE FALCON
Eye color—Brown
Eye size—10mm
Height—15 to 20"
Wing span—3½'

BROAD-WINGED HAWK
Eye color—Brown
Eye size—10mm
Height—14 to 19"
Wing span—3'

RED-SHOULDERED HAWK
Eye color—Hazel
Eye size—14mm
Height—18 to 24"
Wing span—3½ to 4'

RED-TAILED HAWK
Eye color—Brown
Eye size—14mm
Height—2'
Wing span—4½ to 5'

ROUGH-LEGGED HAWK
Eye color—Hazel
Eye size—14mm
Height—2'
Wing span—4½'

BALD EAGLE
Eye color—Brown
Eye size—18mm
Height—3'
Wing span—6½ to 7½'

SHARP-SHINNED HAWK
Eye color—Yellow
Eye size—10mm
Height—10 to 14"
Wing span—2'

COOPER HAWK
Eye color—Straw
Eye size—12mm
Height—15 to 20"
Wing span—27 to 36"

NORTHERN GOSHAWK
Eye color—Hazel
Eye size—14mm
Height—20 to 26"
Wing span—3½ to 4'

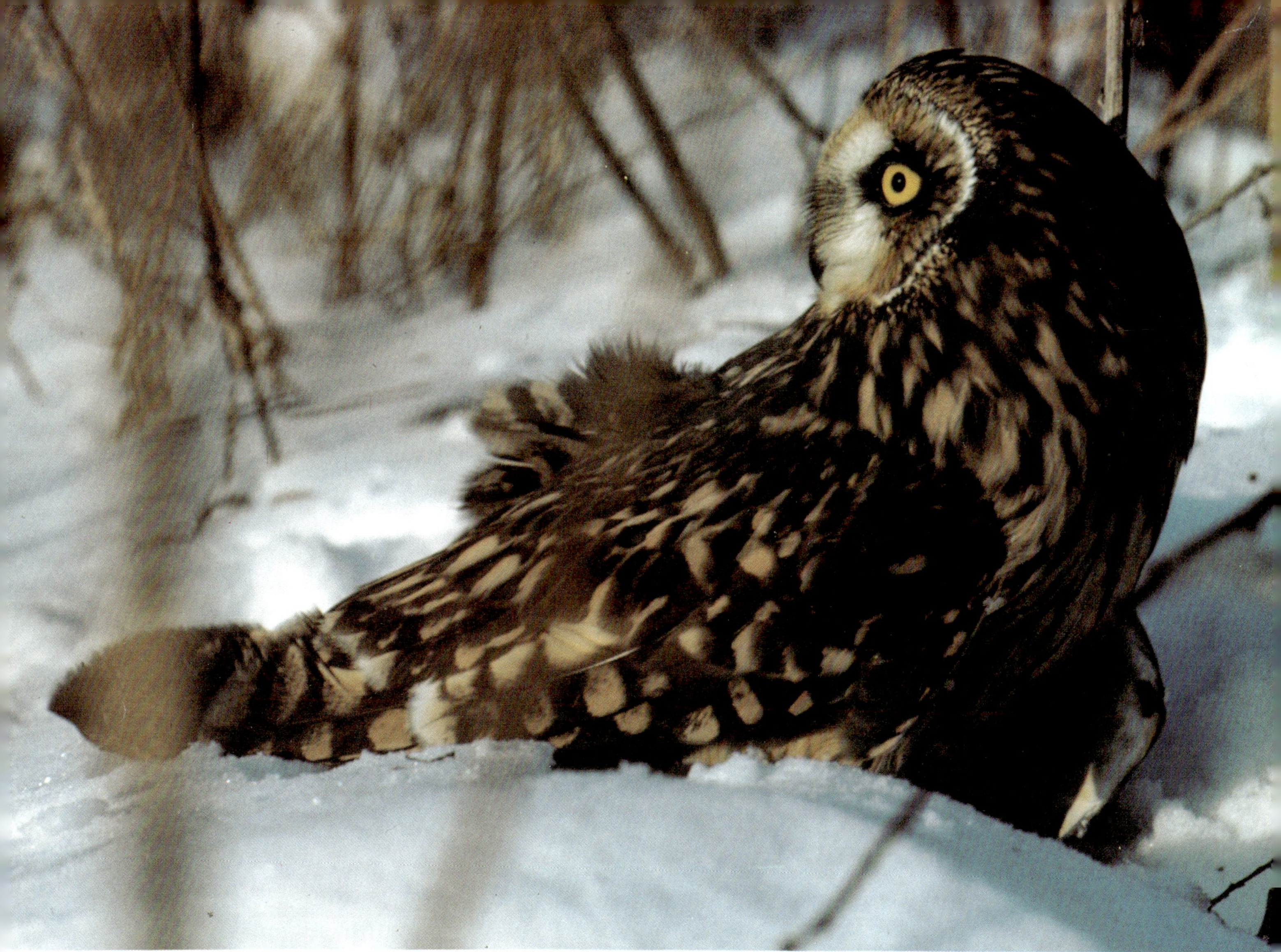

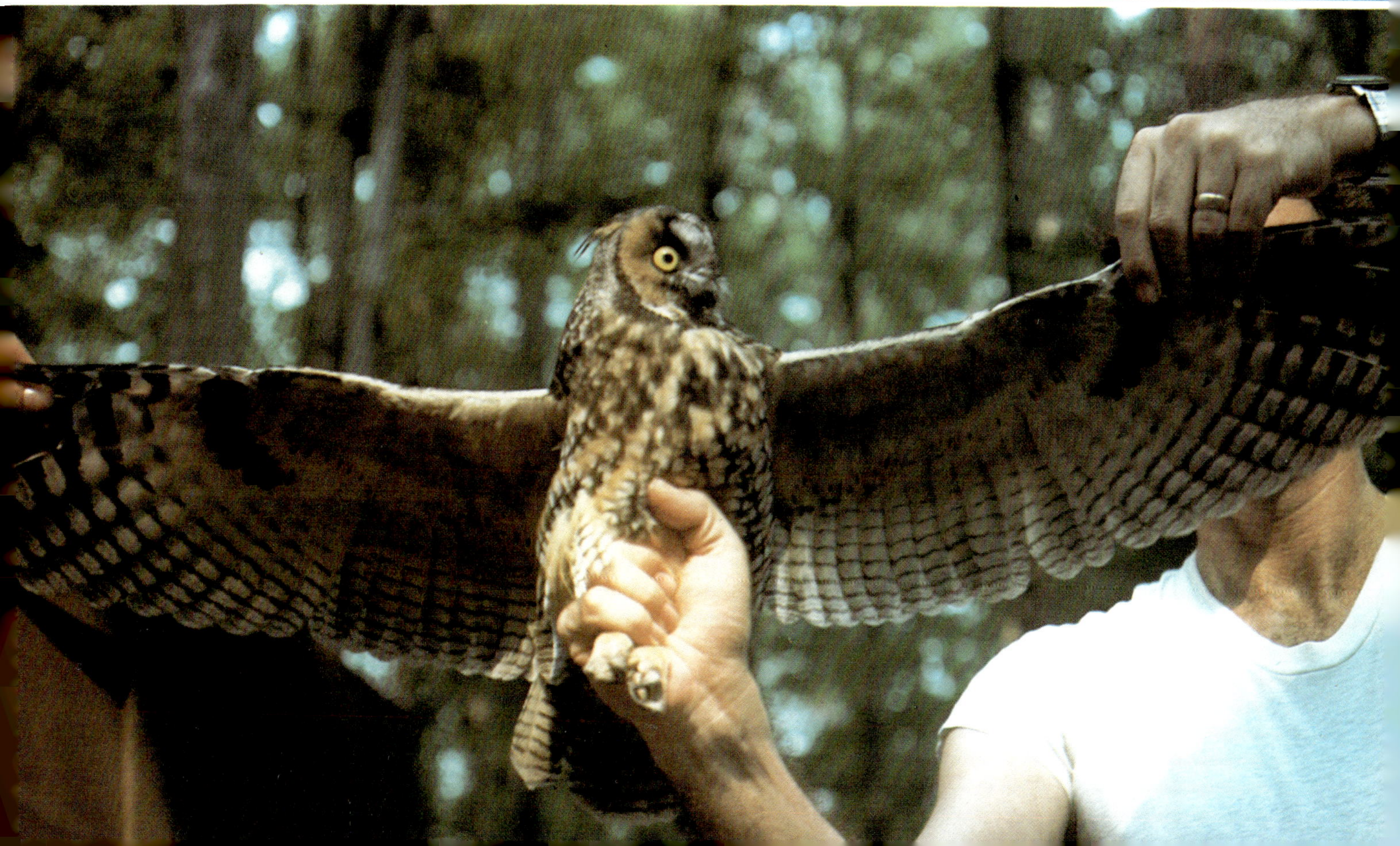

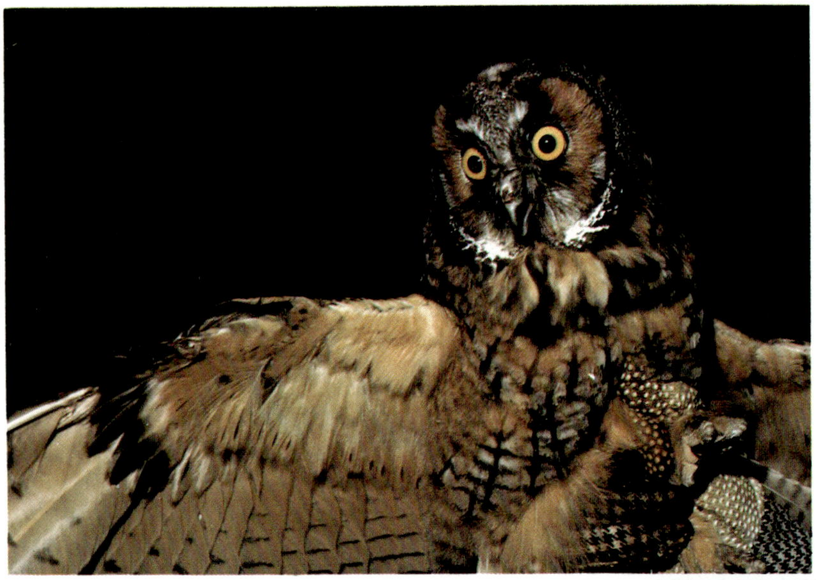

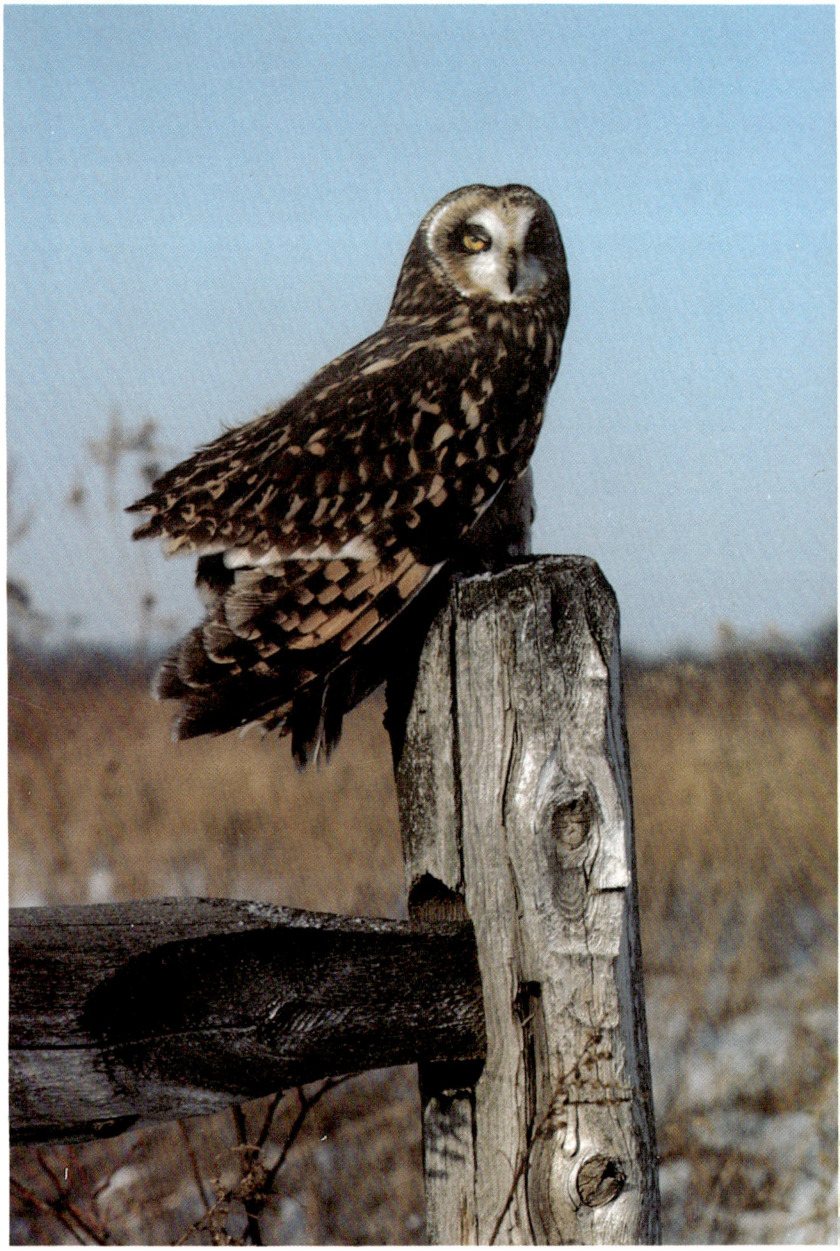

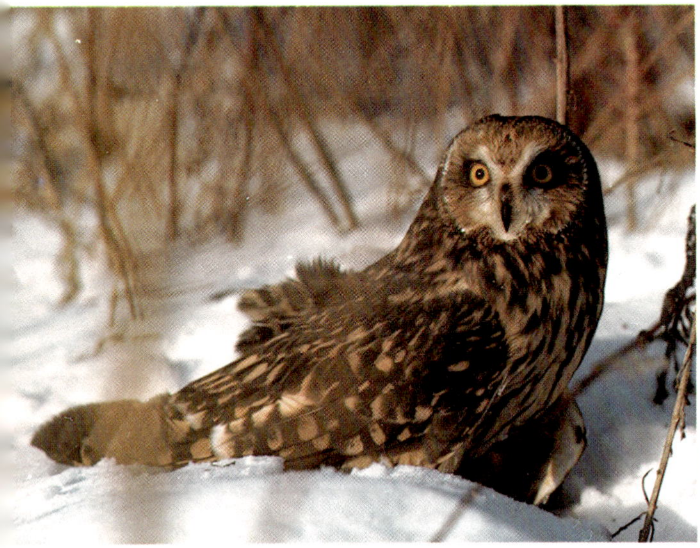

Saw-Whet Owl

Aegolius acadicus

The Saw-whet Owl is New Jersey's smallest bird of prey. Only 7 to 8 inches tall with a wingspan of 18 to 21 inches, this mini-owl weighs a mere 4 ounces. That's about the size of a "quarter-pounder." It has a wide rounded head with no feather tufts, and bright yellow eyes.

Saw-whets are seldom observed because of their small size, their nocturnal habits, and the dense, deep woods in which they live. When discovered, however, they are amazingly tame and easily approached.

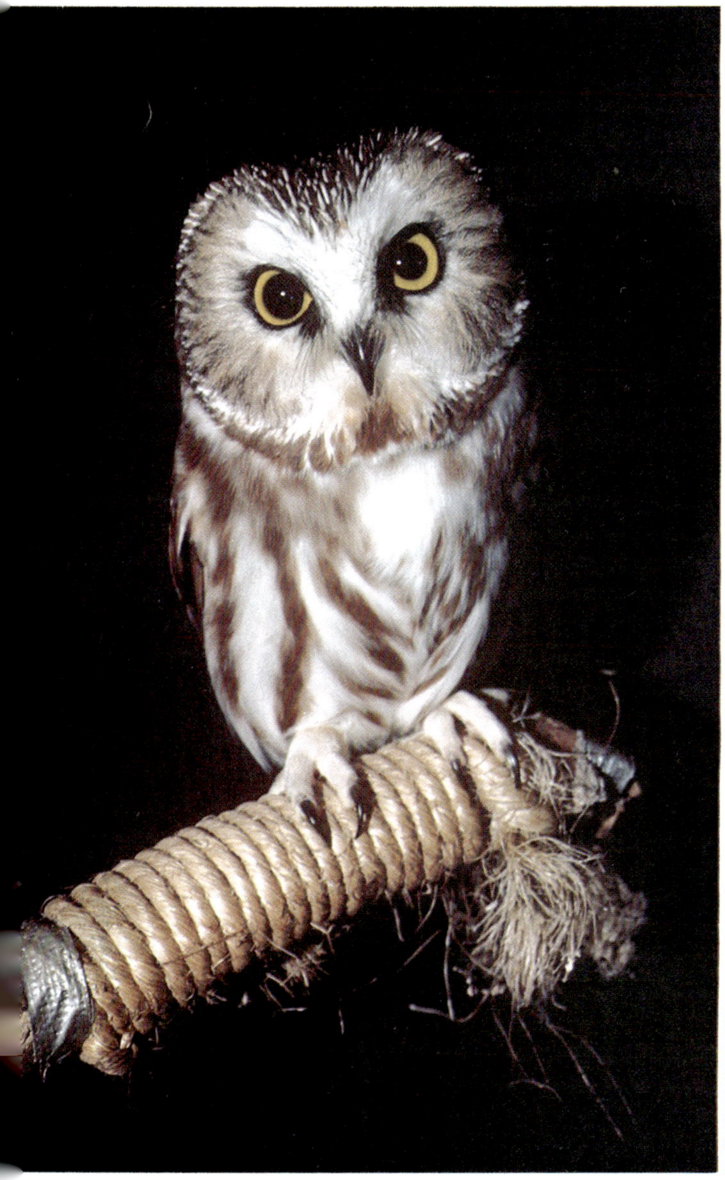

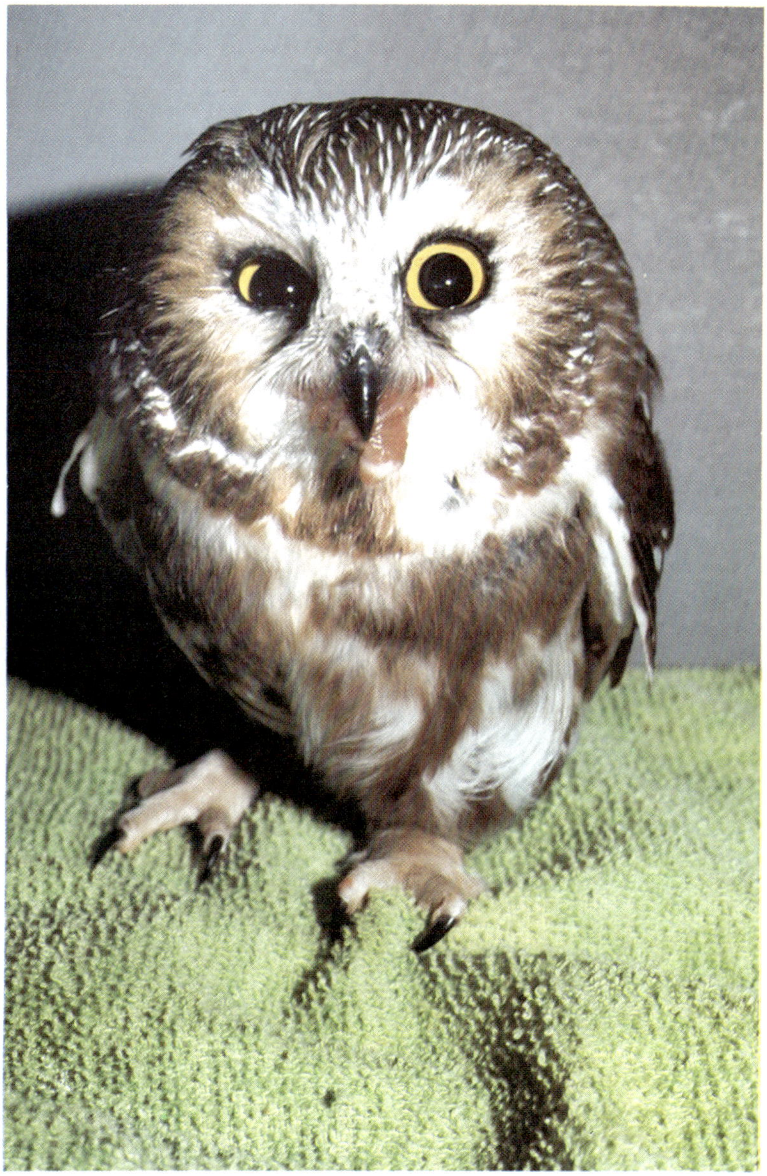

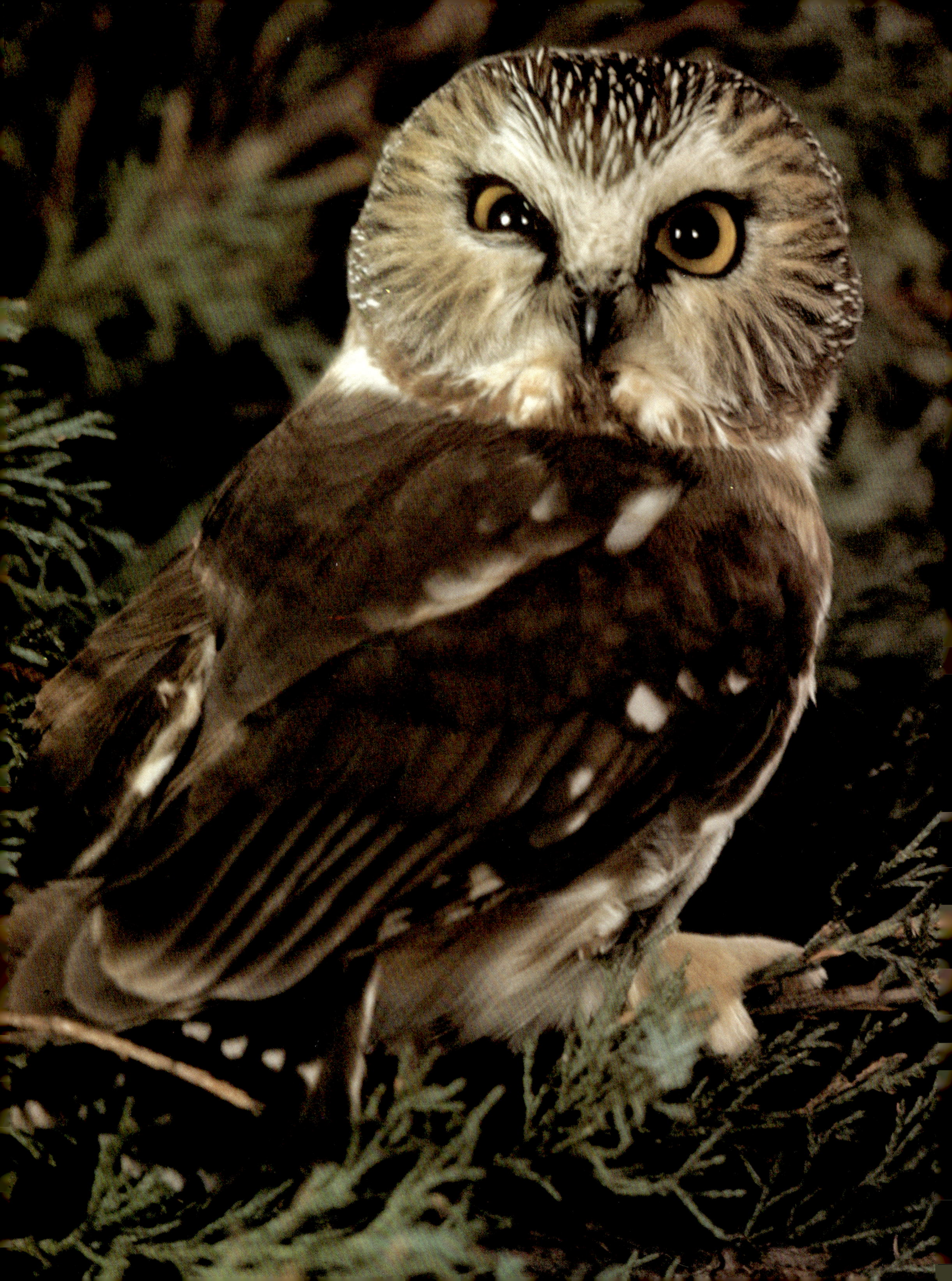

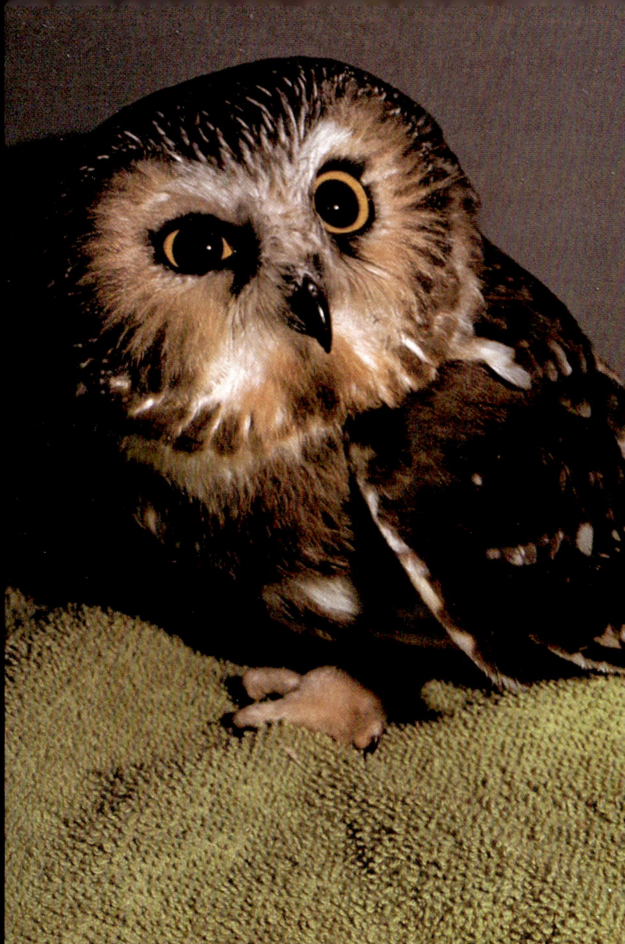
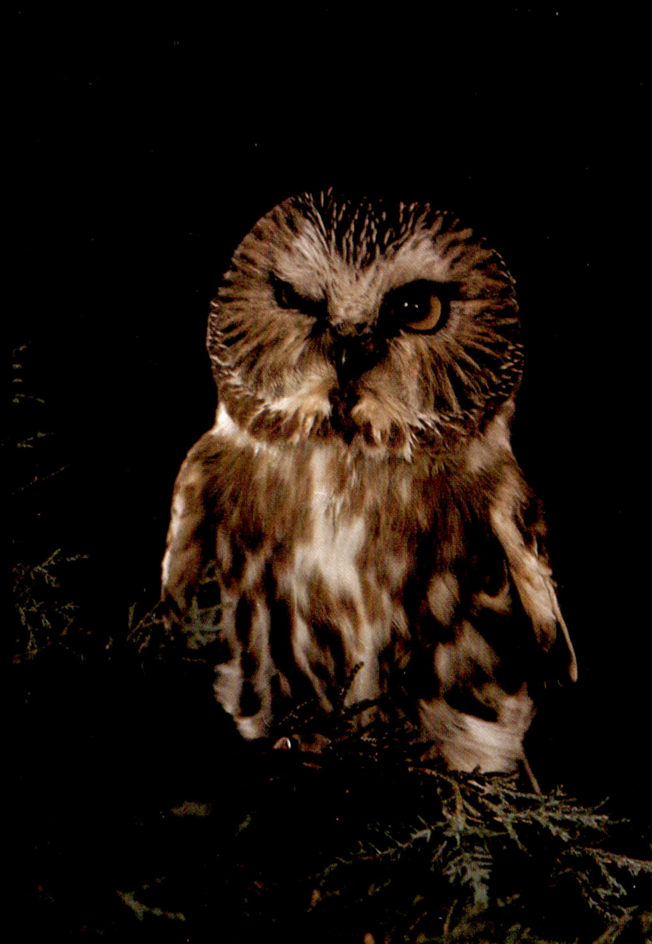
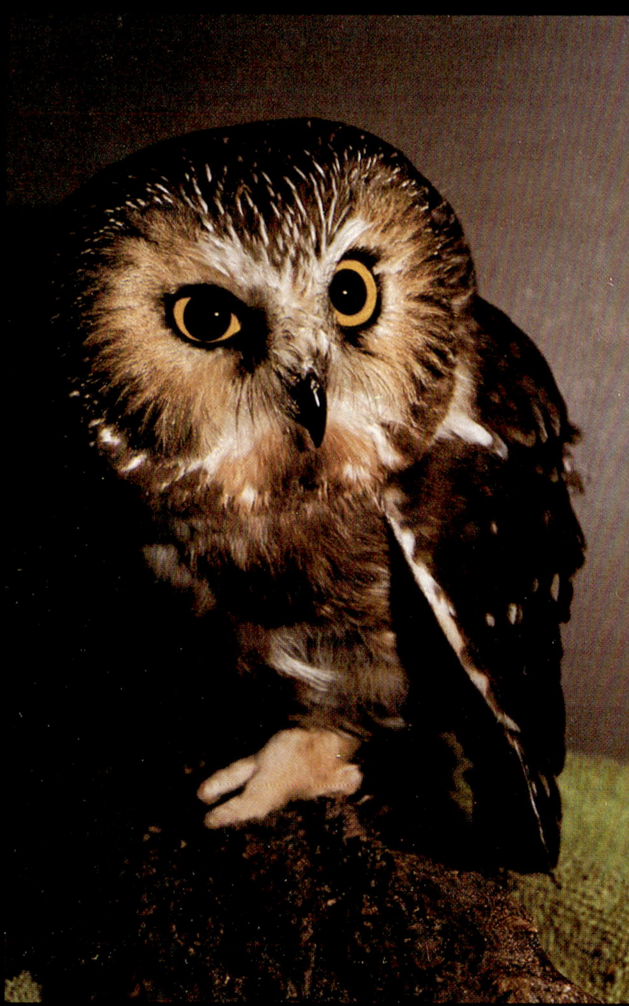
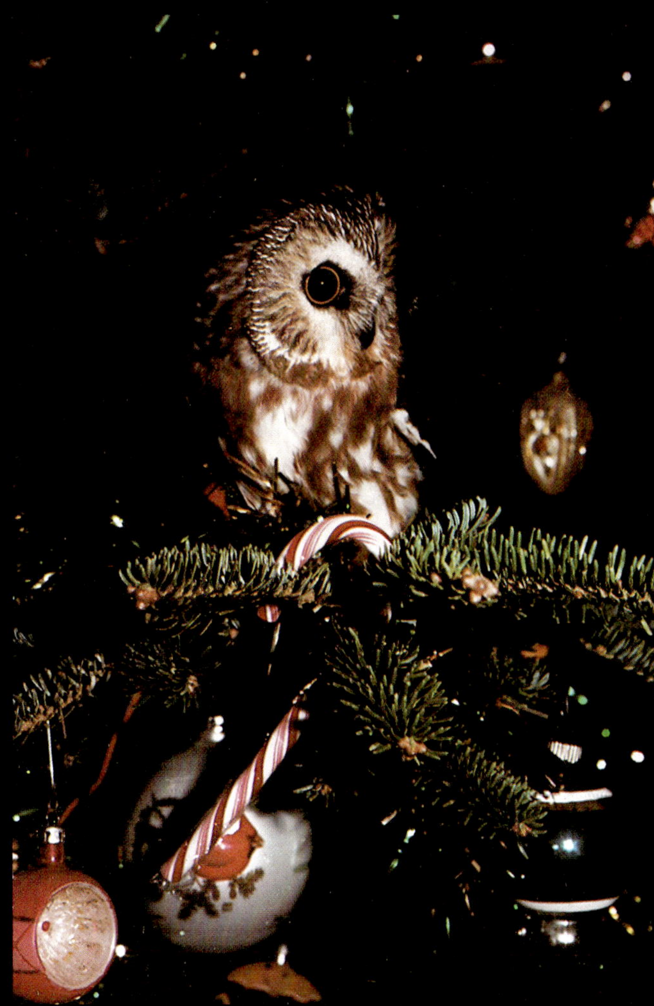

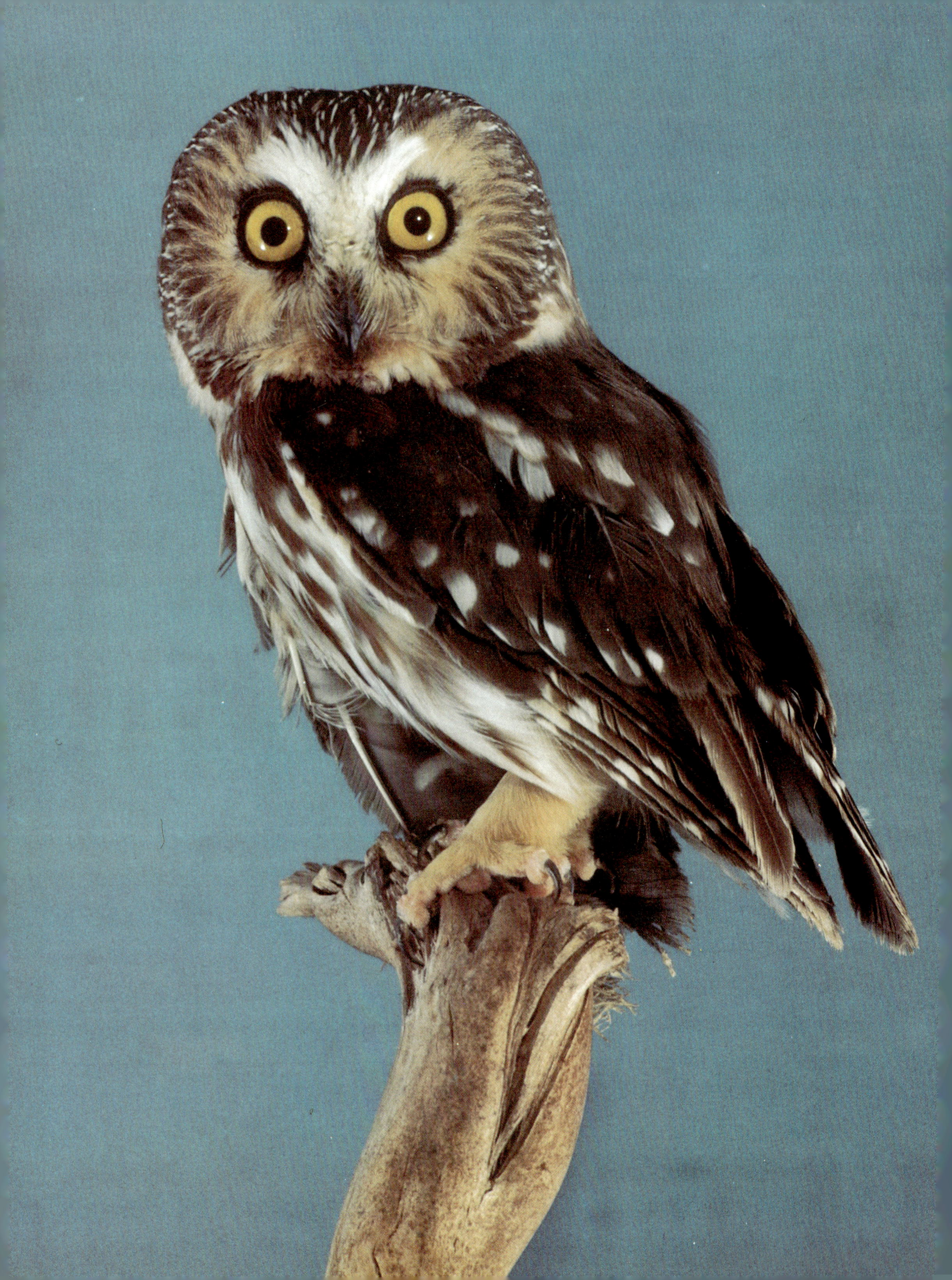

Snowy Owl

Nyctea scandiaca

The Snowy Owl is one of the most beautiful of all birds of prey. It is a large bird, 21 to 28 inches tall, and has a wingspan of 50 to 65 inches. When perched, the bird has a smooth, heavy appearance. Its head is rounded and lacks feather tufts. It has bright yellow eyes, a black beak, and thickly feathered legs and feet.

Male and female Snowys can be told apart, something which is not always possible in other species. The female is larger than the male, as in all owls, but the recognizable difference is that the adult male is almost pure white, while the female has dark, heavy flecking.

The Snowy Owl is a bird of the Canadian tundra. It prefers open country such as fields, pastures, coastal beaches and airports.

These winter visits to our state depend on the availability of food in its Arctic home, not on the severe weather there, which the bird is well equipped to endure. Periodically, in cycles of from four to eight years, the populations of the Snowy's usual northern prey species decline. Then these owls begin a southward movement in search of food, and we are afforded a chance to see one of nature's masterpieces.

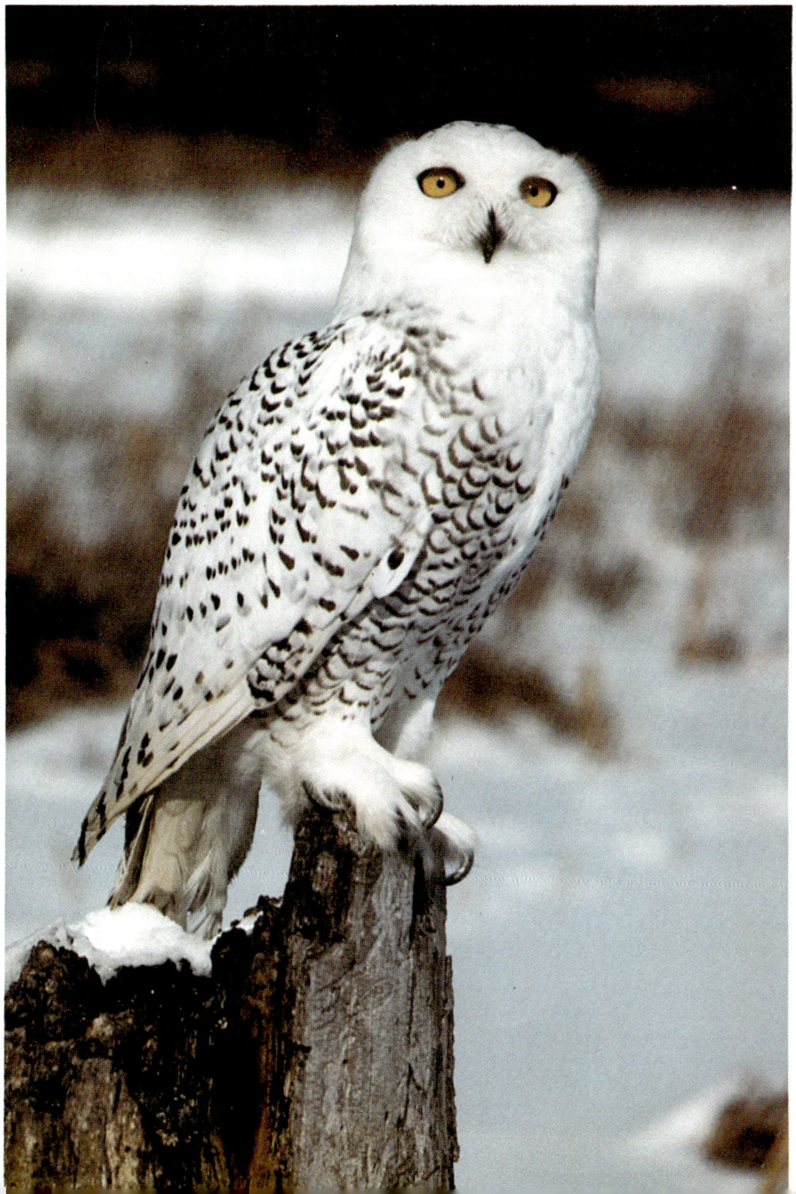

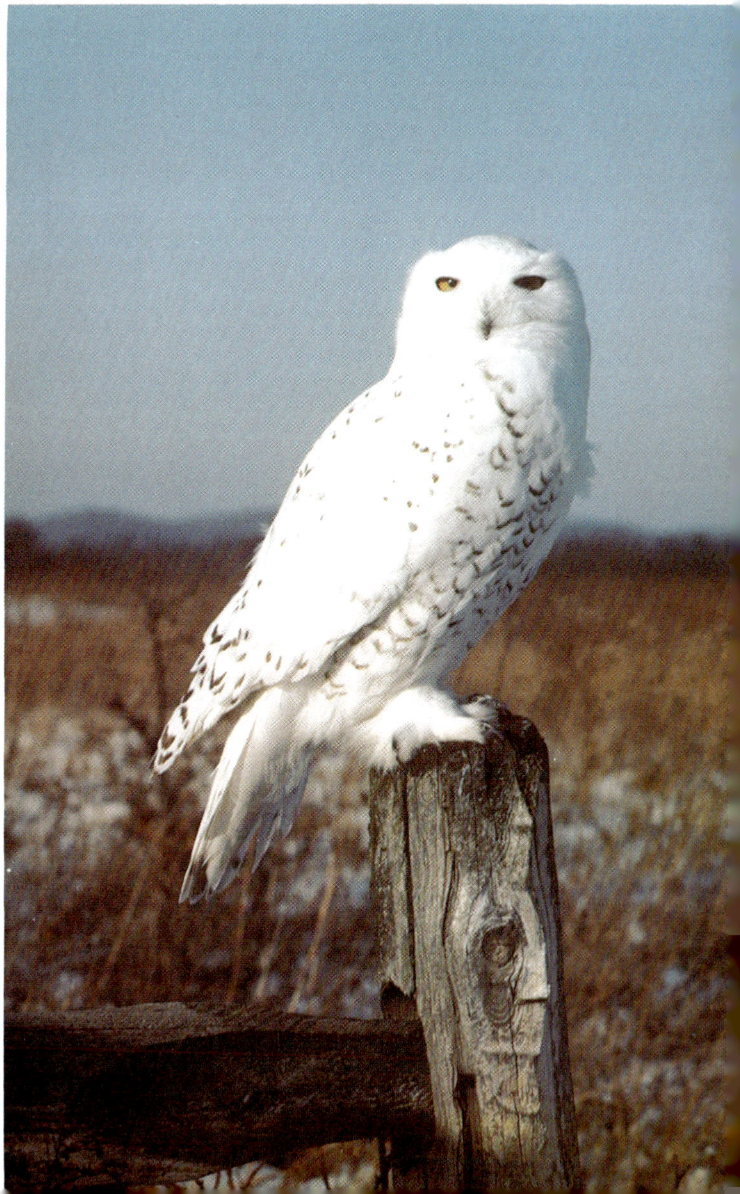

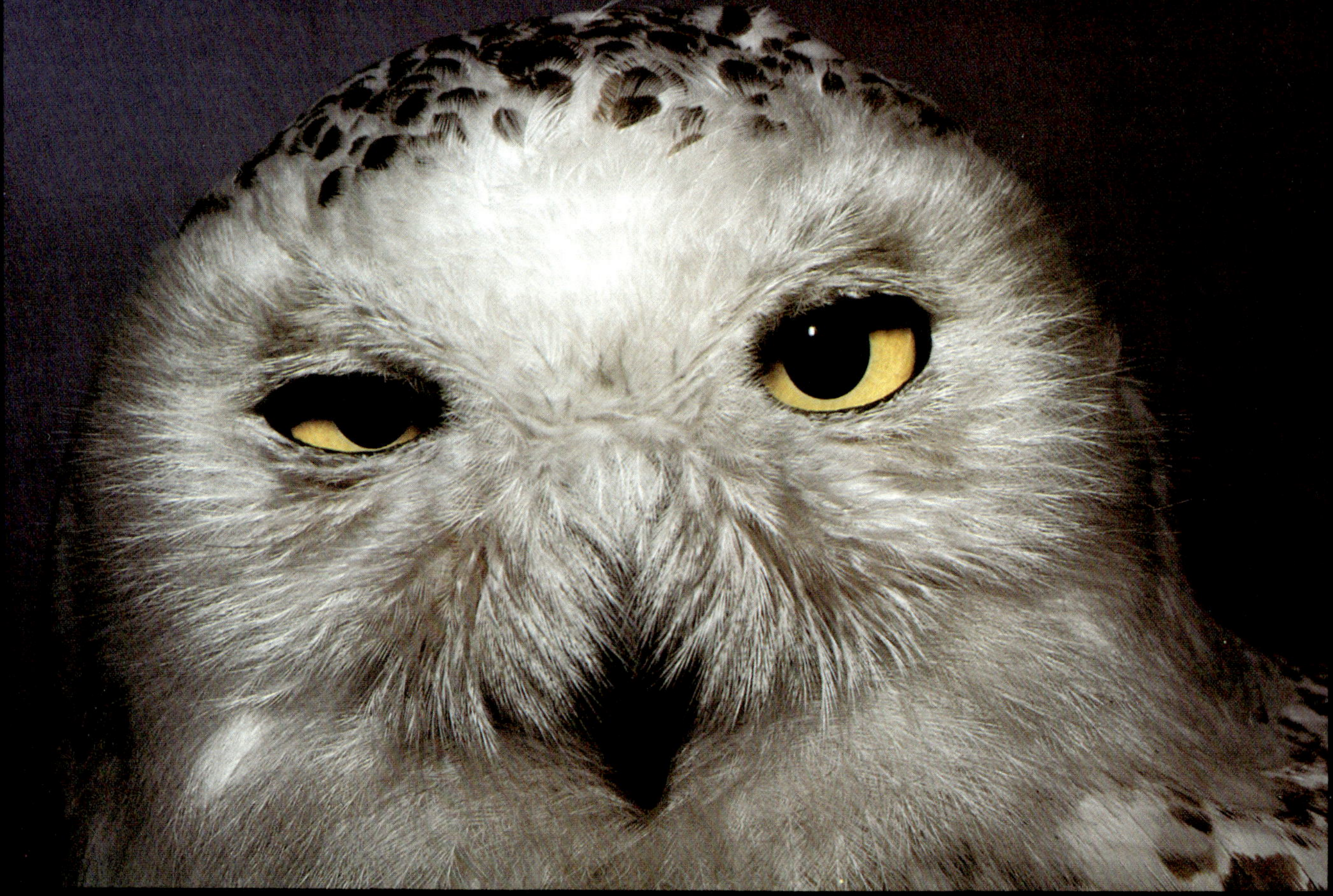

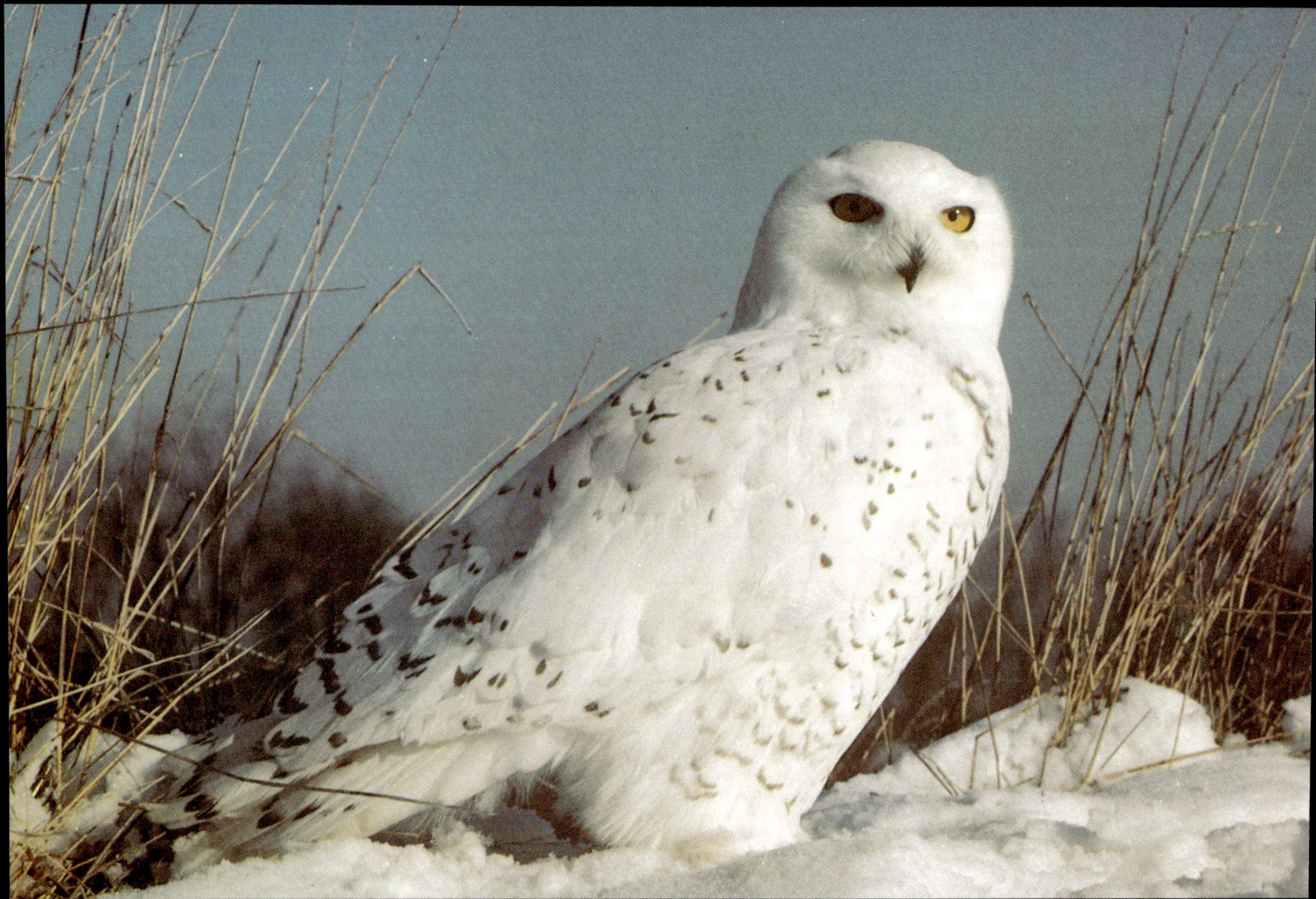

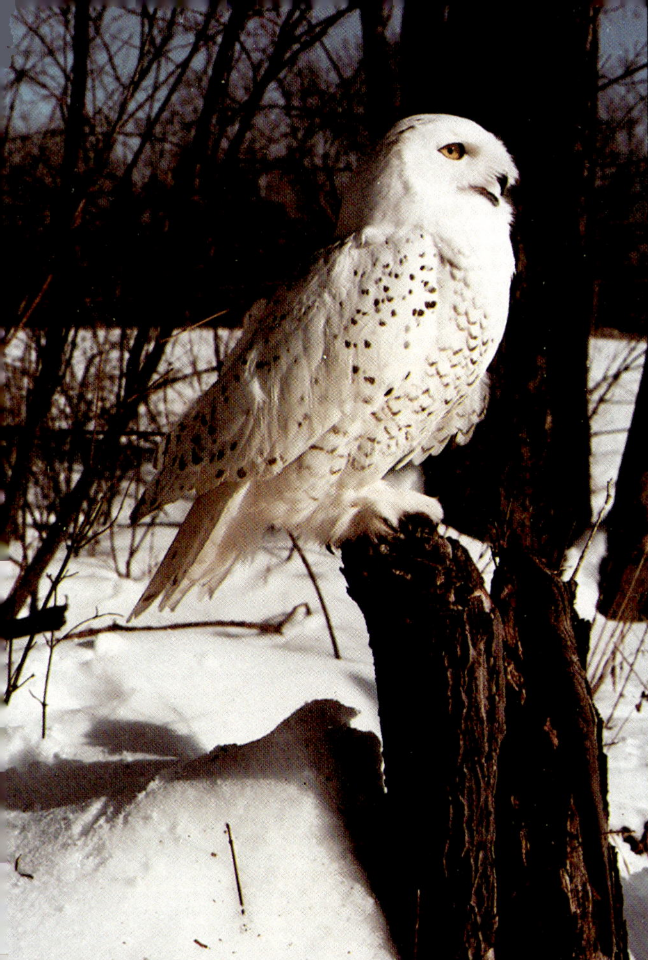
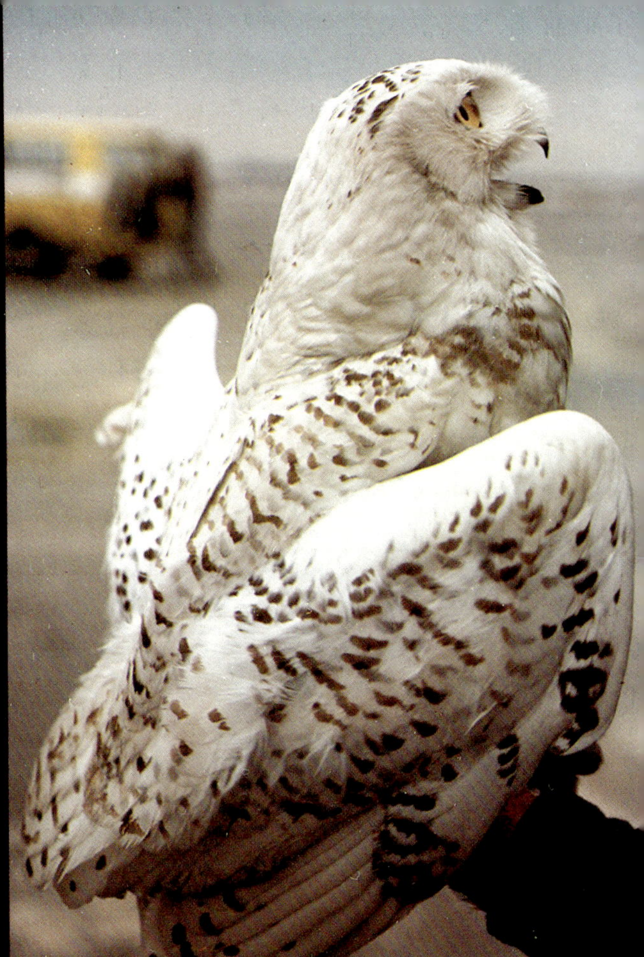
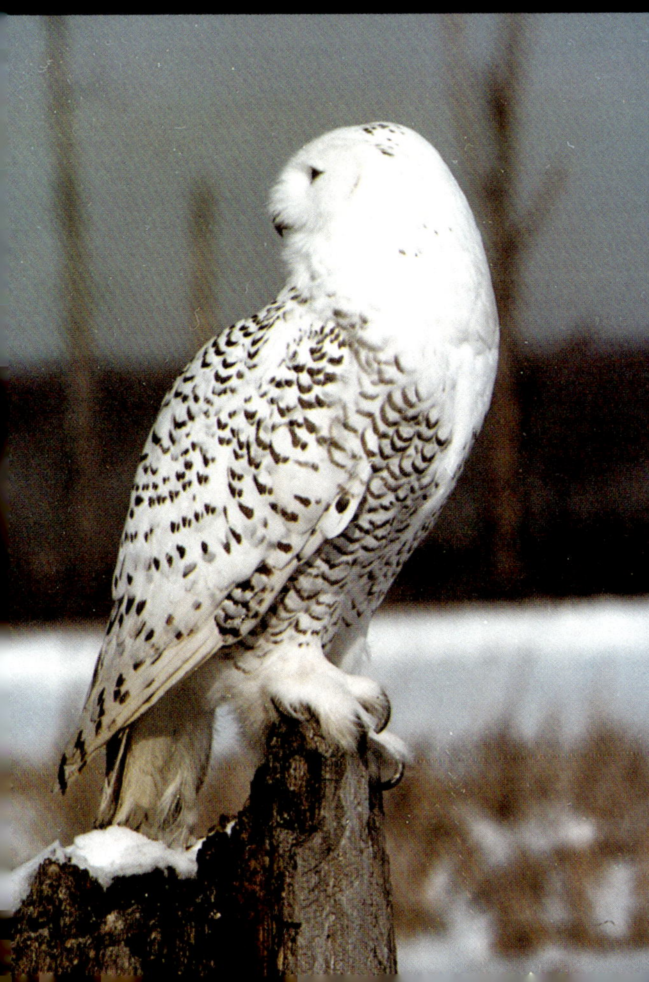
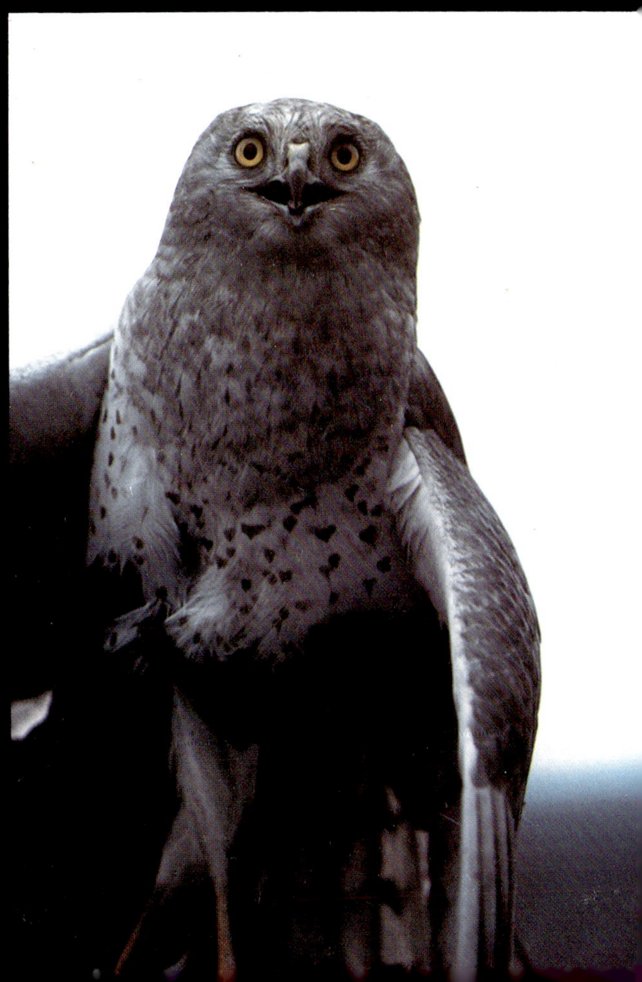

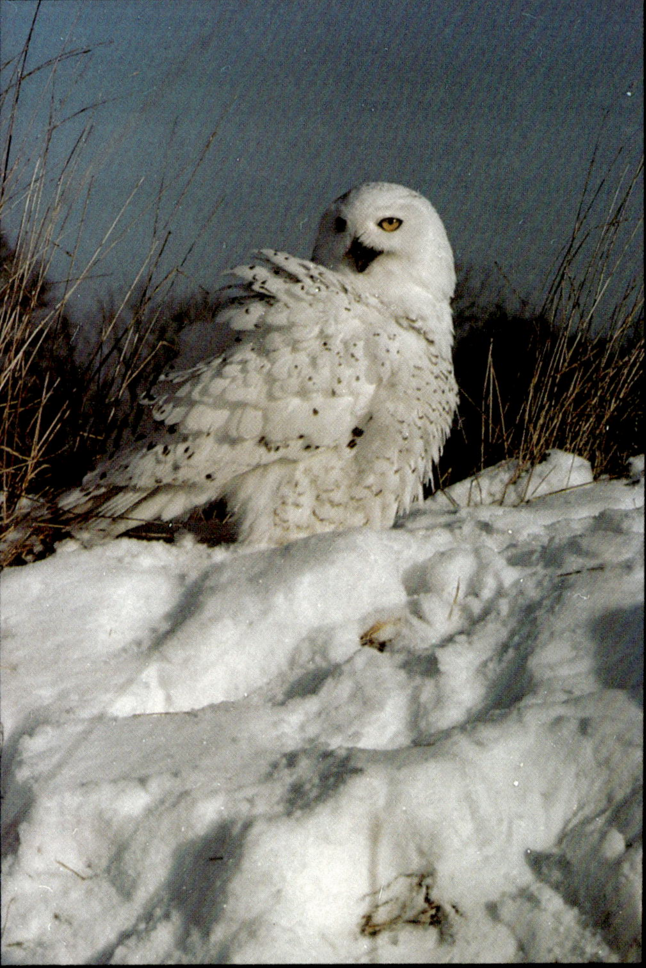

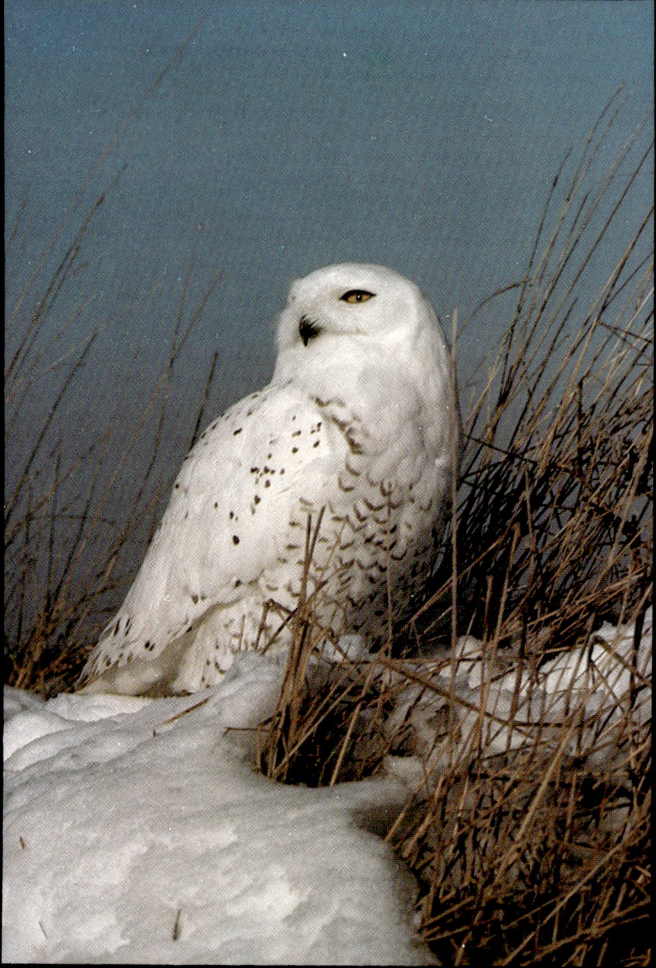

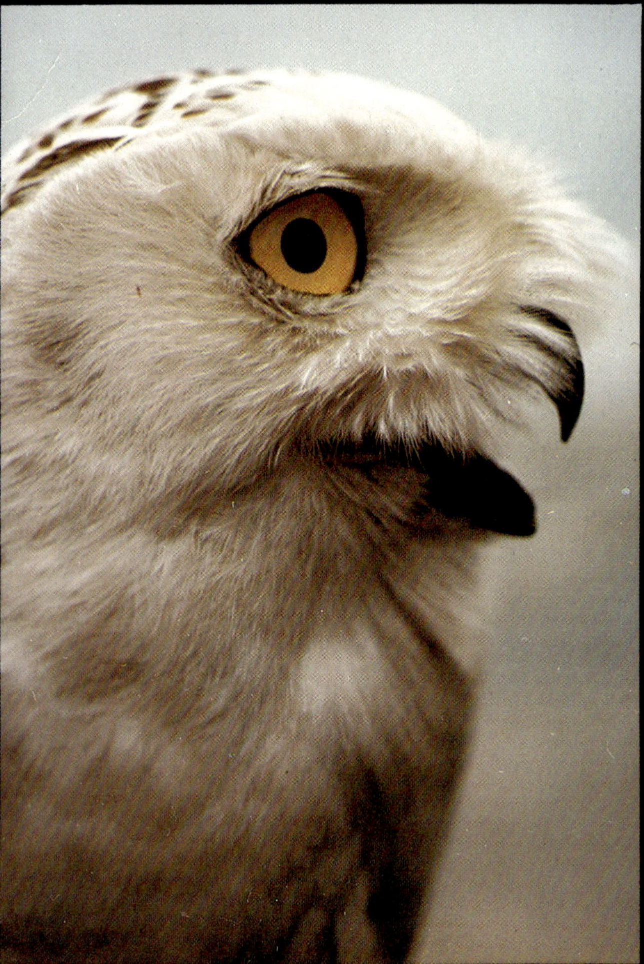

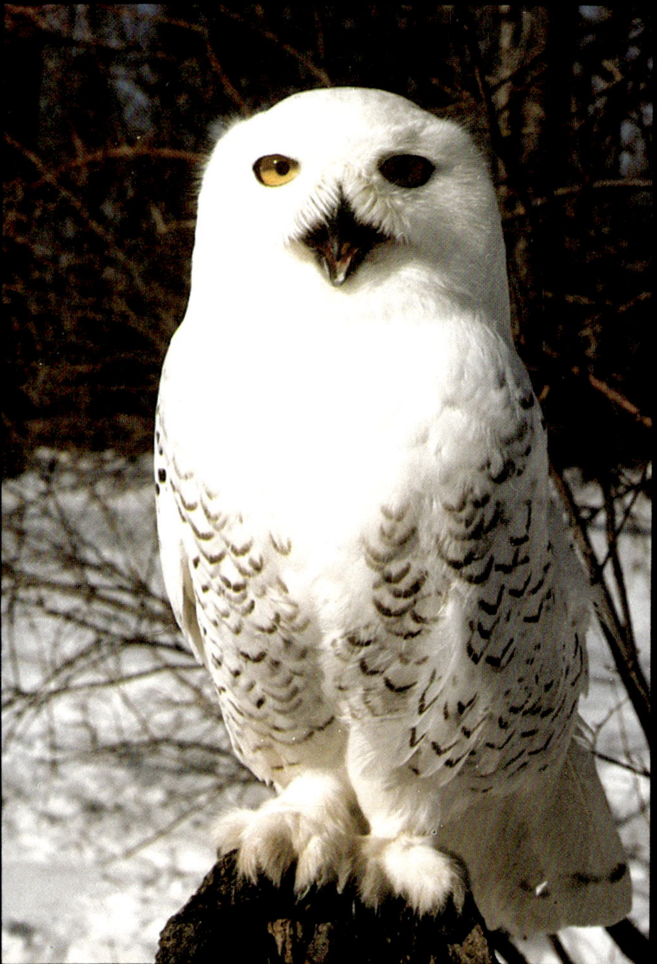

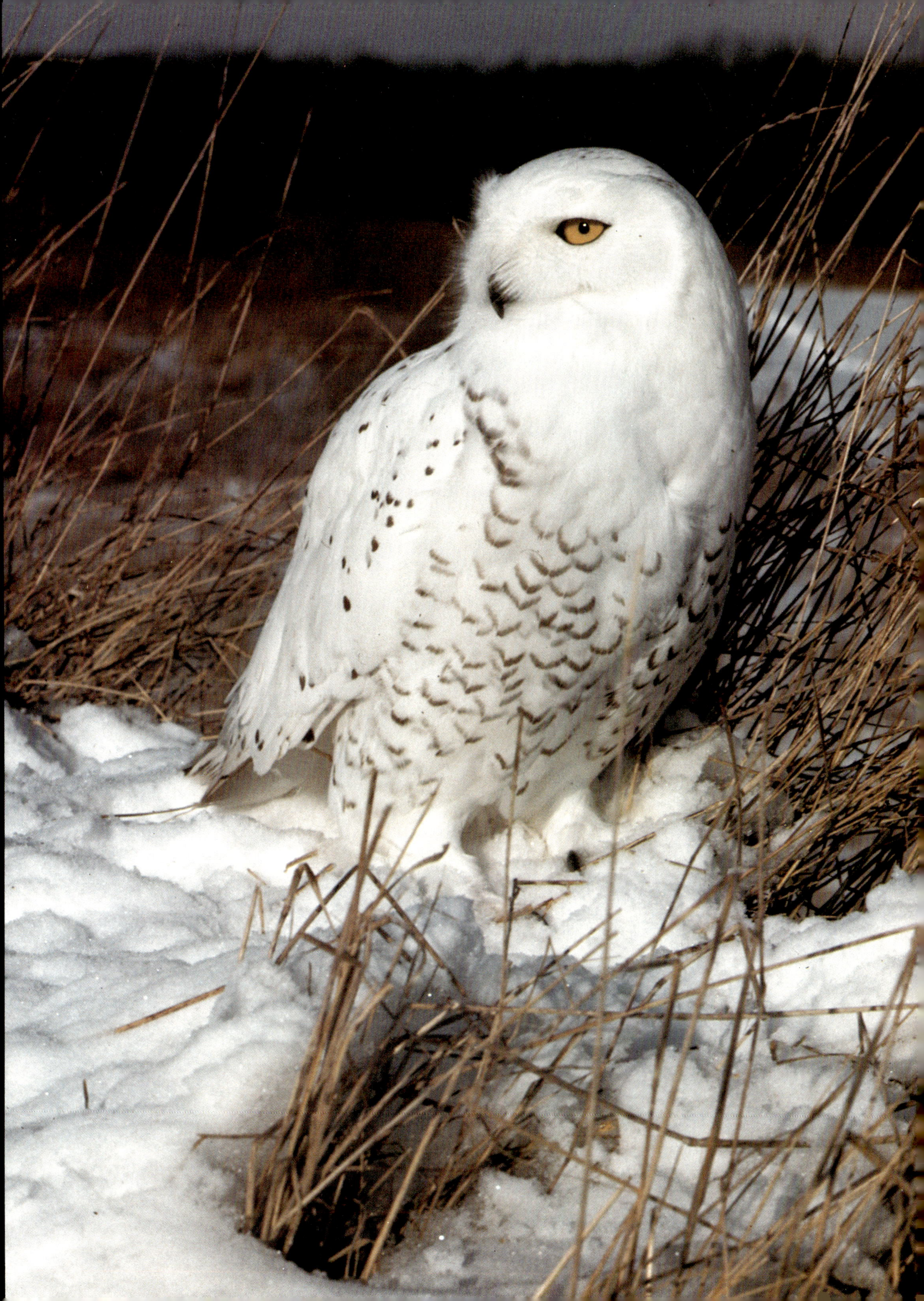

Osprey

Pandion haliaetus

This hawk is a highly specialized fish eater, seldom found far from water. The Osprey plunges feet first into the water to capture fish swimming near the surface. Rough sandpaper-like spicules on the bottoms of its feet allow the Osprey a good grip on slippery prey.

It is a large bird measuring 21 to 24 inches long with a wingspan from 4½ to 6 feet. Soaring in the air the Osprey resembles a gull. Its long, narrow wings are bent in the shape of a stretched out "M." Seen from below, the hawk is white with a black patch at the bend of each wing. Its head is white with a broad dark stripe through the cheeks, and its upperparts are dark brown.

In the past few decades Ospreys have declined in numbers, due mainly to the indiscriminate use of pesticides. Our breeding population has made a striking recovery in recent years. Restricted pesticide use and successful management plans are helping the Osprey to once again attain a healthy status. Their large stick nests, constructed in trees or atop high platforms specially provided for them, are once again visible from major highways along the shore.

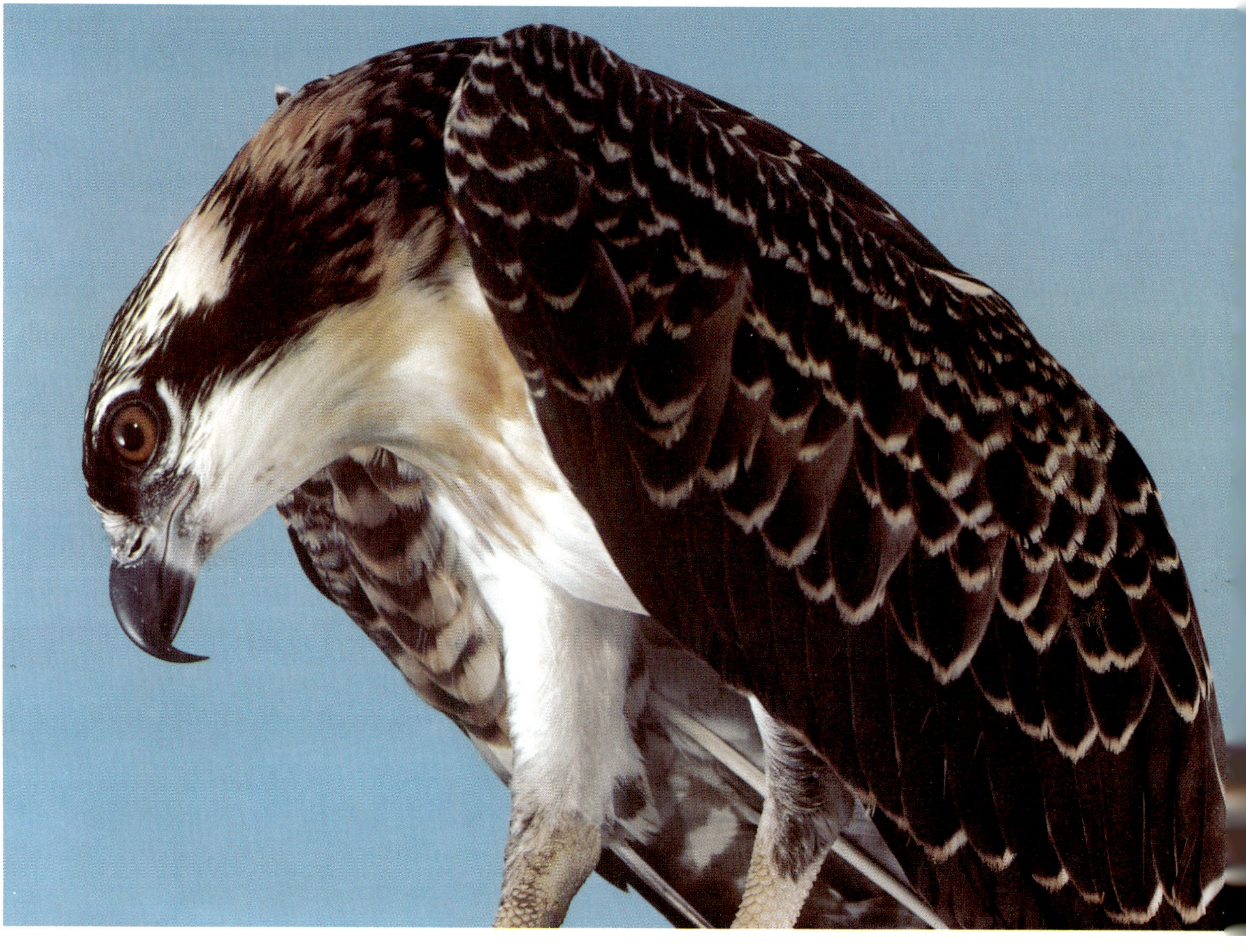

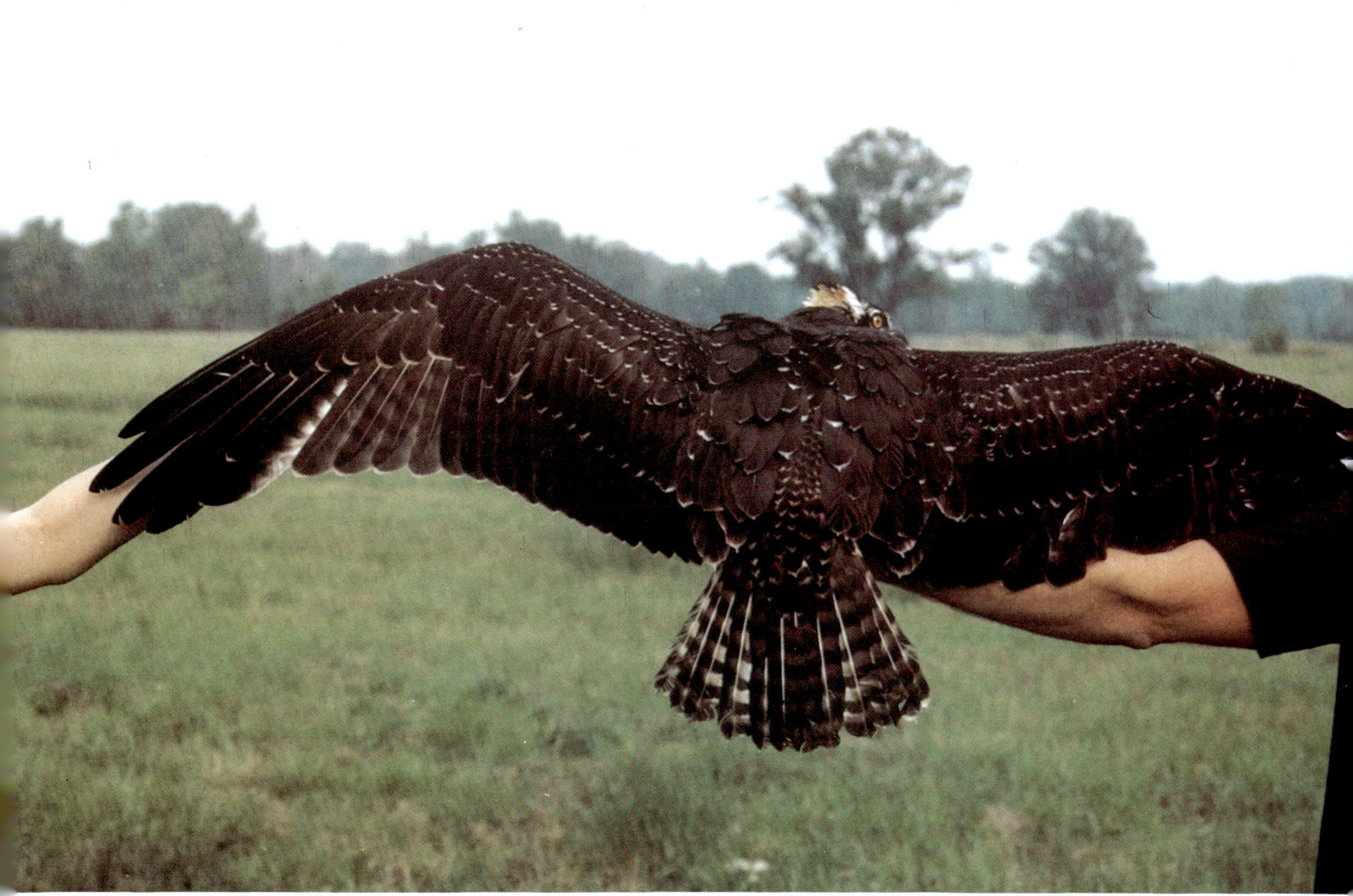

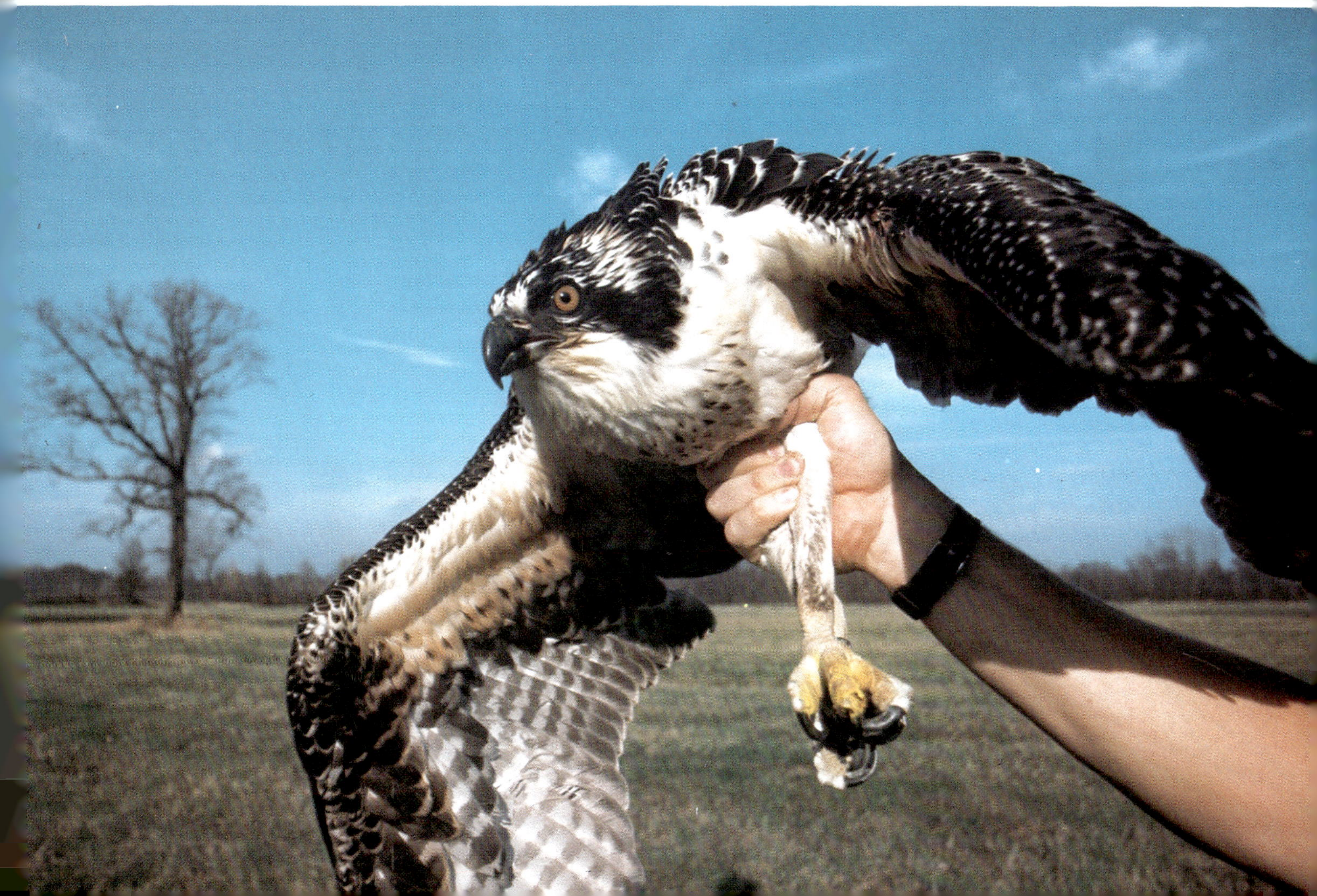

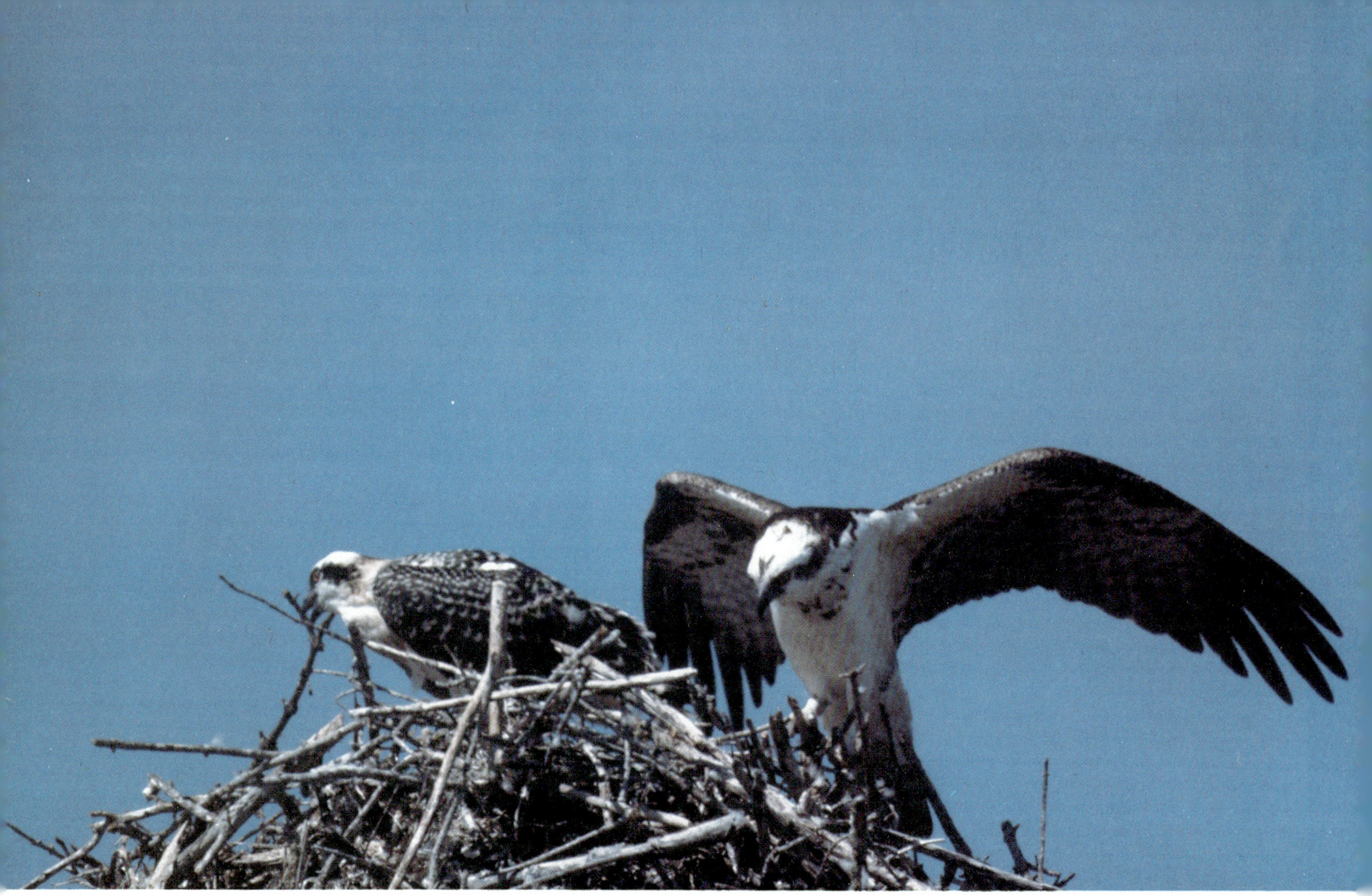

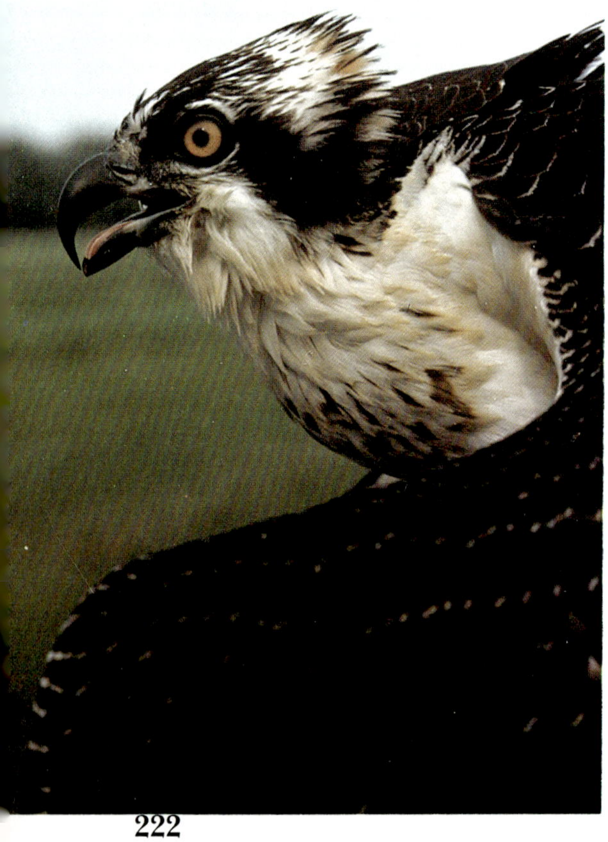

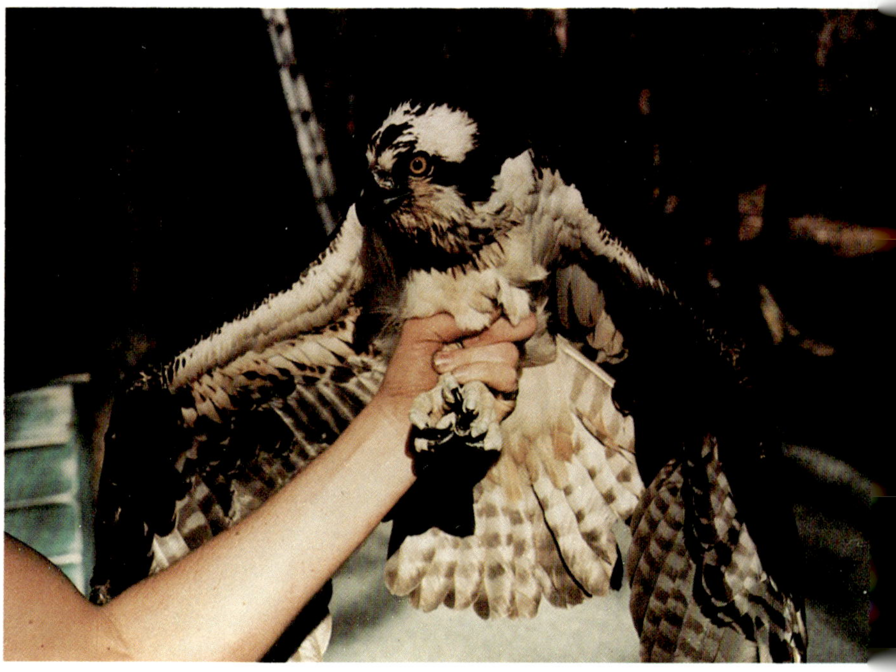

American Kestrel

Falco sparverius

The American Kestrel, sometimes called the Sparrow Hawk, is our smallest and most common falcon. Although this bird is easily seen, it is often not recognized as a hawk because of its resemblance to a songbird. Perched, it is similar to a dove or robin. From head to tail the Kestrel measures only 9 to 12 inches, but its wings are long, spanning up to 2 feet.

Unlike most other birds of prey, in which the sexes are alike, male and female Kestrels have different color plumages. Females have rufous backs and wings, barred with black, while males have rufous backs and blue-gray wings.

Kestrels catch most of their prey on the ground. They are often seen perched on telephone poles and wires, like sentinels of the road, searching the terrain below. They also hunt on the wing, characteristically hovering over grassy areas. Grasshoppers, crickets and other insects are eaten in great numbers when available; but mice, voles, snakes and songbirds are also taken.

Kestrels are unique among our falcons in that they are hole-nesters, using natural cavities in trees and small openings in buildings. They are the only North American hawks that will nest in bird boxes.

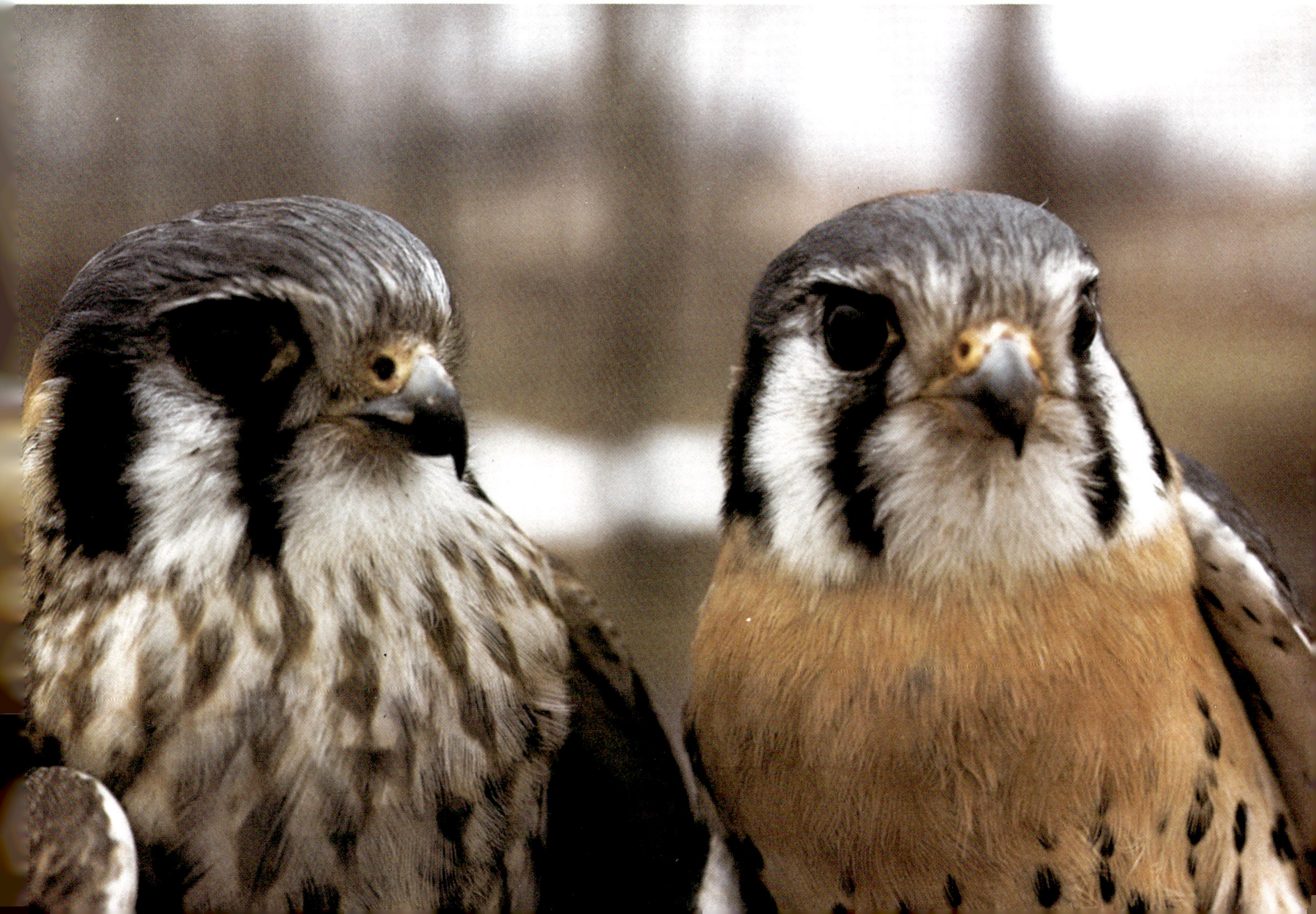

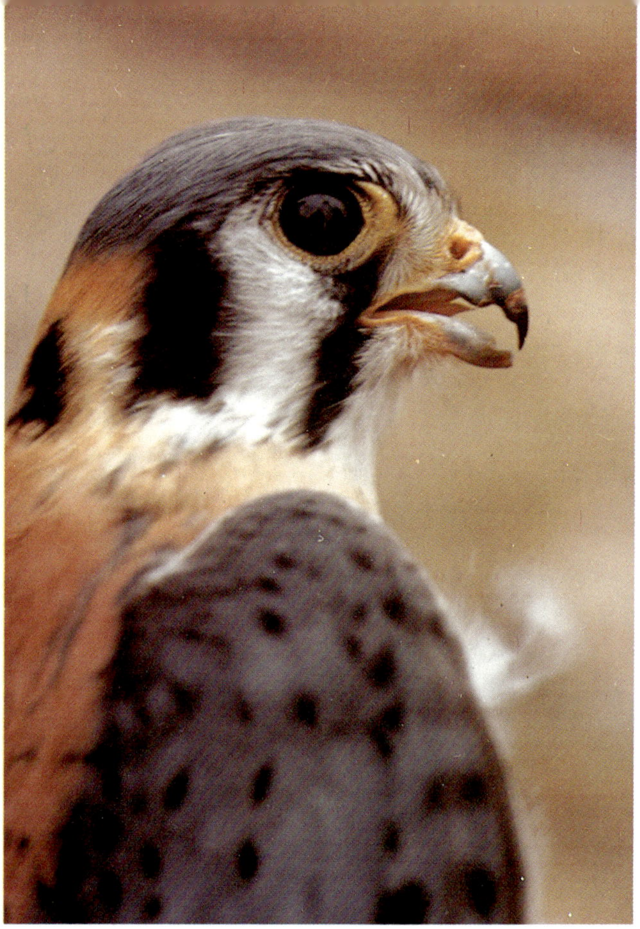

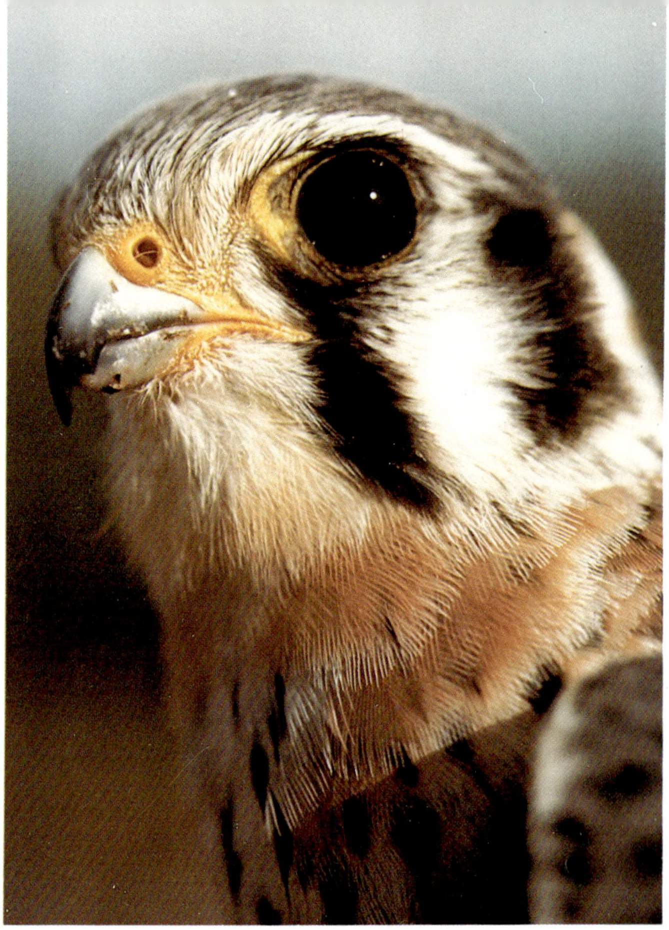

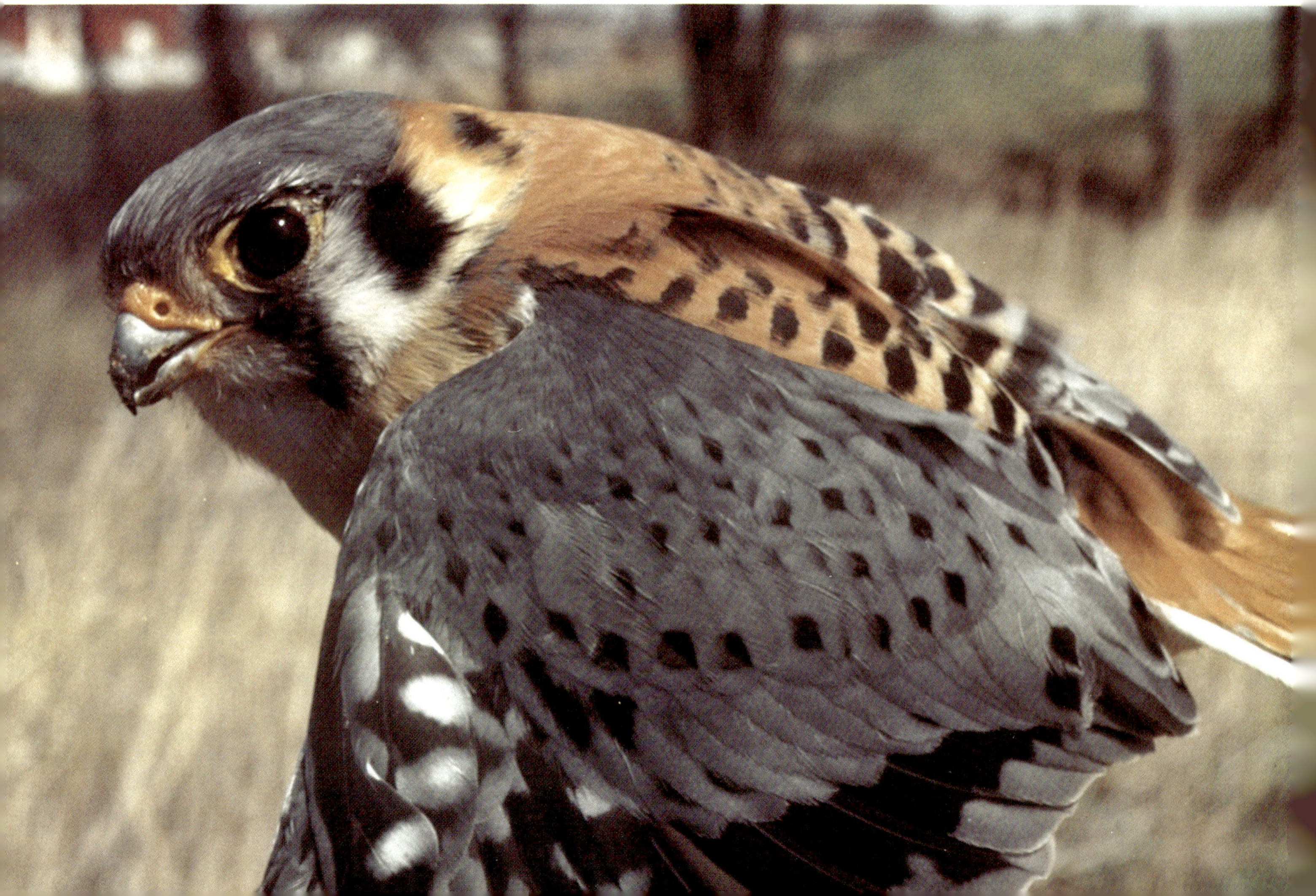

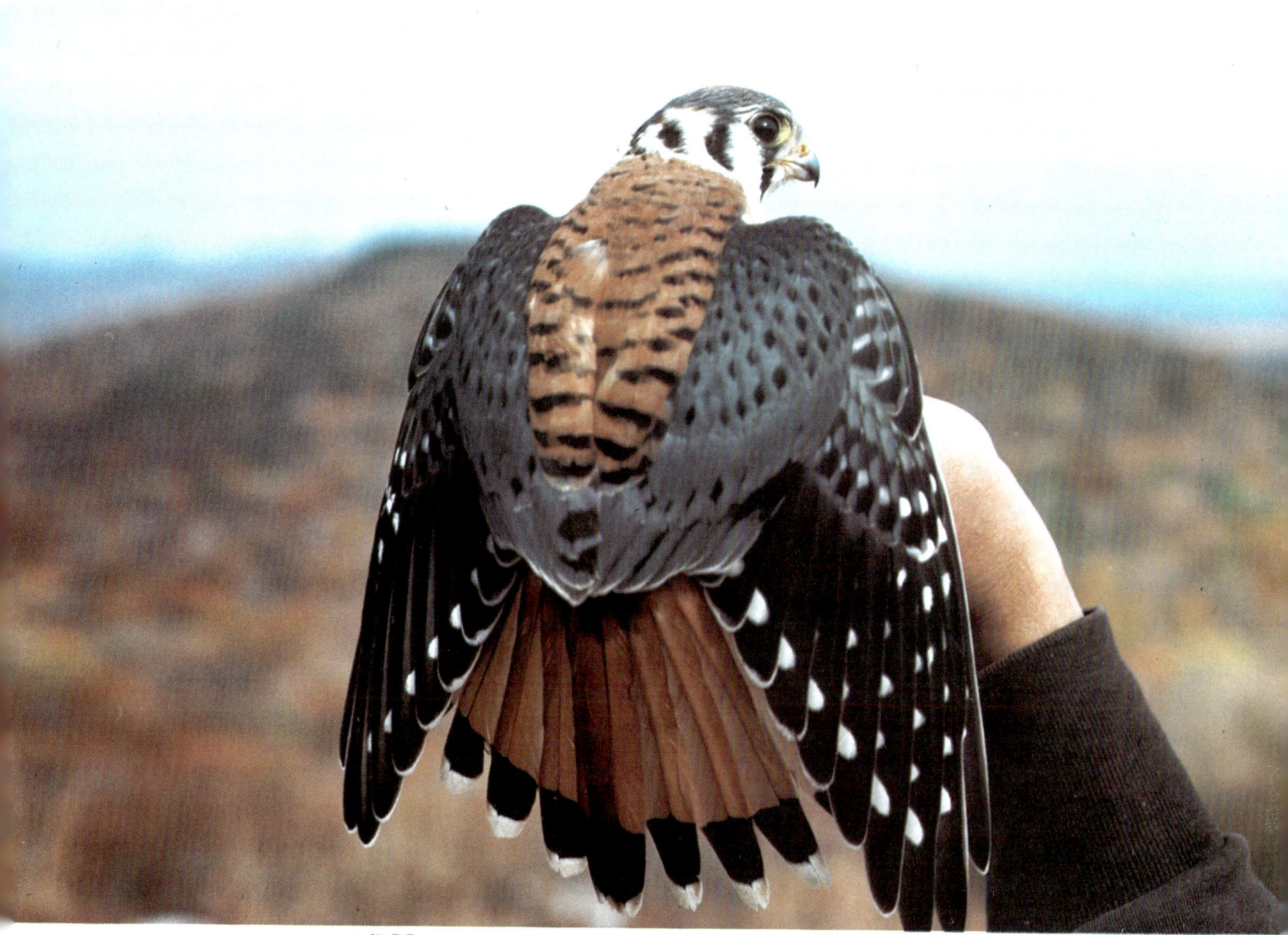

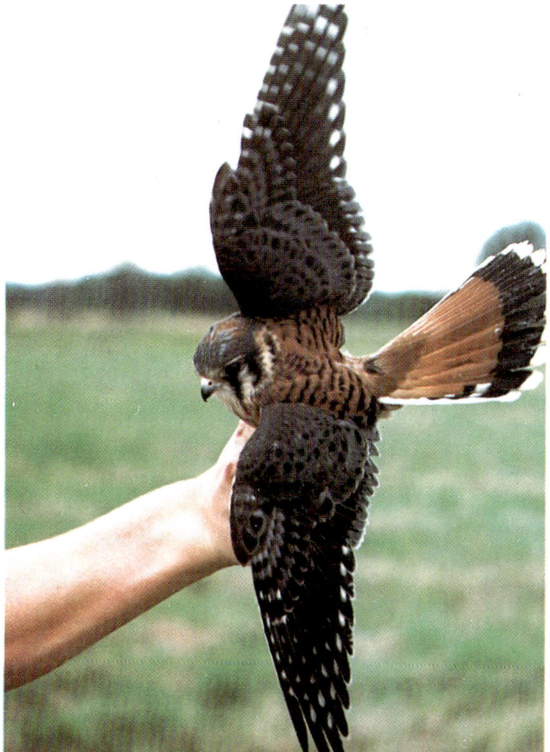

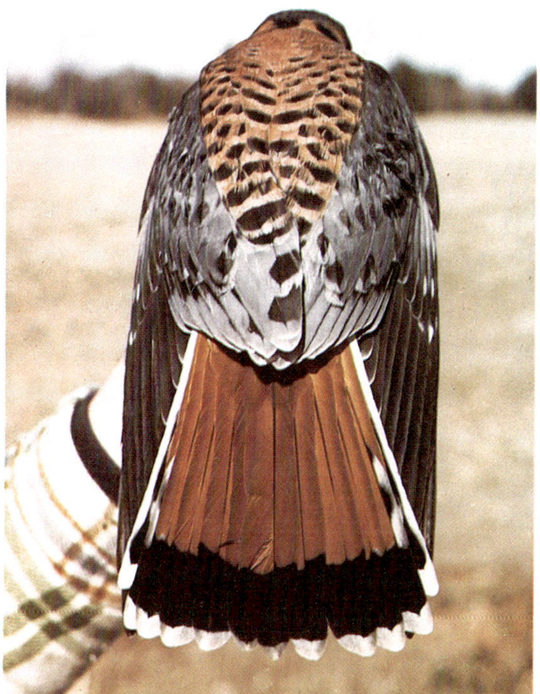

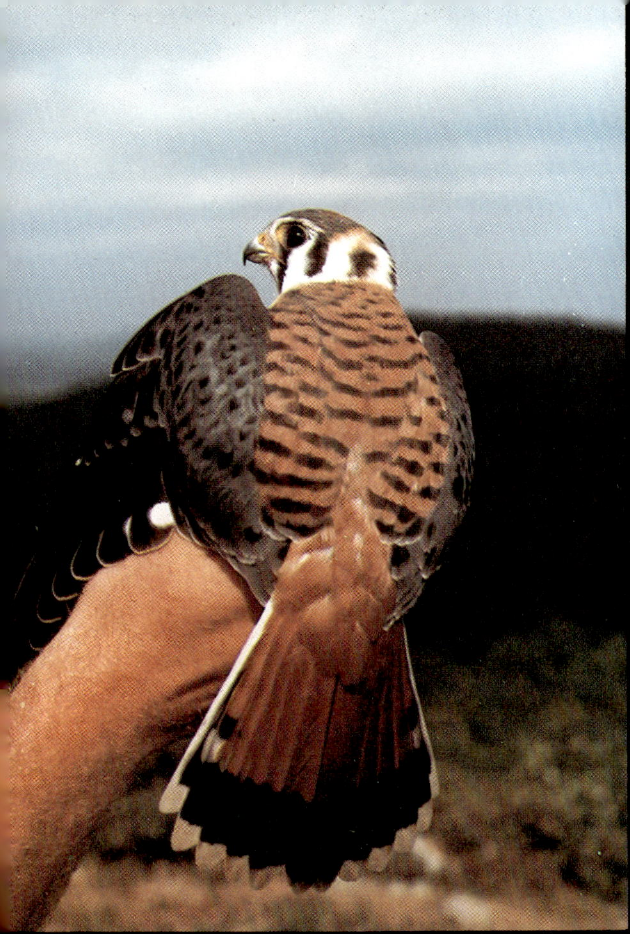
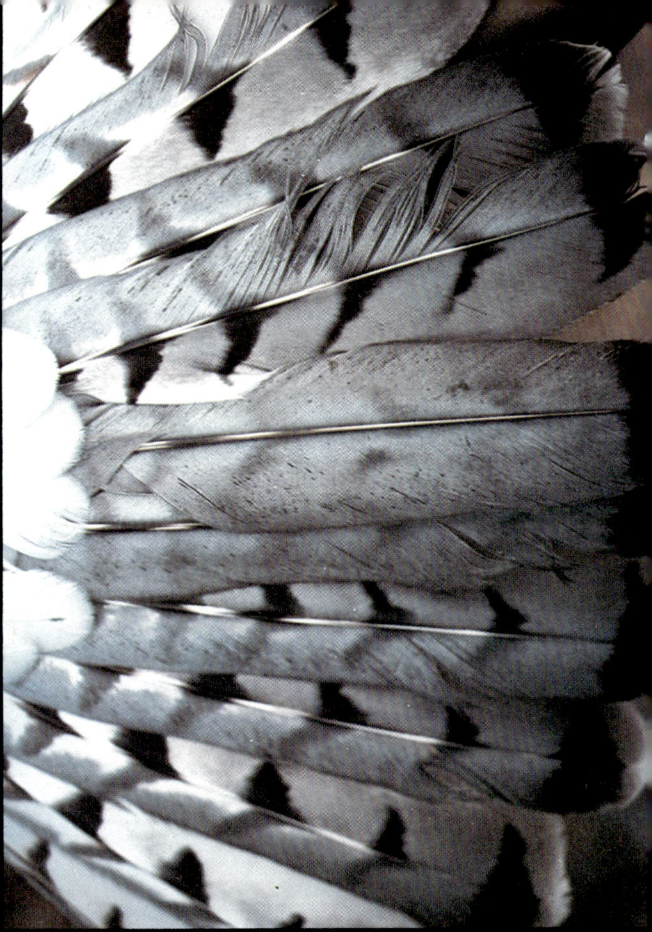
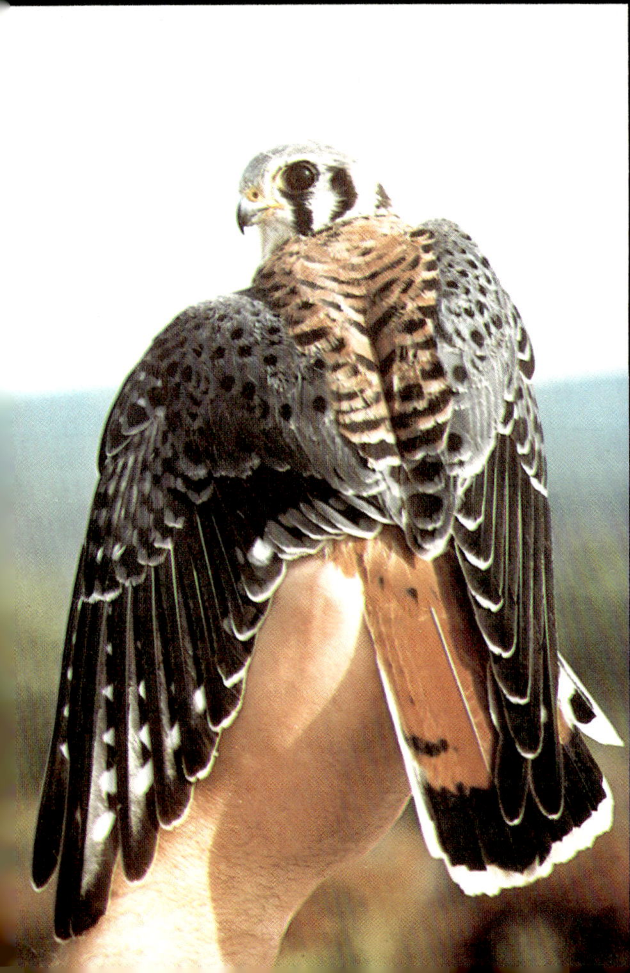
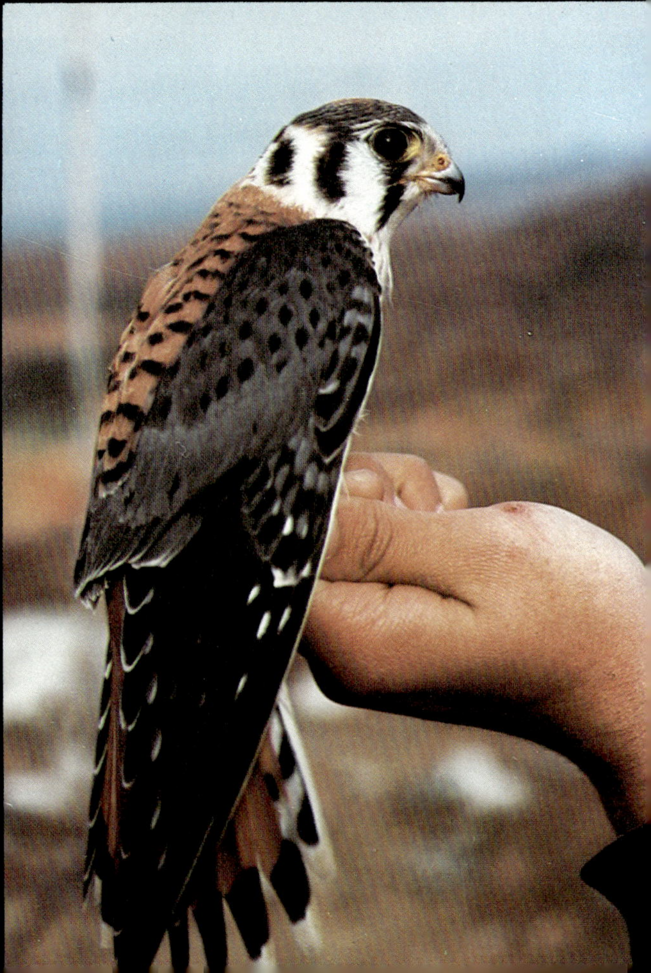

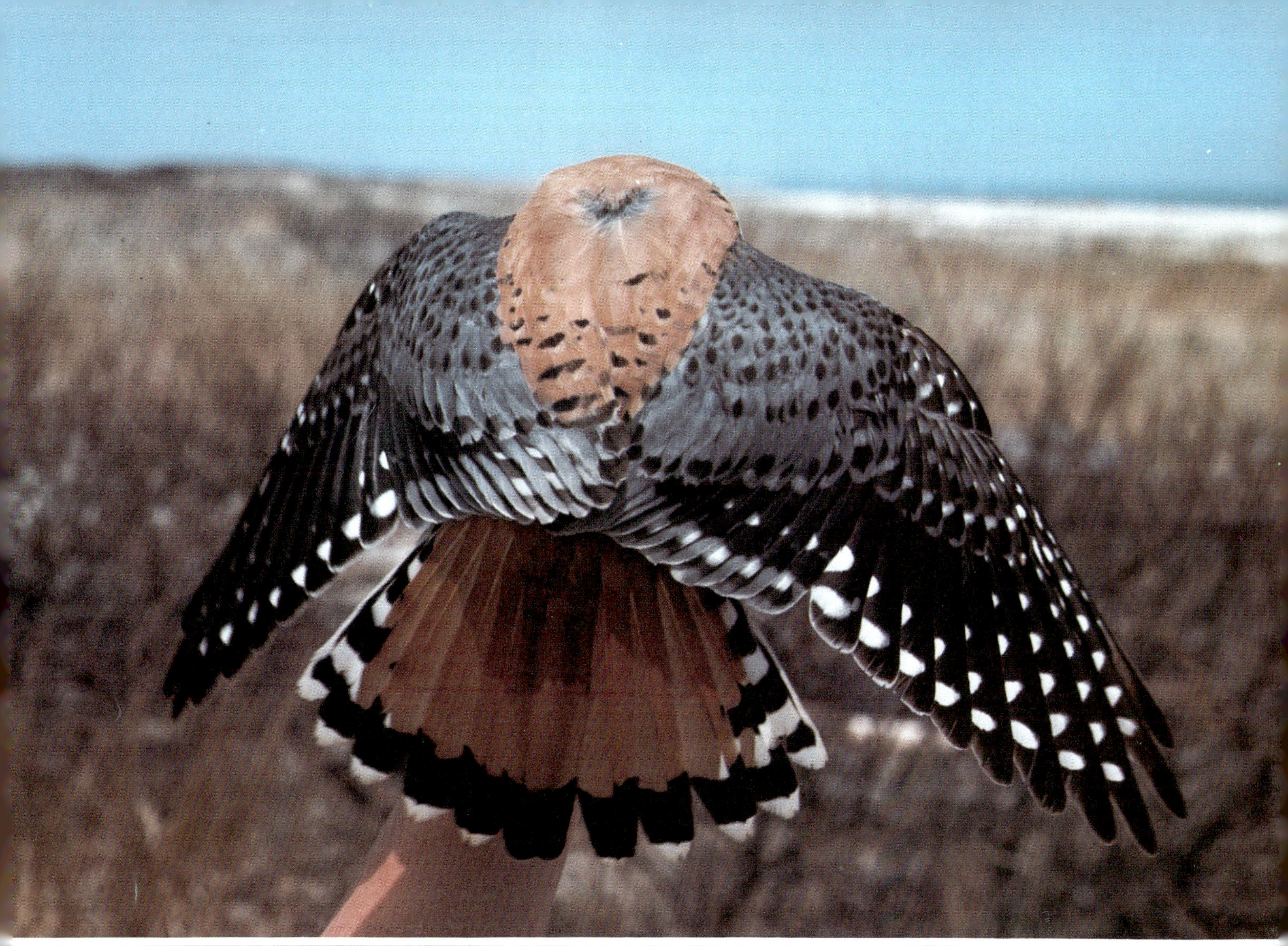
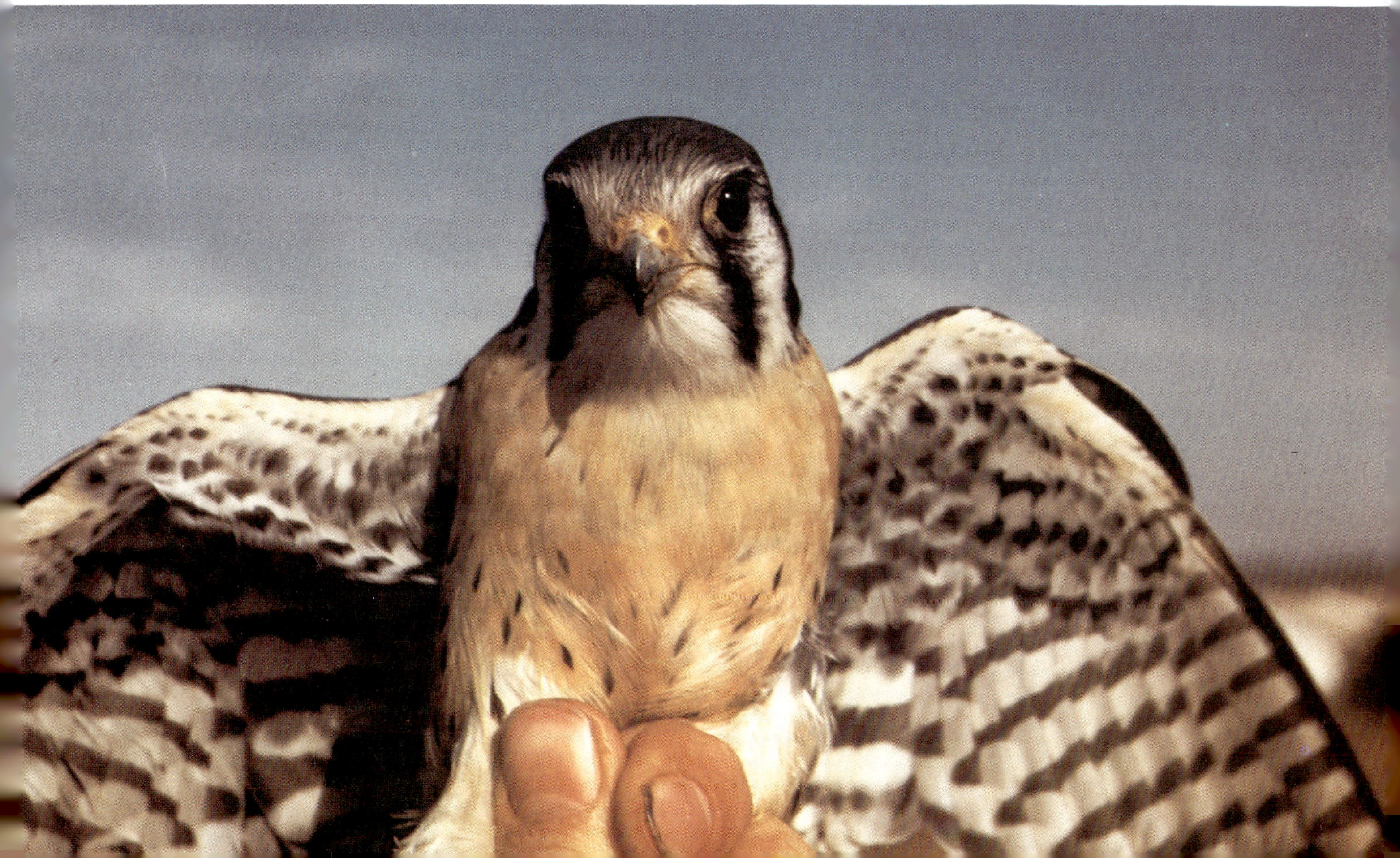

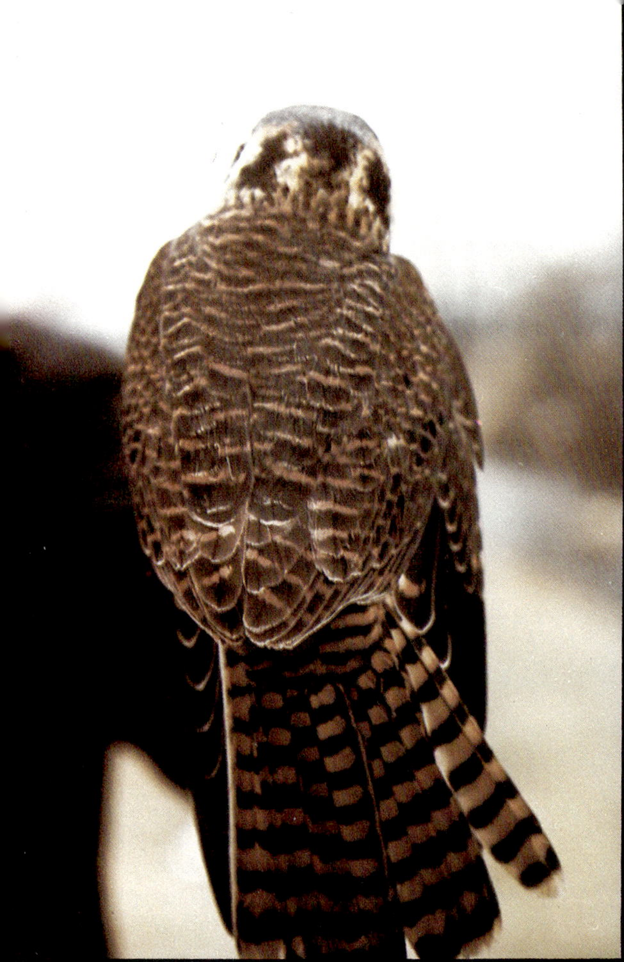
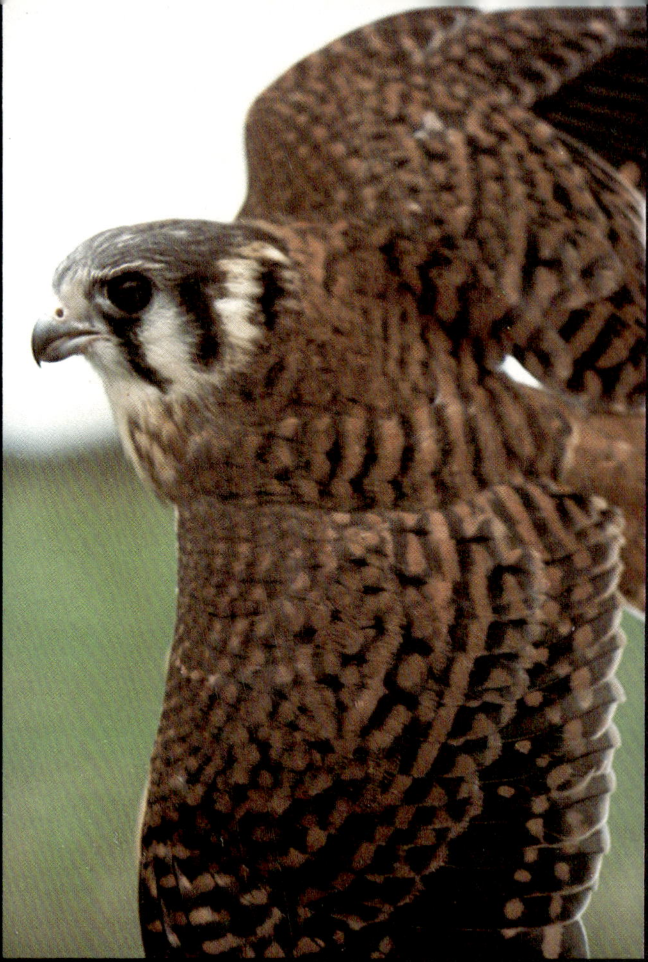
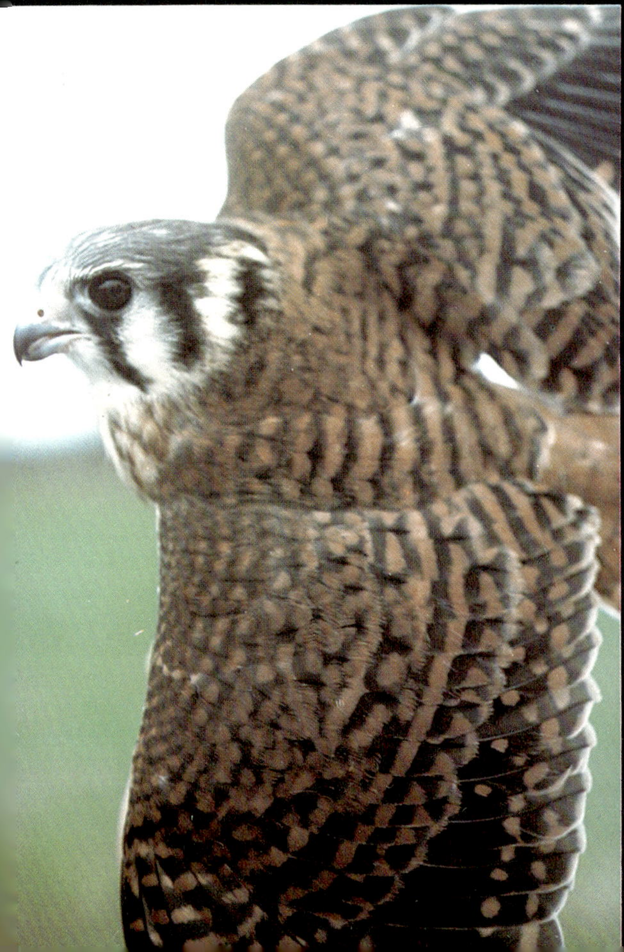
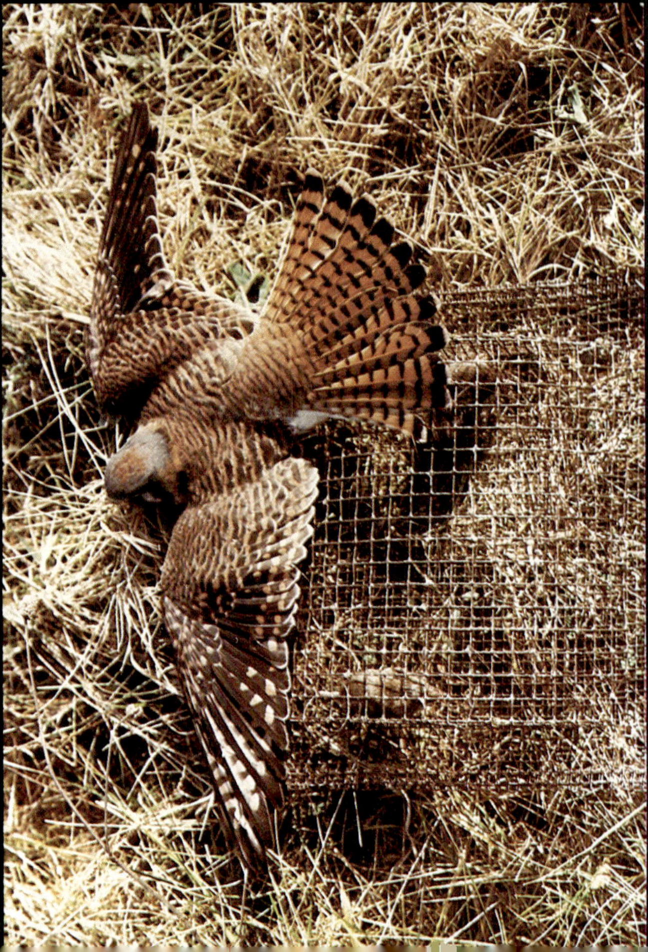

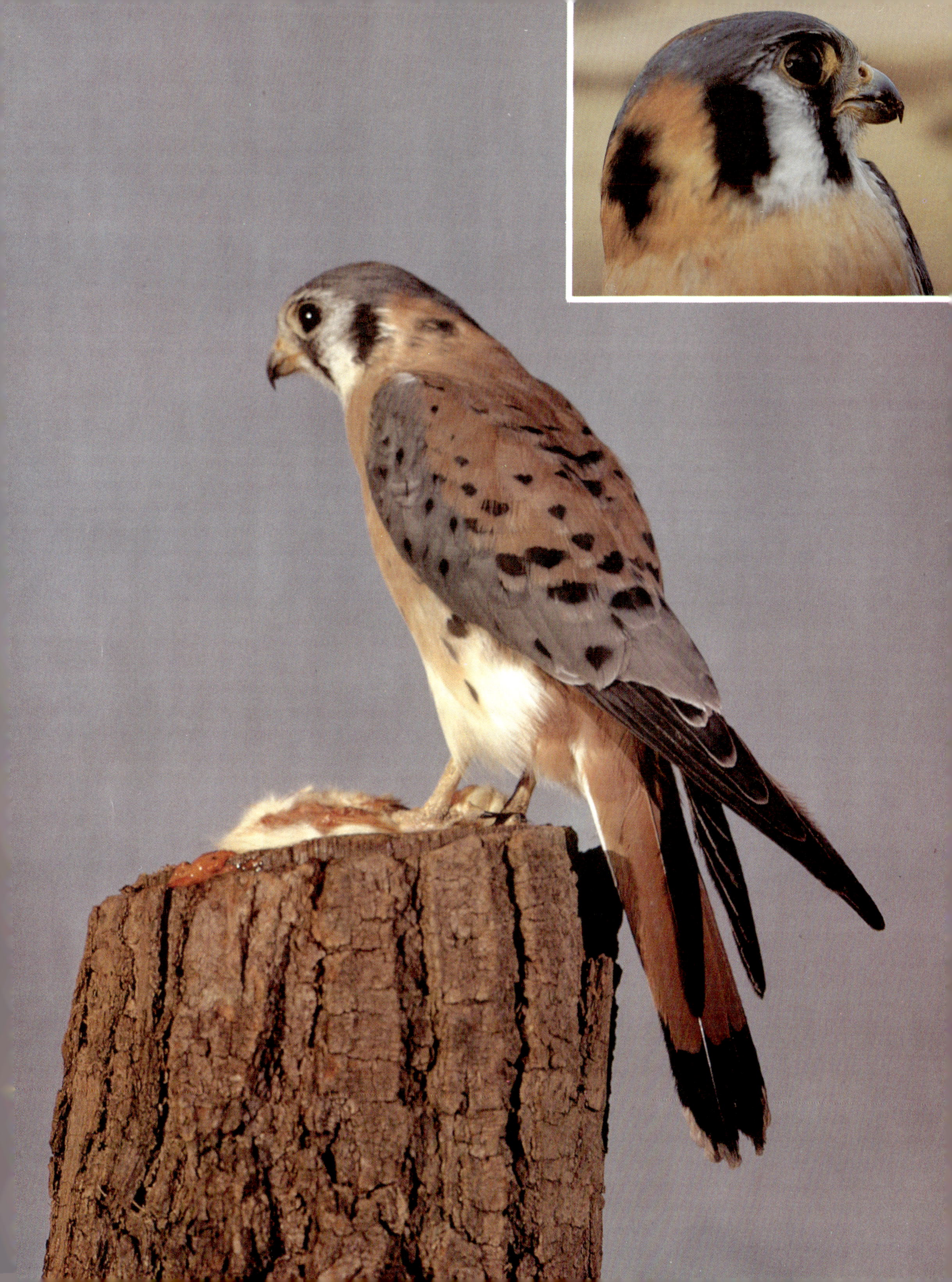

Merlin

Falco columbarius

Merlins are small dark falcons just slightly larger than Kestrels. They measure 10 to 13½ inches long and have wingspans of 24 to 27 inches. Immature Merlins are brown above, while adults are blue-gray; both young and adult birds have heavy dark brown vertical streaks on their underparts. Their tails are long with prominent dark bands. When flying and perched, a Merlin resembles a dark pigeon.

Like other falcons, Merlins are birds of open country and generally avoid wooded areas. They are fast-flying aerial acrobats and hunt primarily on the wing, catching other birds (their main food), some insects and occasionally small mammals.

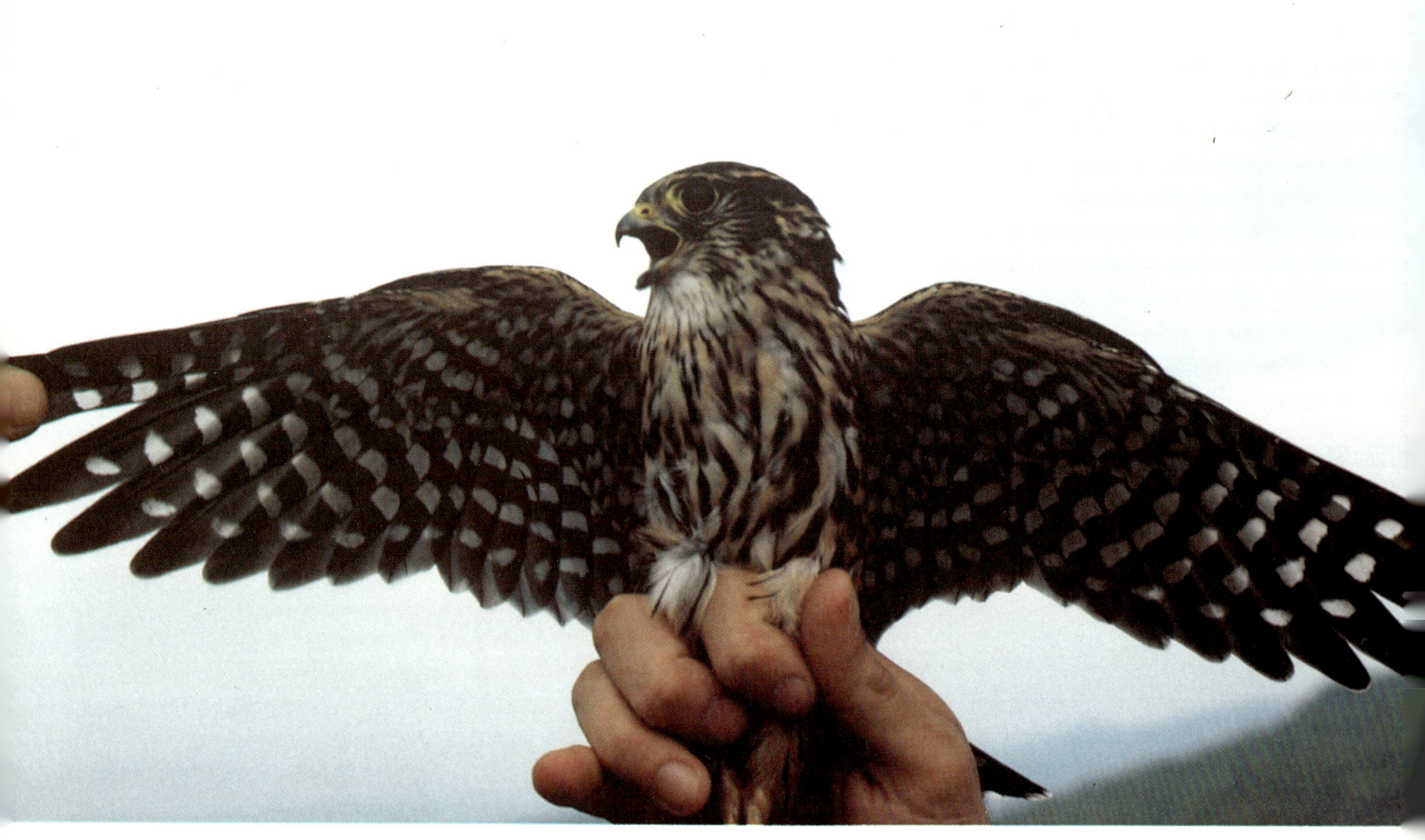

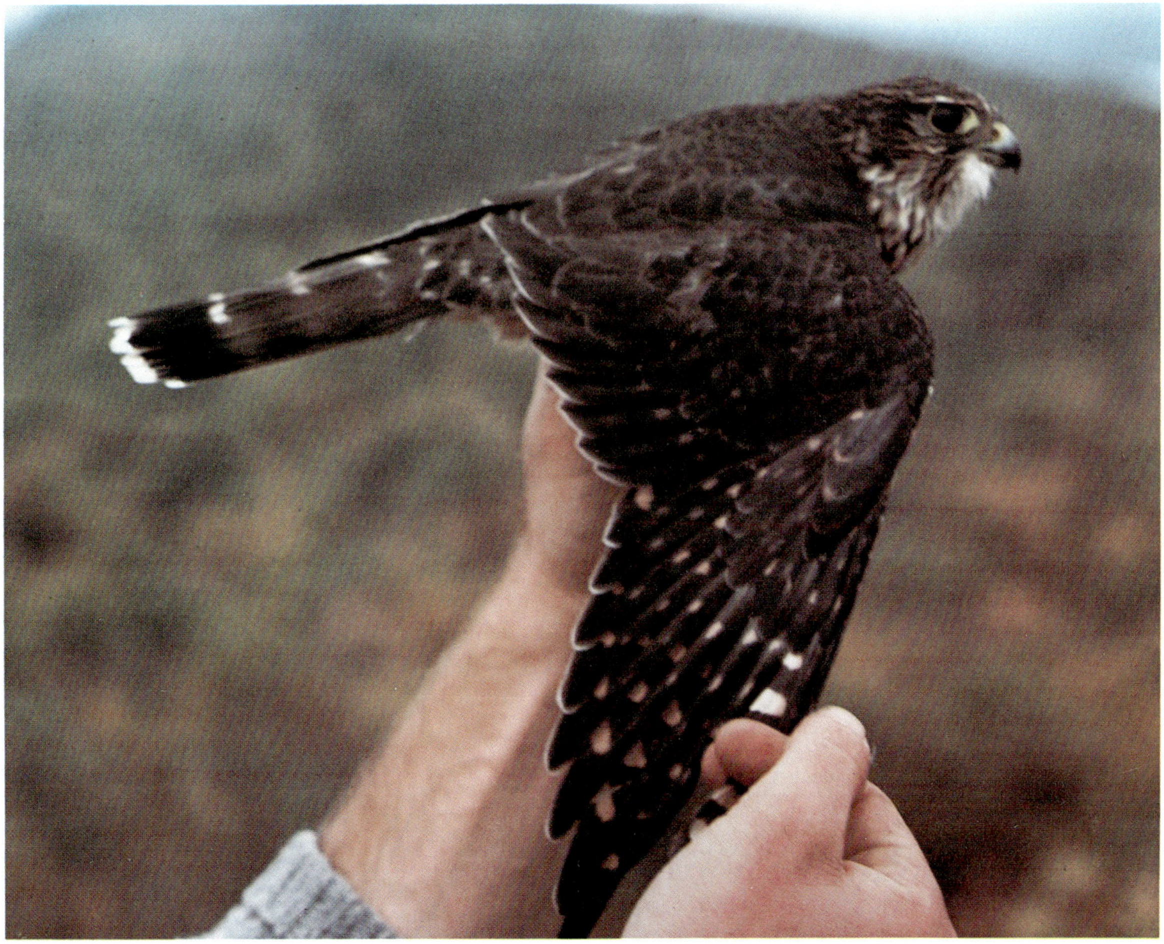

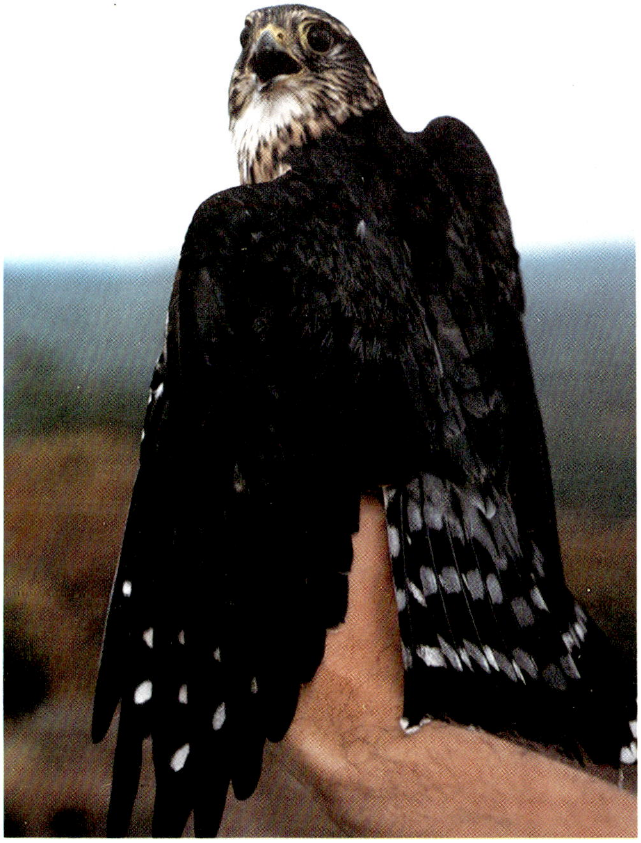

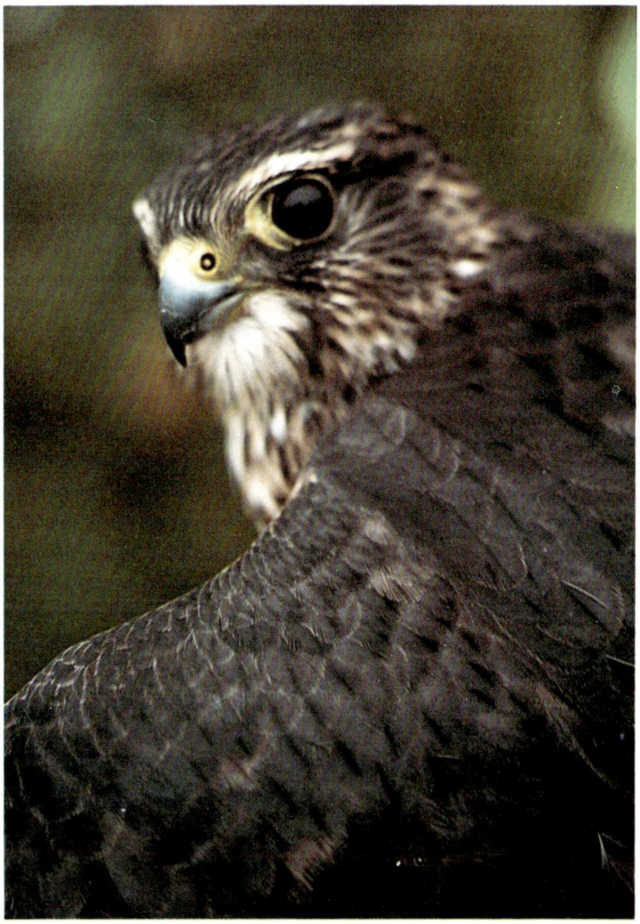

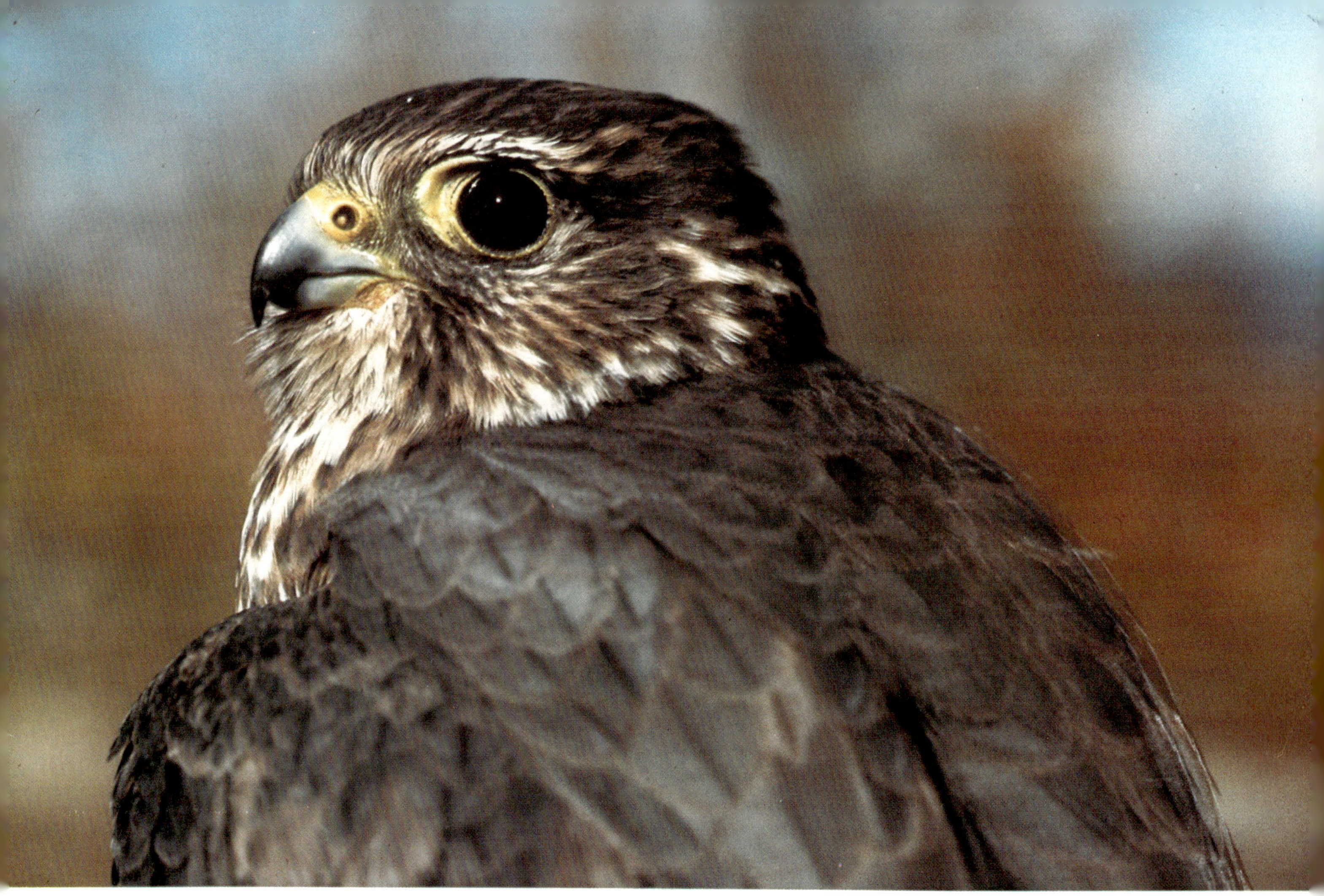

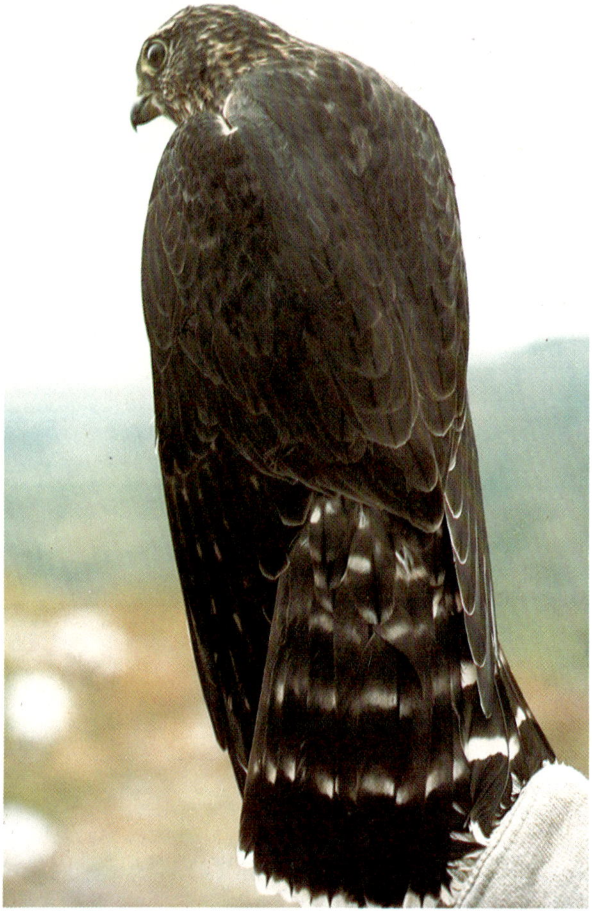

Peregrine Falcon

Falco peregrinus

This mighty falcon's scientific name *peregrinus* means "wandering," and indeed. Peregrines are among the most widely distributed birds in the world. Although they inhabit every continent except Antarctica, Peregrine populations have suffered drastic declines during the past 40 years due to the effects of pesticides. The species is presently classified as endangered throughout the world. Recently, through conservation programs on their behalf, they are making a comeback throughout their breeding range.

Peregrines are large falcons, 15 to 20 inches long, with a wingspan of 3½ feet. They have a distinctive facial pattern with a dark "mustache" mark on the cheeks. Adult Peregrines have slate blue backs.

Their favored nesting sites are generally high, rocky cliff ledges in remote places overlooking a lake, stream, or river, but they have been known to nest on the rooftops or ledges of city buildings and in the steelwork of bridges.

Peregrines feed mainly on other birds, catching whatever is available, from small songbirds to large ducks. They dive at incredible speeds, approaching 200 miles an hour, to capture their prey in mid-air.

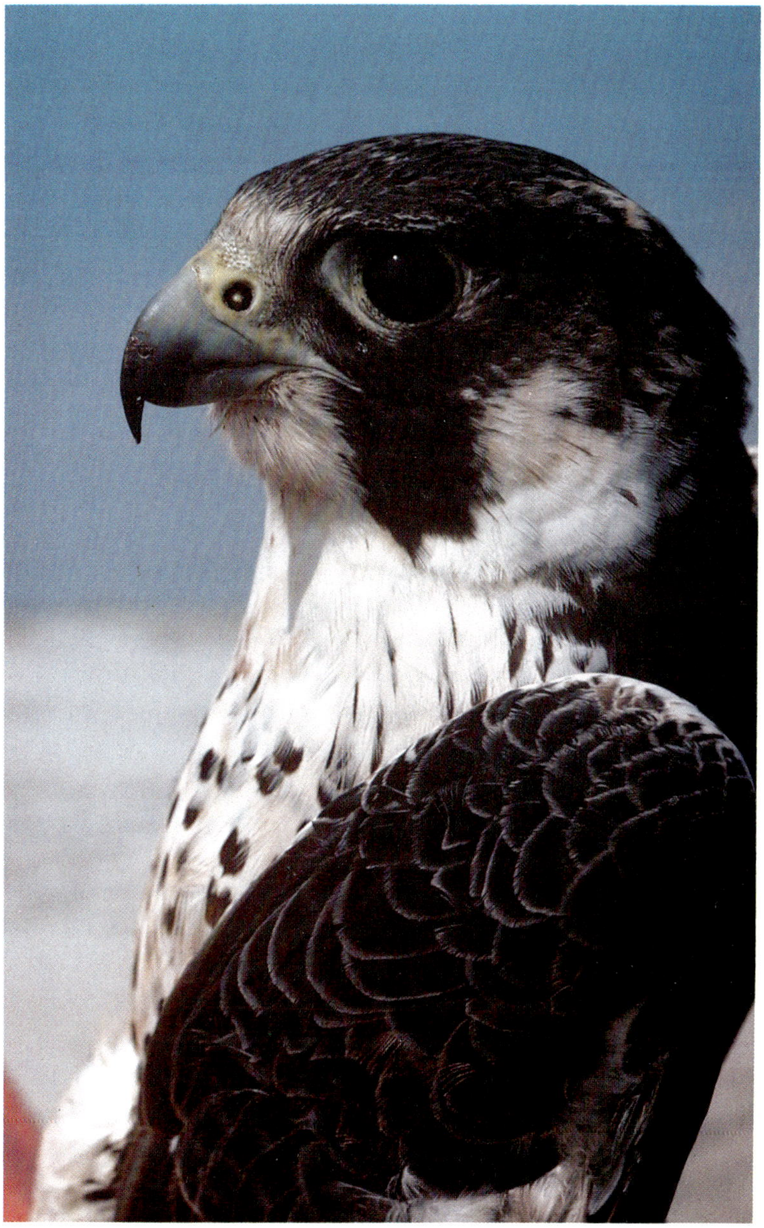

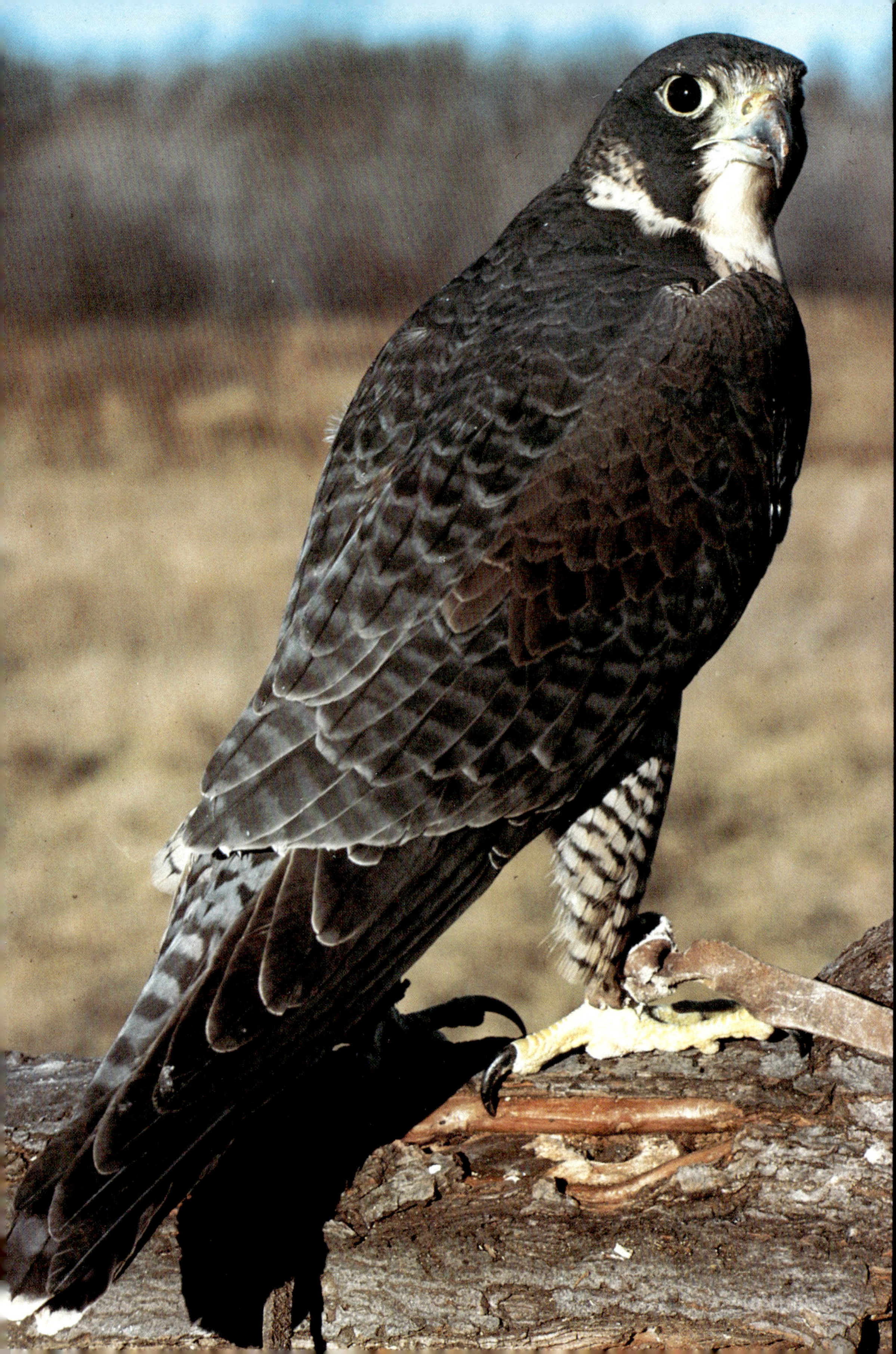

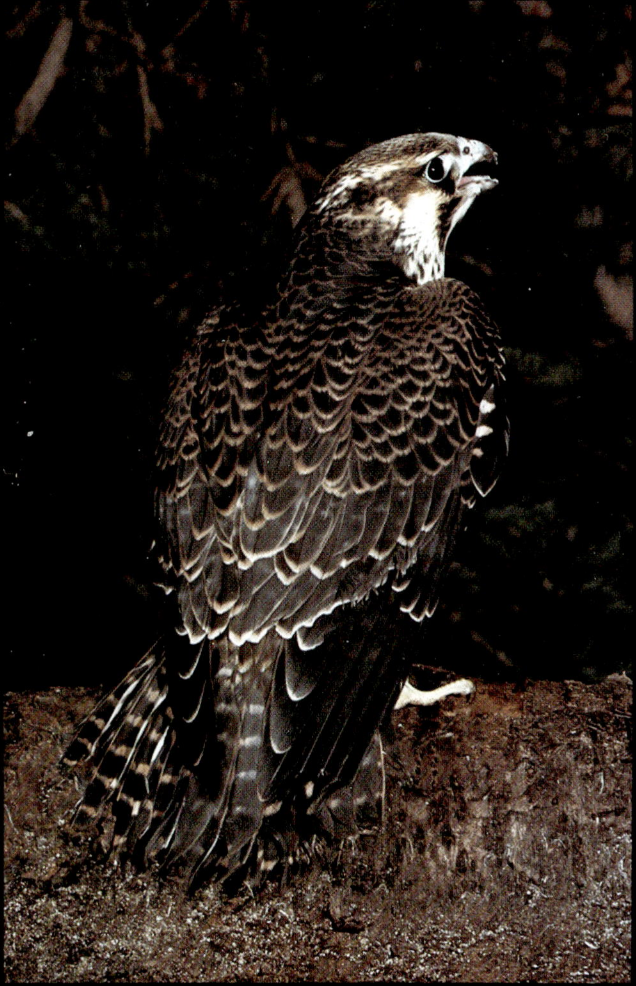
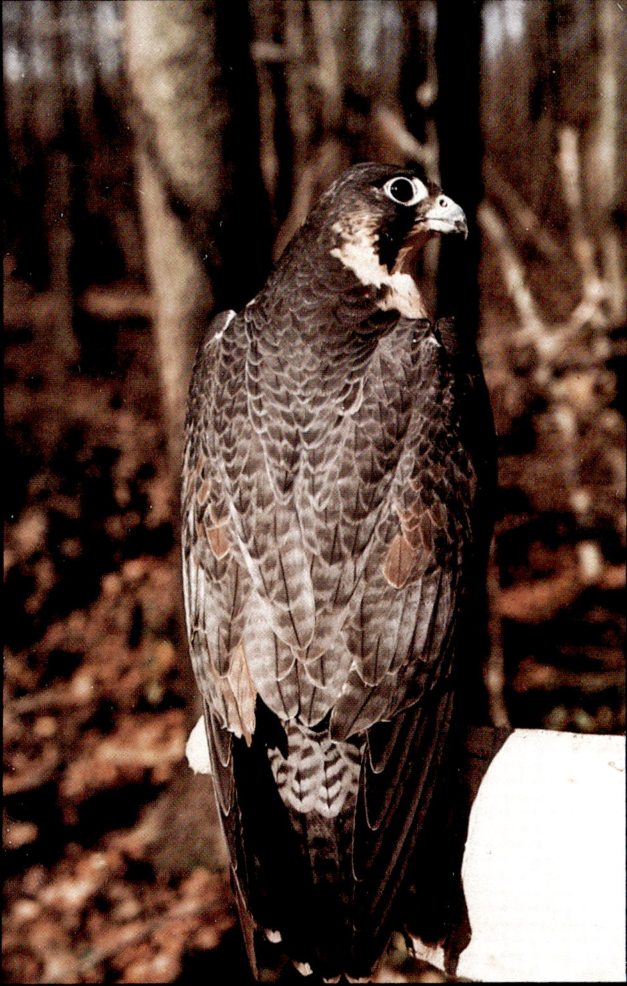
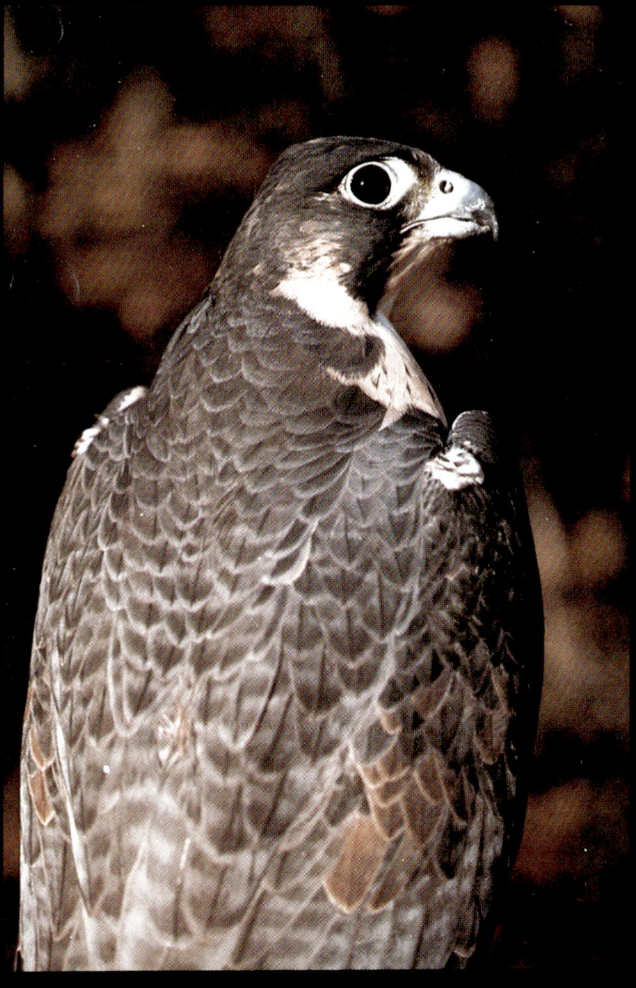
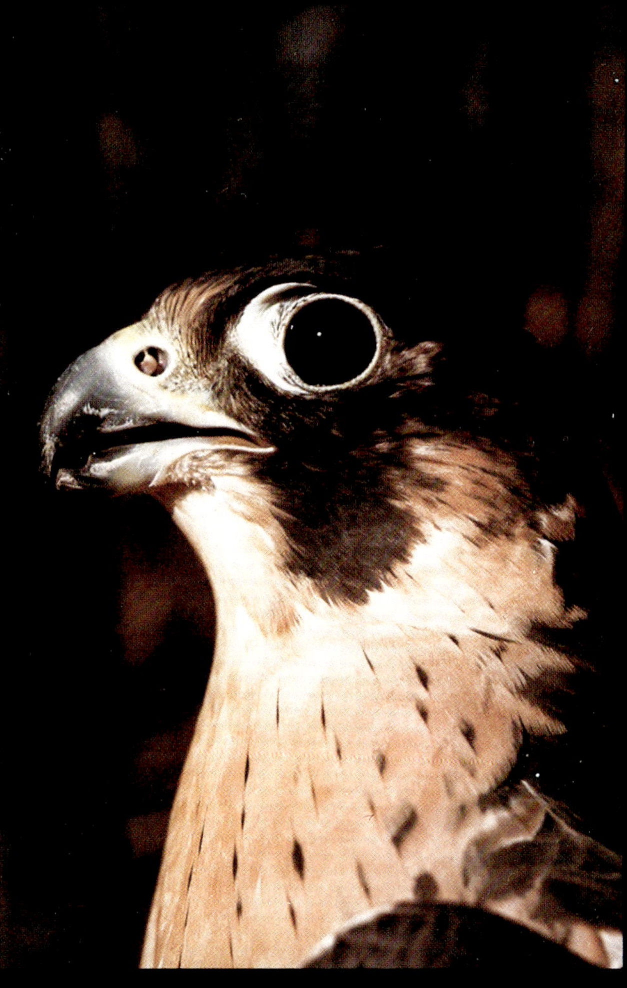

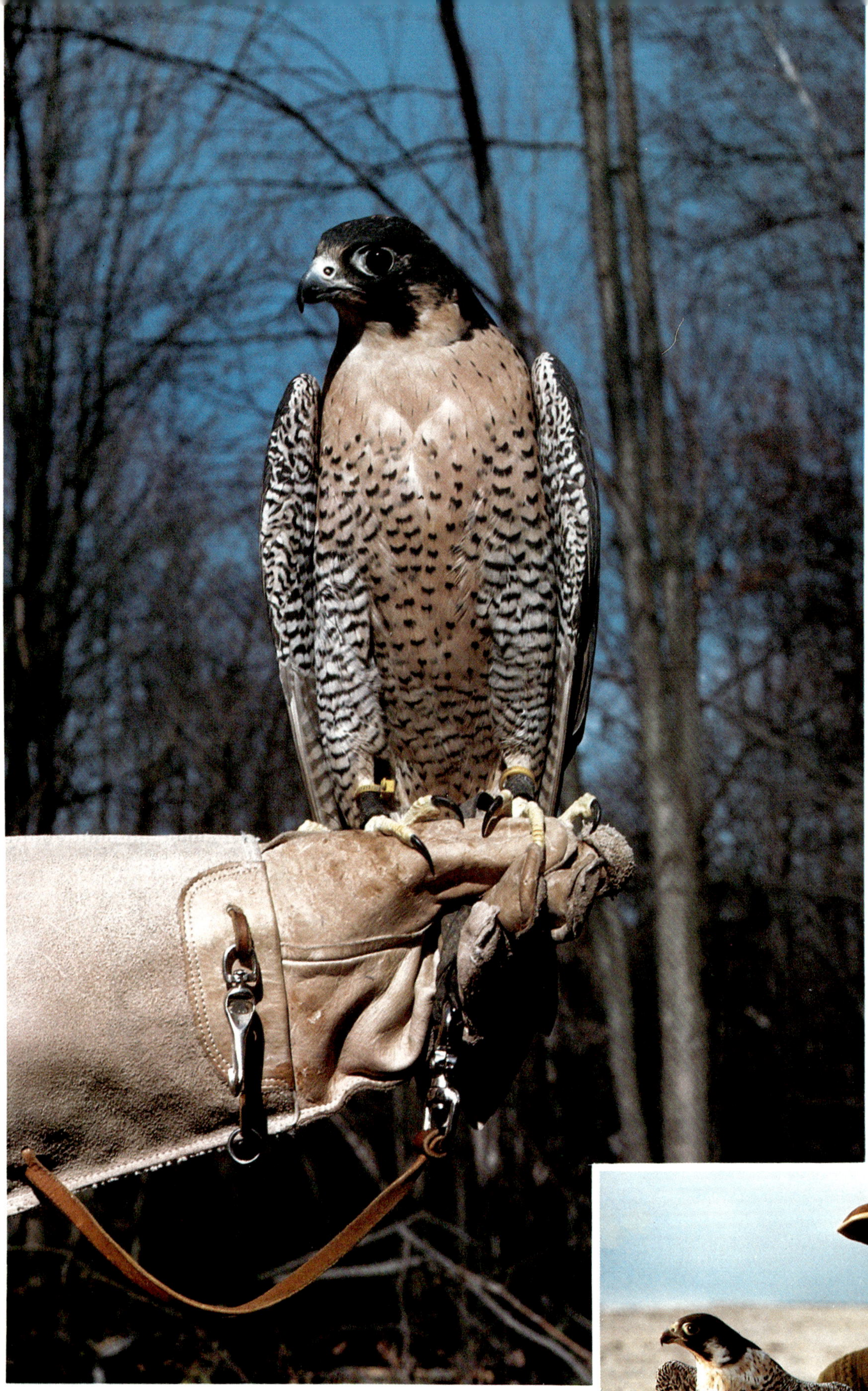

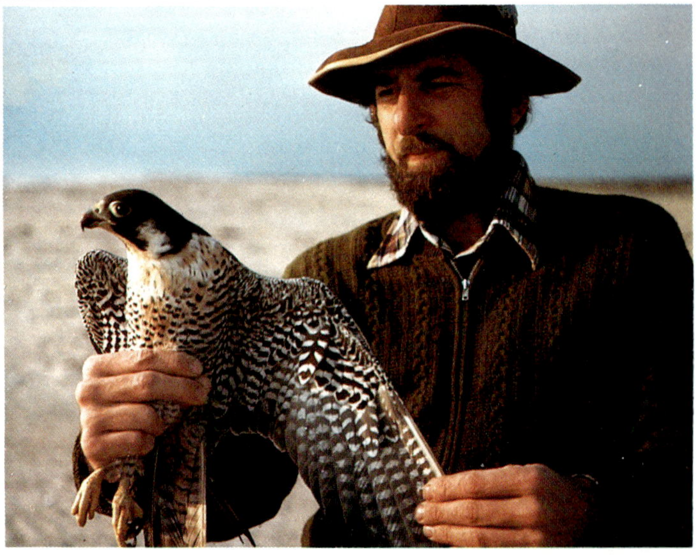

Sharp-Shinned Hawk

Accipiter striatus

Sharp-shinned Hawks are the smallest of the three North American accipiters. They measure 10 to 14 inches long and have wingspans of about 2 feet, yet weigh only 3½ to 7 ounces.

Young Sharp-shins are brown backed and have brown streaks on their white breasts. As they mature, the colors change: their backs become slate-gray, and their breasts become barred with reddish-brown. Even their eye color changes with age — from yellow to deep red.

The Sharp-shinned Hawk gets its common name from the "shins" of its legs which are not round, but oval and rather sharp. The small head is round, and the long, square-tipped tail has narrow black and gray bands.

They are swift, agile hawks well adapted to flying in heavily forested areas. Their prey, predominantly small birds, is captured in dashing, headlong pursuits.

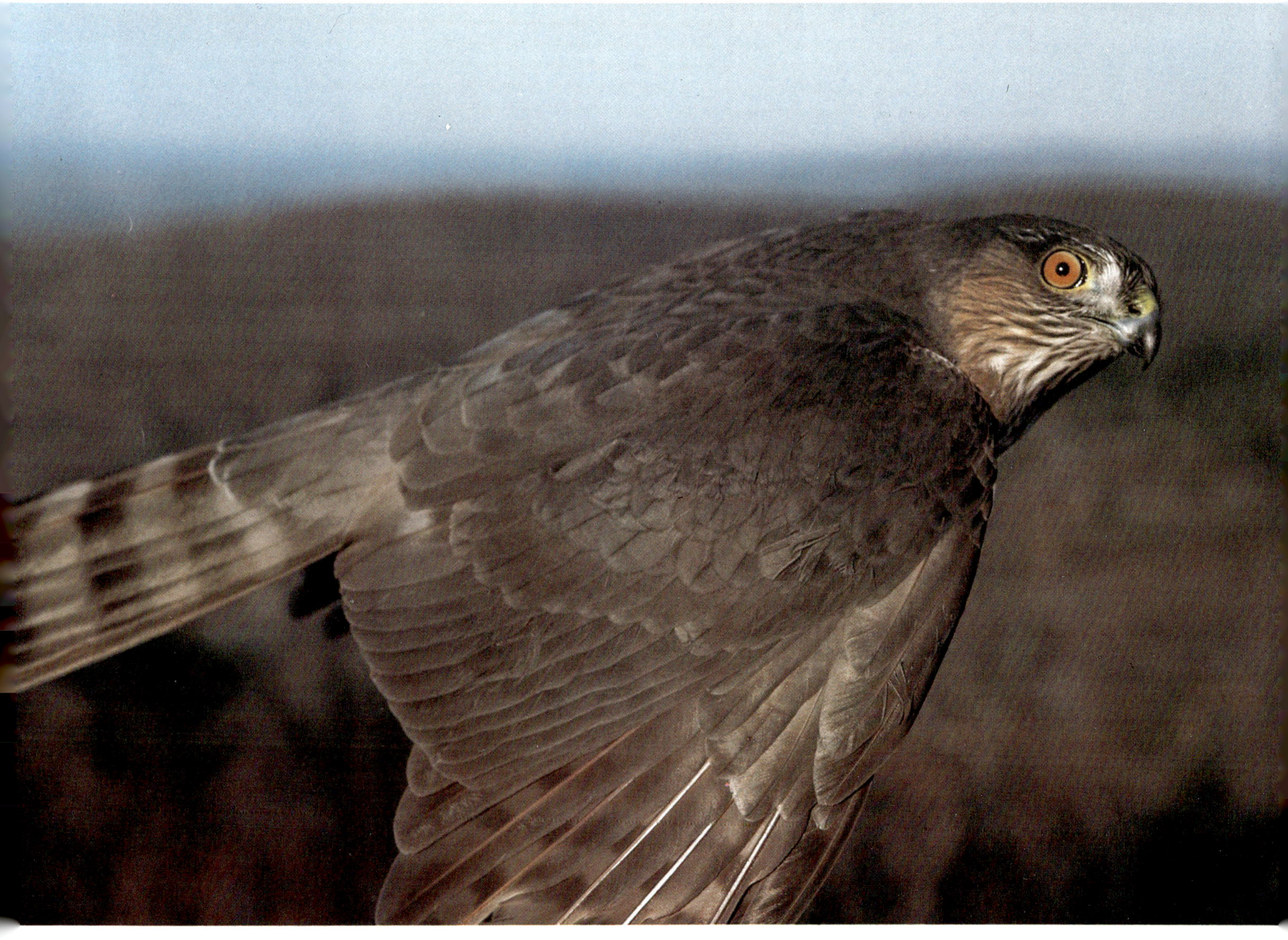

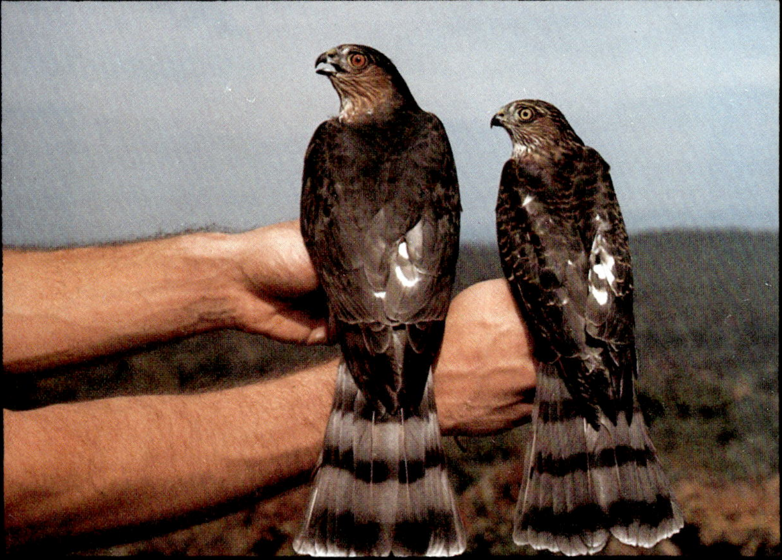

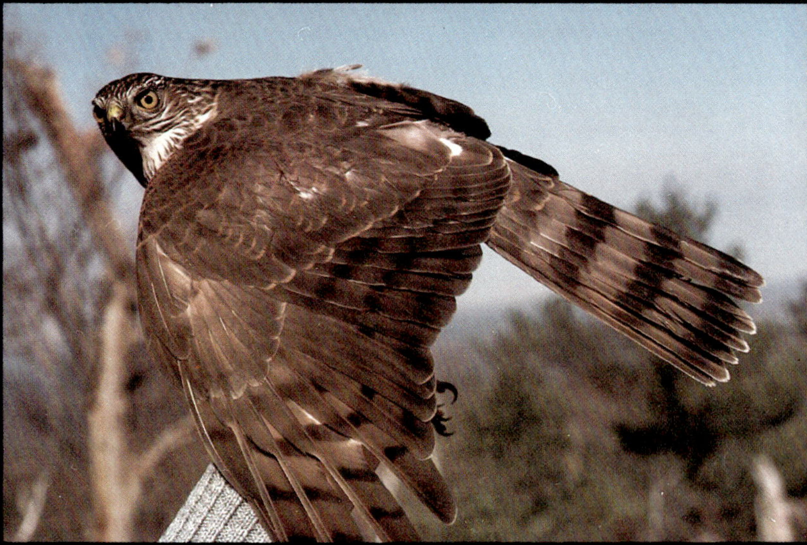

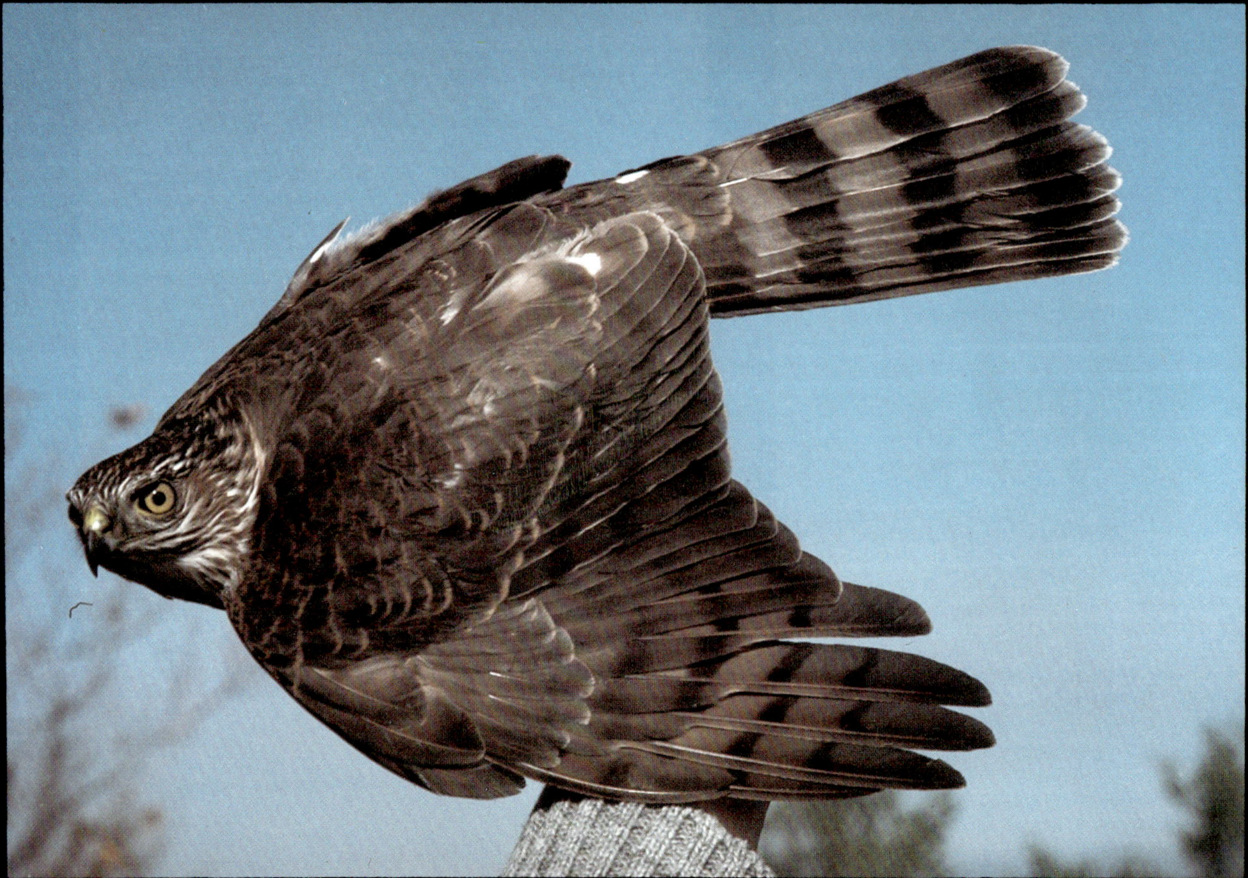

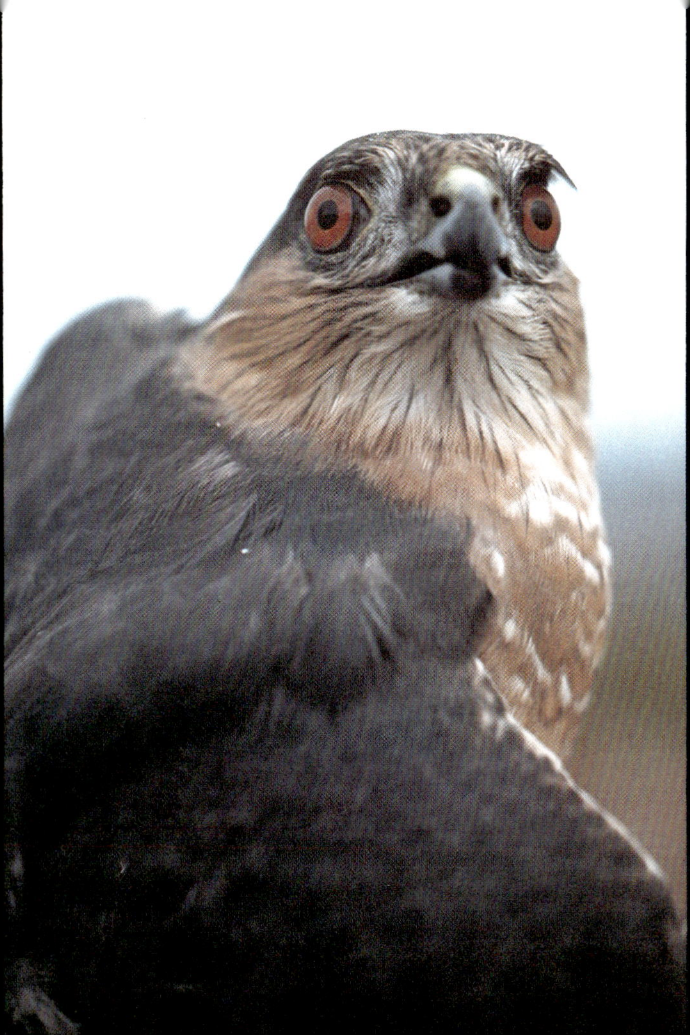

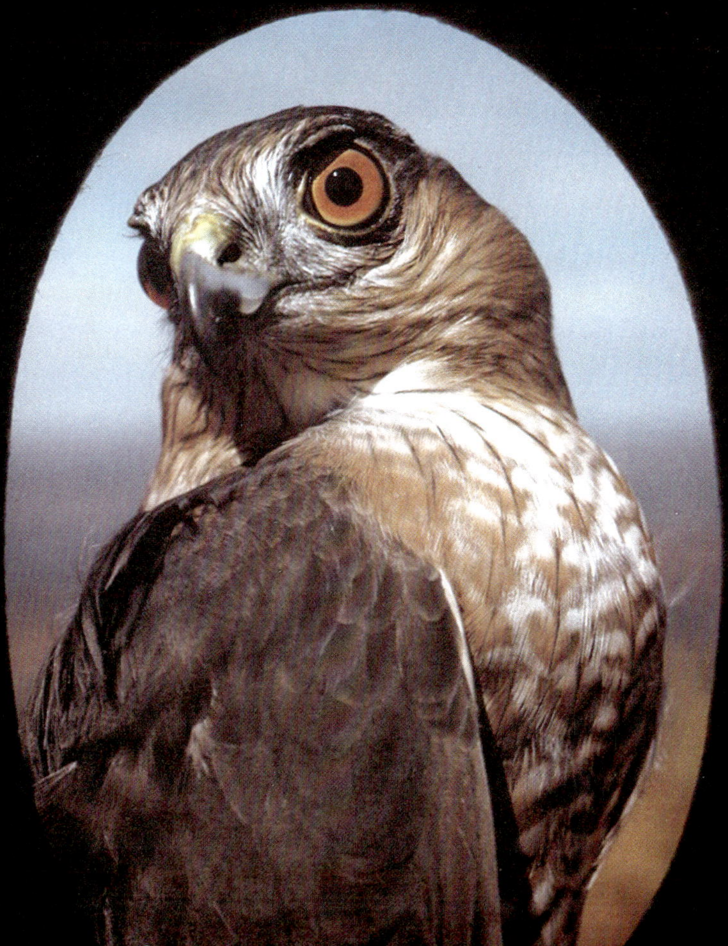

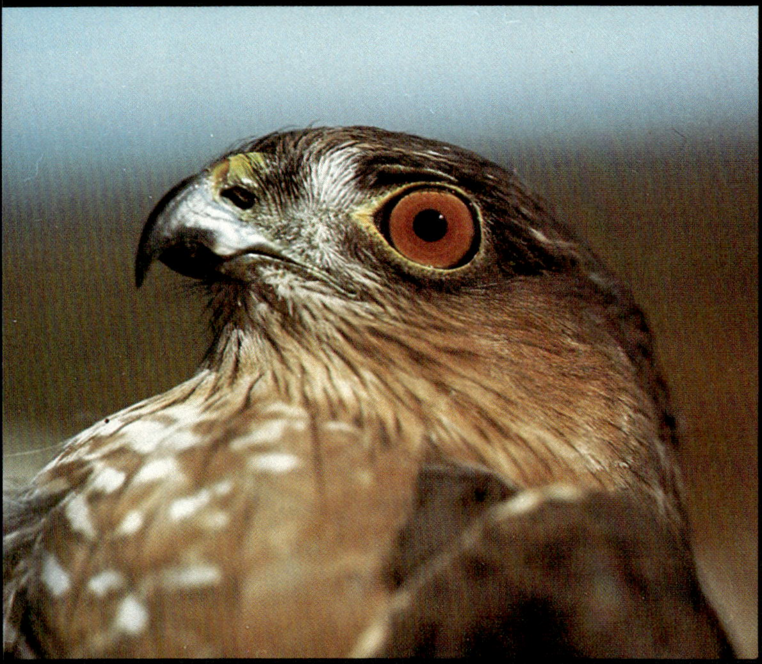
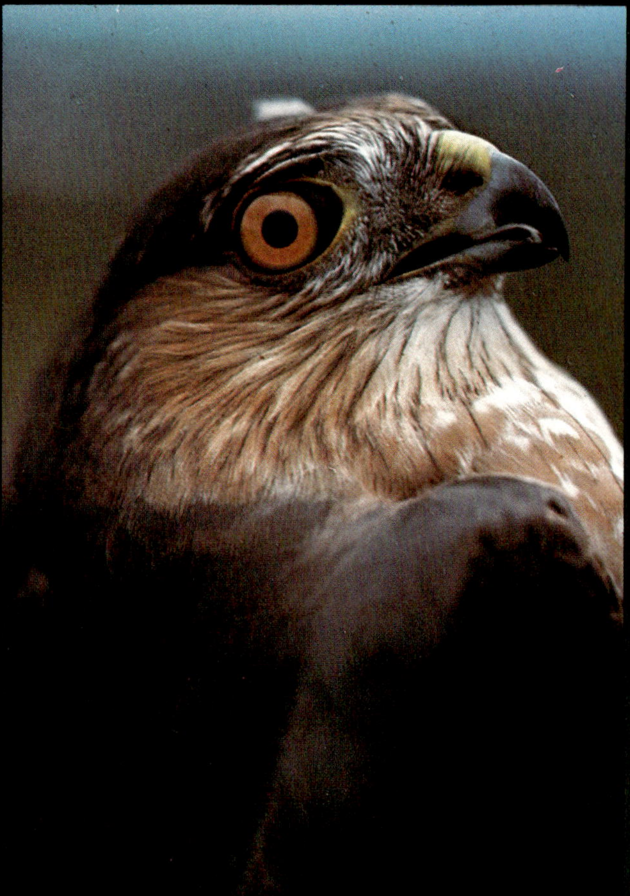
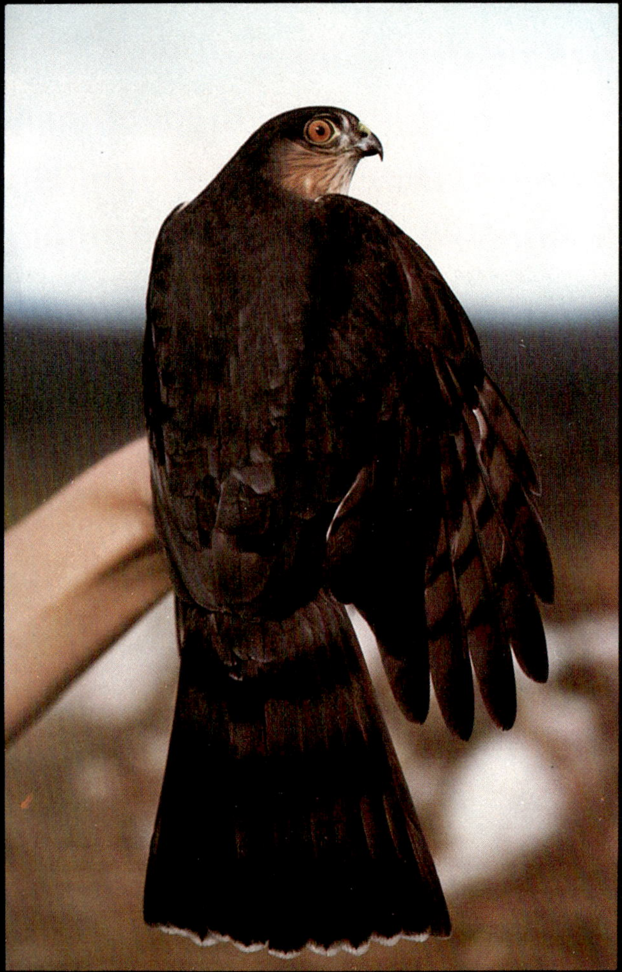
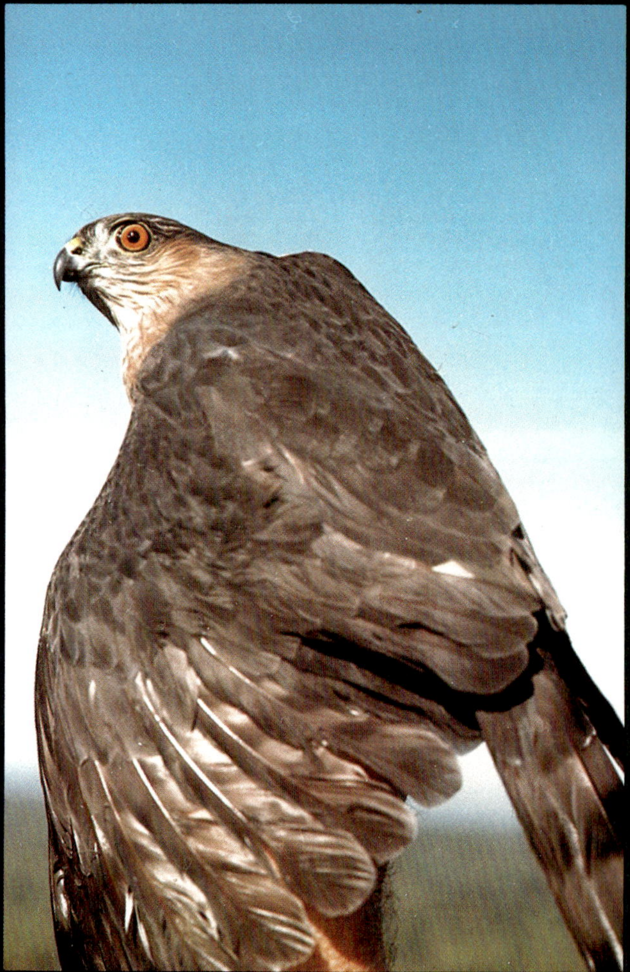

Nothern Goshawk

Accipiter gentilis

The Goshawk is a powerful raptor and the largest of the North American accipiters. It is 20 to 26 inches long with a wingspan of 3½ to 4 feet. The immature is brown above with brown streaking on its white underside, and closely resembles an immature Cooper's Hawk. The adult Goshawk is bluish-gray above, and its underside is white with a fine black herringbone pattern. All have a white streak above the eye.

Their prey consist largely of birds, from songbirds to ducks and grouse. They also capture numbers of mammals, ranging from mice and chipmunks to rabbits and woodchucks. Hunting from perches or on the wing, Goshawks are aggressive and persistent in pursuit of food and have been known to chase prey on foot.

The Goshawk is a norther bird. They are secretive by nature and prefer to live in dense wooded areas; hence, Goshawks are seldom observed.

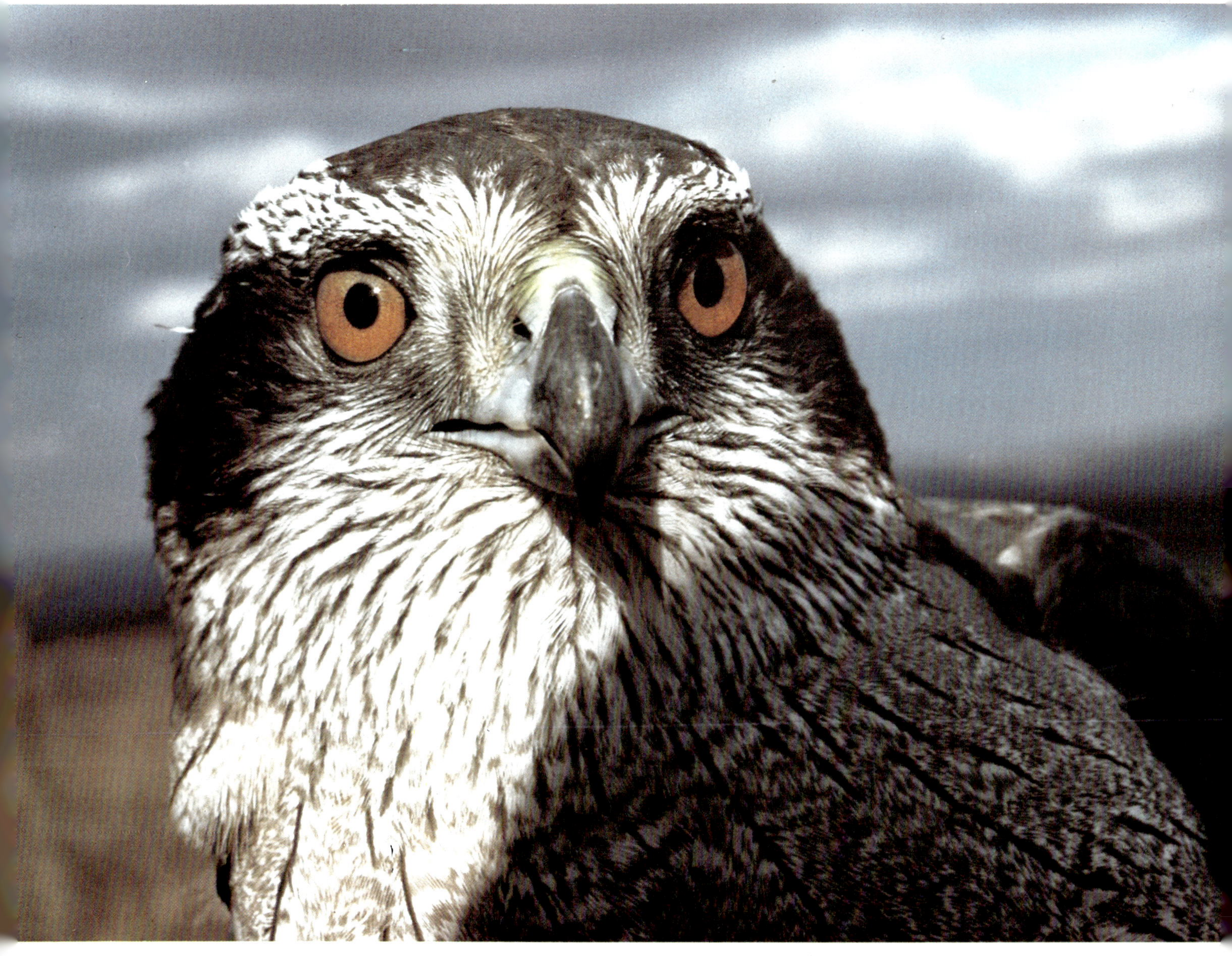

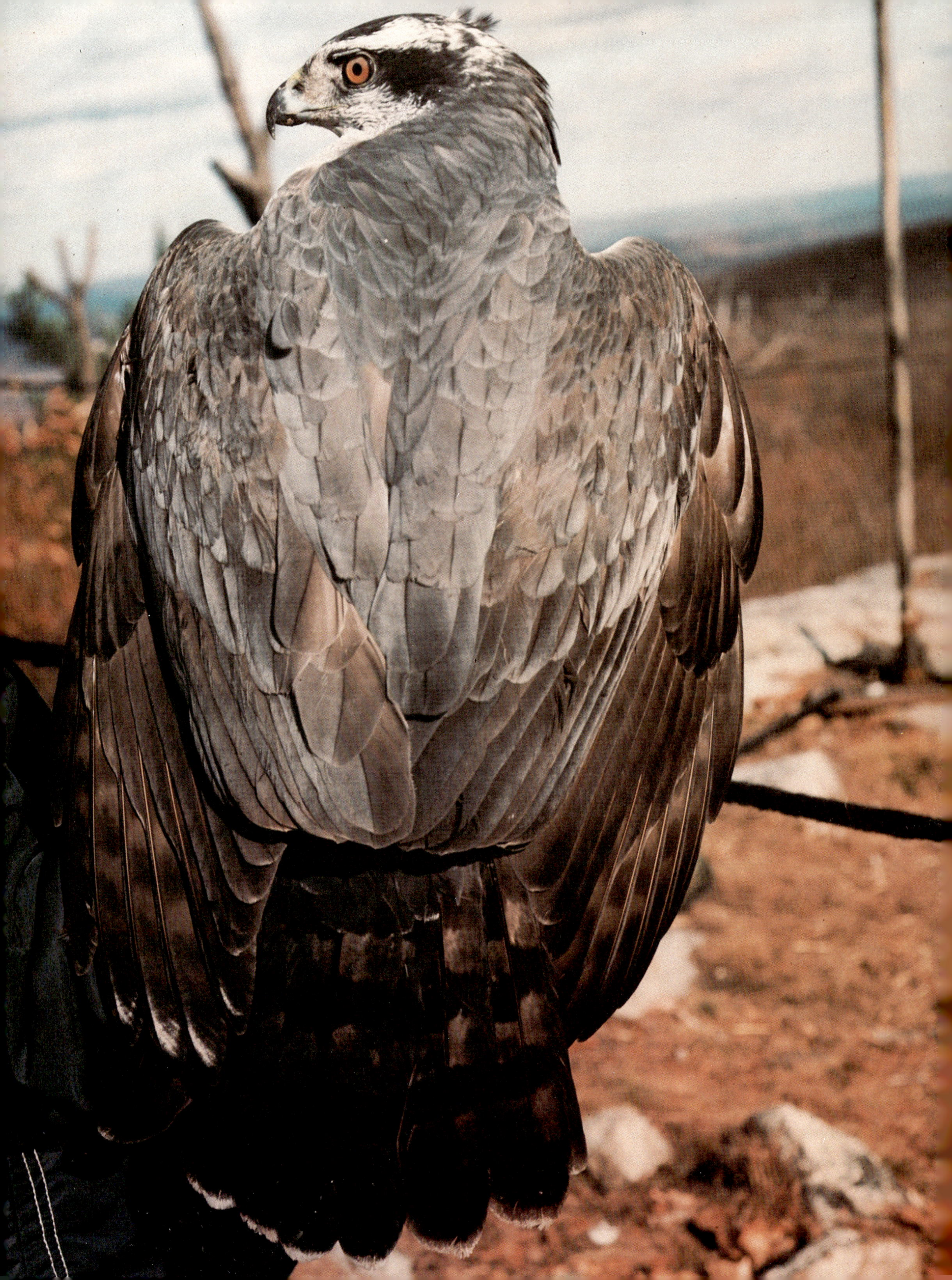

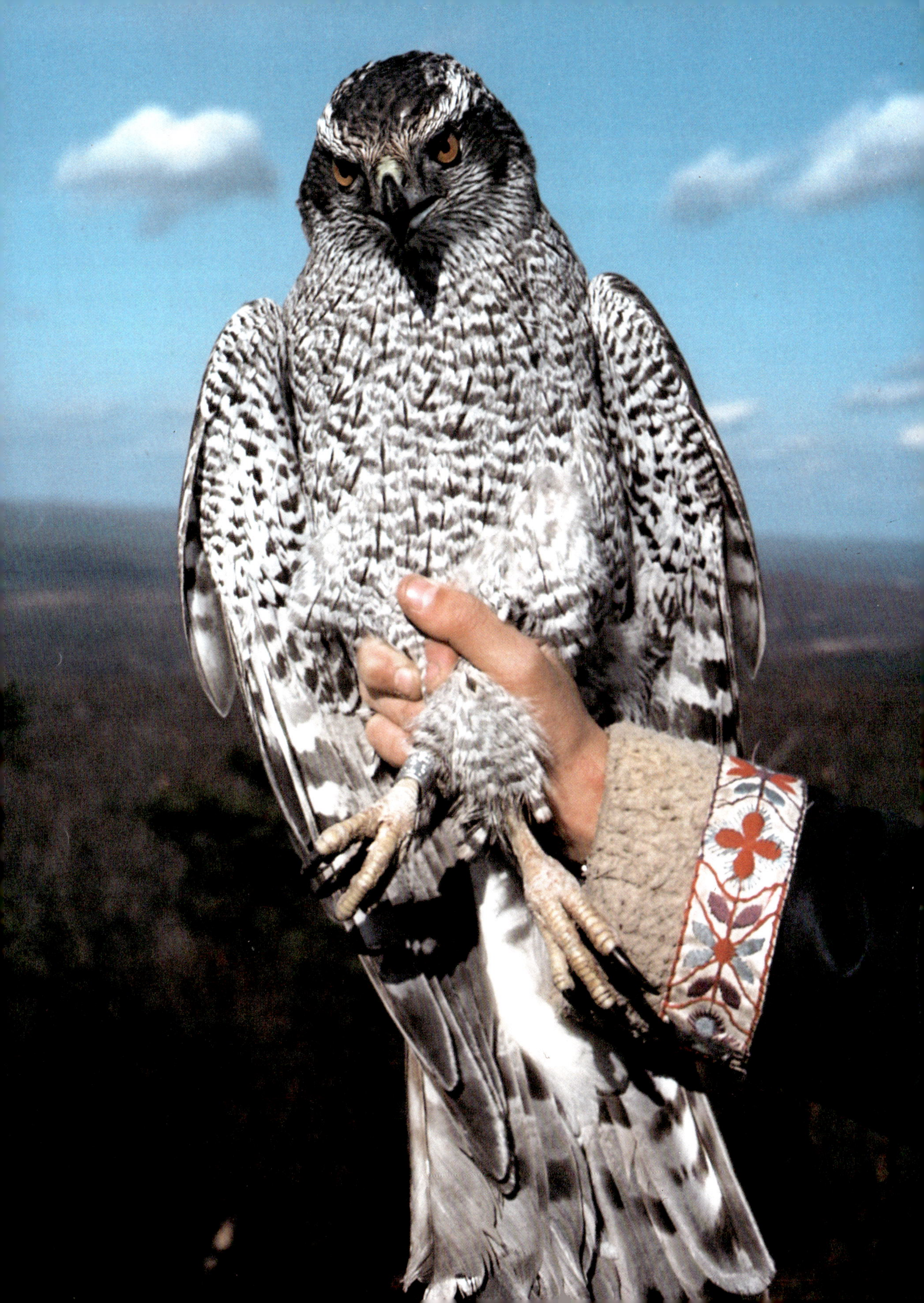

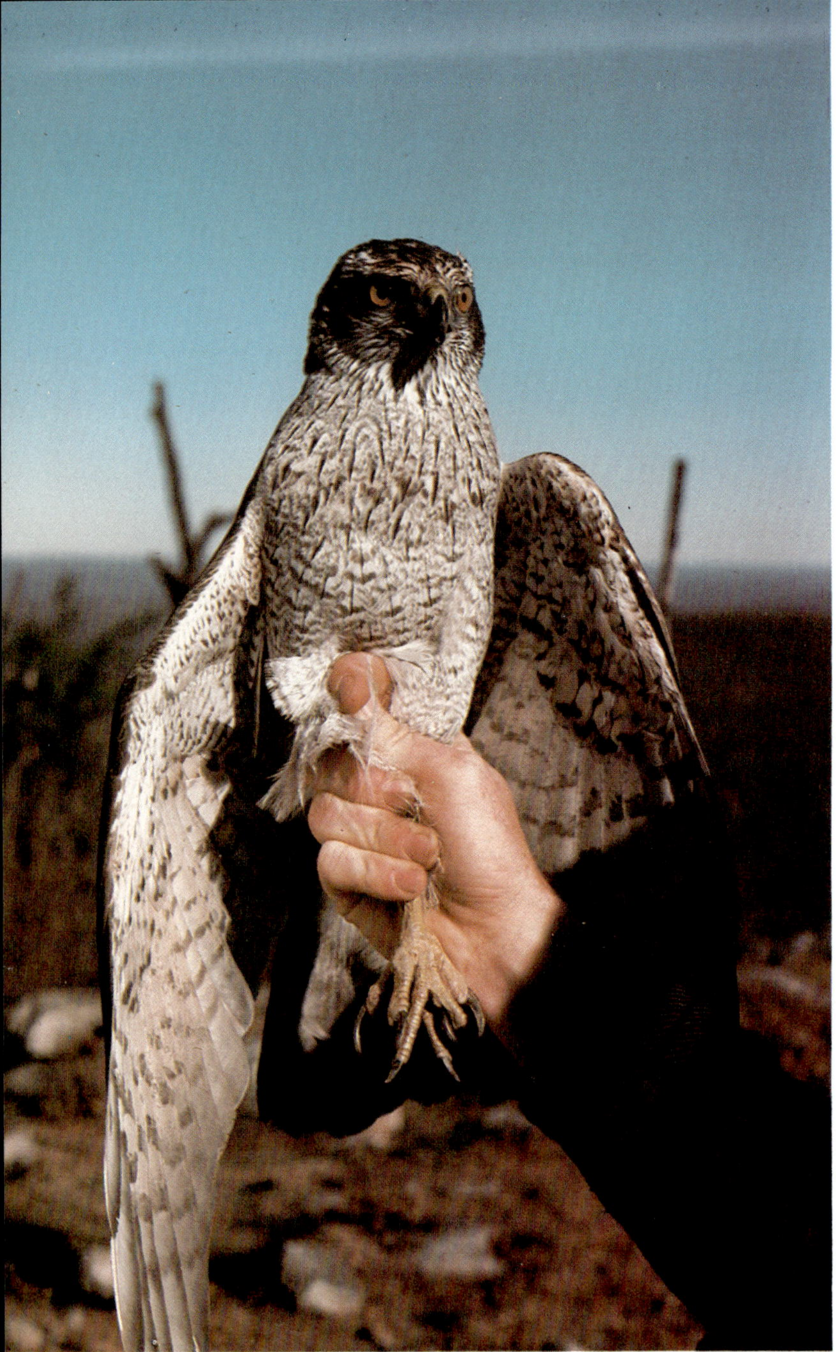

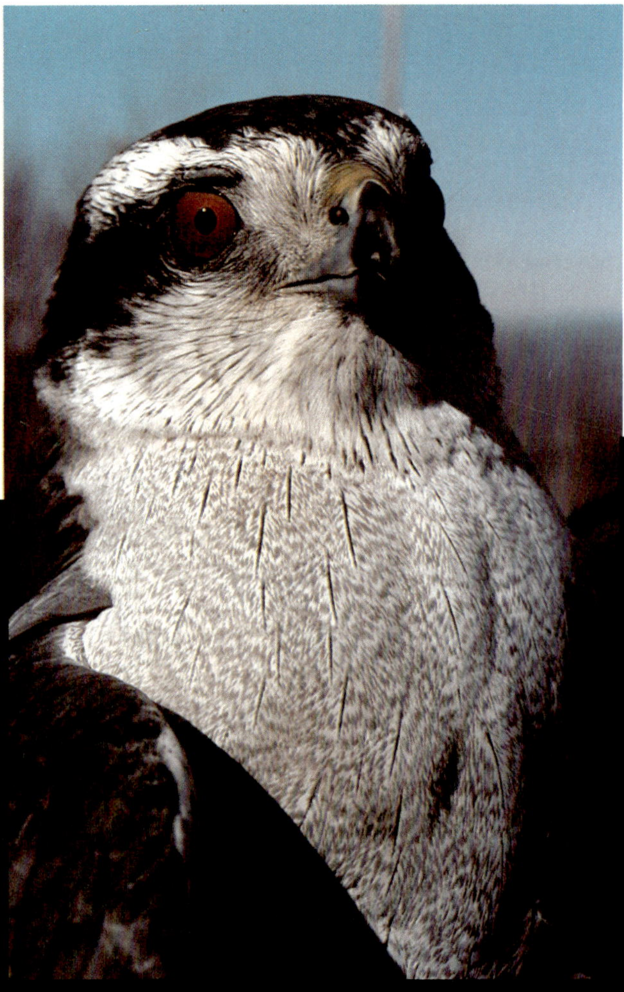

Red-Tailed Hawk

Buteo jamaicensis

The Red-tail is named for the rufous color of the adult's tail. These buteos are often seen soaring in wide circles or perched conspicuously in trees along roadsides. Vocal hawks, their distinctive call — a high, shrill "kree-e-e" — is usually uttered in flight.

Red-tails stand about 2 feet tall and have wingspans of 4½ to 5 feet. They are dark brown above, white to cinnamon below, and usually have a band of dark streaks across the belly. Immature birds are similar to adults in plumage except for their tails — the young have brown tails for their first year. When they molt, these brown feathers are replaced by the characteristic red of the species.

Red-tailed Hawks are found throughout North America. They prefer a habitat of fields and pastures mixed with open woodlands. Their large stick nests are usually built in the tallest available tree. From one to three young are raised each year.

Their diet consists mainly of mammals and includes mice, voles, squirrels and rabbits.

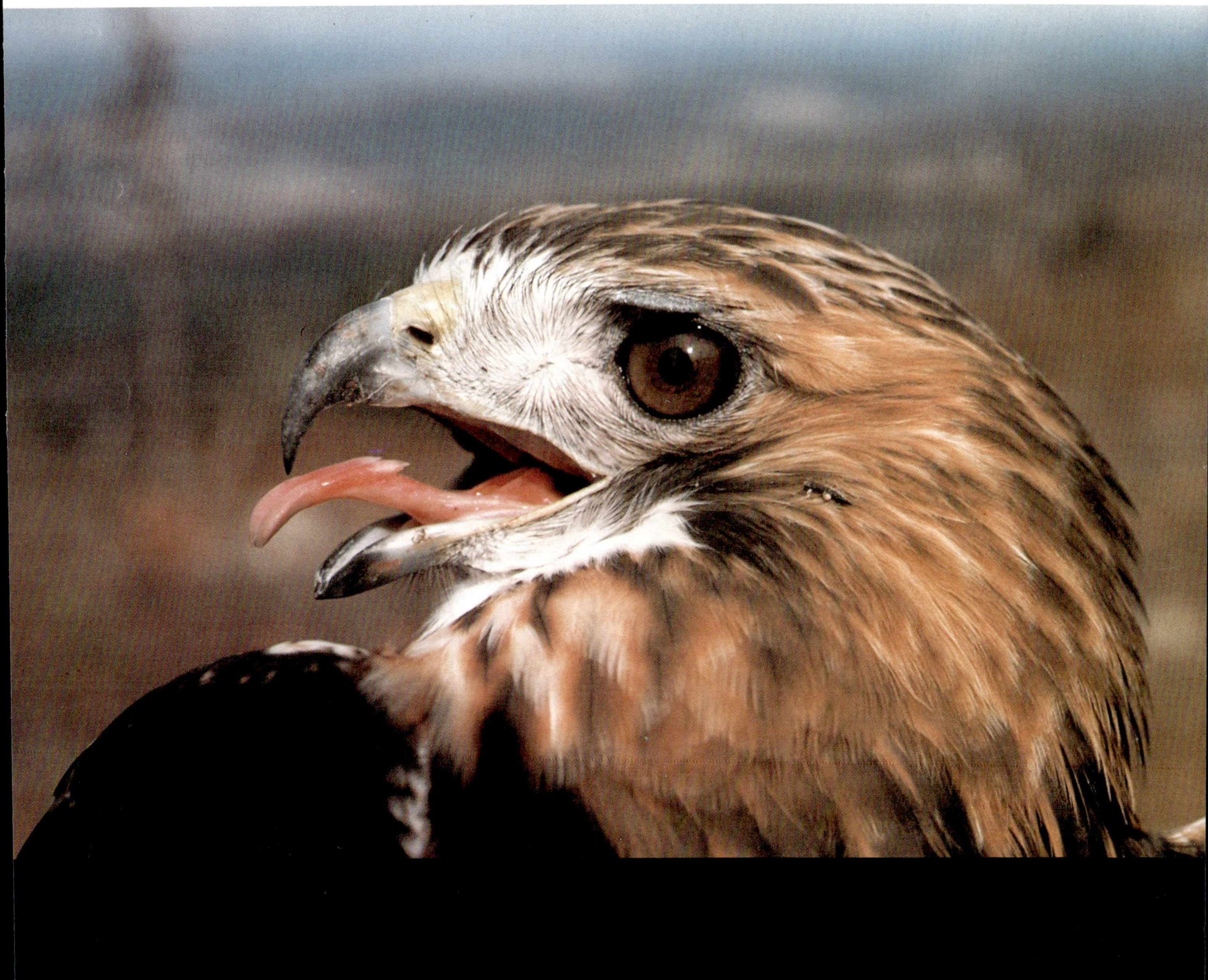

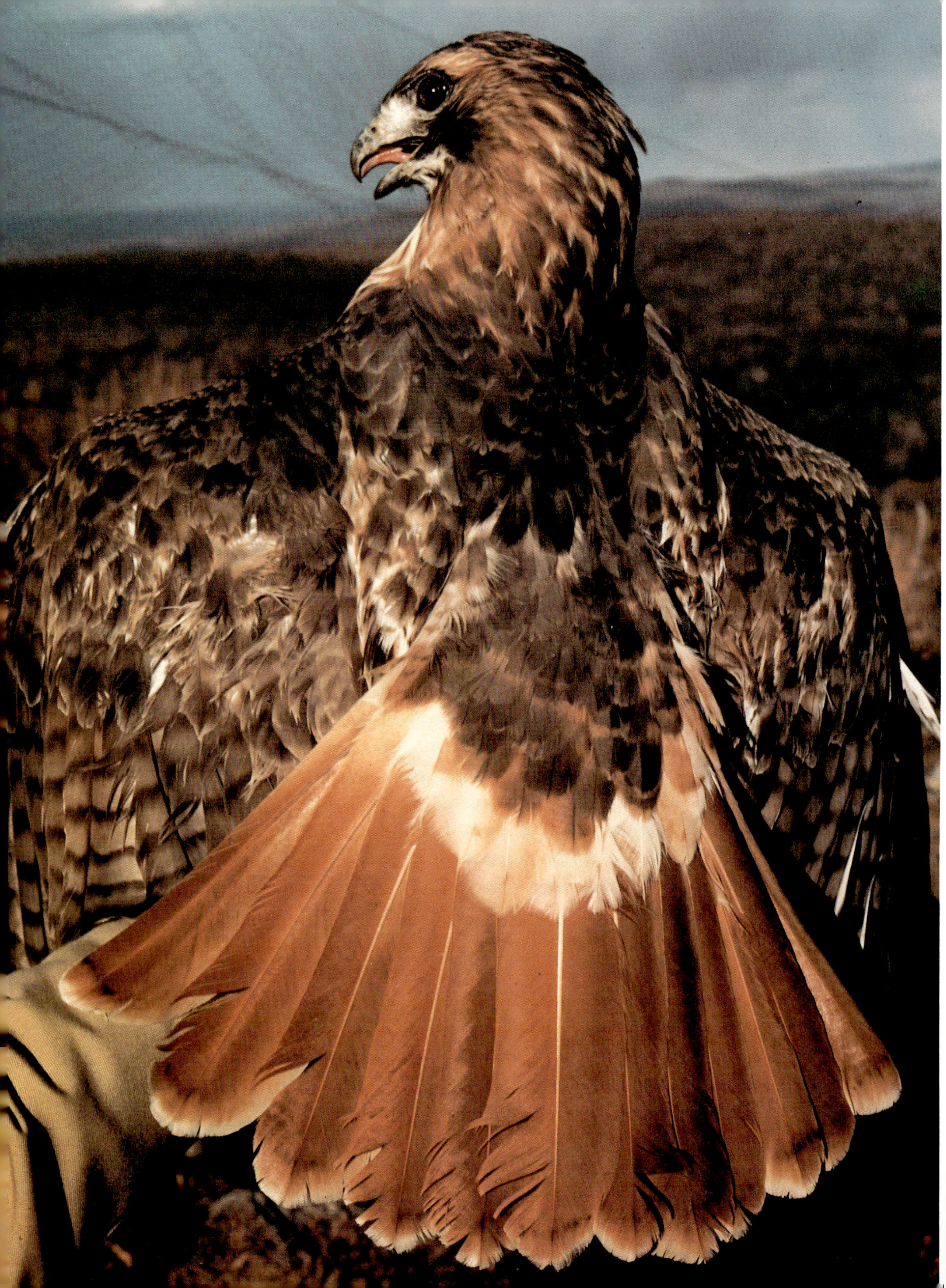

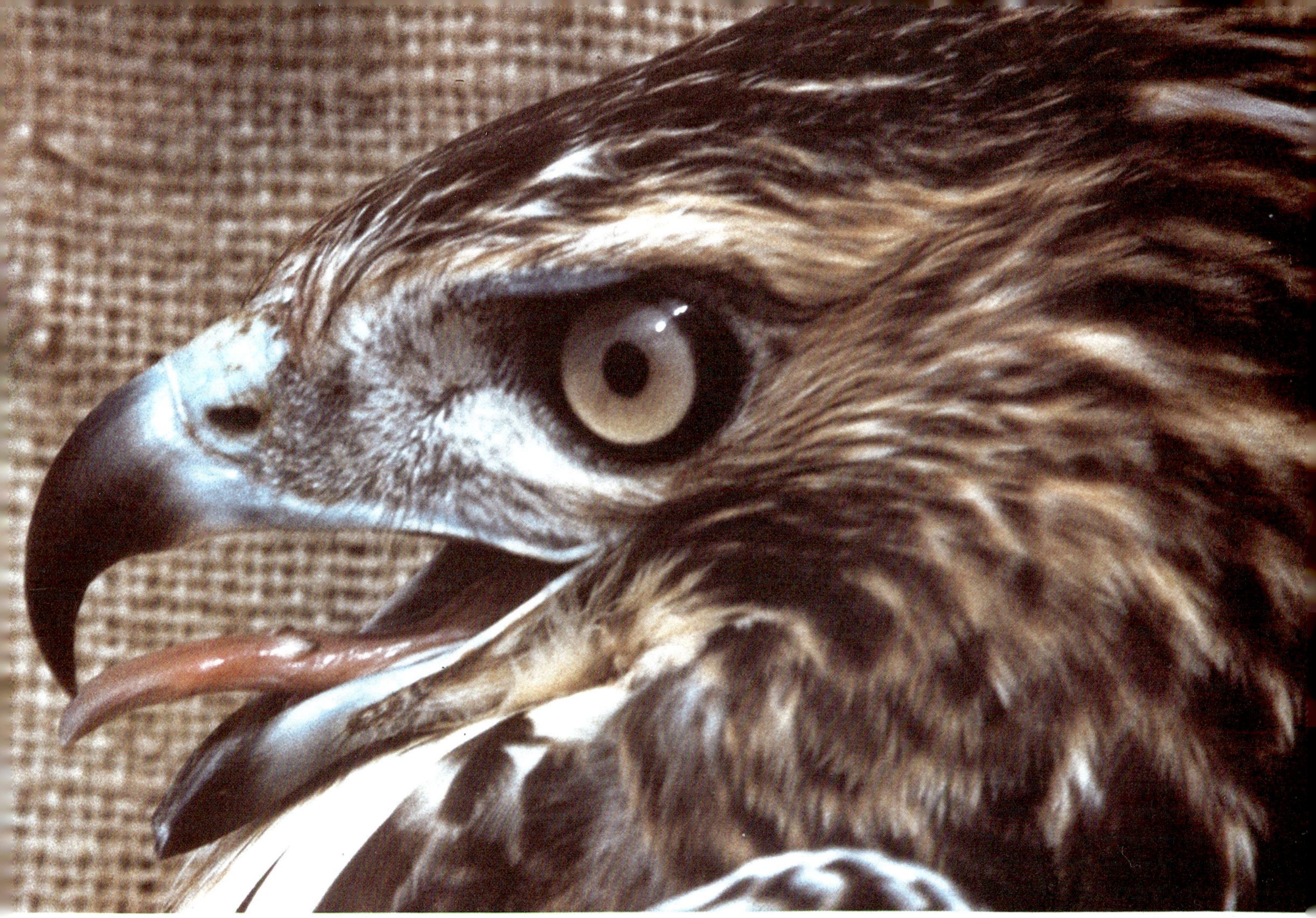
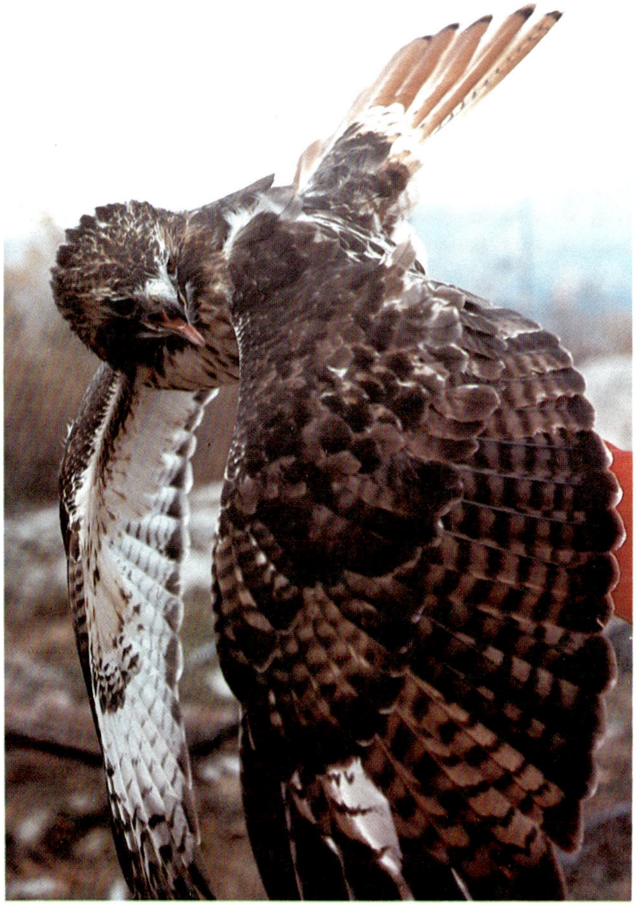
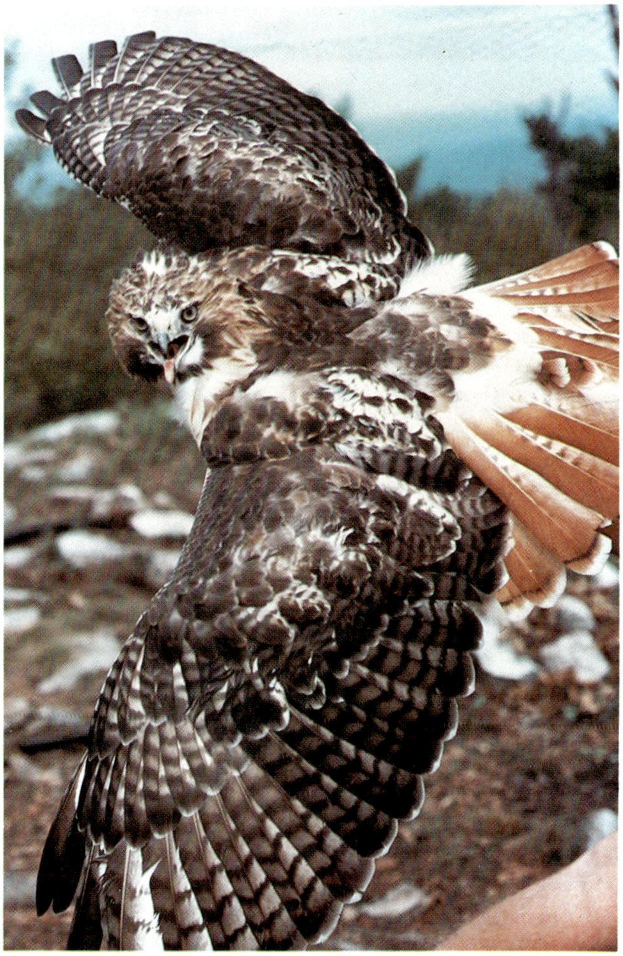

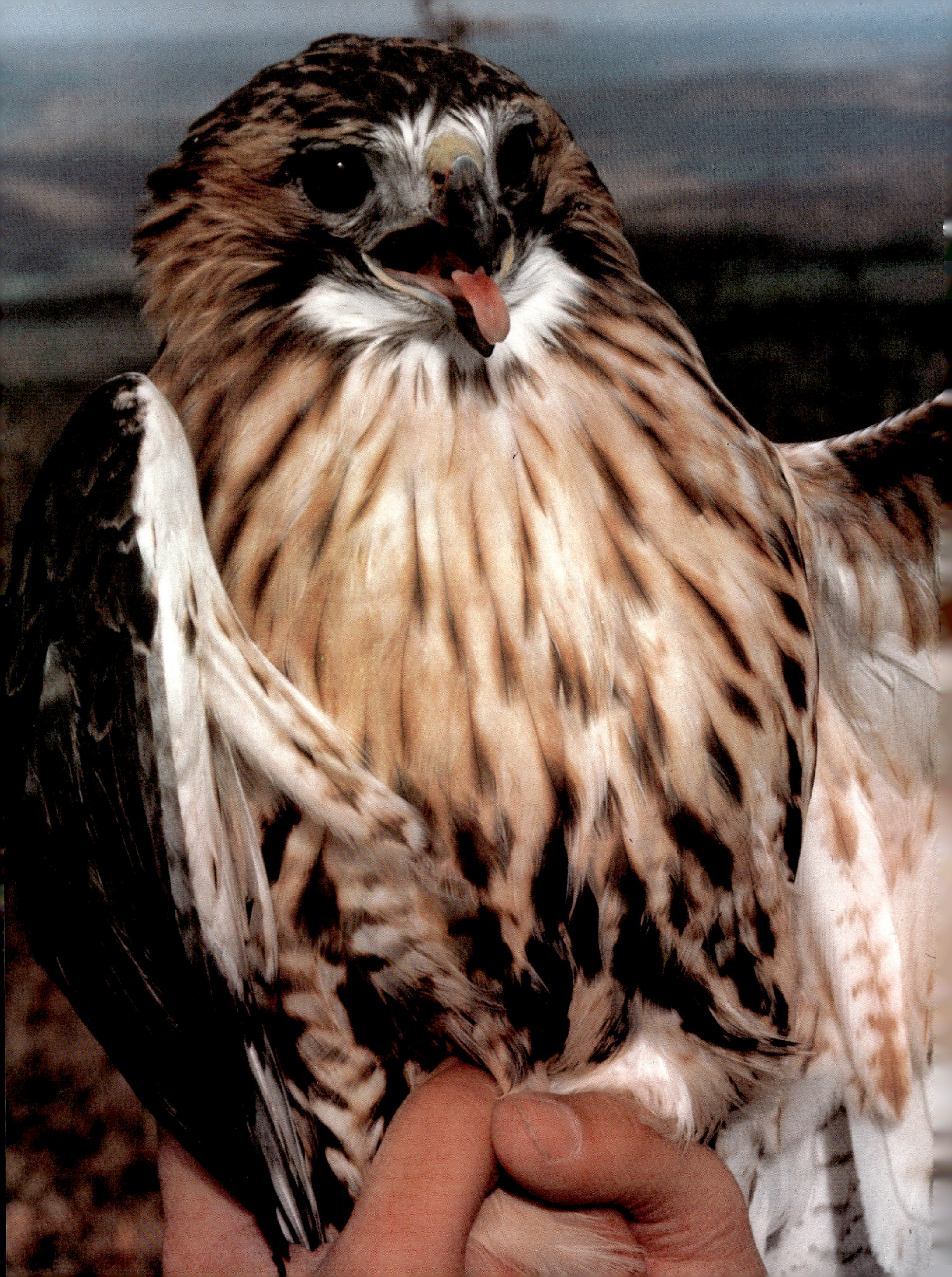

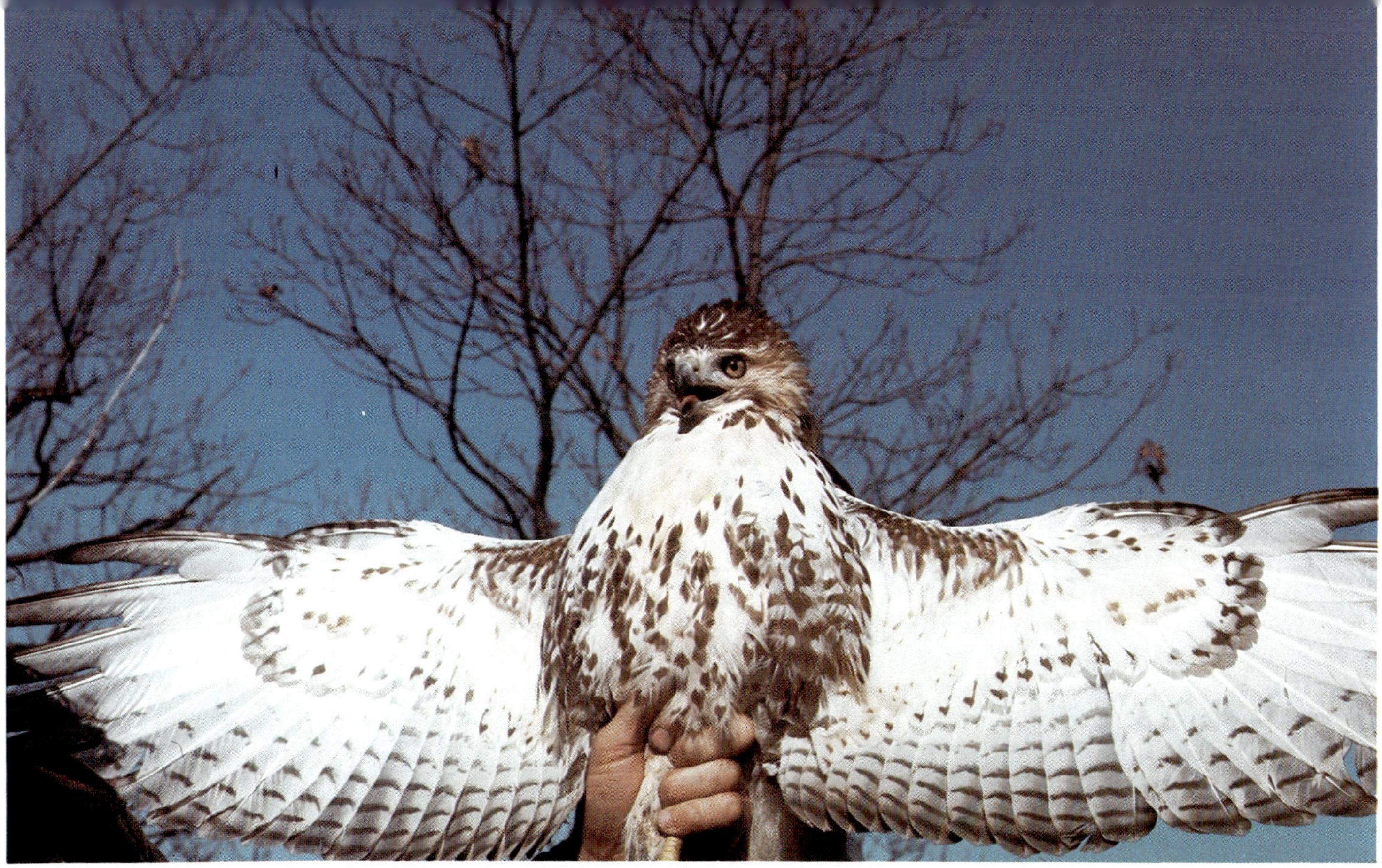

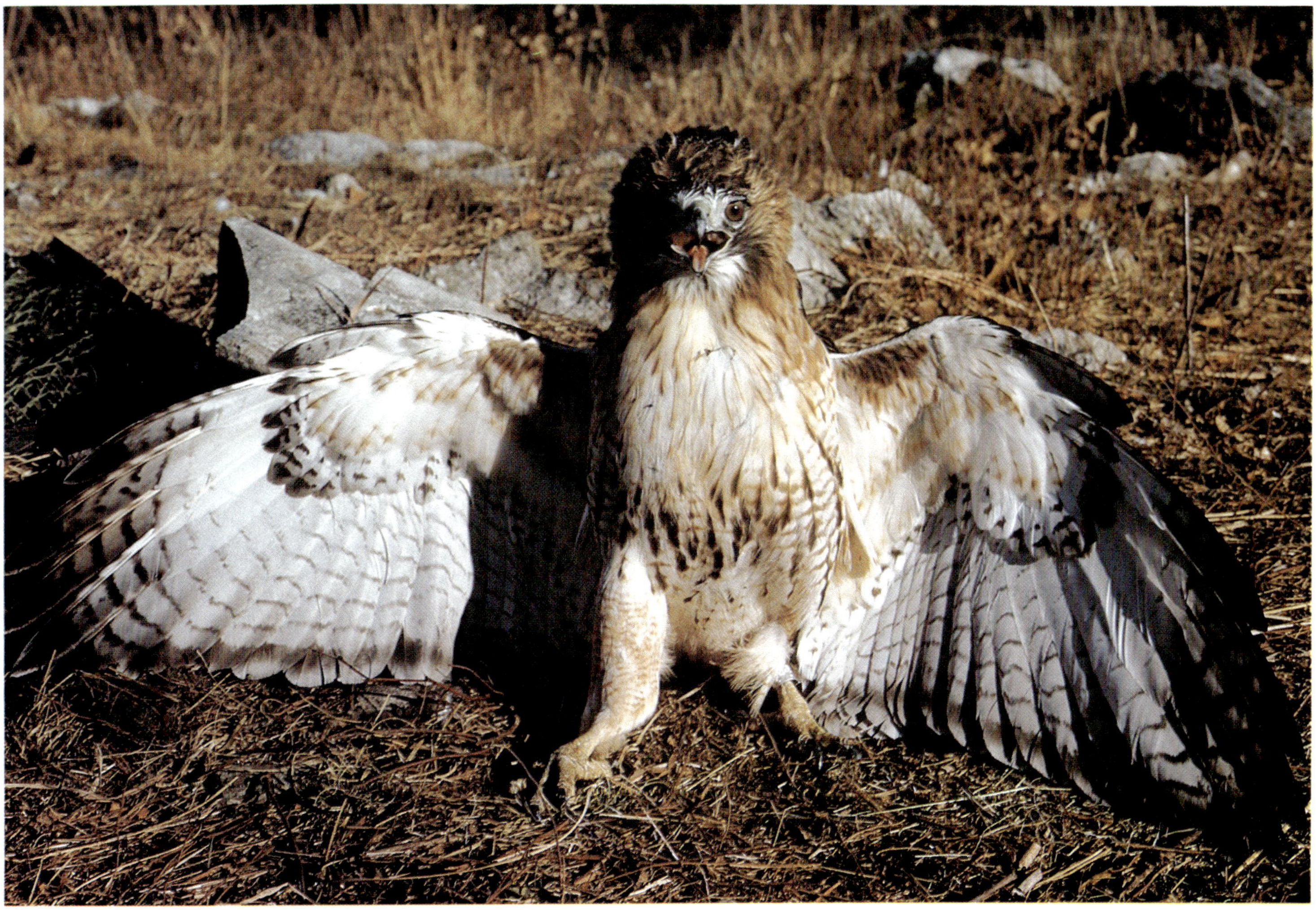

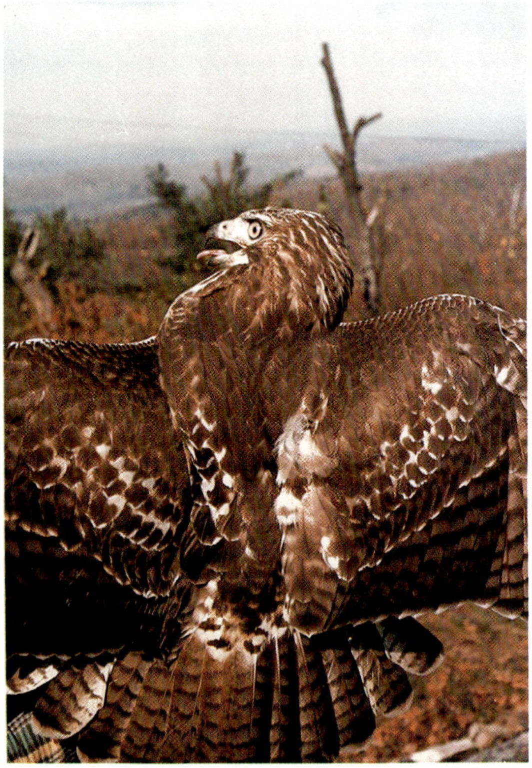
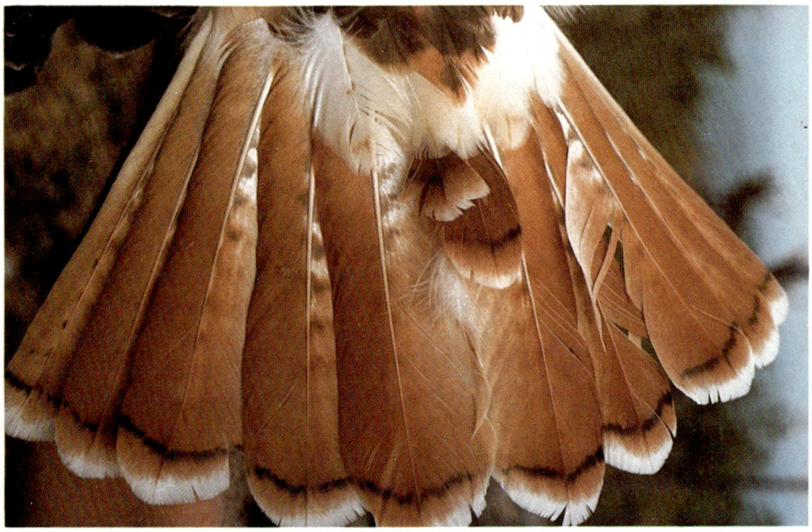
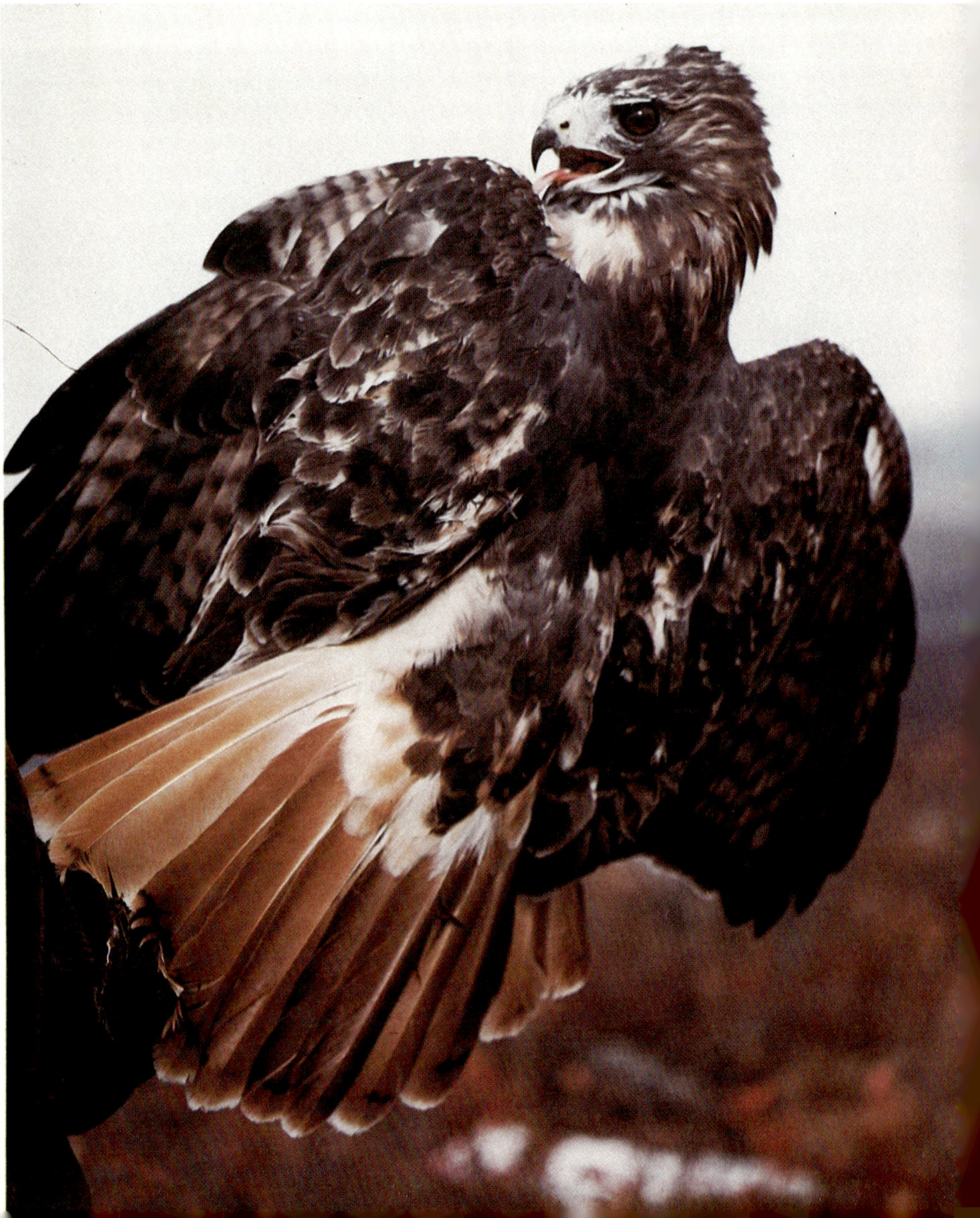

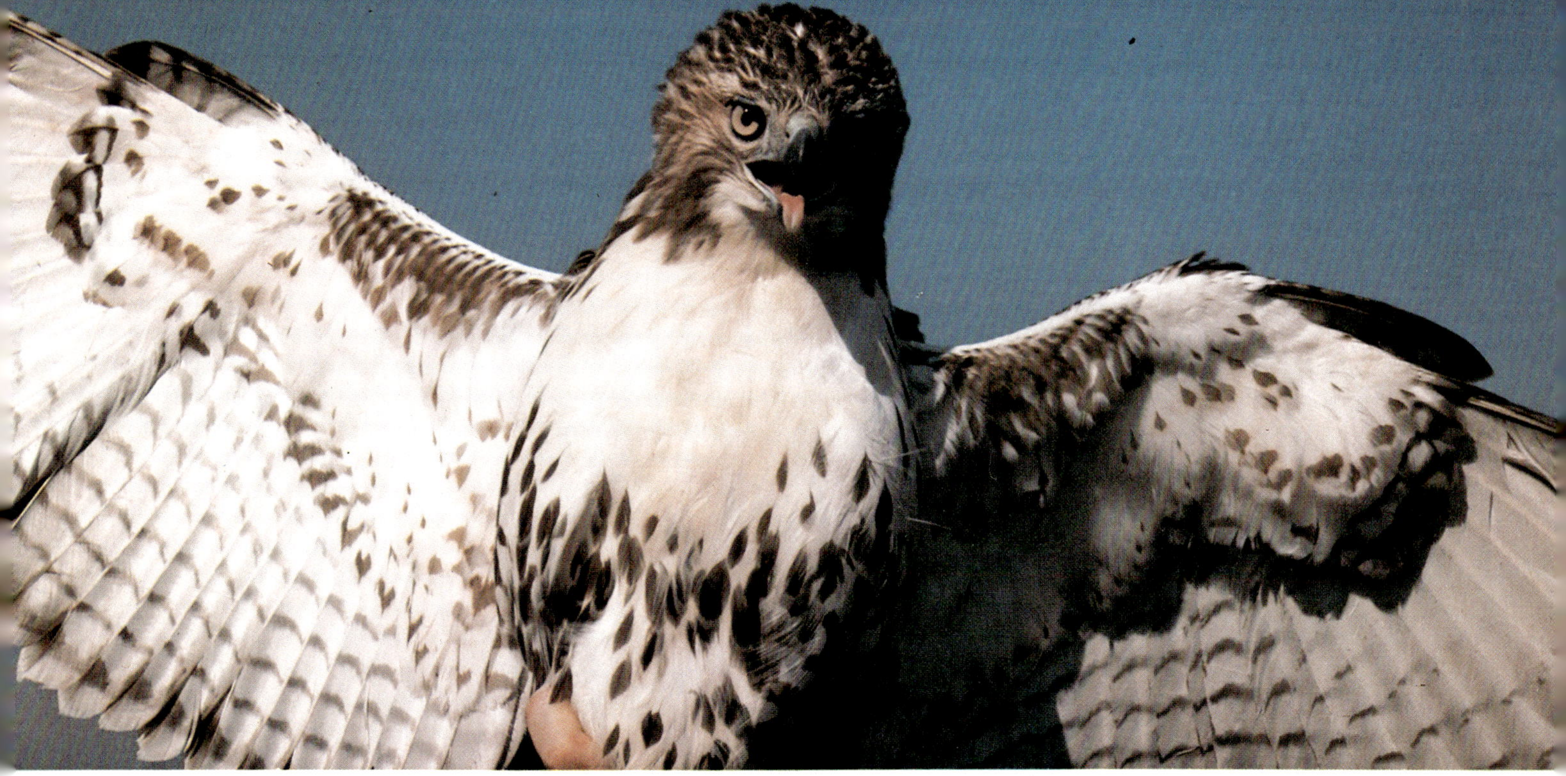

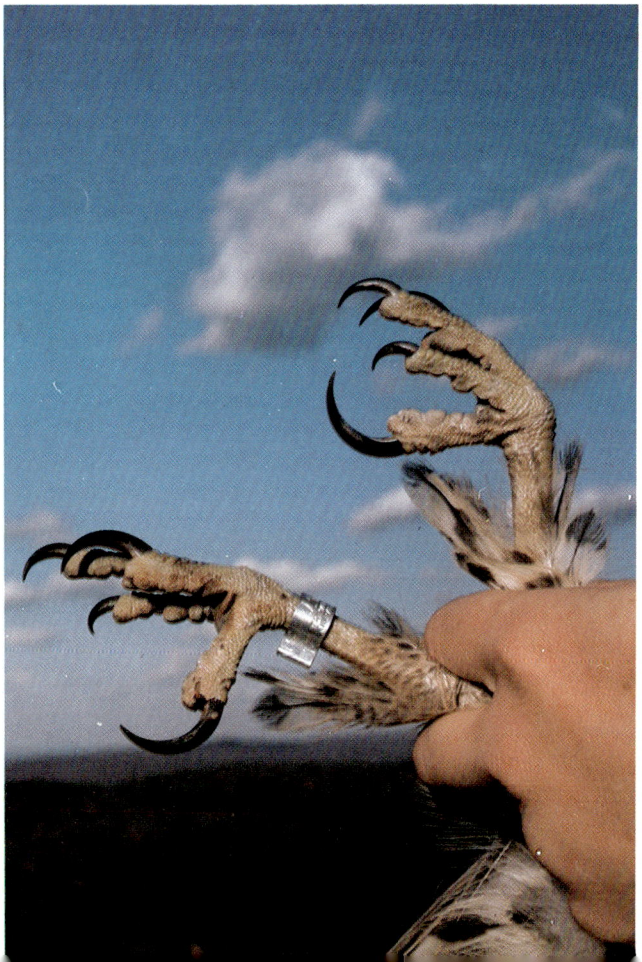

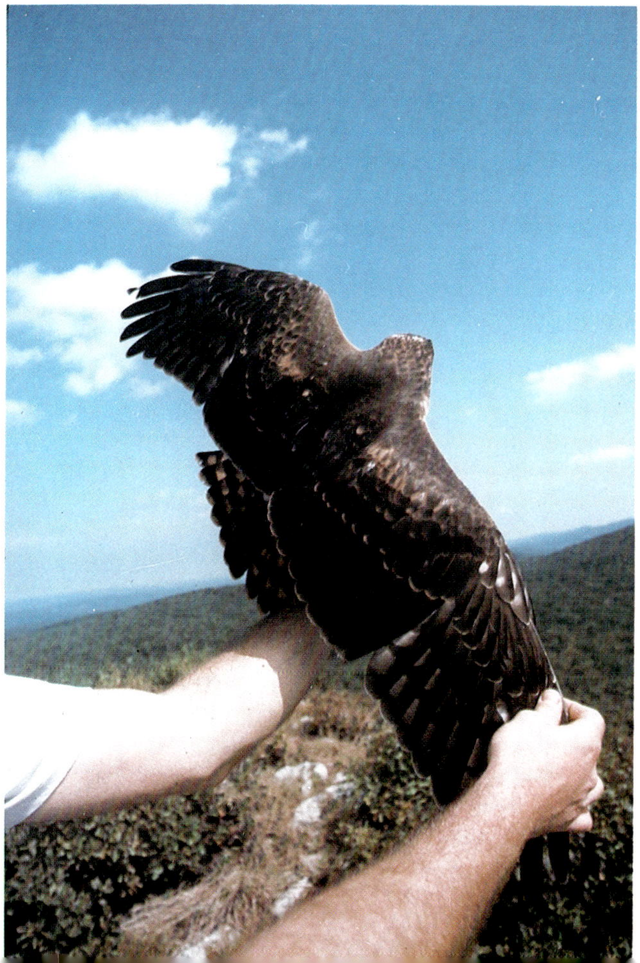

Bald Eagle

Haliaeetus leucocephalus

Our national emblem, the Bald Eagle is familiar to nearly everyone. The adult bird, with its snowy white head and tail and contrasting dark brown body, is unmistakable. The term "Bald" as used here means white, rather than featherless; and its scientific name *leucocephalus* means "white head." The immature Bald Eagle, however, lacks the distinctive white markings of the adult. The young bird is an overall brown color for several years before its head and tail become pure white; for this reason it can be mistaken for a Golden Eagle.

A large bird, measuring approximately three feet high with a wingspan of up to 7½ feet, this eagle is an efficient hunter and also a scavenger. It feeds primarily on fish and waterfowl which it catches alive, but will readily eat carrion when available.

Although a well-known symbol, the Bald Eagle is rarely seen. Its population across North America has drastically declined in the past forty years, due primarily to loss of habitat and DDT poisoning.

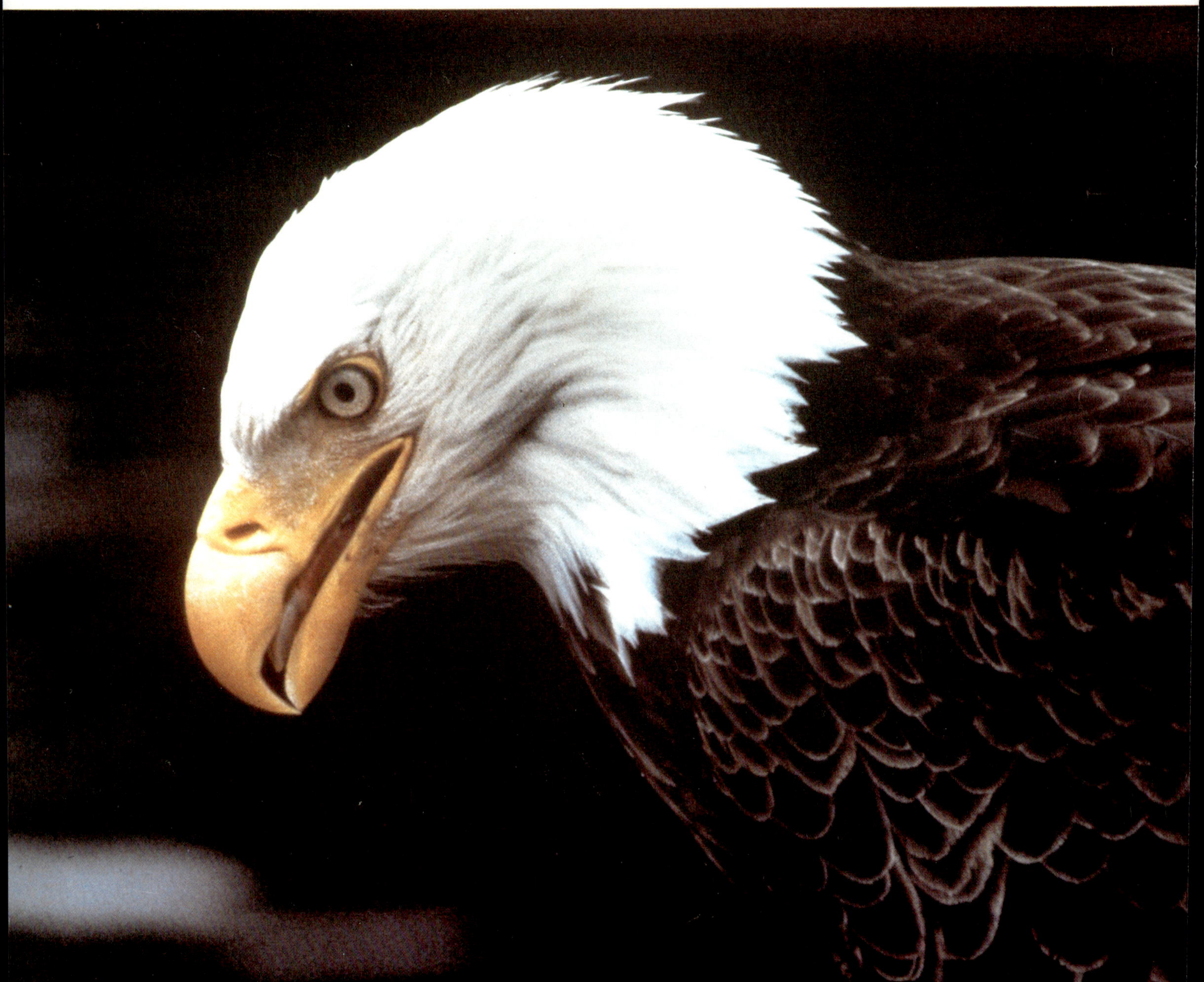

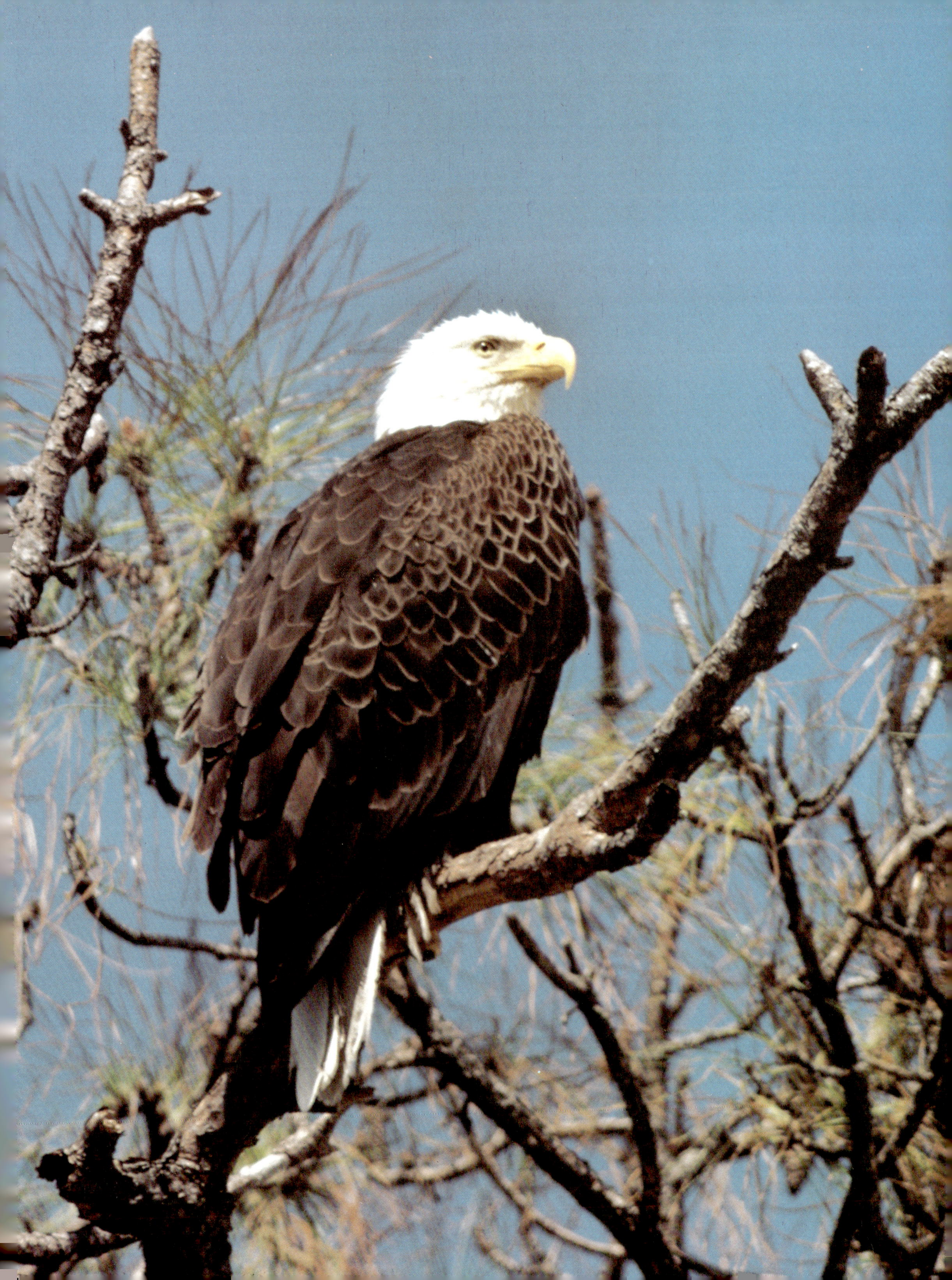

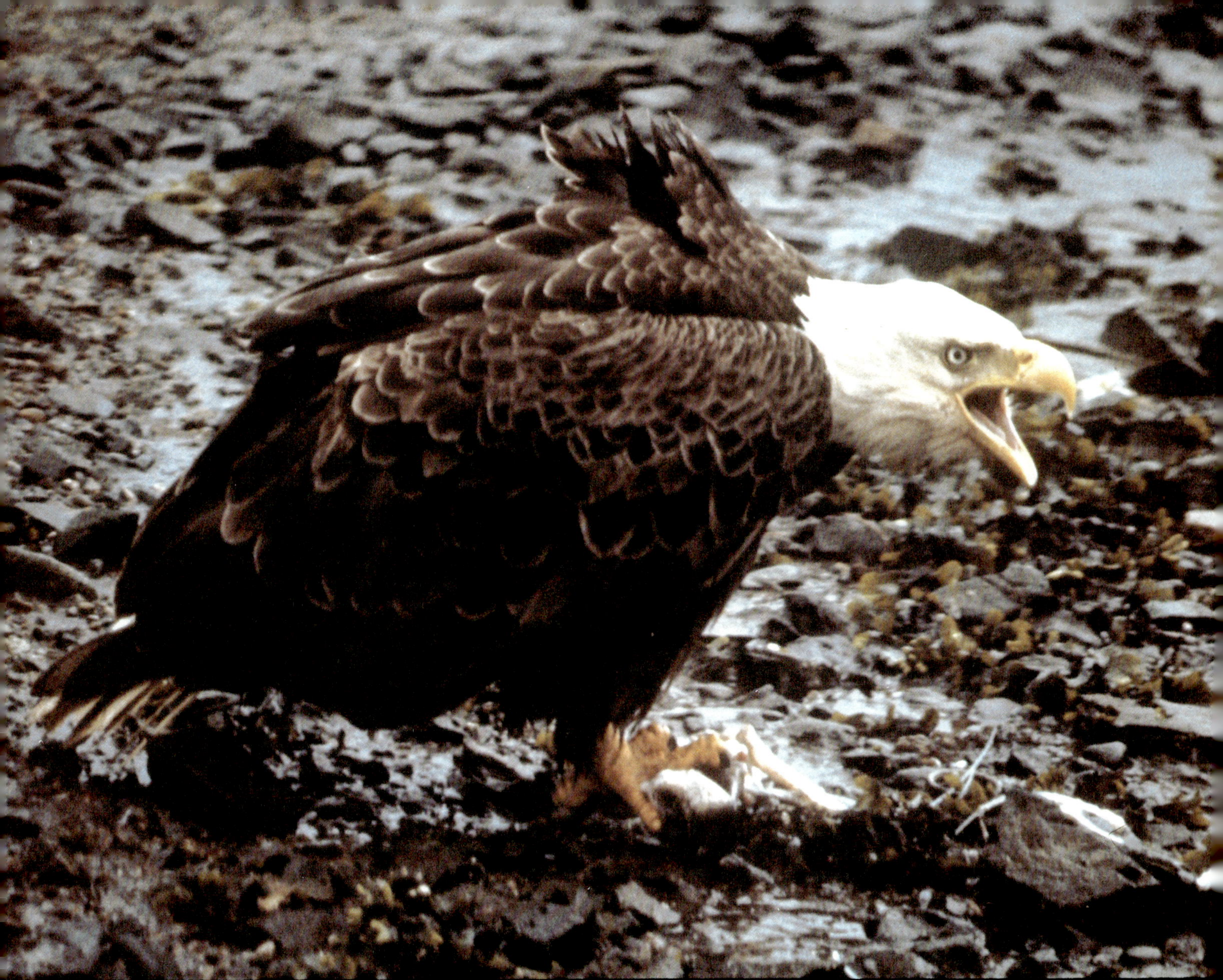
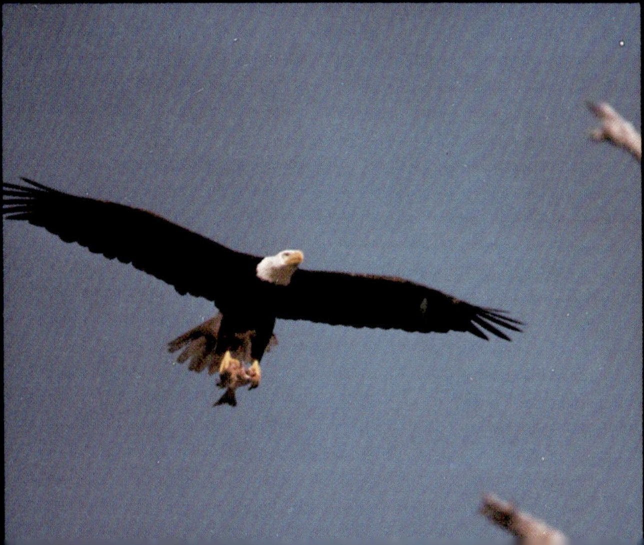
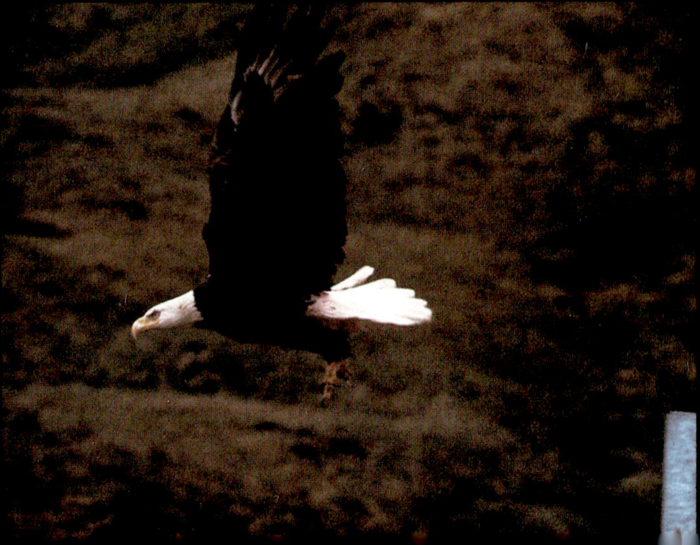

Golden Eagle

Aquila chrysaetos

The Golden eagle is a huge bird weighing up to thirteen pounds, measuring approximately three feet in length, with a wingspan of 6½ to 7½ feet. The entire bird appears dark brown in color, but at closer view a gold wash of feathers on the back of its neck and head can be seen—hence the common name. Young birds can be distinguished from adults by their white-based tail feathers and white patches in their wings.

Golden Eagles range across the entire Northern Hemisphere and in North America they are most common in the west. Their large stick nests are usually constructed on high, inaccessible cliff ledges in remote mountainous areas. The same nest site, or eyrie, may be used year after year.

These large and powerful birds hunt while flying, dropping suddenly on prey which they have surprised in the open. Their diet is varied, but consists mainly of rabbits and other small mammals.

Although primarily a western species, some Golden Eagles do breed in eastern Canada, northern New England, and a few in New York state.

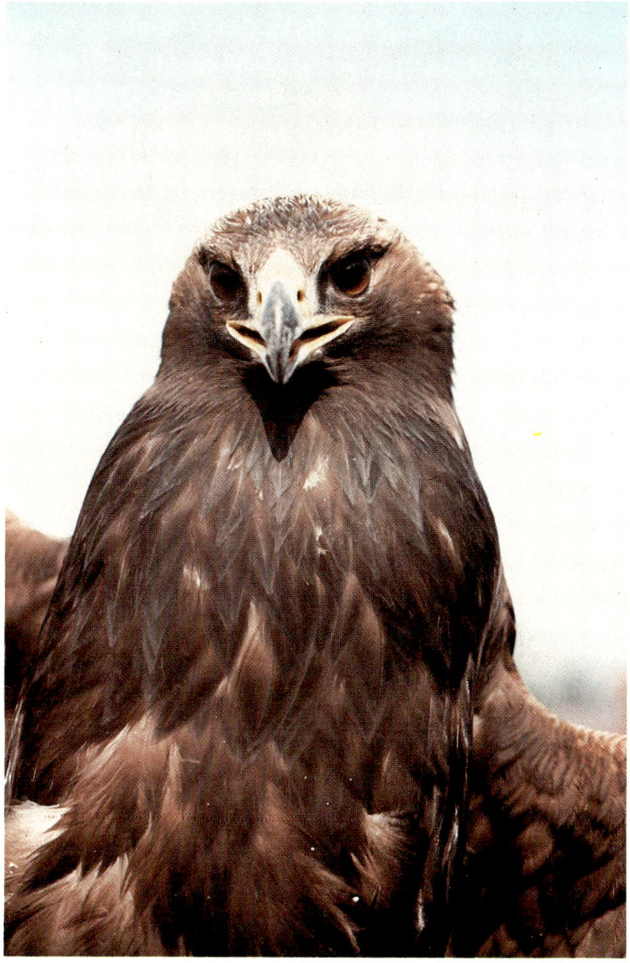

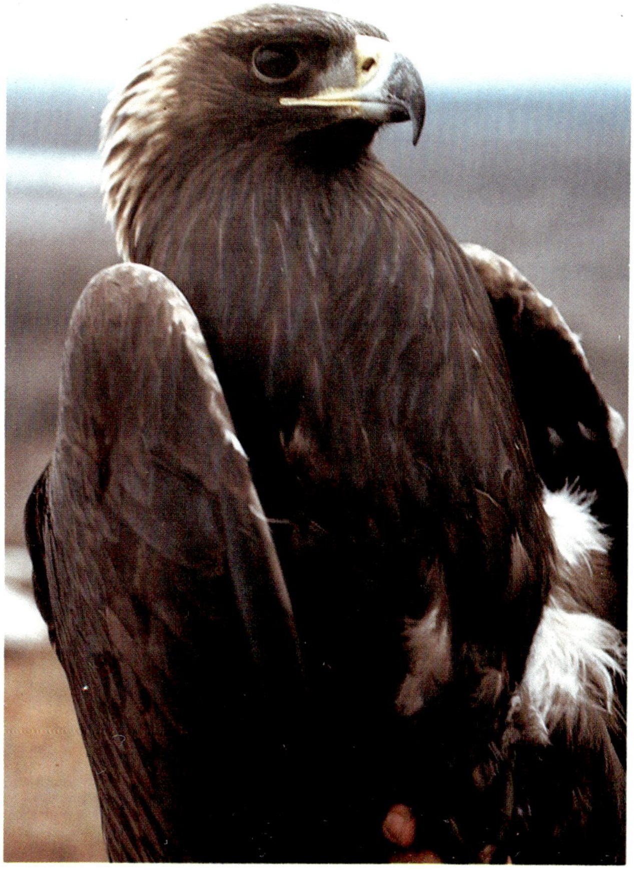

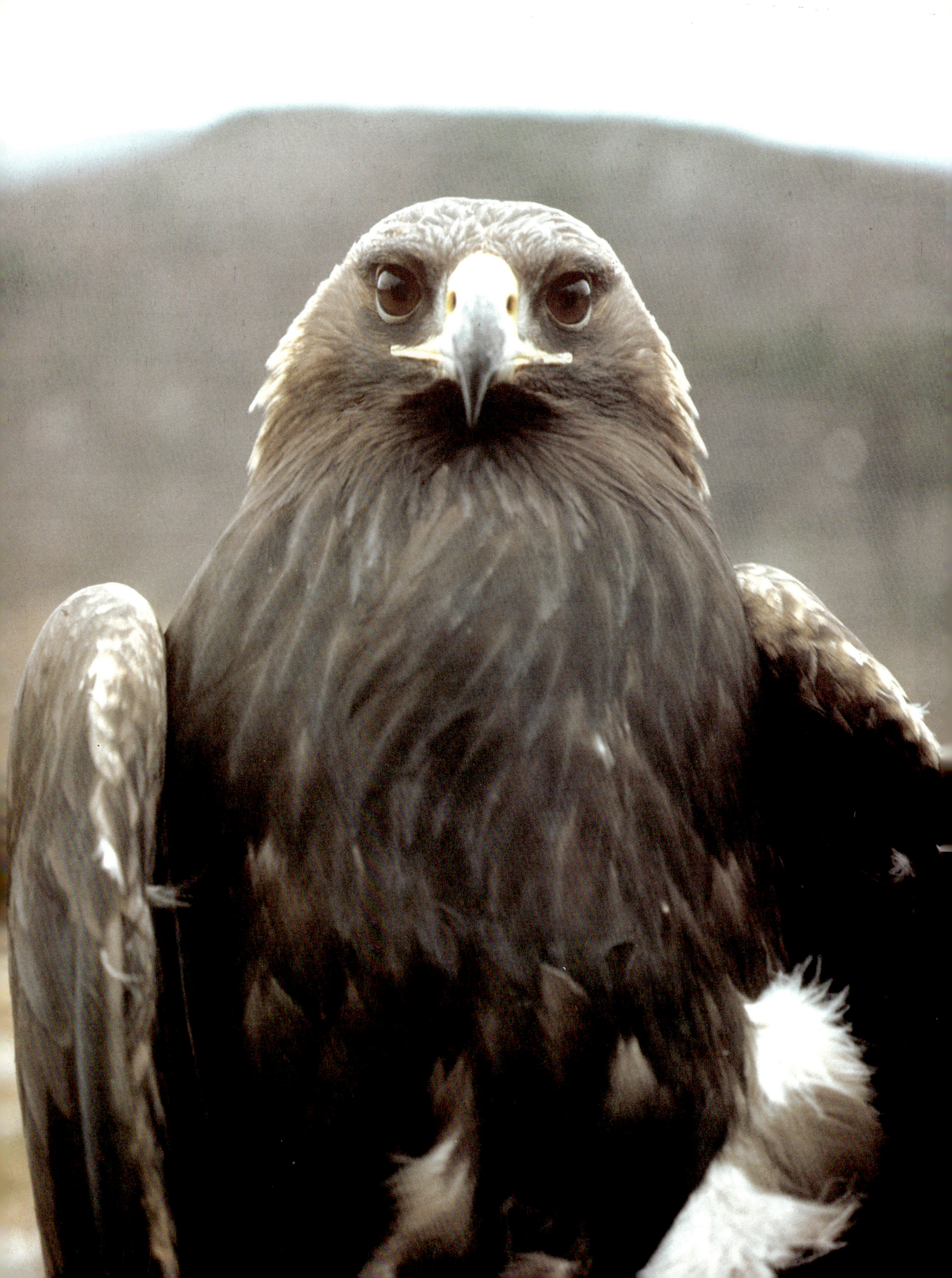

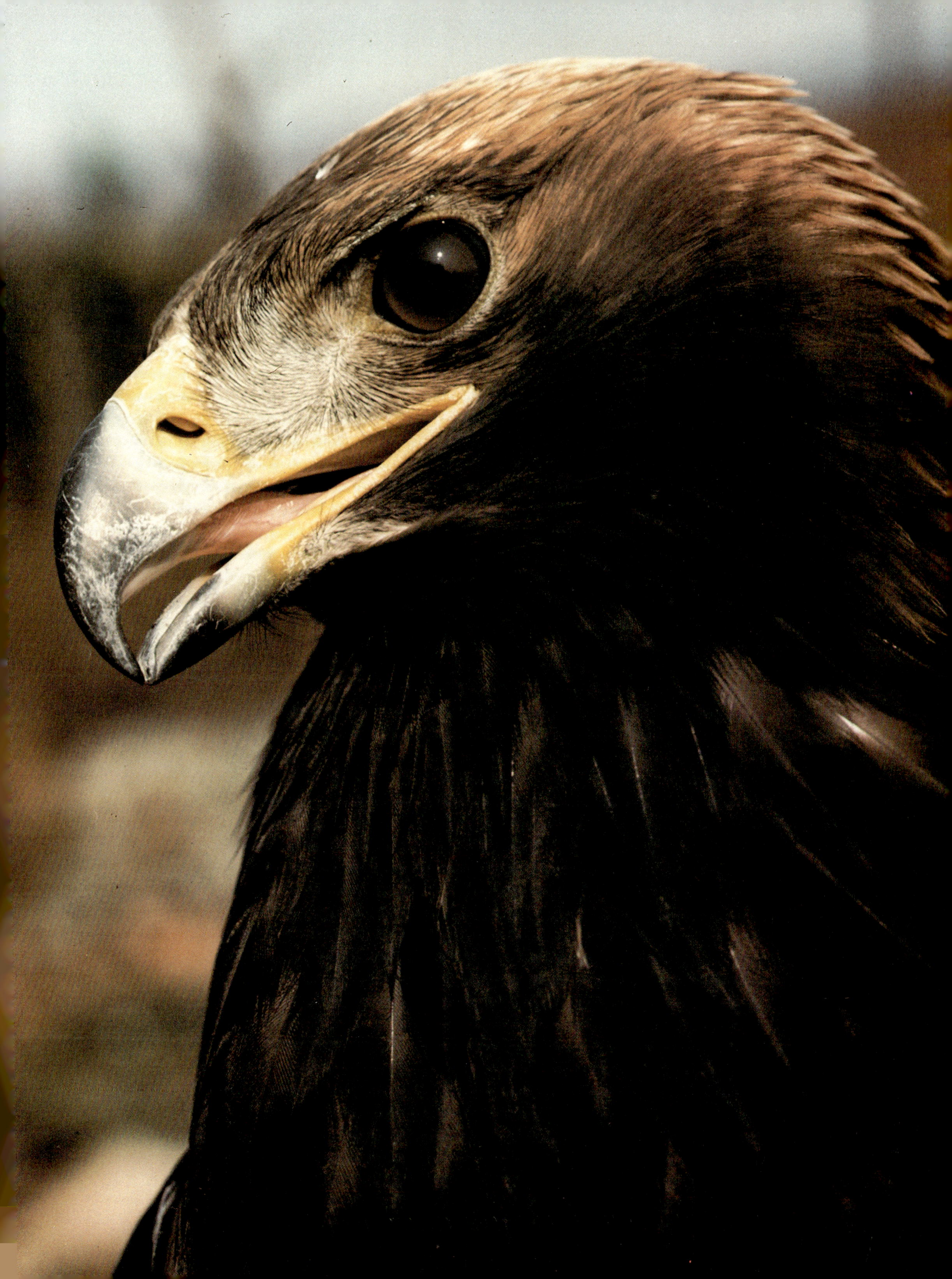

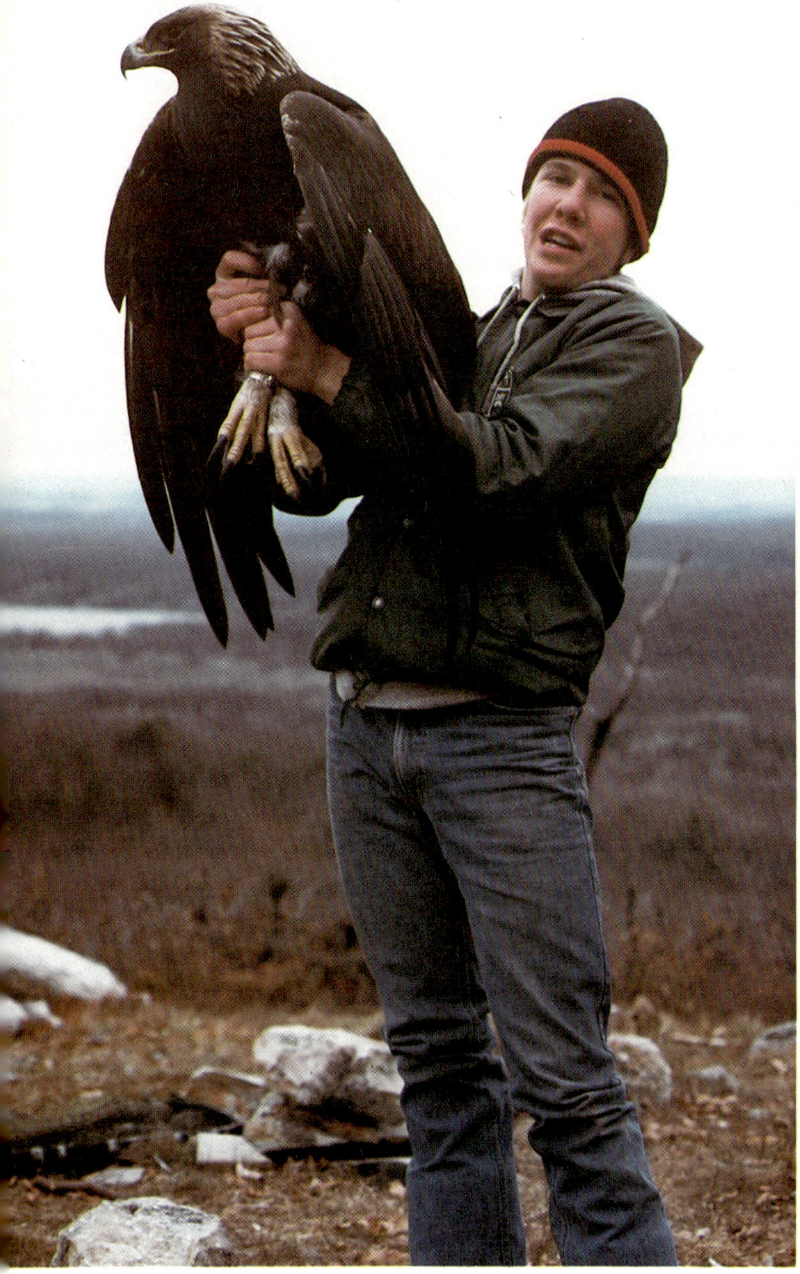

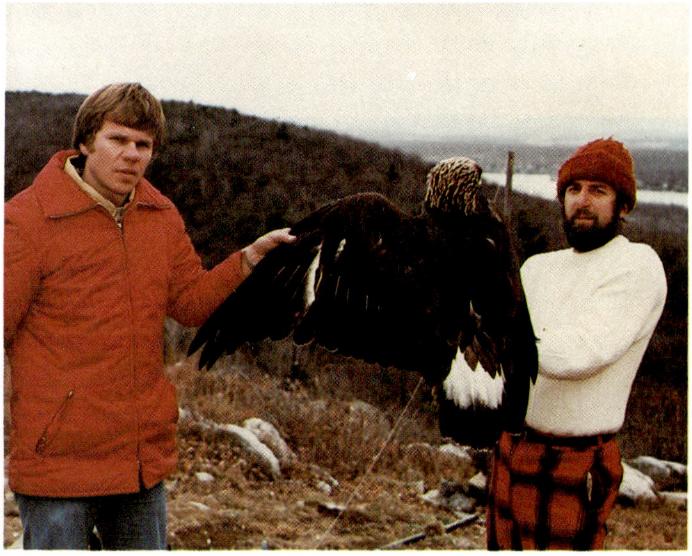

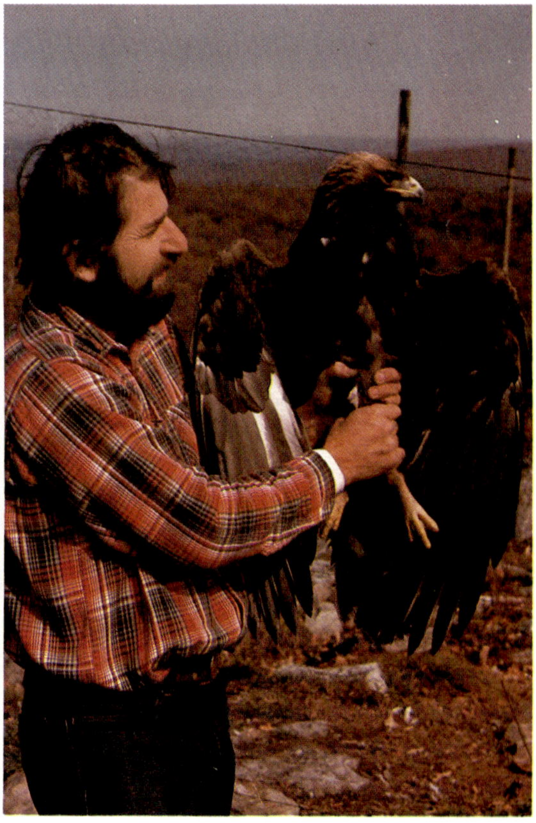

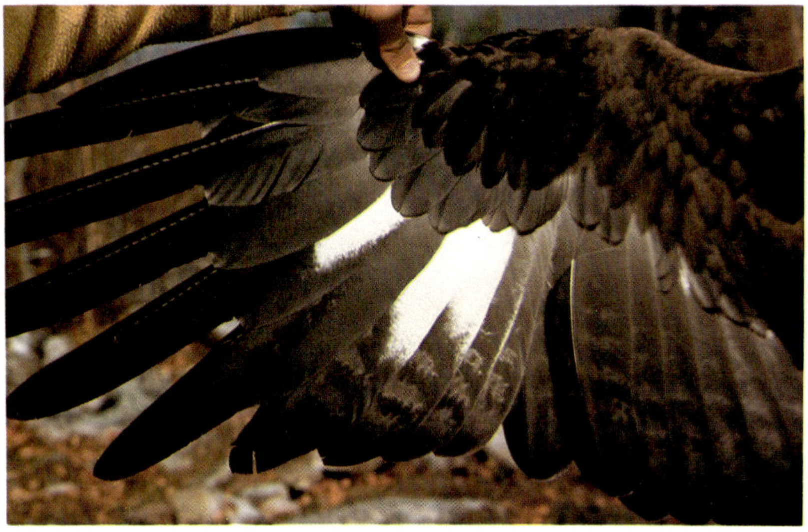

Northern Harrier

Circus cyaneus

Northern Harriers, also known as Marsh Hawks, are long-winged, long-tailed birds of open terrain. They can be seen coursing low over fields, pastures, and marshes in search of prey. Their buoyant, veering flight is very distinctive.

Harriers are slender birds, 18 to 23 inches in length, with wingspans of about 4 feet. Although large, they are light in weight, weighing approximately one pound. Adult male Harriers are silvery-blue with black wingtips; adult females are dark brown above and have streaks on their white underparts. The young (both male and female) resemble the adult females. All Harriers have a white rump patch.

Their diet consists chiefly of small mammals, especially meadow voles, but also include frogs, insects, and small birds.

Unlike most hawks, Harriers nest on the ground. Their nests are built of dry grasses and small sticks and are hidden among the weeds and vegetation of fields and marshes. A few breed in New Jersey, but most Harriers seen here are migrants. They are present in large numbers along the coastline during migration.

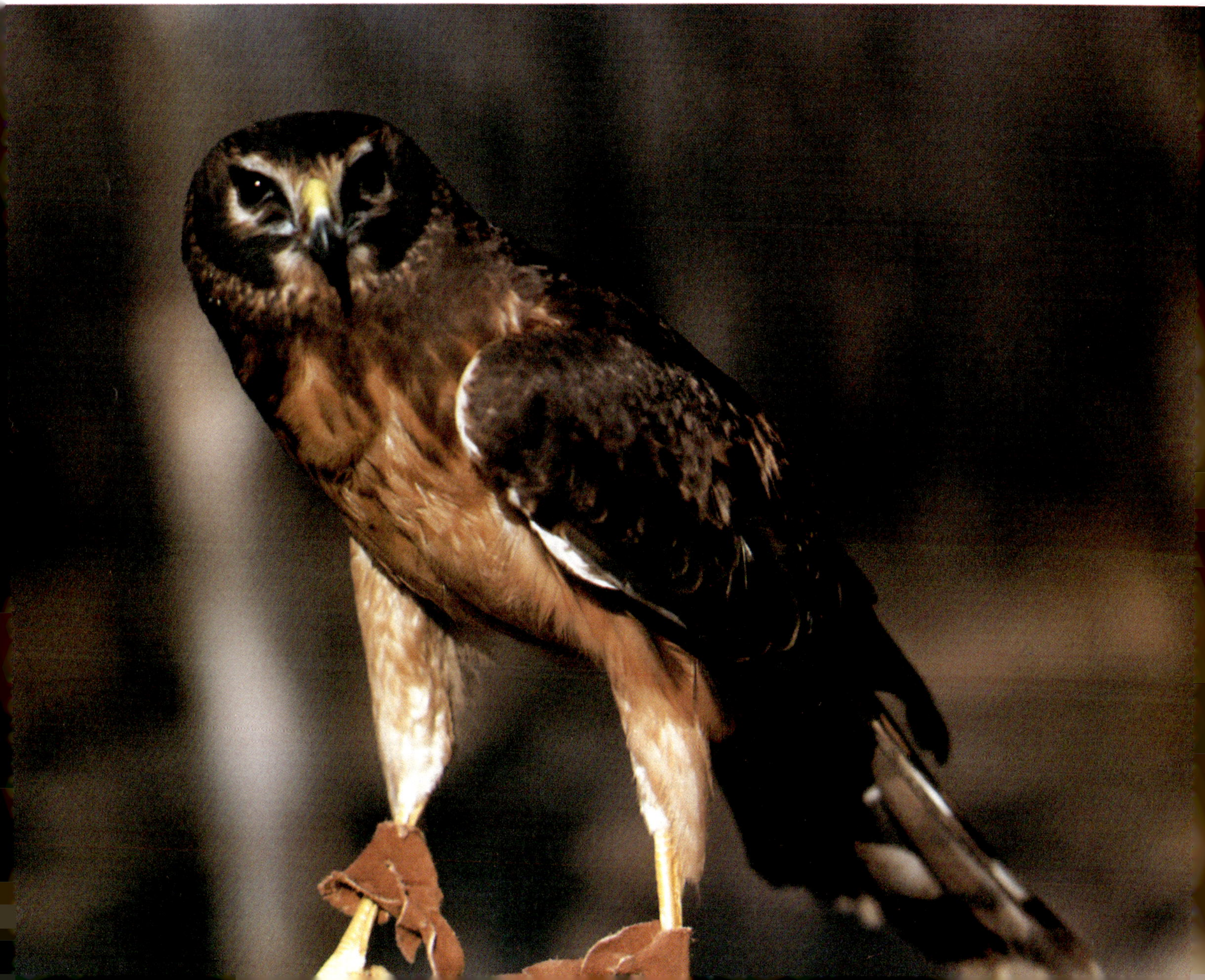

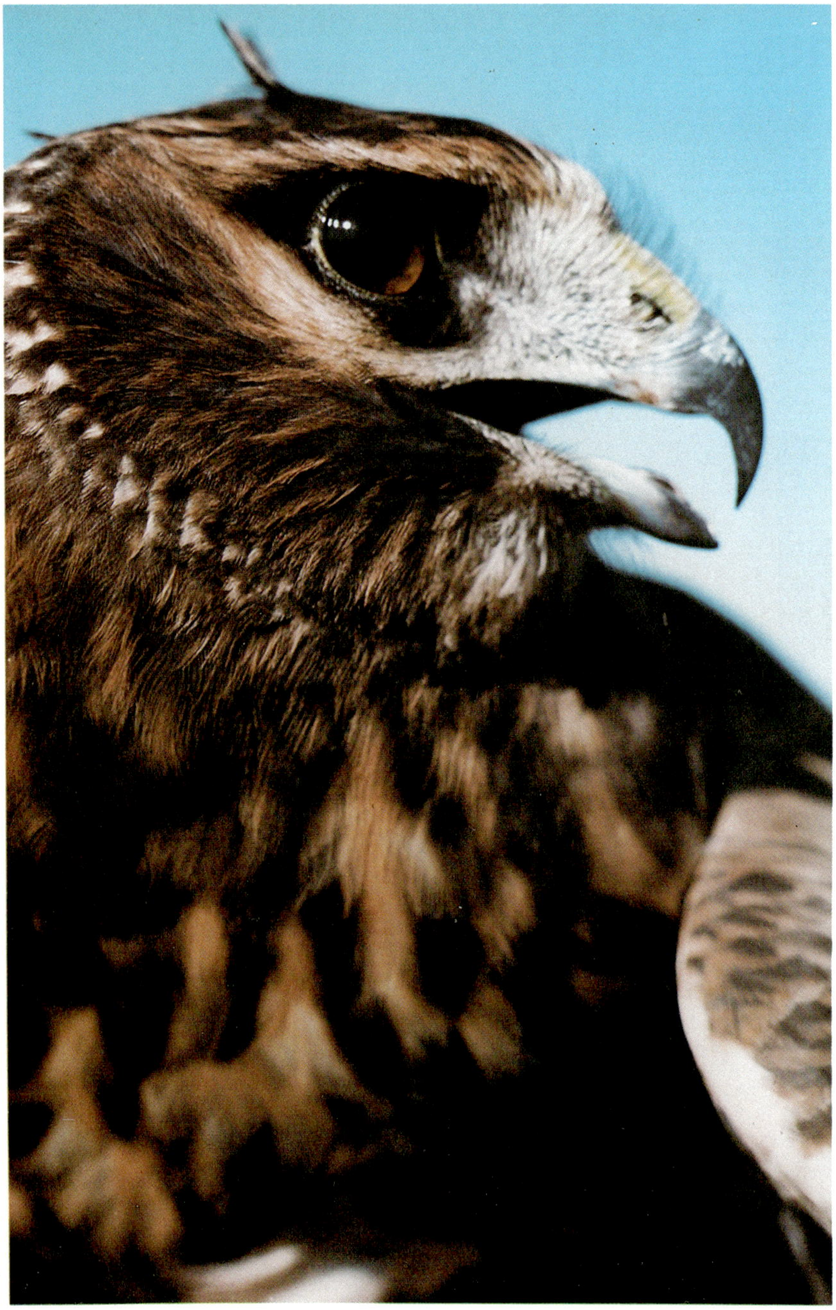

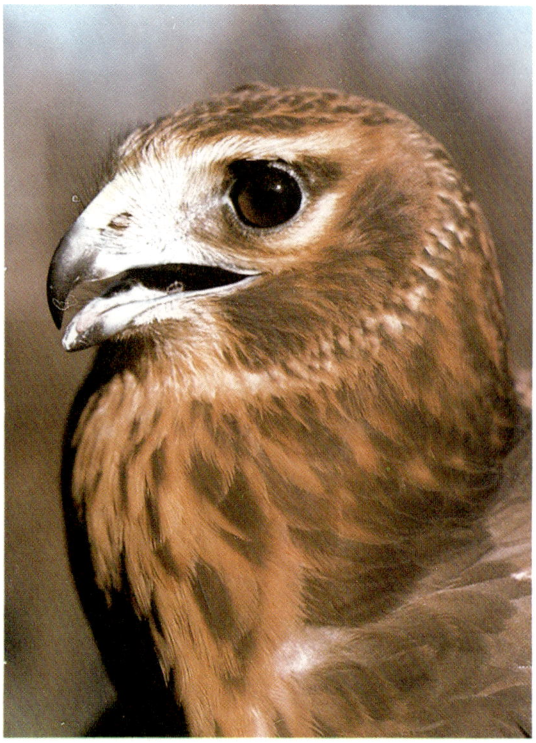

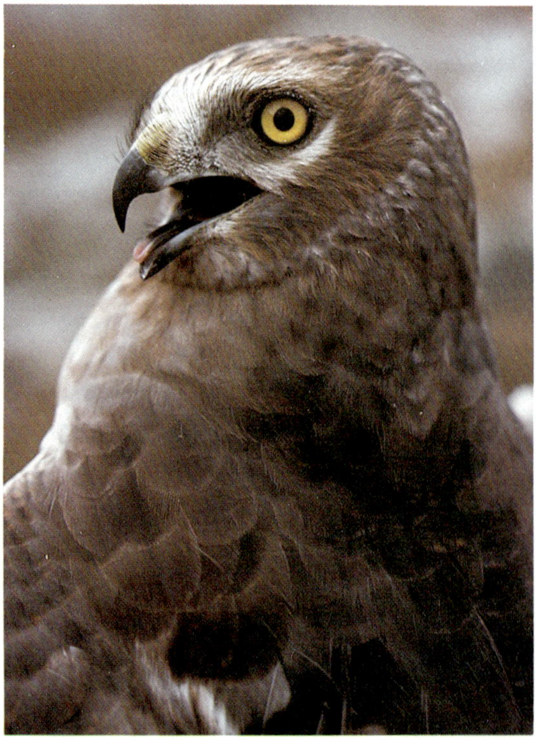

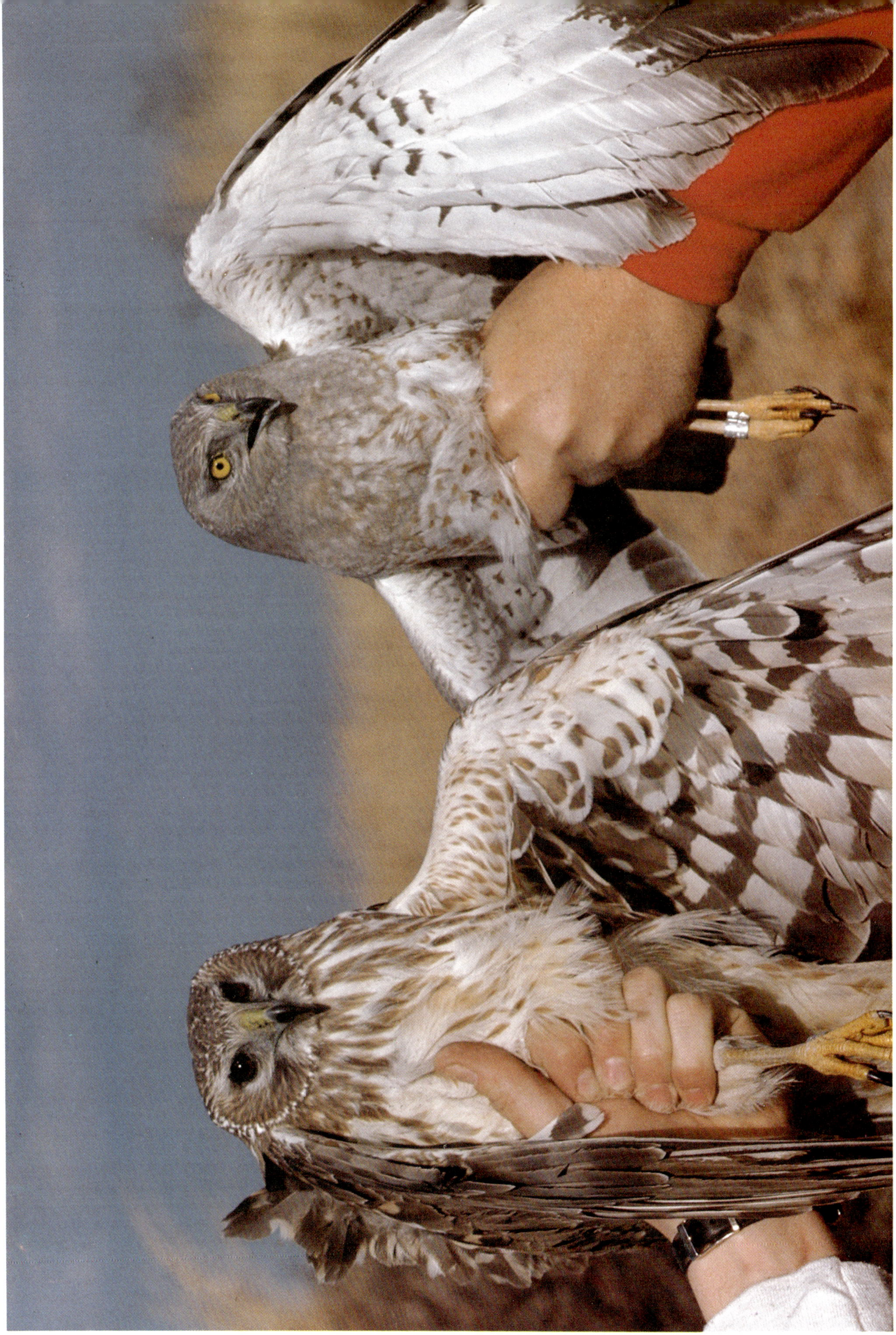

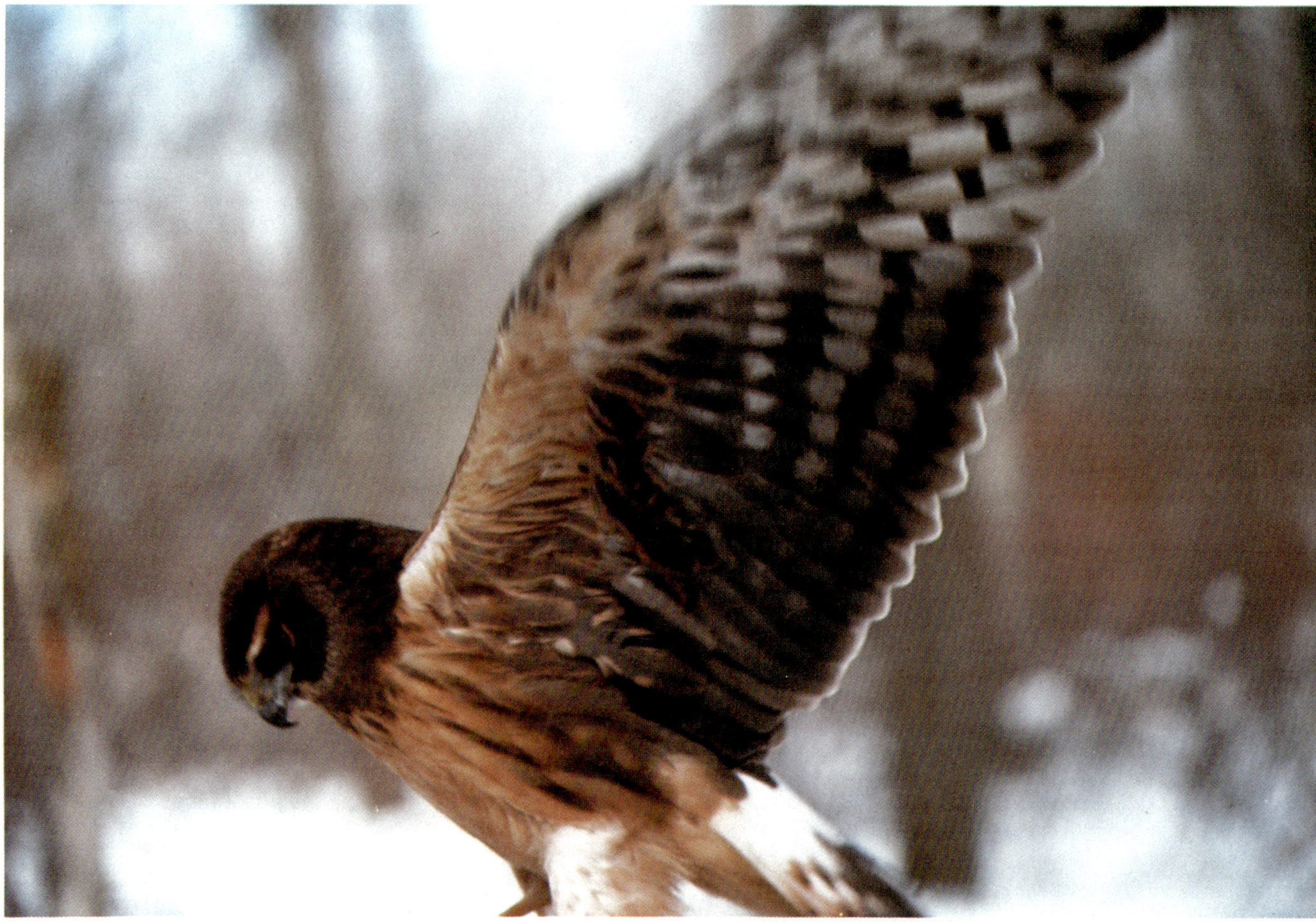

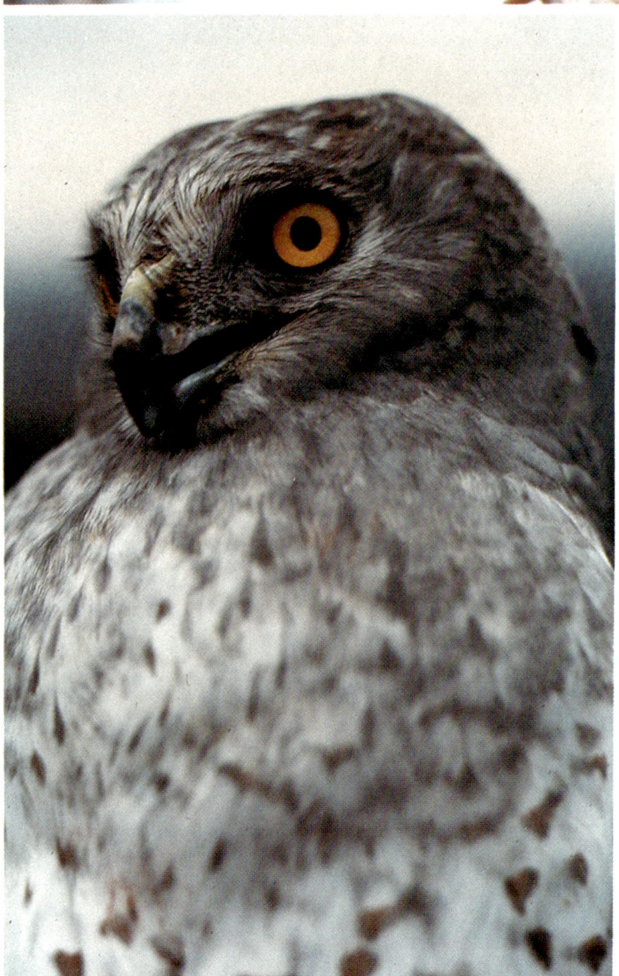

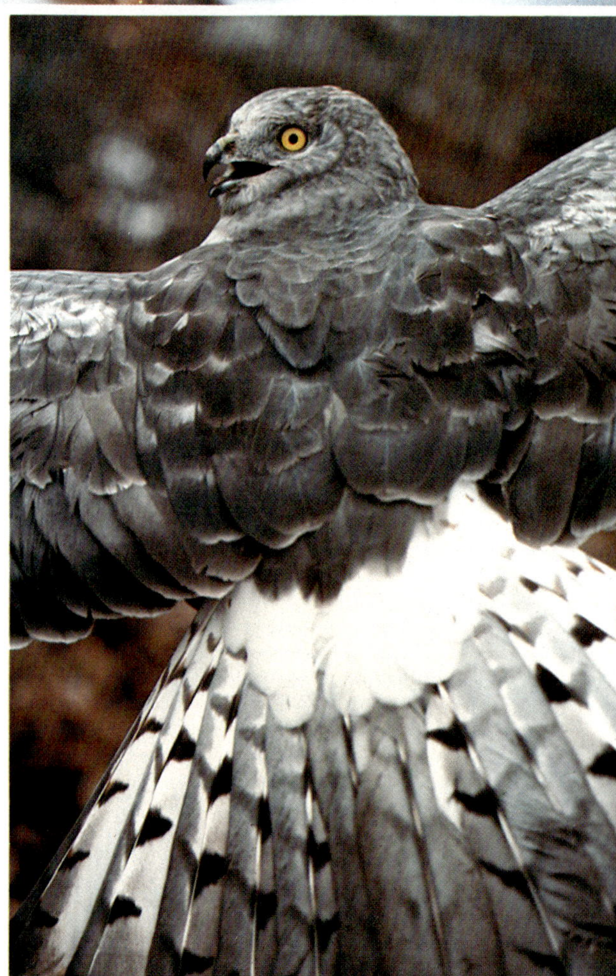

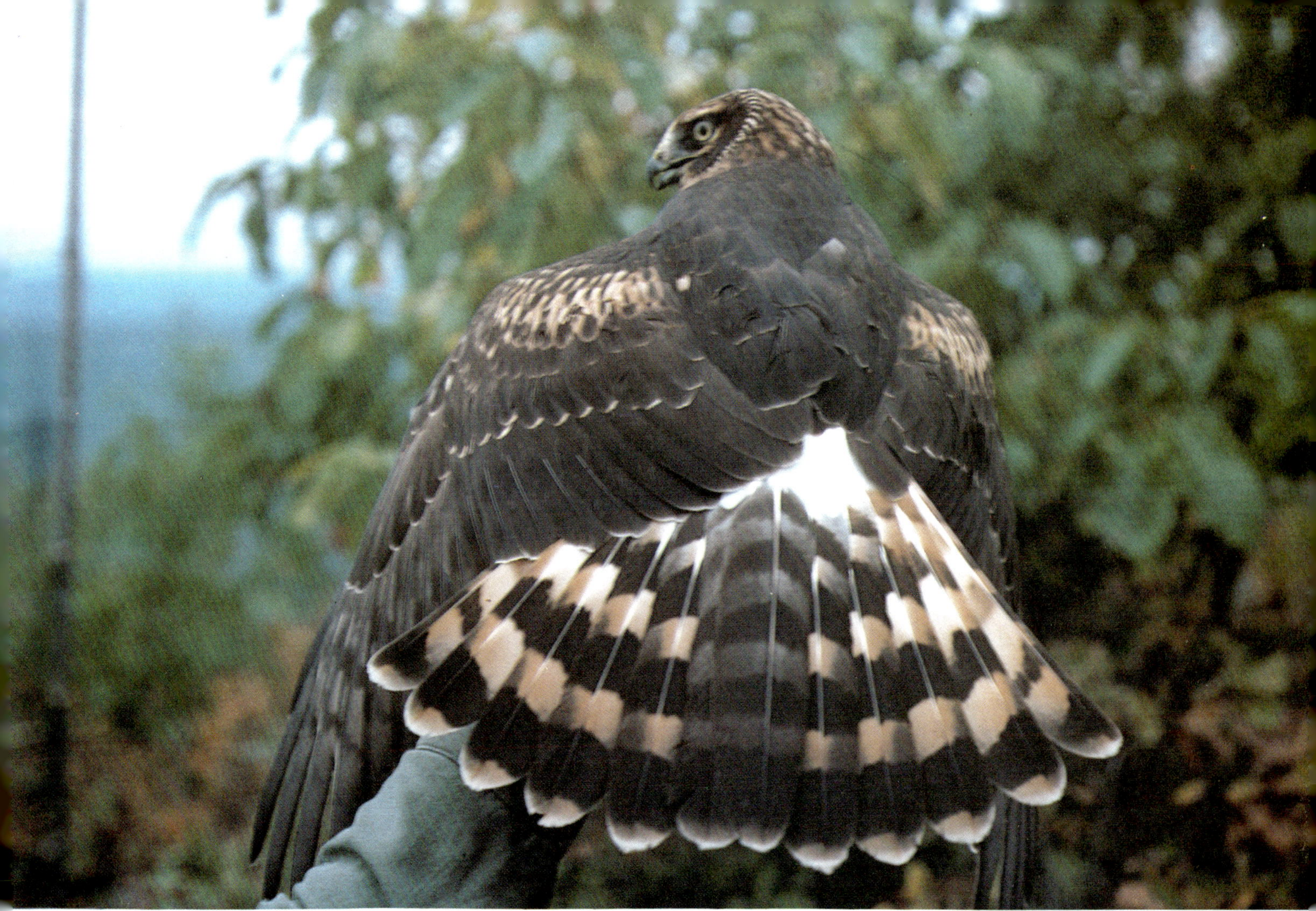

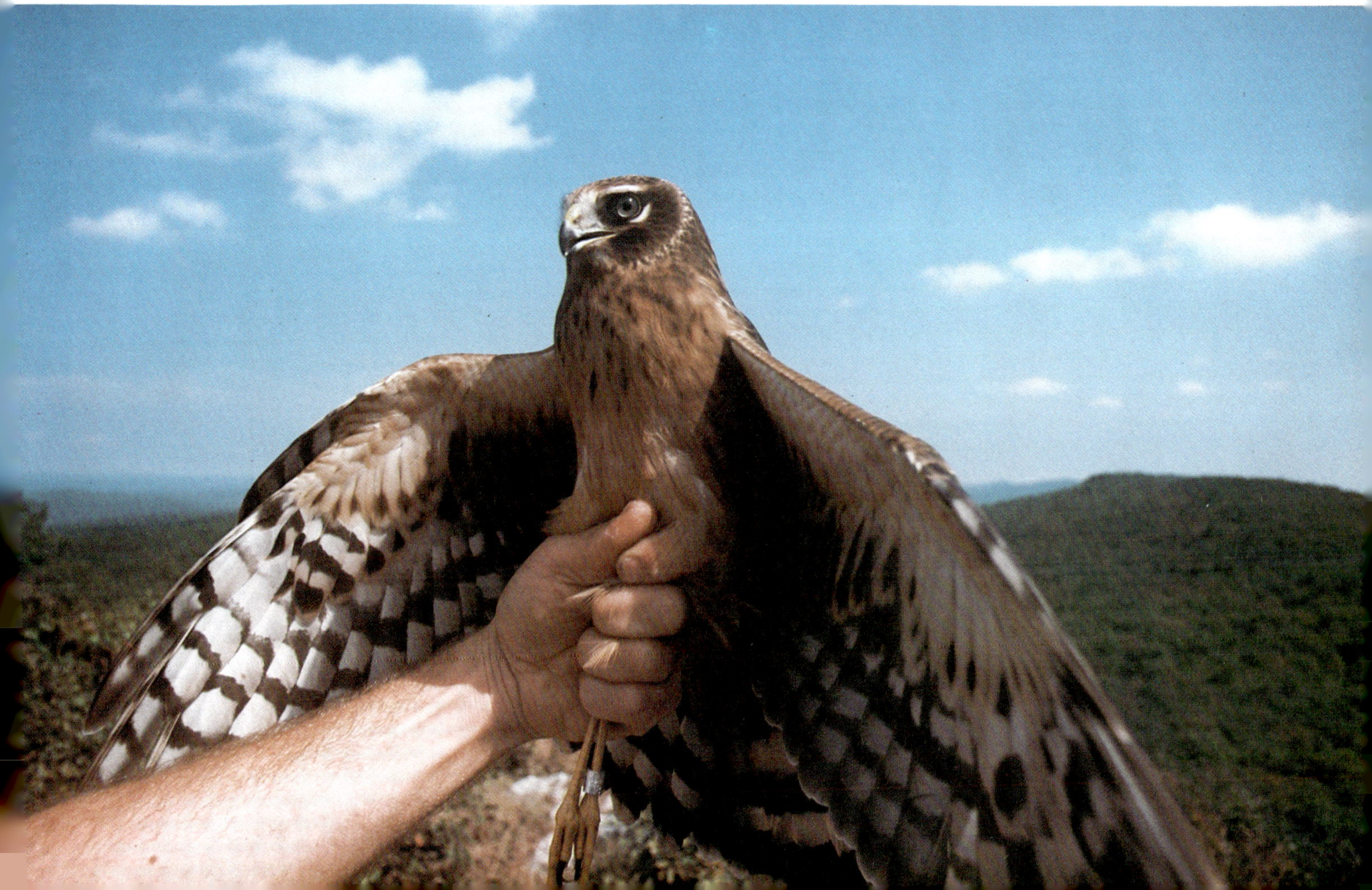

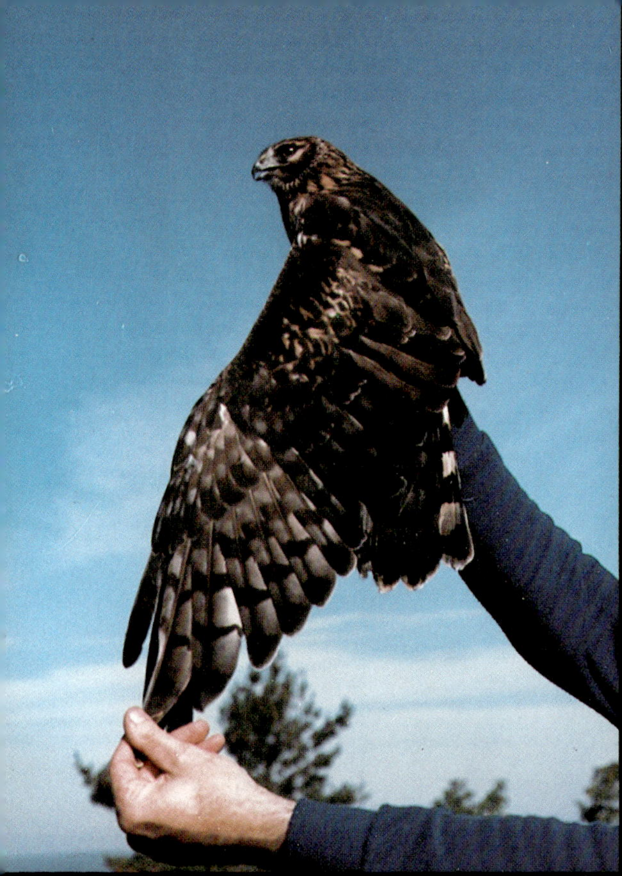
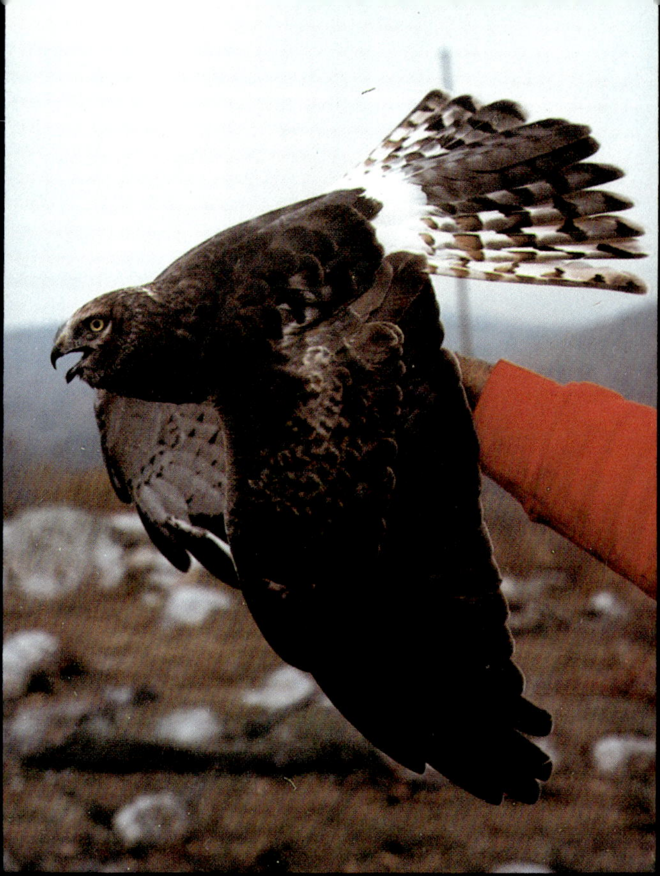
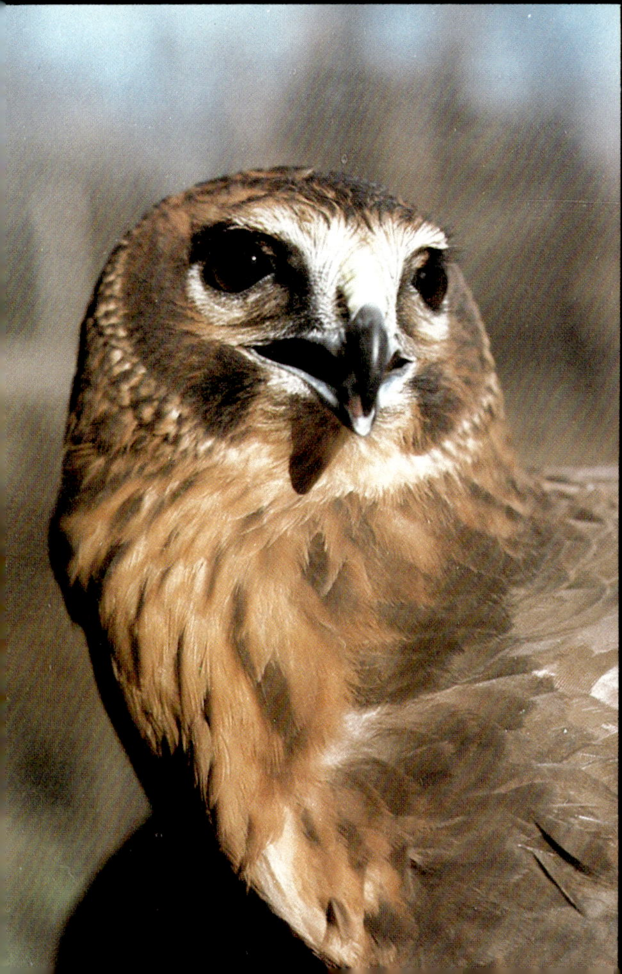
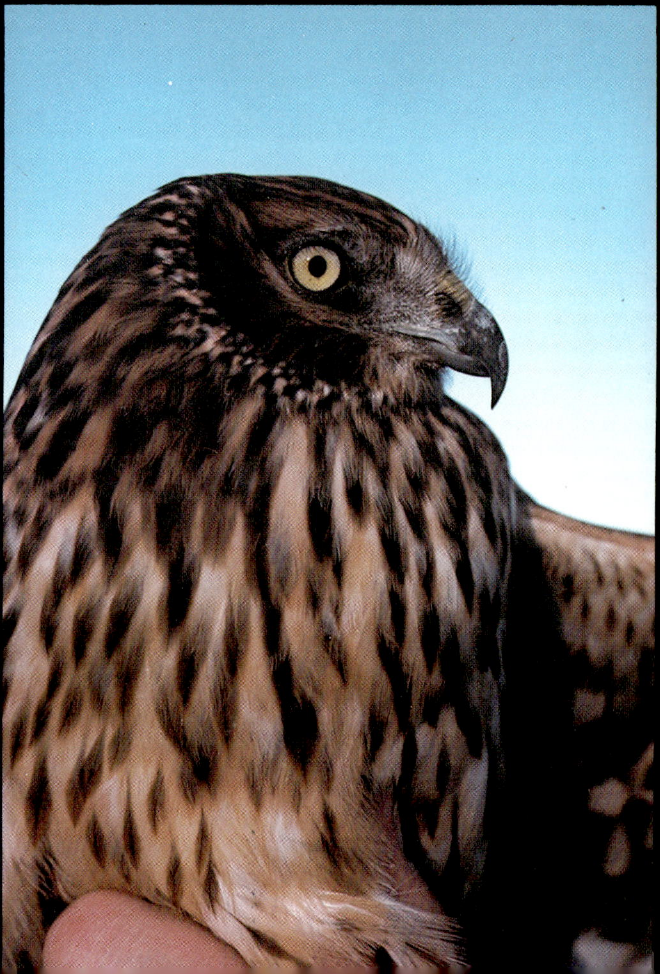

Pattern Series

Included in the following pages are complete patterns for the ten carving projects.

SCREECH OWL PERCHED
Body block—8" x 4" x 3½"
Eye size—12mm
Eye color—straw to yellow
Gray Morph

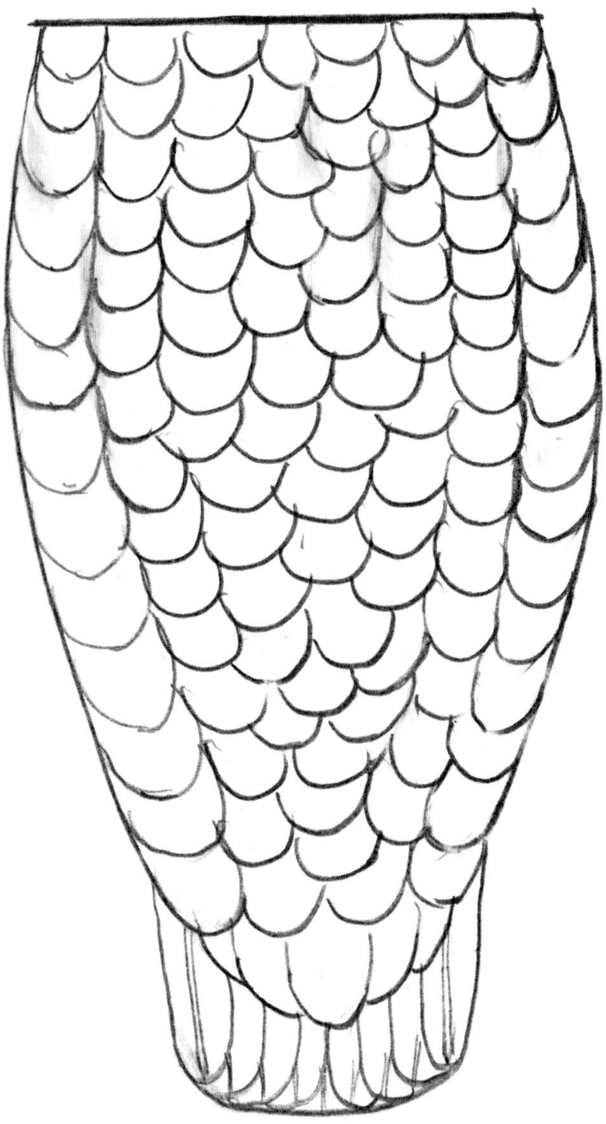

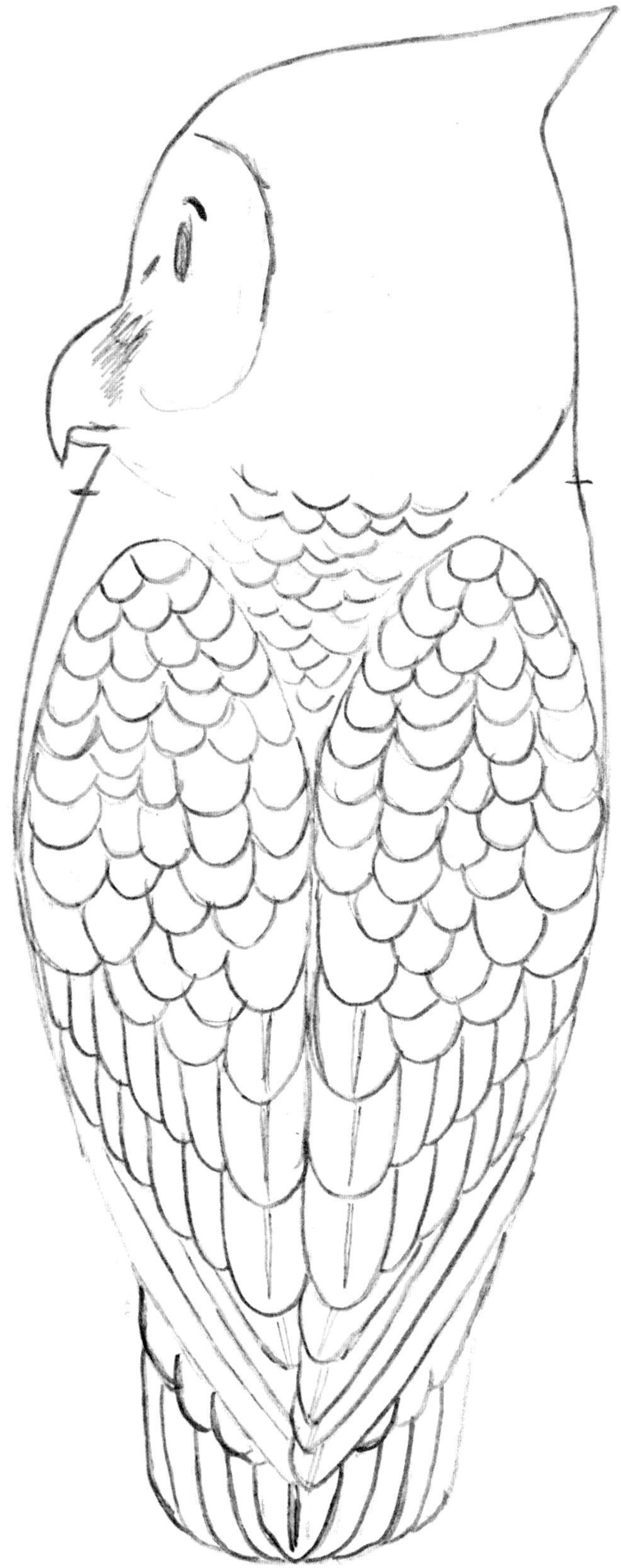

Back view

RED SCREECH OWL

(Debbie) Wingsup
Body block—8½" x 4½" x 4"
Wing blocks—5" x 8" x 2"
Eye size—14mm
Eye color—straw

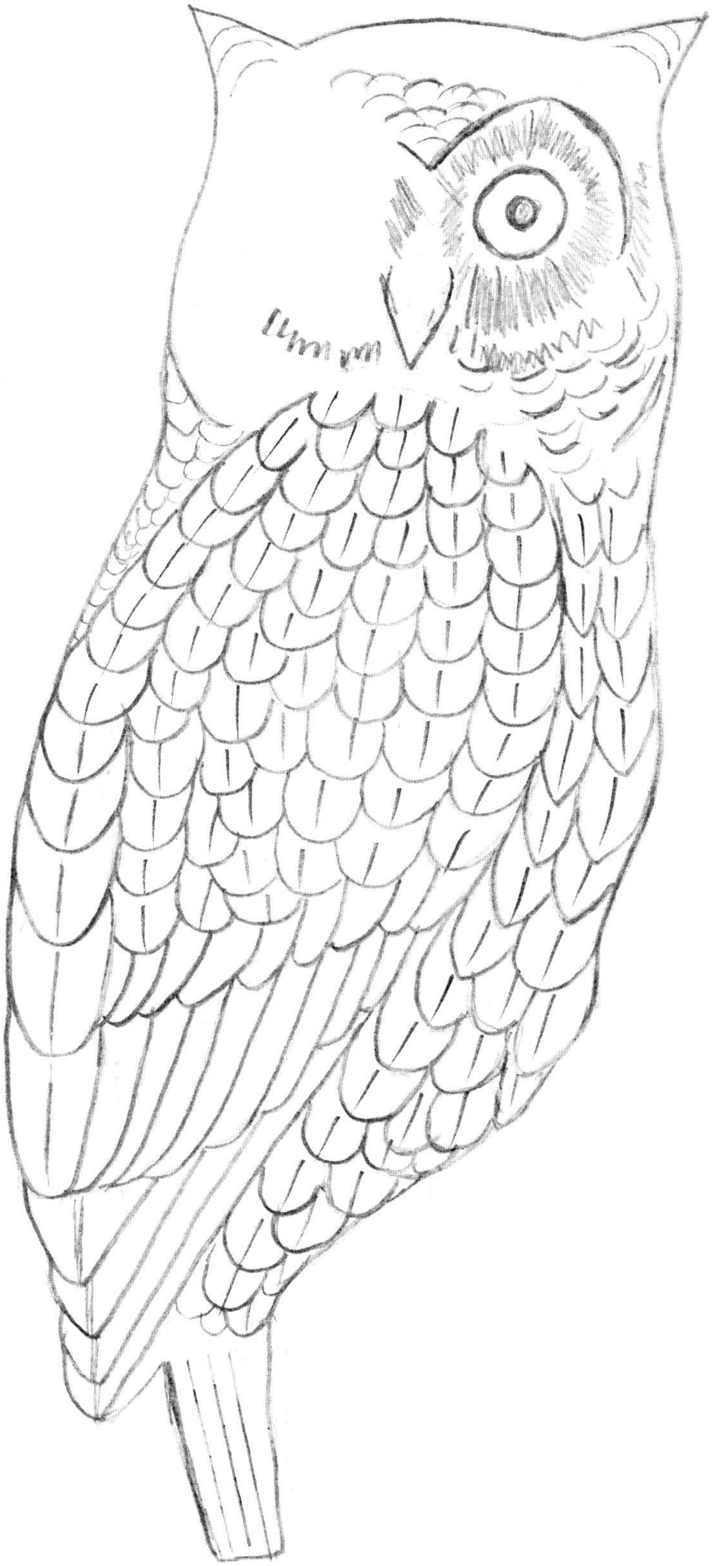

Profile view

Body—top view

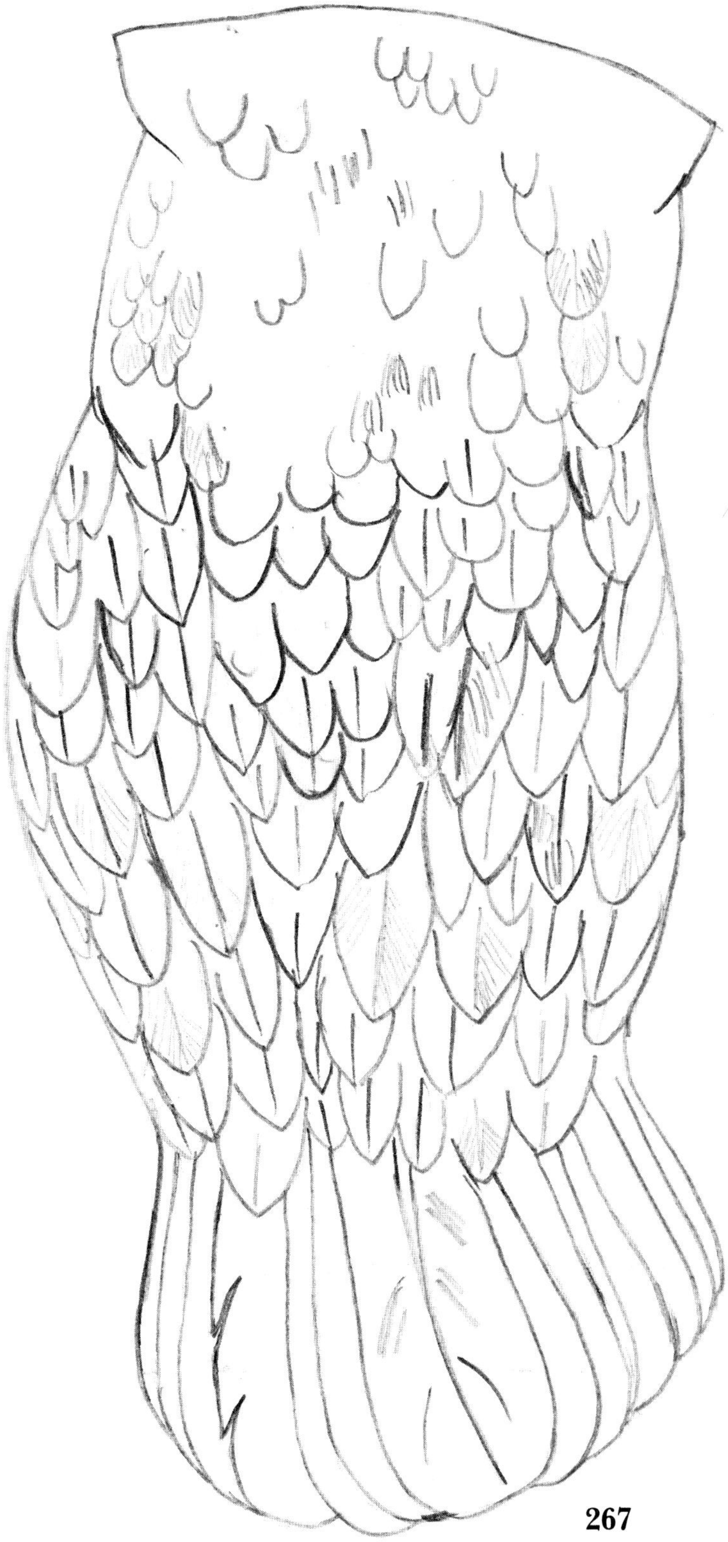

Red Screech Owl

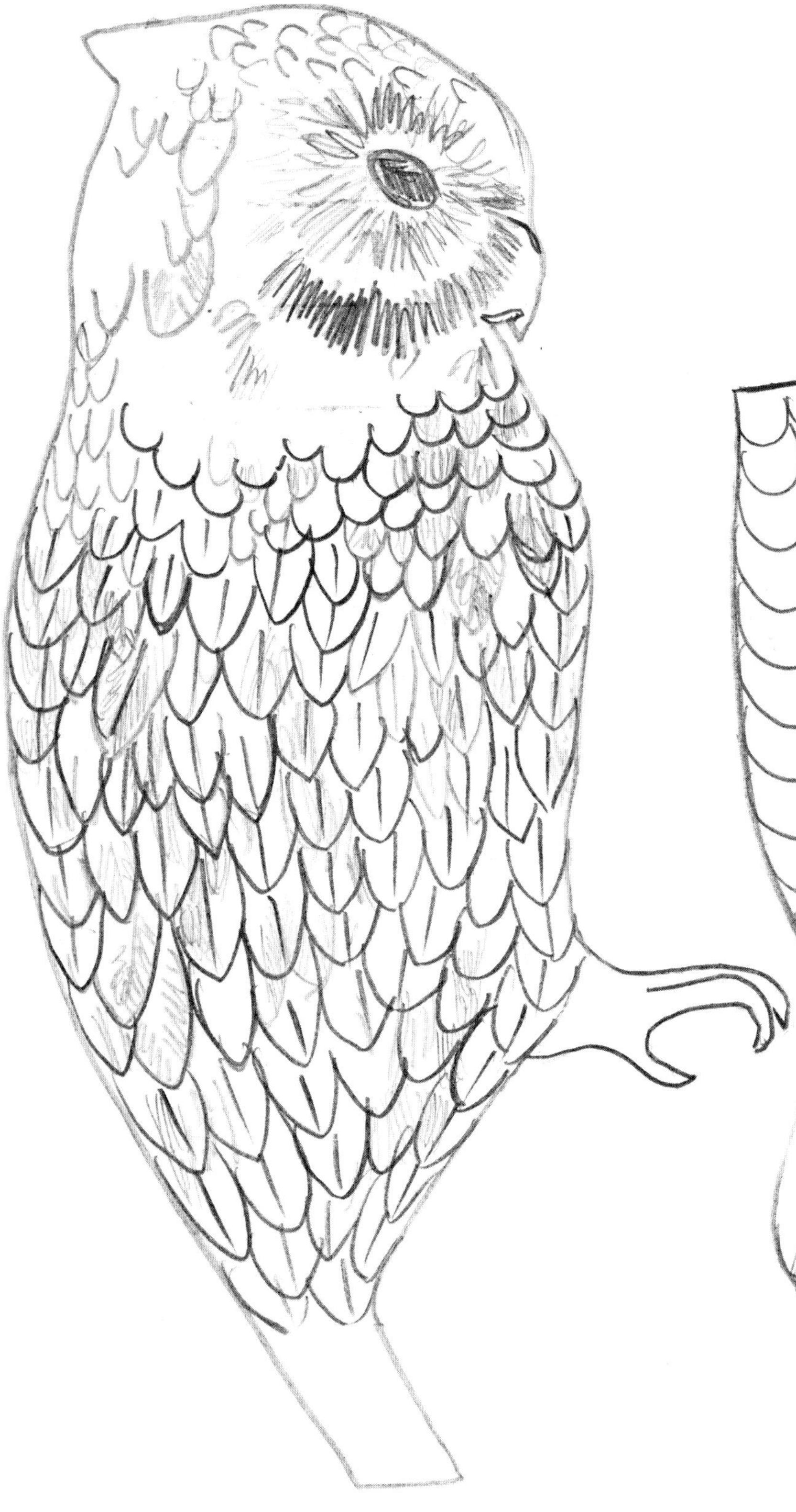

Body—profile

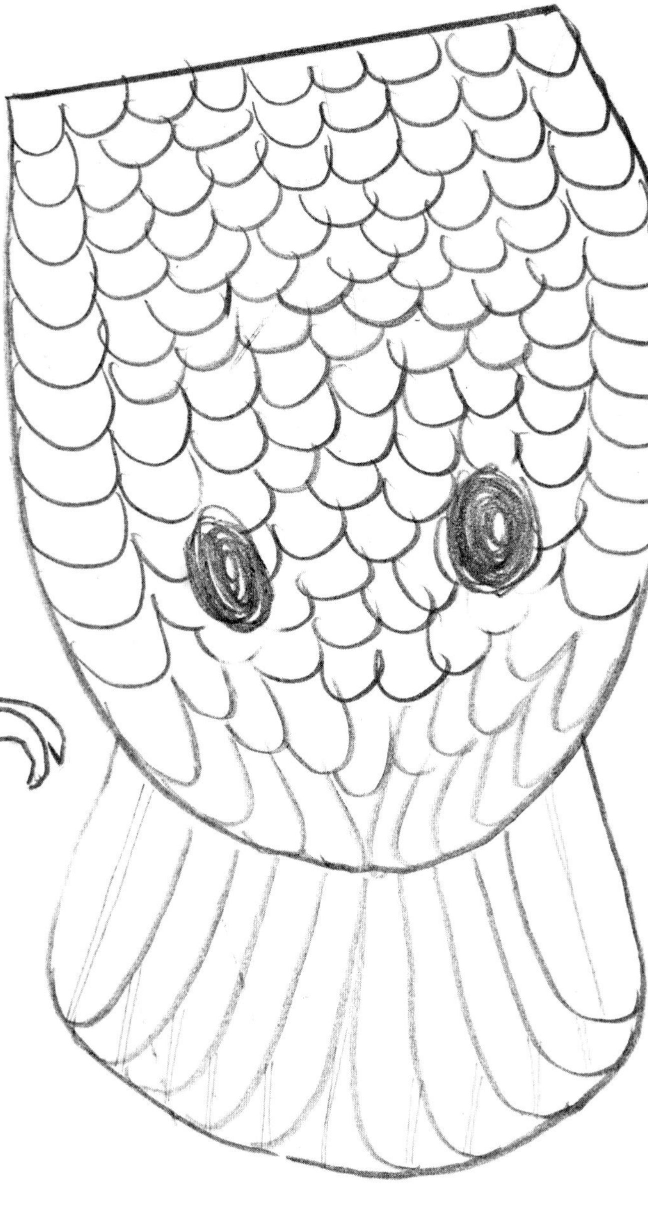

Body—belly or bottom view

Screech Owl Wings

Top view

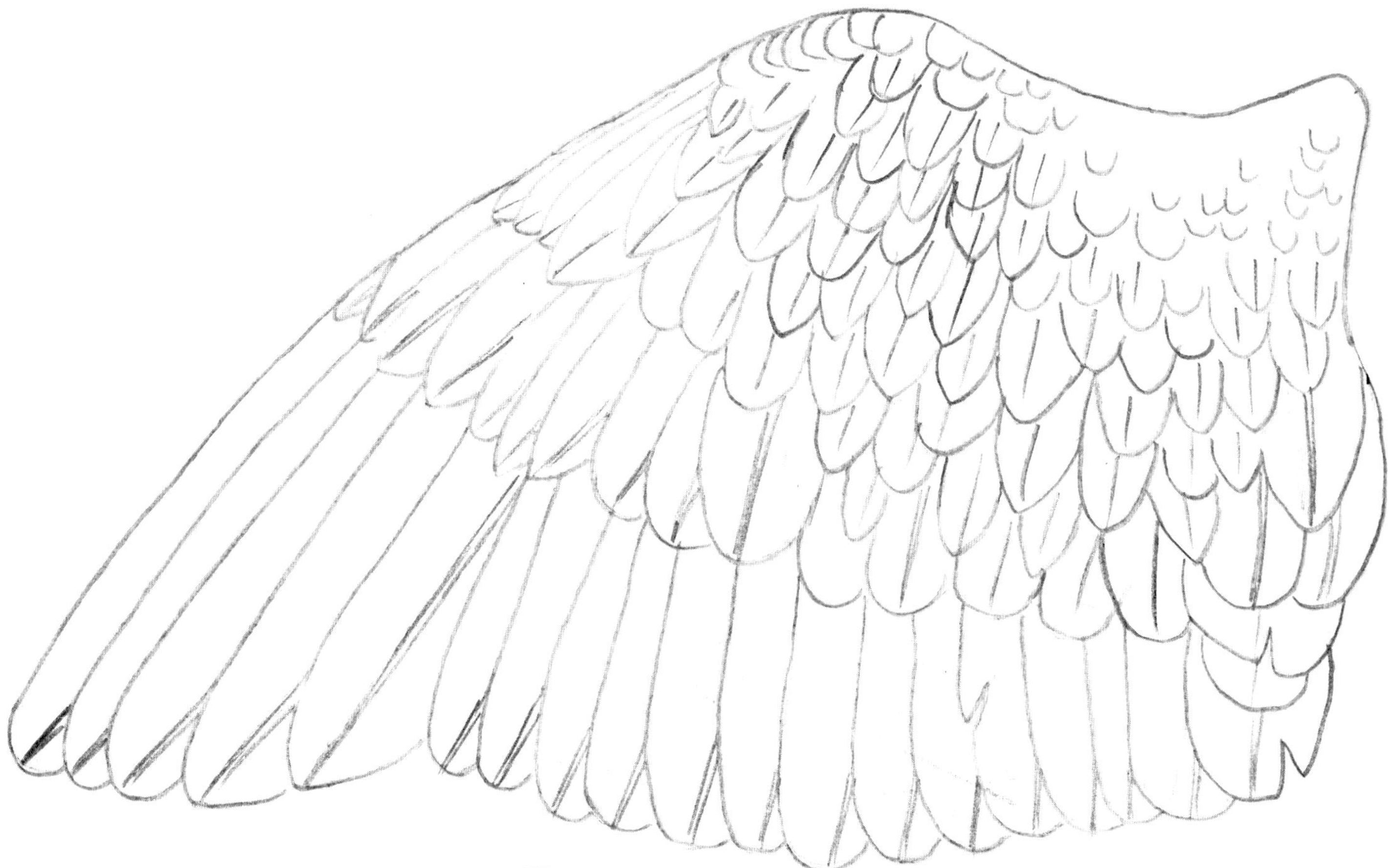

Bottom view

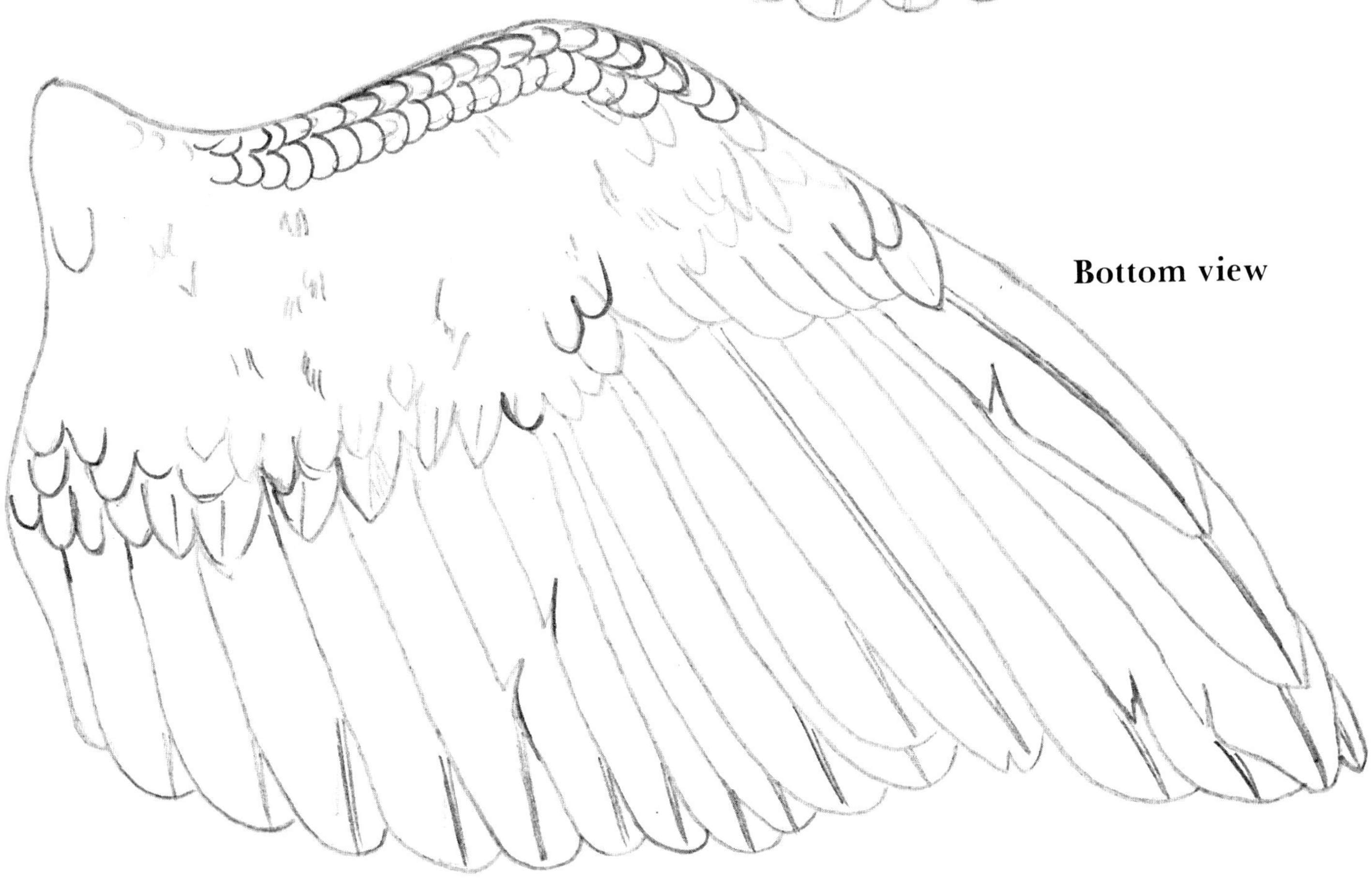

SAW-WHET OWL
Body block—7" x 3½" x 3½"
Eye size—14mm
Eye color—straw
Saw-whet Owl

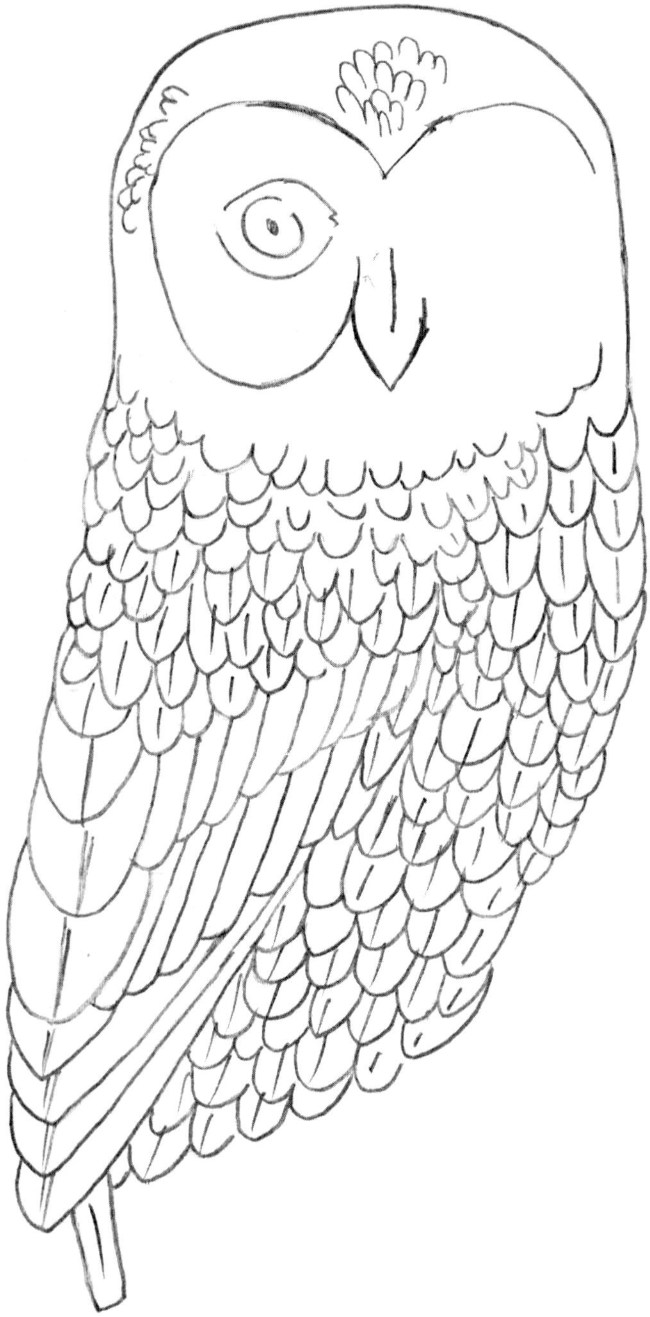

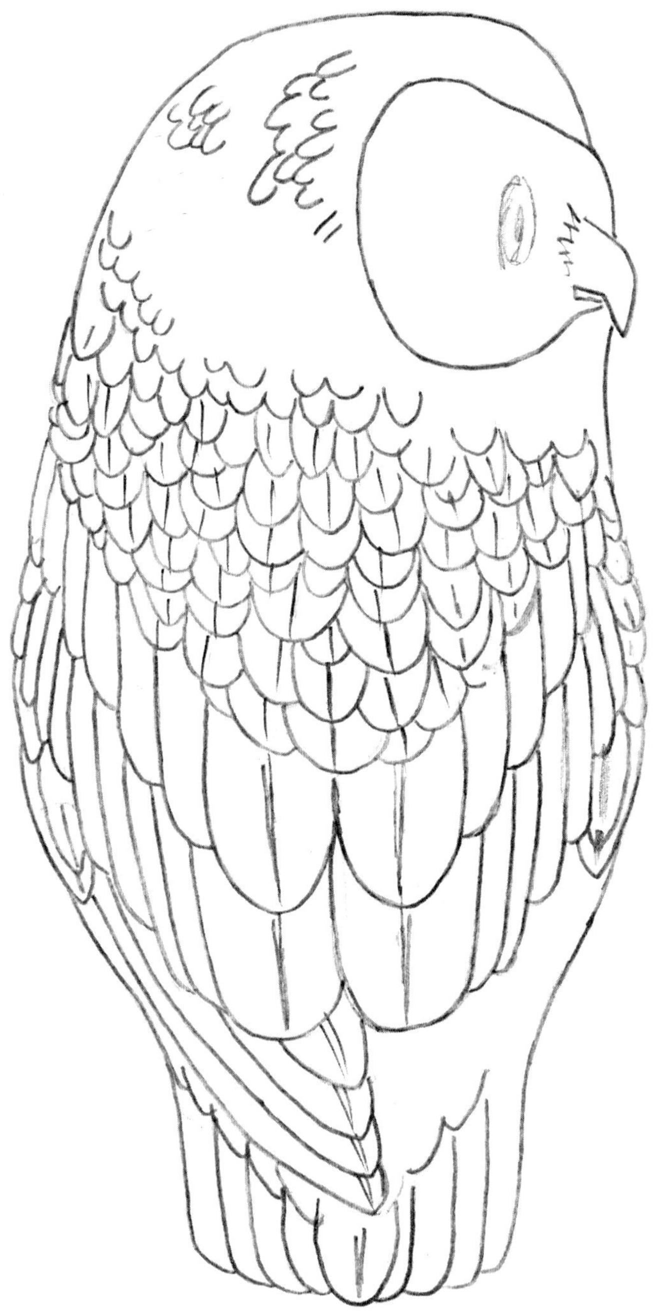

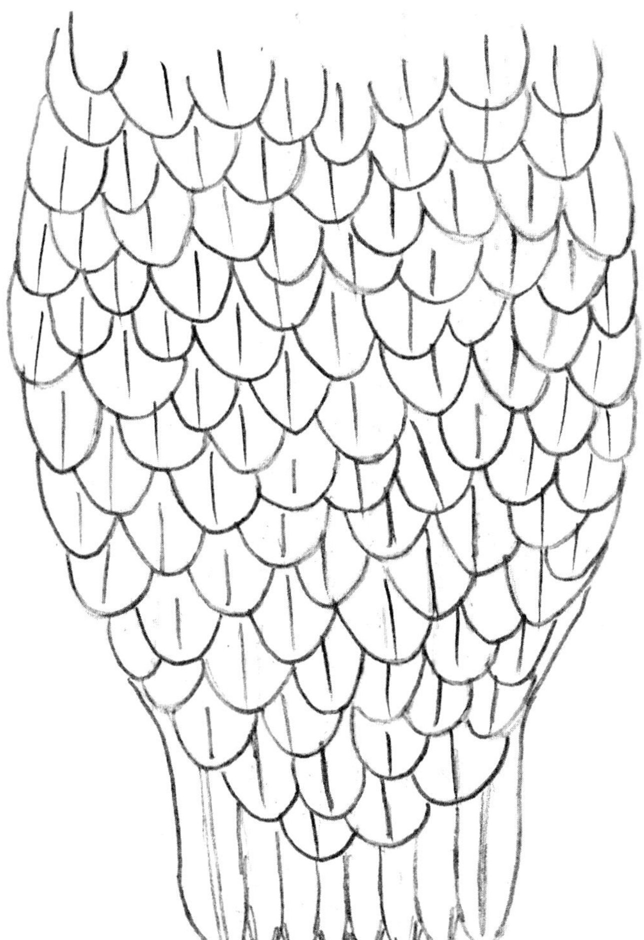

SNOWY OWL
3/4 size
Body block—14" x 7" x 7"
Head block—5" x 5" x 3"
Eye size—12mm
Eye color—straw

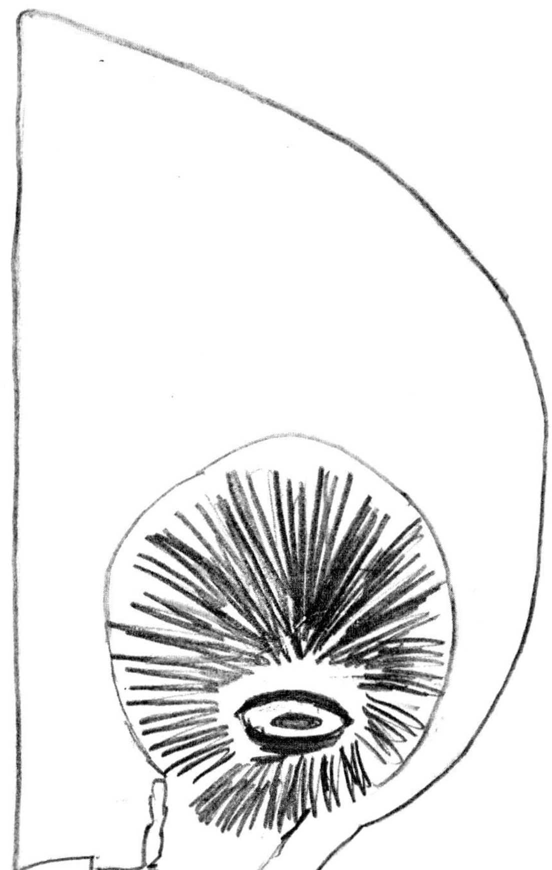

Profile head

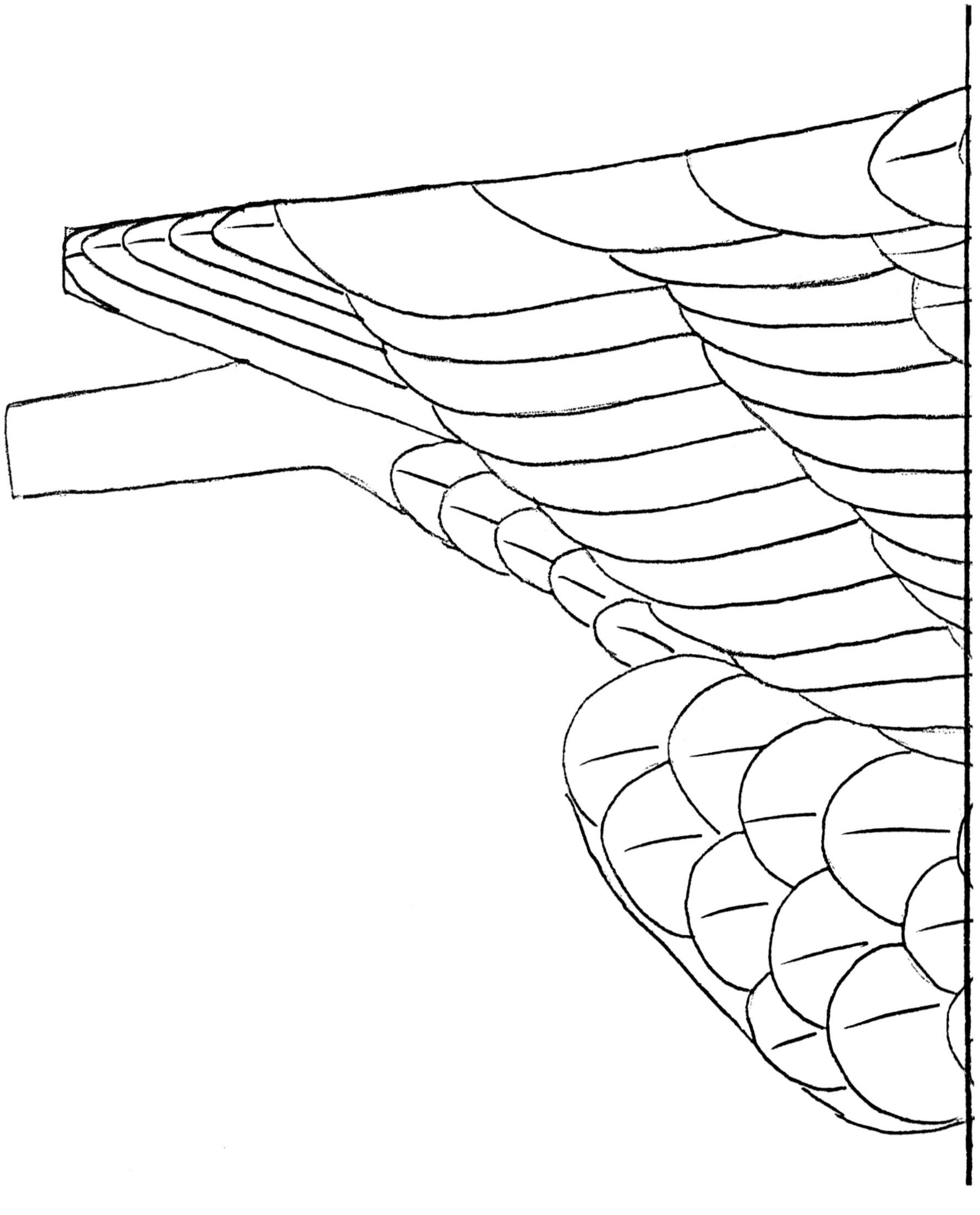

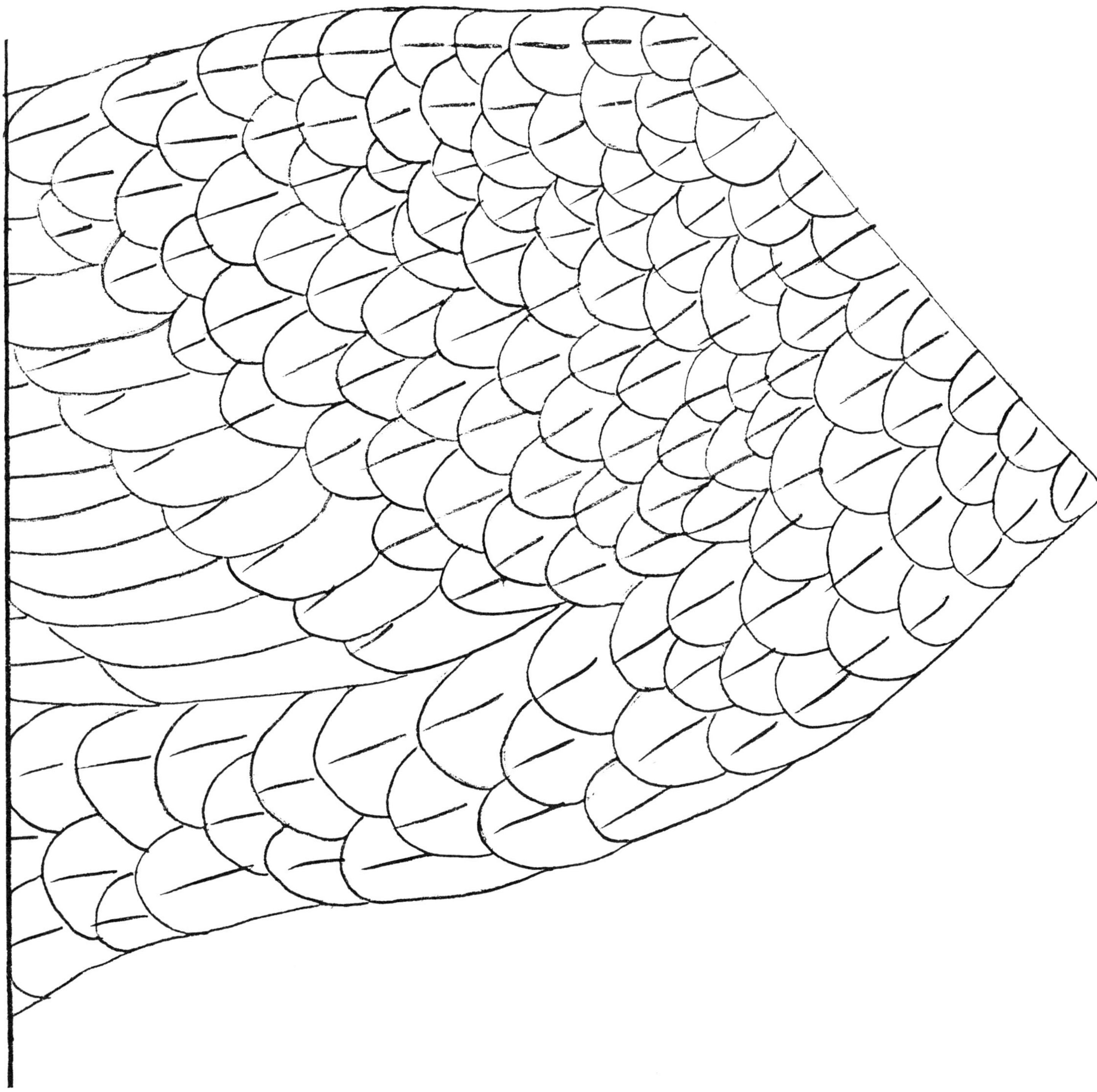

Profile view

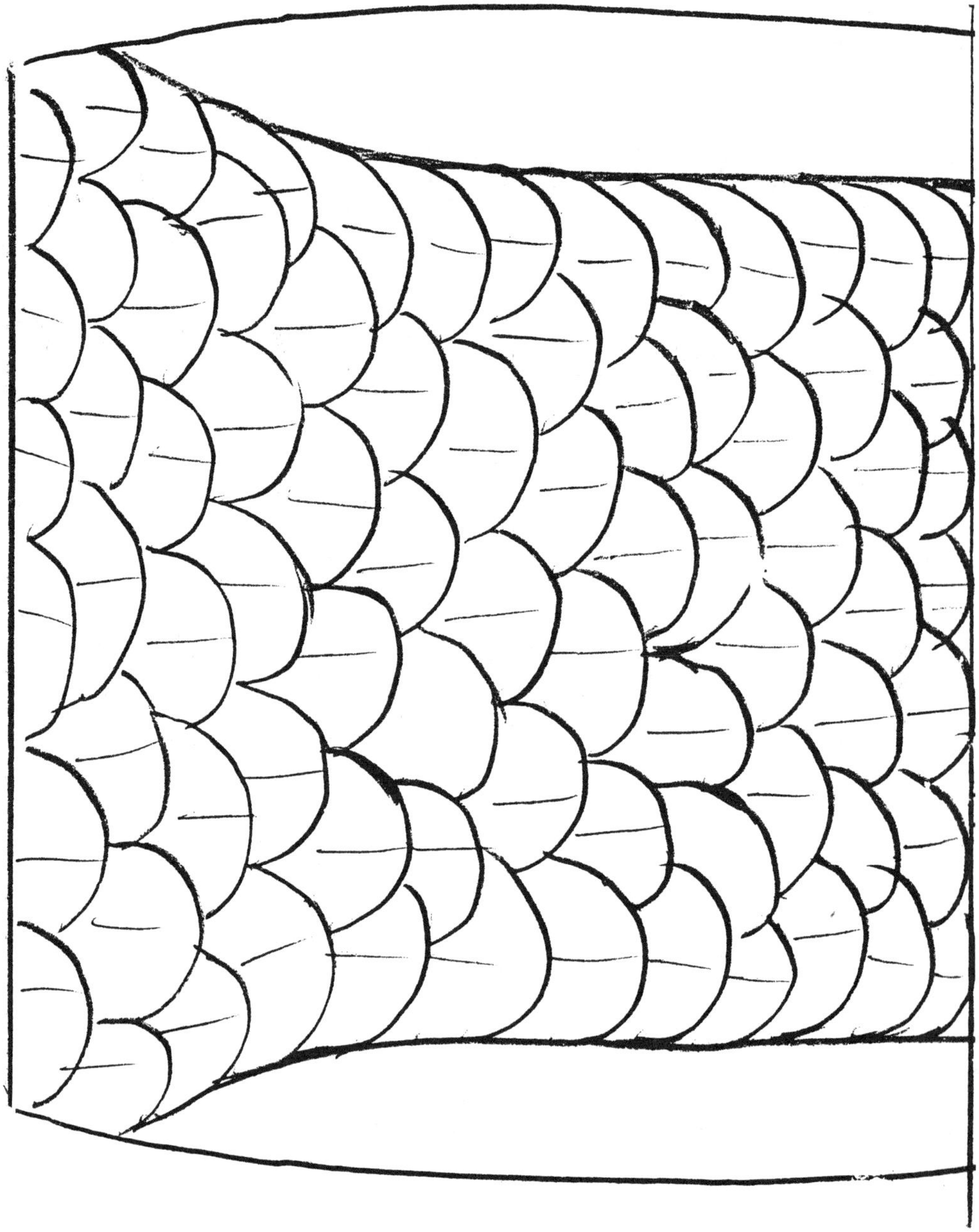

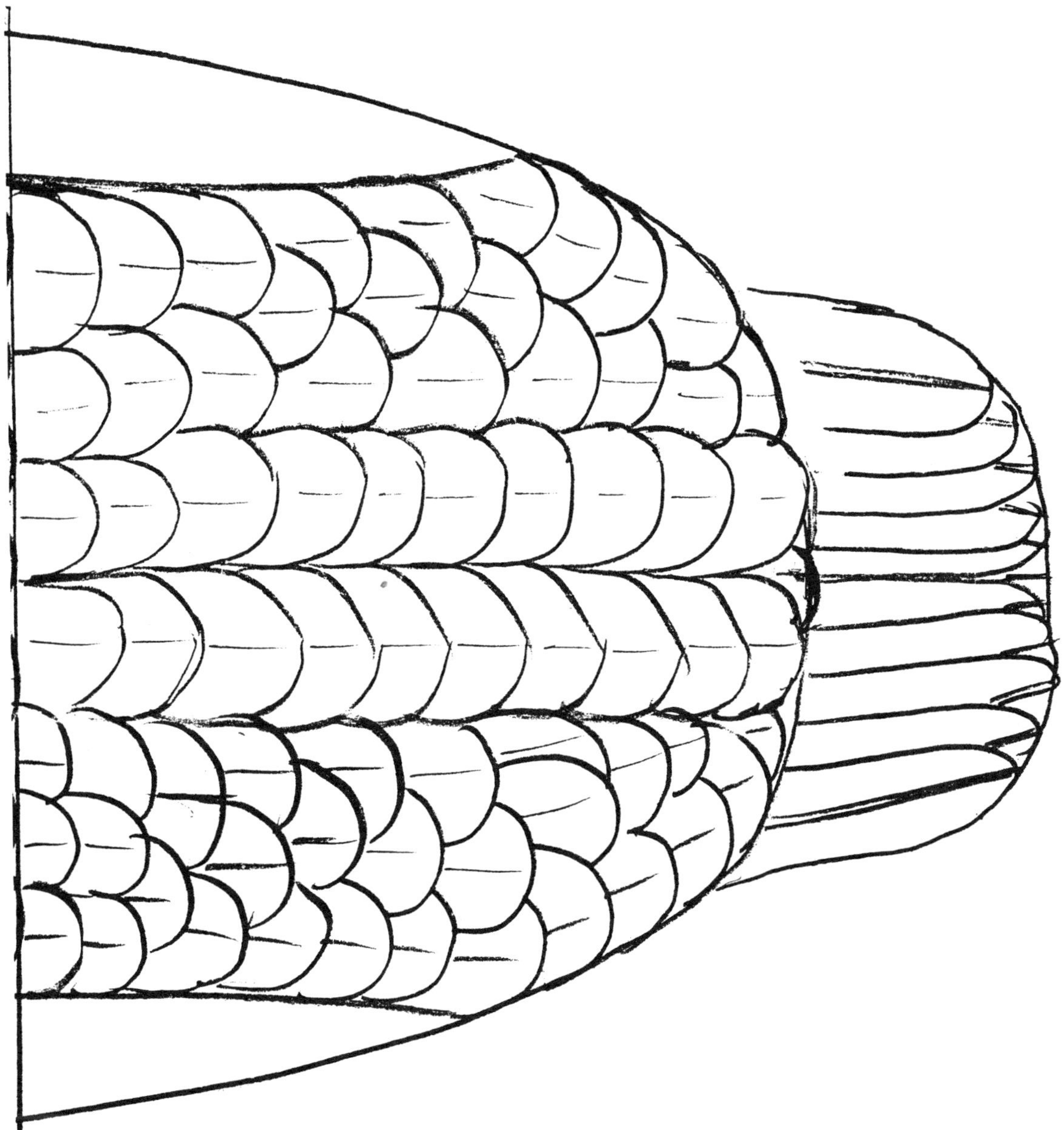

Belly and underside of tail

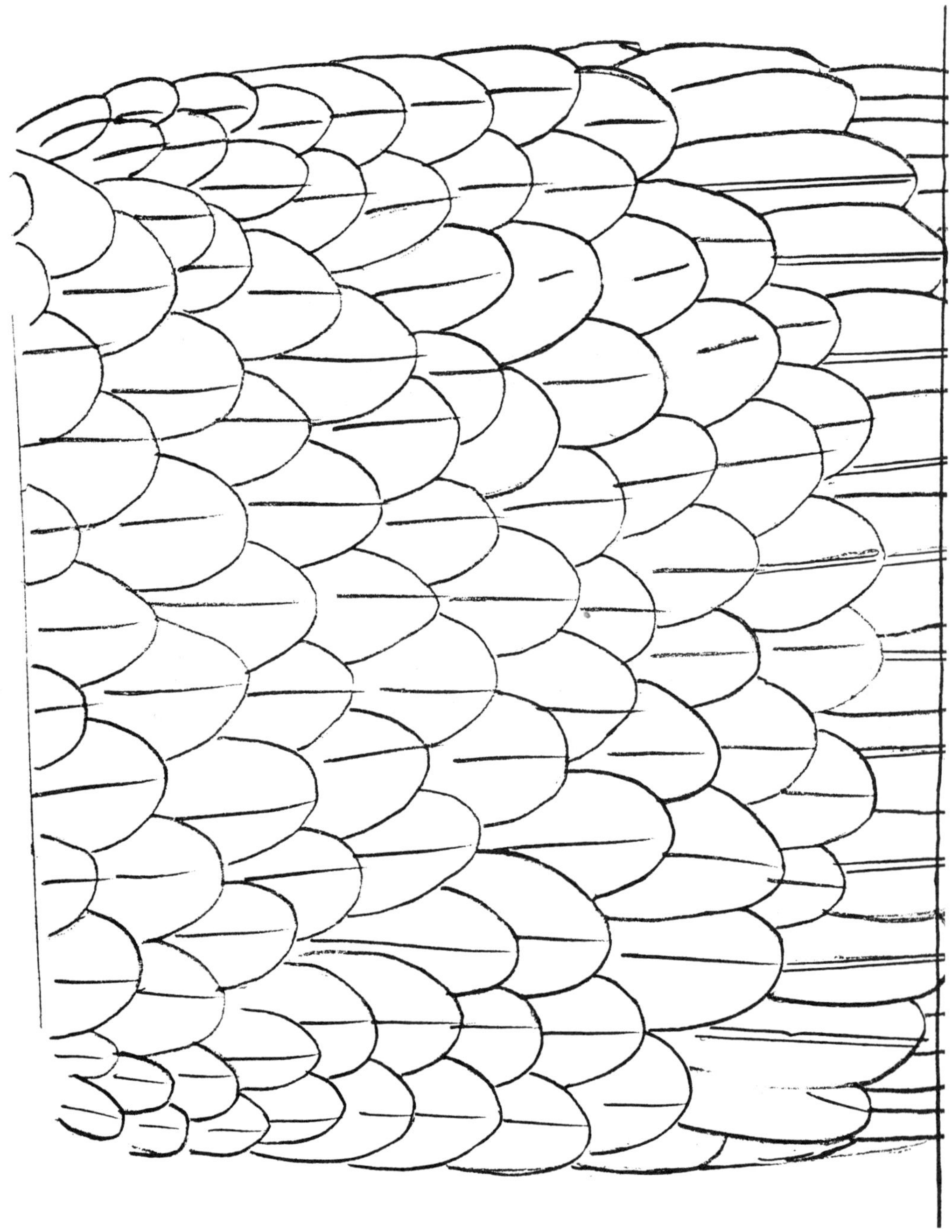

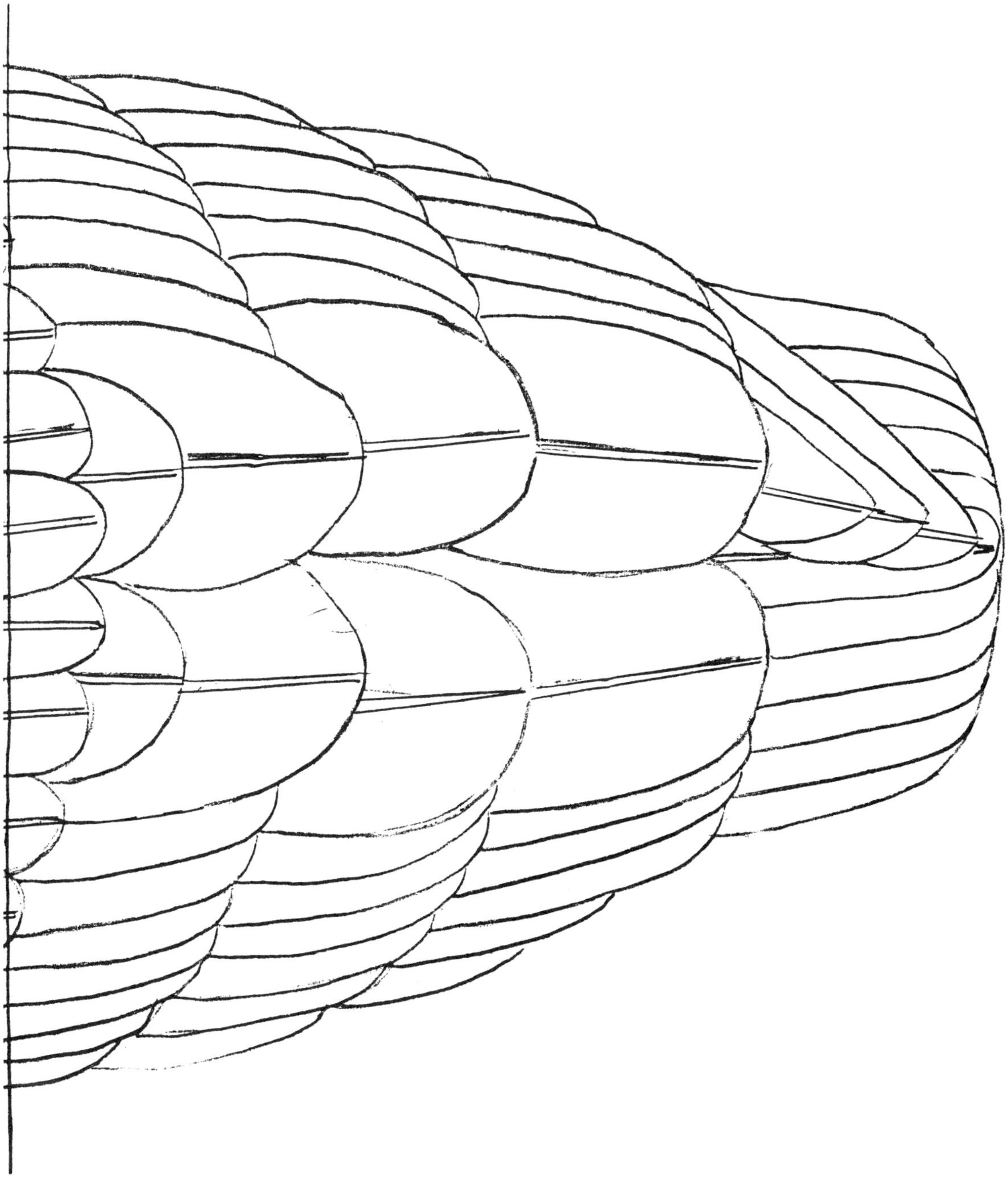

Top view

OSPREY
2/3 size
Body block—12" x 5" x 4"
Wing block—14" x 5" x 2"
Head block—3" x 3" x 4"
Eye size—9mm
Eye color—yellow

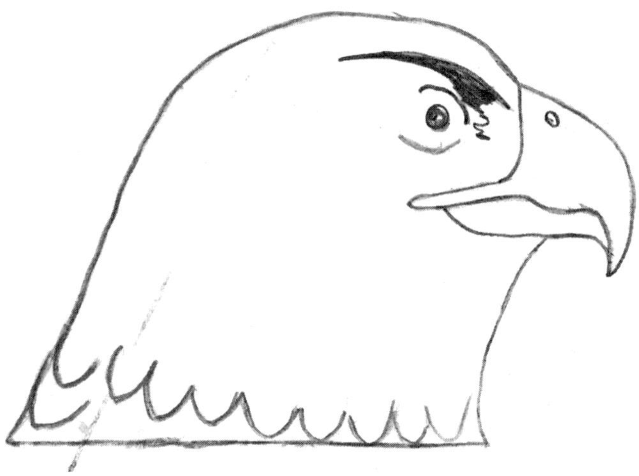

Top view of head
A. Crown line
B. Cheek line
C. Neck joint line

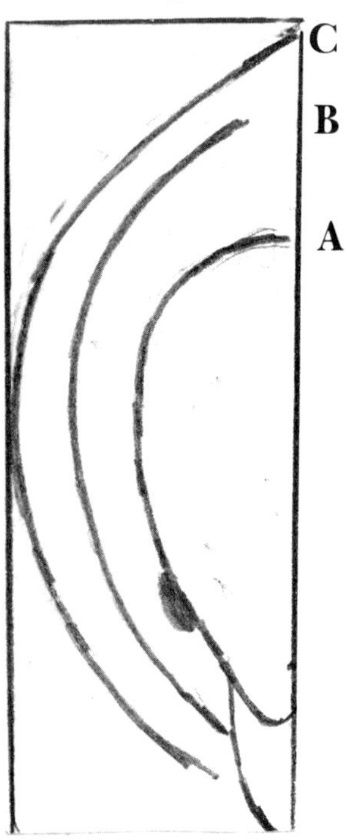

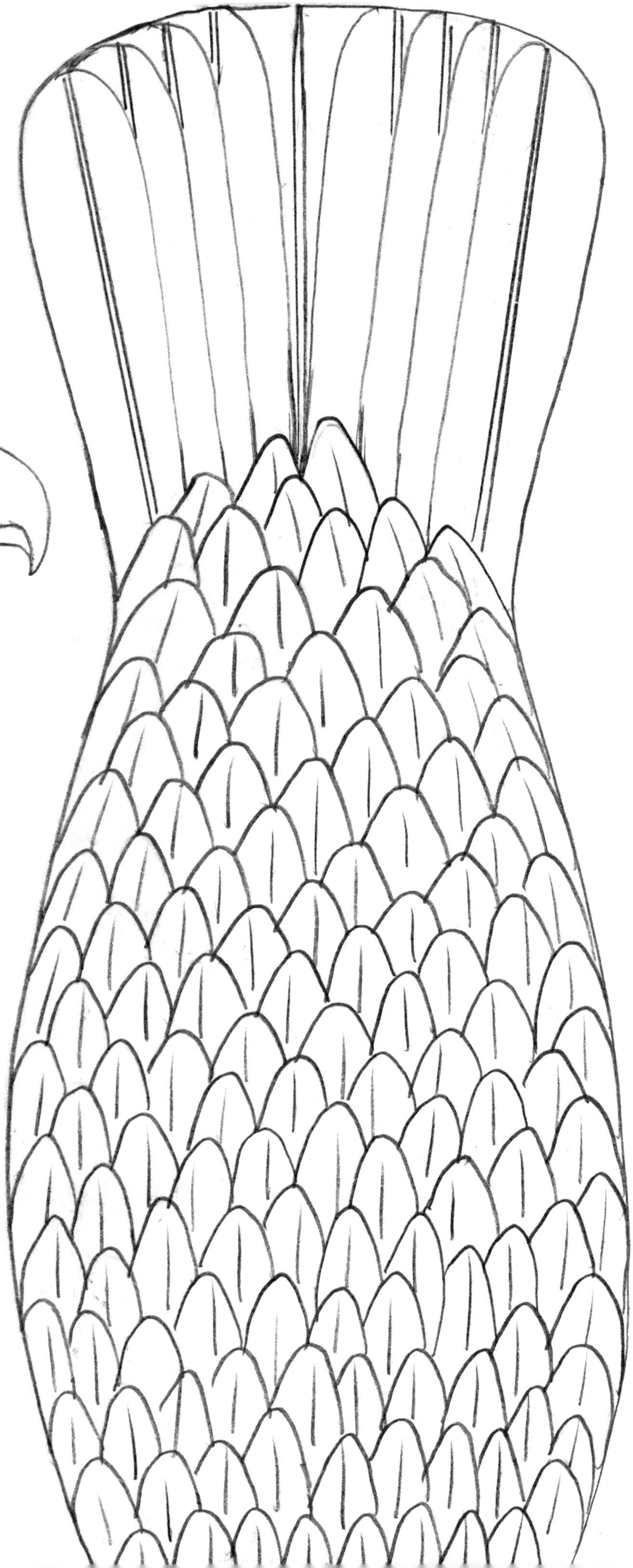

Bottom view

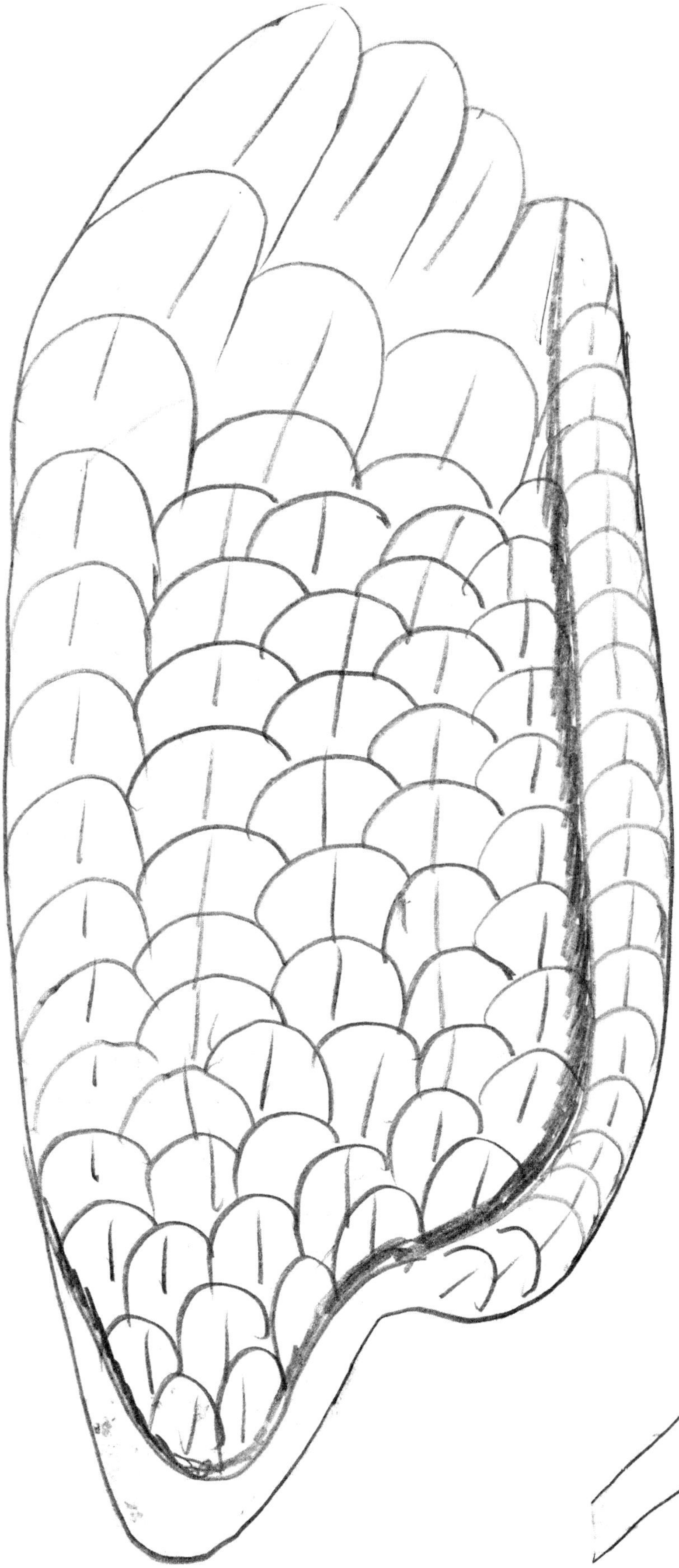

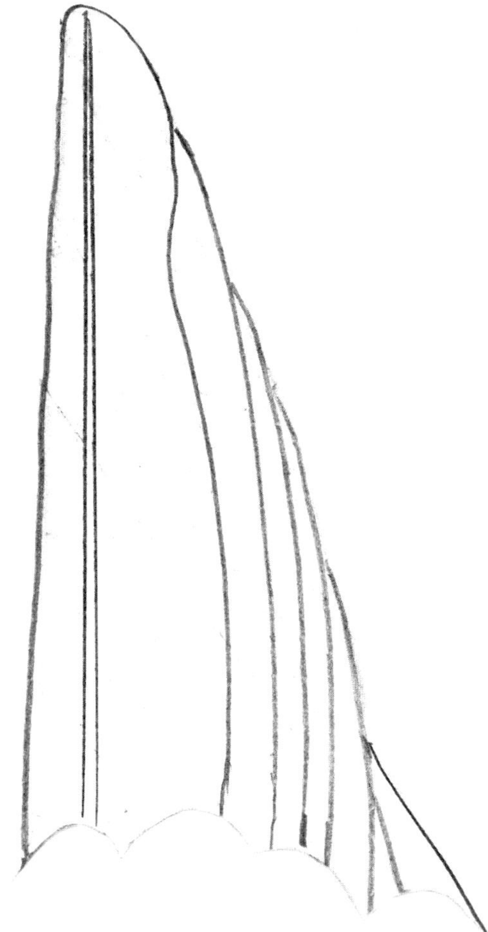

Underside of wing

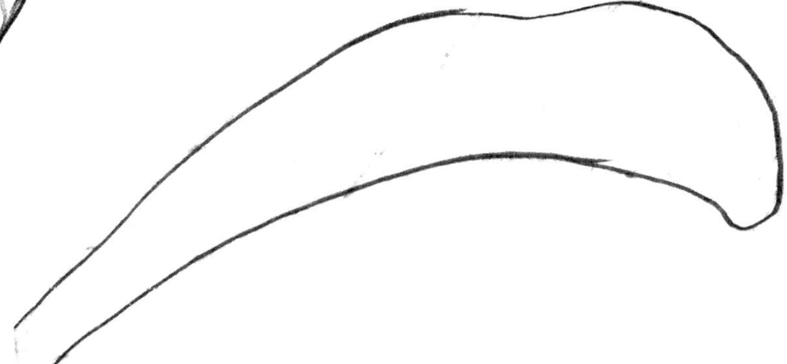

End view of wing

Osprey

Wing top view

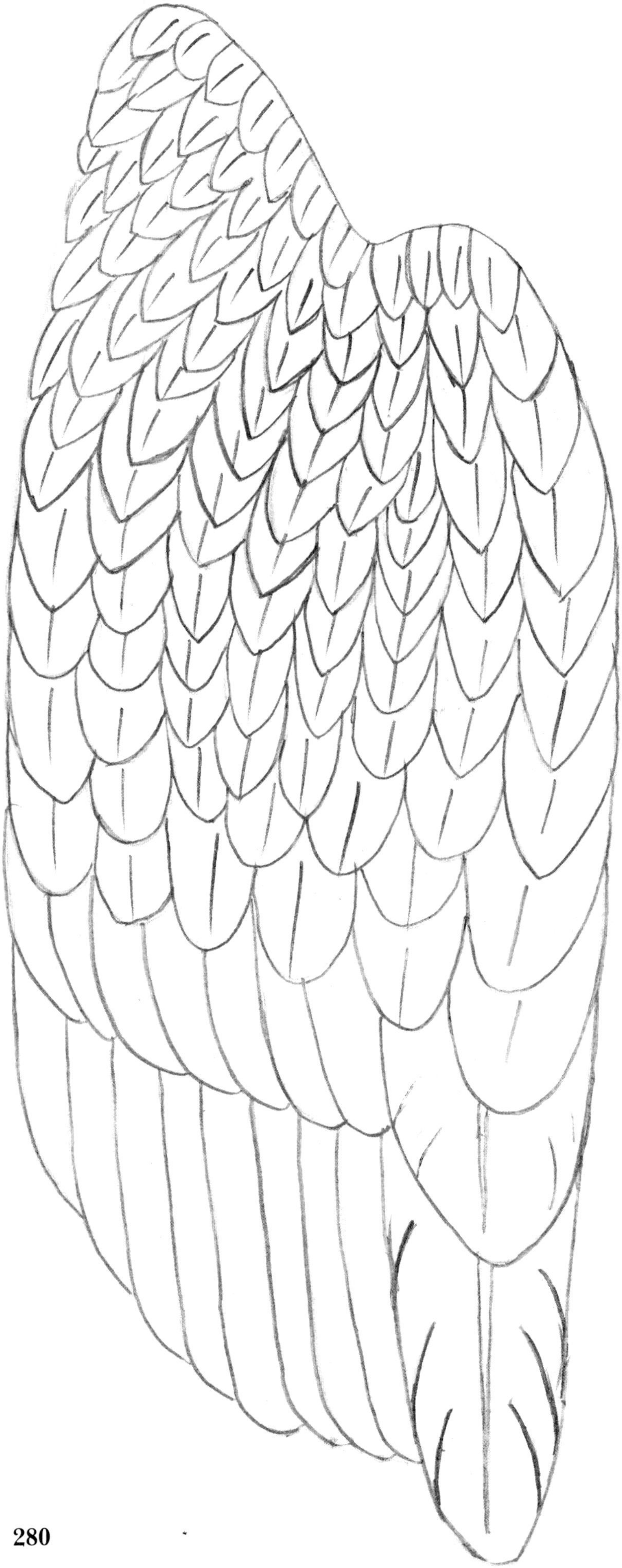

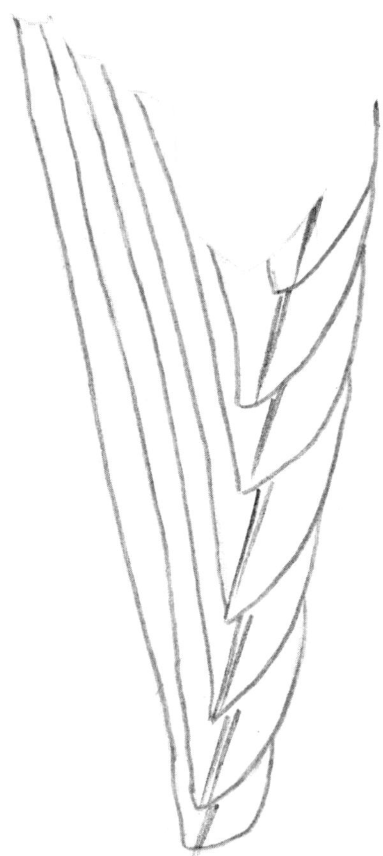

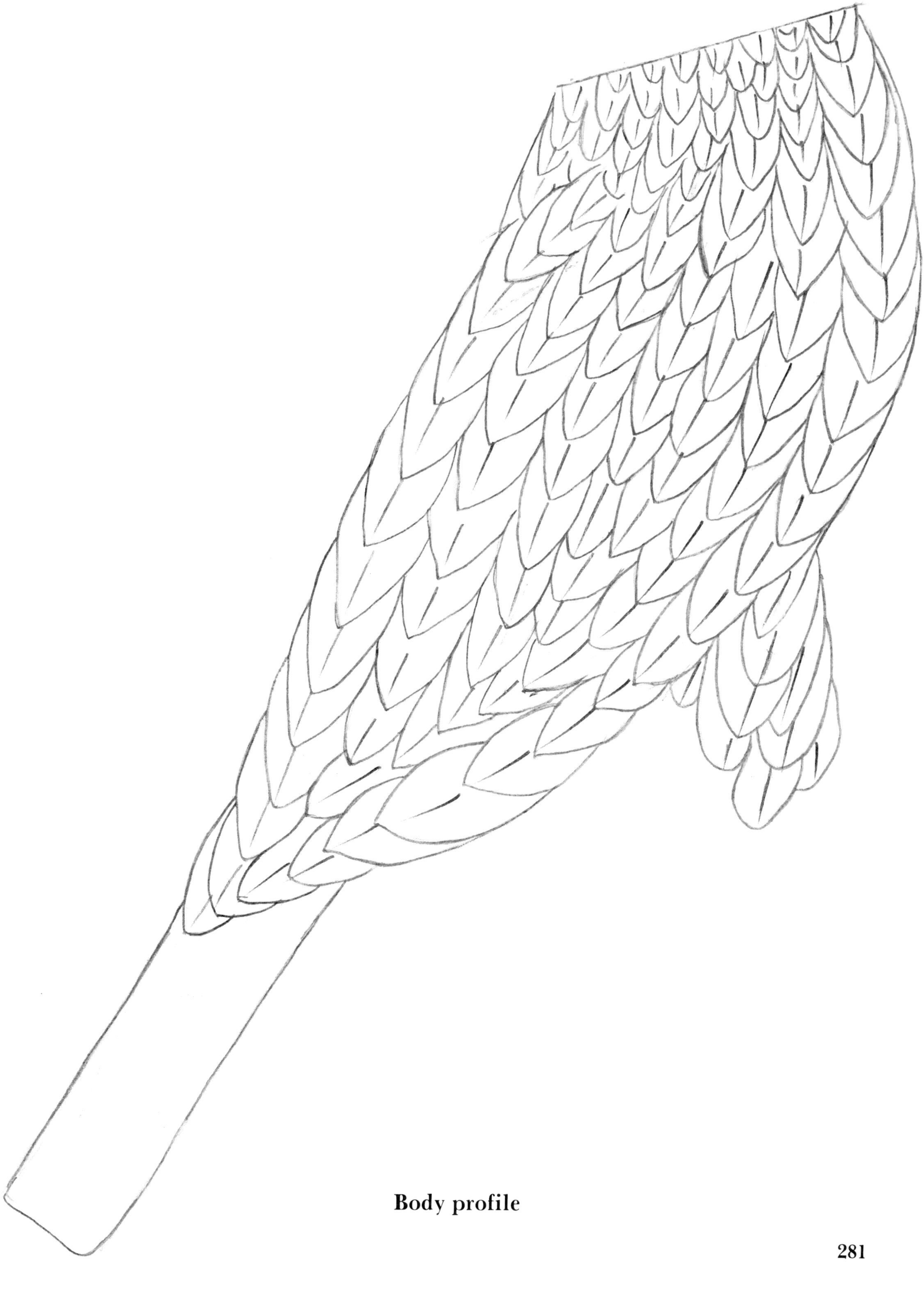

Body profile

Osprey Top view

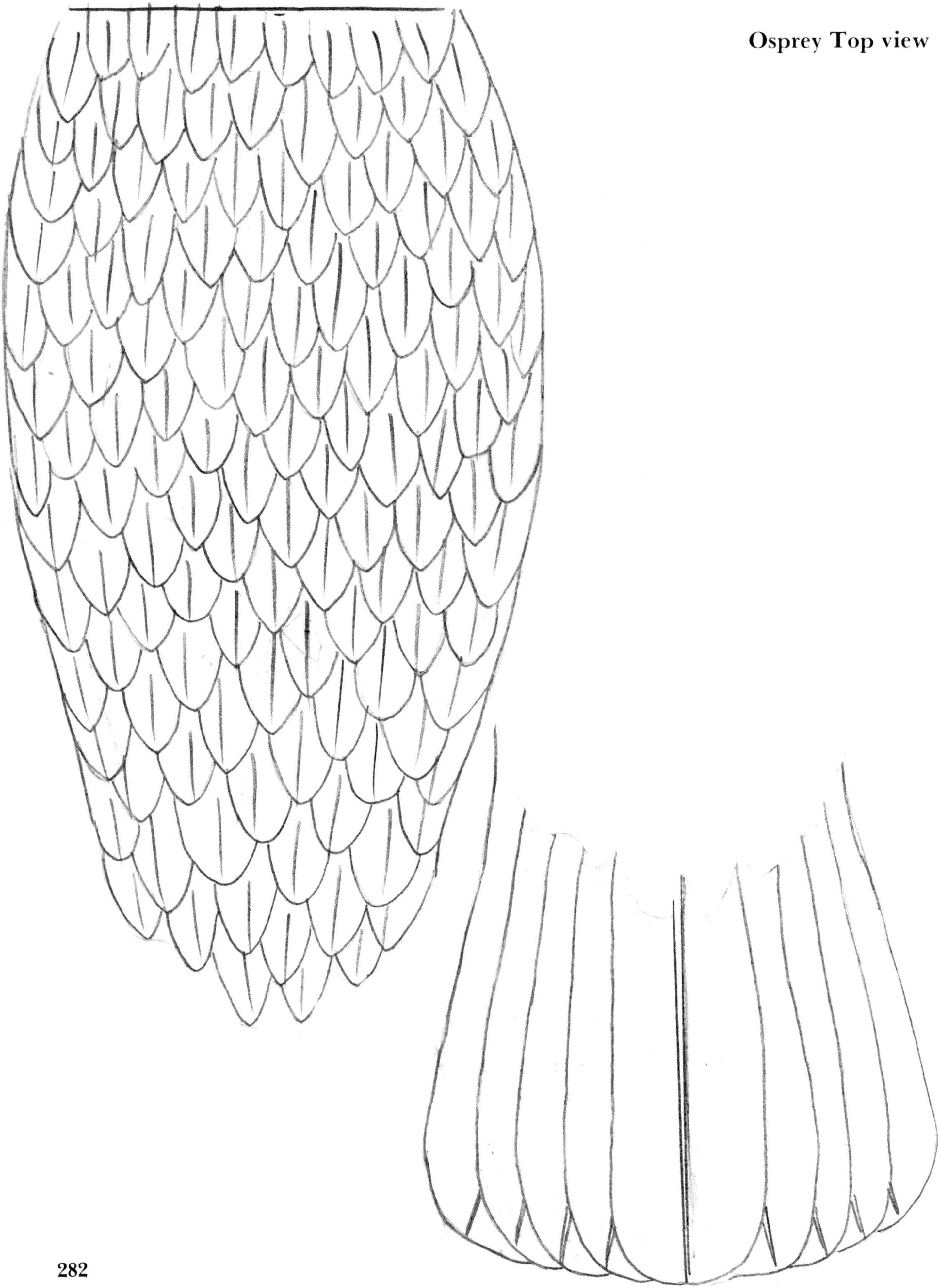

AMERICAN KESTREL
Body block—8" x 6½" x 4"
Head block—3" x 2" x 2"
Eye size—9mm
Eye color—brown

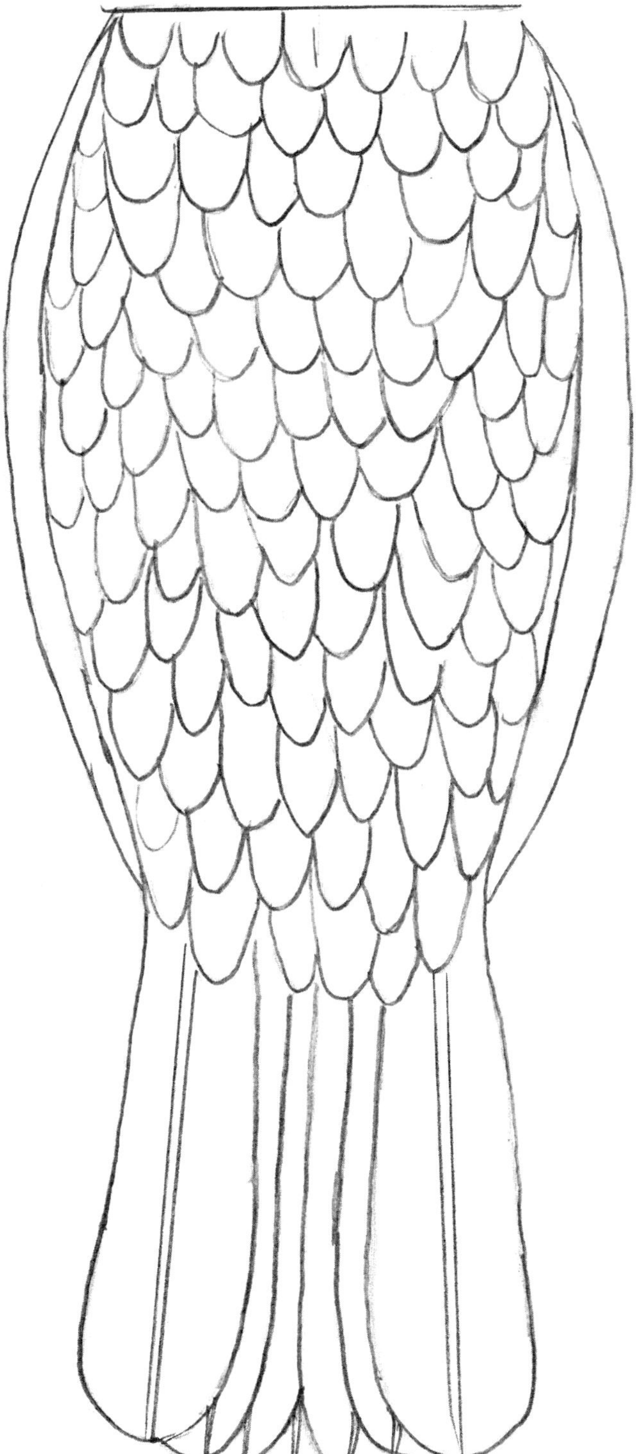

Underside of tail and belly

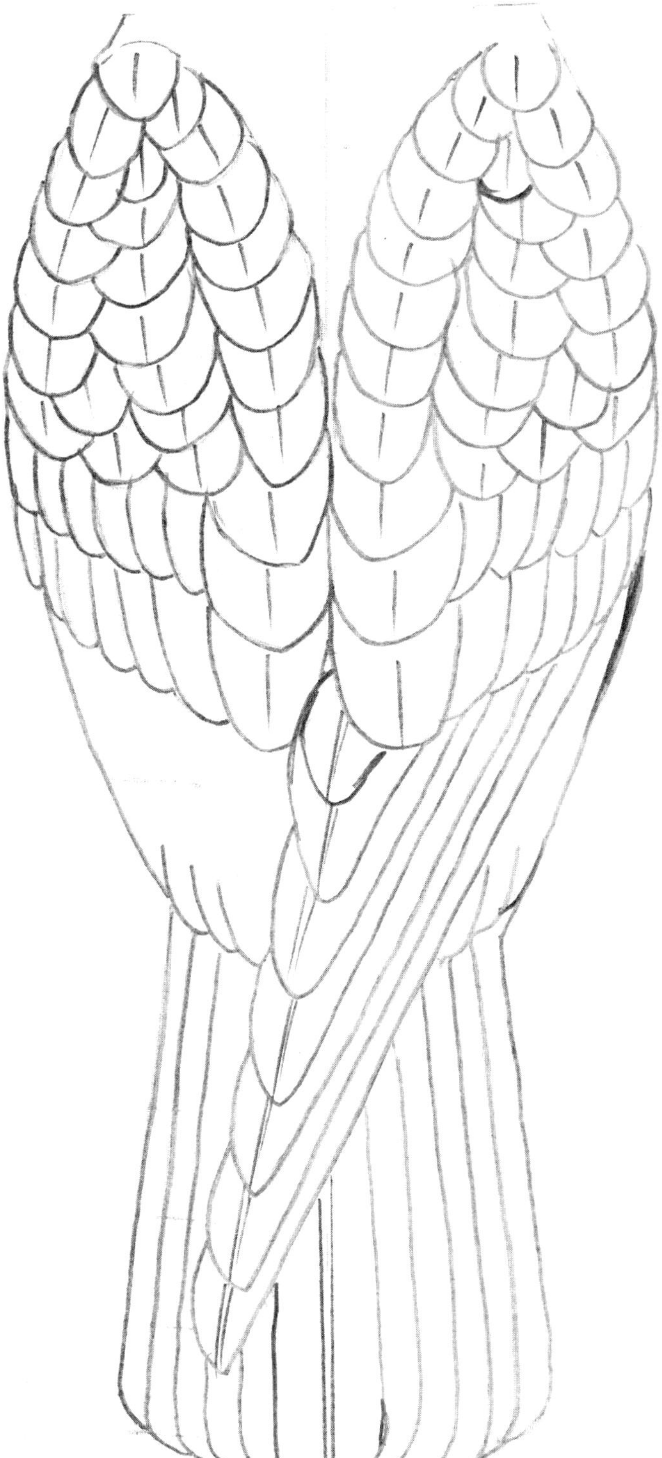

Body top view

Kestrel

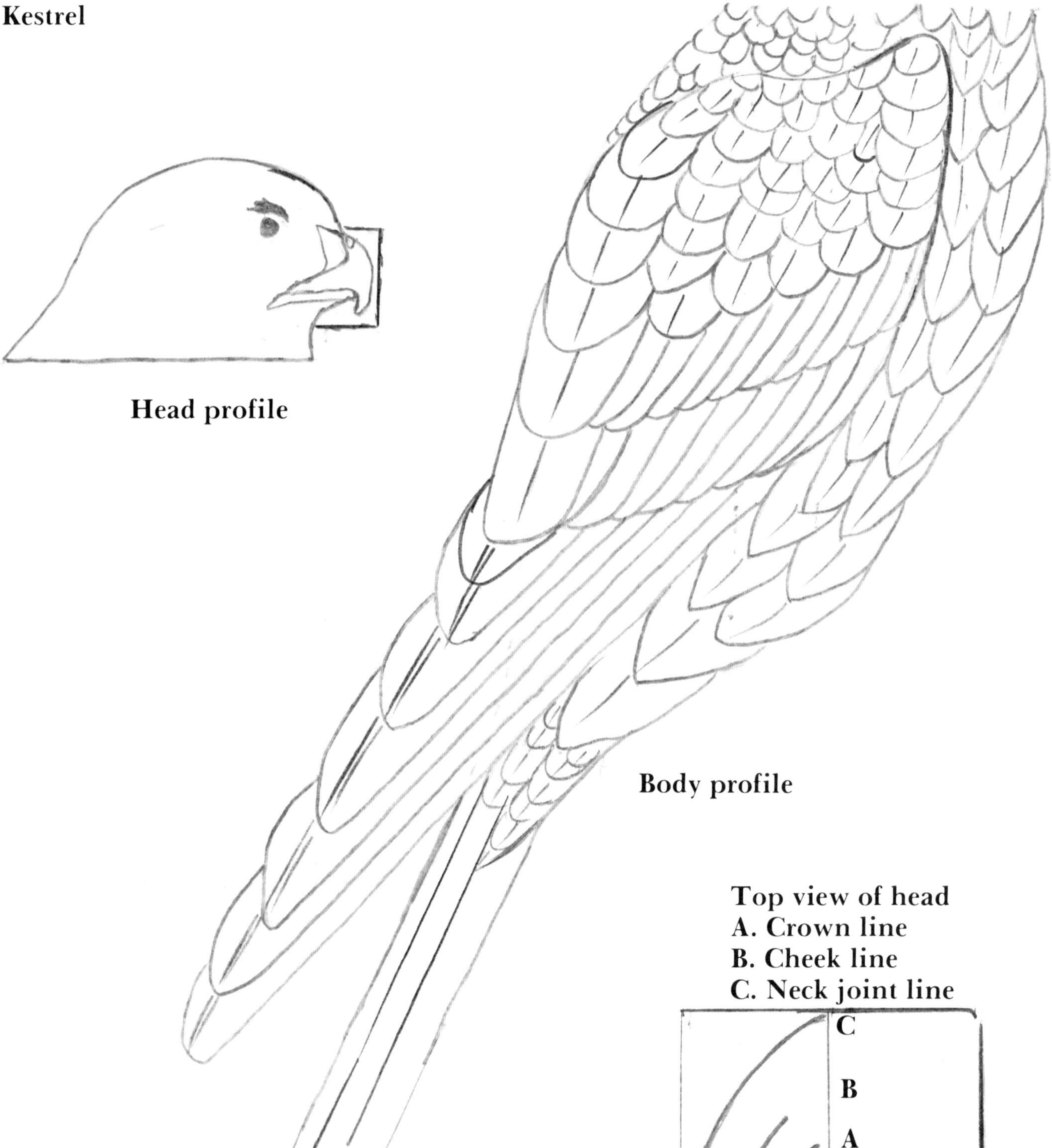

Head profile

Body profile

Top view of head
A. Crown line
B. Cheek line
C. Neck joint line

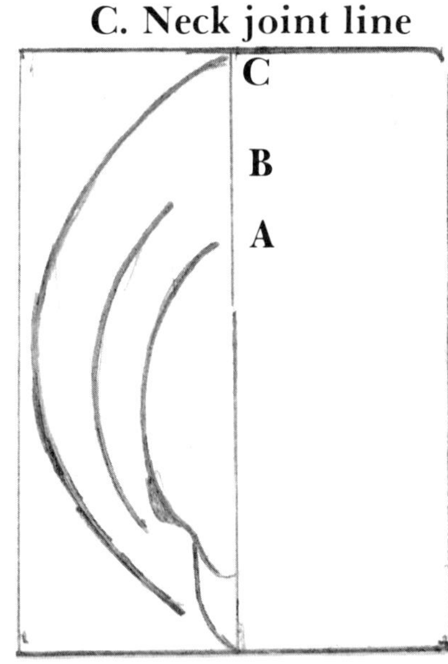

Top view of Merlin

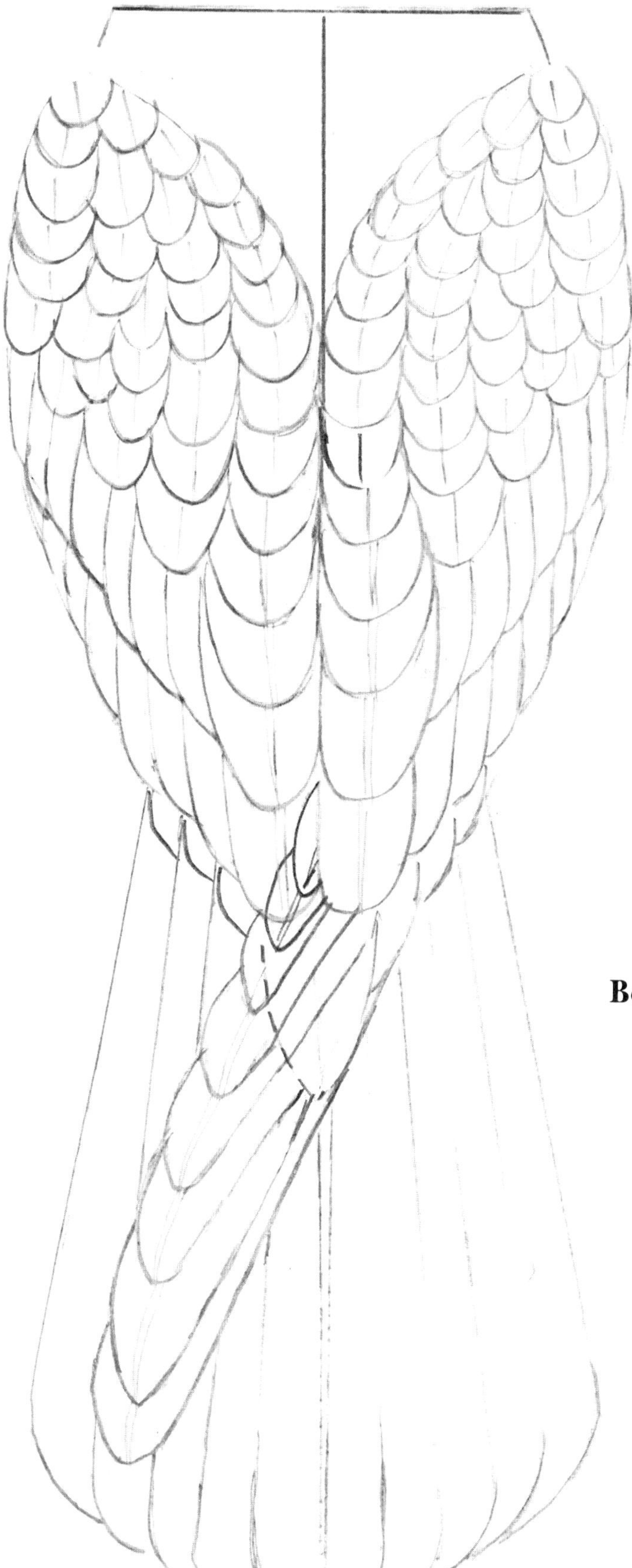

(Male is carved and has same feather layout as female but is different color)

FEMALE MERLIN
Body block—9½" x 4" x 3"
Head block—3" x 2" x 2"
Eye size—9mm
Eye color—brown

Bottom view

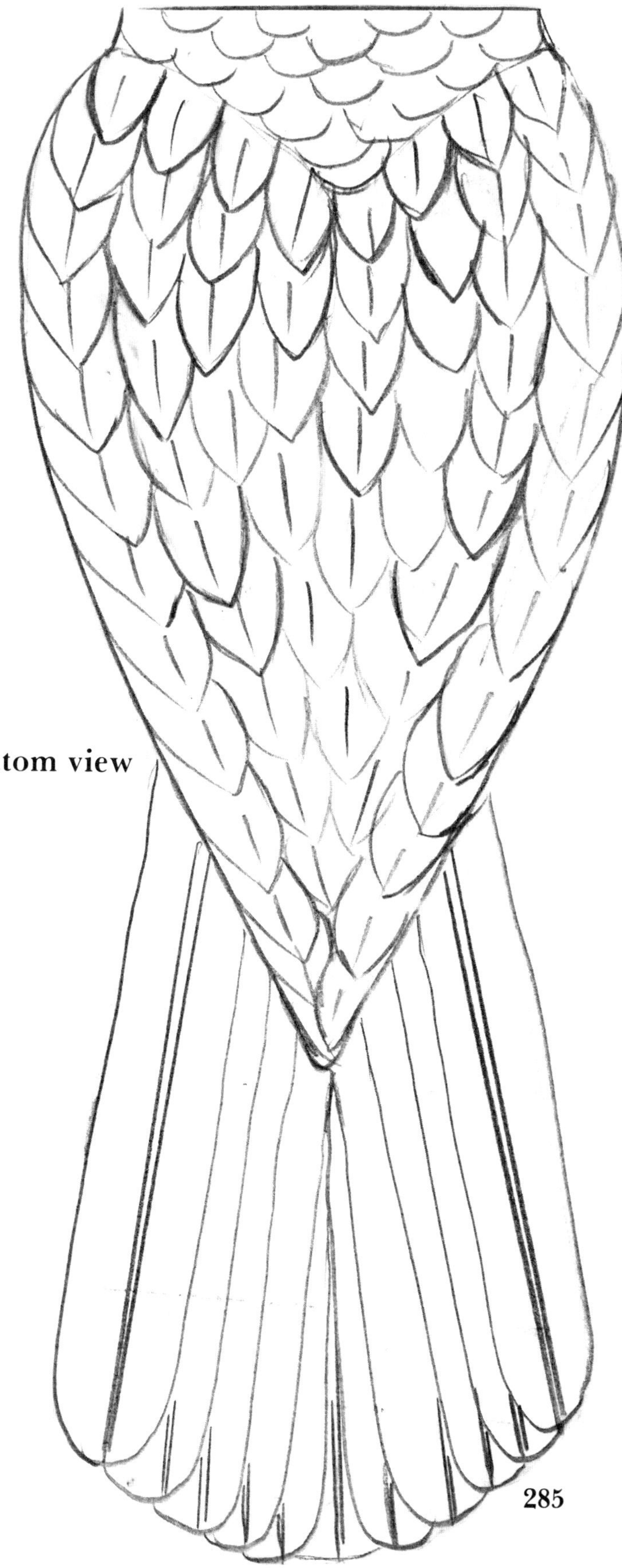

Female Merlin

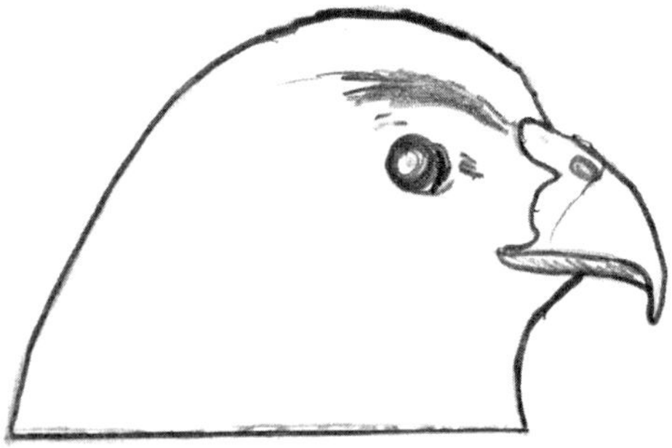

Top view of head
A. Crown line
B. Cheek line
C. Neck joint line

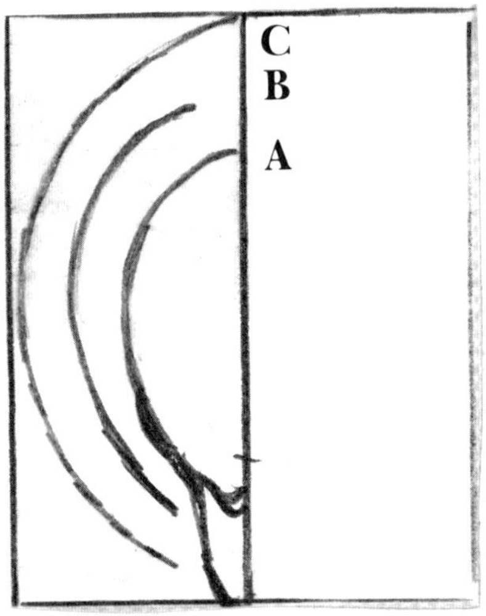

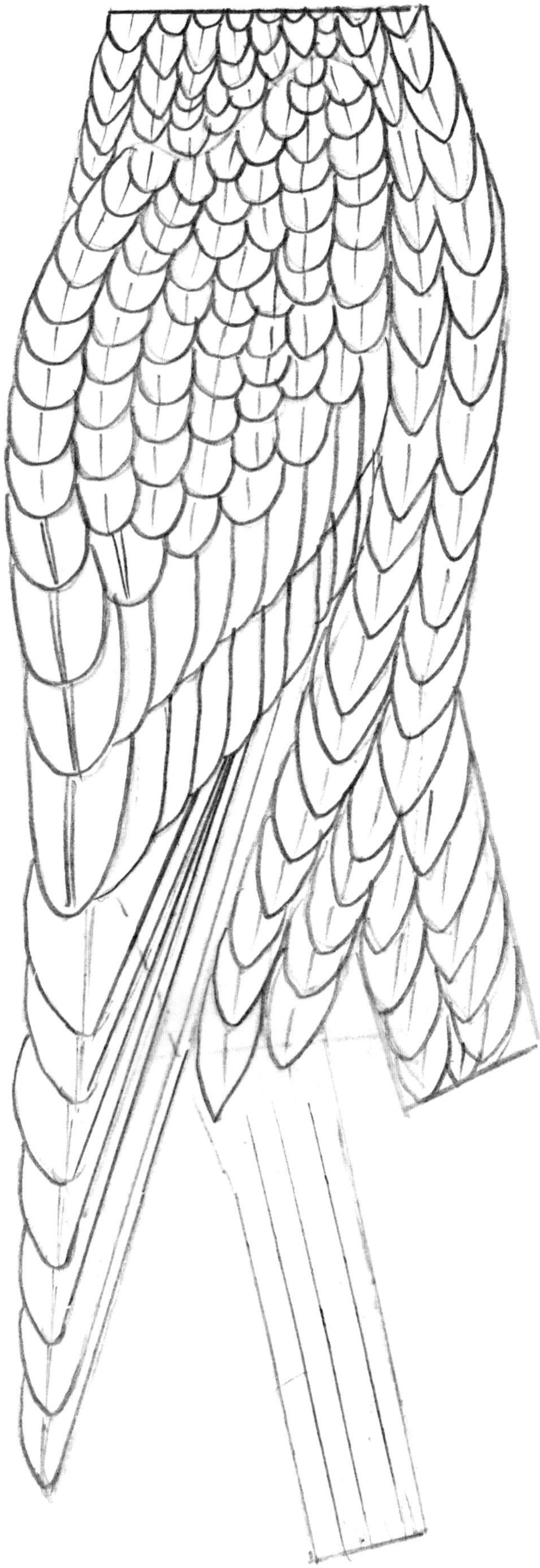

Profile pattern

MINIATURE FLYING PEREGRINE FALCON

Wing block—8" x 3" x 2"
Body block—7" x 3" x 2"
Eye size—5mm
Eye color—brown

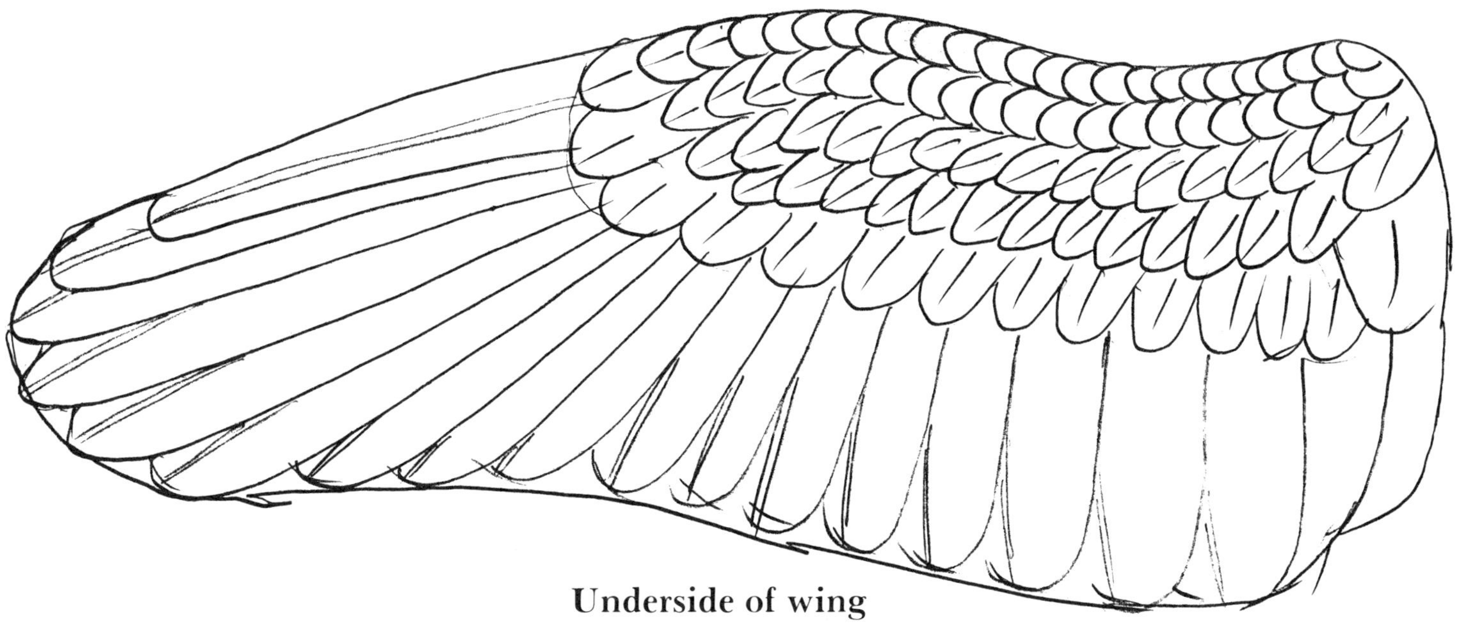

Underside of wing

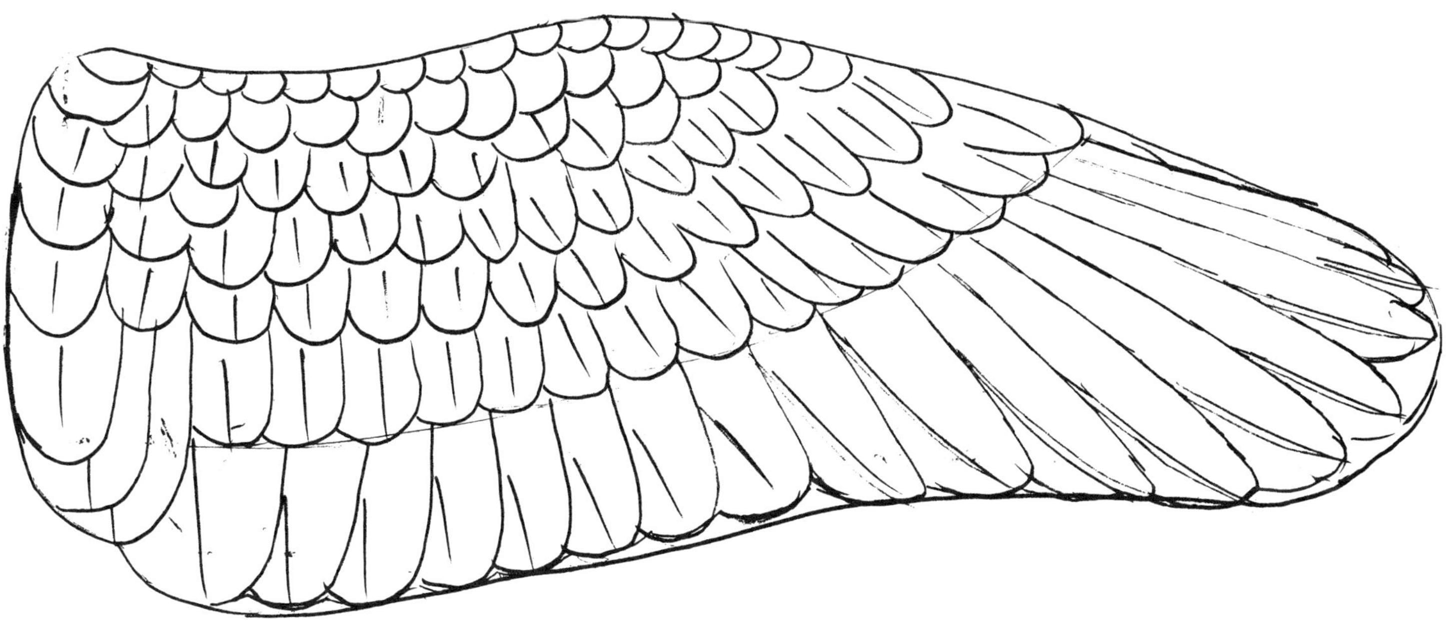

Top side of wing

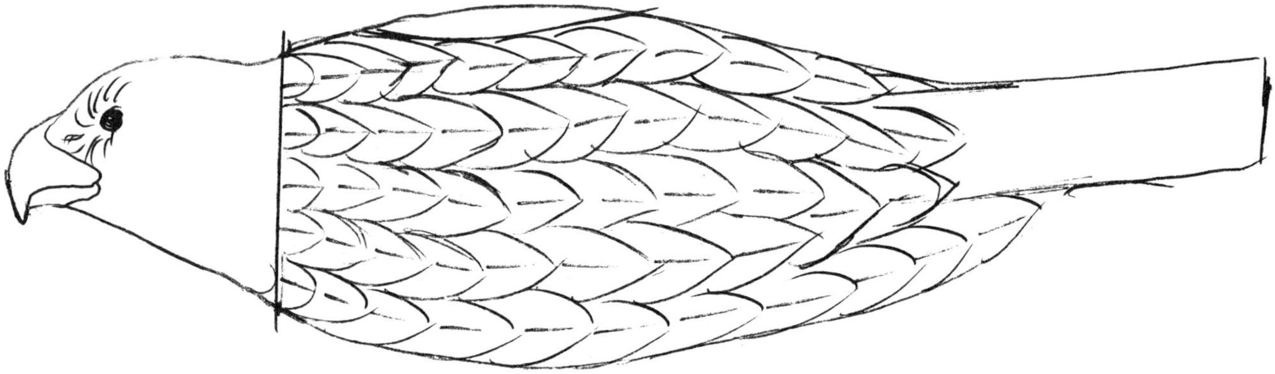

Profile pattern

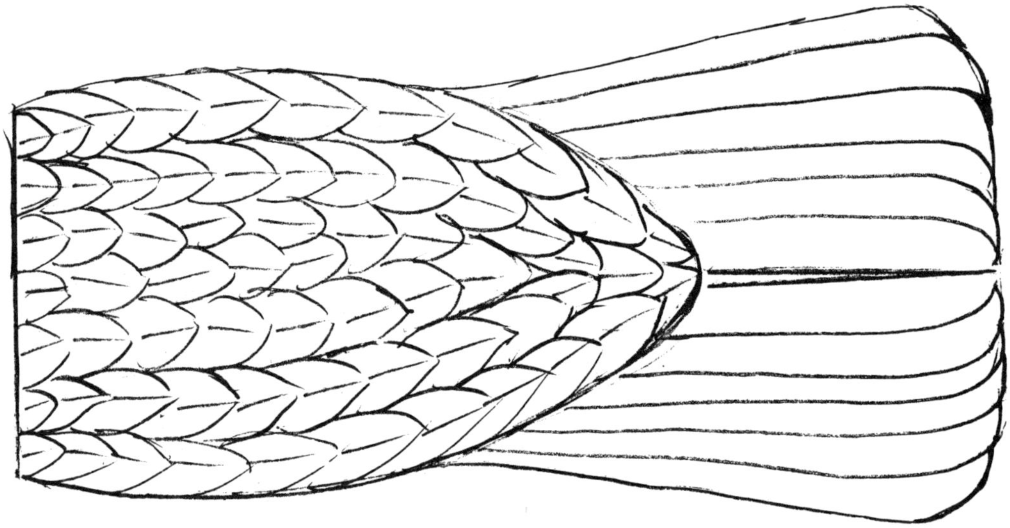

Top view

Top view of head
A. Crown line
B. Cheek line
C. Neck joint line

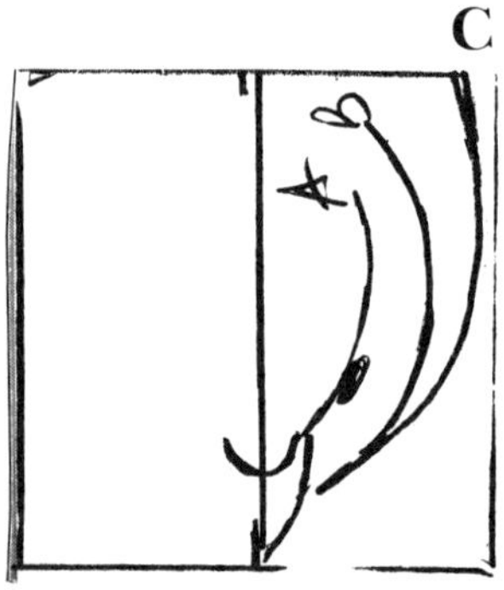

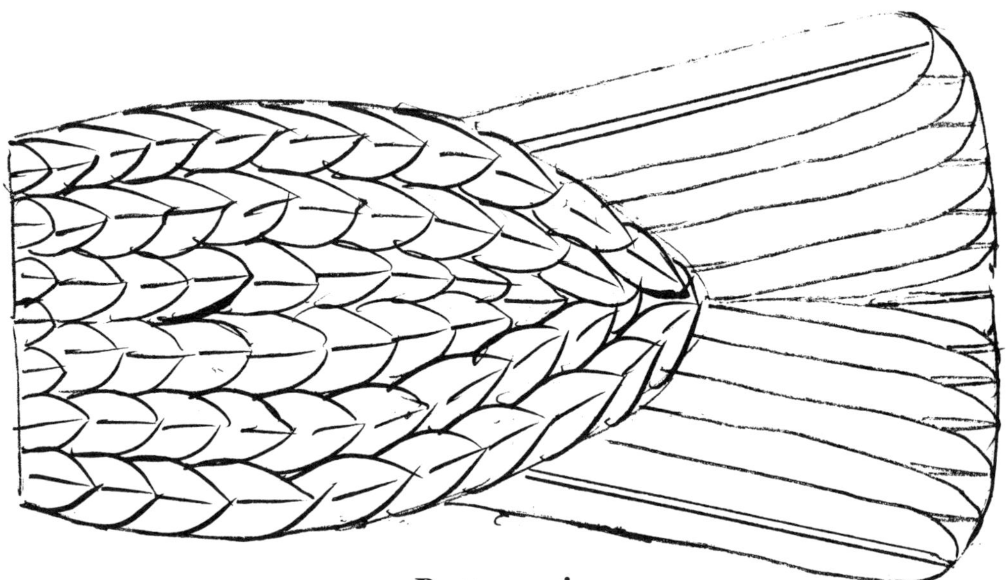

Bottom view

Miniature Flying Peregrine Falcon

ANTIQUED GOSHAWK
Body block—15½" x 6" x 7"
Wing block—15" x 6½" x 2"
Head block—6" x 4" x 3"
Eye size—10mm
Eye color—red

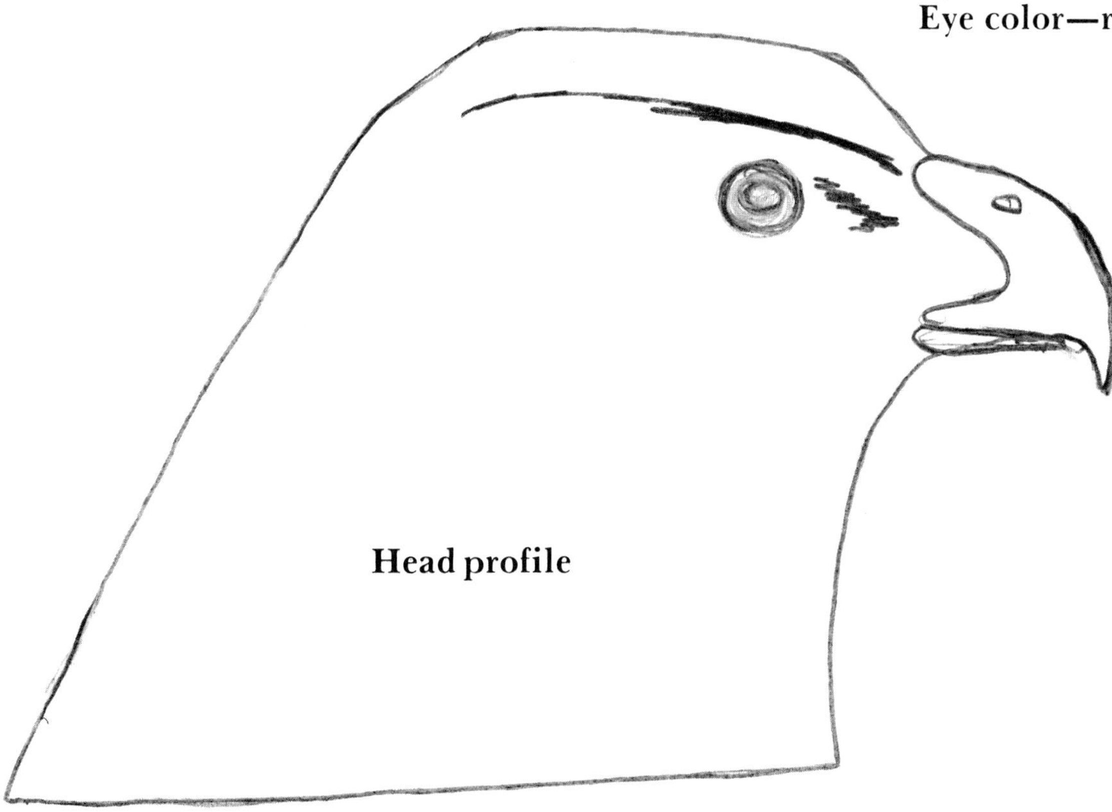

Head profile

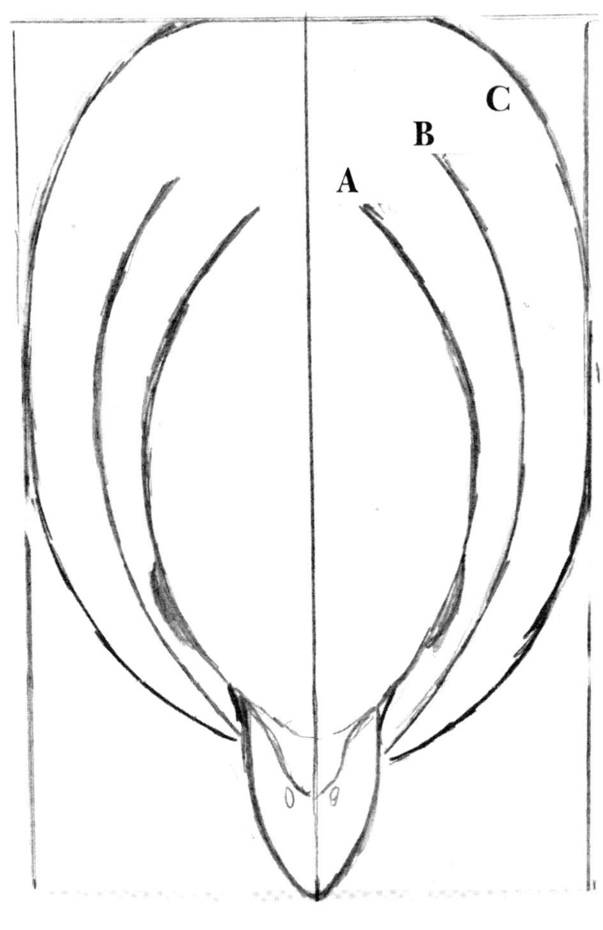

Top view of head
A. Crown line
B. Cheek line
C. Head joint line

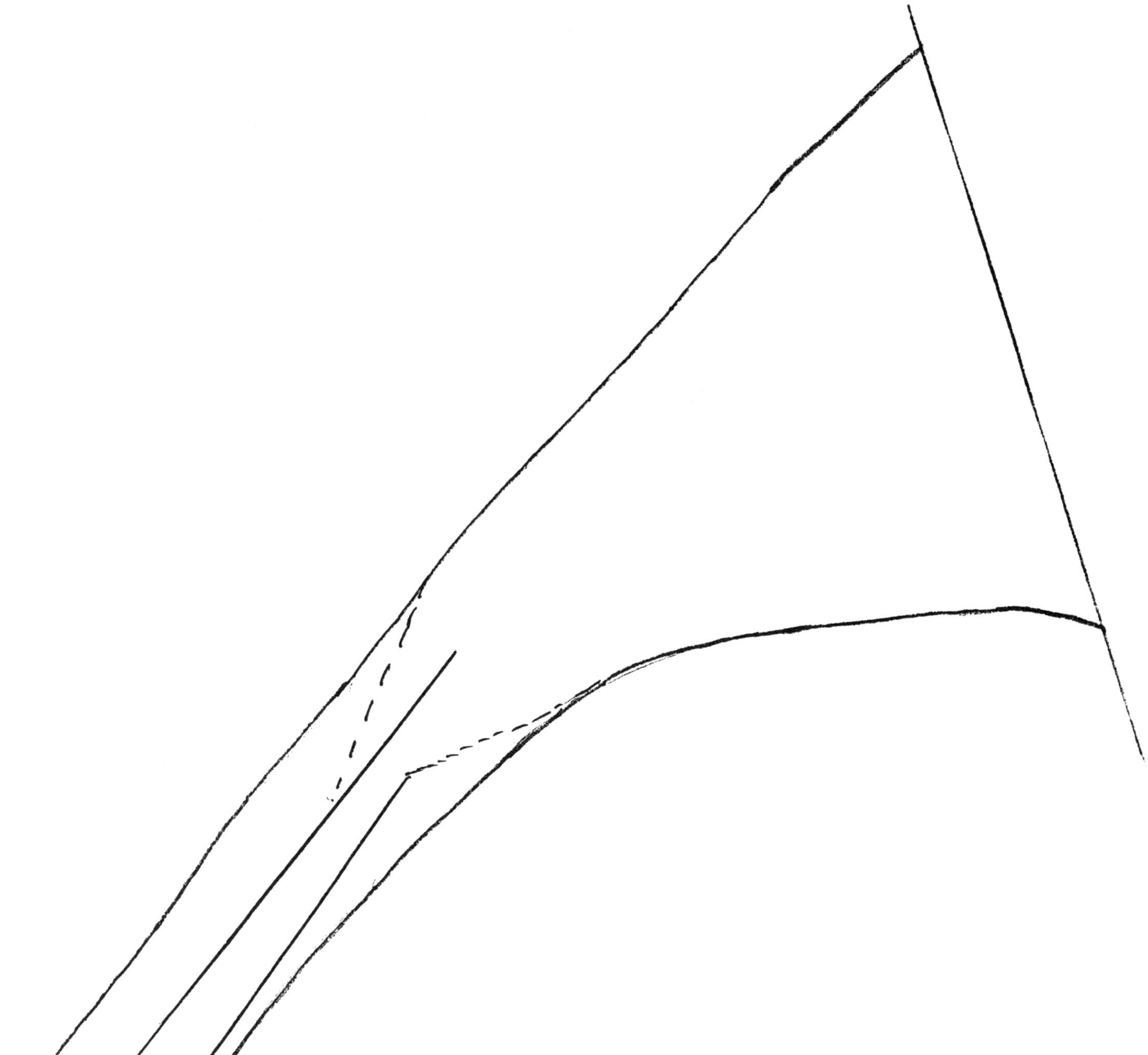

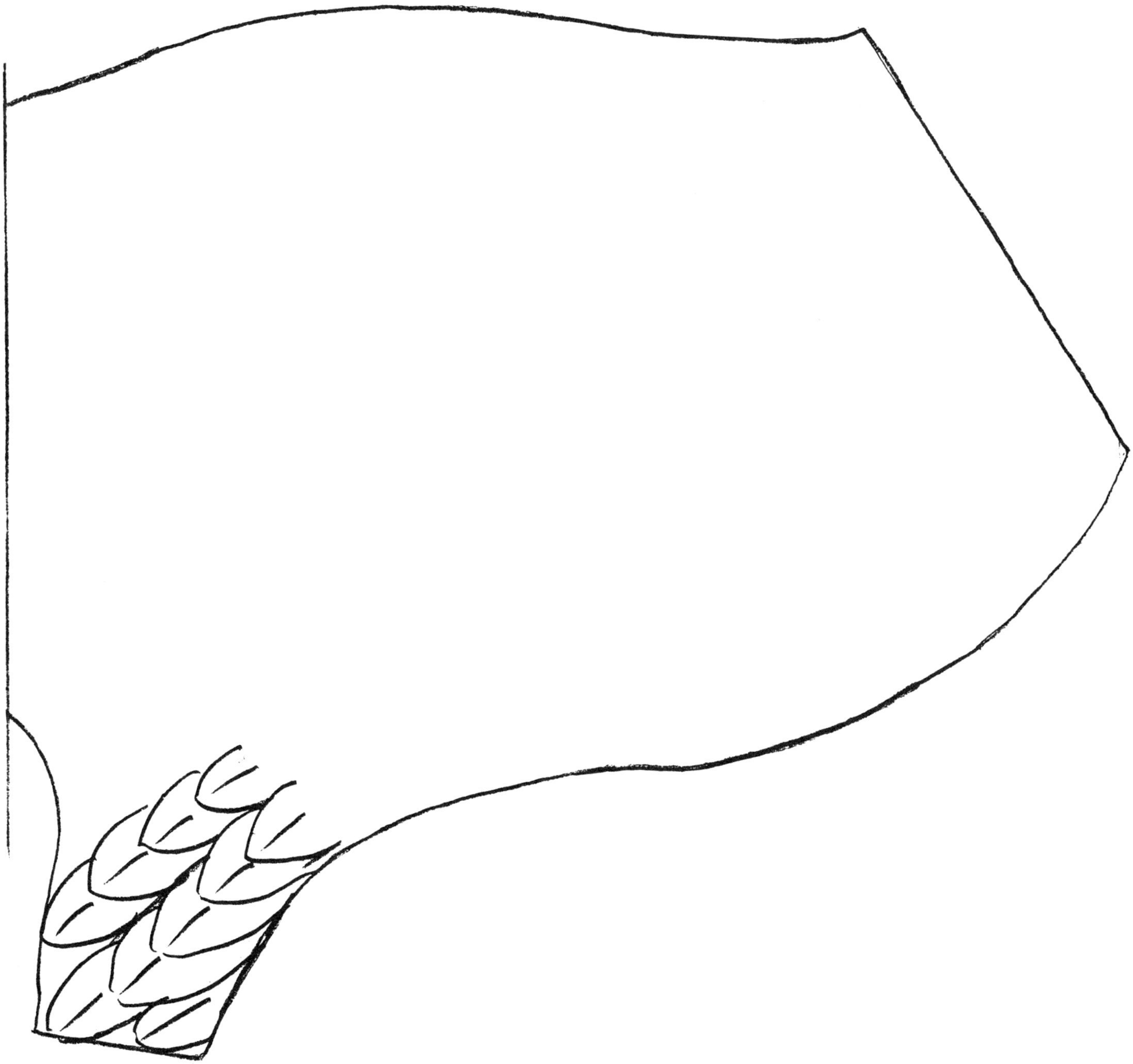

Profile pattern

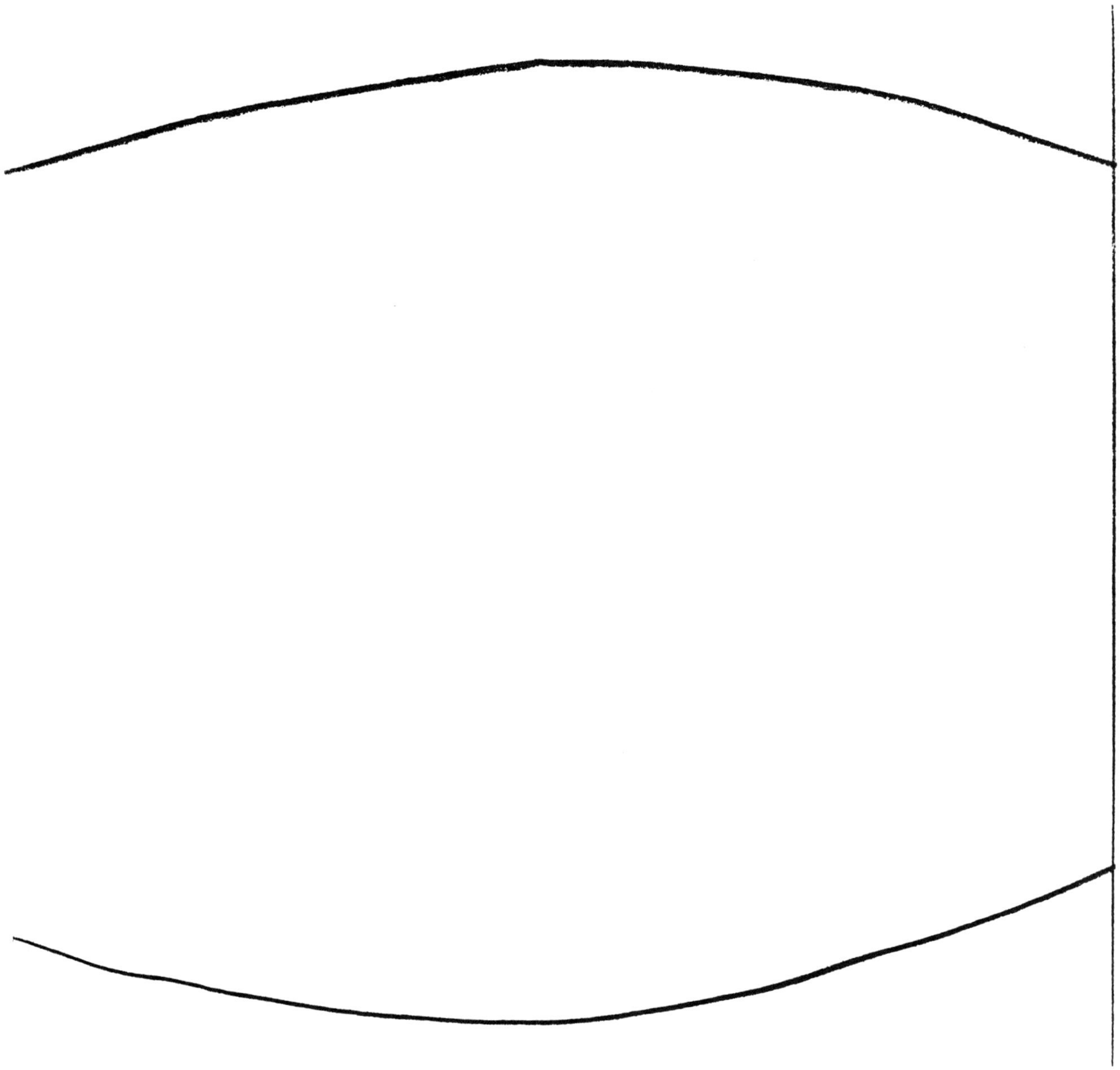

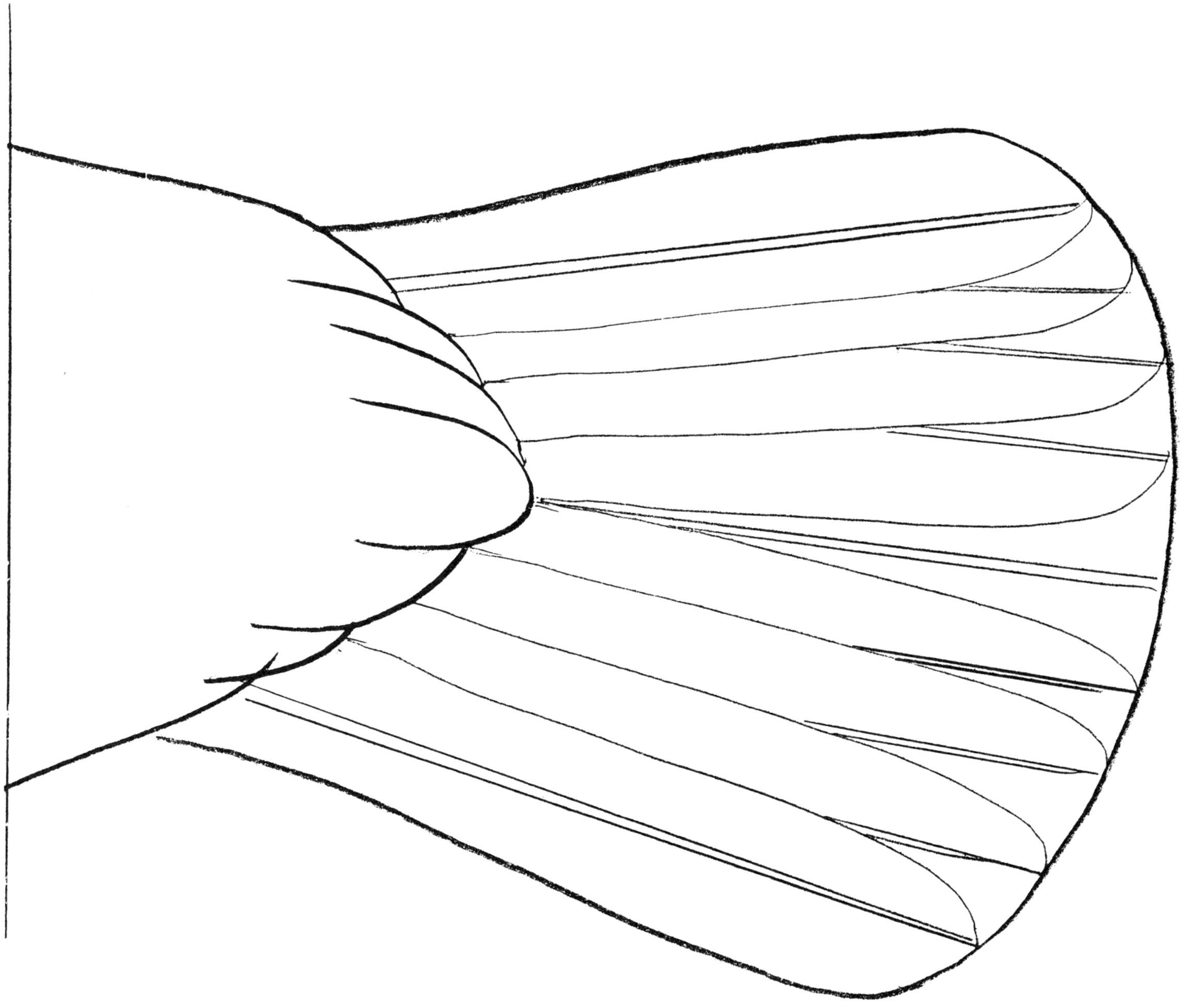

Bottom view

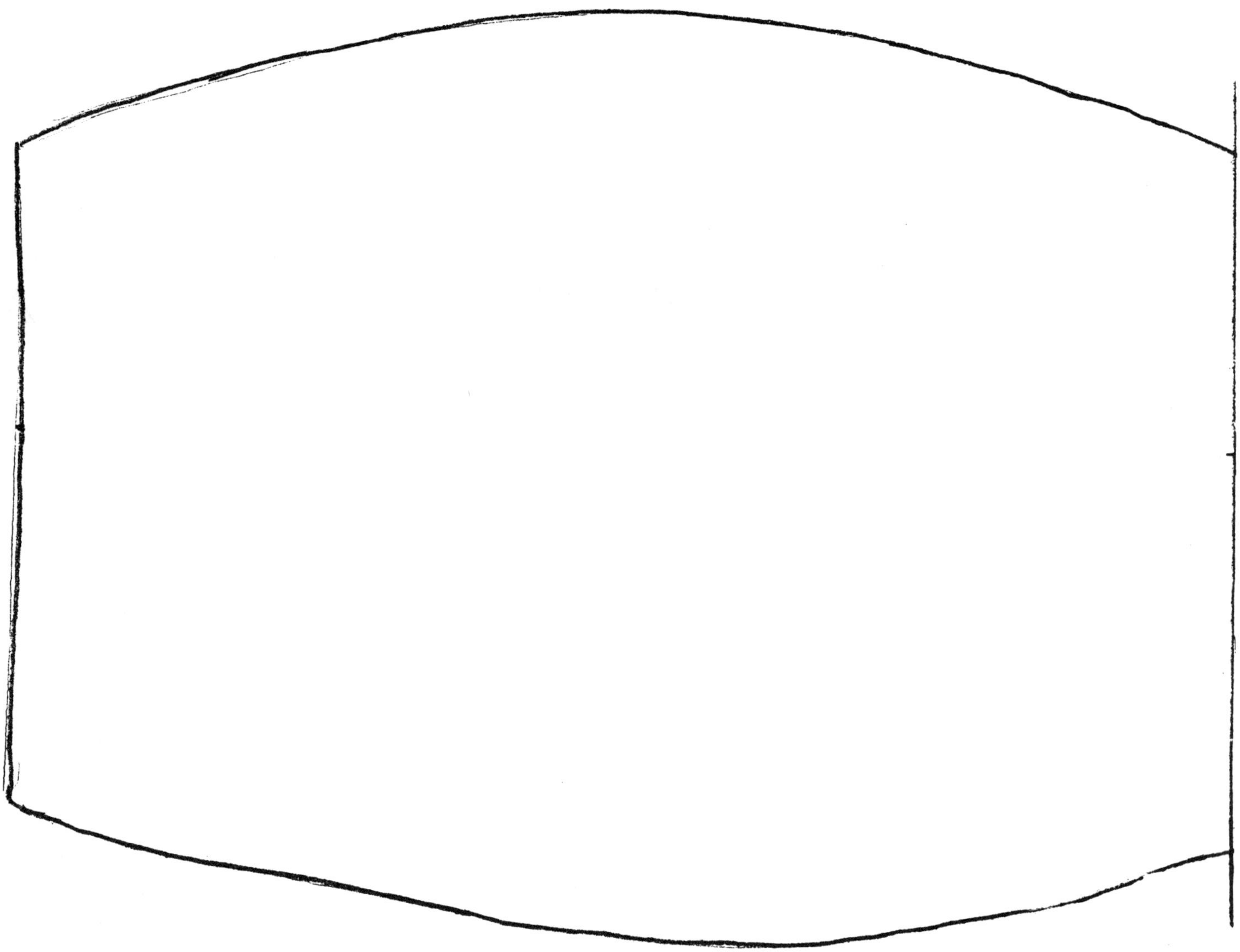

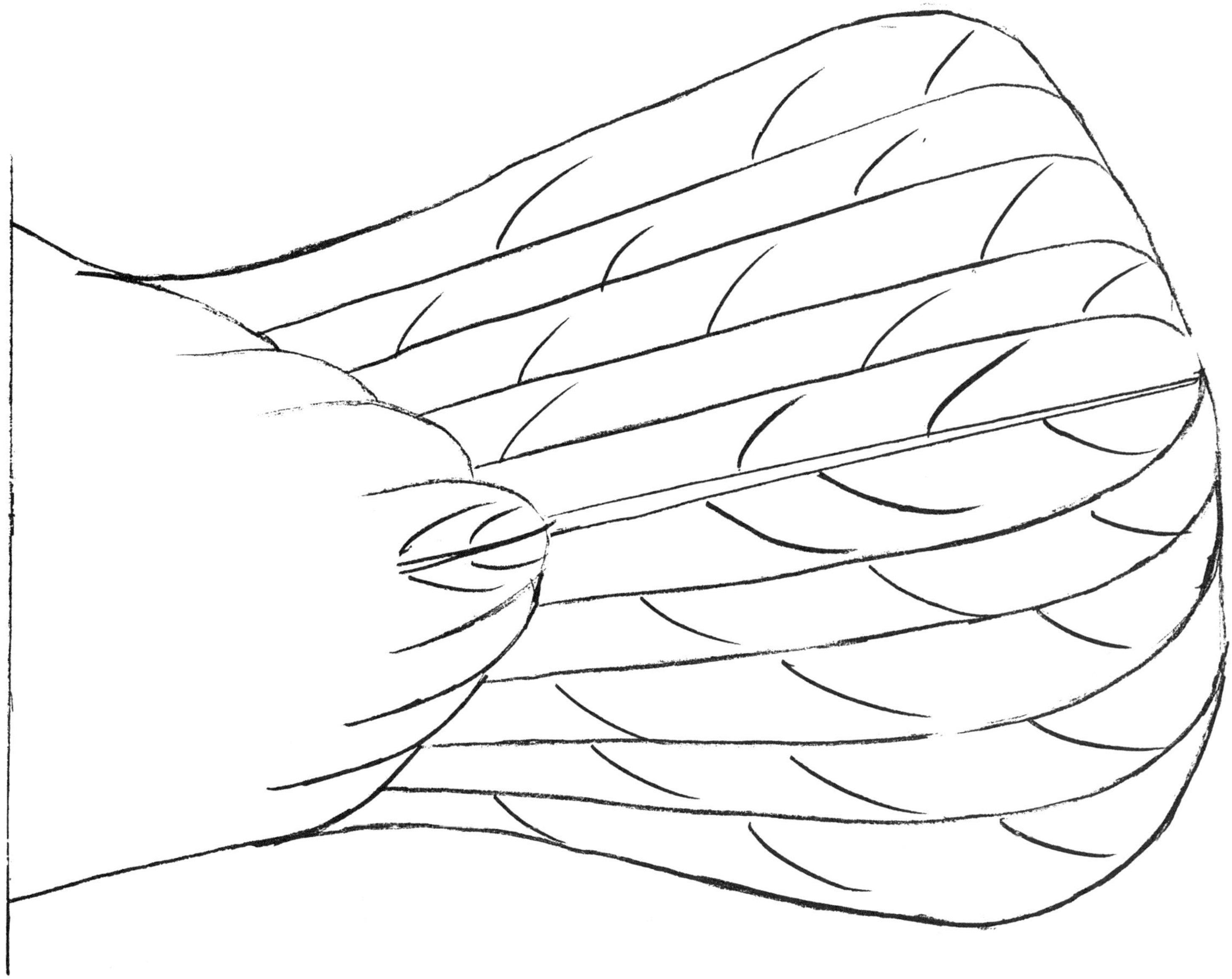

Pattern Top view

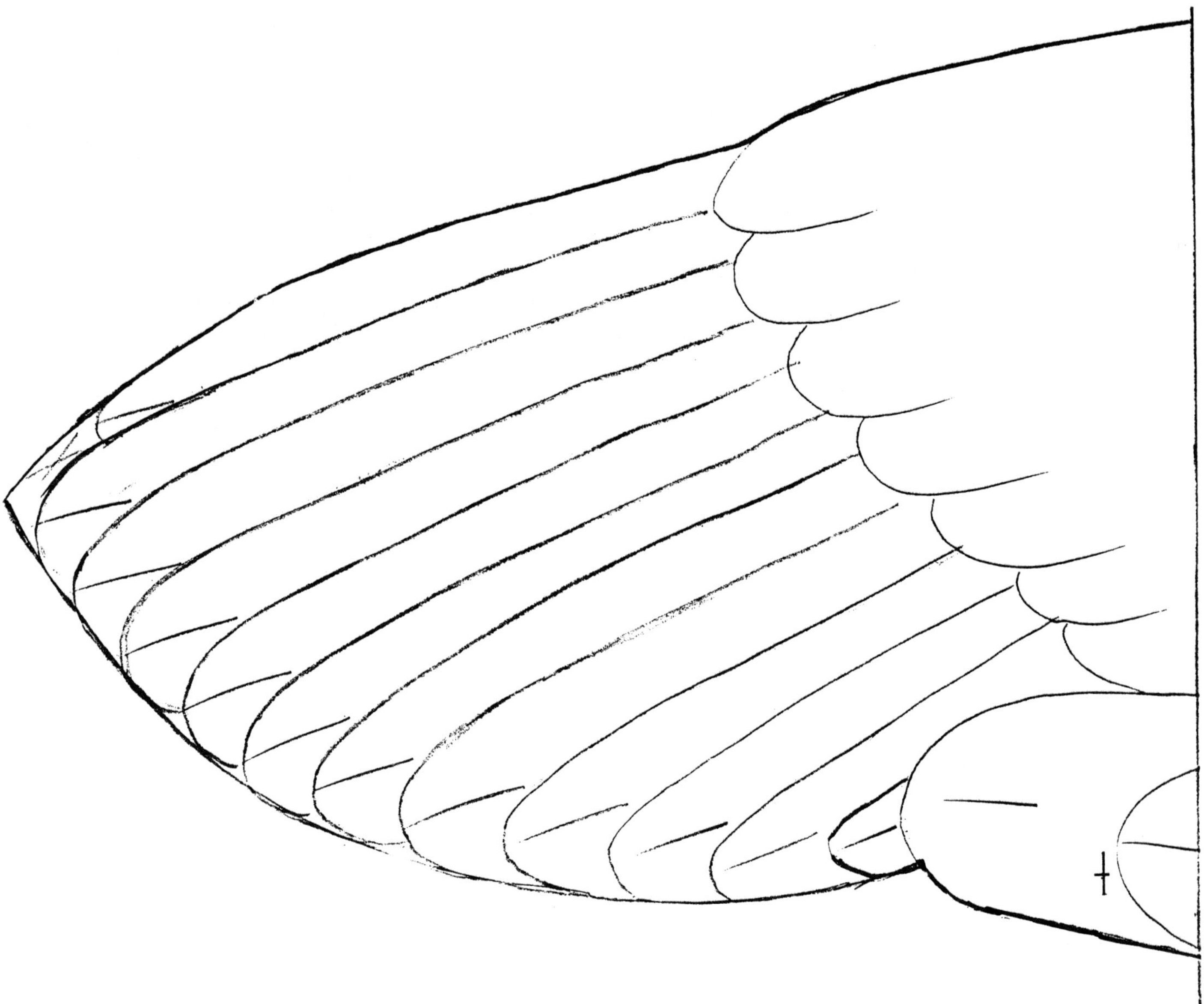

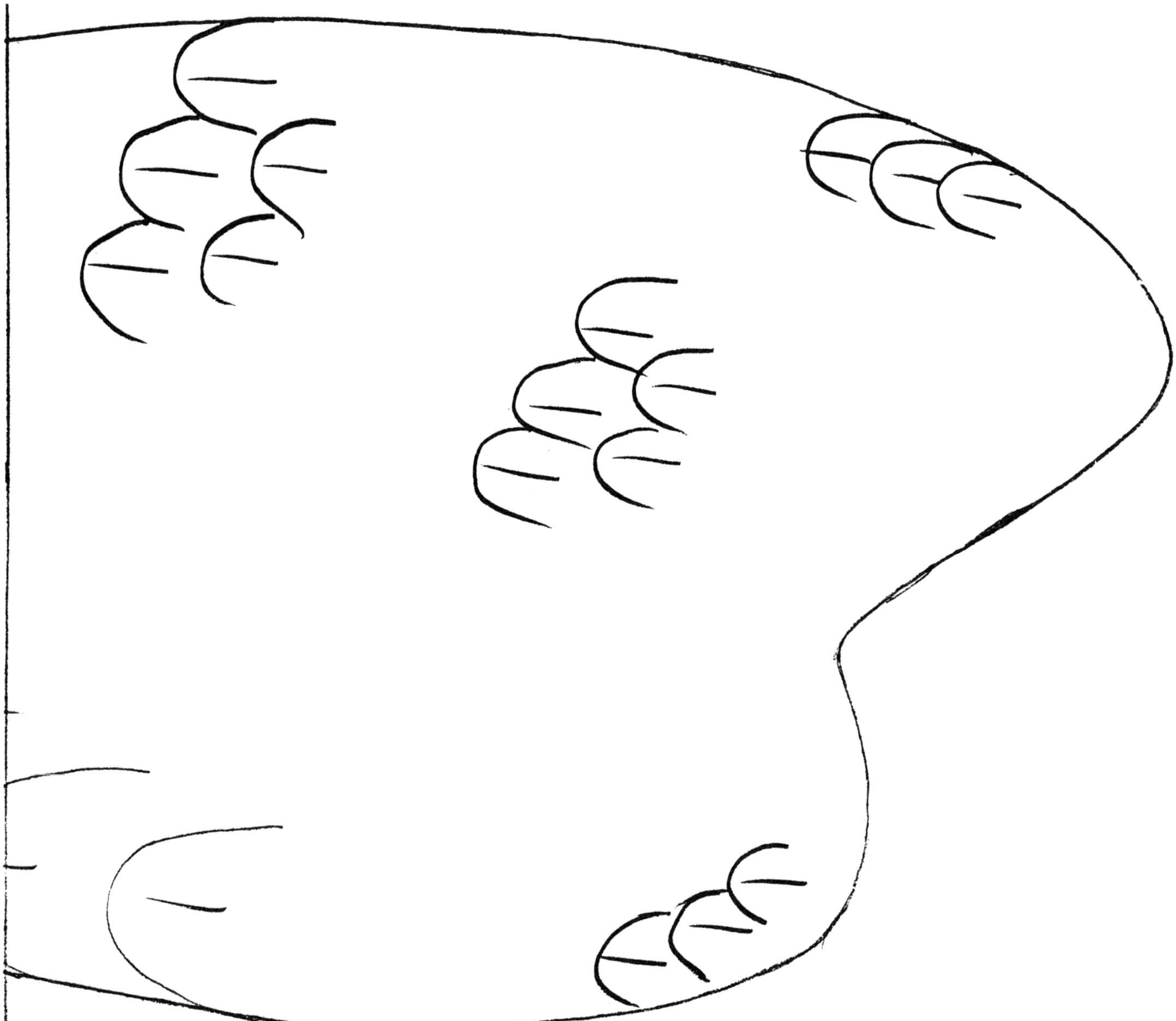

Wing pattern
Top view

REDTAILED HAWK
Body block—16" x 6½" x 5½"
Head block—6½" x 3" x 3"
Eye size—12mm
Eye color—brown

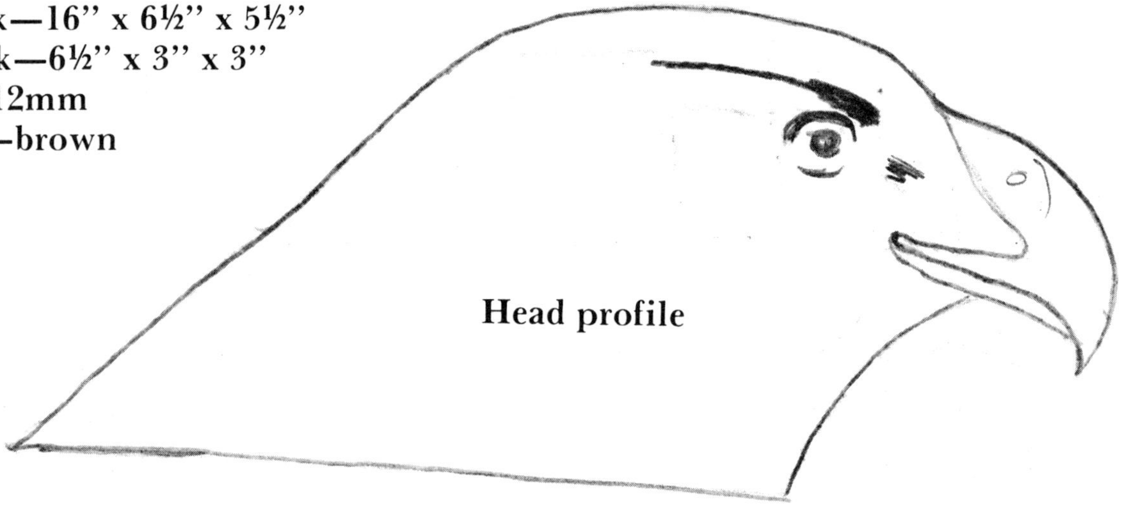

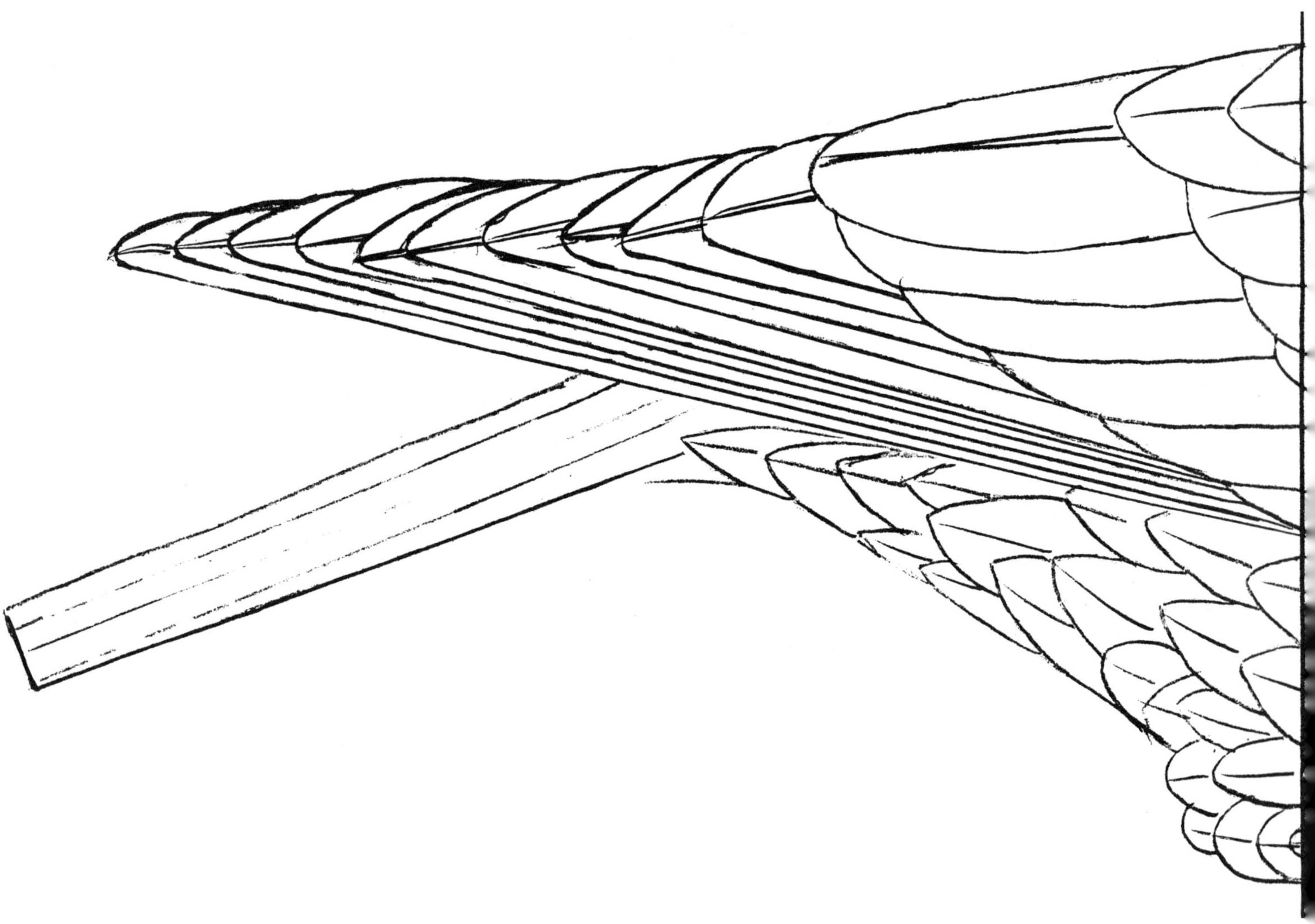

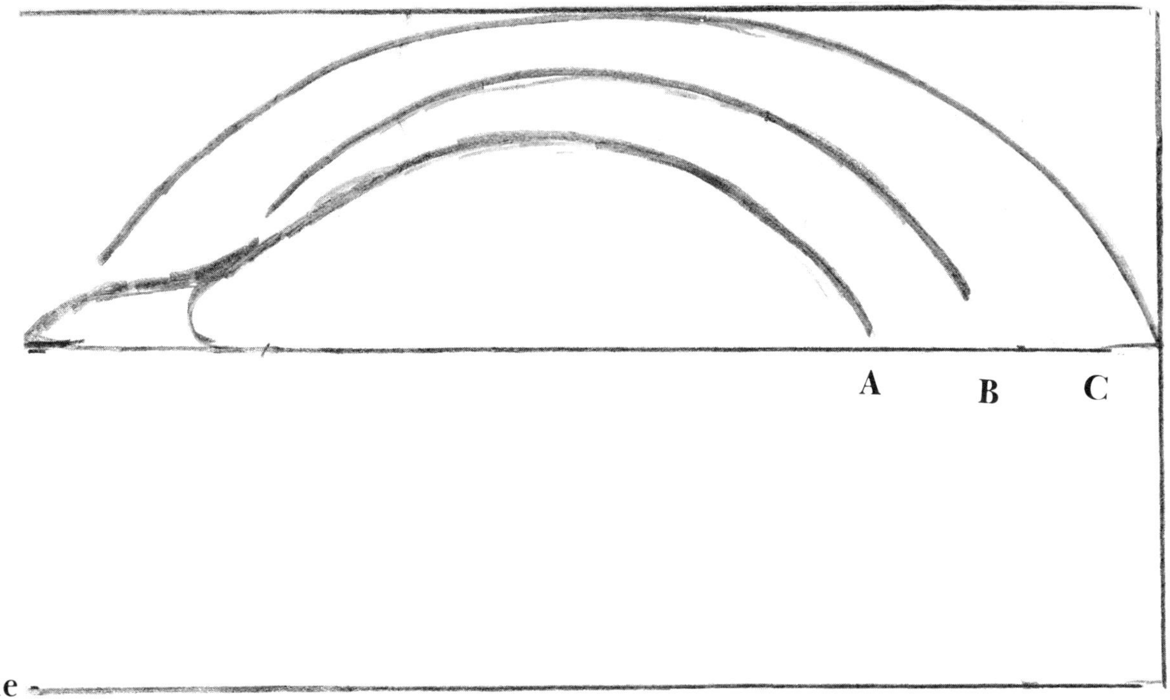

Top view
A. Crown line
B. Cheek line
C. Neck joint line

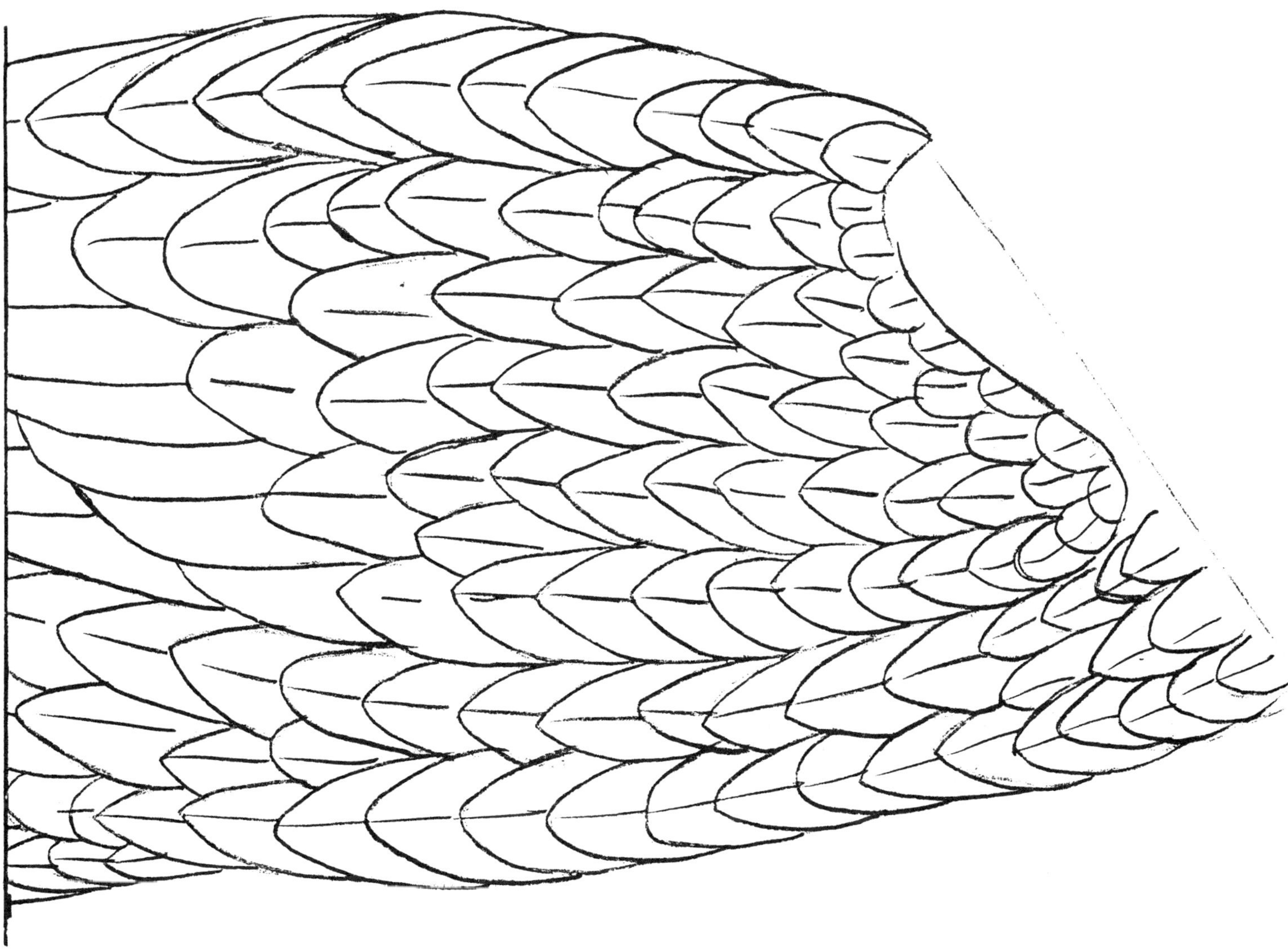

Profile pattern

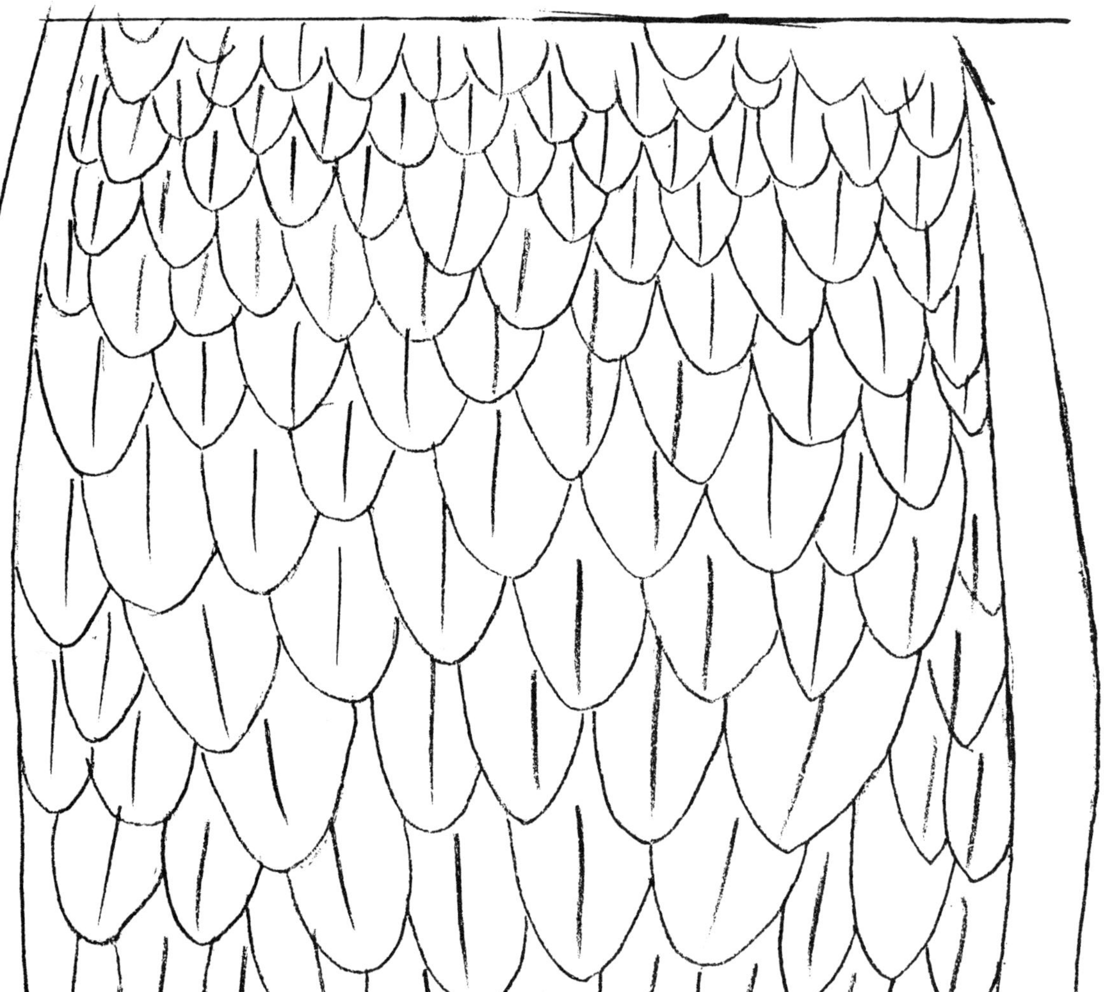

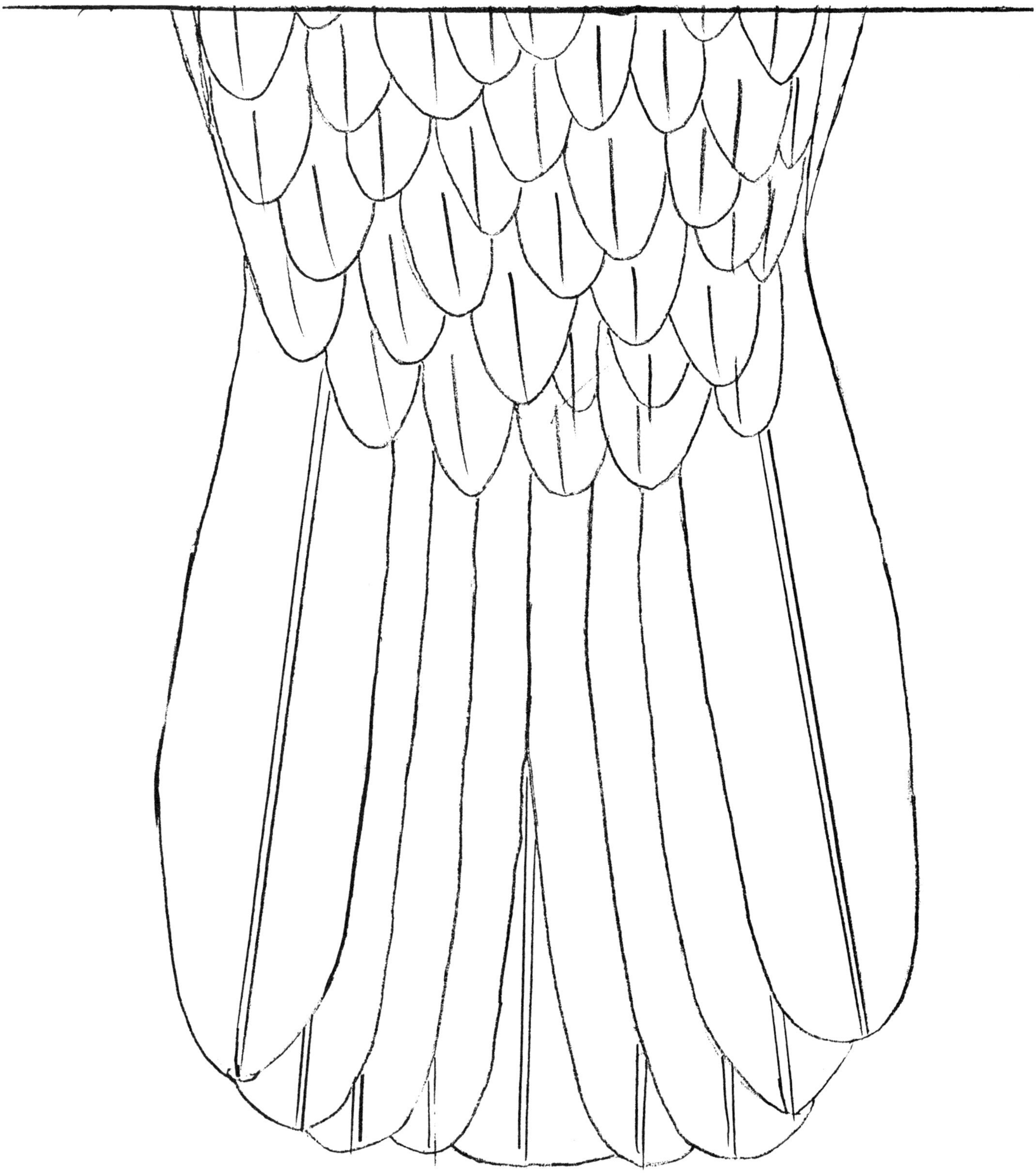

Bottom view

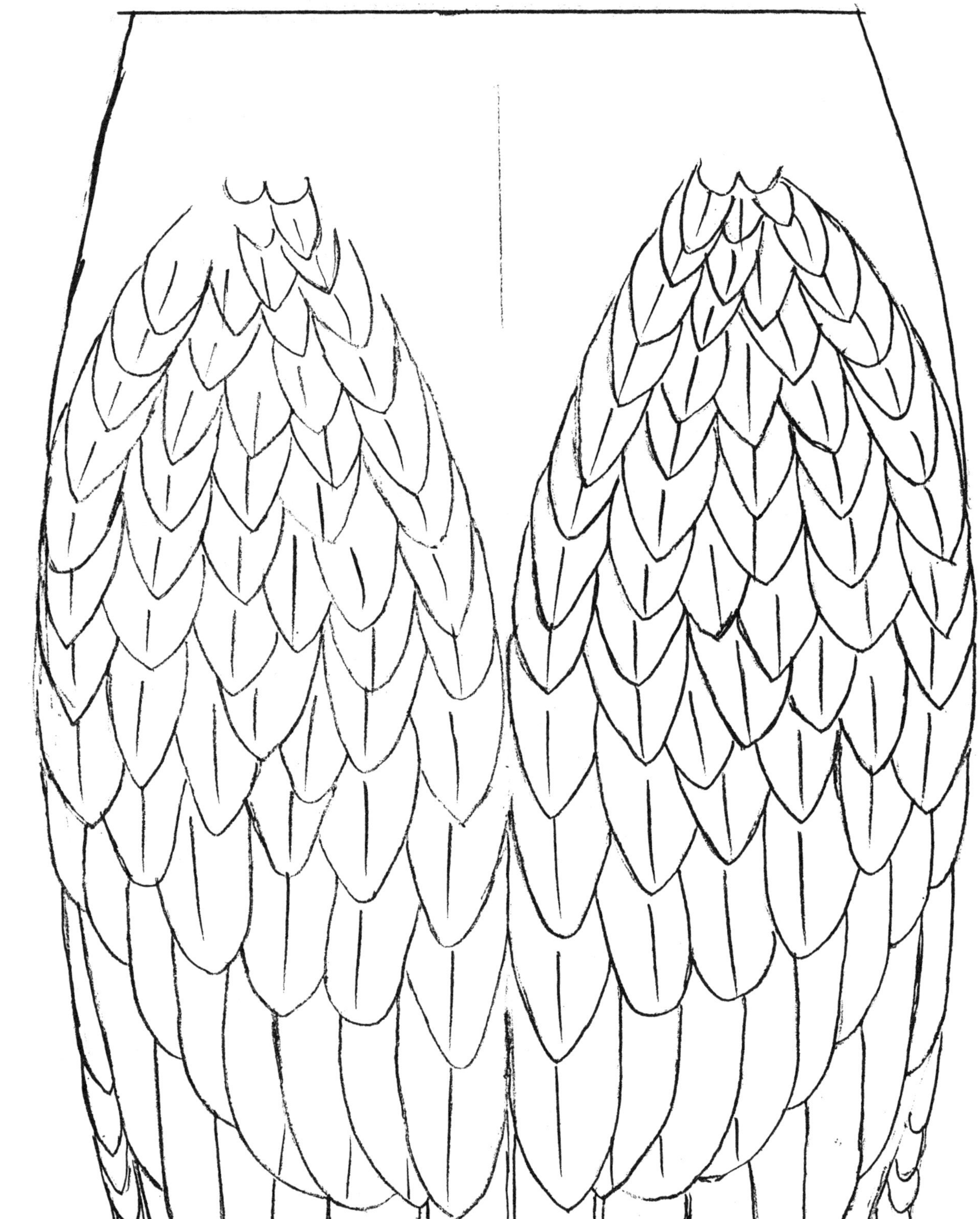

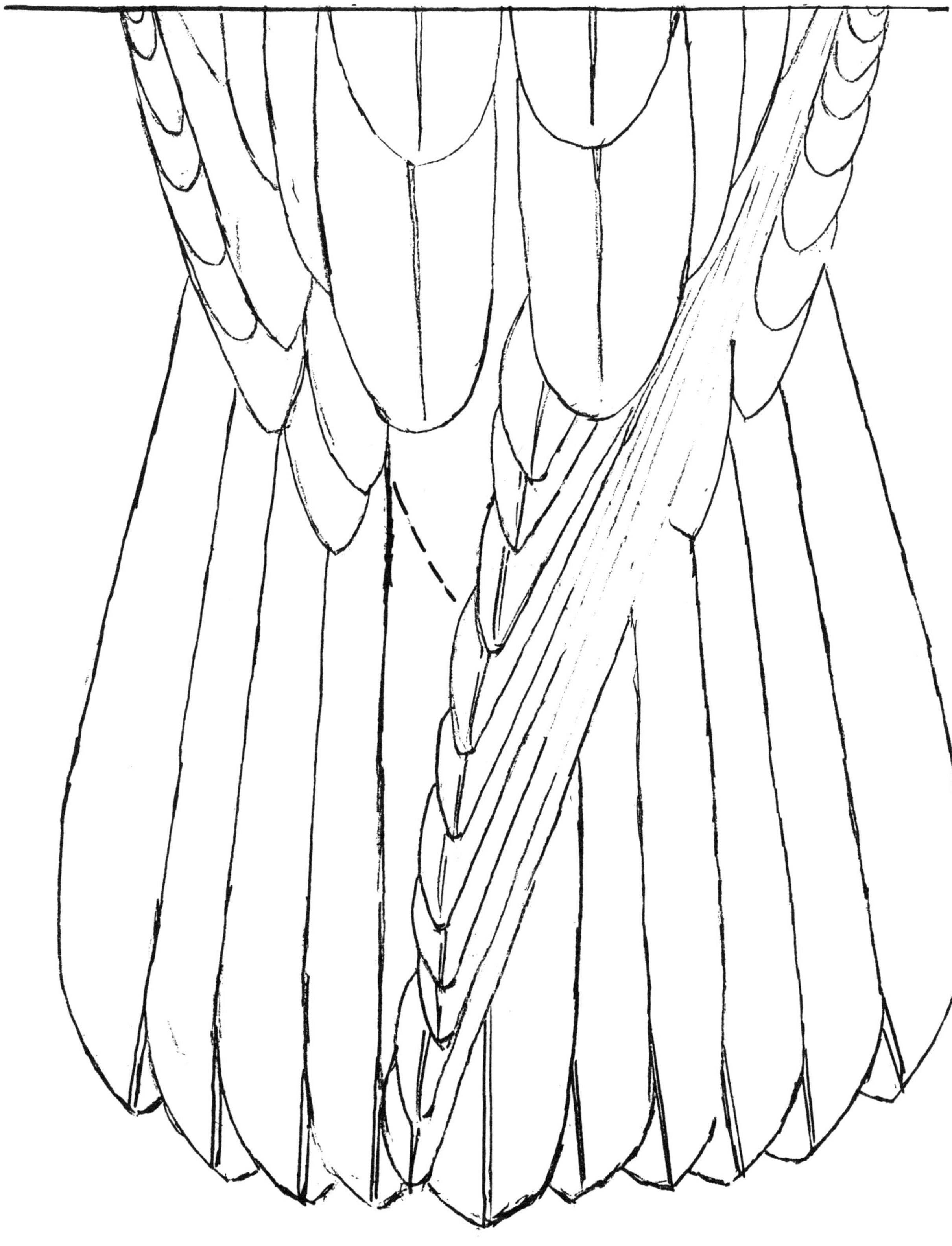

Top view